POLITICS AND GOVERNMENT

THIRD EDITION

With chapters contributed by
Edwin O. Reischauer, Roy Hofheinz, Jr., and Van R. Whiting, Jr.
Harvard University

POLITICS AND GOVERNMENT

HOW PEOPLE DECIDE THEIR FATE

KARL W. DEUTSCH

Professor of Government, Harvard University

HOUGHTON MIFFLIN COMPANY BOSTON

DALLAS GENEVA, ILLINOIS HOPEWELL, NEW JERSEY PALO ALTO LONDON

Library of Congress Catalog Card Number: 79-90262

ISBN: 0-395-28486-4

Printed in the U.S.A.

To the memory of my mother, Maria Deutsch (1882-1969),
one of the first women legislators in her time,
who taught me that politics must serve
the peace and freedom of future generations.

CONTENTS

PART III: TODAY AND TOMORROW

PREFACE

Teachers and students at colleges and universities in the United States, Canada, and other countries have been very generous in accepting the first two editions of this book. Their many searching questions and helpful suggestions, together with my own continuing work on problems of political science, have led me to make this third edition in many ways different from its predecessors.

As in the first two editions, the first nine chapters offer a scheme of political analysis. As in the second edition, this scheme is then applied to the study of particular countries in the second part of the book.

POLITICAL SCIENCE: WHAT THIS BOOK IS ABOUT

This book aims to make clear the principles of political analysis. It seeks to help the reader to learn to recognize the important questions in public life, and thus in the lives of all of us. It also aims to help him or her recognize within each question the crucial facts and conditions that make the main difference to what will happen. The ability to recognize the problems and facts that matter most in deciding our fate is only part of politics. For politics involves both knowledge and action. It is, therefore, in part a science, in part an art, in some small part a gift, and in part a matter of personal decision. But most of it can be learned and taught. Those who care enough to learn about politics as much as can be learned about it have also an excellent chance to decide actively and responsibly about it, and to master in time the art and gift of acting on this knowledge.

The purpose of this book is to help people begin the study of politics. It is written in simple language, in order to make facts plain and ideas clear. It offers a set of basic concepts, like a box of tools, to be used rather than exhibited. Each concept is defined in terms of some operation that can be repeated and tested by different people regardless of their preferences. By demonstrating the meaning and use of concepts, the book also introduces the reader to the development of concepts and encourages him to form his own concepts where they may help his thinking. Relevent concepts and clear meanings will not make all of us agree in politics, but they may help us know what our disagreements are about. They may help us avoid arguments over mere words, and to concentrate on arguments about issues that matter.

To keep track of key concepts, those introduced in each chapter are listed at its end, together with suggestions for additional readings. Some concepts also are highlighted in the chapter section heads and subheads, which have been designed to outline the argument and aid in review. Finally, the index will help readers to trace the different aspects of a concept as it appears in the context of various chapters.

HOW THIS BOOK IS ORGANIZED

The book is divided into three parts. The first presents in nine chapters a set of basic concepts for analysis, together with some comparative data and some classic theories of politics. In Chapters 1 through 5 the emphasis is on the nature of politics; political stakes and participation; the images of politics in terms of political theories and ideologies; and the arena of politics in nations, states, and world affairs.

Chapters 6 and 7 are more technical, in the sense that they try to introduce in simple language such modern concepts as the political system and the processes of political autonomy and self-steering, from the viewpoint of the theory of communication and control. If readers, students, or instructors should find these matters too advanced for their purposes, however, they may skip these chapters, and go straight on to Chapters 8 and 9, which deal with the process and machinery of government, with communication, institutions, and decisions, and with the evaluation of political performance.

Throughout Part I, the main focus of attention is on the advanced countries of the world. There are references, in addition, to problems of developing countries, but it is a central thesis of this book that the political development of the world's major industrial nations is by no means finished.

Part II takes a closer look at seven major political systems: the United States, the Soviet Union, Britain, France, the German Federal Republic, Japan, and the new giant in world politics, the Chinese People's Republic. Each nation is treated at length in its own chapter. A further chapter introduces the world of emerging nations, followed by a chapter on four nations in Africa and Asia—Nigeria, India, Egypt, and Iran—and another on three nations in Latin America—Cuba, Mexico, and Brazil.

The third and final part is brief—a concluding chapter looking to some of the unfinished business of politics that confronts us now and will confront us tomorrow and in years to come.

WHAT HAS BEEN CHANGED

All chapters have been updated through 1979 in terms of events and statistics, wherever appropriate data were found. In Chapter 10, the analysis of the political system of the United States has been still more extended, in addition to the many data and examples from American politics given in the analytic chapters.

In Chapter 4 on "Images of Politics," a substantial section on fascism has been added to the discussions of the ideas of the classical theorists Machiavelli, Hobbes, Locke, Rousseau, Burke, Marx, and John Stuart Mill, together with a discussion of the conditions for a revival of fascist ideas and a possible return to a fascist regime in a major country.

Generally, definitions and discussions of values, ideas, and ideologies, and of valued institutional patterns, such as democracy, have been expanded at many places in the book, including contemporary references to the developing countries.

A new chapter on Japan, the first major industrial power with a non-Western cultural tradition, has been added by a leading expert, Professor Edwin O. Reischauer of Harvard University. The chapter on the People's Republic of China, by Professor Roy Hofheinz of Harvard, has been updated by the author.

The treatment of the world of the emerging nations has been updated in Chapter 17 and greatly expanded by the addition of sketches of two major nations from Africa—Nigeria and Egypt—and two from Asia—India and Iran—in a new Chapter 18, and of three Latin American nations—Cuba, Mexico, and Brazil—in a new Chapter 19 by a specialist on Latin America, Van R. Whiting, Jr., also of Harvard University.

WHAT CAN BE COMPARED

The book thus permits students to develop comparisons among the politics of four highly industrialized market-oriented countries, the United States, Britain, France, and the Federal Republic of Germany; between these and the Soviet Union, which is highly industrialized, with a predominantly Western cultural tradition but a centrally planned economic system; and between all of these and a highly industrialized market economy with a non-Western tradition (Japan). Similarly, students can compare any or all of these political systems with those of any or all of the eight developing countries treated in this volume, or they may wish to compare the three Communist governments of the Soviet Union, China, and Cuba. Other comparisons can be made in terms of political regimes and historic episodes of dictatorship and democracy, or of major civil wars and revolutions, or finally, of foreign rule.

The suggestions "For Further Reading" have been considerably enlarged, most often by references to more recent studies. For the convenience of students, the letters "PB" after any listed book title indicate that it is also available in paperback, although not necessarily in exactly the same edition and from the same publisher.

Despite these many and substantial changes, the original approach and purpose of this book have remained unchanged. It was written from the outset by one teacher, with the aid of hundreds of students and with the help and advice of many colleagues of all ages. The concerned and lively questions, objections, and responses of these students have had the greatest general influence on this book, while the suggestions and criticisms of my academic colleagues have weighed heavily with me on many specific points of fact. Even so, all decisions about the contents of the book were mine, and I alone must be blamed for its weaknesses.

HOW POLITICAL SCIENCE HAS BEEN CHANGING: THE USES OF NUMBERS AND INSIGHTS INTO QUALITIES

Though this is a book for beginners, it seeks to be a modern one. Too often, the time between an advance in research and its appearance in textbooks has been far longer than it should be. Political science includes a good deal of traditional political wisdom of humankind, some of it going back 2,000 years or more. But its main concern is with the world in which we live, and with the political knowledge that may help people make political decisions here and now—decisions about their own fate and the fate of future generations.

Political science in our time is rapidly changing. It is now undergoing the kind of revolution that economics underwent a generation ago, through the work of Lord Keynes, the rise of national income accounting, and the development of the quantitative science of econometrics. The questions "how much? how fast? how soon? and how likely?" that are asked in economics are now also being raised in politics. And increasingly often, they can be answered. To introduce beginners to these new developments in political science and thought, many problems are presented in simple language but from an advanced point of view. Where an argument hinges on figures and series of quantitative data, these appear in the text or in the tables and charts. These often can help to tell more of the truth more clearly and concisely than words alone could do—provided that we appreciate the context of history, institutions, and human values within which each graph or number must be understood, and provided that we remain aware of the limitations of the accuracy and relevance of all such quantitative data.

Numbers can tell us much about politics but by no means all. Votes, budgets, armies, campaign funds, and party memberships are all resources in politics. Health, employment, literacy, increasing life expectancy, and diminishing inequality in the distribution of incomes, or other values can be among the results of the political process. But there is also quality in politics. What other political systems does this one resemble? As we study a current or recent crisis, which crises in other times or countries have shown a similar pattern? Have we seen something like it before? And if so, what are the remaining differences, making the present crisis special in some way, though still comparable in others? As a quantity grows, such as the supporters of a political movement for the freedom of a group, what thresholds does that quantity reach at which new side effects may appear, such as its turning into a majority, seizing power, and perhaps becoming more intolerant of other views? All these are *qualitative* questions. They deal with matters not of number but of kind. What *kind* of a system, a movement, a revolution, a government or an idea are we studying? Here our answers cannot be numbers but only insights—and this book seeks to help students to discover them and to start seeking further insights of their own.

MODERN POLITICAL ANALYSIS: WHY INCLUDE HISTORY?

Qualitative insights depend on our knowing something from history. Often history can tell us what a quantitative change—in the number of peasants, workers, or voters—may mean.

This is why in this book particular attention is paid to history. For history is to politics and government what nature is to biology or physics. It is the source of a major part of all political experience. The comparison of different peoples and political systems or of their structure and behavior requires a knowledge of at least the essentials of their past. It is often quite possible to describe and predict the routine politics of a country without referring to its past. If nothing more is at stake than a minor shift in votes, then such a phenomenon can often be interpreted adequately from a few recent polls. But when a nation faces a major crisis, when great changes seem imminent and fateful decisions are being made, then a nation's past—the memories and character of its people—can be decisive. Thus the United States and Germany responded differently to the Great Depression; France and Britain responded differently to the Nazi attack in World War II; and Russia and the United States are responding differently in some ways to the challenges of modern technology. History does make a difference, and this is why historical information commands extensive attention in this modern comparative and analytical treatment of politics and government.

In addition, relevant interlocking information from other social sciences is presented throughout the book.

ACKNOWLEDGMENTS AND THANKS

Many colleagues and students have helped once again to improve the third edition of this book. Chapter drafts were read and criticized by Sidney Verba, Thomas B. Edsall, and Wayne Koonie on the United States, Adam Bergson on the Soviet Union, Hugh Heclo on Britain, Suzanne Berger on France, and Frieder Naschold on the German Federal Republic. John G. Merriam, Steve Worth, and Gerard Rutan read and commented on the chapters in Part I. Dieter Dux and Roger Benjamin read and criticized various chapters in Part II. For recent data, suggestions, and ideas on particular points I am grateful to Hayward R. Alker, Jr., Atilio Boron, Jorge Dominguez, Shmul Eisenstadt, Bruno Fritsch, Manfred Kochen, John R. Platt, Philip Stone, Nier Yalman, and to Stuart Bremer and Charles L. Taylor and their collaborators in the International Institute for Comparative Social Research at the Science Center Berlin. For valuable assistance in research I am indebted to Robert Grady, David Jodice, and Stephen Livingston. But the decision on what to adopt of the suggestions and data offered has been mine throughout, and so is the responsibility for all errors, gaps, and weaknesses remaining in the text.

I also owe thanks to Harvard University and its librarians and to the Science Center Berlin. The facilities and assistance of these institutions greatly aided in the writing of this manuscript. I should also like to thank the staff members at Houghton Mifflin who helped, often far beyond the call of duty, to produce each edition of this book.

From the beginning, many scholars have influenced my thinking. Some of them are no longer living: Edward Chamberlin, Rupert Emerson, Merle Fainsod, Harold Lasswell, Peter Lindz, Talcott Parsons, Stein Rokkan, Joseph A. Schumpeter, and Norbert Wiener. For me, their thought lives on. To many others I owe intellectual gratitude. I cannot name all, but I must list Hayward R. Alker, Gabriel Almond, Daniel Bell, Robert A. Dahl, Alex Inkeles, Robert E. Lane, Seymour Martin Lipset, Richard L. Merritt, Wolf-Dieter Narr, Ithiel de Sola Pool, Bruce M. Russett, Dieter Senghaas, J. David Singer, Robert Triffin, and Rudolf Wildenmann.

Despite its many changes and additions, this third edition builds inevitably on the second and the first. For these, my debts of gratitude remain. Sheldon Kravitz, John Lunean, and James Chapman checked many details of early research.

Van Whiting would like to thank Jorge Dominguez, Peter Evans, Edward Strasser, and John Womack, Jr. for their help in critically reading all or part of the early drafts of Chapter 19, producing extremely useful suggestions. Errors that remain are in spite of their efforts.

For the second edition, I am grateful for many helpful criticisms and suggestions from my students, and from my correspondents, critics, and colleagues teaching at many colleges and universities, including Dennis Albrecht, William T. Bucklin, Marn J. Cha, Phan Thien Chau, James D. Cochrane, Russell Edgerton, Parris N. Glendening, C. G. Gunter, Andrew Gyorgy, Leroy C. Hardy, Evelyn Harris, Klaus J. Herrmann, Gilbert N. Kahn, Henry C. Kenski, Bernard L. Kronick, Eugene C. Lee, Edward A. Leonard, Roy C. Macridis, John McCully, Catherine McFarlane, Ida Meltzer, E.P. Morgan, John Patterson, Robert L. Peterson, Jeffrey Race, Abdul H. Raoof, Marie B. Rosenberg, Scott Shrewsbury, Edwin B. Strong, Jr., Earl Sullivan, and George V. Wolfe. The administrative and secretarial help of Evelyn Neumark at Harvard and Ina Frieser at the Science Center Berlin, as well as the assistance of Robin Shanus at Harvard, have been essential in preparing the present edition.

Throughout the entire time of writing and revision, the patience, encouragement, and lively insight of my wife Ruth have meant more to me than I can say.

With all these helpers contributing to whatever assets this book may have, I alone am left to answer for its liabilities. I can only hope that, with its weaknesses, this book will encourage others to carry forward the study of politics and government as they are here conceived: as processes of collective human self-direction.

Like its first edition, the present book seeks to help to make political thinking more searching and more comprehensive—in terms of the past and the present, in terms of words and of numbers, and in terms of facts and of values, that is, in terms both of knowing and of caring. If this new edition helps some readers to learn to know more clearly, to care more deeply, to question more widely, and to act more effectively and responsibly in politics, then it will have served its task.

KARL W. DEUTSCH

Cambridge, Massachusetts.

LIST OF FIGURES

LIST OF TABLES

PART I

BASIC CONCEPTS FOR ANALYSIS

I

The Nature of Politics

All of us know that politics affects our lives, but do we realize the full extent of its importance? Clearly, we live in an age of growing *politicization.* Many matters that did not involve politics in the past, or that did not involve it directly, now are seen as political issues. Many decisions that in earlier times did not need to be made, or were made automatically by custom, or were made by private individuals now must be made by public agencies and by the political process.

Our cities are webs of politics. The water we drink, the energy we use, the air we breathe, the safety of our streets, the dignity of our poor, the health of our old, the education of our young, and the hope for our minority groups—all these are bound up with the political decisions made at city hall, in the state capital, or in Washington, D.C. At all levels of government, politics will decide to what extent the problems of the "three big E's" that trouble us today—Employment, Environment, and Energy—will be dealt with or neglected.

What is true of cities is even truer of nations. Almost everywhere, people feel daily the effects of national political decisions. Such decisions go far to determine the lunches eaten by schoolchildren, the level of wages, the prices of many commodities, the cost of credit, the value of money, and the career choices of young people, especially women and members of ethnic minorities. Political decisions also influence the quality of life—its security or insecurity, the ugliness or beauty of the physical environment, as well as its health hazards or safety; and still other political decisions determine the relations of countries with each other and, thus, the likelihood of peace or war.

Politics, in one sense, is the making of decisions by public means, that is, by elections, referenda, laws, court judgments, administrative regulations and decisions, and the like. Here people participate because they have a vote—often by law an equal vote—or because they can exert influence on voters and officeholders. The total of resources and activities that are directly subject to such political decisions is called the *public sector* of a nation's economy. This sector includes national, state, and local governments; public agencies, such as post offices; and publicly owned industries and installations. In our own time, public sectors have been growing in all countries.

In contrast to its public sector, the *private sector* of a nation's economy consists of all resources and activities that are primarily subject to private decisions by individuals, families, business corporations, and similar bodies. Here people often have more leeway to decide to buy or sell or move as they please, if they can afford to pay the price. The results of their decisions come back to them almost immediately. This contrasts with their public votes and decisions, the results of which may come back to them only slowly and indirectly and sometimes may be revealed in unexpected ways. The needs of daily life are such that significant private sectors have survived even in the most collectivistic Communist-ruled countries and are likely to persist.

Finally, there is in many countries a *quasi-public sector* that consists of private business firms that have mainly or only governments as customers, such as pavement contractors or the manufacturers of armaments. And there are publicly licensed firms, such as bars and liquor stores, which are privately owned and serve private customers, but depend on a license granted them by a public, more or less political process, involving many of their owners in local politics.

In all these sectors, people have some freedom of decision, but in none is their freedom complete. In the private sector their "votes" in the market are unequal, depending on how much money or wealth a person has; and the private decisions of individuals and business firms are limited by impersonal market forces, inflation, recession, unemployment, and resource scarcities. Decisions in the public and quasi-public sectors are also limited by these matters, though to a much lesser extent, but each decision maker in the public sector, from the single voter to the chief executive, must cooperate and compromise with others in order to get results. This is why people feel that they can act freely and spontaneously in smaller matters in the private sphere, but must make large-scale decisions by public means.

The larger the public sector, the more frequently political decisions must be made and the more politicized life must become. This has been a decisive part of the story of our century, and this process is still happening throughout the world.

AN AGE OF GROWING POLITICIZATION

The Growth of the Public Sector. One index or measure of increased politicization is the share of the gross national product that passes through the public sector of a nation. The *gross national product (GNP)* is the sum of all goods and services that a nation produces. The growth of the public sector in France over the past two hundred years dramatically illustrates the increased scope of public decision making. One year before the outbreak of the French Revolution, the France of the Bourbon kings collected through municipal, provincial, and national taxes approximately 8 percent of the gross national product (measured in current prices). A hundred years later, the Third French Republic still collected through government taxes approximately 8 percent of the gross national product, although the GNP by then was larger and the spending policies presumably more prudent than those of the Bourbon kings. In 1975, in contrast, the French government—at local, provincial, and national levels and through the publicly owned agencies and enterprises—collected and redirected the spending of 42 percent of the gross national product. Therefore, in terms of the role of politics in allocating the resources of the people, during the past several decades France has become five times more political than it was nearly a century ago.

In the United States in 1976 approximately 35

percent of the gross national product was collected in municipal, state, and federal taxes. Very possibly not all the moneys that flow through the public sector were included in this figure; in countries that depend on private enterprise, governments have tried to minimize the size of their share of the national economy in the mind of the public, even though they cannot reduce it in reality. In 1975 in West Germany, a country well known in the 1960s and 1970s for favoring private enterprise, about 48 percent of the gross national product passed through the public sector. In Sweden under a Social Democratic government, the share of the public sector in the GNP in the 1960s was about 53 percent, including social security and public enterprises. In 1976 the Swedish voters elected a nonsocialist government that extended this sector further. All these figures apply to non-Communist countries. In Communist countries the political sectors of the national economies are still larger, although nowhere in the world do they equal 100 percent (see Figure 1.1).

A World Politicized. Not only every national government, but the world itself has become more politicized. In the late nineteenth century, there were perhaps 50 sovereign states; today there are more than 150, and the number may increase further in the decades ahead. A good deal of the world's trade and its communications are being influenced—indeed channeled—by political decisions. But far more is at stake than economic gain. Strategically, the world has become one: guided missiles with nuclear warheads can be delivered halfway around the globe in forty minutes. What little military security is left now depends on deterrence among those countries that already have nuclear weapons and the means for their delivery. And in the long run it will depend on the proliferation or nonproliferation of such weapons and means among those countries that do not as yet have them. If civilization should be destroyed and most of humankind killed within the next twenty to thirty years, we shall not be killed by plague or pestilence; we shall be killed by politics. Politics has become a matter of life and death.

THE TASK OF POLITICAL SCIENCE

To understand politics means first of all to be able to recognize what is *important*—what things make the biggest difference to the outcome of events. It also means to know what is *valuable*—what difference each political outcome will make to our values and to the people and things we care about. And it finally means to know what is real and *true*—which of our first impressions, our surface guesses, and our popular beliefs will stand up to the tests of systematic verification and practical experience. In sum, we are seeking political knowledge that will be important in predicting and influencing outcomes, that will be relevant to our values, and that will be confirmed by testing and experience.

The last of these three aspects of political knowledge—its *verifiability* and truth—is no less important than the other two. Insofar as such verification is possible, our knowledge can be shared and tested impersonally, independent of our individual likes and dislikes, biases, and personalities. Insofar as we learn to test and control even the partial biases and errors inherent in our own psychological and social situation and in our own assumptions and methods of research, to that extent can there be a *political science* and not a study of politics or a philosophy of politics—which can make their own contributions to our understanding of politics—or a mere airing of our prejudices.

As in every other science, not everything political science deals with can be verified at any moment. But if those findings that can be verified turn out to reinforce one another, if the revisions of earlier findings and beliefs strengthen and enlarge the revised structure of verified knowledge, and if the new findings and the revisions of old ones lead to new questions and eventually to additional verified knowledge, then we are dealing with a living and growing science.

Political action seldom waits for the slow growth

FIGURE 1.1 *Growth of the Public Sector*

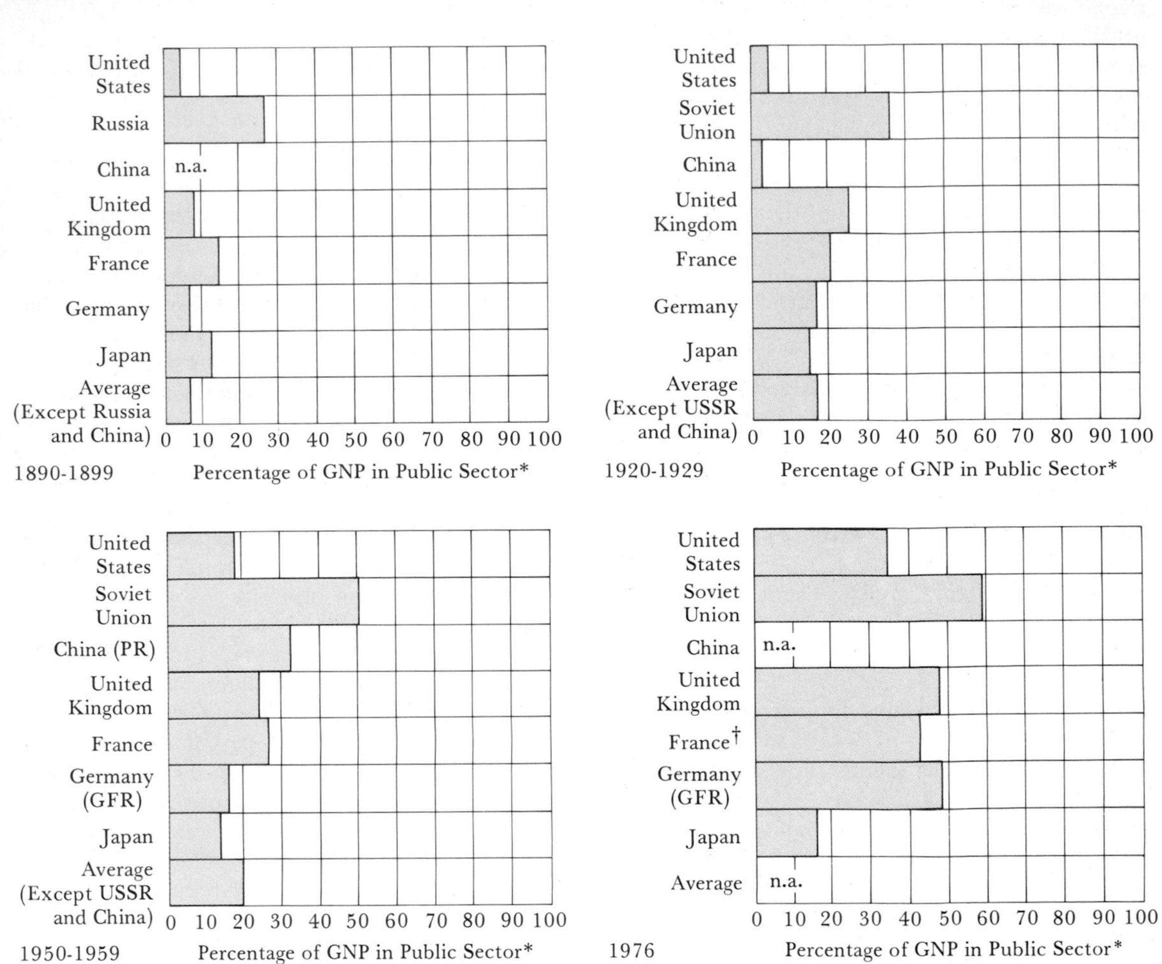

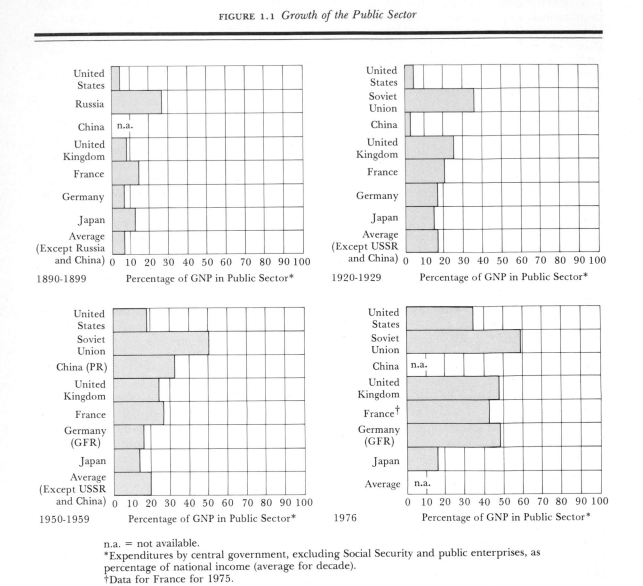

n.a. = not available.
*Expenditures by central government, excluding Social Security and public enterprises, as percentage of national income (average for decade).
†Data for France for 1975.

Sources: W. Zapf and W. Schneider from standard sources, Harvard University, 1969; B. M. Russett et al., *World Handbook* (New Haven: Yale University Press, 1964), p. 63; *United Nations Statistical Yearbook, 1977*, tables 187, 202; *U.N. Yearbook of National Accounts Statistics, 1976*, p. 290.

of knowledge. Decisions often must be made on the basis of whatever incomplete or doubtful knowledge is at hand; and these decisions may later turn out to have been wrong, sometimes entailing vast costs in blood, wealth, and human suffering. But delay of a needed action or decision may prove no less costly. At all times, therefore, both political leaders and plain citizens must weigh the costs of error against the costs of delay. Only with better political knowledge—better knowledge of the consequences of our own attitudes and actions—can we render this choice less painful and less dangerous and make ourselves more likely to be masters, not victims, of our fate.

Politics, then, is a matter of facts and values, of self-interest and loyalties to others, of concern and competence. If it is true that people see most easily what they wish to see, it is also true that in order to survive they often cannot do without the truth. It is the central concern for truth, for knowledge that can be verified, and for policies that work that turns the study of politics into a science and its practitioners into political scientists. Without this concern for evidence, politics remains a clash of opinions, pressures, power, propaganda, or naked force. With a concern for truth, politics can become a search for solutions and new discoveries, for new ways of working together and deciding our own fate.

Insofar as political science is a science, it is an applied one. Its tasks are practical, and its theories are both challenged and nourished by practice. In these respects, political science resembles such other applied sciences as medicine and engineering. Each of these applied sciences draws on a wide range of fundamental sciences for facts and methods to deal with its own tasks. Engineers call on physics, mathematics, chemistry, and other disciplines to help them build bridges that will stand and machines that will work safely. Physicians and surgeons turn to biology, chemistry, physics, anatomy, physiology, psychology, and many other fields for knowledge to help them keep people alive and healthy. Political scientists similarly call on all sciences of human behavior, such as psychology, sociology, economics, anthropology, history, and the theory of communication. They do so to help people keep themselves peaceful, free, and able to cooperate, manage their conflicts, and make common decisions without self-destruction.

FROM POLITICS TO GOVERNMENT

Because politics is the making of decisions by *public means,* it is primarily concerned with *government,* that is, with the direction and self-direction of large communities of people. The word "politics" stresses the process of decision making about public actions or goods—about what is done and who gets what. The word "government" stresses the results of this process in terms of the control and self-control of the community—whether city, state, or nation. Any community larger than the family contains an element of politics. In fact, "politics" comes from the Greek word *polis,* meaning city-state, and to the Greeks the *polis* was the most meaningful community above the family level.

Government: The Helmsman Concept. Government is related to both the old art of steering and self-steering and the new sciences of information and control. The Greek word for the steersman or helmsman of a ship was *kubernētēs.* "Governor" and "government" derive from this term, and so does the word for the science of communication and control, "cybernetics."[1]

[1]*The American Heritage Dictionary* notes that the word "govern" comes by way of Middle English *governen* and Old French *governer* from the Latin *gubernare* (to direct, steer), which, in turn, is from the Greek *kubernan* (to steer, guide, govern). The word "cybernetics," relating to this common character of the processes of steering, control, and government, was proposed in the nineteenth century by the French physicist André Marie Ampère and in 1948 by the United States mathematician Norbert Wiener.

The similarity between the tasks of steering and government has been recognized almost since the beginning of political thought. In the *Republic,* Plato developed this analogy in his "parable of the ship." The man most expert in navigating around reefs, wrote Plato, might fail to win a popularity contest among the crew in the election of a captain. Aristotle also frequently used this analogy. For example, in his *Politics* he wrote that the limits to the size of an efficient state should be the same as those for the size of a ship—neither should be made too large to obey its rudder.

It is not surprising that the image of "the ship of state" should have become firmly entrenched in political thought. The direction of both ships and organizations requires mastery of much the same kinds of knowledge and techniques. The helmsman of a ship must have information about many things. He must know, first of all, where the helm is or where he can put his hand on the tiller. He must know where he himself is in relation to everything in his ship, and he must know what he has to do to stay in control of it; for if he loses control, all other information is irrelevant to him. Second, the helmsman must know where his ship is, where it is moving, and what kind of ship it is. Third, he must know the relevant environment of the ship—where the reefs, sandbars, shoals, currents, and channels are—and where his ship is in relation to all of these. Finally, he must know where he wants to go. He must have some image of his goal, purpose, or preferred course, and he must know at each moment whether the actual movement of the ship is carrying him closer to his objective or farther away from it. Putting together these four kinds of knowledge and acting on them constitute the process of navigation.

Something very similar constitutes the process of government. Those who direct the affairs of a country—or of any large organization or community—must know how to stay in control; what is the basic nature and the current state of the country or organization that they are controlling; what are the limits and opportunities in its environment that they must cope with; and what results they wish to attain. Combining these four kinds of knowledge and acting on them are the essence of the art of government.

Like other complex tasks, steering and government often involve a division of labor. Flying a modern airplane requires two jobs, not one: the manipulating of the controls and the charting of the course. Both the pilot's and the navigator's contributions are essential. This remains true even if modern automatic equipment can replace the navigator or, indeed, the pilot. The two tasks of orientation and control still must be performed.

In politics, too, the task of maintaining control is supplemented by the tasks of *orientation* and navigation. A chief executive and his or her foreign minister must be aware of what their own people will stand for, as well as what the legislature and various important parties and political groups will accept. However, they must also be aware of what foreigners will stand for. They must know, or try to know, what the effect of a national action will be in some distant theater of the world. They must know what policies will be successful at home and what policies will succeed in some strange country ten thousand miles away. In World War II three great countries—Germany, Italy, and Japan—were brought to ruin by their governments because each of these governments, though highly expert in securing and holding power within its national boundaries, proved tragically incompetent in assessing realistically what the rest of the world would stand for and what policies could or could not succeed in the international arena.

Aids to Navigation: Maps and Ideologies. In order to orient ourselves in a difficult and often bewildering world, we frequently make use of maps. Maps present a simplified image of the real world. For example, any map of the New England coastline must be a great deal simpler than the coastline itself, and any diagram of the anatomy of a cat must be much simpler than the cat. The only completely realistic picture of a cat, the mathematician Norbert Wiener once remarked, would have to be a cat—preferably the same cat.

What maps are to the navigator, ideologies are to all of us. An *ideology* is a simplified picture of the world. We may hold such a picture fairly explicitly in our minds, or we may take it more or less for granted and embody it in our feelings rather than in precise thoughts. However explicit or implicit, an ideology serves as a map by which we guide our behavior. Ideologies, therefore, have a direct significance for politics, which seeks to govern behavior. Sometimes we are suspicious of any picture of the world that is labeled an ideology, because we feel that ideologies are by definition misleading. Yet we all have ideologies. Some of us tend to divide them into two categories: "orthodoxy" (which means sound, established beliefs, accepted within a group, society, or school of thought—ours) and "heterodoxy" (meaning different beliefs—the other fellow's) or, more simply, our side and the wrong one.

A *political ideology* may be a general way of thinking about politics, a kind of political folklore that is shared among a group of people, such as most of the inhabitants of a particular country or most of the members of an occupational group or social class. Or else a political ideology may be derived from the theories of some particular thinker, from the particular image of politics that he or she has created. Eventually, perhaps many years later, such a theory or image may find large numbers of adherents who feel that it gives shape to some of their own feelings, experiences, and vague thoughts. These adherents may very well understand the theory differently from the ways its author meant it; but even in its simplified and partly distorted form, the theory will be held by its new adherents as they now understand it because it gives them just what they seek from an ideology—simplicity, orientation, reassurance, and often guidance for their behavior and coordination for their actions. Examples of major political theories that have been used as ideologies at many times and places are given in Chapter 4.

Certainly, we cannot wholly do without ideologies. An ideology is an instrument for making the world look simpler and more consistent than it is. Human beings find it hard to accept and hold in their minds several pieces of information seeming to contradict one another. When we are expected to believe several things that do not fit together, we feel uncomfortable. Psychologists then say that we are suffering from *cognitive dissonance*. Their experiments show that people tend to reduce or abolish cognitive dissonance, either by attempting to reconcile intellectually the seeming contradiction or, more often, by suppressing or forgetting the piece of information that does not fit. Ideologies thus become guides to the selective perception and recall of information. Not only individuals, but also groups of people, organizations, societies, and nations try to reduce or abolish their particular cognitive dissonances by repressing or denying inconvenient bits of information—even if these happen to be true and vital to their prosperity or their survival.

Not all ideologies, however, are equally resistant to new information or equally impervious to truth. We may call an ideology *extreme* when it rejects or resists any piece of information, however true and important, that does not fit. And we may call an ideology *moderate* or *reasonable*—even if we do not happen to agree with it—when it keeps the way open for additional pieces of information that may provide greater realism. Political scientists, like all other scientists, test any item of knowledge by its consistency with many different facts, each of which, in turn, has been verified independently. The difference between extremism and reasonableness hinges on the capacity to recognize reality and to test the truth of opinions. Extremism always involves a tendency toward self-deception, regardless of the virtues of the cause that it is supposed to serve. When running for the presidency in 1964, Senator Barry M. Goldwater overlooked this point when he proclaimed: "Extremism in the defense of liberty is no vice. . . . Moderation in the pursuit of justice is no virtue!"

The question is this: does a particular ideology permit the truth of a piece of information to be tested against a wide range of different kinds of evidence from the outside world—the multiple and interdependent facets of reality that exist whether we like it or not? Or does it test new information only in terms of consistency with a preferred doctrine? To the extent that an ideology permits objective and multiple verification, it is likely to be more *realistic.* Its adherents have a better chance to learn to act effectively, and its values have a better chance to be attained through realistic action.

POLITICS, INTERESTS, AND VALUES

Politics and the Pursuit of Interests. Most of the time, people are interested more in rewards than in sacrifices. One of the fundamental truths about politics is that much of it occurs in the pursuit of the *interests* of particular individuals or groups. In the analysis of politics the concept of interest has played a central role since the early sixteenth century. The word "interest" entered the language at that time. It comes from the Latin word *interesse,* meaning "to be between," like wheat grains among chaff or like meat between bones and gristle. This meaning implies that among (or between) nonrewarding things and events certain rewarding elements can be separated out. To ask "What is my interest?" is a Latin way of asking "What's in it for me?" In this same sense we use the word "interest" for the payment that a debtor makes to a creditor for the use of money. The interest is the reward that the creditor extracts from the financial situation of the debtor. In general, then, anyone's interest in a situation consists in the rewards that he or she can extract from it.

The concept of interest, however, is ambiguous. It implies a claim or *expectation of reward.* But such a claim or expectation has both subjective and objective sides. On the *subjective* side, it describes a *distribution of attention.* People are interested in whatever they pay attention to. If we say that a picture, an advertisement, a book, or a play is holding the interest of its audience, we mean that it has their attention, and usually people pay attention to things by which they expect to be rewarded. When we pay attention to some message, piece of information, or concrete situation in real life, we do so because we think we may derive some reward, even if only by avoiding damage or penalty.

The *objective* side of interest is the actual *probability of reward.* In the behavior of animals, their attention and the likelihood of reward are closely connected. We know that when a cat watches a mouse hole intently, there is usually a mouse in it, for cats are fairly realistic animals. Governments often are less realistic. National and international politics are rich in instances of political groups, parties, and even governments that have paid a great deal of sustained attention to policies and situations that proved to be completely unrewarding. History is full of such examples. The Japanese warlords thought it was in their interest to attack Pearl Harbor; Napoleon and Hitler each thought it was to his interest to invade Russia. Each of these decisions brought about the defeat of a nation and the downfall of its leaders. This pattern goes back thousands of years. King Croesus of Lydia in Asia Minor asked the Greek oracle at Delphi whether he should attack the kingdom of Persia. The oracle replied, "If you cross the river Halys [which formed the border between Lydia and Persia], you will destroy a great kingdom." Croesus attacked, and a kingdom was destroyed—his own.

What is true of governments also has been true of smaller groups, such as labor unions, business investors, and real estate speculators. Though people have often guessed shrewdly about their interests, they also have often guessed wrong. For example, mine workers' unions in many countries have opposed the introduction of automated coal-mining equipment. Yet where such equipment has been introduced in cooperation with the unions, mine workers' wages have risen and mine workers' sons have been absorbed in more attractive occupations. Or the record shows that many business leaders of the 1930s thought that President Roosevelt's administration would greatly damage their interests. Yet American business people controlled a bigger and more secure share of the world's wealth and power by 1945 than they had enjoyed in 1933. Their interests had been well served.

But though national and political leaders, governments, and groups have often been spectacularly mistaken about their interests, in the classic concept of interest the distribution of attention and the probability of obtaining a reward come together. We speak in these cases of a true or *well-understood interest,* in contrast to some imagined or presumed interest that turned out to be unrealistic.

Interests and Needs. True or well-understood interests often are related to the needs of individuals and groups. A *need* is an input or supply of some thing or relationship, the lack of which is followed by observable damage. Our bodies need food, water, oxygen, and many other things; if we do not get enough of these, we die or are severely damaged. In the seventeenth century, sailors were not *interested* in vitamins; they had never heard of them and did not know they *needed* them. But on long voyages, lacking vitamin C from fresh vegetables or fruit, many sailors were damaged by a deficiency disease, scurvy, or died of it. Eventually they learned to carry in their ships adequate supplies of lemons or sauerkraut—good sources of vitamin C—and scurvy was practically eliminated.

Individuals and governments sometimes may desire what they do not need or need what they do not desire. If so, the way from needs to needed actions may be long, as it has been in many questions of environmental protection. Thus, in the 1950s and 1960s, few consumers, business firms, or government officials in the United States desired a redesign of our conventional automobile engines. That desire emerged only with evidence that the exhausts from millions of cars in many big cities were helping create concentrations of smog that were leading to illness or death for increasing numbers of people. The need for unpolluted air and water is a characteristic of the human organism; an objective interest in doing something about automobile exhaust gases has existed in the United States since at least the late 1940s; large-scale public attention began to be directed to the problem only in the late 1950s; effective political interest in issues of pollution became strong only in the late 1960s; effective political action through new legislative and administrative controls became a matter for the 1970s; and the main changes in the majority of the actual vehicles and fuels in use, and thus in the air over our big cities, were aided by the need to conserve energy and reduce oil imports, which emerged in the 1970s. By the late 1970s, average gas mileage of automobiles in the United States was increasing under the pressure of a congressional mandate to reduce the size and weight of new cars. In this case the path from human need to political and industrial remedy may have stretched over nearly fifty years—and the chapter on the critical issue of energy has not yet been finished, despite the passage of the first "energy bill" by Congress in October 1978.

Human needs must be translated into active interests, if they are to be politically effective. Political efforts based on major human needs sometimes may get little backing in the short run, as long as these needs are not yet widely felt and perceived. But in the long run, realistic policies backed by active interests and based on the needs of millions of people may well prove irresistible.

Politics and the Allocation of Values. Politics deals with the interplay of interests—the claiming and distributing of rewards, that is, of values, things or relationships that people would like to have or to enjoy. Acting in politics and pursuing their interests, different individuals, groups, or even countries may cooperate or compete in regard to the *allocation of values.* Indeed, politics has often been defined as the process by which values are allocated *authoritatively* (in a way that will stick and can be relied on) and *legitimately* (in a way that fits people's sense of right and wrong). A famous book on politics by Harold D. Lasswell bore the title *Politics: Who Gets What, When, How?*

In the past, political theories sometimes have been formulated in terms of a single value that the theorist believed various political actors were trying to get. For nearly two thousand years, from the fifth century B.C. until about the fifteenth century A.D., most political theory dealt with politics in terms of *rectitude* or *justice,* that is, in terms of how powers, responsibilities, and rewards in society ought best to be allocated for the common good. From the sixteenth century onward, notably in the works of such writers as Machiavelli and Thomas Hobbes, politics was usually conceived of in terms of *power,* that is, in terms of how powers, responsibilities, and rewards in society were actually allocated; and power was seen as the key value through which all other values could be obtained. In the nineteenth century in the days of Prince Metternich after the Napoleonic Wars and again in the twentieth century after World War II, some political writers tried to see politics mainly as the pursuit of *stability*—the attempt to keep each society and the relations among societies much as they then were. Still other theorists might think of politics as the study of change, growth, and *development.* In general, however, all attempts to view politics in terms of a single value, or a single overriding human concern, have been unsuccessful. They have failed to give an adequate picture of the richness of the political process and of its unending surprises.

Politics and the Plurality of Needs: Eight Basic Values. Perhaps the most realistic approach has been that of Lasswell, who suggests that there exist at least eight basic values, all of which people will pursue—although with varying degrees of interest—and none of which they can do entirely without in either politics or life. Lasswell's eight values are *power, enlightenment, wealth, well-being* (or health), *skill, affection, rectitude* (which involves both righteousness and justice), and *deference* (or respect). People want to be powerful; they have a natural curiosity and want to increase their knowledge; they desire wealth; they value health and the sensual joy of well-being. They enjoy a feeling of skill, of a difficult job done well, and they possess what Thorstein Veblen called "the instinct of workmanship." All people need affection (in fact, psychological research has shown that small children may even die if one tries to raise them without a minimum of affection). People also want to feel righteous in terms of their own conscience and usually also in terms of their religion or philosophy or the system of right and wrong that prevails in their society and that they have made an internal part of their own personality. Finally, most people want to be respected outwardly by their neighbors and to receive due deference from them. People enjoy being permitted to go first through a door, being invited to sit at the head of a table, and having due and respectful attention paid to their communications and messages.

In addition to these eight basic values that most people and groups pursue, people also desire certain ways of enjoying them, such as security and liberty. If we enjoy a value, we want to have it in *security;* that is, we want to be able to count on having it in the future. We not only value health; we want to stay healthy. We not only enjoy power or wealth; we want to keep it. To those who have few or no substantive values to enjoy, such as the unemployed, the very poor, or the desperate, security has little meaning.

The other manner of enjoying values is *liberty* or spontaneity, that is, the ability to act in accordance with one's own personality, without having to make a great effort at self-denial or self-control and without being subjected to external constraints. In short, people like "doing what comes naturally" to them. They enjoy being healthy, but dislike a strict diet or health regime. They may enjoy wealth, but may balk at excessive self-denial or forced savings. Different actions may seem "natural" to different peoples. People tend to act out spontaneously habits or cultural patterns learned earlier. Quarrels over the meanings of liberty, therefore, have been frequent.

POLITICS AND LEGITIMACY: THE COMPATIBILITY OF VALUES

People do not and cannot live by any single value alone, but values are not always wholly compatible—in harmony—with one another. People might be able to increase their wealth only by working so hard that they injure their health. Or they might make money in ways that reduce their feeling of righteousness or diminish the respect they enjoy in the community. This raises the problem of legitimacy. Earlier we spoke of legitimacy as compatibility with one's beliefs of right and wrong. Now we can explore this concept in somewhat greater depth. *Legitimacy* is the promise that the pursuit of one value will prove compatible with the pursuit or enjoyment of other values.

We say that the pursuit of a value is *legitimate* if, and only if, we have reason to expect that it will not inflict intolerable damage on any other value that is also vitally important to us. It is legitimate to make money as long as this pursuit does not involve us in a grave moral wrong or a serious loss of respect in our community or a severe impairment of our health. Of course, to the extent that different people prize different values, their ideas of legitimacy will differ. Some may believe that it is legitimate to be concerned about righteousness, respect, and health only as long as these concerns do not interfere with the making of money.

The problem of legitimacy takes on a particularly terrible form during wartime. Should nothing count but "winning," in the sense of breaking the adversary's capacity or will to resist? Or should there be a restraint on some of the most atrocious practices of war in response to other values, such as rectitude, affection for fellow human beings, or a decent respect for the opinions of humankind? The military laws of the United States impose restraints on permissible methods of warfare, and they aim at protecting civilians; but the massacre of women, children, and old people at My Lai in Vietnam and the subsequent trial of Lieutenant Calley revealed the divided state of American public opinion. Here, as in other urgent and tragic questions, a common view of legitimacy has yet to be achieved.

Legitimacy, then, is a relative, rather than an absolute, concept. It is the promise of a viable configuration (that is, an organized, workable set) of one's values. It is a relationship among values within a situation that makes them compatible or puts them into conflict. As the situation changes, legitimacy may change, too. Since legitimacy may vary with time and place, it may vary among groups, and different views of legitimacy may lead to conflict among groups or may intensify existing conflicts.

Conversely, agreement about what actions or what values are compatible goes far in facilitating the creation or preservation of communities. So long as there is agreement about what is legitimate, politics and government will function more smoothly. When legitimacy is lost, agreements break down or are reduced to matters of expediency and can be disregarded when convenient. The consequences may be tyranny, revolution, secession, or some other form of breakup.

Legitimacy by Procedure. The concept of legitimacy is commonly applied to the manner in which a government, ruler, or officeholder has attained office. The tenure of office is called legitimate if the incumbent has been put into a position or job by a legitimate procedure—a procedure that those whom he or she governs will consider compatible with the configuration of their own values. According to this view, the incumbent's tenure of office is legitimate because of the way the office is obtained, not because of what the incumbent does with it.[2] In some political cultures, rules of hereditary succession determine who is the legitimate ruler; in medieval monarchies there were great disputes about who was the rightful heir to the throne. In the United States or the Soviet Union, by contrast, being a child or close relative of the chief executive does not in itself establish any legitimate claim to political office and may, in the event of one's appointment to office, arouse suspicions of the illegitimate practice of *nepotism*—the unfair favoring of relatives. Such suspicions of nepotism were voiced in the early 1960s when President John F. Kennedy appointed his brother Robert as attorney general and in the 1970s when British Prime Minister Callaghan appointed his son-in-law, Peter Jay, to be ambassador to the United States. President Carter's use of members of his family for international missions was not so criticized, since it involved no paid permanent appointments.

Legitimacy by Representation. Sometimes a political decision is considered legitimate, and therefore binding, for a political community because it has been made by *representatives* of that community. The concept of a "representative," to be sure, is more complex than it seems. It has at least five different meanings. A representative may be similar to the constituents, so that they can see in him or her a sample of themselves. A representative may give voice to their own vague feelings. A representative may deliver their explicit message and do their will. They may trust their representative to use his or her greater competence and wisdom on behalf of their interests. A representative may serve them as a broker who brings together their diverse and divided groups and interests, in order to make them more powerful in combination. Or a representative may combine any or all of these functions.

These different aspects of representative government are discussed in greater detail in Chapter 8. What matters here is that, for any or all of these reasons, people may be willing to identify with their representatives, whose decisions they accept as their own and therefore as legitimate; to comply with these decisions; and even to support them against anyone's resistance. Representation makes discussion and agreement possible among larger numbers of people, at greater length, and in more detail than would the "direct democracy" of face-to-face discussions in an assembly of all members of a small community (or the simplified questions of a large-scale popular referendum). Insofar as people accept the principle of representative government and consider the collectivity of representatives as somehow representative of themselves, these facts will create legitimacy for most or all of the decisions, laws, officeholders, and institutions produced by the representatives, even if not all the prescribed procedures have been observed.

A stricter notion of legitimacy would insist both on the representative nature of the decision makers and on the proper observance of all procedures. In practice, however, neither legitimacy by procedure nor legitimacy by representation is interpreted strictly. People are usually quite willing to accord legitimacy to their rulers and their laws out of habit and childhood memories of obeying parental authority, without asking whether all political procedures have been correct or whom their rulers in fact represent. As a result, most governments are obeyed most of the time by their subjects, and a great deal has to happen before an established government will lose its legitimacy in the eyes of its people. What will count most heavily in the long run are results—what difference, if any, the actions or omissions of the government will seem to make in the lives of those who count in politics and eventually in the lives of the mass of the population.

If a government or a political party should violate the established laws and rules of procedure spectacularly and repeatedly, if its leaders or

[2]For an elaboration of this view of legitimacy as the right to act or to rule, see Carl J. Friedrich, *Man and His Government* (New York: McGraw-Hill, 1963), pp. 258-59.

personnel should be caught publicly in deliberate acts of illegality and deception, then it may lose its legitimacy and credibility in the eyes of a large part of the population. This is what happened in the mid-1970s to President Nixon, Attorney General John Mitchell, and other highly placed members of the administration in the wake of the Watergate affair.

Legitimacy by Results. Legitimacy by results is a broader and a substantive concept of legitimacy, and it is the one stressed in this book. It deals with the substance of what exists or what is done in politics and not just with the procedure by which political power is obtained or the representation through which it is exercised. This broader usage of legitimacy is close to what many writers have called "justice"—by which they mean the compatibility of a political action or practice with the configuration of values prevailing in a particular community.[3] In this book, the terms "legitimate" and "just" will be used interchangeably. People feel that a government is just or unjust, legitimate or illegitimate, not only by how it came to power, but also—and mainly—by what it does. If its actions or omissions violate their basic values, they may conclude, as Saint Augustine did in *The City of God,* that "a government without justice is a great robbery."

Since legitimacy promises a compatibility of values and actions in pursuit of them, it also promises that public goals and practices will be compatible with the private values and personalities of individuals. When this is so, and when government and its laws are held legitimate, individuals cannot break the law without psychological damage to themselves. They will feel the pangs of conscience. When a law, or the government, or the entire political system appears illegitimate, people will defy it without qualms.

Legitimacy among Different Nations and Cultures. To the extent that most people share many basic values within the same culture, they can also share a view of legitimacy. To the extent that some basic values are shared across cultures, international and even worldwide ideas of legitimacy are possible. But this does not mean that there exists only one legitimate set of beliefs. Within most cultures, as well as across them, there are several viable value configurations and several acceptable ways of life. Sometimes these differing views of what is legitimate can coexist. The great world religions, such as Hinduism, Buddhism, Judaism, Christianity, and Islam, as well as various types of philosophy, have existed side by side for many centuries and have all proved viable in practice.

POLITICS AND THE HABITS OF COMPLIANCE

The Probabilities of Law Enforcement. By what means does politics accomplish the direction and self-direction of societies and the allocation of values within them? Primarily it works through the habits of the great mass of the population—the general inclination to comply with the laws and commands of government. These *habits of compliance* are reinforced and strengthened by the probability of *enforcement of the law* against those who may transgress it. Compliance habits are the invisible partner of government, but they do more than 90 percent of the job. If most automobile drivers were not in the habit of stopping at red lights without a traffic policeman being present, the law about stoplights would be impossible to enforce at any reasonable cost. Similarly, the habits of most people *not* to murder their neighbors, *not* to burglarize houses, and *not* to steal cars are what make it at all practical to enforce the laws against the very small minority of people who occasionally do these things.

In order to maintain the compliance habits of the many, it is not necessary to achieve perfect enforcement against the few who are violators. Of

[3]See Friedrich, *Man and His Government,* p. 254.

every ten known murders in major United States cities, no more than three are followed by conviction. Although there are apparently seven chances in ten of getting away with murder, these odds are still not high enough to make murder an attractive undertaking.[4] Something similar holds for most other types of crime. The enforcement rates are imperfect, but they suffice to keep the amount of crime down to some level considered tolerable by the voters.

When the compliance habits of the population decline or disappear, laws may become unenforceable. Generally, laws become difficult to enforce when less than 90 percent of the population will obey them voluntarily. That was the story of prohibition. A little more than 50 percent of the American electorate tried to outlaw the thirst for alcoholic beverages of a little less than 50 percent, but the widespread lack of compliance with the resulting laws made them impossible to enforce; this, in turn, encouraged further disobeying of the laws. Similarly, the apparent increase in the use of marijuana, particularly among members of the middle and upper classes, has resulted in the partial liberalization of criminal penalties in many states and in some pressure for the abolition of laws prohibiting its use. The subject has been poorly studied in the past; feelings about it run deep; and some controversy seems likely to continue into the 1980s.

Certainly the probabilities of enforcement can encourage habits of compliance, though it should not be forgotten that compliance habits are the biggest and strongest part of the combination with enforcement and that the effects of laws and enforcement threats are relatively marginal.

[4]In the United States in 1975 one murder was committed for roughly every ten thousand people. In many advanced countries the frequency is much less: it is less than one-eighth as great in Germany and only one-tenth as great in England and Wales. See U.S. Department of Commerce, Bureau of the Census, *Statistical Abstract of the United States, 1976* (Washington, D.C.: U.S. Government Printing Office, 1977), p. 159.

We use laws to control human behavior because they are cheap to pass and, as long as most people obey them voluntarily, not too expensive to enforce. Laws, the habits of compliance with them, and the probabilities of law enforcement enable a society to continue to function. Within limits, we can change society by changing laws, so long as these will be obeyed. But the greatest changes in society come about through changes in habits of compliance. Slavery was abolished in the nineteenth century not because legislation was passed, but because the entire cultural and social climate of the Western world had begun to change. No one lawmaking body could have legislated such a change, but once the change came, laws took their proper place in hastening the abolition of slavery and in making abolition stick. The great reforms of the world cannot be started by legislation, although they can be helped by it. Legislation is only one of the elements contributing to the deeper change in the thoughts and feelings of individuals, of groups, and of whole societies that transforms one cultural or political epoch into another.

The Concept of Democracy: Some Meanings and Some Tests. Most people obey the government and the laws voluntarily, out of habit or the belief that they are right or legitimate. But what happens when some people think that a law is wrong, or that a particular policy of the government is wrong, or even that many laws or most of the policies of a government are wrong and perhaps immoral, bad for the country and its people?

Under a *democratic* government, the *majority* (directly or indirectly) makes or confirms laws and elects or confirms the government, its officials, and its policies. But the *minority* that disagrees today with these policies or laws may become a majority tomorrow. Under a democratic political system, therefore, a minority must remain free to express its views, to agitate for them, to organize, and to try to win converts to its side. It must have this freedom not only in its own interest, but also in the interest of every member of the majority, in order to protect the chance to get different kinds of information and the right to change one's mind. Thus, the minority opinions may serve as listening aids to the community. When minority views are silenced, the majority is crippled in its ability to compare ideas, to learn new ones, and, if it so wishes, to change its actions.

If majorities and minorities are to learn from each other, government must be open and secrecy must be restricted to a minimum. When a government claims to have made an important decision on the basis of secret information, the parties and spokespeople of the opposition may have to trust it blindly and the voters may be left helpless to decide. The more secrecy there is in government, the fewer democratic decisions can be made by voters, interest groups, and public opinion on a basis of adequate information. This is perhaps why Americans have always disliked secrecy and its accompanying demands for blind trust in government. They have preferred the proverb "Trust your mother, but cut the cards."

A minority, in its turn, usually will obey the laws and the government, in order to permit the political system to function and in order to maintain its chance eventually to convert its fellow citizens. This is why many people say that *majority rule,* the freedom to criticize and oppose the government, the *protection of minorities,* and the loyalty of minorities to the political community and to its basic patterns of government are all essential for a functioning democracy.

In a democracy most citizens are in fact likely to switch back and forth between majority and minority roles or situations. They may find themselves in a minority on one specific issue, but will get their way as a majority on some other; or they may be now in a minority whose view may win majority support later.

Thus far we have spoken of a minority in the numerical sense of the term. But in political practice, the term is often used to refer to any disadvantaged group, regardless of its numbers. Thus, women are sometimes spoken of as a minority. They constitute the numerical majority of the population in most countries, but thus far have been getting only a minority share of power, economic rewards, and political representation. Something similar can and does happen to large ethnic, religious, or income groups in many countries.

When the members of a minority find themselves permanently outvoted on most of their issues, then they may no longer see the prospect of political give-and-take—of reciprocity and change of roles—as realistic. When this happens, the minority status of the group has become *diffuse* (oriented to many issues) and permanent; their identification with the larger democratic community will be weakened, and their feelings of legitimacy and loyalty toward it may become severely strained. As a result, the minority may attempt secession, revolution, or rebellion. Or it may fall back on general nonviolent resistance, or scattered acts of overt civil disobedience, or quiet noncompliance with the law. The government and its supporters then may try to prevail by force or exhortation, or else the minority may succeed wholly or in part in its resistance.

In each case, however, when a minority becomes estranged from the political system, it is worthwhile to ask what motivates the majority of government supporters and, even more, to ask what motivates a minority group—whether distinguished by race, language, ethnicity and culture, class, age, gender, sexual orientation, or any other characteristic—to become politically active and eventually estranged from the supposedly democratic political system. Condemnation is less likely to be effective in dealing with such processes than an understanding of the conditions that give rise to them.

It follows that a stable democracy, legitimate in the eyes of its entire population, must meet not just a few tests, but many. It requires many other characteristics besides the few we have discussed so far. These matters are dealt with in Chapter 9 on the performance of governments. With the help of such multiple tests of political performance, we shall be better able to judge how democratic any particular nation-state or political system is likely to prove and what its chances are to retain or increase its legitimacy and the loyalty of its people.

POLITICS AND PRIORITIES

The Art of the Possible. Politics is indeed what nineteenth-century statesmen called it: *the art of the possible.* To be effective any politician or statesman must know what can be done politically at any particular time and place: what laws and behavior people will accept as legitimate, will permit to be enforced, and will continue to support long enough to achieve the desired results.

What is practical—that is, possible—at any particular time and place depends on people's fundamental habits and values and, to a very important extent, on their *scale of priorities*—their beliefs about which things should come first. As long as Americans in the early nineteenth century thought that the protection of property, including property in human slaves, was more important than the freedom of all individuals, the abolition of slavery was not practical politics in the United States. It took a generation of unruly young people, together with some older ones, to change the limits of the possible. Without their desperate determination, this might not have happened, at least not so soon. For years, abolitionists were called unrealistic and extremist; and from the point of view of their contemporaries, no doubt they were. Indeed, like all extreme political causes, abolitionism attracted the types of people who found it easier to take extreme positions and make extreme demands than to work patiently at the possible. But the extremists—including some angry and violent people like John Brown—did fulfill a mission in history. Their deeds and misdeeds, their crimes and their sacrifices, all contributed to one result: they changed the sense of urgency among their fellow citizens. They helped to rearrange priorities. And they opened the way for responsible leaders and practitioners of the art of the possible, like Abraham Lincoln, to find a practical solution to the problem of abolishing slavery while at the same time keeping the Union together and making the new political arrangements work.

At the beginning of the Civil War, the hero of the Italian National Revolution, Giuseppe Garibaldi, offered to fight for the North if Lincoln would immediately announce the abolition of slavery. Lincoln might well have appreciated the contribution that Garibaldi's military talent and heroism could have made, but he felt, probably quite realistically, that he needed even more urgently the support of Delaware, Maryland, and Kentucky—indeed, of all the border states—and that he could get their support at that time not on the issue of slavery, but on the issue of union. Accordingly, Lincoln waged the Civil War as a war for the preservation of the Union and retained the support of the border states throughout. He had to do without the support of Garibaldi, but he did abolish slavery in 1863—and he won the Civil War.

Reordering Priorities. In our own time, we may occasionally face similar problems and similar decisions. A Brazilian student chafing under dictatorship in his country said that he thought he and his contemporaries had to become a "sacrificed generation." He felt that they would have to sacrifice their immediate political effectiveness by making extreme demands in order to free the way again for a more continuous and evolutionary type of politics in years to come. Whether this will prove true for Brazil remains to be seen, as does the extent to which similar problems may have to be faced at certain times in the United States. If it becomes clear that the wealth and resources of the United States do not permit it to deal simultaneously with, say, political stability in the Middle East or Africa and poverty in South Chicago on the scale that each problem demands, some people may find a role in trying to call on the consciences of their fellow citizens and persuading them to change their sense of priorities and values. But, in the end, if the United States and the world are to be changed constructively, it will be done by people who have mastered the art of the possible, by people who can make coalitions and keep them and who can not only *demand* that the world be changed for the better, but can actually bring such change about.

POLITICS AND LEARNING

The Capacity to Learn. All self-direction is crippled without self-correction. The ability to correct actions and errors is crucial for all self-steering and self-government. To the extent that we are able to correct or improve our behavior by making more complex responses to the world around us, we say that we have the capacity to learn. *Learning capacity* is the ability of a person or group to give a reliable new response when an old stimulus is repeated. (We can even build machines today that have some learning capacity in this sense.) This is the opposite of the kind of nonlearning that occurs when a person or group reacts with the same response to anything that happens. To some members of the John Birch Society in the United States, everything is a Communist threat; and, to some Communist Party secretaries in the Soviet Union, everything is a Western plot.

All learning ultimately requires reallocating some of the resources of the learning person, group, or system. This is often a costly and painful process, because it is often neither cheap nor easy to change old habits and arrangements. The more we learn about the economically disadvantaged in the United States, the more we recognize that our habits need change and that our resources need to be managed and distributed better, although whether or not we are prepared to make the necessary changes and sacrifices is another matter.

The *politics of dogma* tries to avoid the costs involved in modifying old ideas or in accepting new ones. Here the political process serves mainly to defend cherished beliefs and illusions, and here politics is based on the assumption that no new information is either possible or desirable. The politics of dogma usually seeks to preserve existing practices and institutions, but this is not always the case. Those persons or groups who advocate particular forms of change but who have closed their minds to all other forms also practice the politics of dogma. The critical factor is not the attitude toward the status quo, but the attitude toward learning.

In contrast, the *politics of discovery* begins with the proposition that though we know something about ourselves, our needs, and our capacities and about the world in which we live, we do not know all there is to know. We still need additional knowledge and, indeed, actively seek it. We regard the political process as a means of obtaining new knowledge, and we are willing to act on this knowledge, once obtained, despite the price we may have to pay for such action. A similar stress on discovery has characterized the growth of modern science. As the style of thinking and acting that seeks discoveries spreads into political behavior, our politics may become less dogmatic and more oriented toward the making of political discoveries and personal sacrifices.

Viewed over the longer term, politics has the function of coordinating the learning processes of a whole society. When a new problem arises and old answers are useless in coping with it, or when a new response to an old problem becomes necessary because some critical threshold has been passed—as when the forests have been cut down to the point at which soil erosion threatens and new trees have to be planted—then the society has to learn a set of new habits.

Whenever a society has to acquire new habits, it will discover that not all people can learn at the same speed. Some individuals and groups learn very quickly, many learn at more nearly the average or modal speed of the society, and some are particularly slow or resistant. But if the society as a whole has to make a response, its behavior may have to be coordinated. Here the power of government can play a vital role. By offering rewards for the behavior needed, or by using penalties to accelerate the speed of the stragglers, it can help the society to respond more quickly and uniformly than in the absence of such assistance. This function of politics may well be perennial, as long as human societies meet new conditions and have to learn new habits of response to them and as long as human beings differ in their speed of learning. The hopeful theory of anarchists and Marxists that the state someday will wither away and that all government and all politics will become superfluous is not likely to be realized. Even though many present-day tasks of government may one day disappear, in some respects politics and government have a perpetual function in the ordering of human affairs.

Accelerating Social Learning. Politics has the task of coordinating human expectations and social learning in such a way as to help society attain its goals. Attainment of goals, according to the sociologist Talcott Parsons, is one of the basic functions of every social system. But society not only tries to attain the goals it espouses at a particular time; it can set new goals and try to attain them.

This setting and changing of goals is different from merely trying to attain the goals one has. Indeed, it may be crucial for a society not to turn political commitment into idolatry—not to make its current goals into little tin gods to be worshipped. It was a simple psychological process that made the nineteenth-century pioneers in the United States write on the sides of their covered wagons the slogan "California or bust." But when a modern government writes on its flag some policy goal with the invisible postscript "or bust," the situation becomes dangerous. In the nuclear age it may be important for governments to realize that goals cannot be treated as absolutes in either domestic or international politics. Rather, our social and political goals must be thought about, discussed, re-evaluated in the political process, and in time changed—one hopes for the better. Such changes in the goals of a society, however, may also involve some changes in its structure.

Self-Transformation. Eventually it is possible for a society not only to change some of its patterns and a few of its goals, but also to become changed in so many aspects and with respect to so many goals that one may speak of its *self-transformation.* Western societies, in particular, have repeatedly shown this power of self-transformation. Medieval western Europe in the tenth century was transformed as a result of the Roman Papacy's rise to independent political power and the church's acquisition of freedom to run its affairs without undue interference from secular governments. Since that time, Western civilization has been different from anything it was before and from any other civilization in the world. For hundreds of years, the people of the West usually had not one but two authorities above them, and they experienced not only the problems but also the responsibilities and opportunities of making their own decisions.

Centuries later, the American Revolution was described by John Adams as fundamentally a change in the habits and customs of the American people, and Adams felt that this transformation was more important than what had happened on the battlefields of the War of Independence. Great and bloody revolutions have occurred in other countries as well: in England in the seventeenth century, in France in the eighteenth, and in Mexico, Russia, and China in the twentieth. Yet major changes also have occurred without significant violence. British parliamentary and voting reforms transformed the country between 1832 and 1884. In the United States the age of reform between 1890 and 1910 and the period of the New

Deal in the 1930s were epochs in which the political system and, to some extent, political culture became transformed. Whether change comes violently or peacefully, it is likely that any society wishing to retain its vitality must retain its power of partial or far-reaching self-transformation. This is true even though the governments of many societies, and notably of dictatorships, would rather pretend that they and the institutions on which they are based are going to last forever.

SOVEREIGNTY AND THE WORLD COMMUNITY

Peoples, states, and countries change, but they often do so at different speeds and in different directions from those of their neighbors. After World War II, Britain and France nationalized some major industries, but the United States, West Germany, and Japan did not. In the Communist world, the Soviet Union, like the German Democratic Republic and several other Eastern European states, continued to stress the growth of heavy industry, advanced technology, centralized economic planning, and the power of bureaucratic and managerial "cadres" or elites, but Yugoslavia and the People's Republic of China developed in strikingly different directions.

All over the world, people have much in common in their basic human needs and desires, as well as in the necessities and constraints they face in making a living, developing adequate technologies in farming and industry, controlling the growth of their own numbers, preserving a livable natural environment, and helping one another in all these tasks by the exchange or sharing of goods, services, and knowledge. These tasks are worldwide. In facing them, humankind often can be thought of as one community. In these matters we then may ask of each nation whether it is acting as a good citizen of the world community or whether its rulers and citizens are trying to take more from the world than they are willing to give it.

Some people wonder whether we should not all be better off if we were to abolish all nation-states, including their national governments, laws, armies, police forces, and the like, and put all humankind under a single world authority—a *world government*—with a world constitution, a world police force, and perhaps a world electorate.

But would the roughly 4.5 billion people of the world be willing to obey and support a single government? If not, could they be forced to do so, and would any such enforced arrangement be at all likely to last? Would not such a world dictatorship be likely to collapse in even more bloodshed, suffering, and devastation than we find in the world of many independent states and nations that we have now?

The limits of territories and populations that a government can control are closely related to the limits of the population that is willing to obey it and to give it support. The further the claims of a government extend beyond its limits of popular acceptance and support, the more likely they are to become unenforceable.

This is why there are in today's world so many states that are *sovereign,* that cannot be ruled from outside. When we call a country, government, or people sovereign, we are saying that the main decisions about its actions come independently from somewhere within it. *Sovereignty,* as lawyers since the sixteenth century have developed the concept, means the power to make decisions of last resort, decisions that cannot be overridden or reversed by any other human decision maker or agency. In the course of history, lawyers have sometimes argued about where within a state this sovereign power of ultimate decision is located. Does it reside in a single person, such as an absolute monarch in seventeenth- or eighteenth-century Europe or the president of the United States—if that individual should decide on a major undeclared war in the age of nuclear weapons? Or is it lodged in a limited collective body such as the British Parliament, or the United States Congress, or the congresses and top-level committees of the Communist Party of the Soviet Union? Or is it located in the national electorate or in a nation's entire adult population? Or is sovereignty within any modern state distributed among several parts of the political system, so that no one group or agency has all of it and it exists only in the system as a whole?

And finally, are all nation-states that are called sovereign in law also sovereign in fact? What about the small states that may be dependent on the world market for tin, cocoa, coffee, or bananas, or on foreign banks and multinational corporations that may own most of the major assets in the country, or on some powerful political and military ally whose troops may be stationed on their territory and who may partly finance or otherwise control their supposedly national government, army, and police? How truly sovereign were Guatemala, Honduras, the Dominican Republic, Hungary, Czechoslovakia, and the German Democratic Republic in the late 1970s?

These questions will be explored later in this book. The location of decisions—and hence of sovereignty—within a state is discussed in Chapter 6 on the political system, and in Chapter 7 on the self-steering of governments, as well as in Chapters 10 through 19, which deal with particular countries. The question of the degree of sovereignty, or of external dependence, of smaller or less-developed countries is taken up in Chapters 17 through 19, on the world of the emerging nations.

We must note here, however, that even the biggest and strongest nations in the world are limited in the decisions they can make. Compared with the world as a whole, as well as with the powers of modern technology and the problems of the natural environment, every nation-state is small. The worldwide effects of severe nuclear fallout, for example, or of any major deterioration of the atmosphere or of life in the oceans could dwarf the powers even of the United States, the Soviet Union, or China. Nothing less than worldwide cooperation among many governments would offer us a chance for coping with problems of this magnitude.

In international politics, too, the power even of the strongest nation is only relative to the power of the rest of the world. As other nations change and as the international system changes, the meaning of being "number one" also changes. In military matters the United States in 1945 and 1946 had all of the few atomic bombs there were, and military superiority seemed a meaningful notion to many Americans at that time. Today the United States's nuclear monopoly is gone. The Soviet Union by itself has enough nuclear warheads to kill all Americans several times over, and it is little comfort to know that there are enough American warheads to kill Russians even more redundantly. If we all killed one another only once, it would be quite enough. In this respect, national military superiority has become a myth.

National economic power in world affairs has proved no less vulnerable to worldwide changes. Between 1950 and 1970, American automobile production grew substantially. Yet according to a government report, whereas the United States in 1950 was manufacturing about three-quarters of all automobiles in the world, by 1960 its share in world automobile production had declined to about one-half. By 1970 it was down to about one-third and by 1976 to less than 30 percent. During this period the automobile industry in the United States had not declined, but those of the rest of the world had developed faster.[5]

Some such development may well continue in the future. As the world grows, the power of any single nation in world politics will become smaller. Britain, France, Germany, and Japan all had to learn to live with this fact after 1945. The United States, the Soviet Union, and China are learning to live with it in the 1970s and 1980s.

THE UNITY OF POLITICS

The concept of politics has been explored from a variety of perspectives. We have observed that

[5] *United Nations Statistical Yearbook, 1977*, table 137, p. 346.

politics involves the self-direction of communities, the allocation of values, the search for legitimate patterns of compatible values and policies, the art of the possible, and sometimes a fundamental resetting of priorities; it also involves the coordination of social learning, the attainment of the goals of a society, the changing of these goals, the setting of new ones, and even the self-transformation of an entire country, its people, and its culture. But all these are different aspects of a single process: the common decisions of men and women about their fate.

The many different aspects of politics are appropriate topics of the study we call political science. This study inquires into the stakes of politics, the participants in politics, the varieties of political thought, the nature of states and nations, the functions and structure of the political system, the development, administration, and execution of policies, the making of political decisions, and the evaluation of political performance. These are topics to which we turn our attention in the next chapters—without losing sight, we hope, of the unity that gives all these studies purpose and meaning.

KEY TERMS AND CONCEPTS

politicization
politics
public sector
private sector
quasi-public sector
gross national product (GNP)
verifiability
political science
government as steering
ideology
political ideology
cognitive dissonance
extreme ideology
moderate ideology
realism
interest
need
allocation of values
authoritative
rectitude
justice
power
stability
development
Lasswell's eight basic values
security
liberty
legitimacy
nepotism
representative government
habits of compliance
law enforcement and its limits
democracy
majority rule
minority protection
the art of the possible
scale of priorities
learning capacity
politics of dogma
politics of discovery
self-transformation
world government
sovereignty

ADDITIONAL READINGS

Almond, G. A., and G. B. Powell, Jr. *Comparative Politics: System, Process, and Policy.* 2nd ed. Boston: Little, Brown, 1978. PB

Aristotle. *Politics.* Trans. Sir Ernest Barker. New York: Oxford University Press, 1958.

Bernstein, C., and B. Woodward. *All the President's Men.* New York: Warner Books, 1976. PB

Dahl, R. A. *Modern Political Analysis.* 3rd ed. Englewood Cliffs, N.J.: Prentice Hall, 1976. PB

Easton, D. *Framework for Political Analysis.* Englewood Cliffs, N.J.: Prentice-Hall, 1965.

Eayrs, J. *The Art of the Possible: Government and Foreign Policy in Canada.* Toronto: University of Toronto Press, 1961. PB

Festinger, L. *A Theory of Cognitive Dissonance.* Stanford, Calif.: Stanford University Press, 1962.

Lane, R. E. *Political Man.* New York: Free Press, 1972. PB

Lasswell, H. *Politics: Who Gets What, When, How?* Cleveland: World Publishing, 1958. PB

Lieberman, J. K. *How the Government Breaks the Law.* Baltimore: Penguin Books, 1973. PB

Lindblom, C. E. *Politics and Markets: The World's Political Economic Systems.* New York: Basic Books, 1977.

Lipset, S. M. *Political Man: The Social Bases of Politics.* New York: Doubleday Anchor, 1959. Chaps. 1-3. PB

Lockard, D. *The Perverted Priorities of American Politics.* New York: Macmillan, 1971. PB

Merritt, R. L. *Systematic Approaches to Comparative Politics.* Chicago: Rand McNally, 1970.

Plato. *Republic.*

Some More Difficult Books:

Friedrich, C. J. *Man and His Government.* New York: McGraw-Hill, 1963.

Lipset, S. M., ed. *Politics and the Social Sciences.* New York: Oxford University Press, 1970. PB

Mannheim, K. *Ideology and Utopia.* New York: Harcourt Brace, 1955. PB

———. *Man and Society in an Age of Reconstruction.* New York: Harcourt Brace, 1967. PB

Moore, B., Jr. *Injustice: The Social Bases of Obedience and Revolt.* New York: Pantheon, 1978.

Waxman, C. I., ed. *The End of Ideology Debate.* Louisville, Ky.: Touchstone, 1969. PB

PB = *available in paperback*

II

The Stakes of Politics: What Can Be Got and What Can Be Done

The philosopher William James persistently asked one question about an idea or institution: what difference does it make? We would like to know what difference politics makes and, within the sphere of politics, what difference a particular political institution or action may make. But before we can answer these questions, we must ask *to what* does politics make a difference? What is at stake in politics? What can be changed, rearranged, or redistributed by politics? The present chapter deals with these matters. The next chapter then asks *to whom* does politics make a difference? This, in turn, leads to the study of political participants and interests.

THE POLITICAL ALLOCATION OF RESOURCES AND OPPORTUNITIES

What is directly at stake in politics emerges from an examination of the political, or public, sectors of most countries. Generally speaking, in most of the advanced non-Communist countries, the public sector directly involves approximately 40 percent of the national income or 35 percent of the gross national product.[1] Since about one-third of the capital stock of a modern society (roads, school buildings, research laboratories, and the like) is now in the public sector, roughly one-third of the

[1]Roughly speaking, the *gross national product* (GNP) is the sum total of all goods and services produced in a country, measured in current prices. The *national income* (NI; or net national product, NNP) is calculated by subtracting from the GNP the sums required for replacement and amortization of the worn-out capital equipment of the society—amounting to between 10 and 20 percent of GNP in highly developed countries—and by adding or subtracting the net gains or losses from dealings with the rest of the world. In the case of some advanced countries, such as Britain, the gains from foreign trade and services may amount to as much as 5 to 10 percent of GNP. For further discussion, see Paul Samuelson, *Economics,* 10th ed. (New York: McGraw-Hill, 1976).

wealth of society is directly at stake in the politics of highly developed non-Communist countries.

As for employment, the public sector directly controls between one-twelfth and one-eighth of the jobs or the work force. In Communist countries, the public sector involves roughly two-thirds of the national income or the gross national product and often more than half of the work force. But since most Communist countries still have a large agricultural work force (working on collective farms or on agricultural cooperatives, as in the Soviet Union, or even on small owner-operated farms, as in Yugoslavia or Poland), the Communist countries have a mixture of public employment, cooperative employment, and self-employment.

The indirect stakes of politics are larger. Politics can make the difference between inflation and deflation by determining price levels, the values of people's savings, employment levels and employment opportunities, and the chances of vertical mobility, of moving up or down in society. Politics also can make the difference between more racial or religious discrimination or greater equality. Politics affects all aspects of life and even life itself. It affects the look and the smell of our cities. It affects the safety and the dignity of people in the streets. It affects our experience of justice or injustice. It affects our lifestyles and our life expectancies. In 1968 politics in the form of foreign policy was one of the ten principal causes of death in the United States. One of its operations, the Vietnam War, in that year killed about as many Americans as were killed by criminal homicide. For every American killed in 1968 by lawless violence at home another American was sent to his death in Southeast Asia by the lawful operation of the political system. This politically caused death rate, moreover, was highly concentrated among young men between the ages of nineteen and twenty-six. By mid-1975 a combination of political protests and changes in voter opinion had produced an end to the war. If political processes earlier had brought on the war in Southeast Asia and later expanded it, further political processes had ended it.

All these results of politics are produced by the interplay of the political process with the entire society. What happens to all of us happens because of the continuous and pervasive interaction of political behavior and political decisions with the economic, sociological, and cultural patterns of society—those habits, practices, and institutions that we so often and so superficially consider nonpolitical.

POWER: A NET AND A FISH

There are, as we noted in Chapter 1, at least eight values that most people desire: power, respect, rectitude, wealth, health, enlightenment, skill, and affection. Each of these values forms one of the basic stakes of politics. Let us begin with power.

Power can be thought of as the instrument by which all other values are obtained, much as a net is used for catching fish. For many people, power is also a value in itself; in fact, to some people it is often the prize fish. Since power functions both as means and end, as net and fish, it is a key value in politics. But it is a key value only in the context of other values, because people do not live by one value alone.

Power has been defined by Robert Dahl as the capacity to change the probability of outcomes. Another definition is that power is the participation in decisions about severe sanctions, that is, about major rewards or deprivations; this definition is preferred by Harold Lasswell. In either case, *power* is the ability to make things happen that would not have happened otherwise. In this sense it is akin to causality, that is, to producing a change in the probability distribution of events in the world. And since the world is changing already, power deals with the change of change—or second-order change. Thus power involves our ability to alter changes already under way that would continue without our intervention.

Influence and Power. Hand in hand with the subject of power goes the question of influence. If we ask who has power in politics, we also ask who has the most influence. Lasswell defines politics as "the study of influence and the influential," and he defines influence as participation in decisions about relatively milder sanctions. Based on this definition then, influence is a broader and milder form of power. Other writers use the words "influence" and "power" nearly interchangeably. Influence, however, also has a special aspect. Often we think of influence as involving some appeal to the thoughts and feelings of the person to be influenced. *Influence* then tries to get inside the personality of a person, whereas power operates on him or her mainly from without. If either Henry Kissinger, Arthur M. Schlesinger, Jr., or John Kenneth Galbraith were disfranchised in a congressional election because he had moved just before it was to be held, he still could *influence* the results of the election through his writings, but without a vote he would have no *power* to affect the outcome. Although not everyone who has influence has power as well, everyone who has power also has influence.

To say that the essence of politics is power and influence is only partly true. Short-run politics and short-run history are the story of changes among the *elite*—the few who currently hold most power. In the long run, however, the greatest developments in history are brought about by changes among those who are believed to be powerless—by changes in the needs, habits, and actions of the many.

Dimensions of Power. When we study power, we must ask about several things: *who* has what *resources* to exercise power *where* and over *whom,* in regard to *what,* with what probable results, and at what costs to themselves? A careful look will explain this list and expand it to eight points.

First, who are the *power holders?* Or is it just one person, and is that individual single-minded or ambivalent, like Shakespeare's Prince Hamlet? If it is a group—a committee, a party, an elite, or a large body of voters—how well are they united? Do they know how to use their power and for what aims? Can they keep their purpose firm? (More on these questions will be found in Chapters 6 and 7.)

Second, what are the *power resources* or *power bases?* What means of power do the power holders have: soldiers, police officers, weapons, money, means of information and persuasion, control over other matters valued by people in order to make them follow the power holders' wishes or will? (The political theorists Hans Morgenthau, Harold Lasswell, and Klaus Knorr have written on this question.)

Third, over what *domain* is power wielded, that is, over what geographic *area* and what group of *persons?* Is it just a small town or district, or is it an entire country? Does this power apply just to some group of people, such as the members of a particular party or religious denomination, or to everybody in an area? (On this point and on the next three, work has been done by Harold Lasswell and Harold Kaplan.)

Fourth, what is the *scope* of this power? To what sectors of behavior does it apply? Only to preventing violent crimes, or also to paying income taxes, sending children to school, obeying safety laws, and avoiding race discrimination?

Fifth, what is the *range* of this power? What is the greatest reward these power holders can bestow, and what is the worst punishment they can inflict?

And now we come to the results. Sixth, what is the *weight* of this power? By how much can it change the probability of a class of outcomes? If a president supports some bills before the national legislature, but not others, *how much of a difference* does this support make for their chances of passage? (Here the main ideas have been developed by Robert Dahl.)

Seventh, at some point the weight of two contending persons or groups may seem to be evenly balanced, each having about the same chance to win the decision. But where is that point of balance located? We may call this the *issue point* of power. Between 1910 and 1920 in the United States, an issue point was women's right to vote. In the 1970s the issue point promoted was equal treatment in women's right to be employed, paid, and promoted in accordance with their training and their work. The issue point had shifted in their favor, indicating that the political power of women in the United States had to some extent increased. When power holders are strong, they can keep the issue point at questions that do not matter much to them, far away from their more urgent needs. They may keep those arrangements that are very important to them entirely out of the debate. Thus the central desires of strong power holders may be kept off the overt political agenda, and even their marginal desires may prevail over the urgent needs of their weaker rivals. Only when their weaker adversaries gain strength will the latter be able to put their needs high up on the list of public issues. (This aspect of power has been stressed by Peter Bachrach and Morton S. Baratz, and it is included in Jerry Hough's interesting study of the Soviet Union, which includes some comparisons with the United States.[2])

Finally, all power has some *cost.* By how much do power holders have to change their own behavior and their own time schedule and program for action in order to impose the kind of behavior they desire on someone else? Even if the power holders prevail, what does it cost them in resources spent, damage suffered, plans and actions changed, and opportunities missed? In the end, are the costs smaller or larger than the gain?

[2]Peter Bachrach and Morton S. Baratz, "Two Faces of Power," *American Political Science Review,* 56 (December 1962), 947–52, and *Power and Poverty* (New York: Oxford University Press, 1970); Jerry Hough, *The Soviet Union and Social Science Theory* (Cambridge: Harvard University Press, 1977), pp. 212–15.

Power over Nature; Power over People. Power consists mainly in power over nature and in power over people. These two kinds of power often interact. Throughout history it has turned out that when people increase their power over nature, they use this greater power as a means of increasing their power over others. When people learned to tame horses, they became riders and used their new fighting skill as riders to subjugate others. When the Assyrians and Egyptians learned to irrigate and to control rivers, this power allowed the centralized monarchies in Assyria and Egypt to pile up the agricultural surpluses that maintained the bureaucracies and armies of these huge irrigation states. In more modern societies, the development of ships to cross the oceans (and later planes to cross the skies) often was transformed into power over colonies and colonial peoples, and sometimes into power over the poor and oppressed in the home countries of the nations whose rulers set out to conquer the world.

These two kinds of power differ in important ways. Power over nature is something human beings can share. Power over people is something for which people must compete. Machiavelli said that a prince who advances another prince's power diminishes his own. Put in mathematical terms, Machiavelli and thinkers in his tradition have seen power as a zero-sum game. A *zero-sum game* is defined as a game in which the payoffs to all players add up to zero; it is a special case of a fixed-sum game, in which all payoffs add up to a constant sum. Whatever one competitor wins in a zero-sum game, he or she can win only from the losses of a rival, so that any one person's winnings must come out of the losses of others. A zero-sum game is a merciless form of competition. What is good for one player must be bad for some other player. And insofar as power in politics is of this competitive, Machiavellian, zero-sum character, the contest for power is without end or mercy. Fortunately, power is not only of this kind.

Power over nature is something that humankind can collectively increase and has increased for the last half-million years. It is a *variable-sum game,* one in which by definition players compete with one another, but all can win jointly at the expense of the bank, namely, nature. We all have been winners from increased power over nature, from the development of vaccines, irrigation, dams, and other great contributions to human life. By the same token, of course, people also can lose jointly to nature as they have lost in countries depleted by famine, pestilence, pollution, or exhaustion of resources.

Even within human society, people can share in the positive by-products of increases in power over other people. It is possible to increase such power to the degree that people can expand their capacity to act, to do things, to coordinate their behavior, or to comply with other people's wishes. Moreover, a tyrant ruling a million powerless illiterates has less power to affect the outcome of many events than a democratic ruler governing a million high school graduates, because the high school graduates can do more things than the illiterates. It is not merely the greater education that enables the high school graduates to do more. Equally important is the greater experience a democratic country gives its people in making decisions and thinking and acting for themselves.

One of the most important questions of political analysis, therefore, is whether a particular power situation is primarily a zero-sum game or whether it is possible to discover variable-sum aspects within it, so that different players can all win or improve their positions jointly.

Power and Voting. Whether a power situation is primarily a zero-sum game or a variable-sum game, it is useful to know how the chips of power are divided up among the various participants. As a simple example of the distribution of power, we can ask: who has the vote? At the beginning of the century only about 25 percent of the American adult population could vote. In 1976 there were 147 million persons aged eighteen or older in the United States. Registered voters numbered 98 million. Therefore, 49 million adults—or nearly one-third of all adults—were, for all practical purposes, disfranchised. They were unable to vote on election day even if they wanted to. People are effectively disfranchised through a host of different institutional arrangements, registration laws, residence requirements, and time-consuming procedures for registration. Such requirements and procedures in effect disfranchise not only many poor, but also many well-educated professional people, employees, and students, who change their address—as do about one-sixth of the American people every year.[3] The situation has been made worse by the curious habits of southern registrars in the presence of black voters or the habits of northern registrars in such riot-torn cities as Newark, New Jersey, where the majority of the population is black, but the majority of registered voters is white. In addition to the 49 million disfranchised adults living in our country, there are another 11 million adults who are registered voters, but who disfranchise themselves by not taking the trouble to vote.

Those who are enfranchised and do vote are typically members of the upper-income and middle-income groups, particularly those who stay put in their localities and those in small towns and on farms. The actual voters are also the older people. Voting is heaviest among those over thirty-five, and the median age of the American voters is about forty-five. The young may or may not want to trust people over thirty, but to win an election, one must swing people of the median age of forty-five.

[3]Between March 1975 and March 1976, 17.1 percent of the population one year old and above moved to a different house within the United States. The residence requirements for voting in a presidential election have been removed in many states, so these people are not formally disfranchised, but the discouraging effect of cumbersome procedures remains. In many other democracies, voter registration is universal and automatic, and the share of disfranchised adults is much smaller.

It is these voters, then, who may decide whether the United States shall fight a war in Southeast Asia or the Middle East or whether the United States is to outrace the Soviet Union in increasing its supply of intercontinental nuclear weapons. The male students who in 1968 rang doorbells for Senator Eugene McCarthy in the New Hampshire primary had to shave and get haircuts and the female students had to wear dresses in order to win 42 percent of the vote for their candidate and to bring about the retirement of Lyndon B. Johnson from the presidency. They had, in effect, to persuade the economically comfortable, home-owning, white voter of forty-five. Many of these same young workers were instrumental in bringing about the presidential nomination of Senator George S. McGovern in 1972, by providing enough support to help win a majority of delegates to the Democratic convention that year. They did not succeed, however, in winning the trust of a majority of voters, including many Democrats. In the 1976 elections many of the same people worked for Jimmy Carter and later entered his administration on many levels, but by then President Ford had also won appreciable youth support for his campaign.

In a representative democracy the young are a permanent minority. Young men and women between eighteen and twenty-four constitute over 12 percent of the total population and 18 percent of the voting-age population. But because so many of the young change their residence or take jobs or go to college away from home and do not bother to cast absentee ballots or sometimes even to register, only about 13 percent of the actual voters are in this age group. This compares with about 42 percent of the actual voters who are over fifty years of age. Foreign policy is often shaped, therefore, by ideas that were internalized twenty or thirty years ago by voters who are now over forty-five and possibly over fifty. Thus, through the workings of the electoral system, the views and preferences of the older generation enjoy a disproportionate influence over the lives of the young (see Figure 2.1).

This state of affairs is nothing radically new, but in a mass democracy it becomes more serious in a period when international relations as well as domestic politics are rapidly changing. In the 1960s, with draft laws in force during the Vietnam War and no votes for those under twenty-one, young people's lives were at stake in the foreign policy decisions of the United States. After the mid-1970s, with the draft replaced by a volunteer defense force and international tensions reduced (sometimes called *détente*), these stakes were less visible. But they are still there—and some people are talking about bringing back the draft. Politics may change and young people still may think about using their vote: the lives they save may be their own.

If democracy is to be made more viable as time goes on, people will have to find ways of improving such representation. Perhaps the most radical among the young will revive an idea of John Calhoun, a conservative nineteenth-century statesman who developed the notion of *concurrent majorities.* According to this view, a national law should be valid only if it is also backed by a concurrent majority of the representatives of the section most directly affected, such as the South in Calhoun's day; today such groups as the young, the poor, or the big-city dwellers might qualify as concurrent majorities. Perhaps somebody will think of a better idea. But it is clear that the present method of representation, though it has worked well for many things and in many respects, has serious imperfections. Much remains to be improved. Indeed, we may have to look for some improvements quickly.

By 1972, eligibility for voting had been extended to all citizens eighteen years old and over, but many of the cumbersome registration procedures were left unchanged. In 1976, of 12 million newly eligible persons in the age group of eighteen to twenty, 5.7 million, or 47 percent, registered and 4.6 million, or 38 percent, actually reported voting. The effect of their votes seems to have been not very great, but if other conditions should prove favorable, the long-term effects of the addition of this new group of voters might be far-reaching.

Motives and Opportunities for Power. Other inequalities in the distribution of power stem from differences in motivation and in opportunities. Often a group that is disadvantaged and partly powerless will be disappointed when it first tries to exercise power. When its attempts to exercise power prove unsuccessful, many of its members will conclude that such efforts are not worth the trouble. They will either lapse into apathy or turn toward an extreme radicalism that will prevent them from cooperating with others of more moderate views—who are apt to be more numerous. Whether they stay at home and say that there is nothing to be done or isolate themselves at some far end of the political spectrum, the disappointed group will cease to be politically effective. Thus, the very groups that are denied power are the most vulnerable to the loss of motivation needed to get the power they lack and perhaps ought to have.

Of course, among those motivated to claim a share in power, not all have equal opportunities to do so. Even if everyone were sufficiently equal in power to get a favorite candidate automatically placed on the ballot, some of us would be "more equal" in power than others. The candidates of some persons or groups would be more likely to

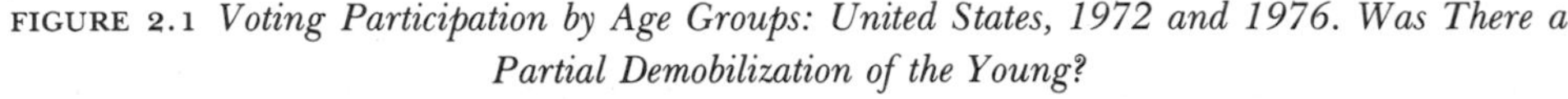

FIGURE 2.1 *Voting Participation by Age Groups: United States, 1972 and 1976. Was There a Partial Demobilization of the Young?*

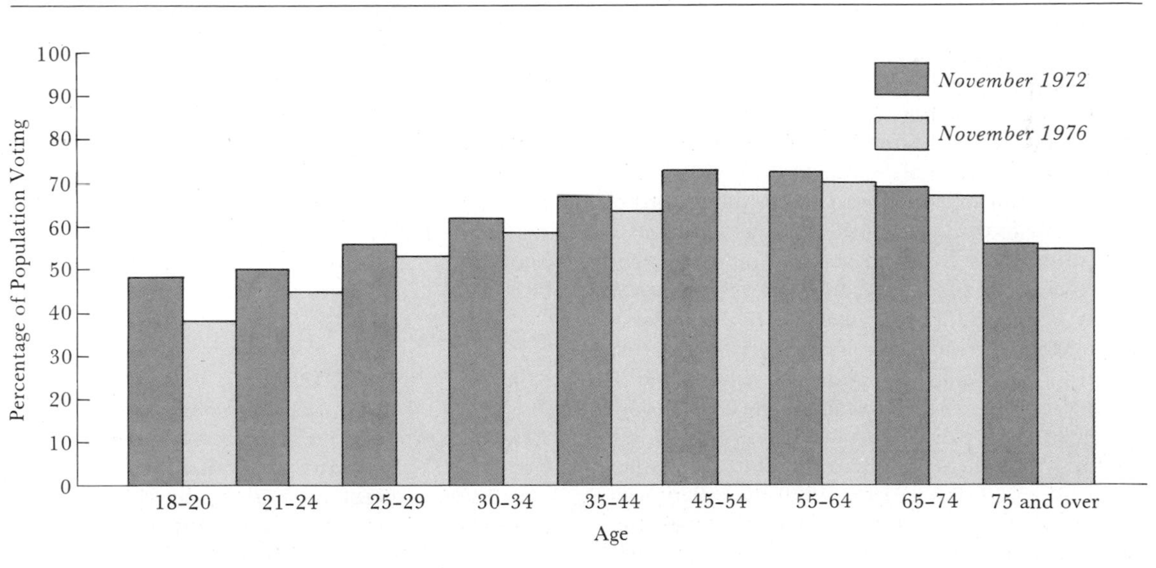

Source: U.S. Department of Commerce, Bureau of the Census, *Current Population Reports*, ser. P–20, nos. 244 (1972), 322 (1978).

win the election because of the power or influence of the persons or groups supporting them. The party machines and party financiers would certainly have their say. The higher costs of television, printing, labor, and many services needed in political campaigns have dramatically increased the potential power of those who control large sources of money.

The mass media would have their say as well, since they determine a great deal of what the voters see and hear and read. The owners of the media, their advertisers, and their staff members (who often have a different point of view from that of the owners or advertisers) would all have a disproportionate influence on the election's outcome. Thus, even within a representative democracy, the political preferences of a truck driver from Jersey City or a stenographer from San Francisco carry less weight than the preferences of a network newscaster or a top executive of Ford or General Motors. Power and influence make that difference.

The Test of Reality. The more powerless a group is, the more important it is for its members to study the significance of power and to seek ways of getting more. But the more powerful its members become and the more power they acquire, the more important it becomes for them to study the limits of power.

What determines the outcome of the actions of all those who can vote, nominate, elect, pass laws, and administer them—in short, of all those who have power? There is an ultimate test: external reality. A government can have the power to pass a tariff, but the world economic situation may determine what actually happens after the tariff is passed. An administration can initiate an economic policy, but the world may produce a run on the nation's currency that may throw national finances into disarray. From 1973 to 1979 the inflationary rise of prices in the United States and the decline of the dollar in the money markets of the world were providing vivid reminders of this possibility. A nation may start a military action in some distant country, but what then happens there may make a great difference to the policy that originally looked so well-conceived. Or a nation's voters and legislators may refuse to reduce foreign oil imports, but the consequences of this kind of nonaction may turn out to be quite serious.

There may also be a difference between the power to force outcomes on other groups and the power to produce change in oneself or one's group. Psychologists have spoken of the difference between power *over* people and power *with* people. The latter is the power to coordinate, to pull a group of people into phase, so that their efforts reinforce each other. So long as the mutinous sailors on the *Bounty* could not coordinate their actions, Captain Bligh was irresistible. Once they managed to coordinate their efforts, Bligh was out of a job. If they could have coordinated their activities even better, they might have reached a more comfortable island than Pitcairn.

The power to promote mutual coordination and cooperation among people may help them to discover their own strength, as well as many other things. In such a widening context of discovery and sensitivity, power can be used to serve creativity, to aid the production of new combinations of thoughts and actions that are relevant to the needs of the people concerned. When this happens, power becomes not a self-narrowing or self-defeating force, but an instrument of human liberation.

SOME OTHER STAKES

Respect. Respect, and the accompanying status, prestige, and authority, is a value that is perhaps even more sought after than power. Relations among races, among cultural, ethnic, or religious groups, between management and labor, between generations, and among nations in the world all involve the allocation of respect. This value seems intangible, but is not. Its results are readily observable. *Respect* involves the precedence given to people, the priority given to their messages, and the preference given to their wishes. Indirectly respect affects employability, trust, career chances, and the likelihood of society's responding to people's needs. The more respected a group is, the better off it is likely to be. The more that respect is denied a group, the worse off the group is apt to be.

In the short run, disadvantaged groups are often denied respect. In seeking to obtain their rights, they, in turn, often deny respect to those who are privileged in relation to them. Thus we find young white policemen calling mature black men "boys" and young black men calling policemen "pigs." Here a denial of respect that was originally one-sided has become mutual. Sometimes the pursuit of respect can be a zero-sum game in which there is very little respect available in the community and every one of the struggling groups despises the other: during the 1960s and 1970s in New York City, Boston, and elsewhere, embattled local black and white groups had screamed insults at each other. But sometimes the pursuit of respect can be converted into a variable-sum game in which a society is able to grant a reasonable amount of respect to everybody and to find ways in which everyone can get a reasonable priority for his or her *urgent* needs and can be heard at least a reasonable part of the time.

Rectitude. Respect (or deference) often is closely related to a third value at stake in politics: that of *rectitude* or morality. Rectitude can be a competitive zero-sum value. In a conflict between two quite different and equally intolerant ideologies, each group of adherents may believe that all members or adherents of the other are heretics, maniacs, traitors, deviationists, class enemies, or spawn of the devil (depending on each group's favorite invectives) to be repressed, expelled, or even murdered. The ability of a more tolerant society to find room for and to maintain several varieties of views of rectitude can convert the pursuit of rectitude into a variable-sum game.

Of course, there are limits to such mutual accommodation. As Abraham Lincoln pointed out, a wolf may have one definition of freedom or righteousness; and a sheep, another. In a modern industrial society, it is very likely that people will develop more than one religion, more than one philosophy, more than one ideology. The problem of permitting people to act righteously in terms of their own conscience in a society in which not everybody shares the same views of righteousness is crucial to the survival of modern societies.

Conflicts over different views of rectitude are frequent in politics. For centuries, many churches, including the Roman Catholic church, assumed a rightful claim on the government for support from public funds. But according to the principles of the United States Constitution and the Bill of Rights, this is wrong; rather, it is thought just that church and state should remain separated. Discussions about the kind and extent of public financial support for religious schools (such as parochial schools) and for services for their pupils (such as school lunches and bus transportation) have involved not only an argument about money from the public budget, but also a clash between principles of rectitude.

Other conflicts about rectitude that have influenced recent politics and legislation abound: is abortion, and hence the various state laws permitting or forbidding it, right or wrong? Is the heart of this problem simply the right of every woman to control her own body, or is the unborn child also a person with a right to be protected? And if the latter is so, at what point in time should such a right of an unborn person start? How stringent should be the ethical standards to which public officials and legislators are held? What activities and sources of income should be considered incompatible with their office? (See Chapter 10.) If a soldier is ordered by a superior to do something that is against the law, should the soldier obey the superior or the law? If citizens believe that their government is waging an unjust war, should they support the government or oppose the war?

Often the black-and-white, either-or logic of conflicting ideas of rectitude tends to make compromises seem immoral, so that political conflicts become intractable. In the complicated gray world of reality, simple crusading beliefs in one's own righteousness sometimes may do more harm than good. Yet many of our feelings of right and wrong—our conscience—are a part of our personality and of our integrity as individuals. We are divided within ourselves if we fail to follow the dictates of conscience, and we may feel diminished as persons if we do not stand up for our beliefs. By contrast, a belief in rectitude may add to one's action more strength of motivation and singleness of purpose than almost any other value. Some great political leaders have been able to retain great moral strength without becoming fatally self-righteous and unrealistic. Gandhi of India and Abraham Lincoln and Martin Luther King of the United States might be examples.

Wealth. Many conflicts about respect and rectitude are intensified by poverty and eased by wealth. Quite often it is possible to create more opportunities for respect and rectitude, and even for power, if there is more wealth in a society. Because it is difficult (and possibly dangerous) for an automobile driver to decide at a traffic crossing whether at any given moment the east-west or north-south traffic should have priority, a society may use a police officer or a stoplight to determine which of the two lines of traffic is to be permitted to move. A richer society can build an overpass, thereby permitting both traffic streams to proceed at full speed, without the presence of a police officer. This is one case that fits Karl Marx's prophecy that in a more abundant economy the government of people would be replaced by the administration of things. Here indeed the enforcement of law is replaced by the maintenance of concrete—and it works.

Wealth, then—the total supply of goods, services, and facilities and resources for production—is a decisive variable for the range of options before a society. In 1976 the world had an estimated average per capita gross national product of $1,651. These data cover 140 countries, or over 95 percent of the world's population. But it is perfectly clear that world income is unequally distributed. The 1976 United States per capita GDP[4] was more than $7,900. At present, one-twentieth of humankind, the people of the United States, has about one-fourth of the world's income; and one-seventeenth, the people of the Soviet Union, has one-eighth (see Figures 2.2 and 6.8). As will be discussed later, this relatively high income for the world has not prevented long-lasting poverty for many of its countries. Even a high average income of people within a highly developed country does not necessarily prevent persistent poverty among the poorest of its regions and social strata, while prosperity often is distributed relatively evenly among the upper and middle strata.

World income is steadily increasing. The average growth rate in real terms—that is, in goods and services—in the world is 2 percent per capita. (In paper money the figures are, of course, often higher, showing the effect of rising prices. After the devaluations of the dollar in 1971–78, the national incomes of Japan, Germany, the Soviet Union, and some other countries did not change in real terms, but their dollar values rose by more than 30 percent.) Although starting points have been fantastically unequal in different nations, present growth rates vary far less. This fact affords some comfort, for it means that in terms of proportionate income levels, world inequality is not increasing rapidly. If one country is only

[4]*Gross domestic product* (GDP) is the same as GNP except that net imported wealth—such as foreign public subsidies and foreign private investments—are excluded.

one-tenth as rich as another and the incomes of both are growing at the same rate, the ratio between the two incomes will remain unchanged. But though there is little or no change in relative terms, the absolute gap between rich and poor countries is widening. If a country with a $200 per capita income doubles its income in twenty-five years, it will have $400, whereas the United States will go from $7,900 to $15,800. Proportionately, the difference will be the same. In absolute figures, the gap will have widened enormously.

It is important to see whether it is possible to achieve a gradual reduction of inequality in the world at large, as has been done inside most of the modern countries. Figures for a dozen countries are given in Table 5.1 (pp. 126–27). For most countries, even some of the highly developed ones, figures have not yet been computed; however, from the mid-1950s to the mid-1960s, the sketchy available data suggest that in many countries the share of the top 10 percent of income receivers has increased to the relative detriment of the poorer 90 percent. In a highly unequal country the top 10 percent receive half the income or more. In the United States the top 10 percent receive perhaps 28 percent of the income if we count families as units and perhaps 34 percent if we count individual income receivers. In India the richest 10 percent of individuals got 40 percent in 1964; in Chile, 41 percent in 1968; and in Brazil, 49 percent in 1970. In a more egalitarian, non-Communist country like Sweden, the share of the top tenth in 1970 was 28 percent. If 2 or 3 percent of the income should continue to move out of the top sector each decade, by the end of the century only about 24 or 25 percent of income in the United States may be going to the top tenth of individual income receivers. (Their relative share of income will thus have declined; however, thanks to general economic growth, their absolute income will have increased greatly.)

Governments and the political process play an ever larger role in the growth and redistribution of income within each country. At the beginning of the century the federal government of the United States received as revenue about 4 percent of the national income, and state and local governments collected another 7 percent, adding up to a total of 11 percent. In 1976 the federal government and its agencies gathered about 20 percent of the national income, and state and local governments got roughly another 15 percent, making a total of about 35 percent. That is, every year during the past eight decades, about one-third of 1 percent of the national income has moved into the government sector. The data for France, Britain, India, China, and the Soviet Union are similar.

Health. Wealth to a certain extent can buy *health* and *well-being.* It is closely related to life expectancy and to the economics of living and dying. In a comparison of sixty-seven countries in the early 1960s, about 75 percent of the variance in life expectancy could be predicted from their respective per capita gross national products. By 1975, with data for 140 countries available (including many very small ones), the variance accounted for by per capita GNP had dropped to 29 percent. It seems that, on the one hand, some newly rich, oil-exporting countries had not yet developed health services commensurate with their *average* income (of which the poor majority of their population still received very little) and, on the other hand, several not very rich Communist-ruled countries, ranging from China and Cuba to Bulgaria and Yugoslavia, already had made considerable efforts to improve public health. In poorer countries life expectancy at birth is low. In 1975 it was forty years in Afghanistan and forty-four in Nepal. For females it was thirty years in Mali during 1970–75 and forty-one in India during 1951–60, in contrast to seventy-eight years for females in Sweden (1970–75). In the United States in 1975 a newborn female had about a seventy-seven-year life expectancy if white, but only about a seventy-two-year expectancy if black. Yet the matter of life expectancy is not entirely dependent on economics alone. The Japanese, whose national per capita income is but four-fifths

FIGURE 2.2 *Power and Income of 119 Nations. 1975*

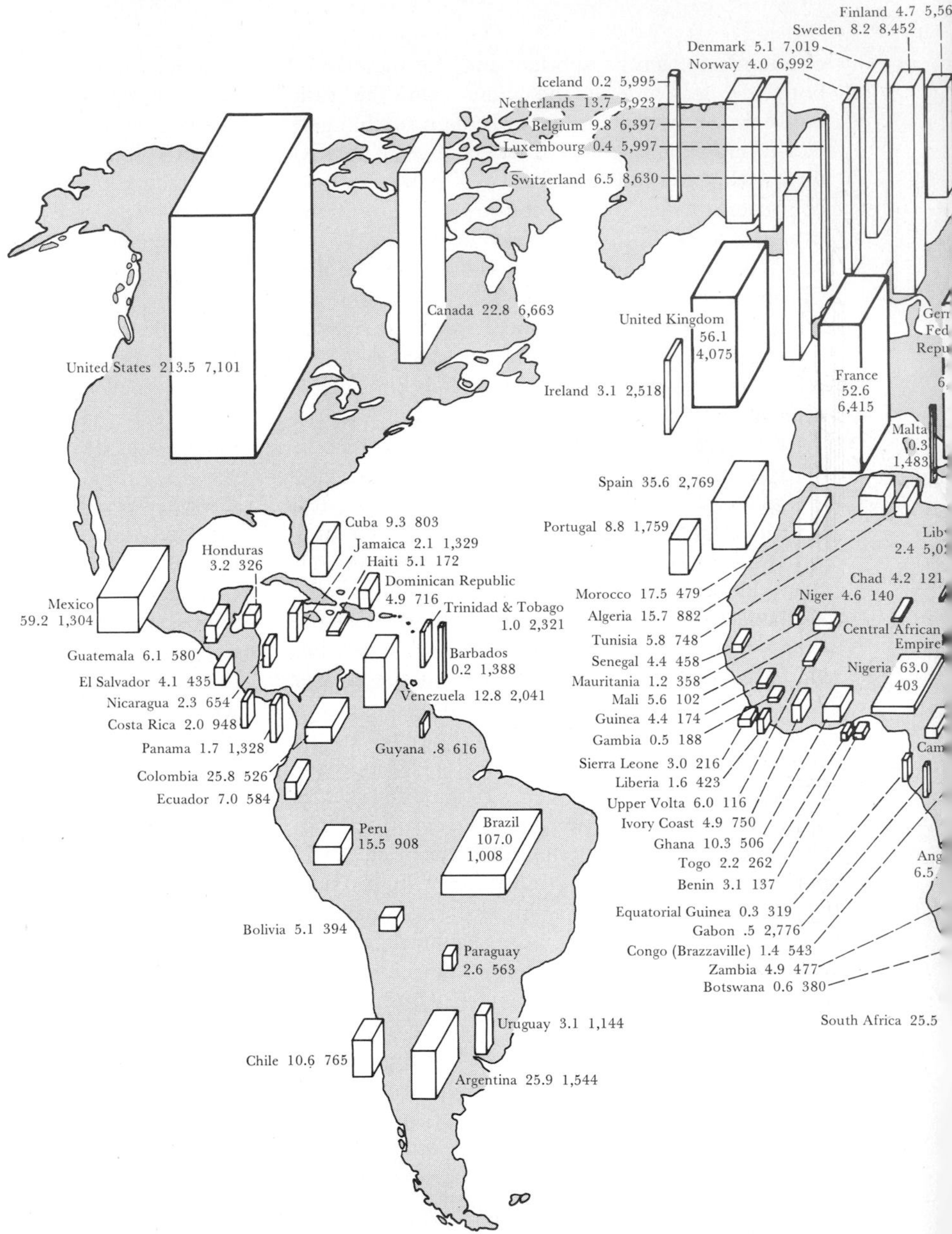

Top area of each brick corresponds to national population; height corresponds to per capita GNP; and volume corresponds to total GNP. With very few exceptions, per capita GNP indicates a nation's level of economic and technological development. Total population *times* per capita GNP gives the total GNP of each country, and it indicates most often its potential power. Each block in the diagram shows at a glance, therefore, the potential power of a nation and its two main components: population and level of development.

Sources: Adapted from K. W. Deutsch, *Nationalism and Social Communication* (Cambridge: MIT Press, 1966), by permission of MIT Press; Ruth Legar Sivard, *World Military and Social Expenditures, 1978* (Leesburg, Va.: WMSE Publications, 1978), pp. 22–29.

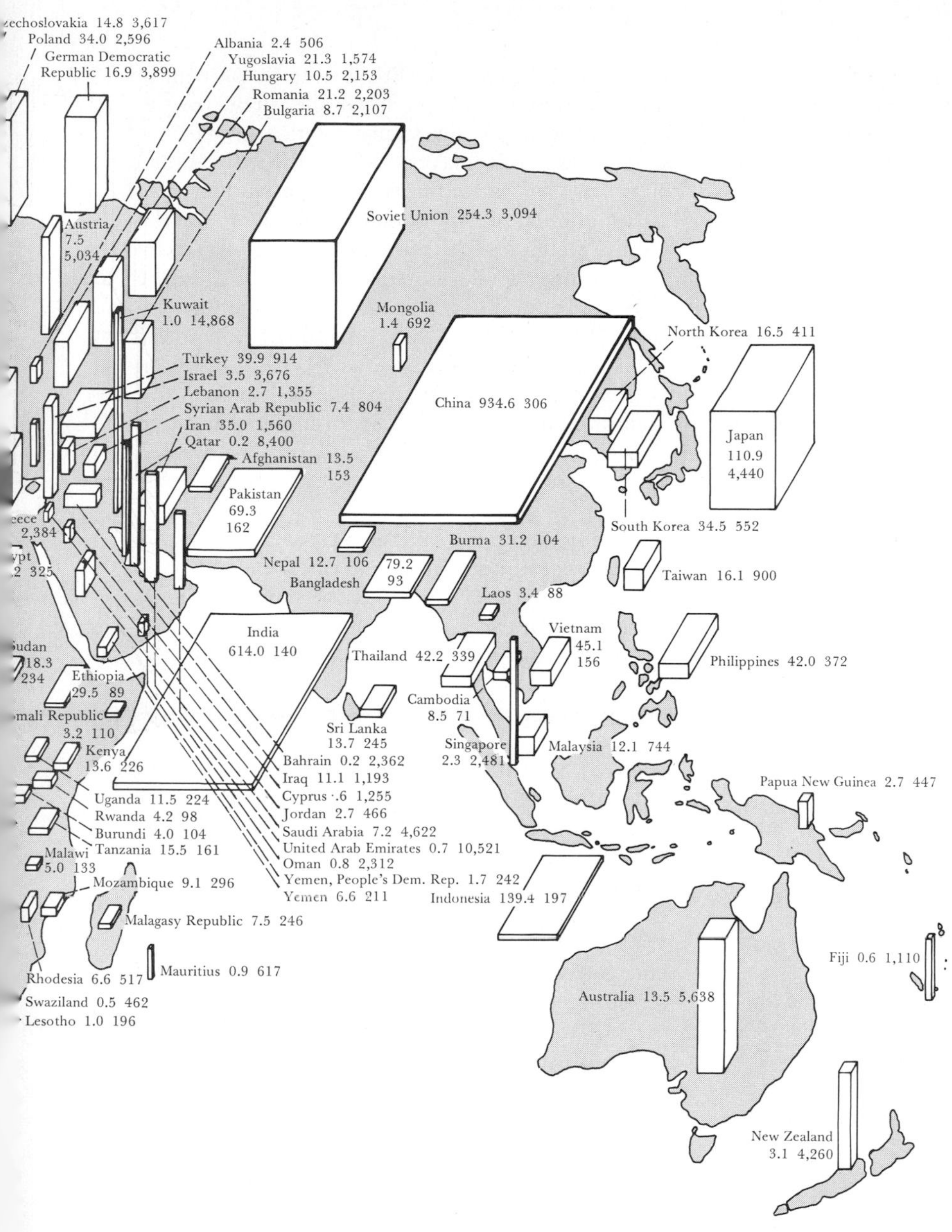

echoslovakia 14.8 3,617
Poland 34.0 2,596
German Democratic Republic 16.9 3,899
Albania 2.4 506
Yugoslavia 21.3 1,574
Hungary 10.5 2,153
Romania 21.2 2,203
Bulgaria 8.7 2,107
Soviet Union 254.3 3,094
Austria 7.5 5,034
Kuwait 1.0 14,868
Mongolia 1.4 692
North Korea 16.5 411
Turkey 39.9 914
Israel 3.5 3,676
Lebanon 2.7 1,355
Syrian Arab Republic 7.4 804
Iran 35.0 1,560
Qatar 0.2 8,400
Afghanistan 13.5 153
China 934.6 306
Japan 110.9 4,440
Pakistan 69.3 162
South Korea 34.5 552
eece 2,384
ypt 2 325
Nepal 12.7 106
Bangladesh 79.2 93
Burma 31.2 104
Taiwan 16.1 900
Laos 3.4 88
udan 18.3 234
India 614.0 140
Vietnam 45.1 156
Ethiopia 29.5 89
Thailand 42.2 339
Philippines 42.0 372
mali Republic 3.2 110
Cambodia 8.5 71
Sri Lanka 13.7 245
Singapore 2.3 2,481
Malaysia 12.1 744
Kenya 13.6 226
Bahrain 0.2 2,362
Iraq 11.1 1,193
Cyprus .6 1,255
Jordan 2.7 466
Saudi Arabia 7.2 4,622
United Arab Emirates 0.7 10,521
Oman 0.8 2,312
Yemen, People's Dem. Rep. 1.7 242
Yemen 6.6 211
Papua New Guinea 2.7 447
Uganda 11.5 224
Rwanda 4.2 98
Burundi 4.0 104
Tanzania 15.5 161
Malawi 5.0 133
Mozambique 9.1 296
Indonesia 139.4 197
Malagasy Republic 7.5 246
Fiji 0.6 1,110
Mauritius 0.9 617
Rhodesia 6.6 517
Australia 13.5 5,638
Swaziland 0.5 462
Lesotho 1.0 196
New Zealand 3.1 4,260

of that of the United States, and the Dutch, whose national per capita income is considerably lower than that of the United States, have higher life expectancies than Americans. The difference can be attributed to politics. Japan and the Netherlands both have national health programs; the United States thus far does not. Since 1975 health care is supplied to all residents of the United States over sixty-five years of age on a voluntary insurance basis under the Medicare and Medex programs. Welfare recipients and poor people can be provided with health services under the Medicaid program. This still excludes, however, most of the employed population of working age and their children. Objections against including the entire population in some national health service center on fears of exploding health costs and inflation and of the creation of a new unresponsive bureaucracy; too, some successful doctors are apprehensive of losing income—in contrast to other (often younger) physicians who hope for better chances of employment through national health care. Significantly, conservative parties in Britain, Sweden, and elsewhere have all accepted national health services once they had been introduced and have administered them with only minor modifications. In no recorded case has a country abolished its national health service once it had tried it—but the changes in political and budgetary habits that a national health service would introduce to the United States still seem considerable.

Enlightenment. Wealth also buys *enlightenment.* A comparison of eighty countries in the early 1960s showed that about two-thirds of the variance in their levels of literacy is predictable from per capita incomes. By the time of a 1975 study of 140 countries, much of that correlation had disappeared. Some of the reasons probably are the same as those mentioned for health. But there is also a simpler reason: much of the world by now has become literate. Greater differences between rich and poor countries now survive mainly at the levels of secondary and higher education. In 1975, however, mass literacy levels among people fifteen years of age and older ranged from 1 percent in Gabon and 7 percent in Ethiopia to 99 percent in the United States and slightly higher in northwestern Europe. There are similar contrasts regarding college and university students—the educational elite. In 1977 the number of these students per 1,000 population amounted to about 46 in the United States, 18 in the Soviet Union, 16 in Japan, 14 in France, 11 in England and Wales, 10 in the German Federal Republic and the German Democratic Republic, 9 in Spain, 8 in Brazil, 4 in India, 1.2 in the People's Republic of China, 0.6 in Ghana, 0.4 in Nigeria, and 0.2 in Ethiopia and Malawi.[5] Thus, the availability of higher education also varies with national income, but less so than the existence of health or of literacy at the mass level.

In short, though wealth is important, it does not decide everything. In the areas of health and enlightenment there are genuine political choices to be made at every level of national income; and the quality of life in each country is determined to a significant extent by the political choices that its people make.

Skill. The availability of *skill* also varies greatly among countries, regions, and ethnic groups. One reason for this variance is politics. Black Americans for a long time have been excluded from apprenticeship in many skilled trades, particularly in the construction industries. Some unions, such as those of the automobile workers, steel workers, and garment workers, have welcomed them and encouraged their training. Since the early 1970s, the full and free access of minorities to all skilled trades in the United States has been an explosive political issue. To a lesser degree, immigrant or foreign labor has been used mainly in unskilled trades in Britain and the German Federal Repub-

[5]Data for 1977 from UNESCO, *Statistical Yearbook, 1978,* table 5.1, pp. 346–89, and *United Nations Demographic Yearbook, 1978,* table 5, pp. 137–41. Only 1962 data are available for the People's Republic of China.

lic, and there, too, political disputes have arisen over the practice.

In a more general sense, skill is involved in the composition of a national work force and is affected by public policy, both directly and indirectly through the educational system. Some nations let their schools teach enlightenment, but neglect skill. Other countries try to make a large portion of their people skilled. In the most advanced countries, unskilled and uneducated labor is becoming unemployable. The training of young high school dropouts is becoming increasingly a task of government.

Affection. An even greater range of choice and uncertainty applies to the last of the basic values that are at stake in politics. This is the value of *affection*—the value that, in the form of friendship, Socrates believed to be at the basis of all politics. (Centuries later, Saint Augustine wrote that a population becomes united into a people by having a common object of their love.) But affection cannot be bought by money, nor can it be compelled by power. It must be given freely; and it can be won only by a process of wooing, communication, help, and understanding. Affection among people from different regions, groups, and backgrounds still is an essential element in making a political community. It can be learned in common experiences that are meaningful and rewarding to all partners, but the speed and nature of its coming cannot be predicted. Politics can do much to destroy it and something—though much less—to encourage it. But where politics does succeed in its efforts at healing, conciliation, and accommodation, the resulting growth of affection among individuals and between them, their government, and their political institutions is one of the most important prizes of the political process.

VALUE ENJOYMENT: SECURITY AND LIBERTY

In addition to these substantive values, people also desire certain ways of enjoying them. One of the primary stakes of politics is the manner in which any value can be enjoyed. There are perhaps two such ways. As we noted in Chapter 1, if individuals enjoy a value, they usually like to have it in *security,* so that they can count on continuing to enjoy it. Ever since the rise of the state, people have used political organizations to protect social arrangements, persons, and property. The more unequal or unjust the society was, the heavier the machinery necessary for protection. Slave-owning societies used the state to protect and perpetuate the institution of slavery. Societies badly divided into rich and poor have used the state in part to preserve this unequal division.

But at the same time, security has required the protection of values other than wealth and power. As cities have grown and population density has increased, public health has needed additional protection, for protection against epidemic is a common interest of all social groups. As industrialization has progressed, the efficiency of the technology and the economy also has needed increased protection. The more elaborate and improbable the methods of production have become, the more important it has been to safeguard the conditions necessary for the continued functioning of this delicate technological and economic structure. In 1979 the earth had approximately 4.4 billion people on it, about twice as many as could be fed by earlier, traditional methods of agriculture. We could not now keep alive a large part of humankind if we did not have modern technologies and modern economies. The control of pollution, the protection of the natural environment, the preservation of clean air and water, and the conservation of needed metals, sources of energy, and sources of food on land and sea—all have been added in recent years to the more urgent responsibilities of governments. Thus, humankind's security, health, and essential supplies of food and energy are now partially a task of the political sector.

We also like to enjoy a value in *equality.* "As I

would not be a slave, so I would not be a master," said Abraham Lincoln. Extreme inequality is distasteful to many of us. Even if we happen to be on the highly favored side, it may cut us off from many human contacts and choices and from the friendship and affection of many people. In this sense extreme inequality functions like a cage, whether it be the iron cage of destitution or the golden cage of privilege. A higher degree of equality offers us a greater chance of mobility—geographic, social, and economic. How young people struggle for the freedom to fall in love across the barriers of rank and class has been a topic of folk tales and world literature for many centuries. Moderate inequality, however, is accepted in most nations and cultures as long as it does not function as a fatally frustrating barrier to choices and communication. Moderate rewards, though inevitably unequal, may serve as recognition of achievement and spurs to further efforts. In this sense, the values of security and equality lead us not to questions of "either-or," but to that of "how much?"

It is easier to praise equality in words than to ensure it in practice. When women and racial minorities are victims of discrimination, they may require *affirmative action* to better their condition. Affirmative action means that governments insist on some observable test of performance by public or private institutions or business firms, proving that they have indeed offered adequate opportunities to disadvantaged groups for employment, promotion, or admission to their services. Affirmative action has been criticized for aiming not merely at equality of chances, but also at somewhat lesser inequality of results. If one picked Olympic teams only by athletic prowess, should we sometimes send an all-black team in certain specialties? Conversely, if one race or group should be particularly good in answering multiple-choice tests, should all other groups be excluded from a particular medical or law school? But what of the weaker students admitted or the slower candidates employed in the name of justice to women or some race, and what of the superior candidate thus by-passed in the competition for scarce jobs or study places? Until the early 1970s, American practice tended to favor the superior candidates regardless of the narrowness of tests for selection. In the 1970s, fixed quotas sometimes were instituted for members of disadvantaged groups in order to make sure the groups received "their share." By mid-1978 an important decision by the United States Supreme Court, *Bakke* v. *University of California at Davis,* pointed toward a compromise. Universities and employers may continue to take racial balance into consideration as one of the factors in their admissions policy—and, by implication, legislatures may continue to demand that they do so—but race (or sex) may not be the only consideration for admission or employment, and therefore no rigid quotas may be based on it. It remains to be seen how this new principle will be worked out in practice; and comparable questions continue to arise in other nations.

Similar questions of "how much?" and "what kind?" lead us to the third and perhaps most important human value: *liberty.* This, too, is not only a value in itself, but also a key to enjoying other values. Whenever we are desperately poor in regard to some other value, we may be inclined to forget liberty or to postpone it. But whenever we are even slightly better off, we will strive for it again.

Liberty may mean many different things to different people. In different times and places, even the same people have felt one aspect of liberty to be more relevant to them than others. (For this reason, the great conservative thinker Edmund Burke claimed that it was more useful to speak of specific "liberties" than of liberty in general.)

In the days of Adam Smith, toward the end of the eighteenth century, the most salient aspect of liberty seemed to be a negative one: the *absence of restraint.* A century later the simple absence of a prohibition sounded to many like a mockery. Thus, the French writer Anatole France noted,

"The law in its majestic equality prohibits the rich as well as the poor to sleep under bridges, to beg in the streets, and to steal bread." France and others realized that the removal of unjust laws did not necessarily lead to justice, particularly when the conditions underlying the laws remained unequal.

Since the end of the nineteenth century, liberty has been defined not merely as the absence of restraint, but as something positive: the *presence of opportunity*. It is not enough to be told that you are not forbidden to drive an automobile: if you are to take advantage of this liberty, there must be an automobile available for you to drive.

Another positive aspect of liberty, stressed by the German philosopher Hegel in the early nineteenth century, is the *capacity to act*. To give a driver's license and an automobile to a blind person would not be helpful. He or she also would have to be given sight. Capacity to act implies at least a minimum of physical health and strength, of sensory equipment and mental health, and of psychic motivation. Individuals, social groups, and whole populations may suffer from malnutrition, disease, or the shock of war or oppression to such a degree that their capacity to act may be temporarily impaired even though they are free from external restraint and are in the presence of real opportunities.

Closely related to the presence of opportunity and the capacity to act is the availability of an effective *range of choices*. The richer, more meaningful, and more rewarding the choices before individuals, the freer they are. These choices must be meaningful to the people who have to choose; that is, they must correspond to their needs and memories. But to be both meaningful and rewarding to most people, such choices must include possibilities of employment, availability of capital equipment, and opportunities to obtain information and enlightenment.

All four of these dimensions of liberty contribute to a fifth aspect that we experience personally and directly. This fifth aspect of liberty is *spontaneity*, that is, the ability to act in accordance with one's own personality, without having to make a great effort at self-denial or self-control and without being subjected to external constraints. This refers to the compatibility of the choices offered with the personality structure of the chooser. It relates to how well the available choices fit one's particular, personal needs and often the particular culture with which that person has become familiar, in which he or she has grown up, and which has become part of his or her personality. Since spontaneity to so many people is the essential part of liberty, and since it is so closely tied up with culture and familiarity, the existence of a sense of spontaneity has sometimes masked the absence of real liberty. Rousseau noted this when he observed that the Poles felt free so long as their nobles were Polish; when their nobles began to emulate French fashions and culture, the Poles called them tyrants. Thus, a regime that was familiar seemed congenial and, therefore, acceptable. But spontaneity means more than acting in harmony with the familiar. It also means the opportunity to change one's mind—and to change it freely, even playfully, without narrowing external constraints of political pressure or economic scarcity and without excessive internal constraints of one's own personal anxieties, ideology, or culture.

In sum, liberty involves the opportunity for *many-sided cumulative growth*. Liberty means a sequence of choices and steps such that one ends up having more choices than before; fewer restraints; more present opportunities; an increased capacity to act, think, and choose; and a wider play of spontaneity. What we call government and politics—the flow of compliance and defiance, of support and opposition, of rewards and penalties, of permissions and prohibitions—play a decisive role, but not the only role, in making possible such a creative or liberating sequence of developments.

Clearly, politics can make a difference. It determines much of the allocation of resources and opportunities, up to one-third or one-half of the wealth of many nations, and corresponding shares in other values. Every major value can be at stake in politics: power, respect, rectitude, wealth, health, enlightenment, skill, and affection. And politics can decide much about the manner in which we may enjoy our values—whether in security and liberty or not.

But politics can do still more. Ideally, politics is engaged in a triple game to maintain humanity's chances of life, to enhance and improve them in this age of ideological rivalry, and to change the unjust distributions of values toward more viable, more just, more ethically acceptable distributions, suited to our growing up in the industrial age and in the age of high information that follows it. Finally, politics has the task of developing forms of coordination and public self-control—forms that will enable people to make sure that what ought to be done, and can be done, will in fact get done while there is still time.

KEY TERMS AND CONCEPTS

gross national product (GNP)
national income (NI)
power
influence
elite
issue point
zero-sum game
variable-sum game
détente
concurrent majorities
respect
rectitude
wealth
health
enlightenment
skill
affection
security
equality
affirmative action
liberty
absence of restraint
presence of opportunity
capacity to act
range of choices
spontaneity
many-sided cumulative growth

ADDITIONAL READINGS

Banfield, E. *The Moral Basis of a Backward Society.* Glencoe, Ill.: Free Press, 1958. PB

Brown, H., et al. *The Next Hundred Years.* New York: Viking Press, 1966. Chaps. 5, 6, 18. PB

Cole, H. S. D., et al., eds. *Models of Doom: A Critique of* The Limits to Growth. New York: Universe Books, 1973. PB

Herrera, A. O., et al. *Catastrophe or New Society? A Latin American World Model.* Ottawa: International Development Research Centre, 1976.

Jain, S. *Size Distribution of Income.* Washington, D.C.: World Bank Publication, 1976.

Lane, R. E. *Political Life.* New York: Free Press, 1959. PB

Lasswell, H. *Politics: Who Gets What, When, How?* Cleveland: World Publishing, 1958. PB

———. *World Politics and Personal Insecurity.* New York: Free Press, 1965. PB

———, and A. Kaplan. *Power and Society: A Framework for Political Inquiry.* New Haven: Yale University Press, 1950. PB

Meadows, D. H., et al. *The Limits to Growth.* New York: Universe Books, 1972. PB

Mesarovic, M. D., and E. Pestel. *Mankind at the Turning Point: The Second Report to the Club of Rome.* New York: Dutton, 1974.

Oppenheim, F. *Dimensions of Freedom.* New York: St. Martin's, 1961. PB

Rapoport, A. *Fights, Games, Debates.* Ann Arbor: University of Michigan Press, 1960.

Russett, B. M. "The Revolt of the Masses: Public Opinion on Military Expenditure." In B.M. Russett, ed., *Peace, War, and Numbers,* pp. 299-319. Beverly Hills–London: Sage, 1972.

Ward, B., and R. Dubos. *Only One Earth.* New York: Norton, 1972. PB

PB = *available in paperback*

III

The Participants in Politics: Who Does What with Whom

Who participates in politics? Let us go back to Lasswell's notion of politics as the study of influence and the influential. The quickest and cheapest way to find out what a country is likely to do when facing a major decision is to ask its top official. In the United States the person to ask would be the president; in Britain it would be the prime minister. But to know what policy countries are likely to adopt, it is not enough simply to ask their presidents or prime ministers what they think they can do politically. One also has to know what support their preferred policy is likely to get from the heads of their executive departments and from the top officials under them.

When the president of the United States wants to get something done, he needs the cooperation of one of his administrative agencies to draw up a plan of action, and he needs people and facilities to put the plan into effect. If the head of the agency and its top-level officials are unenthusiastic about the plan, they can consume a remarkable amount of time going through the motions of carrying it out without actually doing so. Several presidents have ordered the Department of Defense to insist that all major defense contractors follow fair employment practices by allocating a proper share of jobs to qualified blacks and members of other minority groups. Specifically, the department was told to withhold contracts from firms that failed to comply within a reasonable time with the government's standards. To date, these orders are still awaiting full implementation, and many blacks, including people trained in skilled trades by the armed services themselves, are still waiting to be hired.

In many ages and countries, chief executives have similarly depended on the people around them to carry out their wishes. In the 1770s and 1780s, King Louis XVI of France wished to bolster the finances of his government, which was tottering into bankruptcy. Twice he appointed bankers—first Turgot and then Necker—to reduce expenditures and increase government income by collecting taxes from the nobles and clergy. Both men were thwarted by the opposition of these two groups and of the courtiers surrounding the king. Both men were dismissed; the government eventually went bankrupt; France fell into revolution; and the king was beheaded, as were many of the courtiers who had influenced and controlled his decisions.

Monarchs, presidents, and prime ministers thus depend on a number of individuals for advice and for implementation of their policies. They depend on their cabinets, on the permanent undersecretaries in the various departments or ministries, on the top people in the civil service, on the top people in the military, on the top people in the various interest groups, and, under constitutional systems of government, on the heads of important legislative committees. Taken together, all these add up to what we call the *top elite*.

Dictators, too, usually depend on a top elite of key people who surround them. On the surface, one person may seem to rule, as Hitler and Mussolini claimed to and as Stalin appeared to. Or the highly visible rulers may be a small committee, such as the Politburo of the ruling party in a Communist country or a military junta of Latin American officers. Behind the scenes, however, such conspicuous rulers depend on their chiefs of police, the commanders of strategically located military units, the chief propagandists and heads of the mass media, the top-level bureaucrats, the leaders of political and cultural mass organizations, and the heads of the main economic, financial, and technical organizations, firms, and interest groups.

Most of the major industrial and financial enterprises in non-Communist countries are owned, of course, by private corporations. In Communist countries they are owned by the state. But in either type of country their top managers are likely to be influential and, therefore, to belong to the top elite.

TOP ELITES AND MID-ELITES

Who Are the Top Elites? Members of the top elite are frequently identifiable by the so-called *position method*. That is, they fill positions so strategically located in the decision-making system of a country that, unless they are unusually incompetent, they are fairly sure to have considerable influence. These people control the decisive traffic intersections of the message flows and communication streams of government. Those who decide whom the president sees, for instance, his top White House assistants, belong to the top elite. Between 150 and 200 incumbents of such top positions—in government, in the major political parties, in the major interest groups, and in the major occupational divisions—daily make decisions for millions of people.

In Western-style democracies these groups are free to oppose each other openly. In Communist countries, such as the Soviet Union, a single party has all the publicly acknowledged power. In such countries, the people who want more money spent on rockets must bargain behind the scenes with those who want more money spent on artificial fertilizer so that all can unanimously vote an agreed policy at the public session of the Supreme Soviet. Thus, before such public ceremonies, there is a good deal of bargaining, negotiating, and even wire-pulling and applying pressure.

Some non-Communist countries, too, are governed by a single party or else by a party that is so much stronger than the others that it virtually rules the country. The people of Mexico, India from 1947 to 1977, and Turkey between 1920 and 1960 have concentrated most of the visible power in the hands of a single party, whose leaders accordingly hold an important place among the top elite. In all such countries, however, the top elite also includes other members, military or civilian, who owe their position mainly to groups other than the ruling party.

The top elite can also be identified by *reputation*. The question here is not who has the top job, but who has the reputation of making the decisions. It may be that the individual in the top position who signs a particular decision or decree or act or bill, is simply a rubber stamp, signing whatever the first assistant puts before him or her. In time the word will spread among the knowledgeable that the real power in a particular department rests not in the hands of the chief, but in those of the first assistant or of someone even further down the line.

In American history the personal friends and informal advisers of a president have been called, usually by those who did not like them, the president's "kitchen Cabinet," in contrast to his officially appointed Cabinet. Historians and contemporaries frequently have argued among themselves about the membership and influence of kitchen Cabinets, raising such questions as whether Harry Hopkins had as much or more or less to do with the formulation of President Roosevelt's foreign policy than Secretary of State Cordell Hull. Students of the reputed top elite of the United States in the mid-1960s would have had to include in their list the names of two Washington lawyers, Clark Clifford and Abe Fortas, both of whom were said to have had much influence within the administration of President Lyndon B. Johnson. Clifford later became President Johnson's last secretary of defense, and Fortas was appointed by the president to the Supreme Court, where he served for a short time. The influence of some of President Nixon's advisers—such as Henry Kissinger in foreign affairs and H. R. Haldeman, John Ehrlichman, and John Mitchell in domestic matters—was widely publicized in the early 1970s. Kissinger became secretary of state in late 1973. Mitchell served for a time as President Nixon's attorney general. Subsequently Haldeman, Ehrlichman, and Mitchell were convicted on grave charges of illegal actions in the Watergate scandal. In the Carter administration Charles Kirbo, a lawyer from Atlanta, Georgia, and Bert Lance, a banker from the same state, were prominent as close advisers, and Clark Clifford continued in that role, as he had in earlier administrations. In every administration in the United States during this century, people of reputed influence have frequently wielded great power, and the same is true of other countries insofar as we can tell from our knowledge of their political processes.

The set of people identified as the top elite by position usually overlaps with the set of people so identified by reputation. In only a few marginal cases do people in top jobs possess less influence, and others more, than their formal titles would lead one to believe. Taken together, there are roughly fifty top elite members per million people in Western-style democracies such as the United States, Britain, France, and the German Federal Republic. In a country of 220 million like the United States, about ten thousand people constitute a fairly broad *top elite*. Cutting this down by another factor of ten, to five per million, we could try to list the *central elite*—the one thousand most influential people in the United States. Knowing the views of these one thousand would enable us to predict reasonably well what might or might not be acceptable in politics during the next few months or even during the next year or two. Selecting the top one hundred elite members might not be quite enough for a country the size of the United States. Even the most influential hundred people would yield an imperfect prediction, and any number much smaller than one hundred probably would yield little or nothing reliable.

The top elite in the Soviet Union possibly could be similarly determined, but it might be a little broader. About fifteen thousand people would correspond in importance to the ten thousand in the United States. For a nation of 50 million people—or about one-fourth the population of the United States or one-fifth the population of the Soviet Union—the comparable top elite might be between one-third and one-half of the United States figure. For a still smaller country, such as Switzerland or Denmark, with about 6 and 5 million people respectively (or between one-thirtieth and one-fortieth the size of the United States), one still might have to include among the top elite about one-fifth to one-fourth of the American number. In any country, no matter how small, the top elite probably would amount to not much less than 100 or 150 people. We do not know, however, whether a smaller number of elite members would suffice in a small but poor country, such as Ecuador, Cambodia, or Tunisia. There is reason to think that this may be so, particularly if only a small portion of the population took part in politics, but the matter requires more research.

These, then, are the people in every country who already have their hands on the levers of power. They acquire their position and influence because they are acceptable to, and have the confidence of, a good many of the members of a broader elite. In the United States there is a handy yardstick for measuring this latter kind of elite. The people who publish the fat volumes of *Who's Who in America* every two years say they pick 3 people for every 10,000 in the total population. This corresponds to 300 per million population, or 3 out of about 6,000 adults. *Who's Who* lists well-known writers, artists, and other public figures. Its editors make a special point of saying that it lists only creditable achievement. This excellent work of reference is therefore probably deficient in listing the top personnel of the Mafia, although some Mafia members may have considerable power in politics.

We may think of the different layers of the elite as if they were the officers of an army of political influence. In such an army, the voters—about one-half of the population—serve as private soldiers. Political activists function as sergeants, about one for every thirty to thirty-five voters. At the other end, the central elite corresponds to three-star generals who lead corps or armies, and the top elite is equivalent to two-star generals, each of whom leads a division of at least fifteen thousand voters. The larger elite at the *Who's Who* level

FIGURE 3.1 *The Pyramid of Influence, 1976*

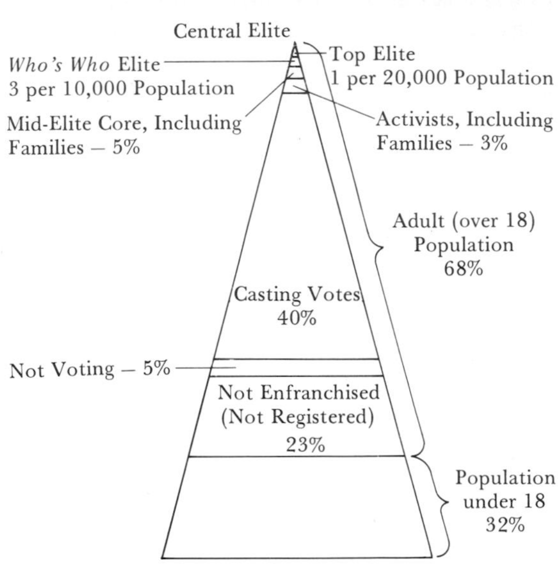

parallels the colonels and lieutenant colonels, with about one for each regiment of about two thousand voters. A lower layer of the elite then corresponds to the lower-ranking commissioned officers. It is these "lieutenants" of the voters and the social system whom we call the *mid-elite*. The *pyramid of political influence* is shown in Figure 3.1.

Is There Really a Mid-Elite? The mid-elite is a statistical artifact. It is obtained by taking a sample of the total electorate such as the Gallup or Harris polls would construct and then, as a result of this sample, selecting the top 5 percent of the adult population in income, education, and occupational status.[1] As shown in Figure 3.2, these three catego-

[1]Occupational status distinguishes professional and managerial occupations, self-employed persons, white-collar and clerical occupations, skilled labor, farmers, unskilled laborers, and other occupational categories. Professionals, managers, and high-level self-employed are potential elite members.

ries will not completely overlap. Those persons who are in the top 5 percent on all three tests form the *core of the mid-elite*; and they have fairly good reason to be content with their condition.

Those for whom one or two of the three tests are negative may be thought of as belonging to a *marginal elite*. In one sense they belong to the elite, but in another they do not; and often they feel somewhat discontented. On the whole, people whose educational rank is much higher than their income tend to be somewhat more critical of existing relationships; they tend to be liberal or radical in their political beliefs. People whose income is significantly higher than their education also tend to be dissatisfied with their status and prestige, but usually they are more to the right of center in their politics.

Allowing for these differences and incomplete overlaps, we can say that the views of the top 5 percent of a country's adult population, as identified by some combination of income, occupational status, and educational level, would tell us a good deal about what was and what was not politically acceptable in that country.

But would these statistical artifacts or constructs help us to discover living, acting groups or strata in politics? How closely do such statistics correspond to reality? The answer is a question of fact, to be discovered by research, and it will vary among different periods and countries. In most countries it is fairly difficult to carry through a policy against the desires of the mid-elite. It can be done, however. A great deal of the reform legislation of the 1930s, together with some of the legislation of the 1960s, was probably rejected by a majority of the core of the mid-elite and by the top 5 percent of income receivers, although significant minorities in these groups may have backed it.[2] The marginal mid-elites, however, were probably divided: the top 5 percent of voters representing the most highly educated people in the United States quite likely were on the side of the reforms. Thus, on these political issues the educational and income elites disagreed. Most of the time, however, when there is no acute crisis or major reorientation, the top 5 percent on all three criteria show a higher degree of consensus, and their views are therefore quite important.

Nevertheless, there is some reason to think that often there is a real difference between the political thinking and behavior of the mid-elite and that of the mass of the voters. When school desegregation was ordered by the United States Supreme

FIGURE 3.2 *Core and Marginal Groups in the Mid-Elite*

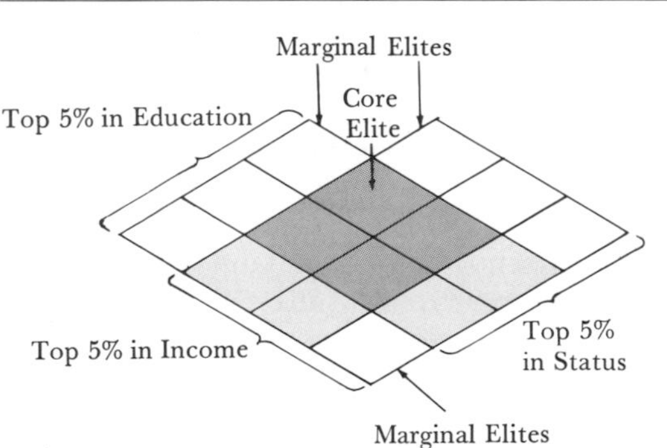

[2]Before the 1936 presidential election in the United States, the *Literary Digest* polled a sample of telephone subscribers (who included most of the mid-elite) about their political preference. *Literary Digest* announced that the Republican candidate, Governor Alfred M. Landon, would defeat President Franklin D. Roosevelt by a landslide. Landon carried only Maine and Vermont; and shortly thereafter the United States had one magazine less. In November 1969 the Gallup poll telephoned 501 people on their responses to President Nixon's speech on the Vietnam War and reported that of the three-quarters of the telephone subscribers who had listened to him, 77 percent agreed with him or about 57 percent of the subscribers polled. This was then reported in some newspaper headlines as indicating the approval of 77 percent of the population—a prize example of inaccurate polling and reporting.

Court in 1954, members of the mid-elite in such states as Arkansas were more willing to comply with the law of the land than were many of the rank-and-file white voters. This limited the power of the mid-elite. Even where there is little or no such difference and where voters and mid-elite agree, this may be because the mid-elite simply shares the feelings of the voters or else because the voters have chosen to follow the lead of their "betters." Either way, it may be important to know what the mid-elite in a country or city will accept, because such knowledge may tell us what the top elite can afford to do today and what the voters may approve tomorrow.

WHO ELSE COUNTS IN POLITICS?

The Relevant Strata. In former times and places one did not have to reach farther down into the social body than the top 5 percent—or at most the top 10 percent—to find out what could not be done in politics. In the last third of the twentieth century this has changed. One must dig more deeply into the social body. For centuries the concept of *politically relevant strata* was important; today it is indispensable. What are the strata of the population that count in politics? Who must be taken into account in order to prevent a policy from turning out to be utterly unrealistic or completely disastrous in domestic politics?

In most countries today, the politically relevant strata include more than just members of the various elites. Dock workers in Lagos or London or New York are not elite members but by going on strike at a crucial moment they can make a major difference to the economic or even the political life of their country. The same is true of railroad personnel or the workers in large enterprises or key industries. During the brief period of liberalism in Czechoslovakia in 1968, it was of decisive importance that the workers in the most important large factories voted in their meetings to support the liberalizing policies of the Czechoslovak Communist government and its dismantling of much of the old Stalinist machinery of repression. They threw their weight to the side of the students and intellectuals who were pressing for preserving and continuing the more liberal course, and they continued to do so throughout the rest of the year, even after these policies were halted from the outside through the entry of the Soviet army into their country. Although policies may change, these strata continue to be relevant.

In representative democracies, registered voters who actually vote are part of the politically relevant strata. In the United States in 1976 about 40 percent of the total population actually cast votes; 5 percent did not vote even though they were registered voters; another 23 percent were not registered; and about 32 percent were below the age of voting. (In developing countries, with higher birth and mortality rates, as much as 50 percent of the population may be less than twenty years old. The 87 million who cast their votes in the 1976 presidential election were politically relevant. And perhaps another million people, although not voting, took part in politics in some other way. They also can be considered politically relevant people. These two groups combined, these 88 million voters and participants, constituted 41 percent of the total U.S. population, then numbering 215 million (see Table 3.1).

In the Soviet Union the 1974 voting-age population was about 172 million, or 68 percent of the total 253 million. About 162 million, or 64 percent, were registered voters, and almost all of them dutifully cast their votes on election day. Thus, the number of voters exceeds the number of people making up that nation's politically relevant strata (see Table 3.2). We can determine these strata through the following calculations: roughly speaking, 60 percent of the Soviet population—or 157 million of the 1978 total of 261 million—live either in cities of over twenty thousand or in small towns. Hence about 96 million voters live in cities or towns. To stay in power, a Soviet regime needs the

TABLE 3.1 *United States: Presidential Election, 1976**

	Numbers in millions (rounded)	Percentage of total population	Percentage of voting-age population
Total population	215	100.0	—
Voting-age population	147	68	100
Registered voters	98	45	67
Actual votes in election	87	40	59
Registered voters who did not vote	11	5	7
Disenfranchised population (population of voting age not registered to vote)	49	23	33
Population below voting age	68	32	46

Source: U.S. Department of Commerce, Bureau of the Census, *Current Population Reports*, ser. P–20, no. 322 (1978).

support of much of this urban population. Within these cities and towns approximately one-sixth of the total population, or 9 percent, may not be capable of forming an effective part of public opinion because of age or health or lack of social connections, and perhaps an additional one-sixth may not be interested. But two-thirds of the urban voters, or 40 percent of total voting-age population in the Soviet Union, are politically relevant adults. By adding to these 69 million relevant urban voters about 20 percent of the rural population—that is, another 23 million—we obtain approximately 92 million people who make up the politically relevant electorate. If a Soviet government is well advised, it keeps an eye on the mood and behavior of those 92 million. Its politically relevant electorate is thus about 35 percent of the total population. Curiously, the share of the total population that politicians need to watch carefully is between 35 and 45 percent in both the United States and the Soviet Union.

In Western Europe, where there is automatic registration of voters, where there are few or no conspicuous racial minorities, where populations are relatively homogeneous, and where high levels of literacy have existed much longer than in either the United States or the Soviet Union, the politically relevant strata are likely to include between 40 and 55 percent of a country's total population (see Table 3.3).

Activities and Activists. Of course, being relevant in politics does not mean being active in politics. Ithiel Pool and his collaborators have proposed six tests for identifying the political activist. An *activist* is a person (1) who is a member of a political organization; (2) who gives money to a political organization or candidate; (3) who frequently attends political meetings, whether of committees or of larger groups; (4) who takes part in electoral campaigns; (5) who writes letters on political topics to legislators, political officeholders, and/or the

TABLE 3.2 *Electoral Participation in the Soviet Union and China (Elections to the Supreme Soviet, 1974–USSR; Local People's Council Election, 1956–China)*

	Numbers in millions (rounded)		Percentage of total population		Percentage of voting-age population	
	USSR	CHINA	USSR	CHINA	USSR	CHINA
Total population	253	628	100	100	—	—
Voting-age population	172	356	68	57	100	100
Actual voters (= registered voters)	162	308	64	49	94	86
Nonvoting adults	10	48	4	8	6	14
Population below voting age	81	272	32	43	46	76

Sources: *Current Digest of the Soviet Press*, vol. 26, no. 25 (1974); *Statistical Yearbook 1976 for Member Countries of the Council for Mutual Economic Assistance*, table 3, p. 10; Leo A. Orleans, *Every Fifth Child*, pp. 62, 126 (adjusted); *Union Research Service*, vol. 9, no. 22 (1957), p. 335.

press; or (6) who talks about politics to people outside his or her immediate circle of family or friends. Pool and his collaborators consider a political activist to be anyone who fulfills at least three of these six conditions. Employing these not very stringent tests, we can count 3 percent of the population in most countries as political activists. This seems to be the case in a number of Western countries. Not all activists are members of the elite, however. On the other hand, all political activists belong to the politically relevant strata—unless their views are so far removed from current opinion that they cannot find any significant group of supporters or allies.

In China, the Soviet Union, and other Communist countries the situation is somewhat different, since the Communist parties try to encompass the great majority of political activists. At the beginning of the 1960s, Communist Party membership ranged from 2.5 percent of the total population of China to more than 15 percent in North Korea. The Soviet Communist Party in 1976 contained about 16 million members, about 6 percent of the Soviet population. In these countries party members are expected to talk politics to their coworkers, donate money in the form of party dues, and attend meetings—frequently. In short, they fit all the tests proposed by Pool and his collaborators. Their numbers are more than doubled by the inclusion of members of the Communist youth organizations, an additional 7 percent in the Soviet Union and 20 percent in demographically more youthful China. Of course, few Communist countries can equal the degree of activism shown by the 17 million Red Guards during China's Great Proletarian Cultural Revolution of the late 1960s; but at the very least, when some of the young men and women and all the party members are included, about one out of every ten persons in these countries can be counted in the activist ranks.

This high proportion of activists shows, in part, what makes Communist systems different in so many ways from other political systems. Communist governments encourage more intense politici-

TABLE 3.3 *Electoral Participation in the United Kingdom, France, and Germany (Parliamentary Elections, 1974–United Kingdom; Presidential Election, 1974–France; Elections to the Bundestag, 1976–German Federal Republic)*

	Number in millions (rounded)*			Percentage of total population			Percentage of voting-age population		
	UK	F	GFR†	UK	F	GFR†	UK	F	GFR†
Total population	56	52	62	100	100	100	—	—	—
Voting-age population	40	34	45	72	65	69	100	100	100
Registered voters	40	31	38	71	60	64	99	91	92
Actual voters in election	31	26	34	55	50	55	77	76	80
Registered voters who did not vote	9	5	4	16	10	6	22	15	9
Disenfranchised population (population of voting age not registered to vote)	0.5	3	7	1	6	11	1	9	16
Population below voting age	16	18	17	28	35	27	39	53	38

* All calculations based on raw data, not rounded figures.
† All figures exclude West Berlin.

Sources: UK: *Whitaker's Almanack,* 1978; *United Nations Demographic Yearbook, 1976,* table 7, p. 94. France: *Annuaire Statistique de la France, 1975,* chap. 10, table 2A, p. 122; *Annuaire Statistique de la France, 1976,* chap. 3, table 2, p. 20. GFR: *Statistisches Jahrbuch die Bundesrepublik Deutschland, 1978,* chap. 4, table 4.1, p. 82; *U.N. Demographic Yearbook, 1976,* table 7, p. 91.

zation and draw many more people into political life, particularly at the middle and lower levels of the social structure. Even though this political life is high in activity, however, it is modest in variety: there is less encouragement, it seems, for persons of top talent to compete for political leadership since there is only one effective political party, one acceptable policy or party line at any moment, and one path to the high levels of leadership—namely, co-optation by those who are already there.

The high level of activity, together with the unceasing demand for it by the ruling party and government, causes some discontent among some people who would like to have more time for their personal affairs or who would prefer to write their poetry, paint their paintings, or pursue their scientific research in a less political manner. But this same high level of activity may produce some valued results for the Communists and some personal rewards for many of the activists. Such rewards may range from promotion up the employment ladder in government or industry to gains in social standing and prestige and to the personal feeling of doing important work and of being needed and wanted. For these reasons, much of this political activism is voluntary. If we ask why the governments of the Soviet Union, China, North Korea, or Vietnam in critical times have shown political and organizational capabilities higher than many foreign observers had expected, part of the answer may be that they have more than three times as many political activists, mobilized by the ruling party or government, as do Western countries.

All this applies to a far lesser degree to countries where a Communist party or regime has failed to become popular with any major section of the population. Where a minority is small and politically isolated, even the most intense activity cannot make up for the lack of popular support. Communist or pro-Communist regimes collapsed easily in northern Iran in 1946 and in Guatemala in 1954, just as Communist guerrillas were defeated in Greece, Malaya, and the Philippines in the 1940s. A comparison of these failures with Communist successes elsewhere, such as in Yugoslavia, Cuba, North Korea, Vietnam, the Soviet Union, and China, suggests that the presence or absence of popular sympathies can be decisive for the success or failure of activist zeal.

Another condition, in addition to the rewards or encouragement that a society gives those who participate in political life, may very well influence the levels of political activity, particularly in highly developed Western countries. Political activists habitually spend time and attention (as well as other resources) on politics. The lower the opportunity cost of this time to them, the more willing they are to spend it on a political activity. *Opportunity cost* is the value of the alternative uses to which resources could be put. On the whole, a substantial business executive, a highly skilled surgeon, a successful lawyer, or a research scientist usually has very attractive opportunities for allocating his or her energy and working time. Very often a reasonable income affords that person attractive opportunities for allocating leisure time. Thus many members of the middle- and upper-income groups in most countries have a high opportunity cost of time. Moreover, in Western-style democracies, where personal affairs, consumer choices, and spontaneous and free behavior command a vital sector of activities, the pressure on people to do what the government wants them to do is less than in Communist dictatorships.

For these reasons, not many of the highly educated and well-to-do in affluent Western countries ordinarily put much time into politics. Neither do many of the poor, because they either lack motivation (having suffered too much, knowing too little, and being too busy keeping body and soul together) or lack rewards (having received too little satisfaction out of politics, as their earlier efforts were too often ineffective or the results disappointing). And even the poor take opportunity cost into account: a poor person might prefer watching television or visiting a bar to talking politics—particularly if politics in the past had not produced any speedy and visible improvements. The result is that only a minority of people become ward heelers, machine politicians, local committee members, or persons who run the affairs of small towns. Thus, the professional people on the one hand and the poor on the other are underrepresented in the day-to-day political process in many Western democracies, whereas many members of the lower middle-class, particularly long-time residents of local communities, choose such routine politics as one of their favorite indoor games.

Spurs to Political Action. In times of national emergency, real or imagined, the picture changes. Now the stakes of politics seem high indeed and may include survival. Many people, including some of great ability, put other things aside and transfer their attention and and energies to politics and public service. If the emergency is sufficiently dramatic, the old politicians and political machines may let the new talents enter because they need them. In other cases there may be a failure of response to the new situation: politics goes on as usual until things get drastically worse.

Of course, many people who usually do not put much of their time and attention into politics can be stirred up to do so even short of an all-out national emergency. As long as they are reasonably contented or only mildly discontented with the outcome of the political process, they will pursue nonpolitical interests. If, however, they find themselves seriously disturbed, these people may shift very large blocks of their time and resources into political activity. In this way the political process may become transformed. Mass unemployment in the 1930s pushed many industrial workers who had not been politically active in the mid-1920s into political activity. In response to the Great Depression and to the new political opportunities provided by the New Deal in the United States, there was not only increased union activity, but also a growth of labor political education committees, voter registration drives, and union voting in factories. As a result, a new element now had to be reckoned with in the American political process—the influence of labor.

Similarly, an acute wave of fear about urban riots or, in the words of the Republican campaign slogan of 1968, about "crime in the streets" moved a great many ordinarily nonpolitical middle-class and upper-class voters into politics and politicized an even broader stratum of suburbanites and lower-middle-class voters. One of the most powerful instruments ever invented for the politicization of students was the draft; some people might consider General Lewis B. Hershey, head of the U.S. Selective Service System during the Vietnam War, as one of the founding fathers of student politics in the United States.[3] Many students who ordinarily would have given much time and attention to other matters entered into politics because so many things of importance in their lives clearly depended on the outcome of the political process. With the end of that war and the abolition of the draft, student concern about war and peace became less active. Restoration of the draft might revive it again.

[3]Likewise in China, students in 1966 entered Red Guard groups in droves perhaps as much because career channels seemed closed to them as because Chairman Mao Tse-tung selected them to be his "small generals" in his struggle against bureaucracy.

The reduction of activism based on opposition to war among young people was shown in the 1972 election, in which, according to the Gallup poll, Senator McGovern, the clear-cut antiwar candidate, received only 48 percent of the vote from persons under thirty, while President Nixon, who had promised to end the war very soon but "with honor"—that is, while retaining his political objectives in Southeast Asia—received 52 percent.

If many different groups move into politics, they may use their new activities to paralyze and checkmate one another so that the outcome does not significantly change, or else they may succeed in coordinating their activities so that what one group does reinforces the activities of another group. Coordinated activities can transform, sometimes very radically, the outcome of the operations of a political system. To a considerable degree, they can even transform the structure of the system itself.

"POLITICS AS USUAL": A PLURALITY OF INTEREST GROUPS

Most of the time, most people are not highly active in politics. They leave this to specific interest organizations to which they delegate their representation. Many years ago student governments existed to represent the interests of students who were not active in politics, to complain from time to time about the food in the campus cafeteria and to exert some pressure for a bigger student activity building or for a marginal relaxation of dormitory rules. Recently, student governments have been doing a bit more. Farmers, union members and business organizations, as well as students, all have their own interest groups.

Indeed, most of the more elaborate political

systems from ancient times onward have contained some interest groups. The ancient kingdoms in the river valleys of India, Mesopotamia, and Egypt took into account two interest groups: warriors and priests. The warriors sought to become nobles, and the priests, or more exactly, their monasteries or temples, sought to become landowners. Similarly, ancient Chinese civilization distinguished scholar-bureaucrats from warriors. In many European countries further developments in the Middle Ages led to the rise of merchant interest groups and guilds of artisans. Occasionally, as in Britain, Norway, Sweden, and Switzerland, yeomen, free farmers, or peasants organized as interest groups with some representation in the political process.

From the nineteenth century on, industrialists have been a powerful interest group, first in Britain and eventually in most private enterprise countries, corporate managers often replacing the old-style owners. In modern private enterprise societies under constitutional governments, industrialist groups are paralleled by farmer organizations and labor unions. As people become more politicized, the number of interest groups tends to rise. In recent years, at one end of the social scale the poor and, at the other end, university students and faculties have formed new interest groups.[4]

Women constitute a large potential interest group, and many of them have become increasingly active. For over a century women have demanded equal rights with men in property and family law and effective access to education and professional training, to employment and promotion in jobs and careers, to voting and holding political office. Before the end of World War I in 1918, they had been denied many of these rights in many countries. Between 1920 and 1980 they won most of these rights in legal form, but much less in substance. "Token" women were admitted, appointed, and sometimes even promoted, but at the high levels of most public and private organizations they remained few and far between.

In the 1970s the women's movement became prominent in several advanced industrialized countries. Its spokeswomen demanded not only equal rights, jobs, and careers, but far-reaching changes in culture, family life, and even language. In earlier decades one part of the women's movement had long been close to the world of labor unions and social work, even though some of its leaders were college-educated. This earlier branch demanded special protection for women against night work, and health hazards, particularly during pregnancy and maternity, and help for working-class women in caring for their children. A more recent development in the women's movement has now mobilized younger, college-educated women from professional and middle-class backgrounds, individuals who are less interested in special protection than in open and equal careers and in a new division of labor between men and women in the home.

Both branches of the women's movement express real needs of their adherents, but they may press for different kinds of law. Whereas one group insists on special protection, even if this should bar women from some kinds of employment, some members of the second group, more highly educated and affluent, would prefer to sweep away all special protections and barriers. In the United States the *Equal Rights Amendment (ERA)* to the Constitution, not yet ratified by three-quarters of the states, is vaguely worded. Yet if it should be adopted, it would be a sign of the direction in which the American people want to go and of the priorities they seek to establish. The practical meaning of ERA for both working-class and professional women will have to be worked out by legislation and through the courts, taking into account the experiences of those states that already have incorporated equal rights clauses in their legislation.

Within other large interest groups, too, there

[4]In the United States today, there are more staff and students occupied full-time in the universities than there are people occupied in farming.

are smaller, special interest groups. The cotton farmers of the South, who favor the lower-priced spreads that usually contain cottonseed oil, have different views from the dairy farmers of Wisconsin, who seek to promote Wisconsin's own natural product, butter. In four states, at least, farmers' interests are closely tied to tobacco, whereas in other states farmers might rather not court lung cancer.

The Politics of Bargaining. The political process then, in one sense, is the result of the bargaining among different groups. This definition furnishes the basis of Robert Dahl's model of a *polyarchy,* that is, his conception of a modern Western political system.[5] In such a pluralistic society, any number can play. Each special interest can set up its own group, its own office, its own organization; each can hire secretaries; each can buy mimeograph machines and begin to churn out releases; each can retain lobbyists in Washington to provide legislators with ample, though one-sided, information and to take legislators to lunch or find more substantial inducements for legislators to vote the way the interest group desires.

But in a society like that of the United States, where almost every substantial interest group is organized, three serious problems arise. First, the strongest interest groups, those with most money and most skills and ruthlessness in using them, are most likely to get their own way, often without regard for the national interest. There is no certainty that an opposing coalition of weaker groups can constrain them.

Second, if most interest groups are organized, heaven help the residual groups that are not—the tenants in the slums, the poor, and some of the ethnic or racial minorities. Until recently, none of these was organized in an effective manner. Lacking organization, they got the worst in most of the political bargaining, and many of the older interest groups were quite content to keep it that way.

Third, when almost everybody is organized, society reaches a point at which almost nothing can be done. Groups with limited power usually find it easier to veto someone else's proposal than to push through any positive policy of their own. When this happens, politics becomes negative, and interest groups turn into veto groups. Even where positive policies are possible, any substantial proposal has to be cleared with every relevant interest group. And the larger the number of organized groups, the more of them that must be consulted, the longer are the resulting delays, and the harder it becomes to turn any idea into action. The problem is vividly illustrated by the long, drawn-out difficulties of President Carter, the secretary of energy, Congress, and the various interest groups in the years 1977–79 in agreeing on an energy policy for the United States or on a policy to defend the international value of the dollar against further decline.

From Immobility to Emergency. Pluralistic interest organization can lead, therefore, to creeping immobility. The society becomes harder and harder to move, and attempting reform or innovation becomes as frustrating as swimming in a sea of molasses. Eventually it becomes so difficult to get things done that some device must be found for breaking the deadlock. This device is the emergency. In an emergency, we cannot spend time consulting all the interest groups: we must do something quickly. If there is a real emergency, we greet it with relief. If there is none, we sometimes invent one. Thus, the politics of a polyarchy—a highly pluralistic, highly organized society—becomes a cycle of *alternating states of immobility and emergency* (see Figure 3.3).

In recent years in the United States the emergency usually has been a foreign policy emergency. Since World War II, presidents have presented Congress with images of cold war emergencies or dire threats to national security, in order to induce

[5]See Robert A. Dahl, *Modern Political Analysis,* 3rd ed. (Englewood Cliffs, N.J.: Prentice-Hall, 1976), and his more detailed books, *Who Governs?* (New Haven: Yale University Press, 1961) and *Pluralistic Democracy in the United States* (Chicago: Rand McNally, 1967).

the legislators to appropriate funds for foreign economic aid and other aspects of foreign policy. However, if a minority group inside the country finds that foreign policy emergencies, by distracting attention away from domestic matters, do not work in its interest, such a group may be desperate enough to create its own emergency at home. Then suddenly things get done. The black poor and urban slums got much more attention and a little more money after the riots in Watts (Los Angeles), Detroit, Newark, and other cities. In this case the original outburst was a real emergency, not a fabricated one. Thereafter, the fear of a "long hot summer" resulting in mass rioting was used by civil rights groups to obtain desired programs and funds.

Universities, and not just governments, have exhibited the immobility-emergency pattern. By the spring of 1968 a report on the role of students in the university had lain on the desk of the president of Columbia University for eight months. Then the emergency created by a student revolt on campus greatly accelerated the speed with which pieces of paper moved through the system. Alumni, trustees, corporations, faculty members, students, and a new president enacted in months changes that had been talked about for years—albeit at a grievous cost in time, in effort, and in estrangement, conflict, and bad feelings within the faculty and university community.

But there are limits to the degree to which such a tactic can be used. Nothing is as destructive in politics as a mood of permanent emergency. To be sure, the group that creates an emergency finally

FIGURE 3.3 *The Emergency-Immobility Cycle: A Danger in Polyarchy*

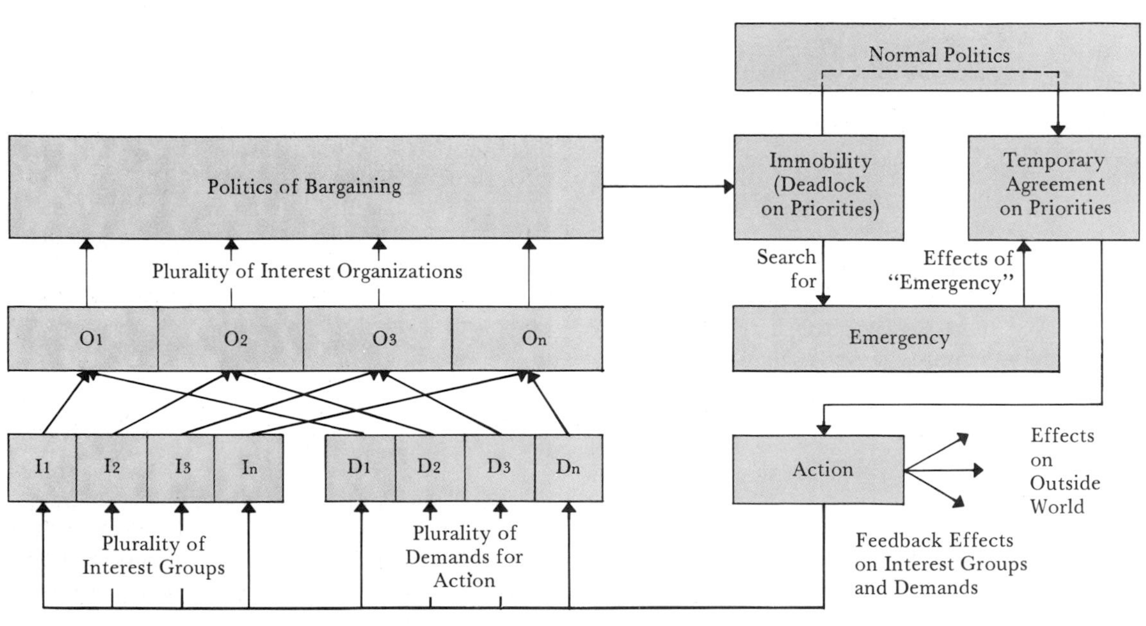

will get some action, but it may not be the action it wanted. It may arouse numerous people who were previously nonpolitical and who now may be hostile to the aims of the group. In 1968 the percentage of votes cast for Governor George Wallace, a spokesman for racial discrimination, was higher than the total percentage of black people in the nation's population. The continuing strength of the race issue among white voters was still shown both in the success Governor Wallace encountered in 1972, when he defeated opponents in several Democratic primaries, and in the support during the 1970s for antibusing legislation. Only gradually did resistance to busing decline, from President Carter's victory in 1976 onward. In 1978 Governor Wallace announced his retirement from politics, but at least some resistance to integration seemed likely to continue into the 1980s.

From Interest Elites to an Establishment. Most of the time, a moderate amount of intergroup interacting, bargaining, and piecemeal decision making goes on between emergencies. To carry out these activities, almost every interest group, sooner or later, develops leaders, secretaries, professionals, or people whose names have become prominent among its members. In this sense, each interest group tends to develop an elite of its own. If *interest elites* become used to working with each other, to knowing each other, to exchanging views and small courtesies among themselves, they may coalesce into an establishment. One may call an *establishment* the ensemble of those interest group elites who have learned to work together. Union leaders and management may learn how to conduct negotiations with each other. Leaders in the mass media may come to know leaders in most other fields, from literature to finance, and to work with them.

This cooperation can sometimes be a good thing; it makes things smoother and gets things done. But it may sometimes be a very bad thing. These groups, used to each other's needs, may become increasingly preoccupied with each other, insensitive to the needs of outsiders, and impervious to new recruitment and to new ideas. Or the members of various interest group elites may identify more and more with one another and less and less with the interests of the groups they represent. Thus some labor leaders, whose incomes and styles of life have set them apart from their own union members, may feel that they have more in common with the representatives of management than with the workers whose interests they are supposed to protect.

POLITICAL PARTIES AND PARTY SYSTEMS

Political Parties: Stable Coalitions among Interests. Interest groups *articulate* the interests of their members. They put into words the vaguely felt needs, fears, and expectations of their constituents and translate these feelings into specific demands for legislation or other government action. Once individuals are aware that they share a common concern with an interest group, many of them move from a passive audience of potential adherents into the group's active members and supporters. In the 1930s Dr. Francis Townsend aroused the concern of many elderly Americans about their lack of security for their old age. Large numbers of them joined his Townsend clubs and engaged in political agitation for a federal old-age pension of "thirty dollars every Thursday," until social security legislation was enacted in 1935. Then as now, the average levels of benefits were much lower than the elderly had demanded, but the most urgent needs of most older wage earners were eventually covered. It was not the Townsend groups, however, that enacted social security. It was the Democratic Party through its majority in Congress under the leadership of the Roosevelt administration that did so, and it was the Republican Party in the Eisenhower administration that twenty years later extended social security coverage to additional millions. Interest groups may raise a demand, but political parties transform the demand into action.

Political parties are key organizations for getting social and political results. They do so by *aggregating* several different interest groups into a stable coalition that is stronger and more powerful than any single interest group by itself. Every major political party represents a combination of such interest groups. In some parties the main component groups are held together only loosely by *logrolling*—that is, by the trading of political favors. Other parties from time to time proclaim dramatic slogans in order to rally support in a manner acceptable to all their interest groups. The Republicans of McKinley's day promised their voters a "full dinner pail." Britain's Conservatives under Stanley Baldwin in 1935 campaigned for "safety first." West Germany's Christian Democratic Union under Konrad Adenauer in 1957 insisted on "no experiments." Each of these was a conservative slogan on which a wide range of different interest groups could agree as long as each of them wished to preserve some particular set of existing arrangements. On the other hand, such slogans as Franklin D. Roosevelt's offer of a "New Deal" in 1932 or John F. Kennedy's vision of a "New Frontier" in 1960 were general appeals for change, designed to unite a wide variety of different groups, each desiring some particular change.

In contrast, the Republican slogan in 1972, "Re-elect the President," appeared to be purposely vague in an effort to draw on a multitude of bases of support, ranging from liberal approval of his tension-reducing foreign policy innovations in relation to China and the Soviet Union to conservative approval of the administration's "benign neglect" of civil rights and poverty issues. Similarly, President Nixon benefited from two informal slogans associated with his policies on the Vietnam War: "Peace with Honor," which reassured some of the "hawks" among the voters, and Henry Kissinger's televised "Peace Is at Hand" speech, reassuring the more "dovelike" voters about the alleged success of his negotiation—a reassurance taken back by both the president and Kissinger within six weeks after the election and restored only in 1975. In 1976, Jimmy Carter was elected by a majority of voters who had grown tired of too simple slogans and overstated promises. They accepted his promises of open and moral government in close touch with the people. The whimsical symbol of the peanut and his serious promise "I will never lie to you" served him well, and by late 1979 the promise did not appear to have been broken.

Party Principles and Ideologies. Still other parties seeking to hold their coalitions together go beyond slogans to more permanent principles, such as liberalism or conservatism. "A party," said Edmund Burke, "is a group of men united to promote the common good in accordance with a principle upon which they are agreed." In Burke's view one such principle was *conservatism,* which implied, first, that any changes attempted should be extremely small, slow, and cautious and, second, that property should be overrepresented in politics, "out of all proportion," as opposed to talent. Burke's principle seemed well designed to unite noblemen, landowners, established churches, favored business interests, and other interests profiting from existing conditions in late eighteenth-century Britain. This kind of conservatism, however, was not an excuse for simply doing nothing. It demanded slow but constant change after the necessity and practicality of change had been demonstrated by experience. "A conservative," said a later writer, "is someone who will never do anything for the first time."

More or less elaborate *ideologies,* as well as simple principles, may unify a party. Some major political theories have become linked to party ideologies. In various countries, conservatives have drawn on Machiavelli, Hobbes, and Burke; liberals on Locke and Mill; radicals on Rousseau and Marx. Some parties have combined ideas from several thinkers into an ideology of their own. Thus American conservatives also invoke the "natural rights" ideas of John Locke; and the Labour Party in Britain has been influenced by the practical gradualism of Edmund Burke. These and other thinkers are discussed in Chapter 4.

Party ideologies, however, must also unite the main interest groups on whom the party depends. Britain's Labour Party's socialist platform serves to link trade union members who mainly want higher wages; intellectuals and white-collar workers who want more government planning, nationalized industries, and public enterprises; women and older people who want more public medical and welfare services; and young voters who are opposed to armaments and compulsory military service. A far more complex and rigid ideology was professed by the Russian Communist Party in the days of Lenin and by the latter-day Communist parties ruling the Soviet Union and the People's Republic of China. Communist ideology, too, is aimed explicitly at maintaining a coalition of workers, peasants, and intellectuals. In practice it must also accommodate some of the interests of the large bureaucracies and military establishments that have developed in Communist countries.

Party Systems and Participation. In some countries a single party has a monopoly of legal political activity. Under such *one-party systems,* almost anyone who wishes to participate effectively in politics must join this party and try to rise in its ranks. Often a one-party system is combined with a dictatorship; competing parties are suppressed by force, and the founding of new parties is punishable as a crime. If a one-party government is also willing and able to control all other organizations affecting public life, from labor unions to sports clubs and young people's groups; if it controls all mass media, all education, and even much of the leisure time of its people; and if it accepts no exception from its claim to power, then it is often called *totalitarian.* The Fascist Party of Mussolini's Italy, the National Socialist (Nazi) Party of Hitler's Germany, and the Communist Party of Stalin's Soviet Union exercised power in this manner. Totalitarian parties and regimes differ according to the main policies and purposes that their total efforts at political mobilization and control are meant to serve. The chief aim of the Fascists and the Nazis was military conquest; the major aim of Soviet Communists was rapid industrialization. But some of their political methods—and the resulting human costs—were similar.

In milder cases a one-party system may give the ruling party its formal political monopoly, but tolerate a number of other long-established interest groups with political potentialities, such as landowners, industrialists, the military, and some major church organizations. It may then also respect a sphere of privacy for its citizens. These less extreme one-party systems are sometimes called *authoritarian.* Franco's Spain (1939–76) with its Falangist Party and Peron's Argentina (1943–55) with its Peronistas are examples.

A third group of one-party systems is involved in rapid change. Such systems are most often found in developing countries. Some of them have a legal monopoly, as did Mustapha Kemal's People's Party in Turkey from the 1920s through the 1940s. Others tolerate small opposition groups, but in fact predominate, controlling most government jobs and wielding most of the influence in public matters. Mexico's Institutional Revolutionary Party (PRI) is a ruling party of this kind, as was India's Congress Party until 1977, and France's Gaullist Party might have liked to attain this status.

One-party systems tend to be most successful—and most likely to be accepted by the population—when the national supply of activists, top level political talent, and of leaders and managers is small relative to the size and urgency of the tasks that a country faces. When there is much to be done quickly and few people to do it, the doers are likely to be organized as a single team of leaders, that is, as a single governing party. If much of what has to be done is backed by popular consent and the ruling party does it tolerably well, the one-party system is likely to enjoy public support.

When the number of political activists and potential leaders and the number and variety of active interest groups are much larger, not all participants can be accommodated within a single party. Under these conditions, a *two-party system* may offer twice as many opportunities for political participation. Each major party may represent a full team of potential leaders for the nation in its struggle against domestic or foreign difficulties. In a sense this resembles the two-platoon system in football. One set of players is on the field while the other platoon is in reserve, sitting on the bench. When the first platoon is temporarily retired, the other platoon takes over. Thus the game may be pursued with unceasing vigor before either platoon gets exhausted. The platoons have special skills—one for offense and the other for defense—and their joint performance can be formidable. A two-platoon team is stronger, not weaker, than a one-platoon team.

In a two-party system, one party may specialize in initiating change and the other in slowing or consolidating it. Or one party may press for a more active foreign policy and the other may emphasize affairs at home. Again, one party may stress the need to develop public services or public enterprise and the other may speak for the private sector. One party may speak for producers, both management and labor, who want higher prices; the other for consumers, such as creditors and housewives, who want lower ones. For a two-party system to work well, there must be a great deal of overlap among the different specialties and interests. Both teams must still play for the same side, and both players and spectators must know it. When this does not hold true, the two-party system may deteriorate into mutual hostility and even into civil war, as it did in Austria between Socialists and Catholic conservatives in 1934 or in Colombia between liberals and conservatives in the 1950s.

The United States and Britain have long provided examples of functioning two-party systems. When it was revealed in 1973 that highly placed members or employees of the Nixon administration and of the Committee to Reelect the President had conspired to burglarize the national headquarters of the Democratic Party in the Watergate building in Washington, D.C., and that efforts had been made to use federal agencies, such as the Federal Bureau of Investigation (FBI), the Central Intelligence Agency (CIA), and the Internal Revenue Service (IRS), against political opponents of the administration, these tactics were widely interpreted as a serious potential threat to the two-party system and were repudiated by many Republican leaders.

Under a two-party system, a large number of interest groups is aggregated into only two major parties. Most interest groups may find, therefore, that neither party fits their needs perfectly. Almost every group will have to compromise in order to squeeze under the umbrella of one of these big *parties of action.* The costs of compromise are the frustrations the interest group accepts; its rewards are what the party can get done for it. If the party can accomplish much, many different groups will be likely to stay within it. If either major party or both of them achieve only little, a large number of interest groups will become intensely dissatisfied. Each of them may then back a smaller party custom-tailored to its needs and prejudices. Smaller specialized parties may accomplish little for their clients, but may serve them at least as *parties of expression.* They may voice their members' interests and act them out symbolically, thus making their members feel better even if they gain little else (see Table 3.4). When parties of action fail, parties of expression are likely to become more visible or frequent.

A *multiparty system,* such as is found in many countries of Western Europe, is a mixture of parties of action and parties of expression. Its largest parties can get enough done to keep operating, but not enough to unite as many as half the voters and interest groups of the country. Its small parties voice sufficient protests and de-

TABLE 3.4 *A Typology of Party Orientations*

	METHODS	
	Action to get results	Expression of feelings and desires
Gain power	Republican and Democratic parties (US) Conservative Party (UK) CDU (GFR) Gaullists (France)	Liberal Party (New York City) Liberal Party (UK) Free Democrats (GFR)
Determine policy	CPSU (USSR) CPCPR (China) Labour Party (UK) SPD (GFR)	Socialists (Norman Thomas, US) American Independent Party (George Wallace, US)

mands, interspersed with occasional bits of accomplishment, to hold the support of their specialized constituencies—regional, occupational, religious, or ideological. To govern the country, several parties, usually both large and small, must form a coalition. Such a coalition then agrees on a program of legislation and on a distribution of government offices to be filled. *Coalition agreements* on these matters often are made in writing even though they are not always publicized. When the program of the coalition has been carried out, or when agreement among members ceases for some reason, the coalition is dissolved and another is formed in its place. France, Germany, Switzerland, and Italy have been governed by changing coalitions for almost a century.

In substance, formal coalition governments among several parties resemble the informal coalitions of interest groups within one- and two-party systems. They differ from the latter two in the relative ease with which coalition governments can be dissolved and re-formed. Multiparty systems may be more flexible and less stable than one- or two-party systems, and they may offer a wider range of opportunities for political participation. This openness to participation, however, much like stability, flexibility, and accomplishment, may depend more on the organization and quality of each party than on the particular party system in effect. The differences in openness and effectiveness among political parties often are as great as or greater than those among party systems as a whole.

Party Membership, Finance, and Administration. The character of any political party is primarily determined by seven things: (1) the interests it serves; (2) the aims it professes; (3) its real aims; (4) the size and nature of its membership; (5) the main sources of its voters and other political support; (6) its chief sources of money; and (7) the internal bureaucracy and administrative machinery that run it.

We have already discussed the first two points, the coalition of interest groups within a party and the party's professed aims and principles. Sometimes the professed aims of a party and its actual aims are the same. Such parties are mainly *policy oriented.* Their leaders and members want to make sure that certain laws are passed or certain policies implemented, regardless of who wins the legislative or administrative power to do these things. They want to determine *what* gets done, no matter *who* gets the job to do it. Minority parties in the United States often have been of this type. In the course of a long life Norman Thomas ran six times for the presidency of the United States on the Socialist ticket. He was always unsuccessful in the sense of never winning an election. But when he died in 1968, the newspapers pointed out that nearly all the reforms for which he had campaigned had become law; over the years they had been enacted by the major parties that had defeated him. If Norman Thomas ever had ambitions of power, then they failed, but his policy aspirations were in large part successful.

Other parties, as well as many individual politicians, are mainly *power oriented.* Their professed aims, in the form of policy statements and platforms, frequently are different from their real ones. These parties care little what laws and policies are enacted, as long as *they* are assured of being in charge of them. If a policy-oriented person would rather be right than be president, a power-oriented party will change many of its policies and even, discreetly, its principles in order to get elected or to stay in office (see Table 3.4). In such cases it may do less for some of the interest groups it has served in the past, while doing more to win the favor of others. Thus it may change in part the nature of the interest coalition it represents. (Conversely, a party may hold fast to its policies and principles, but the actual interests of some of its constitutent groups may change. In the past, southern Democrats in the United States favored free trade, since their region had little manufacturing industry and imported most industrial goods from the North or from abroad. After 1950, as industry grew in the South, an increasing part of southern interests turned protectionist and sought tariffs and quotas to keep out competing foreign goods. Southern legislators then had to choose between changing their policies or losing their support.)

Parties also can be characterized by the size and nature of their membership (see Table 3.5). Some parties are primarily *membership parties.* If these are also mass parties, they will organize a substantial part of their voters as members on a more or less permanent basis. Thus the German Social Democratic Party (SPD) in 1976 had a core of about 960,000 members, while drawing about 15 million votes in national elections. These core members paid regular dues; many attended monthly meetings and volunteered to carry on the routine tasks of the party, such as addressing envelopes, ringing doorbells, distributing handbills, turning out for larger meetings and parades, and taking voters to the polls. With such a large and dependable body of volunteer labor, a membership party needs less money to hire campaign staffs at election time and to buy publicity and advertising space in the mass media. The popularity of membership parties holds fairly steady in public opinion polls between elections.

TABLE 3.5 *A Rough Typology of Party Structures*

	Stable mass membership	Intermittent supporters and skeleton membership
Bureaucratic "machine-ruled"	SPD (GFR) Labour Party (UK)	CDU (GFR) Conservative Party (UK) Republican and Democratic parties on national level (US)
Open	Membership parties in early stages, e.g., New Democratic Party (Canada)	FDP (GFR) Gaullists (France) American Independent Party (US)

In contrast, a *skeleton party* maintains only a small membership and a small staff between elections. On the eve of an electoral campaign, however, skeleton parties recruit a much larger staff, some volunteer and others paid, in order to run a big campaign and to rally its potential voters, who have heard little from the party during the period between elections. Such parties rely much more heavily on posters, newspapers, radio, television, and other forms of mass publicity. As a result, skeleton parties need a great deal of money.

A membership party can afford to run relatively colorless candidates who have proven their dependability and party regularity over many years. The voters will elect these individuals, not because of any personal qualities, but because of trust in the party that has nominated them: "A lamppost could be elected to Parliament from Bombay on the Congress Party ticket" ran a popular Indian saying. The colorful Winston Churchill, turned out of office in 1945 by the colorless Clement Attlee, was left to complain bitterly that he had been defeated by "a sheep in sheep's clothing." In fact, he had been beaten by Attlee's British Labour Party, which had won the confidence of Britain's voters.

Skeleton parties usually nominate candidates who can rapidly gain the attention, respect, and confidence of the voters. Thus they frequently seek candidates who are attractive as well as colorful or who are already well known. Since the voters' impressions of its candidates are so important to the success of a skeleton party, the party may often emphasize its candidate's image, sometimes to the exclusion of his or her ideas. At the end of the 1940s both the Democratic and Republican Parties sought General Eisenhower as their presidential candidate. Neither party knew for certain the general's ideas on government or his political leanings, but they were sure that the voters would find him irresistible. And they were right.

In the United States both the Republican and Democratic parties are largely skeleton organizations on the national level, but maintain more permanent machines in state and local politics. Some regions also have party organizations and clubs in which a somewhat larger number of members meet regularly. Most Republicans and Democrats, however, are registered by party preference without paying membership dues or attending meetings. Individual voters become members of parties by simply indicating their party preference at the time they register to vote, and they may change this preference at any time they please. In many states all such registered members of a party have the right to vote in party *primaries* that nominate the party's candidates for public office, and they often elect the delegates to the party's national convention, which then selects its candidates for president and vice president of the United States. (In other states the election of convention delegates is left to the regulars in the local party clubs.)

Parties differ not only in the varying amounts of money they need, but also in the sources from which they get it. Since membership parties get much of their money in small but regular amounts from their members, they are less dependent on individual "fat cats" or party donors. Moreover, such membership parties as the British Labour Party or the German SPD and liberal parties in general get financial support from other mass organizations, such as labor unions and cooperative societies. Conservative parties frequently obtain financial support from big business and industrial organizations, as well as from particular business firms and individuals. Most of these funds, whether given to liberal or conservative parties, are given in expectation of some favors in return. In politics, as in business, there is no such thing as a free lunch.

With the growth of mass electorates and the mass media, the cost of large political campaigns is steadily rising. In effect, the entrance fee for major candidates is getting steeper. In the United States this has favored the persistence of millionaires in politics, such as Franklin Roosevelt, Herbert Lehman, Averell Harriman, Stuart Symington, and the Kennedy brothers among the Democrats and Robert Taft, Barry Goldwater, Charles Percy, and Nelson Rockefeller among the Republicans. Politicians who started out with smaller personal fortunes included Harry Truman, Lyndon Johnson, Hubert Humphrey, George McGovern, and Jimmy Carter among the Democrats and Thomas E. Dewey, Dwight D. Eisenhower, Richard M. Nixon, and Gerald Ford among the Republicans; they had to attract millions of dollars from private individuals, business interests, and, to a lesser extent, organized labor.

If this trend continues, fewer people will be able to participate effectively in politics and special interests will prevail more often over the common good. A possible remedy would be the public financing of campaign expenditures, perhaps in proportion to the number of votes polled by each party at the previous election or to the number of bona fide signatures on the nominating petitions of a new party. Legislation of this kind was enacted in the German Federal Republic in the mid-1960s and resulted in a markedly greater independence of political parties from the main sources of private financial support; and it may well lead to broader and more varied opportunities for political participation.

Since 1976, presidential election campaigns in the United States have been financed to a large extent from public funds. Contributions from interest groups, business firms, or private individuals—the well-known "angels" or fat cats of political cartoons—are restricted, and fairly stringent accounting standards and controls of campaign financing are now in force. Under these rules, candidates may even apply for public *matching funds* for their primary campaigns for the presidential nomination of their party, as soon as they first can show a minimum amount of voluntary contribution, but from then on they must observe the law's standards of accounting and disclosure.

No such provisions exist as yet in the United States in regard to electoral campaigns *for Congress or in state or local politics*. On all those levels fat cats still play. The political activities of millionaires were conspicuous in some of the 1978 congressional and state elections, as well as in some of the primaries preceding them. Reforms in the financing of campaigns and parties have greatly advanced in Britain, Norway, Sweden, Austria, and the German Federal Republic, but in these matters the United States still has far to go.

Parties can be more or less open or machine-ruled (see Table 3.5). Within every party there is a difference between the members who devote only their free time to politics and the full-time professionals on the party's staff. The latter, together with some holders of political office who in fact devote much time to party matters, form in each party the bureaucracy—the *machine*, as it is called in American cities, the *apparat* as it formerly was termed in Communist countries. In general, the bigger and more self-contained the party bureaucracy, the less is the influence of rank-and-file members. "In other clubs," wrote the playwright Bertolt Brecht about the Communist Party, "the members elect the secretaries. In our club the secretaries elect the members." In the United States, too, the desires of party members often take second place to those of the bureaucracy. The rank-and-file Democrats in the primaries of 1968 gave strong support to Eugene McCarthy and Robert Kennedy as presidential candidates, but the party professionals at the machine-dominated Chicago convention nominated Hubert Humphrey, who led the party to defeat. In so doing, they may have remembered the old politicians's rule: If you must choose between losing control of the party and losing the election, lose the election.

In 1972 they did lose control of the party. After the narrow defeat of the Democrats in 1968, the rules for electing delegates to the party's national convention were changed in order to reduce the powers of the traditional machines and to increase the representation of young voters, women, and racial minorities, particularly blacks—groups whose votes, it was thought, could have given victory to the Democrats in 1968 if they had been mobilized in larger numbers. The new groups played a major role in the 1972 Democractic Party primaries and at the convention in giving victory to the left wing of the party and winning the nomination for its candidate, Senator George McGovern of South Dakota. Within the Democratic Party the activism and enthusiasm of a few seemed to have triumphed over the routine of the professionals and the habits of the many.

This triumph of the new politics at the convention proved hollow on election day. Nearly one-third of normally Democratic voters turned to the Republican candidate and incumbent president,

Richard M. Nixon, who seemed to offer reassurance against radical changes; and additional numbers of Democratic voters stayed home. President Nixon was elected with 61 percent of major party votes cast, the second largest majority of any U.S. president (in 1964, Lyndon Johnson received 61.1 percent).[6]

In the same election, the voters returned a Democratic majority of legislators to both houses of Congress, as they had in all but two elections since 1930.[7] Neither in national nor in state elections did they repudiate the Democratic Party—that loose collection of varied political traditions, policy preferences, and interest groups. What the voters rejected in 1972 was a presidential candidate and the convention majority that had nominated him. But by 1976 the old art of building a political coalition solid and broad enough to win both within the Democratic Party and among the voters was demonstrated once again by Jimmy Carter.

It has been asserted, contrary to the exception noted above, that party bureaucracies almost always prevail over the rank-and-file membership. An *iron law of oligarchy,* claiming just this, was proposed in 1911 by the Italian sociologist Roberto Michels. But such a law would hold true only if old political parties were immortal and no new ones could be founded. In fact, however, the more rigid a monopoly becomes in politics or in business, the more likely it is to lose control. Although party bureaucrats may prefer losing one or several elections, rather than making concessions to new developments and new voters, they cannot go on losing too long or their party will decline and other parties will arise to take its place. Individuals who wish to reform an existing political party must judge carefully whether they will do better to continue participating within the party or to leave it and try to form a new one. Party leaders, in turn, must decide whether to discourage and drive out opposition or to accept enough reforms to keep participation attractive to the young. And both sides may have to take care not to drive out too many of those members and voters with whom they disagree, but on whose support they depend for winning an election.

Other Channels of Political Participation. People often make use of other types of organizations and activities besides political parties in order to influence political and social outcomes. First, there are interest groups and organizations, such as labor unions, associations of manufacturers, chambers of commerce, farm groups, and the like. Race relations may be influenced through such organizations as the National Urban League, the National Association for the Advancement of Colored People (NAACP), the Southern Christian Leadership Conference (SCLC), or smaller but more militant organizations such as the Black Muslims or the Black Panthers. Other ethnic or religious groups have their own associations; Jewish, Italian, Polish, and Irish groups all have been active in American politics. Women are pressing their demands through the National Organization for Women (NOW) and similar groups, thus far with few divisions within their own ranks.

Still other groups are designed to promote particular policies, such as the Urban Coalition and Common Cause, which seek to promote reform legislation in regard to urban problems and welfare and national political processes. More recently, several groups opposed to nuclear energy and proenvironmentalist, have entered the political process.

Often a movement brings with it the rise of a plurality of organizations. The women's movement seeks changes not only in legislation, but also

[6]On election day in 1972, about one-third of Americans over eighteen years of age were not registered to vote. Of those who were registered, about one-fifth did not trouble to cast a ballot. President Nixon's 61 percent majority of votes was figured on only the 54 percent of adult Americans who actually voted; it thus represented the explicit support of less than 34 percent of the adult population of the United States.

[7]The exceptions were 1946 and 1952.

in the hiring policies, pay, and promotion of women in private and public employment. The environmentalist movement seeks changes in laws, public administration, and industrial practice to reduce pollution and protect the resources and beauty of the environment. The consumers' movement—led in the United States in the late 1960s and 1970s by Ralph Nader—strives to get better legal protection for consumers against inferior products and services, misleading advertisements, and needlessly high prices. There is also a student movement pressing for some share of influence on the curricula, teaching methods, disciplinary rules, and other policies of universities and, more recently, of some high schools as well. Even informal movements oriented toward forms of popular art, self-expression, and lifestyle may acquire a political dimension.

None of these movements is likely to become all-powerful or to reach all its major goals quickly. Yet they all have had some successes. They have brought about some changes in politics and law and perhaps even more in the climate of political opinion, thus preparing the ground for the next advance of the reforms they advocate. Movements of this kind offer an alternate way for people to take part in politics, and the established political parties are likely, sooner or later, to offer their services to the potential constituencies that these new movements represent. Conversely, the leaders and followers of such movements are increasingly likely to find themselves in situations in which they must act politically, that is, decide on priorities, seek out allies, form coalitions, and assess the power they have, the power they need, and the power they can get within a reasonable time. In countries where people are free to found such movements and organizations and to choose the policies they desire to promote, these seemingly nonpolitical channels are in fact a valuable supplement to the political system, provided that people learn to work realistically and effectively with the constraints and opportunities provided by the channels.

SCOPE, DOMAIN, AND PARTICIPATION: KEY DIMENSIONS OF A POLITICAL SYSTEM

Thus far the chapter has been a quick sketch of some of the things one might want to ask when looking at any political system: Who are the elites? Which are the politically relevant strata? What is the party system and which are the important interest groups and parties within it? If we consider these matters together with the changing stakes of politics, the changing volume of activities controlled, and the benefits or values redistributed by the political process, we begin to get a rough notion of different kinds of political systems. This set of dimensions points up the radical difference between the political systems discussed by the great political theorists of the past and the political systems of today.

The Greek city-state was a state large in *scope*—that is, in the variety of human activities that it tried to control. The government may have allocated 15 percent or more of the income of Athens. The Athenian state was concerned with theater and art, with education, with religion, as well as with politics and law. Its *domain*—the territory and people it controlled—was small. Athens may have had only 270,000 inhabitants, and the people who were theoretically citizens may not have exceeded 50,000 in number. Active participation in its government was even more limited. In fact, not more than one-tenth of its citizens was politically active. At the Athenian plenary meeting that condemned Socrates about 1,500 votes were cast for the prosecution and a smaller number for the defense, so the total number of votes cast in this trial must have been below 2,500. The political activists in Athens may actually have been only 0.5 percent of the total Athenian population; the politically relevant strata, the citizens who could have been stirred up, may have been about 20 percent.

Rome of the Caesars had a much smaller scope.

TABLE 3.6 *How Big Is "Big Government"? The Government's Share*

Country	Population 1978 (millions)	Total GDP 1976	Per capita GDP 1976 (in US dollars)	GDP in public sector 1976 (approximate, in billion US dollars)
United States	220	1,701	7,912	595
Soviet Union	261	1,136	4,351*	670
German Federal Republic	62	449	7,249	216
France	53	347	6,552	138
United Kingdom	56	220	3,936	104
China	950	290	306	325†
India	650	94	144‡	23

* Estimated by Abraham Bergson and K. W. Deutsch at 55% of the U.S. figure, taking into account the ratios of Soviet to United States GDP in dollar prices and in ruble prices. See references in Chapter 11, note 5, p. 326.
† Estimate.
‡ Estimate, excluding brigade and team agricultural production.

Sources: Ruth Leger Sivard, *World Military and Social Expenditures, 1978* (Leesburg, Va.: WMSE Publications, 1978); *United Nations Statistical Yearbook, 1977,* tables 186, 193, 195, 202.

It did much less for the education of the mass of the people, much less for their arts, much less for their religion. It mainly kept the peace, built a few roads, collected taxes, and maintained Roman law in one-half of the empire. (In the other half of the empire the government left the local laws alone.) The Roman government may have allocated not more than 5 percent of the national income of the Roman Empire. If so, its scope was only one-third that of the Athenians (see Figures 3.4 and 3.5).

The domain of the Roman Empire, on the other hand, was fifty times larger, or more, in terms of both land and people. Adding all the dependencies of Athens at the peak of its power still leaves the population of the Athenian empire at less than 1 million people. The Roman Empire at its peak contained 50 to 60 million people, and it maintained much of its size for centuries. This was an unprecedented extension of domain, purchased only partly by a much lesser reduction in scope. The domain had grown fifty times, while the scope had shrunk by two-thirds. Participation was very low. Probably less than 0.5 percent of the adult population in the empire was involved in politics. The politically relevant strata were probably less than 5 percent of the total. Roman government was based on the political indifference of the mass of the population.

Fifteen hundred years later, in 1785, we find that the scope of the government of the Bourbon kings of France was larger than that of Rome, though smaller than that of Athens. About 8 percent of the national income was redistributed through government taxing and spending. The

TABLE 3.7 *How Big Is "Big Government"? The Government's Job*

Country	Population 1978 (millions)	Total GDP 1976	Percentage of GDP in public sector
United States	220	1,701	35
Soviet Union	261	1,136	59
German Federal Republic	62	449	48
France	53	347	40
United Kingdom	56	220	47*
China	950	290	40†
India	650	94	25

* Public revenues and social security contributions. Expenditures for the entire public sector were reported at 61% of British GDP.
† Estimate, excluding brigade and team agricultural production.

Sources: Sivard, *World Military and Social Expenditures, 1978; U.N. Statistical Yearbook, 1977,* tables 186, 202.

domain, 25 million people, was fairly large, though less than that of Rome. The dependencies were negligible in 1785, since the French had just lost most of their empire. The politically active population before the French Revolution was approximately 0.1 percent, roughly about one-fifth of what it had been in Athens. The politically relevant strata in 1785 were about 1 percent of the population—only the nobles and the clergy. This situation did not last. Four years later, a great many more people became politically relevant.

If we compare the France of the Bourbon kings with the France of 1978 we find striking changes. The scope of government, measured by the share of national income distributed by the political process, has risen five times, from 8 percent to about 40 percent. The domain has nearly doubled. France has 53 million inhabitants. The politically active population of France, as in other Western countries, is at least 3 percent. Since about one-fifth of French voters favor the Communist Party, and since there is a fairly high level of union and other activities, the proportion of activists may be slightly higher. French student unrest may have contributed another 100,000 activists or so. Since about 50 percent of the French population (about 76 percent of all adults) actually votes, the politically relevant strata today are eighty times as large as they were in the Bourbon era.

In the United States about 35 percent of the gross national product goes to the political sector, and 220 million people reside in one federal union. The United States in 1980, moreover, was in a sense the central or *metropolitan power* for a still larger area and population. Another 200 million people in Latin America and some parts of Southeast Asia still depend fairly directly on the political will of the U.S. citizenry. The United States has thus become a quasi-empire, deciding the fate of

FIGURE 3.4 *How Big Is "Big Government"? The Government's Share*

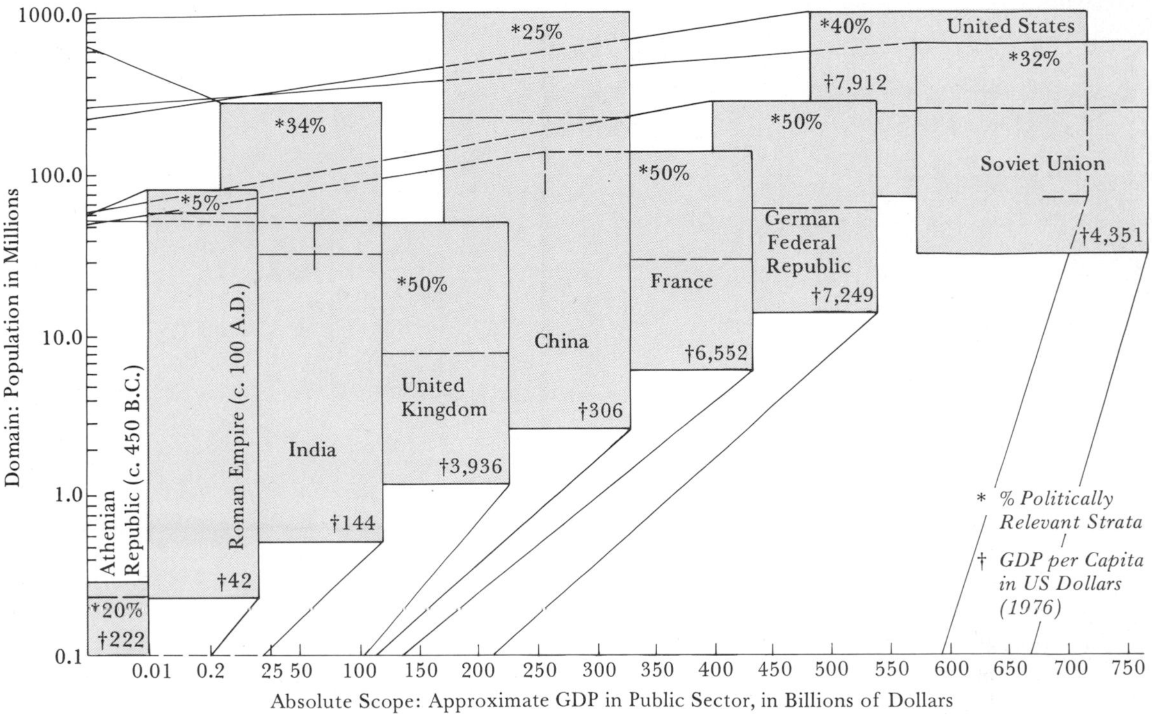

The height of each slab shows the total population within the domain of each state. The width of each slab indicates through the GDP of each slab the approximate amount and variety of the total human activities under government control at all levels of administration. (Note, however, the effects of perspective in the drawing. Who had a bigger job to do: the Roman emperors or the government of the United States?)

For India: Combined central and state government expenditures.

For France: Estimates for all public expenditures, including local, provincial, and public agencies and enterprises; central government expenditures alone were reported as 20 percent and $69 billion, respectively.

Sources: Ruth Leger Sivard, *World Military and Social Expenditures, 1978* (Leesburg, VA.: WMSE Publications, 1978); *United Nations Statistical Yearbook, 1977*, tables 186, 193, 195, 202.

Note that there is a possible discrepancy due to the fact that the GDP figures are for 1976 and, therefore, possibly understated in relation to the 1978 population figures.

FIGURE 3.5 *How Big Is "Big Government"? The Government's Job*

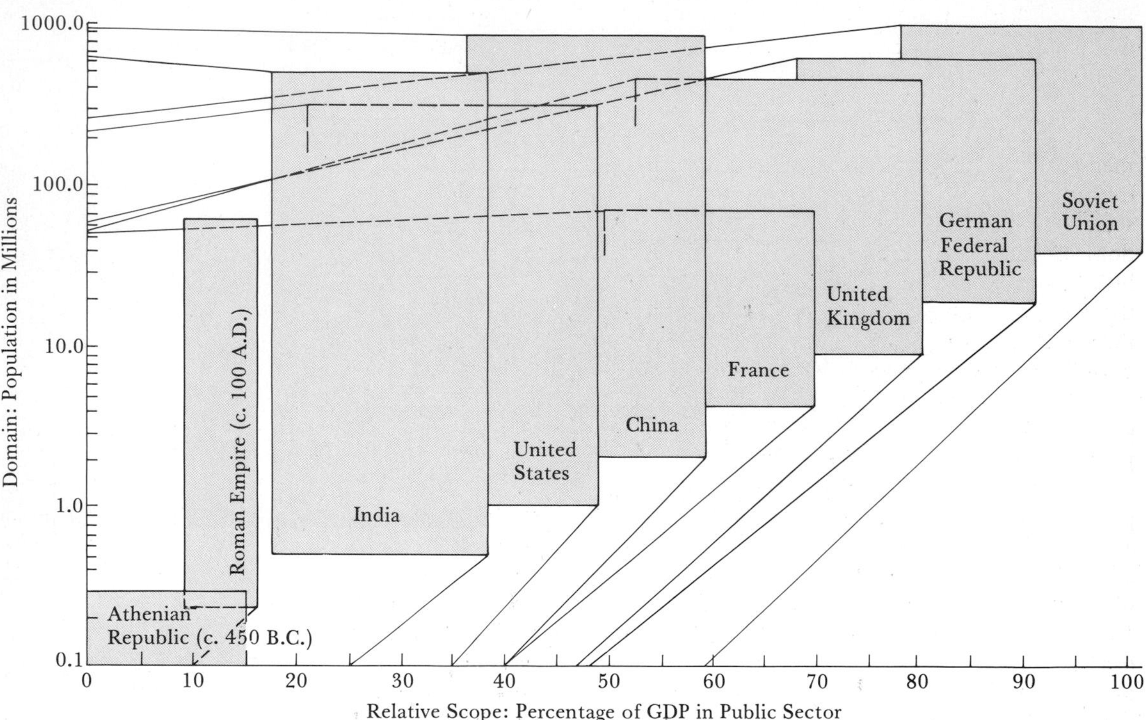

The height of each slab shows the total population within the domain of each state. The width of each slab indicates through the GDP of each slab the approximate amount and variety of the total human activities under government control at all levels of administration. (Note, however, the effects of perspective in the drawing. Who had a bigger job to do: the Roman emperors or the government of the United States?)

For India: Combined central and state government expenditures.

For France: Estimates for all public expenditures, including local, provincial, and public agencies and enterprises; central government expenditures alone were reported as 20 percent and $69 billion, respectively.

Sources: Sivard, *World Military and Social Expenditures, 1978; United Nations Statistical Yearbook, 1977*, tables 186, 202.

about 400 million people in the world. Its political activists currently are about 3 percent of the metropolitan population, and its relevant strata are 36 percent.

In the Soviet Union the scope of the government sector is even larger. The central government alone spends more than 59 percent of the income. Added to this, the budgets of the constituent republics, the other subdivisions of the government, and the municipalities bring the portion of the Soviet GNP that goes through the political sector to roughly 75 percent. The direct human domain, about 261 million people in 1978, is a little larger than that of the United States, and there are another 80 to 100 million people in the satellite countries—East Germany, Poland, Czechoslovakia, Hungary, and Bulgaria—who are fairly directly dependent on the will of the Soviet government. The activists are 13 percent and the politically relevant strata about 45 percent.

Clearly, the one thing that is changing the politics of the world is a huge shift from mass apathy to mass participation. Ancient, medieval, and even absolutist eighteenth-century politics were based on the participation of between 1 and 10 percent of the population. In Western Europe during the first half of the nineteenth century, only 10 percent of the adults of a country could vote. Today approximately three-quarters of a percent of the population in every developing country every year is shifting into mass communication, activity, and modernity and thus is likely to become relevant in politics. More will be said about these changes in Chapter 17 on the developing countries, but the process of change is at work everywhere. By the end of the twentieth century, more than three-fourths of all adults in the world's highly developed countries, or more than one-half of their total population, will be relevant in politics. This shift to broader participation is under way today. It already has transformed the entire nature of politics and has engendered vast new hopes and dangers. Now begun, it will be almost impossible to stop.

KEY TERMS AND CONCEPTS

top elite
position method
reputation method
central elite
mid-elite
the pyramid of influence
core of the mid-elite
marginal elite
politically relevant strata
activist
opportunity cost
Equal Rights Amendment (ERA)
polyarchy
immobility-emergency cycle
interest elite
establishment
articulate
aggregate
logrolling
Burke's definition of conservatism
party ideology
one-party system
totalitarian system
authoritarian system
two-party system
parties of action
parties of expression
multiparty system
coalition agreement
policy-oriented party
power-oriented party
membership party
skeleton party
primaries
matching funds
party machine
party apparat
iron law of oligarchy
scope
domain
metropolitan power

ADDITIONAL READINGS

Adamany, D. W. *Campaign Finance in America.* North Scituate, Mass.: Duxbury Press, 1972. PB

Agger, R., D. Goldrich, and B. Swanson. *The Rulers and the Ruled.* Rev. ed. North Scituate, Mass.: Duxbury Press, 1972. PB

Alexander, H. *Campaign Money: Reform and Reality in the States.* New York: Free Press, 1976. PB

———. *Financing Politics: Money, Elections and Political Reform.* Washington, D.C.: Congressional Quarterly Press, 1976.

Berry, J. M. *Lobbying for the People: The Political Behavior of Public Interest Groups.* Princeton, N.J.: Princeton University Press, 1977.

Blondel, J. *Comparing Political Systems.* New York: Praeger, 1972. PB

Dahl, R. A. *Congress and Foreign Policy.* New York: Norton, 1964. PB

———. *Polyarchy: Participation and Opposition.* New Haven: Yale University Press, 1972. PB

———. *Who Governs? Democracy and Power in an American City.* New Haven: Yale University Press, 1961. PB

Deutsch, K. W., L. J. Edinger, R. C. Macridis, and R. L. Merritt. *France, Germany and the Western Alliance: A Study of Elite Attitudes on European Integration and World Politics.* New York: Scribner's, 1967.

Heard, A. *Costs of Democracy.* Chapel Hill: University of North Carolina Press, 1960. PB

Hoopes, T. *The Limits of Intervention.* New York: McKay, 1969. PB

Horowitz, I., ed. *Power, Politics and People: The Collected Essays of C. Wright Mills.* Oxford: Oxford University Press, 1967.

Keller, S. *Beyond the Ruling Class: Strategic Elites in Modern Society.* New York: Random House, 1963. PB

Lane, R. E. *Political Life.* New York: Free Press, 1959. PB

Lasswell, H. D., and D. Lerner, eds. *World Revolutionary Elites.* Cambridge: MIT Press, 1965.

Lipset, S. M. *Political Man: The Social Bases of Politics.* New York: Doubleday Anchor, 1959. PB

Mills, C. W. *The Power Elite.* Oxford: Oxford University Press, 1956. PB

Polsby, N. *Community Power and Political Theory.* New Haven: Yale University Press, 1963. PB

Pool, I. de S., et al. *Candidates, Issues and Strategies: A Computer Simulation of the 1960 and 1964 Presidential Elections.* Cambridge: MIT Press, 1965. PB

Prewitt, K., and A. Stone. *The Ruling Elites.* New York: Harper & Row, 1973. PB

Reid, T. R. "Public Trust, Private Money." *Washington Post Magazine,* November 26, 1978, pp. 12–31.

Rejai, M., ed. *Decline of Ideology?* Chicago–New York: Aldine-Atherton, 1971. PB

Rose, R. *People in Politics: Observations Across the Atlantic.* New York: Basic Books, 1970.

Verba, S., and N. H. Nie. *Participation in America: Political Democracy and Social Equality.* New York: Harper & Row, 1972.

Verba, S., et al. *Participation and Political Equality.* Cambridge: Cambridge University Press, 1978.

Waxman, C. I., ed. *The End of Ideology Debate.* New York: Funk and Wagnalls, 1968. PB

PB = *available in paperback*

IV

Images of Politics: Some Classic Theories of Behavior and Community

People respond to events not only in terms of what happens, but also in terms of what they think is happening. They respond according to their perceptions of each situation, and hence they respond in part to the memories and images that they already have been carrying in their minds.

Each *perception* is the child of a message and a memory. With our eyes we may see a red blob, while our memory may help us recall earlier experiences with a red necktie, and so we now may perceive this blob as a necktie of similar shape and color. We may even perceive it as being fashionable or unfashionable, cheap or expensive, appropriate or inappropriate for this particular social occasion, if our memories or images are rich enough to permit such a complex act of recognition. If we had never seen a necktie before, we might not recognize the first one we saw; or if we had seen only bow ties, we might not recognize a four-in-hand. Finally, we may recombine some of our memories into new images, and later we may perceive something in the outside world that seems to correspond to what we have imagined.

If we receive a large and confusing jumble of messages and impressions from our environment, such remembered images may help us to sort them into some kind of order and to perceive more clearly those elements or patterns that seem familiar. Images, ideas, theories, and ideologies are all different, but partly overlapping, aspects of the process of *orientation*—the process by which we judge where we think we are and what we ought to do.

In the often confusing world of politics, political images and theories help us orient ourselves. Those thinkers and writers who shape our ideas and images today may shape our perceptions and decisions tomorrow. In this way, the classic Greek political philosophers, such as Plato and Aristotle, both expressed and molded the thinking of the ancient Greeks about their city-states.

With the rise of modern states and nations, from the sixteenth century onward, modern political theorists have played a similar part. In the sixteenth and seventeenth centuries Machiavelli, Hobbes, and Locke developed theories of politics and the state that stressed reason and interest as motivating forces; in the eighteenth century Rousseau and Burke added an emphasis on emotions and the concept of local or national community; in the nineteenth century Mill proposed a more refined theory of freedom, and Marx developed a theory of revolution and world community; and in the first half of the twentieth century Lenin and Mao Tse-tung adapted Marx's ideas to the realities of their own vast but, at that time, less-developed countries. Each of these men was a political philosopher who created an impressive image of what he thought politics was all about and of what political outcomes he saw as desirable. Yet each man also tried to be a political scientist whose assertions could be tested not only for their consistency and logic, but also for their veracity, using the empirical evidence of observation and experience. Despite their important disagreements, each of them greatly contributed to the growth of political science.

"THE PRINCES" VERSUS "THE VULGAR": THE TWO-TRACK MODEL OF MACHIAVELLI

Niccolò Machiavelli (1469–1527) was the first modern political scientist. He was a man of considerable practical political experience, gained during fifteen years of diplomatic service for the small Italian city-state of Florence. In 1513 he wrote his best-known work, *The Prince,* which described not what rulers ought to do, but what in fact they were doing. By-passing questions of morality, he tried to describe politics entirely in terms of causes and effects. His ideas have been so influential that they deserve to be examined in some detail.

Like the great natural scientists of the sixteenth and seventeenth centuries, Machiavelli was a daring simplifier. He reduced the vast complexity of political events to the behavior of a few basic units, interacting in accordance with a few fundamental laws. These few units and laws would suffice, he hoped, to account for the whole rich array of observable political events.

Competitors for Power: Princes and Would-Be Princes. The world, as Machiavelli saw it, consisted of only two kinds of people, each with its own kind of goals. A minority consisted of *"princes"*—that is, rulers—and of those who were trying to become princes through intrigues, conspiracies, or revolts. All such princes and would-be princes were striving primarily for power, or at least they should have been doing so. Any prince who was too lazy, ignorant, or benevolent to struggle for power would be eliminated sooner or later by a more active and ruthless competitor who would take his power. In the long run, therefore, princes were selected by a ceaseless competition for power in which they had to struggle for survival. The ideas of the struggle for survival and the selection of the fittest—albeit strictly limited to princes and would-be princes—were clearly implied in Machiavelli's thought, long before Charles Darwin applied them generally to the animal kingdom in the nineteenth century.

In this sense Machiavelli was the first great theorist of *power politics.* The more power a prince had, the more likely he was to survive, provided that he used his power to get still more power, for to fall behind one's competitors in this contest would be fatal. This was true, Machiavelli suggested, of all politics, including both the unending rivalry among states and the contests among ambitious leaders and would-be leaders within them.

Objects of Power: "The Vulgar." The great majority of people, however, were not princes. Machiavelli called them *"the vulgar"* and had little respect for them. "The vulgar," he wrote, "are cowardly, fickle, and ever ready to be deceived." Princes could rule them easily by means of force and fraud. There were only two things that the vulgar seriously cared for—their property and their women—and these a prudent prince ought to leave undisturbed. As long as their taxes remained moderate and their property and families secure, the vulgar would obey the prince and care little about what else he might be doing. As long as the vulgar remained basically content, conspiracies by would-be princes posed no serious danger to the ruler, for they would always be betrayed by some conspirator or by some chance informant.

Machiavelli believed in an ethics of power as well as in power politics. A prince had only one essential "virtue," as Machiavelli understood the word *virtù*. He had to be prepared to do anything in order to get power and to keep and enhance it. He thus needed sufficient prudence, skill, resources, and singleness of purpose to make this virtue effective. All other more conventional virtues, such as honesty, generosity, courage, and piety, must be subordinated to the search for power, and even as subordinate virtues Machiavelli called them desirable, but not essential. If the prince had them, so much the better; if not, his seeming to have them would suffice. If a prince did not really wish to pray in church, he should still take care to be seen in church. For the same reason, a prince should bestow rewards in person, slowly and as publicly as possible, but should mete out penalties quietly, quickly, and indirectly, through subordinates. By such methods he might make himself appear better and kinder to his subjects than he actually was—and they would believe him.

A Double Standard of Morality. Just as there were two kinds of people in Machiavelli's world, the princes and the vulgar, so were there two kinds of morality. Ordinary people—the vulgar—should be taught to follow traditional morality with its obligations of honesty, truthfulness, loyalty to friends and allies, peaceful and unselfish behavior, and obedience to legitimate superiors and commands. But for the princes, and for any state or government functioning in the role of a prince, this ordinary morality was not binding. States and their rulers might rob and kill, lie and deceive, whenever *"reasons of state"*—that is, their prospects for increasing their power—made this seem advisable. In Machiavelli's world, princes and states had only one duty, self-preservation; one rule of conduct, selfishness; one fundamental goal, the increase of their power. They recognized no legitimate superior, no binding law, no outside judgment over their decisions. Yet they expected their subjects, the vulgar, to retain the traditional morality that they as rulers disdained for themselves; and they used secrecy and deception to maintain the separation between these two moralities.

How to Increase a Prince's Power: Force, Fear, Splendor, and Diplomacy. Both the honesty of the subjects and the duplicity of the rulers were to serve one and the same ultimate purpose: the maintenance of the power of the state. For Machiavelli, power was primarily the capacity to employ force. It was created by military, financial, and diplomatic means; and it was supported by the control of territories and populations and the motivation of one's troops. Soldiers were to be recruited from the prince's own territories, so that in serving him they would be defending their own country.

The direct means of force were most important. Gold and bread, according to Machiavelli, accomplished less in politics than men and iron. It was more likely that men and iron would win control over gold and bread than the reverse. The same principle was supposed to hold for prophets and ideas: unarmed prophets, like the Florentine monk Savonarola, had perished; but armed prophets, like Muhammed, had prevailed. (By this logic Machiavelli might have been alerted to the potential power of Lenin and Mao Tse-tung, but he might have expected Luther and Gandhi to fail and Adolf Hitler to succeed.)

A prince should use his wealth to expand his military power and his time to increase his military skill. His major pastime should be hunting, in order to prepare him for military campaigns. A prince should be miserly, not liberal, in paying out financial rewards to anyone, since otherwise he would diminish his future financial resources. A prince should rule through fear, rather than love, for he could not control the feelings of love in his subjects, but could increase their fear. He should take care, however, not to be hated. Finally, he should learn how to dazzle the multitude by conspicuous deeds and brilliant spectacles.

How and When to Break One's Word: The Concept of the Balance of Power. Diplomacy could enhance the power of a prince by providing him with allies and by isolating his current enemy. But a prince had to know when to break an old alliance and when to make a new one, often with his enemy of yesterday. In Machiavelli's world every prince, or every contender for power, was the potential enemy of every other. Since all were equally competitive and aggressive, the chief difference among them lay in their relative strength. The greatest threat to each prince came from his strongest competitor or coalition of competitors. Hence, a prince should never remain neutral in a war among his neighbors. If the strongest among them should prevail, the winner would be a dangerous threat to the prince who had remained neutral. By intervening on the side of a weaker contender, the prince might win and get a share in the spoils, and he would need to worry only about having to fight later against the strongest among his own allies; or, if he should lose, he would at least have an ally in his misfortune. In any case, one's allies today are one's likely enemies tomorrow, and one's current adversaries are one's likely future allies. Part of the art of politics, in Machiavelli's view, consisted in knowing just which ally to betray, just when, and under what conditions.

Machiavelli discussed these matters in the famous eighteenth chapter of *The Prince,* entitled "How Princes Ought to Keep Their Word." His answer was simple: only as long as it is in their *interest* to do so—that is, as long as it helps to preserve or enhance the prince's power vis-à-vis all possible competitors. From this principle he derived something like a calculus of double-crossing. As an ally or neighbor grows stronger, he becomes more of a potential threat; as soon as this potential threat outweighs his usefulness as an ally (or merely as a neutral neighbor), he should be betrayed; an alliance should be formed against him and perhaps an armed attack made. If both princes had studied Machiavelli, of course, neither of them ought to be surprised at this sudden change of political alignments, for each would know exactly what to do and what to expect at each moment. In later centuries this type of reasoning became known as the concept of the *balance of power,* and to this day it has continued to have considerable influence in international politics, although subject to increasing criticism.

Some Possible Outcomes of Machiavelli's Model. In the long run the political system pictured by Machiavelli could have two types of outcomes. If many princes were about evenly matched in skill and resources and if their competence were high, no one prince would ever become much stronger than the rest, since any serious candidate for supremacy would soon be stopped by an opposing coalition. In that case such timely balance-of-power tactics would preserve a plurality of contenders for an indefinite time.

Conversely, if any one contender were sufficiently favored over his competitors by superior resources, skill, or mere chance, or by some combination of these, then he might well end up absorbing the lands of his rivals, one by one, until he would have unified under his single rule the entire contested area. Since Machiavelli in his personal feelings was an Italian patriot, he hoped for the second outcome for Italy and the first for Europe. Some particularly energetic and ruthless prince, he hoped, would unify Italy by a series of conquests and expel the foreign powers—France, Spain, and Austria—from the peninsula. At the same time he hoped that continuing inconclusive competition among the European powers might keep each of them too weak to invade Italy again.

What a single prince could accomplish also could be achieved by a united people. If all jointly had the single-minded virtue, drive for power, that ancient Romans had shown in the days of the republic, a people, too, could form a republic that might defeat kings and princes in the contest for power.

In Machiavelli's lifetime, things did not work out this way. Italy was not united, nor were the foreign armies driven out, until three and a half centuries later. Even the immediate purpose of *The Prince* was not achieved. Machiavelli had written it as a "how to" book, hoping to impress a prince of the Medici family and thereby return to government service. The effort failed, perhaps because the prince and his advisers were frightened by this formidable display of intelligence and ruthlessness. In any case, Machiavelli never got another government job, and he died in obscurity. After his death his influence increased, and his ideas have continued to claim the attention of practical leaders, as well as students of politics, until our time.

Was Machiavelli Realistic? If posterity has agreed that his work was important, it has not agreed on much else about him. Many critics have called him immoral; his defenders have called him realistic. But how realistic was he in the face of the events of his own time?

Machiavelli's model of politics was mechanical. The princes and the vulgar did not change their nature, and they always interacted in accordance with a few unchanging rules. In such a model all history was contemporary. A prince might learn a political trick from Hannibal or from some ancient Greek or Roman as easily as from an Italian of his own day. But is the real history of humankind so unchanging and repetitive?

Since he saw the vulgar as passive and only the princes as active, Machiavelli overlooked the significance of some of the great economic and social changes that were occurring before his eyes. Ever since the Turkish conquest of Constantinople and the eastern Mediterranean in the middle of the fifteenth century, the trade of the Mediterranean, and particularly of Italy, had been declining. This change undercut the economic basis of the prosperity and power of the Italian states. A second change reinforced this effect. Within three decades after Columbus discovered the New World, its gold and silver greatly increased Spain's power; and the main routes of world trade soon thereafter began to shift to the Atlantic Ocean, turning the Mediterranean and Italy increasingly into one of the backwaters of world affairs. Finally, in 1517 a German monk, Martin Luther, started the Reformation, which soon reduced the flow of pilgrims and pious gifts to Rome, a flow that for so long had been one of the sources of Italian prosperity. For most of the next three centuries, Italian states were weak, and Italy remained an arena for the contest of foreign powers.

Machiavelli's *Prince* showed no particular awareness of these three vast changes—the Turkish conquests, the shift of trade to the Atlantic and the New World, and the Reformation—that transformed so profoundly the politics of Italy. In ignoring these basic changes, Machiavelli's realism was a failure. Preoccupied with power and realistic in regard to many of its details, he still overlooked what was happening to its foundations.

EVERY MAN A PRINCE: THE POLITICAL MODELS OF HOBBES AND LOCKE

One of Machiavelli's fundamental assumptions was that there are two radically different kinds of human beings in politics: a small, active minority of princes and other persons of ambition and a large, passive mass of "the vulgar." This assumption was realistic in Machiavelli's day for Italy and, indeed, for much of Europe. But one and a half centuries later, in the England of the mid-seventeenth century, it was patently false. There a half-century of revolution, civil war, and political upheavals had begun in 1640; armed commoners in the armies of Parliament had defeated the king and his noble cavaliers; Charles I had been beheaded in 1649; and the turmoil of revolution and counterrevolution did not finally subside until the Glorious Revolution in 1688 and the Act of Toleration in 1690, which left Britain a constitutional monarchy. During this period a substantial part of the English people was politically active at one time or another.

Thomas Hobbes's work *Leviathan,* which appeared in 1651, continued Machiavelli's scientific approach in terms of fact-mindedness, rationality, and simplification, but it reflected the new situation. Hobbes's title was biblical and poetic: leviathan, a monster of the sea, was a suggestive symbol of England's rising seapower. The frontispiece of the first edition shows a giant whose body is formed by the bodies of ordinary men: it is they, the picture suggests, who jointly make up the state (see Figure 4.1). How and why they do so was to be explained rationally by Hobbes's theory.

Hobbes's model assumed that every man was likely to behave like one of Machiavelli's princes: active, aggressive, and driven by an insatiable greed for power. Hobbes (1588–1679) had a single-minded view of human nature: man is a wolf unto his fellow man. All of us, he suggested, are proving this view when we travel armed on highways, lock our houses at night, lock our cupboards and larders against our servants and children, and accept as normal the competitive and often warlike relations between sovereign states.

Hobbes's Image of the State of Nature. What would happen if people were left without any ruler and were unrestrained from acting in accordance with their wolfish nature? They would return to the *state of nature,* said Hobbes, and this state of nature would be a war of everybody against everybody else. In this endless war no one ever would be safe. The strongest man could be killed in his sleep by a weaker enemy or overwhelmed by greater numbers. Everyone would live in fear, and his life as Hobbes put it, would be "solitary, nasty, brutish, and short."

Life without government would be so intolerable that people would submit sooner or later to a ruler or group of rulers strong enough to keep them from one another's throats and to enforce peace and security among them. Any ruler who had the power to do this would be legitimate and would deserve to be obeyed, as long as he was strong enough to enforce peace among his subjects. No matter how unjust or immoral his rule otherwise might be, it would still be preferable to the horrors of the state of nature. Thus Hobbes defended *absolute monarchy.*[1] He justified tyranny in the name of order.

The Sovereign. Being the strongest of all, the ruler had to obey no will but his own. Accordingly, Hobbes called him *the sovereign* and included in this term both kings and parliaments or other collective bodies as long as they acted in this role. Only for one cause would a sovereign forfeit his claim to be obeyed: if he became too weak to

[1]A monarch was called "absolute" if he was held to be "absolved" from all human laws. His pleasure was the supreme law in his realm. As to divine law, only the monarch ruling "by the grace of God" was entitled to interpret its meaning. An absolute monarchy existed when a monarch already had forced his nobles to obey him, but had not yet been compelled to share power with the middle class or the masses of the people. Absolute monarchy survived until the seventeenth century in England, until the nineteenth century in the rest of western Europe, and until 1917 in Russia. During the 1970s it survived in Saudi Arabia, but was overthrown in Ethiopia and Iran. A somewhat similar theory asserted that a chief executive, such as the president of the United States, has the right to override ordinary laws and even constitutional safeguards in any situation that he or she decides involves the "national security"; further, this individual alone has the right to make such a decision without consulting anyone else. Any action then undertaken in such a case by the president or staff, according to this theory, should be presumed legal. Reasoning along these lines was expounded by John Ehrlichman, a former high White House aide, at a televised hearing of the United States Senate in August 1973.

FIGURE 4.1 *Title Page of Hobbes's* Leviathan, *1651*

Source: The Bettmann Archive, Inc.

enforce his commands. But if weakness should cause his downfall, the state of nature simply would return and soon become intolerable; sooner or later a contender for power would emerge, stronger than the rest; and people would obey the new sovereign in order to have peace.

Since all human beings, in Hobbes's view, were insatiably aggressive, the basic choice of politics was between anarchy and order; and the basis of order was the power of the ruler, reinforced by the need of his subjects for his order-keeping services. By Hobbes's logic, obedience to any government was justified in domestic politics, as long as it had the power to keep order; but no less justified was obedience to any more powerful successor who, having overthrown the government, could establish himself in its place. Applied to international affairs, as it was by some later writers, Hobbes's line of reasoning would justify any type of world empire or world government, regardless of whether it was based on conquest or consent and regardless of whether it was exercised by one nation or several, as long as it could enforce some sort of peace and international order.

Hobbes's Version of the Social Contract. To escape the terrors of the state of nature, Hobbes thought, people would make a contract to hand over all their powers to some person, or body of persons, to rule them. By making such a *social contract,* people would create an organized political society to enforce peace among them; that is, they would create a state. This contract, however, according to Hobbes, bound only the people, not the ruler; the latter was doing the people a favor in ruling them and saving them from the state of nature. Within this state, therefore, the ruler's powers would be unlimited; any attempt to limit his powers or resist his commands either would fail, if the ruler were strong enough to suppress it, or would risk bringing back the state of nature with all its terrors, if he were not. Later generations of people in such an organized political society or state would be considered parties to the same social contract; they were held to have joined it tacitly, by having chosen not to leave it.

Hobbes's model of politics was simple and elegant, powerful and terrifying. By focusing almost entirely on power, greed, and fear, Hobbes achieved an admirable economy of means for a model that seemed to account for a wide range of political events. But the model was a caricature of reality.

Hobbes's theory went too far and left out too much. It was too simple and elegant to be realistic. Greed, fear, and power are not the only motives that impel people to comply with laws, obey rulers, and give support to governments. As we have seen, people have many needs and pursue many values for which they may turn to their government. Nor do people always have such great fear of their fellow men, or such little confidence in themselves, that they will entrust unlimited power to any tyrant strong enough to keep them from fighting one another.

Hobbes's arguments in some ways fitted the mood of many English people in the early 1650s, when they accepted, until his death, the dictatorship of Lord Protector Oliver Cromwell, and in the 1660s, when they accepted the restoration of the monarchy and the return of a Stuart king, Charles II. But in the 1680s that mood changed. In 1688 the English people overthrew the Stuart monarchy once more and drove Charles II's successor, James II, into exile. The English Parliament invited another ruler, William of Orange, to the throne, and England became a limited monarchy with power divided between Parliament and the king. (For details, see Chapter 12.)

Locke and the Law of Nature. During those years another English thinker, John Locke (1632–1704), developed a more sophisticated theory of politics. People were moved by self-interest, he argued, but they did not always have to fight one another like wolves. Rather they were also capable of rational thought and of moderate, practical behavior even with no ruler or government above them. Indeed, those foolish enough to do nothing but fight would be less likely to survive than those who behaved more reasonably. The state of nature, therefore, was subject to the *law of nature,* and hence it did not seem as frightening to Locke as it had to Hobbes. If a Frenchman and an Englishman, both armed, should meet "in the woods of North America," as Locke put it, they need not fight each other; they might prefer to trade.

Eventually, Locke added, they might find it more convenient to establish a common government with laws, but they would do so only if life under such a government would be better than their life in the state of nature, in which they had managed tolerably well.

Here was a key point in the argument. Hobbes had seen life without government as well-nigh unbearable, but Locke saw it as practicable and acceptable. For Hobbes, any government was better than none. For Locke, government had to be an improvement on the state of nature, a state that, according to him, was already fairly livable.

A Reasonable Social Contract—and a Constitution. Locke, like Hobbes, saw the state as founded by a contract, but in Locke's view the ruler was a party to the contract. People would promise to obey him in the expectation that he would not merely keep domestic peace, but would also protect property and maintain the laws of the land. If the ruler should fail in his duties, his subjects would have no further obligation to obey him. They could now legitimately depose him—even if he were a king—and make a new contract with another ruler who would have to promise to keep his part of the contract as a condition of staying in office.

Such a fundamental contract, binding on the ruler or the government, is in effect a *constitution*—a fundamental law that lays down the powers and limits of government as well as the rights and duties of citizens, and states what kinds of laws can be made, by whom, and by what procedures. Locke was thus a theorist of *constitutionalism*—that is, of limited government based on fundamental law.

Locke was aware, of course, that the British constitution was for the most part unwritten; and it has remained so to this day. It consisted, then as now, largely in the memories, habits, and expectations of the British elites and of ever broader masses of the British people and in the past decisions of their governments and courts of law, which had created precedents for later generations to follow. These memories, precedents, and expectations, however, amounted in Locke's view to a tacit contract of English citizens with their kings and magistrates and with one another. Each king, in accepting his coronation, accepted his obligations under this contract, and so did every British subject so far as rights and obligations were concerned, simply by *not* emigrating and *not* renouncing allegiance to the crown. Any subject who broke this contract by refusing to obey the laws was liable to the penalties for crime, treason, or rebellion, as the case might be. But the king, too, in this view, had to keep the contract and obey the laws. As long as he did so, his rule was *legitimate* and could not be changed or ended, even if a majority of the people should so desire, for the contract was binding on them while the king kept it. Only if the king failed to keep his obligations could he be lawfully resisted and deposed. These views of Locke's prevailed in Britain and became an important part of its political tradition.

Individualism, Property, and Natural Rights. Were men really as normally moderate and prudent, as self-interested and relatively self-sufficient, and as rational and tolerably well endowed with property as Locke's politics required? Locke believed so, at least as far as those men were concerned who counted in the politics of his own time, that is, the property-owning upper and middle classes. In his view, men thought and acted as individuals, and rights belonged to individuals, not groups. As he saw it, every man had a *natural right*—that is, an inborn right that nobody could give away, even if he wanted to—to claim as his *property* any part of nature with which he had "mixed his own labor." All other titles to property, through inheritance, purchase, and the like, were legitimate by natural right insofar as they were derived from this original foundation. Liberty was another natural right of individuals. It was legitimate and it was to be expected that men claim their natural rights sooner or later, always and everywhere, and resist or overthrow any government that denied such rights. If, but only if, their rulers broke the social contract or violated natural rights, men had the right to revolution.[2]

Locke's political theory fitted reality best where real life came closest to fulfilling these conditions. In a world of at least moderately propertied and self-sufficient individuals, no one who mattered would long be in desperate poverty or in desperate need on any other grounds. Such a world would not require a closely knit community to bind individuals together in common cares and feelings in order to share one another's gains and burdens through understanding, aid, and solidarity.

But reality eventually created just such needs. In one country after another, people began to participate in politics, even without having the property, education, and status that Locke had more or less taken for granted. Living often under greater stress, facing deeper poverty and the need for more desperate efforts, such people could not rest content with only the individualistic political philosophy of Locke or Hobbes or Machiavelli. Rather, they yearned for a deeper, warmer, more protective, and more powerful community, and in time new philosophers of political community arose to meet their needs.

[2]In line with this way of thinking, the Declaration of Independence in 1776 accused King George III and his government of a series of such violations, in order to justify the American Revolution.

THE CONCEPT OF COMMUNITY

Many people look on their nations as more than instruments. They seek a sense of community and of belonging to something bigger than themselves. To feel that one truly belongs to a group of people, and in particular to the society in which one is living, means far more than merely being mechanically included in it. An outside observer may lump people together in the same census category because they share some superficial characteristic, such as "unmarried" or "born before 1930," but they will not necessarily feel that they belong to each other in any deeper sense. Indeed, they may look on one another as strangers and on their society as a strange land in which they see themselves as outsiders. This is the feeling of *alienation,* so well known to modern poets, philosophers, and young people in many lands—the feeling of being alone in a world that is unintelligible, unpredictable, and unrewarding.

The sense of *belonging* is the very opposite of such feelings of alienation. It means looking in a special way on one's society, that is, the group of people among whom one lives and makes one's living by taking part in the division of labor. We look on our society as a community which we accept and within which we feel accepted. We are at home in it; and home, as Robert Frost once wrote, is where they have to take you in.

A *community* is a group of people whom one understands and by whom one is understood. It promises—and often delivers—a breakthrough in communication from person to person. It is *particularistic* rather than universal, for only its own particular members—and not everyone—belongs to it. A community is *ascriptive* rather than achievement-oriented, for a person is accepted in it for what that person is rather than for what he or she does; and once an individual is in it, he or she does not have to earn membership again and again. Finally, it is *diffuse* rather than specific, for it accepts a wide range of responsibilities rather than being limited to a single task. Its members can turn to it in whatever respect they may need its aid. A ski club is a specific organization that takes no interest in its members in summer, but a community, like a family, cares for its members at any time and tries to help them meet their needs.

Could there be a community large enough to have the powers of a nation and yet small enough to be a kind of larger family? And could enough of these true communities be set up to include all humanity? People have sought answers to these questions for many years, both in thought and in practice. Some of the great political thinkers of the last two centuries have proposed some answers, based on their own points of view. Their efforts may suggest insights applicable to our own problems in this day.

ROUSSEAU: A PROPHET OF INDIVIDUALISM AND COMMUNITY

Perhaps the most relevant eighteenth-century thinker for the problems of nationality and community was Jean Jacques Rousseau (1712–1778), the watchmaker's son from Geneva. Rousseau was an itinerant, sometimes a hippie, and sometimes a man bent on making a career. So sensitive was he that a contemporary called him "the skinless man." He could be incredibly diligent, but he quarreled prodigiously and at times was illogical. The author of major books, he was the herald of the most elaborate doctrine of civic duties we have had in the world.

Discovering the Individual and Human Emotions. Rousseau was perhaps the first writer to rebel against the rationalist and Enlightenment-oriented climate of the eighteenth century. By emphasizing the profound importance of human emotions, he brought back into politics and social thought a consideration of the whole personality of human beings, not only their rational parts. He was, among other things, a theorist of education. Before Rousseau, most of the breed from Plato to Locke and Hartley and the theorists and psychologists of association had thought that the task of education was to find some perfect, desirable pattern that one could impose on more or less defenseless children until they were formed and shaped to fit their culture. In other words, education had been considered the knowledge of the shaping, forming, and molding of children. A Quaker theorist wrote in the seventeenth century, "children are accursed creatures." The only good thing many people could say about children then was that they were getting older every day.

Rousseau took a different view. One would have to go all the way back to the New Testament and its words, "Unless you become like little children . . ." to find a parallel outlook. He believed that there was something very important in being young and that education should consist of bringing out what was already inside young people rather than impressing upon them what was in society. Inside every individual, according to Rousseau, was something original and unique that made him or her different from everyone else and from the standardized beliefs and habits that society taught people to copy from each other. Education, for Rousseau, was a process that occurred not from the outside in, but from the inside out. For that reason he thought that education should be based on sincerity and spontaneity and that it should encourage self-activity, autonomy, independence, and genuine personal experiences among the young.

From the Individual to the Community. In education Rousseau was a radical libertarian, but in politics he was a theorist of community. In his opinion, the more often people are allowed to live as individuals, developing their whole personalities and following their emotions, the more they discover their need for community and the more salient and urgent the problem of community becomes. Clearly, Rousseau could not try to be a thoroughgoing theorist of individualism without realizing the crucial importance of the problem of community. Human beings are so built that they can be individuals only with the help of and within communities. Communities, on the other hand, can make human individuality richer and freer or they can stifle it. Not surprisingly, many of the great theorists of individualism were also the great theorists of the search for more promising or more hopeful forms of community.

Rousseau tried to make his theory of community wholly rational and logical. His famous book, *The Social Contract,* is a heroic effort at such rational, logical thinking. He based it on the assumption that communities are created by an act of human will. Rousseau had every reason to think this way. He was a citizen of Geneva, which had been a city in the Holy Roman Empire and had become a republic through a political revolution—an act of the political will—in 1526. The independence of Geneva had been confirmed by alliances with Bern and Zurich, by the voluntary conversion of the city to Calvinism, and then by its success in fighting off the efforts of its former overlords, the princes of neighboring Savoy, to reconquer Geneva and make it part of their state. By voluntary political ties to Switzerland, Geneva had also avoided being incorporated into France. Thus, by an act of the political will Geneva had become a republic, and by sustained acts of political will the republic had been preserved.

Rousseau was aware of other states similarly created. Eastward from Geneva, the city-states of Bern and Zurich and the entire Swiss Confederation were also political entities created by acts of will. In Rousseau's own time, of course, there were the American colonies, not yet independent, but clearly rooted in voluntary efforts and agreements. Most of the first colonists had chosen to go to the New World. And by acts of will, by treaties—that is, by social contracts—the Massachusetts Bay Colony and the colony of Connecticut had been formed.

The Sovereignty of the People. Rousseau assumed, therefore, that a state came into existence by explicit or tacit agreement. Explicitly, people said, "We want to be a state, a community"; by tacit agreement they chose to stay inside such a community and not emigrate. Up to this point, Rousseau's idea of the social contract did not look so very different from the social contract theories of Thomas Hobbes and John Locke. But Rousseau developed the theory of the social contract in a radically different direction.

For Rousseau, the state and the people were one. The people, in turn, were one through common customs and habits. Rousseau assumed that whenever individuals decided that they belonged to a people, they already had decided that this people should be sovereign and that, being sovereign, this people should run its own affairs. The people, therefore, constituted the state. Having created the state, the people ought to control it and change it as they pleased. This is the doctrine of *popular sovereignty.*

Under this doctrine, the people owe nothing to the magistrates, the rulers. Legislators are merely enactors or messengers of the popular will; civil servants are servants of the people. The people can decide whether to continue the present political institutions or to change them. An echo of Rousseau's thought appears in Lincoln's first inaugural address: "This country, with its institutions, belongs to the people who inhabit it. Whenever they shall grow weary of the existing government, they can exercise their constitutional right of amending it, or their revolutionary right to dismember or overthrow it." This is Rousseau's popular sovereignty theory in radical form.

To be so powerful against its officials, a people also must be powerful in relation to its own members. Accordingly, Rousseau argued that in order to have such a sovereign people that completely controlled the state and guaranteed the same freedoms to all its members, the people had to make very great claims on the individual. Rousseau asserted that in the social contract every individual surrendered himself or herself totally to the community. This formally unlimited surrender was limited in its effects, however, by every other individual's doing likewise. And no individual, reasoned Rousseau, would make more oppressive demands on a neighbor in the name of popular sovereignty than he or she would personally accept. Moreover, he thought, since any sane person's will could only accord with his or her own interests, the state would never make unwarranted demands. It would use its claim on the person, time, loyalty, and property of its citizens only as necessary. Uniformity in the outlook and interests of its citizens, mutuality of their claims, rationality in their thought, and realism in their perception of what was necessary thus would assure that the unlimited claims of the state would be moderate and limited in practice.

Political movements stressing the unlimited right of popular majorities to impose their will on the entire community, over and against any elites, experts, minorities, and dissenters, have been called *populism,* and their language has often resembled Rousseau's—although usually without his conditions and qualifications. Such movements usually have been simple in thought and short-lived in politics, while Rousseau's own more carefully thought-out theories have had a lasting influence.

The General Will versus the Will of All. The state, as Rousseau saw it, would be steered and controlled by the general will of the people. The *general will* is the sum of all those interests that people have in common. Yet, most individuals also had some interests that were private or personal or special for themselves or for their families and that were different from their neighbors'. These different special interests, constituting the *particular will* of individuals, could not be the basis of government, according to Rousseau: they could be the basis only of some political faction. As long as their common interests clearly were more important to individuals, these persons could form a community and make it work. Within such a true community, each individual had both a higher and a lower self. The former was the source of the general will, and the latter was the source of the particular will. The majority of these particular wills, not based on the common interest of the whole community, Rousseau called the *will of all.* To Rousseau, obedience to the general will both represented a higher moral duty and was more in line with an individual's true interests than indulgence of the particular will, as long as he or she lived in a genuine community.

Rousseau assumed that in any group of persons there would be an overlap of interests. But the overlap could be small or large. If it were large enough, the general will would be strong. If the overlap were small and the special interests greater, the general will would be feeble. Thus, any group of persons who had enough interests in common to permit the establishment of a general will could form a people; but if the overlapping interests were too few or unimportant, then one people could not be formed. At this point, reality would decide. The size and significance of a group's common interests, as opposed to the permanence and the power of its divergent ones, is an empirical question. Hence, Rousseau's notion is tied to a potentially verifiable question: do these persons truly have common interests?

Rousseau believed it possible to have many such groups of persons, those with enough common interests to form a general will. However, the formation of a general will seemed to require relatively small communities of about the size of the city-state of Geneva or a small republic. Rousseau was not sure that large unions, such as communities of millions of people, could have an overwhelming body of common interests.

The general will could not be forcibly obtained. It had to be achieved by the independent judgment of its citizens, as each saw his or her own interests. In order to form the general will, said Rousseau, each individual had to vote quite independently from all others. Because individuals differed from each other, their views were also likely to differ to some extent. But since these views were all based on the same common interests, they would all be scattered around some mean or middle value that also would be the most popular.

Modern statistics has long had technical terms for these three magnitudes. The *mean* is the arithmetic average of a collection of measurements. The *median* is the measurement that falls exactly in the middle of the collection, so that there are as many larger findings above it as there are smaller ones below. Finally, the *mode* of a collection is that group of measurements within it containing the largest number of cases. Many observations in nature and society produce findings that show a bell-shaped *normal distribution,* or *standard error curve,* in which mean, median, and mode all coincide (see Figure 4.2). Approximate examples are the height of men, the height of women, the distribution of "intelligence" (or rather, expected success in college, as measured by college aptitude tests), the scattering of rifle shots around the bull's eye of a target, the numbers that come up in a crap game with two dice (unless they are loaded), and the distribution of attitudes in a community whose voters are in fundamental agreement. It is the last of these situations that politicians refer to when they say that they wish to keep to the "mainstream" or to the "middle of the road."

FIGURE 4.2 *Bell-Shaped and Skewed Curves*

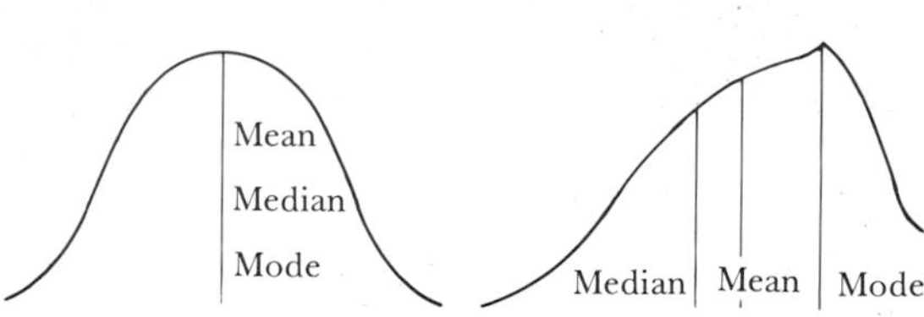

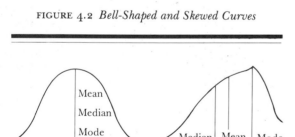

The bell-shaped curve depicts a normal distribution. There can also exist a skewed curve which reflects an asymmetric distribution.

Rousseau, it seems, was beginning to think in terms of this new science of statistics, which had been developed by Blaise Pascal, Jacques Bernoulli, and others. He was particularly attracted to the theory that large numbers of people or large samples will cancel many inaccuracies or accidental errors, thereby providing a more accurate total result, and that measuring something not once but ten times, and measuring each time independently, makes the resulting average figure more accurate than the result of a single measurement. Rousseau hoped for a precise, accurate, sensitive perception of common interests or the general will through the creation of a people sufficiently uniform and small enough in number to have common interests and yet sufficiently independent from one another and large enough not to be swayed by the accidental passions or mistakes of a few individuals.

If people formed factions or cliques, this hope could no longer be fulfilled. Common interests and a general will would prevail only *within* each faction, but not *among* the factions. No longer would there be as many votes as individuals, but only as many votes as there were parties or factions. These votes would then be moved not by the common interest of all, but by the special interests of each faction, group, or party. In such a faction-ridden society even a majority vote would no longer represent the general will, but merely the *will of all;* and the will of all might be both unjust and unrealistic for the community as a whole.

By contrast, the general will was always right by definition, said Rousseau, because it consisted in discerning what should be done in the true interests of the community. Given realistic, well-educated, well-informed, thoughtful, and independent citizens, the vote would very likely reach just such a verdict. On the other hand, if citizens were not as well informed as they should be, there might be a wide gap between what the majority of the people wanted and what was good for them.

The Logic of Reality and the Logic of Coercion. Of course, the real people of the eighteenth century—and for that matter of the twentieth century—were not all that well educated or that wise. Very often even the outcome of a popular vote might not be in the popular interest. In seventeenth-century Brandenburg, poor farmers had tried to eat potatoes raw and had suffered stomachaches as a result. It would have been easy to get a majority of these peasants to agree that potatoes were no good and to vote against cultivating and eating them. It was only after a tyrannical Prussian king had marched soldiers with fixed bayonets into the villages to force the peasants to boil the potatoes before eating them that the German farmers took to potato eating on a grand scale. Ignorance has often been more popular than knowledge. For several centuries the equivalents of Gallup polls would have registered landslide majorities for the proposition that the world is flat. These examples show that it is possible to obtain popular majorities based on grievous misperceptions of fact. However, if we accept the proposition that there can be emergency situations in which the majority of people cannot discern their true interests or form an adequate picture of reality, we open the way for an emergency dictatorship by an enlightened minority.

This is precisely what Rousseau's theory did. Rousseau spoke of the logic of facts—*la logique des choses.* He said that things had a logic of their own and that it might be necessary to act in accordance with the *logic of reality* rather than with the logic of popular illusion. In this sense the French revolutionary leader Maximilien Robespierre was a true disciple of Rousseau. He thought he knew what had to be done to save the French Revolution. Those who did not share his "enlightened" insight had to be constrained to obey; if necessary, they had to be beheaded. Rousseau had furnished the arguments for Robespierre's line of reasoning.

It was quite possible, Rousseau said, for a man to have a common public interest while also having a conflicting private interest. The government and the people then had the right and duty to constrain him, and by doing so, they would force him to be free. This sounds like casuistry, but it is not. Consider a young man in a sports car in a great hurry; he would like to pick up his date and get her to the theater in time. He speeds through a dangerous intersection; a policeman stops him and hauls him off to jail. Rousseau, looking down from heaven, would say, "The young man has been forced to be free." Rousseau would explain to the listening archangels that the young man, most of all, wants to be alive; indeed, his date wants him to be alive, too. To be sure, the young man has a personal, transitory interest in hurrying up, but he has a fundamental and enduring interest in staying alive. He also has an enduring interest in not killing other people. Another example is seen in the laws of several states and countries requiring motorcyclists to wear helmets. Since falls from this form of transport are highly dangerous, the community tries to force the riders not to crack their skulls.

The general will, then, once it is joined with an assumption of superior knowledge, opens the way to an emergency dictatorship. It can be used to justify compulsion, constraint, the draft, and the forcing of people to die for the good of the community. Rousseau would say that since the state defended the lives of its citizens every day by maintaining security, it was only taking back the lives it had preserved in the preceding months and years in drafting men for military service. Nothing but the collectivity's own self-restraint could limit its claims against the individual; and such claims could be made not only by a majority that thought it represented the general will, but also by any minority that regarded itself as so enlightened as to know a people's true interests better than the people itself. Thus Rousseau the libertarian, Rousseau the emotionalist, Rousseau the individualist became, perhaps unwittingly, Rousseau the apostle of almost unlimited collectivism. Here he moved from a community that unites individuals toward a *collectivity* that prevails over them.

BURKE: CONSERVATISM, EXPERIENCE, AND CONTINUITY

Rousseau's thought found its counterpart in the philosophy of a man who shared his view of the political importance of emotions and customs, but who temperamentally was his opposite—Edmund Burke (1729–1797). A brilliant Irishman, a great orator and writer, Burke rose to prominence through his association with some of the leading noblemen and political leaders of eighteenth-century England. He saw the world from their point of view and presented their case with power and conviction. Indeed, he went them one better: few members of the corrupt English nobility of the age of George III were as profound, enlightened, and responsible conservatives as he would have liked them to be, although some later English political and military leaders came close to his ideal.

Rousseau was an ideological forerunner of the French Revolution and its aftermath. Burke became the ideologist of the counterrevolution. But Burke did not differ much from Rousseau in some respects. He shared Rousseau's doubt about the perfection of rationalism and rationality. He also shared Rousseau's view of the importance of popular feelings and traditions. Where Burke differed decisively from Rousseau was in his view of human knowledge.

Burke's Theory of Knowledge. Burke, following the philosopher David Hume, assumed that the truth could be only tentatively proposed by convention and only imperfectly confirmed by experience. Truth was never established by being self-evident; it was never fixed and immutable. People's abilities to discern reality and to recognize their own interests were quite weak.

Humankind, said Burke, is wise; the individual is not. Therefore, people should never demand liberty in general, but only specific liberties that have stood the test of time. When a madman has burst his bonds, asked Burke, should I congratulate him on the recovery of his liberty? This image is indicative of Burke's view of human nature. The average person was feeble, weak, giddy, and comparable to a madman. Thus, the common people—and, of course, the young—must be constrained for their own good.

Popular sovereignty was abhorrent to Burke. In a democracy people assumed that anything was moral if their neighbors considered it to be moral: "Nothing is as shameless as a democracy." (History does not wholly contradict him. If the Athenian democracy thought that unwanted babies should be left to starve in the marketplace and the Athenian people walking by found this perfectly acceptable, this was what the Athenian democracy considered moral. A majority of voters in some parts of the Deep South might condone murders by the Ku Klux Klan. Between 1933 and 1945, there were majorities in parts of Germany for some of Hitler's crimes—against peace, against the Jews, against other peoples, and against his domestic opponents.)

Aristocrats, said Burke, have more of a sense of shame because they must ask themselves what posterity will think of their actions; anonymous citizens in a popular majority have no such thoughts. (In fact, Burke's division between nobles who think of the future and commoners who do not has not proved to be valid. When Churchill spoke to the British electorate in 1940, he said, "Let us . . . so bear ourselves that [later generations] will . . . say, 'this was their finest hour.'" Churchill treated every British voter as a person with a stake in posterity.) But Burke assumed that all peoples and all governments—monarchies and aristocracies as well as democracies—were fallible. Because they all would make errors and be inconsistent, they needed to follow experience, beaten paths, and ancient precedents.

Institutions as Makers of a People. If Rousseau assumed that a people could be created all at once by an act of the will, Burke thought that a people could be produced only slowly. Rousseau thought that a people made its *institutions*—that is, its more permanent organizations and practices, such as property, government, or class distinctions—and could change them freely. Burke asserted that the institutions made the people. Changing the institutions quickly and greatly would destroy the people.

Burke said, "The idea of a people is the idea of a corporation. It is wholly artificial and made, like all other fiction, by common agreement. The particular nature of that agreement is collected from the form into which the particular society has been cast. When men break up the agreement which gives its corporate form and capacity to a state, they are no longer a people." Therefore, by deduction, if the French made a revolution against a Bourbon king, they would no longer be French.

In Burke's view, property institutions and social arrangements were the essence of a people. Rousseau's view, on the contrary, was that once a people decided to be together, all political institutions were mere instruments that could be changed at pleasure. If Rousseau's ideas lived on in the thought of Lincoln, Burke's ideas survived in the beliefs of those southerners who fought for states' rights and for their "peculiar institution" of slavery. Burke said that when people gave up their corporate agreement or changed their social system, they became a number of "vague, loose individuals." Many a weary step was to be taken before they could once again form themselves into a mass that would have a true political personality. For individuals to act with the weight and character of a people, they had to be in that state of habitual social discipline in which the rich, the wise, and the expert led the less wealthy, the weaker in judgment, and the less able. That is, class rule and class privilege were the very essence of a people.

Slow Human Learning versus Fast-Changing Reality. Burke's reasoning—his political philosophy of *conservatism*—contains some strong points and some weak ones. He argued that a state and a people were not just a partnership for a few limited purposes, like the trade in pepper or salt, but that they were a corporation for all memories, for all art, for all science, and for all perfection in the community of the living and the dead. Burke thus assumed the people to be a general-purpose community in the broadest possible sense; and there are some good reasons to think that he was largely right.

Another strong point of Burke's was his awareness of the weakness of people, of their difficulty in recognizing reality. Only very slow learning processes through long periods of practical experience, he assumed, would help people to recognize reality; and the experts, specialists, and various privileged classes would play a decisive role in guiding them. People's needs were not abstract, but concrete; and so were the remedies for them, if any existed. For food, one should turn to the farmer; for health, to the physician; but neither health nor food would be provided by abstract theories. Government, too, had its experienced practitioners: the nobles, the bureaucrats, the rich, and other rulers who had long been in power.

Burke also assumed that the elite in a society would be more realistic than the common people. This assumption does not seem to have been warranted; in many cases it is the poor in a society who know at what points the social system does not work. If one wants to know what is wrong with the slums, one does not run an opinion poll in the suburbs. There are two kinds of expert knowledge: knowing where the shoe pinches and knowing how to make shoes. Burke underestimated the first kind of knowledge, and he underestimated motives. For even when the members of an elite have seen at first hand the need for some urgent change, they often have refused to make it, for fear of losing some income, property, or privilege.

Burke's own view of statesmanship was different. Unlike many conservatives since his time, he was no stand-patter. He accepted the need for change, but he insisted that change come slowly and gradually, in small doses. He saw change as a process similar to the task of rebuilding one's own house while continuing to live in it and depending

Machiavelli

Hobbes

Locke

Rousseau

Burke

Marx

FIGURE 4.3 *Seven Political Philosophers*
Sources: Machiavelli, Hobbes, Locke, Rousseau, and Burke—Culver Pictures, Inc.; Marx and Mill—The Bettmann Archive, Inc.

Mill

on its uninterrupted protection against snow and rain. To the impatient radical, Burke would have pointed out that even if the roof leaked, one could not afford to tear it down. To the complacent conservative, he would have suggested that one could not forget that the roof was leaking and that repairs had to be started soon. Burke was a true *conservative;* he wanted to conserve things even while changing them. In the main thrust of his thought he was not a *reactionary;* he did not try to reverse the changes that had gone before and to turn back to some real or imagined past. And he would have been utterly amazed at some people in our own time who call themselves "conservatives" and advocate the use of nuclear weapons that might blow up the world.

But Burke believed that the rate of learning for a society had to be very slow; and, without proof or examination, he assumed that the needed rate of learning, and also the actual rates of change in technology and in the economic, technical, and political environment of a community, would all have to be slow.

A Burkean type of state, therefore, is at best slow changing and slow adapting. In a fast-changing world it cannot survive. It will quickly fall behind, and if it cannot speed up, it will perish. In this sense, Burke's counsel for being infinitely slow and cautious in making changes is a counsel of perfection. It may be too good for the wicked, fast-changing world in which we live.

A Permanent World of Nations. Burke himself, of course, had no such fears. He thought that since changes would be slow, most states and nations could be strong and wise enough to survive them indefinitely, unless they ruined themselves by their own folly. Since each state differed from all others by its unique history and interests, Burke believed that clashes among such states would be inevitable and war among states would remain a normal part of politics forever.

Like Burke, Rousseau thought that nations might survive indefinitely. Unlike Burke, he believed that war among them could be abolished. The main movers toward war, as Rousseau saw it, were the princes of Europe. Once their power was taken away, peace among the nations of Europe might be preserved. But that would require that all states become true democratic communities. Moreover, each sovereign community would have to be small and homogeneous in language, culture, class, and status, so that no groups of ambitious and undemocratic rulers could arise and push their countries into new wars.

Both Burke and Rousseau contributed to the ideas of nationalism. But Burke's adherents thought that aristocracies and wars would have to be preserved, whereas Rousseau's followers hoped to abolish them. The conflict between these two basic views of politics played a part in the wars and revolutions of the first half of the nineteenth century. And it contributed to the development of the mind of a theorist who was to advance a new proposition: that the previous history of humanity was no more than prehistory; that it would soon come to an end; and that it would be replaced by a new era of true history that would be radically different.

MARX: A THEORIST OF WORLD COMMUNITY

For most of his life, Karl Marx was a German intellectual in exile, writing page after page in the library of the British Museum in London. Often ridiculed in his own day, almost ninety years after his death an American journalist called him "the least funny of the Marx brothers." At the end of the 1970s, over a billion people—close to one-third of humanity with nearly one-third of the world's income—were living in sixteen countries under governments that revered his name, and the governments of several others described themselves as Marxist.

Marx (1818–1883), the son of a lawyer, was born in Trier in western Germany. His parents had been Jewish, but the family adopted the Lutheran faith when he was a child. Marx studied philosophy and became an adherent of the great German philosopher of change and conflict, Georg W. F. Hegel, but he soon developed ideas of his own that in time became an elaborate philosophy and political doctrine.

Motives and Sources of Marx's Thought. One of Marx's early concerns, like Rousseau's, was the alienation of individuals from their neighbors and from the society in which they lived. From the plight of the individual, Marx soon turned to the evils of society and politics and to the possibility of revolution as a remedy for them. For the rest of his life he was an ardent revolutionist. Even many lost revolutions won his sympathy; but unlike some recent revolutionists, he never willingly urged people to risk their lives in uprisings he knew to be hopeless. He wanted to be the theorist of a successful revolution, one that would produce more fundamental changes than any that had gone before.

For this purpose he turned to science. Just as Newton had discovered the laws of motion of physical bodies, so Marx proposed to discover the laws of motion of society. Like most scientists, he made ample use of the work of his predecessors. He cheerfully expropriated ideas that he found useful. He took his economics from the English and the Scots, most of his politics from the French, and most of his philosophy from the Germans. Like Burke, he insisted that truth was concrete and that past historic developments determined much of present reality. Also like Burke, and like Alexander Hamilton in America and Victor du Pont in France, he believed that people's attitudes and actions were determined by economic interests and class position. Marx added to this doctrine two further propositions: first, that the strength and interests of classes would change rapidly with technological and economic change; and, second, that the interests of the chief classes of every society were necessarily opposed to each other, so that the struggles between classes form the foundation of all history and politics. There is a touch of irony in the fact that Marx's revolutionary doctrine of class struggle was partly derived in this manner from conservative ideas.

If all past history were the history of class struggles, as Marx believed, then it was not meaningless chaos. Like British economists Adam Smith and David Ricardo, Marx assumed that there were objective economic tendencies and laws, similar to the laws of supply and demand, and that these laws would work themselves out despite (or even because of) the struggles and confusions of individuals.

A New View of Human Development. These considerations led Marx to a new view of human history. Originally, he thought, what differentiated human beings was their inventing tools and using them in a process of labor that suggested still additional inventions. Thus, the invention of tools was what had contributed to the transformation from tree dwellers and cave dwellers to the machine users of his time and ours. Through millennia of prehistory, men had lived under a system of *primitive communism,* in hordes or tribes that knew neither social classes nor private property in land or in persons. They knew no slavery because no slave could produce enough to make it worthwhile to keep him or her in bondage. Only later, as labor became more productive, did slavery begin to pay. At that stage it became worthwhile for some to claim land as their own and to exact tribute from others for the opportunity to work it. Property, slavery, and social classes were thus not rooted in human nature; products of progress in the past, they would be done away with by further progress at some time in the future.

In Marx's sweeping view, humanity's development would thus lead from the small, classless, and propertyless communities of primitive communism through a sequence of property-based and class-divided social systems to a future worldwide community of economic abundance. In this new and enlarged community, property distinctions and class divisions would once again disappear or become insignificiant. But even this worldwide community of abundance, which Marx called "communism," was not to be the end of human development. Once people had moved from the age of economic scarcity to a worldwide age of plenty, they could aim at the full and free development of all the potentialities and powers of every individual. This human development, said Marx, was "an end in itself." But he frankly conceded that neither he nor anyone else could foresee what this future development actually would be like. He felt sure only that it would mark the leap from "the realm of necessity into the realm of freedom." At that point, he believed, prehistory would end and true history begin. What this true history would be, Marx did not know, but he was certain that it would be more interesting and worthwhile than all the centuries of "prehistory" in the past.

Marx saw this "prehistory"—which most historians call "history"—divided roughly into four major stages: primitive communism, feudalism, capitalism, and socialism. After the last of these four, a fifth stage, communism, would mark the transition to economic abundance, classlessness, and the beginning of true history.

After a period of primitive communism and the first appearance of relatively large-scale private property and social classes, a privileged group of landowners, chieftains, and warriors had arisen to lord it over their poorer neighbors, in time reducing many of the latter to bondage as debtors, serfs, or slaves. The masters had desired to transmit their wealth and power to their children. Class privilege then had become inherited like the property on which it was based; and it had been glorified by the dubious claim of superior descent or blood, such as the proverbial "blue blood' of European aristocracy.

In many times and places, Marx thought, societies had shared certain broad characteristics. They had had a class of large landowners that served as the basis of a warlike aristocracy while exploiting the tillers of the soil. Although the detailed arrangements of such social systems might have varied a great deal across different countries, periods, and cultures, Marx called them all "feudal." He thus used the concepts of *feudalism,* derived from medieval European history, in a broader sense than many historians use it.[3] The stage of feudalism in the political and social history of most countries, as Marx saw it, corresponded to a particular stage in the development of their technology. A hand mill corresponded to a society of nobles and serfs; a steam mill, to a society of capitalists and workers.

In Marx's view, as technology progressed from muscle power to machine power and from handicrafts to factories, capital became more important than land, cash and credit more important than blue blood and nobility, and a bankbook more important than a coat of arms. Once these changes had occurred, a new middle class of merchants, business owners, and capitalists would rise in power and prestige and eventually take the leadership of society away from the nobility. Society would then pass from the stage of feudalism to the stage of *capitalism.* This was what Marx believed had happened in many countries of his time.

The new ruling class would now consist of "burghers" or, in the French term that Marx preferred, of *bourgeois,* who collectively made up the *bourgeoisie.* (If they still preferred to call themselves "middle class," Marx would have thought them excessively modest.) Within the bourgeoisie the rich and the super-rich would make up the top layer of bankers, large factory owners, and the like—the *big bourgeois.* Beneath them would be their far more numerous, far less affluent colleagues, the *petty bourgeois,* who shared much of the outlook of the richer businesspeople, but, alas, neither their security nor their prestige. These small businesspeople, shopkeepers, artisans, and other small employers of labor might envy and resent their big competitors, but they would quarrel even more with the wage earners whom they employed and whose demands for higher wages or shorter working hours threatened their own slender profits.

[3]See Rushton C. Coulborn, ed., *Feudalism in History* (Princeton: Princeton University Press, 1956).

In Marx's image of the world, however, these wage earners were the chosen people or, rather, the chosen class of destiny. They owned no significant property in land, machines, or major tools and thus no substantial "means of production." The clothes, household goods, and other personal articles they owned did not make other workers dependent on them and thus did not count in the distribution of economic and political power. The ancient Romans had called such poor, propertyless citizens mere "offspring begetters" or *proletarii;* hence their kind became known in the nineteenth century as *proletarians* and their class as the *proletariat.* Marx accepted this usage with enthusiasm, but reversed its values. A bourgeois existence tied individuals to the present and the past; a proletarian condition gave them a stake in the future.

Being propertyless, the proletariat had to be international in its point of view. "The workers have no fatherland," he wrote, "one cannot take from them that which they do not possess." The interests of workers in all countries were the same: better wages and working conditions in the short run, but, beyond that, a rise to political power, the overthrow of the old order of property and privilege, and the establishment of a new society. "Proletarians of all lands, unite!" Marx and Engels wrote in the *Communist Manifesto* in 1847; "You have nothing to lose but your chains. You have a world to win."

If the workers were predestined to become internationalists in outlook and action, the middle classes were apt to become nationalists, at least for a time. As capitalism replaced feudalism as the chief social and economic system, local markets gave way to national markets, local dialects retreated before the standardized national languages, feudal or absolute monarchies were replaced by constitutional governments that safeguarded private property and competition, and the nobility was replaced by a national bourgeoisie as the leading class in society, politics, and culture. In ousting feudalism, according to Marx, capitalism thus built modern nations. All this, however, was merely transitional. National markets would give way to a world market and national literatures to a world literature. Nation-states were destined to become obsolete.

Within each country the effects of merciless competition were sure to turn most members of the middle class and the peasantry into proletarians. "One capitalist," Marx noted gleefully, "ruins many." In time, almost the whole population would be proletarian, united and disciplined by the experience of factory labor, and motivated by increasing misery to end the capitalist system that kept them poor and oppressed. Opposing them would be an ever smaller handful of ever richer capitalists, who would become ever easier to overthrow. In the end, as Marx envisioned it, "the knell of private property sounds. The expropriators are expropriated."

In each country the workers would seize power. During a transitional period they would exercise a *dictatorship of the proletariat,* "by the vast majority and in the interests of the vast majority," and would be advised, no doubt, by helpful intellectuals like Karl Marx and by "the best elements of the bourgeoisie," who by then would have come over to their side. Since the proletarians were internationalist by nature, the countries they now ruled would all cooperate in a fraternal community of socialist nations. This state of *socialism* would still know scarcity, social classes, and the state. But these, too, would soon pass. Technology would have progressed under capitalism, and this progress would be accelerated in the socialist stage. Soon, therefore, an economy of abundance would usher in the next stage—*communism*—and with it the stateless and classless future of humankind.[4]

[4]This usage of the words "socialism" and "communism" was referred to by Lenin and became established long after Marx's death in the writings of many authors in the Soviet Union. Marx himself spoke of a "first phase of the communist society" and of a later "higher phase," in expressing the same two-stage conception.

Some Second Thoughts. This entire vision seems to have been present in Marx's mind by 1847, before he reached the age of thirty. But in 1875, about a generation later, Marx put down some careful second thoughts.[5]

Economic and political development were taking much longer than had been expected. The development of capitalism and the path toward socialism and communism seemed far longer and more complex—steeper, more winding, and more fogbound—than had been anticipated. The distinction between *socialism* (the expected first stage after capitalism) and *communism* (the later stage) now loomed much larger and more important.

Capitalism, Marx now saw, could last a very long time. It could reach high levels of development in some countries while still in its beginnings in others. The growth of imperialism appeared to be increasing the longevity of capitalism. It now seemed possible that for a time there should be entire "nations of capitalists," such as England, profiting from the exploitation of entire nations of peasants, such as India—and doling out some of these profits to the English workers as a payment for their cooperation in this scheme of things and for their failure to play the revolutionary role that Marx earlier had predicted for them. Only after many years, Marx now thought, would capitalism collapse and would an eventual chain of world wars, depressions, and mass suffering bring the workers of the privileged countries back to the revolutionary path.

In addition, Marx now saw that socialism would still be a social order of scarcity and partial injustice. It would demand work from everyone "according to his abilities," but it would pay only according to the work performed and not in accordance with needs. The skilled worker would earn more than the unskilled (Marx considered skilled labor a multiple of unskilled labor, so that one hour of a skilled worker's time might be worth several hours of an unskilled worker's—but he did not say how many). Highly skilled work, such as that of professionals, engineers, or scientists, by this principle might have to be paid still more highly—regardless of how each had acquired his or her skill in the first place. Parents who could give their children a better education could equip them with a chance for a better income than the children of their less fortunate neighbors. And these differences in income might find expression in differences of personal property, such as clothes, furniture, and housing—though not in the major means of production.

The reason for Marx's second thoughts is clear. To escape forever from economic scarcity, humanity had to produce much more than it did. Labor had to become vastly more productive. New capital equipment and skills had to be created and accumulated by vast efforts. For all this, people had to be motivated, not only by words, but also by tangible rewards that were distributed unequally, in proportion to the work they actually did. At the same time, skilled and professionally trained personnel also would be scarce, and so would people willing to make the prolonged effort to acquire such training. As long as this scarcity persisted, it might be in the interest of socialist governments to offer higher wages to labor with these scarce qualifications and, thus, to maintain differential incomes high enough to ensure a continuing supply of trainees and professional specialists with the requisite qualifications.

During this stage of socialism, with its inevitable residual injustices, the state would still be needed. It would be needed not only against external threats from surviving capitalist countries, or against domestic efforts of the old capitalist classes to restore their rule; the socialist state would also be needed to enforce its own laws and its own partly unjust distribution of incomes and opportunities even against members of the proletariat and the working population.

Only later, after this socialist stage had accomplished its task (and Marx did not say how many

[5]He did so mainly in a critique of the program of the German Social Democrats, called *Critique of the Gotha Program* (1875).

decades or generations this might take), only when the productive equipment of society had been vastly increased and when the "springs of wealth [flowed] more freely," would it be possible to enter the more highly developed stage—that of communism. In that stage, most goods and services would be so abundant that they would not have to be distributed by being priced and sold unit by unit. In the distant communist economy of abundance each person would work according to his or her ability; but now at last the individual would receive—or rather take—according to his or her needs. Marx's notion was that eventually most consumer goods would become so abundant that the question of allocation would become irrelevant. Nations would disappear, allocation problems would vanish, and we would have a single unified humankind.

In the twentieth century, Marx's ideas were taken up and considerably modified by democratic socialists in Western Europe, by various theorists in developing countries, and in more elaborate and radical form by Lenin and Mao Tse-tung and their respective followers. (These last two developments are discussed in Chapters 11 and 15.) In 1979 more than twenty countries were ruled by governments calling themselves "Marxist" in one form or another, and like other countries they were encountering many unexpected difficulties.

WHAT THE THEORISTS DID NOT FORETELL: THE TENDENCY OF STATES AND COMMUNITIES TO SPLIT

Machiavelli, Hobbes, and Locke had been concerned with what held states together; Rousseau, Burke, and Marx all centered their attention on what united people into communities and on how these communities were developed and maintained. None of the six thinkers concerned himself much with the splitting up of larger states and communities into smaller ones. But by focusing only on the integration, and not on the division, of communities, the six theorists overlooked an important part of the political and social process.

Their Limited Treatment of Conflict. This is not to say, of course, that these theorists were not aware of political and social conflicts. Machiavelli's whole theory was based on his notion of perpetual conflict among competing princes (and would-be princes or conspirators). Hobbes saw conflict as ever present among all people, overt in the state of nature, latent within each state when restrained by the power of an individual or collective ruler. Locke sought a prudent balance between conflict and cooperation in the law of nature and in the limited mutual obligations of constitutional government. Rousseau tried to overcome all possibility of serious conflict by having individuals surrender all powers to the general will of the small, like-minded community; and conflicts among such communities would disappear, he thought, once the rule of ambitious warlike princes was abolished.

Burke thought that conflict was normal and inevitable, both among states and among interest groups within them, but that patient, prudent leadership usually could keep it within tolerable bounds, even in the case of war. He also believed that immoderate policies were likely to end in failure and perhaps eventually in the elimination of the governments and leaders who persisted in them. Marx, of course, wholeheartedly believed in conflict as a major moving force in the history of all class-divided societies, but the conflicts he considered most important were those between classes, not among states or nations. To him, the national state, the national market, and increasingly the world market were the natural arenas in which these class conflicts would be fought out.

None of these six thinkers expected that established states would split up into smaller ones (except in quite unusual cases) or that the seemingly predominant trend, from the seventeenth to the mid-nineteenth century, toward larger states and empires would be reversed. None of them, to be sure, lived to see the reversal. But it did begin in the late nineteenth century, and between the 1890s and the 1970s it swept the world.

What Has Been Learned More Recently. We know now that there is probably a law of cultural, national, and political differentiation that holds true very generally. If communication within a small group is much larger than external communication, then the internal group will in time develop a communication code of its own. This is the mathematics of the Tower of Babel. If people in a mountain village speak frequently to each other and rarely to strangers for hundreds of years, the dialect of the peasants will become unintelligible to people from other valleys. If the programmers in a computer center at Harvard talk mostly to each other and rarely to outsiders, their programming conventions will become unintelligible to the people working the same IBM computers at other centers.

These thoughts have major implications that most of Marx's followers have overlooked. His principle of socialism—payment according to amount of work—also applied to the international division of labor among socialist countries. A rich socialist nation like the Soviet Union, well equipped with skills, capital, and improved land, will expect to be paid for its exports in accordance with their value, even if they go to a poorer socialist country. A poor country of this kind, such as the People's Republic of China, lacking skills and equipment, can produce only exports of much lesser value, even if they should require greater human effort to produce. There is, therefore, a likelihood that a significant degree of inequality and potential injustice will persist among socialist countries. If their states and armed forces have the task of defending these unequal socialist patterns of distribution at home and abroad, they may also have to defend them against each other. What seemed to be only a theoretical implication in Marx's writings in 1875 became an ominous reality in the clashes between Soviet and Chinese Communist troops on the Ussuri River in 1969. Marx's seemingly complete theory will remain highly vulnerable so long as it is not developed considerably further toward dealing more realistically with its unfinished problems.

But the followers of the other five have done no better. States have arisen, split up, and been replaced by others much faster than Machiavelli's strategies for princes, or Hobbes's or Locke's versions of the social contract, or Burke's theories would have predicted. The trend toward popular participation in politics has become more powerful than even Rousseau expected, but the size and power of many states are much vaster than anything Rousseau foresaw for his small republics. Conflicts among states ruled by governments with mass support have been more bitter and frequent than Rousseau envisaged, and the risks habitually taken by great powers in the nuclear age are vastly greater than anything Hobbes, Locke, or Burke would have considered prudent or, indeed, sane. The problems of nationalism and international conflict—of national community and world community—are still a challenge to society's understanding and leadership.

FASCISM: AN IDEA OR A STATE OF MIND?

After World War I, small groups of war veterans were organized in several countries to fight class-oriented labor movements of all varieties—communist, democratic socialist, and independent labor union. These groups broke strikes and broke heads, using force and terror in organized and disciplined maneuvers. They got money from some employers, weapons from some military commanders, and benevolent protection from some police chiefs and judges. Above all, they seemed to offer reassurance to the frightened upper and middle classes of their countries against the feared threat of leftist revolution and the less dramatic pressure of labor union demands for higher wages, shorter working hours, and more comprehensive welfare benefits. Accordingly, in times of crisis they could count on considerable open and covert middle-class support. In some countries these groups were integrated into organizations and a political party and later were equipped with an explicit ideology.

Fascism in Italy. Initially fascism was not an idea, but a technique, an organizational and psychological technique for winning and holding power. Its basis was the application of the methods of military warfare to domestic politics—including violence, deception, surprise, concentrated force, intimidation, and terror. Its early adherents began as scattered strong-arm squads and semimilitary forces, but soon they acquired a uniform or at least a colored shirt—black in Italy, brown in Germany and Austria, green in Hungary—as well as a party organization, an authoritarian leader, and an ideology.

In Italy their leader was Benito Mussolini, a self-taught, former socialist editor who had turned Nationalist in 1915. He organized the first *fasci di combattimento* (combat groups), whose members became known as *fascisti,* the movement as *Fascism.*

At first, Mussolini had been disdainful of ideology. The slogan "I don't care," written by a squad man on his bloody bandage, was more important than all programs, wrote Mussolini. Fascism was more than a program, he said; what mattered was that people died for it. In 1922, after a wave of strikes and labor unrest had waxed and waned yet again, Mussolini became prime minister of Italy. He came to power legally, with the help of the king and the connivance of the middle-class government that had preceded him, but simultaneously he had ordered his black-shirted troops to the dramatic March on Rome, unopposed by army and police. (He followed the troops in a sleeping car.) Once in power, however, he began to suppress mercilessly Socialists, Communists, and eventually Liberals and free labor unions, using both the formal force of the state and the informal, but effective, terror of the Fascists, ranging from severe beatings and forced drafts of castor oil to assassination. After the assassination in 1924 of a Parliament member, the Socialist Giacomo Matteotti, the rule of Fascism was well-nigh complete.

Mussolini lacked one thing. "The time has come," he wrote in 1927 to the philosopher Giovanni Gentile, "for Fascism to equip itself with a philosophy. I can give you three months for this task." Gentile promptly delivered, and the treatise appeared in the *Italian Encyclopedia,* entitled "Fascism" and bearing Mussolini's name, which guaranteed its authority.

Fascist Views of Equality and Reason. Fascist ideas were more often expressed in brief slogans than in longer treatises. "Fascism affirms the eternal, immutable and beneficial inequality of man" was one such statement. In this way, Mussolini—now called *il Duce* (the Leader)—rejected the traditions of equality and rationality that the ages of the Renaissance and the Enlightenment had established in Western thought. Opposing equality, Fascism proclaimed the principle of *hierarchy:* men were held to be superior to women, officers to soldiers, employers to employees, Fascists to non-Fascists, leaders to followers, Italians to non-Italians, and Mussolini, the supreme leader, to all others. Other slogans drove home the point: "The Duce is always right" was one; "Believe, Obey, Fight!" was another.

The Total State. The state was to be total, irresistible, and all-embracing. "Everything within the State, nothing without the State, nothing against the State!" was the corresponding slogan. Thus, Italy became one of the countries in which this notion of *totalitarianism* developed.

The Fascist View of Population Policy. In the Soviet Union the new party-state was gaining even greater comprehensive power. But, at least in theory, it was destined to "wither away" in some age of abundance. The Fascist state, on the contrary, was to last forever, and so were the world's poverty and wars. On population, Fascism accepted the old and dubious theory of Thomas Malthus (1766–1834): human beings always multiply faster than their food supply unless the "preventive checks" of restraint (chastity) or "vice" limit their increase or else until the "positive checks" of war, famine, or disease reduce their numbers. Fascism, however, did not count on virtue, vice, or birth control; it expected that at some future time peoples would fight wars of survival for land and food in a starving world. "Overpopulated countries," such as Italy, Germany, and Japan, "are like bursting bombs," Mussolini wrote; hence, Italians should have as many children as possible now, in order to leave more soldiers for those wars to come. People who liked war were ready to believe in the need to prepare for it, with babies, weapons, and ideas.

Cult of War and Death. As part of the same preparation, war itself was proclaimed ever more insistently to be beautiful and good. "War alone," Mussolini wrote, ". . . puts the stamp of nobility on peoples. . . . I do not believe in perpetual peace. . . . I find it depressing and a negation of all the fundamental virtues of man. . . . I consider the Italian nation in a permanent state of war." Uttered on different occasions, these phrases fit together. He meant what they said, he repeated them often.

In some of its symbols, Fascism became a death cult. Its black shirts, uniforms, and impressively designed pseudo-chapels in which the dead Fascist street fighters were reporting *"Presente!"*—"Present!"—to visitors were all designed to play on that combined appeal of death and immortality that often has attracted young people. At the same time, many Fascist hymns and slogans exalted youth and the future. "The twentieth century will be the century of Fascism," said Mussolini in 1934.

Ambiguous Attitudes Toward Property and the Middle Class. Fascism claimed to defend private property and upper- and middle-class privileges, but at the same time its leaders and spokespeople expressed contempt for "square" or bourgeois values. In theory, their models were the soldier and the artist. Most of their leaders and key personnel came from the lower middle class and particularly from its marginal groups threatened by failure: unsuccessful journalists, intellectuals, and small businesspeople, failed students, and demobilized officers and sergeants after World War I. Many of them had lost social status and income or feared their loss. Fascism encouraged them to transmute their anxiety and frustration into rage. Its ideology offered them scapegoats—parliamentarianism, democracy, Freemasons, Marxists, ethnic minorities, foreigners, and, eventually, Jews. The jobs and property of such groups often became fair game and their members easy targets for denunciation.

In addition, many middle-class values were rejected or destroyed. For Fascism, truth was unimportant, and right was whatever was held to be useful to the regime; humanitarianism was unrealistic and sentimental; friendship, family, and privacy were to be subordinated to the total state.

Big business, however, was protected. Mussolini and, later, Hitler were as solicitous of it as a dairy farmer would be toward a herd of cows. Big business and industry were to furnish first some of the money for the Fascist party and later most of the weapons for the war machine of the Fascist state. Fascism abolished independent labor unions and declared all strikes illegal. In theory, each branch of industry was to be administered by a corporation, uniting employers and employees, and to be headed by an official appointed by the Fascist government. This arrangement was called *corporativism* or the *corporate state,* and it was supposed to replace both capitalism and socialism as a way of running an industrial country. In practice, however, the corporations meant nothing, and the corporate state remained a paper entity. Owners and managers ran their factories much as before, but were no longer disturbed by union demands. The Fascist notion of hierarchy, according to which responsibility ran only upward from subordinates to superiors—a concept that the Nazis adopted under the name of *Führerprinzip,* or *leadership principle*—further glorified the employers' position.

In response, many businesspeople in both Italy and Germany supported Fascism. But the dictatorships that "protected" them in this manner also destroyed the individual liberties, legal rights, and opportunities for critical and realistic information that the businesspeople had had before. In the end, Fascism only dragged them blindly into a world war that destroyed their cities and killed their children, too. Thus, those who had seen themselves as Fascism's beneficiaries often ended up among its victims. After World War II, most businesspeople quickly abandoned their links to Fascism as an experiment that had failed.

Religion: Another Double-Faced Relationship. Fascism at heart was as anti-Christian as it was antirational. Christianity praised the weak and meek; Fascism had only contempt for them. Christianity preached mercy, pity, and compassion; Fascism rejected such feelings. Christianity exalted peace; Fascism despised it, except as a brief maneuver for deception.

Fascist rulers were quite willing, however, to make deals with Christian churches about money, land, and legal rights. Popes signed *concordates*—agreements of collaboration—with Fascist Italy in 1929 and with Nazi Germany in 1939. Many Protestant churches in Germany collaborated with the Nazis, as did Orthodox churches with fascistic regimes in their own countries, such as Rumania and Greece. Fascism often could deal with organized churches, even if it rejected the Sermon on the Mount.

Authoritarian and Fascistic Regimes in Other Countries. Italian Fascism had arisen out of a legacy of war, a crisis of a weak parliamentary regime that had preceded it, and a preference of the upper- and middle-class voters and parties for an alliance with the Fascists rather than an anti-Fascist alliance of the middle classes with the democratic labor parties and the Communists. During the 1920s similar conditions surfaced in several other countries, such as Spain, Portugal, Poland, and Lithuania. In 1923, General Primo de Rivera established a military dictatorship in Spain with the consent of the king. In 1926 the Portuguese army undertook a March on Lisbon, modeled on the March on Rome; there it abolished party government and after a few years of turmoil Antonio de Oliveira Salazar emerged as dictator. Also in 1926, Józef Pilsudski marched with some regiments on Warsaw and made himself dictator, and a military coup in Lithuania installed a dictatorship under Augustinas Voldemaras.

All these new regimes rejected democracy, calling it miserably weak, dangerously soft toward labor, socialism, and communism (which they held to be much alike), and criminally negligent of the national interest in providing armaments, in quarreling with neighboring countries, and in preparing for war. But they were less uniform in ideology and less developed in social and political organization than Italy had by then become. Landowners, members of the clergy, and to some extent businesspeople supported these dictatorships, but retained much in the way of their own voice and organization. Hence, it seems more accurate to call these four regimes *authoritarian,* rather than totalitarian in character, despite their sympathies for Fascism. Other movements sympathetic to Fascism arose in several countries, but remained minor.

This situation changed sharply in the early 1930s with the deepening of the Great Depression. In Austria an authoritarian regime with some fascist traits was installed in February 1934 by Chancellor Engelbert Dollfuss and his middle-class government, after breaking the power of the Social Democrats who had taken up arms to defend the constitution. In Latvia and Estonia authoritarian and semifascist regimes seized power in the same year. In Greece, General Metaxas in 1936 set up a dictatorship complete with a black-shirted party, the fascist stiff-armed, flat-handed salute, and the promise of a "Third Hellenic Civilization." Also in 1936 an extreme militarist faction acquired major influence in the government of Japan.

In the same year, 1936, Colonel Francisco Franco challenged the elected constitutional government of the Republic of Spain. His rebellion was supported by most army officers, the fascist party (the Falange), many Roman Catholic priests in central and southern Spain (many priests in the Basque region sided with the Republic), and various monarchist factions. The Republic, in turn, was defended by many Liberals and Democrats, as well as by Socialists, Communists, and Anarchists, but was weakened by their many disagreements. The Civil War was long and bloody, claiming about 1 million lives. It was decided by massive foreign intervention on Franco's side—ample military equipment from Germany and Italy, several Italian infantry brigades, and a German air corps (the Condor Legion)—in addition to the Spanish Foreign Legion and Moroccan mercenary troops. Compared with all these, the leftist International Brigades were small and their effect was minor. In early 1939, Franco prevailed and installed his authoritarian and semifascist regime; but he did then keep his exhausted country out of World War II.

A British Union of Fascists was organized by Sir Oswald Mosley in 1932. Other fascist movements were introduced in Norway under Major Vidkun Quisling, in the Netherlands under Anton Mussert, in Belgium under Léon Degrelle, in France under Jacques Doriot and others, and in the United States (called the German-American Bund) under Fritz Kuhn. Indeed, by the late 1930s it seemed as if Fascism in one form or another might become a worldwide movement.

From Fascism to National Socialism. A still more ominous result of the depression years was that their political and economic crises had a devastating effect on two major powers, Germany and Japan. In both countries, memories of war were fresh and veterans were active: in Germany, those of World War I; in Japan, those of the new war in Manchuria that started in 1931. Large parts of the upper and middle classes in these two countries feared the power of liberals, socialists, and communists, backed the military, and shared dreams of military power and imperial expansion over conquered lands and peoples. As in Italy in 1922, so now in Germany and Japan these conditions fostered the rise of fascistic movements and regimes, albeit with important variations.

A German National Socialist Workers Party had been founded in about 1910 in the old Austro-Hungarian monarchy, in the German-speaking and highly industrial Sudetenland areas of Bohemia, Moravia, and Silesia; and after 1918 the party survived there under the Czechoslovak Republic, the monarchy's successor state in those regions. Young Adolf Hitler, an Austrian living in Vienna during the years before World War I, could hardly have failed to know this party, which already was advocating many of his later views.

The main idea of *National Socialism* was that workers should seek their social betterment through nationalist cooperation with their employers of the same ethnic group and not through internationalist solidarity with workers of different nations or ethnic groups. The richer and more powerful Germans became, and not least German employers, the better off German workers would become. By this reasoning workers' interests lay with their German employers and not with, say, the Czech workers who might compete with them for employment and promotion. The same situation applied to German sales and office employees and to the German lower middle class of shopkeepers and artisans. All were said to be threatened by Jewish, Czech, and other "alien" competitors, and they were urged to look to national solidarity for their rescue. Jews provided a particularly prominent target, because they won many middle-class positions, for which lower-middle-class persons envied them.

It may have seemed a long way from this primitive German national socialism and *anti-Semitism*—"the socialism of morons," as Austrian labor leader Victor Adler called it—to the coldly calculated techniques by which Italian Fascism had seized power, yet that way was traversed in just a few years. In 1919, Hitler founded the National Socialist German Workers' Party (NSDAP) at Munich with seven members. Soon it had grown into a full-fledged organization with brown-shirted and jackbooted Storm Troops and black-uniformed Elite guards with death's head insignia on their caps, all of whom gave the stiff-armed salute of the Italian *fascisti*. By 1924, the movement had its explicit ideology in Hitler's book *Mein Kampf* ("My Struggle").

Population Theory Once More. Hitler's book was muddled and unoriginal, but more thoroughgoing and fanatically dedicated to its own weird logic than Mussolini's slogans and philosophy. Hitler fully accepted the dubious logic of Malthus, the nineteenth-century social Darwinists, and the Italian Fascists: in the future, inevitably, there would be too many people and too little food; hence, ever new wars would be unavoidable, and each far-sighted nation should seek to have not fewer children, but more, in order to ensure having enough future soldiers to prevail in the coming wars among peoples threatened by starvation. Nineteenth-century believers in these pseudo-Darwinian ideas had ignored—as did Mussolini—the possibility that food supplies could be expanded, as they have been from Malthus's time to our day, or that there would be a worldwide spread of birth control and resulting lower birth rates. They did not imagine that the world population might ever become stabilized, much less decrease, by about 2075, as is expected now.

It was left for Adolf Hitler to take the old Malthusian theories to their extreme consequences. Hitler blindly accepted this distorted picture of nature, which he called "the cruel queen of all wisdom." With insane logic, he rejected all mercy or pity and any compassion for the weak in the struggle for survival. He concluded that the coming conflicts had to be struggles for extermination. The vast crimes and mass murders of the Nazis later grew from this basic perspective.

Racism and Anti-Semitism. Mussolini had accepted social Darwinism, but did not at first adopt its implied stress on heredity and racism. Hitler, however, had learned anti-Semitism as a young man in Austria, before he had ever heard of biology or population theory. He naively defined Jews as a race—which they are not, being a people descended from many kinds of converts to their religion—and he fanatically applied his ideas of survival and extermination to them, but not to them alone. Later, in World War II, he tried to exterminate the Gypsies and the Jews and to wipe out the educated strata of the Poles, in order to leave the rest of the Polish people as ignorant and obedient servants for the German "master race."

Hitler's hatred for the nonwhite races was even greater. (For political reasons he excepted the Japanese, whose military leaders became his allies after 1939.) The notion that a black person could flourish at a university only enraged him. Should not that university place go instead to a deserving German?

Despite a penchant for carrying some seemingly logical implications of his thought to extremes, Hitler and his fellow Nazis shared Mussolini's distrust of reason. Rationality was "bloodless," they insisted; real men should "think with their blood." Claimed Hitler's minister of propaganda, Joseph Goebbels: "I do not have to prove that Jesus was not a Jew. It is so." Even more than Italian Fascism, German National Socialism was anti-intellectual.

It was also far more cruel. In its concentration camps, people were tortured for months. Often even death was made to linger. Hitler watched films of his enemies' execution after the failure of the 1944 coup against him. A high-ranking chief of the Gestapo (the Nazi secret police), Ernst

Kaltenbrunner, enjoyed watching the dying agonies of victims in the gas chambers through a small glass window.

Fascism as a State of Mind. Like the Italian Fascists, the Nazis accepted no moral restraints on the means they used to gain their ends. This was not new in politics. Machiavelli had known that princes were using force, fraud, lies, cruelty, and treason, and he advised them to do just that, preferably in secret, when it would serve their aims. Lenin had urged his Bolsheviks to use any and all means to win, and they had acted on his advice. Mussolini, in turn, may have learned from them. But Hitler carried ruthlessness and amorality, or the perversion of morality, to new extremes.

Yet, millions followed Hitler, as they followed Mussolini. For about two decades, many people sincerely believed in fascism. Many even became fanatics in its cause, ready to kill and die for it. Fascism offered many individuals the props for faltering self-confidence: uniforms, parades, stiff drill and ceremonies, opportunities for "legitimate" brutality, inclusion in a national community, superior roles to play in a ruling party and master race, symbolism and a vague political mystique, and, finally, a leader with a hazy creed on which one's personal dreams could be projected. For many people, all this added up to a new sense of personal identity and meaning for their lives—and they followed it often to their death.

It is this element of fanaticism and active dedication on a mass scale, organized in a single ruling party and giving life and force to it, that distinguishes genuine *fascism* from mere *authoritarian* regimes. Authoritarianism means persistence and acceptance. Fascism to its own adherents meant activity and action. It tapped the roots of human longing to belong to a strong group, of rage at frustration, of passion for meaningful action or even sacrifice, and it carried these feelings to extremes.

Ultimately, the extremes became self-defeating. Every kind of *extremism* eventually impoverishes the capacity to learn and to use information. Hitler and Mussolini swept their countries into a war they could not win. They made lesser, but still fateful, errors on the tactical level. They could trust ever fewer people and felt constantly surrounded by betrayal. Their armies were pounded to bits on the battlefields of World War II; their countries were defeated and their movements crumbled; they died miserable deaths; and the great majority of their peoples rejected their memories.

Could Fascism Return? At the level of individual psychology, many of the feelings that favor fascism are to be found scattered in many countries under both democratic and authoritarian regimes. According to votes and surveys, perhaps between 5 and 10 percent of the people in many democratic industrial countries had such feelings between the late 1940s and the late 1970s. In quiet times these persons are isolated or form small groups, here and there, with limited means and competing would-be leaders. Elements of fascist ideology are similarly scattered. Some people still believe in war as desirable and permanent, and others fear that soon there will be too little food and too many people in the world. There are still anti-Semites and many more racists and opponents of equality for women. Some people feel alienated, enraged, and impatient with morality, and other people feel unsuccessful, marginal, and insecure. Some business executives dislike labor unions. Nowadays such feelings are not integrated into a coherent ideology, nor organized in a large party, nor widely propagated by the media. To produce a big fascist movement in any country, these scattered persons and notions would have to be collected, organized, and given considerable material support. Moreover, it would be necessary for a large majority of people not to know or care how the last big fascist experiments ended.

But someday and somewhere the eight conditions that gave the original fascists their chance could come together again. Let us recall them:

1. a severe crisis within a liberal-democratic political system;

2. vivid war memories or large-scale war preparations;
3. fear among the upper and middle classes of left-wing radicalism and/or democratic but expensive demands for higher wages and welfare benefits; hence, willingness of strong groups among the upper classes, particularly property owners, businesspeople, and the military, to establish or support a fascistic movement or dictatorship;
4. recruitment of ex-radicals or other experts in appealing to crowds, manipulating mass communication media, and exercising techniques of actual control;
5. rekindled hopes for nationalist and/or racist expansion and conquest;
6. strong antiscientific, antirational, and anti-intellectual currents of thought;
7. widespread moods of frustration and impatience with all doubt, disagreement, and diversity of views;
8. large numbers of marginal individuals and widespread feelings of frustration, alienation, meaninglessness of life, and latent rage among them.

Fascism rose and fell before the age of nuclear energy, so its creed of mass destruction was still limited in its means. Thus far the two creeds of fascism and mass destruction have never come together. It is only now that the means have vastly grown, and at present no powerful government exists that truly worships both creeds.

At the end of the 1970s no out-and-out fascist regime, no governing death cult, existed in any country in the world. There is a small neo-Nazi party in the German Federal Republic, a small neo-Fascist party with some military and police connections in Italy; some small neo-militaristic groups in Japan; and a small American Nazi Party in the United States. None of these groups receives large-scale financial support, and none seems likely to win power.

There are authoritarian dictatorships of the political right in many countries, some of which are terroristic and cruel, and similar cases of cruelty and terror tactics may still persist in some Communist regimes.

All this is a far cry from the fascist regimes of sustained mass passion and mass murder and their pseudo-biological creeds of race extermination that threatened the world until 1945. Those regimes committed political suicide about five to ten years before they could have acquired nuclear weapons. If another truly fascist regime should ever rise again in a major country, humanity might not be so lucky.

Fascism was the most extreme and desperate effort on the part of individuals, groups, and, for a time, even whole nations to stop long-run change and to refuse to learn. It was the very opposite of what humanity needed: more knowledge, more understanding, more compassion and morality, more skills for continuing habit change and innovation. To produce and maintain such knowledge and such skills in the long run, freedom seems likely to prove a major condition. For these reasons, as well as many others, theorists of freedom, such as John Stuart Mill, are important not only for their time, but also for ours.

GROWTH THROUGH DISSENTERS AND MINORITIES: THE CRITICAL COMMUNITY CONCEPT OF JOHN STUART MILL

The concepts of community of the six classical theorists we have surveyed all stressed the need for cohesion and agreement, treating disagreements and divisions as undesirable or relatively unimportant. Each of these thinkers put the greatest stress on what he thought was known and then advocated some political actions, practices, or institutions based on this knowledge. In comparison to them, John Stuart Mill (1806–1873) seems very moderate, not to say limited, in many of his ideas. He did not share the simple and merciless logic of power of Machiavelli and Hobbes; he lacked Locke's trust in the wisdom of a majority of reasonable people, Rousseau's faith in the general will of the sovereign people, Burke's reliance on tradition and authority, and Marx's sweeping vision of a revolutionary future.

Utilitarianism: The Greatest Happiness of the Greatest Number. Mill did not care for assertions about natural rights or about historical necessity. His concern was with utility. Anything that increased the sum total of human happiness—"the greatest happiness of the greatest number"—was to be fostered; anything that diminished it was to be rejected. In order to calculate or estimate the greatest happiness of the greatest number, every person was to be counted as one, and no one as more than one.

This was the doctrine of *utilitarianism.* It proposed to apply to all political and social institutions, habits, and practices the test of usefulness on a basis of the equality of all human beings. Any individual, by this reasoning, could legitimately claim special treatment or privileges only insofar as that person was more useful than others to his or her compatriots. If in a shipwreck there were not enough seats in a lifeboat, a consistent utilitarian would have to give preference to taking aboard a physician and someone competent in navigation, since persons with these skills were most likely to save more lives than their own. From this viewpoint, the best that could be said of anyone at the end of his or her life would be that that person had been useful to humankind.

This philosophy of usefulness was invented by a genius in the late eighteenth century. Young Jeremy Bentham (1748–1832) had entered Oxford University at the age of thirteen, winning his bachelor's degree at fifteen. Later, he was influential in many reforms in various countries. He won a devoted follower in James Mill, whose son, John Stuart Mill, was another genius, reading Greek at the age of three. A modern psychologist has estimated John Stuart Mill's IQ at about 200. John Stuart Mill himself maintained that his personality and work had been saved by his wife. She had made him human, he insisted, and he reported that she had made major intellectual contributions to his thought.

John Stuart Mill's ideas went beyond those of Bentham in several directions. Bentham had defined human happiness simply as the quantifiable length, intensity, or uncertainty of any kind of pleasure, regardless of its source, be it from playing a game of pushpin or from reading poetry. John Stuart Mill broke with this view and insisted on the importance of the quality of pleasure—what today we might call "the quality of life." There were "higher pleasures" and a "sense of dignity," he wrote; it was "better to be Socrates dissatisfied than a pig satisfied." His ultimate concept of utility was "utility in the largest sense, grounded on the permanent interests of man as a progressive being." What ought to count for most in politics, therefore, was not merely the security and material welfare of a state and its population, but the quality of life in it and the kind of persons who would develop under its regime.

Above all, Mill saw human communities as ever liable to ignorance and error, and these most often were but hardened and deepened by the authority of the few and the conformity of the many. Other writers before Mill, such as John Milton in England, Voltaire in France, and Roger Williams and Thomas Jefferson in America, had defended freedom of expression as something to be tolerated. Mill's philosophy of *liberalism* went deeper. He treated freedom of opinion and expression as constituting something to be cherished, as performing a vital and indispensable function in society and politics. Therefore, every community always needed criticism and self-criticism. It needed minorities and dissenters to look on the world differently from their neighbors, to try out different opinions, and to discover new ideas and perhaps new truths or new aspects of old ones.

Dissenters and minorities, in short, were fundamentally useful. Seen from Mill's viewpoint, they are the decisive instruments for the discovery and application of new knowledge; they are the intellectual reserves of the community today and perhaps its pioneers of tomorrow.

Governments and public opinion, Mill said, most often tend to suppress dissent; and of the two, public opinion often is the more oppressive, since the pressure of its social sanctions is likely to be more omnipresent and more unrelenting than the formal penalties of the state. Freedom of opinion and expression must be defended against both.[6]

Such freedom was not primarily a convenience for the dissenters, no matter how outlandish their views might be. It was a vital necessity for the whole community, most of whose members did not share these strange, new opinions. This entire community needed their critical contribution, their challenge to received opinions—even true ones—in order to impel people to think them through once more, for themselves, instead of merely accepting them unthinkingly, with "no need of any other faculty than the ape-like one of imitation." Where conformity prevails, even the best-organized system will eventually stagnate and decline. The freedom of our dissenters today is the basis of our own right to change our minds tomorrow, someday turning a minority into a majority. Only in this way, Mill maintained, could a community remain vigorous and able to cope with its collective tasks and meet the unknown difficulties of the future. Above all, only in this way could it foster the growth of individuals; and this, to Mill, was its crucial test: "The worth of a State, in the long run, is the worth of the individuals composing it; and . . . a State which dwarfs its men, in order that they be more docile instruments in its hands even for beneficial purposes—will find that with small men no great thing can really be accomplished. . . ."[7]

The images drawn by these seven theorists—power politics, absolutism, constitutionalism, populism, conservatism, socialism, communism, and liberalism—are still each in its own way, among the dominant political ideas of our time. Millions of people still derive from them, directly or indirectly, their political rallying cries and battle flags and their more or less serviceable maps of political reality.

But how does this reality of our most effective large political communities—of states, nations, and world politics—look to the political scientist who wants to understand their inner workings and who asks for evidence that can be verified? It is to this range of questions that we turn in the next chapter.

KEY TERMS AND CONCEPTS

perception
orientation
"princes"
power politics
"the vulgar"
"reasons of state"
interest
balance of power
"leviathan"
state of nature
absolute monarchy
sovereign
social contract

[6]Individual opinion or action could be legitimately suppressed, in Mill's view, only when it was clearly likely to injure other persons or when the government must defend itself against an undoubted and immediate threat. The burden of proof in each case, however, was to be on those who advocated repression. And sane adults should never be protected against themselves. They might not know what was good for them, Mill thought, but those who would restrain them were no less liable to error. All that should be done for their protection would be to provide warnings, such as the requirement to sign a register when buying a poison or dangerous drug.

[7]J. S. Mill, *On Liberty* (New York: Dutton, 1951), p. 229.

law of nature
constitution
constitutionalism
legitimate rule
natural right
property
alienation
belonging
community
particularistic
ascriptive
diffuse
popular sovereignty
populism
general will
particular will
will of all
mean
median
mode
normal distribution
logic of reality
collectivity
institutions
conservative
reactionary
primitive communism
feudalism
capitalism
bourgeois
bourgeoisie
big bourgeois
petty bourgeois
proletarian
proletariat
dictatorship of the proletariat
socialism
communism
fascism
hierarchy
Malthusian population theory
totalitarianism
corporativism
leadership principle
concordate
authoritarianism
national socialism
anti-Semitism
Mein Kampf
extremism
utilitarianism
liberalism
Mill's test of the worth of a state

ADDITIONAL READINGS

Aristotle. *Politics*. Trans. Sir Ernest Barker. New York: Oxford University Press, 1958. Book 5.
Bell, David V. J. *Resistance and Revolution*. Boston: Houghton Mifflin, 1973. PB
Bottomore, T., and P. Goode, eds. *Austro-Marxism*. Oxford: Clarendon Press, 1978. PB
Burke, E. *Reflections on the Revolution in France*.
Burns, James M. *Leadership*. New York: Harper & Row, 1978.
Ebenstein, W. *Political Thought in Perspective*. New York: McGraw-Hill, 1957.
Friedrich, C. J. *Nomos II: Community*. New York: Liberal Arts Press, 1959.
Hobbes, T. *Leviathan*.
Lipset, S. M. "Issues in Social Class Analysis." In Lipset, *Revolution and Counterrevolution: Change and Persistence in Social Structures*. New York: Basic Books, 1968.
Locke, J. *Two Treatises of Government*.
Machiavelli, N. *The Prince*.
Marx, K., and F. Engels. *Communist Manifesto*.
Mill, J. S. *On Liberty*. New York: Dutton, 1951.
Rousseau, J. J. *Considerations on the Government of Poland*.
Sabine, G. N. *A History of Political Theory*. 4th ed. New York: Holt, Rinehart and Winston, 1973.
Tucker, R. C., ed. *The Marx-Engels Reader*. 2nd ed. New York: Norton, 1978.

PB = *available in paperback*

V

The Arena of Politics: States, Nations, the World

Anyone can participate in politics as an individual, but most people participate through groups and organizations. When the labor union leader Joe Hill was executed in 1925 in Salt Lake City on a charge of murder that he insisted was a frame-up, he had these last words for his friends: "Don't mourn me; organize!" Before and since that day, millions of people have known that strength grows from organization.

The most powerful kind of organization in the world today is the modern nation-state. To understand the nation-state—its origins, its nature, the ways in which it is partially controlled by interest groups, and the ways in which it tries to control itself as a political system—is to understand much of the heart of politics.

STATES AND NATION-STATES

A *state* is the organized machinery for the making and carrying out of political decisions and for the enforcing of the laws and rules of a government. Its material appendages include not only officials and office buildings, but also soldiers, police officers, and jails.

In the classical theory of nineteenth-century laissez-faire liberals, as well as of Marxists, the enforcement function was the essence of the state. Everything else was thought to be peripheral. Whether or not this view was true one hundred years ago, it does not fit the facts today. Most modern states spend less than one-third of their budgets on law enforcement, including the maintenance of criminal courts, police, and the national defense. About two-thirds of the activities of the *general government sector*—national, provincial or state, and local—are now devoted to social services, welfare, education, economic aid, and the maintenance of the economic infrastructure, such as schools, roads, airports, and other parts of the transportation system. (The *economic infrastructure* is the collection of all facilities necessary to make the economy function.) Even in Communist states the tasks of production planning, economic regulation, allocation of investments, and provision of social services, education, and public health take a larger amount of money and personnel than the mere enforcement function.

Nonetheless, the enforcement function remains important. If an ethnic group—usually called a *people*—tries to acquire enforcement capabilities in order to police the compliance habits of its members, it becomes politicized. Such a politicized people is often called a *nationality*. If some members of this people control a *sovereign state*—that is, a state that recognizes no higher decision-making power outside itself—we speak of a *nation* or *nation-state*. All these concepts will be examined in greater detail later in this chapter.

The Changing Relevance of Race. At some times and places and, most strikingly, in some Western countries since the eighteenth century, the visible and inheritable physical marks that distinguish a race became associated with the formation of a people. Where this has happened, we often can tell at a glance to what people an individual belongs and thus, often, his or her political majority or minority status in the state. At other times and places, the lines of nationality, loyalty, language, and culture all cut across the lines of race: in such cases, race may have little or no relevance in politics.

In all cases, *race* to the anthropologist means a collection of persons who have some similar inheritable physical characteristics. Most of our physical characteristics, of course, are common to all humankind. We are one single biological species, not several. Unlike lions and tigers—or horses and donkeys—human beings of all races can produce fertile offspring when they interbreed. We are divided into blood groups, but these cut across all races and all political views. Moreover, our heredity is combinatorial. Two or more of our inheritable traits may go together in some individuals, but need not do so in others. Some tall people have poor coordination and awkward reflexes, but others do not and excel at basketball. After centuries of argument, no conclusive evidence has been found that intelligence or creativity goes with having a long or short nose, being fat or thin, having blond or dark or straight or curly hair or having skin that is white, black, brown, red, or yellow. There is even less connection between inherited physical traits and such human qualities as kindness, honesty, or competence in politics.

Observable physical traits often do make a difference, however, in how people are treated. In Egypt and Morocco they make little difference; in Brazil and India, only a little more. In the United States they matter a good deal; and in Rhodesia and South Africa they matter most of all. What is most significant about many such physical traits is that they furnish us with an automatic signaling device for identifying a collection of persons with great speed and without cost or effort. We then can file in one place in our mind—we can *associate*—all our experiences with persons of similar physical appearance. By these means we can quickly produce stereotypes and prejudices that eliminate the need for thinking. If in some country many black people are poor and unschooled, we may quickly associate blackness with poverty and lack of education.

If a racial group has a distinct culture in common, then it is an ethnic group as well. Its members would be an ethnic group even without any similarities in physical appearance. If American blacks all became white tomorrow and resembled a group such as the Irish, having no predominant physical traits, most blacks would still form an ethnic group—and they might still be subject to the same sort of discrimination faced by poor Irish people in English and American cities in the nineteenth century. Furthermore, many members of this now white group might well retain a sense of ethnic cultural cohesion and identity, much as many Irish have done.

The importance of race in American politics today derives in part from this coincidence, in the case of blacks, of racial traits with genuine cultural and historical distinctiveness—indeed uniqueness—as a people. In addition, this particular people, vulnerable to easy discrimination through physical appearance (and association with the stigma of poverty), has been the victim of severe economic and social inequality and often of outright political oppression.

"Race" is the label under which this combination of conditions is perceived. But race need not be associated only with the difficulties of being a black in the United States. Assets and sources of pride are also perceived in this manner. What other people would call their history, their culture, their songs, and their sense of belonging together—all this many American blacks may experience as pride of race.

Old Peoples and Young States. These distinctions among peoples, races, nationalities, states, and nations are relevant in our own time because of the rapid changes world politics has undergone. Most peoples in the world are reasonably old, in the sense that their average age as a people can be measured in generations. Most of them go back several centuries and some, such as the Chinese, have had a recognizable identity for more than 2,000 years. The major western European peoples, too, go back a millennium or more. By the year 1000 A.D., a recognizable Italian language and Italian people had emerged. The French similarly trace their continuity back at least to the ninth century A.D., and so do the Germans. The American people go back at best about 350 years if we consider the first pilgrim stepping ashore at Plymouth Rock as a 100 percent American. If we assume more realistically that this people came fully into existence in the middle of the eighteenth century, approximately fifteen years before the American Revolution, then we must consider the American people as a little more than 200 years old.[1] The Ghanaian people within Ghana's present borders is only twenty or thirty years old (although some peoples within Ghana have a much older tradition). Many other peoples are as young or even younger. But on the whole, the age of most peoples in the world, and certainly of the major peoples, can be measured in terms of centuries.

States are much younger. So are political regimes. (By political *regime* we mean the basic political order under which persons live, such as a monarchy or a republic, a despotism or a democracy, or capitalism or communism in their political aspects.) New states have arisen, and some states that have existed for a long time have become thoroughly transformed in their political arrangements. The China of the emperors and the China of Chiang Kai-shek were both very different from the China of Mao Tse-tung or Teng Hsiao-p'ing. If we consider such differences as radical changes in regime, then we discover that the majority of all persons throughout the world over thirty years of age are older than the political regimes under which they live.

In this world of rapid political change, the United States is a striking exception. No other major country has changed its constitutional form so little since 1791. To most outsiders its politics may seem remarkably conservative. Other countries whose present constitutional forms are old, though younger than that of the United States, include Britain (since the Reform Bill of 1832), Sweden, and Switzerland. These countries, too, are exceptions in the modern world.

For there has never been a period like ours. In past recorded history, changes of states and regimes were slower than the changes of generations. The political system under which most

[1]See Richard Merritt, *Symbols of American Community, 1735–1775* (New Haven: Yale University Press, 1966). Another interesting work on this topic is Max Savelle, "Nationalism and Other Loyalties in the American Revolution," *American Historical Review,* vol. 67, no. 4 (1962), 901-23.

persons in most places lived was older than the individual. It is only in our time that most of the world's adults over thirty are older than their political regimes. At a time when states and political systems are changing so quickly, it is important to distinguish the slower-changing *habits* of peoples and language groups from the faster-changing *institutions* of politics, economics, national sovereignties, national identities, basic political regimes, and even social systems.

The Changing Number of States. A state is to a people as a suit of clothes is to a man, a German nationalist once wrote. Just as a healthy man will wear out many suits in his lifetime, a people should survive many states and political regimes. (Of course, he was writing before the age of nuclear weapons.) What he said is not quite true, but there is some truth in it. Not only have political regimes come and gone faster than the peoples living under them, but the number of states, too, has changed strikingly.

In the years 1815 to 1871, the number of sovereign states tended to decline. In Asia during these years, many principalities in India, Indochina, and elsewhere were replaced by the colonial rule of a few European powers. Between 1871 and 1900, much the same happened in Africa: a few colonial empires replaced a multitude of petty principalities, small tribal communities, and states. Earlier, in the Western hemisphere, the empires of the Aztecs in Mexico and of the Incas in Peru, together with many independent tribes in South and North America, had been swallowed up in the vast expansion of the Spanish and English colonial empires from about 1500 to 1775. In the latter year, most of the Western hemisphere was under the flags of only these two powers. In Europe the smallest number of modern sovereign states—15—was not reached until about 1871; and in Asia and Africa, not until about 1900. For the four centuries from 1500 to 1900, the replacement of many small and backward political units by ever fewer, larger, and more modern states seemed to be the general historic trend (see Figures 5.1 and 5.2).[2] The successful independence movements of a few small nations, such as the Swiss, the Dutch, the Belgians, the Norwegians, and the American colonists, appeared to be but minor exceptions to the general rule; and the United States in the end seemed to confirm the apparent pattern by expanding clear across its continent and absorbing whatever peoples lay in its way.

But this general picture is deceptive. From 1810 onward, republics, finally reaching 18 in number, replaced the Spanish empire in Latin America. From the Ottoman Empire, 5 Balkan states emerged between 1804 and 1912: Serbia (now the core of Yugoslavia), Greece, Rumania, Bulgaria, and Albania; since World War I at least 10 Arab nations have done likewise, leaving behind a much smaller and more nationalistic Turkish republic. Scandinavia, which in 1800 contained 2 sovereign states, Sweden and Denmark, now has 5, as Norway, Finland, and Iceland emerged into sovereignty in the interim. Europe consisted altogether of about 15 sovereign states in 1871, approximately 25 shortly before World War I, and over 30 by the 1930s. The world at large reveals a similar pattern. In Africa and Asia a plethora of new states arose from the French and British empires. Indeed, since 1945 the number of sovereign states around the world has more than doubled to well above 140 at the last count (see Figures 5.3 and 5.4).

The historic trend has now reversed itself. Whereas before many premodern states were giving way to a few half-modern ones, more recently a few partly modern states and empires have been giving way to many that in some respects are still more modern. But this has not been a mere swing of the pendulum. The many states and statelike units that were submerged and swallowed up in the past were economically back-

[2]Our maps in Figures 5.1 through 5.4 show only this more modern type of state. Most of the ancient premodern empires and states, such as the Moghul and Ottoman empires, are not shown.

ward and their populations politically apathetic. The many new states have all experienced at least some touches of economic modernization, industrialism, and mass communications. Their populations are far more numerous and politically active than their forebears were, and they feel a greater need for that high degree of mutual communication, understanding, and solidarity that turns populations into peoples and, eventually, peoples into nations.

An Age of Nationalism. It is these developments that have made the twentieth century an age of nationalism. *Nationalism* is an attitude of mind, a pattern of attention and desires. It arises in response to a condition of society and to a particular stage in its development. It is a predisposition to pay far more attention to messages about one's own people, or to messages from its members, than to messages from or about any other people. At the same time, it is a desire to have one's own people get any and all values that are available. Extreme nationalists want their people to have all the power, all the wealth, and all the well-being for which they can possibly compete. They want their people to command all the respect and deference they can possibly get from others; they tend to claim all rectitude and virtue for their country, as well as all enlightenment and skill; and they give it a monopoly of their affection. In short, extreme

FIGURE 5.1 *The Growth in the Number of Sovereign States: Modern States Independent before 1770*

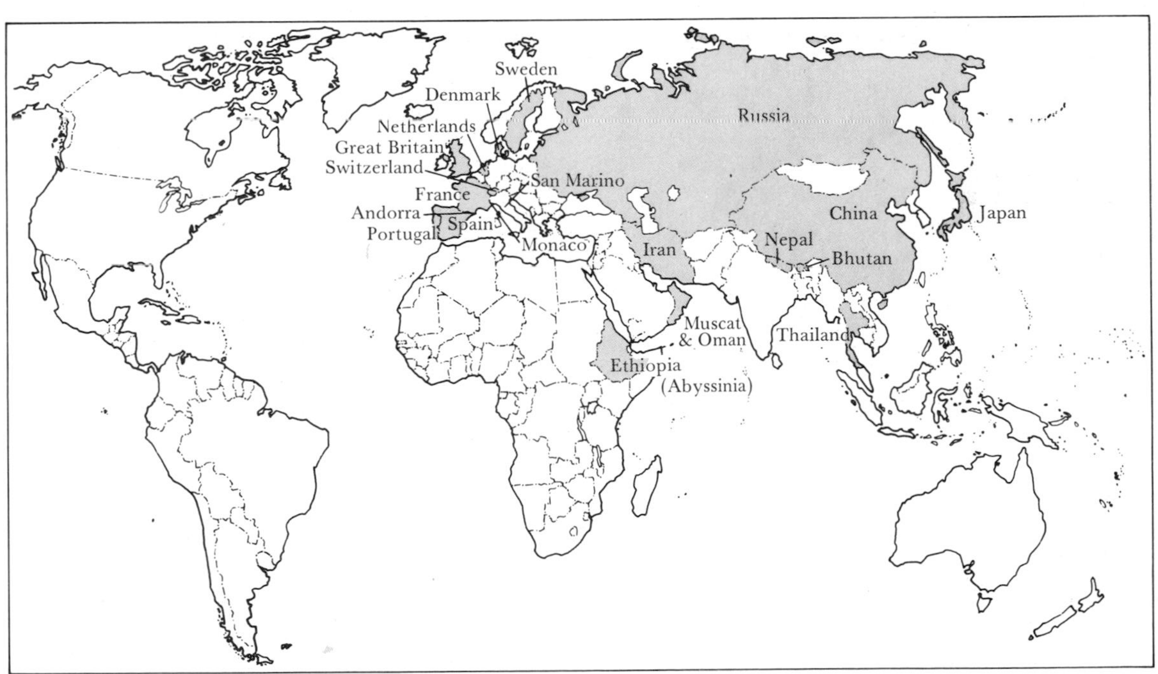

nationalists identify totally with their nation. Though they may be willing to sacrifice themselves for their country, their nationalism is a form of egotism written large.

Although nationalism today is a pervasive state of mind, it is in partial conflict with human nature. Children are not born with it; they have to be carefully taught. In most periods of history, nationalism has been weak or nonexistent. It bids us to prefer distant strangers who share our language and culture to any of our next-door neighbors who do not. It stresses a community of outlook and interest across class lines, but denies any such community across ethnic or national divisions—and stigmatizes a sense of international community as treason to the nation.

Actually, most people do not think in a nationalist way. In a mass survey undertaken by UNESCO (the United Nations Educational, Scientific, and Cultural Organization) respondents in nine countries were asked, first, whether they felt they had much in common with people in their own class but from other nations and, second, whether they thought they had much in common with people in their own nation but in other classes (see Figure 5.5). According to the doctrine of nationalism,

FIGURE 5.2 *The Growth in the Number of Sovereign States: Modern States That Became Independent Between 1770 and 1890*

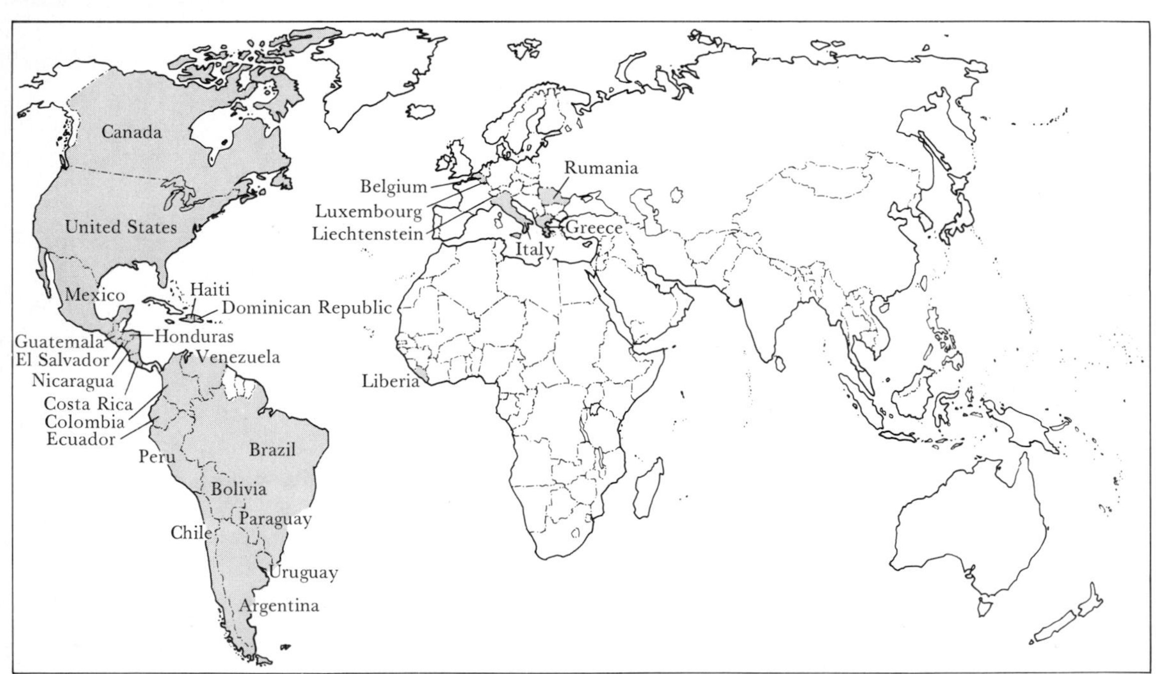

most people should have answered yes to the second question and no to the first; according to theories of class conflict, they ought to have answered the other way around. In fact, they did neither. Their answers revealed their individual personalities. Those who liked and trusted people did so across both class lines and national boundaries. Those who disliked and distrusted foreigners thought little better of their own compatriots.

Even if most people are not extreme nationalists, this attitude has altered the world in many ways. Nationalism has not only increased the number of countries in the world, but it has helped to diminish the number of inhabitants. All major wars in the twentieth century have been fought in its name. This is true even of the limited wars since 1945, though the ideologies of both communism and anticommunism have played a role in many of these. In a speech at Montreal in 1966, Secretary of Defense Robert McNamara stated that more than three-fifths of the 149 conflicts that the Defense Department had counted since 1945 had occurred *within* the non-Communist world. These were primarily conflicts engendered by nationalism.

Nationalism is in potential conflict with all

FIGURE 5.3 *The Growth in the Number of Sovereign States: Modern States That Became Independent Between 1891 and 1945*

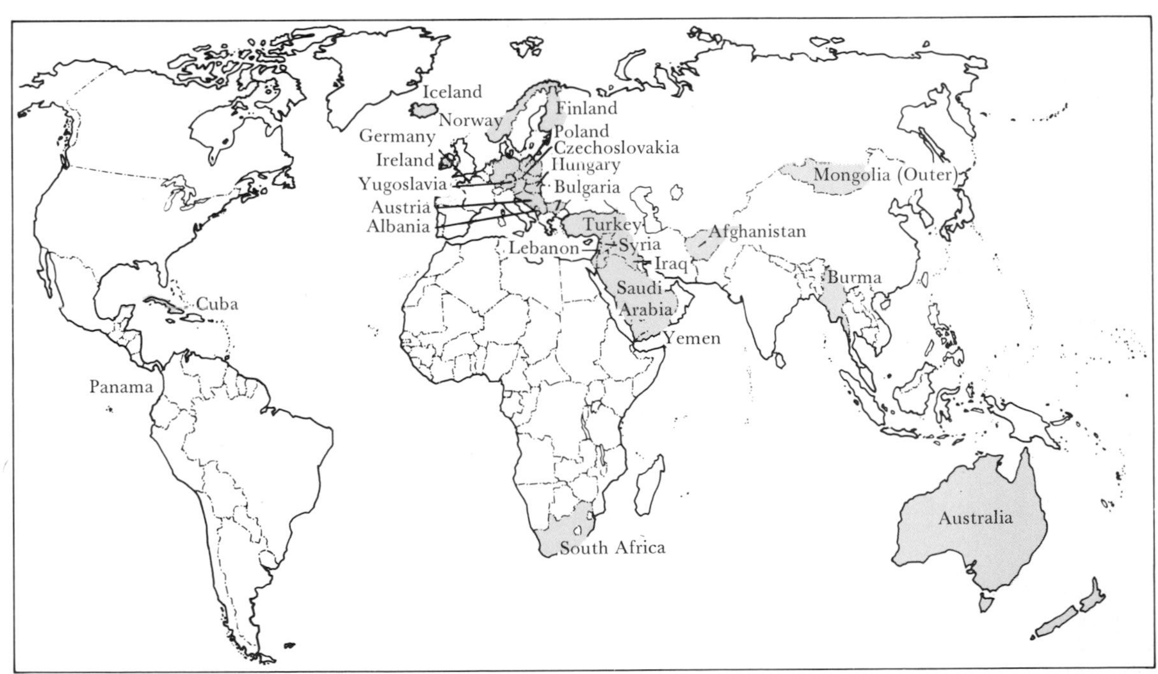

FIGURE 5·4 *The Growth in the Number of Sovereign States: Modern States That Became Independent Between 1946 and 1979*

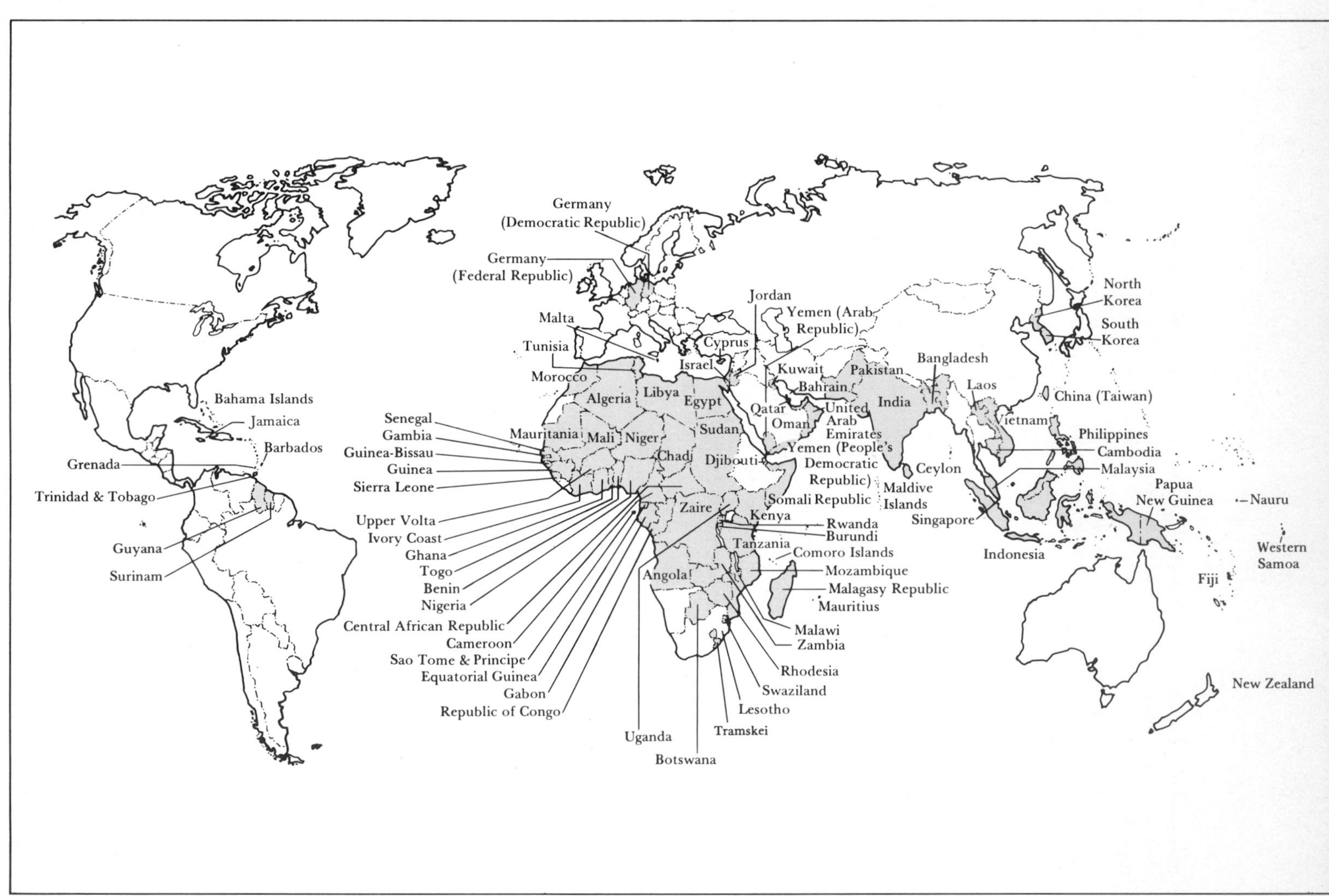

philosophies or religions—such as Christianity—that teach universal standards of truth and of right and wrong, regardless of nation, race, or tribe. Early in the nineteenth century a gallant American naval officer, Stephen Decatur, proposed the toast, "Our country! In her intercourse with foreign nations, may she be always in the right, but our country, right or wrong." Nearly 150 years later the United States Third Army, marching into Germany following the collapse of the Nazi regime, liberated the huge concentration camp at Buchenwald. Over the main entrance to that place of torture and death, the Nazi elite guard had thoughtfully inscribed "My Country, Right or Wrong."

FIGURE 5.5 *National and Class Solidarities: Nine Nations, 1949*

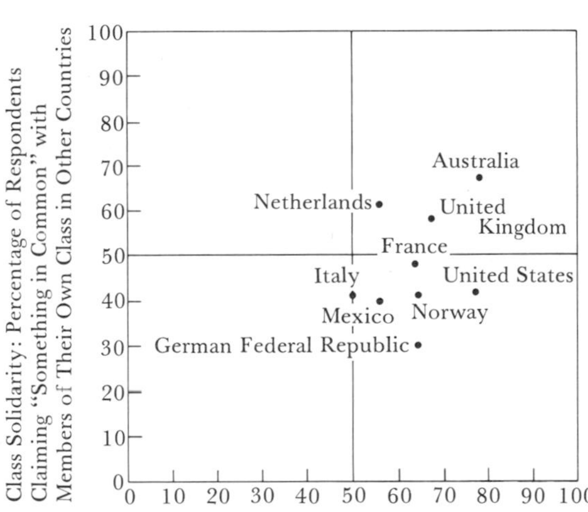

Note that people identify both with class and nation, though national solidarity is higher, and that top left-hand quadrant—high loyalty to class, low loyalty to nation—is empty.

Source: W. Buchanan, *How Nations See Each Other* (Westport, Conn.: Greenwood Press, 1972).

FROM COUNTRIES TO PEOPLES

The Concept of a Country. For those who live in it, a country is an area of multiple interdependences. In economic terms a country is a multiple market for goods and services. An increase in the price of bread or of textiles, an increase in wages, a change in employment, or even a natural catastrophe has a tangible effect on the lives of all its inhabitants. This is true in emotional as well as material terms. To an American, a hundred Americans killed in a mine explosion or landslide represents a disaster. But to most American newspaper readers, ten thousand Iranians killed in an earthquake is a statistic.

A *country* is a geographic area of material, economic, physical, and psychological interdependences. This is why leaders of different states at a conference table cannot arbitrarily make a country that will endure. The Congress of Vienna in 1815 and the Paris Peace Conference in 1919 tried to redraw the boundaries of many countries and to create some new countries, but not all of these lasted.

Some political geographers have tried to find natural frontiers to define a country, but frontiers that seem natural to one country may seem quite unnatural to another, particularly if both covet the same frontier. The French, for instance, asserted for centuries that the Rhine was a natural frontier of France, because they wanted the German-speaking territories on its left bank to be incorporated into their nation. German patriots, however, countered that the Rhine was a German river, not a German boundary.

By and large, there are few natural frontiers. A natural boundary at most imposes major obstacles to transport and frequently is characterized by thin settlement. And yet a thinly settled boundary region can become a heartland when people have learned to drain its swamps, clear its forests, or irrigate its dry pastures. Similarly, a mountain chain separates two countries only as long as people do not know how to build bridges over its gorges and roads over its passes. Thus, in the early Middle Ages, Switzerland was not a country, but a frontier region. As roads or passes were built and pass traffic made Saint Gotthard the medieval equivalent of the Panama Canal, Switzerland became a country.

Depending on changes in settlement and in technology, a geographic feature can be either a barrier or a bridge. Centuries ago, the skin-and-wicker boats of the ancient Irish were unable to cope with North Sea navigational conditions, and Ireland was sharply separated from England and Scotland. But after the English and Scottish learned to build better boats and the Vikings and Normans started sailing the seas, Ireland eventually became part of Britain. Nowadays, reinforced by differences in religion and general culture, the most critical Irish boundary is on land, not at the seashore: Ireland is divided in two, six counties forming British or Northern Ireland and twenty-six in the south forming the Irish Free State. In the 1970s the most bitter divisions were within Northern Ireland, between the favored Protestant two-thirds majority and the disadvantaged Roman Catholic one-third minority of that strife-torn region. These two nations, the British and the Irish, are, as Bernard Shaw put it, separated by the same language to which they tend to attach different political meanings

A country need not be inhabited by only one set of people. It can be populated by several races speaking different languages and having different cultural traditions. Nevertheless, all these groups live in the same country. To the extent that they do, their fates are linked. Until World War II, Bohemia was a single country of two peoples, Czechs and Germans. India was also a single country before its partition into India and Pakistan in 1947. Today the United States includes persons who call themselves the Negro or black people, others who feel a certain affiliation with the Jewish people, and still others who point with pride to their Irish, Scottish, Spanish, or other roots. It is thus evident that one country can contain or include several peoples.

It is also possible for the same person to belong to more than one people. A Scottish native is a Scot and a Briton; a black militant American belongs to both the black people and the American people. Many an American Jew will feel both a special kinship to Israel and a patriotic loyalty to the United States. Multiple loyalties are not rare occurrences and may remain compatible indefinitely.

Patriotism: Solidarity by Territory. Usually in the past, a country was inhabited largely by people who had been born there. Most people did not distinguish between their country of residence and their country of birth. The country of birth in a patriarchal society was called the fatherland, the *patria*; and ever since the days of the Romans, people have been told that it was sweet and honorable to die for their *patria*. Loyalty to a fatherland, however, was not strong in the early Middle Ages, when people had loyalties mainly to their tribes. It emerged in western Europe only in the thirteenth century and at that time was assiduously fostered by the church. The key change came when Pope Honorius III decreed in 1240 that a kingdom, like a diocese, could not be divided nor could any part of it be alienated or sold off to someone else.[3] Applied first to Hungary and then to France, the decree established the notion that kingdoms were indivisible, that a

[3]See Ernst Kantorowicz, "Pro Patria Mori in Medieval Political Thought," *American Historical Review*, vol. 56, no. 3 (1951), 472-92.

kingdom was a unit, and that the crown united a country regardless of the whims or policies of the king who happened to wear it. These views became accepted in much of western Europe between 1240 and 1500. Eventually they formed a major principle of European politics: a country belongs together and, though rulers may come and go, a country remains intact.

If we think of a country as the place where we were born, we attach to it many of the warm sentiments that we attach to childhood and to the memories of our parents; and we begin to have strong feelings of loyalty to the country and to anything to which the symbols of the country are attached. Those who believe that the interests of their compatriots ought to take precedence over the interests of others are called patriots. *Patriotism* means giving preference to the interests of inhabitants of one's country regardless of their race, language, nationality, or religion.

Patriotism sometimes leads to rather striking interpretations. After World War II, a chapel in Philadelphia was to be dedicated to the memory of four chaplains of various creeds. On a sinking troopship these men had given their lifebelts to some GIs and had gone down with the ship. The architect for the chapel proposed an auditorium in which the congregation would sit before a fixed podium decorated by an American flag and the flag of the State of Pennsylvania, and a rotating stage would present the appropriate altar or sanctuary for a Roman Catholic, Greek Orthodox, Protestant, or Jewish service. At the push of a button, a machine would interchange the religious symbols before the fixed flags. The promoters considered this architectural scheme perfectly normal and sensible. Not a voice was raised against it. But think of what would happen if somebody built a church with a fixed altar and a rotation device that would exchange national flags! Quite likely, a number of patriotic societies would accuse the promoters of political blasphemy. It seems that in the last quarter of the twentieth century we are more inclined to worship the gods of the tribe and the nation-state than the universal symbols of religion.

If successful, patriotism can unite people of different languages, different races, different religions, and different backgrounds to serve the interests of one country. Let us remember that by "interest" we mean both a distribution of attention and an expectation of reward. A patriot will pay attention to the things that concern his or her fellow citizens and will try to work for the rewards that they are expected to receive.

PEOPLES AND NATIONALISTS

Nationalism: Solidarity by Language, Culture, or Descent. People sometimes do not attach their main allegiance to a geographic unit. Instead they think mainly of their social group and their ancestors. Such people do not ask *where* they were born or where they are living. They ask *who* their parents were. Very likely these people are nationalists. In its classic form, *nationalism* stresses one's origin by descent and birth; it involves the belief that one's people share a common descent. In actual fact, the bloodlines of humankind have been mixed up a good deal. This holds true not only in such "immigrant" countries as the United States, Canada, and Australia. If we go far enough back in history, it is equally true of all European countries. Ultimately, it is true of the entire world. As we have learned from experience with blood transfusions, there are indeed different blood groups; but these do not coincide with any particular race or nation.

It has been said in central Europe that a nation is a group of persons jointly misinformed about their ancestry and jointly hostile to their neighbors. Nevertheless, if people believe that they belong together through ancestry, their belief is likely to be reinforced by something observable. They often "prove" their ancestry by producing pieces of paper. When the Nazis introduced elaborate race legislation, they gave rise to a brisk trade in documents, some genuine and some less so. Language, too, is observable; we know what language people speak. We also can observe the culture that has become part of people's personality and habits. We can observe people's associations in terms of friendship and relatives, whether these are relations by blood, adoption, or marriage. We can even observe the probabilities of intermarriage. If the memories of ancestors, subject to error as they may be, coincide with the language group, the culture, the group of friendship and associative ties, and the probabilities of past and future intermarriages—that is, if all these pieces fall into place—then we can say with confidence that we have identified a people.

The Concept of a People. Probably the simplest way to define a *people* is to call it a group of persons who share complementary habits of communication. The individual members of the group have a wide range of common ideas and notions and can communicate on many topics. A French Communist and a French nationalist may, for instance, differ on many points about politics, one of them perhaps admiring General de Gaulle or President Giscard d'Estaing and the other deploring him, but they might nevertheless find common ground on many things: the definition of a good dinner, the proper way to win a lover, and whether to wear a hat or a beret. French men and women of different ideologies still can communicate clearly on thousands of topics with a high degree of mutual understanding and responsiveness. They recognize each other as French regardless of their politics.

A people, then, is a group with complementary communication habits whose members usually share the same language and always share a similar culture, so that all members of the group attach the same meanings to words. In that sense a people is a community of shared meanings. The word *liberté* to a French Swiss means much the same thing—local self-government—as *Freiheit* means to a German Swiss. But to a North German, *Freiheit* might easily mean subjection to a familiar tyranny, as in the days of the German emperor or of Hitler; and to a French person, *liberté* might mean membership in a highly centralized republic governed by a charismatic general as president. What distinguishes the Genevan from the Parisian, or what makes the Swiss a people, is the group with whom each shares the meaning of words rather than those with whom each shares the mechanics of grammar and vocabulary.

The individual who believes that the interests of his or her own people should take precedence over the interests of other people is an *ethnic nationalist.* German nationalists in World War I hoped that Americans of German descent would side with the emperor against the United States on the grounds that blood was thicker than water. This calculation proved to be mistaken. There were millions of Americans of German descent, but they functioned just like any other group of American citizens. The assimilation of people of German ancestry to the language and culture of the United States had succeeded. They had become members of the American people. Thus the Nazis obtained little pleasure from the ancestry of Dwight David Eisenhower when he led the United States armies into Germany in World War II. Again and again, the process of assimilation has triumphed thoroughly over mere ties of ancestry.

In one sense the process of assimilation is repeated in each generation. Children, in growing up, learn not only the general language and culture, but also the *political culture,* of the people to which their parents belong and of the people among whom they are raised. (Usually, these two are the same, but if their parents' cultures differ from that of most of their schoolmates, they may have to choose one or the other, or else learn both, at the risk of remaining somewhat marginal in both.) As they grow up, they learn about order and authority, command and obedience, choice and freedom, rank and privilege, equality and solidarity, and many other human relations that occur in politics. They learn how to feel trust or suspicion, respect or contempt, generosity or enmity, and they learn when to expect each of these feelings or responses from others.

All these, however, are not just isolated traits. They interact and interlock; and they most often add up to a pattern of political culture that indicates expectations about politicians and administrators, votes and elections, judges and police officers, legislators and the chief executive or head of the state.

Political culture suggests what is and what is not done in politics, what would be shocking, and what is expected. When in the 1920s the comedian Will Rogers said that the United States had "the best politicians money can buy," his listeners were not shocked. Would you be if someone said it about the United States today? Or what would be your feelings? The answer will tell you something about the particular political culture to which you have become accustomed. And it may lead you to another question: to what extent is this particular culture a fair or unfair sample of the general political culture of the United States?

Growing up in a political culture, being taught its ways explicitly or implicitly, by hints and suggestions from parents, teachers, contemporaries, and mass media, learning its do's and don'ts, and coming to share the feelings and expectations appropriate to it—all this is called *political socialization.* Most people experience it during the period of adolescence, when so much of their whole personality is still in the process of formation. To some extent, however, it may happen to people in very early childhood and again in primary school. More rarely, others experience it later in life, perhaps after immigrating to a new country, or while going to college, or after moving into a new town or a new social environment. In any case, political socialization is the process by which individuals acquire their habits of political behavior and their images of politics in such a manner that these images and habits become a part of their personality, which will change but little in the future or only over a long time and with difficulty. There are rare cases of political "resocialization," to be sure, in connection with religious or ideological conversion, but even here many of the traits of political behavior may be preserved and only be turned in a different direction. Radicals of the left have turned into radicals of the right, without becoming more tolerant of divergent opinions or less sure of the authority of their own current views. Political socialization thus tends to have long-lasting results for many individuals; and the prevailing patterns of political socialization tend to have long-lasting effects on the predominant political culture of a country.

The political culture of a country is not fixed and unchangeable. Men and women make it and remake it by their attention or indifference, their actions or omissions. When, at the time of the Watergate scandal, former Cabinet officers and high White House staff members were accused of illegally manipulating large political campaign funds, committing political espionage, planting paid agents and electronic listening devices, organizing burglaries, forging documents, and suppressing and destroying evidence, several writers and spokespersons rushed to their defense by asserting that such practices long had been customary in American politics—in other words, that they were a normal part of our political culture. By August 1974, public opinion had rejected these propositions, and Richard Nixon resigned from the presidency.

Politicization and Ethnic Self-Rule. Governments today are engaged in such widespread activities as providing vaccines, old-age pensions, medical care, roads, and many other things and services. As a result, the governmental sector has become bigger, and a larger part of human life has been *politicized* (see Chapters 1 and 2).

As government becomes more important to it, as more and more of society's goods and services become subject to allocation through the political process, a people may wish to associate with a state that its members can call their own. They may find that it is essential to live in a state that is staffed by their own kind, administered in their own language, and run in terms compatible with their basic culture. They want it to be *their* state, in a sense, regardless of whether the state is democratic or not.

Arabs living under the dictatorship of President Sadat in Egypt will find that their government at least is predictable. They can look into their own hearts and say, "Well, the man who's governing me is an Arab, and I can find out what he will do next by thinking what I would do if I were in his place." Back in the 1920s, Egypt was governed by English officials who were efficient and law-abiding. Most of them were incorruptible; and since the government was constitutional, there were fair chances for a hearing of complaints. Yet the English were not predictable to the Egyptians because they did not react as Egyptians would in a given situation, nor could Egyptians identify with their rulers. Moreover, they were not accessible to them through other than legal channels. By contrast, even under dictatorship, Egyptian officials are likely to have cousins who know the cousins of ordinary citizens. They are thus accessible to many Egyptians through family ties, through friendship, and, if need be, through bribery.

People want to be governed by an accessible, predictable government that is compatible with their values and functions in congenial ways. Then they can say "our government," even if this government does not permit free debate or free discussion. And they are likely to defend it against any attack by foreigners.

Nationalities: Peoples Moving Toward Nationhood. If a people tries to acquire a state or gain political power at the local, district, or regional level, its members form a *nationality*. Poland was a nation in a very limited sense in the eighteenth century. The petty nobles, who thought of themselves as Poles, were running the country, but most of the peasants under them had no share in administrative affairs and few had an active interest in gaining power. Although the country of Poland was geographically large and the Polish people were numerous, the Polish nationality was small and shallow. It involved only a thin social layer of people who sought and obtained political power. Then the country was divided in the late eighteenth century among three of its neighbors: Prussia, Austria, and Russia. And for the next 150 years Polish patriots tried to make Poland a single entity both as a country and as a nation. Since Polish groups were always trying to attain political power, and since they did exercise some pressure or control over their members, it is fair to say that at least certain of the Poles constituted a nationality in those days. Indeed, many Poles insisted on saying they were a nation even though they did not have a state. They regained their state in 1918; and since that time Poland has been a full-fledged nation-state.

A *nation-state* is the strongest organization for getting things done. Usually it commands a good deal of popular support and can count on a fair amount of popular compliance. The government's orders are couched in words the people can understand, communication is fast, and common cultural patterns facilitate teamwork. Where there exists a single people, nation-states—whether capitalist or Communist—have become the normal instruments of running modern industrial societies.

MULTI-ETHNIC STATES

Many sovereign states are not composed of only one ethnic group, however. More than half of the world's states for which we have information include linguistic or ethnic minorities amounting to more than one-fifth of their population. Such *multi-ethnic states* are liable to become politically divided in their domestic affairs. If their population is also sharply divided into social strata, the risk of such conflict increases.

Double Trouble: Ethnic plus Social Cleavage. Most societies are in fact divided into social strata. Even the United States is stratified, despite its historic reputation of having greater social mobility and a wider distribution of wealth than most other countries. Of the six social classes listed by such sociologists as Lloyd Warner and Morris Janowitz, the three top strata combined—upper upper, lower upper, and upper middle—contain about 10 percent of the U.S. population. (By way of contrast, however, these three strata accounted for only 3 percent of the populations of many European countries, such as Germany, in the 1930s.) Below these three top strata, sociologists frequently find a large lower middle class, but hardly anybody wants to admit membership in it. Nevertheless, it is quite numerous, composed of small entrepreneurs, small businesspeople, small craftspeople, and white-collar workers. The upper lower class consists of skilled workers and such, comprising about 30 percent of the population, and the lower lower are the unskilled workers and the poor. Middling farmers would be among the upper lower class or the lower middle class, depending on farm size and income, and the farmer who owned a two-thousand acre wheat farm and a private airplane would qualify for the narrow upper strata.

Where nationalities are divided, they are not likely to be evenly split by social strata. Switzerland is the one country whose different language groups are about equally divided on all social levels. But in most countries one language or ethnic group is much "more equal" than the others. In the days of the Austro-Hungarian Empire, for example, about 80 percent of the upper level in Bohemia were German and 20 percent were Czech. In pre-1960 Algeria, 90 percent of the top jobs were held by French people and 10 percent, at most, by Arabs. The farther down one goes in the social scale, the smaller becomes the percentage of the favored group until at the bottom there are only very few of the favored. In its sociological profile the disfavored group looks like a pyramid; the favored group looks like a pyramid standing on its head. Such profiles have long been observed to reflect the condition of blacks and whites, respectively, in the South of the United States and to a growing extent in the big cities in the North.

Modernization, Mobility, and Ethnic Conflict. Now consider what happens when a country with this kind of profile becomes modernized. All the children begin to go to school. Mass media, shop windows, advertising, and all the rest begin to exercise a powerful demonstration effect.[4] Everybody begins to discover what life could be like. Industry lures people from the countryside and offers them more attractive jobs in the cities; and how can you keep them down on the farm once they have seen Scranton, Pennsylvania!

Once people want to move, they also want to move upward in society. The modern industrial society teaches people not to take their class as a God-given position but as somehow the result of their own efforts. Class status becomes achieved rather than ascribed or inherited. This means that energetic young individuals now want to move up and feel resentful if they fail to do so. However, when they try to move up in a multi-ethnic country, they often bump heads with another nationality group occupying the next higher level in society. And nationality groups, by definition, tend to be exclusive, for a people (or nationality group) acts not only as a community of communication and a community of mutual predictability of behavior, but also as a community of mutal trust. When we know exactly what someone will do, we trust that person. As Rudyard Kipling once said of his compatriots, we "know the lies they tell."

When a young Arab in Algiers wanted a job from a French employer, the latter usually found

[4]*Demonstration effect* is the sum of the effects that the demonstration of modern products, practices, and living conditions have on the aspirations and habits of people previously unfamiliar with them. Prominent among these effects are a rise in economic demand for new goods and a rise in political demands for new rights, services and opportunities.

that he could trust another French person more (unless the work was menial). This is an example of overt *ethnic discrimination,* but discrimination can take more innocent forms. In the United States today, someone decides that having a rich vocabulary in French is excellent proof of good college material and that a university that requires a knowledge of French for admission has "high standards." On the other hand, an excellent knowledge of the vocabulary of "black English" is considered irrelevant for college studies (even though it might suggest a good deal of "verbal aptitude"). Enrolling black Americans who do not know French but who possess a rich ghetto vocabulary is considered, therefore, a lowering of the standards of a university. Thus, college board exams examine people in French, but not in black culture, even though the latter may be more useful for future teachers or principals in urban schools; and in the name of higher standards, such examinations may keep many otherwise qualified blacks out of the better colleges. (This is not to say, of course, that all students, white and black, will not need a good command of standard English for their careers in the United States. They will need it, since it is the common speech of the great majority of the people among whom most of the students will have to make their living.)

What people regard as objective standards are usually in large part culture-bound. For disfavored peoples and races these *culture-bound standards* may become tremendous obstacles in the way of social elevation. They may even hurt the psychic self-image—the sense of personal worth—of the members of the disfavored nationalities. The result is social conflict, often long and bitter, driven by disappointed hopes and deep personal emotions.

A favored nationality may sometimes also be motivated by the vision of *upward social mobility.* It may think that if it could conquer another country or colony, it could spread itself out like a tree over even more populations. And by adding a new colonial area, it could broaden the opportunities for middle-class jobs for its own people. This is what the French and British peoples did to some extent during the hundred-odd years before World War II and what the German, Italian, and Japanese peoples were urged to try by some of their leaders from the 1890s onward. In each case, an upper layer of colonial bureaucrats, military officers, business executives, and professional people from the ruling colonial power was spread over the underlying native population. To the extent that it succeeds in doing this, the favored nationality acquires a sociological profile resembling a mushroom cloud with a thin stem and a wide crown, overshadowing the chances of others. It may then further impoverish the people in the conquered country, pressing them or their children down into lower-level jobs. The nationalist movement of the natives seeks to prevent this stratification or to reverse it.

In such ethnic or racial conflicts there is no built-in stopping point. We begin with nationality A, the favored one, prevailing over the other. But suppose that B, the former underdog, gets on top of A through some combination of events. Then B will try to corner most of the top jobs for its own people and turn the people of A into the drawers of water and the hewers of wood. This can be done by outright discrimination, by examination and selection of candidates according to the standards of the now dominant culture. Whereas North African Arabs once were examined in French for civil service jobs, both they and the children of French settlers now may be tested in Arabic.

In many countries nobody is as solicitous for equality and social justice as the spokesperson for an oppressed nationality. And nobody is as callous as the same spokesperson once his or her nationality succeeds in getting on top. Such nationalists have interchangeable attitudes toward justice. Touchingly concerned for it as long as their own group has been trampled on, they often show utter unconcern for others when positions are reversed.

A Curve of Inequality. Such ethnic or racial struggles are expressions of underlying social conflicts. Their intensity grows with the extent of economic inequality and social tension in a society. We can measure the inequality of income among individuals, families, or classes by drawing a so-called *Lorenz curve* (see Figure 5.6). In this diagram the percentages of population in a country are measured along the horizontal axis and the percentages of income along the vertical axis. If every percentage of people had exactly the same percentage of income, the curve of distribution would be a straight line, coinciding with the diagonal. The more bent the Lorenz curve, the greater is the area between it and the diagonal and the greater the economic and social inequality. In a country that manages to move toward more equality, the Lorenz curve will flatten and the area of inequality will shrink. The area between the Lorenz curve and the diagonal thus permits us to calculate a single number called the *Gini index,* after the Italian economist Corrado Gini. This number is a measure of the extent of social or economic inequality prevailing in a country.[5]

The greater the inequality among classes or strata, the greater the motivation of ethnic groups to compete for improvement. The less inequality, the less driving force for conflict. Lack of employment and gross inequality of opportunity are two engines that accelerate conflict among nationalities.

Within most of the advanced countries, stratification has been declining. The richer and more advanced a country is, the closer it moves toward reasonable equality. Very well-to-do countries have a Gini index of about 0.4; very poor countries have a Gini index of about 0.5 or higher, but they may keep these data hidden (see Table 5.1). As the table also shows, Communist countries enforce a higher degree of equality, but they do so at the cost

[5]For details of calculation, see H. R. Alker, Jr., and B. M. Russett, "Indices for Comparing Inequality," in R. L. Merritt and S. Rokkan, *Comparing Nations* (New Haven: Yale University Press, 1966), pp. 349-72.

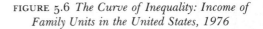

FIGURE 5.6 *The Curve of Inequality: Income of Family Units in the United States, 1976*

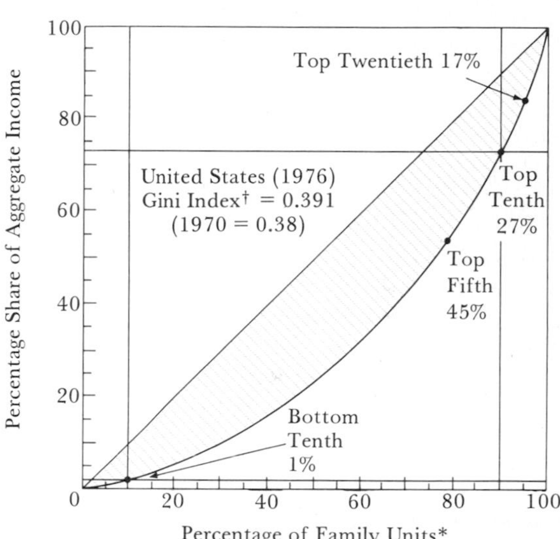

Note: Calculation is made on the basis of share of each fifth of population. Top fifth's share of income is 44.7%; bottom fifth's is 3.8%. Estimate from figures given by Shail Jain is that top share is now 28%, while bottom share is closer to 1%. See S. Jain, *Size Distribution of Income*, World Bank series (Baltimore: Johns Hopkins University Press, 1976).

*A family unit is two or more people living in the same dwelling unit and related to each other by blood, marriage, or adoption. A single person unrelated to the other occupants in the dwelling unit or living alone is a family unit" (see source note).
†The Gini index is the ratio of twice the shaded area (between the Lorenz curve and the diagonal) and the area of the square. The greater the inequality of incomes, the more steeply curved will be the Lorenz curve and the larger will be the shaded area, and hence the larger will be the Gini index. (See discussion on pp. 124–29)

Source: U.S.Department of Commerce, Bureau of the Census, *Current Population Reports*, "Consumer Income," ser. P–60, no. 14 (1978) p. 56.

TABLE 5.1 *Distribution of Income Before Taxes in Twenty-One Countries: A World Bank Study, 1975*

Rank of Gini Index Inequality	Country	Year	Type of Data Sample*	% of Income Going to		Ratio of Top to Bottom	Gini Index of Inequality	Average Net Change in Gini Index per Decade	Average Net Change in Incomes Share of Top Decile per Decade
				Top Decile	Bottom Decile				
1	Brazil	1960	IR	49.1	1.2	40.9	.59		
		1970	IR	54.3	1.1	49.4	.65	+.06	+5.2%
		1970	HH	48.6	0.9	54.0	.61		
2	Peru	1961	EAP	49.6	0.9	55.1	.61	−.02	−4.5
		1971	EAP	45.1	0.4	112.8	.59		
3	Mexico	1963	HH	42.2	1.5	28.1	.55	+.05	+11.0
		1969	HH	48.8	2.0	24.4	.58		
4	Malaysia	1960	HH	45.7	1.2	38.1	.57	−.05	−4.6
		1970	HH	41.1	1.2	34.3	.52		
5	Philippines	1956	HH	38.9	2.1	18.5	.49	+.02	+3.2
		1961	HH	40.5	2.0	20.3	.50	−.01	−3.4
		1971	HH	37.1	1.3	28.5	.49		
6	France	1956	HH	34.3	0.7	49.0	.48	+.07	+4.8
		1962	HH	37.2	0.5	74.4	.52		
7	India	1960	HH	36.7	1.1	33.4	.47	+.01	0
		1968	HH	36.7	1.8	20.4	.48		
8	Finland	1952	IR	29.0	0.9	32.2	.41	+.06	+3.9
		1962	IR	32.9	0.5	65.8	.47		
9	Netherlands	1952	IR	33.9	1.1	30.8	.45	−.01	−0.3
		1962	IR	33.6	1.1	30.5	.44	+.02	−0.6
		1967	IR	33.0	1.0	33.0	.45		

10	Japan	1962	HH	28.8	1.7	16.9	.39	+.03	+2.0
		1971	HH	30.6	0.5	61.2	.42		
11	German Federal	1968	HH	28.6	2.4	11.9	.39	0	+2.5
	Republic	1970	HH	29.1	2.2	13.2	.39		
12	United States	1960	HH	26.7	0.8	33.4	.39	0	+1.2
		1972	HH	28.1	0.8	35.1	.39		
13	Sweden	1963	IR	28.5	1.3	21.9	.41	−.03	−1.4
		1970	IR	27.5	1.5	18.3	.39		
14	Denmark	1955	IR	26.9	1.3	20.7	.39	−.02	−1.3
		1966	IR	25.5	1.6	15.9	.37		
15	Norway	1957	IR	27.9	0.9	31.0	.39	−.05	−4.8
		1963	IR	25.0	0.8	31.3	.36		
16	Yugoslavia	1963	HH	26.2	2.5	10.5	.35	0	−1.8
		1968	HH	25.3	2.3	11.0	.35		
17	United	1960	HH	25.8	2.3	11.2	.35	−.01	−2.4
	Kingdom	1968	HH	23.9	2.3	10.4	.34		
18	Israel	1956–57	HH†	20.7	3.3	6.3	.25	+.11	+5.3
		1968–69	HH†	27.0	1.3	20.8	.38		
19	Canada	1961	HH	23.4	2.4	9.8	.32	+.03	+1.5
		1965	HH	24.0	2.3	10.4	.33		
20	Hungary	1967	POP	19.3	2.8	6.9	.25	−.05	−1.0
		1969	POP	19.1	3.3	5.8	.24		
21	German	1967	HH	16.9	4.1	4.1	.20	0	0
	Democratic	1970	HH	16.9	4.0	4.2	.20		
	Republic								

* HH-households; IR-income recipients; EAP-economically active population; POP-population.
† Urban households only.

Source: Jain, *Size Distribution of Income*, World Bank series (Baltimore: Johns Hopkins University Press, 1976).

of other values. On the whole, economic growth works better with higher equality, up to a Gini number of perhaps 0.3. What happens beyond that, no one as yet knows. A country may have, therefore, a high *average* income and fairly high *average* equality and yet have some severely disadvantaged small groups (see curve B in Figure 5.7).

The Gini index measures the entire amount of inequality in a country across all income classes. A country may therefore have a relatively low Gini index, due to a low degree of inequality among 70 or 80 percent of its income receivers, and yet have much more inequality in regard to the poorest 10 or 15 percent of its population. Thus, in Figure 5.7, curves A, B and C all include the same area and hence have the same Gini index. Curve A shows inequality distributed more or less evenly over all income levels. Curve B shows a relatively high degree of equality among the upper- and middle-income levels, but severe inequality to the detriment of the poorest income groups. Curve C shows the reverse, the middle-income groups being more equal to the poor and inequality favoring mostly a small layer at the top.

FIGURE 5.7 *What the Gini Index Does Not Measure: Distribution of Equality/Inequality*

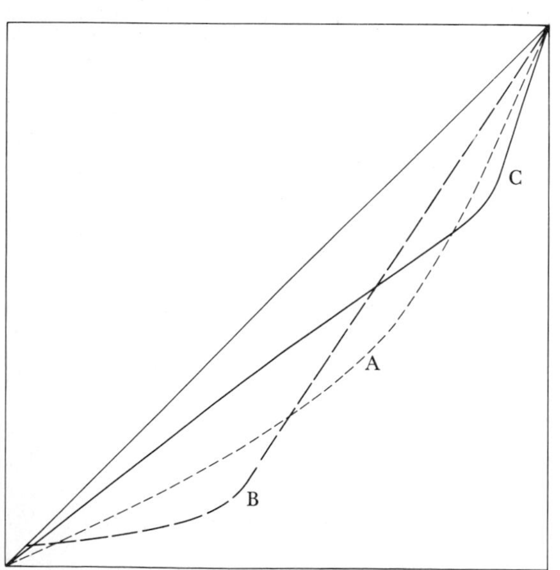

Curves A, B, and C all include the same area and hence have the same Gini index.

If the real situation in a country should resemble curve B in Figure 5.7, the middle-income groups may feel that they have much in common with the top strata and be somewhat conservative in politics. If the facts, on the contrary, should resemble curve C, the middle-income strata might have more in common with the poorer levels and might be more willing to join them in political coalitions for redistribution and reform. Which curve, if any, do you think most resembles the situation in the United States? Which one resembles conditions in Russia in 1917, or in China in 1949, or in Cuba in 1959?

A Lorenz curve and a Gini index can also be made for the world as a whole (see Figure 5.8). International inequality has so increased since 1910 that the world of nation-states is now about as unequal as the worst-governed nation-state within it. In the United States the richest state, Connecticut, has three times the per capita income of the poorest state, Mississippi. In the world as a whole, the difference among countries is not three to one, but sixty to one. The world is extremely unequal and thus, if economic equality is at least one criterion of good government, extremely badly governed.

A multi-ethnic nation-state with high inequality and high stratification is unstable; it invites major conflicts among language groups, nationalities, and races. A world that is highly unequal does the same. Western Europe, the United States, Canada, the Soviet Union, and the few Eastern European Soviet-bloc countries have among them more than 80 percent of the world's income; all the other countries of the world must scramble for the less than 20 percent remaining. If large nation-states such as the United States are racked with tensions, then how explosive is the rest of the world?

DOES THE EARTH HAVE ENOUGH RESOURCES FOR ALL PEOPLES?

In the 1970s, about one-fourth of humankind had over four-fifths of the world income. What would happen if the poorer three-fourths should claim the same living standards and material facilities? What would be their chances of getting these, either through the international *redistribution* of existing wealth or through *increases in* the economic *productivity* of their own peoples and countries? They could not get these directly from the richer countries—certainly not soon or quickly. Most voters in the latter countries would not stand for it; and any attempt to redistribute among nations a large part of the world income by force would involve unacceptable risks of war and impoverishment for all.

What seems more likely in the long run are some moderate transfers of capital and productive equipment from the richer countries to the poorer ones. In the 1970s, 1 percent of GNP was considered a target figure for economic aid, but many rich countries—including the United States, which had urged this figure on other nations—persisted in falling short of it. This 1-percent level of aid had not been reached by the late 1970s—the United States contribution was about 0.5 percent of GNP per year—but in the 1980s and 1990s economic aid levels of 3 or 5 percent of GNP may sound less unlikely than they do now.

The main steps toward economic betterment, however, will have to be taken by the poor countries themselves; and this will require major political efforts toward raising the productivity of

FIGURE 5.8 *Gini Indices for Unequal Distribution of Power and Wealth: (a) The Unequal Economic Power of Nation-States; (b) The Unequal Distribution of the World's Wealth*

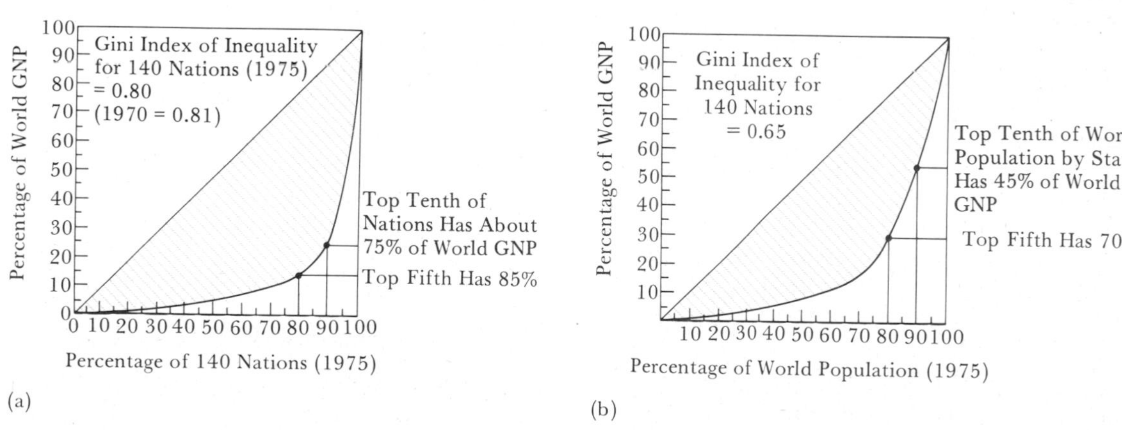

Source: Ruth Legar Sivard, *World Military and Social Expenditures, 1978* (Leesburg, VA.: WMSE Publications 1978). Figures computed by Sheldon Kravitz and Robert Grady.

their own economies and populations. These efforts will include government-aided increases in the rate of domestic savings and basic investment; development of transport, public utilities, and the entire economic infrastructure; development of basic industries, including fuels, steel and other metals, building materials, machines, fertilizers and other chemicals; as well as development of so-called light industries producing articles of daily life, such as fibers, textiles, shoes, processed foods, containers, and the like.

At the same time, or earlier, there will have to be investments in the invisible capital of each poor country: the health, skills, and education of its human resources. Such undertakings will require hospitals, nurses, and physicians; schools and teachers; universities, laboratories, scientists, and scholars; and the necessary material facilities for all these.

If we suppose that most of the world's poor countries and their 3 billion present-day inhabitants were to make such a sustained effort, would there be enough raw materials, energy resources, and relatively unpolluted environment in the world to permit the industrialization of all countries up to the present-day levels of the United States, Western Europe, and the European Soviet bloc?[6]

Some scholars claim that it cannot be done. There are simply not enough known deposits of metals and fuels in the world, they believe, and the necessary expansion of industries in today's poor countries would produce an intolerable amount of pollution in the world's atmosphere and oceans. Moreover, population growth will continue for some time and will make all these effects much worse. Some social scientists have incorporated a number of assumptions of this kind into mathematical models on computers; and the computers then have duly returned to them the implications of the assumptions fed into them. Unless population growth is stopped quickly, these computer printouts suggest, and unless the poor countries give up their efforts to reach the economic levels of today's rich ones, or unless today's rich countries stop growing richer and even consent to make themselves poorer, a bleak future lies ahead: population, pollution, and consumption of scarce metals and fuels will build up to a point at which the whole system will collapse in the ruin of the environment, with famine, disease, and perhaps war destroying a large part of humankind, leaving at best only fewer and much poorer survivors on an impoverished planet.

Other scholars disagree. The earth's resources are "enough and to spare," they say, for the needs of 12 to 14 billion people, about three times today's world population. Moreover, the real progress of technology will teach us to do more with less, much as modern transistors permit us to build radios, television sets, and computers with much less copper in them than they required earlier. If we learn to operate our common "spaceship earth," some more optimistic economists and engineers suggest, we will find that we all can live together in peace and relative plenty on our planet, provided only that we summon up the political will and skill to agree on the necessary action.

The discussion is still going on. New discoveries and experiences will bear on its outcome. But all our political contests and conflicts, within nations and among them, are indeed being made against this background. Our politics will decide much of our large-scale behavior and, with it, the future habitability of the only planet that we have.

[6]This bloc, sometimes called the Warsaw Pact countries after an alliance treaty among them, includes the Soviet Union, Poland, the German Democratic Republic, Czechoslovakia, Hungary, Rumania, and Bulgaria.

KEY TERMS AND CONCEPTS

state
general government sector
economic infrastructure
sovereign state
nation-state

race
regime
nationalism
country
patria
patriotism
people
ethnic nationalist
political culture
political socialization
nationality
multi-ethnic state
cleavage (social, ethnic)
demonstration effect
ethnic discrimination
culture-bound standards
upward social mobility
Lorenz curve
Gini index
redistribution vs. increased productivity
limits to growth

ADDITIONAL READINGS

Black, C. *The Dynamics of Modernization.* New York: Harper & Row, 1967. PB

Buchanan, W. *How Nations See Each Other.* Westport, Conn.: Greenwood Press, 1972.

Cole, H. S. D., et al. *Models of Doom: A Critique of* The Limits to Growth. New York: Universe Books, 1973. PB

Deutsch, K. W. *The Analysis of International Relations.* 2nd ed. Englewood Cliffs, N.J.: Prentice-Hall, 1978. PB

———. *Nationalism and Social Communication.* Rev. ed. Cambridge: MIT Press, 1966. PB

Forrester, J. W. *World Dynamics.* 2nd ed. Cambridge: MIT Press, 1973.

Fuller, B. *Operating Manual for Spaceship Earth.* Carbondale: Southern Illinois University Press, 1969. PB

Geertz, C., ed. *Old Societies and New States.* New York: Free Press, 1963.

Jain, S. *Size Distribution of Income.* World Bank Series. Baltimore: Johns Hopkins University Press, 1976. PB

Lijphart, A. *Democracy in Plural Societies: A Comparative Exploration.* New Haven: Yale University Press, 1977.

Mather, K. *Enough and to Spare.* New York: Harper and Brothers, 1944.

Meadows, D. H., et al. *The Limits to Growth.* New York: Universe Books, 1972. PB

Miller, S. M., and P. Roby. *The Future of Inequality.* New York: Basic Books, 1970. PB

Myrdal, G. *The Challenge of World Poverty.* New York: Random House, 1971. PB

Rustow, D. A. *A World of Nations.* Washington: Brookings Institution, 1967. PB

Ward, B. *Rich Nations and the Poor Nations.* New York: Norton, 1962. PB

———, and R. Dubos. *Only One Earth.* New York: Norton, 1972. PB

PB = *available in paperback*

VI

The Political System: What Holds It Together

Theorists have interpreted the world of politics in many ways. In this age of nuclear energy and space navigation, however, our first task is to survive in this promising and dangerous world of politics. Our second is to change it for the better. For both tasks, we must understand how this world works, what makes it go, and what persons, groups, or relationships produce its outcomes, good or bad. What knowledge is crucial if we are to predict political events or possibly to control them? In the course of time many answers have been proposed to this question, but most of them have been unsatisfactory. The most recent answers, and perhaps the best ones available, have been organized around the concept of the political system.

In studying a political system, we must ask first what it is and then what it does. A *political system* is a collection of recognizable units, which are characterized by cohesion and covariance.

Cohesion means sticking together, or forming a whole. It is related to causality. Two units cohere if many of the operations on one of the units have definite effects on the other. Thus a tug at one end of a chain will be transmitted to the other links, and the turn of a key will open a lock. Symbols may cohere in a system, such as the alphabet, so that changing a letter in a word changes the meaning of the entire word. People may cohere in a society or a state so that changing the lives of some of them is likely to change the lives of others.

Covariance means changing together. If one unit changes, the others do, too. In social science, as in all science, discovering covariance is one step toward discovering not only what goes together, but also what causes what. An individual and his or her shadow move together, but we must find out separately whether a change in the individual causes a change in the shadow or whether we can move the individual by moving the shadow—which of course we cannot. Covariance is in some sense a weaker relationship than cohesion. Wherever there is cohesion, there will also be some observable covariance; but where there is covariance, there need not be any cohesion. Benjamin

Franklin forcefully advised his fellow signers of the Declaration of Independence that even if they lost cohesion, they most certainly would not lose covariance: "We must, indeed, all hang together," he told them, "or most assuredly, we shall all hang separately."

To the extent that units appear to be covariant, and on closer investigation turn out to be cohesive as well, we say that they are *interdependent* and that their fates are tied together. The relation of interdependence may be *asymmetrical;* engineers would say that the *coupling*—that is, the transfer of effects—from A to B was strong, but that from B to A was weak or even negligible.

In any case, we may call the interdependent units the *components* or parts of a system—bearing in mind that some or all of them may be capable of existing outside the system. Thus keys and locks can exist separately, but work together—as do the parts of more elaborate systems, such as an automobile or a stereo system. An interest group, a political party, a city, a national government, and the United Nations are examples of interdependent systems of this kind.

THE FREQUENCY OF TRANSACTIONS AND THE INTERDEPENDENCE OF PEOPLE

The Concept of a Transaction. A system is held together from within, in contrast to a mere *collection,* which can be held together from outside by some external means. A system is made by interdependence; and, among people, interdependence is made by transactions. A *transaction* is a chain of events that begins in one place or unit and ends in another. The units thus connected are partners in this transaction, but their influence on its result need not be equal. Such transactions may involve the transfer of material objects, as in the trade of wheat, iron, or textiles; or the transfer of energy, as in the transmission of electrical power; or the transfer of services, as in the repair of automobiles or watches. An important class of transactions involves the movement of people, such as those who commute to work every day or otherwise travel for business, pleasure, education, or migration. Another important class of transactions comprises primarily the transfer of information, as in letters, telegrams, telephone calls, in newspaper circulation, and in radio or television broadcasts.

The transactions among the parts of a system can be observed and measured. In principle, therefore, they are accessible to the methods of scientific investigation, which requires repetition and verification of results by different observers regardless of their prejudices. A system usually can be recognized by the fact that some kinds of transactions occur much more often among the parts within it than between some parts of the system and the world outside it. If we wish to find out whether there are any particular friendship groups or cliques in a college class, we might start by observing which students most often see one another, talk to one another, and exchange letters or telephone calls and which students seem partly or wholly excluded from these partnerships. The *relative frequency of transactions* is thus a test for the existence of a system and for deciding whether a particular unit belongs to it.

Boundary Lines and Boundary Zones. The fact that certain transactions are more frequent within a system than outside it gives rise to the concept of boundaries. *Boundaries* consist of those components, groups, persons, or areas in space where the frequency of transactions falls off to an observable degree. If this frequency falls off suddenly, the boundary will look like a *line;* if the transactions fall off gradually, we may speak of a *boundary zone.* We can observe such boundary zones in the density of settlements, in the frequency of traffic, around local shopping centers, or even between countries. When students hitchhike northward from New England to Quebec, or westward from Cologne in Germany to Paris in France, they will notice the automobile traffic thinning as they near the border or frontier of each country. These frontiers are areas that have been thinly settled for centuries and have formed historic boundary regions. A country, in general, is a good example of this type of frequency system; it is held together by many kinds of transaction flows that are most frequent at its center, but fall off toward its boundaries.

Boundary zones of this kind are more or less automatic, since they work through the thinning out of traffic or settlements, caused by natural obstacles or by historical, social, or economic reasons. *Political boundaries* are much different. They are set by the political decisions of states, sometimes after wars and usually by treaty. Often they are established in some natural or historic boundary zone, where they are more convenient and easy to maintain. At these boundaries, states collect customs payments, admit or reject goods, letters, travelers and immigrants, and sometimes prohibit their own subjects from leaving the country without official permission. All these controls tend to slow down traffic and reduce it still more. Nonetheless, most governments insist on maintaining boundaries and boundary controls around their territories, because they see in them a necessary instrument for exercising some control over what goes on within their countries.

Something similar can apply to a group of individuals. It, too, may have a core and a periphery with a boundary zone. The members of a nuclear family—husband, wife, and their young children—usually have much more to do with one another than with people outside this closely knit group. In contrast to past centuries, today the importance of the extended family has declined. The nuclear family may have few or almost no transactions with great-aunts or second cousins. Aunts and first cousins fall somewhere in between. As a rule, the members of the nuclear family see them less often than they see each other, but in many cases more often than strangers or more distant relatives. These closer relatives thus form a kind of boundary zone around the nuclear family: they are its marginal members.

Many large groups, such as a people, often show a similar pattern. Most Americans carry on more transactions with other Americans than with other persons. This is even true of many of the "overseas Americans" who may be living abroad in military garrisons or business enclaves and orienting their lives to their compatriots around the PX facilities or the American Club.

Most boundaries are relatively stable over time. They stay in the same place, and we can easily remember where they are. Some frontiers among European nations have not changed for centuries. The main part of the frontier between the United States and Canada has remained unchanged for 150 years, and the frontier between the United States and Mexico has stayed the same for more than 100 years. But this is not true of all boundaries. If a system is growing, its frontiers may be moving and expanding rapidly, through settlement, conquest, or conversion, although its frequent transactions will continue to maintain internal cohesion. Thus the United States, Canada, the Soviet Union, China, and many Latin American countries have continued to expand their boundaries without most of their people's feeling that they had to give up their national cohesion or their identity.

The relationship between the frequency of transactions and the boundary of systems is illustrated in Figures 6.1, 6.2, and 6.3. In all such cases—whether they involve geographic areas, small groups, or whole peoples—the frequency of transactions is a source of cohesion that holds together a system of human relations. (A country is thus not held together by its "rocks and rills," but by the relations among the people who inhabit it.) Insofar as people are held together by frequent transactions, they are likely to matter more to one another in politics. They are likely to make a greater difference to one another's political behavior, either in conflict or in cooperation.

The Importance of Transactions: Who Gets Rewards. Not all transactions are equally important. Indeed, some very frequent ones may be politically trivial. (For instance, in most countries sports have little direct political significance, although they may acquire it under particular conditions, such as the Czech-Soviet hockey game following the U.S.S.R.'s occupation of Czechoslovakia in 1968.) The importance of any transaction to any person depends on the difference it makes to the *values* that person gains or loses or expects to gain or lose from it. The greater the rewards or penalties that people get from certain transactions, the more important these transactions are to them.

More generally, the importance of transactions depends on their *side effects*. These are effects that accompany some events or transactions and vary with their amount just as traffic has the side effect of noise. The size of a district, for example, may influence the availability of candidates for elective office. In a large district, canvassing requires much time, staff, and money, making candidates more dependent on private means, donors, or machine support.

Some side effects may occur only above certain levels of frequency. A road or railroad may be worth building if there is a sufficiently high level of traffic or business for it; but below this amount of traffic, no road will be built. Similarly, a secondary school may be worth building in a community if there are a sufficient number of schoolchildren; but below this number of schoolchildren, no secondary school will be built. Such numbers, frequencies, or levels of demands are called *critical levels* or *thresholds*. Below any such threshold, some important side effect is negligible. Above this threshold, it becomes significant. Thresholds mark those stages in a process at which small changes in one kind of thing or event make a big difference in another. Below a certain frequency of traffic, innkeepers cannot make a living. Below some level of population, prosperity, tax yield, civil obedience, and perhaps strategic importance, a piece of territory may not be worth the costs of administering and defending it, and its government may willingly leave it to a neighboring country that values it more highly. Where such thresholds exist, they may influence the boundaries of a system, even if the frequency of transactions itself is changing only very gradually. Some relations of this kind are shown in Figures 6.4, 6.5, and 6.6.

FIGURE 6.1 *Boundary Line I*

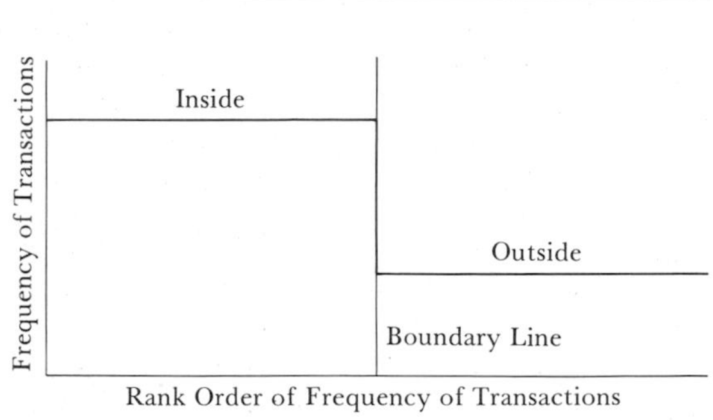

Discontinuous change in frequency.

FIGURE 6.2 *Boundary Zone I*

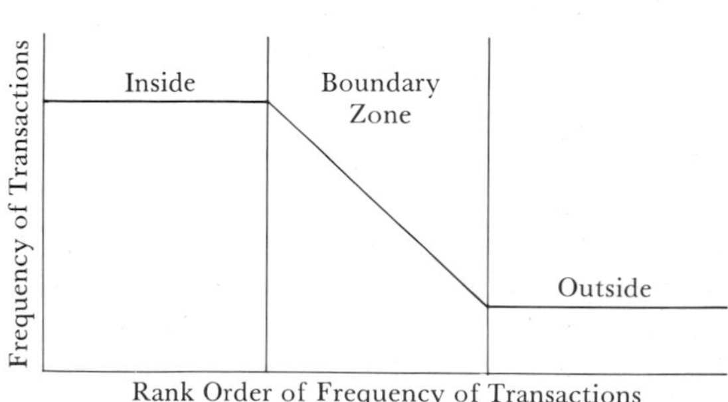

Discontinuous change in frequency at edge of zone: continuous change within zone.

THE COVARIANCE OF REWARDS

In addition to being connected by transactions, the components of systems are linked by a second

FIGURE 6.3 *Core and periphery I*

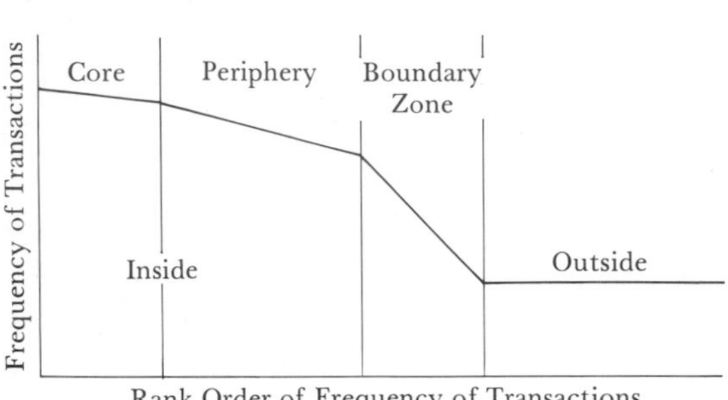

Plural zones: discontinuous change among frequency zones: continuous change within zones.

FIGURE 6.4 *Boundary Line II*

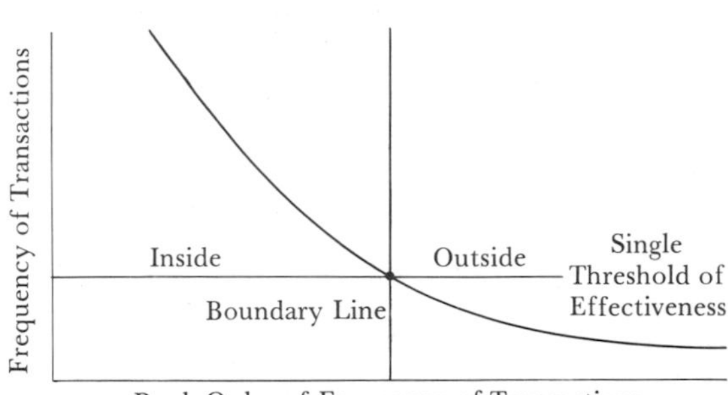

Continuous change in frequency: discontinuous change in effect.

relationship: the *covariance of rewards.* Such covariance exists if, when something rewarding to one component changes, the rewards to other components are also likely to change. This is another example of how the fate of one component is tied to the fate of other components if all belong to the same social or political system. A reward is *positive* if it increases the values enjoyed by a component or if it reduces that component's inner disequilibrium or tension. It is *negative* if it reduces the values received by a component or if it increases the component's inner disequilibrium or tension.

Positive Covariance: Solidarity Systems. Some systems are connected by a *positive covariance* of rewards. What is good for the United States is also likely to be good for General Motors. The reverse of this proposition—that "what is good for General Motors is good for the country"—does not follow with compelling necessity, though in the 1950s this statement was attributed to a former General Motors executive, Charles E. Wilson, when he was secretary of defense. Systems whose components are connected by a positive covariance of rewards may be called *solidarity systems.* The interests of wage earners are solidary if they all stand to gain from a better union contract. Conversely, if all employers in a wage negotiation join forces to gain or lose together, their interests, too, are solidary. If people act in accordance with the saying "all for one and one for all," we say that their behavior shows solidarity. In international relations, allies act in solidarity if each allied government feels that the gains of the others will bring gains to itself, that its interests are closely linked with theirs, and that it has to act accordingly. Since national states often think that they have distinct national interests, the degree of solidarity found in their alliances is often slight and relatively unsatisfactory. The Duke of Wellington is supposed to have said that Napoleon was not really a very great general because he had won only against alliances.

If several individuals or groups experience high frequencies of transactions with a positive covariance of rewards, they may wish to increase their ties to one another, at least to a moderate degree. We may speak of them as being favorable candidates for *integration* into a common system that includes them all. The states of Western Europe, for instance, are already connected in many re-

FIGURE 6.5 *Boundary Zone II*

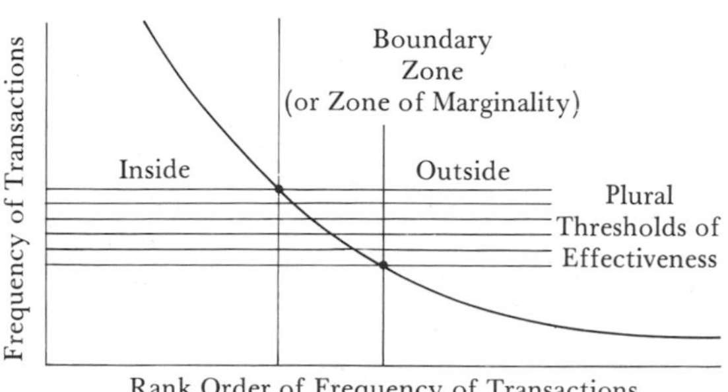

Continuous change in frequency: discontinuous change in effect at edge of zone.

FIGURE 6.6 *Core and Periphery II*

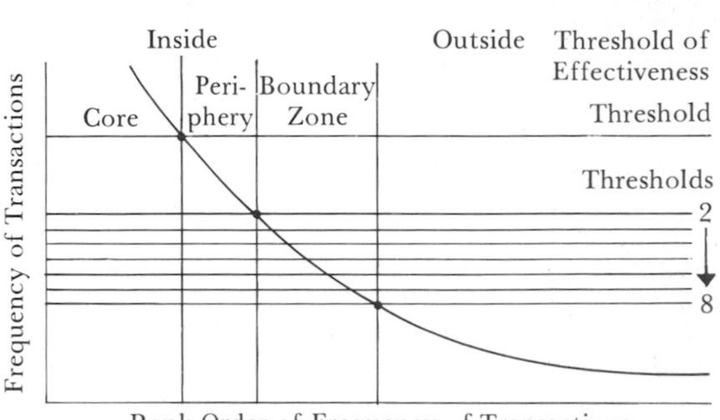

Continuous change in frequency: plural thresholds for discontinuous changes.

spects by a high number of mutual transactions and a positive covariance of rewards. To the extent that this is the case, it should be easier to promote further integration of these countries into a single political system, such as a confederation of Western Europe.

Negative Covariance: Conflict Systems. The covariance of rewards, however, may be negative. In a very frequent flow of transactions—or in a single transaction of great consequence—something may be rewarding to one partner in the system, but penalizing to others. If students are made to compete for rank in class, the ability of one student may be rewarding to that individual but may penalize those students who cannot do equally well. When several people apply for the same job, hiring of one of them will certainly be rewarding to that person, but will penalize the other applicants (unless they can get better jobs elsewhere).

When several units are closely connected by a negative covariance of rewards that suggests the relationship of a cat to a canary or a wolf to a sheep, we speak of a *conflict system.* Groups locked in conflict are part of one system. The fate of one cannot be understood or predicted without knowing something about the actions of the other.[1] They belong together, but in a rather unhappy sense. During World War I, the French war veteran Henri Barbusse wrote, "Two armies fighting each other are one great army in the act of suicide."[2]

A system is likely to be more stable and durable if the transactions that maintain it are not only high in number, but also consist of many kinds. For the system to last, these transactions must on the whole be rewarding rather than penalizing to the subsystems and individuals composing the system. Systems torn by conflict, therefore, are less

[1]A conflict system is thus a type of zero-sum game. See Chapter 2 for a discussion of zero-sum games.

[2]Henri Barbusse, *Under Fire: The Story of a Squad* (New York: Dutton, 1917). When the book was first published in French in 1916, Barbusse was a pacifist. Later he became a Communist, hoping that communism would abolish war. He did not live to see Russian and Chinese Communists fighting each other at the Ussuri River in 1969 (see Chapter 11, pp. 344–46) or the fighting between Vietnamese and Kampuchean Communists in early 1979.

likely to endure. When conflicting groups remain together in one system for a long time, they are likely to have some common interests that make them want to continue their association despite the conflict. Karl Marx and his followers have made much of the antagonism of interest between employer and employee, property owner and propertyless. However, Marx himself implied the possibility of a degree of common interest between the two. In a famous sentence in the *Communist Manifesto* he spoke of the "class struggle" as ending either in the victory of one of the two classes or in the common destruction of the contending classes. Since neither class wishes to be destroyed, both have a common interest in survival, even if it means continuing the struggle. Out of this consideration, Soviet Communists, and even Chinese ones, have found it necessary in the nuclear age to think about coexisting peacefully in a single international system with capitalist countries.

Mixed Covariance: The Dilemmas of Political Reality. Barbusse's comment about two armies illustrates the mixed nature of rewards in most situations of interdependence in the real world. Though their soldiers fight for opposed countries or causes, when victory for one implies defeat for the other, they share a common desire to stay alive. In this respect, a cease-fire without victory would reward both sides, and peace would let all soldiers return home to their families.

This example is typical of many situations of political interdependence. The rewards of both partners in an interdependent system vary together positively in some respects, but negatively in others. Some rewards for one also reward the other, but other rewards for that person may penalize his or her partner. On the other hand, if something penalized both partners, it would again join them in solidarity. In these situations of mixed covariance it would be naive for any partner to act as if the other were nothing but a friend; it would be equally naive to treat the other as nothing but an enemy or rival. Both must find patterns of *competitive cooperation* or of *cooperative competition.* Each must learn to foresee the consequences of his or her own actions for the actions of the other; and both must learn to coordinate their behavior.[3] Practical people have developed such patterns of behavior through hard-won experience. Rival department stores like Macy's and Gimbel's, major league baseball clubs, large automobile manufacturers, major radio and television networks, and major political parties in constitutional democracies have been able to work out patterns of competitive cooperation or cooperative competition. Unfortunately, we have not done very well in developing viable strategies of this type between blacks and whites in the United States; and we have done even less well in the international arena where conflicts among the great powers are most conspicuous and where the common penalties for war are most terrible.

The more we study situations of mixed covariance, the more we realize how inadequate were the old models and theories of politics, which all too often divided humankind neatly into "friends" and "enemies." But we also realize the inadequacy of the idealism that thinks that all people can become friends simply by ceasing to be enemies, as well as the inadequacy of one old rule of practical politics: "If you can't lick 'em, join 'em!" None of these strategies is realistic enough or good enough, but in politics better ones have yet to be adopted.

AN OVERVIEW OF SYSTEM LEVELS

To say that a system is linked by covariance of rewards, and that a solidarity system is linked by

[3]See Thomas C. Schelling, *The Strategy of Conflict* (Oxford: Oxford University Press, 1960); Anatol Rapoport, *Fights, Games, and Debates* (Ann Arbor: University of Michigan Press, 1960); and Anatol Rapoport and Albert Chammah, *Prisoner's Dilemma: A Study in Conflict and Cooperation* (Ann Arbor: University of Michigan Press, 1965).

positive covariance, is another way of saying that members of such a system are connected by a *community of interest.*

But the interests of a system or a subsystem are not always the same as those of the larger system of which it may be a part. Neither are they the same as the interests of the smaller subsystems that it may comprise. To weigh and, if possible, to balance the interests of large political bodies against the divergent interests of the smaller subsystems that they include—down to the individual—has always been a central problem of politics.

To analyze such problems, we speak of *system levels.* Three tests indicate what these levels are. The first test is the test of logical *inclusion.* Virginia is a part of the United States, but the United States is not a part of Virginia. Virginia is thus a lower-level system, and the United States is a higher-level one. The second test is the test of *size.* If the larger system is at least twice as large, we can clearly say that the larger one is on a higher system level. Virginia has approximately 4.5 million inhabitants; the United States, 220 million. The third test, related to the first two, is the *probable outcome of a conflict.* If the two systems should clash, the bigger system would (as sports writers say) "outclass" the smaller one. When the state of Arkansas in the 1950s tried to defy the judgment of the United States Supreme Court on school desegregation, the presence of federal troops in Little Rock ended the defiance within a short time, but the governor of Arkansas may have felt unfairly outclassed.

A TEN-STEP SCALE OF POLITICS

In analyzing politics we may think of as many as ten system levels. These levels are shown in Figure 6.7. Organizations at each of these levels may include very roughly between two and ten times as many persons as organizations at the next lower level.

Direct Relationships. The *smallest system* in politics is the individual, comprising all the different memories, drives, and complexes carried in that individual's body and personality. The physical and psychological subsystems within the individual are studied mainly by doctors, psychologists, and psychiatrists. The subsystems have much to do with why some individuals take part in politics while others do not, even though their outward circumstances are similar.

The next largest, or *second smallest,* group is the nuclear family and other so-called primary groups, most often comprising between two and fifteen members. These are often studied by group psychologists, sociologists, and some management experts. Many of the latter believe that no individual can supervise closely more than six subordinates. Significantly, too, psychologist George A. Miller has suggested that the human capacity for close attention and discrimination is ordinarily limited to "the magical number 7, ± 2." Miller's limit is thought to apply to almost anything that we can remember distinctly, from lecture outlines to team patterns to multiparty systems.

The *third system level* corresponds to the small settlement or hamlet, or the extended kin group, clan, or small tribe in developing countries, or the immediate neighborhood in cities. The membership of each such group can be counted in the hundreds. These groups are studied by cultural anthropologists, ethnologists, social psychologists, and sociologists.

At the *fourth level,* we find thousands of people, aggregated in large villages and small towns, middle-sized factories and other business enterprises with about five hundred employees (which approximates two thousand people, including dependents), small colleges, and the like. Here sociologists have a field day, and some political scientists get a piece of the action.

Where Politics Becomes Impersonal. At all larger system levels, intimate face-to-face knowledge of all participants in a system is no longer possible. Relationships now become more indirect. Psychologically, they are often more superficial, but their effects may be very powerful. Seeing a candidate on television or reading a commentator's discussion of his or her personality, is not the same as knowing that candidate well from many evenings at one's own home, the local tavern, or the neighborhood clubhouse. The *fifth level* comprises units of tens of thousands of people in towns and small cities, counties and districts, large tribes, large factories and firms, and the large universities. Here authority tends to become more formal. Rules of behavior are often written down, and many tasks of management and administration are carried out by full-time specialists working according to increasingly elaborate rules. What we call *bureaucratization* is thus in part a function of the level of political system to which an organization corresponds. This level is studied less by psychologists than by sociologists, management experts, and to some extent political scientists.

The *sixth level* deals with hundreds of thousands of people. It includes big cities, more populous districts, large counties, large tribes, and many fairly large organizations. (Nearly a dozen small states in the United States, such as Vermont or Nevada, and some small sovereign states, such as Iceland, Luxembourg, and Guyana, are on this level in terms of numbers, but their institutions correspond to those of higher system levels.) Most

FIGURE 6.7 *A Ten-Level Political System*

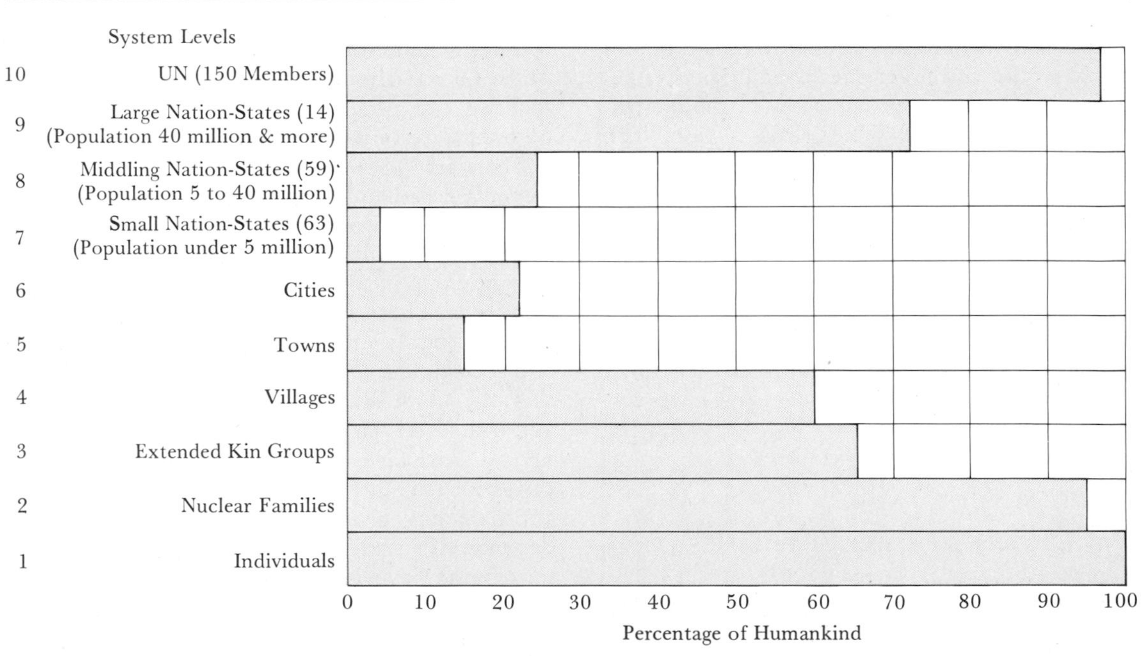

Sources: U.N. Office of Public Information: *Membership in the United Nations, 1969*; Population Reference Bureau Information Service, *World Population Data Sheets* (Washington, D.C., 1968); K. Davis, *World Urbanization, 1950-1970*, vol. 1 (Berkeley and Los Angeles: University of California Press, 1969).

of the research at this level is conducted by political scientists and to some extent by economists, though sociologists still do a good deal of work here, and a few psychologists and anthropologists are active in the field.

Units on the *seventh level* count their members in the millions, up to an upper limit of ten million. Here we encounter thirty-one of the fifty states in the American union and roughly one-half of the approximately 140 sovereign nations of the world. At this level we also find all but two of the world's fifty largest metropolitan areas.[4] Organizations at this and at all higher system levels are primarily the province of political scientists and economists, although important contributions are being made by a small number of social psychologists, sociologists, and cultural anthropologists.

A sizable minority of large sovereign nations (fifty-one in 1970), six states in the American union (California, New York, Pennsylvania, Ohio, Texas, and Illinois), and two of the largest metropolitan areas (New York and Tokyo) form the *eighth level* and count their populations in the tens of millions. Here we are clearly in the realm of politics and economics on a national and quasi-national scale.

Giant States and World Affairs. The *ninth level* brings us to the largest powers and to much of international politics. Here the numbers of people within each unit run in the hundreds of millions. Only seven giant nation-states have populations of this size, but these seven comprise nearly 60 percent of the world's population and income. In the population rank order of 1970 these are the People's Republic of China, India, the Soviet Union, the United States, Brazil, Indonesia, and Japan (see Figure 6.8). No metropolitan area and no private business organization is even remotely close to entry into this category. But a few religious organizations, notably the Roman Catholic church, have constituencies of this size. By contrast, practically all major international alliance systems, such as NATO and the Warsaw Pact, are of this order of magnitude.

The *tenth level* includes organizations that deal with more than a billion people. The principal organization at this level is the United Nations, together with the specialized organizations affiliated with the UN. These include the World Health Organization (WHO), the International Labor Organization (ILO), the Food and Agricultural Organization (FAO), and many more. Paradoxically, though world peace and world order are most important to the survival of humankind, the actual organizations, human resources, budgets, and legal powers are much weaker at this level

FIGURE 6.8 *The World's Chief Nation-States, 1975*

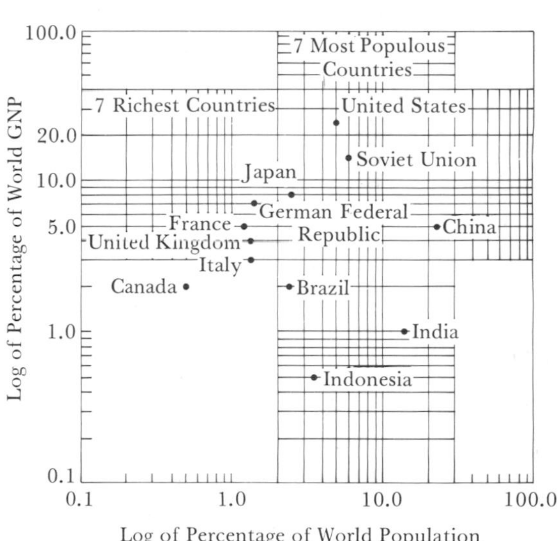

Source: Ruth Leger Sivard, *World Military and Social Expenditures, 1978* (Leesburg, Va.: WMSE Publications, 1978).

[4]*World Almanac and Book of Facts* (Garden City, N.Y.: Doubleday, 1973), p. 625. The dates for the estimates of urban areas vary between 1958 and 1971.

than the corresponding facilities at the nation-state level. While national governments allocate about 30 percent of the gross national product of humankind, world organizations control less than 1 percent.

SYSTEM LEVELS AND THE INDIVIDUAL

In politics, as in other fields, the whole may be greater than the sum of its parts. Systems may have different characteristics from the components or *subsystems* they comprise. It is certainly possible to organize sane motorists into the pattern of a crazy traffic system that has gone haywire. Likewise, it is possible to take small, petty, mean, cowardly, unimaginative bureaucrats, who are not particularly bloodthirsty—only eager to do exactly what they have been ordered to do—and organize these people into tiny links of a huge machine that will send millions of men, women, and children to their deaths. In this way a large number of petty Nazi bureaucrats were organized to send millions of Jewish men, women, and children to extermination camps. When one of the top bureaucrats of death, Adolf Eichmann, pleaded mere "obedience to orders," at his trial in Israel, philosopher Hannah Arendt was appalled by "the banality of evil" that his case epitomized.

Modern large states lend themselves to organizing people into vast bodies that can be much stronger, much more knowledgeable, much more persistent, and, as in the case of Nazi Germany, sometimes much more evil than the individuals who compose them. But the size or system level of an organization is not necessarily related to its capacity for evil. A hospital is more tireless and persistent in saving lives than even the most dedicated doctor on its staff. Perhaps humankind can yet learn to make political systems that increase its power only for good.

Moral Responsibility and System Levels. A recurrent problem in the politics of all countries is the moral responsibility of individuals for taking part in large organizations that do things that they as individuals would not do. On the level of a village, Friedrich Dürrenmatt's play *The Visit* raised the question of the responsibility of individuals for the cruelties committed by a village as an operating system. On the level of a much larger system, the state, some Russian intellectuals have raised the question of individual responsibility for the cruelties committed under the Stalin regime and for the continuing acts of Soviet repression.

Similar questions have arisen in other major countries of the Western world. "To throw a baby into the fire," said an Englishman recently, "is a crime. To throw fire on a baby is a military operation." When students demonstrated on American university campuses against recruiters for the Dow Chemical Company, spokespeople for the company replied that it bore no responsibility for the use of one of its products, napalm, in throwing fire on settlements in Vietnam and burning to death many civilians, including babies and children. It was not the company's business, Dow asserted, to question the policies of the government. Dow was merely supplying a weapon. It was the government's responsibility to determine how, when, and if that weapon should be used.

In the end, Americans may have to decide whether it is enough for citizens to carry out unquestioningly whatever orders their government may give or whether they should pursue a more active interest in what the government does—in the actual means, methods, and results of its policies. Such a decision may take years to reach. But it will have a profound effect not only on the policies but also on the very nature of the United States and on the character of the American people.

In short, individuals and small groups are often merely small cogs in the large machines of bigger interest groups or national governments. To what extent do these cogs retain the capability of understanding what the machine is actually doing?

How far does their responsibility go for the acts of the machine? The answers to these questions will decide how much governments of the future will display the blindness and moral insensitivity of still bigger and bigger machines and how much they will resemble the behavior of sentient, self-conscious communities of human beings. The thing to remember is that our biggest machines are not only made by people, they are also composed of people. Thus, there is a moral interdependence between individuals and the large organizations they compose. Our most fateful decisions, therefore, will not be technological, but political. They will deal with changes in our patterns of communication, obedience, criticism, and responsibility among people.

A Scale of Political Values. Scholars often forget that the individual is at the basis of all large systems. One reason for this oversight is the arbitrary division of organizations into small and large system levels. Students of political science will note the break in the scholarly interest in a system that comes at the seventh system level, the unit size of approximately one million people. Microeconomics deals with the decisions made by individual firms and small groups. Above the level of a million, macroeconomics replaces microeconomics and deals with problems of national economies and problems of the world economy. Similarly, *micropolitics* deals with the political behavior of individuals and small groups of voters and the affairs of small communities. Above the level of a million, *macropolitics* replaces micropolitics, dealing with the political behavior of large interest groups, cities, states, and nations and the affairs of the world. Though the systems below the seventh level are of interest to almost all social scientists, the large-scale organizations containing a million or more people are studied more by political scientists and economists—and, after the event, by historians—than by the specialists in the other behavioral sciences.

This is the prevailing situation, but it is not an ideal one. It hampers our knowledge. Scholars studying small-scale processes often take too little account of the large-scale changes that influence profoundly the background conditions for all the matters they study. And the students of large-scale processes often pay too little attention to the methods and findings of behavioral scientists concerned with the small-scale processes that can modify profoundly the outcome of large-scale events.

For centuries, political leaders have called on individuals to sacrifice themselves for the presumed good of the state, the party, or some other large-scale organization or cause. In contrast, they have rarely called on a state to sacrifice itself for its people. Yet it is a fundamental characteristic of human organizations that the smallest components—individuals—are more complex and in a certain sense more important than the large organizations that they form. The best thinkers always have recognized this and have refused to treat human beings as disposable or expendable. Theorists of democracy, from Pericles to John Stuart Mill, have seen the test of a good government in the quality of the individuals that grow up under it. This test is still relevant today.

POLITICAL STRUCTURES AND POLITICAL FUNCTIONS

Up to this point we have been talking about systems as structures. The *structure* of any situation or organization consists of those of its aspects that change relatively slowly and whose change can be modified or accelerated only at considerable cost. The rocks and mountains in a landscape and the skeleton of a human body are structures. Likewise, the size and level of a political system are structures, for ordinarily there is no quick or easy way to change them. (Our definition of structure is worth remembering when people speak of "structural" changes in colleges, cities, or nations. Regardless of their merits, such changes require much time, or great efforts and costs, or possibly all of these.)

In contrast to slow-changing structures, those aspects of a situation or organization that change relatively quickly and easily are called *processes* or functions. The movement of winds and water in the mountains are processes, and so is breathing in the human body. When we wish to stress the effects of one process on other processes or on structures we speak of its *function.* Wind and water may have the function of leveling mountains by erosion. Breathing has the function of maintaining life in the human body.

We are now ready to understand why structures change with such relative slowness and at such high cost. Structures, no matter how motionless they look, are formed by interlocking processes. Within each structure we can find a large number of processes interlocked in such a way that they are not only mutually reinforcing, but also mutually self-preserving and often also self-repairing and self-reproducing. Any attempt at changing any one or several of these processes would have to overcome the interlocking effects of all of them. What we call the function of a process, then, is just this contribution it makes to the relatively self-sustaining, interlocking pattern of processes that we call a structure.

Thus a structure of social and political inequality is often reinforced, maintained, and reproduced in each generation by the interlocking processes of unequal property acquisition and inheritance; unequal access to education and educational success; home backgrounds producing unequal attitudes, skills, and motivations for learning; ethnic, racial, and class discrimination; the preferences of potential employers and business partners for particular patterns of speech, dress, subculture, and lifestyle; and differential probabilities of intermarriage and acceptance into social clubs, informal friendship circles, and that borderland where social contacts and professional and business contacts overlap. One function of property and a high income may then be to enable an individual or family to keep up an elite lifestyle and the educational opportunities and social contacts that go with it; and these, in turn, may also make it easier for this person or for members of this family to earn a high income.

Changing any one or two of these interlocking processes or functions may produce very little change in the overall outcome of social, economic, or political stratification. After some temporary disturbances, the structure of inequality may appear much as it was before. Only a more comprehensive change of many of these interlocking processes would be likely to change such a structure, and usually this would require a longer time and higher costs.

A single structure may support many different processes or functions. The human skeleton and the general structure of the human body sustain the play of muscles, the circulation of blood, and the movement of impulses through the nervous system. The government of a city sustains the regulation of traffic, the operation of public schools, the administration of welfare, and a host of other tasks. The multiplicity of functions of the modern nation-state is still larger. Most structures are thus *multifunctional.*

The same function, however, may be fulfilled by more than one type of structure. Railroad service may be provided by private companies, as in the United States, or by the nation-state, as in Switzerland or Britain. Elementary public schools can be run by the national government, as in France; by the state governments, as in the German Federal Republic; or by cities, municipalities, or local school districts, as in the United States. To the extent that different structures can fulfill the same function, and can thus be substituted for each other, we say that they are *functionally equivalent.*

Political structures are first of all governments, from the local level all the way up through the international level. Political structures also include those organizations specifically designed to influence governments in regard to many matters, such as political parties. In the United States political parties range over many system levels, from the local political club to the municipal, state, and national party organizations. Similar but more tightly knit hierarchies are found in the major parties of Britain, the German Federal Republic, and Italy and, with a much lesser degree of party regularity and discipline, in France. Other organizations, though not primarily political, may have large political interests, as do labor unions, employer organizations, and other interest groups (as noted in Chapter 3). For organizations of this latter kind, political activity is obviously only one among the many tasks they perform; it is one among their several functions.

The same is true, however, of all the major systems discussed in our ten-step model. The most important organizations at each level are multipurpose systems: the individual, the family, the small community, the city, the state, the nation, and humankind. All these are social systems. (Even the individual may be thought of as a society of the components of his or her personality.) Politics is only one function of each of the systems. If political activity fits well into the context of the other functions; it will derive strength from them, both for itself and for the social system as a whole. If politics fits badly, it may become *dysfunctional.* It will then tend to weaken the system and ultimately to weaken and destroy itself.

THE POLITICAL SYSTEM AS A COMPONENT OF THE SOCIAL SYSTEM

Functions of a Social System. So far we have been dealing mainly with systems as *political* systems at various levels of organization. We now turn to the larger *social system,* which we shall examine in terms derived from the sociologist Talcott Parsons. According to Parsons, there are four basic functions of every social system. First, it must *maintain* its own basic patterns, particularly those of its own governing and control, so that the next day or the next year finds the social system still recognizable and responsible for its own actions. Second, it must *adapt* itself to changing conditions in both its physical environment in nature and its human environment in terms of other systems. Third, it must *integrate* its different tasks and functions. Fourth, if it has specific goals beyond mere adaptation, integration, and the maintenance of its patterns, it must move to *attain* its goals. Accordingly, pattern maintenance, adaptation, integration, and goal attainment are its basic tasks. From Parsons' approach we can derive a way of looking at politics and the subsystems of society in the context of these basic functions.[5]

Pattern Maintenance. *Pattern maintenance* is a task that can be carried on by many actors, but some structural (or multipurpose) subsystems spend much more of their time and resources on this task than on any other. The main subsystems devoted to pattern maintenance in Western society are *families* and *households.* They maintain the bodies of their members by cooking their meals and giving them a place to sleep. More subtly, they maintain the motivation of their members by a process of mutual support and encouragement. Finally, these subsystems maintain the culture of the society by transmitting it to children, sometimes with interesting variations and with unexpected results.

Adaptation. The main *adaptive* subsystem of the society is the *economy.* Economic activities enable us to transform our somewhat inhospitable natural environment into one in which people can survive and from which they can draw sustenance and resources. The economy is reinforced in this function by the technological and scientific subsystem. At more primitive levels, science and technology are not separate from the efforts of farmers and artisans. As societies become more complex, science and technology become full-time occupations carried on by specialized institutions. Even

[5]See Talcott Parsons, *The Social System* (Glencoe, Ill.: Free Press, 1951). The responsibility for the application of this general approach in this book is, of course, my own.

here, however, they are effective only if their findings are eventually applied in economic life. The basic adaptive function of the economy holds true equally for societies characterized by a large element of private enterprise and for societies characterized by the predominance of central planning.

Integration. The *integrative* subsystem of every society consists mainly in its *culture,* or cultural sector, including education, religion, philosophy, and art. Education not only has the task of reproducing yesterday's culture in the young people of today and the older people of tomorrow; it also has the task of making the different elements of society somewhat more compatible with each other. Religion and philosophy have the same task to an even greater degree. All the world's great religions ask people whether their pursuit of short-run values or goals is compatible with their long-run interests. Religion and philosophy teach the long-run nature of the universe, the long-run values of humankind, and, perhaps, the long-run purpose for which humankind itself exists. And in their own way, artists either integrate different elements or aspects of the world or, in the case of the artists of despair or protest, tell us in some powerful way about some lack of integration that may need our attention.

Goal Attainment. Finally, the typical *goal-attaining* subsystem of society is the government or, more generally, the *political sector.* It is the government that organizes the society for the pursuit of whatever goals the society has chosen. Pursuing a goal involves forming an image of it, which we may call an *intention,* and then finding the means to implement the intention or a course toward the goal. The Spanish government in the fifteenth century organized Spain first for the reconquest of the peninsula, then for the expulsion of the Moors from Granada, and still later for the conquest of the New World. In our own time the governmental sector has organized Americans for a variety of purposes, including resolving the race problem, maintaining full employment, making higher education available to an ever larger number of young people, and putting an American on the moon.

Interchanges among Subsystems. In the context of Parson's four basic functions of a social system, then, four classic subsystems can be identified: the family and household sector, the economic sector, the cultural sector, and the political sector. Each of these classic subsystems of society has interchanges with all of the others and depends on all of them. Members of households, for example, perform labor in the economy and eventually receive consumer goods from that subsystem. In most advanced societies this is done not directly by barter, but by a generalized medium of exchange. Individuals working in the economy get paid in money, then spend their wages in the supermarket to get goods and services for the household. And this exchange between work inputs, on the one hand, and goods and services, on the other hand, is mediated by money, a generalized and abstract medium that is accepted as a currency by both sides.

Something similar goes on between the household sector and the government. The population usually makes specific demands on the government. The government, in turn, reaches decisions that serve to coordinate people's expectations and are often backed with the promise of enforcement. In the early stages of a political relationship, specific demands are exchanged for specific decisions. This is political logrolling; but as time goes on, the government may take on a generalized role of responsibility. The government says to the population: "We are in charge. If you need something done that you cannot do yourselves, the government is here to do it." If individuals find that governmental decisions are acceptable to them and that living under the government is rewarding, they are likely to develop a generalized loyalty. They no longer give their support to specific decisions. Instead, they give to the government a general loyalty in exchange for the government's general assumption of responsibility.

Just as money is the generalized medium of economic interchanges, so *power* serves as the generalized medium of interchange between a government and its people.[6] Power functions as the currency of politics. Just as money is worth no more than the things it can buy, so power is worth no more than the teamwork it can procure. Economics is really not about money, but about wealth; and politics is really not about power, but about the changing ways people find to work and live together. A government uses its power to enforce some of the decisions the people want enforced, but in reality the power of the government comes from the support of the population. A government that is not supported by its people is in a precarious position. The less popular a government is, the less likely it is to endure. If a government is popular at home, but seems alien to the people of a distant country, its power to control the latter will be precarious as well.

Of course, where populations are apathetic, ignorant, unarmed, or powerless, minority governments based on small bodies of armed soldiers have long maintained themselves in power. Thus colonial rule has endured longest in the world's most backward colonies, such as Portuguese Angola and Mozambique in Africa. However, the more educated, active, and capable a population becomes, the harder it is to neglect it in politics and the harder it becomes to rule it against its will. Everywhere in the world, industrialization and modernization have increased the interests, communication levels, needs, knowledge, demands, and capabilities of populations. These changes may well be irreversible. Since they have made all countries in the world harder to govern against the will of their populations, a politician's lot is now a less happy one than it may have been fifty or a hundred years ago. And since all countries are now even harder to govern from a distance, the job of a would-be world ruler is hopeless.

[6]Other aspects of power are discussed in Chapters 2 and 7.

HOW SOCIAL SYSTEMS CHANGE

The four classic subsystems are found in all social systems of which we have knowledge, according to Parsons. But the four functions that these subsystems perform deal mainly with keeping societies as they are and do not tell us enough about the way societies change. So Parsons seems to suggest that all social systems have an inclination to behave in accordance with the way they are set up. We know, however, that many social systems in the world have changed, some of them very thoroughly indeed.

It is important, therefore, to ask what are the basic functions in systems in which change is a major part of their behavior. There are two such functions (see Table 6.1). The first is *change of goals,* and the second is *self-transformation.*

Goal Change. Systems not only pursue old goals, but they may also from time to time abandon old goals and replace them by new ones. Societies that cannot change goals either fossilize or perish. Sparta and ancient Rome largely refused to change their goals and thus became extinct. Modern societies, on the other hand, have changed their goals again and again.

All major powers in the world have gone through periods of major goal change. England in the Middle Ages had as a major policy goal the maintenance of power on the European continent. Its rulers kept garrisons at Bordeaux, Calais, and other strategic places. In the sixteenth century, England give up all military footholds on the Continent and turned its attention to sea power and to colonial empire. Four centuries later, Britain's goals changed again. In 1947, England conceded independence to India and dropped the pursuit of empire to concentrate on the modernization of technology and the improvement of the human condition within the British Isles.

Similar examples of goal changes can be found in the histories of other nations. Switzerland and Sweden at certain times in their history were great

TABLE 6.1 *Ways to Basic Change in Social Systems*

SUBSTANTIVE CHANGE	POLITICAL METHOD	
	Reform	Revolutionary
Goal change	Britain gives up Empire Britain shifts to welfare state, 1945–	France quits Algeria, but Fifth Republic preserves partial continuity at home 1958–62
Self-tranformation	Britain's Reform Bills, 1832–67 Japan, 1868 Turkey, 1920– US, 1933–	US, 1776–1830 France, 1789–1830 Russia, 1917– China, 1911– Mexico, 1912–40 Algeria, 1954–62 Cuba, 1959– Iran, 1979–

military powers with major foreign policy ambitions. At later stages they substituted for these schemes the goals of internal progress and peace. The United States pursued as a major goal for many decades isolation from the politics of Europe. During World War I and after the late 1930s American goals changed to worldwide intervention and involvement. The 1980s find the United States once again engaged in redefining its goals, this time perhaps with greater emphasis on domestic affairs, energy policy, and the control of unemployment and inflation. It is not enough, therefore, to consider only a country's current goals or interests; one must also ask these questions: How long will they last? When, how, and under what conditions will they change?

Self-transformation. The other basic change function of a social system is *self-transformation.* A system may transform a good part of its own structure that ordinarily is slow to change. Every one of us has gone through at least some self-transformation as we moved from infancy to childhood and again from childhood through the storms of adolescence to adulthood. Countries also transform themselves, sometimes violently, sometimes gradually. In either case, they end up not only with different goals, but also with different basic structures and patterns of behavior. Even so, important elements of their identity may remain unchanged.

In political systems, violent self-transformation involving a large part of society is called *revolution,* as distinct from coups d'état or palace revolutions, which merely change the people in power or a few laws, without changing the fundamentals of social living. Daniel Boorstin's brilliant book entitled *The Genius of American Politics* emphasizes the ways in which colonial America and present-day America are alike. But no less important, as Charles Beard and other historians point out, are the many ways in which America after the Revolution was radically different from America before the Revolution. A period of revolution occurred in Britain during the forty-year interval between Oliver Cromwell in the 1650s and the Act of Toleration in 1690. A similar period occurred in France in the forty years between the storming of the Bastille in 1789 and the acceptance of the formerly subversive red, white, and blue as the national colors of France in 1830. Revolutions in Mexico, in China, and in Russia are other examples. Each of these has usually involved its society in roughly a half-century of self-transformation.

In nonviolent cases we may speak of *reform.* In many of these respects England transformed itself during the period of the great Reform Bills between 1832 and 1884 and again during the time of the new wave of social reforms between 1945 and the 1960s. In the United States, the year 1933 may well have ushered in a period of reform legislation that, with some interruptions, has been going on until the present and may not yet have ended.

Change and Integration. A modern adaptation of Parsons's system would probably include these basic functions of political and social change. Goal change and self-transformation are always closely related to the problem of the *integration* of society. A social system changes its goals or its inner structure because some elements or functions within it are no longer compatible with other elements or functions. That is, every problem of goal change and self-transformation begins with a severe strain on the integrative system. Because a system can no longer live with itself or with its environment, it then begins to change its goals or transform its structure. Goal change and self-transformation are, therefore, more complex and more elaborate aspects of the basic function of integration. If we include them in the integrative subsystem in more highly developed societies, the remarkable economy and simplicity of the Parsonian scheme become still more useful for analyzing the basic problems of political systems.

A SECOND LOOK AT THE POLITICAL SYSTEM

Thus far we have looked at politics in the context of multipurpose systems. We saw that families, villages, cities, nations, and the world all have their political aspects, but they deal with more than merely politics. It is time now to look at specifically political systems at various system levels and to examine the concept of the political system somewhat more thoroughly.

A *political system* is a particular kind of system. It maintains coordinated expectations among the people who live under it and coordinates a good deal of their actual behavior by means of their cooperation and compliance habits, which are reinforced by rewards and penalties.

Since human beings tend to learn more from rewards than penalties, this implies that most political systems must contain at least a significant probability of some rewards for those who accept their rules and regulations. The less rewarding a political community or a government is to those living under it, the less likely it is to endure. Habits of cooperation are reinforced not only by the specific rewards or penalties offered by the government, but also by the general rewards implied in living within the political community. American governments have not often given specific rewards to their citizens beyond such items as congressional medals, presidential citations and occasional veterans' bonuses. But the American economy has produced a living standard so markedly higher than many other countries and American life has been so much freer and more permissive that immigrants from dozens of places and many different backgrounds have found themselves closely tied to and eventually integrated into the multifarious American political community.

Political systems are based on other social systems. From four conceptual bases we can identify four types of political systems. First, a political system usually is based on a territorial community. Thus, a nation-state is often based on a *country.* Second, a country may contain one or more peoples. So a political system usually has an ethnic as well as a territorial base, and we have the concept of a political system as a *people.*

A third concept often associated with political systems is that of a *citizenry* or *body politic* or *polity.* Here we speak of persons who have acquired a common set of political behaviors and civic loyalties. A person we call a *fellow citizen,* in the true sense of the term, is one whom we trust and by whom we are willing to let ourselves be outvoted. Those whom we do not trust and by whom it would be intolerable to be outvoted we consider as *aliens,* in effect, even though they may have a legal right to vote.

Finally, we may speak of a *state* as an organized body of citizens, some of them armed and some of them wielding other instruments of administration, all engaged in the business of government. The classic definition of a state used to emphasize its responsibilities for deterring enemies from without and repressing disorders from within. Liberal followers of Adam Smith and radical followers of Karl Marx agreed: the main task of the state was the exercise of force. Adherents of laissez-faire liberalism pictured the state as a night watchman who stood by while the "invisible hand" of the market ran the economy. Marxists viewed it as a committee to look after the interests of the bourgeoisie as a whole. Engels and Lenin considered the state primarily a body of armed men, weapons, and prisons.

The actual development of the modern state has taken a somewhat different direction. Today, in every modern industrial country, more than half of the resources and activities of the government tend to be devoted to civilian services and facilities that involve functions other than the exercise of force. In the United States, government at all levels—municipal, state, and national—spends about 35 percent of the gross national product and at least 20 percent or more of that gross national product for activities not related to force, such as public education, public health, traffic and transport, science and research, and a host of other services.

It is the coincidence of these four types of systems—the country, the people, the body politic, and the state—that make the modern nation-state such a powerful instrument for so many different kinds of action. In districts and countries where this coincidence is weak, the nation-state is likely to be weak. Where the coincidence is strong, the nation-state is likely to be strong.

One characteristic of political systems, perhaps the most remarkable of all, has yet to be mentioned: their ability to steer themselves. The capacity for self-steering, for autonomy, makes governments and political communities vital and effective, and it is this capacity that we shall discuss in the next chapter.

KEY TERMS AND CONCEPTS

political system
cohesion
covariance
interdependent
components
collection
transaction
relative frequency of transactions
boundaries
boundary line
boundary zone
political boundaries
side effects
threshold
covariance of rewards
positive reward
negative reward
positive covariance
solidarity system
integration
negative covariance
conflict system
mixed covariance
competitive cooperation
community of interest
system levels
ten-step scale of politics
bureaucratization
subsystem
micropolitics
macropolitics
structure
processes
function
multifunctional
functionally equivalent
political structure

dysfunctional
pattern maintenance
adaptation
integration
goal attainment
intention
change of goals
self-transformation
revolution
coup d'état
reform
body politic
fellow citizen
alien
state

ADDITIONAL READINGS

Almond, G. A., and G. B. Powell. *Comparative Politics: System, Process, and Policy.* 2nd ed. Boston: Little, Brown, 1978. PB

Bertalanffy, L. "General System Theory." In J. D. Singer, ed., *Human Behavior and International Politics.* Chicago: Rand McNally, 1965.

Deutsch, K. W. *The Nerves of Government.* 2nd ed. New York: Free Press, 1966. PB

———, ed. *Ecosocial Systems and Ecopolitics.* Paris: UNESCO, 1977.

Easton, D. *Framework for Political Analysis.* Englewood Cliffs, N.J.: Prentice-Hall, 1965.

———. *The Political System.* New York: Knopf, 1953. PB

———. *Systems Analysis of Political Life.* New York: Wiley, 1965.

Parsons, T. *The Social System.* Glencoe, Ill.: Free Press, 1951. PB

———. *Societies: Evolutionary and Comparative Perspectives.* Englewood Cliffs, N.J.: Prentice-Hall, 1966.

Young, O. *Systems of Political Science.* Englewood Cliffs, N.J.: Prentice-Hall, 1968. PB

PB = *available in paperback*

VII

Self-Government: How a Political System Steers Itself

In general usage, the word *self-government* has two meanings. Sometimes it refers to a political unit that governs itself in all respects, including its relations with the outside world. But sometimes it may refer to any unit that decides about its internal affairs by its own processes, even though its external affairs are managed by some larger political system. In this latter sense, New York City is self-governing in many of its local affairs, even though it is certainly not wholly independent. And sometimes the word self-government is used ambiguously, straddling the two meanings; or it is used to indicate a matter of degree, of more or less self-government, rather than an all-or-nothing quality. Politicians have found these ambiguities of usage convenient, permitting them to use the same word to build support by promising different things to different people.

THE BEHAVIOR OF SELF-GOVERNING BODIES

The difference between self-government and political dependence resembles the difference between driving an automobile and being towed. A car with its own steering wheel and driver can go in many directions; a towed car goes where the towing truck takes it. Similarly, a piece of driftwood must float with the current; a motorboat can move across it or against it. Together with their human operators or their automatic piloting devices, automobiles, motorboats, airplanes, and some types of guided missiles and space vehicles, are all examples of *self-steering systems.* Ordinarily their course cannot be predicted from knowing only their environment. To know where they will go, we must also know something about what is going on inside them.

Self-Rule and the Environment. Much the same is true of political systems, large or small. For if we can predict completely what a group, a party, a city, or a nation will do, without knowing anything about its inner processes—if we can predict its behavior completely from knowing its environment—then this system is entirely dependent on something outside itself and is therefore not self-governing. In contrast, to the extent that a political system's behavior is determined by structures and processes inside itself—whatever these may be—we call such a system *independent.*

Self-government can exist at different system levels, as shown in Table 7.1. In the case of a self-governing country or nation, we say it is *sovereign;* that is, it obeys no outside command and it recognizes no law higher than its own. When such a country obeys international law or an international treaty, it does so voluntarily for reasons of prudence or morality. But it is possible for a country to be dependent in international affairs and still have effective autonomy in domestic matters. (*Autonomy,* as defined by Rousseau, is "obedience to the law which we prescribe for ourselves.") Thus the island of Antigua in the Caribbean is wholly dependent on Britain in its foreign policy, but politics within the island is largely in the hands of its 73,000 people. Real political arrangements can be much more complex than the simple distinctions shown in Table 7.1. Near Antigua, the much larger Commonwealth of Puerto Rico is associated with the United States by a special arrangement that gives the islanders no vote in American policy, but gives them a special tax status, permits unlimited migration to the United States, and leaves the internal affairs of the island to Puerto Rico's own political processes.

Subsystems within a self-governing system may not necessarily be self-governing or autonomous. A nation-state could be sovereign in international affairs and yet dominate most groups and individuals within it. It could deny any significant autonomy to its subsystems, such as its regions, provinces, or cities, or to political parties, labor unions, and other interest groups. At the end of the 1970s this was the case in many dictatorships, such as in Saudi Arabia, Pakistan, South Korea, many Latin American regimes, and the Communist countries, to varying degrees, from Yugoslavia to China.

TABLE 7.1 *Self-Government at Different System Levels*

SYSTEM LEVEL	EFFECTIVE SELF-GOVERNMENT* Yes	No
Nation in foreign affairs	US USSR People's Republic of China France German Federal Republic	Czechoslovakia German Democratic Republic Dominican Republic
Nation in domestic affairs	Canada, 1867–98 Commonwealth of Puerto Rico	India, 1857–1947
State or province	Any of the 50 states in the US	Any French department Any state in Brazil, 1964–
City	Hamburg in German Federal Republic	Washington, D.C., until 1968
Interest group	Any labor union, or business organization, or student organization in the US	Any labor, industrial, or student organization in the USSR

* Test: Not subject to superiors, or free to oppose them.

Self-Rule and the Past. There is more to self-government, however, than mere independence from outside domination. The course of a high-velocity rifle bullet over short distances is practically independent of much of its environment; no wind is likely to deflect it. But once it has been fired, its course is almost completely dependent on the bullet's momentum and, therefore, on its past. It has no freedom. It is enslaved to its own weight, speed, and direction and hence to what happened to it earlier, when the gun was pointed and the trigger pulled.

Larger systems, too, can be imprisoned by their past. A car going at sixty miles per hour cannot stop in less than two hundred feet, no matter how hard the driver may step on the brakes. A large ocean liner takes about one and one-half miles to come to a stop from full speed ahead, after its engines have been reversed.

Human organizations may have a kind of momentum of their own. How long does it take to stop a traditional political or social practice in a local community, after it has become clearly outdated? How long does it take to change a major national policy? How long does it take to stop a war? Political systems evidently also can be prisoners of their past, as well as of their environment.

Real self-steering differs both from the past-determined path of a bullet and from the environment-determined path of driftwood. The behavior of a self-steering system cannot be predicted wholly from its environment or from its past. Self-steering consists in combining the effects of the past of a system with those of its present and the effects of its environment with those of its own inner structure and processes. But just how is this done?

THE FEEDBACK CYCLE, STEERING, AND GOAL-SEEKING

The Processing of Information and the Feedback Cycle. Self-steering in any system requires, first, an intake of information from the outside world. In the simplest case the information comes in directly; more often there are special subsystems called *receptors*. In the human body these are eyes, ears, and other sense organs. In an airplane or ship they may include radio receivers and radar sets. In a government the receptors may be foreign service officers sending in reports from abroad, or they may be organizations, polling groups, the press, or public hearings that tell the government what the voters think. Regardless of its original source, information comes in through receptors.

Eventually information results in an output of action or behavior by the system that receives it. Usually, this behavior is accomplished by specialized *effectors*. In the human organism these are arms, legs, muscles, teeth, the tongue, and vocal cords. In an airplane they are engines, the rudder, and control surfaces; and in a warplane, rockets, guns, and bomb release mechanisms. In a government the effectors are officials, bureaucrats, the army, the navy, social security administrators, tax collectors, or whoever else performs services for the government.

The important thing about any self-steering system is this: its effectors send back new information about the results of their actions. This new information is added to the information already in the system, and it is used to correct the output in the next cycle. Results from this corrected output are again fed back, cycle after cycle. Each such cycle of output, feedback, and corrected output is called a *feedback cycle.* All goal seeking, all steered or controlled behavior, depends on feedback cycles.

Feedback is a process that requires a structure to carry it. It is based on a return flow of information, but every flow of information needs a *channel* by which it is transmitted. In every feedback process, information flows in a loop; and the channels carrying it must form a *circuit.* In electronic devices these circuits may consist of wires or invisible beams. In politics they may consist of standardized procedures or informal habits of reporting and listening. Thus in dealing with a bureaucracy, we usually are told to "go through channels." A more informal feedback circuit consists in the habit of members of Congress of sending news of their speeches and votes to the residents of their districts or states, by whom they want to be re-elected, and of listening to their responses as a guide for future actions.

Amplifying Feedback Processes. Feedback, however, can be of two kinds—amplifying or negative—with important differences in their operation and results. *Amplifying feedback* adds a signal to preceding behavior that says, "Do more of it; increase the behavior." If the amplifying feedback signals add about the same proportion to the output in every cycle, the effect is comparable to compound interest or to the explosion of a stick of dynamite. Both are described by the same type of exponential curve. The graph of amplifying feedback seems to grow slowly and then takes off and seems to go through the roof (see Figure 7.1).

For instance, let us assume that countries A and B each have 100 missiles and that they are engaged in an arms race with each other. A government official or a political candidate in country A says, "We must have clear-cut superiority over country B." The government of A then agrees, "Yes, we do need clear-cut superiority"; to its joint chiefs of staff this may mean 10 percent more, or a total of 110 missiles. But the joint chiefs of country B are just as patriotic. They must now have clear-cut superiority for their country, and 10 percent more than 110 is 121. Country A rejoins by seeking 133, and B responds with 146. Unless this attempted outdoing of each other ends, the graph will soar. If we fit the differential equations that describe this process to the arms budgets of the major powers up to and during World War I, we get a remarkably good match. From 1914 to 1918, however, the process described by these equations put a considerable number of people into cemeteries.

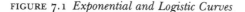

FIGURE 7.1 *Exponential and Logistic Curves*

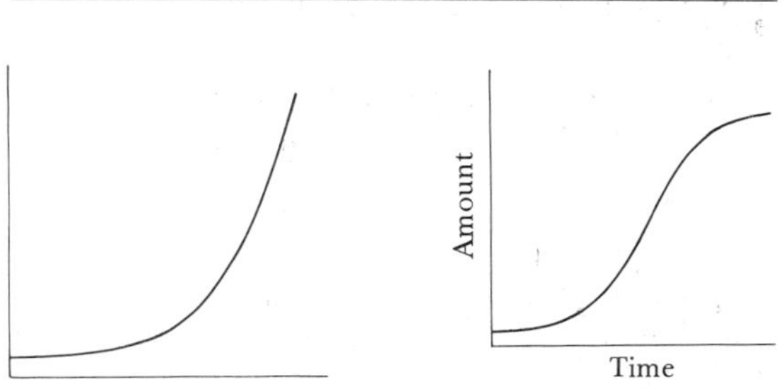

An amplifying feedback process, if continued with a constant rate of increments, is likely to run out of control. If the increments decline, however—if, for instance, fuel, personnel, or resources dwindle—the process becomes exhausted after a while. Instead of an exponential curve, a *logistic curve,* which is S-shaped, is formed, and the output flattens out (see Figure 7.1).

The amplifying feedback principle is worth knowing because it is the basic pattern of *escalation.* It occurs not only in international politics, but also in domestic politics. Suppose that scandalous neglect of the poor and of racial minorities in a city eventually causes a riot. The national guard is called up, it shoots into the crowd, and there are thirty-four dead, as in the 1965 Watts riot in Los Angeles. As a result of amplifying feedback, great resentment spreads among the ghetto dwellers, which, in turn, results in clandestine attacks, more arson and rioting, more violence against the police, more armed soldiers, more armored trucks patrolling the streets, more outbreaks of violence, more heavy-handed repression, and therefore, a spiral of bloodshed on both sides. Ultimately, it is recognized that this has to be stopped. Efforts are then made to improve the situation and end the bloodshed and the misery on both sides. Unfortunately, we know very little about how to prevent the escalation of violence or hatred, even of the verbal kind. But perhaps by spotting amplifying feedback processes early, we may someday be able to stop the growth of hostility or at least to bring it under control before it gets out of hand.

Negative Feedback Processes. In *negative feedback* the signal reporting the results of a previous action says, "Oppose this action; change it or modify it."

Negative feedback is in essence critical. It says no to those in charge of the preceding operation. A negative feedback system is at the heart of all controlled situations. A thermostat is a negative feedback system. The thermometer reports the temperature of the room; the setting of the control determines the desired level. If it is set at 65 degrees, for example, and the temperature falls to 62, the furnace will turn on, the registers will open, and hot air will come into the room. When the temperature reaches 65 or 66, the furnace will shut off. In effect, the 65-degree temperature had been made a *goal state* for the system. The goal state of any system is that relation of the system to its environment in which its inner imbalance or *disequilibrium* is at a minimum. In negative feedback, whenever the system departs from its goal state, the preceding operation is opposed or reversed.

A control system of this sort maintains a constant steady state. Processes that tend to maintain some particular state of affairs are called *homeostatic*. In the human body, for instance, a homeostatic or negative feedback system makes sure we do not have too much carbon dioxide in our blood. Every time the CO_2 concentration in our blood gets too high, the system turns on the breathing mechanism and we breathe. A similar, slower-working system makes us hungry when we have too little blood sugar and makes us feel sated when we have enough. In the body politic a similar conservative or homeostatic feedback system exists to induce the Council of Economic Advisers in the American government to recommend the manipulating of credit rates in such a way that unemployment is not less than 2 and not more than 6 percent of the work force. However, the idea of using one overall feedback circuit on the whole employment level of the economy may turn out to be an oversimplification, for it may ignore the significance of pockets of unemployment in ghettos and depressed areas. Nevertheless, the basic principle of maintaining a certain state of affairs by reversing any behavior leading away from it has been tested in many different cases. It is as applicable to a government or to politics as to the nerves in an organism.

Critical Aspects of Steering: Load, Lag, Gain, and Lead. Negative feedback systems can, of course, also be used to make an object home toward a moving target. A greyhound racing after a rabbit is homing toward a moving target. The rabbit may rapidly change its course, whereas the greyhound, which runs faster but is heavier, has more difficulty in controlling its own momentum. Thus, although the greyhound is faster, many rabbits survive by imposing a greater load on the steering system of the greyhound than that system can handle. This leads to a concept of power that is fundamentally different from the traditional one. The greyhound surpasses the rabbit in sharpness of teeth, strength of body, weight, and speed, but cannot match it in cybernetic capacity—the capacity for self-steering.

So the rabbit frequently changes course, imposing a load on the steering system of the greyhound. Generally, the *load* on a steering system is the amount of behavior change per unit of time that is demanded by the changes in the system's course of target. The interval between the moment the rabbit turns and the moment the greyhound notices the turn and slows down its own body in order to turn is the *lag* in its response. The extent to which the greyhound corrects its action is the *gain,* that is, the change that is accomplished by the response to a new input signal. But if the gain is too large, the greyhound will overcorrect and overshoot the target. Unlike a duck hunter, the greyhound ordinarily does not lead the target. Duck hunters and antiaircraft artillery, on the contrary, both lead their targets, by aiming at the target's probable future position, instead of at its present one. Thus, the amount of *lead* is the amount of advance time by which a steering system can predict and respond to the future state of a target, within an acceptably small margin of error.

These four measures of performance—load, lag, gain, and lead—are relevant to politics as well. They apply to all negative feedback processes and hence to all self-steering systems. They can be used, with appropriate qualifications, to study and evaluate the performance of electronic control devices, business organizations, and governments. To return to the example of the developing riot situation in a slum, we know that sensitive observers often can see that life is becoming intolerable for certain people under certain conditions. In the past they have sent out warnings of trouble; but sometimes, as in Chicago, it has taken bloody riots in the streets for a city government to authorize turning on the fire hydrants during a heat wave so that slum children could enjoy a shower. A little more intelligence would have cut down this *lag.* Indeed, it should be possible for governments to *lead,* to know when it will get hot and, thus, to know when the hydrants should be turned on.

But governments tend to *lag;* and the greater the lag, the greater is the temptation to use heavy-handed overreaction—and repression, in particular—as a way of *gain.* Unfortunately, overreaction may merely result in replacing one error with an equal or bigger error in the opposite direction. When a dictatorship first purges left deviationists and then, with the same elephantine thoroughness, purges right deviationists, only to reverse itself to purge leftists once again, it is behaving much like a novice driver who notices too late that the auto is heading for a ditch and overcorrects the steering wheel in the opposite direction. Governments are perfectly capable of oversteering, and frequently they are deficient in the ability to lead events, to foresee the action that will be needed.

The Nature of Goals and Goal-Seeking. Negative feedback systems are usually goal-seeking systems. A goal-seeking system that is in internal disequilibrium is likely to change; when it is in equilibrium, it is likely to be at rest. So long as it is in disequilibrium, and therefore is changing, it is also likely to change in its relation to the outside world. If its new relationships to the environment preserve the system's inner disequilibrium, changes will continue; in effect, the system will act as though it were searching for still other relationships. If, however, the system's internal disequilibrium is reduced in some new relationship, its drive to change will be reduced. If the system's inner disequilibrium is brought to a minimum in some particular relationship to the environment, then the system will tend to remain in this relation; it will have reached a goal. Systems that behave in this manner—as negative feedback systems ordinarily do—are called *goal-seeking systems.* If negative feedback signals tell a system to change or reverse any behavior that moves it farther away from a goal situation—though confirming or reinforcing any behavior moving it closer to a goal situation—we have a *goal-seeking system* in the proper sense of the term.

Goals or goal states, as we have seen, are those relationships between a goal-seeking system and its environment in which the system's disequilibrium is minimal. If more than one such relationship has this effect for a system, then the system has several goals. A *goal* is thus not a thing, but a relationship of a system to its environment. When such a goal relation has already been attained by a system and has only to be preserved against disturbances, we speak of a *homeostatic* system. When the goal situation is distant or the target is moving, we ordinarily speak of goal-seeking in its narrower sense. The word *purpose* applies when a more distant goal is approached by a longer and more complex course around obstacles. Purposeful behavior requires the steadfast pursuit of a goal through a sequence of changing moves. In all these cases the basic relation is the same.

Goal-seeking and homeostatic behavior turn up almost everywhere in life. If we have set our thermostat at 65 degrees, the disequilibrium in the heat control system will be at a minimum when the room is at 65 degrees. A hungry greyhound will be at a relative equilibrium when it has caught and eaten the rabbit. Governments may be under disequilibria owing to their internal political setups, but they may reduce these disequilibria by conquering a colony or a border province or by acquiring a favorable political or economic treaty. Thus governments tend to pursue foreign policies that are likely—or expected—to relieve domestic tensions and the pressures of rival interest groups. In other words, what governments seek as political goals are in essence responses to internal disequilibria.

ENVIRONMENT AND THE NATURE OF DECISION MAKING

Two Kinds of Environment. Any self-steering system has two kinds of environment. The first is obvious; it is the world outside the system. The second should be no less obvious, but is often overlooked; it is the environment within the system. The inner world, and its effects on the disequilibrium of the system, can influence decisively what the system does. What people do depends not only on the world around them, but also on the state of their bodies and minds. An automobile driver must take into account not only the condition of the road, but also the state of the car's brakes and engine.

The existence of two separate environments, both of which a system must take into account, has a significant effect on decision making. If a system could pay attention to its external environment alone or its internal environment alone, it might have very few decisions to make. Decisions become frequent and important whenever information from one kind of environment must be confronted with information from the other.

Something like this has been happening to our universities: important current information about donors and alumni, about local, state, and national governments, and about the local community has been confronted with urgent current information about internal problems of the university and particularly about the needs and feelings of students and faculty. In many such cases, current messages from both environments have called for decisions. (Often the addition of messages from the past, recalled from memory, introduces a third element into the decision problem. This matter will be discussed later in this chapter.)

Decision Making on the National Level. For a national government, too, there are two kinds of feedback of current information. There is an external feedback about foreign policy and an internal feedback about what goes on inside the country. The latter is usually more important. Domestic politics tends to outweigh foreign policy in most countries most of the time, particularly in the modern age of mass politics. It is a commonplace of political experience that politicians ignorant of foreign policy who make gross mistakes in foreign affairs can get re-elected if they correctly gauge the realities of domestic politics. Today most government policies are domestically determined more often than internationally determined, although most political decisions are a mixture of the two.

When all the information comes in from the different streams of current intake, a decision must be made by the government. The more diverse intake streams of information a system has, the freer it is in making decisions. In this sense, the replacing of the four intelligence agencies that existed under Franklin D. Roosevelt by a single one, the CIA, impoverished the decision-making latitude of the president of the United States. It reduced the president's degree of freedom and increased the risks of error. The task of reconciling different and conflicting streams of information is one of the highest-level tasks of government. Delegating this responsibility to a lower level of authority may have resulted in a weakening of the country's intelligence and decision-making capabilities, as seen in the abortive invasion of Cuba's Bay of Pigs in 1961, in the war in Vietnam, and in the fall of the shah of Iran in 1979. Having subordinate officials reconcile or "consolidate" contradictory streams of information from different sources often may look like efficient preparation for decision making. But their work may prejudge the decision; indeed, they, in effect, may make the decision, without their superiors' being fully aware of it. Many aspects of the Watergate affair revealed in 1973 the damage that the government of the United States, and in particular the presidency, had suffered from such practices.

Decision Points and Decision Areas. To a casual observer, a decision point is something in the environment that forces a decision, like a fork in the road or a soda fountain menu. On closer inspection it turns out that a *decision point* is a point where two different streams of feedback information are confronted. Since information is carried in channels—whether they are copper wires, electronic beams, nerves, or human chains of reporting and command—a decision point is the meeting place of at least two channels. Where several channels meet and many decisions have to be made, we may speak of a *decision area.* The judge—or the jury—stands at a decision point in a lawsuit. The court is a decision area for many lawsuits. The United States Congress is another kind of decision area; and the presidency is still another. President Harry Truman dramatized this fact when he put a sign on his own desk that read: "The buck stops here."

Decision points and decision areas are junctions in the flow of information where organizations—and especially governments—are vulnerable to damage and exposed to influence for good or ill. Knocking out a crucial junction may paralyze a government. Filling, infiltrating, or occupying this junction with one's own friends or adherents may give a leader or a group influence and power out of proportion to its numbers. Such considerations played a part in the "court-packing" controversies of 1937 and 1969 about the composition of the Supreme Court of the United States. Conversely, the incumbents of a decision area can be rendered powerless if the information streams leading to their junction are cut off or if they are rechanneled so as to by-pass them. Finally, the incumbents of a decision area also may become powerless when one stream of information so predominates over all others that there is nothing left to decide. In this case the incumbents of the formal decision area can only make gestures of agreement; they are reduced to being rubber stamps.

FROM MEMORY TO AUTONOMY

Among the most important junctions in the flow of information are those where messages from the present meet with information recalled from the past. As a function, *memory* is the storage and recall of past information. As a tangible structure, memory consists of those parts of a self-steering system where past information is stored, together with the channels and facilities for its recall. Any large computer must have such a memory to store the information required for its calculations. The facilities for such storage may include magnetic cores, tapes, disks, or drums. These are supplemented by channels and devices to search the stored information, pick out items for recall, and apply the recalled data to decisions about current operations.

In the human body, information is stored in the brain; it is recalled and applied with the help of other parts of the brain and the nervous system. The human personality resembles a long single run on the thinking and storing facilities of our nervous system. But, unlike a computer, a human mind cannot be "cleared" or emptied of the past. To the day we die, some of our past will stay with us and will make us the unique individuals that we are.

Selfhood and Autonomy. In this sense, memory is the source of selfhood and identity. To have a *self* means to have a memory, together with the facilities for intake, output, and decision and with the feedback circuits linking them.

An ethnic or cultural group of people can be said to acquire a self when it acquires a common memory and a common set of channels of social communication that links its members into a self-steering system. At first, such a self is often cultural, based on common memories, communication habits, and ease of understanding. It often becomes a *political self,* however, when it is applied to political actions and decisions. The Irish people in the nineteenth century, when they followed the slogan *"Sinn Fein"* ("We Ourselves"), and the American blacks in the 1960s, when they proclaimed "Black Power" and "Black is Beautiful," directed their movement toward this kind of political selfhood and identity.

Identity, then, is the recognition and awareness of one's own memory and of one's self. It is the ability to remember that one can remember. "This is I, myself," says the individual. "This is we ourselves," say the members of a group that is attaining a sense of its identity. And from this sense of group identity it is only a short step to the asserting of political preferences and the taking of political actions. Often these eventually culminate in demands for political self-government and self-determination.

In terms of action, memory is the source of our autonomy. To be *autonomous* means to be able to apply information from the past to a decision in the present. Without memory, without an effective past, there can be no autonomy. Not every feedback system, therefore, that already is self-steering will necessarily have full autonomy. To have full autonomy, a system must have a memory; it must have stored information from the past that can be recalled and fed back into the decisions of the present. If a system has such a memory, if it is truly autonomous, then even the most exhaustive knowledge of its environment will not predict with complete accuracy what it will do next, since it might act in terms of its memories as well as in terms of its current intake.

What Locke and Orwell Overlooked. Here is the fundamental error in the otherwise great and liberating theories of John Locke and his followers. Locke believed that the mind of a child was like a blank piece of paper. The child's associations and environment would become associations in his or her experiences; these experiences would then become associations in memory; and future action would be governed by the associations of the past as recorded in memory. Eighteenth-century social scientists were quick to draw the conclusion that complete control of a human being's environment would in time completely control the content of his or her mind and, therefore, behavior.

The writers of the Enlightenment were optimists. They believed that governments on the whole would be reasonable and benevolent. Princes, they thought, could be educated, and even despots could be made enlightened. If these rulers could control the environment of their subjects and shape their minds, the results were likely to be good. Two and one-half centuries later, knowledge of totalitarian governments and of the horrors of World War II seemed to support the opposite view. Some writers, such as George Orwell, expressed the belief that there was much evil in all people and that evil had freer rein among those persons in power. Governments, therefore, were likely to be both dishonest and cruel; and the more power they had over the environment and the minds of their subjects, the worse the results would be. Orwell's imagined world of *1984* is a world of horror. Watched by the ever present television cameras of "Big Brother," the individual's environment and actions are totally government controlled. At the end of the novel, the hero has become a walking robot. He believes what government tells him to believe, fears what he is told to fear, and hates what he is told to hate. In both the optimism of the Enlightenment thinkers and the pessimism of George Orwell we find the same view that people's thoughts can be determined from the outside: control of the environment controls the intake and the memories of human beings; hence it controls their personalities and thus their future behavior.

In its one-sided form, this "environmentalist" theory is demonstrably false. One's behavior is strongly influenced not only by what one learns from the environment, but also by the autonomous processes and combinations inside one's mind, particularly inside one's own memory.

Dissociation and Recombination: Elements of Human Freedom. The important point about the human memory is that it is dissociative and combinational. The ability to *dissociate*—to separate pieces of information and to sort them out—is essential for critical thinking; the ability to *combine* them into new patterns is essential for creativity. Human beings are capable of breaking into pieces the patterns that they perceive in their environment. The most obvious example was the human ability to see a bird and, by detaching its wings in the imagination and putting them on the body of a person, to conceive of human flight, something radically new, thousands of years before the flight of an airplane. By dissociating what he or she sees and learns and hears and then by recombining it in an almost infinite variety of ways, a person achieves degrees of freedom that no creature with a less complete memory can match. Even if a dictator completely controlled everything his or her subjects saw and heard, that individual could not control the many ways they might piece together inside their minds the things that they had seen. If the dictator shot every adult in the world who expressed a certain idea, there would be no guarantee that a bright sixteen-year-old might not put the idea together again. It is impossible to fix the human mind in an individual or a group by controlling that individual's or group's environment, for there is an ineradicable element of combinational freedom in the human mind and in human society.

Dissociation and recombination occur in the memory, usually below the level of our awareness. Not all memories are recalled and not all of them prevail, but those that are recalled can have a great effect on the decision area of a human being or of a government. We interpret riots at home or new foreign policy crises in the Middle East in the light not only of what we remember, but also of *how* we remember it and of what new ideas we can combine. In this sense, societies are autonomous, as are the individuals of which they are composed; and the collective memory of societies—as embodied in their history, literature, language, and general culture—is often decisive for their autonomous behavior.

Governments, too, have memories, and these often are decisive for their actions. In foreign affairs many of the effective memories of a government are in the files of its foreign office or state department and in the minds of its senior officials. What the files record and what these men remember about the past actions of foreign governments or leaders may make all the difference to how they respond to current messages from them. Different elements from a government's memory also may be combined into a new policy. What many American scientists remembered about the effects of radioactive fallout on the bones of children was combined in a significant step in 1963 with what American military and diplomatic experts knew about military strategy and international relations. A similar intellectual and political effort was made in the Soviet Union. The result was a new departure in world politics: the Partial Test Ban Treaty of 1963, banning all nuclear explosions in the open air and signed by the United States, the Soviet Union, and about eighty other countries.[1]

[1]France and China refused to accept this treaty and produced in the 1960s a small number of nuclear test explosions in the open air; but the amount of fallout produced was much smaller than that which would have occurred if there had been no test ban treaty and the major nuclear powers had continued open air testing. There seems little doubt that by 1979 the Partial Test Ban Treaty had saved the lives and health of many children around the world. The test ban treaty thus is an example of an innovation in world politics that seems to have worked well.

The two Strategic Arms Limitation Treaties between the United States and the Soviet Union are further examples. The first, SALT I, was ratified in 1974. The second, SALT II, was still being negotiated in 1979.

Memories of voters, or of people in local communities, may make a major difference to how they respond to later political challenges. In Spain there are small peasant proprietors in the province of Navarra in the Pyrenees, as well as in the nearby Basque provinces on the Bay of Biscay. But in Navarra, loyalties to the Spanish monarchy have lived on for generations, whereas the Basque provinces have not only more industrial workers, but also long memories of local self-government and of an equalitarian and almost republican political tradition. At the outbreak of the Spanish Civil War in 1936, most of the men of Navarra joined Colonel Francisco Franco—later, the Generalissimo—in his insurrection against the Spanish Republic; the Basques, together with the majority of the Spanish people, supported the Republican side.[2] Historical memories thus had a major influence on the political alignments of important parts of the Spanish people at a critical moment in world history.

Reassertion of Memories: Fundamentalist Movements. Sometimes a recent flood of information may be incompatible with many of the memories of a people. This may happen, for instance, when a developing country is suddenly overwhelmed by massive and rapid modernization in the surface texture of its life and in the behavior of many of its elites; this happened in Iran under the shah from the 1950s through the 1970s, leaving many people with a sense of bewilderment and outrage. When such modernization is associated with many individual cases of social injustice—when it seems that the rich get richer and the poor get poorer and when the older ethics of religion, family, and community solidarity seem to be overwhelmed by a pitiless calculus of money making, debt, and usury—then many people may long for a return to the old-time religion and try to reassert its literal teachings. This is the response of *fundamentalism* as a viable way of defending one's individual and collective memories and the clearly or dimly remembered ethics of tradition and the group. In this manner, populism and fundamentalism together perhaps served as a collective response for William Jennings Bryan and many American farmers in the age of rising big industry and the "robber barons" during the 1890s and for decades thereafter. Such fundamentalist responses are not limited to Christian traditions. A fundamentalist revival of Islamic traditions played a conspicuous part in the revolutionary events in Iran in 1978 and 1979.

[2]Franco won after three years, thanks to massive aid from Hitler and Mussolini, which dwarfed all aid given to the Republic by the Soviet Union and other countries.

WILL: THE HARDENING OF DECISIONS

Ordinarily, there is a good deal of change and variation in the current information that a self-steering system takes in from the outside world, as well as in the current information it receives from within itself. Similarly, there may be much change in the stream of past information, recalled from memory. Since complex decisions are produced by the combination of current information with information recalled from the past, such decisions are apt to vary frequently with the changes in the information streams from which decisions are produced. Decisions, thus, often may change faster than they can be carried out.

To be acted on, a decision must be sustained long enough to take effect. This is accomplished by the screening out of information that might change the decision or change it too soon. *Information screens* or filters are thus essential for the function of a complex self-steering system, such as the political system of a country. In order to get anything done, there comes a moment when a society must stop taking more and more and more information into account and must make a decision. After it has been made, the decision must hold. Sticking to a decision means rejecting information that is incompatible with it. The decision makers reach a decision in the light of all the information available until the moment at which the policy is set. They then stop considering information contrary to this decision. Political *will*—the capacity to subordinate postdecision information to predecision information—is an essential aspect of any sustained political action.

This capacity, however, is a two-edged weapon. Will is the capacity not to learn. It is the ability to ignore any messages that would modify a decision previously taken. Although will is needed to get things done, it is a danger of the first order, for it is the temporary and deliberate cognitive impoverishment of an acting organization or organism. The more a government is likely to stress will, the more its leaders speak of "a test of will" (as former Secretary of State Dean Rusk called the Vietnam War), or the more a political movement proclaims itself a "triumph of will" (as the Nazis did in the 1930s), the more the system is apt to be deficient in cognitive performance. The more a government or a political system becomes completely oriented toward will, the more likely it is to suffer a cognitive catastrophe.

We can picture will as a system of screens (see Figure 7.2). Certain information is not taken in from the receptors. Certain information is not recalled from memory. In the individual, this is called repression by Freudians. It also happens in countries and nations. Some countries censor their history books; other countries just select what they care to remember and censor their memories without being fully aware of doing so. For instance, American history books imply that the United States never lost a war; they play down the fact that the War of 1812 failed in its major objective: the conquest of Canada. Every nation has such blind spots in its memory. But if these blind spots become too large or too serious, they may deprive the nation of much-needed information; they may prevent the timely correction of mistakes; and they may let government and nation move blindly toward disaster.

Making these blind spots smaller may improve the mental, political, and moral health of a people. In the late 1970s, tens of millions of Americans were reminded by the television series *Roots* of the effects of slavery and the slave trade on their country's past and on the fate of black Americans. In early 1979, tens of millions of Germans—many more than expected—chose to watch the television series *Holocaust,* recalling the real and deliberate murder of 6 million Jews by the Nazi government of Germany in World War II. In both cases, acknowledging previously half-ignored and hidden memories was painful, but led to a sense of relief: facing the evils of their respective pasts and breaking emotionally with them, both Americans and Germans may have felt somewhat better. Such unlocking of memories, however, does not occur often. More frequently, the governments and the entire political and cultural system of a nation will tend to filter the transmission and recall of memories from the past and the intake of information of the present, in order to make people's behavior somewhat more easily predictable and controllable.

One form of screening the intake of information is accomplished by controlling the flow of messages and persons across a nation's boundaries. Boundary control by a government may have serious effects. It may enable the government for a time to stop or slow the growth of those opposition movements—and of many other initiatives toward innovation—that might clash with established policies or be troublesome to control. But if necessary amounts of such resources as information, personnel, or equipment cannot be found at home, some importing of them may be needed from abroad. And boundary control works to inhibit such imports.

Tight control at the boundaries makes governments more secure over the short run, at the price

FIGURE 7.2 *A Functional Diagram of Information Flow in a Political System*

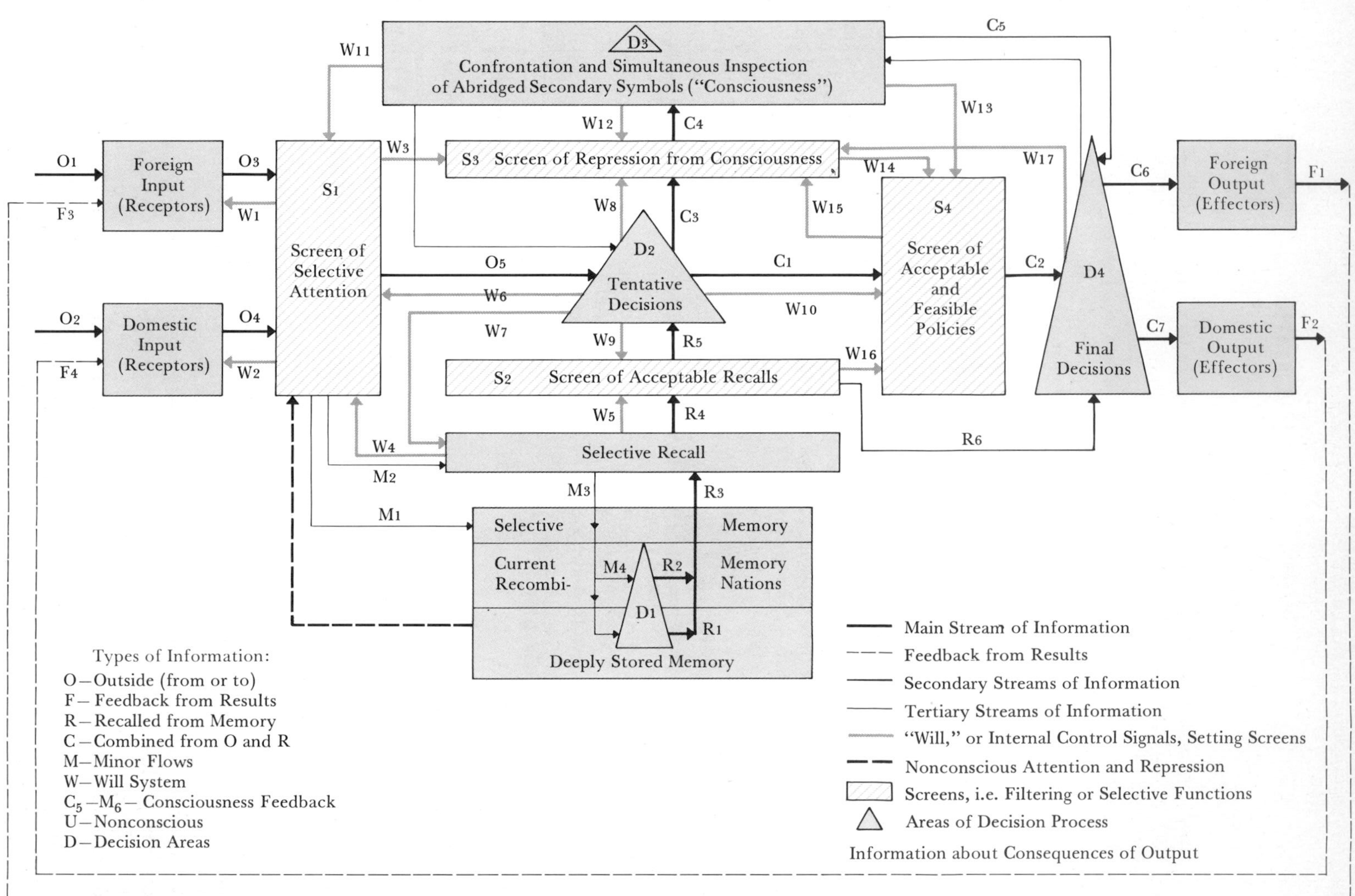

Source: Adapted and redrawn with permission of The Macmillan Company from *Nerves of Government* by Karl W. Deutsch, Copyright© 1963 by The Free Press of Glencoe, a division of The Macmillan Company.

of making their societies more conservative, sluggish, and backward over the long run. Open societies, with a free flow of transactions over their borders, are harder to rule, but they are more likely to innovate, adapt, and grow and are thus ultimately more likely to survive.

CONSCIOUSNESS: SELF-MONITORING FOR COORDINATION

A complex system may have to try to compare what goes on in its receptors, screens, and decision areas and then try to assemble highly abbreviated excerpts of all this information at one place for simultaneous inspection, coordination, and decision. The situation room in the White House is such a place. In this situation room highly condensed and abstracted information from many parts of the world is put before the president and his top advisers. Another such place was the plotting room for the defense of London during the Battle of Britain in 1940. A room-sized map pictured the south of England. Little wooden toylike replicas showed every German plane coming in and every British fighter plane available. Soldiers with long rakes moved these replicas over the map, and the marshal in charge of the air defense of London could see at a glance what was going on and could make the best decision for deployment of British planes.

This is consciousness. *Consciousness* means the processing of highly simplified and condensed summaries of second-order messages (that is, messages about first-order messages) for simultaneous inspection and decision (see Figure 7.2). A society that lacks consciousness lacks complete control of itself.

But like will, consciousness has its own costs and risks. Its most serious cost probably is delay. It takes time to monitor the first-order messages going through a system, to abstract them into shorter second-order messages, and to assemble them in one place for side-by-side inspection and decision. When quick action is needed, the risks of such delays must be weighed against the risks of error from insufficient information, inspection, and coordination. Consciousness also requires tangible facilities, such as monitoring circuits and display screens. In governmental, military, or business organizations it requires human monitors, abstractors, and other personnel, often together with briefing rooms and display facilities. It requires costs in money and resources.

Together, the costs and delays can be crippling. According to an old story, a centipede was immobilized when asked which foot he planned to move next: the creature became lost in thought. Governments, no less than centipedes, can become entangled in their own complexity. Moreover, political decisions can be slowed down as more people become aware of them. More individuals and agencies may try to get into the act; more interest groups may insist on being heard; more logrolling politicians with veto power may demand a price for allowing the project to go through. No wonder that it is a rule of practical politics to arouse as little attention as possible about any plan that has enough support to pass.

Added to these costs are special risks of error. A society that has consciousness risks three things. First, it runs the risk of a false consciousness. At the end of World War II, Adolf Hitler in his command bunker in Berlin was ordering the advance of German divisions that had ceased to exist. The symbols were still on the map, but the divisions no longer were in existence. In a less consequential error, President Carter's administration in December 1978 and January 1979 treated the government of the shah of Iran as stable when it was not.

Second, a society runs the risk of an incorrect estimate. Something that is mildly important may be overrepresented; something significant may be underrepresented. The history of black Americans has been underrepresented in the awareness of historians for many years, much as the needs and aspirations of black Americans have long been underrepresented in our politics. This is one of the many deficiencies that now are crying out for remedy.

Third, condensation and simplification are fraught with dangers of their own. The U.S. State Department gets about a thousand cables a day. Each week it gets several hundred messages and reports, averaging ten to twenty pages each, in the diplomatic pouches. No secretary of state could possibly read all these dispatches. Condensation is thus indispensable. Highly abbreviated one-page summaries are drawn up by lower-level officials and affixed to the longer reports. Cables of half a page are summarized in a sentence. These summaries then go to one official who quickly scans all of them and summarizes the summaries. By the time the world situation is condensed into what can be discussed with the secretary of state or the president in a one-hour briefing session, it has been fantastically simplified and sometimes dangerously oversimplified.

In every large political system, all politics must pass between the twin dangers of being blinded by superficiality and being drowned in detail. What is true of the consciousness of the State Department about world politics, or the Air Force about airplane and missile dispositions, or the Navy about the location of its own and other countries' ships is equally true of our knowledge of our cities, our economy, our educational situation, and our domestic politics. The Senate investigations of 1973 revealed how often some parts of the government were kept in ignorance of what other parts or officials were doing. The U.S. Defense Department admitted that it had concealed from Congress, as well as from the American people, the dropping of more than 100,000 tons of bombs on Cambodia while publicly claiming to respect that country's neutrality. President Nixon claimed that he had been kept in ignorance of the true extent of the Watergate affair by his White House staff until March 21, 1973, approximately nine months after the original burglary of the Democratic Party's national headquarters. Both incidents were dramatic reminders that societies must have consciousness, but must be critical toward their consciousness lest they become prisoners of their own illusions.

SELF-GOVERNMENT IN PERSPECTIVE

At its core, self-government is based on self-steering; at its boundaries, it is founded on relative independence from the outside world. The legal doctrine of *sovereignty* stresses the latter aspect in its extreme form: a state is held to be sovereign if it obeys no laws or commands from outside itself, except those it accepts voluntarily by its own internal decision processes. This legal concept of sovereignty says little, however, about the ability of a government, a nation, a city, or any other organization to control its own affairs.

To control its own affairs, a government or any other organization must first be able to direct its own behavior. All self-direction—and hence self-government—is a process of steering. It must combine several streams of information: past information about what its goal or target is; current outside information about where the goal or target is; and internal information about where the system itself is in relation to its goal. All these streams of information are based on cycles of feedback. These report back to the system the results of its own previous behavior. If this behavior has brought the system closer to its goal, it is continued; if not, it is reversed or modified until the goal is reached.

Self-government implies the ability to set goals and to keep to them; to make decisions and keep them stable long enough for action; and hence to screen out or suppress postdecision information that might jeopardize stability. This is the function of the will, which is a subsystem of information filters performing this service.

In complex systems the coordination of many subsystems and decisions is facilitated by internal monitoring. The voluminous primary messages moving through the system are abstracted and condensed into much shorter secondary ones that are then presented for simultaneous inspection and decision. This process corresponds in its essentials to what we call consciousness.

All these processes have their particular costs and risks. Together, however, they make it possible for individuals, small groups, and large nations to govern their own actions and to win a greater share in controlling their own fate.

KEY TERMS AND CONCEPTS

self-government
self-steering
independent
sovereign
autonomy
receptors
effectors
feedback cycle
amplifying feedback
escalation
negative feedback
goal state
disequilibrium
homeostatic process
load
lag
gain
lead
goal-seeking system
goal
purpose
decision point
decision area
memory
self
political self
identity
autonomous
dissociative
combinational
fundamentalism
information screens
will
consciousness
sovereignty

ADDITIONAL READINGS

Ashby, W. R. *An Introduction to Cybernetics.* London: Chapman and Hall, 1956. PB

Brecher, M. *The Foreign Policy System of Israel.* New Haven: Yale University Press, 1972.

Deutsch, K. W. *The Nerves of Government.* 2nd ed. New York: Free Press, 1966. PB

Halberstam, D. *The Best and the Brightest.* New York: Random House, 1972.

Haley, A. *Roots.* Garden City, N.Y.: Doubleday, 1977. PB

Hoffmann, S. *Gulliver's Troubles.* New York: McGraw-Hill, 1968. PB

Janis, I. L. *Victims of Groupthink.* Boston: Houghton Mifflin, 1973. PB

Kennedy, R. *Thirteen Days.* New York: Norton, 1971. PB

Orwell, G. *1984.* New York: New American Library, 1971. PB

The Pentagon Papers: As published by The New York Times. New York: Bantam Books, 1971. PB

Snyder, R. C., H. W. Bruck, and B. M. Sapin, eds. *Foreign Policy Decision-Making.* New York: Free Press, 1962.

Wiener, N. *The Human Use of Human Beings.* Boston: Houghton Mifflin, 1950. PB

Wildavsky, A. "The Empty-Head Blues: Black Rebellion and White Reaction." *Public Interest,* vol. 2, no. 1 (1968), pp. 3-16.

PB = *available in paperback*

VIII

The Process and Machinery of Government

The two preceding chapters have presented an abstract model of the political system. They have focused on the system's main functions—how a system keeps itself together and how it steers itself—and on the general processes by which these tasks are attained. Let us look now at the specific processes and machinery by which the work of government and politics gets done.*

Politics and government refer to a single complex of activities viewed from different, but overlapping perspectives. Politics stresses competing demands and the allocation of values—that is, of valued outcomes, resources, and opportunities—among them. Government emphasizes steering and control. Politics deals with Harold Lasswell's classic question: "Who gets what, when, how?" Government deals with this question: "Who controls what, when, and how?" One distinction between politics and government is that between getting and controlling.

*For some of the material in this chapter I am indebted to Professor Carl J. Friedrich.

Politics and government interact, necessarily and closely; and both need specific institutions, organizations, channels, and procedures in order to operate. It is these specific arrangements, and some of the main similarities and differences among them in different countries, that we shall study in the present chapter. Thus we can find out what is subject to political and governmental decisions, who makes them, how they are made, how they are put into effect, in what ways they are limited, and what opportunities they offer.

DECISIONS AND THEIR LIMITS

One of the most difficult and most important features of politics is how one makes decisions—especially decisions on policy. In any organization some mystery always surrounds the decision-making process. This is as true of big commercial companies as of universities, governments, and other kinds of organizations. And yet, because of the importance of decision making, many organizations establish elaborate rules, which seem to tell us how decisions are supposed to be made. In fact, many of these rules are observed mostly in the abstract and frequently not at all. For example, if you buy shares of stock in an American company, you may go to the annual meeting at which the stockholders are supposed to reach basic policy decisions. Actually, they do nothing of the kind. If somebody should have the temerity to suggest a policy decision, the stockholders are informed that management opposes the proposal; and, as you might expect, an overwhelming majority of stockholders roundly defeats it. Of course, most of the people making this decision are in no way aware of its significance, nor do they really care, as long as management is earning 7 percent or more on the investment. Something similar is characteristic of all kinds of organizations: as long as things seem to go well, most people are happy to "let George do it"—to let someone else make the decisions.

Many people have the illusion that something important is accomplished in the change of a rule about decision making. Curiously, these decision-making processes have an inner dynamism with which we cannot cope effectively by formal rule making. *Thirteen Days,* Robert Kennedy's memoir of the Cuban missile crisis in October 1962, is a revealing case study of a particular type of decision-making process. It describes step by step how President Kennedy arrived at a series of decisions that were precipitated by the Soviet Union's attempt in the summer of 1962 to install intermediate range ballistic missiles (IRBMs) in Cuba. The Soviets may have intended their action as a move to deter another United States–supported invasion of Cuba, similar to the one that had failed at the Bay of Pigs in April 1961; or they might have wanted to match the positioning of similar United States missiles since the 1950s in Turkey, near Soviet territory, and at a somewhat greater distance in southern Italy. Another possibility is that the Soviets might simply have wanted a bargaining card to trade for some United States concession, such as an American promise not to attack Cuba again. Or they might really have thought that their intermediate-range missiles in Cuba could change the strategic balance of power in the world.

We will not know what the true purpose of the Soviet move was, or indeed whether it had a single purpose, until the Soviet archives are opened. But we do know the impression that this move made on the American government and public. Most Americans interpreted it as a direct threat against various countries in this hemisphere, particularly the United States. As President Kennedy saw it, American domestic politics left him very little choice about how to interpret the Soviet move. It left him very little *decision latitude.* A majority of his advisers considered the installation of Soviet missiles in Cuba a possible change in the world's balance of power. A small minority denied this; they thought these missiles would make little or no difference and saw no need for action. But, as President Kennedy later said, if he had not acted in some way, "I would have been impeached."

The account of another White House adviser, Theodore Sorensen's *Decision-Making in the White House,* provides an interesting supplement to Robert Kennedy's story. Both Robert Kennedy and Sorensen suggest that the very word "decision" often is deceptive. Sorensen says at the outset, "The President is in his decisions very much affected by basic forces and factors which will shape his decisions." He adds, "The President may ignore these forces or factors, he may even be unaware of them, but he cannot escape them. He may choose to decide in solitude, but he does not decide in a vacuum." In other words, you may think you are deciding something; however, your decision is partly determined by forces and factors over which you have little or no control, but which must be taken into account if you want to make a good decision. If you ignore them, you are likely to make a bad decision that will not accomplish any of the things you want.

Thirteen Days is an exciting and dramatic illustration of this point. During those thirteen days in October 1962 some very important decisions were made. At one stage there was an intense debate over whether to respond to the threat of the installation of the missiles in Cuba with a relatively mild measure, such as a blockade, or with military force. Robert Kennedy strongly opposed a massive surprise attack by a large nation on a very small nation, because he believed that the immorality of such an action was contrary to America's traditions and ideals. Secretary of Defense Robert S. McNamara later wrote in his introduction to *Thirteen Days:* "The air and ground strikes favored by so many would have brought death to thousands of innocent Cuban civilians and to thousands of U.S. military personnel." The expected number of Cuban civilian casualties alone was put at twenty-five thousand. Thus, the conscience and moral tradition of the American people constituted one of the forces acting on President Kennedy's decision. In addition, President Kennedy decided in favor of the milder measure rather than military attack for still another reason: the latter might have precipitated a nuclear confrontation and possible nuclear war between the United States and the Soviet Union.

Once the decision for the blockade was made, United Nations Secretary General U Thant appealed to Nikita Khrushchev, who then was chairman of the Council of Ministers, to order all ships from the Soviet Union en route to Cuba not to proceed until some adjustment had been reached between the United States and the Soviet Union. Khrushchev responded to this appeal and thus avoided a particularly dangerous confrontation. On both sides, in the United States and in the Soviet Union, crucial decisions led to the course that eventually emerged. Large-scale loss of life was avoided, and all three governments remained in power.

In the first stage of the crisis President Kennedy's decision latitude was small. He could not choose to wait. Had he done nothing, he would have risked a deterioration in the international power and prestige of the United States and, in any case, serious political troubles with Congress and the public. At the same time, he could not do very much. If he had chosen to attack Cuba, he could not have prevented Soviet retaliation against Berlin and the risk of World War III. At a later stage President Kennedy's decision latitude increased. Within the limits of his decision to blockade Cuba, he had a range of options for the manner of carrying it out. These limits were wide enough for him to act forcefully and yet to remain at all times in control of his own actions. They permitted him to reach his main objective, the removal of the missiles, and yet preserve peace.

Soviet Chairman Nikita Khrushchev also had to face his own limits of decision making. He could not choose to defend Cuba locally with any prospect of success against a full-scale American attack, since neither the U.S.S.R. nor Cuba had enough forces on the spot. He could decide at most to apply counterpressure elsewhere, such as on Berlin, and risk all-out war with the United States. Or he could choose to respect the American blockade and to negotiate. Once he decided on the last course, his options improved. In exchange for removing the missiles, he obtained an informal American pledge not to attack Cuba; in addition, the aging American IRBMs were removed from Italy and Turkey, in tardy fulfillment of an order given by President Kennedy long before the crisis.

In the handling of the Cuban missile crisis, both Kennedy and Khrushchev acted like true statesmen, for part of the art of statesmanship consists in recognizing the limits to decision making at a particular time and place and in making the most of the opportunities within those limits.

Decisions are often broken into sequences. First, a decision is made about the general preferences, purposes, or goals in regard to some class of problems. This is called a *policy* decision. Later decisions deal with the means and methods of carrying out the policy. The difference between policy and its execution resembles that between strategy and tactics. *Strategy* consists in setting a long-run series of goals or targets; *tactics* consists in choosing and applying the short-run means to attain them. Generally, strategy looks farther ahead into the future and involves setting a larger class of goals, whereas tactics denotes choosing a more limited class of intermediate steps within the larger class. This orderly progress from policy to tactical decision occurs when there has been an accurate assessment of the consequences of each step. In practice, the decision-making sequence may easily degenerate into muddle, drift, and worse, as in the United States involvement in the Vietnam War: the failure of early strategic and tactical decisions to produce the desired effects resulted in progressively widening the scope of the initial policy decision to provide limited support to the government of South Vietnam.

Policy also often implies the setting of a relatively distant goal or purpose that may have to be approached by a zigzag course of short-run moves around several intervening obstacles. Since these moves seem to contradict each other, much as in the tacking of a sailboat into a tricky harbor entrance, the notion of policy sometimes connotes a devious sequence of actions aimed at a single goal. So does the word "purpose." As we discussed in Chapter 7, it refers to pursuing a goal through a circuitous sequence of steps around obstacles. The French, Shakespeare wrote in *Henry V,* "with pale policy seek to divert the English purposes."

In modern politics, "policy" is a very controversial word. Before World War II, people did not talk much about policy. From the age of John Locke to the beginning of the twentieth century, people talked about "legislation." When Locke divided power among several authorities, he was primarily concerned about the power of legislative decision, not the power of policy making. He wanted each legislative decision to be made very carefully, at the appropriate time. He did not concern himself with setting policy as a general guide for the future conduct of the government. Nowadays people demand just that, for they have become increasingly preoccupied with policy. Those in public life are very keen about being involved in policy making. This has become the really important task of government; legislation is looked down upon as a technical matter. The concern of important people is to decide policy. They then leave it to lawyers to work out the technicalities of the legislation involved.

At this point the interests of the "important people" coincide with those of thc "man in the street." He, too, knows little about technicalities of legislation, and he is impatient with them. But he knows what he likes and often knows what he wants. He can make clear which goal or outcome he prefers. He can express his support for a policy, or his opposition to it; and he can vote for a candidate or party that appears to stand for the policies he likes.

But something else is characteristic of policies besides their generally accepted importance. Policy decisions involve particular objectives; and the more important the objectives are, the more important the decisions are. The security of the United States is an extremely important objective. Consequently, any decision involving the security of the United States is an important decision. But somebody could raise this question: What *is* the security of the United States? Wherein does it consist? Some Americans might think themselves secure if nobody could shoot them without being shot at in return. But it is not as simple as that. When a government seeks security in national armaments, other nations are provoked to arm, possibly leading to the dangers of an arms race. As Henry Kissinger is said to have remarked about security through superior armament: Absolute security for any one nation is absolute insecurity for any other.

The definition of objectives, or goals, is a critical stage in policy making. Goal definition has all kinds of ramifications. For example, much of the criticism directed against the universities in recent years has stemmed from differing views of the goal of higher education. On this point there is a wide range of opinion among those immediately or indirectly affected, whether as students, teachers, administrators, residents of the local community, or citizens and taxpayers of the state and nation. Some see a university's main task as the education of undergraduates. Others see it as service to the community or to the community's poorest members. Still others view the university primarily as a means of training students to fill the economy's current needs for specialized personnel and of indoctrinating them with the society's current beliefs and mores. And again others variously see the university's main task as questioning and criticizing existing practices and institutions; or discovering and applying new knowledge; or providing its graduates with hunting licenses for better-paying jobs. Deciding on the goals of a university is typically a policy matter, because agreement on policy means that we have decided on our goals.

The goal of President Kennedy during the Cuban missile crisis was, above everything else, to avoid an all-out war. (Giving in to the Soviet Union, he thought, would not accomplish this. It would only usher into power a more warlike American administration and invite further Soviet aggressiveness.) Robert Kennedy wrote of his brother: "The thought that disturbed him the most, and that made the prospect of war much more fearful than it would otherwise have been, was the specter of the death of the children of this country and all the world—the young people who had no role, who had no say, who knew nothing even of the confrontation, but whose lives would be snuffed out like everyone else's." A little further on in *Thirteen Days* he repeats this and says, "It was this that troubled him most, that gave him such pain." Then comes the crucial point—how to make certain that the Soviet Union would not misunderstand the goals of the United States or vice versa: "And it was then that he and Secretary Rusk decided that I should visit with Ambassador Dobrynin and personally convey the President's great concern." Robert Kennedy in effect was to say to Dobrynin: Look, you know you are really playing with fire and you are marching right into a war—an uncontrollable conflagration—with the United States. Is that what you really want? Dobrynin came back the next day after having communicated with Moscow and in effect answered: This is not what we want; we want some other things; our goals have been misunderstood. Understanding the significance of this conversation is very important for the understanding of the meaning of policy.

Policy, in short, means goal setting or goal definition. It is a decision about what one's goals should be. One reason that discussions about foreign policy are usually unenlightening and futile is the lack of definition of the concept of foreign policy. If you ask people, "What do you mean when you say you are displeased with foreign policy?" you usually do not get a specific answer because they do not really know what they are displeased about. The reason is not that they are stupid. Rather, the term "foreign policy" is not a clearly defined proposition.

What does foreign policy really mean for a country like the United States? If you say, "I am displeased with its foreign policy," you may mean, "I am displeased with the goal definition of a particular aspect of its foreign policy." Many people meant by such an assertion that the proclamations of Secretary Rusk and President Johnson on Vietnam contained a goal definition with which they totally disagreed. They in effect said, "We do not want to turn the Vietnamese into little Americans. If that is your goal, we do not like it, and hence we do not like your policy." Other people, however, said, "We accept this goal provided it can be reached at a price that does not reduce our chances to reach other and more important goals."

Often people have several goals that they find hard to reconcile but cannot put into a clear and agreed-on rank order of importance. Many American voters considered the Vietnam War a mistake and wanted the United States to disengage from it, yet they did not want the United States to appear to be a loser. In the presidential election of November 1972, the majority seemed to reject the choice offered by the Democratic candidate, Senator George McGovern, between an early peace and the preservation of the nation's military prestige. They re-elected President Nixon, who promised them both. After the Vietnam War and the Nixon presidency were over, Presidents Ford and Carter moved toward a more cautious balance between the twin goals: they reduced the risk of American involvement in distant wars, but maintained a rough parity of American and Soviet military power.

As a rule, it is difficult to say what is the goal of American foreign policy or, indeed, of the foreign policy of any modern democratic nation. The reason that Richelieu, Bismarck, and Napoleon could make such "good" foreign policy in their day was that they had perfectly simple, clear-cut, aggressive imperialist goals. Moreover, no groups in their countries were strong enough to assert other goals for the state that might be partly or wholly incompatible with the acknowledged ones. Richelieu told Louis XIII in 1625, "We must smash the power of Habsburg." The king agreed. No one else with real power objected. All Richelieu had to do was to direct his efforts at smashing the power of the Habsburg dynasty. Unfortunately or luckily, in a democracy nobody can effectively decide to seek such clear-cut, simple, and aggressive goals for foreign policy (whether or not they could be carried out in today's world). All sorts of people in a democracy have different kinds of needs and orientations and, hence, different preferences for national goals; each will try to make his or her definition prevail, and many have enough power to compel at least some consideration. Thus, by the very nature of the democratic process, long-range foreign policy will only rarely be real policy, since usually it will lack an agreed-upon, clearly defined goal. More modest short-range goals sometimes command easier agreement, because different groups may interpret them as steps toward different long-range policies and support them for different reasons. Of course, we can proclaim general formulas like "peace" or "security," but these are not goals that define operations.

Something similar holds for domestic policy. Only if widespread agreement can be reached on well-defined, specific goals—such as maintaining nearly full employment or speeding the end of race discrimination in housing, education, or employment—and only if such goals are realistic, will domestic policies have a chance to succeed. Here again, the same policy may be supported by several groups for different reasons. Some groups, for example, may support fairer treatment for black people through *affirmative action*—the demand that more minority persons be admitted to universities or be hired and promoted in public or private institutions until they reach some proportion that is defined as fair; and they may do so because they want to increase the general role of government in promoting social justice. Others may support the same policy in the hope that it will integrate black people more fully into the private enterprise system. For a considerable time, both groups may be able to cooperate and bring about a significant reduction in discrimination. But at some later time they may quarrel decisively about this matter—or else the main problems of policy may change.

Conversely, in domestic as in foreign policy, people may seek to attain several goals without being able to agree on which one to put first. Many American voters may want to abolish or diminish discrimination and racial strife, increase equality of opportunity, maintain an ethic of hard work and competition, keep taxes low, and preserve the predominantly white, middle-class character of many of our suburbs. They may then defeat new taxes or bond issues to build better schools in black neighborhoods, vote against busing black children to better school buildings in the white suburbs, believe that black young people have just as good a chance to rise in our society as do white ones, and demand from government that it ensure civic peace and security in the streets of our big cities, as well as produce a moral and spiritual renewal—all this, once again, without increasing taxes. These goals are in part mutually inconsistent, as well as being inconsistent with the needs and desires of many black Americans. So far, no one seems to have succeeded in shaping a consistent and workable policy out of these contradictory, but very real, wants and goals. Voters have tended to hit out at whatever particular threat to their goals seemed most salient at any given moment. "High taxes," "government spending," and "inflation" headed the list of such issues in 1979 throughout most of the nation and delivered political success to those parties and candidates who knew best how to respond to them. But for the more distant future, the piecemeal approach will not be good enough. To keep the array of problems that forms the tangled complex of "poverty," "race," "housing," "unemployment," "crime," "inequality," "neighborhood," and "education" from getting worse, better policies sooner or later will have to be invented and applied.

DELIBERATION: DECIDING ABOUT ENDS AND MEANS

The Deliberative Process. Deliberation goes on in any political organization, even a dictatorship, but it is at the heart of democratic politics. *Deliberation* is the chief process by which policy is determined. It is a continuous process of debate. Like any genuine debate, deliberation not only lets the participants promote their own views and interests, but also permits them to adjust their own views of reality and even to change their values as a result of this process. All policy decisions involve deliberation, which is directed toward the same two distinct ends as policy. First, as we have seen, deliberation and policy seek to set common ends or goals. Second, all policy debates and deliberations concern the choice of *means* to achieve the defined goal.

These twin aspects of deliberation and policy are illustrated by the debate over social security in the United States. In the 1930s extensive debate prevailed throughout the United States over what is now known as social security, the term itself testifying to the great skill of Franklin D. Roosevelt as an inventor of catchwords. Until that time the concept had always been talked about as "old-age pensions" or "public assistance," that is, in terms that were hostile to the traditional imagery of Americans. Why should red-blooded Americans need any help from the government to provide for their old age? Indeed, why should anyone admit to being old or to no longer having a job? By defining as his goal the achievement of "social security" through a government-run administration, Roosevelt was able to broaden the support for his policy. Once the decision had been made about the goal to be achieved—government provision of social security—the debate then focused on the means to be used to achieve the desired end, on the way in which the government was to set up old-age insurance, unemployment insurance, and other related security arrangements. Through the years and under both major political parties, the system of providing social security set up under Roosevelt has been revised, modified, and improved.

Thus, the graph of this process of deliberation is a jagged line. First, before a goal is determined, nothing happens; then there is a great outburst of activity to set the general goal; then again for a time nothing happens; and so on, until both the general policy and its practical implementation are set. The deliberation goes on all the time, but at certain key points it crystallizes into a decision. And then immediately after a decision has been made, the deliberation begins again. People come along and say, "Did we make the right decision? Look—this is a consequence we didn't anticipate. What are we going to do about it?" For example, in connection with social security, something ultimately had to be done—a new decision had to be made—about the enormous financial reserves that soon piled up in the hands of the Social Security Administration because nobody had foreseen that these large accumulations of money would affect the economy. Later, another decision became necessary. As people lived longer and as inflation created a need for higher social security contributions and payments, a federal law was passed forbidding compulsory retirement before the age of seventy, in order to reduce the burden of retirement claims on the system. This law took effect on January 1, 1979, with a delay for universities until 1982. Thus, in the short run, "to deliberate" means "to stop and think," but in the long run we can never stop thinking. The deliberative process is continuous, with ups and downs and culminating points at which crucial decisions occur. It is a process that goes on and on, unceasingly.

Procedures Safeguarding Deliberation. It has always been agreed that political deliberation should be carefully institutionalized because of its importance and continuity. An *institution* is an orderly and more or less formal collection of human habits and *roles*—that is, of interlocking expectations of behavior—that results in a stable organization or practice whose performance can be predicted with some reliability. Governments, universities, hospitals, law courts, planning boards, and business firms are such organizations; voting, marriage, property, and law are such practices. To *institutionalize* a practice, process, or service is to transform it from a poorly organized and informal activity into a highly organized and formal one.

Attempts to institutionalize the practice of political deliberation have led to the development of the elaborate codes of parliamentary procedure that pervade the Congress of the United States, the House of Commons, and the other parliaments of Europe. This is one of the areas in politics in which the people of the West have been most significantly innovative. *Jefferson's Manual of Parliamentary Practice* and *Robert's Rules of Order,* although they might look rather dull now, represent the accretion and culmination of a long struggle to cope with the intense practical problems of deliberation and decision making.

The history of parliamentary government is in a sense the history of parliamentary procedure. In England such procedure is particularly impressive, because the British have been especially alert to its importance and have been remarkably inventive in connection with it. A whole range of procedures that we now consider matters of course, such as referring to a committee, putting a motion, and amending a motion, were developed in the course of the last seven hundred years. One reason that democratic schemes of government sometimes do not function in emergent nations is that these peoples have not yet developed these habits of parliamentary procedure. Also, the frequent failures of parliamentary government in continental Europe have been due in some part to a lack of sound procedural rules for getting at the work of deliberation in parliamentary bodies.

The word "parliament" comes from the French *parler,* which means "to talk." European theorists sometimes have said of European parliaments, "Parliamentary government is government by talk." A German theorist called it *"Das ewige Gespräch,"* the eternal dialogue. Those who hold such views forget that English parliamentary procedure developed continually not in terms of talk, but in terms of ways to reach decisions. It is important to understand that in decision making through deliberation one cannot wait indefinitely. The business of government must get on. The English House of Commons until the last century afforded unlimited protection for all people who wanted to talk, including protection for speakers expressing minority opinions, and was able to get its business done. But then the Irish Independence Movement produced a group of members of Parliament who were not at all interested in arriving at any decision. They wished to sabotage decisions, to prevent them from being reached. Accordingly, they applied the technique of deliberately wasting time, the *filibuster,* which the United States had originated in 1825 and has since perfected.[1] What could Parliament do? It was supposed to reach a decision, yet certain members used the rules of procedure not to get the job done, but to prevent it from being done. At the crucial point, the speaker of the House of Commons, its chairman, made a decision, as he could because of an old tradition in English procedure. He exercised his right to recognize. He decided not to recognize any more speakers from the Irish contingent, and that was the end of legislative filibustering in England. Only in England would this have been appreciated as being the decisive political step it actually was. This step, of course, has since developed into a variety of rules for ending debate and bringing the matter to a vote, the so-called rules of closure or *cloture,* which operate in all parliaments and which play an important part in getting things done.[2]

On the other hand, the decision-making process works best without extreme limitations of time. Robert Kennedy pointed out the critical role that time plays in decision making in *Thirteen Days* under the heading "Some of the Things We Learned." The Kennedy group learned that if they had had "to make a decision in twenty-four hours, I believe the course that [they] ultimately would have taken would have been quite different and filled with far greater risk." The alternative of taking military action was the most obvious way to respond to the threat. Thus, if the group had had only twenty-four hours, they would have supported military action. But having time to talk and to deliberate, they could consider a wider range of consequences and options. This made it possible for them to arrive at a better decision. Group experiments, simulating the making of major decisions, confirm this view. The greater the pressure of time and the more simple-minded the participants, the more extreme and warlike the decisions are likely to be. Similar experiences from real life are summed up in a proverb: "Decide in haste, repent at leisure."

The Pros and Cons of Secrecy. Another lesson that Robert Kennedy said he learned was the importance of keeping such deliberations entirely secret. If the deliberations had been publicized, he claimed, the final decision would have been hastily made and would have entailed far greater risks. Very often the need for secrecy while deliberating is forgotten by those who believe that publicity is always a good thing. Publicity can be an obstacle and can lead to bad decisions. When you publicize discussions, some politicians or officials will no longer stick to the job at hand, but will play to the galleries. They will talk with a view to what is going to be said in print rather than pertinence to the discussion. For this reason, in most parliaments today deliberations have been transferred from the publicized general debate to committees that can bar publicity. Few people realize that the British Parliament deliberated entirely in secret until the nineteenth century, not because of disdain for the general public, but because Parliament still saw itself as essentially opposed to the

[1]The custom of filibustering began in the United States Senate in 1825, when John Randolph of Virginia began making long speeches that John C. Calhoun refused to rule out of order. Prior to then, by custom, it had always been the chair's privilege to limit debate. By 1872, filibustering had itself become such an established custom that Vice President Schuyler Colfax ruled that the chair could not restrain a senator from remarks that the senator considered pertinent. The practice is definitely American by invention as well as by extent of use. A filibustering senator will speak at inordinate length—for days, if necessary—until he or she is exhausted or is relieved by another filibustering colleague. The method is impractical for a single individual, but can be quite effective for a dozen senators of adequate endurance.

[2]The real basis of the filibuster is the tolerance of the majority, whose members usually refrain from voting cloture. Until 1967 the rules of the Senate provided that cloture could be voted only by a two-thirds majority of all members of the Senate, that is, sixty-seven votes. In that year the requirement was lowered to a two-thirds majority of those senators present and voting—generally a much smaller number. In 1975 the majority needed for cloture was changed to three-fifths of the entire Senate, that is, 60 votes, if no Senate seats are vacant.

monarchy and believed that the monarch and his or her councillors should not know who had said what in Parliament. As Parliament became stronger, this need for secrecy declined, but secrecy still has its uses in modern deliberative processes.

Something similar holds for the practice of tape-recording confidential conversations or conferences by one party alone, one who keeps control of the tape and who may not even tell the other participants that their words have been recorded. In 1973, President Nixon revealed that he had arranged for just such tape recordings of all his conversations in the White House, although he did not inform his interlocutors of this practice. If his partners in these conversations did not suspect that their words were being recorded, they may have spoken more incautiously and laid themselves open to possible political pressure and embarrassment; if they did suspect the secret taping, they would have spoken less freely.

President Nixon long refused to make any of these tapes available either to a Senate investigating committee under Senator Sam Ervin or to Special Prosecutor Archibald Cox, whom Nixon himself had appointed to ascertain the truth in the Watergate affair—even though certain tapes could have thrown light on instances in which President Nixon's statements were in conflict with the sworn testimony of former members of his staff. Eventually, Nixon dismissed Cox, although he had earlier promised the prosecutor a free hand; thereupon, Attorney General Elliot Richardson and his deputy, William Ruckelshaus, resigned. When Nixon finally let the courts have the tapes, two crucial tapes turned out to have been "missing" and a third one had a long gap where a key passage had been erased, it was claimed, "by accident."

To make matters worse, tape recordings can be cut, spliced together, changed by insertions, and otherwise edited. Clumsy frauds of this kind can be easily detected by experts, but expert forgeries may pass as genuine; they might deceive public opinion and even courts of law. The physical custody of tape recordings of confidential conversations by only one of the interested parties thus creates a situation of inequality and risk—in contrast to the older practice of having stenographic transcripts of such conversations typed out, read, and signed or initialed by all parties, each of whom would then retain a copy.

Sometimes the power of governments to carry out policies and to make decisions secretly has been used to delude the public. The publication in 1971 of *The Pentagon Papers*—a Defense Department study that described the decision making of three administrations about Southeast Asia—disclosed instances of false information, or none at all, given by the executive branch both to the public and to members of Congress, although information was critical to an understanding of the probable consequences of the decisions for which their support was being asked. (Subsequently, public attention was largely diverted to the legality or illegality of publishing the papers and away from the poor methods of governmental decision making that they revealed.)

An even more blatant instance of the practice of secrecy came to light in mid-1973 when some United States Air Force pilots revealed that they had been bombing targets in legally neutral Cambodia and falsifying the coordinates of their targets in order to misreport them as located in South Vietnam. This practice, it was finally disclosed, had continued for about four years, from 1969 to 1973, and included the dropping of 100,000 tons of bombs on that legally neutral territory. President Nixon and Secretary of Defense Melvin Laird—who both had ordered these bombings—during that period had made public statements denying them, asserting their "scrupulous" respect for Cambodia's neutrality and insisting that "our hands are clean."

After the facts had come out, President Nixon and spokespeople for his administration explained that the bombings had been directed against North Vietnamese troops who were operating on Cambodian soil; that these bombings had been secretly approved at the beginning by the head of state of Cambodia, Prince Norodom Sihanouk; and that they had been kept secret to avoid "diplomatic embarrassment." The four years of secret bombings, said Assistant Secretary of Defense Clements, had been "a first-class military operation" for which no apology was owed to anyone.

Prince Sihanouk denied that he had given any foreign power any permission to bomb any part of his country. But by then his rule in Cambodia had been overthrown by a U.S.-backed military group under General Lon Nol. The prince was speaking from exile in Peking, but his adherents were fighting inside Cambodia against the Lon Nol regime and apparently with the support of some North Vietnamese troops. By that time, United States bombs were unlikely to distinguish between Sihanouk's Cambodian partisans and their North Vietnamese allies, if the bomber pilots had ever tried to make such distinctions. In any event, American intervention proved ineffective, and Lon Nol's regime fell. By the late 1970s it had been replaced by a particularly repressive Communist regime, friendly to China but hostile to Communist Vietnam, which in turn signed a treaty of friendship with the Soviet Union. The further spread of Communist regimes in Southeast Asia seemed more likely to be slowed by divisions within the Communist camp than by United States bombing.

The real targets of the secrecy and of the falsification of air force reports, it seems, were the United States Congress and the American people. Certainly, the Cambodians knew that they were being bombed, and the facts were obviously known fairly soon to the Communist governments in Hanoi, Peking, and Moscow, as well as to major neutral nations, such as India. Only Western opinion, particularly American opinion, was kept in the dark. But if Congress and its competent committees could thus be kept ignorant and misinformed, what remnant of its constitutional powers over war and peace could Congress still retain? If the four years of secret bombing in Cambodia should become a precedent for future practices of this kind and for the right of an American president to engage in them while keeping Congress uninformed or misinformed, how would this development rearrange the distribution of information, power, and decision making within the American political system? To some observers, this issue far overshadowed, in potential importance, the question of "diplomatic embarrassment." The end result was deeper congressional distrust of the executive power, an attitude that persisted throughout the 1970s.

The Representation of Special Interests and the Deliberative Process. According to some classic theories, deliberation should be carried out by wise persons impartially pondering the *common good,* that is, the collection of objective interests or expectable rewards, direct and indirect, that all participants have in common. No selfish thoughts or special interests are supposed to distract them. In practice, however, few politicians are that wise, or unselfish, or free from links to special interests. Indeed, if they were any or all of these, they would not be representative of most of the people whom they are supposed to represent.

In the United States most people believe in representative government and also in government by deliberation. They rarely notice the tension between these two concepts. Calling legislators the *representatives* of their constituents may be interpreted in four different ways. First, the representative may be a true *sample* of the voters electing that representative in his or her opinions, personality, and circumstances. Without any special instructions from the voters, and with neither more nor less knowledge than they have, the legislator may represent perfectly his or her constituents' passions, prejudices, and experiences. The ancient Athenians sometimes chose representatives of this kind by casting lots among the voters, and even today some old-line American politicians, representing relatively homogeneous constituencies, try to look and sound like perfect samples of the folks back home.

Second, a representative may simply be a *messen-*

ger or deputy carrying out the instructions of his or her constituents. The legislator will then vote exactly as he or she has been instructed; the legislator's own knowledge or judgment on the matter will be irrelevant. In the 1820s the former president, John Quincy Adams, indignantly refused to serve in the House of Representatives as this kind of messenger for his constituents, who elected him just the same. Third, a representative may serve his or her constituents much as a doctor or a lawyer serves patients or clients. He or she may act as a *trustee* for the voters' best interests, but use his or her own superior knowledge and experience to judge what the voters' true interests are and how they should be served. Edmund Burke insisted on this role in his famous letter to his constituents in Bristol: "Your representative owes you, not his industry only, but his judgment; and he betrays you, instead of serves you, if he sacrifices it to your opinion." Burke, too, was an elected representative. Finally, if a constituency includes a wide variety of groups and interests, the representative's role may be that of a *broker*. Ever mindful of the need to be re-elected, he or she will then arrange coalitions and compromises among the voters, carry out whatever consensus emerges, and keep a shrewd eye on his or her most influential and powerful supporters.

A real representative must be a mixture of all four of these roles. Unlike a doctor or lawyer, a representative has much greater power to bind by his or her decisions those whom the representative represents. The constituents cannot easily or quickly recall him or her or change the laws that representatives have passed. The voters will feel safer, therefore, if their elected representative's habits and interests are similar to their own—or at least seem to be so—and if their elected legislator is willing to carry out their will whenever they express it clearly and explicitly. The voters will be pleased, however, if their legislator can help them to reach a higher degree of consensus and can use his or her superior competence to serve their interests and to ensure that their will prevails.

But only one of these four views of the role of a representative—that of a trustee or professional counselor—is compatible with the idea of government by deliberation. The other three concepts of a representative—as a sample, messenger, or broker—are not. The actual process of representative government, therefore, and particularly of legislation, resembles a bubbling stew of occasional calm deliberation and frequent struggles among interests.

In a viable democratic state, the many special interests of different groups will overlap to such a degree that the notion of a common good will have real meaning for all or most of them. Conversely, groups whose diverging interests are so numerous that they dwarf the few interests they have in common cannot be kept together in a well-functioning democracy. This is one of the reasons that the United States was pulled apart in the decades before the Civil War. The divergent interests of slavery versus free labor, free trade versus protection, cotton and tobacco growing versus industry, and debtor versus creditor, and the competition between rival transcontinental railroad projects—all these causes for quarrels outgrew the social and political bonds between the North and South, but left intact the unity of each section. Both presidents between 1852 and 1860 were weak because there was no strong coalition to support them.

Similarly, the French in the late 1930s became badly divided between the leftist coalition led by Léon Blum and the rightist groups who later united behind Pierre Laval and Marshal Pétain. Many conservatives were quoted as saying: "Rather Hitler than Blum." When in 1939 the left coalition split again, France was ready to fall before the first Nazi armored column that entered the country in the following year.

These instances are not only matters of history. They could happen again in any country, including the United States. The American people could become deeply divided between conservatives and radicals, blacks and whites, affluent suburbanites and impoverished slum dwellers, militarists and pacifists, Protestants and Catholics, old-stock Americans and those of more recent immigrant descent, the hip and the straight, the young and the old. None of these cleavages coincides exactly with any other. Between them, they could split and cross-divide the American people so thoroughly that no common political will could be formed. In that event, no coalition strong enough to bring about reforms could be organized, and nothing could be done to maintain the paralyzed political system.

To ensure a happy political outcome, what is needed is not only the skill of political leaders, but also a genuine community of interests. When interests overlap sufficiently, their pursuit is compatible with true deliberation and compromise in the framework of representative government. In such cases the decisions arrived at are likely to have the authority of law.

One Product of Deliberation: Law. A *law* is a general rule deciding not a single case, but a whole class of cases. Under the English and American tradition a vote of a legislature to penalize a specifically named individual—a *bill of attainder*—cannot be a law. In the United States it is forbidden by the Constitution (Article I, Section 9, Paragraph 3). The main tasks of law are three: to make the operations of government predictable, technically consistent with each other, and morally legitimate—that is, consistent with the main value patterns of the community.

Not every general rule, therefore, is a law. Even though it is general, it may not be enforced by the government or, more importantly, complied with by the people or even by the government's own officials. In any of these cases the effects of the government's operations cannot be reliably predicted. The rule then will be obeyed sometimes, and sometimes not; and no one will know which to expect. Thus the Volstead Act of 1920, prohibiting the sale of alcoholic beverages, was disobeyed by a large part of the American people and by many government officials, while other officials tried unsuccessfully to enforce it. The legal restrictions imposed on those who use electronic surveillance devices such as wiretaps also have been disregarded frequently by law enforcement officials, including those within the federal government, sometimes with the approval of Cabinet officers and even of the White House. On the other hand, most of the laws in the world's highly developed countries are complied with and enforced to a remarkably high degree. In the 1950s and 1960s, the United States collected more than half of its revenue by means of a federal income tax on corporations and individuals, for which only one individual tax return out of twenty was checked each year. (Since then, as computers have been used more and more extensively in tax collection, the proportion of returns that are checked has increased.)

Effective laws limit the actions of the government itself, so that people can know what the government will and will not do. In contrast to governments dependent on the whims of absolute princes or of modern dictators, constitutional governments are meant to be "governments of laws, not of men."

A whole array of political machinery has been created to ensure predictable and lawful rule. The role of the lawmaker in most countries has been made a specialized full-time job. Legislators are subject to election and re-election, so that they must win and retain the confidence of the voters of their constituency. In most advanced countries, national legislators are adequately paid in order to keep legislative office from being a monopoly for those rich enough to afford it or for those subsidized by special economic interests.

The laws that legislators make must pass through a repeated process of deliberation. In the United States, Britain, France, the German Federal Republic, and even the Soviet Union, the national legislatures are divided into two chambers, most of the proposed legislation being scrutinized by each. (In the Soviet Union most of the scrutinizing occurs within the top echelons of the Communist Party.) In addition, in most countries, proposed laws are first submitted as drafts, then discussed and amended in committees of each legislative chamber, then debated, possibly amended, and finally voted on by each full legislative body. In many countries this final vote has to be repeated. In the British House of Commons and the German Bundestag, bills are required to pass three separate readings; and in the United States House of Representatives, money bills must pass once as an *authorization* for the government to spend the money and a second time as an *appropriation,* allocating to the government the actual money to be spent—often in a less generous amount. Before final passage, the different versions of a bill passed by the two chambers have to be reconciled; in the United States this is done by *joint conference committees* of the Senate and House of Representatives. Finally, in many countries the bill still must receive the signature of the chief executive, or else it must be passed once again over the latter's veto by a larger legislative majority. Only then is the bill ready for promulgation to the public, usually in print—which is the last step in the making of a law.

Separation of Powers. The elaborate machinery of the law-making process is meant to ensure that laws will be considered and formulated carefully and that the bulk of the population—as well as the major interest groups in the country—will recognize the laws passed as legitimate. Inevitably, this process consumes a great deal of time, except in war or other rare emergencies, when legislatures may quickly pass laws delegating sweeping powers to the executive. In constitutional governments of the Western type, however, such delegation of emergency powers is exceptional.

The separation of the deliberative process, the legislative and the judicial, from the execution of laws has remained the basic rule. This is the famous *separation of powers:* the principle according to which the legislative, judiciary, and executive powers are to be separate and independent from one another in order to provide a system of *checks and balances* that limits the powers of the government and safeguards the rights of individuals. Under this arrangement the legislative power deliberates and decides about making general laws; the judicial power—that is, the courts—deliberates and decides about applying these general laws to particular cases; and the executive power carries out the decisions of the two other branches.

This doctrine is well designed to protect individuals from the police, civilians from the military, and property owners from expropriation and the tax collector. It encourages governments to wait rather than to act and to do less rather than more. It was formulated in the eighteenth century by Montesquieu and other theorists of the Enlightenment who sought to protect the rights of relatively rich or self-sufficient individuals against absolutist rule, at the risk of making government slower and sometimes weaker. Poorer people who urgently needed the help of government often preferred quick public action at some risk to their liberties—and many still do so. The best balance between liberty and speed is thus a matter of group interest as well as of political design.

If the separation of powers is sometimes attacked from the left by partisans of more rapid social change, it is also attacked on other occasions from the right by social and political conservatives. In the United States from the mid-1950s to the early 1970s the courts often were more liberal, and more mindful of the claims of minorities and the rights of defendants, than were the contemporary local or national majorities of voters. In this context, efforts sometimes were made to pass federal laws to limit the jurisdiction of the courts, such as a federal bill proposed in 1972, but killed in the Senate by a filibuster supported by northern Democrats and liberal Republicans. If this bill had become law, it would have banned the busing of schoolchildren for the purpose of improving the racial balance in the schools. A companion bill attempted to limit the courts in reviewing legislation and practice in this matter, but the bill died in committee in both houses. (For a brief history of the increasing extent of school busing over the past four decades, see Table 8.1.) Similarly, a 1972 California referendum, passed by a majority of votes cast, attempted to override the limitations on the death penalty that had been introduced by recent court decisions and also attempted to bar the courts from reviewing this law itself and its application to cases. If accepted as law, the results of this referendum and of similar measures passed by legislative or popular majorities would go far to destroy the separation of legislative and judicial powers embodied in nearly two centuries of American constitutional practice.

If these trends should prevail and the separation of powers be drastically weakened, both the courts and the rights of individuals would become more thoroughly subordinated to the popular sentiment and all its changes over place and time. If courts could be legally barred from reviewing legislation, the constitutional protection of property rights, of human rights, and of the due process of law itself would be in large part destroyed.

Another attack on the constitutional separation of powers has come from the executive. President Nixon *impounded* a considerable number of substantial appropriations passed by Congress in the form of law. That is, he refused to spend them, on the grounds that in his judgment these particular appropriations—for health, education, and the like—were less important than the need to reduce public spending and to reduce inflation, while other appropriations, such as those for air force activities in Southeast Asia, continued to be spent in full. Earlier presidents had impounded smaller amounts on less frequent occasions, mainly on the grounds that some particular need or opportunity for this or that expenditure had in fact disappeared. What seemed new in Nixon's practice was the large scale of the *impounding power,* its deliberate use as an instrument of policy to override the policies voted by Congress, and its repeated use in clear defiance of the will of the congressional majority that had passed the original law. The matter soon came into the courts. In the first round the federal courts found in most cases in favor of Congress and against the president; and in 1974 a bill passed by Congress severely restricted presidential ability to impound funds. Finally, in February 1975 the Supreme Court ruled that President Nixon had exceeded his authority in refusing to spend funds that had been appropriated by Congress to curb water pollution. The congressional "power of the purse" survived.

A parallel doctrine was put before a congressional committee by President Nixon's Secretary of Defense, Elliot Richardson. If Congress should cut off the funds for continued United States bombing in Cambodia, Richardson said, then he would take the money from other items in the budget in order to continue the operation. In the end, Congress passed a law positively forbidding as of August 15, 1973, the use of any United States funds for military, naval, or air operations in, off, or over Cambodia; and it was then announced that United States bombing of Cambodia had ceased as of that day. The specific issue had been resolved in compromise; Congress had voted the president permission to bomb Cambodia for six weeks beyond the July 1 cut-off date that its members had originally envisaged. But the question of principle, raised by Secretary Richardson, remained unresolved: how far may a president go in diverting public funds from the specific appropriations for which Congress has voted them and in spending them instead on purposes that Congress has refused to back—perhaps even explicitly so—but that the president prefers?

If President Nixon's initiatives in these matters had succeeded together with his stated view that the president may override ordinary laws in the light of his personal view of "national security," this would have drastically enhanced the powers of the president and greatly reduced those of Congress. The United States then would have come closer to being governed by a single man than it had ever been in its history as an independent nation. In 1974 and the years that followed,

TABLE 8.1 *A Thumbnail History of Busing in the United States*

President	Years	Total school enrollment (millions)	Students transported at public expense (millions)	% of total enrollment	Average % shift per year*
Hoover	1929–30	25.7	1.9	7.4	—
Roosevelt	1933–34	26.4	2.8	10.6	0.8
	1943–44	23.3	4.5	19.4	0.9
Truman	1945–46	23.3	5.1	21.7	1.2
	1951–52	26.6	7.7	29.0	1.2
Eisenhower	1953–54	26.6	8.4	32.8	1.9
	1959–60	32.5	12.2	37.6	0.8
Kennedy	1961–62	34.7	13.2	38.1	0.3
Johnson	1965–66	39.2	15.6	39.7	0.4
	1967–68	40.8	17.1	42.1	1.2
Nixon	1969–70	41.9	18.2	43.4	0.7
	1971–72	42.3	19.5	46.1	5.4
Nixon/Ford	1973–74	41.4	21.3	51.5	10.8
Ford	1975–76	41.3	22.8	55.1	7.2

* The shift toward busing has been continuous over a long time, proceeding at a moderate rate from year to year under both Republican and Democratic administrations. Political resistance to busing seems to have arisen mainly where it carried children across boundaries of both social class and race, but until the 1970s such protests do not seem to have stopped the gradual spread of busing in general.

Source: *Congressional Quarterly*, vol. 30, no. 31 (July 19, 1972), 1883; Department of Health, Education and Welfare, Office of Education, National Center for Education Statistics, December 20, 1978.

Congress and the American people clearly rejected that prospect.

Despite these recent trends, separation of powers has been formulated most thoroughly in the Constitution of the United States, as well as respected in practice. It has been used less in Britain, where the prime minister is merely the leader of the House of Commons, dependent on its confidence, and where the Cabinet is in effect a committee of the House. Each branch of the American government is limited in its lawful powers. In Britain, by contrast, as legal scholar John Austin saw it, there was not a thing between heaven and earth that Parliament could not do. In fact, however, Britain's *unwritten constitution*—that is, the political habits and traditions of the British people—limits the powers of governments and parliamentary majorities more effectively than appears on the surface. In the German Federal Republic there is a greater separation of the three powers of government than in Britain, but less than in the United States. And the Fifth Republic of France concentrates a large proportion of power in the hands of the president as chief executive.

The Merging of Powers: The Soviet System. Under the Soviet system of government the principle of separation of powers has been explicitly rejected. According to Lenin, the Soviet state was to be the instrument of a social revolution, directed by a highly disciplined party of professional revolutionaries who could foresee in part the course of future history. This revolution was to get its power from the backing of Russia's industrial working class and the much larger mass of Russia's poor and "middling" peasants. In Marxist theory the result of this coalition of workers and peasants was to be a "dictatorship of the proletariat," that is, "the dictatorship of the vast majority in the interest of the vast majority." In practice, it meant the predominance of the workers over the peasants and, very soon, the predominance of the Communist Party, many of whose leaders were intellectuals, over the working class. Within a decade after the Communists' seizure of power in Russia in 1917, the Soviet regime had become in effect the dictatorship of a small group of party leaders and officials over the bulk of the Communist Party membership and the Soviet people. The circle of persons exercising decisive power thus had become much smaller than Marx and even Lenin had envisaged. But the manner in which power was wielded was close to Lenin's conception in at least one respect. "Dictatorship," he had written, "is a rule based directly on force and unrestricted by any law."

In setting up the government of the Soviet Union, Lenin adopted the institution of councils, or *soviets,* of deputies of workers, peasants, and the local population. Such soviets had sprung up spontaneously in the unsuccessful revolution of 1905, and they had reappeared in greater strength in the revolutionary turmoil of 1917. Some soviets were formed for large factories or other economic enterprises; other soviets were formed for city blocks or neighborhoods and for villages and rural districts. Deputies for each soviet were often elected publicly in meetings of workers in factories or in meetings of their neighbors in local units. These local soviets in turn elected higher councils of deputies for larger cities and regions. This ladder of indirect elections eventually culminated in an all-Union Soviet, which was formally the highest organ of the Soviet government. The whole procedure lent itself very well to the leadership and eventual domination by the Communist Party. The hierarchy of councils served as a multistage amplifier—or, as the Communists called it, a "transmission belt"—by which a few tens of thousands, and later hundreds of thousands, of Communists could govern a country that in 1917 numbered 150 million people.

This view of government excluded a separation of powers. Each soviet not only was to deliberate about what was to be done within its area of control, but also was to carry out whatever acts its members agreed on. It was to be both a legislative and an executive body. The courts, of course, likewise were to be an instrument of soviet power with no independence for judges. "All powers to the soviets!" ran the 1917 revolutionary slogan. When power shifted from the soviets to the Communist Party, legislative and executive tasks remained merged.

In the half-century that followed, the Soviet Union was transformed into a modern industrial country, exhibiting increasing specialization of political, administrative, and judicial roles and growing pressures toward some separation of its governmental powers. Since the mid-1950s the demands for greater respect for judicial independence and "socialist legality" have been increasing. The limits and prospects of these trends will be discussed in Chapter 11, but they suggest in any case that some degree of separation of powers may not result from a mere middle-class prejudice, but may fit some of the needs of any highly advanced society.

Cabinet Solidarity and Democratic Centralism. To some extent, however, there are in most political systems some bodies that both deliberate and execute. The British Cabinet deliberates about policy and then must carry it out. Hence, its members are free to oppose a policy before it has been decided on and to advocate another course of action. But once the decision has been made, all Cabinet members are obliged to support it in public, even if they had opposed it earlier. If any member should be unwilling to do this, that member would be expected normally to leave the Cabinet. The National Security Council in the United States shares a similar practice.

The Communist Party in the Soviet Union, as well as Communist parties in other countries, extend this obligation to all members. Members may debate freely a proposed policy, at least in theory, before a decision has been made. After the decision, however, they must support the official policy that has been set, even if it runs counter to their own judgment. In Communist parlance, this practice is called *democratic centralism.* British writers speak of *Cabinet solidarity.* To the more limited practices in the United States, people apply such looser terms as "party regularity" or "loyalty" to the administration and the president.

In all cases the practice derives from the union of deliberation and execution in the same body. (Members of a legislature—or of the electorate—usually are free to continue criticizing a majority decision and to agitate for its reversal.) It clearly makes it easier to get things done, but it exacts a price. Those who opposed the decision now must support it, perhaps against their own convictions; and since they may no longer crticize it, a mistaken decision is less likely to be corrected or reversed.

If problems are very urgent, and weakness is a greater danger than error, then Cabinet solidarity or democratic centralism may seem preferable. If problems are less urgent, if resources of wealth and power are abundant, and if the risks of error are great and its likely consequences serious, then separation of powers and its continuing opportunities for debate and reconsideration might seem preferable. In the short run, therefore, American institutions may not fit the needs of poor countries, which face as their most critical task an increase in the actual power of the government to deal with urgent social and economic problems. But in the long run, increasing wealth as well as the increasing costs of large errors in a highly politicized and technological society may make the separation of powers desirable for a larger number of countries.

Decision Making by the Judiciary. Another important aspect of the concept of separation of powers relates to the deliberations and decisions carried on by the judiciary in most countries. The courts have developed an elaborate procedural law or custom about how to arrive at decisions. In most countries the rule of secrecy in the deliberations of the judiciary, after hearing arguments in open court, has always been observed. If Americans were to insist that what the Supreme Court justices say to each other be made public—or what jurors say to each other in the jury room—the outcry from the legal fraternity would be loud and clear. Most lawyers and judges would argue that it would not be possible to arrive at good decisions in this way. Hence, how judges or juries arrive at their decisions is much less well known than how presidents or legislative bodies arrive at theirs.

People who talk about deliberating on decisions and policy must not limit themselves to the executive and legislative branches, but should bear in mind that in free societies the judiciary is also involved in the deliberative act. The deliberative process of judges to some extent is organized within the open court. The so-called *adversary procedure,* by which lawyers present their cases, is an organization of deliberation. Each lawyer cites the cases and data that support his or her position. Then the court (or the judge) withdraws into private chambers and tries to sort out the arguments for the purpose of eventually arriving at its decision. This is the process that Justice Benjamin Cardozo emphasized in his book, *The Judicial Process,* which undertook to analyze how judges arrive at their decisions.

In the United States the substance of judicial decisions can be far-reaching, indeed. Back in

1803, the case of *Marbury* v. *Madison* established the right of the Supreme Court to review the actions of Congress and the executive branch. In 1810 the case of *Fletcher* v. *Peck* extended *judicial review* to the acts of legislatures, and in 1819 the *Dartmouth College* case put the charters of private corporations anywhere in the country under federal protection by declaring them to be a kind of contract and thus including them under the protection of the Constitution. In time this decision had far-reaching effects on the development of business corporations and private universities. Since that time, the United States judiciary has always been a machine for the production of "judge-made law" to supplement and correct or balance the laws made by the Congress and the state legislatures and by the rule-making power of administrative agencies.

Judicial review offers an additional opportunity for redress to citizens whose needs and rights as individuals or members of minority groups have found no adequate response in the legislative process. In *Plessy* v. *Ferguson* in 1897, the Supreme Court established the "separate but equal" doctrine, which permitted railroad companies to segregate black passengers in separate, but supposedly equal, accommodations; later this doctrine was extended to education and stated that separate public schools for black children were legal if they were equal—in theory at least—to schools for white children in the equipment, teaching staffs, and educational opportunities they offered. More than half a century later, in the 1954 *Brown* v. *Board of Education of Topeka* decision, the Supreme Court found that there was in fact no possible equality for black children in segregated schools. *Segregation by race,* the Court held, in itself was doing an injury to children; and it had to be ended in all public schools "with all deliberate speed." Fifteen years later, in 1969, perhaps 90 percent or more of black children in the five states of the Deep South of the United States were still attending segregated schools, as compared with the virtually 100 percent in 1954 when the Court first issued its decision. In October 1969 the Supreme Court under a new chief justice, Warren E. Burger, broke with the doctrine of "deliberate speed." Dual school systems—that is, segregated ones—were to be terminated "at once" in public education everywhere in the United States. Local authorities were to put into operation "immediately" unitary public school systems "within which no person is to be effectively excluded from any school because of race or color." Enforcement of this order was slow and uneven. In several parts of the country—not just in the South—there was some flight of white families to racially segregated private schools for their children, and in 1978 the federal government began to question the right of such schools to tax exemption. The ending of race discrimination in education will continue to be a critical test of American government in the 1980s.

Though the direct impact of the Court on actual practice was slow and limited, its impact on the climate of American thought and on the long-term trends of politics was profound. In 1957, 86 percent of southern white voters in a poll said that school integration would never come. Six years later, only 46 percent still clung to this thought. In nationwide polls, 67 percent of voters in 1962 said they could not accept a black as president of the United States. Seven years later, only 34 percent still held this view. A more recent survey by the Louis Harris organization, published in February 1979, reported a further decline of racist attitudes.

At the same time, however, some respected spokespeople for blacks and other minorities denied the validity of these findings. Of course, they said, people would deny racist feelings when asked, but at home and after a drink they might still reveal them. Perhaps both sides are right. In public discussion and, more importantly, in many matters of hiring and promoting, racism has ceased to be respectable, even though much of it lives on "in the woodwork." But this still means change. While in the 1970s many members of minorities have moved "out of the closet," many racists have moved in.

All this has changed much of politics. A series of Supreme Court decisions, supported by the mass media, by important political groups, by the efforts of black Americans themselves, and by the spontaneous responses of millions of young people, have transformed overt race discrimination from a majority prejudice into a minority one. The main direction of American thought seems to have been set on a new course of speed and urgency; and the new setting seems irreversible.

The politics of the 1970s revealed once again the complex relationship between decision making by the judiciary and assimilating those decisions into public thought. A majority of white American voters, it appeared, were willing to accept their black compatriots in a wide range of new roles, as elected or appointed officeholders, as fellow guests in hotels and restaurants, as fellow employees at work, as schoolmates for their children, and, increasingly, as neighbors on their streets—provided, however, that such black people should differ from them only in color, and not at all significantly in income, lifestyle or culture, and status or social class. The well-to-do do not welcome in their neighborhoods the arrival of large numbers of poor people of any color. The highly educated have misgivings about sending their children to schools dominated by large numbers of students from families in which books are rarely used, correct speech is considered snobbish or servile, and education is held in low regard. Those who like quiet, neatness, and self-discipline object to neighbors whose lifestyle seems to be noisier, more relaxed, and more tolerant of litter. Many people work hard and willingly at regular full-time jobs that, after a considerable time, will reward them in terms of pay and promotion; they resent being looked on as "square" or "uptight" by people who appear to stick rarely to any regular job or career or who despise unskilled manual work as menial, but somehow rarely acquire any craft skill or formal education—be it for lack of opportunity to learn or for lack of motivation or ability to put in the years of sustained effort that such training requires. Informal social pressures and seemingly nonpolitical *zoning laws*—such as permitting only expensive one-family houses on large lots—in many suburbs have the effect of keeping people with such different lifestyles apart. The practice of *redlining*—the refusal of mortgage loans and insurance contracts by financial institutions in racially mixed neighborhoods—sometimes has the same effect.

All these conflicts would exist regardless of color; all have been observed at many times and places in all-white (or all-black) communities. They become aggravated, however, when nature has made the sides to such a conflict highly and permanently visible. And they become still more serious if new public policies bring these different, mutually distrustful and potentially hostile racial groups into close and frequent contact in neighborhoods and schools.

Such situations can produce social dynamite. What was remarkable of the late 1960s and early 1970s was not that there were serious social and racial conflicts in many localities, South and North, but that there were so relatively few of them. Rather, white lower-middle-class and working-class protest had, by 1968, found some expression in the movement headed by the former governor of Alabama, George Wallace, who in that year polled about 13 percent of the presidential vote. In 1972, with Governor Wallace's being confined to a wheelchair by a would-be assassin's bullet and not running for the presidency, his followers appear to have voted almost solidly for President Nixon, whose *"southern strategy"* and publicly stated opposition to busing had been widely interpreted as a bid for just these votes. The president's 1972 majority of 61 percent of votes cast exceeded by 4 percentage points the 57 percent formed by combining the votes cast for Nixon and Wallace in 1968. This extra gain by Nixon then could be ascribed to the personalities of the candidates, the incidents of the campaign, Nixon's advantage of being the incumbent, and the more popular aspects of his recent policies, including the withdrawal of United States troops from Vietnam, the improvement of relations with China and the

Soviet Union, and the dramatic announcement in October 1972 that peace was "at hand" in Vietnam. But the hope of some Republicans that 1972 would prove to have been a "critical election in which a combination of incidents and realignments would produce a long-lasting new majority in American politics" turned out to be an illusion.[3] In 1976, President Carter was elected by a combination of southern voters, blacks, liberals, labor, organization Democrats, and former Wallace voters. Against a candidate from Georgia, no Republican southern strategy could work.

The moods and events of 1972 were transitory, as were those of 1964 when the far-right Republican candidate, Senator Barry Goldwater, was defeated by a similar landslide. The appointments of several conservative Supreme Court justices by President Nixon during his second term had somewhat longer lasting, but limited, effects. All these twists and turns seemed likely to prove eddies in the stream of American politics, not its main current. Such eddies are real. They can drown some people and policies, but in the end the stream will dwarf them. Americans will come to terms with their races, their cities, their divergent groups of voters, and their courts, if they want to keep theirs a free country. In time, they will insist on preserving freedom, and their Constitution with its separation of powers may prove a serviceable instrument to help them reach their goal.

FEDERALISM: A POLITICAL INVENTION

Unitary versus Confederal Governments. Every government has two major tasks that may be in competition with each other. The first of these is to concentrate most of the forces and resources of its population on a single common goal or the pursuit of several such goals. *Common goals* may be the achievement of independence, the victory in war, the purchase of a large territory, the rapid industrialization of the country, the removal of some major external or internal threat to the integrity of the system of some valued institution, or, on the contrary, the accomplishment of some desired major political, social, educational, or economic change. In all such cases the government has to mobilize, unify, and apply the power of the people. It must organize them so that they can form a common will that they are collectively capable of carrying out.

An equally important task of every government is to respond to the needs of its population. The more diverse the population is, the more different will be the needs and wishes of various groups and regions. The more powerful we wish a government to be in order to do the things on which most people agree, that is, in order to achieve common goals, the more unified and centralized the government should be and the larger the population and geographic area under its direct control. Such a centralized government is known as a *unitary* form of government. But the more we want the government to respond quickly and adequately to the needs of many different groups and localities, the more decentralized and localized it has to be; the more it must be a *confederal* form of government. The Swiss Confederation, a government of many diverse ethnic and political elements, was almost totally decentralized for over five hundred years. Each canton, or self-governing region, was a small sovereign state, well suited to respond to the needs of its inhabitants or, at least, to the needs of the most influential among them. In contrast, although respected for their success in unifying power, the great centralized monarchies—from ancient Rome to eighteenth-century Britain, France, Russia, and Prussia—were deficient in the ability to respond to diverse popular needs.

When the American colonies declared their independence, their leaders were familiar with both types of government, unitary and confederal.

[3]See Kevin Phillips, *The Emerging Republican Majority* (Garden City, N.Y.: Doubleday Anchor, 1970), and the analysis of voting data in Jack Rosenthal, "Kennedy is Found Popular in '76," *New York Times,* November 12, 1972, p. 40.

They knew the large monarchies of their time; they knew the small republics such as Venice; they knew the confederation of the Swiss. But they needed a government that would combine the strength of both types of government, and in due course they invented it. They started out in 1776 with an alliance; seven years later they turned it into a confederation, being somewhat like that of the Swiss, but having stronger provisions for common interests and actions; and still later, in 1787, they started drafting a federal constitution. The Constitution was ratified in 1791 and to this day has remained in essence the basic United States charter of government.

Federal Unions versus Confederacies. A *federal union* of states differs from a *confederacy* in four main respects. First, a federal government is relatively strong in regard to organization, personnel, budget, and jurisdiction. Ordinarily, it is stronger in all these respects than the government of any of its constituent states. In a confederacy the common institutions are weak or nearly nonexistent in some or all of these respects. They are much weaker than the corresponding institutions of the major states that make up the confederacy.

Second, whereas federal governments act directly on individuals in all matters within the scope of the national government, the government of a confederacy ordinarily deals with individuals only indirectly, through the state governments and their administrations. A federal government can collect taxes, raise armies, and enforce its own decisions, but a confederacy depends for all these matters on what the states will do for it or what resources the states will give it.

Third, states often may secede from a confederacy, if their own governments or voters so desire, whereas such secession is not permitted in a federal union. In the Soviet Union the major republics have in theory the right to secede. The actual structure and distribution of power, however, which resembles that of a federation or even of a unitary state, has made secession impractical, and few, if any, Soviet citizens appear to mind.

Finally, within the sphere of federal jurisdiction the laws of a federal union usually prevail over those of the states, and the state governments are expected to obey them and carry them out. In a confederacy, however, a law or decision of the confederal authorities becomes valid in a state only if the state government endorses it or at least does not exercise its right to veto its application within the state. (The latter doctrine is known as *nullification,* since it holds that each state can "nullify" at will within its own territory any federal law of which it disapproves. This doctrine was advocated mainly between 1798 and 1830 by some southern leaders in the United States and was finally buried by the outcome of the Civil War.)

All four differences make it likely that, among countries comparable in size and in military and economic power, a confederacy will be much weaker than a federation. In the American Civil War, some southern states withheld at critical moments needed troops, weapons, and supplies from the Confederate Army. The leaders of these states believed so thoroughly in *states' rights* that they were more concerned with upholding this doctrine than with preventing the defeat of their own confederacy and the victory of the North.

If a country is too large and diverse to accept a unitary government, and if it needs more effective power and performance than a confederacy can produce, then federal union seems to be the most effective form of government so far discovered. If people in the various states are not ready politically, socially, culturally, or economically to accept a federal union, then a confederation may be the best that can be organized and made to work for the time being, and it may prepare the way for federation at a later stage.

The Dual Nature of Federalist Government. *Federalism* consists in putting every individual under two governments at one and the same time. As far as the individual is concerned, these governments coincide in domain, but differ in scope. Each of them has a claim to the individual's obedience in some respects, but not in others. One of these governments, the national or *federal,* governs the entire country. The other—the *state* in the United States and India, the *province* in Canada, the *union republic* in the Soviet Union, the *canton* in Switzerland, and the *Land* (plural *Länder*) in the German Federal Republic—usually governs only a relatively small part of the country. Each of the two most populous states in the United States, California and New York, has less than 10 percent of the total population. Together, however, the several states of the Union include most of the country's population and only a small part lives in federal districts or territories.

Some of these other small political units may include a larger part of their country's national population than do their counterparts in the United States. The provinces of Quebec and Ontario each include more than one-quarter of the Canadian population; the *Land* of North Rhine-Westphalia includes nearly one-third of the population of West Germany; and the Russian Soviet Federal Socialist Republic (RSFSR)—itself a federation—includes more than one-half the population of the Soviet Union.

Throughout the national territory the scope of the federal or national government includes jurisdiction in foreign affairs and other matters assigned to it by the country's constitution or through subsequent usage. In the United States these matters include national defense, interstate commerce and transport, and protection of contracts; the states have primary jurisdiction over civil and criminal law, public order and the police power, education, and—a peculiarity of the United States—the conditions for voting in both state and federal elections.

In some areas, federal and state jurisdictions overlap. In the United States, both levy taxes, but the state governments are restrained by the practical fact that if their taxes become too heavy the richer taxpayers and business firms may move into another state. This has been one of the reasons for the migration of the textile industry from New England to the South. It explains why many New York business executives prefer to live in Connecticut or New Jersey and why some Californians establish legal residence in Nevada. It also explains why some national corporations maintain headquarters in Delaware. In contrast to state taxes, federal taxes cannot be easily avoided in this manner; any large sums needed for public purposes must be raised by the federal government on a nationwide scale. When taxpayer organizations cry "states' rights," they are in reality trying to keep the federal government from effectively collecting large amounts of tax money and are thus opposing the domestic programs for which these funds are required.

Sometimes economic interests may work in the opposite direction. Most expenditures at the municipal and state levels may have become accepted as necessary and unavoidable. No one now seriously proposes to abandon traffic control, abolish street lighting, close the public schools and hospitals,[4] and leave the old, the ill, and the mothers and children on welfare unprovided for. Nor do any reputable private corporations bid to do these jobs just as well and more cheaply. They must be done or paid for by governments, because there is no one else to do them; and they should be controlled locally because people and conditions differ from place to place in a country as large and varied as the United States. As the amount and kind of public services needed vary among states and localities, so does their cost, and it often does so in a manner that differs greatly from the variations in their financial resources.

If a city is too poor to educate its children properly, to control its criminals, to treat its sick, to provide welfare, or to control the smoke and chemical wastes from its factories, the resulting ill effects will not stay within its boundaries. Its grime

[4]There are many excellent private hospitals, but most of them depend on direct or indirect government subsidies—such as tax-free municipal services—for their continued existence.

and crime will invade neighboring communities. Its neglected children, inadequately educated and almost unemployable youngsters, and juvenile delinquents may eventually end up anywhere in the country. At the same time, its business corporations, middle-class residents, and richer citizens and taxpayers may not wish to pack up and go as local taxes rise. They may have too large fixed investments in their businesses and homes. Moving and starting over elsewhere might cost too much and so might paying for the new roads, sewer systems, schools, and other facilities of the additional infrastructure that would be needed at their new location.

It seems more reasonable to stay where one is and face the problems instead of trying to run away from them. And it may be preferable to draw on the taxing powers of the federal government to collect from the entire country the sums necessary to deal properly with the common tasks of traffic control, education, health and welfare services, wherever they may be needed.

Using the national power of effective tax collection for local spending is the basic idea of *revenue sharing* between the national government and state and local authorities. Long practiced by such European states as Britain and West Germany, this device was introduced during the 1970s in order to bring at least partial relief to the hard-pressed states and cities in the United States. The federal government, this plan envisaged, would use its centralized power to collect taxes everywhere, mainly but not exclusively through its income tax, more or less graduated according to each taxpayer's capacity to pay. Some part of these revenues, in the amount of several billions of dollars, then would be transferred to the state and local governments, with no strings attached—except, since 1976, that these funds be spent free of any race discrimination—in order to permit them to spend these amounts in accordance with local knowledge and local needs. It was to be understood, however, that these federal funds were meant to help these governments perform their tasks while reducing or reversing the pressure for ever higher state and local taxes. Home owners in particular—over 54 percent of the American people—were to be relieved by this federal action from the ever-mounting burden of property taxes that had gravely hurt many of them during recent years. This last objective was not achieved, and the voters' *tax revolt* in 1978 indicated the continuing seriousness of the problem. Even so, it appears that revenue sharing is on the way to becoming a new and important aspect of federalism in the United States.

The Assignment of Residual Powers. No constitution and no tradition can provide for every specific situation. Which government, federal or state, has the *residual powers*—that is, the responsibility and legal power for dealing with those tasks that have not been assigned to either?

Canada and India, following British tradition, have reserved such residual powers to the national government. In the Soviet Union, of course, the powers of the national government are overwhelming. For this reason, some writers doubt that these governments should be called "federal" in the strictest sense, since the balance between the nation and the smaller political units seems to be heavily weighted in the national government's favor.

In the United States the ratifiers of the *Tenth Amendment* of the Constitution (Article X of the Bill of Rights) tried to reserve these powers explicitly to the states: "The powers not delegated to the United States by the Constitution, nor prohibited by it to the states, are reserved to the states respectively, or to the people." In the Preamble to the Constitution, however, the framers had listed among the purposes for which the federal union and its government were being founded the promotion of the "general welfare" of the people of the United States. From the days of Alexander Hamilton to those of Franklin D. Roosevelt and the present, national leaders and federal courts have held that this *general welfare clause* in the Constitution empowers the federal government to deal with a wide variety of tasks of which the nation's founders never even dreamed. The constitutions of Switzerland and of West Germany in their own ways achieve a similar balance between the powers of the federal government and those of the states.

The Sovereign Equality of States and Nations. Another mark of federalism is the far-reaching degree of equality among the smaller political units composing a federal system. All the states, large and small, are legally equal. In some federal systems the states also have equal representation in one house of the national legislature, as in the United States Senate or, in somewhat different form, in the Soviet of Nationalities in the Soviet Union. Such equal representation of states implies, of course, an overrepresentation of the voters of the smallest states. As most Americans know and many city dwellers lament, the 406,000 people of Wyoming, as well as the 633,000 people of Nevada, have as many senators in the United States Senate as the nearly 20 million people of California. If all the senators from all the small states should vote together, less than one-fifth of the American people would command a majority of the Senate. Similar problems exist elsewhere. Switzerland follows the same principle of equal representation for large and small cantons, though some small units are defined as "half-cantons." The German Federal Republic compromises; it gives the larger *Länder* a somewhat larger representation in the federal council, but still overrepresents the smaller ones.

In genuine federal systems the national government cannot legally abolish any state or remove its officers or judges. Neither can any state or group of states abolish the federal government or secede from it. (This last point was disputed in the United States from 1781 to 1861, but was settled by the Civil War. In Switzerland it was also settled by civil war—a minor one in 1847.) A federal constitution can be amended only by the nation as a whole, acting through a substantial majority and by procedures that each constitution provides.

In emergencies a federal government may determine that some state government has become temporarily incapable of functioning and may take measures to appoint officers for the duration of the incapacity. It may also send federal marshals or troops into a state in order to enforce laws or court decisions, as the United States did in the 1950s in Little Rock, Arkansas, and Tuscaloosa, Alabama. In a genuinely federal system, however, all such actions are subject to review by independent courts. These safeguards contrast with the practice of some Latin American republics, which have federal "paper" constitutions, but in which the national government and army intervene freely in the affairs of the states.

The element of equality distinguishes the powers of states in a federal system from the important, but lesser, powers of local and city governments within the states. In day-to-day administration the governments of towns, cities, countries, villages, and districts form a third layer of government, which is by no means equal to the other layers. To a greater or lesser degree, these local units are the creatures of the states in the United States, the cantons in Switzerland, or the *Länder* in West Germany. In the United States a state can revoke or amend the charter of a city; acting through its legislature or a state constitutional convention, it can merge cities or counties or abolish them. In other federal systems, local governments are similarly subject to decisions by the states, and in unitary states they are ruled by the national government. Nowhere in modern countries do local governments enjoy to any significant degree sovereign equality with the other layers of government.

If the proof of a pudding is in the eating, the proof of federalism is in the administering and in

the spending of money. Although many taxes have to be collected nationally (for reasons discussed earlier), in any system of "living federalism," a large part of the money collected as taxes has to be spent in states and localities by governments closer and more responsive to local needs than the national government. National budgets and bureaucracies have grown spectacularly with the increase in the scope of government; state and local personnel and budgets have not declined, either. They have grown along with those of the national government, albeit sometimes more slowly. State and local governments are now spending a smaller slice of the political pie than formerly. In the United States between 1900 and 1960 their share declined from nearly 70 percent to only 40 percent, increasing slightly to 48 percent in 1975; the comparable Swiss figures show a decline from 75 percent in 1900 to 56 percent in 1975.[5] But the whole political pie is now much bigger. Gross national products have increased and so has the share of the public sector in them. State and local governments are therefore likely to play a large and vigorous role for many years to come in most of the world's existing federal systems. And such systems are quite likely to spread.

GETTING THINGS DONE: EXECUTIVE RESPONSIBILITY AND PARTY GOVERNMENT

In his memoirs Winston Churchill recalled a remark he made to Stalin and Roosevelt during the conference at Teheran. They had to remember, he told them, that they could go home and whatever they had agreed to at Teheran would stand, whereas if he brought back anything unacceptable to Parliament, he could be overthrown on the day of his return to Britain. What Churchill sought to indicate to Stalin and Roosevelt was that he was directly responsible to the majority in the House of Commons and therefore was not quite as free as they to yield on points that might be controversial. In a way this was true; and it does represent a conventional view of the difference between the British government, on the one hand, and the American and Soviet governments, on the other. But in another way, at least as far as Roosevelt was concerned, it was not quite accurate. Fundamentally, there are two kinds of political power, closely controlled and relatively uncontrolled, and there are two kinds of executives, those with wide powers of decision and those with only narrow powers.

Executive Discretion. The word "executive" suggests by its derivation that someone executes what has been decided either by that person or by others, but more particularly by others. The decisions to be executed are primarily laws that need to be enforced. In the language of the United States Constitution (Article II, Section 3), the chief executive "shall take care that the laws be faithfully executed." From this point of view, executives have little choice but to carry out the general commands of lawmakers and voters.

In government as in business, however, executives have a good deal of *discretion*—that is, a range of choice—about what they put into effect. In business corporations or universities, executives execute what they as directors or trustees first have decided on as policy. This practice to some extent also holds true for governments. Although government officials are formally called on to execute what others have decided, they actually propose a great deal of what is decided and then execute it afterward. When others have chosen a policy for the executives to carry out, the latter may choose to delay or not to act at all, citing various reasons for procrastination.

In the United States the Constitution in effect

[5]For the United States: U.S. Department of Commerce, Bureau of the Census, *Statistical Abstract of the United States, 1977* (Washington, D.C.: U.S. Government Printing Office, 1978), table 455, p. 276. For Switzerland: *U.N. Handbook of National Account Statistics, 1976,* table 14 b and c, pp. 1039–41.

increases the discretion of the chief executive by providing the power to *veto* bills passed by Congress and sent to the Oval Office for signature. If the president vetoes a bill while Congress is in session, it goes back there and must be passed again by a two-thirds majority to override the veto in order to become law. If it fails to get this majority or if it has been vetoed near the end of the legislative period, when the old Congress is no longer in session and the newly elected Congress has not yet met, the bill dies. This latter practice is called a *pocket veto,* since during those last weeks the president in effect puts the bill in a pocket, allowing it to die through inaction. It is then a matter for the new Congress to start the bill all over again, with or without modification, and to find out whether the president will veto it again and, if so, whether there will be enough Congressional votes and time to override the veto.

During his period in office, 1969 to 1974, President Nixon vetoed forty-one bills that Congress had passed. On three of these, his veto was overridden by the necessary two-thirds majorities of both houses; and seventeen were pocket vetoes on which Congress could not vote. Twenty-one were "sustained"; that is, the votes to override fell short of a two-thirds majority in one or both houses. From 1974 to 1976, President Ford vetoed sixty-one bills, but was overridden by Congress on twelve of these—a record since the days of Andrew Jackson. Sixteen of President Ford's vetoes were pocket vetoes. From 1976 to 1978, President Carter vetoed only eight bills (three by pocket veto), and none of those vetoes was overridden.

In 1972, President Nixon asked Congress for an extension of this power in the form of an *item veto.* Under the present law the president must veto a bill entirely or not at all and cannot pick and choose, in order to let pass certain parts, or items, of a bill and to stop others. (Sometimes an item that is likely to be vetoed will be added by Congress to a bill that the president urgently needs, such as a major budget appropriation, in order to increase the likelihood of its passage.) This power sought by President Nixon, on the grounds of combating inflation, would have given him the right to select those items in the budget that he wished to stop, despite their having been voted by Congress, and at the same time would have allowed him to select and save from excision from the same bill those items and expenditures that met with his approval. Congress rejected this presidential proposal on the grounds that it would alter the balance between Congress and president too much in favor of the latter. After Nixon's resignation in 1974, demands for a presidential item veto subsided.

Regardless of the results of this dispute, a great deal of executive discretion is here to stay. Executing a decision inevitably involves unforeseen difficulties and problems that require some changes in the original policy or rule. So there is some range of discretion, large or small, that must be granted any executive. The range of discretion given to that individual goes far in determining the extent of his or her power before a decision, as well as the magnitude of the reward or penalty that the executive may receive as the result of a decision (see Table 8.2).

Responsibility and Power. Power that is subject to control is different from power not subject to such restrictions. In a famous dictum a distinguished nineteenth-century British liberal, Lord Acton, said, "All power tends to corrupt and absolute power corrupts absolutely." But in a very real sense, power is hardly ever absolute. Even the power of Stalin and Hitler, though very great, was not absolute. All executives and all rulers, even in dictatorships, are limited by what their subjects and subordinates can do and will stand for. As these capabilities and compliance habits change, the ruler's power changes with them.

To be *responsible* is to be controlled by someone else: those to whom an actor is responsible are the controllers. In the language of our model of a political system in Chapter 7, responsibility depends on a circuit of communication channels, and responsible behavior is a feedback process. To say that an individual or group that holds power is responsible to some other person or group is to say

TABLE 8.2 *Executive Discretion and Responsibility*

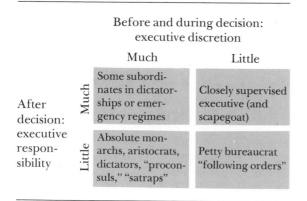

		Before and during decision: executive discretion	
		Much	Little
After decision: executive responsibility	Much	Some subordinates in dictatorships or emergency regimes	Closely supervised executive (and scapegoat)
	Little	Absolute monarchs, aristocrats, dictators, "proconsuls," "satraps"	Petty bureaucrat "following orders"

several things all at once. First, it means that there is a channel of communication through which signals about the behavior of the responsible actor are transmitted to the controllers, that is, to those to whom the actor is responsible. Second, it means that the controllers are receiving and interpreting these signals, checking them against their own memories to determine which of the actor's actions or omissions they will reward or penalize and within what limits. Third, it means that the controllers have a channel through which they actually can apply these rewards or penalties to the actor whom they control and that they are able and motivated to do so.

Thus, in most situations discretion does not mean arbitrary power. Although it seems to be part of the nature of discretion to leave individuals free to decide what they have to do, executives who have been granted some discretion do not have license to do whatever they please. In theory, executives are bound by the goals that have been defined. (If they act for reasons irrelevant to the goals, we may condemn their actions as *arbitrary* or capricious.) In practice, executives are bound by the persons and organizations to whom they must report: by their necessity to keep the people in the organization informed of their actions; by their superiors' ability to reward or punish them for their conduct or to remove them from office; and by their superiors' memories and motivations to supervise the executives and sanction their actions effectively.

Although no executive power is unlimited, not all rulers know the limits of their power, nor do they all know the persons and groups on whom these limits depend. It is this knowledge that makes the difference between responsible and *irresponsible power.* A political actor may in fact be responsible to someone else without knowing it. We then say that that individual acts irresponsibly, but that in the end responsibility may be brought home to him or her, perhaps quite painfully. A hot rod driver may careen irresponsibly through traffic until forcibly reminded either by a police officer or by an accident of a responsibility to other drivers and to his or her family. After the Japanese attacked Pearl Harbor, President Franklin D. Roosevelt said that the warlords of Japan had "started this war but the massed angry forces of humanity will finish it." The famous words of Louis XV of France, "After us, the deluge," are a supreme example of political irresponsibility; his successor, Louis XVI, paid for it with his head. Some of our present-day advocates of preventive nuclear war, too, do not seem to have progressed much beyond the level of the Bourbons.

To act responsibly means to act with the knowledge that one is going to be held accountable for one's actions and to know in what ways and to whom one is accountable. A power holder may be responsible to some group or individual outside his or her immediate establishment; for example, a United States president is responsible to Congress and also to the people. Or a power holder may be responsible to insiders, the superiors in his or her own organization: officials within the federal executive establishment ordinarily are responsible in the United States to the president. There may also be a pattern of responsibility beyond the boundaries of a power holder's national establishment—a responsibility that Adolf Hitler and others like him did not understand.

Party Government and Power. We may now return to the remark of Churchill to Roosevelt and Stalin. There is indeed a difference between executive responsibility to Congress in American government and executive responsibility in a so-called parliamentary government. The *theory of parliamentary government* says that at any time the prime minister, the cabinet, or any individual minister may be confronted with a vote of "no confidence" and be obliged to resign. In other words, the ministers are responsible to the parliament. This theory was most thoroughly put into practice in Britain and France throughout much of the nineteenth century. The parliaments of this period consisted of freewheeling individuals, legislators who had to obey only their conscience or their special interests. All this changed with the growth of the *party system.* Responsibility shifted from the parliament as a body to the majority party within it. This happened not only in England, but also in other countries.

Between 1919 and 1933 the Weimar Republic was run somewhat like the governments of Britain and France. The government had to resign when a majority in the parliament expressed its lack of confidence. Since the Weimar Republic had a great many parties with changing coalitions, this system led to the frequent fall of cabinets, much as it did in France. Often quite disparate elements in the parliament would get together and pass a vote of no confidence, not because they were agreed on anything positive, but merely because they were opposed to the incumbent cabinet and chancellor (or prime minister). Many people in Germany attributed the fall of the Weimar Republic to this arrangement.

After World War II, many Germans looked forward to something better. Therefore they invented in 1949 a rather ingenious device. An article in the basic law introduced a *constructive vote of no confidence,* which provided that a parliamentary vote of lack of confidence in a government could be entertained only if coupled with the election of a new chancellor. The result of this provision was that during the next thirty years there were no votes of lack of confidence, because the deputies opposed to the old government could not agree on a new one to take its place.

Nevertheless, although the provision for a constructive vote of no confidence has never been invoked, its existence—that is, the threat of its being used—has fostered changes in West Germany's government. When the party that Chancellor Ludwig Erhard was supposed to be leading lost confidence in him, Erhard resigned because he realized that it was only a matter of days until his party would get together with one of the opposition parties in the choice of a new chancellor. Erhard's successor, Georg Kiesinger, then governed for two years with a coalition of the kind that Erhard had been unwilling to entertain, namely, a coalition between the Christian Democrats and the Social Democrats.

There has also been a curious transformation as a result of the development of the party system in the United States. In one way, the development in the United States has been exactly the opposite of that in Britain. The major parties in Britain are highly disciplined; legislators from the same party usually vote together. But legislators in the United States cross party lines quite often in voting for or against a proposed law. In another way, developments in the two countries have become more alike. The British prime minister has come to depend more and more on the support of the majority party rather than the support of Parliament; and, owing to the looseness of the American party system, the president has come to depend more and more on the support of a working majority coalition in Congress rather than the support of a majority of the party. Thus, in a sense, the United States now has more of a parliamentary government than it ever has had, perhaps even more than in Britain. How has this come about? It originated in the fact that the American Constitution requires Congress—more particularly, the House—to grant money for the affairs of government. More and more, policy decisions and their execution depend on these grants. And the increasing costliness of government has produced the increasing dependence of the government on maintaining majority congressional support.

Yet there is still at least one major difference between American and parliamentary government. In the United States the government need not resign when it loses the support of Congress. By announcing his decision not to seek re-election several months before the nominating conventions, Lyndon Johnson in effect resigned his office as of January 20, 1969. Even if Johnson had said, "Since I have lost the effective control of Congress and the support I need, I can no longer carry on," even if he had resigned as of April 1, this would not have meant that the government would have been taken over by another party or party combination. It would have only meant that the government would have been taken over and carried on by the vice president. American voters seem content with this arrangement. In November 1972 they not only elected President Nixon by a large majority of votes cast, but they also elected a House of Representatives with a clear majority of Democrats, and they even increased the Democratic majority in the Senate. The voters had preferred President Nixon to his opponent, but they refused to give him a blank check for his policies. In "an orgy of ticket-splitting," as one newspaper called the 1972 election, they insisted on a politics of checks and balances. Only in 1976 did both the presidency and the majority in both houses of Congress once again come under the control of the same party.

In recent years in the Soviet Union, maintaining the support of top Communist Party leaders has been the major limitation on executive power. This curtailment of executive power is a reaction to the period between 1934 and 1953 when Stalin was so strongly entrenched that no one, in effect, seemed to be able to call him to responsibility. The success of his policies of forced high-speed industrialization, together with the victorious outcome of World War II, gave him a measure of continuing popular support; his relentless use of police repression and mass propaganda did the rest. His successors, however, never gained such power. Each of them remained to some extent responsible to the majority of the Politburo and the other top-level committees of the Communist Party. Without their support no Soviet leader after Stalin has been able to remain in office—as Chairman Nikita Khrushchev discovered when he was deprived of power in November 1964. To what extent the Communist Party and the Soviet leaders collectively are held responsible to the people of their country is another question. It seems certain that their power is not unlimited, but their people—even those strata that count in politics—seem far from controlling them closely or effectively on day-to-day matters.

STAFF AND LINE: THE IMPORTANCE OF ADMINISTRATION

Parties are organized to decide what things should be done. Executives are put into office to decide how they should be done. But it is the people on the spot, the administrators, who must do them.

No policy can be put into effect without administration. But the administrative machinery can continue to function by routine—and often does—even when there is no carefully thought-out policy. Only in the long run do decisions about consistency and policy become inevitable.

Even the business of thinking about policy needs to be administered. The type of administration that serves this task is called *staff*. Officers or officials on the staff of an organization—private or public, civilian or military—collect and process current information and past memories that are relevant for the decisions to be made. On the basis of all this information the staff then advises the *line executive* who makes the actual decision.

The Structure of Administration. Most administrative services in government or economic life are organized as hierarchies or chains of command. In such pyramids or chains, small numbers of superiors give orders to larger numbers of subordinates who, in turn, give more detailed orders to still larger numbers of their own subordinates and so on down the line. This *one-way downward flow of commands* continues through link after link of the chain or layer after layer of the administrative pyramid, down to the lowest clerk in the last local office, who then carries out the instructions of those above in dealing with the public. In perfect bureaucracies of this kind the "man in the street" runs a great risk of being treated as the lowest of the low.

As commands flow down the line, responsibility is demanded from above. Each subordinate is responsible to a superior who is expected to supervise that person's performance and usually has means to reward or punish him or her for it. However, in this generally *one-way upward flow of responsibility* it is unusual for superiors to be made responsible to their subordinates. In this sense, armies, political bureaucracies, priestly hierarchies, and business organizations are all quite different from democracies in which lines of command are circular—from the government to the people and back again from the people to the government. In a democracy responsibility is often mutual, and ultimately it must be to the people—provided that they do not forget their own responsibility to humankind and to the future. A key problem of modern administration is to reconcile the built-in tendency of every line organization toward one-way chains of command with the essentially *two-way circular process of democracy*.

In coping with this problem, line executives may be aided by their staffs. The staffs may include not only specialists in various matters of substance, such as transportation, finance, and safety, but also specialists in communication with subordinates, clients and other people. Through such personnel the needs and responses of the latter groups can be brought effectively to the executives' attention.[6] From the days of Franklin D. Roosevelt to those of Jimmy Carter, this has been one of the many tasks of the growing staff of presidential advisers. Similar tasks have developed among the staffs of state governors and other executives at lower levels in the United States, as well as among the staffs of prime ministers and other political executives in Western Europe, and albeit more informally, in the Soviet Union and other Communist-ruled countries.

Policy at the Mercy of Administrators. Administration can make or break a policy. Bureaucrats can go through the motions of carrying out a policy or law while actually sabotaging it. In the eighteenth century such enlightened despots as Catherine II of Russia and Joseph II of Austria tried to abolish a large part of the institution of serfdom in their countries. But the landowning nobles who controlled the administration of their governments took care that the policies remained ineffective. In the 1930s many generals of the Spanish army pretended to obey the Republican government while preparing the uprising of Colonel Francisco Franco that eventually overthrew the Republic. In the United States, laws have long specified equal rights for black voters and equal educational opportunities for black children,

[6]Or the staff members may shield them from what they may not want to hear. Even though President Nixon told the country in 1973 that his high-level staff had kept him uninformed about the Watergate affair, he had high praise for the two former key assistants—H. R. Haldeman and John Ehrlichman—who had held main responsibilities for keeping him informed, or uninformed, about political matters and were later sentenced to prison terms.

but local registrars, school boards, and other administrative agencies have long prevented the exercise of many of these rights.

If a policy is to work or if a leader or party is to have real power, it must have the support of a body of administrative personnel that is loyal and competent enough to give effect to its orders. But while policies, leaders, and parties change, bureaucrats remain. Bureaucracy may be an unmoving anvil that wears out many hammers of reform. If a new policy is to be implemented, can the old bureaucracy be expected to administer it?

This question has provoked four main competing answers. The first answer is provided by the concept of a *civil service*. This notion goes back to the time of European monarchies, when government officials were supposed to be primarily loyal to the king and not to any policy, party, or special interest group. Civil servants were expected to be equally loyal and competent in serving any minister or policy that the king commanded. Later this loyalty of civil servants became oriented not to the king, but to the crown—that is, to the state—for even kings come and go or make mistakes. Civil servants then were expected to be loyal to the interests of the state and its constitution, if need be against the errors of kings and cabinets. Under this tradition a Labour government or a Conservative government will expect to be served equally well by the nonpartisan professionals of the British civil service.

Recruitment and promotion of such professional civil servants are usually carried on by means of some *merit system* in accordance with supposedly objective standards of training and performance. In practice, however, such standards often favor members of particular social classes or particular ethnic, racial, or religious groups. As Sir Dennis Brogan has put it: "The British Civil Service is open to rich and poor alike—like the Ritz Hotel." Certainly no fully objective standards for the hiring and promoting of government personnel have been discovered yet.

A strikingly different theory developed in the United States in the nineteenth century during the days of President Andrew Jackson: government offices were a matter not for specialists and experts, but for ordinary men. In those days, any right thinking—and right voting—man was good enough to fill an office after his party had won the election, for "to the victor belong the spoils." This *spoils system* permitted the victorious party to fill administrative posts with its own adherents, who were expected to carry out its policy, if it had one, and to be grateful to the party for getting them their jobs. Such officeholders, of course, were not politically neutral, but intensely partisan. Benjamin Franklin's old practice of filling postmasterships with political supporters thus was extended for a time to most of the American government. Few other countries went as far, but a part of the practice lingers on in the machine politics of many American cities.

A third notion of administration is a *class theory*, as elaborated by Marx, Engels, and, particularly, Lenin. As they saw it, professional bureaucrats would serve different masters or policies equally well as long as the latter remained within the same ruling class and social system. As soon as a new policy or government went radically beyond the old class limits, however, the old bureaucracy could not be expected to serve it loyally. (In fact, democratic socialist governments in Britain, Sweden, Norway, and Denmark experienced no crippling difficulties with their civil servants.) According to Lenin, however, socialist or Communist governments, on coming to power, would need to dismiss most of the old officials and replace them by new ones recruited from the working class and its allies. Even this new bureaucracy would have to be watched closely and purged often, in order to prevent it from becoming a new middle class. Finally, the Communists would have to reorganize the whole machinery of government, making it so simple that eventually, as Lenin put it, "any cook could rule the state." The practical experience of the Soviet Union and other Communist countries shows that Communist bureaucracies have a way of becoming large and persistent. Dissident Communists have complained bitterly of the rise of a "new class" of Communist bureaucrats and managers.[7] Clearly, the administrative machinery of Communist countries has not yet become simplified enough, nor their cooks sophisticated enough, for Lenin's words to be fulfilled.

The fourth answer to the question of administrative competence and loyalty is a *compromise* between the merit and spoils system, a compromise that has been gradually emerging in the United States. Currently somewhat more than two thousand top positions in the federal government are defined as "policy making" or political. Their incumbents are expected to resign whenever the administration changes. The new administration then may fill these positions with its own personnel, either to ensure the faithful execution of its policies or to reward some of its supporters with the spoils of victory.

The bulk of federal jobs, however—more than 2 million—has been put under the protection of civil service laws and regulations. Accordingly, their incumbents are to be promoted by merit and are to be discharged only for cause and under carefully safeguarded proceedings. During World War II and in the heyday of the Cold War, some of the safeguards were weakened seriously. A large number of security regulations and requirements made it possible for many officials to be denied *security clearance* and to be discharged from office on the basis of anonymous accusations and with no chance to face their accusers.[8] The recurrent purges of administrative personnel, so characteristic of Communist dictatorships, thus found a minor, but disquieting, counterpart in the United States.

Despite these tensions the American administrative machinery has on the whole worked well. Since World War II it has carried out a greatly expanded range of responsibilities and policies. Compared to its size and the vast sums of money it has handled, the federal bureaucracy has remained remarkably free from corruption. It has been efficient in many of its tasks, both old and new, ranging from building roads and installing rural electrification to putting men on the moon. Despite the ominous powers given to the security system, it has not turned the country into a police state. Congressional and popular defense of civil liberties has provided an effective counterweight.

America's administrative machinery has been least successful when it has had to change major habits and practices among the American people, such as in race relations, poverty, and the crisis of the cities. Here neither line nor staff has been able to provide a substitute for the needed reorientation of the will of the American people. Individuals and small groups can urge this *reordering of national priorities* or goals, but only the people can bring it about. Only they can decide which things they want done first. They must decide on the kind and size of the new jobs to be done and on the machinery with which to do them. As this reorientation develops and popular support increases for new policies, it will be an important task for citizens to see to it that the administrative machinery of the American government—in the nation, the states, and the cities—will prove adequate to its new tasks.

[7]See Milovan Djilas, *The New Class* (New York: Praeger, 1957).

[8]For a good study of the legal implications, see Ralph S. Brown, *Loyalty and Security: Employment Tests in the United States* (New Haven: Yale University Press, 1958).

KEY TERMS AND CONCEPTS

decision latitude
policy
strategy
tactics
affirmative action
deliberation
institution
role
institutionalize

filibuster
cloture
common good
representative
law
bill of attainder
authorization
appropriation
joint conference committee
separation of powers
checks and balances
impound
unwritten constitution
soviet
democratic centralism
Cabinet solidarity
adversary procedure
judicial review
segregation by race
zoning laws
redlining
southern strategy
unitary government
federal union
confederacy
nullification
states' rights
federalism
revenue sharing
tax revolt
residual powers
Tenth Amendment
general welfare clause
discretion
veto
pocket veto
item veto
responsibility
arbitrary actions
irresponsible power
theory of parliamentary government
party system
constructive vote of no confidence
staff
line executive
one-way downward flow of commands
one-way upward flow of responsibility
two-way circular process of democracy
civil service
merit system
spoils system
security clearance
reordering of national priorities

ADDITIONAL READINGS

Crozier, M. *The Bureaucratic Phenomenon.* Chicago: University of Chicago Press, 1967. PB

Dogan, M., and R. Rose, eds. *European Politics: A Reader.* Boston: Little, Brown, 1971.

Friedrich, C. J. *Constitutional Government and Democracy.* 4th ed. Waltham, Mass.: Blaisdell Publishing Co., 1968.

———. *The Pathology of Politics.* New York: Harper & Row, 1972.

Heclo, H. *A Government of Strangers: Executive Politics in Washington.* Washington: Brookings Institution, 1977.

———. *Modern Social Politics in Britain and Sweden: From Relief to Income Maintenance.* New Haven: Yale University Press, 1976. PB

Hersh, S. M. "Laird Approved False Reporting of Secret Raids." *New York Times,* August 10, 1973, pp. 1, 8.

Huntington, S. P. *Political Order in Changing Societies.* New Haven: Yale University Press, 1968. Chaps. 1, 2. PB

Merton, R. K., et al., eds. *Reader in Bureaucracy.* New York: Free Press, 1965. PB

Neustadt, R. E. *Presidential Power.* New York: Wiley, 1960. PB

Rourke, F. *Bureaucratic Power in National Politics.* 2nd ed. Boston: Little, Brown, 1972. PB

Schubert, G. A. *The Judicial Mind.* Evanston, Ill.: Northwestern University Press, 1965.

Scott, J. C. *Comparative Political Corruption.* Englewood Cliffs, N.J.: Prentice-Hall, 1972.

Sheehan, N., and E. W. Kenworthy, eds. *The Pentagon Papers.* Chicago: Quadrangle Books, 1972. PB

Simon, H. A. *Administrative Behavior.* 3rd ed. New York: Free Press, 1976. PB

Suleiman, E. N. *Politics, Power and Bureaucracy in France: The Administrative Elite.* Princeton: Princeton University Press, 1974. PB

Wilson, J. Q. *Political Organizations.* New York: Basic Books, 1973.

PB = *available in paperback*

IX

The Performance of Political Systems

Some people adapt their attitudes toward political change simply according to their prejudices, as they have learned them from others or as they may fit the needs of their own personalities. "Every boy and every gal that's born into this world alive is either a little liberal or else a little conservative," claimed a song in *Iolanthe* by Gilbert and Sullivan. Some people are born conformists. They simply favor the existing political order, whatever that may be. In a small town in the American Midwest they would cheer for the American Legion; in a small town in the Soviet Union they would be supporters of the Communist Party. If they had been born in a New Guinea tribe, they would be loyal headhunters or cannibals. Other people are dissenters by nature, such as the nineteenth-century immigrant from Ireland who arrived in America on election day, got off the ship, and went straight to the polling place. Asked whether he knew anything about the candidates or issues, he replied: "No, I don't. But I want to vote against the government." A Philadelphia taxi driver of the 1960s said the same thing: "I pay no attention to politics, but I always vote against the gang that's in."

In fact, there is no good evidence that either conformism or dissent are inborn attitudes; but they can be learned at an early age from one's family, associates, personal experiences, and social and cultural environment, until they become part of one's personality structure, sense of identity, and self-respect, seriously restricting one's later perceptions of reality and freedom of decision. If we are not to remain prisoners of our past attitudes, we must reach out for something better. In our time, politics is such a serious matter that neither unthinking conformism nor blind nonconformism will suffice. In order to decide intelligently whether a political system needs changing, and in what respects, we must know how it performs. We must know whether it produces the outcomes we want and how well it does in producing them.

If we know how to analyze the workings of

political systems and the machinery of government, we may feel less naive and uncritical about politics. We also may feel less helpless and bewildered by the actions of the governments under which we live. Systems theory and systems analysis may make us less inclined to search for demons and villains in political life and to see it as a simple crusade of good against evil. Our questions may then become more pointed toward reality and more likely to lead us to effective action.

THE USES OF SYSTEMS THEORY

Some years ago a student radical (who has since become an expert labor lawyer in the complicated field of workman's compensation) asked, "Who really determines American foreign policy?" The question was a little like that of the small child who asks, "Where in the refrigerator is the little man who turns on the light when you open the refrigerator door?" Or the questions of primitive peoples: "Where is the god within the hurricane? Where is the spirit within the earthquake?" In effect, most such questions are attempts to personify the workings of systems.

A hurricane is a revolving disk of air, one mile high and five hundred miles across, which is fed by streams of air in two dimensions and by the rising of air in a third dimension all the way to the stratosphere. It is a complicated, but understandable, system of storms that is part of a larger system of storm tracks. An earthquake is a system. And so is a war. Systems analysis thus may help us to see that the great catastrophes in history as well as in nature are products of systems.

Systems do not always work for human good. Quite the contrary, the outcome of a system may be pernicious and destructive. Systems can be traps. They have a logic of their own, which goes even beyond the interests of the individuals whom they may temporarily reward. Many slave owners, for example, benefited from the social system of slavery. Hence, they learned to believe in it and to defend it. They persisted in acting in accordance with this system even when it led to economic stagnation and civil war, the destruction of their homes, the loss of their property, and the death of their children.[1]

Whether we speak of the catastrophes of nature or of people, the workings of a machine, or the slower changes in human politics, it is important to see that many developments in each of these cases are produced by systems. As we saw in Chapter 6, a *system* is a collection of recognizable units or components that hang together and vary together, in a manner regular enough to be described. Political systems consist of political units and are connected mainly by political processes. We can try to analyze each system to see how it works, how its outcomes are produced, and how it can be changed. With the help of systems analysis we can try to separate the properties of systems from individual interests, group interests, and the shares of persons in making decisions.

The political systems analyst uses his or her skill to understand how wide must be the *decision latitude* of an individual, office, organization, or government, so that it can make a real difference to the outcome. The analyst also tries to recognize when and where the momentum of a system is so great that officeholders become rubber stamps or "dependent variables," making very little difference to the outcome. For it is always important to know whether you can change the outcome of a system by appealing to the judgment of an individual, or by replacing one officeholder with another, or only by changing some or most of the structure of the system. The political analyst also tries to learn who would help make the change, who is interested in it, how to build a coalition big enough and motivated enough to produce the change, and

[1]For detailed accounts, see William C. Dodd, *The Cotton Kingdom* (New Haven: Yale University Press, 1919); and Eugene D. Genovese, *The Political Economy of Slavery* (New York: Pantheon, 1965).

how to aim one's resources with sufficient precision to bring about the change desired.

THE CONCEPT OF PERFORMANCE

Systems analysts are aided in their work by the concept of performance. Performance tests occur everywhere. Automobile firms take part in races to test the design and performance of their cars and to improve them in the light of experience. But automobile races are tests not only of machines but also of drivers. A first-rate driver may win even with a less than first-rate car. Moreover, every race also involves track or road conditions, weather, chance, and luck. Performance, in government as in automobiles, is thus determined jointly by systems, the individuals who operate them, and the environment in which they must function.

Effectiveness and Efficiency. *Performance* is the name we give to any outcome that is desired but improbable without an effort to produce it. Performance achieves some result that otherwise would not occur. If an outcome is certain, no one has to act to bring it about. No human being or organization has to perform anything to make the sun rise. By contrast, a room that is cold in winter may be warmed by the performance of a stove. Any performance is measured by the outcome attained as against the costs and other adverse conditions that make its attainment unlikely. Performance thus includes two dimensions: *effectiveness*—that which makes an unlikely outcome more likely to happen; and *efficiency*—the ratio between change in the probability of the outcome and the costs incurred in producing it. The effectiveness of an automobile may be measured by the speed it can attain; its efficiency, by its consumption of gasoline. (Another kind of effectiveness might be the automobile's freedom from the need for repairs in over 100,000 miles of normal use; the corresponding efficiency would be measured against the higher cost for stronger and better original parts.)

A similar distinction between effectiveness and efficiency applies to the performance of governments and entire political systems. We ask not only how likely a government or political system is to attain some value we are interested in, but also at what price. The American government of the 1920s gave free rein to private business enterprise, with a minimum of government intervention. The enormous cost became evident in the 1930s when 10 million people were thrown out of work for years by the greatest of depressions. The semi-developed Soviet Union was transformed into a modern industrial state by Stalin's iron-fisted methods, at vast cost in human suffering.

Emergency Politics: Pursuit of a Single Value. Performance is measured, first of all, by specific values. If there is a single overwhelming goal, the primary emphasis will be on effectiveness in reaching it. A leader of a political movement, a party, or a government may ask what headway is being made toward this particular goal. The leader may then give this goal priority over all others. Even democracies do so in time of war. After the attack on Pearl Harbor there was overwhelming agreement in the United States that the war against Nazi Germany and imperial Japan had to be won. Everything else for a time was subordinated to this goal. Similarly, when the Nazis invaded the Soviet Union and Stalin's dictatorship was at war with Germany, Winston Churchill promptly offered Stalin an alliance. The prime minister was asked in the House of Commons how he could justify allying Britain with such an immoral dictatorship as Stalin's. Churchill replied that if Hitler's forces should invade hell, His Majesty's government would offer the devil a treaty of alliance. This, incidentally, was a paraphrase of the statement by Lenin a generation earlier that the Bolsheviks would enter an alliance "with the devil and his grandmother" if it would bring about the victory of the Russian Revolution. With victory in war or revolution as the overriding goal, the best system of government is that which appears most likely to win.

If there is more than one major value, however, the question of cost and efficiency cannot be ignored. If justice and other conceptions of the national interest are equally or more important to people than the military effort, if a large part of the people do not believe in the war's being just or being in the national interest, then the issue of priorities arises. Thus in the early 1970s many Americans felt, "Carrying on this war is not our paramount goal. Vietnam is not the most important problem facing the United States. It is more urgent to improve our own society right here at home."

In the long run no single goal, no matter how just or admirable, can be pursued completely. The methods of emergency thinking and *emergency government*—the argument that one would do anything, override any scruples, make any arrangements, pay any price to get a goal—are psychologically and organizationally tolerable only for limited amounts of time. The pursuit of a single overwhelming goal year after year will change and distort the personalities of individuals, the behavior of small groups, and the structure of a government. It can even destroy the moral fabric of a society. If it is justifiable to use any means to achieve a desired end, if violence or concealment is acceptable, as in a wartime crisis, then why not use the technique of the "Big Lie"? If you want followers, why not gain them by deception? If someone disputes your leadership or disagrees with your goal or your methods, why not jail that individual or assassinate that person's character?

In every great emergency, people are tempted to set aside the basic rights of individuals and groups, such as free speech, freedom of assembly, or due process of law. In the late 1960s, General Lewis B. Hershey, then director of Selective Service in the United States, ordered active protestors against the draft to be inducted forthwith into the army. His involuntary retirement followed. If basic rights are set aside briefly, the damage is limited. If emergency rule violates them for a longer time, the damage to constitutional government will be severe and may prove fatal.

Multiple Goals and Open-Ended Values. Over any longer period of time it is vitally important for people to learn to preserve or restore to their governments the capacity to pursue many goals without neglecting any of them. A good political system is able to balance different values, to accept the possibility of error and to correct it, and to accept the likelihood that there are many questions to which the exact answer is not yet known. The poet Bertolt Brecht, a lifelong believer in communism, once said to his Communist audience, "Shouldn't we ask our friends to make a list of all those questions to which they do not yet know an answer?" Brecht was reminding them of a general truth, valid for all ideologies. It is important to keep open the frontier to the unknown so that we know where we must still seek for answers. *Multiple goal-seeking capacities* and research capabilities must be included, therefore, among essential performance criteria for any government or political system that is to endure.

It was in this frame of mind that Thomas Jefferson worked on the draft of the American Declaration of Independence. At one stage the draft document spoke of "unalienable rights" and went on: "These rights are life, liberty, and property." Jefferson then changed the text. He crossed out "These rights are" and substituted "Among these rights are," making it clear that unalienable rights were not necessarily limited to any particular number. He also struck out the word "property" and substituted "the pursuit of happiness." Some scholars think he did so believing that in future centuries people might be less concerned with property, but would always search for happiness. In any case, "happiness" included much more than "property," and it was more open to the changing needs of future generations. Thus amended, the declaration was signed and published, giving shape to the spirit of the new nation. It became one of America's greatest documents and a testimony to the open-ended nature of the American dream. When President Franklin Roosevelt in the 1930s said "human rights come before property rights," he spoke in the same tradition.

THE BUDGET: FIRST TESTS OF PERFORMANCE

"For warfare, three things are needed," wrote the Austrian general Montecucculi in the seventeenth century: "money, money, and once again, money." Much the same is true for government. To get anything done anywhere, a government is likely to need money in the amount required at the time and place it is needed. The ability of a government to raise money, and then to spend it wisely, is a major test of its performance. If a government has to do several things, it must plan to have money available for all of them and it must plan how to get it. A summary of these plans is called the *budget.* Every modern national government needs a budget, and so does each of its administrative subdivisions. What a government plans for in its budget will reveal its values. How well it plans and executes its budget is a first test of its performance.

Anyone who knows how to read a budget can discover the goals of a government. If a government plans to build many highways, its budget for road construction will be large. If a city plans to increase opportunities and facilities for education, its education budget will increase. If a national government decides to acquire expensive new weapons, its defense budget will rise—and so may those of other nations. *Budgetary analysis* is the art and skill of reading a budget so carefully that the analyst can tell for what purposes the government's financial resources will be spent and usually also how its spending pattern will have changed from those of the previous years. Budgetary analysis thus may serve as a test of both political intentions and performance.

Revenue Budgets and the Art of Collecting Taxes. What holds for public expenditures also holds for public *revenues*—the way the government expects to get the money that it plans to spend. The revenue budget—the income side of a budget—will reveal which groups the government is willing to burden more heavily and which ones will be let off more lightly. Governments favoring the rich at the expense of the poor tend to use poll taxes, which are collected in equal amounts per head of population or, as in past decades in the United States, per head of voters. Governments that are solicitous of special groups—such as mothers, churches, universities, or oil producers—may grant them special tax exemptions or allowances. Governments that want to collect revenue in accordance with ability to pay tend to use *progressive taxes.* These taxes, such as corporate and individual income taxes in most modern countries, progress to higher tax rates as the taxpayer's income increases. *Regressive taxes* have the opposite effect: a uniform sales tax on bread tends to fall most heavily on the poor. Poll taxes usually are regressive in their impact, too.

Since wealth is much more unequally distributed than income, *wealth taxes* or *property taxes* would fall much more heavily on the upper- and middle-income groups, but just for this reason they encounter much more resistance. (Besides, taxes on real estate, which are one kind of wealth tax, often hit older people after their incomes have dwindled, so they may cause much hardship and injustice.) Perhaps the best way to build an equitable tax system consists in not relying on any one kind of tax, but on combining several kinds, within the limits of keeping the system relatively simple. At best, however, this results in equitable taxes, not necessarily in equal taxes.

The revenue side of a budget will also reveal much about the capabilities of a government or an entire political system. The less income a government gets, the less it can do. Generally the art of collecting taxes, as J. B. Colbert once said, resembles the art of plucking a goose: it consists in getting the largest amount of feathers with the fewest squawks. The tax system of a country thus depends in part on which groups can squawk loudest and most effectively. Politicians anticipating the reactions of such groups—on whose support they may depend—tax them lightly, if at all. This is what happens in many underdeveloped countries. Extremely underdeveloped countries collect most of their revenue at their borders, generally at ports of entry. Tariffs and export taxes—and foreign grants and loans—tend to be the major sources of income for their governments. Somewhat more highly developed countries collect much of their income through *indirect taxes* on trade within their borders, and sometimes through excises at the boundaries of their cities. Highly developed countries collect most of their revenue through *direct taxes* on individuals, households, and business enterprises. (The Soviet Union raises most of its tax revenue through a combination of *turnover* and profit transfer taxes at the factory level.) Progressive direct income taxes tend to be more just and humane—and they bring in more money. The ability to use taxes effectively, therefore, is an additional test of government performance.

Deficit Financing. Governments have another potential source of income besides taxes, loans, and what they earn from public services. They can deliberately spend more money than they take in, and unlike private citizens and business firms they can get away with it. For governments can create money—and most of them do—and they can compel anyone in the country to accept this money as legal tender for paying taxes or settling debts. In spending a billion dollars more than it has collected, a government may borrow the money and pay interest on it or it may print it or create it in other ways. These practices are known as *deficit financing.*

If a government prints or otherwise creates money, the purchasing power of the remaining money in the country will be somewhat diluted. When this happens there may be some *inflation*—more money purchasing the same amount of goods. Inflation acts like an indirect tax that falls unequally on different groups. People hurt by inflation—consumers, creditors, white-collar workers, civil servants, the military, pensioners, and others living on fixed incomes—may turn against the government. In contrast, debtors, farmers, manufacturers, and skilled union labor will be little troubled or may even be quite satisfied with the government's policy. Whether the government then stays in power will depend less on the amount of the inflation and more on the strength and attitudes of these contending interest groups. Inflation may not necessarily occur, however. If there are unemployed people and resources within the country, the new money created by the government may stimulate demand and induce the production of additional goods and services that might counter the inflation wholly or partially. The government, of course, will get its money whether there are idle resources in the country or not. But if there are unemployed resources, deficit financing may actually promote employment and prosperity. How skillfully a government foresees the effects of its financial policies, and how well it controls its own actions, constitutes another test of its performance.

Budgetary Planning and Control. Ordinarily budgets are prepared for one year ahead. In the case of large public expenditures or investments, however, some countries use capital budgets or development budgets that are planned for several years ahead. The five-year plans of the Soviet Union and other countries are the most elaborate form of such budgeting, covering much of the country's national economy. The art of *budget forecasting* aims at predicting how much money each of a government's several activities will receive in next year's budget or in the budgets of other future years. A rough rule of thumb seems to be that most items in a large government budget will not differ by more than 10 percent from the sums budgeted in the preceding year. Changes of more than 10 percent, either upward or downward, are no longer matters of routine; they are likely to require relatively substantial political decisions.

A budget is a tool not only of action, but also of control. It enables a government to control its own actions, by making sure that subordinate offices and agencies spend their budgetary allocations on the purposes intended and that the amounts spent stay within budgetary limits. Most countries assign this control function to special national accounting offices or comptrollers general. The United States also has a Bureau of the Budget, which controls the requests of the various agencies for future appropriations to make certain that they are compatible with each other, with government policy, and with expected income.

The budget can be a tool for controlling the government from outside. Whoever controls the budget can control most of what a government can do. Countries whose budgets are controlled by foreign powers or creditors are not fully sovereign. In sovereign countries, on the other hand, legislatures or the people can use the budget to control executive power. When in the seventeenth century the British Parliament gained full control of this *power of the purse,* it wrested effective power from the Crown. Even in the twentieth century, the day on which the British chancellor of the Exchequer presents the government's annually proposed budget to Parliament for its approval remains one of the high points in British political life.

In the United States, the double process of authorization and appropriation of each major budgetary item is intended to strengthen congressional control over the executive.[2] It is partly counteracted by the skill of some executive departments in concealing their specific expenditures under vague budgetary headings and in exceeding or not fully spending budgetary estimates. Sometimes, under systems of direct democracy, as in some Swiss cantons, certain budgetary items must be approved directly by the voters.

In the muted contest between the controllers and the controlled in any country there is no substitute for the vigilance of informed legislators and voters. In all modern countries the need for some executive discretion must be balanced against the need for some political control of the bureaucracy through the budget. How well this balance is maintained is yet another test of performance. But all such budgetary tests do not tell what quality of life a government buys for its people. Here we must ask not how much money is collected and spent, but what qualitative and quantitative results the combination of money and politics produces.

SOME QUALITATIVE TESTS OF PERFORMANCE

The performance of government relates to both the present and the future. It must aim at *attaining* as much as possible of each of the many values that people now desire, and it must keep the pursuit of all these values as *compatible* as possible. But it must also preserve and enhance the capacity to seek *new* values in the future and to attain these, too. Serving these three tasks, governments must often work for subtle configurations of values that are not easily spelled out, but that people can sometimes recognize by intuition. People then speak of the quality of a political system or of the *quality of life* in a society. We all know some simple tests for this kind of quality: how breathable the air still is, how often the garbage gets collected, how safe it is to walk home after dark, how many children are properly fed and how many go hungry, how many sick are well attended and how many are not attended at all, how many people lead meaningful lives and how many lead "lives of quiet desperation."

[2]On the significance of President Nixion's attempted impounding policies for the congressional power of the purse, see pp. 182–83, above.

The Quality of Leaders. A more profound test of the quality of a political system was stressed by Pericles in ancient Greece and by John Stuart Mill in nineteenth-century England. It consists in the kinds of individuals who grow up under it and in the kind of persons it elevates to leadership. Clearly, in all countries the personalities of leaders will vary as they succeed one another over the course of time. But the personalities and actions of Britain's prime ministers and Cabinet ministers since 1945, such as Winston Churchill, Clement Attlee, Anthony Eden, Harold Macmillan, Harold Wilson, Edward Heath, James Callahan, and Margaret Thatcher, say something about the quality of British politics since World War II. Similarly the personalities and acts of Adolf Hitler, Joseph Goebbels, Hermann Goering, Heinrich Himmler, Ernst Kaltenbrunner, Franz Hoess, and Adolf Eichmann say something about the quality of the Nazi political system.

A look at the personalities of American leaders reminds us of the great variety of political life in the United States. American leaders have included persons of vast accomplishment and great humanity, like Franklin D. Roosevelt and Dwight D. Eisenhower. They have included leaders of great promise cut off before their time, like Martin Luther King, and John and Robert Kennedy; and they have included many men and women of lesser stature, each stubbornly doing his or her best as he or she saw it, from Frederick Douglass, Carl Schurz, and Harriet Tubman to Frances Perkins, Eleanor Roosevelt, Margaret Mead, Jonas Salk, and Earl Warren. In American history the roster of presidents is composed of great leaders like Washington, Jefferson, Jackson, and Lincoln, as well as of lesser men like Martin Van Buren, James Buchanan, Chester A. Arthur, and Calvin Coolidge. But in nearly two centuries the American political system has seldom elevated to high office any person who was outstandingly criminal, cruel, or insanely ambitious. When in the period of 1973–74 President Nixon was suspected of having either ordered or condoned illegal acts by his subordinates, public protests, congressional investigations, and mass opinion polls compelled his resignation. Americans are still not willing to let even the president elevate himself above the law.

The Quality of Ordinary People. Another test for the quality of a political system is in the types of personality and behavior it produces among ordinary men and women. How numerous are the drunks, drug addicts, and suicides? How many murders are committed? How frequent are other crimes of callousness or cruelty? Some answers can be found in the crime statistics of each country and in its surveys of social attitudes and mental health (see Table 9.1).

But the quality of life under a political system does not depend solely on crime and acts legally defined as antisocial. How many persons suffer from race discrimination, and how many people practice it? How many "authoritarian personalities" do we find and how many petty tyrants of the office or the breakfast table? What is the most frequently found personality type among the people—the *modal personality*[3]—which accounts for so much of what is called "national character"?

And the quality of life is determined as much or more by the presence of good things as by the absence of bad ones. How many people volunteer to help those in need? How many will help their neighbors, shelter refugees, or donate blood? How many acts of interracial decency do we find? In how many cities can people leave their coins on unwatched newspaper piles without the money being stolen? In how many homes are the doors left unlocked? How many jurors and judges treat the accused as innocent until proven guilty? And how many taxpayers are honest in filling out their tax returns?

Every reader may apply this list of questions to

[3]For a discussion of modal personality and national character, refer to A. Inkeles and D. Levinson, "National Character: The Study of Modal Personality and Sociocultural Systems," in Gardner Lindzey, ed., *Handbook of Experimental Psychology,* 2nd ed. (Reading, Mass.: Addison-Wesley Publishers, 1969), vol. 4, pp. 418–506.

the community in which he or she lives. American readers may find that their country is seriously vulnerable to homicide, carelessness, intermittent corruption, and the destructive overuse of stimulants. They will also find evidence of remarkable generosity and openness, respect for people, and confidence and trust in them.

Political Culture: The Sum of Qualities. Taken together, all these qualitative aspects of a political system add up to the political culture underlying a country or a people. The notion of "culture" is used here similarly to the way it is used by anthropologists. The *culture* of a people means the collection of all its traditions and habits, particularly those transmitted by parents to children and by children to each other. It includes their common stock of images and perceptions of the world in which they live. It thus includes their views of what is practical and possible and what is not; what is beautiful and what is ugly; what is good and what is bad; what is right and what is wrong. Culture functions like a traffic code for behavior. It tells people where to go ahead and where to stop and where and how to make detours.

Culture has implications for political behavior. All cultures, say the anthropologists Florence Kluckhohn and Fred Strodtbeck, can be compared in terms of a few basic questions.[4] Three of these are most relevant here. (1) Does a culture teach people mainly to submit to their environment, to work along with it, or to master it? (2) Is it oriented chiefly toward the past, the present, or the future? (3) Does it see human relations primarily as *lineal*—that is, in terms of fathers and sons, mothers and daughers, superiors and subordinates—or as *collateral*—that is, in terms of brothers and sisters, equals and colleagues?

People who are used to submitting to their environment will readily submit to rulers, foreign or native, and may feel frightened and bewildered when faced with the task of ruling themselves. People accustomed to working along with their environment in constant two-way communication also may favor compromise and decisions by unanimity, even at the cost of much delay; they may dislike quick decisions by majority rule. (This trait, common among many of the emerging peoples in Asia and Africa, often has exasperated Western economic development experts.) People taught to master nature will resort more readily to power and manipulation. They will seek quick decisions overriding all doubts and obstacles, disregarding the needs of dissenting opinions, minorities, and the less obvious consequences of their actions. Such masters of nature will win many triumphs in technology and politics, but in their rush ahead they may leave a trail of neglected vital problems such as eroded soil, polluted air, careless wars, and ill-treated minorities. Those who have learned to work *with* nature—learning from it as often as imposing their will on it—may learn from their dialogue with nature the art of working through dialogues with their fellow people.

Likewise, people's basic view of the relative importance of the past, the present, and the future will shape their attitudes toward economic growth, political reform, and the needs of old and young. A culture looking more to the past than to either the present or the future may be better in preserving monuments than in accelerating innovations. It may enact laws for old-age pensions many years before expanding large-scale public higher education for the young. Britain passed legislation for old-age pensions in 1908, but legislation for greatly expanded public higher education appeared only after 1960. A culture looking to the future, such as that of the United States, passed these kinds of legislation in reverse order: land grant colleges came in the 1860s and social security in 1935.

Finally, if a people tends to regard its members as equals, as many Americans and French do, its

[4]See Florence R. Kluckhohn et al., *Variations in Value Orientations* (New York: Harper & Row, 1961).

politics will be fairly different from that of a people which tends to divide its members into superiors and subordinates, as the Japanese, the Germans, and, to a lesser extent, the English have done during many periods of their history.

Political culture is related to the *frequency* and *probability* of various kinds of political behavior and not to their rigid determination. England has had its great forward-looking reformers; Germany and Japan have had their democrats; the United States has produced its share of conservatives and conservationists. Nonetheless, the different political cultures of these countries can be seen in the record of their past behavior and will not soon disappear completely from their future actions.

THE NATURE OF AUTHORITY

The culture of a country is the basis for the concept of authority prevailing in its politics. In some countries and ages, political leadership is attained through ascription, such as by noble birth. At other times and places, leadership must be won by achievement, as in public service, war, or electoral contests. The English get their authority from who they are and what they are. They *stand* for election and *sit* for their exams. Americans get their authority from what they do. They *run* for office and *take* exams. One concept of authority is static and bound by status and *ascription*—what people are labeled to be, the other is dynamic and oriented to *achievement*—what people actually accomplish. As Britain transforms itself to meet the modern age, its image of authority, too, will grow more dynamic—but it may be an uphill struggle.

Behind these differences the concept of authority has a common meaning in all countries. *Authority* means, first, the credibility of a source of communication: its messages will be believed almost regardless of their content. If a scholar has become an "authority," that person's views will be believed even when the evidence for them is weak. "The authority of a scientist can be measured," wrote a disillusioned colleague, "by the number of years for which he can retard progress in his field." (Real science, of course, is antiauthoritarian in its essence. The youngest instructor or student can contradict the most senior professor when the evidence is on the younger person's side. When Charles II of England joined Britain's first organization of scientists—the Royal Society—the awkward problem arose of how any other scientist could presume to contradict the scientific theories of His Majesty. The Royal Society thereupon put into its seal *nullius in verba*—"on the words of no man." Its members thus proclaimed their decision to believe not in authority, but in facts.)

In political and military matters, too, people often pay more attention to who is talking than to what is said. This tends to save much time and effort since no one person can test the evidence for everything he or she hears. But this easy acceptance of authority can lead to catastrophic error. Many civilians have believed the word of a general who told them that the war in prospect would be short and easy. The bombed-out cities of Germany and Japan and the military cemeteries of many other countries bear witness that authority can err. In politics, voters often have trusted the authority of leaders who assured them of the safety or success of some financial or economic policy or who asserted, on the contrary, that some reform could not possibly work. President Hoover predicted that grass would grow in the streets of American cities if Franklin D. Roosevelt's New Deal policies were adopted. But the voters repudiated Hoover's authority, which had been discredited by previous unsuccessful predictions. The New Deal program won, with Hoover making very little hay from his pronouncement.

Why do people so often believe an authoritative voice without testing what it says? Convenience is not the only reason. A deeper motive is emotional. As children we all had to learn to trust authority. Our fathers and mothers had to tell us of many dangers too serious to be tested by our own bodies. When they told us about reality, we had to take their word about it. In the same years we learned to love our parents and to identify with them. Thus most of us made a three-way association in our minds that was deep and lasting. We learned to associate the commands of our parents with reality and both the commands and reality with someone we loved. In later life the commands or instructions of a teacher or superior may remind us of the voice of our parents. This kind of childhood experience is normal in many societies. People who have had it can easily obey the commands of their superiors and government and feel happy about it. They may gladly volunteer to do more than is asked of them. Glad to obey, they may also be glad to command. When they themselves become parents or are promoted in business or to political or military office, they will speak with the voice of authority and expect to be obeyed.

Authority in this sense is *internalized;* that is, it has become part of the innermost feelings and the self-image of each individual. If such an individual should violate the commands of what he or she takes to be authority, that person can do so only at the price of psychic conflict. He or she will feel pangs of conscience, as they used to be called, or experience "neurotic guilt feelings," as a more fashionable phrase would put it. An active conscience, like a sense of pain, may seem an inconvenience to many of us. How simple life would be if our bodies could feel no pain and our minds no inhibitions and scruples. But people who cannot feel pain are cripples. They lack the essential warning devices for their bodies; they may continue to hold something hot rather than drop it immediately and are therefore more susceptible to burns and to infections following from those burns. Persons who lack all internalized sense of authority and all conscience are social cripples. They lack an essential warning system that would keep them from damaging themselves and others, as well as their community. Under many political systems they may become criminals or tyrants. If they stay clear of the law and rise to power in the system, the hidden damage they do may be greater still.

Therefore, all individuals and all political systems need some sense of authority. But authority must not be accepted blindly, uncritically, or unrestrictedly. Much of what is called *conscience* is whatever we were taught before the age of six. It is in part a matter of accident in our biography, a matter of the family and country in which we grew up. (In Mark Twain's novel, southern-born Huckleberry Finn had a bad conscience when he helped his black friend Jim escape from slavery.) But *legitimate authority* also has an objective character. It implies the promise that its commands will remain compatible with other values that we personally hold and with the needs of the persons and communities that we hold dear. Such a promise may be true or false. It is our responsibility to test it against facts and to make sure that we do not follow false authorities no matter how long established or how recently in fashion.

To say that authority must be tested against fact is to say that it must be tested by performance, for authority is both the product of a political system and a condition for its future functioning. The way a political system has performed in the past goes far toward determining what authority it has among its people; but the kind of authority a system has at any one time will have great effects on what it can do in the future. The performance of political systems can thus be tested by the authority relationships that they create and by the loyalties that they evoke. These authority relationships and loyalties, in turn, will determine some of the capacities of these systems for future performance.

The effectiveness of authority can be measured by the frequency and dependability with which it is obeyed in the absence of supervision or coercion. Conscience, said a Greek philosopher, is what controls our acts when nobody is watching. Wherever data are available on a population's rate of compliance with the laws or commands of a government, we can learn something about authority. When authority disintegrates, compliance will decline. The ratio of prisoners to casualties among combat troops is a rough-and-ready indicator of their loyalty. In World War I both the German-speaking and the Hungarian regiments of the Austro-Hungarian army were very loyal to the Empire. On the average there was one casualty among them for every soldier who surrendered. The Slavic regiments in the same army had little sympathy for the Empire and its war. For every casualty among them, more than three others were taken prisoner. In the war in Vietnam, figures published by the United States Department of Defense showed many more desertions than fatalities among South Vietnamese troops, but among the Vietcong they showed persistently many more fatalities than prisoners or desertions. It is obviously difficult to compile accurate figures for a guerrilla war, but the message of these Vietnam data over several years is clear. The actual rates of compliance or obedience, by soldiers as well as by civilians, are a kind of voting-by-action on the commands of those trying to rule them.

WHAT ONE MAY LEGITIMATELY DEMAND FROM THE STATE: THE TEST OF HUMAN RIGHTS

Authority and loyalty determine what the state may demand of its people; *human rights* sum up what people may legitimately demand of their state. Authority and loyalty define one's duties toward the government; and if one does one's duties, one should not expect to be thanked for it. (It is only for courage "above and beyond the call of duty" that members of the United States armed forces receive the Congressional Medal of Honor.) The same applies to rights. Whatever is yours by right is not a privilege or a gift. You should get it without owing thanks to anyone, and you may take it if need be.

In 1976–78, human rights became a major theme of United States foreign policy, with some explicit exceptions for "strategically important" states, such as South Korea and Iran under the Shah. In his State of the Union Address on January 19, 1978, President Carter declared, "The very heart of our identity as a nation is our firm commitment to human rights." He reiterated this theme in a speech at Memphis, Tennessee, in December 1978 and urged congressional ratification of the United Nations Human Rights Convention. Early in 1977 a private organization, *Amnesty International,* was awarded the Nobel Peace Prize for monitoring the human rights performance of many governments around the world.

With so much stress on human rights, the concept deserves closer examination. Through the centuries many writers, from Cicero and Saint Augustine to Saint Thomas Aquinas and to the great liberals like John Locke and John Stuart Mill, have held that certain rights are *natural.* By this they have meant that these rights are inborn. Any younger brother or sister seems to demand quite naturally equal rights with an elder sibling. But "nature" is a difficult concept to apply. The more that scientists have discovered about nature, the less freely have philosophers been able to use it in their theories. Some rights that were considered natural in the past, such as the right of revenge or the right to own slaves or large estates of land, have turned out not to be rights at all in other times and places, and societies function fairly well without them.

Nevertheless, we may ascribe to the concept of natural rights an operational meaning. Natural behavior is probable behavior. It is likely to occur whenever it is not prevented by "artificial" obstacles, that is, by obstacles that are less probable and that can be maintained only by special efforts or arrangements. *Natural rights* are rights that people are likely to claim whenever not specifically restrained from doing so and likely to claim again as soon as the restraint ceases. Whether a particular right is a natural right in this sense—one that is claimed spontaneously at many times and places—is a question of fact. And it is a task of political scientists to look at the facts and to see whether and to what extent this is the case.

Insofar as any human right is natural in this sense, it cannot be sold or signed away. By definition, people will automatically claim it again as soon as no one stops them; and they will claim it anyway if they are strong enough. From this point of view, no one can legally sign away his or her right to live. Neither can anyone sign away the right to be free. Nor can such rights be lost by "prescription"—that is, by long usage, habit, or passage of time. They are "imprescriptible," in the language of eighteenth-century lawyers, or "unalienable," in the language of the Declaration of Independence.[5]

In the two centuries since the American and French revolutions, the demand for human rights has spread around the world. England has had a Bill of Rights since 1674, dealing mostly with legal procedures that safeguard individuals against the abuse of power by the government. In the United States a Bill of Rights forms the first ten amendments to the Constitution. In the German Federal Republic, similar rights are embodied in the country's Basic Law. The constitutions of most countries, including that of the Soviet Union, contain some provisions of this kind. It is a task of political scientists to observe and report how well such rights are respected in practice.

Many of the early lists of human rights are *negative* in character. They state what the government may not do to individuals. It may not mutilate or torture them, or kill or imprison them without due legal process, or deny them equal protection of the law. It may not stifle their freedom of speech, or stop them from worshipping according to conscience, or force them to worship against their will. The limits and margins of these rights vary with time and place, but their core is the same in many countries.

In our own century demands for *positive* human rights have come to the forefront. It is not enough to treat all people equally before the law. The right to life, it is now argued, implies the right to food and shelter and in more recent views, the right to medical help when needed. Freedom of speech implies the freedom to read; it implies the right to knowledge and education. Generally the absence of restraint is useless without the presence of opportunity and the knowledge and capacity to act.

All human rights and freedoms thus have their positive aspects; and when these are not automatically supplied by social and economic life, people are turning increasingly to their governments for them. President Franklin D. Roosevelt expressed this new perception of freedom in 1941 when he spoke of the "Four Freedoms" that were to be established everywhere in the world: freedom of religion, freedom of speech, freedom from want, and freedom from fear. The first two are primarily negative, demanding restraints from governments. But freedom from want—which has not yet been achieved even in the United States four decades later—requires a vast positive effort of both production and distribution within each country and among countries as well. Freedom from fear may require the most complex action. It implies nothing less than the abolition of war—and in the long run, the end of all tyranny and persecution. And the abolition of war requires the peaceful management of conflicts. It requires, therefore, a great deal of positive coordination of the behavior of governments and nations, of which the United Nations is only a beginning.

President Roosevelt later presented a more detailed list of positive human rights. In his message to Congress in January 1945 he called for a "Second Bill of Rights" for the American people. As a whole, such a bill has yet to be passed. The full employment legislation and the medicare and

[5]Not all political thinkers have shared this view. Burke, the great conservative, thought that all rights were artificial, made only by convention and experience. Natural rights, he once suggested testily, were nonsense; natural and imprescriptible rights, nonsense on stilts.

medicaid bills in the United States are steps in this direction. President Nixon's proposal for a guaranteed minimum income was another, until it was lost from sight within his own administration; it may well re-emerge some day in the policies of one or both of the major parties. Similar principles and practices have been adopted in many Western European countries. Long catalogues of positive rights are also found in the constitutions of the Soviet Union and other Communist countries.

But it is one thing to promise human rights and another to deliver them. Later in this chapter we shall see how the performance of government in many of these matters can be measured. First, however, we must ask another set of questions. *Who* is to implement these rights? Is it to be the central government alone that will do these things for its people? Or can the people do them for themselves, by joining together in their localities and neighborhoods and in a multitude of groups and self-governing associations? Organizing autonomous groups is itself a human right, but it is also a matter of capacity, opportunity, and motivation.

The Ability to Form Self-Governing Groups. Whether a political system enables its population to form many self-governing associations is another test of its performance. The more capacity and opportunity it produces for the formation of such groups, the better will be its performance for its people. But the capacity of the people to form such groups and to govern themselves in conducting the affairs of these groups is in itself an important condition for the performance of a political system. Indeed, this capacity may be one of the most important aspects of the political culture of a country. Thus, when the Japanese political theorist Masao Maruyama set out to understand the political changes in his own country, he developed a scheme for comparing political systems of different periods and countries in terms of their capacity to form self-governing associations[6] (see Figure 9.1).

Maruyama proposed two ways of comparing different political systems. First, he would determine whether they were centrifugal or centripetal. The decentralized or *centrifugal system* attempts to allocate power outward to regions and not inward to a single center of decision making, whereas the

[6]Masao Maruyama, "Patterns of Individuation and the Case of Japan: A Conceptual Scheme," in Marius B. Jansen, ed., *Changing Japanese Attitudes Toward Modernization* (Princeton: Princeton University Press, 1965), pp. 489–531.

FIGURE 9.1 *Maruyama's Typology of Political Systems*

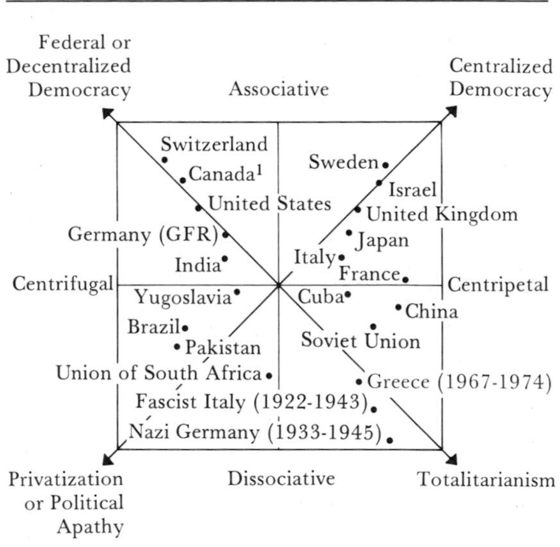

[1]On paper, the Canadian constitution gives more powers to the central government than does the American. In practice, French-speaking Quebec has more effective "states' rights" than Alabama or Mississippi.

centralized or *centripetal system* tends to draw power together to a single center. Second, he would determine whether they were associationist or dissociationist. An *associationist* society contains traditions and skills for forming autonomous, small, self-governing groups on matters of substantive relevance. Such groups include local governments, labor unions, cooperatives, churches, and the like. A *dissociationist* society reveals the opposite pattern of behavior. Here individuals think that in all important matters they cannot trust other individuals very much, and on the whole they withdraw from permanent, direct self-government.

It is important to note that not all nations in which people join organizations are associationist. Joining powerless associations has no political effect. What counts is how important these associations are, how seriously people take their self-government within their groups, and how tenaciously they will defend it. If the organizations joined deal mainly with trivial affairs, then there is no associationism in that society. The German people in the 1920s and early 1930s, for example, were remarkably rich in numbers of organizations. They joined everything in sight: stamp collectors' clubs, garden clubs, rabbit breeders' clubs, and all kinds of similar *Vereine*. But when it came to really important matters, they deferred to authority and reorganized their associations in line with Nazi policies.

Maruyama suggests that a highly associationist, centripetal political system fosters a particular type of *centralized democracy*. In the United Kingdom a great deal of government is carried on by all sorts of voluntary associations. We may think of British local government, of the trade unions or cooperative societies, or of the British clubs that organize a good part of the elite of Britain's political parties, whether Conservative, Liberal, or Labour. One might further include among the many voluntary associations the Briton's local castle, the neighborhood pub. Besides encouraging voluntary organizations, Britain tends to give most power to Parliament as a single center of decision making. Thus the United Kingdom rates high on both the associationist and the centripetal scales.

The United States, on the other hand, is markedly more centrifugal, with its distribution of power between the federal government and the states, its promotion of states' rights, and its continuing allocation of a little more than one-third of the government sector to spending by states and municipalities. The recent policy of revenue sharing, introduced on a large scale by the Nixon administration, caters to this tendency by transferring relatively large lump sums of federal tax money to the states and municipalities to be spent locally in accordance with the prevailing needs, habits, and political power relationships within each community. At the same time, the United States is strongly associationist. Switzerland is even more associationist and more centrifugal than the United States. Maruyama calls this combination "individualism." We would probably call it pluralism. *Pluralistic individualism* might be an even better term.

Another type of government is heavily centripetal, giving all power to a central decision maker, but dissociationist in that its subjects or citizens do not trust each other. This pattern is characteristic of *totalitarian* regimes. Such a government resembles a wheel with strong spokes, but no rim. People do not trust each other, but they trust the central government, a government that strongly discourages voluntary and spontaneous groups (except those run by the government). Nazi Germany (1933–45) and Fascist Italy (1922–43) are telling examples.

At some stages in its history the Soviet Union fitted into such a scheme, but even then the fit was a poor one. The Soviet Union's collective farms, labor unions, cooperatives, and various local and factory councils all brought about a considerable increase in associationist skills in that nation. Most likely a Soviet citizen of today, or even of the 1920s and 1930s, is a member of many more organizations in which he or she has more of a share at least in minor decisions than was his or her grandparent in the days of the czar. On the other hand, these organizations usually are not free to differ in fundamental policy from the national government. Their members do not get much experience in discussing or deciding fundamental matters. The U.S.S.R. is also still dissociationist in part. Its citizens are always exhorted to look for "bourgeois remnants," deviationists, agents of counterrevolution, and similar foes of their society. And the more one looks for all these wicked people, the less one can trust one's neighbor, since, after all, that person might be an agent of capitalism in disguise.

To some extent the People's Republic of China fits a pattern similar to that of the Soviet Union. Many Chinese now take more part in decision making and in the administering of villages, communes, factories, and cooperatives than ever before. Yet they are told in many ways to be "vigilant," which means, in effect, to distrust each other. One document from a Chinese Communist Party Congress denounced the Communist president of Communist China as a "scab." Apparently a really loyal Communist Chinese cannot trust anyone else, not even the president of the country. Almost anyone, with the possible exception of Mao Tse-tung, might be revealed as a "deviationist" in the course of the next campaign, and suspicion among Mao's successors does not seem to have abated much. Such suspicion leads to real difficulties in building lasting trust or lasting cooperation among individuals in a political system that again and again teaches each person to look upon his or her neighbor as a potential traitor, heretic, or enemy.

Finally, a country may be both centrifugal and dissociationist, with people trusting neither their government nor one another. This somewhat dismal state of affairs fits what Maruyama calls the pattern of *privatization*. Edward Banfield has found this pattern in a southern Italian village. In his book entitled *The Moral Basis of a Backward Society*, he speaks of the "amoral familism" dominating the life of a Calabrian village and relates how it was impossible for this village to organize a cooperative ambulance service to the nearest hospital a few miles away. It could not be done because every villager was convinced that all other villagers would steal the gasoline from the vehicle. When it was proposed that the village priest should have charge of the gasoline, the villagers, pointed out that he might steal it, too. As a result, people who needed emergency medical care continued to suffer and possibly to die without a chance of getting to the hospital in time.

Maruyama points out that none of these patterns are eternal. Japan, he finds, during the last century has passed through all of them. So, to some extent, has Germany. In appraising the political performance of other countries, we may ask where they are now in terms of centralized power and of self-governing associations and where they seem to be going.

THE EFFECTIVENESS OF GOVERNMENT: SOME QUANTITATIVE INDICATORS

In sum, the efforts of the national government, the effects of laws, the functioning of administration, the services of state and local governments, the activities of voluntary groups and associations, and the behavior of individuals all add up to the general performance of a political system.

We may also ask a more specific question: how well does a government or political system perform in attaining particular values? If a system promises life to its people, what does it deliver in terms of life expectancy? If it promises enlightenment, how does it perform with respect to primary and secondary school enrollment and higher education? For every major set of values we can find some measurable indicators of this kind and test the performance of the country's political system against them (see Table 9.1). Of course, such performance also involves the effects of the country's social and economic systems, but it is the

TABLE 9.1 *Some Indicators of the Quality of Life*

	Per capita GNP, 1976 (U.S. Dollars)	Infant mortality in first year per 1,000 births, 1975	Suicides per 1,000, 1973	Homicides per 1,000, 1973	Students in higher education per 100,000 (all institutions) 1973–75
United States	7,890	16.1	12.1	12.4	4,825[5]
Soviet Union	4,340[1]	27.7[5]	[7]	[7]	1,908[6]
United Kingdom	4,020	16.0			
England and Wales		15.7	7.8	3.3	1,111[4]
Northern Ireland		20.4	4.6	25.5	948[4]
Scotland		17.2	8.5	5.0	1,449[4]
France	6,550	11.3[3]	15.6[2]	18.4[2]	1,884[5]
German Federal Republic	7,380	19.8	20.2[3]	3.2[3]	1,602[5]

[1]Computed in dollar prices, the Soviet per capita income is about 55 percent of the corresponding United States figure, according to Professor Bergson. Estimates in ruble prices give a much lower Soviet figure, but are less appropriate. See note to Table 3.6, above.
[2]1970. [3]1972. [4]1973. [5]1974. [6]1975. [7]Not available.

Sources: For GNP (except the Soviet Union): World Bank, *World Development Report, 1978,* table 1, pp. 76–77. For mortality: *United Nations Demographic Yearbook, 1976,* table 14, pp. 305–9. For suicides and homicides: *United Nations Demographic Yearbook, 1974,* p. 399. For students: *UNESCO Yearbook, 1976,* table 5.1, pp. 349–89; *United Nations Demographic Yearbook, 1976,* table 5, pp. 137–41.

political system through which these other aspects of life can be preserved or changed. If the conditions of life are bad and a political system lacks the power or motivation to change them, this would be worth knowing. If conditions are good and getting better, a political system would deserve much of the credit—and in practice would be likely to get it from many of the people living under it.

Life Expectancy. Perhaps the first value of politics is the value of *life*—the value that both John Locke and the Declaration of Independence put first among the rights of people. If we consider the life expectancy for women (which is higher than that for men), we find that in this respect the best performance by any political system in the world was turned in by the governments of Norway, Sweden, and Iceland, which in 1976 provided for their female populations a life expectancy of nearly seventy-eight years. These were followed in a tight group by all the world's highly developed countries, both Communist and non-Communist: about seventy-seven years for the Netherlands; seventy-six years for the United States, Britain,

France, Denmark, Canada, Japan, and Switzerland; seventy-five years for Italy and West Germany; seventy-four years for Australia, the Soviet Union, and East Germany; seventy-three years for Czechoslovakia and Ireland; and seventy-two years for Hungary. The American life expectancy of seventy-six years constituted an average of seventy-seven for whites and about seventy-two years for blacks. (In the 1970s it still cost one-fifteenth of one's life to be born black in the United States, a bitter statistic worth repeating.) Among the world's poor countries the average in the 1950s and 60s was forty-one years for India and about thirty-five years for some of the sub-Saharan African states; some of the countries with still worse life expectancies cagily do not publish statistics. We do know, however, that in some African countries in recent years half of the babies born have died before they reached the age of two.

Where statistics of infant mortality are available, they offer the chance to further substantiate data on life expectancy and on the incidence of human grief and pain. Table 9.2 compares the infant mortality rates for a few countries, in order to show the large inequalities between rich and poor countries, the more modest but real gains in many countries from 1960 to 1975, and perhaps some effects of more or less efficient public health services provided by different governments with countries on roughly the same level of per capita GNP.

Compare in Table 9.2 the per capita GNPs, infant death rates, and rates of improvement for the Netherlands and Switzerland; Japan and the United Kingdom; France, the two Germanies, Czechoslovakia, and the United States; Mexico and Chile; India, Turkey, and Saudi Arabia. Are these facts and data "nonpolitical"? What would you expect the mothers and fathers of young children in these countries to think of the performance of their governments, once they discovered that the deaths of so many children were unnecessary?

The protection of life is the first performance requirement of governments because whether people live or die is a political question. If we leave living and dying to the ballot of the dollar bill and to the forces of the market, the poor and their children will die like flies. There is no way in which any modern country can keep the mass of its people alive except by public, civic action. No country in the world that has introduced socialized medicine in some form has ever given it up. The ledger now contains about thirty countries in the world with comprehensive low-cost public medical care.[7] The concept of a government's responsibility for the health of its people began with conservatives like Bismarck in Germany and liberals like Lloyd George in England, but now cuts across all ideologies. Public health services have become important parts of the responsibility of government.

Wealth and Economic Growth. A second value almost universally desired is *wealth*. Except for a few saints or philosophers, most people do not like to be poor. In 1976 the gross national product of the United States was close to $1,700 billion, or $7,890 per capita (that is, for each individual in the population). Poor countries such as Ethiopia, Somalia, Cambodia, Laos, Mali, Bangladesh, and Nepal had per capita incomes below $120; Tanzania, India, Burma, and Pakistan were below $200. Switzerland's per capita income in 1976 was $8,880, and Sweden's was $8,670; both of these surpassed the United States, despite their modest natural resources. Somewhat below the United States were Canada with $7,510 and West Germany with $7,380 (but by 1978 the West German per capita income was reported to have overtaken that of the United States). Then followed, in 1976 figures, France with $6,550, Japan with $4,910, the Soviet Union with $4,340, East Germany with

[7]About thirty countries have subsidized or nationalized medicine (or a nationwide state insurance program) that absorbs at least 80 percent of the cost of treatment and covers the great majority of their population. At least another forty-five countries have assumed some of the burden of public medical care.

TABLE 9.2 *Wealth and Infant Death Rates in Selected Countries*

Country	Per capita GNP, 1976	Infant mortality in first year per 1,000 births 1960	1975	Net reduction in annual infant deaths per 1,000 1960–75
Sweden	8,670	17	9	8
Japan	4,910	31	10	21
Netherlands	6,200	18	11	7
Switzerland	8,880	21	11	10
France	6,550	27	11	16
United Kingdom	4,020	23	16	7
German Democratic Republic	4,220	39	16	23
United States	7,890	26	16	10
German Federal Republic	7,380	34	20	14
Czechoslovakia	3,840	24	21	3
Italy	3,050	44	21	23
Poland	2,860	57	25	32
Soviet Union	4,340[1]	35	28[5]	7
Mexico	1,090	74	50	24
Chile	1,050	125	56	69
India	150	139[2]	122	17
Turkey	990	[6]	153[4]	[6]
Saudi Arabia	4,480	500[3]	[6]	[6]

[1]See note on Table 9.1, above. [2]1951–61. [3]1964. [4]1967. [5]1974. [6]Not available.

Sources: *United Nations Statistical Yearbook, 1967,* pp. 100–2, and *1976*, p. 414; Charles L. Taylor and Michael C. Hudson, *World Handbook of Political and Social Indicators,* 2nd ed. (New Haven: Yale University Press, 1972), p. 255; World Bank, *World Development Report, 1978,* table 17, pp. 108–9, and table 1, p. 76.

$4,220, the United Kingdom with $4,020, and Italy with $3,050.[8]

Per capita income figures do not mean that the individual consumers in these countries have these amounts to spend. Less than two-thirds of these sums were available in 1976 for private consumption in all the industrial countries: 66 percent in East Germany, 65 percent in the United States and the Soviet Union, 63 percent in Switzerland, 62 percent in France, 60 percent in the United

[8]For Soviet per capita income, estimated at 55 percent of the U.S. figure, see note to Table 3.6 below. Other data come from World Bank, *World Development Report, 1978.*

Kingdom, 57 percent in Japan and Canada, 55 percent in West Germany, and 53 percent in Sweden. The rest of the gross national product in these countries was spent on capital formation in private or public enterprises, on national defense, and on other government expenditures. In very poor countries much less is available for public purposes. In such countries as Bangladesh, Lebanon, Sierra Leone, and Portugal, over 80 percent of the gross national product went in 1976 to private consumption, and their people are still poor.[9]

The higher the per capita income of a country, the more its people can do, either privately as individuals or collectively through public institutions. Very rich countries can permit a great deal of waste and error and still not be too badly off. Poor countries must spend their financial resources more carefully if they are to buy for their people a tolerable amount of other values. Thus, Britain, with less than half the per capita income of the United States, still secures for its people the same life expectancy as the United States does for Americans.

People want to know not only how rich they are at any one moment, but also whether they are going to get richer. Therefore, another performance test that most people consider important is that of *economic growth.* The normal performance for governments was growth in gross national product of 4 percent per year in the 1950s and about 5 percent during the 1960s. These were the median rates for the whole world; and since the world's population grows at about 2 percent per year, this means that per capita income should grow at about 3 percent per year. In countries with prosperous economies and vigorous governments, per capita growth rates of between 4 and 8 percent per year can be attained, as they often have been in Japan, France, Israel, and China. In countries where things go badly, per capita growth rates can sink to 1 or 2 percent or less. Such stagnating countries included Chile, India, Uruguay, Egypt, Ghana, and Zambia in 1969–76. The United States grew at a 2.3 percent average between 1960 and 1976 and at only a 1.8 percent rate in the 1950s. (America's years on the golf course during the Eisenhower era were characterized by one of the lowest growth rates in the world at the time.) Of course, averages can be computed for long periods of time. If we count the long-range growth of the United States since the 1890s, per capita income has grown at 3 percent per year, which means it has doubled every twenty-three years. The Soviet Union has grown at about the same rate over the same period, despite the devastations of revolution, civil war, and two world wars. The performances of both the United States and the Soviet Union are clearly better than the average performance of the rest of the world. (These growth rates are given in "real" terms, that is, on the basis of fixed prices. Since prices in dollars have been rising since the 1930s, the "nominal" growth rates in paper money have been higher.)

The Extent of Inequality. But whether income grows or not is not the whole story. There is an anecdote about a man eating a roast chicken in a room with a hungry man looking on. A statistician looking in through the window reported that "on the average" there was half a chicken per capita in that room. That did not help the hungry man. Thus we also want to know how equally or unequally the benefits of life are distributed within a country.

As we noted in Chapter 5, the best method for reporting the equality of distribution and for measuring this performance in regard to equality, is the so-called *Lorenz curve* (see Figure 5.6, above). If everybody received exactly the same amount of income, 10 percent of the population would get 10 percent of the income, 20 percent would get 20 percent, and the line connecting all these groups

[9]Source: *United Nations Statistical Yearbook, 1977,* table 187, pp. 703–17.

of people would be absolutely straight. The more unequal the distribution of income, the smaller is the share of the poorest group, the higher is the share of the richest, and the more steeply curved becomes the line of income distribution. The more bent the bow is on the Lorenz diagram, the greater may be the tension in a society.

In reasonably decently governed countries the top 10 percent tend to get approximately 20 to 30 percent of the income, and this is usually borne without great social unrest. Israel distributes 27 percent of its income among the top 10 percent of receivers; Sweden, 27 to 28 percent; England, about 24 percent; and the United States, 28 percent. In India the figure rises to 37 percent; in Puerto Rico it is 35 percent. In Brazil, Peru, and Mexico it exceeds 48 percent; and in Bolivia the figure is a state secret or unknown information, but obviously the inequality there is grim.

If we take the area under the curve, double it, call the sides of the square one, and subtract the area under the double curve from the area of the square, we get the *Gini index* of inequality (see Figure 5.8, above). This index shows how unequally anything is distributed—voting rights, representation, income, and many other things. As yet there is no experience of any large society with a Gini index of less than 20 percent. It would be interesting to know what such a society would be like. In the meantime, it is worth noting that the more advanced and richer countries have less inequality. Countries with more inequality, as shown by a higher Gini index, also have less economic growth. For our time, at least, the old view that great inequality is essential to progress has turned out to be a myth.

The Gini index of inequality may indicate a society in which the poor are relatively well off, but the middle class has been shortchanged. Or it may describe a society in which the middle strata do fairly well, but the poor are treated very badly. The United States, on the whole, has an income distribution that distributes prosperity well in the middle groups. The third, fourth, fifth, and sixth deciles of income receivers, and probably also the seventh decile, still are well off in the United States. Human misery begins in the eighth decile; the last 20 percent of Americans are miserably treated, and the last 10 percent, which include of course many people from broken homes and families, live in conditions that no self-respecting northwestern European country would tolerate. Thus, in providing for its poor, the United States is behind many countries in the world because of the scandalous conditions that it tolerates. United States citizens became more aware of and sensitive to these conditions in the 1960s, and efforts were made to speed up the slow pace of improvement. President Johnson's "poverty program," President Nixon's proposal for a "family assistance plan" and President Carter's urban assistance program have not yet produced any major changes in the situation, but it seems likely that efforts at more substantial improvements will occupy much of the attention of both Congress and the president in the 1980s—if enough Americans should care to press for them.

A country can do something about inequality if it wants to and if its people know how income is distributed and on whom suffering is inflicted. We can, therefore, judge the performance of a political system not only by the quality of life it provides for its people, but also by the specific figures that measure it; and specifying those figures, we can begin to see whether things are getting better or worse and whether some particular political changes make a difference.

At the same time, equality of income has proved practicable to only a limited extent. The data from eight Western and four Communist countries, as given in Table 9.3, show a moderate span of incomes of 1:2 or less between unskilled manual workers and lower administrative and professional personnel, spans of between about 1:2 and 1:4 between manual workers and higher administrative and professional staff in the United States and

TABLE 9.3 *Another Indicator of Inequality: Incomes of Unskilled, Skilled, and Professional and Managerial Personnel*

A. WESTERN EUROPE AND UNITED STATES*

OCCUPATIONAL STRATA	West Germany (1957)	West Germany 1965	Norway (1956)	Norway 1964	United States (1939)	United States 1959	Sweden (1953)	Sweden 1963
Unskilled manual workers	(1.0)	1.0	(1.0)	1.0	(1.0)	1.0	(1.0)	1.0
Skilled manual workers	(1.3)	1.3	(1.1)	1.2	(1.5)	1.6	(n.a.)	n.a.
Clerks	(1.0)	1.0	(1.0)	1.0	(2.1)	1.8	(1.3)	1.3
Lower administrative and professional staff	(1.5)	1.4	(1.2)	1.3	(n.a.)	n.a.	(1.5)	1.8
Higher administrative and professional staff	(2.1)	1.8	(2.2)	2.4	(3.2)	2.4	(2.0)	3.1

	United Kingdom (1935)	United Kingdom 1960	Denmark 1965	France (1956)	France 1964	Italy 1959
Unskilled manual workers	(1.0)	1.0	1.0	(1.0)	1.0	1.0
Skilled manual workers	(1.5)	1.5	1.2	(1.4)	1.5	1.2
Clerks	(1.5)	1.3	1.3	(1.4)	1.5	1.5
Lower administrative and professional staff	(2.4)	1.6	2.1	(2.4)	2.8	2.0
Higher administrative and professional staff	(3.8)	3.5	4.3	(4.9)	5.5	7.0

*Earnings of unskilled manual labor in each country = 1.0.

B. EASTERN EUROPE†

	Czechoslovakia 1970	Czechoslovakia 1974	Hungary 1970	Hungary 1974	Poland 1970	Poland 1974	Soviet Union 1970	Soviet Union 1974
Manual workers	0.96	0.97	0.96	0.98	0.95	0.97	0.98	0.99
Engineering and Technical personnel	1.17	1.15	1.45	1.38	1.43	1.36	1.34	1.24
Administrative personnel			0.93	0.89	0.98	0.94	0.84	0.81

†Income of industrial workers and employees only. Average wage in industry in each country = 1.00.

Source: *United Nations Economic Survey of Europe, 1975,* chap. 5, p. 127.

northwestern Europe, and spans of 1:5.5 and 1:7 between the earnings of manual workers and those of higher staff personnel in France and Italy, respectively. (Would you care to guess in which of these eight Western countries Communist parties get a substantial portion of the vote in free elections?)

In the four Communist countries, the occupational stratification data are not readily comparable to the Western ones. However, the figures suggest that there, too, for the large bulk of income earners in industry, transport, and distributive services there are moderate but significant differences in earnings, perhaps not much smaller than in West Germany or Norway, but starting from a lower basis of consumer goods and living standards.

Though these moderate income differentials in East and West may well hold for the great majority of income earners, there seem to be in most countries a few top income receivers whose earnings make excellent targets for political attack. Western writers point to the 1,500–2,000 rubles earned monthly by top Soviet scientists and government leaders, which may correspond to thirty or forty times the monthly earnings of unskilled workers in Soviet industry; and Communist and other critics of the United States may point to the reported $1,000,000 annual incomes of a few American corporation executives, which amount to about 150 times the federal minimum wage for unskilled labor. All this makes for attention-getting rhetoric; but most of the everyday work of modern industrial nations is carried on within a much narrower range of economic incentives and inequalities. Within this modest range, still more nearly complete equality may prove difficult and costly to establish; but outside this range, spectacular inequalities may persist mainly by the sufferance of the political system. They depend on its protection; they can be reduced or abolished by political change; or they may be preserved in part and in modified form in the service of other values desired by the community.

The Relevance of Facts and Figures. We could present a much longer list of indicators for the performance of political systems (see Table 9.4). Some of these might be indicators of performance in regard to values shared by most political systems in the world, such as literacy and mass education. Others might be indicators of performance in regard to matters highly valued by some nations, but much less by others, such as the concentration of political power, the growth of big cities, the size of the state, or the nation's military strength. A recent study of the Swiss political system used more than forty indicators of performance. The task of this book, however, is only to introduce the reader to various methods of political analysis. It will suffice to present only a limited number of examples of empirical and quantitative research data if the ways in which these data are used are explained fully.

Facts and figures can tell us what the world is like and to what extent it is being changed by the actions of others or ourselves. If we say we are against the death of children, this is as helpful as saying that we are for home, God, and mother and against the man-eating shark. However, if we can say that child mortality in Mississippi has been cut by one-third, then we have said something meaningful. We have said that there now exists a visible number of children who would not have survived otherwise. Our general sentiments of value and good will are taking on the cutting edge of specific fact. If such facts are lacking, sentiments and values are likely to remain meaningless. Values and facts, qualities and quantities, must be put together if political analysis and action are to be effective.

QUANTITY AND QUALITY: POLITICAL SYSTEM PERFORMANCE AS A WHOLE

The measurement of quantities and the transformation of the quality of life are two aspects of one and the same reality, of a single social process. When we ask what something *resembles*, we refer to

TABLE 9.4 *Some Quantitative Tests for the Performance of Political Systems*

Test or Criterion	Quantitative Indicator (per 1,000 population)
1. Quality of leaders	How many criminal acts? How many people in prison?
2. Quality of common people	What is the life expectancy, Gini index, number of suicides, number of homicides?
3. Provision of rights	What guarantees exist? How much freedom to speak, read, publish? Are the guarantees positive or negative? To what extent are they respected in practice?
4. Opportunity to form self-governing associations	How many and how important self-governing associations or major informal groups? How much mutual trust? How many persons report sense of belonging and of political effectiveness? How many have right to oppose government on specific issues? On general policy?
5. Protection for minorities	How many children taught in mother tongue? How many people belong to minority religions or philosophies protected by law? How many cases or complaints of group discrimination? How great a difference among the occupations and values attained by different racial or ethnic groups?

its quality. When we ask *how often* have we recognized it, we refer to its quantity.

We can now see that much of what happens in politics and government is the result of the workings of a political system rather than the plottings of a few villains or conspirators. We can gauge the effectiveness of such a system by the extent to which it is likely to attain its main goals, and we estimate its efficiency by the the ratio of its successes to their costs. Such judgments are easily made in political emergencies, when a single goal or value predominates; they are more difficult to make in normal situations, when goals are multiple and open-ended.

Quantitative tests for government performance begin with the budget. Qualitative tests begin with the quality of leaders and of ordinary people, as well as of the political culture and authority, as produced by the system. A key test of such qualities is the ability of a people to form self-governing groups dealing with matters of genuine importance.

The results of political performance become visible through a host of quantitative indicators about the life of the people. These include life expectancy, infant mortality, per capita gross national product, economic growth, literacy and access to education, voting rights and actual political participation, and extent of inequality in regard to these and other values. Together with indicators of political violence, executive stability,

and popular compliance with the laws, these indicators can tell us much about how well a political system works.

But they do not tell us enough. There is more to the performance of a political system as a whole than a mere sum of quantitative tests. It is this something more to which we refer when we speak of the quality of life.

Quality of life means a chance of fulfilling one's possibilities, an ability to grow. On the one hand, it means acting out what we are and have right now; but it also means the possibility of reaching beyond what we have and are at any one moment. As the philosopher Nietzsche once said, "Man is a transition and a perdition." We are reaching beyond what we are because we can become more. And this openness is one of the essential aspects of the quality of being human.

Quality of life also involves whether people have to be afraid of one another or can trust and count on one another. Political systems that destroy trust and political movements that deny all trust produce political paralysis. Without a minimum of mutual trust, people cannot cooperate and cannot control their fate.

The fate of the people is the people themselves. We are each other's fate; and if we can do something about getting control not only of our own lives but also of our larger environment, and if we know what to do with that control, we can improve the quality of our lives and our own quality as persons and as a community. This can be done only if competence and compassion are united. Competence without compassion could turn us into executioners, whether we know it or not. And compassion without competence could turn us into well-meaning quacks. When illness is serious, a quack is a menace. The difference between medicine and quackery is defined by the tests of facts. We had better not offer ourselves as surgeons for appendicitis if we do not know where the appendix is.

KEY TERMS AND CONCEPTS

system
performance
effectiveness
efficiency
emergency government
multiple goal-seeking capacities
budget
budgetary analysis
revenue
progressive tax
regressive tax
wealth tax
property tax
indirect tax
direct tax
turnover tax
deficit financing
inflation
budget forecasting
power of the purse
modal personality
culture
lineal human relations
collateral human relations
ascription
achievement
authority
internalization
conscience
legitimate authority
human rights
Amnesty International
natural rights
Maruyama scheme
centrifugal system
centripetal system
associationist
dissociationist
centralized democracy
pluralistic individualism
privatization
wealth
economic growth
quality of life

ADDITIONAL READINGS

Almond, G. A., and G. B. Powell, Jr. *Comparative Politics: System, Process, and Policy.* 2nd ed. Boston: Little, Brown, 1978. Chap. 8 PB

Aristotle. *Politics.* Trans. Sir Ernest Barker. New York: Oxford University Press, 1958. Books II and IV.

Banfield, E., and L. F. Banfield. *The Moral Basis of a Backward Society.* New York: Free Press, 1958. PB

Bauer, R. A., A. Inkeles, and C. Kluckhohn. *How the Soviet System Works.* Cambridge: Harvard University Press, 1956.

Boulding, K. *Ecodynamics: A New Theory of Societal Evolution.* Beverly Hills–London: Sage, 1978.

Brzezinski, Z., and S. P. Huntington. *Political Power: USA/USSR.* New York: Viking Press, 1963. "Conclusion." PB

Deutsch, K. W. *Ecosocial Systems and Ecopolitics.* Paris: UNESCO, 1977.

Lipset, S. M. *Revolution and Counterrevolution: Change and Persistence in Social Structures.* New York: Basic Books, 1968. PB

Maruyama, M. "Patterns of Individuation and the Case of Japan: A Conceptual Scheme." In M. B. Jansen, ed., *Changing Japanese Attitudes Toward Modernization.* Princeton: Princeton University Press, 1965.

Parkin, F. *Class Inequality and Political Order.* London: Paladin (Granada Ltd.), 1972. PB

Pitkin, H. F. *The Concept of Representation.* Berkeley and Los Angeles: University of California Press, 1967. PB

Singer, J. D., and M. Small. *The Wages of War.* New York: Wiley, 1972.

Data Resources

Russett, B. M., H. R. Alker, Jr., K. W. Deutsch, and H. D. Lasswell. *World Handbook of Political and Social Indicators.* New Haven: Yale University Press, 1964.

Sivard, R. L. *World Military and Social Expenditures* (annual). Leesburg, Va.: WMSE Publications, 1978 et seq.

Taylor, C. L., and M. C. Hudson. *World Handbook of Political and Social Indicators.* 2nd ed. New Haven: Yale University Press, 1972

United Nations Demographic Yearbook (annual).

United Nations Statistical Yearbook (annual).

World Bank. *World Development Report, 1978.* Washington, D.C.: International Bank for Reconstruction and Development, 1978.

PB = *available in paperback*

PART II

SEVEN MODERN COUNTRIES AND AN EMERGING WORLD

X

The United States

Nobody really understands the United States—neither foreigners nor its own people. Winston Churchill once spoke of the Soviet Union as "a riddle wrapped in a mystery inside an enigma." Much the same might be said about the United States by any harassed Kremlin specialist in American research. If American "Kremlinologists" find it hard to forecast the Soviet Union's moves, Soviet "Pentagonologists" or "Washingtonologists" find it equally difficult to forecast United States behavior.

Let us try to see whether we can make at least some progress toward understanding American politics by applying the main analytic tools with which we became acquainted in Part I. Accordingly, we shall ask first about the particular nature of politics in the United States, as it has developed in the course of the history of the American people. We shall inquire what "government" and "governing" have meant to Americans at different times in the past and what they mean now. We shall ask what values have arisen here; how and to what extent expectations of legitimacy and habits of compliance have developed; what priorities in the political decision process have tended to prevail; and how far and in what ways the American political system has shown capacities for learning and self-transformation.

After this excursion into history, we shall look more closely at present-day American politics. What are its stakes, and who are its participants? What major images and theories or ideologies have people formed about its working? And what is now the arena of American politics, both domestic and worldwide? These questions will have been answered in good part by our historical discussion, so briefer remarks should suffice.

After these concerns, we shall take a closer look at the structure of the American political system. What holds it together, at which system levels do the main political processes occur, and which institutions have been most important and enduring? How does the system steer itself? What channels and processes of communication, corrective feedback, and decision making are most effective? To what extent does the political system of the United States—or, put differently, of the American people, Union, and nation—show processes similar to memory, consciousness, and will? Who or what—which persons, groups, institutions, or organizations—most often or most effectively remember, are aware, harden or change their will and that of the nation? What particular political processes and pieces of machinery seem to be most relevant for the outcome? What is the outcome of American politics, and what are its costs—when, where, for whom, in what respects? What, in short, is the performance of the American political system in regard to which tastes, which values, and which groups of people?

Most of these questions can be answered only with difficulty, in part, and with ever present risks of error. Even if we could answer all of them, we should only have begun to understand the politics and policies of the United States. But even a start will be well worth undertaking.

THE NATURE OF AMERICAN POLITICS: THE ROLE OF HISTORY

The political system of the United States has been marked by a large land area, a short history, a young and mobile people, a succession of moving frontiers, and vast resources in wealth and opportunity. It also has been marked by competing individuals and interest groups; uneven and uncertain images of legitimacy and habits of compliance; great influence and power conceded to money; conflicting ideas and values, often held by the same people; tolerance of a wide variety of surface fads and fashions; serious readiness to learn and change quickly and boldly in particular sectors; and widespread insistence on visible overall continuity of the nation's basic morality and culture.

Political moods in America often swing back and forth between optimism and pessimism; trust in education and distrust of the educated; a confident faith in the improvement of human beings through knowledge and kindness and a hardheaded claim that most people can be moved only by wealth or force. In such a system and such a political culture it is often hard to agree on priorities and to set a consistent course of action, yet in major crises in the past this usually has been done. Despite its diversities and inner conflicts, the political system has preserved its unity; despite tragedies and errors—some past, some still continuing—it has often been a force for good in the world; and there is reason to think that it retains the capacity to renew itself and develop into something still better.

SOME WAYS IN WHICH AMERICA IS DIFFERENT

The United States has much in common with other modern industrial nations. The whole point of this book is comparative political analysis; if the United States were incomparable, it could not be included here, and Americans and people from other countries would have little or nothing to learn from each other in regard to politics. But many aspects of American politics, both assets and handicaps, are indeed peculiar to this country, and we must look to history for help in understanding them.

In American history a few background characteristics stand out. The United States is the first of the world's new nations. Emerging in the 1760s and early 1770s and taking shape in an anticolonial revolution, the American people faced many of the problems of nation building that the world's emerging nations are encountering today. But since 1791 the United States also has been the oldest steadily functioning constitutional political system in the world. In contrast to the United States, every other political system has undergone more radical changes in recent times. This includes Sweden, Norway, Denmark, and Switzerland, whose written constitutions all date from the first half of the nineteenth century; and it is certainly true of all other large countries. Compared with the rest of the world, then, the changes in the American political system have been moderate, and the continuity of its tradition has been remarkable. This has not always been a blessing: the United States was the last modern country in the world to abolish slavery. But for good or ill, the historic facts of early anticolonialism and political traditionalism very likely have contributed to the traits of impatience and conservatism so evident in American politics.[1]

Second, in terms of economic capability the United States is the largest political system in the world. For a brief time after the end of World War II, it had more than one-half of the world's income and productive machinery. After the war the United States continued to grow, but as other countries recovered from the war and often grew faster, the relative share of the United States declined. In 1978 the United States still had nearly 25 percent of the gross national product of the world, together with nearly as large a share of the world's capital equipment. The United States also has on a per capita basis one of the highest average living standards in the world. In population and in area the United States is the world's fourth largest political system. Only three countries—the Soviet Union, Canada, and China—are bigger in area, and only three countries—China, India, and the Soviet Union—are larger in population.

In less than two centuries the American political system has succeeded in organizing a country on the scale of a continent. Only religious ideologies have done comparable jobs of organization on such a vast scale, and they did so much earlier in history. The religion of Lao-Tse, together with the Confucian philosophy, helped unite Chinese culture; Hindu religion kept India together; and Byzantine Christianity was the basis of the Russian state. The United States is the child of the eighteenth-century Enlightenment, the only secular ideology that has *created* a huge country and kept it intact. Varieties of communism have taken over large existing countries, such as Russia and China, but the United States started off with a bundle of colonies with 3 million people and parlayed this population into a country of over 200 million—close to what Benjamin Franklin predicted at its start.

At present the United States is perhaps the largest country in the world in capabilities for good and evil, insights and errors. It did more than any other country in relieving famines after World Wars I and II and again in the 1950s and 1960s. Its economic aid under the Marshall Plan in 1948-52 was crucial in the reconstruction of Western Europe. Its technological contributions—from Edison's electric light and the Wright brothers' airplane to nuclear energy and the landings on the moon—have changed the world. But its errors can be more devastating, shattering, and damaging than those of any other country because they have had more power behind them. Only slowly are some other countries drawing closer to the United States in their national power and their capacity to do vast damage to themselves and others by their errors.

Government by Design. To be sure, the United States was intended not to commit errors, but to be the world's first truly rational government. Its political system was shaped by the ideas of applied social scientists who were familiar with the most advanced theory of their time. Franklin, Jefferson, Hamilton, James Wilson, and especially Madison—all were men who had studied carefully

[1]For two fascinating books, each exploring a different aspect of this paradox, see Seymour Martin Lipset, *The First New Nation* (New York: Basic Books, 1963); and Daniel Boorstin, *The Genius of American Politics* (Chicago: University of Chicago Press, 1953). For the emergence of the American people, see the quantitative evidence from the colonial newspapers, presented by Richard L. Merritt, *Symbols of American Community, 1735-1775* (New Haven: Yale University Press, 1966).

what was then called "the science of government."[2] These founders of the Republic were deliberately trying to set up the United States as a government founded on reason—today we might say as a piece of social engineering. They *designed* the American political system with several tasks in mind. It was designed for expansion across a continent and, in some minds, at least, for further expansion across the oceans. It was also designed to attract capital from abroad and from within the country and to promote its investment in advanced technologies. And it was meant to give its inhabitants a better opportunity for spontaneity, freedom, and self-expression than could be found anywhere else.

People by Development. Unlike its political institutions, the American people, of course, was not produced by anyone's design. It was formed by history and by the decisions of millions of immigrants. The American colonists were molded into a new people by their common experience in the New World, the growing communication among the colonies, the distance from Europe, and, finally, their growing revolutionary movement. They learned to think of themselves as Americans, and of the colonies as one country, before the first shots were fired at Lexington and Concord.[3] The experience of the American Revolution deepened this sense of a common identity and made it more widespread, but it had been clearly established before 1776 in the press, in the flow of many transactions of everyday life, and in the minds of such leaders as Benjamin Franklin.

Americans became recognizable as a people as they became more and more associated with certain distinctive traits. One of the persistent characteristics of the American people has been its great geographic mobility. About one-third of Americans live outside the state of their birth, and there is reason to believe the proportion has been this high since the Revolution. This figure is much higher than the exchange of population among the states of Western Europe. Even within Germany, as late as 1870 only 5 percent of the inhabitants of Bavaria came from outside Bavaria. Benjamin Franklin commented on the ability of Americans, thanks to a plentiful supply of land, to move freely in order to take up farming or other work in new locations. This mobility put a limit on what anyone could do to people. If local government or conditions of work became oppressive, they could pick up their possessions—which for most of them were sparse enough to be mobile—and move on. Mobility dispersed them, first along the eastern seaboard and then across the continent, but this constant flow of migrants kept Americans uniform in culture. In the late eighteenth century, British travelers reported that the speech of the American people was almost identical over a thousand miles' distance, in contrast to the speech of the English rural population, which differed by dialect every hundred miles.

Another shared characteristic of the American people was a relatively high degree of literacy, which was uncommon in eighteenth-century Europe and is yet to be reached by many developing countries. A third was the high degree of political participation, in rural areas as well as in towns. A fourth trait was the habit of self-government and the widespread ability to form and maintain self-governing groups for a variety of political, economic, and social purposes.

Two final common conditions, in part underlying the others, were the facts that most farmers owned their land and that they did not feel bound by tradition in choosing their methods of tillage. As a result, American farmers were more independent, innovative, and prosperous. Unlike their European counterparts, they owned guns and horses; they wore felt hats and leather boots; they

[2]The reading lists of these men have become available. See Douglas Adair and Walton Hale Hamilton, *The Power to Govern: The Constitution, Then and Now* (New York: Norton, 1937); and Douglas Adair, "'That Politics May Be Reduced to a Science': David Hume, James Madison, and the Tenth Federalist," *Huntington Library Quarterly,* 20 (1957), 343-60.

[3]For the growing use of the words "American" and "Americans" in the colonial press, see Merritt, *Symbols of American Community.*

were free to hunt and fish; and most of them never had been subject to large landowners or nobles. In short, they were not *peasants*. Their mobility and their resources gave them far greater capabilities to escape oppression or frustration or to resist them successfully. Thus the Constitution did not *give* freedom to the American people. Rather, it helped them to make more effective use of the freedom that was already woven into the fabric of their lives. This point is often forgotten by those who would transplant political institutions and constitutions from one society to another.

If American farmers were far more free than the peasants of Europe, the black people in America were slaves, having neither freedom nor mobility. But the model of free farmers and free workers was set for everybody; and once the slaves were liberated, their descendants sooner or later would insist on claiming the same freedom in full measure.

Above all, most Americans discovered that much in their lives was not irrevocably fixed by past tradition, long-entrenched institutions, or immemorial usage. Within the limits of practicality and of their own resources, they could choose their place of residence, their line of work or line of business, their religious denomination, their patterns of family life and community relations; and they often could change any or all of these by simply moving on or by combining with their neighbors to make some changes where they lived.

In many places they could get land, claiming it formally or informally for settlement or buying it cheaply from some owner, since land was abundant. There was no one to deny it to them; no king, no aristocracy, no powerful state church monopolized much of the land, as so often had been the case in the Old World. Neither were mineral rights a royal or state monopoly; mining claims often were not difficult to stake. Established class barriers rarely seemed insurmountable. Nor was there a stifling weight of well-nigh unchangeable cultural tradition, for too many Americans had come from too many different countries and backgrounds.

More than people in most other countries, Americans felt free to innovate, unhampered by tradition. It was an attitude well expressed by Mark Twain in *A Connecticut Yankee at King Arthur's Court,* and it has found more recent expression in government-financed American footprints and car tracks on the moon.

The Underlying Premise: Economic Abundance. American politics has been based on a belief in optimism, spontaneity, harmony of interests, readiness to experiment, and willingness to compromise. For over two hundred years, these traits have stood out more strongly and continuously in American politics than in those of, say, Germany, France, or Russia. Why did these beliefs prevail and why did the political system succeed? Perhaps most important, the American political system was superimposed from the beginning on a highly prosperous economy. For a long time this economy was nearly automatic. At the start of the Republic there was no dogmatic taboo against government's acting in economic matters, but most of the expansion of the frontier was done by individuals, not government. Most of the nation's farming, manufacturing, mining, and transporting was undertaken spontaneously by individuals seeking profit and was guided automatically by the market mechanism.

In most markets people vote not with ballots, but with dollar bills or their equivalent. In the United States the distribution of income is such that the top 10 percent of individual income receivers hold about 28 percent of the income, the second 10 percent hold about 15 percent, and the third 10 percent have at least 10 percent or more (see Figures 5.6 a and b, and Table 10.1). That is, 30 percent of the American people have more than 50 percent of the dollar votes in the market. One must never forget that in voting with dollars there is a differential franchise that makes a permanent minority of over two-thirds of the American people. But in voting with ballots these two-thirds

TABLE 10.1 *Income Distribution in the United States, 1977 and 1971 (in 1977 Dollars)*

CLASS	YEAR				CHANGE	
	1971		1977		1971–77	
	All Families	Black Families	All Families	Black Families	All Families	Black Families
Poor (under $5,000)	9.9	23.5	9.4	23.8	−0.5	+0.3
Unskilled Labor ($5,000–7,500)	8.6	15.1	9.0	15.6	+0.4	+0.5
Skilled Labor and Lower Middle Class ($7,500–15,000)	29.7	33.3	27.5	31.7	−2.2	−1.6
Middle Class ($15,000–25,000)	29.6	18.6	31.7	20.9	+2.1	+2.3
Upper Middle and Top Class (over $25,000)	22.2	9.5	22.4	9.1	+0.2	−0.4

Sources for Figures 10.1(a) and 10.1(b) and Table 10.1, above:
U.S. Department of Commerce, Bureau of the Census, *Current Population Reports,* ser. P-60, no. 116 (July 1978); ser. P-60, no. 85 (1972).
For conversion of 1971 incomes to 1977 incomes: U.S. Department of Labor, Bureau of Labor Statistics, *The Consumer Price Index for January 1972* (April 1972).
Ibid., *CPI Detailed Report–November 1977* (Washington D.C.: U.S. Government Printing Office, 1978).

have a better chance of making their needs known and their voices heard, provided that they use their ballots effectively and combine them with other forms of political participation.

The American economy worked as well as it did because the energy and diligence of its people were further supported by a number of visible and invisible subsidies.

The first of these subsidies was land. It was abundant, much of it being of good quality, well watered and timbered, and had a favorable climate and excellent natural facilities for communication, such as lakes, rivers, harbors, and a long coastline. It was virtually free for the taking. Dispossessing the British Crown and a few Indians was relatively cheap. Ground rents were lower, and the ratios of land to labor—and hence the potential economic rewards available for labor and capital—were higher than in any other advanced country. Accordingly, more labor and more capital streamed into the United States for many decades.

The country also was unusually well supplied with highly skilled personnel. From the beginning, American settlers had many more skilled craftspeople among them than did Latin American settlers from Spain or settlers in Canada or Australia.

Second, immigrants to the United States between 1775 and 1875 came with more capital. The average covered wagon with which pioneers—

FIGURE 10.1 *Income Distribution in the United States: (a) For 1977; (b) Recent Changes*

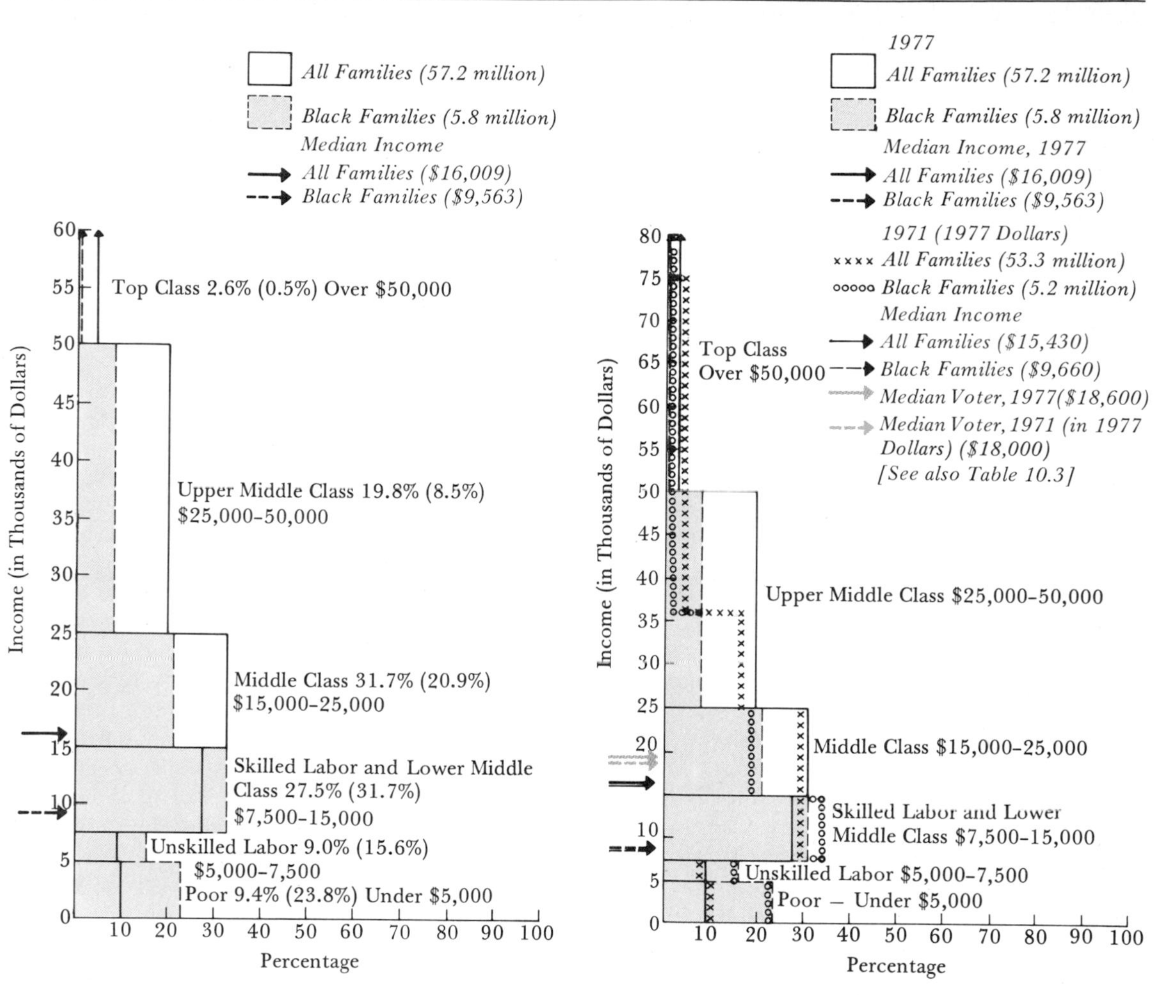

Source: See Table 10.1

many of them foreign born—crossed the prairies in the mid-nineteenth century contained in current prices about $5,000 worth of axes, rifles, blankets, ammunition, and other things. New capital was found and new labor kept arriving through immigration from Europe. Most of the new arrivals were of prime working age, whereas the babies and the aged stayed in the Old World. The cost of raising babies until they were husky twenty-year-olds was borne by the European economies. The *dependency burden* stayed in Europe, and the working personnel came to America. In this sense, throughout the nineteenth century the rest of the world subsidized the United States—perhaps to a larger degree than the United States has subsidized the rest of the world in the twentieth.

Added to this voluntary subsidy by adult immigration was a grim involuntary subsidy. The import of black slaves until 1808 transported net labor power from Africa to the United States. It left the terrible cost of this traffic mainly in Africa and took some of the economic growth of the country out of the bones of the slaves.

Additional capital, too, was accumulated in the outside world and then imported here. Alexander Hamilton's policies specifically aimed at making capital import attractive to foreign investors. But the United States not only attracted more capital than other countries: it squandered less. Both American and foreign observers in the nineteenth century often commented on American wastefulness and corruption. They overlooked that the proportionate cost of all such scandals was much less than the regular cost of maintaining monarchies, aristocracies, and large standing armies, as the European powers did. The large amounts European nations spent on the splendor of monarchs and on cannons and barracks were spent in America on factories, fields, and mines. The United States had the smallest standing military force among nineteenth-century powers and the highest rate of economic growth—something that might remind us of Japan's small military expenditures and spectacular economic growth between 1948 and 1978.

The result of this uniquely productive, uniquely prosperous, and invisibly subsidized economy with its vast resources of land, labor, and capital was a steady growth of living standards. At the time of the American Revolution the American people used more iron per capita than any other country in the world. They were using more tonnage of shipping than any other country in the world as well. On the average, and for most people, the American living standard was ahead of the European as early as the 1840s and 1850s. It has never lagged.

This prosperity—fostered by the presence of the frontier until 1890, by business growth until 1929, and by the revival of business growth in the years following the prosperity of World War II—produced a popular belief in private enterprise. The American economy was characterized by what the economist Gunnar Myrdal has called a *spread effect*. Since there was so much capital and so much managerial talent available, these factors of production often spread into the less-developed regions. In this manner, capital and managerial talent in the 1970s also flowed in increased measure into the "sunbelt states" of the southwest and the south. This effect is the opposite of the *backwash effect* in areas where skilled personnel, management, and capital are rare and where economic growth elsewhere leads to a draining of these resources out of the poorer regions and into richer ones. Appalachia, Mississippi, West Virginia, and South and North Dakota long were examples of regions and states where wealth flowed out rather than in. But in most other states the American economy pumped wealth in rather than out, and the exceptions—the poor regions, neighborhoods, and strata—were frequently forgotten.

Although most Americans enjoyed the fruits of their economic practices, they had a hard time finding a precise name for them. Since economic activities within a country are independent in many ways, it seemed natural to think of them as forming an economic system. An economic system, however, is far more complex than the simple labels—"capitalism" and "socialism"—that nineteenth-century economic thought made current. *Capitalism* is the name for a system in which factories and land are privately owned and economic development is directed by the automatic working of supply and demand in the market. *Socialism,* by contrast, is a system in which land and factories are owned publicly, either by the state or by large cooperatives, and economic development is directed by plan.

The American economy from the beginnings of the Republic has been mixed. It was clearly much more capitalist than socialist; but from the Erie Canal to the Panama Canal and from the original land grants (to railroads) to the current vast public activities in education and research, the government's share has never been negligible.

Since capitalist elements clearly predominated, however, and since most Americans approved of the results, businesspeople were proud until 1929 to call themselves capitalists and the United States a capitalist system. In 1929 the national treasurer of the Democratic Party, John J. Raskob, listed his occupation in *Who's Who* as "capitalist." The Great Depression, with its mass unemployment, then made capitalism unpopular. Whether or not businesspeople privately thought of themselves as "capitalists," their public relations advisers preferred the words "business" or "private enterprise" or "management" to the term "capitalism." Radicals enthusiastically used the words "capitalist" and "capitalism" for persons and practices they did not like. Many moderates began to shun these words as potentially misleading or divisive. Only in the 1960s did use of the terms revive in the United States. Conservative leaders like Barry Goldwater and a few writers, including William F. Buckley, Jr., and Ayn Rand, stressed them again as something that they liked; at the same time their negative use became much more widespread among social critics from the left half of the political spectrum. Since the words "capitalism" and "capitalist" thus still tended to divide Americans, their use in United States politics declined once more in the 1970s.

At present, both conservatives and their critics think of capitalism not only in terms of an economic system, but also in terms of a social class and of the power that it is supposed to have, or ought to have, within the political system. Some political scientists have taken part in this debate, but others have preferred the use of the term "elite" as permitting a more discriminating and precise analysis. By "elite" they have understood a group that gets on the average substantially more of the good things in a country—such as wealth, power, status, and the like—than do most other people living there. Moreover, usually members of this group tend to transmit most of their privileges to their children. (For a more detailed discussion of elites, see Chapter 3, pp. 44-48, above.) Many political scientists agree, however, that at the heart of the debate stand two important questions: Which groups in the United States have the most power? And how is the unequal distribution of power related to the economic system?

THE STAKES OF POLITICS IN A MOBILE SOCIETY

Just because human behavior in the United States was less rigidly controlled than in other countries by long-standing sociological and cultural mechanisms, a greater burden of social control fell on the economic mechanisms of money and the marketplace and, since these often did not suffice, on the political process. Politics had to produce the laws that determined land grants to railroad companies, homestead farmers, and universities; regulated municipal zoning for land use in cities, suburbs, and towns; first backed and later abolished slavery; regulated industries, public utilities, the rights of workers, and the activities of labor unions. Indeed, politics in alliance with religion produced laws that for a time permitted a man to have more than one wife, as it did in nineteenth-century Utah, and later politics denied this permission even to the most sincere of Mormon believers. Politics decided at one time that no Americans should be permitted to drink alcohol and that a beer brewer who continued business in the United States would be a criminal; later politics reversed all this. At one time, politics forbade Americans in several states to practice birth control or even to give or receive information about it. At another time, politics provided public money to make such information more widely available. In some other countries people have tried to change many matters through new laws or decrees, but they have done so usually only during a few years or decades of revolutions. In some respects, such as labor-management relations, government control of industry, and the provision of medical services, the United States has tended to leave more to the market than most other industrial countries have done. In such matters, the United States government has less control over the private sector. But in many other regards, it is doubtful that any other country in the world has used its political system—its legislatures, laws, and courts, as well as the administrative agencies of government—so continuously and extensively to control and change its own life and that of other nations as the United States has done.

Some political decisions are invisible. Often they are *nondecisions,* that is, decisions *not* to discuss a problem or *not* to put a project on the agenda of the council, committee, or administrative agency that has the legal power to deal with it. For many years the problems of inferior and segregated schools for black children were not discussed by many local school boards. Projects of publicly owned hydroelectric power stations faded from the national agenda after the 1930s. For many years projects for a national health insurance plan, such as have long existed in many modern countries, got little effective attention from Congress and the White House. Such selective inattention often is convenient for those groups whose interests it suits to keep these matters outside the arena of practical politics, but it works to the detriment of the persons and groups who might be helped by government attention and action, but who are not strong enough to obtain them.

Other concealed decisions may consist in scheduling for an early part of a meeting a question one favors, so that it is likely to be discussed and passed, while putting some other item one dislikes so far back on the agenda that it is likely to fail for lack of time to consider it or for lack of funds not yet committed to other purposes. Such techniques of deferring political intervention or making it selective tend to benefit those groups who have the power and organizational skills to use them, and they hurt those groups who have not.

Almost every political decision or nondecision makes someone richer or poorer, more or less free to follow his or her desires, more powerful or less so. Highway construction, zoning laws, building permits, and land values; government subsidies and grants; tariffs and import quotas; interest rates and monetary policy; government purchases and contracts at federal, state, and local levels; minimum wage laws or exemptions from them; bans on or permissions for the use of chemicals and pharmaceuticals; welfare payments and rules of eligibility; regulation of the rates charged by railroads, airlines, telephone, gas, and power companies—all can make someone's fortune in the marketplace or ruin someone else. When politics has decided to raise the postal rates for magazines, some periodicals have ceased publication, as *Life* magazine did when faced with the prospect of a sharp rate increase in 1972; a change in postal and tax policies might have saved many of these magazines and, with them, a valuable source of free and diversified information and opinion.

In a similar manner, American politics decides about the level of our defense expenditures, although this is accomplished partly in interplay with the arms decisions of other major powers, as in President Carter's 1979 agreements on partial arms limitations with the Soviet Union. American politics decides to a large extent about the intervention or nonintervention of the United States in the affairs of weaker nations; and it decides about the risks of a larger war that are to be accepted or avoided.

Political power also includes the power to be noticed, for politics also decides which problems are to be neglected or ignored, which ideas can be expressed with a chance of getting serious attention, which questions are not to be discussed, and which groups of people are to be forgotten or persistently overlooked, as if they were invisible—often for years or decades. Occasionally, when politics changes at some later time, these formerly invisible groups and unmentionable questions then move into the focus of attention, and public opinion suddenly becomes aware of some flagrant facts about race discrimination, or discrimination against women, or the neglect of the social, cultural, and economic needs of the *Chicanos*—the Spanish-surnamed Americans, mainly of Mexican origin—even though these facts had long existed.

In all these ways, American politics decides about much more than the spending of the more than one-third of American gross national product that passes through our public sector. It decides about the fortunes and careers of millions of private individuals, about their social and economic status, about the physical quality of our environment, and about the cultural and moral quality of our lives. Short on traditions and long on geographic and social mobility, the United States perhaps has made the stakes of day-to-day politics higher than have most other countries.

These stakes, to be sure, are not equally high for everyone, nor are they equally visible to everybody. These considerations lead us directly to the problem of political participation.

POLITICAL PARTICIPATION, INFLUENCE, AND POWER

In the presidential election of November 2, 1976, almost 46 percent of adult American citizens did not cast a vote. Nearly one-third had not been registered voters, and of those registered, about one-fifth, or about 13 percent of all adults, had not cared to vote. Mr. Indecision and Ms. Apathy, it seemed, represented more Americans than did the candidates of either of the major parties.

The actual voting turnout in 1976 was about 54 percent of the population of voting age of eighteen and above; and this was a lower level than had been customary during most of the past 120 years. (The main exception had been in the years 1920–28, which gave the presidencies of Warren G. Harding, Calvin Coolidge, and Herbert Hoover to the Republic.) The turnout figures are shown in Table 10.2, and they suggest that American voting in the twentieth century has tended to be substantially lower than it was in the second half of the nineteenth.

Part of the explanation for this trend may consist in the enfranchisement of women from 1920 onward and in the temporary increase of eligible voters of relatively recent immigrant stock after 1900, but it seems that these conditions do not suffice to account for the magnitude of the observed changes. According to Walter D. Burnham, the figures rather suggest a considerable degree of alienation of part of our adult population from the existing political system. These men and women, it is suggested, have found casting their ballots unrewarding, and they expect from further voting little, if any, improvement in their lot.

Participation through Money. The relative decline in the *participation by voters* has been paralleled by an increase in the political role of money. Even though popular participation in the 1972 campaign was low, the *participation by money* was conspicuous. Total campaign expenses, raised by the need to use expensive television time, were estimated at $400–500 million, or roughly $6 for each of the approximately 74 million votes cast. In the 1976 campaign the Federal Election Campaign Act of 1971, with its amendments of 1974 and 1976, had some effect in limiting spending, at least

TABLE 10.2 *Mean Levels of National Voting Turnout by Periods, 1848–1972*

Period (presidential) years	Mean estimated turnout (%)
1848–1872	75
1876–1896	79
1900–1916	65
1920–1928	52
1932–1944	59
1948–1960	60
1964	63
1968	62
1972	55
1976	59

Sources: W. D. Burnham, "The Changing Shape of the American Political Universe," *American Political Science Review*, 59 (March 1965), 10; U.S. Bureau of the Census, *Statistical Abstract of the United States* (Washington, D.C.: U.S. Government Printing Office, 1972) U.S. Bureau of the Census, *Current Population Reports*, ser. p–20, no. 322 (March 1978). Cf. also Richard Scammon, "Electoral Participation," Annals, no. 371 (May 1967), pp. 59–71.

for the presidential contest, for which $72 million were paid out from public funds to all major party candidates and national committees.[4] In the congressional elections of 1978, however, money again was talking, loud and clear. In the future the need for campaign money is likely to increase, for a larger share of voters will be scattered in the suburbs, where they can best be reached by costly television advertising, supplemented by radio and print.

Interest groups expect a return on such financial investments, particularly from an incumbent candidate or from one very likely to win. In 1972 the dairy industry was reported to have contributed more than $400,000 to President Nixon's campaign for re-election, beginning with a visit by dairy industry representatives to Nixon on March 23, 1971, and a $25,000 contribution on March 24. On the next day the Nixon administration reversed its earlier policy and permitted a 30-cent increase per hundredweight in the federal government's support price of milk. In 1971 as a whole, wholesale milk prices per hundredweight were 16 cents higher than in 1970. With United States consumption per year totaling about 500 million hundredweight, this price rise increased the annual gross income of the dairy industry by more than $30 million or, on an annual basis, by about 200 times the amount of its total reported contributions to Nixon's campaign.[5]

Such practices are not restricted to national politics, nor are they the monopoly of any one political party. In state and local politics, perhaps four-fifths or more of the larger campaign contributions come from individuals, firms, or interest groups who have business pending or planned with the government office that is being contested in that campaign. Such contributions are paid either directly to the candidate or to one of the organizations and committees working on the candidate's behalf; and the amount of each contribution often tends to be roughly 1 percent of the sum or value of the contract, permit, or other favor in which the donor has a direct financial interest.[6] When very large amounts of money are

[4]See Herbert E. Alexander, *Financing Politics: Money, Elections and Political Reform* (Washington, D.C.: Congressional Quarterly Press, 1976).

[5]Some of these campaign contributions by the dairy industry were publicly reported only after the election. See "Dairy Industry Gifts to Nixon Campaign Disclosed," *New York Times*, December 29, 1972, p. 23. The calculation of price changes and the sales volume of the dairy industry are based on U.S. Department of Agriculture data, reported in *The 1973 World Almanac and Book of Facts* (New York: Doubleday and Newspaper Enterprise Association, 1972), pp. 975–81.

[6]For data for a single state that may well be representative of others, see Thomas B. Edsall, "The Governor Raiseth," *Washington Monthly*, February 1972.

at stake, those willing to pay money for political favors may get something like a quantity discount; in such cases, one-half of 1 percent or less of the sums at stake may suffice to purchase the candidate's favor. Since such contributions may pay at a rate of 100:1 or more, the donor may find it to his or her interest to give some money to a candidate who is not certain to win or even to make campaign contributions (discreetly if possible) to two or more of the contending candidates.

Some large contributions, of course, come from wealthy individuals who agree with the candidate on ideals or issues, or are related to the candidate by family ties, or would like to have closer ties and easier access to the government after "their" candidate has won.

Another source of campaign financing is the aggregate of smaller individual gifts of up to fifty dollars, which in 1972 for the first time could be deducted from the donor's income tax. Although this tax concession had little meaning for the poor, it made small-scale political giving easier for the middle class. Most often, however, unless the middle- and low-income supporters of a candidate are numerous and unusually highly motivated, small contributions make up somewhat less than half of the moneys collected—let alone needed—for a modern political campaign. Candidates have generally found the *"fat cats"*—the large contributors—indispensable to winning and have felt obliged to pay some current or future price for their support.

Since money can be invested in this manner to buy influence, it increases the political power of those who have it. As long as a substantial part of campaign expenditures is still financed from private funds, the need for money in campaigning will tend to distort the political market, which in a democracy counts all ballots as equal, and to move it appreciably closer to the commercial market, which allots purchasing power to individuals and groups in proportion to the dollars they own or control.

Participation Through Activity. Luckily, money is not the only way of exercising influence in American politics, nor is it always the decisive one. Since 1930 the presidential candidates with more money behind them have been defeated seven times: in 1932, 1936, 1940, 1944, 1948, 1960, and 1964. In at least some of the four years in which the better-financed candidates won—1952, 1956, 1968, and 1972—they won primarily for other reasons than merely the advantage of more money and more television time. What often weighed more heavily in deciding the outcome were major events and the experiences that citizens derived from them, such as depressions, wars, inflation, race conflicts, and the like; the autonomous interests, attitudes, beliefs, and convictions of voters in matters of economic policy, but also of religion, culture, and morality; and the political activities of men and women in trying to make the casting of their own votes effective and in working to influence the political decisions and actions of others.

Political activities, however, are also distributed unequally, including considerable inequalities by class. A large and careful survey, made in 1967 by Sidney Verba and Norman Nie and published in 1972, showed consistently higher-than-average activity levels among those Americans who were in the top one-third of income and *socioeconomic* status and consistently lower-than-average activity among the socioeconomic lowest third of citizens. Within each third on the socioeconomic status scale, political activity likewise increases in the direction of the higher status levels. The findings of Verba and Nie in this regard are summarized in Figure 10.2. Altogether, their results, as well as those of another major study by Almond and Verba, show that "social status has a closer relationship to political participation in the United States than in all but one of nine other countries" for which comparable data could be found. As Table 10.3 shows, only in India, caste-ridden in the past and still partly so in the present, is the correlation between social status and political activity slightly higher.

Who Is the Median Voter? The effect of income and status—that is roughly, of class—on voting is considerable. During the period 1952–79 in the United States these effects seem to have increased. Back in 1952, studies showed that among given income classes of potential voters only about 53 percent of those receiving less than $2,000 a year had voted, as against 76 percent in the middle group, receiving between $3,000 and $4,000, and 85 percent in the highest income category, receiv-

FIGURE 10.2 *Who Puts Effort into Politics: Status Composition at Varying Levels of Participation*

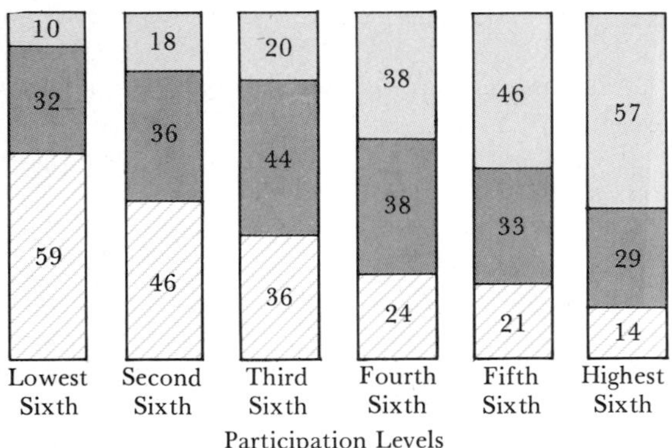

Numbers on bars refer to the percentage of each participation group coming from a particular socioeconomic status group. All figures have been rounded to the nearest significant digit. Percentages may not add up to 100 for this reason.

Source: S. Verba and N . H. Nie, *Participation in America: Political Democracy and Social Equality* (New York: Harper & Row, 1972), p. 131.

TABLE 10.3 *Correlation of Social Status and Participation in Ten Countries*

Civic culture data		Cross-national program data	
United States	.43	India	.36
United Kingdom	.30	Yugoslavia	.36
Italy	.28	United States	.35
Mexico	.24	Netherlands	.23
Germany	.18	Nigeria	.22
		Austria	.12
		Japan	.12

Note: Verba and Nie say: "We present two separate sets of correlation because the data come from two different studies. In each column the measures are comparable, but not across the columns, because different measures are used. This explains the two different figures for the U.S.

"The data in the left column . . . are discussed in Nie, Powell, and Prewitt, 'Social Structure and Political Participation'; those in the right column in Verba, Nie, and Kim, *Participation and Political Equality*. Data such as those . . . cry out for further analysis along the lines suggested in this book. Such remain on the agenda for the future.

"For comparative data, see Gabriel A. Almond and Sidney Verba, *The Civic Culture;* Sidney Verba, Norman H. Nie, and Jae-on Kim, *The Modes of Democratic Participation: A Cross-National Comparison* (Beverly Hills: Sage Publications, 1971); and Norman H. Hie, G. Bingham Powell, and Kenneth Prewitt, 'Social Structure and Political Participation,' *American Political Science Review,* vol. 63 (June and September, 1969), pp. 361–378."

Source: S. Verba and N. H. Nie, *Participation in America: Political Democracy and Social Equality* (New York: Harper & Row, 1972), p. 340; S. Verba, N. H. Nie, and J. Kim, *Participation and Political Equality* (Cambridge: Cambridge University Press, 1978), p. 64.

ing $5,000 or more. In the two decades since 1952, both average incomes and the value of the dollar have changed, so that, roughly, the bottom third now gets less than $5,000 annually, the middle third about $5,000-$9,000, and the top third above $9,000. But the voting frequencies are still highly unequal among socioeconomic status groups. For the top one-third in the presidential election of 1968, the percentage of regular voters was 90 percent; for the middle group, 77 percent; and for the bottom third, 61 percent; while the average for all three groups was 76 percent. In 1972 the average probability of voting for all income levels was 55 percent; estimates for the probability of voting at each level are given in Table 10.4.

This unequal frequency of voting has a significant effect on American politics. If one wants to win an election, one must gain the vote of, say, 51 percent of the voters actually voting. If all adults voted, and if the issue was one in which they might line up according to their relative wealth or poverty or, more generally, their socioeconomic status, then the voters around the fiftieth income percentile, say from the forty-seventh to the fifty-third percentile, would constitute the pivotal middle group with the *swing vote* to decide elections between the "big money" and the "little people" parties or factions above and below them. Success in politics would depend on pleasing and persuading this midway group, and political and economic compromises would have to be tailored to suit it. The *median income voter* would be the kingpin of the system.

In fact, this is not so, even though some people have imagined that it is. If, for example, only 60 percent of the voters in the bottom third of the income scale are actually voting, while 76 percent in the middle third, and 85 percent in the top third do so, then the voting turnout will be 73 percent of adults, and 37 percent will suffice for a majority. Since 28 percent out of the 33 percent of top income receivers still will vote, they will need the votes of only another 9 percent to win. If, as we are supposing, the issue is an economic or otherwise class-related one, these votes may well be found among the top percentiles of the middle third of income receivers, say, those between the forty-first and the forty-ninth percentile of income. Since at least 76 percent of these upper-middle level individuals are likely to vote, the small group between the thirty-third and the forty-sixth percentile will suffice to produce the additional 9 percent of votes that the top income receivers need to prevail. The new swing group with the power to decide the election, and hence the group to be accommodated in the policies proposed, will now be the voters around the forty-fifth income percentile, counting from the top downward. The middle-middle level voters between the forty-eighth and fifty-second percentiles will have lost much of their former power, since they no longer can form a majority by siding with the voters who are poorer than themselves.

Something like this may have been the situation in 1952, if the survey data in our sources are to be trusted. (They may actually overstate *voting frequencies* for 1952, either because survey respondents tend to overreport their having voted or because voting ratios may have been reported on the basis of registered voters only, rather than on the basis of all citizens of voting age; but our sources are not clear on this.) For the 1960 election, we do have a figure for the percentage of voting for the entire adult population. In that year, 64 percent of adult Americans voted; so if we allow for differential frequency of voting at different income levels, as shown in Table 10.4, we find that the pivotal midgroup may have moved up to the thirty-seventh percentile.

Finally, we recall that in the 1972 presidential election only about 55 percent of adult Americans voted. The midgroup needed to win might have been up at the twenty-eighth percentile, at the edge of the top one-third of income receivers, if the election had been closely contested. In fact, of course, Nixon received 61 percent of the votes cast, corresponding to nearly 34 percent of all adult Americans. But even this landslide majority could have been produced largely within the more affluent half of the American people. From these

TABLE 10.4 *Some Schematic Models of Voting Participation at Different Income Levels in the United States: The Location of the Pivotal Middle Group of Voters: 1952, 1967, 1968, 1972, and 1976*

Percentile of income receivers		Expected votes cast if everybody votes	Midpoint	1952 Probability of voting (%)	1952 Expected votes cast (%)	1952 Midpoint	1967 poll ("regular voters") Probability of voting	1967 poll ("regular voters") Expected votes cast (%)	1967 poll ("regular voters") Midpoint
Top	1-33	33		85	28		60	20	
	34-41	8			6			*4*	*24*
	42-49	8		76	*6*	*36*	47	4	
Middle	50-57	*8*	*50*		6			4	
	58-65	8			6			4	
Bottom	66-100	34		53	18		38	13	
Total		100			71			49	
Average probability of voting		100		71			48		

Note: All percentages are rounded. All percentages refer to the total of citizens of voting age. All midpercentiles and midpoints are italicized.
[1]In 1972 the bottom third of families received less than $6,600, the top third of families, more than $12,400.
[2]In 1976 the bottom third of families received less than $10,800; the top third of families, more than $19,300.

Sources: For voting behavior: U.S. Department of Commerce, Bureau of the Census, *Current Population Reports: Population Characteristics*, "Voting and Registration in the Election of 1972," ser. P–20, no. 253 (October 1973); U.S. Department of Commerce, Bureau of the Census, *Current Population Reports: Population Characteristics*, "Voting and Registration in the Election of 1976," ser. P–20, no. 322 (March

examples it seems that in practical American politics the "middle" is above the middle: the key group to be convinced, the typical or "middle" voter in the United States, is somewhere between the twenty-fifth and thirtieth income percentiles, with a 1978 income of nearly $18,000 per year. As long as many millions of Americans do not change their political habits, it will be these solid citizens who must be won over by anyone who wishes to win a national election.

Other Forms of Political Participation. Americans are more active in politics than many people think. Only about 22 percent seem to do practically nothing. Another 21 percent limit their activities to voting. For at least one-half of the American people, however, there are three other major ways in which they participate in politics. They can take part in political campaigns; in the 1967 Verba and Nie survey, 15 percent were classified as having done so. They can form groups that cooperate in regard to some local political problem; this activity was recorded for 20 percent of the respondents. And they can initiate direct contacts with public officials at the local or national level in regard to some specific matter; this seems to require the most effort, and only 4 percent appeared to

1968			1972[1]			1976[2]		
Probability of voting	Expected votes cast (%)	Midpoint	Probability of voting	Expected votes cast (%)	Midpoint	Probability of voting	Expected votes cast (%)	Midpoint
90	30		85	22		67	22	
	6			5			*5*	*27*
77	*6*	*38*	45	*5*	*28*	54	5	
	6			5			4	
	6			4			4	
61	21		35	14		44	14	
	75			55			54	
76			55			55		

1978). For income levels: U.S. Department of Commerce, Bureau of the Census, *Current Population Reports: Consumer Income,* "Money, Income and Poverty Status of Families and Persons in the United States: 1972," ser. P–60, no. 89 (July 1973); U.S. Department of Commerce, Bureau of the Census, *Current Population Reports: Population Characteristics,* "Money, Income and Poverty Status of Families in the United States: 1976," ser. P–60, no. 114 (July 1978). For 1952: Robert E. Lane, *Political Life* (New York–Glencoe, Ill.: Free Press, 1959), p. 49. For 1968: computed from University of Michigan Survey Research Center, 1968 Presidential Election Data. For 1972: *New York Times,* November 12, 1972, p. 40. For the frequencies of voting at different income or status levels, see Lane, *Political Life*; Verba and Nie, *Participation in America,* pp. 31-37, 132; and *Time,* November 6, 1972, p. 47.

specialize in actions of this kind. Verba and Nie call them "parochial participants," but *contact specialists* seems a better name for them. While one-fifth of the people engage in none of these forms of participation, about 11 percent all-round *activists* engage strongly in all, except in initiating contacts on specific matters with particular officials.[7] As Table 10.5 shows, these four types of political participation are distinct in practice.

[7]The types of participators were computed by scoring each survey respondent on several reported acts for every activity type. Thus, talking to people to influence their vote, attending meetings, giving money, working for a candidate, being a member of a political party, and working actively in it all turn out to be highly correlated with each other, and this is confirmed by factor analysis. They are counted, therefore, as elements of a single overall *campaign activity,* for which a score is computed. These scores are then standardized in order to show the extent to which each respondent is above or below the average of all others in the survey. Finally, each respondent is grouped into a type or "cluster" with all other respondents who are most like him or her in having high or low scores on all four major ways or "modes" of political participation. See Verba and Nie, *Participation in America,* pp. 79-81, 127-33, and 350-57 for the survey data on particular activities. The latter seem to tally well with the earlier data reported in Lane, *Political Life,* pp. 46-56.

TABLE 10.5 *Participatory Profiles of the American Citizenry*

Groups produced by cluster analysis	Voting	Campaign activity	Communal activity	Particularized contacting	Percentage of sample in type
1. Complete activists	98	93	92	15	11
2. Campaigners	95	70	16	13	15
3. Communalists	92	16	69	12	20
4. Parochial participants	73	13	3	100	4
5. Voting specialists	94	5	3	0	21
6. Inactive	37	9	3	0	22

Source: From data in Verba and Nie, *Participation in America,* p. 79. Italics supplied.

These data already suggest that political participation in the United States is not narrowly concentrated in the hands of a few. Only 53 percent of the American people in the sample were inactive in regard to the six activities studied in the model (though many were politically active in easier ways, such as voting). Reality, in other words, showed that although no one of these six rarer types of political activity was reported by more than one-fifth of the respondents, they were so well dispersed that nearly one-half of the respondents had been engaged in at least one; but they still were so well concentrated that almost 6 percent reported having engaged in more than four of these activities, ten times more than the sixth-tenths of 1 percent who should have done so if the distribution had been random.[8]

Participation in American politics thus shows a good deal of openness but also a considerable amount of structure. Almost any number can play, but if they do, what are their chances of winning?

[8]See data and analysis in Verba and Nie, *Participation in America,* pp. 35-40.

The Effects of Participation—and Who Benefits from Them. The various modes of political participation have their greatest effect when they are applied in combination. Voting applies pressure to the holders of elective offices and to all those who aspire to leadership in a democracy. It is the pressure of a threat, the sanction of political failure: not to be re-elected or never to be elected at all. But voting for or against some candidate or party usually expresses only a general trust in or distrust of a candidate or party and their promises. At most it registers a response of the voters to what these present office seekers may have done in the past, or failed to do. But in most instances voting conveys no precise information about which problems and issues are most important to which groups of voters, what their priorities are, and just what each group wants done. High on power, but low on information, voting by itself is a blunt instrument indeed.

It is the other modes of participation that convey more specific information about who wants what.

The activists in a campaign can influence the promises and policies with which candidates identify themselves. The active groups in a local community can help to translate general policies and budget categories into specific decisions about particular school construction, police and welfare procedures, zoning laws, municipal wages, health and safety standards, interracial employment policies, and much else. And the initiating of particular direct contacts with elected officials and administrative officers at each level of government—national, state, or local—can pinpoint the interest of individual groups in obtaining some specific decision in a particular case. Together, these three modes of participation at their best can convey much of the precise target information about public policy decisions that voting fails to give.

Without the present or potential pressure of voting, however, such information and the mode of participation conveying it would remain powerless. This is, in fact, the case in communities where voting turnout is low or where no effective voting power is available to those concerned. Hearings are useful for letting all interested groups and persons have their say and for making legislators or administrators listen to them for a while, but mere hearings lack the power to compel responsiveness. That can be done only by the pressure of some negative or positive *sanction:* electoral, administrative, judicial, or financial. Examples of negative sanctions are the flight of industry and high-income families from a city or town where the crime rate or the taxes are too high or where the amenities of life have declined below the level that they find tolerable. Positive sanctions are getting re-elected or gaining increases in the local tax base through the inflow of capital, industry, service establishments, or high-income residents. When information about voter and group interests is working together with some known likelihood of sanctions, the responsiveness of government is likely to be higher—but it will remain unevenly distributed.

How can we measure the responsiveness of political leaders and public officials and agencies? *Responsiveness* in general can be defined for any person, organization, or technical device as its average probability of producing a response of acceptable content and quality within an acceptable time limit in answer to some input or request for service. Thus, a telephone system that gives us a 90 percent chance to reach a called station within one minute is more responsive than one that would take an average of two minutes to do so or would offer us only 80 percent chance of success. Such a measure also could be developed for public service systems and political administrations. What is the average delay time and likelihood of success for some particular type of request directed to each of them?

This procedure, however, would give us only specific measures for particular organizations and types of service. How could we get a more general indicator of responsiveness that could be applied over a variety of issues or types of service and over a large number of different communities or agencies? Verba and Nie proposed an ingenious answer for their analysis of politics in sixty-four local communities chosen to be representative of American politics in general. They compared the order of priorities in public policy, as expressed by different groups of voters, with the priorities expressed by the political leaders and decision makers in the community. Every instance in which a leader concurred with the order of priorities expressed by a group of voters was then counted by Verba and Nie as a *concurrence statement* obtained by that group; and they found that the more closely the priorities of the leaders agreed with those of a particular group of citizens, and hence the larger the proportion of concurrence statements, the more responsive were the local leaders to the desires of that group. Thus if a group of poor voters put housing and welfare first on their agenda and the leaders also put these items first, then the leaders were counted as responsive to the demands of that group. But if the leaders had put law and order first, they would have been counted as unresponsive to that group and as more responsive to the views of some other group of voters. Furthermore, at the local level at least, the citizens' activities seem to be much more powerful in influencing the leaders' priorities than the other way around; indeed, the effect of the leaders' activities on citizens' political priorities was so small that it did not rise significantly above the chance level. And once the leaders have accepted the agenda and priorities set by some interest group, the substantive content of the leaders' or officials' decisions is also likely to fit in with the desires of that group. Accordingly, the statistical measure of the extent to which the policy agenda of leaders corresponded to that of some particular group of citizens was regarded by Verba and Nie as a good indicator of what this group would actually get from government in terms of the decisions and services it wanted.[9]

Who Gets the Day-to-Day Rewards? In these terms, who, then, gets what out of the American political process? The first answer is those who put in most by way of participation and who have the resources or allies. A second answer tells us who these people—the most actively participating and most likely to succeed—are: they are the members of the upper income groups.

The members of the top one-third of the people by status and income furnish about three-fifths of the activists at the top level of participation; and as Figure 10.3 shows, they get 38 percent of the total of concurrence statements—that is, responsiveness—from community leaders that go to that most active group. The middle-status one-third of citizens furnish about 30 percent of the top activists and get 30 percent of responsiveness; but the bottom one-third by status furnish only 10 percent of the most intensive participation and get about 20 percent of responsiveness. In short, the top one-third of citizens, by status and income, participate six times as much at the top level of activity as does the bottom one-third, and they get nearly twice as much responsiveness from government.

FIGURE 10.3 *Who Gets Influence out of Politics: Participation and Concurrence for Three Socioeconomic Groups: Individual-Level Data*

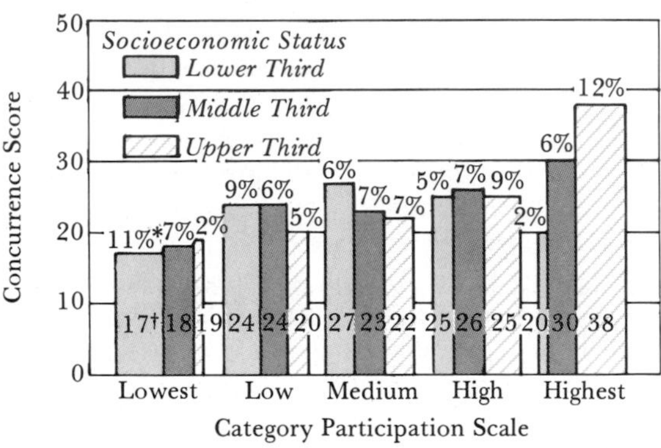

*These percentages are the proportion that the particular group is of the population as a whole.
†The circled figures are the average concurrence scores of that group, indicating roughly the influence it is likely to exercise.

Source: Verba and Nie, *Participation in America,* p. 337.

By contrast, the few lower-status citizens who participate most actively get less concurrence—and presumably less responsiveness—than do less active lower-status citizens.[10]

Other conditions have minor effects. Catholics and older people rank higher on voting, but lower on other modes of political activity. Local participation is higher in relatively isolated or well-bounded communities than in small suburbs, especially those of the "dormitory" type, in which

[9]Verba and Nie, *Participation in America,* pp. 328, 332.

[10]See Figure 10.3, above, and Verba and Nie, *Participation in America,* p. 337.

most residents commute to work elsewhere. Some political belief systems increase participation beyond the effects of status and income: strong Republican convictions—that is, conservative beliefs—seem to double steadily the rate of activity; recently, black militancy has had a similar effect, but its long-term steadiness and strength remain to be seen. Despite these modifications, the inequalities of income, education, and status remain the most important influences on the extent of political participation and on the distribution of its rewards. Small numbers of highly active lower-status citizens, about 2 percent of the population, together with a few upper-status converts to their views, may use highly visible and dramatic tactics; but, as Verba and Nie report, "they are counterpoised against the almost glacial pressure of a much larger number of conservative activists. The latter group may not speak as dramatically, but as our data . . . make clear, they speak very effectively."[11]

If this is the case in day-to-day politics at the local level, who holds most power in regard to the larger political decisions in the states and the nation?

LOCATIONS OF POWER OVER LARGER ISSUES

Where does the power lie in the United States? Some people think that it is concentrated in the hands of a small group, perhaps even an anonymous one. Others think that power is widely dispersed among the people or that in a democracy it ought to be. Our concern is with the actual *distribution of power* in the United States, which lies somewhere between. Though this distribution is highly unequal, it is by no means fully concentrated in any one group—and it is subject to continuing change.

In order to study this distribution more closely, one might make a distinction between *general purpose elites* and *special elites*. The former have influence in regard to many matters; the latter have influence in some narrower field.

The Core of the American Establishment. Probably the greatest single concentration of influence and power for general purposes in the United States comprises the credit, banking, and investment communities. Since money is needed for many purposes, those who control its flow will have power in many matters, if they choose to exercise it. The sociologist Robert Lamb proposed that one could find the leading families of any small American town by looking up the names of the board of the local bank twenty-five years earlier. Insofar as these families had not left town, they would be the leading families today.

It is safe to say that the banking-financial community—which is fairly broad, reaching from the small-town banker all the way to the president of the Chase Manhattan Bank—has the greatest amount of influence. Studies of congressional mail show that a letter from a small-town banker weighs more with a representative in Congress than a letter from most other people.

Also at the core of the establishment is the top political leadership of the country. This includes the leaders of both major parties, in or out of office. The political scientist Ralph Huitt recounts how an ambitious graduate of Yale and the Harvard Business School went to work for the Wall Street firm of Morgan Guaranty Trust. After a time he concluded that the decisions were no longer made by financiers, but by politicians. Accordingly, he moved to the Midwest and in due course became Senator William O. Proxmire of Wisconsin.

The interchange between bankers and the government is extensive. Andrew Mellon as Secretary of the Treasury under Hoover, Douglas Dillon in the Kennedy and Johnson years, and the executives of Dillon, Read and Company and other investment houses in New York as major officers in the Defense and State Departments after World War II—all reflect the close ties between the

[11] Ibid., p. 339.

investment interests and the federal government. After Carter's election in 1976, however, bankers became rare in the administration, and the press commented on a decline of business confidence.

A second large group influential in government is manufacturing. A list of the ten biggest industrial corporations in the United States ranked in order of their advertising budget was published some years ago. Included in this list was General Motors in first place, Procter and Gamble, and the Ford Motor Company. In the late 1950s and early 1960s, when these firms were among the ten top advertisers in the United States, the American secretaries of defense were Charles Wilson of General Motors, Neal McElroy of Procter and Gamble, and Robert S. McNamara of Ford. More recently, advertising methods played a major part in the presidential campaigns of 1968 and 1972.[12] Ties of this kind were much less prominent in the administration of President Carter, but both his first and second secretaries of the treasury, Michael Blumenthal, founder of the Bendix Corporation, and William Miller, formerly of Litton Industries, represent a continuation of the practice on a diminished scale, and the power of the oil and energy interest groups in Congress has been growing.

The law firms are another major link in connecting the financial community, the industrial community, and the government. Such firms as Sullivan and Cromwell, in which the late Secretary of State John Foster Dulles was a partner, is a good example. President Nixon's law firm is another; his law partner, John Mitchell, ran his presidential campaign in 1968, became his attorney general, then was active again in President Nixon's 1972 campaign. Such influence, however, has its limits. By early September 1973, Mitchell was out of office, had pleaded guilty to a charge of perjury, and had served some time in a federal prison.

An important development in American law is the rapid growth of law practice in Washington, D.C., and particularly the founding and expansion of Washington branches of law firms based in such cities as New York, Chicago, and Houston. This recent change reflects the increasing importance of the national government in the daily lives of American citizens and corporations, as well as the awareness by clients that federal legislation and bureaucratic regulation are today the major determinants of their well-being. Resort to litigation in the courts remains a key element in American economic life, but increasingly pervasive federal regulation and control have enhanced Washington's status as a center of influence in the high-stakes game of economic activity. Whereas businesses previously were content to allow their regional law firms in New York or Texas to contract with Washington firms specializing in administrative law in order to handle affairs relating to the federal government, these same clients today are urging such regional firms to open their own branches in the capital, staffed by lawyers with expertise in dealing with bureaucratic agencies, regulatory commissions, and Congress.

Since 1942 the military establishment has become a major force in the economic community. A United States senator recently pointed out that two thousand high-ranking former military officers now occupy high-level executive posts in American industry, usually in firms that have had and continue to have contracts with the Defense Department. The late General Douglas MacArthur was board chairman of Remington Rand, and General Omar Bradley is on the board of Bulova Watch Company. The list of eminent military alumni is long. It should be remembered that good generals are competent executives, that business firms are perfectly willing to hire good executives whenever they can get them, and that generals know very well what kind of goods the armed forces are likely to buy.

[12]See, for example, Joe McGinniss, *The Selling of the President* (New York: Simon and Schuster, 1968); and E. R. May and J. Fraser, eds., *Campaign '72: The Managers Speak* (Cambridge: Harvard University Press, 1973).

There has also been an interchange of military and financial judgment. For instance, in World War II an investment banker, Robert Lovett, was undersecretary of defense in charge of bombing strategy. The selection of targets for investment and the selection of targets for strategic bombing are intellectually analogous processes. In each case, one is trying to find key facilities—in one, to buy; in the other, to destroy—but in both the same type of judgment is involved.

Then there are the information and communication services: the advertising and public relations complexes on Madison Avenue and the mass media empires, such as the Henry Luce papers and the Scripps-Howard and Hearst chains. In recent years the major television and radio networks—NBC, CBS, and ABC—have outgrown the newspaper chains in importance. Still more important are the great news agencies, Associated Press (AP) and United Press International (UPI), which supply news to newspapers and news magazines, as well as to radio and television. Some great newspapers, however, such as the *New York Times* and the *Washington Post,* sometimes can exercise great influence, aided by a powerful tradition of investigative reporting.

Putting these five groups together—banking, large industry, the military complex, law firms, and fringe services such as advertising and mass media—we get the core of *the establishment.* Somewhat more dependent at the fringes are the large foundations and major private and public universities.

Conflicts within the Establishment. Though the members of the establishment often have been united by interest, lifestyle, intermarriage, and social life, there have been some substantial conflicts among its components. Big-city financial and real estate interests stand to lose from prolonged situations of intense threat of nuclear war, which might induce industries and people to migrate to the hinterland. Consumer industries and department stores stand to lose, rather than gain, from protracted large-scale United States wars in Asia, which divert customers and friends from their sectors. Rentiers and persons on fixed incomes stand to lose from war-induced levels of inflation and taxation. All these are readers of or advertisers in the metropolitan press; and in becoming more critical of the Vietnam War, the major newspapers were also speaking to their concerns. Though most of the press and the electronic media supported President Nixon against his rivals in the presidential campaigns of 1968 and 1972, Nixon continued to believe that the media were against him; and a minority of them did indeed take the lead in drawing attention to difficulties and scandals in his administration, such as the Watergate affair, and persist in reporting such matters in detail. Public attacks by President Nixon, Vice President Spiro T. Agnew, and other administration spokespeople—speaking for a government with some power over broadcasting licenses, newsprint imports, postal rates, and the like—sometimes tended to depress in the stock market the value of shares of those newspapers and of radio and television networks that had incurred the government's displeasure.

An even broader split in the establishment was indicated in 1973 by the list of "enemies" of the Nixon administration, drawn up in 1972 by President Nixon's White House assistant, John Dean, and revealed in the course of the Watergate investigation by a Senate committee. The list included well-known journalists, writers, scholars, former officials of the Johnson administration, and the presidents of Harvard, Yale, and the Massachusetts Institute of Technology. A memorandum accompanying the list suggested that the persons could be punished informally through the minute examination of their income tax returns, through changes in "grant availability" to themselves and to their institutions, and in other ways. Much of this plan remained a paper project, but some persons listed were in fact subjected to harassing income tax examinations and had to establish their innocence at considerable cost in time and legal assistance. Whether such divisions within the establishment—and particularly between its older East coast–oriented elements and the more recent oil and defense interests of such states as Texas, Florida, Arizona, and California—will prove to be a passing episode or whether they indicate a deeper and more lasting split remains yet to be seen. Yet, united or divided by conflict, the five major establishment groups—banking, big industry, the defense complex, top law firms, and advertising and mass media—carry more general influence than any other group.

The Power of Special Interests. The establishment interests must be distinguished from special interests; the five groups named above are so diversified that they are interested in many things, not only in one. General Motors and Du Pont are involved in dozens of products in dozens of lines. Rarely will they exert all-out pressure on one particular law because their interests are so diversified. One division of General Motors or of Du Pont may want a protective tariff for its specialty, but another division, making a product for export, may want free trade.

Special interests have much clearer configurations. First, there are the aircraft and electronics industries. The military effectiveness of strategic bombing was discredited after World War II by the strategic bombing survey, after the Korean War by the failure of the air force to stop the flow of ammunitions to the Korean front, and again in Vietnam. But the belief in air power does not stop, since the aircraft industry continues to sustain it. Just as smoking does not disappear with a report from the surgeon general, but is more related to the persistence of popular habits and to the advertising budget of the tobacco industry, so the belief in air power is related in part to the persistence of military traditions and popular habits of thought, as well as to the public relations budgets, organized *lobbies,* and *lobbyists* of the aircraft and electronics industries. Their large social and economic interests will continue to have an input into the political and communication systems of the United States.

The oil companies form another obvious major interest group. The old oil interests of Standard Oil have now merged with the general financial community, through such institutions as the Rockefeller interests and the Chase Manhattan Bank. More recent, special oil interests, such as those formed by some Texas oil drillers, are on the fringes. They are more inclined to express their grievances against the Eastern establishment through support of raucous, superpatriotic groups and to suspect all of Wall Street as "unpatriotic."

The mineral interests in the southeastern states and the copper and tin interests in overseas operations are also special interest groups, having strong views on Latin American affairs. Cotton, tobacco, and sugar interests are located mainly in the southern states. Large-scale farming is more prominent in the Midwest and in California. Control of the import of bananas from Central America and of sugar from Cuba and the Caribbean, together with the plantations producing these commodities, long has been concentrated in Boston and New York. There are declining interest groups, such as the railroads, and rising interest groups, such as road building, heavy construction, and urban redevelopment—all of which have very close ties to local political parties and to state and local governments. Building and road contractors are usually involved in politics. The electronics industry is growing, and so is the research industry; they have many common ties and form a rising interest group.

Labor unions also form a powerful complex of interest groups. On some issues they are united. Unions of all types tend to support a federal minimum wage and higher wages in general. On other issues, such as the maintenance of a restrictive apprentice system that can almost close a trade to newcomers and thus tends to work to the disadvantage of black people and other minorities, only some highly skilled craft unions will commit their efforts. In contrast, proposed laws against race discrimination are more likely to be supported by industrial unions, comprising both skilled and unskilled workers, such as the United Automobile Workers of America.

Special interest groups tend to use their power only in regard to matters of specific concern to them. On these matters they may form shifting coalitions; and for their particular objectives they usually get fairly good service from the political system.

Interest groups are highly unequal in their ability to mobilize their members for political action, to arouse larger constituencies to their support, and to coordinate their activities in an effective manner. Some interest groups have strong permanent organizations with professional staffs; quick access to relevant information; large financial resources; well-defined channels of communication to their membership; well-established habits of political participation, activity, and discipline; and a tradition of rapid, large-scale, and coordinated action. Intensity of need or size of reward is thus only one, and not always the decisive, factor in the power of an interest group. Often its capabilities to organize and act will count for more.

Usually, members of the middle and upper strata of society have greater capabilities along these lines. They have more time and money, better education and information, greater skills of communication and organization, and stronger self-confidence and expectations of success. Often they do not choose to invest these capabilities in political action, since they often are not too dissatisfied with their lot and since most of them usually have more rewarding uses for their time; but when their fears are aroused or some major interest of theirs is touched, their political power can be formidable. Their old interest organizations will gain new strength from their increased support, and new committees and organizations may spring up spontaneously to supplement or surpass these.

Poorer people, by contrast, may have intense needs and potential interests, but they are often less aware of them, less united, less active, and less organized, and they generally have lower capabilities for long-sustained effective action. Hence, the poorer groups most often lose out in the competition among a plurality of interest groups; and those better-organized interests who have greater capacities for taking an effective part in the pluralistic contest will get and keep more of its spoils. Here, too, as an old saying puts it, "to those that have is given."

There is, however, one large exception. The capabilities of interest groups are not unchangeable. The unaware can gain awareness, the inexperienced and unskilled can learn to become steadfast, and the weak can become strong. When these things happen to a group, its position in politics changes. When they happen to several groups that comprise large numbers of people, they will change the distribution of political influence and power. And if these changes are large enough, they may change the operation—and even the structure—of the political system.

Such changes often take time, but sometimes new coalitions form quickly, cutting across classes and strata. Property taxes, assessed on all or part of the market value of real estate, long had been the mainstay of local finances, paying for schools and a growing array of municipal services. By 1978, however, rising land prices and municipal budgets were pushing up these taxes, threatening to drive many older or poorer people out of their homes, for their incomes were rising at a much slower rate or even not at all. Together with wealthier voters who always had disliked paying high taxes on their larger houses, many of these distressed voters joined in a *"tax revolt"* that swept much of the United States during that year. In California, Proposition 13 was passed by referendum, putting a legal limit on the level of local property taxation. Similar referenda passed elsewhere, and still further measures of this kind were introduced for future action. It seemed that state and local services would have to be cut back or else municipal finances would have to be based less on property taxes and more on a combination of other sources, including new service charges for garbage removal and other municipal services, sales taxes, and state income taxes, in order not to hurt any large group of voters quite so badly. The tax revolt of 1978 contributed by the end of that year to a general mood of budget cutting and economy at all levels of government. Beyond this, it offered an example of *macropolitical intervention,* that is, the large-scale shift of ordinarily passive groups into political participation and activity, checking and sometimes changing the normal power of the "establishment" of routinely active and influential groups.

Social Strata and Their Power. Below the interest groups are the social strata. The middle class, or what can be called the middle class in the United States, has been steadily growing. Today the United States probably has the broadest middle class in the world. Depending on how one defines it (and whether one includes what is called the *lower* middle class, to which nobody wants to belong, but which always turns up in the statistics), the American middle class goes down from the ninety-fifth to at least the sixtieth percentile of income and possibly to the fortieth percentile. This group overlaps in part with the clerical and service occupations, the white-collar occupations that also have grown. Most mass media cater to the tastes and views of the middle class, and so does much of the advertising they carry. Politicians bow to middle-class mores and values; those who do not rarely are elected to national office. Almost the only ones who sometimes purposely offend it are its children—but often with the opposite political results from those intended.

Though the middle class is generally respected in matters of form, it may fail to get its way on some large matters of substance, such as ending an unpopular war or keeping America's central cities habitable. Nevertheless, although most of the political coalitions among interest groups change from issue to issue, they remain within a general middle-class setting. Civil rights legislation in the 1960s was put through by a coalition of liberals, conservatives, labor groups, businesspeople, intellectuals, and others who felt an injustice was being done. Last, but not least, was the pressure of the black Americans themselves. This pressure, too, was motivated in no small part by the desire of blacks to win access to middle-class living standards on equal terms.

Labor as a social stratum is less powerful. As a rule, it can prevail politically only in coalition with other groups. Production-line labor has not grown for twenty-five years. The skilled workers, insofar as they are union members, are now in the middle third of the income distribution in the United States. Unskilled and nonunion labor are well below this level. Farmers have been reduced to 5 percent of the work force; less than 2 percent produce major surpluses of food; the remaining 3 percent are subsistence farmers. Then come the forgotten Americans, the 20 percent who are poor and the 10 percent who are very poor.

This inequality in income, status, and power is greater in the United States than in any other highly advanced industrial country. Some of the poor are urban blacks, but at present at least half and possibly more than half of the very poor are not black. There is poverty in Appalachia, and there is poverty in the hillbilly neighborhoods of Chicago as well. A second group is less poor, but still forgotten: the hard-working whites at the fringe of poverty and at the edge of respectability. These are tense and worried people who resent the increase in attention given to the poor. A third forgotten group is the mobile disfranchised. These are the professional people, the students, and in part the young—all those who for one reason or another do not make it into the ranks of stable, organized interest groups and registered voters. They number many millions. Together, these three groups get far less political influence and consideration than their needs and their numbers should entitle them to.

This unequal distribution of power—from the core establishment to the most disadvantaged—will not change quickly, but it *is* changing, and larger changes are on their way. Later in this chapter we shall ask whether these changes can add up in time to a transformation of the American political system. First, however, we must look at some other aspects of that system, beginning with one that in the past has been a force for both stability and change: the major images of the American political community that have developed in this country.

SOME IMAGES OF THE AMERICAN POLITICAL COMMUNITY

"Who is this new man, the American?" asked an eighteenth-century Frenchman, J. Hector St. John (Jean de Crèvecoeur), who had been farming in America at the time of the American Revolution. His question has not been fully answered to this day. Many Americans agree that they somehow belong together and that they have some important things in common. They often find it harder to agree on what these things are and what their felt *community* consists in.

It is not blood and descent. No nation on earth has had a wider variety of ancestors. It is not the land as such. There is little in common between the geographies of Maine and Hawaii, Iowa and Florida, Nevada and Maryland, or Texas and Vermont. It is not even will. The nineteenth-century southerners who wanted to secede from the United States in the Civil War were still Americans, whatever they might have become if they had succeeded. Perhaps, more than anything else, it is the common culture and communication habits of the people, the ability of each to foretell much of what his or her compatriots will do, and their knack of joining quickly into teams or crews that can cooperate effectively at any time or place, on wagon trains or airlines, whaling ships or space ships.

Political Culture: Standardization, Novelty, and Pragmatism. Americans are a people of survivors from the frustrations and shipwrecks of the Old World, from which their ancestors came. Ours is a *culture* of simplification, like the household goods of people who had to move on often by sea or land and who could take only the essentials with them, sifting and repacking them often. But it is also a culture of practical boldness and innovation; its simplified components have been made more uniform, but also more suitable to being disassembled and put together again, probably in new configurations. It is a culture of ever present tension and potential conflict between conservative standardization and combinational novelty and change; and the contest between these two cannot be won by either, since each depends on the other for effectiveness.

A third element in the culture is its stress on performance, on efficiency, and on practicality. "American gadgets have one peculiarity," a European writer once observed; "they work." So did the floating American harbors brought to the coast of Normandy in World War II, and later the American vaccines against polio, and the American landing vehicle on the surface of the moon. The early American settlers had to be practical in order to survive on their new continent, and those who came in later generations had to be practical in order to survive among the descendants of the earlier settlers. Out of this necessity came *pragmatism*—at the popular level, roughly the notion that "true is what works"—and a readiness to accept whatever seemed to be the realities of the American environment.[13] This practicality, however, is often culture-bound, and it causes difficulties in foreseeing the long-run consequences of actions. Popular pragmatic attitudes also often include a propensity to ignore or override the realities of foreign countries or of minorities in the United States if they do not seem to fit the general pattern.

[13]For the far more subtle and flexible views of the original American pragmatic philosophers, see John E. Smith, *The Spirit of American Philosophy* (New York: Oxford University Press, 1963); and for some legal and political applications, see Max Lerner, ed., *The Mind and Faith of Justice Holmes* (New York: Halcyon House, 1948).

Some Basic Value Orientations: Mastery, Equality, and Performance. There are other themes that hold American culture together. Three of these were touched on briefly in the discussion of political culture in Chapter 9 (pp. 211-12). Americans expect to master their environment, natural or political; failing that mastery, they tend to ignore it or to withdraw from it. They will refuse to submit to it or even to work *with* it on a basis of genuine understanding and mutual give-and-take. Many of us are descendants of people who were so impatient with the frustrations of the Old World that they left it and moved to the New. Later Americans would leave the stony acres of New England for the fertile plains of Iowa and Kansas and the sunnier sky of California. When topsoil and timber were exhausted, when lakes or rivers became polluted—a condition that was rare in the early years when there was much clean water and few people—it was often possible to move on or to tap a new source of supply. But now, with about 220 million Americans and an economy using vast amounts of water and other natural resources, American practicality will increasingly demand a more responsible treatment of the ecology and the environment, even against the opposition of some short-range interest groups.[14]

Similar problems arise in politics proper. Many Americans leave the centers of their big cities when too many black or poor people arrive, and they prefer to ignore in the temporary safety of the more affluent suburbs the mounting problems of their central cities. And in international politics we tend as a nation to reduce our interest and participation in the United Nations if the other 150 countries will not see things our way. (But what place could we use as a suburb of retreat from the problems of this planet?)

While one major theme in American culture suggests that the alien environment is to be mastered rather than listened to, another theme insists that people, if they are at all real to us, must be treated as equals. When this theme predominates, American human relations are *collateral,* like those among peers or brothers and sisters, and not *lineal,* like those between superior and subordinate, officer and soldier, or father and son in a patriarchal (that is, father-dominated) family. But though the theme of equality is a general demand of American culture and most Americans feel uncomfortable if they must act contrary to it, some major institutions in the United States require them to do just that. Not only the armed forces, now much larger than they were before World War II, but also the civil service and most of the middle-sized and large business organizations are *command systems* in which orders flow down and mainly reports of obedience are expected to move up. The promise, often implied in American culture, that anyone can work to the top, does not work often enough or fast enough in practice to overcome this command character. Many educational institutions also resemble command systems: school boards and superintendents give orders to grade school and high school principals, principals give orders to teachers, and teachers give orders to students. Even at some colleges and universities, the high school pattern is repeated; and even when there is no intent to have this happen, the necessary difference between the level of knowledge of the faculty and the relative ignorance of the students puts special difficulties in the way of creating and maintaining a more collateral educational relationship.

There is some built-in conflict and tension between the themes of equality, or collaterality, on the one hand, and of efficiency and performance, on the other. Often competitive and supposedly equal opportunity is expected to resolve the conflict. "Never mind his color—can he pitch?" asked a small white boy on a World War II poster about a

[14]*Ecology* refers to the mutually supporting and/or balancing network of physical processes and life forms in an area, such as water, wind, moss, grass, trees, fish, insects, birds, animals, and often also human beings. In a broader sense, ecology then refers to the knowledge or study of such interdependent life systems, often linked to a concern for their conservation.

black youngster at the forming of a sandlot baseball team. It was the same question, in essence, that was asked by the whalers in Herman Melville's novel *Moby Dick* when the copper-colored and richly tattooed Maori Queequeg was hired as a harpooner. But in present-day politics, economics, and social relations, competition and opportunities are still in significant part unequal and limited. This is a growing problem in American life, as a larger proportion of young people reach out for higher education and for freer and more meaningful jobs and career chances thereafter; and it seems likely to play a larger part in the politics of the 1980s.

Doing and the Future. The themes of performance and achievement in American culture are also linked to the theme of action, of *doing,* in contrast to mere *being,* or *being-in-becoming,* which is an anthropologist's term, roughly, for development. Americans usually esteem other people and themselves according to what they do, or have done just recently, or are likely to do in the near future. They might well agree with Goethe's *Faust:* "In the beginning was the Deed." Doing, for most Americans, is a value in itself.

Past deeds and achievements count for little, however, if those who accomplished them do not seem likely to do as well or better in the future. "What have you done for me lately?" is the proverbial answer of an American politician to an appeal for gratitude; and to call a person a has-been in politics is to dismiss him or her from serious consideration.

At this point, the American orientations toward *action* and toward the *future* meet. "I do not know who my grandfather was," Abraham Lincoln is supposed to have said; "I am much more concerned to know what his grandson will be." On the stock exchange, in publishers' contracts, in university appointments, almost everywhere are present decisions guided by expectations of future performance. In contrast, protecting the works of the past—such as landmarks of earlier styles of architecture in American cities—is perennially difficult and requires much effort.

Human Nature: Good and Partly Manageable. A final theme in American culture—and one that apparently every culture must define for itself—concerns the view of human nature. Are human beings predominantly good, bad, or mixed? And is human nature basically capable of improvement, or is it fundamentally unalterable? The mainstream of American culture treats human beings as basically good and as capable of further improvement. A conservative minority view asserts that "human nature can't be changed." Here again is a tension between two partly conflicting assumptions. Belief in the goodness of people leads to the corollary that they should not be too closely controlled and directed by government. At the same time, belief that people can be improved has often been interpreted to mean that they can be changed in quite specific ways, in a very short time and without fundamental disturbance, if only the government or some other controlling agency will push them hard enough and skillfully enough. This view leads to a belief in manipulating people to make them do what we want them to, because we think it moral, or advantageous to ourselves, or both. In their time, American public and private agencies have tried through intensive programs to Americanize European immigrants; alter the sex-and-family behavior of Asian peasant populations; improve the future school performance of black preschool children; teach college students and others how to read and comprehend a thousand words per minute; abolish poverty; end race discrimination; wipe out alcoholism, prostitution, and drug abuse; train corporation executives to greater sensitivity; and free people from loneliness—in short, to channel human behavior into directions that these agencies held to be desirable, often with good reason.

The methods used often showed a common pattern. A mechanical or chemical device or a special psychological or social procedure was applied to a narrow aspect of the life of the target population or group, in order to change that particular aspect, but otherwise to leave essentially undisturbed their personalities, lifestyles, culture, housing, and other social and economic circumstances.

Sometimes these methods were successful. But more often, success proved transitory or did not materialize at all, particularly when the behavior to be changed was embedded in a larger structure of interlocking, mutually reinforcing, and self-restoring conditions. Thus, unemployed adults or adolescents from broken families, when moved from slums into public housing, often stayed unemployed; their home environment stayed damaged; and the concentration of similarly disadvantaged neighbors in the same low-income housing projects often re-created an even greater resentment and despair than had prevailed in the slums from which they had been moved. To gain and consolidate major improvements would have required a sustained attack on a whole cluster of conditions, but such an attack would have required more resources, more personnel, more help toward self-rule and self-development, and, last but not least, more political support and power than usually were available. Yet, though the widespread American confidence in simple, quick solutions often led to conflicts and disappointments, perhaps at least it kept alive the efforts at improvement until better methods, larger resources, and broader and more steadfast political support could be mobilized. Perhaps even the failed attempts made it less likely that the bad conditions would be accepted indefinitely under the cloak of a philosophy of resignation.

Conflict and Unity among American Values: A Sense of Direction? In each of the major orientations and themes of American political culture we have found not only much that is admirable, but also profound inner tensions and contradictions, many of which are likely to persist for a long time and to generate recurrent conflicts. But they also keep the political culture of the United States alive, changing and developing. Together with the effects of mobility, transport, communication, and continuing economic prosperity—of relative plenty for most Americans, compared to most other peoples in the world—the common culture orientations and themes have kept the American political community together. Any political creed or idea that could win a substantial following in the United States would have to stay somewhere within these basic orientations of American political culture.

This might even apply to the identity and unity of the American people. The French, English, and Germans have remained distinctive peoples under a wide variety of political regimes. Americans, except for a scant dozen years before 1776, have lived under the same set of basic political principles and orientations ever since they emerged as a distinctive people. If these principles were abandoned or destroyed—if, as we might imagine, the "self-evident" truths of the Declaration of Independence and the principles of the Bill of Rights should ever be explicitly rejected, perhaps under some fascist or authoritarian regime—then the American people as we now know them might well disintegrate. In abandoning their own basic political principles and value orientations, the American people might have more to lose, therefore, than other nations. Even if we should not perish in a nuclear war that a genuinely fascist regime would be likely to bring about, we should still be apt to lose our cohesion and existence as a nation.

Luckily, such dangers do not seem close at hand. What is more likely to happen, and has happened often in the past, is that we should retain the American principles and value orientations, but visibly fail to live up to them. In that case, however, our political culture and its aspirations would continue to live in our memories, and they would be apt to become salient time and again in periods of crisis and decision.

More than a hundred years ago, Senator Stephen Douglas taunted his opponent in debate, Congressman Abraham Lincoln, by saying that a statement in the Declaration of Independence, "all men are created equal," was not a self-evident truth, as the Declaration had asserted, but by now (1858) was a "self-evident lie," since slavery had been and was being practiced in the United States. Lincoln answered that the Declaration did not describe past or current practice, but stated the direction in which the American people wanted to go; and he suggested that that direction would prevail. He was right; slavery was abolished five years later, in 1863. Aided by an array of cumulative changes in the political, social, and economic fabric of the American people, the basic ideas of its political culture triumphed eventually over the practices that had so long denied them.

Much later, in the 1930s, the Swedish social scientist *Gunnar Myrdal* made a similar prediction about the future of racial discrimination in the United States, which then was far more massive and brutal than today and seemed solidly entrenched. The main thrust of American ideals and values was against racial discrimination, he suggested, and together with the large ongoing social changes in the lives of black and white Americans, they would eventually defeat racial oppression and its defenders. He may well have been right, for the following decades brought a succession of legal, administrative, and judicial changes in racial politics and practices and, not least among them, a broader political awakening of black Americans and a change in attitudes among many of the young of all races. But these struggles and changes still are going on; and all of us in the United States are still writing by our actions and behavior the current chapter of the story related to Gunnar Myrdal's prediction.

SOME PATTERNS OF RESPONSE

In response to the tensions and conflicts in American political culture and to the different experiences and interests of various groups, at least four major types of political outlook have emerged. They can be found in every region of the country, in almost any town, large place of employment, university, or other large community, albeit in different proportions. Which configuration each individual will pick deliberately—or grow into without noticing, or conform to in deference to friends, family, and neighbors—will depend not only on that person's social and economic circumstances, experiences, and interests, but also on his or her family and personal associates, and not least on his or her own personality. We can predict reasonably well, therefore, which views will be more widespread among which social groups and classes. But we shall do much less well in predicting which smaller groups will hold what images of politics, and we can predict very little about which particular individuals will end up holding what beliefs. Moreover, each of these outlooks has been presented by major philosophic spokespeople in highly differentiated and subtle terms, although the bulk of its present-day adherents are likely to hold their particular view of politics in a much simplified form. It is with these popular political outlooks that we shall be concerned here.

American Liberalism. The first popular image of American politics is a kind of traditional *liberalism,* which goes back in its roots to the Declaration of Independence, the Bill of Rights, and the works and presidency of Thomas Jefferson. It continues in the writings of Ralph Waldo Emerson, later in the abolitionists and Abraham Lincoln, and then in the philosopher William James, Justice Oliver Wendell Holmes, Franklin D. Roosevelt and Wendell Willkie, in such poets as Carl Sandburg and Archibald MacLeish, and in the liberal Democratic and Republican spokespeople of our time. In this view, America is mainly a country of self-employed small businesspeople, farmers, lawyers, physicians, and other professional people; and those Americans who are employed by others and work for wages or salaries ought to model themselves on the self-employed group.

Opinions, works of art, and varieties of entertainment, like commodities, are to be free to compete in the marketplace. Education is to offer students free choices and to aid their self-development. Economic competition is to be encouraged; public utilities should be supervised and regulated to prevent any misuse of "national" monopolies; and antitrust laws should be enforced, or one should threaten to enforce them, in order to curb the formation of new monopolies and limit all restrictive arrangements "in restraint of trade."

Legal race discrimination must be abolished, but the private preferences of people in their personal and social arrangements should be left undisturbed as much as possible. Unions have their place in helping those wage earners who join them freely; they should not acquire too much power, but their internal arrangements and membership policies should not be disturbed by any uprisings of a majority of the current members. Welfare legislation and institutions should help the needy who cannot provide for their own needs, and experts should tell the clients of these welfare institutions what to do in order to become self-supporting. Taxes should be kept low, but may be raised if essential welfare needs or national security demands it. Simultaneously, government spending should be closely watched for any signs of graft, inefficiency, or waste.

Above all, the American political system is rational, despite some local or temporary distortions; and most voters are rational, too. They know their true interests, and in the long run they will vote accordingly. They will support reasonable new experiments, but they will want their leaders to be practical, not doctrinaire. One must have patience. Perfection can never be expected. Politics is the art of the possible, and in the long run it will produce a reasonable approximation to the good.

American liberals believe in human dignity and equality, as well as in mobility, initiative, and self-control as means to master nature and one's own fate. They put human rights above property rights, but see the two as normally compatible. They trust human nature as good and have faith in our ability to build a better future, but in any case they see the meaning of life in doing the best one can here and now. If years of efforts should dim their confidence, the best among them still may say what William the Silent said centuries ago in the long Dutch War of Independence: "It is not necessary to hope in order to persevere."

The American Conservative Tradition. *Conservatism* in the United States goes almost as far back as liberalism does: to Jefferson's great contemporary, Alexander Hamilton. If the spirit of the Declaration of Independence of 1776 was primarily liberal, parts of the federal Constitution, drafted in 1787 and ratified in 1791 (albeit together with the liberal Bill of Rights), express a more conservative mood. Later notable conservative thinkers and writers include, between 1830 and 1860, John C. Calhoun and George Fitzhugh in the South; around 1900, the sociologist William Graham Sumner; at mid-century, Senator Robert Taft; in the 1960s, Senator Barry M. Goldwater and the writer William F. Buckley, Jr.; and in the 1970s, former California Governor Ronald Reagan.

American conservatives used to be more inclined toward abstract principles than their British counterparts. Only in the early 1970s did some of President Nixon's advisers publicly recall the very flexible methods of Britain's nineteenth-century Conservative prime minister, Benjamin Disraeli, and did President Nixon himself show a comparable tactical flexibility in changing his own earlier positions. Thus he moved to improve relations with China and the Soviet Union, effectively devalued the dollar twice by an aggregate of about 20 percent in foreign trade and international finance; instituted temporary wage and price controls in the domestic economy; suspended military conscription; and withdrew most American ground troops from South Vietnam. Despite these striking changes in tactics and methods, however, President Nixon gave no indication that he had changed in any way his commitment to the general principles of American conservatism in economic life. Many of these policies and principles were then continued in 1975–76 by President Ford and, to some extent, in 1977–79 by the Democratic and avowedly populist administration of President Carter.

What are these principles? The first principle deals with the relation of politics to economics. Government should not interfere with the activities of individuals and the rights of property, particularly the latter. In most conflicts between government and some existing business interest, American conservatives tend to oppose the government—the tax authorities, the regulatory agencies, and the like—and to side with the individual or corporation, if these represent interests of substance. However, in many conflicts between some individual and the police, American conservatives are inclined to side with the police, particularly if the individual happens to be nonwhite, poor, or young. And whenever government activities and power are likely to benefit property interests, conservatives, from Alexander Hamilton onward, have tended to favor them.

American conservative thought is often relatively theoretical and explicit. It tends to accept Locke's view of property as an inalienable natural right of individuals; and it extends this notion of natural rights to large private business corporations, which other schools of thought might view as highly artificial organizations, created by the laws under which they are chartered. American conservatives also often share Adam Smith's trust in the benefits of economic laissez faire and Herbert Spencer's belief in the "survival of the fittest" in society and nature. Sometimes this latter theme is developed along the lines of social Darwinism; that is, human nature is seen as fundamentally bad, or at least aggressive, and a highly simplified image of the process of natural selection in the jungle is turned into an image of human relations in society. The members of the richer and more powerful social strata and classes, together with their families, are then said to be biologically superior and likely to transmit their superior genetic traits by heredity to their offspring. By the same logic, the weak and poor are seen as inferior; the ethic of the New Testament (and of many religions other than Christianity), which commands that they should be loved, helped, and respected, is often suspected as bad biology and unsound economics. Once this view is accepted, it seems unreasonable to give voting rights and civil liberties to the socially and biologically inferior majority, instead of keeping them firmly under the rule of "the rich, the well-born, and the wise." Accordingly, many conservatives have traditionally viewed democracy with a good deal of suspicion; and some of them have continued to insist that the United States ought to be called not a "democracy"—which it should not be—but a "republic," in which unequal political rights should be preserved in perpetuity.

The basic appeal of conservatism, in America as elsewhere, goes deeper than mere attachment to habits, family, social position, and possessions. While all these play an important part as sources of reinforcement and support, conservatism at bottom is also a strategy for defending one's identity and self-respect. To be proud of what one is and has can be a source of emotional security. To hope that family, position, property, and reputation will survive beyond one's own life is a way of seeking reassurance against death—even though some major religions have been skeptical about it. And if some form of traditional religious assurance and credible ritual can be added to the conservative system of beliefs, the combination may be powerful, indeed.

In foreign relations, conservatives usually stress power politics, ideological anticommunism, the pursuit of national security through large armaments, and the vigorous defense of the property rights and creditor interests of American corporations in foreign countries.

At the same time, the American conservative tradition has its generous and imaginative aspects.

Herbert Hoover in the late 1920s was the first American president to speak of the abolition of poverty within the United States as a national goal. Under Hoover's administration, too, Secretary of State Frank B. Kellogg negotiated the Kellogg-Briand Pact of 1927, which formally renounced war as an instrument of policy—a principle that many nations, including our own, still have to live up to in their actions. Senator Robert Taft was a champion of public housing; and the principle of a guaranteed minimum income for every American family was first proposed officially under President Nixon's administration. In international affairs many conservatives supported American economic aid to war-devastated Europe under the Marshall Plan and later, within more stringent limits, some economic aid to developing countries. Many conservatives also have supported or accepted United States membership in the United Nations, and some have favored a federal world government (though often on the assumption that such a world authority would be primarily influenced by the United States and would limit itself mainly to the protection of law, order, and property along conservative lines).

Despite many differences, there usually has been enough overlap between conservative and liberal values and interests in American politics to preserve a dialogue between the two traditions in the realm of ideas and values and to permit agreement on the forming of coalitions and support for specific common policies, regardless of the philosophic cleavage between the two systems of belief. The result has been an intermittent and limited consensus between conservatives and liberals that often has provoked radicals to bitter criticisms against both.

The Classic Radical Tradition. Like the preceding two traditions, American *radicalism* is as old as the United States. It is a tradition that has included such early patriots as Samuel Adams, Patrick Henry, and Tom Paine; the abolitionists and the radical Republicans before and during the Civil War, such as John Brown and Thaddeus Stevens; some populists and muckrakers of the 1890s and 1900s, as different from each other as William Jennings Bryan, Lincoln Steffens, and Upton Sinclair; the Socialists such as Eugene V. Debs and Norman Thomas; the leaders of the farmer and labor movements of the 1920s and 1930s, such as the brothers La Follette in Wisconsin, and later Henry Wallace and Wayne Morse; and in the 1960s such writers as Michael Harrington and religious spokespeople such as the brothers Daniel and Philip Berrigan. For a time in the mid-1930s the small number of American Communists seemed part of this varied and contradictory current of opinion, but their attempts to direct and control it, their rigid defense of Joseph Stalin, and their complete commitment to the changing foreign policies of the Soviet Union eventually made them unpopular even in radical circles. Most of the individuals of radical temper who had joined them in the 1930s sooner or later left the Communist Party, some because of the hostile pressure of public opinion, congressional and other investigatory committees, employers, and the like, but perhaps more often because of genuine disappointment with a party and an ideology that seemed so manifestly ill fitted to the moral and political concerns of most Americans. The trials of the dissidents in the Soviet Union during 1978, essentially for what Americans in the United States would have considered as expressions of political opinion, once more highlighted the contrast between the political values of the two countries.

Radicalism in the classic and American patterns stresses the work ethic, performance, competence, and practical results. But it also insists on the rights and dignity of all working people, not only of an elite of competence or merit. Radicals often favor far-reaching social and political changes, including changes in economic structure and property relations. They distrust people in positions of power and prestige. They attack oppression, fraud, hypocrisy; they are quick to raise such accusations, even on incomplete evidence. Even then the classic radicals are sincere, not cynical; most of them would reject the use of deliberate political deception. They tend to be puritans and to take themselves rather seriously. When they resort to laughter, it is apt to be closer to satire than to clowning. Most of them have rejected drunkenness, drugs, and sexual promiscuity. They live for the future; they work to do good as they see it and to change the world. In the experience of solidarity with the men and women of their time, in taking part in the transformation of the world, and in making their own lives a part of the emerging future, radicals, too, can feel that death cannot really touch them because it cannot stop this larger movement of humanity or the movement—as many radicals believe or feel—of the entire universe of which humankind is just one part.

All three classic American traditions, then—liberalism, conservatism, and radicalism—offer not only an image of politics, but also an implicit philosophy of life, hidden but discoverable. What new elements, if any, have the "new politics" and the counterculture of the late 1960s and 1970s brought into the contest among these American images of politics and human nature?

A New Kind of Radicalism. During the 1960s a new pattern of political and social beliefs and values seemed to be emerging among some groups in the United States, and similar views found adherents in several other highly developed countries. Most of the ideas involved had been put forward earlier, most often by older people, but by the late 1960s they had found their strongest echo among the young, particularly the fifteen- to twenty-four-year-olds. The new attitudes went by many names, ranging in the late 1960s and 1970s from *"the new politics"* and "the new left" to *"the counterculture"* and, less formally, to "being with it" or "tuning in, turning on, and dropping out," but in any case to "doing one's own thing." Doubtless the slogans and the names would change, but the underlying moods and images might last a good deal longer. What are some of these feelings and images?

Perhaps most visible is the longing for sincerity and authenticity, for the undistorted expression of one's needs and feelings, for the freedom to express one's impulses as spontaneously and directly as possible. Most young people have to inhibit their impulses, from their childhood onward, in homes, schools, universities, offices, and factories and in the society dominated by their elders. This society, as the new radicalism sees it, is both manipulative and repressive. It prescribes and forbids endlessly what people may or may not do. Its pervasive commands and prohibitions thwart and frustrate everything—sex, love, music, art, one's very speech, body, dress, and hair style, the arrangement of one's room, one's time, one's plans, and one's desires. Why not use any "unprintable" word whenever and wherever one feels an impulse to do so? Moreover, what this repression cannot command it tries to govern through manipulation and suggestion, which come from everywhere—from parents, teachers, advertisements, and television sets. For the new radicals this whole system of repression and manipulation is the main enemy; it must be resisted and dismantled whenever possible.

To get rid of manipulation, this same ideology suggests, one must get rid of the notion of linking differences in rewards to differences in effort, competence, and performance; one should break or weaken the links between achievement and rewards. The pursuit of achievement leads to inequality, to elitism, to envy and unhappiness. Those who reject achievement can be equal, fraternal, and serene. Not only the achievement of money, careers, or academic grades should be rejected. Even the achievement of beauty is sometimes suspect. "We cannot all be beautiful," said a student in all seriousness, "but we can all be ugly."

People should be rewarded, not for what they do, but for being what they are—human. In the language of some social scientists, achievement is replaced here by ascription; specific rewards, by diffuse good will; and preferences for particular nations, races, or classes, by universal solidarity.

People should not only avoid competing for rewards, but they should not even strive for them. To disdain consumer goods, money, and economic security will make one happier through living simply, close to nature, and devoting oneself to human relations, art, and contemplation. If work must be done to earn one's sustenance, let it be simple work, such as carpentry, in preference to a career in science, business, medicine, or law; in the 1970s one could find quite a few former brilliant undergraduates who were trying to live in accordance with this prescription.

This new lifestyle can become practical for all, many of the new radicals believe, because we are now living in a "postindustrial" age, in which the production of wealth is no longer important for society. The machines are already now producing most of this wealth automatically. Hence, production is no longer a major task or problem; only distribution and enjoyment are.

In addition, this belief system has room for exploration and experiment, provided that these are not conducted in a too controlled, precise, and "uptight" manner. People should strive less to add to the stock of accurate and verified knowledge (which is already vast and unimportant) and rather seek more vivid and intense ways of enjoyment and experience, without any confining commitments for the future. In this lifestyle, people do not study subjects deeply, but rather say that they are currently "into" some subject—be it astrology, extrasensory perception, organic gardening, or Zen philosophy—until their changing interests get them "into" something else. And if these half-playful explorations should not lead to enough intellectual and emotional excitement, there is still the chance to borrow some sense of ersatz excitement from drugs, much as some people in earlier generations borrowed it from alcohol (often ending up, however, not in a new freedom, but in a new dependency).

What do these feelings and beliefs add up to? They often imply serious concerns with human frustration, a sincere desire for human sympathy and warmth, genuine indignation at the lies, oppression, injustice, cruelty, and inclination toward war found in many of the political and social practices of many countries. Like the classic liberals and radicals, the adherents of these new protest movements want to change the world. But they often want to do it here and now, when their mood moves them, and not through the long commitment to the hard work of a lifetime. If they are more skeptical of the status quo and of the views of their elders, they are often touchingly willing to believe the things they want to. Many of them will believe in the effectiveness of whatever tools they are currently using—whether flowers, bombs, or votes—until they get around to trying something else. They will even try sustained political activity, provided that the experiment does not last too long and does not require them to adjust too many of their current habits or to trouble too much about the risks and costs of their own errors.

Despite its occasional bizarre language and trappings, the new radical ferment is still connected with many elements of American political culture. The belief in the essential goodness of people and the desire for equality and friendliness are characteristic of the mainstream of the American tradition. Henry David Thoreau would have understood the new radicals' interest in living with nature rather than conquering it and their interest in nonviolent and noncoercive forms of politics.

The weakest points in this new radical set of beliefs were perhaps its distance from reality, its partially built-in resistance to reality correction, its underestimation of the feelings of other groups in the population, and its underestimation of world poverty and of the consequent need for more, not less, widespread productivity and competence. By 1978, more than a decade after its rise, the movement seemed to have declined throughout most of the United States, but it had caused some changes in the political landscape.

On the surface the college generation of "the

movement" was replaced by "the *me generation,*" as the journalist Thomas Wolfe called it. Jobs, careers, grades, and personal advancement seemed to be the center of its members' attention. Some of this change was genuine and necessary in a time of declining employment opportunities for young people. But many attitudes had changed for good. Racists and haters of minorities had become themselves a minority in the country and particularly among the young. Lifestyles had become more informal. Women's needs and rights had gained political weight and had to be taken into serious consideration. Many of the young activists of the 1960s had re-entered mainstream political life, and some of them had won important public office by election or appointment.

One small fringe sect that had started amid the counterculture went on to bizarre extremes that ended in horror. This was the People's Temple of the Reverend Jim Jones, who in November 1978 led over nine hundred of his tightly controlled followers to mass murder and suicide in his settlement at Jonestown, Guyana. But most of the recent small religious movements in the United States eventually found an accepted place for themselves and their members. As long as a religious movement did not strive to control totally the minds of its converts, nor try to cut them off from all contacts with their families, friends, and people with different beliefs, and as long as its members retained the chance to leave freely, they seemed likely to remain in the future within the larger community of the American people and humankind.

A Neoconservative Challenge to the Liberals. In the 1970s, a new kind of conservatism began to emerge, less rigid than the traditional ideas of such Republican leaders as Senator Goldwater and Governor Ronald Reagan. The new version appealed to both Republicans and Democrats, with such leaders as Democratic Senator Henry Jackson and Republican Governor John Connally as its vague symbols, and with a range of academic advisers as its increasingly explicit spokesmen. Not all members of this school of thought agree with each other on all points. Yet many of their ideas overlap. They are in debate among themselves; they are beginning to be seen as a group; and though their views doubtless will undergo further development and change, they appear already as one of the trends of the 1980s that will have to be reckoned with.

The following are some of the propositions that can be found in neoconservative thought or are implied in it.

Stability and institutions are more important than activity and participation.

Legitimacy should be a major goal of government, loyalty and duties a major concern of citizens. These are more important than any quick increase in the demands and rights of citizens and minorities.

The economic and social matters, the habits, liberties, and property rights of individuals and corporations should be strengthened against the state, but in matters regarding crime, subversion, and foreign influence, the power of the state, as well as its liberty of action, should be increased against individuals. Courts and police forces should be given more power and discretion to supervise, search, and arrest potential suspects, and more discretion to sentence them to varying lengths of imprisonment.

The United States should remain "Number One"—paramount in military strength with both conventional and nuclear weapons. It should be ready and able to intervene anywhere in the world to protect its national interests and those of its allies. Proposals for arms limitations and arms control should be viewed with great skepticism, and considered only within the limits of preserving or restoring the preponderance of United States power in the world. Nuclear wars need not be avoided at any price. If necessary, the United States should seek to win them by "first strike" tactics or in any case, to prevail in them.

The main enemy of the United States is and remains the Soviet Union, with China and the claims of the Third World as a lesser threat. All these countries must be watched with tense alertness. Any mood of *détente* or relaxation of tensions in regard to these threats would be a dangerous illusion.

Welfare policies, social reforms, and improvements in the lot of minorities do not have a high priority as ends in themselves, but they should be advanced mainly as instruments to the extent that they increase political and social stability and support for the government and the present American political and economic system.

Similarly, economic aid to poorer countries and the promotion of human rights abroad should be used to the extent that these programs realistically serve as instruments of United States foreign policy, strategy, and power.

Some of the policies may be unrealistic. Long-term imprisonment as a way to control may be more expensive and less effective than its neoconservative advocates believe. More freedom for market forces may not suffice to reduce unemployment and inflation. Greater military force and an unrestrained arms control competition may reduce, not increase, the security of the United States.

Nonetheless, all these proposed policies have deep psychological roots in the feelings of substantial parts of the American people. Even traditionally liberal voters from some previously disadvantaged groups that now have become well established, such as many Americans of Irish, Italian, or Jewish background, may now find these ideas more appealing. Inflation and fear of crime hurt almost everyone. If an American consensus on public policy is to emerge in the 1980s, the neoconservative views and the feelings to which they appeal cannot be wholly disregarded.

Liberals and Radicals in Search of a Response. Neoconservatism posed a serious challenge to liberals and radicals, for two reasons. For one, it had taken over some of their own appeals to freedom, spontaneity, and security. Some neoconservatives called themselves "libertarians" in attacking bureaucracy and the welfare state in the United States and other countries; but neoconservatives also promised more law and order, stability and security, for individuals, property, and familiar patterns of morality.

Second, some of the liberal trust in progress had proved disappointing; and some of the radical experiments had failed in practice. "Progress" sometimes had meant bulldozers, superhighways, crowding, and a decline in the felt quality of life. Radical school experiments sometimes had not lived up to the hopes of their proponents; many communes had broken up, with members staying only an average of perhaps eighteen months and then drifting away; dropping out often had ended in poverty and boredom; the counterculture had produced few impressive works, if any.

Above all, the old evils—poverty, unemployment, inflation, and the risk of war—had not been abolished, although liberals had set the tone in the decades of effort to that end, from President Franklin D. Roosevelt in the 1930s to President Jimmy Carter in the late 1970s, and various kinds of radicals had enjoyed some permissive latitude during most of that time. Would they be able to do better in the 1980s?

Perhaps liberals would have to regain some of the spirit of experimentation of the early 1930s without losing some of the more sophisticated understanding gained from almost 50 years' additional experience. Perhaps radicals may have to become more interested in the realistic and the practicable, in developing consistent policies, coherent coalitions, and habits of patience, tenacity, responsibility, and competence, while widening and deepening their compassion and imagination. In any process of that kind, the boundaries between liberalism and radicalism would become blurred. Liberalism, one recalls, has long meant faith in people and in the goal of freedom, but it often has changed in its views of particular institutions and instruments to promote these values.

Perhaps in the 1980s liberal thought will have to reach further and cut deeper than before, if it is to survive as a major intellectual and moral force.

Thus far, adherents of all of the five major political belief systems—liberalism, conservatism, classic radicalism, the new radicalism, and neoconservatism—in the United States—in contrast to, say, Germany in the 1930s—have remained on speaking terms with one another. Indeed, most persons are not pure representatives of any single one of these configurations. Rather, most individuals are drawing on all five as resources in the development of their thoughts and feelings about politics and life, even though each may draw most heavily on the view he or she finds most congenial. In their interplay and overlap, these five systems of political images, together with the American political culture in which they are embedded, go far to determine the arena of American politics.

THE ARENA OF AMERICAN POLITICS

The images of American politics and the inputs and outputs of the American political system are all part of the arena of American politics. Most immediately they touch those people who live in the United States. But these images reach out much further, into foreign countries and international relations.

An arena is to politics what a market is to business. Two businesspeople are in the same *market* if they receive to a large extent the same information about prices and offers to buy and sell and if they take this information into account in making their own decisions—or, differently put, if this information then makes an observable difference in their economic behavior. Two political actors are in the same *arena* if they are members of the same domain, subject to the same power holders, and if they receive to a large extent the same information about who is demanding power over whom and in regard to what activities.

In the modern world the arena of politics is, first, the national state. During the history of the United States its political arena has changed with its geographic expansion: beginning with a strip of states along the Atlantic coast in the late eighteenth century, spreading over the midwest and adding Texas and California during the nineteenth century, and reaching out across land and sea to add Alaska and Hawaii as full-fledged states and Puerto Rico as an associated commonwealth in the twentieth century. Correspondingly, the non-self-governing possessions of the United States have dwindled to a few islands in the Pacific and the Caribbean.

In another sense, however, the American political arena is much larger. It comprises many areas not directly governed by the United States, but in many ways clearly subject to its overwhelming political, economic, and military power. In effect, they are part of the domain of the United States, but they have relatively little influence on American political decisions. In 1979 these areas included such countries as the Dominican Republic, Haiti, Nicaragua, and the other Central American republics; South Korea and Taiwan; and Singapore, Israel, Jordan, and Liberia. Other countries under lesser, but still considerable, United States influence were Turkey, Greece, Pakistan, Bolivia, Paraguay, and Spain. By 1979, United States influence seemed lost in five minor countries: Vietnam, Laos, Cambodia, Ethiopia, and Afghanistan, as well as in the more important oil-producing Iran. It had somewhat weakened in America's old friend, Israel, and in its quarreling allies, Greece and Turkey. But American influence had increased in Egypt, Somalia, and Bangladesh, to some extent in India, and perhaps slightly in China. On balance, the reach of American influence had not been diminished. It was striking to note, however, that United States influence usually fell short of effective control; that after decades of American involvement most of these countries remained poor; and that the governments of many of them remained authoritarian, military, and dictatorial.

Some critics concluded from this state of affairs that such announced United States policy goals as independence, prosperity, and democracy for all countries should be viewed with skepticism. Others felt that American purposes were more divided and that American capabilities to achieve national policy goals in foreign countries were far more limited than had been expected. Still others suggested that some American voters might be willing to support a limited effort to defend some or all of these countries against what they perceived as the threat of communism, but that most voters were unwilling to do much else for them. Yet a sudden crisis in any one of these countries might bring the United States to the brink of war; and any such war might escalate to a world war with thermonuclear weapons, endangering the survival of the American people.

Other countries, though allied with the United States, were much less subject to direct American political influence. These included France, Britain, the German Federal Republic and the other members of the European Economic Community, Japan, Canada, Australia, and New Zealand. In most of these countries, United States influence had been very high in the early 1950s. By early 1973, however, it had dropped dramatically. When President Nixon, shortly before Christmas 1972, ordered the massive bombing of the city of Hanoi in order to influence the peace negotiations with North Vietnam, his use of large-scale bombing as an instrument of diplomacy was condemned by political leaders and public opinion in most of these countries. The moral prestige of the United States improved again after 1975, with the end of the Vietnam War, and even more in 1977 and 1978, with President Carter's international campaign for human rights.

Finally, the United States political arena in the mid- and late 1970s included two countries, the Soviet Union and China, whose actions, demands, and probable responses had to be taken into account in the making of major American policy decisions.

The American political arena thus consisted of a central portion, the United States itself; a periphery of about two dozen less developed countries, subject to much influence from the United States, but exercising little in return; and more than a dozen democratic countries—many in Western Europe, but also Canada, Australia, and Japan—that in earlier years had often been treated as partners of the United States, but whose views had come to be increasingly disregarded and whose political ties to the United States in many ways were weakening. The vision of an Atlantic community of North America and Western Europe, so confidently proclaimed in the 1940s, now was dimmer than it had ever been.

Yet the fates of all these countries remained tied together and, to a considerable degree, dependent on the political processes and decisions of the United States. Perhaps never before in history has there been such widespread political interdependence combined with such limited capabilities for common consultation, decision, and control. By 1978, some common institutions had been created for these tasks, such as annual economic summit meetings among the heads of chief industrial "Western" countries, including Japan. Whether these meetings would lead to common actions, however, only the legislators and voters of these countries could decide. Alternatively, the arena of political interdependence and the domain of American political influence might well start shrinking again, reaching the level of the large, but limited, capabilities of the American political system.

THE AMERICAN POLITICAL SYSTEM: THE MACHINERY AND PROCESSES OF GOVERNMENT

In our look at the American political system, we shall change somewhat the sequence of topics outlined in the earlier parts of this book. We shall ask first what holds the system together. Then we shall look at the specific machinery and processes of government and then ask how, and how well, this large and complex system manages to steer itself. Finally we shall focus on two key dimensions of political performance: how much freedom and self-development the system permits to the individuals living under it, and what capabilities the system has developed for its own growth and self-transformation.

The Roots of Its Cohesion. The American political system is being held together, perhaps first of all, by the high *mobility* of the population. As people move from place to place and job to job, they keep much of their character, memories, loyalties, and habits of communications, so that they then still have ties to the people they have left behind and to the people among whom they have come to live now. If they keep moving often, and often back and forth, they weave a web of common memories and habits that makes them more coherent, that is, more apt to understand each other and more reluctant to be separated. This seems true of many people but even more so of Americans. About every third American lives in some state of the Union other than the one in which he or she was born. Along with this geographic mobility has gone also a remarkable degree of mobility among occupations and even among roles and positions in society.

Second, the American political system is held together by the experience and expectation of *joint rewards* from the high national income, living standards, and educational and social opportunities that have been shared in some form and to some extent by perhaps 85 to 90 percent of the population.

And third, the political system of the United States is held together by the *social and cultural cohesiveness* of the American people—by the interlocking of social roles, the similarity of expectations and experiences, and the community of habits, values, character, and culture. The legal rules and the political and administrative arrangements that provide for the formal and institutional unity of the system derive most of their strength from these underlying social, economic, and psychological conditions.

All three of these basic conditions are somewhat older than the Constitution of the United States, as it was ratified in 1791. However, the Constitution was designed to fit these conditions and the needs and resources of the American people that went with them; and once the Constitution was in force, its design influenced the further development of the nation.

Federalism and the Separation of Powers. One of the primary characteristics of this design for the government of the United States was its basic pattern of *federalism,* which was then a radically new idea in its application on a continental scale. (Prior to the establishment of the United States, the only successful large republic had been that of ancient Rome, which was not federal. Since Rome's collapse, only small republics like Venice, small confederations like Switzerland, and the small-scale federal institutions of the Dutch had flourished.)

This federal design combined a legislative congress, representing the diversity of the states, and a single chief executive—an "elective monarch," as this individual has been called—to direct the power of the nation. In such a federal union, as discussed in Chapter 8, every person is subject at one and the same time to two governments that are partly independent of each other. The federal government and the government in each state are separated in scope—in *what* they are supposed to govern—but united in domain—in *whom* they are governing. In the United States the federal government and the state governments each operate directly on the individual, within their respective spheres of powers. Those *residual powers* not explicitly given by the Constitution either to the Union or to the states are now held to belong to the federal government. This usage has been confirmed by several decisions of the U.S. Supreme Court, despite the long-lasting opposition of states' righters who would have preferred the opposite outcome.

Here federalism in Canada differs from that in the United States. In Canada the residual powers—those not explicitly allocated to provinces—were left by the British North America Act to the federal government. However, that act also included an "illustrative" list of central government powers and a vaguely defined power of the provinces in regard to "property and civil rights." Later court decisions have tended to expand this power of the provinces into a "sort of residuary competence . . . and to treat the Centre's residuary power as confined to the listed matters, matters similar to them, and national emergencies."[15] Under this arrangement, in Canada or the United States, no small region or group nor any individual has been able to dictate to the rest.

Some theorists have claimed that government is based on two monopolies: the monopoly of violence and the monopoly of legitimacy. The American experience casts doubt on this view. During its formative decades the United States was relatively decentralized. For many decades after the ratification of the Constitution there was no federal monopoly of violence and, indeed, no federal monopoly of legitimacy. In part, this was due to a physical fact: the army of the United States federal government in the 1790s had fifteen hundred soldiers strung out over almost as many miles along the Indian frontier. The state militia of a single state such as New York, on the other hand, had twenty thousand men. Therefore, the federal government in the early years of the republic had no way of coercing the states. Only if the states backed the federal government could the federal government make its will prevail.

The American system also offers remarkable freedom to opposition. Americans traditionally have refused to believe that anything was right merely because the government said so. Some Americans even held that rebellion was legitimate. Jefferson said of Shays's Rebellion (1786) that it might be necessary for the United States to have such an uprising every twenty-five years. These views did not prevent him from being later elected president of the United States.

In its essence, then, the American federal system has always tended to permit searching criticism of basic practices and institutions by the people, as well as by their elected representatives. Again it was Jefferson, this time after his tenure of office, who said of slavery, "I tremble for my country when I reflect that God is just." Serious criticism of one's own country is as old as the republic. Through freedom of criticism the United States has remained cohesive and its federal system has remained strong, and both have become more so in the course of time. The argument that criticism is divisive, or that dissent weakens national unity, runs counter to the mainstream of American experience.

America's federalist scheme has been imitated widely, but not always with the same degree of success as in America. Federalism worked as a political system in the United States for a combination of two basic reasons. First, as we noted, Americans early became a single people and identified themselves as such. Being highly mobile, they perceived of their needs and interests as shared, more often than not, and thus were willing to commit themselves to supporting a national government. Second, and equally important, America had a long tradition of independent and self-governing states. If either of these factors had existed alone, federalism might not have succeeded. The existence of both of them in combination helped provide the workable balance between local and national government that is the essence of federalism.

A System of Checks and Balances. Another characteristic of American government is that it is based on a *separation of powers,* that is, a sharp separation of legislative power from executive power and of judicial power—the power of judges and courts—

[15]Geoffrey Sawyer, *Modern Federalism* (London: Watts, 1969), p. 31.

from both. This concept was advanced by eighteenth-century theorists like Montesquieu, but the United States was unique in the thoroughness with which it put it into practice. To ensure the independence of all three branches of government, and at the same time to ensure that these three branches made up one coherent government, a system of *checks and balances* was developed (see Figure 10.4).

For nearly two centuries, separation of powers among the legislative, executive, and judicial branches has worked remarkably well. For the stronger and better organized groups, at least, it has provided a framework within which their different interests could be expressed and brought together into acceptable programs for action.

Pluralism versus Populism. American government is also characterized by an informal separation of powers, which some political scientists call *pluralism:*

FIGURE 10.4 *The Separation of Powers: A Simplified Sketch*

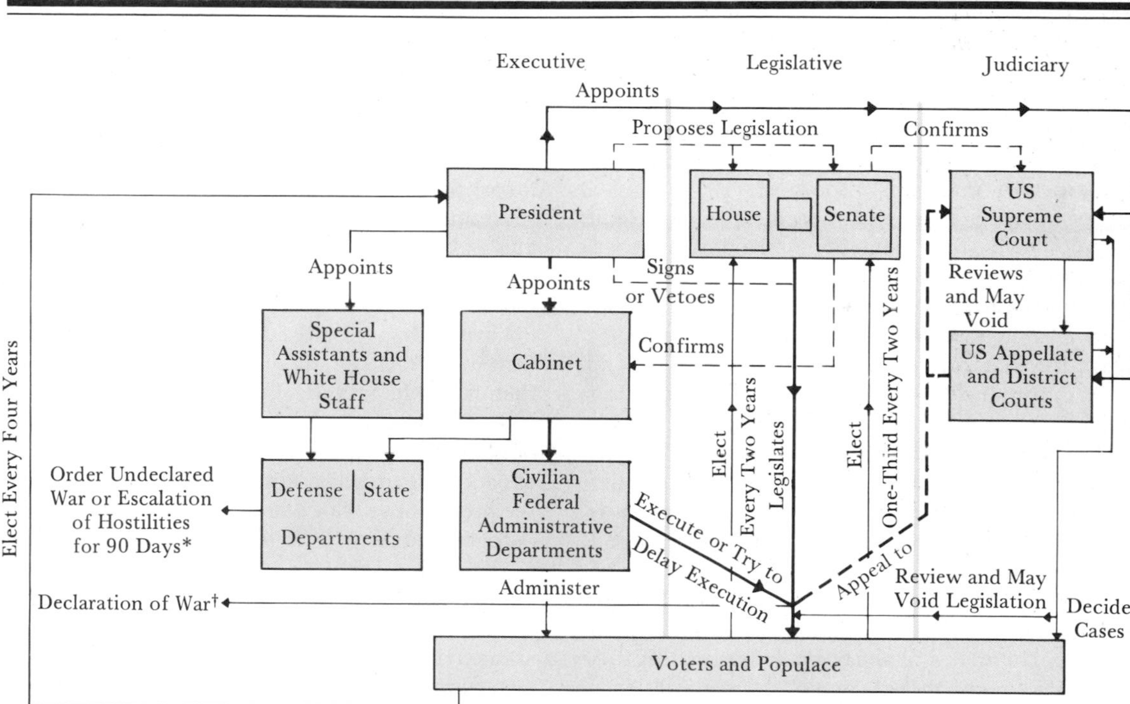

*If Congress directs by concurrent resolution, such forces shall be removed by the president before the 90 days are up.

†Note that there are two separate war powers: the power to declare war, which the Constitution reserves to Congress, and the power to wage undeclared war, which has been claimed by the president.

a plurality of competing interest groups and a diversity of rival interests—regional, social, economic, religious, and psychological. As James Madison pointed out in the "Tenth Federalist Letter," no special interest commands a majority in the United States: no one religion, no one economic interest, and no one region. Madison was confident that this fact would prevent the rise of tyrannical popular majorities for a long time. In the short run, he thought, there could be a tyrannical popular majority, but even that would be difficult to achieve and it would soon vanish. The view that the will of a popular majority should prevail in all matters, including science, art, and morals, and that neither experts nor minorities ought to have any valid claims against it became known in nineteenth-century American politics as *populism.* The quick decline of populism in the 1890s and McCarthyism in the 1950s (the demagogic and intolerant kind named after Senator Joseph McCarthy of Wisconsin) can be taken as examples of Madison's wisdom.

Populism can, at least, produce a consistent political will for limited populations, regions, periods of time, and small sets of issues. Here the popular *initiative* to move matters toward legislation and the *referendum* to decide on a new law by popular vote can be highly effective. The passing of Proposition 13 by referendum in California is a recent example. If populations become large, areas more diversified, time perspectives longer, and issues more varied, then populist majorities risk falling apart. In 1976, President Carter was elected on a quasi-populist platform. He appealed to the resentment of many voters against the distant bureaucracies and elites in far-off Washington, against costly foreign policy adventures in remote countries, against the long-standing neglect of some of the economic and medical needs of ordinary people, and against injustices between races, sexes, and age groups, and he represented a revival of a fundamental morality in public life that was based on more than mere expectations of pragmatic success.

By late 1978 the Carter administration had made some major advances in all these respects, but its supporters had returned to their old quarrels among themselves. Whereas many younger voters demanded more permissiveness, many older voters demanded a reaffirmation of traditional morality. *Feminists* asserted each woman's right to maintain control over her own body, including the right to have her own pregnancy terminated on demand, but other voters, including many women, asserted a *"right to life"* for an embryo in the first weeks and months after conception, even against the mother's will. A practical *trimester solution* was handed down by the Supreme Court. It treated the embryo as a part of the mother's body during the first three months and as a person to be protected in his or her own right thereafter; but even this decision did not still the controversy.

Some of President Carter's supporters backed his attacks on the abuses in the organization and practices of Congress, including the trading of favors for local projects among members of Congress and its so-called *porkbarrel politics,* that is, the grant of federal money to local projects. However, senators and representatives remembered that most of them had been elected in 1976 with higher majorities than the president had received in their districts, and they remembered Carter's attacks on them when he had to come to them later for their votes to pass his legislation. Some groups in and out of Congress pressed Carter for higher defense expenditures, while others pressed for lower ones; the president's policy of a 3-percent increase of the defense budget in real terms did not give much satisfaction to either side. Some groups wanted the United States to intervene secretly or openly with its forces in Africa and elsewhere, but others warned that such a course might lead to dangerous escalation and perhaps to World War III. By late 1978, President Carter's refusal to send new troops or even "instructors" abroad and his postponement of a decision on the production of the neutron bomb had displeased the former side, but not fully reassured the latter. Again, some interest groups and senators wanted to improve America's energy supply and reduce oil imports by increasing the profit margins of oil producers in the United States, but other groups and senators opposed this; so President Carter's energy program passed Congress only in late 1978 and in strongly modified form. In short, President Carter continued to depend on a semipopulist coalition for his strength during 1978–79, but by then that coalition was weaker and less united than it had been on election day. American politics seemed more pluralistic than ever.

Does Pluralism Give an Equal Chance to Everybody? Pluralism, however, is not an unmixed blessing. In its early stages, half the interest groups of a political system may be unorganized and the other half may run the show. In that case, pluralism helps the strong, but can be merciless against the weak. Later, when everybody is organized, the political system may become immobile, as seemed to be the case for a time during the long debate about a national energy policy in 1977–78. Unless political leaders play a brilliant role in discovering workable policies and organizing broad coalitions to carry them out, this immobility may lead to weak compromises that fail to meet the larger issue at stake or it may persist. But such diplomacy and leadership happen rarely. If they do not happen, then the immobility-emergency syndrome discussed in Chapter 3 will set in, and some leaders may start looking for emergencies—foreign, military, or other—to force quick action.

Pluralism and the Distribution of Political Opinion. The danger of immobility may be compounded by the dangers of *polarization,* the risk that many voters may desert the middle ground on several important issues and move to one or the other extreme pole—far left or far right—in regard to all of them. But if voters shift attitude to the left on one issue and to the right on another, the two shifts might balance or cancel each other out and the voters might still vote for a candidate in the political middle. This is what advocates of pluralism usually hope for, but it does not always happen. When it exerts its full power, political polarization implies that voters move to more extreme attitudes on several issues consistently; that is, some voters move on several issues to the left, and others move on several issues to the right. The plurality of opinions then is reduced to two, directly opposed to one another.

Just this has happened in the United States from the 1950s to the 1970s. In 1956 only 25 percent of American voters had such consistent attitudes: 12 percent leftists and 13 percent rightists in their views. A vast majority, 75 percent, were in the middle: 41 percent were centrists, and the remaining 34 percent were divided between the moderate left and the moderate right. The whole profile of voters' attitudes resembled the capital letter *A*, or a curve of normal statistical distribution. But by 1973 this profile had changed to one resembling a capital *W*. The centrist group had shrunk greatly, to 27 percent; the moderate left had declined from 19 to 12 percent, and the moderate right had grown slightly, from 15 to 17 percent, so that the three middle groups together now totaled only 56 percent. But at the extreme ends of the political spectrum, consistent leftists had risen from 12 to 21 percent and consistent rightists from 13 to 23 percent.

The changes from 1956 to 1963 are shown in Figure 10.5, and the 1973 situation still seems to be reflected by the results of the 1978 congressional elections. The three center groups still constitute a majority, but there is no majority either to the right or to the left of center. The difficulties for President Carter, and for any national leader, are now larger than they would have been twenty years ago.

Two-Track Legislation for the Nation. Another political invention has given America's national legislature its distinctive cast. This invention deals with the relation of large and small states and their representation in Congress. The legislature was organized into two chambers. In the House of Representatives, equal representation was given to the people. In the Senate, equal representation was given to the states. England had long had a two-chamber legislature comprising its House of Lords and its House of Commons, but the use of the two-chamber system to accommodate the interests of large and small states in a federal union of continental dimensions was an American invention.

FIGURE 10.5 *Distribution of Population by Political Beliefs, 1956 and 1973*

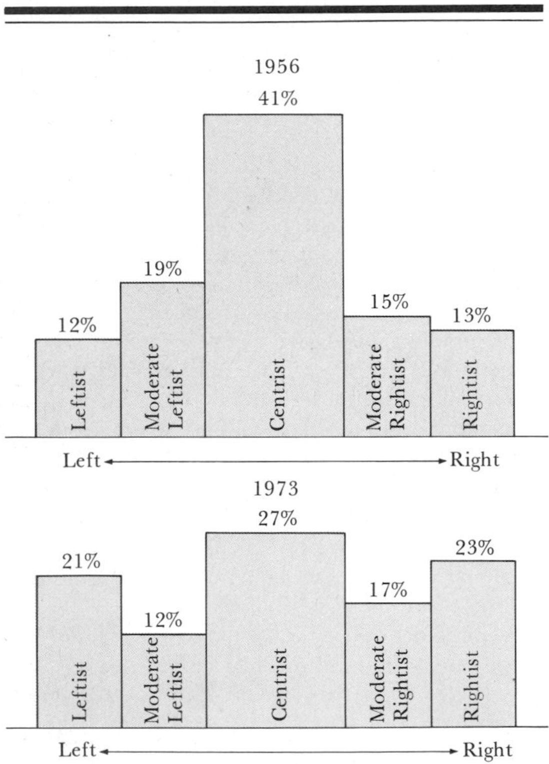

Source: Norman H. Nie, Sidney Verba and John R. Petrocik, *The Changing American Voter* (Cambridge: Harvard University Press, 1976), p. 143.

Representing the People by Numbers: The House. In the House of Representatives the people are represented by one representative for every equal number of inhabitants as fixed by law—originally one for every 30,000, now one for almost every 500,000.[16] The representatives are chosen directly by the people for two-year terms. They are elected from congressional districts, all intended to be equal in population. To ensure this equality, congressional districts are supposed to be readjusted, both among and within states, after each decennial census. The manner of adjustment within each state, like the qualifications for voting, is left to the state's legislature, while allocation of districts among states is entrusted to Congress. All these provisions were intended to ensure equal representation of the people in the House of Representatives.

In practice the representation in the House has turned out to be much less equal. Although congressional districts are supposed to be readjusted every ten years, at the start of the 1960s there were some state legislatures that had neglected this duty for as long as half a century. Many legislators from rural districts were benefiting from this neglect because they did not have to share power with representatives of the faster-growing urban areas. In the eighteenth and nineteenth centuries a similar neglect to provide adequate representation for the rapidly growing cities of Britain led there to the evils of the *"rotten boroughs"*—thinly populated rural districts overrepresented in Parliament. These were abolished by Britain's Reform Bill of 1832, although Britain today is still far from

[16]Until the abolition of slavery in 1865, only free persons were counted fully: according to Article I, Section 2, Paragraph 3 of the Constitution, each slave, though without vote, was to be counted as three-fifths of a person, for the benefit of the state in which he or she was held in bondage. Nowadays representation is by the number of people who live in a state, even if they are not registered to vote. Southern states have increased their seats in the House by counting many blacks to whom, nevertheless, they denied the right to vote.

achieving absolutely equal representation for all its people. In the United States, major efforts to provide just apportionment of congressional districts gained momentum only in the 1960s and then with the aid of the courts. By that time it was charged that rural voters in some sparsely settled Illinois districts had nine times the voting power of citizens in some of Chicago's crowded precincts. Moreover, the new suburbs on the edge of many big cities had long remained underrepresented in Congress.

By the end of the 1960s, the doctrine of *"one man one vote"* had been established by decision of the United States Supreme Court, and the courts were beginning to demand that redistricting plans, in order to be constitutional, had to provide for districts that would vary by no more than 10 percent in their number of voters. This principle was also applied by the courts to state legislatures, with far-reaching implications for the distribution of political power within the states and, indirectly, throughout much of the country. These developments promised to wipe out the last elements of representation by wealth or ownership of land.[17] During the 1970s the effects of redistricting—or *legislative reapportionment*—in accordance with the "one man one vote" principle facilitated substantial changes in the congressional system of seniority and in the structure and operations of congressional committees, reducing the power and length of tenure of committee chairs. Similarly, it facilitated changes in the structure of the executive, reducing the secrecy of its operations and extending the areas of congressional oversight. Beyond this, however, reapportionment mainly strengthened the power of suburban voters whose districts had grown most rapidly in population. While the overrepresentation of rural districts had helped to make the House more conservative than the Senate—contrary to what the nation's founders had expected—the suburban voters and their representatives in Congress favored reforms in some areas, such as openness of government, protection of the environment, and a low-risk foreign policy, while also developing more conservative attitudes in regard to taxation, affirmative action, and federal pressure for racial integration of local public schools. On these issues the voting records of newly elected surburban representatives in the 1976–78 period furnished striking evidence.

The two-year term for representatives may have had a similar effect. Intended to keep representatives close to their constituents, this provision has involved many legislators in contested districts in expensive and almost permanent campaigns for re-election, giving them little time for what was to have been their first responsibility, legislating for the people. This same provision, of course, gives disproportionate influence to those of their colleagues who are virtually unopposed in their rural districts or in urban districts dominated by a single ethnic group or political machine. Legislators from such safe one-party districts get re-elected time after time; and through the congressional custom of *seniority* (which allocates committee chairs to legislators with the longest continuous term of service) they dominate the important committees of the House and thereby much of the legislative business (see Table 10.6). These conditions have condemned many urban voters in contested districts to a feeling of powerlessness. Even if they succeed in electing a representative of their choice, he or she rarely seems to get anywhere in Congress. Although voters can change their representatives in Congress every two years, it would take them ten to twenty years to get their representative to head an important House committee. In 1968, Shirley Chisholm, the first black

[17]Conservative opponents of thoroughgoing equality among voters have backed a constitutional amendment proposed by the late Senator Everett McKinley Dirksen of Illinois that would explicitly permit the allocating of districts and, in effect, the weighting of votes by standards other than the equality of voters. In 1972 the Supreme Court refused to review the decision of an appellate court that permitted the departure from the "one man one vote" principle in a case involving the election of local judges. In fact, however, the principle prevailed.

TABLE 10.6 *Democratic Representatives, January 1964 (in percentages)*

	NORTH		SOUTH	
	Rural	Urban	Rural	Urban
All Democratic representatives (255)	21	42	29	9
Major committee chairs held by Democrats	18	29	53	0
Safe seats occupied by Democrats	7	30	52	11

Source: R. E. Wolfinger and J. Heifetz, "Safe Seats, Seniority, and Power in Congress," *American Political Science Review* 59 (1965), pp. 337–49.

woman elected to Congress, represented a crowded urban area in Brooklyn, but was promptly assigned to the House Committee on Agriculture; her refusal to accept brought her a change of assignment—to the Veterans Affairs Committee. By early 1973, however, she had become one of the best known and most widely respected members of Congress.

Representing the People by States: The Senate. If one branch of Congress was intended to represent the people in all regions of the country more or less equally as individuals, the other branch was designed to represent them unequally as individuals, but equally as states. For this reason the small states of the Union, inferior to the large ones in population and effective political power, have the same representation in the Senate as their large neighbors: two senators for each state.

Those small states that are virtually one-party states, such as Mississippi, Arkansas, and, until recently, Maine and Vermont, can gain disproportionate influence in the Senate through the seniority system that in time tends to put their senators at the head of major Senate committees. The effects of the seniority system, still accepted by many senators from industrial or urban states, make it harder for a senator from New York or California to head a key committee. However, this power of seniority is declining. As two-party competition spreads to formerly one-party states, senators from two-party states may be gaining in influence.

The framers of the Constitution expected the Senate to serve as a counterweight to the House. They believed that senators would be older, more conservative, and more representative of the established elites of their states—those whom an eighteenth-century writer called "the rich, the well-born, and the wise." As we shall see, this is not quite what eventually happened.

Senators are elected for a term of six years, in order to have a greater measure of stability and independence for their term of service. At every congressional election, every two years, only one-third of the Senate faces re-election, in contrast to all the members of the House. This is to protect the composition of the Senate from quick changes in the mood of the voters.

Originally, the senators were elected indirectly by the legislatures of their states. But in 1912 the *Seventeenth Amendment* to the Constitution changed this to direct election by majority vote of those voters who "have the qualifications requisite for electors of the most numerous branch of the state legislatures." The effect of this change has varied somewhat by regions. In most northern and western states the registered voters make up a large part of the adult population, though by no means all of them. In some southern states, owing to various discriminatory practices against blacks and the poor, less than half of the adult population have been registered to vote and less than one-fourth have actually voted. Yet the sharp increase in the registration of blacks in the South after the Voting Rights Act of 1965 suggests the beginnings of a change.

Since the Senate is supposed to represent the states equally, regardless of population, it has been particularly sensitive to regional or sectional differences and more distrustful of simple national majorities. The still continuing practice of the filibuster—or its threat—and the long struggle for workable rules of *cloture* confirm this built-in bias (see Chapter 8, footnotes 1 and 2, for a discussion of the filibuster and cloture).

Despite the conservative role intended for it by the nation's founders, the Senate in many matters has become more liberal than the House. Senators must be elected by the voters of an entire state, so the unequal apportionment of voting districts has no effect on them. Voters from urban and industrial areas within each state have their full share of influence on the election of their senators. It is also much more difficult for any political machine, ethnic group, or special interest group to dominate an entire state, compared with the relative ease with which such groups can hold sway over a congressional district. There are, to be sure, a few senators with well-known concerns for the interests of cotton or tobacco growers, dairy farmers, aircraft manufacturers, or defense contractors, but they make up a relatively limited part of the Senate, and even seniority cannot put them in charge of *all* Senate committees.

To get re-elected, therefore, most senators must be responsive to both rural and urban interests in their states, to many different ethnic groups and economic interests, and to the independent voters who may hold the balance in many two-party states. The smaller size of the Senate makes individual senators more highly visible. The mass media, particularly television, have reinforced these opportunities and have made it easier for many senators to entertain ambitions for higher office—at the Cabinet level, on the Supreme Court, or for the presidency—all of which, at one time or another, have been attained by former senators. These conditions often favor the selection of more statesmanlike candidates, and the six-year term gives them a better opportunity to build a record of accomplishment. Although many legislators in the House as well as in the Senate have done their best to serve the public good as they saw it, the prestige of senators has usually been higher, perhaps with good reason.

Beyond the prestige of its members, the Senate as a whole and its committees have certain powers: to direct national attention to particular problems, to put new issues before the public, and to become a potentially important source for new legislation and political initiatives. To what extent these opportunities are used may depend in part on the political situation and the public mood, but also on the individual senators, on their staff assistants, and on the particular Senate committees, staffs, and philosophy under which they operate. In any event, according to a recent study by David Price, these senatorial committees and their staffs have become a major part of the real legislative process in the United States.

Latent Tensions: Congress and the Chief Executive. A brilliant conservative theorist of American politics, Willmoore Kendall, once remarked that many American voters, when stepping into the polling booth, develop a split personality. First, they think of themselves as far-sighted and generous. They consider the problems of the nation as a whole, both in domestic matters and in world affairs, and like to think about world leadership by the United States. Willing to accept some American responsibilities toward humankind, they then cast their votes for the presidential candidate most likely to represent these aspirations. As soon as they have done this, says Kendall, our voters turn around and ask themselves this question: what about *my* district, *my* locality, *my* special economic interest, and *my* ethnic group? All the grand, costly, national and international policies go out the window. Now they seek the most distrustful, tightfisted, narrow-minded, intensely parochial candidates they can find—and in this mood they pick their representatives to Congress. Once their president and representatives reach Washington, they must try to work out the conflicts that the voters failed to resolve in their own minds.[18]

Kendall's sketch may be overdrawn, but there is some truth in it. Congressional and presidential candidates of the same party rarely receive the same number of votes from a particular district. In districts where one party is strong enough to win at least 65 percent of the vote for a congressional seat, the victorious legislator tends to run ahead of the presidential candidate of the same party. In all other districts, on the average, the opposite tendency prevails; the representative, more often than not running behind the presidential ticket, tends to benefit from the pulling power of the leader's coattails. Once elected, however, the entire Congress is likely to approve less than one-half of the president's proposals, as Lewis Froman has shown.

The Making of a Crisis: A Critical Congress and a Single-Minded President. After 1968, and especially after 1972, this situation began to change. Both times, President Nixon was elected, although the voters at the same time refused his party a majority in either house of Congress. As a result, the latent tension between the presidency and the legislature became increasingly manifest, since each of these two branches could claim to have received a mandate from the voters.

The crisis had been long in the making. The exclusive *right of Congress* to declare war in full legal form had gradually fallen into disuse during the decades of the Cold War after 1945; and the president's power to order units of the armed forces into battle had correspondingly increased. President Jefferson early in the nineteenth century had ordered a small force of marines into action against the Algerian pirates. But by the 1960s this executive power was being exercised on a grand scale: President Kennedy sent 16,000 "advisers" into South Vietnam, and President Johnson raised this force to over 500,000. By early 1973, President Nixon had reduced the American ground troops in that country to less than 30,000, but kept more than 100,000 in the area, on ships, and on bases in neighboring Thailand, while ordering unprecedentedly heavy bombing raids on the North Vietnamese cities. All these actions were taken without any explicit vote of Congress—some of them in the face of explicit congressional opposition. Only later in 1973 were all American ground troops evacuated from Vietnam, and on August 15, 1973, all American bombardment of Indochina officially ceased. In April 1975 the last American troops and personnel were evacuated from South Vietnam, which later was merged with North Vietnam under Communist rule. As such, Vietnam is now a member of the United Nations, recognized by the United States.

At the same time, President Nixon began to "impound" moneys specifically authorized and appropriated by laws passed by Congress. He refused to let his administration execute these laws and spend these moneys, claiming as his reason that these expenditures—some of them quite moderate—would contribute to inflation. At the same time he continued to spend public moneys for the military, naval, and air activities that he had ordered on his own authority. In this manner the priorities of spending preferred by the chief executive were made to prevail over the duly enacted decisions of the legislative branch—a practice very different from that which the Constitution had ordained; and it became explicitly illegal in 1975 under a new law passed by Congress and signed by President Ford.

In late 1972, President Nixon requested Con-

[18]In recent years, the opposite of Kendall's surmise sometimes was true. Repeatedly, voters have elected liberal representatives and senators from their districts and states, while electing at the same time a strongly conservative president, as happened in the 1972 election. But the split in the inner attitudes of many voters remained, giving both Congress and the president an equal, but incomplete, mandate.

gress to delegate to him the right to suspend, at his discretion, the execution of specific items in any law that Congress henceforth might pass. Congress, however, refused to vote in favor of this request on the grounds that such a general authorization would take away the power of the purse from Congress and shift it to the president, thus destroying the constitutional separation of powers and the balance among the three main branches of government. Thereupon, some spokespeople from the White House told the press that the requested congressional authorization really had not been needed: the president, they said, already had these powers. Had he not already impounded sums that Congress had appropriated to be spent, and was not this in effect the same kind of item veto over money bills that the president had requested? (According to Article I, Section 7, of the Constitution the president may refuse to sign a bill passed by Congress. This refusal—usually called a *veto*—will prevent this entire bill from becoming law, unless it is passed once more by a two-thirds majority in each house of Congress. But the Constitution does not give the president the power of an *item veto*, that is, the power to strike out just one part of a bill, while letting the rest of it become law, perhaps with a drastically altered balance.)

By early September 1973 it seemed that neither the president nor Congress wanted the conflict to reach extremes, and several bills had been permitted to pass in a spirit of compromise. However, the basic conflict of views remained unresolved. It still seemed that a constitutional crisis was in the making, if president and Congress should continue on their collision course. In the end, the Supreme Court, with four Nixon-appointed and Senate-confirmed judges among its nine members, voted against Nixon in deciding that he had to turn over to a judge the tapes that he had made of White House conversations and that he had wished to define as executive secrets.

Throughout his term Nixon had insisted that any action whatsoever was lawful if the president ordered it to be taken "in the national interest" and that he had the right to make such decisions by himself alone. For a long time top members of his staff had shared this view. One of his aides was asked by a congressional committee whether he thought that a presidential order would justify his committing murder; he replied that a line would have to be drawn somewhere, but he did not wish to be the one to draw it.

Defenders of President Nixon pointed out, truthfully, that similar cases could be found during the preceding two centuries of American history for almost all the abuses of which President Nixon and his staff were accused. But it seems also true that never before had so many abuses been committed on so large a scale within so short a time. In the feelings of many American voters a "critical mass," or body of violations large enough to threaten an explosion in one direction or another, had been reached.

At last, in August 1974 a congressional committee voted to impeach President Nixon for his crimes and misdemeanors, and the president resigned rather than risk a vote on the House floor or a trial in the Senate. This outcome was ratified by the voters in the elections of 1974 and 1976.

Earlier, Vice President Agnew had resigned and been convicted in court for corruption and tax evasion, and President Nixon had appointed Gerald Ford as his successor in the vice presidency. After Nixon's resignation President Ford pardoned him for all offenses committed during his term of office, left him his presidential pension, and then proceeded to rescind or modify many of Nixon's policies. Many of Nixon's highest associates, however, were sentenced to jail terms by the courts.

The 48.9 percent of the popular votes cast for major-party candidates received by President Ford in 1976 (as opposed to President Carter's 51.1 percent) showed that after years of intense conflict the candidate of the Republican Party had retained the confidence of only slightly fewer electors than his Democratic rival, President Carter, had won. The social and economic underpinnings of both major parties in the United States seemed to have remained more solid than observers might have expected.

If President Nixon had prevailed in the final conflict, the political system of the United States might have become very different indeed. But in a major collision between the Constitution and the president, the American people had decided to keep the Constitution, and they had done so without fatally tearing the country apart. By mid-1978, ex-President Nixon seemed no longer a significant figure in American politics, but his best-selling memoirs were making him financially more secure than he had ever been.

Another Kind of President—But the Same Kind of Congress? In Jimmy Carter the American people elected a president who was no less individualistic than some of his recent predecessors, but markedly less assertive. He had won his office as the builder of a popular coalition (see p. 274, above); he never forgot the wide differences among its components; and he was frequently reminded of them. But in his first year in office he underestimated the power of Congress and its peculiarities. When he proposed to veto the pet projects of many of the members of Congress, when he sometimes failed to consult congressional leaders before making important decisions, and when he appointed many people from his native state of Georgia to important positions in the White House and elsewhere, by-passing possible candidates whom some representatives and senators had suggested to him for these posts, then by all these measures he laid a solid foundation for conflict. During the same first year President Carter had proposed to by-pass or override important interest groups, such as big industry and banking, the oil interests, the armaments and aircraft industry, the leaders of George Meany's AFL-CIO, the backers of local water projects, and others. It seems that these interest groups soon transferred additional lobbying efforts and political support to Congress, where they found willing allies for their views. Carter's proposal to increase and improve provisions for registration and disclosure of lobbying activity never cleared the Senate Governmental Operations Subcommittee, and soon a considerable part of his legislative program was delayed or stalled, including his important program on energy, which finally passed in a weakened version in November 1978. In the public mind these many instances of congressional resistance seemed to outweigh the president's legislative successes, such as the Senate's ratification of the Panama Canal Treaty, which would return the canal to Panama by the end of this century and on which the president had risked much of his international prestige.

How Legislators Vote and Work. Once in Congress, legislators try to represent their constituencies as well as their own convictions. The votes cast by representatives are shaped by what their constituencies are like and by what they themselves are like; by what the voters in their constituencies think and by what they think their voters think; by the events that impinge on both the voters and their representatives; by the legislative system, which offers them specific choices; and by their perceptions of these options. These seven conditions and the way in which they shape the votes cast by legislators are shown in Figure 10.6.

An eighth consideration is not represented in this diagram. Many legislative decisions have a technical or economic dimension to them and are likely to have consequences that cannot be estimated without expert knowledge. In the days of George Washington, such expert knowledge was perhaps equally scarce in Congress and in the executive and perhaps even scarcer in the rest of the country. But from the 1930s through the 1950s, the executive branch of the American government grew vastly in personnel and also in the number and quality of its experts. Presidents and Cabinet members could present their legislative proposals, backed by an impressive array of arguments and data compiled by the specialists on their staffs, which neither representatives nor senators nor even congressional committees could match. During these decades a knowledge gap was beginning to open between the executive and legislative branches of government. Though lobbyists for special interest groups were eager to supply data to both bureaucrats and legislators, their evidence was often biased and at best was of limited help.

From the 1960s onward, however, this situation began to improve. Representatives and senators acquired their own professional staffs, which are now usually between eight and twelve persons and at salary levels permitting the employment of adequately trained and competent individuals. Gifted young lawyers, economists, political scientists, and others found rewarding careers on these staffs. In addition, Congress greatly strengthened important governmental accounting and supervisory institutions, such as the *General Accounting Office (GAO)*, endowing some of them with important additional research functions. It even created new research and analysis bodies, such as the *Congressional Budget Office (CBO)*, through which Congress could improve its chances for balancing the impact of the executive branch's Office of Management and Budget on the drafting of budgets, the analyzing and monitoring of programs and expenditures, and the manipulating of the general flow of legislation.

FIGURE 10.6 *Why Representatives Vote as They Do*

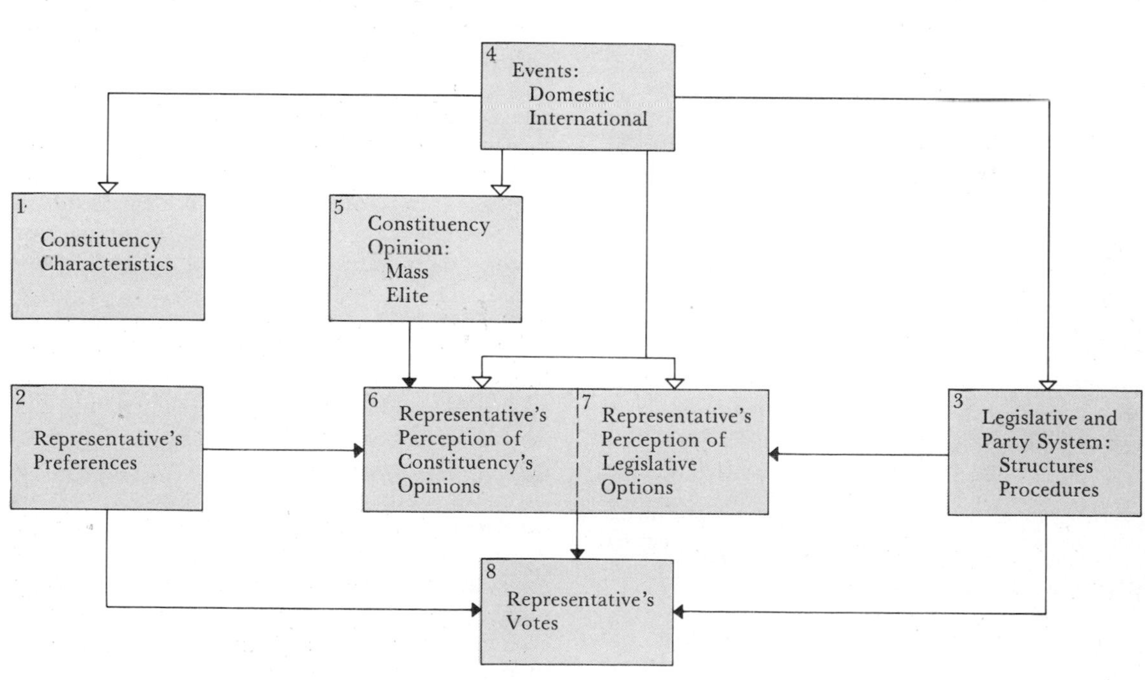

The House and Senate work in strikingly different ways. Having 435 members, the House is larger, more impersonal and formal in its proceedings, and more hierarchically organized. It is governed by more rigid rules, but is geared to quicker action. Power in the House is more unevenly distributed, and apprentice periods for first-year legislators are longer. With shorter terms and smaller and less important constituencies, House members carry less prestige. Because they more often represent local and small-town interests, their politics tend to be more conservative.

The 100 members of the Senate run their smaller chamber in a less formal manner. The Senate is less hierarchical, its rules more flexible, its actions slower, and its politics more personal. Power in the Senate is more evenly distributed, and apprentice periods for new members are shorter. Often the Senate has been called a "club". With longer terms and larger and more important constituencies—entire states—senators carry more prestige. Representing statewide interests, they are often politically more liberal.

Even within their chambers senators are likely to be more powerful than members of the House. In 1964, as Lewis Froman has shown, four out of five Senate Democrats held at least one committee or subcommittee chair, while in the House only two out of five Democrats held such positions.[19] When the Republicans are in power, similar proportions tend to apply to them. In either case, the power that comes from holding a chair—to expedite, delay, or sidetrack legislation—is twice as accessible to senators. By 1979, each member of the Senate had at least one subcommittee to chair, and with it a national forum for gaining attention.

[19]Senate committee chairs are appointed by the meeting—called a *caucus*—of all senators of the majority party, in accordance with seniority. The caucus of the minority party chooses the "ranking" minority member of each committee in the same manner. Nearly the same procedures prevail in the House.

The Work of Congress: Passing Legislation. For both branches of Congress the workload has grown. The first Congress (in 1790-92) passed one law for every five of the few days it was in session. In the 1960s, Congress met much longer and worked much faster: it passed about nine times as many laws, or nearly two laws per day. In such a crowded calendar, a bill's chances of becoming law are uncertain. Its hopes of passage depend first on its substance—the interests at stake. It is more likely to pass if more members support it, if their support is more intense, if its supporters are influential, and particularly if support comes from congressional leaders and the president. Its chances further improve if its supporters are strategically located, such as on the committee or subcommittee to which the bill is assigned or on the Rules Committee, which determines which committee will be assigned the bill. Finally, the bill is more likely to succeed if its opponents are few, lukewarm, lacking in influence, and poorly located.

Most bills are neither so popular in Congress as to be certain to breeze through nor so unpopular as to be hopeless. Proponents of such uncertain bills must win additional support for their proposals, and they do so by bargaining. Some of this bargaining may occur without overt negotiation. Legislators seem to go ahead and act, but in fact they take into account what they anticipate will be the reaction of their colleagues. In other cases there is more direct negotiation, explicit or implied.

The simplest technique is *logrolling.* Legislator A votes for legislator B's project, expecting or arranging that B will reciprocate. Legislator A expects B to be an "honest politician," that is, one who never fails to repay favors. Sometimes logrolling may extend over time. A legislator will vote for a colleague's project in return for an invisible legislative IOU to be cashed in at some future date. A raft of well-rolled logs is found in the omnibus rivers and harbors bills, which comprise a large number of separate and independent projects, each one dear to a particular legislator, but all of them as a package appealing to a sufficient number to ensure the support of a majority of legislators.

Sometimes logrolling involves large interest groups. In 1964, when the House passed the Cotton Bill, the Senate tacked on a wheat section. When the Cotton-Wheat Bill was returned to the House and still needed additional support for passage, the rural Democrats supporting it made a deal with urban Democrats who wanted a food stamp plan. As part of the bargain, the Food Stamp Bill had to be reported to the floor of the House first, but eventually both bills became law.

Another form of bargaining is the making of *compromises.* The proponents of a bill settle for less than they had originally demanded and then modify the bill to meet their opponents halfway. Compromises may end up exactly halfway between different positions or at some other highly visible or prominent solution that is acceptable to both sides; or else a compromise may give much to one side and little to the other, reflecting perhaps their unequal power or bargaining skills.

Finally, bargaining may involve *side payments*—advantages distinct from the content of the bill. Positive side payments to legislators may consist of federal judgeships, postmasterships, or other patronage appointments being placed under their control in exchange for their support of legislation important to the president. Other side payments may come from within Congress, such as desirable committee assignments or subcommittee chairs. Still other side payments may come from outside the government—from the national party or from special interest groups—and may include campaign contributions, well-paid speaking engagements, and the like. Influential legislators have reported annual income from such sources in excess of $100,000.

Outside pressures on Congress—such as from voters, interest groups, or the executive branch—clash or mesh in a changing balance with *inside influences* from congressional leaders or ordinary members. Inside influences tend to prevail and inside strategies are more likely to succeed, according to Nelson Polsby, when (1) the pending decision can be made a matter of procedure rather than substance; (2) one side has much greater inside strength, while both are evenly matched outside; and (3) the members are shielded from surveillance by outsiders. When these conditions are reversed, outside forces and the strategies designed to marshal them are likely to predominate.

Miniature Legislatures: The Congressional Committees. Congressional committees resemble small cross sections of Congress. They often are selected in a biased manner favoring some groups in Congress at the expense of others. Nonetheless, their contribution is indispensable. They permit bargaining, compromising, and logrolling with a minimum of publicity, until a workable majority coalition emerges. After a bill is reported out of committee, other members of Congress know more readily how to vote on it; they can pick up cues from committee members who are familiar with the measure and who have outlooks and interests similar to their own. A bill that passes in committee has a good chance to pass on the floor. Without the work of the committees a larger percentage of legislation would be defeated. While making legislation more acceptable to their fellow legislators, the committees tend to make it also less ideological, as abstract and sweeping provisions are whittled down and specific points are changed or added. Finally, by involving diverse interest groups outside Congress through formal hearings or informal communications, committee work makes the ultimate legislation more acceptable to the country.

The House Committee on Appropriations performs a particularly important task: it deals with money. Its decisions shape the federal budget and over the course of time much of the national government. Most of the increases or other budgetary changes that it makes when voting on the budgets of federal agencies are marginal; and the overall pattern of its decisions is balanced and conservative. Within this pattern, says Richard Fenno, most increases go to those agencies that have much support in the House outside the committee and in the country at large or that have won the confidence of the committee in the course of time. A very few agencies, such as the Federal Bureau of Investigation, meet all three tests. The Appropriations Committee is greatly trusted by the House; from 1947 to 1962, by Fenno's count, 90 percent of its recommendations were accepted.

Representation in the committees is heavily weighted on the rural and conservative side. Rural representatives made up half of the House Democrats in 1964, but held nearly three-quarters of the House's major committee chairs; and rural representatives from the South contributed less than 30 percent of the House strength, but had more than one-half the chairs. Significantly, southern representation among major committee chairs corresponded almost exactly to the proportion of southern safe seats in the House (see Table 10.6). On the important House Rules Committee, the giving of half the Democratic seats to southerners had become traditional.

In 1972 a somewhat more liberal House and Senate were elected by the same voters who refused to vote for Senator George McGovern for president and voted for President Nixon without sharing his entire political outlook. The new House of Representatives included about fifty younger and more liberal members, and about a half-dozen of the most senior—and often conservative—committee chairs did not return. The election of 1974 reinforced this trend, and those of 1976 and 1978 did not reverse it. However, the new members of Congress from suburban districts depended less on their national party organizations or on favors from the executive. They were more responsive to local opinion from their constituencies and to the pressure of local interest groups, ranging from environmentalists and pacifists to local bankers and businesspeople, alarmed patriots and members of ethnic groups of European descent—despite the slowly declining influence of the latter. Neither a liberal president nor the traditional conservative coalition of Republicans and southern Democrats could take their support for granted. It seemed that congressional members and measures were becoming harder to predict and more difficult to manage than they had been for many years.

In *roll-call votes* (when each legislator present publicly records his or her vote by name), a Democratic president could count within the House committees on an average support of 73 percent from the Democrats and 37 percent from Republican committee members. The same held true for Senate committees. For a Republican president in a Congress dominated by Democrats, the proportions might be reversed if the presidential program were not shaped to attract more bipartisan support. Conversely, a Republican president might choose to try to by-pass Congress and to enhance the powers of that office. President Nixon's choice of the latter course ended in disaster. President Carter, facing an unruly majority from his own party in Congress, was still trying in the late 1970s to find a viable strategy of compromise.

The Favored Elements in Congress. In matters of procedure Congress is dominated by two parties. Democrats and Republicans compete to organize Congress to determine its majority and minority, its committee chairs, and within each party the committee assignments. But on matters of substance many writers have seen four parties at work in Congress: northern Democrats, mostly urban and liberal; southern Democrats, mostly rural and conservative; liberal Republicans, mostly from northeastern cities, suburbs, and rural areas; and conservative Republicans, mostly from the rural Midwest, suburban California, and parts of the urban South. None of these four has a majority in Congress. On many issues an informal coalition of conservative Republicans and southern Democrats has commanded a majority. (No such coalition was able to control the 1965-66 Congress; much of the program of social legislation that it passed had been held up for decades.) A still more detailed division would add two more groups to the four listed: middle-of-the-road Democrats and middle-of-the-road Republicans. These two are minorities, but they are likely to be needed in helping majorities to form, and thus their influence is often great.

All told, Congress has come a long way from the days when Ralph Waldo Emerson called it "a standing insurrection." In its operations it is slow, conservative, and compromising in domestic matters. It is replete with lawyers, farmers, and businesspeople. Of some of its members it must be said that their prejudices seem more rigid than their ethics. In foreign affairs after World War II, Congress drifted into the habit of backing a vast expansion of foreign involvement and military expenditure with little supervision or criticism, reserving its distrust mainly for the foreign economic aid programs that are now allocated about $2 billion (less than one-quarter of 1 percent of the GNP), or about one-tenth the share that foreign aid had in 1949. Nevertheless, domestic expenditures for health, education, welfare, housing, and urban development had become about three times as large as defense spending by mid-1978. And these expenditures, rather than defense spending, had become the target of protests by middle-class taxpayers. Real increases in defense spending of about 3 percent per year seem to be acceptable once again to Congress, public opinion, and the press; and although some congressional committees have made some gestures toward increased supervision of the armed services and particularly of the Central Intelligence Agency (CIA) and the National Security Agency (NSA), their impact on the practices of these institutions is not yet clear.

Despite its continuing problems, Congress has enacted a vast program of legislation since 1933—one that has in many ways transformed the country—and it is likely to go on doing so in the decades ahead. Congress remains one of the broadest and most essential channels of communication between the American people and their government; it is an essential instrument for translating communication into agreement and agreement into action.

Legislative Representation and State Politics. On the state level, as on the national level, bicameral legislatures are the rule. (Only Nebraska still has a single-chamber legislature.) In the states, too, the twentieth-century trend has been toward direct election of both chambers.

Unlike politics on the national level, state politics have been characterized more often by unequal districts or districts of bizarre shape, deliberately drawn to favor one party at the expense of the other. The first such district was drawn in the early years of the republic with the advice of Elbridge Gerry of Massachusetts; because it was elongated like a salamander, Gerry's opponents called it a new monster, the *gerrymander,* thus adding both a noun and a verb to the language of politics. Together with restrictive residence requirements and other voter registration laws and practices, these conditions have favored the domination of many states by political machines well entrenched at the state, county, and municipal levels. In recent years, industrialization, mass migration, and the growing participation of large numbers of people in politics have put mounting pressure on these ancient practices. Struggles over voter registration, equal representation, legislative reapportionment, and the breaking or limiting of the power of state political machines now loom large in American politics and may continue to do so for some time.

The struggle for political control on the state level has been a persistent factor in American government, for state politics is critical to the working of the federal system. There are four basic ways by which it affects the federal system. First, it indirectly controls the nomination and election of all United States senators and, thus, the composition of one branch of the federal legislature. Second, the major political parties in the nation are actually little more than federations of state party organizations. The state organizations of each party control more personnel and resources than each party's national committee. Each national party, therefore, depends heavily on influence and patronage within each state. Control of national parties is often won or lost at the state level. Without control of jobs and favors at the state level a party cannot hold together much of its organization. With such control a party can survive for many years out of national office.

Third, the party organization in each state often plays a decisive part in the nomination and election of candidates for the United States House of Representatives. And finally, state politics, state parties, and sometimes state *primaries*—"first-round" elections in which the candidates to be nominated by a party for a public office are chosen by members of that party—often determine the nomination of major party candidates for president of the United States. In this respect, the party machine in each state sometimes has been more important than the party voters. In 1968 both Republicans and Democrats nominated presidential candidates who seemed to be more popular with the regular party organizations than with the mass of voters, but in 1976 the opposite happened after primaries had become more open in both major parties. Even near the end of the 1970s, however, state politics continued to exercise a direct influence on the composition of Congress and an indirect, but powerful, influence on the selection of the chief executive of the United States. This influence, however, has its limits. When conservative Republicans in 1964 captured the party machine and the presidential nomination for Senator Barry Goldwater, and in 1972 when well-left-of-center Democrats, young activ-

FIGURE 10.7 *Woodrow Wilson*

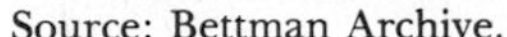

Source: Bettman Archive.

ists, and some adherents of new lifestyles captured the Democratic national convention and the presidential nomination for Senator George McGovern, these candidates were in each case badly defeated at the polls. On the average, voters are more moderate in their views than party activists, despite some increase in political polarization (p. 275, above) and the activists and machine controllers forget it at their peril. Remembering this fact of life enabled Jimmy Carter and Gerald Ford to fight their closely matched campaign in 1976.

The Presidency and Executive Power. The most demanding job in federal government is the presidency of the United States. It is always wearing, often thankless, and sometimes deadly. Abraham Lincoln once remarked that his position reminded him of a comment by a man being ridden out of town on a rail: "If it were not for the honor of the thing, I would rather walk." For more than a century there has been a bitter reality behind Lincoln's quip. The presidency has killed many of its incumbents, four by assassination—Lincoln, Garfield, McKinley, Kennedy—and others, such as Wilson and Franklin D. Roosevelt, by strain and overwork (see Figure 10.7). When it has not killed them, the presidency has certainly worn them down (see Figure 10.8).

Yet the office has never wanted for occupants; there has never been a need to put a "For rent" sign on the White House lawn. The presidency has always been the most powerful office within the United States, and with the coming of nuclear weapons it has become one of the most powerful on a planet that no single country, office, or officeholder can control. But today the president of the United States could be both the nation's chief executive and its executioner: the president shares with the rulers of the Soviet Union the power to destroy civilization and to kill most of humankind. At the same time, with the coming of

FIGURE 10.8 *Jimmy Carter*

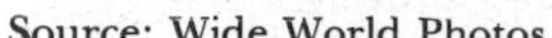
Source: Wide World Photos

the welfare state and of international economic aid, the United States presidency has become crucially involved with a growing range of human needs. Its potentialities for good, too, are vast and are still growing. But while the powers of the office have grown vastly, the mental and moral capacities of its incumbents have not. Inevitably, they have remained ordinary human beings, each of whom, as one politican put it, "has to put on his trousers one leg at a time."

In the past some American presidents have chosen not to use their full powers. They have been passive in office. When the writer Dorothy Parker was told that President Calvin Coolidge had died, she asked: "How could they tell?" But just as the passive presidents of the 1850s—Fillmore, Pierce, and Buchanan—were followed by the Civil War, the passive presidents of the 1920s—Harding, Coolidge, and Hoover—were followed by the Great Depression. Again, during the 1950s many voters wanted President Eisenhower to preside over a relaxed nation and a passive government, and some of the things left undone in those years may have borne bitter fruit in the unemployed young, the neglected minorities, and the urban riots and crises of the 1960s. The presidency is the primary place from which unified leadership can be offered to the American people. The costs to the country are high when presidents neglect their opportunities—but also when they underestimate the limits to their power.

The President's Election. The American president and vice president are elected for a four-year term, and the president is limited to two terms in office. Both are elected by all the people, and in their election the people's votes have more nearly equal weight than in the election of any other branch of government.

Even here, however, the weighting of votes is not completely equal. As a matter of form, the president is elected indirectly by an *Electoral College*. Each state has a number of electors equal to the sum of its senators and representatives; and its state legislature may provide for the appointment or election of these electors in any manner it sees fit. This arrangement favors somewhat the smaller states, since even the smallest ones must have at least two senators and one representative in Congress and thus cannot have fewer than three votes in the Electoral College. Nonetheless, in 1972 the massive electoral votes of the seven most populous states—California, New York, Pennsylvania, Illinois, Ohio, Texas, and Michigan—accounted for 211 of a total of 538 electors. These states have been decisive in past elections, and they are likely to continue to be decisive in the future.

Despite the intentions of the framers of the Constitution, the election of the president has, in effect, become the result of a popular vote, and most voters so perceive it. Electors are usually *pledged* to vote for a particular candidate; most voters neither know nor care who the electors are, but vote for a slate of electors because these electors promise to cast their ballots for the candidate whom the voters favor. In some states, however, it is legally possible for a slate of electors to present itself *unpledged* to the voters, perhaps with the promise to strike the best bargain in the Electoral College in regard to some issue of particular importance to the voters of that state. Electors pledged to the candidate of a minority party might play a similar role if no major party candidate were able to command a majority of electoral votes. It is also legally possible for an elector to break his or her pledge to his voters and cast a ballot for another candidate. The Constitution provides no remedy against such a breach of party discipline or of faith to the voters.

As the only officer of the United States government elected from a nationwide constituency, the president is expected, therefore, to act as president of all the people. And in practice the presidency often has been the branch of the government that is most responsive to urban and industrial voters and to the needs of ethnic, religious, or racial minorities. The mechanism ensuring this responsiveness rests in the present composition of the Electoral College and the crucial role of the seven largest states within it. These seven are highly urban and industrial; each includes a high concentration of minorities; and the votes of each state must be cast as a unit. A presidential candidate therefore must win or lose each state as a whole; and for winning, that candidate depends heavily on the urban, industrial, and minority group voters within it. In 1972, Senator McGovern counted on this base of support, but his personality, associates, platform, and changing style and tactics did not represent the feelings of many traditional urban Democrats, blue-collar workers, and ethnic groups. Accordingly, he lost many big cities or carried them by small margins, while President Nixon was widely perceived as a safe and sound peacemaker, retained the substantial support of the countryside, the suburbs, and the South, and added the votes of some of the disaffected Democrats.

This winner-take-all provision for the electoral votes of each state represents in one sense an injustice against the voters of the losing party. Their votes are not counted, and they might well prefer some scheme of proportional representation among the electors of their state. But in another sense the winner-take-all arrangement is a countervailing injustice. Often it balances the overweighting of the small states and of the rural areas and old stock elements in the population; as we have seen, this overweighting has long characterized the way in which the House of Representatives and, to a lesser extent, the Senate are elected.

In the late 1960s, various proposals for reforming the procedure for presidential elections were discussed. There seemed to be widespread agreement that the Electoral College should be replaced by the direct vote of the people, but there was disagreement whether to retain majority rule within each state or whether to replace it by some scheme of proportional representation. If the latter device were adopted, voters from urban and industrial areas and from minority groups might find their influence drastically reduced. Lacking any compensating change in other aspects of political representation, such voters might then feel permanently underrepresented in the American political system and become alienated from it. Under the present arrangement, voters disappointed with their representation in Congress often still look to the presidency for redress. Conversely, of course, voters dissatisfied with the policies of a president may find some help for their concerns in Congress. A constitutional amendment to abolish the Electoral College was proposed by Senator Birch Bayh, but interest in the matter declined during the 1970s when the prospects of a strong third party faded and Governor George Wallace in 1978 announced his withdrawal from political life.

Since the president is an essential part of the system, he or she must be promptly replaced in case of death or disability. Detailed rules for the succession to the presidency have been worked out to guarantee a rapid and peaceful transfer of power. If the president dies in office, he or she is succeeded by the vice president. After the assassination of President Kennedy, the transfer of his office to Vice President Lyndon B. Johnson was accomplished within an hour. If both the president and the vice president should die, the speaker of the House would become president; after that individual the office would go to the president pro tempore of the Senate, and then to the secretary of State, the secretary of the Treasury, and the rest of the Cabinet. There are also specific provisions for succession in case of the president's illness or incapacity. These seem unique, and they contrast strikingly with the practice of dictatorships. They also appear as reasonably safe as can be expected. Even in the age of nuclear weapons, when one large hydrogen bomb could wipe out Washington, D.C., it seems unlikely that all these persons could be killed at once. Some continuity in the office of chief executive thus seems to be as well assured as anything else in the American political system under conditions of modern weaponry.

The President's Many Roles. Once elected, the president must fulfill many different roles that may be only partly compatible with one another. In military matters he or she is *commander in chief* of a peacetime defense force of 2.5 million people in uniform (not counting another 1.1 million civilian Defense Department employees)[20] and of the entire nation in times of war. In recent years the increasing power of modern weapons systems has made this individual responsible for more destructive power than any human being should have. The same modern technology has made the president potentially more helpless. On the eve of an all-out war the president would have to depend on radar echoes and other types of electronic information, hard to interpret and subject to error. The president would have to make decisions under extreme constraints of time and would then have to live on the bull's eye of a target, with Washington and the White House exposed to the thermonuclear weapons of an enemy. There might be only a few minutes to decide, and the president might have to use much of this short time just to move to some presumably safer shelter; and any orders given to American aircraft and missiles might soon prove impossible to recall. The military technology that has so vastly increased the president's power also has tended to make him or her its prisoner.

In regard to conventional weapons and troop commitments, the president has a wider range of discretion. According to the Constitution, only Congress can declare war. But tradition has long permitted American presidents to commit troops and ships—and more recently aircraft—to smaller "police actions" on their own authority. Such precedents reach from Jefferson's sending a few ships against Algerian pirates to numerous skirmishes on the Indian frontier of the United States and to various interventions by the American Marines in the Caribbean and Mexico during the first two decades of the twentieth century. In recent years these police actions have tended to become much bigger in such places as Korea, Lebanon, the Dominican Republic, and Vietnam. They have involved not only professional soldiers and volunteers, as in earlier police actions, but also large numbers of drafted citizen soldiers, including many reluctant or unwilling ones; and the size and duration of some of these undertakings have proved increasingly difficult to control. These powers of the president were reduced, however, in 1976 and afterward by new legal restrictions voted by Congress and originally designed to prevent United States military intervention in Angola without express congressional approval. The War Powers Act of 1976, in particular, was an attempt by Congress to gain the power to declare peace, though how it will work in practice is not yet clear.

Although the president's role as commander in chief was intended primarily to provide powers against foreign threats, the law has long been vague about what the president could order the armed forces to do if he or she personally chose to perceive the danger of a domestic insurrection. The power of the president to have the governor of a state removed by federal force was made subject to judicial review in the famous judgment *ex parte Milligan,* when the Supreme Court reversed such a decision made by President Abraham Lincoln at the time of the Civil War. But what would have happened if the president had ordered the soldiers to arrest not a governor, but the Supreme Court, perhaps stating that he perceived the justices as constituting a danger to national security? Or if a president someday should order the armed forces to disperse or arrest the members of Congress?

Luckily, the problem has not arisen in the more than two-hundred-year history of the United States. But when President Nixon was about to resign in August 1974, Secretary of Defense James M. Schlesinger issued an order to all armed forces of the United States not to carry out any order from their commander in chief without Schlesinger's countersignature. The formal legal basis for this order seems unclear, but its basis in common

[20]Data from *Statistical Abstract of the United States, 1972,* p. 259.

prudence seems self-evident. By the late 1970s, however, no formal legal procedure for dealing with such problems had been established.

At home the president is the country's bureaucrat in chief. As head of the executive branch of the government, he is in charge of more than 2 million civilian employees. Many of these are now protected by Civil Service regulations designed to prevent their hiring and firing on political grounds. About 2,000 top-level government jobs are defined in various ways as *policy-making appointments* and are in the president's gift, and so are another 1,800 high-level jobs somewhat farther down the line.[21] President Carter has proposed to enlarge this number, but his Civil Service reform thus far has not been passed by Congress. The president also appoints the *White House staff,* which has grown substantially in recent years, both in numbers and in the scope and importance of affairs entrusted to it. This growth continued under President Carter despite his earlier campaign declarations to the contrary. The president also appoints members of *presidential commissions* to report on matters of fact or policy, and a variety of informal advisers and associates can be selected. For the appointment of ambassadors, federal judges, and the members of the official Cabinet, which comprises the heads of the major departments of the government, the *advice and consent* of the Senate is required. Such consent is only rarely refused to Cabinet nominees. Generally, the president anticipates the probable response of the Senate in nominating such persons for appointment or else, if possible, entrusts the task to a member of the White House staff who is not subject to Senate confirmation.

The president is also the party leader, and dispenser in chief of federal patronage and favors. Through these powers the president can exercise not only moral, but also material, influence on the votes of representatives and senators. The more responsive they are to the wishes of the president the more receptive the executive may prove to the needs of their districts, states, party organizations, and personal acquaintances. Some presidents have been more vigorous than others in reminding members of Congress of their presidential powers. Franklin D. Roosevelt was a master of such methods; and so, more bluntly, was Lyndon B. Johnson.

A major source of presidential power is the role as the symbol of national unity and as media manipulator in chief. Anything the president does makes news if he or she so chooses and sometimes even if he or she does not. The president often can define a situation and thus can predetermine much of the response of American opinion. After taking over the presidency in 1963 Lyndon Johnson chose to define the fighting in South Vietnam as a case of simple foreign aggression by the North Vietnamese, and in August 1964 he defined an ambiguous incident in the Gulf of Tonkin as an attack on the United States Navy. These definitions went far to prepare Congress and the voters to accept the escalation of the American commitment in South Vietnam from 16,000 "advisers" in late 1963 to over 540,000 troops in late 1968. By contrast, the Johnson decision *not* to define the capture of the American electronic intelligence ship *Pueblo* by the North Koreans in 1968 as an act of war kept public opinion relatively quiet and permitted the government to obtain the return of the ship and its crew through negotiation. From 1972 on, President Nixon calmed public feelings by his visits to China and the Soviet Union and his conduct of peace negotiations with North Vietnam, and later he stressed the relaxation of tensions when he received the Soviet leader, Leonid Brezhnev, in Washington and when he completed the official withdrawal of United States troops from South Vietnam. On the whole, this presidential policy of détente was continued—though not always under this name—by Presidents Ford and Carter.

Beginning in 1970, President Nixon and Vice President Agnew stressed heavily what they considered to be the obligation of the mass media to

[21]From data in Hugh Heclo, *A Government of Strangers: Executive Politics in Washington* (Washington, D.C.: Brookings Institution, 1977).

support the policies of the administration, particularly in all matters of foreign and military policy. By early 1973, radio and television stations had been reminded of their dependence on federal licenses, publishers of newspapers and periodicals had been made aware of the difference that postal rates and regulations could make to their revenues, and prosecutors and judges had been encouraged to cooperate in sending journalists and scholars to jail for refusing to name the sources of their information, as the latter had often been permitted informally to do in the past. In the short run, at least, this tactic of heavier administrative pressure produced more opposition, rather than more conformity. In mid-1973 the major mass media did not fail to report in detail the revelations of administration scandals and of the Watergate affair; and members of Congress seemed well aware that the destruction of the independence of the press and the electronic media would also wipe out much of the power of Congress itself. Congressional investigations would lose much of their effect if the press, radio, and television were no longer free to report their results. The mass media are an essential link to the American people for Congress, as well as for the president, and they are an essential link for the people to their elected representatives. The mass media must balance their freedom and their responsibility; but if in doubt, it is perhaps best for the country if they take their chances on the side of truth. The issue is not simple, however, and it is likely to play a role in American politics throughout the 1980s.

The president's power to define issues and direct public attention is scarcely less in domestic affairs. Presidential support and leadership, or their lack, have decided the success or failure of many a civil rights or social welfare program.

Despite all these assets, the president's powers are severely limited. He or she cannot allocate any major amounts of money without congressional support. Even some of the major official appointments depend on senatorial good will. Beyond Congress, the president depends on the courts, which may declare his or her acts unconstitutional—even though they usually are reluctant to do so. Yet the Supreme Court did exactly this when it threw out some of the early acts of Franklin D. Roosevelt's New Deal. Major executive acts, such as President Harry S Truman's seizure of the strike-bound steel industry in 1952, likewise may be subject to court scrutiny. Beyond the courts, the president depends on the voluntary cooperation of the government officials and the people. Only if the great majority of them comply can presidential decisions be enforced on the rest.

In regard to these many elements, the president often must act as a political broker, striving to put together a coalition that is like-minded enough to agree and strong enough to act. As a rule, a chief executive can be no stronger than the coalition behind him or her. But even if backed by all elements of the American political system, the president is not all-powerful in world politics. The actions of many foreign nations cannot be controlled. Nor is power over nature and technology unlimited. Inescapably, the president is human and fallible—and so are the American people. One test of greatness for both consists in the ability to recognize these limitations.

Finally, the president also is supposed to be something of a human model for the nation. Ideally, he or she should unite the moral virtues of goodness, honesty, and truthfulness with the worldly skills of shrewdness, energy, and competence. Even a well-publicized divorce is a liability for a presidential candidate. If all these virtues cannot be found in equal excellence in a single candidate, American voters have more than once elected presidents whose moral virtues had been open to criticism. Grover Cleveland was the admitted father of an illegitimate child; some of Warren G. Harding's close associates were deeply involved in corruption; yet both were elected. But American voters have always insisted on an image of competence in chief executives. Like passengers of a ship at sea, they want their captain to be virtuous, but they insist on competence in navigation. But if the American people, for one reason or another, should want to get rid of an unsatisfactory president, how under the Constitution could they go about it?

Emergency Exit in Slow Motion: The Procedure of Impeachment. By mid-1973, President Richard M. Nixon had become the target of twofold pressure. The Watergate scandal had thrown grave doubts on the integrity of some of the highest and closest associates of the president; and it had led many voters to doubt the veracity of the president himself. (Only 11 percent in a Gallup poll in August 1973 said they believed President Nixon's claim that he had not known for a long time either of his associates' share in the Watergate burglary and other illegal actions or of their later attempts to cover up the whole matter.) Simultaneously, the president's competence in halting inflation and managing the American economy came under attack as prices continued to rise.

At the same time, however, Nixon reminded the American people that he was the only president they had. Indeed, the Constitution provides no means for removing a president from office except through the cumbersome and divisive procedure of *impeachment*. A president of the United States can be impeached—that is, formally accused and put on trial—only for "treason, bribery, or other high crimes and misdemeanors" (U.S. Constitution, Article III, Section 4); and such impeachment must be voted by the House of Representatives. If the House so votes, the president then must be tried by the Senate with the chief justice of the United States presiding; and conviction is possible only "with the concurrence [the vote] of two-thirds of the Members [the senators] present" (Article I, Section 3). If convicted, the president would be removed from office, which then would devolve upon the vice president. If both president and vice president should be removed or otherwise incapacitated, the speaker of the House of Representatives would succeed to the presidency, followed by the president pro tempore of the Senate and the members of the Cabinet in order of seniority of their departments, beginning with the State Department. Further details are regulated by the Twenty-fifth Amendment to the U.S. Constitution, passed in 1967.

In the history of the United States only one president, Andrew Johnson, has been impeached, and his conviction in the Senate failed, being one vote short of the required two-thirds majority. In 1974, however, the removal of a president again came close to fulfillment when a congressional committee voted to impeach President Nixon. He then resigned and later was pardoned by his successor (see page 281, above).

Federal Powers and the Judiciary. Federal powers, characteristic of the American system, are very great over credit, commerce, and contracts. These powers were crucial for the integration of the United States into one country. The first large step in the development of federal power was taken by the states under the Articles of Confederation with the *full faith and credit clause.* Under this clause each state had to give full faith and credit to the public acts, records, and judicial proceedings of every other state. The Constitution now embodies this principle, but it shifts the main integrative task to federal institutions.

A major channel of federal influence is the institution of *judicial review:* the right and duty of the courts to decide whether any law or act is valid under the Constitution. It does not appear in the Constitution, but grew up as an interpretation of it. In no other country in the world has the Supreme Court as much power and as much respect as in the United States. The Court has functioned in a very important way, beginning in 1800 with Chief Justice John Marshall's opinion in the famous case of *Marbury* v. *Madison.* Ever since, the courts have had the right to review the executive acts of the federal and state governments and the laws of the national and state legislatures.

The power of the judiciary to determine the

constitutionality of legislation and executive acts has five major consequences. First, the courts settle many serious political conflicts peaceably. Second, they are one of the chief instruments of balance in the American political system, by limiting the power of the other branches of government and by protecting individuals and minorities. Third, they often slow down change until it becomes acceptable to a larger proportion of the people. Fourth, they sometimes accelerate change, or they bring about immediate changes that the other branches of government have failed to produce. Fifth, the courts offer in all these respects an additional channel of communication between the people and their government and a long-term feedback circuit by which the American political system can steer itself.

The courts contribute an important check and balance by their practice of judging acts of the legislative and executive branches of government in the light of the judges' understanding of the Constitution. As Charles Evans Hughes said before he became chief justice, "The Constitution is what the judges say it is." Though the Constitution looks like a simple document, it is often not at all clear how it should be applied to the many complex problems that have arisen since its enactment. The judges' latitude in interpreting it is great indeed, and their decisions, in particular those of the Supreme Court, have become an important part of *"judge-made" law.* Because most Americans habitually respect and obey their courts and because the lower courts accept the overriding decisions of the higher courts, the entire judiciary system has important powers over what happens in government and throughout the country.

The courts have thrown out important acts of Congress, such as the National Recovery Act in the 1930s. They also have declared illegal some major acts of the president, including some taken in the name of national security. Thus the Supreme Court in the decision *ex parte Milligan* held illegal certain emergency powers assumed by the Lincoln administration during the Civil War. A later Supreme Court took a very critical view of the compulsory internment of Americans of Japanese descent during World War II. In both cases the Court acted, however, only after the emergency had passed; and the compensation finally paid to the illegally and unjustly interned Japanese-Americans for their lost properties amounted to about ten cents on the dollar.[22]

The courts cannot act quickly. In times of emergency they are reluctant to stop the other two branches of the government from acting; and even later they cannot always ensure full redress to victims of injustice. Nevertheless, they can provide at least partial redress. They can free individuals from prison; they can restore rights that were denied; they can clear people's names; and they can make clear what individuals and agencies of government cannot do within the law. In serving these functions, the courts protect individuals as well as the soundness of the American political process. "The brain is an organ of inhibition," said an Austrian labor leader many years ago; the Supreme Court has long been a vital part of the brain and conscience of the American republic and its people.

As an agency of inhibition, the Supreme Court has often acted as a brake on change. On the average, Supreme Court justices in the twentieth century have held that position for twelve years; ordinarily they cannot be removed against their will. No president has been able during a single four-year term to appoint a majority of Supreme Court justices. So the justices often represent the memories and standards of a somewhat earlier day and, at least intermittently, the view of an older generation.

For this they have often been chided. Justice Oliver Wendell Holmes criticized his colleagues for clinging too closely to nineteenth-century doctrines of government nonintervention in the labor market when they held that sweatshops and night work for women should not be interfered

[22]See Morton Grodzins, *Americans Betrayed* (Chicago: University of Chicago Press, 1949).

with by state governments. The Constitution, said Holmes, did not enact the prejudices of Herbert Spencer, the nineteenth-century British laissez-faire writer. (Later, Justice Holmes's views on this point were accepted by the Court's majority.) In the 1930s, President Franklin Roosevelt complained of the "nine old men" of the Supreme Court who in his view were going too far in defending property rights and thwarting the will of the voters.

At their best, however, the courts also represent some of the more enduring values and long-term points of view. During the decades since 1945 the Supreme Court has particularly stressed the rights of individuals. It has often opposed or limited the new controls over individuals introduced by the government in the name of national security. In the face of congressional legislation and administrative practices the Court has limited the requirements for security clearances, and it has tended to favor the traditional rights of Americans to keep their jobs, to travel abroad freely, to face their accusers, and to be held innocent until proved guilty by due process of law.

Sometimes the courts have been important instruments of change. They have struck down laws that no longer had the backing of the majority of voters, but were so intensely defended by influential minorities that no legislative majority could be found for their repeal. Since these laws no longer corresponded to the convictions of the majority, they threatened penalties for what Burke might have called "artificial crimes"; yet there seemed to be no practical legislative remedy. This was the case with the legal ban on birth control information that in the early 1960s was still on the books of Connecticut and Massachusetts and made almost all local doctors and druggists into lawbreakers. When the courts finally struck down these laws as unconstitititutional, no politician made any serious effort to resurrect them, and doctors and druggists could breathe more freely.

Finally, the courts function as a major communication channel both to the memories and traditions of the past and to the felt needs of the present and future. The Supreme Court, said Finley Peter Dunne's Mr. Dooley, follows the election returns. In one sense this is true, but the Court often follows these returns with a time delay of one or two decades, during which it becomes clear whether these earlier returns reflected a passing mood or a genuine trend of development.

In this manner many Supreme Court justices have followed the advice of Roscoe Pound to view law as an instrument of social control and to use it as such. Some justices have been eminent lawyers, whereas others have been highly skilled in practical affairs, often having served as governors of states, Cabinet members, United States presidents (Taft), or presidential candidates (Hughes and Warren). Whatever their background, many of them have had a refreshing sense of the practical. In the early 1920s a Court majority confirmed a lower court decision that barred an immigrant grandmother, Rosika Schwimmer, from citizenship on the grounds that as an avowed pacifist she would not "bear arms" in defense of the Constitution. Justice Holmes dissented. For three centuries, he wrote, the Quakers had been pacifists, refusing to bear arms, yet they had done well by their country. Besides, he added dryly, the United States would be in a perilous position indeed if it needed the armed service of a grandmother to defend it. In later years this dissent of Justice Holmes, too, became the Court's majority doctrine. Pacifism is not a bar to United States citizenship any longer; and the 1969 verdict of an appeals court, throwing out a lower court's conviction of Dr. Benjamin Spock (for allegedly having "conspired" to thwart the draft for the Vietnam War), was in the Holmes tradition.

Another problem of reconciling legal, moral, and practical considerations occurred at the time of the sit-down strikes in the late 1930s when striking auto workers occupied the factories of several major auto manufacturers. Some business and conservative interests called on the governor of Michigan, Frank Murphy, to use military force to defend property rights and evict the strikers, regardless of the bloodshed that could be expected. Governor Murphy refused to do this. His refusal compelled both sides to negotiate. In time the strikes were settled; the union was recognized; the strikers returned to work; and Governor Murphy was appointed to the Supreme Court. Some lawyers said that the Court henceforth would offer "justice tempered with Murphy," but the balance between property rights and human rights, between strict law and the politically practical, has remained among the Court's significant concerns—as such cases as *Baker* v. *Carr,* favoring legislative reapportionment, have demonstrated.

In one respect the role of the judiciary is unique. Both legislation and administration are processes designed primarily to deal with human beings in large numbers. Inevitably, they are most often concerned with mass legislation and mass administration. The courts alone are primarily designed to deal with individuals and with specific cases. It is this ability that we have in mind when we say that every person ought to have a right to "a day in court"—the day when the legal and political system is focused on that person's problems as an individual. This function of the courts has often been obscured in practice by the enormous costs and delays of court procedures. Carrying a case through the trial court, the higher courts, and the Supreme Court by now usually costs upward of $50,000. "A poor man has a chanst in coort, . . ." said Mr. Dooley more than half a century ago. "He has the same chanst there that he has outside. He has a splendid poor man's chanst."

In recent years the Supreme Court has handed down several decisions that are beginning to make a difference to a poor person's chances. Indigent defendants in federal felony trials have won the right to a free lawyer, and in *Gideon* v. *Wainwright* the Court extended this right to the state courts, where most of the actual felony trials are held. A suspect in police custody has long had the right to ask for a lawyer if the suspect can pay for one or can get one free. In *Escobedo* v. *Illinois* the Court ruled that the police must honor such a request for consultation; and in *Miranda* v. *Arizona* it said that before being questioned in police custody individuals must be told of their right to keep silent and to have a lawyer (free, if they are poor) and they must be warned that anything they say may be used against them—a warning customary in federal practice and long-standing in Britain. Together these decisions give the same protection of legal rights to the innocent suspect and the ignorant lawbreaker as the professional criminal and the large-scale operator of crime have had for many years. The effects on actual police practice have thus far been moderate. Nonetheless, these decisions have been charged with hampering the work of the police and endangering the victims of future crimes. Recent decisions by a somewhat more conservative Supreme Court have once again tended to increase slightly the powers of the police. Despite such back-and-forth shifts of opinion, a basic problem has remained: what risks would people rather run—those from unchecked crime or those from an uncontrolled police? In making its rulings, the Court has had to decide between these conflicting viewpoints and values—the rights of individual citizens as opposed to the convenience of administration and the fears of the community—and during the last thirty years it has decided more often in favor of the individual.

In the long run such Court decisions require the backing of the people if they are to be effective. But these decisions show that the Court may sometimes try to lead opinion rather than merely follow it. This is the important question of *judicial activism:* how far should the courts go in leading opinion and deciding on public policy? In the days of Chief Justice Marshall between 1800 and 1820, and again during the last thirty years, the courts have been more active in deciding matters with large political implications than they were during most of the decades in between. How the courts act continues to make a difference to politics. Leading or following, the judiciary helps to decide where the American people and their government will go next; and the size and importance of its contribution to this self-steering process make the American political system different from all others in the world.

HOW DOES THE AMERICAN POLITICAL SYSTEM STEER ITSELF?

In its domestic politics the American system has more effective channels for the intake of information than does the political system of any other large industrial country. American political culture, too, places high value on listening to people and on paying attention to the views at the grassroots. At the same time, intake channels for information from abroad are poorer: far less well coordinated, more handicapped by inattention and secrecy, and often overridden by the streams of messages from major domestic interest groups that command a higher priority in the attention of political decision makers.

Domestic Intake Channels. There are more than a half-dozen groups of major intake channels bringing to the various levels and agencies of government a wide variety of information about domestic conditions, popular feelings, specific needs and demands of large interest groups, and the problems of numerous small groups and individuals. Every senator and member of Congress, every state legislator, every member of a municipal council is a potential listening device: people approach or write to him or her to present their problems and requests for legislative or administrative help or, in the case of less than 3 percent of the population, simply to express their views on some political issue; moreover, the members of the staffs of legislators and committees can search out information and bring it to bear on the legislative work.

Administrative officers and agencies—from the president and the governors of the fifty states to the various specialized administrative agencies, federal, state, and municipal—receive a similar stream of information. Some of this information may be aggregated in regional conferences, such as those of the governors or legislators from the resource-rich western states or of the governors of depression-sensitive New England; or they may aggregate information from the nation's urban areas, such as the U.S. Conference of Mayors.

A third system of intake channels is the court system, through which complaints about alleged violations of legal and constitutional rights of individuals and groups can be raised and often brought to a decision. And a fourth ensemble of information-carrying agencies and individuals consists of the lobbying organizations and lobbyists representing large corporate enterprise, industry, agriculture, and various labor unions and public interest groups.

In all four of these systems of channels—legislative, administrative, judicial, and lobbying—messages can be and often are initiated by parties at interest, that is, by individuals and groups outside the government. They can also be initiated, however, by some part of the government that is in search of information. Congressional committees can use their staff members to look into a variety of matters, and they can initiate formal investigations, using—and sometimes abusing—their powers to compel witnesses to testify before them. Administrative agencies, such as the Federal Trade Commission and the Civil Aeronautics Board, can initiate their inquiries. Lobbyists are legally required to register and reveal their employers or clients, but so far little information has been obtained and made public about their activities. Courts and grand juries can investigate and compel testimony; and in the early

1970s this long-existing power of judges and grand juries was being used more vigorously than had been the long-established practice, as prosecutors and other government authorities put pressure on journalists and scholars to reveal sources of information to whom they had promised anonymity in return for cooperation.

Three other systems of intake channels bring information into the political system and up to the higher levels of government. These are the press, television, and other mass media of communication; the universities, foundations, and research organizations, such as the Ford Foundation, the Carnegie Corporation, the Brookings Institution, the Rand Corporation, and the Battelle Institute; and, finally, the churches and religious organizations. All these can raise questions, gather information, stimulate attention, and at times suggest possible answers or solutions.

This wide variety of potential information-intake sources is one of the essential strengths of democracy and government in the United States. Any attempts to cut down the range and freedom of these flows of information; to intimidate the universities, the foundations, the television networks, and the press; to make the government listen less and talk more loudly—all such efforts, if successful, cut down both the intrinsic values and the long-run operational effectiveness of the American political system.

Information Intake from Abroad. If the facilities for the intake of domestic information are relatively good, the facilities for getting information about the rest of the world are less so. Today only a few American newspapers and periodicals maintain news-gathering staffs abroad. Universities and research organizations do more than they did a quarter of a century ago, but the scholarly books, articles, and research reports they produce are not read widely, nor usually at high levels of government. Diplomatic reporting has been long constrained by nonrecognition policies: in 1979 there still were no United States embassies in, and hence no continuous diplomatic reporting from, such countries as Cuba, North Korea, and Vietnam, all of which were important to the security and other interests of the United States. A United States mission was established in China only in 1973 (and this was raised to embassy status in March 1979), after a lapse of twenty-four years, but it would take time to overcome the results of such a long period of mutual ignorance. From countries where United States diplomats were stationed, reporting often had been constrained by pressures within the government to report only or mainly facts confirming the wisdom of the official policies of the day and to play down or omit all facts that might have suggested their revision.

The reports from abroad by the large intelligence organizations, such as the CIA, suffered in part from similar pressures toward conformity with current policy and perhaps still more from the secrecy that usually protected such reports from comparison with information known to the press or the scholarly community, which might have led to re-evaluation or correction. Secret information is often better than none, but is usually inferior to information that can be publicly discussed and tested. During the last two decades, crises in Cuba, Angola, Zaire, and Iran revealed that the CIA knew little about the real state of affairs in these nations and that it had passed on even less than that to Congress and the president.

Many American or "multinational" business organizations, of course, have a distinct interest in getting realistic information from abroad; but this information often is limited to their special fields of activities or distorted by some specific conflict of interest with a foreign government, as in the conflict between the International Telephone and Telegraph Company and the Allende government in Chile. Moreover, much of the limited information obtained by a business corporation is held confidential in order to deny its use to potential competitors.

In general, the information coming from the rest of the world into the American political system is inferior to the domestic information arriving there, in quantity and in quality, and the attention that it receives is less widespread and knowledgeable. Consequently, domestic maladjustments and errors have a better chance to be detected earlier and mitigated or corrected than errors in foreign policy and military matters. This disproportion has had its heavy costs in blood and treasure from the intelligence failure at Pearl Harbor in 1941 until the present day, and it involves even more serious risks of error in a nuclear crisis or confrontation in the future.

The Distribution of Memories. The imbalance in information intake is reinforced by an imbalance in the distribution of memories. Many Americans, inside and outside government, have rich and relevant memories about domestic conditions. With the aid of these memories they can evaluate relatively quickly and effectively much of the new information about domestic political, social, and economic problems; but their memories about the rest of the world usually are far more unrealistic, inaccurate, and incomplete.

In addition, many of the memories of individual Americans, as well as of public or private agencies and organizations, are specialized and limited. Some persons or groups may know how to manage the economy in good times in order to produce an unemployment rate of 5 to 6 percent, and they may know what effect this measure, more or less by itself, may have on the rate of inflation in order to keep the general rise in prices below, say, 6 or 8 percent per year. But they may not know how to keep the economy working within these limits when an economic depression deepens, or when events abroad push up radically the price of imported oil, and then indirectly the price of domestic fuels. And even in times of relative prosperity, they may remember little, nor care much, about the differential impact of unemployment on young people or black people and on young people who are black, 12 percent or more of whom now may be unemployed. Nor would they necessarily remember or care much about connections between unemployment among young people and the frequency of crimes, violence, political alienation, and divisiveness in the political system.

Rich and diversified as the memory facilities of that political system are, they often suffer seriously from the lack of cross-connections and coherence among the different specialists and special agencies. A few agencies, such as the president and the Cabinet, then are supposed to put and keep all these memories and information streams together—an overwhelming task for anyone to assume. In fact, of course, those charged with this responsibility are just human, and they react to their overloads by coping as best they can with whatever decisions are most immediately pressing, putting off the rest. The result is once again the immobility-emergency cycle described earlier in this book (pp. 55-57).

Decision Points and Institutions. In this matter of memories, the American political system—like that of other countries—is also vulnerable in another way. Memories held today are potential premises for decisions made tomorrow. These memories may seem unimportant now, but the future decisions swayed by them may be fateful. Relatively small rewards or penalties prevailing at one time may influence the acceptance of such memories—the articles and books that are published, the ideas and symbols that are accepted as normal and sound, and even eventually the later books that are written; the persons who are employed in government or promoted therein to higher office; the problems that are investigated and the questions that are asked. But this seemingly harmless manipulation of the accepted doctrines and assumptions today is in effect a process of *cognitive corruption.* It is a manipulation of the future memories of the population and of the political community, which may go far in controlling some major decisions in a subsequent crisis.

Compared to these weaknesses of American political memories in regard to international affairs, the *decision points* in the government of the United States are relatively clearly defined. The presidency, the governors of the fifty states, the United States Congress and the state legislatures, the federal and state courts—all have relatively well defined tasks. In emergencies they can decide relatively fast; and if any one agency or decision point should become incapacitated, others quickly can take over its functions. In recognized emergencies this system is less well protected against the risks of error than against the risks of delay. (In nonemergency situations, however, this situation tends to be reversed.) The risks of error through ignorance, time pressure, overburdening of decision makers, and inappropriate decision premises are further aggravated by secrecy and the pressures of "group think" or group conformity, which tend to slow down or screen out the processes of self-correction through feedback information from reality.

Effectors and Outputs of the System. The effectors of the American political system are varied and powerful, and some of them are formidable. Among them must be counted the armed forces and their weaponry, having vast forces of destruction, but only limited capabilities for control of foreign areas with unwilling populations, and having even more limited capabilities for protecting American cities against thermonuclear missiles in the event of all-out war against a major power. Other effectors of the political system are United States diplomats, information services, and economic aid agencies abroad and the entire array of government agencies and employees at home. Most of these function well in discharging their special tasks, but the unified direction and coordination of their efforts are more likely to be relatively weak or intermittent.

The Problem of Consciousness and Coherence. It is difficult to find in the political system of the United States a single center of comprehensive awareness or *consciousness*—a point at which abridged and summarized information about all significant political, social, and economic processes in the United States and in the world at large is being currently assembled for simultaneous inspection, comparison, and decision. There are "situation rooms" and "big boards" for strategic information at various high-level command posts of the armed forces and in the White House, but all these deal primarily with foreign countries, forces, and events, and with the deployment of American and allied forces in relation to them. Though American intake channels of information from abroad are relatively weak, serious efforts are made to coordinate the information that they do yield.

The situation seems to be reversed in regard to domestic politics. The strong and rich information streams from domestic affairs are not well coordinated, except in the head of a very busy president or through the competing efforts of a few assistants. There does not seem to be a comparable situation room in the White House, or in any other high-level government agency, currently showing the interacting amounts and effects of poverty, malnutrition, unemployment, labor conflicts or settlements, race conflicts, drug addiction, crime, campus unrest, protest activities, environmental improvement or deterioration, and the like. It seems that we have made more progress in the United States in coordinating our poor knowledge of foreign affairs than our rich knowledge in domestic matters.

Awareness of many of these problems and of their possible joint effects seems to be low or intermittent at the top of the political pyramid. Special agencies seem to be knowledgeable about some of these problems and events, but not about others. Some awareness of the overall picture is embodied in certain nongovernmental organizations, such as the major political parties, the National Industrial Conference Board, the universities and the major foundations, and some of the better newspapers, periodicals, and television programs; but it is often less deep and accurate than necessary because of the pressures of time, special interests, and limited staffs and equipment. Despite these handicaps, a network of such organizations and facilities, intercommunicating more or less freely, may supplement the very incomplete consciousness of political and social reality available at the top of the pyramidal structure of formal government, whenever cognition and awareness within this pyramidal structure should fall short or fail. Any successful attempt to reduce the intake and free communication and evaluation of information within this informal nongovernmental network would have its very real cost in reducing the capabilities of cognition and awareness for the entire political system.

The Maintenance of Will. The situation is quite different in regard to the political *will,* its formation, and its maintenance.

Once established, popular images and political, economic, or strategic doctrines are likely to be defended tenaciously by interest groups who benefit from them and by officials who associate them with a rise in their careers. Persons and groups with dissenting views usually are less united and less motivated to bring about a change in policy. This may help us understand why the United States, which tends to innovate more quickly in some sectors of technology and business methods than many other countries, often is conspicuously slower in changing some of its policies.

In domestic affairs, legislation for social security and for medical care for the elderly was adopted much later than in most of Western Europe; and a national health service or health insurance scheme—long established in Western Europe, Canada, and other countries—has yet to be adopted in the United States. In international affairs the United States took ten years longer to recognize the Soviet Union than did the anti-Communist governments of France and Britain and more than twenty years longer to recognize the government of Communist China. In 1972, President Nixon impressed Americans and world opinion by his official visit to China, which changed a nonrecognition policy of more than two decades, and by 1979 Chinese-American relations had become relatively friendly, even though characterized by some continuing ups and downs.

There are some advantages in this capacity of the American political system to hold fast for a long time to a policy once it has been adopted. The powers of the United States, both at home and in world affairs, are very large, though not unlimited; fickle, erratic behavior in a giant might be even more dangerous than relatively rigid resistance to any major change of course. But both drifting and rigid persisting are deficiencies in the process of steering. If the United States is to live safely with its own large resources and powers, its capabilities for steering itself will still need major improvements.

Creativity and Innovation. There are many points in the American system at which different items of information can be separated from each other, then selected and recombined into patterns that did not exist before, at least not at that particular time and place. These twin operations of breaking down old patterns of information into smaller components and of recombining them in new ways are at the heart of the process that we call *creativity.* In politics, creativity involves perceiving the needs and demands of individuals and groups; the known material resources and technical possibilities for meeting them; the legal, technical, and administrative requirements for making each of these possible arrangements work in practice; and the political conditions for obtaining acceptance and support for any one of them, as well as the interests and groups likely to be arrayed in opposition in each case. Analyzing this information into its elements and trying out new combinations of these elements may then lead to proposals of new solutions, perhaps in the form of proposals for new legislation, such as the Social Security Act of 1935, or the G.I. Bill of Rights after World War II, or Medicare in the 1960s. Often it also may produce proposals for new administrative agencies, such as the Tennessee Valley Administration in the 1930s, the National Aeronautics and Space Administration in the 1950s, the National Science Foundation and the National Endowment for the

Humanities in the 1960s, or the Family Assistance Plan or "negative income tax"—not yet enacted—of the 1970s.

The places in the political system where such new proposals are worked out are those where different streams of information meet and where the people at work there—be they legislators, legislative staff members, federal, state, or local bureaucrats, or persons working for nongovernmental research organizations, such as the Brookings Institution—have the time, the motivation, and the resources to engage in this work of analysis and recombination of information into tentative "candidate solutions" and then to critically re-examine and reshape these tentative projects or political inventions into more fully developed versions that can be proposed for action to major elements in the political system.

Turning an invention into large-scale practice is the essence of the process of *innovation.* It involves often the changing of existing habits and arrangements among relatively large numbers of people, the overcoming of the resistance that usually goes with change, and the mobilizing and arraying of positive expectations and support, broad enough and strong enough to help the innovation to prevail in the political decision process and eventually in the daily practice of the society. The more far-reaching and fundamental the innovation is, the more habits and institutions it requires to be changed, and the more likely it is to affect noticeably the structure of the political and social system. The more flexible the larger system is, the more likely it will be to succeed in accepting and accommodating even major innovations without losing its own cohesion and the sense of continuity and identity of its populations.

Judged in these terms and compared with other nations, the political system of the United States in the last sixty-plus years has not done badly. During that period it accepted first the eight-hour working day and then the forty-hour week; industrial labor unions, grievance committees and collective bargaining in the factories; votes for women and, more recently, significant pressures for their equal pay and promotion; a federal minimum wage; widespread unemployment compensation and a large array of welfare services; nearly universal old-age pensions through social security; publicly financed medical care for persons aged sixty-five and older; publicly supported education for nearly one-half of all young people of college age; public legal assistance for needy defendants; and the large—though still inadequate—reduction of racial discrimination and oppression. Many of these changes were long and bitterly resisted, evoking dire predictions that each of them would ruin the nation or destroy its cherished way of life—predictions that so far have not come true. Rather, most often a majority of Americans has agreed that *not* to have made these changes would have threatened greater damage to the country.

But what if the United States should confront even graver problems, both foreign and domestic, and if it should face the need for even more surprising political and social inventions and for even greater and more rapid innovations and reforms? What if such needed changes should seem to require more serious transformations of the present American political and economic structure? How would the American republic and its democracy respond to such a challenge?

A Key Test of Performance: Capabilities for Change and Self-Transformation. Such improvements in the American political system may require major structural reforms that may add up to a process of more or less far-reaching self-transformation. In the end, these capacities for survival through adaptation and self-transformation, more than current wealth and power, will constitute the most important test of the performance of the American political system. But what are the resources, forces, and capabilities of American politics for such a process of continuing change?

The Elements of Change. To discover something about the future of American politics, we must study the processes of both change and resistance to change at work. Many of these processes occur on a large scale, beyond the power of any individual or small group to speed or slow them. Nonetheless, these processes are important for the limits and opportunities they pose for the actions of individuals and groups. A man who wants to sail a boat may not be able to create the wind and the currents; but if he knows how to navigate, he can make use of them, and if he has an engine in the boat, he can do even more. But he still must know the speed and direction of the current and the wind.

Currents of Change in American Society. Two major elements of change in America are the continuing shifts in occupation and residence. In 1940, 20 percent of the American people were in agriculture; today there are less than 5 percent. Yet more than 40 percent of the members of Congress still list rural or small-town addresses, and a majority of the heads of the important congressional committees, such as the Appropriations Committee in the House, comes from small towns and rural neighborhoods. The nation, therefore, stands at the threshold of a structural change in its representative system. A nonagricultural majority of more than 95 percent is still partly represented—or misrepresented—by a heavily agriculturally oriented and overweighted Congress.

The second shift is from rural residence to urban. Only about 20 percent of the American people still live in rural areas; four-fifths live in cities, towns, and suburbs. Indeed, more than half the American people live in cities over 50,000 in population. These metropolises would be the most endangered targets in a nuclear war. Yet their representatives have little influence on foreign policy. In the meantime the majority of small-town legislators believe in "deterrence" and legislate accordingly.

Another population shift now in progress is that from the central city into the suburbs. Currently this is favored by the tax system, which still puts part of the national welfare burden for migrants and other needy groups on the taxpayers in the central cities.

A fourth shift in process is from the rural South into southern cities. This has had a definite effect on southern politics. Observers in the North and West tend to believe that American youth is moving in a liberal, humanitarian direction. They do not see the movement, like that in South Africa or Rhodesia, of rural and young ex-rural southern whites into the cities, a shift that may be producing a more militant racial conservatism in southern cities. This trend resulted in 1968 in a vote for George Wallace in southern cities amounting to 20 percent—and over 30 percent among the South's young people. In 1972 in many southern areas, as in the nation, President Nixon ran ahead of the combined shares of votes that had been cast for him and Governor Wallace in 1968. Other southern whites have remained in the countryside, but have shifted to greater political participation and greater use of mass media. During the 1970s many southerners became more tolerant, and fewer remained racist or stayed indifferent. In time the *"white backlash"* and the Wallace movement faded, and with the campaign of Jimmy Carter a more liberal southern tradition came to the fore, resulting in the election of the first president from the Deep South since the Civil War.

In addition, there was a large movement from the rural black South to the central cities of the North. The mechanization of cotton picking and other changes have driven black people from the countryside, and low southern relief rates have driven them north. Gradually, this shift slowed down as the pool of black rural southerners declined and as more jobs opened in southern cities and industries. In the North, however, this slowdown was balanced by the rise in black births in its cities and the entry into the adult job market by black youths. Together these changes are causing a revolution in northern city politics.

While poor blacks long have been moving to the North, white skilled and professional personnel and other members of the white middle class (and in the late 1970s even some poor or black people), working or retired, have been moving to the South, settling particularly in the Sun Belt states, which stretch from Florida to Arizona and southern California. As a result, these states have become less typically southern or western. They have become more tolerant with regard to race relations, but perhaps somewhat more conservative with regard to taxes and inflation.

There are four further shifts. From grade school to high school and college, a radical change is underway in the educational level of the American people. Women have entered the work force in much greater numbers than before, and in many cases their attitudes have changed. They demand access to a wider range of jobs. They want to be not only hired, but also paid equally and promoted on the strength of their performance. They are taking a new look at many of the traditional roles of women and are beginning to change some of them, sometimes with good results, sometimes at considerable human cost—and with many of the results not yet apparent.

In the highly filtered news media there is a great shift from newspapers, which simply do not print what they think is not fit to print, to television, in which the pictures on the camera let through a great deal of information that was not intended to be seen. Television is more difficult to censor, and it entails more total involvement and immersion by its audience. This creates new opportunities for criticism and independent thought. Perhaps this explains why people seem to resent discovery of a lie on television more than an untruth in print. Newspapers, on the other hand, can offer depth, follow-up, summary, and coherence, if their editors and publishers choose to do so; and a number of newspapers and periodicals are continuing to perform this essential service.

Finally, a new kind of lobby has appeared. These *public interest lobbies* speak, or claim to speak, not for business, farmers, or labor, but for non-profit causes, among which are consumer protection (such as Ralph Nader's "Raiders"), conservation of the natural environment (such as the Sierra Club), and improvement in government. Not all of their causes are compatible (as is the case with common cause), nor are they often agreed on the priorities among them. But on the whole they make a start toward counterbalancing the older pressure groups and to assist at least some processes of change in political and social values and practices.

The Resistances to Change. Resistances to change come from many sources. Some are habitual, for the habits of millions of people are hard to change. Other resistances are based on age groups. In the United States there are nearly three registered voters over fifty years of age for every two registered voters under thirty, and older voters are more reluctant to accept change. At the end of the 1960s on many issues American voters over fifty years of age were more conservative—by 20 percent—than voters under thirty. In 1972, in particular, many voters over forty and fifty were repelled by much of the new lifestyle associations and images surrounding the McGovern nomination and campaign. President Nixon's victory in that election represented in part a cultural backlash more than an economic or political one.

Resistance also comes from special interest groups. In the late 1960s there was a food stamp scandal. Food stamps, it was reported, were being manipulated in the interests of the farmers who wanted to sell their produce and not in the interests of the hungry children who needed adequate food. Reformers urged transfer of the program from the Department of Agriculture, which serves only the producers, to the Department of Health, Education, and Welfare, which presumably has a greater interest in children. Many changes of this kind are technically possible, but they require the substantial weakening or removing of certain conservative bulwarks. The overrepresentation of rural areas, small towns, and voters who never move is such a bulwark, as is the electoral underrepresentation of the young, the educated, and the mobile. Still other obstacles survive in the congressional systems of committees and seniority, despite recent reforms. When the powers of the presidency and of the Supreme Court majority are added, at least temporarily, to these forces of conservatism, the array of forces against change may look formidable, indeed—perhaps as formidable as it looked half a century ago, in the days of presidents Harding, Coolidge, and Hoover. But as experience has shown, the power of such coalitions against change does not last forever. Some groups opposing change eventually decline in strength or lose popular backing. Other groups find that some kinds of change may be in their own interest. The food stamp program has changed substantially, and it has been one of the more successful public programs significantly to reduce hunger.

Opportunities for Change. To some extent the mass media are sensitive to needs for change and to communications from individuals. Partisans of change can help to increase the popularity of those persons and programs that promote newer attitudes. Any individual can write to newspapers and broadcasting stations, although the person who always writes is often discounted, whereas the many who occasionally write are much needed. Individuals can gain even more influence by founding groups that have cohesion, political know-how, and capacity to form coalitions. Coalitions get more results than does mere rhetoric.

But can the American political system change far enough and fast enough to cope with the mounting problems that confront it? At a slower pace it has always been changing since the first days of the republic. In some periods and in some sectors it has changed very rapidly. The entire population has become more politicized, and this process is continuing. Today Americans of southern and eastern European ancestry are just as active in politics and as insistent on their rights as old-stock Americans have ever been. Millions of black Americans, too, have become aroused to political concern and participation and so have many of the poor of all races. Large professions whose members used to think themselves too genteel to join a labor union—such as teachers, journalists, actors, and radio and television personnel—are all becoming unionized in many cities. So are the poorest and most often forgotten groups of labor, such as the hospital orderlies and garbage collectors. Also awakened to political participation are large parts of another previously passive group—the young.

As more Americans have become politically active, the political system has accepted a wider range of responsibilities. Medical care for those over age sixty-five is no longer disputed in principle. It is now law, and the discussion turns on the best ways to make it work. Public aid to low-rent housing and scholarships or loans to students seeking higher education have become accepted principles. Broader voter registration and fairer apportionment of legislative districts are now under way. The abolition of race segregation in public schools has become national policy and the law of the land, and beginnings have been made to put these into practice. In some of the big cities a search has started for methods of decentralization that will give different ethnic groups and neighborhoods a greater share in the decisions affecting their lives and the education of their children. City politics may be rediscovering in some respects the principle of "concurrent majorities" that John C. Calhoun proposed more than a century ago for the politics of the nation. If accepted, this principle would mean that decisions directly affecting a black urban region, such as Harlem in New York City, would require majority support in Harlem as well as in New York City as a whole. There have been many political inventions and innovations in the American past; there may be more in the future.

The American political system has the capacities for change if its people have the will to use them. There is a gap between the interests that are already organized and the potential ones that are not. The great majority of the American society has nothing to gain from perpetuating poverty or war. It is passionately interested in its own survival and that of its children. But these majority interests have yet to be organized. There is a vast opportunity for discovering and developing strategies of *coalition building* and action to this end. If reformers can recover the commitment, the dedication, and the intellectual and political skill to keep people of good will working with each other instead of against each other, then the most powerful country in the world can turn itself around and move in the direction selected by its founders. Such an outcome would require more openness from moderate conservatives and liberals, more self-control and willingness to compromise from radicals and adherents to new lifestyles, and more patience and perspective from perfectionists. But the possible results might well be worth the effort.

One part of such a reorientation and renewal of American politics would be a rethinking of United States foreign policy. No nation could go on indefinitely thinking itself omnipotent and invincible, least of all in today's world. When its people were told their country "never lost a war," they increasingly suspected that some historical evidence had been stretched a little. Or else they thought that earlier administrations had been wise enough not to involve the nation in wars that could not be won or were not worth winning. History knows no nation that was never defeated, but it knows the vital difference between those nations that survived their defeats and learned from them and those that failed to do so.

As every nation must learn to survive its setbacks in world politics, it also must learn to cooperate effectively with allies. The United States did so with spectacular success in two world wars and in the great reconstruction of Western Europe after World War II under the Marshall Plan. Since that time, however, the sheer size of the population and economy of the United States has often tended to dwarf the interests of America's allies, unless these allies were able to find strong American domestic interest groups to speak for them. During the first decade after World War II, the impoverished nations of Western Europe were glad to follow American policies, particularly as long as these coincided with their own needs for European reconstruction. In the 1960s, however, such newly more prosperous nations as France, West Germany, and Britain demanded more independence for themselves, more consideration for their views. They wanted less Western involvement in Asian wars and more American attention to European needs.

The Western alliance was further tested in 1973, when the Organization of Petroleum Exporting Countries (OPEC) imposed drastically increased oil prices on the world, despite American protests. When the United States let the international value of the dollar decline between 1971 and 1979, regardless of the objections of its foreign allies and its trade partners, the OPEC countries threatened to refuse to accept dollars alone in payment for their oil. The European powers announced efforts aimed at creating a European currency that might replace the dollar in much of international trading; and the private bankers and traders of the world lowered the value of the dollar against the yen, the Swiss franc, the Deutsche mark, and the price of gold. Only time will tell whether the United States government and electorate will be able to preserve international economic stability and renew a meaningful Western alliance through the 1980s.

In the meantime, the domestic experience of the United States has much to offer the rest of the world. The American social and political habits that emphasize equality and mobility, respect for all kinds of work, including manual labor, and interest in discovery and practical solutions could be of real help to many societies whose politics have remained bound by more rigid barriers of class and status, tradition, or ideology. And other nations may secretly admire the American optimism that undertakes impossible technical tasks, such as a series of voyages to the moon, and completes them not only with great success, but on schedule.

Foreign nations may be less enthusiastic about the American unconcern—in practice, if not in theory—for the conservation of natural and human resources. They watch the wasteful American use of energy and the extraordinary difficulties of the American political system in attempting to control it. They know that Americans easily discard old things rather than mend them, that they like to use throwaway packages and containers. They fear that this habit may carry over into an American inclination to have throwaway cities and perhaps even throwaway people. They note that Americans are quick to use things and people and, sometimes, foreign countries, without knowing them well. And they are worried by the occasional American propensity to see foreign people as so many dominoes blindly falling with each push of power. Foreigners watching pictures of American race riots or urban blight on their television screens may feel in no particular hurry to imitate American politics or institutions. In times such as these, the United States perhaps needs more constructive innovators working at home and fewer political propagandists traveling abroad. It needs to advance its ideas in the world arena more by example than by attempts at persuasion. If the example is good enough, other nations will find their own ways to respond to it.

KEY TERMS AND CONCEPTS

government by design
dependency burden
spread effect
backwash effect
capitalism
socialism
nondecisions
Chicanos
political participation (participation by voters)
campaign financing (participation by money)
"fat cats"
socioeconomic status
swing vote
median income voter
voting frequencies
contact specialists
activists
sanctions
responsiveness
concurrence statement
distribution of power
general purpose elites
special elites
the establishment
lobbyists
"tax revolt"
political community
political culture
pragmatism
basic value orientations
ecology
collateral
lineal
command systems
action orientation
future orientation
Gunnar Myrdal's prediction
liberalism
conservatism
radicalism
the new politics and the counterculture
the me generation
market
arena
mobility
joint rewards
social and cultural cohesiveness
federalism
residual powers
separation of powers

checks and balances
pluralism
populism
feminism
"right to life"
trimester solution
porkbarrel politics
polarization
"rotten boroughs"
"one man one vote"
legislative reapportionment
seniority
Seventeenth Amendment
cloture
rights of Congress versus rights of the president
veto
item veto
General Accounting Office (GAO)
Congressional Budget Office (CBO)
caucus
logrolling
side payments
roll-call votes
gerrymander
primaries
Electoral College
pledged electors
commander in chief
policy-making appointments
White House staff
advice and consent
détente
impeachment
full faith and credit clause
judicial review
Marbury v. *Madison*
"judge-made" law
ex parte Milligan
Baker v. *Carr*
Gideon v. *Wainwright*
Escobedo v. *Illinois*
Miranda v. *Arizona*
judicial activism
cognitive corruption
decision points
consciousness
will
creativity
innovation
"white backlash"
coalition building

ADDITIONAL READINGS

American Politics: General

Barber, J. D. *Citizen Politics.* 2nd ed. Chicago: Rand McNally, 1972. PB

Barone, M. et al. *The Almanac of American Politics 1980.* New York: Dutton, 1979.

Dahl, R. A. *Democracy in the United States.* 3rd ed. Chicago: Rand McNally, 1976. PB

Lockard, D. *The Perverted Priorities of American Politics.* 2nd ed. New York: Macmillan, 1976. PB

Mitchell, J. M. and W. C. *Political Analysis and Public Policy: An Introduction to Political Science.* Chicago: Rand McNally, 1969.

Historical Background

Adair, D. "'That Politics May Be Reduced to a Science': David Hume, James Madison, and the Tenth Federalist." *Huntington Library Quarterly* 20 (1957), 343-60.

Boorstin, D. *The Genius of American Politics.* Chicago: University of Chicago Press, 1953. PB

Elkins, S., and E. McKittrick. "The Founding Fathers: Young Men of the Revolution." *Political Science Quarterly* 76 (June 1961), 181-216.

Genovese, E. *Roll, Jordan, Roll: The World the Slaves Made.* New York: Random House, 1976.

Hofstadter, R. *The American Political Tradition.* New York: Knopf, 1973.

Lipset, S. M. *The First New Nation: The United States in Historical and Comparative Perspective.* New York: Basic Books, 1963. PB

Potter, D. M. *People of Plenty: Economic Abundance and the American Character.* Chicago: University of Chicago Press, 1954. PB

Woodward, C. V. *The Strange Career of Jim Crow.* 3rd rev. ed. Oxford: Oxford University Press, 1974. PB

———. *Tom Watson: Agrarian Rebel.* London and New York: Oxford University Press, 1973.

Participation and Power

Agger, R., D. Goldrich, and B. Swanson. *The Rulers and the Ruled: Political Power and Impotence in American Communities.* Rev. ed. North Scituate, Mass.: Duxbury Press, 1972. PB

Alexander, H. A. *Financing Politics: Money, Elections and Political Reform.* Washington, D. C.: Congressional Quarterly Press, 1976.

Bachrach, P. *The Theory of Democratic Elitism.* Boston: Little, Brown, 1967. PB

———, and M. S. Baratz. "Two Faces of Power." *American Political Science Review* 56 (December 1962), 947-53.

Dahl, R. A. *Who Governs? Democracy and Power in an American City* New Haven: Yale University Press, 1962. PB

Heard, A. *The Costs of Democracy.* Chapel Hill: University of North Carolina Press, 1960.

McGinniss, J. *The Selling of the President.* New York: Trident, 1969. PB

Prewitt, K., and A. Stone. *The Ruling Elites: Elite Theory, and American Democracy.* New York: Harper & Row, 1973. PB

Verba, S., and N. H. Nie. *Participation in America: Political Democracy and Social Equality.* New York: Harper & Row, 1972. PB

Wilson, J. Q. *Varieties of Police Behavior.* New York: Atheneum, 1970. PB

Images and Ideologies

The Conservative Papers. With introduction by Melvin R. Laird. Garden City, N.Y.: Doubleday Anchor, 1964. PB

Harrington, M. *Socialism.* New York: Bantam Books, 1973. PB

Hartz, L. *The Liberal Tradition in America.* New York: Harcourt, 1962. PB

Hofstadter, R. *Anti-Intellectualism in American Life.* New York: Random House, 1966. PB

Lasch, C. *New Radicalism in America.* New York: Random House, 1967. PB

Lipset, S. M., and E. Raab. *The Politics of Unreason: Right-Wing Extremism in America, 1790–1970.* 2nd ed. Chicago: University of Chicago Press, 1978. PB

Lowi, T. *The End of Liberalism: Ideology, Policy, and the Crisis of Public Authority.* New York: Norton, 1969. PB

Roosevelt, J., ed. *The Liberal Papers.* Chicago: Quadrangle Books, 1962.

Steinfels, P. *Neoconservatism.* New York: Simon and Shuster, 1979.

Wise, D. *The Politics of Lying: Government Deception, Secrecy, and Power.* New York: Random House, 1973. PB

Political Machinery and Processes: *Congress and Voting*

Campbell, A., P. Converse, W. Miller, and D. Stokes. *The American Voter: An Abridgement.* New York: Wiley, 1964. PB

Fenno, R. *Congressmen in Committees.* Boston: Little, Brown, 1973. PB

———. *The Power of the Purse: Appropriations Politics in Congress.* Boston: Little, Brown, 1966.

Froman, L. A., Jr. *The Congressional Process: Strategies, Rules and Procedures.* Boston: Little, Brown, 1967. PB

Matthews, D. *U.S. Senators and their World.* New ed. New York: Norton, 1973. PB

Nie, N. H., S. Verba, and J. R. Petrocik. *The Changing American Voter.* Cambridge: Harvard University Press, 1976. PB

Polsby, N. "Policy Analysis and Congress." *Public Policy* 18 (Fall 1969), 61-74.

Price, E. *Who Makes the Laws? Creativity and Power in Senate Committees.* Cambridge: Schenkman, 1972. PB

Redman, E. *The Dance of Legislation.* New York: Simon and Schuster, 1973.

Rieselbach, L. N. *Congressional Politics.* New York: McGraw-Hill, 1973.

Truman, D., ed. *The Congress and America's Future.* 2nd ed. Englewood Cliffs, N.J.: Prentice-Hall, 1973. PB

Political Machinery and Processes: *The Presidency*

Barber, J. D. *The Presidential Character.* Englewood Cliffs, N.J.: Prentice-Hall, 1973. PB

Berger, R. *Impeachment: The Constitutional Problems.* Cambridge: Harvard University Press, 1973.

Bernstein, C., and B. Woodward. *All the President's Men.* New York: Warner Books, 1976. PB

———. *The Final Days.* New York: Simon and Schuster, 1976. PB

Burns, J. M. *Roosevelt: The Lion and the Fox.* 2 vols. New York: Harcourt Brace Jovanovich, 1970.

Carter, J. *Why Not the Best?* New York: Bantam, 1976. PB

Eisenhower, D. D. *The White House Years.* 2 vols. New York: Doubleday, 1963–65.

Johnson, L. B. *The Vantage Point.* New York: Popular Library, 1972, PB

Kearns, D. *Lyndon Johnson and the American Dream.* New York: New American Libary, 1977. PB

Miller, M. *Plain Speaking: An Oral Biography of Harry S. Truman.* New York: Putnam, 1974.

Neustadt, R. *Presidential Power: The Politics of Leadership.* New York: Wiley, 1976. PB

Nixon, R. M. *Memoirs.* New York: Grosset and Dunlap, 1978.

———. *Six Crises.* Garden City, N.Y.: Doubleday, 1962.

Schlesinger, A., Jr. *The Imperial Presidency.* Boston: Houghton Mifflin, 1973.

———. *A Thousand Days: John F. Kennedy in the White House.* Boston: Houghton Mifflin, 1965.

Sorensen, T. *Kennedy.* New York: Harper & Row, 1965.

White, T. H. *The Making of the President, 1972.* New York: Atheneum, 1973. PB

———. *The Making of the President, 1968.* New York: Atheneum, 1969. PB

Witcover, J. *Marathon: The Pursuit of the Presidency, 1972–1976.* New York: Viking Press, 1977.

American Performance and Prospects

Arlen, M. J. *An American Verdict.* Garden City, N.Y.: Doubleday, 1973.

Barnet, R. J. *Roots of War: The Men and Institutions Behind U.S. Foreign Policy.* Baltimore: Penguin Books, 1973. PB

Beer, S. H., and R. E. Barringer, eds. *The State and the Poor.* Cambridge: Winthrop, 1970. PB

Galbraith, J. K. *Economics and the Public Purpose.* Boston: Houghton Mifflin, 1973.

Harrington, M. *The Other America.* Rev. ed. New York: Macmillan, 1970.

Hoopes, T. *The Limits of Intervention.* 2nd ed. New York: Longman, 1974. PB

Jencks, C., et al. *Inequality.* New York: Basic Books, 1972.

Kail, F. M. *What Washington Said: Administration Rhetoric and the Vietnam War, 1949–1969.* New York: Harper Torchbooks, 1974. PB

King, M. L., Jr. *Why We Can't Wait.* New York: Harper Torchbooks, 1964. PB

Kitagawa, E. M., and P. M. Hauser. *Differential Mortality in the United States.* Cambridge: Harvard University Press, 1973.

Malcolm X (with Alex Haley). *The Autobiography of Malcolm X.* New York: Grove Press, 1965. PB

Miller, S. M., and P. Roby. *The Future of Inequality.* New York: Basic Books, 1970. PB

Moynihan, D. P. *The Politics of a Guaranteed Income: The Nixon Administration and the Family Assistance Plan.* New York: Vintage Books, 1973. PB

The Pentagon Papers: As Published by The New York Times. New York: Bantam Books, 1971. PB

Perloff, H., ed. *The Future of the United States Government: Toward the Year 2000.* New York: Braziller, 1971.

Pressman, J. L., and A. B. Wildavsky. *Implementation.* Berkeley and Los Angeles: University of California Press, 1973. PB

Russett, B. M. *What Price Vigilance? The Burdens of National Defense.* New Haven: Yale University Press, 1970. PB

Sampson, A. *The Sovereign State of ITT.* New York: Stein and Day, 1973.

PB = *available in paperback*

XI

The Soviet Union

After a look at the length of the preceding chapter, obviously we cannot apply the scheme of analysis that was proposed in Part 1 in such detail to the other nations covered in Part 2 and expect this book to remain portable. Accordingly, only much briefer sketches can be presented here, and it will be the reader's responsibility to work out a more nearly full-scale analysis with the help of the further readings indicated at the end of each chapter.

One topic, however, deserves full treatment for each country, because it furnishes the essential setting and background for all the other information that we may find out about it. This is the section on the general nature and historical background of politics in the particular country. For the sake of brevity a discussion of the most important images and ideologies of politics, as they have developed in the history of that country, will have to be merged with this section, rather than being treated separately and more extensively (corresponding to the separate Chapter 4 in Part 1). Again, the Additional Readings will suggest a fuller treatment of the ideas that have come to mark the main processes of politics in each country.

THE NATURE AND BACKGROUND OF SOVIET POLITICS

Perhaps the best way of getting a sense of the nature of the Soviet political system is to take a look at its similarities to and differences from the political system of the United States. In this way we may get a first impression of what these two huge countries may have in common, in what ways each is unique, and in what direction each may be going. Such a comparison is not easy to make; and some of our preconceptions make it harder. Most studies of the Soviet Union available to Western readers resemble descriptions of hell that were written by fair-minded theologians. It is particularly hard for Westerners to understand that most Russians are loyal to their government and will fight to defend it against foreign attack. Russians have a similar difficulty in understanding political loyalties in the West. But anyone who thinks that either Americans or Russians would not defend their government against any direct attack has been deceived. The Japanese military discovered this when they attacked the United States at Pearl Harbor. So did Hitler when he attacked the Soviet Union. In the 1980s it would be madness for either Russian or American leaders ever to forget that fact.

TWO EXPANDING PEOPLES— TWO IDEAS OF GOVERNMENT

Like the United States, the Soviet Union has been shaped by a unique combination of vast historical development and deliberate political design. The United States is the product of an outpouring of largely English-speaking (followed by non-English-speaking) people westward across rivers and mountains and then across a continent and onward to Hawaii and Alaska. This had made Scottish and Irish Americans, Pennsylvania Dutch, Louisiana French, Minnesota Swedes, Slavic and Italian Americans, Spanish and Indian Americans, Jews, Puerto Ricans, and black Americans all members of the American people. The Soviet Union, now a nation of about 261 million, is the product of an eastward outpouring of Slavic-speaking peoples, mainly Russians and Ukrainians, across the land mass of Eurasia all the way to Vladivostok and Sakhalin Island. To an even greater extent than the United States, the Soviet Union emerged from its expansion as a *multilingual* country. Russians accounted in 1971 for only about 52 percent of the Soviet people, while twenty-one major minorities composed another 43 percent and more than a hundred ethnic splinter groups made up the rest.[1] Yet each of these large countries—the United States and the Soviet Union—grew out of a revolution and out of a deliberate political design at a decisive stage in its history.

A Common Dream. Out of each revolution came a political system engineered by theorists who had tried to master what they held to be the social science of their day. These theorists were desperately determined to make their blueprints practical. The purpose of each design was no less than the liberation of the people and the creation of the political conditions for their happiness. Now, over two hundred years after the event, we can see the good and bad that have come out of the vision of the American revolutionary theorists: the triumphs, the disappointments, and the hopes deferred, but perhaps not quite forsaken. It is difficult to realize that the Soviet system was also created by theorists with no less idealistic a vision—even though Lenin and his Bolshevik comrades would have bridled with indignation at the very word "idealism," which they considered bourgeois.

The word *idealism* has many meanings, among which three stand out. In common speech "idealism" means, first, a selfless aspiration to make things better, particularly for others; here it is opposed to the common meaning of "materialism"—a preoccupation with tangible rewards, often with overtones of selfishness. Second, also in common speech, "idealism" sometimes means an inclination to see things as better or more perfect than they actually are; here it is opposed to the ordinary meaning of "realism." A third meaning pertains to the philosophy of knowledge. Here "idealism" means the doctrine that thoughts, abstract forms, or ideas are more real and enduring than tangible things and events and that individuals' inner lives are more real than the world

[1]For these and other recent data I am indebted to Professor Ellen Mickiewicz, and to the work edited by her, *Handbook of Soviet Social Science Data* (New York: Free Press, 1973), and to Steven Livingston, Harvard University.

around them. It was this third, philosophic meaning of "idealism" that Marx and Lenin opposed. They contrasted it with philosophic *materialism,* which taught that the outside world was real, independent of the wishes of observers. To put ideas first, they believed, was to stand knowledge on its head. Only by putting its feet on the ground and seeing the world as it was, they argued, could the world be changed for the better.

Philosophic materialists, of course, may be quite capable of unselfish—or idealistic—behavior. Lenin, the revolutionary, and Krasin, the economic planner, Stalin and Trotsky, Radek and Budharin, even perhaps Khrushchev and Kosygin—all had their vision of a better social order. Each attempted to transform his vision of the good society into reality for a vast, poor, and backward country in order to implement human happiness there. But if the underlying visions and aspirations were similar in the Soviet Union and in the United States, there were nevertheless profound differences between these nations' attempts to realize their dreams and between the outcomes each attempt produced.

Two Revolutions and Their Differences. The American Revolution had five characteristics that distinguished it from the Russian. It began with a vision of *plenty.* Not only were the 3 million colonists of the 1770s and 1780s at the edge of a rich continent; on a per capita basis they also had the richest capital equipment in the world. Thus, in that sense, the Americans were already at the time of their revolution the most advanced people in the world.

Second, the American people at the time of the revolution had had a long tradition of local *self-government,* of spontaneous organizations in small, self-governing groups, such as church congregations, town meetings, and committees of correspondence. By the end of the eighteenth century the English-speaking world had had at least a century-old tradition of local self-government and of voluntary agreements.

Third, the American revolutionaries envisioned the possibility of harmony or at least of a workable *compatibility of interests* within the country. Divergent interests would be accommodated not through factionalism or violence, but through accepted and legal channels of government. These ideas later found expression in James Madison's "Tenth Federalist Paper." On the whole they also felt that if America stayed out of international entanglements after winning its independence and remained reasonably well defended, no foreign countries would have a major motive to harm the United States. Such thinking pervades George Washington's farewell address.

A fourth basic characteristic was the American trust in the *spontaneity* of individuals. Setting people free to pursue their happiness, as the Declaration of Independence put it, implies having automatic trust in their knowing what will be good for themselves. Both before and since the Revolution the mainstream of American culture has trusted the spontaneity of men and women.

Finally, from the American Revolution onward, there has been an American tradition of *moderation.* This might now be called into question by some, but there seems to be a fair chance that it will endure. Extremist episodes always have been short-lived. In major emergencies the American people have tended to move toward the middle, whereas some of the European populations, such as those of Russia and Germany, have tended to move toward the extremes. Comparing the extreme German responses to the Great Depression of the 1930s with the American responses shows the American tradition of moderation, which is sometimes frustrating and irritating, but which has stood the country in good stead.

In contrast to the American experience, the Russian tradition began with *scarcity,* in a poor country with many people and little capital. At the time of the Russian Revolution the peasants of Russia had long been among the poorest of all the poor peasantries of Europe. The revolution occurred at the end of a bloody world war that had exhausted the country and ruined its economy. Food was scarce in the big cities before the first shots of the revolution were fired. And scarcity remained a critical factor even after the end of the revolution. A Soviet teamster at the building of the Dnieper River dam in the late 1920s exhorted his helper to take good care of the horses: "You can always make a man," he said, "but just try to make a horse." Twenty years and two five-year plans after the Russian Revolution, only half as many pairs of shoes were being made each year as there were Russians, amounting thus to one shoe per individual. This was seen by many Russians as an improvement; in the days of the czar the normal winter footwear of 100 million peasants was burlap rags tied around their feet.[2]

Second, for many centuries, self-government was very limited at the village level and almost nonexistent at any other. *Violent conflict,* like scarcity, had long been a basic assumption of Russian politics, and the Russian Revolution merely reinforced it. Revolutionary Russia saw itself in the position of a besieged fortress. And, indeed, from its start in 1917 the new Soviet government faced foreign conflict. Fourteen foreign countries made war on the Soviet government in the first four years of its existence. They did so ineffectively and half-heartedly, but they still killed many people, and the intervention prolonged the Russian civil war to 1921. The situation of the Bolsheviks resembled that of the embattled Jacobins in the French Revolution of 1793, who were besieged by more than a half-dozen European monarchies and who resorted to a terrorist dictatorship to save the republic. A similar mood of desperate determination was characteristic of the Russian Revolution. In contrast, the American Revolution had strong foreign allies: France, Spain, and the Netherlands.

Whereas the leaders of the American Revolution believed in spontaneity, the experiences of the Russian revolutionaries led them to a different conclusion. Prior to the revolution, Lenin and the members of his conspiratorial Bolshevik party had had an almost full-time job dodging the czarist secret police. The leaders who emerged from these struggles believed in *discipline,* direction, and organization. The Soviet leaders distrusted spontaneity and do so to this day.

Finally, whereas the American tradition stressed moderation, the Russian tradition stressed desperate *ruthlessness.* In order to get things done, any means were acceptable. Lenin said he would make an alliance "with the devil and his grandmother" if it would help the revolution. It is tempting for Westerners to sit back and criticize the tactics of the Russian revolutionaries. Living where and when the Soviet leaders did, they regarded ruthlessness as the only realistic way of completing their revolution. But we should not forget that even when a price seems inevitable, it still has to be paid. Bertolt Brecht, the pro-Communist German poet, said that even righteous indignation will make one's voice hoarse. And the Soviet people and their government have paid with more than hoarseness of voice.

THE BASIC THEORY: MARX

Not unlike the United States, the Soviet Union is a child of an encounter between a developing nation and an international idea. In each country the images and values accepted by its governments and people had a significant influence on what they did in politics and on what they thought they were doing. And if the two nations and their histories were different, the crucial ideas adopted by each differed still more. The American Revolution had adopted the international ideas of the eighteenth-century Enlightenment, stemming largely from John Locke, and supplemented them to a lesser extent with notions of populism, resem-

[2]Around 1970 the U.S.S.R. produced annually 560 million pairs of leather shoes, or 2.4 pairs per person.

bling some of the ideas of Jean Jacques Rousseau. (Both Locke's and Rousseau's ideas were discussed in Chapter 4.) The ideas that became dominant in the Russian Revolution and in the Soviet Union that emerged from it came from another age and setting. They are the ideas of nineteenth- and early twentieth-century Marxism and Leninism.

Essentials of Marxism. The originator of the theory that was taken over by Lenin and the Bolsheviks in Russia was Karl Marx. Marx's theory was rooted in a profoundly pessimistic evaluation of the nineteenth-century private enterprise system, based mainly on the experience of England (where Marx spent much of his adult life) in the first half of that century. As we have seen in Chapter 4, Marx assumed that the conditions that he had seen were not unique characteristics of a particular society at a specific time, but general tendencies of an entire economic system. Among these tendencies, as he saw them, were increasingly frequent wars and depressions, increasing oppression, increasing misery of working people, and increasing alienation of people who were being treated more and more like things or commodities. Marx assumed that the only response to this experience would be a struggle among economic classes, out of which the industrial wage earners would eventually emerge as the most numerous—and eventually the dominant—class. Indeed, the middle classes would disappear; the children and grandchildren of the peasants and artisans would overwhelmingly end up as factory workers or unemployed wage earners, only a tiny minority becoming property owners. These workers would become increasingly dissatisfied and radicalized. Factory work would teach them organization and discipline. They would learn to form unions and fight for higher wages. Communists would teach them class consciousness and the need for revolution. The resulting class struggle, Marx asserted, would determine the future course of history.

Marx believed in stages of historical development. After the stages of primitive communism and of feudalism, there would be a stage of private enterprise in which middle-class capitalist rule would replace the power of the nobles and the landowners. Only after this stage had reached its height would social revolution and socialism follow. Marx believed that socialism would be an outgrowth of capitalism: socialism would grow under the surface, within the husk of the private enterprise society, so that one would have only to remove the shell and the full-blown industrialized socialist economy would emerge, nearly completed.

At this point the working class would be united, Marx believed. Workers would, on the whole, accept the Marxist ideology; and since they would be united and enlightened and would constitute the vast majority, they would exercise a dictatorship over the remaining few former members of the owning classes. This new regime somehow would not be a dictatorship over the workers themselves, because there would be so many of them and they would all know what they wanted. They would be able to be dictators and yet act spontaneously. It would be the rule of the many over the few.

Socialism: How Long a Period of Scarcity and Inequality? Two economic stages would follow capitalism. The first, which Lenin later called *socialism* (Marx just called it a lower stage of communism), would be an *economy of scarcity,* in which land, machines, and means of production would be owned collectively, but the society would still be poor. In this society people would work according to their ability and be paid according to their performance. Those who worked more or did more complicated or more urgently needed work would be paid better regardless of their needs or those of their families. The society of socialism, therefore, would be unjust, and the state machinery would still have to be used to defend the higher incomes of what we now would call the *meritocracy,* the more productive or more skilled workers, technicians, and managers.

Marx's logic vis-à-vis this question could be

extended to the relation between highly productive and less productive regions of any large country at this still poor stage of economic development. Each region might be expected to contribute according to its economic capacities and to receive from the exchange of goods and services no more than corresponds to its limited capacities; the power of the socialist state will regulate and limit the migration of the poorer population to the richer and more advanced cities and regions. Transfers of resources from these more advanced regions to the poorer ones will be limited, despite genuine beliefs in solidarity. Only slowly will greater skills be learned by the unskilled or their children, will capital be invested at an increased rate in the less developed regions, will the economic inequalities decline or become less important. But during this time of transition the socialist state will continue to defend the basic injustices and inequalities of its present condition, offering only the hope and promise of overcoming them in the future. And that future has turned out to be much more distant than Marx's followers originally expected.

The same inherent logic of Marx's thought applies on the international level to the exchange of goods and services among socialist states. Here again, highly developed socialist countries would tend to export high-priced products of high technology, skilled labor, and intensive capital investments, whereas less developed countries would be more likely to export farm goods, raw materials, and goods produced with less capital and cheaper, less skilled labor. Thus, the international market among socialist countries, according to the implications of Marx's logic, will continue for a long time to show many of the inequalities and inequities that critics have pointed out in today's capitalist world markets. And each socialist state is likely to defend its national advantages in capital, natural resources, skilled labor, and technology against other socialist states, making only very limited modifications in the name of international solidarity. The possibility of economic disputes, military threats, and even warfare among socialist states should have been predictable from Marx's own theory, as he wrote it down in 1875,[3] long before some of these possibilities became realities a century later in the bloody clashes between the troops of different Communist states, at the borders of Russia and China in 1969 and at those of China and Vietnam in 1979.

Marx tried to be a genuine scientist, to see reality whether or not it would please himself or his adherents. If the first stage of socialism still was to include much poverty, scarcity, and injustice and if a repressive socialist state was to exist during this stage, he did not shrink from making this fact clear in his writing. But most of his followers, and most of the adherents of socialism in general, expected something very different. They expected socialism to be the fairly prompt fulfillment of all their hopes for universal freedom, friendship, and plenty—in short, all their moral, political, and economic aspirations for humankind. Once the socialist revolution had triumphed and large estates and factories had become collective property, they expected workers, peasants, and intellectuals to rule together in freedom. At most they might be willing to work and wait for ten or twenty years, but then surely the "vast productive forces" of modern industry would bring about that economic abundance on which a free, rich, and nonrepressive socialist society would be based. They would have been appalled to learn that the transition to this hoped-for state would take not merely years or decades, but several generations and perhaps one or two centuries.

The Soviet leaders may have shared some of these impatient illusions. (Estimates of time always have been a weak point in Marxist theory.) In any case, they did not dare to disillusion their followers. Rather, they used the Soviet state, its mass

[3]See Marx's *Critique of the Gotha Program* (of the Social Democratic Party).

media, and the Communist Party to assert that much of this freedom and fellowship already had arrived in their country and that the Soviet government was not repressing anyone except the members of the former enemy classes, the landlords and capitalists. In short, they claimed that Soviet society was much richer and freer than it actually was. They still are caught in this pretense today: they still must claim that much of what Marx hoped for in the future is existing in their country here and now.

Measured against this claim, even their real successes must fall short. Many people must notice that things are not as good as the government says they are. Some persons go on working, defer their hopes, and are reinforced by limited, but visible, improvements; others become disillusioned and respond by opportunism and cynicism; still others focus their attention on their private lives; and a few respond by some degree of opposition to the regime, try to emigrate, or become *dissidents.* Such dissidents seek to spread their critical dissenting views within the country by means of "self-published" writings, called *samizdat,* and also with the help of foreign newspapers, radio stations, and personal contacts. Often they are targets of official efforts at repression. They risk jobs, careers, and prison terms, but from the 1960s onward they have persistently turned up in Soviet life. Though many an ordinary Soviet citizen may think of them as "foreign agents," they are a product of Soviet society and perhaps of the clash between the hopes and the realities of the unexpectedly long Marxist path to which the Soviet Union remains committed.

This path still is expected to lead to Marx's vision of the more distant future, regardless of whether it should turn out to be decades, generations, or centuries away.

Marx's Vision of the Long Run Future. However long it might take, this early stage—socialism—would have only one purpose: to put itself out of business. It would amass ever more wealth, ever more capital, and ever more machines until finally production would become efficient and goods plentiful. The symptoms of the transition to the age of plenty would be clear to see, Marx thought: the differences between worker and intellectual and between town and countryside would disappear.[4] He held similar hopes for the economic differences between regions and nations. Ultimately, economic abundance would make these differences unimportant, too.

Marx expected a society of plenty to emerge, first within a few highly advanced countries and eventually as a worldwide phenomenon. Within such a society the government of people would be replaced by the administration of things. Marx's notion was that a great deal of the productive equipment of humankind would eventually become semiautomatic or automatic. It would have to be maintained, but the business of government would be replaced by the business of maintenance.

Thus, sitting in the library of the British Museum behind his bristling beard, Marx envisioned a society of freedom and generosity for all people. In the middle of a long economic discussion in the third volume of *Das Kapital* there is a revealing throwaway sentence in which he speaks of "that full development of all human capacities and powers which is an end in itself." This is what Marx wanted to live for: the full realization of human capabilities, the end of the subordination of human beings to the division of labor, a new age of the all-sided development of individuals. After the revolution, all this would depend on economic growth. Only after people had made the transition from poverty to plenty would they move "out of the realm of necessity into the realm of freedom."

[4]It is ironic to think that these predictions have been most nearly fulfilled in the world's least Marxist country, the United States. Whether you call a laboratory technician or a television repair person a worker or an intellectual is a moot question; they are both likely to be skilled and intelligent. And whether you call a suburb a town or a countryside is again debatable. Contrary to Marx's theory, these blurrings of age-old categories in the United States have been the result of industry, not of revolution.

Only then would the prehistory of humankind end and the real history of human beings, the interesting history, begin.

Some of His Predictions—and the Facts. Marx assumed the existence of a high degree of technological determinism: a hand mill meant a society of landlords and serfs; a steam mill meant capitalists and wage workers. His assumption has turned out to be partly false, for modern machines have served a variety of social systems. Henry Ford's tractors have worked on Soviet collective farms as well as on American private enterprise farms.

Second, Marx foresaw automatic growth of all the elements for a socialist economy under the capitalist surface. This has not materialized. Countries that have wanted public planning agencies and skills have had to create them by deliberate political effort.

Third, he thought that the advanced countries, and particularly their urban and industrial sectors, would be the most likely areas for Communist success. He had blistering phrases of contempt for peasants and for what he called "the idiocy of rural life." The best thing Marx might have said about peasants was that their children or grandchildren might someday become honest, upstanding proletarians. Here reality has differed from this prediction in a crucial way. Indigenous Communist revolutions have triumphed thus far only in semi-developed or underdeveloped countries, such as Russia, Yugoslavia, China, Cuba, and Vietnam, and then only with the help of peasant uprisings.

Fourth, Marx predicted that the proletariat—the wage-earning factory workers—would become the vast majority. This has not been the case. In the United States, for instance, production-line jobs have not increased in numbers since the end of World War II. The main increase in the work force has been in services and clerical work, not in manual labor. The same is true of all other highly industrialized countries, including those ruled by Communists. Some dissident Communist writers, such as the Yugoslav Milovan Djilas, have attacked this growth of bureaucracy and management as heralding the rise of a "new class." Some Communist regimes have tried to slow the trend or at least play it down in their published statistics, or they may define as a "proletarian element" any government or Party official who was once a worker, even many years ago. More recently they have begun to define office workers as proletarians. None of this necessarily proves the rise of a new hereditary class of privileged persons in these countries but rather indicates the pressure of modern technology, which requires fewer people in performing manual work and more in handling information.

Finally, Marx expected the workers in the highly industrialized countries to move spontaneously toward revolution and proletarian dictatorship. All efforts at reform and real wage increases would fail in the end, he thought; history would drum revolution into the heads of most workers. This, too, has not happened. The majority of factory workers in the advanced Western countries have benefited from reforms and higher living standards; and most often they have become attached to labor unions committed to further reforms, further wage increases, and constitutional government.

THE MODIFIED THEORY: LENIN

When Marx died, his most important follower in Russia was only twelve years old. His name at birth was Vladimir Ilyich Ulyanov. He came from a family of professionals that included some petty nobles. He earned a law degree and might have become a civil servant. But in 1887 his older brother was hanged by the czarist authorities for conspiracy against the monarch. This act of deterrence proved counterproductive for the czar. Young Ulyanov, at sixteen, became a revolutionist and within a decade turned to Marxism, seeking in the social conditions of his country an explosive more powerful than dynamite. By the end of the century he had been banished by the czarist government to Siberia, and soon after 1900 he went into exile into western Europe. After his Siberian banishment he called himself "Lenin," or "the man from the Lena River." Years later, in 1912, a large strike in the gold fields at the Lena River was smashed by czarist forces who killed about two hundred workers. From then on, Ulyanov's chosen name, Lenin, had a more ominous ring: the man from the Lena River, like a ghost of the slain, would come back to claim the czar and the entire social order that he stood for.

Lenin's Theoretical Contributions. Marx's assumptions were partly modified and changed in several ways by Lenin. First, Lenin believed in *uneven development* among the countries of the world. Some countries would become highly industrialized, but others would stay far behind. Modern technology would increase the political choices open to a society rather than completely determining the outcome through economic influence alone.

Second, like Marx, Lenin thought there was an automatic tendency in most societies toward weakening the power of landowners and replacing it by the power of industrialists and businesspeople. This is what he called the *bourgeois revolution.* Unlike Marx, however, he expected far less support for this revolution from the bourgeois proper—the big and middling businesspeople—except in colonial and semicolonial countries, where a native business class might struggle against foreign rulers or competitors. Major support for a bourgeois revolution would come from the peasants, Lenin believed, particularly from tenants and landless laborers who would revolt to make themselves owners of the land they tilled. Also unlike Marx, Lenin no longer maintained that the tendency toward socialism would be automatic.

Third, Lenin felt that the countries particularly well suited for a revolution were those that formed the *weakest links* in the chain of capitalist countries. They had to be backward enough to keep the workers poor and disgruntled, but advanced enough to keep them numerous and concentrated at strategic centers. In these countries, Lenin predicted, bourgeois revolutions would break out, but they would remain weak and incomplete; out of them, however, proletarian revolutions would emerge and finish the job. The best bets for such combined revolutions were Russia, China, and Spain.

Lenin saw two alternatives. Once revolution had triumphed in one country, it either would spread quickly throughout the whole world, in which case Lenin would preside over a *world revolution,* or else one or a few countries would have to set up their own Communist regimes, and try to establish *socialism in one country* (as Stalin later called it). These regimes would then hold out as long as needed, even for decades or for generations, until the rest of the world would accept the new doctrine. Sooner or later, revolutions in colonial countries would destroy imperialism and much of the capitalist world market, making capitalism in western Europe unworkable. This is the thought behind Lenin's reported remark that the way to Paris might lead through Peking. Such expectations were behind Lenin's "new economic policy" in 1921, in which he made major concessions to private enterprise among the peasants. At the same time he tightened authoritarian control over the Russian Communist Party at the Tenth Congress, which forbade the forming of groups or factions within the Party and prohibited any criticism of a policy after the Party had adopted it.

Fourth, Lenin assumed that *peasant-worker alliances* would be extremely important, whereas Marx had relegated the peasants to the fringes of his intellectual universe. Lenin believed there would be peasant revolutions against the landowners in all developing countries and that the art of Communist revolution would consist in synchronizing the strikes and uprisings of disgruntled urban workers with the uprisings of disgruntled peasants. (Later Mao Tse-tung in China went one step further by putting the major weight of revolution on the peasantry.) Lenin assumed that the peasant revolution would result in the minority rule of workers, who would be allied with the peasants, but exercise power over them. The Communist Party in each country, in turn, would lead the working class. It was to be the *vanguard* of the workers, thinking and acting today in the way most workers would act tomorrow. (In theory, it would *not* become, therefore, a permanent *elite*, different from the workers. Maintaining this principle to any extent in practice has been one of the continuing and acknowledged problems of the Soviet regime, as we shall see later.) In Lenin's view the resulting "proletarian dictatorship" would no longer be spontaneous; it would deliberately direct further economic development. In effect, it would be a dictatorship of the Communist Party, but it would have to be skillful enough to retain enough popular support among the peasants and workers to stay in power.

Finally, Lenin made a more radical psychological break with the existing order than had his ideological forerunners. Lenin was thoroughly alienated both from his government's bureaucracy and from western Europe. Both Marx and Engels were the most radical revolutionists of their day, but they felt very much at home in western Europe. In contrast, Lenin—who spent many years in the West—in many ways remained a stranger in the Western world. Yet Lenin put great stress on maintaining close contacts with the workers anywhere; and it is recorded that, unlike many other radicals, he spent considerable time listening to peasants and plain people when in Russia.

This psychological distance from the mainstream of Western tradition had something to do with Lenin's fifth basic contribution to Communist theory, his *distrust of spontaneity*. When left to their own initiative, Lenin thought, workers would always try to behave like the American Federation of Labor, getting higher wages, but not really questioning who was running the economy or whether their wages came from a war contract. It was the intellectuals, the Bolsheviks, the revolutionaries, who had to supply the sense of historical mission. But only individuals fully committed to this mission could do so, and they had to devote their lives to it. Such intense commitment had occurred also in the West, briefly and exceptionally, during the revolutionary period of Cromwell in England and of Robespierre in France. In Russia, however, this style of leadership proved more lasting and significant.

Lenin's distrust of spontaneity had a practical side as well. A spontaneous, loose, liberal organization, such as a Western-type political party, he felt, would be a sitting duck for the police forces of the czar, the most elaborate secret police organization of the time. Dodging the police would be a full-time job; and being a revolutionary, a profession.

As a result of these ideas, Lenin developed a concept of a tightly disciplined, small party of full-time *professional revolutionists*. The czarist regime, like other anti-Communist dictatorships, unwittingly aided this development. By denying alternative employment to intellectuals who opposed it, it turned additional numbers of them into such professional revolutionists. Party members of the Leninist kind were much less likely to express themselves spontaneously, but might develop a sense of common pride and dedication. In the long run, however, these professional revolutionists could turn into a kind of underground bureaucracy, which was dedicated to the revolution and later to the regime that its victory created, but which in time often became rigid and one-sided in its thinking.

Lenin's Tactical Contributions. The quarrel between the two concepts of a party—the loose and the tight—came to a head in 1903 at a congress of Russia's Social Democratic (SD) Party held in

Brussels and London. Lenin's followers were defeated on this issue. But the withdrawal of some members of the SD Party during the congress enabled Lenin's minority to become a majority at the end of the congress when elections were held for the central committee. From the Russian word for majority, they were henceforth called *Bolsheviks*, and the "minority," their more Western-minded opponents, became known for a similar reason as *Mensheviks*. Until 1952 the full name of the ruling party of the Soviet Union was Communist Party of the Soviet Union (Bolsheviks)—CPSU(B).

In order to keep his small party disciplined, doctrinally pure, and uncontaminated by the capitalist environment, Lenin insisted on authoritarianism both in matters of party strategy and in terms of doctrine. At the same time he exhibited a mastery of coalition tactics and tactical retreats and topped it all off with a ceaseless demand for what he called "Bolshevik tenacity." In some ways one might compare the social organization that Lenin built with an organization developed for entirely different purposes by Saint Ignatius of Loyola in the sixteenth century. Jesuit fathers were taught to be masters of compromise, masters of adjustment, masters of practicality, and yet to have the utmost devotion to both the general teachings of the church and the specific authority of the head of the Jesuit order. This combination of external flexibility and intense internal commitment was something that the Jesuits had successfully incorporated into their religious organization. Lenin tried to do something similar in the name of a secular doctrine.

Lenin died in 1924. He lived long enough to see that his plans for world revolution would have to be put off and that for some time his followers would have to hold out in a single country. But should they concentrate their efforts on internal development or on foreign revolutions? This unresolved question in Lenin's thought surfaced as a fateful quarrel among his successors.

THE STALINIST YEARS

With the death of Lenin a struggle for the control of the Communist Party and of the future of the Soviet Union began. This struggle ultimately centered on two men: Leon Trotsky and Joseph Stalin. Trotsky was a revolutionist who, far more than Lenin, saw revolution as attractive for its own sake. He believed in permanent revolution and in using military methods to accomplish it. A brilliant writer, he was better at commanding than at listening. Trotsky was a highly effective organizer of the Red Army during the period of civil war, and as late as 1920 he advocated organizing all of Russian industry on the Red Army model.

Trotsky versus Stalin. Trotsky was much more cosmopolitan than either Lenin or Stalin. He was more at home in the West emotionally and intellectually than in Russia. He distrusted the Russian base of the revolution; Russia, to him, was uncouth and backward. Like Marx, he regarded Germany in particular, and France and England to a lesser degree, as the predestined countries for revolution. He strove, therefore, to push revolution in the West as fast as possible. Suspicious of the Russian peasants, Trotsky wanted to tax them. He also advocated the rapid build-up of Russia's military industry. These were not policies likely to appeal to most Russian Communists or to most of the Russian people; and they contributed much to Trotsky's political defeat within the Russian Communist Party, to his exile in 1929 (which eventually was followed by his assassination in Mexico in 1940), and to Stalin's ultimate victory.

Stalin took the opposite tack. Born in Georgia in the Caucasus as the son of a shoemaker and a washerwoman, educated for a time on a scholarship in a seminary for Orthodox priests, he joined the Marxists at the age of nineteen and soon became a professional revolutionary. His personality has remained a riddle, even to his daughter. He was an early member of Lenin's faction and soon became an insider in its organization, in contrast to the individualist Trotsky, whom the old-line Bolsheviks distrusted.

Both Stalin and Trotsky sought power. Stalin got it, partly because of his old Party connections and partly because he chose policies that suited his nation. Stalin's most important decision, and probably the prime cause of his success, was his commitment to the possibilities of the Russian base. Unlike Trotsky, he insisted from late 1924 onward that a collectivistic economy could be built in Russia, with Russian workers (few as they were), Russian industry (backward as it was), and Russian peasants (numerous as they were). After years of political maneuvering, Stalin came out strongly in support of *socialism in one country* and gave up the notion of expecting an immediate world revolution. The fact that world revolution did not take place in the 1920s also encouraged Stalin's action, since one of Lenin's options had turned out to be ineffective.

Second, Stalin wished to make a much greater attempt to industrialize the country than Trotsky ever considered. Trotsky planned to tax the peasants quickly for a relatively small-scale industrial effort. Stalin envisaged a much bigger plan, though he developed the details only later. He wanted to permit the peasants to engage in private enterprise several years longer, in order to squeeze them much more thoroughly at a later date. This would enable him to build up greater resources for the big industrial push. He therefore looked like a "rightist" (in Communist parlance) until 1927 and like a "leftist" afterward. In actual fact, he used a fairly consistent argument: he wanted to build up a large backlog, surplus, or war chest for an internal campaign of industrialization that he knew would be very costly. Finally, more than Trotsky, Stalin believed in a type of centralized planning that would be neither militarist nor permissive, but would require a new set of institutions.

Planning: The Second Russian Revolution. Once in power, Stalin began organizing the Soviet Union and developing the new planning apparatus on a massive scale. He decided to transform the peasantry, not just tax them, and this transformation was successfully undertaken in two five-year plans from 1927 to 1937. First, he began the *mechanization of agriculture,* largely with the help of American tractors. Second, he pushed the peasants into *collective farms.* These were farms in which the home, the household, the kitchen, and, in practice, the garden plot remained in private hands, while the fields were held in common and the tractors were owned by the government. It was a compromise system that worked for several decades. Third, he *industrialized* the country by moving a large portion of the work force from the fields into the factories. Progress was slow: when Stalin started, 80 percent of the work force was in agriculture, but by the time he died it was down to approximately 50 percent. Thus, about one-third of the Russian work force was transferred from agriculture into the industrial sector, but at fantastic cost.

In effect, the first two five-year plans marked a second Russian revolution, hardly less desperate and costly than the first. As collectivization proceeded, the peasants slaughtered much of their livestock; it took over ten years to get back to pre-1927 levels. Indeed, about 5 percent of the peasants, or approximately 5 million people, including the wealthier, or more tradition-minded, or more independent, resisted to the bitter end. Their defiance was ultimately broken by brutality and by deportations to Siberia. But the graves of collective farm chairmen who were killed by the peasants in model collective farms tell a harsh story. It was a second civil war in the countryside.

Stalin insisted on squeezing every last bit of the available grain from the collective farms. If somebody had to starve, it was not going to be the cities and the workers on whom the Soviet regime depended. There followed in 1932–33 a man-made famine that cost the lives of several million peasants in the Ukraine and elsewhere in Russia. The next spring, the Soviet regime provided additional incentives for the surviving peasants to work harder, which they did, to produce a bumper crop. But a price had been paid. The famine had hit women and children, producing unimaginable suffering. It had produced a death toll estimated at 5 million, comparable to the toll of the civil war.

The Stalinist defense was that until that time there had been natural famines in Russia every ten years; that everybody had said they were catastrophes about which nothing could be done; and that Stalin's ruthless policies had ended them. The fact is that although crop failures have recurred there, in no peacetime year since the mid-1930s has there been a famine. Stalin's reforms eventually left agriculture sufficiently productive to yield food and industry for exports in order to buy additional food abroad when needed.

Costs and Achievements. The achievement of the Stalin era was, on the whole, an unprecedented success in rapid industrialization. Never before was so agrarian a country transformed into so industrial a state in so few years. Agriculture became capable of feeding the entire country even though there were many fewer people in the rural work force, and the youngest, most energetic, most able people had left the villages. In no other country did literacy spread so fast or science and technology grow so rapidly and extensively. The nearest parallel in the non-Communist world is the industrialization of Japan in the late nineteenth and early twentieth centuries, which took longer and was also accompanied by dictatorship—and, incidentally, by very warlike, military regimes for a large part of the time. The last test of Stalin's regime was perhaps the most grueling—World War II. On the whole, when that test came, most of the Soviet population, with its many different languages, fought for the Soviet regime, often displaying great heroism.

But the cost of Stalin's ruthlessness was high. A balance sheet would probably suggest that in the long run Stalin's ruthlessness saved more lives from famine than it cost. But such a method of rationalistic analysis may be shallow. We must also ask what this ruthlessness, this willingness to sacrifice millions for some future good, does to the minds of the people who practice it, wherever and for whatever reason. When Stalin and his followers actively accepted ruthlessness and dictatorship, they agreed to go to any lengths to reach their goals. They also learned to expect hostility everywhere. As a result, they learned to fear each other. Indeed, one of the most dangerous security risks to the Soviet government has been the secret police, and a police chief's lot in Russia has not been a happy one. At least three of them, Yagoda, Yezhov, and Beria, were shot by the government. At other times the accusations by such men sent others to their doom. Thus, in the end the dictatorship of Stalin became a dictatorship of suspicion and paranoia.

The hidden costs of his paranoia—the inability to tell friends from enemies, reality from fantasy, and an honest difference of opinion from an attempt at sabotage and subversion—were, perhaps, even more serious. The memoirs of Stalin's daughter, Svetlana Alliluyeva, are a poignant illustration. There were losses of life and liberties far beyond the costs inherent in the policies themselves. Most of the Bolsheviks who preached ruthlessness in the name of revolution ultimately perished at the hands of other Communists who had been reared in the same creed. Stalin's purges, which began after 1934, went into high gear after 1936 and 1938; and, as the Soviet government has publicly stated since 1956, a large number of these purges were completely innocent. They were the victims of frameups, manufactured evidence, forced confessions. In this manner Communists killed each other in large numbers.

In September 1972 one could see near the motion picture theatre Udarnik, located on one of the main streets of Moscow, a plaque in memory of Soviet Marshal Mikhail N. Tukhachevsky, who was tried and executed for treason in one of Stalin's purges. After Stalin's death it was revealed that Tukhachevsky had been completely innocent, and a laudatory biography of him was published. None of this could bring him back to life, but it may have helped his family and perhaps some of his surviving fellow officers, and the plaque continues to remind Russians of the bloody errors a powerful government can commit.

Others suffered more slowly. Alexander Solzhenitsyn's book entitled *One Day in the Life of Ivan Denisovich,* published in the Soviet Union in 1962, is a former inmate's description of one day in a labor camp in Stalin's era. These camps at their peak in 1950 had 10 million people in them; and since many died there and others were released, probably over 20 million Russians got into these camps at one time or another. Nearly every second family in the Soviet Union had somebody who was touched, brushed, or hit by the Stalin terror in the years between 1934 and 1953. In the years after Stalin's death in 1953 the number of political prisoners has declined to less than 150,000, but the memory of those terrible years remains vivid among the present generation of Soviet citizens.

A MEASURE OF PROSPERITY—AND THE NEW STAKES OF POLITICS

The Stalin era laid the basis for the second largest concentration of economic power in the world. The Soviet Union has almost 17 percent of the world income, whereas the United States has 25 percent. American per capita income in 1976 was about $7,900; Soviet per capita income was around $4,350, if the Soviet output of goods and services is valued in 1976 dollars. This corresponds to about 58 percent of the United States figure. This Soviet level was below that of the German Federal Republic and France, but, according to some data, perhaps a touch ahead of Britain (however, it depends on whose figures you use[5]). About 1920, however, United States per capita income already was close to $1,000, while Soviet per capita income—after years of foreign and civil wars—was below $100. Even in 1928, Soviet per capita income was only one-fifth of that in the United States. The American-Soviet income gap, therefore, has shrunk from 10:1 to 5:1 to 1.75:1. In regard to the total GNP, which is important for assessment of potential power in world affairs, the American-Soviet ratio in 1979 was about 3:2.

A per capita income of $4,350 does not mean that the Russians live or eat better than the British. Part of the Soviet per capita income is circling the globe in the form of Sputniks and assorted space hardware. Other parts of their income are buried in hardened intercontinental missile sites in the Ural Mountains. Thus, a fair degree of Soviet income does not get to the consumers. Russian consumer standards are much lower than those of the Western European countries. Back in 1955, when Soviet total per capita income was only 38

[5]The figures in the text are based on the work of Abram Bergson of Harvard. The estimate by American scholars of the 1976 per capita income of the Soviet Union at $4,350 is based on the dollar valuation of the Soviet output of goods and services. Valuing the same output in rubles and then translating the rubles into dollars at official rates would understate the cost of producing the goods and services comprised in the Soviet GNP, if we should try to produce them in the United States. Attempts to take some mean or other intermediate figure between the dollar and ruble valuations still would understate the Soviet GNP. I agree with Professor Bergson's view that the dollar valuation of the Soviet GNP—and hence the $4,350 per capita figure for 1976—is the best approximation available for the purposes of comparative analysis. The data presented by Ruth Sivard for 1975 give the Soviet per capita income as $3,094, compared to a United States figure of $7,101. There the estimated ratio of Soviet to U.S. income is apparently based on a comparison of the two incomes at *ruble*—not dollar—prices, so all Soviet income figures will appear much lower and the Soviet Union's share of world income would shrink to 12.5 percent.

For data up to 1965, see Abram Bergson, "Comparative National Income of the USSR and the States," in D. J. Daly, ed., *International Comparison and Output* (New York: National Bureau of Economic Research and Columbia University Press, 1972), pp. 145–93, 216–24, especially p. 182, table 14. For extrapolations since 1965, from the ratio of Soviet to U.S. per capita incomes at dollar values, I am indebted to Professor Bergson, oral communication, January 29, 1973, and December 4, 1978. See also Bergson, *Productivity and the Social System* (Cambridge: Harvard University Press, 1978), p. 49.

percent of the United States level, Soviet *consumption* spending per capita totaled only 37 percent of the corresponding United States amount, but the total for *nonconsumption* items, such as capital investments and defense, already then amounted to 63 percent of the American level. By 1978, when total Soviet per capita income had reached nearly one-half of the United States amount, Soviet consumption levels were still well below—and Soviet defense and investment expenditures were well above—that overall Soviet average.[6]

These high and sustained rates of growth and this consistent favoring of investments and defense spending, as opposed to consumption, have been among the large stakes of Soviet politics. How much to spend how fast on what is never a purely technical question in any country or under any system. What people want and value, what messages they respond to, how they perceive or misperceive reality, and which persons or groups have the power to make their current values and perceptions prevail over those of everybody else—all these are also largely political questions, albeit within the limits of given economic and technological constraints. In the Soviet Union these questions and decisions are more political than anywhere else.

The political aspects of what might look like purely economic decisions are highlighted by the Russian tendency to concentrate efforts on *decisive sectors,* as the Russians call them. This now means space technology; earlier it was intercontinental rockets and nuclear energy; during World War II it was the tank program and earlier still the tractor program. Coming decisive sectors may well be automation, agricultural biology, and the chemistry of fertilizers. Even if the leaders should misjudge the next decisive sector, however, Soviet industry now has a productive capacity that can survive a great deal of error and difficulties.

[6]See Bergson, "Comparative National Income," p. 178.

Nevertheless, certain critical economic problems remain as yet unsolved. First, Soviet planners have not resolved the problem of recurrent *disproportions in investment.* They invest heavily in industry, which gives *increasing returns to scale:* the more you make, the cheaper you can manufacture each additional product. Agriculture and mining, in contrast, produce *diminishing returns:* the more crops or minerals you need, the poorer the soils or deposits you must go to and, ultimately, the more expensive it becomes to produce each additional item. To some extent the force-feeding of capital into industry and the underinvesting in agriculture occasionally have led to bad years in which economic growth has slowed down or sometimes has even stopped. These are not cyclical depressions, as in the West, but they look like depressions and can be as serious, if not more serious. After more than four decades, Communist planning is still neither perfect nor smooth.

The second disproportion is between investment goods and *incentive goods,* that is, goods for which people are willing to work harder, such as better clothes, washing machines, and television sets. Communist ideology thinks of consumer goods as luxuries; in this belief the Communists are almost like the Puritans of the seventeenth century and Adam Smith in the eighteenth. They do not realize that many consumer goods are also incentive goods. A color television set is not a luxury, but an incentive good that makes a plumber show up on the job on the next day in order to meet the installment payments on his television set. The Russians have not yet fully discovered the tremendous power of consumer goods as incentives to further productive effort.

Moreover, the Communists have not resolved the problem of the tension between *equalitarianism* (making wages relatively equal) and *performance payments* (paying more to people who do important or good work than to people who work less, who do less important work, or who work less well). Much of the emotional appeal of socialist or Communist ideas comes from their implied promise of greater equality. Much of the motivation to work, in the Soviet Union as elsewhere, comes from material incentives, such as better pay, that are unequal for unequal work. At present, inequality among Soviet wages and salaries is not very different from such inequalities in the United States. On the whole, more than 90 percent of the Soviet wage structure falls within a span between ten and one; that is, the highest paid people get about ten times as much as the lowest paid. In the United States probably 85 percent of the wage structure falls within that span.

Nonetheless, these inequalities are still large. Both in Russia and in the United States they create a lasting tension between what may be a good incentive for production and what is likely to be accepted by almost everyone in the country as legitimate and just. In the Soviet Union this tension is potentially enhanced by the promise of social justice that is inherent in so much of Soviet thought and in the broader socialist tradition from which it is in part derived.

Reliable data on Soviet income differences are not easy to obtain. Some old data from 1960 are presented in Table 11.1. Less detailed data for 1973, by economic sectors, are shown in Table 11.2. The incomes in the 1970s are certainly higher, and the improvement may be greater at the lower levels, but much of the substance of inequality has remained. The extent, distribution, and future increase or decrease of these income inequalities are among the continuing stakes of Soviet politics.

Neither the United States nor the Soviet Union as yet understands human *motivation* thoroughly. The American stress on material incentives perhaps slights many less tangible motives, as well as the quality of life; and the Soviet stress on exhortation and ideology underrates the incentives of consumer goods and choices and of greater scope for individuality and spontaneity. So far, however, neither society has been able to manage without the incentive of markedly unequal rewards.

With inequalities of income often go inequalities in education, lifestyle, chances of success in primary and secondary schools, and, hence, opportunities for higher education, other advanced training, and subsequent careers—all of which contribute once more to the inequalities in the income structure of the next generation. A comparison of the education aspirations of secondary school graduates from different social strata in one Soviet district with their successes in continuing their education is presented in Table 11.3.

Since the different occupational and educational strata are not quite evenly distributed over all the regions and ethnic groups of the Soviet Union, there are also observable inequalities in the levels of income and education among its different regions and the peoples that live in them. According to some estimates, the Baltic Union Republics—Estonia, Latvia, and Lithuania—and the territories inhabited mainly by Russians and organized as the Russian Soviet Republic within the Soviet Union are about 25 percent better off in some of these respects than are the non-Russian territories and populations in Central Asia.

The uneven incidence of new investments could either reduce or increase these inequalities. Since many investments were in fact channeled into the Siberian part of the Russian Soviet Republic, rather than into such older European, but non-Russian, regions as the Ukraine and Byelorussia or into such Asian Soviet areas as the Kazakh or Uzbek republics, the effect was to enhance the relative advantages of the Russian areas and populations. The arguments about where to direct such large investments most often were couched in terms of economic or technological rationality, but this made their social and political implications no less real; and Soviet decision makers and plain citizens often are well aware of them. The professed overall aims of Soviet policy remain, of course, the full and equal development of all Soviet peoples and regions, but the lag of equality behind development has persisted. Its extent is illustrated by the estimated per capita income ratio of roughly 2:1 between the most highly developed region, Latvia, and the least developed one, the

TABLE 11.1 *Income Inequalities in the Soviet Union in 1960: Some Representative Occupations*

Occupation	Monthly income (in rubles)
INTELLIGENTSIA (EXECUTIVE LEVEL)	
Top party or state leader	2,000
Opera star	500–2,000
Scientist (academician)	800–1,500
Professor (science)	600–1,000
Plant manager	300–1,000
Minister or department head	700
Professor (medicine)	400– 600
Docent (assistant professor)	300– 500
INTELLIGENTSIA (OTHERS)	
Engineer	100– 300
Technician	80– 200
Physician (chief)	95– 180
Bookkeeper	110– 115
Physician (staff)	85– 100
Teacher (high school)	85– 100
Teacher (primary school)	60– 90
WORKING CLASS	
Skilled worker	100– 250
Office clerk	80– 90
Semiskilled worker	60– 90
Unskilled worker (cleaning woman, cook)	33– 50
Peasant	27– 50

Source: From data in V. Aspaturian, "The Soviet Union," in R. C. Macridis and R. E. Ward, eds., *Modern Political Systems: Europe,* 3rd ed. (1972), p. 543, with reference to U.S. Bureau of Labor Statistics, *Monthly Labor Review,* vol. 83, no. 4 (April 1960), pp. 359–64. Adapted by permission of Prentice-Hall, Inc., Englewood Cliffs, N.J.

TABLE 11.2 *Average Annual Earnings of Workers in the Soviet Union, by Economic Sectors, 1958–1973 (rubles)*

Rank 1973	Sector	Number Employed, 1973 (million)	Woman as % of Workers, 1969	Average Earnings 1958	1965	1969	1973	% Change, 1959–73
1	Construction	6.65	27	1040	1308	1680	1968	89.2
2	Transportation	7.80	24	988	1266	1572	1884	89.7
3	Science	3.13	47	1271	1387	1596	1764	38.8
4	Industry	31.16	48	1045	1236	1536	1764	68.8
	AVERAGE*	—	50.5	934	1144	1440	1620	73.5
5	Administration	1.83	60	1010	1256	1440	1512	49.7
6	Credit/Insurance	0.36	77	865	1030	1284	1476	70.6
7	Education/Culture	7.78	72	833	1122	1248	1440	72.9
8	Agriculture	9.08	43	637	883	1116	1428	124.2
9	Communications	1.26	67	696	886	1128	1284	84.5
10	Trade	7.29	75	697	907	1116	1224	75.6
11	Housing, communal	2.93	51	665	871	1092	1224	84.1
12	Art	0.40	42	—	—	1116	1200	—
13	Health	4.93	85	707	944	1092	1188	68.0
Range from highest to lowest earnings				634	516	588	780	+23%
Approximate ratio of highest to lowest				2:1	1.6:1	1.5:1	1.7:1	−15%

*Averages based on a total of 87.92 million workers, include 2.90 million other workers.

Source: From data in V. Aspaturian, "The Soviet Union" in R. C. Macridis, ed., *Modern Political Systems: Europe,* 4th ed. (1978), p. 369 (Table 5.3, q.v. for full citation), with reference to *Narodnoye Khozyaisto . . . v 1969 Godu,* pp. 538–40, and *. . . v 1974 Godu.* Adapted with permission of Prentice-Hall, Inc., Englewood Cliffs, N.J.

TABLE 11.3 *Personal Plans of Secondary School Graduates. Their Successes, and the Social Status of Their Families (Novosibirsk Oblast, 1965)*

Occupational status of family	Percentage of graduates who said they wanted to continue studies	Percentage of graduates who succeeded in continuing studies	
		Those desiring further study	All graduates
Urban nonmanual	93	88	82
Manual, industry and construction	83	73	61
Average of all students	83	73	61
Manual, services	76	78	59
Rural nonmanual	76	76	58
Manual, transport and communications	82	55	45
Manual, agriculture	76	13	10
Others	38	66	25

Source: From data in V. Aspaturian, "The Soviet Union," in R. C. Macridis and R. E. Ward, eds., *Modern Political Systems: Europe,* 3rd ed. (1972), p. 553, with reference to V. N. Shubkin, "Youth Starts Out," *Voprosy Filosofii,* no. 5 (1965). Adapted by permission of Prentice-Hall, Inc., Englewood Cliffs, N.J.

Kazakh Republic. This is comparable to the similar current 2:1 ratio between the richest state and the poorest state in the United States—Connecticut and Mississippi.

In the longer run there are still bigger things at stake in Soviet politics. For in the Soviet Union, even more than in many other countries, political decisions can influence the entire direction of its economy and culture and the course of the continuing transformation of its society.

Such political decisions also shaped the responses of the Soviet regime to such external challenges as the foreign anti-Soviet interventions of 1917–21; the Nazi threat of 1933–41; the all-out onslaught of the Cold War, particularly in 1946–55, and its continuation, though less intense, until at least President Nixon's visit in 1972; and, since the late 1960s, a certain pressure from China after the Mao government's resurrection of territorial disagreements over—though not yet outright claims to—present Soviet territory. The challenge from China increased with the establishment of more friendly relations between China and the United States and the brief war between China and the Soviets' ally, Vietnam, in 1979. Finally, the stakes of Soviet politics also include the degree of attention and support, if any, that will continue to be given to the ideological, missionary, and world-political ambitions and aspirations of those Soviet interest groups and leaders who are concerned about international affairs beyond a mere general interest in national security. The extent of aid given to such countries as Cuba or Vietnam and the risks accepted for their protection also will be determined largely by the political processes within the Soviet system.

PARTICIPATION IN POLITICS AND THE MACHINERY OF GOVERNMENT

A Persisting Element: Government by Pyramid. In politics, as well as in economics, the Soviet system depends on the guidance of a *pyramid* of political authorities and on the intense efforts of millions of activists—nearly one adult out of every five—organized in the Communist Party or its youth organization, the Young Communist League (Komsomol). All these organizations call for civic efforts, yet try to channel and control these efforts closely. Periods of somewhat greater liberality and scope for differences of opinion in politics and culture have alternated with calls for more conformity and discipline. These swings have characterized much of Soviet politics during the last three decades, but they have not changed the basic structure of Soviet government.

All modern countries, in a sense, are governed by pyramids of administration and decision making, but the Soviet system is more pyramidal than most. It consists of a multiplicity of pyramids. There is the pyramid of local and territorial government, from villages, towns, and districts all the way up to the Supreme Soviet. There is the pyramid of the Communist Party, from the primary units to the All-Union Secretariat and the Politburo (see Figure 11.1). There is a military pyramid and another pyramid of economic planning and management. Finally, there are several lesser pyramids of mass organizations, such as trade unions, consumer cooperatives, sports organizations, youth organizations, and the like.

In the Soviet Union all these pyramids interlock at every level. Directly or indirectly, the Soviet government reaches into every nook and cranny of social life. At the same time the system offers many opportunities for participation; it has many ties to the life of the population and many opportunities to win popular support. Last but not least, despite its multiplicity, complexity, and popular connections, it is well suited to centralized direction from above.

The National Government. The Soviet Union as a whole is formally governed by a *Supreme Soviet* of over 1,500 delegates. This body is so large, and meets for such a limited time each year, that its main tasks consist of confirming and ratifying legislation produced by smaller groups. The Supreme Soviet is divided into two chambers of roughly equal numbers, the *Soviet of the Union* (one deputy for every 300,000 people) and the *Soviet of Nationalities* (deputies elected by each union republic, autonomous republic, or other territorial unit based on nationality or ethnic group). In the former, voters are represented in proportion to their numbers; in the latter, similar to the United States Senate, the smaller republics, areas, and nationalities are deliberately overrepresented (see Figure 11.2).

The Supreme Soviet elects a *Presidium,* which we shall abbreviate PSS, to function as the collective chief of state of the Soviet Union. The chairman of this Presidium, L. D. Brezhnev in 1979, fulfills on ceremonial occasions a role analogous to that of president of the Soviet Union. Besides the chairman the PSS in 1976 had 37 members including a secretary and seventeen deputy chairmen (one from each union republic). Between sessions of the Supreme Soviet, the Presidium exercises all the state powers of the Supreme Soviet, including the passage of legislation, as well as far-reaching executive powers.

The PSS, however, is not the government of the Soviet Union. It directly controls neither the execution and administration of policy nor the Soviet bureaucracy. These tasks fall to the *Council of Ministers,* which the Constitution of the U.S.S.R. calls "the highest executive and administrative organ of state power." In 1976 the Council had 114 members, including a chairman, eleven deputy chairmen, and representatives of sixty-two ministries, fifteen state committees, four specialized agencies, fifteen union republic premiers (*ex officio*), and six others. The decrees and orders of

FIGURE 11.1 *Democratic Centralism in the Soviet Union, 1976*

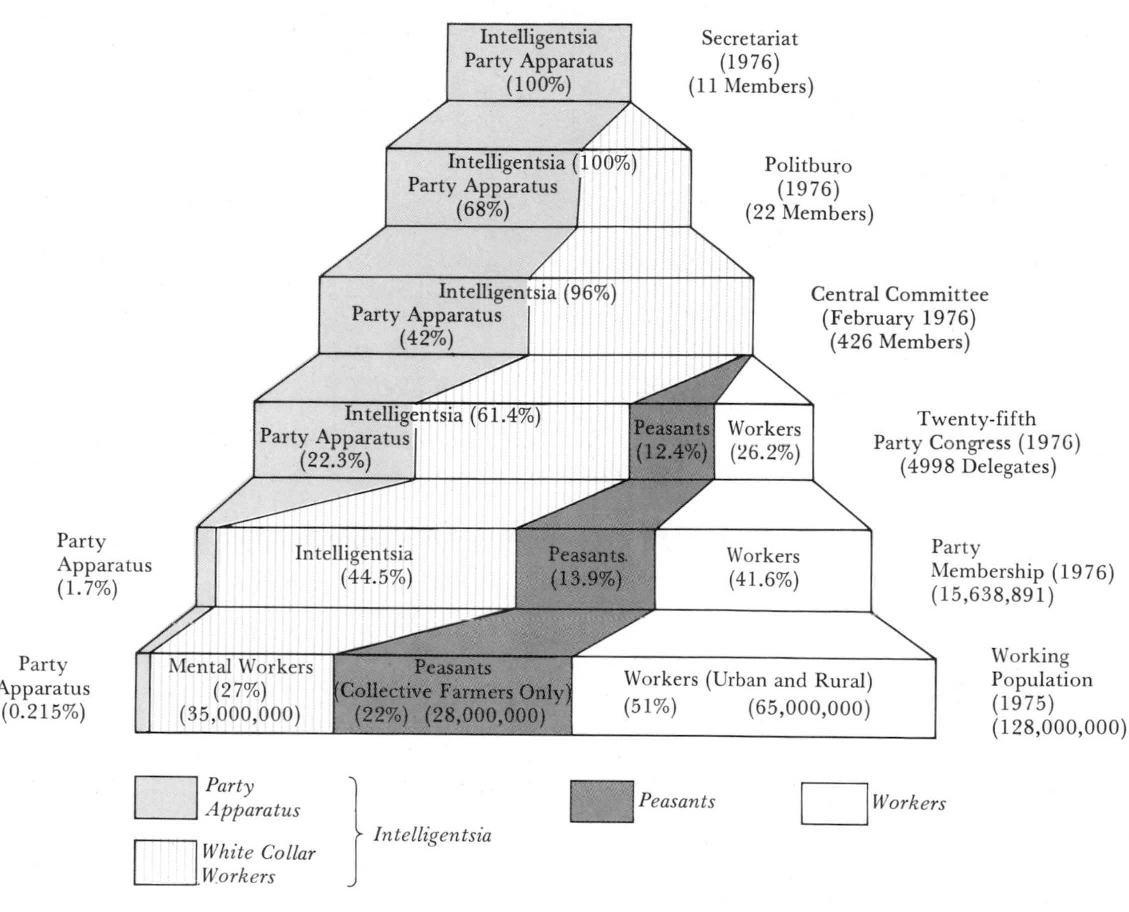

Source: V. Aspaturian, "The Soviet Union," in R.C. Macridis, ed., *Modern Political Systems: Europe*, 4th ed., 1978. Adapted by permission of Prentice-Hall, Inc., Englewood Cliffs, N.J.

FIGURE 11.2 *Constitutional Structure of the Soviet Union*

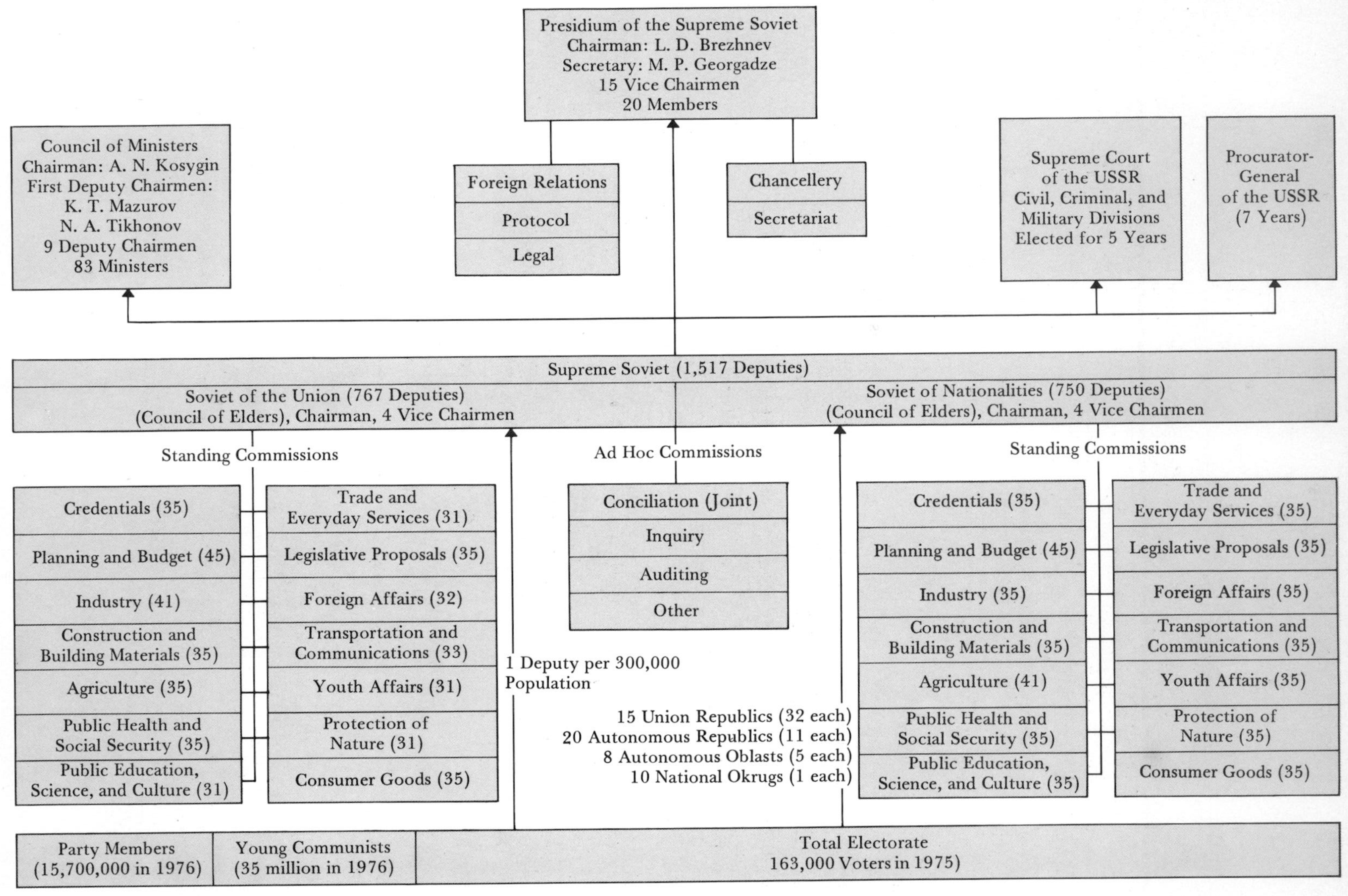

Sources: V. Aspaturian, "The Soviet Union," in R. C. Macridis, ed., *Modern Political Systems: Europe*, 4th ed., 1978. Adapted by permission of Prentice-Hall, Inc., Englewood Cliffs, N.J. Also R. J. Mitchell, "Union of Soviet Socialist Republics," in Richard Starr, ed., *Yearbook on International Communism, 1977* (Stanford, Calif.: Hoover Institution Press, 1977).

the Council are binding throughout the Soviet Union and form the great mass of Soviet legislation. Since the Council of Ministers is much too large for efficient deliberation, its principal administrative decision making powers are entrusted to the much smaller *Presidium of the Council of Ministers* (PCM). The chairman of the PCM has always been a top-ranking member of the Communist Party, ranging from such early leaders as Lenin, Molotov, and Stalin to such more recent incumbents as Khrushchev and Kosygin. The office of *chairman of the Presidium of the Council of Ministers* somewhat resembles that of prime minister in Britain or France.

Territorial Units and Ethnic Groups. Below the all-union level there are fifteen *union republics*, each with its own constitution, soviet, council of ministers, and prime minister. By far the largest union republic is the Russian Soviet Federal Socialist Republic (RSFSR)—itself a federation—which includes the majority of the population and land area of the Soviet Union.

Within the republics there are twenty *autonomous soviet socialist republics* (ASSR), sixteen of them within the RSFSR. Each autonomous republic has its own constitution and, though subordinate to the union republic in which it lies, enjoys within it an autonomy similar to that of the union republic vis-à-vis the national government.

Below these three tiers of government—the national government of the Soviet Union, the union republic, and the autonomous republic—is a fourth layer formed by regions called *oblasts*. Some *oblasts* are autonomous, lacking constitutions of their own, but electing deputies to the Soviet of Nationalities in the Supreme Soviet. Others are purely administrative divisions and lack such autonomy. In two large union republics, the RSFSR and Kazakhstan, there is an alternative regional unit called an "area," or *kray*. Altogether in 1977 there were 8 autonomous *oblasts*, 148 administrative *oblasts*, and 6 *krays*. Historically, many of the regional units have inherited some of the tasks of the czarist provinces, and in addition the various units provide graduated degrees of national autonomy for ethnic minorities on a manageable, territorial basis.

A fifth layer of government is formed by the district, or *rayon*. In 1977 about 2,900 of these were rural, including small towns; about 815 were urban; and about 760 were municipal subdivisions of large towns. The sixth and lowest tier comprises about 3,800 "settlements of an urban type" and about 41,000 rural soviets that correspond to rural villages (see Figure 11.3).

Each of these units down to the smallest village is entitled to elect a local council or soviet. Each soviet has a limited amount of legal authority (less impressive than it looks on paper, but nevertheless significant), and each also serves as an instrument for some local participation. Much of the work is delegated to the executive committee of each soviet and to a large number of local commissions; in the 1960s there were about 230,000 such commissions involving about 1.3 million Soviet deputies and another 2.3 million activists drawn from the people, and the figures have not substantially changed.

At all levels, deputies to the soviets are elected directly. However, the nomination of candidates at every level is closely controlled by the Communist Party, and there are no competing candidates. Even so, the elections and the work of the soviets serve to solidify the connections between the people and their government. They help the government to present its policies to the people; and, as in other countries, the experience of local government provides many opportunities for the training of local political talent and its recruitment for higher office. Unlike the process in many other countries, all this happens in the Soviet Union under the initiative and surveillance of the Communist Party.

The Party Pyramid. The Communist Party of the Soviet Union, in its organization and ideology, is itself one of the major political inventions of the twentieth century. As we saw earlier in the chapter, it grew out of a tightly knit body of professional revolutionists. These were organized into small conspiratorial groups that were well suited to escape the persecutions of the Okhrana, the czarist secret police. Each small group was so self-contained that its discovery by the police was unlikely to expose other groups. These groups—sometimes called *cells,* but now called *primary units*—were organized secretly where the people actually worked and lived. Most often they were formed in factories, offices, institutions, and towns or within military units or other mass organizations; sometimes they were organized in villages or urban neighborhoods. The extent to which the Party now penetrates the different Russian social and occupational groups is shown in Table 11.4.

Though no longer secret, primary units still exist largely in this compact form. Now, as in the past, every Communist Party member is expected to work actively under the control of the primary unit and to report his or her activities to it. This basic organizational design seeks to combine the personal commitment of each individual with the

FIGURE 11.3 *Administrative Structure of the Soviet Union*

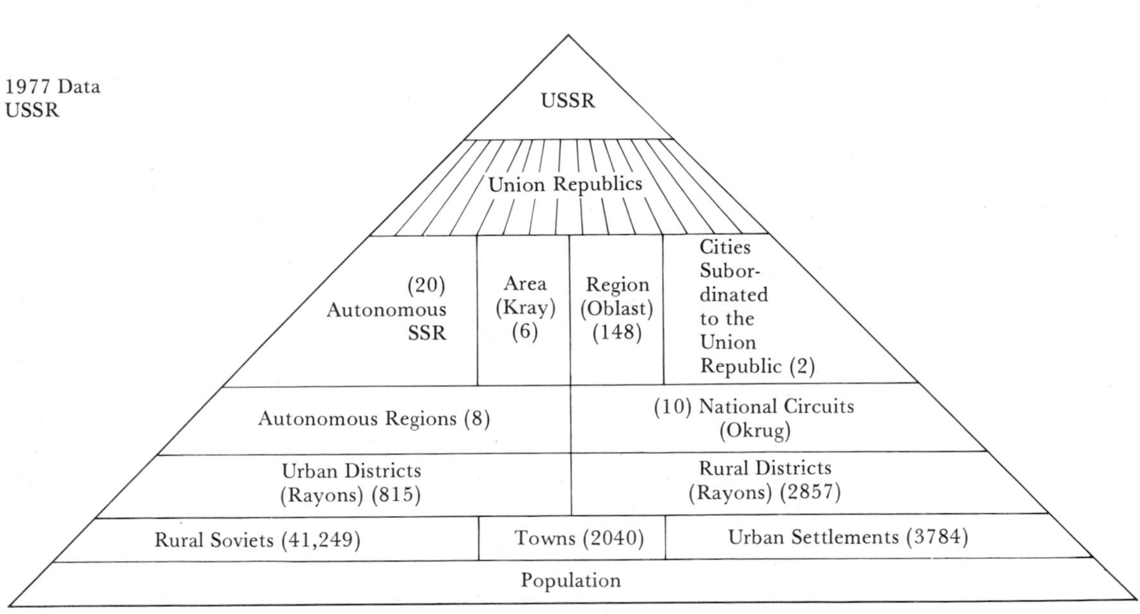

Sources: Adapted from *The Government and Politics of the Soviet Union,* Revised Edition, by Leonard Schapiro. Copyright © 1965, 1967 by Leonard Schapiro. Reprinted by permission of Random House, Inc. 1977 data from R. J. Mitchell, "Union of Soviet Socialist Republics," in R. Starr, ed., *Yearbook of International Communist Affairs* (Stanford, Calif: Hoover Institution Press, annual); "Union of Soviet Socialist Republics," in *Europe Yearbook* (London: Europa Publications), vol. 1; and J. Paxton, ed. *Statesman's Yearbook: 1978–79* (New York: St. Martin's Press, 1978).

TABLE 11.4 *Social Composition of the Communist Party of the Soviet Union, 1905–76*

	1905	1917	1920*	1932	1956	1961	1967	1971	1976
Workers	61.7%	60.2%	33.2%	64.5%	32.0%	34.5%	38.1%	40.1%	41.6%
Peasants	4.7	7.6	36.9	27.8	17.1	17.5	16.0	15.1	13.9
Intelligentsia	33.6	32.2	22.1	7.7	50.9	48.0	45.9	44.8	44.5
N =	8,400	23,600	612,000	3,172,215	7,173,521	9,176,005	12,684,133	14,455,321	15,638,891

*The 1920 column adds up to only 92.9 percent. In that year, the last of the civil war, a large number of individuals from other groups may still have been in the Red Army.

Source: V. Aspaturian, "The Soviet Union," in R. C. Macridis, ed., *Modern Political Systems: Europe,* 4th ed. (1978), p. 394, with reference to *Partiinaya Zhizn,* no. 7 (April 1967), pp. 7–8; *Pravda,* March 31, 1971; and *Partiinaya Zhizn,* no. 10 (May 1976), pp. 13–22. Adapted by permission of Prentice-Hall, Inc., Englewood Cliffs, N.J.

sustaining and motivating power of small groups in which members all know each other personally. A modern American psychiatrist, Stanley Elkes, has called the small group "the engine of society"; the Communist Party, by its design, seeks to harness this engine to its purposes.

Since Lenin's time the number of primary units has grown and so has Party membership—more than a hundredfold (see Figure 11.4). In 1976 there were about 15.7 million Party members in the Soviet Union—nearly 6 percent of the total population, or about 9 percent of those of voting age. Yet Party membership remains restrictive. Party members must first serve for a time as *candidates* under the supervision of a primary unit, and each candidate must be sponsored by three Party members for admission. Members are dropped for failing to pay dues for three consecutive months; they may be reprimanded or expelled for inactivity or deviation from Party policy. In 1951–56 an annual average of about 100,000 members were expelled; in the more permissive period of 1956–64 this dropped to about 50,000 or less than 0.5 percent of the total membership per year.

Communist Party members are closely supervised and are supposed to be unceasingly active—often at some cost to their families' and their own peace of mind.[7] They gain improved chances of promotion and careers and sometimes of power and prestige. Less tangibly, they may gain a sense of belonging to a "vocation of leadership," to a band of persons committed to a historic mission, which may give added meaning to their lives. Such commitment exacts a price. The more intensely members respond to motives of this latter kind, the more bitter will be their disputes in case of disagreement, and the more painful will it be for them to be reprimanded or expelled for disagreeing with the party line or to support it silently against their personal convictions.

The interplay of Party practices and individual motivations has produced a Party membership that is markedly more intellectual, or at least more oriented to white-collar work, more urban, better educated, more managerial, and more predominantly Russian than the general Soviet population (see Table 11.5).

[7]Some members, of course, join just to get a job and then only go through the motions needed to keep it.

Party members were organized in 1976 into almost 380,000 primary units, averaging roughly 41 members per unit. The primary units in each locality report to local Party committees, of which there were more than 28,000 in 1976, averaging 13 primary units per locality. Each local Party committee has its own secretary, who forms a part of the formal "apparatus" of the Communist Party of the Soviet Union. The primary units also report to and elect delegates to the *rayon,* city, and borough (city subdivision) Party conferences. In 1976 there were approximately 5,500 Party conferences at this level.

The next higher tier is formed by the regional Party organizations. These are Party conferences at the *kray, oblast,* and ethnic unit levels, which number less than 200. Each of these again is composed of elected delegates and has its own Party committee, bureau, and secretariat. The next level up consists of the Party organizations for each union republic and for the autonomous republics within the RSFSR.

FIGURE 11.4 *The Growth and Social Composition of the Communist Party, 1924–76*

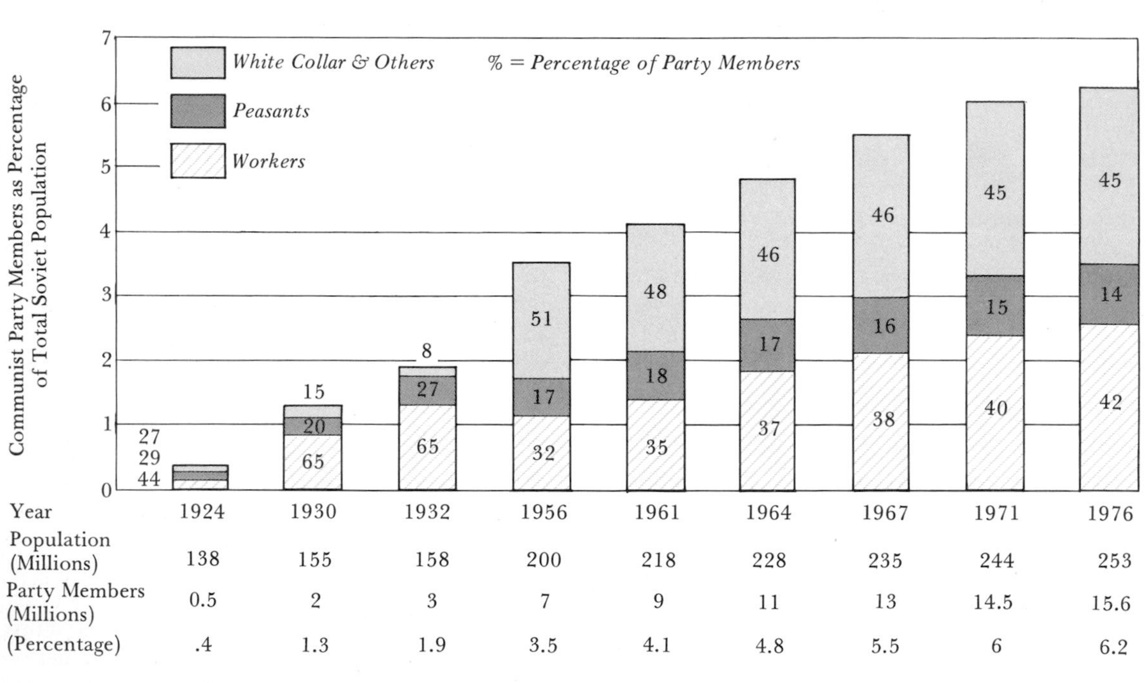

Year	1924	1930	1932	1956	1961	1964	1967	1971	1976
Population (Millions)	138	155	158	200	218	228	235	244	253
Party Members (Millions)	0.5	2	3	7	9	11	13	14.5	15.6
(Percentage)	.4	1.3	1.9	3.5	4.1	4.8	5.5	6	6.2

Sources: F. Lorimer, *The Population of the Soviet Union: History and Prospects* (Geneva: Economic, Financial, and Transit Department, League of Nations, 1946); United Nations, *Demographic Yearbook, 1966* and *1967*; T. H. Rigby, *Communist Party Membership in the U.S.S.R., 1917–1967* (Princeton: Princeton University Press, 1968); *Pravda,* March 31, 1971; *Partiinaya Zhizn,* no. 10 (May 1976). Note that in recent years the definition of "workers" has been expanded to include some clerical and service occupations.

TABLE 11.5 *The Communist Party and the Soviet People, 1932 and 1976 (in percentages)*

	Stalin Era, 1932			Brezhnev Era (1976 data)		
	Share in population A	Party members B	Overrepresentation or under-representation B/A	Share in population C	Party members D	Overrepresentation or under-representation D/C
Intelligentsia	4	8	2.0	27	45	1.7
Urban dwellers	n.a.	n.a.	n.a.	61	80	1.3
Russians	n.a.	n.a.	n.a.	52	61	1.2
Workers	14	64	4.5	51	42	0.8
Peasants	78	28	0.3	22	14	0.6
Women	52*	15†	0.3	54	24	0.4

*1939 data
†1937 data

Sources: V. Aspaturian, "The Soviet Union," in R. C. Macridis and R. E. Ward, eds., *Modern Political Systems: Europe,* 3rd ed. (1972). Adapted by permission of Prentice-Hall, Inc., Englewood Cliffs, N.J. *The USSR in Figures for 1975* (Statiskika Publishers, USSR 1976). This latter source includes some 1976 figures.

At the top of the pyramid is the single *All-Union Party Congress* with its Central Committee, its *Politburo* of thirteen full and eight candidate members, and its *Secretariat.* The latter is headed by the *general secretary of the Communist Party* of the Soviet Union, who by virtue of this position sits atop the pyramid and is one of the most powerful individuals in the country (see Figure 11.5).

In theory the constituent body of Party members or Party organizations—the primary units, Party conferences, and Party congresses, respectively—should each be the highest authority at its level. Though these bodies meet only rarely, they create Party committees and central committees at each level to act for them as governing bodies between sessions. These committees meet more frequently and, in turn, elect the bureaus or presidia to act for them between their sessions. Together, the committees and bureaus at each level supervise the secretariat. At the same time, the committees and bureaus are responsible to the Party conference or congress at the next higher level, and each Party secretary or secretariat is responsible to the next higher secretariat.

In theory, too, this design is meant to balance a democratic control from below by Party members and their elected delegates with centralized supervision and direction from above in a pattern called *democratic centralism* (see Figure 11.6). This pattern supposedly permits Party members to discuss political issues freely—though usually within the Party—before a Party decision is reached, but

FIGURE 11.6 *Organizational Structure of the Communist Party, 1976*

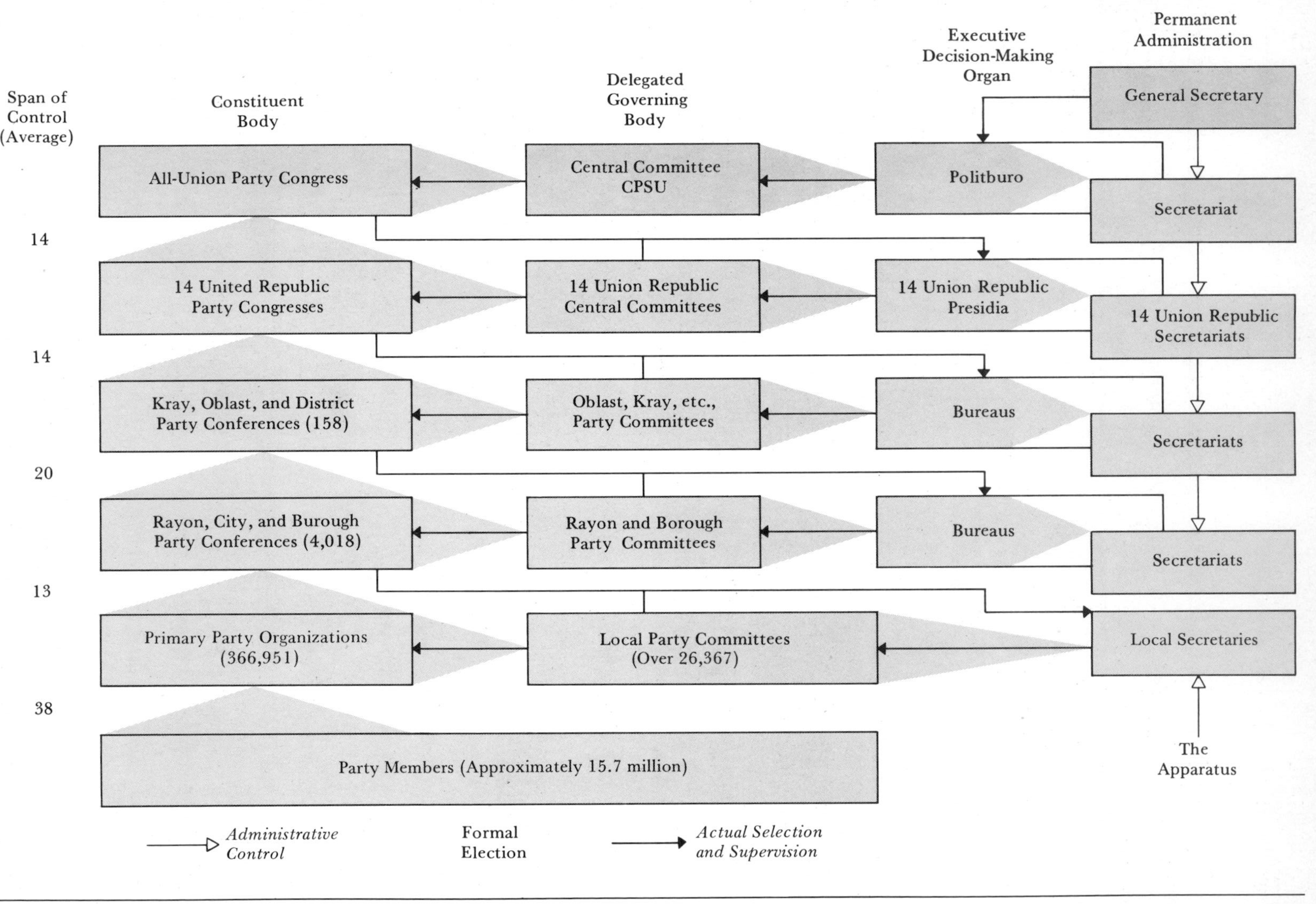

Sources: V. Aspaturian, "The Soviet Union," in R. C. Macridis, ed., *Modern Political Systems: Europe*, 4th ed., (1978). Adapted by permission of Prentice–Hall, Inc. Englewood Cliffs, N.J. Also from data supplied by Mickiewicz, *Handbook of Soviet Social Science Data.*

FIGURE 11.5 *The Central Organs of the Communist Party, 1977*

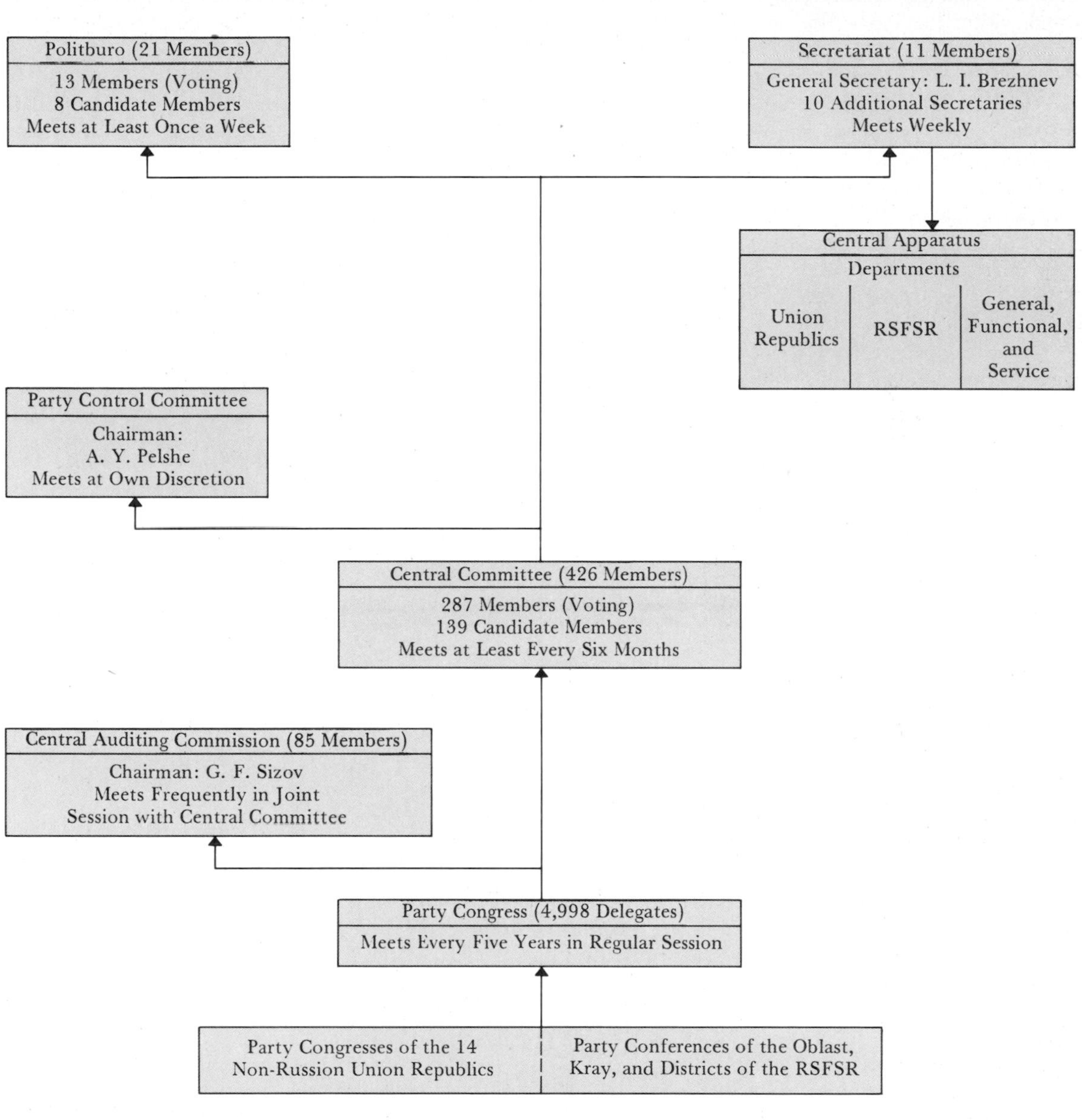

Sources: V. Aspaturian, "The Soviet Union," in R. C. Macridis ed., *Modern Political Systems: Europe*, 4th ed., (1978). Adapted by permission of Prentice-Hall, Englewood Cliffs, N.J. Also from data from the Russian Research Center, Harvard University, 1978.

obliges them to execute and defend both outside and within the Party any decision that has been reached, even if they had opposed it earlier. Moreover, no Communist may deviate from a decision once made or from the *party line* once laid down, nor—since the Tenth Party Congress in 1920—may a member reopen an issue for reconsideration. Finally, neither before nor after a decision may Communists organize in separate groups or factions to promote their views within the Party. These last two provisions may have been meant as emergency measures in 1921, but they still remain in force.

Practice differs from theory, however. Party secretaries alone are full-time Party officials. Their influence prevails in the bureaus, whose other members have other responsibilities and cannot devote their full energies to bureau work. The secretaries also prevail in committees and the constituent bodies, which meet only infrequently. In theory the members of the constituent body elect the members of the committees and the committees elect the members of the bureaus. But in practice the secretaries pick the candidates who are then duly elected to these bodies. Party secretaries are not elected, but are chosen by the next higher secretary; this is the hierarchy to which they tend to look for guidance and instruction, which they then transmit to their own committees. As permanent links between higher and lower organizations, the secretaries form a chain of power that in effect controls the Party.[8] An old Soviet joke distinguishes three epochs of human history: the matriarchate, the patriarchate, and the secretariat. Since the days of Stalin, the dictatorship of the proletariat has turned, in many ways, into the dictatorship of the secretariat.

But despite its bureaucratization the Communist Party continues to be the heart and soul of the Soviet system. The Party is the chief source of legitimacy. It is the chief formulator of political and social goals and of the policies by which they are to be pursued. In all these ways it is the Communist Party that makes the Soviet system work. In the Soviet Union, as in all countries, the bureaucrats, the police, and the military apply power in the execution of policy, but in no country have they shown themselves capable of formulating policy over long periods of time. They cannot create fundamental goals. In non-Communist countries, such as the United States, they depend on interest groups and on competing political parties to set these goals, whereas in the Soviet Union they depend to a crucial degree on the Communist Party alone. Not surprisingly, in every major clash between military leaders, police chiefs, or state bureaucrats, on the one hand, and Party secretaries, on the other hand, the Party secretaries thus far have always won.

Party and State: The Interlocking Pyramids. The Communist Party penetrates the government at every level (see Figure 11.7). The government in turn runs the economy, of which nearly 90 percent is government-owned and much of the rest is owned by cooperatives. The government also runs the armed forces and police, as well as the educational system, the mass media, and almost all means of support for artistic and literary life. These enormous powers of the government enhance the power of the Communist Party and, particularly, the power of the Party leaders over their own members as well as over the rest of the people; this, in turn, enhances the Party's control of the state.

At the top the All-Union Party Secretariat and the Politburo interlock closely not only with each other, but also with the Presidum of the Supreme Soviet and the Presidium of the Council of Ministers. In 1979, Leonid Brezhnev, the general secretary of the Communist Party, was also a member of its Politburo and chairman of the Presidium of the Supreme Soviet. The chairman of the Presidium of the Council of Ministers, Aleksei Kosygin, was also a Politburo member. Sometimes the names of the incumbents change (though no faster than in

[8]See Aspaturian, "The Soviet Union."

FIGURE 11.7 *Interlocking Party and State Structures in the Soviet Union*

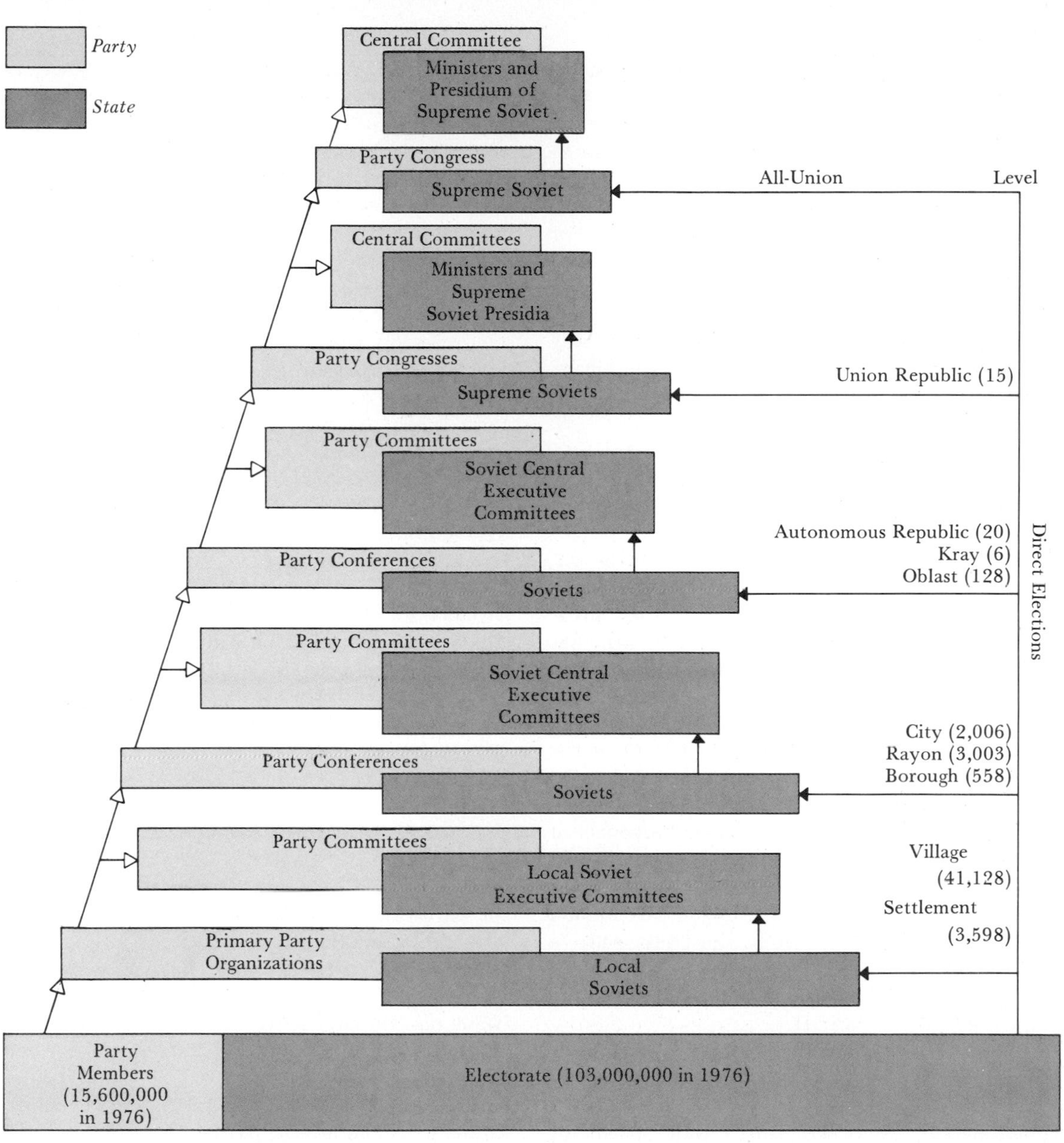

Source: V. Aspaturian, "The Soviet Union," in R. C. Macridis, ed., *Modern Political Systems: Europe*, 4th ed., (1978). Adapted by permission of Prentice–Hall, Inc., Englewood Cliffs, N.J.

the United States), but the tight interlock among Party and government jobs persists.

Something similar holds true down the line. At the all-union level, the Party Congress interlocks with the Supreme Soviet. In the union republics the central committees of the Party interlock with the ministers and presidia of the supreme soviet of each union republic, and the party congresses interlock with the supreme soviets. There are similar interlockings at all lower levels—from the autonomous republics, *krays*, and *oblasts* all the way down to the primary Party units and the village soviets (see Figure 11.8).

THE PERFORMANCE OF THE SOVIET UNION

After the preceding discussion, it should be unnecessary to summarize the performance of the political system of the Soviet Union in any great detail. On the positive side, the Soviet regime has done things that had been thought impossible. Within forty years it transformed a less-developed country into a highly developed one, despite the intervening devastations of World War II. It has demonstrated that a highly developed industrial economy can be run by a decision system of politics and planning without any major influence of private enterprise or a Western-style market system. It has transformed the educational and cultural levels of what now are over 261 million people. And it has done all this with a considerable—though not complete—amount of social solidarity and popular support, tested in the crucible of World War II.

On the negative side, the persistence of dictatorship or government-decreed uniformity in many fields of opinion, culture, and expression are manifest for all to see. But a wide variety of communications and of new recombinations of information are not just a luxury or a consumer good. Like freedom, they are in the long run conditions for the production of new knowledge. Consequently, after more than a half-century of existence the Soviet Union still must import—mainly from capitalist countries—much more knowledge in science, technology, styling, and design, as well as in culture, films, and other arts, than it creates and exports to the outside world.

Finally, the Soviet system has paid for its achievements with vast human costs. The memory of the terror of the Stalin years remains to testify to its vulnerability to many degrees of potential deformation and distortion away from its own goals and standards. In the past this deformation was brought about by the behavior of some of its own rulers; the Soviet system then had no adequate counterweights or correctives against this trend; and it is not clear to what extent, if any, it is now better protected against a possible repetition of the domestic crimes and tragedies of the Stalin era at some future time.

Perhaps more important than striking an exact balance for the past is assessing the prospects of the Soviet system for the future. Here we turn to its unfinished business: its unresolved problems and its potentialities for future growth, self-transformation, and preservation of identity.

SOME UNRESOLVED POLITICAL PROBLEMS

To the Soviet Communist leaders the interlocking of party and state has been a great source of strength within their own country. In international politics, however, the close linkage between a supposedly internationalist party and a national state has threatened to create almost as many liabilities as assets.

International Polycentrism. In the international arena of Communist parties and regimes the Russians now face a continuing problem of pluralism, or *polycentrism,* as it is called by writers on the Communist world. The Russians no longer form the only Communist country. There are now sixteen of them, and the big ones like China cannot be dictated to. Indeed, neither can some of

FIGURE 11.8 *Interlocking Government and Party Institutions and Personnel, 1978*

Mass Organizations	First Party Secretaries of Republics and Local Organs	Premiers of Republics	Presidium of the Supreme Soviet	Council of Ministers	Communist Party Politburo	Communist Party Secretariat
			Brezhnev (Chairman)		Brezhnev	Brezhnev (General Secretary)
				Kosygin (Chairman)	Kosygin	
					Suslov	Suslov
					Kirilenko	Kirilenko
					Chernenko	Chernenko
				Gromyko (Foreign Affairs)	Gromyko	
				Ustinov (Defense)	Ustinov	Ustinov
Shibayev (Trade Unions)			Shibayev			
				Andropov (State Security)	Andropov	
					Pelshe*	
	Romanov (Leningrad)				Romanov	
	Grishin (Moscow)				Grishin	
	Kunayev (Kazakh)				Kunayev	
	Shcherbitsky (Ukraine)				Shcherbitsky	
	Rashidov (Uzbek)		Rashidov		Rashidov	
				Demichev (Culture)	Demichev	
		Solomentsev (RSFSR)			Solomentsev	
	Masherov (Byelorussia)		Masherov		Masherov	
					Ponomarev	Ponomarev
	Aliyev (Azerbaidzhan)				Aliyev	Aliyev
			Kuznetsov (First Deputy)		Kuznetsov	
						Kapitonov
						Dolgikh
						Ryabov
						Zimyanin
						Rusakov
				Tikhonov (First Deputy)	Tikhonov	
	Shevardnadze (Georgia)				Shevardnadze	
						Gorbachev

Note: Those Party leaders who hold important positions in the all-union government, in mass organizations, or in the union republics are indicated by shaded backgrounds.

*Chairman, Party Central Commission

Sources: V. Aspaturian, "The Soviet Union," in R. C. Macridis and R. E. Ward, eds., *Modern Political Systems: Europe*, 3rd ed., 1972, adapted by permission of Prentice-Hall, Inc., Englewood Cliffs, N.J.; Russian Research Center, Harvard University, 1978; *Current Digest of the Soviet Press*, vol. 28, no. 14 (May 5, 1976), and vol. 29, no. 21 (June 22, 1977); *New York Times*, November 28, 1978, p. 2.

the smaller ones, like Yugoslavia, Cuba, Albania, North Korea or Vietnam. Nor do French or Italian Communists always follow Russian policies, as they did in earlier days. In Czechoslovakia in 1968 the will of the Russian Communist leadership could be made to prevail over that of the Czech and Slovak Communists only by the physical invasion of the country by Soviet and Soviet-bloc troops. Overall, then, the Russian Communist government has lost absolute control of the international Communist world.

Though less powerful outside their country than formerly, the Soviet leaders have not become much more tolerant.[9] There is growing national diversity in the Communist world. Yet inside each country Communists tend to claim that they are infallible and that anybody who is not with them is against them. When two Communist regimes differ in opinion, their discussion resembles that of two medieval would-be popes. It is a discussion between two sides in which both insist on being right. For the last five hundred years the Catholic church has been most careful to avoid schismatic elections. Communism, on the other hand, has built-in schisms. Although these schisms have become increasingly evident, the Communists have not yet discovered that tolerance is not a luxury, but a necessity.

A Gap in Communist Ideology. Another unresolved problem faced by all Communist countries involves the question of the property of nations. Communists agree that, in regard to means of production, individuals may not retain private property against the claims of the nation-state. But they are not clear whether a nation-state may legitimately retain the capital and land within its borders as its collective quasi-private property against the claims of poorer nations or of any international community. Most Communists have not thought through the question of whether a Communist state owns property collectively and has the right to deny its use to poorer Communist nations. If the Russians own some empty real estate in Siberia and the Chinese are overcrowded in China, is the Russian government right in closing off all its land as its own property, or is the Chinese government correct in thinking that this is a bourgeois way of behaving? The quarrels between the haves and have-nots of the Communist world pose at least as serious a problem as whether the rich free-world countries owe anything to the poor free-world countries. There is a difference, however. In the free world, people occasionally try to see the other person's point of view. In the Communist world, disagreement itself often is considered a deviation.

The Soviet Military-Industrial Complex. The Soviet Union shares another problem with the Western world. It, too, probably has a *military-industrial complex* of its own. A Red Army officer or an admiral, as a professional soldier or sailor, is as keen on getting the best modern hardware in the largest possible amounts as is any professional military or naval officer anywhere. This individual will probably be as skillful in lobbying and forging connections to the political decision system as any general anywhere in the world.

But the Soviet system is not a monolith. Within the limitations set by the political system, groups vie for influence and power and their share of the nation's resources. A manager of a heavy industrial plant may want priorities in investment money for factories, yet there is sure to be a department store manager clamoring for more consumer goods. In other words, there is a political process in the Soviet Union behind the facade of unanimity and common will—hidden, but real.

Where will this political process lead? Will escalation in the conflict between East and West make Russian society more and more rigid, its military-industrial sectors more powerful, its ideology more intolerant, and intra-Communist

[9]For the limited increases in diversity permitted among Soviet-bloc countries, see *New York Times,* May 14–16, 1979.

quarrels—as well as quarrels between Communists and non-Communists—more tense and more likely to lead toward war? Or will a de-escalation of international tensions necessarily lead toward more discovery, more experimentation, and more freedom in the Soviet Union? Whether world affairs grow more tense or more relaxed depends on the actions of the West as well as those of the Eastern European powers. But what will happen within the Soviet Union will hinge on the flexibility of the Soviet system, on its ability to accept criticism and change.

The Limited Responsiveness to Criticism. Often one hears this question: "How do individuals or small groups make their views felt in the Soviet system?" To find the answer, one must distinguish the channels provided by official theory and doctrine from the way things actually work.

A look at Soviet ideology shows important differences from the ideas underlying the defunct dictatorships of Nazi Germany and Fascist Italy. The word *totalitarian,* applied to all three of these regimes, stresses only what they have in common (single-party control, concentration of leadership, and mobilization of all efforts of the population toward a single goal, with no tolerance for opposition). But it is seriously misleading, because it fails to show their differences in goals (forced-speed economic growth in the Soviet Union versus military conquest for the Fascists and Nazis) as well as in some of their methods. The Nazi and Fascist regimes were based on the *leadership principle:* authority flowed only from the top down. The leaders were supposed to be always right and did all the talking; the people only had to listen and, as Mussolini put it, to "believe, obey and fight." In Soviet ideology, greater stress is put on flexibility, tactical retreats, self-correction of mistakes, collective authority, and listening to the people. Soviet tradition pictures Lenin not only addressing revolutionary crowds from the top of an armored car, but also patiently sitting down for hours and listening to peasants. In practice, however, Soviet listening has been highly selective.

In theory, there are at least four channels through which individuals can make their views felt. First, they can write letters to the press, and the Soviet press has been quite diligent in printing such letters; however, in practice, these letters are screened. The decision to print the letter is itself treated as a political decision. A letter that is compatible with current policy or that offers only minor modifications has a fair chance of being printed. A letter that says "Reverse basic policy" does not.

A similar channel is what used to be called *Bolshevist self-criticism.* Such criticism is encouraged and permitted by doctrine; the people at small Party unit meetings and larger meetings are supposed to speak up and criticize the practices of their own unit, their own group, the management of their factory, the local government of their village or town, or the way their collective farm is being managed. They may criticize themselves, the local Party secretaries, and others. In practice, such criticism is used to prepare and mobilize opinion for changes in policy, to loosen bureaucratic rigidity, and to provide a safety valve for accumulated tensions. In general, however, criticism suggesting how basic policy can be better carried through is more acceptable than criticism attacking basic policy.

The Soviet Union is run to this day by people who think in the style of emergency politics, the style in which its political system was founded. They will not permit opposition to basic policies that, rightly or wrongly, they consider necessary. As a result, criticism is muzzled and limited to details of policy, to personalities, and to methods of carrying out programs. Sometimes initiatives from below are encouraged, but only if they fit into the general plan. Thus, an initiative movement among central Asian farmers to dig more irrigation canals was picked up by the mass media and greatly amplified, increased, and backed. Similarly, in the 1930s the Stakhanovite movement of people who proposed improvements in production was widely publicized. This is somewhat like the kind of freedom of speech that employees have when they are permitted to drop suggestions to management into specially designated suggestion boxes. Bolshevist self-criticism is a relatively limited kind of freedom, to put it mildly.

A third channel is the particular units of the Party in which candidates are picked. For a time after Stalin's death there was talk of permitting more candidates to run than there were offices so that the voters would have some degree of selection. Yet this latitude has in fact been limited to some trade union elections and does not seem to have been applied in elections to the soviets or to Party posts. The right to nominate has not been given to the people, and there is no right to organize interest groups, factions, or opinion groups within the ruling Communist Party. Nor is there any other party that has the right to contest an election. To some extent, then, a major link of control of the society inheres in the control over the nomination process and the control of personnel policy, or *cadre policy,* as the Communists call it—that is, in deciding who gets promoted, appointed, or moved around. Here, too, there is only a very limited degree of freedom for the individual.

Poetry and literature provide a fourth, although indirect, channel. Because free political discussion is not possible and a free political vote does not exist, some of the people's desire to express their views has shown up in aesthetic judgment. If it is not permissible to say that the policy of the Party secretary is stupid, it is permissible to say that an officially approved play praising that policy is boring. Similarly, it is possible to find that certain poetry is beautiful and exciting even if it happens to stress emotions not completely accepted in the Party program. The Russian poet Yevgeny Yevtushenko pointed out that in the Russian language the words for "poet" and "fighter" are phonetically very similar; from this notion he developed the idea that it was the task of poets and writers in Russia to take upon themselves the role of fighting for a better expression of popular moods.

In the early 1960s thousands of people would gather at street corners to attend a recital of poetry. Part of the explanation is that Russians like poetry. But part of it also is that poetry has become a substitute for other forms of expression that are banned. A similar attitude exists toward movies and plays. Again, there is political control, but when the party line changes or weakens or when there is a period of freer discussion, a good deal of material gets through that otherwise would be prohibited. For example, in the mid-1950s the Russian film entitled *The Rumyantsev Case* showed a truck driver whose load of textiles was highjacked, thereby conceding that there are highjackers and robbers in the Soviet Union after forty years of Soviet government. Railroaded by the police through a trial, the man is promptly clapped into jail, whereupon his fellow workers in the factory hold a meeting, march on the police station, and protest against what has happened to their comrade. This was a film made at the height of the *de-Stalinization* campaign. This is the kind of loosening up that sometimes occurs, but since 1965, and still more since the intervention in Czechoslovakia in 1968, Soviet cultural policy has again become more oppressive. A nationwide exhibition at Moscow of young Soviet painters in the fall of 1972 showed less of the varieties of art than the uniformity of bureaucracy; these young painters had aged before their time. In 1978, harsh sentences against dissidents in the Soviet Union once again aroused worldwide attention. No one can tell how long this stifling climate in many sectors of Soviet life will continue.

Yet the real picture is more complex. There is a fifth channel toward greater autonomy and variety in present-day Soviet culture. This is the rediscovery of the works of the longer historic past and the increase in direct access to them. The great writers of the world and of Russia are being published and read again—not only Leo Tolstoy and Maxim Gorki, but also Fyodor Dostoyevsky and Anna Akhmatova, of whose political views the Bolsheviks had not approved. Similarly published and read in translation are such writers as Shakespeare, Dickens, Hemingway, and many others. Each of these writers conveys to his or her readers a world of images, ideas, human characters, feelings, and actions far richer than any single group of ideologists or censors could control. Many Russian high school graduates have a more thorough grounding in this wider literary tradition than have some of their counterparts in the United States; and with this knowledge they have major potential resources for independent thought.

A similar process is occurring in the world of art. Many Russians in the 1970s were engaged in the rediscovery of the great artistic and architectural traditions of their country. They can be seen standing in long lines in the Kremlin to view the beautiful sixteenth-century images of saints, called *ikons,* by such great masters as Andrei Ryublev, or to tour the eighteenth-century palaces of the czars at Peterhof and Pavlovsk near Leningrad, destroyed by the Nazis in World War II and now restored again by the painstaking efforts of Soviet scholars and craftspeople (whose pictures sometimes are on exhibit next to explanations of their difficult labors).

These are not trivial matters. After decades of effort and struggle, large numbers of Soviet citizens are discovering beauty; and with it they discover a deeper pride in the achievements and capabilities of their peoples, even decades and centuries before the revolution. Clearly, this revolution and its results are here to stay. But like every great revolution, it must reach a stage at which it will reincorporate the longer past of its country and its people, giving them added resources for richer and more varied responses to the problems of the future. Some time after the French Revolution, the French became proud of the royal palace at Versailles and of the castles of the nobles in the valley of the Loire River, without having to remind themselves constantly that the kings and the nobles had been oppressors of the people. Russia, it seems, is now approaching this stage. The old social order will not come back, even though a gifted writer in exile like Alexander Solzhenitsyn remembers it with nostalgia; but its heritage of artistic and literary achievement is now being shared more widely and deeply than before.

There is one other element that may make for more independent thoughts and feelings: the universal experience of the tragedies and sufferings of World War II, together with the profound desire for peace that is found on all levels of the society. In the Piskarevsky cemetery at Leningrad, which President Nixon visited in 1972, lie nearly half a million Leningraders, victims of bombardment and starvation during Hitler's siege of the city in World War II. "We cannot list your names here," says the inscription on a granite slab, "but nobody is forgotten and nothing is forgotten." It goes on to recall their proud saying during the great siege: "Let death become afraid of us, rather than that we should be afraid of death." But the cost is fully remembered. There is the scrawled diary of a small girl, Tanya, who recorded the deaths by illness and starvation of every member of her family during the siege, ending with the entry "Now I am all alone"—written just before her own death. Today the cemetery has become a place of commemoration to the people of the city and the nation. Crowds come out to visit it; brides on their wedding day lay their bouquets on the graves.

Soft background music is broadcast over loudspeakers throughout the cemetery grounds. On the day that I was there, it was the second movement of Beethoven's Seventh Symphony. The victims of a German war were being remembered with the music of a German master. This is a people who will not start war lightly, nor will they encourage any leaders to take them into war.

SOME RESOURCES FOR CHANGE

In Czechoslovakia in 1968, Communist Party members in relatively high standing argued that intraparty factions should be legalized, discussions should be free, and groups defeated in one Party congress should have the right to ask for a reopening of the issue at the next Party congress. (Of course, they argued, such groups would have to offer new information or new experiences relevant to the issue and have majority support for getting it back onto the agenda.) After the Russian tanks rolled into Prague in the summer of 1968, these proposals were silenced and some of those who had made them, or supported them, were demoted.

Nevertheless, the Czech experience shows that such lines of thought can arise under the crust of a totalitarian system and that nothing but a foreign occupation may be able to stop them—at least for a time. Hannah Arendt's theory of totalitarianism argued in the early 1950s that Communist dictatorship was like death: permanent and irreversible. Her view of this matter has been proved false. Politics, human beings, aspirations, and efforts at self-expression all exist even under Communist dictatorship. Thus, there is a degree of uncertainty and potential openness about the future even in Communist-ruled countries. Just the same, residents of the Soviet Union cannot expect many opportunities for individual political self-expression, and they must be circumspect indeed in the ways in which they try to make their views heard.

Yet, as far as anyone can judge, the bulk of the Soviet people continues to be loyal to a collectivistic economy. There is no mass support of any kind for giving the country back either to the czar or to the private corporations. People have grown used to the way that basic industries are being developed, and they seem to like it. Despite the devastations of World War II they have seen the steel output of their country rise from less than 10 percent after World War I to more than 100 percent of that produced in the United States today. An economic system that in peacetime doubles industrial output every twelve years or so they reason, cannot be all bad. At such rates of growth, sooner or later some appreciable improvements will trickle down to the consumers, first in the cities and eventually in the countryside. This has already happened in the fields of basic nutrition and public health. By lengthening life expectancies and lowering infant death rates, the Soviet Union has now reached the level of the United States. In the meantime, many of the young people continue to find careers in the expanding industrial and technological sectors of their society. Still larger numbers can derive a sense of pride from the visible accomplishments of their country, ranging from the spectacular growth of its cities (see Figure 11.9) to its continuing share in the exploration of the moon and the planets.

The very successes of Soviet industrialization in the past are now creating new kinds of problems for the future. As consumers become more affluent, they will insist on a wider range of choice. They will demand a better combination of planning and a market in which choices can be made.

Other problems will arise on the production side, through the growing need for innovation. Until recently, the Soviets could apply inventions and innovations developed and tested abroad at the expense of other countries. Henceforth they will need not only to apply new inventions and innovations, but also to produce them by their own efforts. However, bureaucracy, dictatorship, and rigid official ideology are not conducive to the creation of new knowledge that fosters invention or to the repeated breaking of old habits that is essential to innovation. In many ways the Soviet Union and its people were more inventive and innovative between 1917 and the mid-1930s than they have been since. Some of this intellectual slowdown may be attributable to the effects of Stalin's purges, but it has long survived his death. To an increasing extent, bureaucracy, conformity, and dictatorship are hampering the future economic, scientific, and technological development of the country. They do not impede the production of more pig iron, but they will curtail the introduction of new ideas and practices. Soviet leaders now speak of the new *scientific-technical revolution*—that is, the transformation of economic life through the development and large-scale application of new methods of science and technology—that their country must undergo in

FIGURE 11.9 *Urban Growth in the Soviet Union, 1920–76*

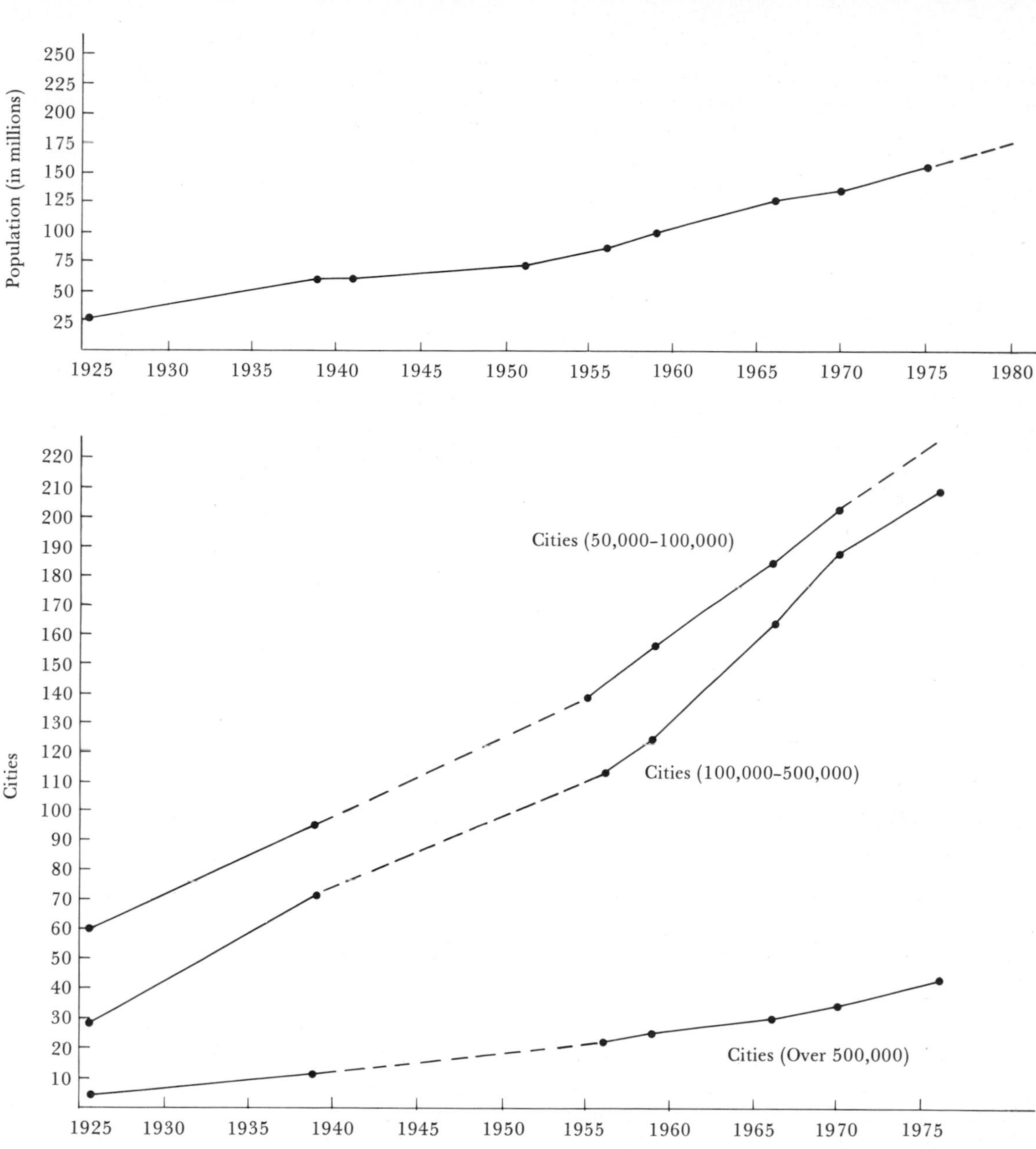

Sources: V. Aspaturian, "The Soviet Union," in R. C. Macridis, ed., *Modern Political Systems: Europe*, 4th ed. (1978), adapted by permission from Prentice-Hall, Inc., Englewood Cliffs, N.J.; and *United Nations Demographic Yearbook, 1976.*

order to cope with its vast future economic tasks. But without more room for experiment, criticism, nonconformity, innovation, and freedom it seems unlikely that this new peaceful revolution will be able to develop its full potential. Eminent Soviet scientists like Peter Kapitsa and Andrei D. Sakharov have repeatedly pointed to these problems.

Similar problems are arising in the work force, in human relations, and in Soviet culture. One cannot tell people for thirty years to admire only one officially approved style in painting and poetry and also expect them to remain resourceful and eager for change in industry and science. There will be other ideological difficulties. The ideological image of the Soviet Union as a country of workers is clashing increasingly with the fact that its proportion of manual workers in the work force is becoming constant and seems destined to decline. As in all industrial countries, manual labor in the Soviet Union is being replaced by automation, and the clerical and professional occupations—the so-called white-collar personnel—are expanding, taking in perhaps another 5 percent of the work force every decade. These groups are peripheral in Marxist theory and Soviet ideology, but they are becoming central in Soviet life.

Industrialization requires mass education as well as a large expansion of higher education. The success of the Soviet government in promoting both will eventually create another set of political problems. A good deal of research shows that, in general, people with little education prefer to be told only one side of a problem. When presented with two conflicting views, they tend to become confused and angry. This fact has contributed to the observed tendency toward an "authoritarianism of the poor" in many countries. It has also contributed to the success of the one-sided indoctrination methods of the Soviet government during the decades when a large part of its people were illiterate or had only a primary school education. Now the Soviet people are becoming a nation of high school or college graduates, particularly in the younger generation. Such better-educated people tend in most countries to feel angry and insulted when presented only one side of an issue. They want to hear all sides and make their own decisions. In the years to come, a growing proportion of the Soviet people may press for far-reaching changes in the cultural and information policies of their government.

The change in generations may well bring these pressures to a head in the 1980s. Many people form their basic political ideas around the age of twenty—more broadly, between fifteen and twenty-five—but these people tend to attain most power around the age of fifty-five, when they become heads of departments or organizations. The present Soviet leaders, now in their late fifties, formed their political ideas in the 1930s at the height of Stalin's purges, but also at the time of the successes of his economic development and military preparedness policies. The Soviet leaders of the 1980s will be of the generation of the poet Yevtushenko, who was born in 1933. They will have been in their early twenties when de-Stalinization was at its height and Stalin's crimes were revealed to the Soviet people. When this generation comes into control, it may be more willing to cooperate with popular demands for change and liberalization.

The path to liberalization will not be straight, easy, or certain. Periods of greater permissiveness will alternate with seasons of increased repression. But life, group experiences and interests, human spontaneity, and the political process will go on beneath the surface. As the Soviet people become more prosperous and confident, their needs and views will make themselves felt at unexpected points in the system.

All these considerations suggest that the Soviet Union will need, first, leaders who will seek to improve their own society and government. Beyond that, they will have to improve their ability to accept other nations—both Communist and non-Communist—as neighbors deserving genuine cooperation and equality. The Soviet Union will have

less need for missionaries to press or persuade other nations to copy current Soviet policies and institutions. To be able to say that a few more nations have adopted some type of Communist government might be a convenience for the Soviet rulers of the 1970s and 1980s, but to develop their own society, and to improve it thoroughly, will be a necessity.

KEY TERMS AND CONCEPTS

multilingual
idealism
materialism
socialism
economy of scarcity
meritocracy
dissidents
samizdat
uneven development
bourgeois revolution
"weakest link" theory
world revolution
socialism in one country
peasant-worker alliances
vanguard versus elite
distrust of spontaneity
professional revolutionist
Bolsheviks
Mensheviks
collective farms
decisive sectors
disproportions in investment
increasing returns to scale
diminishing returns
incentive goods
equalitarianism
performance payments;
motivation
government by pyramid
Supreme Soviet
Soviet of the Union
Soviet of Nationalities
Presidium of the Supreme Soviet (PSS)
Council of Ministers
Presidium of the Council of Ministers (PCM)
chairman of the PCM
union republic
autonomous soviet socialist republic
oblast
kray
rayon
Party cells (primary units)
Party candidate
All-Union Party Congress
Politburo
secretariat
general secretary of the Communist Party
democratic centralism
party line
polycentrism
military-industrial complex
totalitarian
leadership principle
Bolshevist self-criticism
cadre policy
de-Stalinization
scientific-technical revolution

ADDITIONAL READINGS

Alliluyeva, S. *Twenty Letters to a Friend.* Trans. P. McMillan. New York: Harper & Row, 1967. PB

Aspaturian, V. "The Soviet Union." In R. C. Macridis, ed., *Modern Political Systems: Europe.* 4th ed. Englewood Cliffs, N.J.: Prentice-Hall, 1978.

Brzezinski, Z. *The Soviet Bloc.* Rev. ed. Cambridge: Harvard University Press, 1967. PB

———, and S. P. Huntington. *Political Power: USA/USSR.* New York: Penguin Books, 1977. PB

Fainsod, M. *How Russia Is Ruled.* Rev. ed. Cambridge: Harvard University Press, 1963.

Fleron, F. J., ed. *Communist Studies and the Social Sciences.* Chicago: Rand McNally, 1969. PB

Friedrich, C. J., ed. *Totalitarianism.* 2nd ed. New York: Grosset and Dunlap, 1964. PB

Hough, J. *Soviet Prefects: The Local Party Organs in Industrial Decision-Making.* Cambridge: Harvard University Press, 1969.

———. *The Soviet Union and Social Science Theory.* Cambridge: Harvard University Press, 1977.

Inkeles, A. *Social Change in Soviet Russia.* Cambridge: Harvard University Press, 1968.

———, and R. Bauer. *Soviet Citizen: Daily Life in a Totalitarian Society.* New York: Atheneum, 1968. PB

Kassof, A., ed. *Prospects for Soviet Society.* New York: Praeger, 1968. PB

Lenin, V. I. *State and Revolution.* San Francisco: China Books, 1965. PB

Lipset, S. M., and R. B. Dobson. "Social Stratification and Sociology in the Soviet Union." *Survey,* no. 388 (Summer 1973).

Medvedev, R. *Let History Judge.* New York: Random House, 1973. PB

Mickiewicz, E. *Handbook of Soviet Social Science Data.* New York: Free Press, 1973.

Reed, J. *Ten Days that Shook the World.* New York: International Publishing Company, 1967. PB

Sakharov, A. D. *Progress, Coexistence and Intellectual Freedom.* Trans. The New York Times. New York: Norton, 1968.

Schapiro, L. *The Government and Politics of the Soviet Union.* Rev. ed. New York: Vintage Books, 1978. PB

Solzhenitsyn, A. *One Day in the Life of Ivan Denisovich.* Trans. M. Hayward and R. Hingley. New York: Praeger, 1963. PB

Ulam, A. *The Rivals: America and Russia Since World War II.* New York: Penguin Books, 1972. PB

———. *The Unfinished Revolution.* New York: Random House, 1960. PB

Yevtushenko, Y. *Bratsk Station and Other New Poems.* Garden City, N.Y.: Doubleday Anchor, 1967. PB

———. *A Precocious Autobiography.* Trans. A. R. MacAndrew. New York: Dutton, 1962. PB

PB = *available in paperback*

XII

The United Kingdom

Some years ago, a popular book by a Frenchman bore the title *The English—Are They Human?* Many foreign observers long have wondered just what the English—and, since the eighteenth century, the British—people are like. Some, like Hitler's air force in World War II, found out the hard way. Now once again, when Britain has entered the European Common Market and is coping with the different and new world of the 1980s, people are asking this question: what makes the people of England—and of Britain—act in politics the way they do?

THE BACKGROUND OF BRITISH POLITICS AND THE CONTINUING DEVELOPMENT OF POLITICAL INSTITUTIONS

Two conditions, perhaps more than any others, have long influenced English politics and the behavior of the English people. These two major influences are their class structure and their history. Class distinctions in Britain—and particularly in England—are more marked and pervasive than in almost any other highly industrial nation. Some English people like it that way, and they are found not only among those who are personally favored by the class system. Such persons think that the different social classes complement each other, providing greater security and strength for all. They seek progress within and through the traditional class system, which they consider, broadly speaking, just and fair; and they tend to support one of Britain's two major parties, the Conservatives, who since 1979 once again have been entrusted by a majority of voters with the government of the country. Another group of people feel that the traditional British class system is unjust, frustrating, and oppressive; that it is bad for the development of individuals and the progress of the nation; and that its barriers and distinctions should be reduced and, whenever possible, abolished. Persons holding these views are more likely to support Britain's other major party, the Labour Party, which was the governing majority party in 1945–51, 1964–70, and 1974–79. In the last period, however, it was dependent on the support of smaller parties, the Liberals and the Scottish Nationals. These nationalists, too, represented a protest vote, but their defection in 1979 from the informal coalition with Labour forced a new election, resulting in a Conservative victory and a virtual elimination of the Scottish Nationals from Parliament.

One thing most British voters will not do is to ignore class. The Liberal Party, whose leaders tried to do just that, has long been limited to about one-tenth of the national vote or less.

Later in this chapter we shall look at these matters in more detail. Here let us cast only a quick glance at the British class system and at the long history that has produced it.

Such a glance at English society shows that at least four strata have long existed, like the layers of a cake. At the top there has long been an aristocratic and imperial group—the *establishment,* constituting with their families less than 1 per cent of the population. Many of its members are self-assured and relaxed about their pleasures, much as their ancestors were in the unblushing days of Fielding's *Tom Jones.* Beneath the aristocracy, but still in the establishment, there is a mixed layer of the *upper middle class.* amounting to about 6 percent of the population and including military officers, professional people, employers and managers in large industrial or business enterprises, and high civil servants. Inheritors of large fortunes in commerce, industry, and finance also fit into this layer, and so do well-educated white-collar workers. The diverse members of this group all have been molded into *gentlemen.* They are taught their excellent manners in *public schools,* which are private, and they have accepted the morals of Victorian responsibility, which is an extension of the middle-class Protestant ethic of self-control.

Below these two elite groups comes the third layer: the employers and managers of small firms (5 percent) and farms (1 percent), some of whom are sometimes called *tradespeople,* and—often linked to them by family ties—the intermediate (6 percent) and junior managerial personnel and nonmanual workers (22 percent) in semiprofessional sales and clerical occupations. Together, all these individuals make up the *middle middle* and *lower middle classes,* totaling with their families about 34 percent of the population. Many of these own property and employ or supervise labor, but they lack the full education and manners of gentlemen. Here we also find the more simply educated white-collar employees. Some of these adhere to tighter standards of hard work and success; others try to imitate the gentility of their "betters"; but still others have grown impatient and angry with upper-middle-class manners and respectability, which seem stuffy and pretentious to them. Whatever the attitude, most of them are likely to stay trapped in this middle stratum. In the eyes of many English people the abyss between gentlemen and tradespeople has remained: an engineer is a kind of plumber and a plumber is not a gentleman.

The fourth layer consists of *manual workers.* Such workers and their families total about 58 percent of the population. They include both skilled (23 percent) and semiskilled (15 percent) personnel, together with those working in personal service jobs (5 percent), such as those dealing with drink and clothing, and manual foremen and supervisors (3 percent). At the bottom of the stratum are the very poor (12 percent), consisting of the least skilled and lowest paid workers, state pensioners, and other severely disadvantaged persons. (See Table 12.1.)

From this society the English have produced a *four-layer culture:* at the top a libertarian culture of the avant-garde in the style of Virginia Woolf and the Bloomsbury set of artists and writers; next the Victorian respectability of the upper middle class;

TABLE 12.1 *Socioeconomic Structure in England and Wales, 1966*

	Percentage	
ESTABLISHMENT AND UPPER MIDDLE CLASS		
Employers and managers, large enterprises	3	
Professional workers, self-employed	0.5	
Professional workers, employees	2.5	6
MIDDLE CLASS		
Employers and managers, small enterprises	5	
Farmers (employers, managers, and owners)	1	
Intermediate nonmanual workers	6	12
LOWER MIDDLE CLASS (EMPLOYEES)		
Junior nonmanual workers (clerical, sales, communications)	22	22
MANUAL WORKERS		
Personal service (food, drink, and clothing occupations)	5	
Foremen and supervisors, manual	3	
Skilled manual workers	23	
Semiskilled manual workers	15	
Unskilled manual workers	8	
Agricultural workers	1	
Self-employed workers (not professional)	3	58
Armed forces		1
Unclassified		1
Total		100

Sources: Data in Sample, 1966 Census, *Social Trends* (London: HMSO, 1973), table 18.5; S. E. Finer and M. Steed, "Politics of Great Britain," in R. C. Macridis, ed., *Modern Political Systems: Europe,* 4th ed. (Englewood Cliffs, N.J.: Prentice-Hall, 1978), p. 41, table 2-2; Central Statistical Office (U.K.), *Annual Abstract of Statistics, 1977* (London: HMSO, 1977).

then a tight lower-middle-class respectability; and at the bottom an irrepressible working-class hedonism that is reflected in the writings of Alan Sillitoe and many others. Thus, there is no simple single English character.

For more than a century this class structure has changed with only glacierlike slowness. But since the late 1950s the rate of change has accelerated, and as the British enter the 1980s, they may see radical alterations take place. Material living standards have greatly improved for much of the population (see pp. 377–78, below). But many workers still feel that much of this general improvement has passed them by, and they have become increasingly impatient and more militant in claiming their share, often engaging in union-led strikes or in *wildcat strikes* without union authorization.

At the same time, about three-fourths of the middle and lower middle classes—the 28 percent of the work force earning modest salaries and wages in nonmanual or service occupations—have come to feel that they, too, are wage earners, but that their salaries have risen very little in real purchasing power. Here they see a contrast to the limited, but real, gains that most manual workers have made, often aided by their unions (see pp. 381–82, below). These clerical and service employees have begun to demonstrate a new militancy, going out on large strikes in hospitals and government offices, two work places in which their salaries have not kept pace with inflation, the cost of living, or the rise of wages in industry. Some members of these groups may come to identify with the cause of labor and the working class. But others among them may see themselves as part of the "general public," may feel annoyed by the inconvenience caused by the strikes, and may shift their support at least temporarily to the Conservative Party—as they did in the 1979 election. Still others may feel disenchanted with unions as well as with management and with both big parties, Labour and Conservative, that represent them; their response may be to retreat into nonvoting or to support minor parties as a gesture of protest.

This series of actions and reactions explains much of the ebb and flow of current British politics, but behind it may be an even bigger change: the search of almost one-third of the British population—the salary earners and service employees—for their social identity. If they choose to identify themselves with Labour, then British society and politics may become different in the 1980s, now that some of these groups have taken a more conservative middle-class position.

The variety of possible nonclass and third-party options and identities is enhanced by the ethnic and cultural diversities among the British peoples, for the peoples of Scotland and Wales, who together with the English and the Northern Irish form the United Kingdom and the British nation, have their own distinct characteristics. They are less class-ridden within, but more disadvantaged as a group and more likely to engage in social or national protest. In 1974 some of their voters backed nationalist parties, but in 1979 most of them returned to the Labour Party and thus reduced the Conservative majority in the new Parliament. All these peoples somehow have remained cohesive around the English core; and the different kinds and strata of British citizens have remained a single people of remarkable energy, endurance, and political resourcefulness.

A UNIQUE POLITICAL ARENA: THE ISLANDS THAT SHAPED A STATE

In Britain more than in any other country, politics can be understood only against a background of history. It is the history of a state that changed its major tasks five times in nine hundred years—and of a people that became stronger with each change.

Openness and Isolation. The English state is in some ways a unique combination of a response to given conditions and a political inventiveness. The British state derived its flexibility from its geography, rich in its variety of coastlines, plains, and mountains. Geography permitted options of basic policy: the British could choose whether they wanted the state to be strong or weak, centralized or decentralized.

The *Celtic* culture of England and Ireland was native. Later it fused with Christianity brought by Roman missionaries. Between 500 and 800 A.D., Ireland was the most learned country in Europe. More Irishmen knew Greek at that time than did Frenchmen; and it was the Irish who sent out missionaries to civilize the Swiss. After the Celtic and Roman influence in Britain came the *Saxon* tribes and, still later, the Scandinavian or Viking culture. The civilization and knowledge that the seafaring Vikings brought from Byzantium and the Arab countries also found their way to England. In the Middle Ages, England was at one and the same time the end of the road and the crossroads of Europe, where many cultural influences met. With its long coastline and high hills and mountains, the country was suited both to receive and to shelter people and ideas. Many habits could persist unchanged for centuries in mountainous seclusion, yet all the world could come by boat.

The whole tradition of the moving frontier and the savage Old Testament practice of meeting other cultures with the edge of the sword are built into British history. There were four frontiers in the British Isles—the Cornish, the Welsh, the Scottish, and the Irish. England also had a continental frontier in Europe. From the thirteenth century on, it held territories on the European continent. Bordeaux was under British rule for two hundred years. Calais may have been to Mary, the Catholic queen who died in 1558, what Saigon became to some American policy makers in the 1960s: a beachhead and guarantee of long-standing involvement and aspiration on a continent that was increasingly ungrateful and inhospitable.

From 1497 onward, starting in the days of Henry VII, England turned to sea power. In the middle of the sixteenth century, the turn was completed: on ascending to the throne, Queen Elizabeth I gave up Calais, thereby liquidating the commitment on the Continent. Beginning with a modest business partnership between the queen of England and the pirate Sir Francis Drake, this new policy led to four centuries of dominion of the seven seas.

But before England could extend its frontiers, it first had to become united at home. At a crucial time, much of this unity was imposed by outsiders.

The Conquest That Lasted. In the eleventh century Saxon England was economically advanced, having many towns and widespread use of money. But politically weak and internally divided, it was conquered by recently Frenchified Scandinavian roughnecks. In 955 a Scandinavian with the expressive name of Hrolf the Ganger (fairly close in meaning to the modern word "gangster") had settled with his followers in Normandy. He soon became Rollo, le Duc de Normandie. In 1066 a descendant, William the Conqueror (since he was of illegitimate birth, the Saxon appellation of William "the Bastard" is technically not inaccurate), conquered England with the blessings of the pope. The conquest was shattering and thorough, though precarious. There were a million Saxons and not very many Norse in the country. The result was a high degree of solidarity among the *Norman* rulers. They had to stand together to defend their lives and to control their Saxon subjects.

POLITICAL INSTITUTIONS AND INVENTIONS: THE CREATION OF CHARACTERISTIC ELEMENTS OF BRITISH GOVERNMENT

The First Modern State. To strengthen their solidarity and control, the Norman conquerors built up a highly centralized state with the aid of the latest administrative techniques provided by the church. For its day their state was very modern. In the twelfth century the Normans established a sophisticated administration of royal taxes and spending, called the *exchequer.* This was the first modern office of the treasury in Europe outside of Italy. Out of the old Roman roads the Normans developed a network of king's highways; the king's law applied everywhere within arrowshot of both sides of the highways. Another statute of the time specified that contracts everywhere in England could be enforced in the king's courts. This action shifted the attention of everyone interested in merchandising, trade, and money away from the local powers and toward the king and the central state. Thus, by the thirteenth century there were king's courts, king's highways, and the king's law (which soon become the *common law,* because the king's law largely adopted customary law). In this manner the English genius combined bold innovation with deeply rooted elements of tradition. The king's courts and king's highways were new. The use of customary law linked old law to a new political system.

Centralization and solidarity were the unique gifts of Norman administration, and they became two of the key aspects of British government. In the thirteenth century French nobles paid an average of 3 percent of their income as taxes to the Crown. English nobles paid 6 percent. As a result, the English monarchy, though ruling a less populous country, had more money than the French, and the Hundred Years' War eventually was fought on French soil. Without this superior political and financial performance England's sea power and island position would not have kept the war from its shores, any more than they had been able to prevent the Norman conquest. From the days of the tax assessments of the thirteenth century to the rationing system of World War II, the English have made a point of obeying their laws and paying their taxes. Thanks in part to the more dependable compliance habits of its elites and of its common people, England was able to achieve more power than many larger states or kingdoms.

Soon after the Norman conquerors set up their state, they began making peace with the different elements of English society. At the time of the conquest William depended completely on his Normans. Thereafter he and his successors worked with several diverse groups, often playing them against one another. When some of William the Conqueror's Norman barons rose against him in 1086, he promptly turned around and called out the Saxon territorial militia against them. Step by step, the Saxons were brought into the English system; and by the fourteenth century their language had come back into respectable use in the courts and in public administration.

The story of England is the story of the refusal of a people to assimilate to its conquerors. Rather, things worked the other way around. The conquerors were assimilated to the people. For three hundred years England was governed in French, but eventually the beer brewers and then other guilds in London brought the use of English back into the courts after 1362. By the time of Chaucer a common language had been restored, albeit one with 48 percent of its vocabulary taken from Latin and French.

A Legacy of Institutions. Perhaps most important, the interplay of Normans and Saxons created in England a set of political institutions that continued to grow and function long after the differences between Normans and Saxons had faded. An *institution* is a pattern of interlocking habits and expectations of behavior—and hence a configuration of social roles—such that these roles, habits, and expectations tend mutually to preserve and reinforce each other and to produce a more or less consistent and systematic effect on the society.

Such an institution may be limited at any time to a unique set of persons: the Roman Catholic church is an institution, but it is unique, and there is only one legitimate pope at a time. Similarly, there is only one British monarchy with one legitimate monarch. But the word "institution" also may refer to a class of such institutions. If we call Christian churches "institutions," we find that there are many different denominations. So, too, with the institution of monarchy, or of marriage, or of private property, or of central planning—each exists in many countries and in many specific circumstances.

English institutions of this kind included from an early time the centralized monarchy, the exchequer, and the common law. Others, as we shall see presently, were the tradition of enquiry and eventually of commissions of enquiry; inquests; Parliament; and the new tradition of the gentleman. Later stages of English, and later British, history were to add still other institutions of their own. More than those of many other countries, English institutions, once established, tended to be preserved and carried on for centuries, but they also tended to be modified and developed with greater boldness and flexibility, making them at one and the same time carriers of continuity and instruments of innovation.

The Tradition of Enquiry. Another key aspect of English politics from early times onward—in addition to centralization and solidarity—has been the *tradition of enquiry,* that is, the systematic asking of questions, listening to evidence, and searching for facts. William the Conqueror, foreshadowing the best modern practice in government and social science, began his reign with a statistical survey. The results were recorded in his *Domesday Book,* which counted every piece of real estate and every potential taxpayer as well as the population as a whole. It was an inventory of the national resources of England at the end of the twelfth century, a report that surely could have gone to a national resources planning board, had one existed at the time.

The notion of enquiry lies at the heart of British political and administrative tradition. Among its major points the *Magna Carta* in 1215 required that when a dead body was found anywhere in England, a board of enquiry had to be set up and an *inquest* held by a coroner. This was not an inevitable position. The conquering Norman elite might have said that when a dead Norman body was found, the next Saxon village would be burned. They could have introduced hostage systems, massacres, or other reprisals, leading to escalating hatred. Instead they chose to start specific inquests, which turned out to be a more civilized and durable way of coping with murder. The Magna Carta marked the rise of the secular tradition that every individual's life and death matters. The English poet W. H. Auden said that it is not wholly accidental that there is a detective story tradition in English-speaking countries. If a person dies in most parts of the English-speaking world, it is not something one takes for granted, as part of an Oriental fatalism or as the result of mute historic forces; it is considered a matter of human importance and thus gives rise to searching curiosity.

Parliament, too, developed from a tradition of enquiry. Arising out of the king's great council around 1240, it was based on the principle that "what touches all should be approved by all." This is still a reasonable principle of government. Hearings, consultations, and eventually the grant to people of a widening share in decision making are characteristic of the English tradition of government and have had a profound effect on British society. *Royal Commissions* of Enquiry in the nineteenth century produced the facts and recommendations that led to the legislation abolishing chattel slavery, child labor, and exploitation of women in mines and factories. Similar commissions laid the foundations for Britain's present-day "cradle-to-grave" social security system and for the humanizing reform of British penal law. The principle of enquiry spread to other English-speaking countries. In Canada, a Royal Commission on Bilingualism and Biculturalism has opened the way for improving relations between French-speaking and English-speaking Canadians. The essential contribution of all such commissions is not advocacy, but discovery. They see their task not primarily as bargaining between parties for some compromise, nor as a public relations job to arouse support for some preconceived policy, but as a probe of the facts of the problem before them in order to discover new and genuine solutions.

A Link Across Two Classes: The Gentleman. Another part of the English tradition has been the building of human and communication bridges between groups. One of the forces helping to break the barriers between the nobles and commoners was the concept of *the gentleman*—the person who carried his gentle breeding wherever he went. Gentlemen sending their younger sons into towns to become guildsmen was typical of fifteenth-century England. Most other European nobles would rather have been found dead than have had their children join guilds of artisans or merchants. Only in England did one-third of the apprentices in the tailors' and skinners' guilds in 1485 turn out to be the sons of gentlemen. In Berne and Zurich there was a touch of social equality, but in most of Europe an abyss separated commoners from nobles. In England, in contrast, the upper middle class and the lesser nobles merged in the new elite of gentlemen.

The English *law of primogeniture* aided this development. It reserved the noble title and the family estate to the oldest son of the family. It made all other sons commoners, and the latter then were free to intermarry with commoners, to engage in business ventures, and to profit from the wool trade or from shipping—all of which they did.

The social, cultural, and psychological unity between the upper middle classes and the nobility took more than four centuries to develop fully. In the ninteenth century, great public schools were founded to mold the sons of aristocrats, successful businessmen, and some professional men into a single class of gentlemen. This class was expected to rule every major aspect of British life by its example, charm, upper-class manners and accent, and the social, political, and economic power of the "old boy" network, through which the graduates of public schools find jobs for each other.

This far-reaching consolidation of the nobility and the upper middle class was paid for by a wider gap between gentlemen and tradesmen (or the lower middle class) than is found in many other countries. England long has been more democratic on top, but more class-ridden in the middle and bottom layers of society. There one finds more deference and more resentment than in the United States. While some English voters are more responsive to the snob appeal of voting for their betters, others have long responded to the class appeal of the Labour Party and its promise to change the social system. The basis for the power of both appeals is rooted deeply in English society and history. Polite British taxi drivers still may call high-tipping passengers "governor" and "sir" and then vote for the Labour Party with its program to nationalize the coal, steel, and transport industries.

Links Across Localities and Classes: Members of Parliament. During the reign of Queen Elizabeth I, in the mid-sixteenth century, England abandoned the tradition of completely local representation, which is still the formal law and usual practice in the United States. Any constituency, borough, or shire in England became free to elect anyone as its *member of Parliament,* whether or not he was a local resident. In the words of Edmund Burke, Parliament was no longer "a congress of ambassadors from different and hostile interests . . . but . . . a deliberative assembly of one nation, with one interest, that of the whole. . . ."

By the middle of the sixteenth century about one-fifth of Parliament was made up of country districts represented by rural nobles, called knights of the shire. Another fifth consisted of *burghers*—local citizens—from the boroughs, and three-fifths came from urban communities that were represented by noblemen elected by middle-class voters. This was the political tradition that later pervaded George Washington's Virginia. A political elite of noblemen by birth, upbringing, and education had enough leisure time in which to master the art of politics; and such an elite won and retained the confidence of the English burghers—and later of the Virginia frontiersmen. This was the tradition of building *cross-class coalitions.*

THE FIRST GREAT MODERN POLITICAL REVOLUTION, 1640–90

From Person to Institution: The Differentiation Between King and Crown. The Crown function, as well as the parliamentary function, was firmly established quite apart from the existence of a given monarch by the end of the fifteenth century. During the century before Elizabeth, in the civil wars between the houses of Lancaster and York, the English learned to keep the institution of the Crown functioning even without knowing who was king. The *Crown* became the symbol of a continuing impersonal organization: the public administration and bureaucracy and the property, treasury, and machinery of the state. All these somehow kept working, usually in cooperation with Parliament, no matter what happened to the person of the monarch. When strong absolute monarchs, like Henry VIII and Elizabeth I, increased their power against the great nobles, these powers soon shifted to the Crown. But inevitably, the separation of the Crown from the monarchy weakened the power of the British king. In reaction, as the government became increasingly able to function without him a monarch might be tempted to assert his or her power more, trying to balance the loss of real power by an effort of his or her political will.

King James I, succcessor to Queen Elizabeth, succumbed to this temptation. James, perhaps a genius, was a man of tremendously high intelligence, but of such bad political judgment that his contemporaries called him, "the wisest fool in Christendom." A strong proponent of the *divine right theory*, according to which a monarch ruled by the will of God and was answerable to no one else for his or her actions, James tried hard to block or reverse the spread of power to Parliament and the growing independence of the courts. And for twenty to thirty years he succeeded in halting the increase of Parliament's power.

James also carried out constructive reforms, some with lasting effects. He introduced the name "Great Britain" for England and Scotland, and he persuaded the English Parliament to vote citizenship for all Scotsmen born after 1603 and the Scots Parliament to do as much for Englishmen. Thus, he laid the foundations for the British political system and people.

James's son, Charles I, was less bad as a ruler than his father, but it was Charles who paid the price for both. His fate reminds one of a principle mentioned by Saint Thomas Aquinas in the thirteenth century. Aquinas said that if a country has an unusually bad prince, one should not overthrow him; in the nature of things he will die sooner or later, and a less bad one is likely to succeed him and make the system work. But if the ruler is of average or better quality (as Charles proved to be), and if life is nevertheless intolerable under him, then there is something wrong with the system of government itself; in that case the government must be overthrown, because an improvement in the incumbent will not cure a bad system. Four centuries later, the Engish revolution seemed to corroborate Aquinas's views.

Charles was conscientious, good-looking, and almost charismatic. He tried to govern England as it once had been governed, but could no longer be, and set off a revolution in the process. The revolution against him was led by a cross-class coalition. Country gentlemen, mainly from the shire of Cambridge and the east of England, were at first the main sources of the armies fighting him, but Parliament raised armies, too. The issue was decided by the actions of the mass of the people. A painting in the House of Commons still shows the shuttered shops in London when the City of London voted to close them all so that apprentices and journeymen could go out and take up weapons "until the city of Gloucester be relieved." Commanded by Oliver Cromwell, the armies of country gentlemen from Cambridgeshire and of Parliament—the *roundheads,* or "ironsides," as they were known—swept away the royalist *cavaliers.* The king was tried and beheaded, for as Cromwell's secretary, the poet John Milton, noted in *The Tenure of Kings and Magistrates,* kings had their office only as long as they kept their agreements with the community; otherwise they became public enemies and had to be treated as such.

Milton's doctrine was grim and perhaps more extreme than most English people were completely willing to accept at the time. After Cromwell's death his generals, the "military complex" of the time, brought back a Stuart king, Charles II; Cromwell's bones were disinterred and scattered. England, having had twenty years of Puritan dictatorship and publicly enforced morality, went to the other extreme. After the Battle of Naseby in 1645, Cromwell's soldiers had slashed the faces of women camp followers of the Royalist Army so that they should not endanger the virtue of Puritans in the future. Twenty years after that inhuman outbreak of instant righteousness, restoration comedy began to introduce plays that to this day cannot be advertised in a family newspaper without changing their titles; these plays became popular and were widely performed.

In 1688 the Stuarts were thrown out once more, and England settled down in 1690 to an Act of Toleration and parliamentary supremacy. In the military sphere, standing armies, which were considered a threat to liberty, were abolished. The British began to concentrate on building up the navy, though keeping the army relatively small. A strong navy could dominate the seas, but not the English people. In 1707, England and Scotland were formally united under a single Parliament, and the country formed was henceforth to be called Great Britain—the name that James I had introduced a century earlier.

The English revolution took more than half a century to run its full course. It was a real *revolution,* for it did not merely replace some rulers by some others, but it also changed the habits and political culture of the people, the structure of many political and social institutions, and the structure of the relationships among them. It made England the first great modern nation. Its first phase—the war of Parliament against the king—and the days of Cromwell are often called in England "the Great Rebellion"; its second period, the almost bloodless expulsion of the last Stuart king in 1688, is called "the Glorious Revolution." The relative importance of these events in the minds of the British seems clear: it is Oliver Cromwell's statue that now stands in front of the House of Commons to commemorate his role as protector of parliamentary power. The two waves of revolution also left their invisible but real monuments in the world of ideas. The political theories of Thomas Hobbes and of John Locke (as discussed in Chapter 4) are responses to the experiences of the times, but they have influenced political thought and action, directly and indirectly, at many times and places ever since.

In 150 years the reforms of absolute monarchs and two waves of revolution had merged England into Britain and made it the most modern country of the world. In the course of these events, kings lost power to the Crown, and the Crown lost most of it to Parliament (see Figure 12.1).

A LASTING RESULT: GOVERNMENT BY PARLIAMENT

There is not a thing between heaven and earth that Parliament cannot do, said English jurist John Austin. This is largely true. Under the British system there are no legal limits on the power of Parliament. Nor has Britain a written constitution. Nor is there a separation of powers as in the United States. Indeed, Britain has no such thing as judicial review of the acts of Parliament.

The Emerging Power of the House of Commons. For a time, power in Britain was divided among three parties: the Lords, the Commons, and the Crown. The *House of Lords* and the *House of Commons* were the two chambers of Parliament. The House of Lords represented and was composed of the high nobility, the peers of England, as they were called. These were the barons, viscounts, earls, marquises, and dukes, each of whom took his seat by heredity as soon as he inherited his title. By contrast, the members of the House of Commons were elected, each representing one of the boroughs or shires of the kingdom (much as they now represent the 600-odd parliamentary constituencies—that is, electoral districts—of the country).[1]

In the course of time, power shifted increasingly to the House of Commons. The revolutions in the seventeenth century accelerated this process, which was completed by the middle of the twentieth. The seventeenth-century revolutions destroyed many of the old families of peers. Their places were taken by new peerage created by

[1]Until 1963 no peer of England could renounce his title in order to represent a constituency in the House of Commons. For this reason Winston Churchill refused a peerage after World War II: he wanted to remain in the House of Commons.

James II and his successors from courtiers and successful speculators. As the monarch became increasingly obliged to choose ministers only with the advice of the House of Commons and then to follow the advice of these Parliament-controlled ministers in his or her own political actions, the House of Commons—or, more exactly, the prime minister and the Cabinet—gradually acquired the powers of the Crown. In consequence, the House of Commons became ever more likely to prevail in any conflict with the House of Lords.

Other circumstances strengthened the hand of the Commons. Governments always need more money, and from early days the Commons alone could introduce money bills. In the nineteenth century it gained exclusive control over appropriations; this was formally recognized by law in 1911. Other types of legislation had to be passed by majorities in both houses, so the Lords had, in effect, a right of veto. This right gradually eroded. The Crown could create new peers by bestowing appropriate titles on whomever it chose. The threat to create many new peers often was used to make a recalcitrant majority in the House of Lords temper its resistance to the monarch and to the Commons majority and Cabinet advising him or

FIGURE 12.1 *Parliamentary Government, ca. 1600*

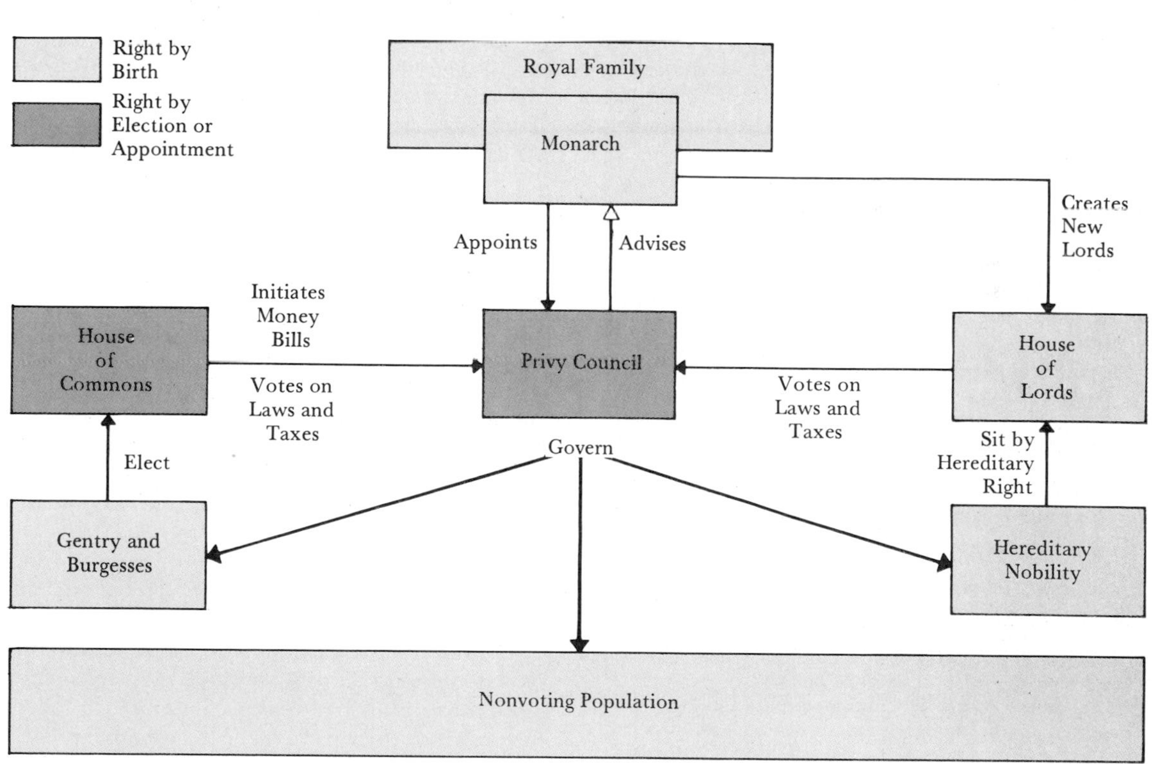

her. Finally, in 1911 the House of Lords lost its absolute power of veto over legislation, retaining only the right to delay legislation by two years. In 1919 this was reduced to only one year, and the power to delay at all has since applied only to non-financial legislation.[2] A final reason for the increase in power of the Commons was the consent of the governed. Ordinary people became less inclined to obey the Lords, but remained willing to support the Commons.

The Cabinet and the Party System. The primary result of these shifts in power has been the transformation of the *Cabinet* from a council of advisers to the king or queen, chosen by and responsible to the monarch, into an instrument of the House of Commons. Today the Cabinet, the chief executive power headed by the prime minister, is a committee of Parliament. In theory, it is Parliament's creature. Parliament can make it or unmake it; if Parliament votes "no confidence" in the Cabinet, the Cabinet must resign. This has remained settled policy in England for several centuries. This power is taken for granted so unquestioningly that Parliament has rarely exercised its prerogative. In March 1979, when the House of Commons voted out of office Prime Minister James Callaghan's Labour Cabinet, it was the first time a Cabinet had been overthrown by Parliament since 1924. A prime minister who discovers that he or she is about to lose a majority may choose instead to step down in advance. Neville Chamberlain did so in 1940, in favor of Winston Churchill, whom all parties trusted. Over time, however, the Prime Minister's power vis-à-vis Parliament has grown.

In practice, the prime minister and the Cabinet depend on the support of their party. To function well, the British system requires political parties and *party discipline.* Parties began to emerge among the still narrow political elites in the late seventeenth century. The *Whigs* (who took their name from Scottish lowland opponents of the monarchy) favored increasing the power of Parliament and reducing that of the monarch. They drew their support from urban and mercantile interests and a minority of the great landed families. The *Tories* (named after bands of outlaws favoring Catholicism and the traditional monarchy) formed the court party. They stressed the claims of the hereditary nobility and the divine right of kings. Their supporters were a majority of the landed nobles and a minority of urban and commercial groups interested in monopolies and court favors. The Whigs were more inclined than the Tories to favor freer competition and more permissive government, at least for the educated and the well-to-do. Neither party advocated revolution.

In the eighteenth century both parties were deeply entangled in the inefficiency and corruption that characterized British politics at the time, and for a while the Tories were practically defunct. In the course of the nineteenth century the revived Tories became the modern *Conservative Party,* and the Whigs became the *Liberals.* In the twentieth century the *Labour Party* was founded, and after World War I it became one of the main pillars of the two-party system, relegating the Liberals to a minor role.

As time went on, candidates for the Commons came to depend on party support for election and re-election. They had reason, therefore, to follow the orders of their party while in Parliament. Each

[2]To compensate somewhat for this final loss of power, the Conservative government after 1945 introduced the practice of having the monarch make distinguished persons peers for their own lifetime, but without any hereditary title for their descendants. It was hoped that these lifetime peers would increase the quality and prestige of the House of Lords. In addition, the monarch has continued to create hereditary lords from among meritorious commoners, including nowadays deserving trade union leaders as well as business executives. In 1971 there were 838 hereditary peers and 19 hereditary peeresses, together with 157 life peers and 23 life peeresses. Since 1964 no new hereditary peerages have been created.

The ordinary rank of knight, with its title "Sir," is still bestowed by the monarch as a governmental honor on British subjects in many walks of life. It implies no peerage, is not hereditary, and does not bar its bearer from membership in the House of Commons.

party organized its members in the House into a disciplined group called the *parliamentary party,* in contrast to the *national party* outside Parliament. The parliamentary party elects floor leaders, called party *whips,* to instruct members how to vote. *Free votes,* left to the discretion of each member, are rare.

The majority party designates the *prime minister,* who is then formally entrusted by the monarch with the task of forming a government. Specifically, the prime minister chooses the members of the Cabinet and assigns them their tasks. He or she may change their assignments or drop them from the Cabinet and replace them by others. In all this, the prime minister needs the support of Parliament and, above all, the support of his or her own parliamentary party. Parliament can overthrow this official by an adverse vote if a majority strongly opposes his or her Cabinet choices or policies, but, as we have seen, this is rare. (The prime minister may even draw some Cabinet members from the House of Lords, provided that the House continues to back this government.)

Thus, Britain is governed by a double feedback process. Parliament can give instructions to the government that exercises leadership in the House of Commons and can be overthrown by the House. But the Cabinet can also dissolve the House of Commons and can appeal over its head to the voters in a general election. The voters then elect a new Parliament, and a new Cabinet may emerge as a result (see Figures 12.2 and 12.3).

The same double feedback process includes the parties. A prime minister ordinarily is the leader of his party both within and outside Parliament. But a parliamentary party may revolt against a prime minister, or a national party may induce the members of the parliamentary party to do so. When Parliament is dissolved by the prime minister, perhaps because no new majority can be formed, elections must be called, and the former majority is very likely to lose. Members of the House of Commons do not like to risk their seats and, hence, do not overthrow governments lightly.

The British system, thus, has two feedback cycles: a short one between Cabinet and Parliament during normal times and a long one from the Cabinet to the voters via the new House of Commons to the new Cabinet. What the United States would call the "executive branch" is one part of the process. What it calls the "legislative branch" is the other part of the process. In Britain the two are on the same feedback cycle. Both systems, British and American, most often have worked well in providing constitutional and democratic government.

This comparison of the British and American governments shows that background conditions limit the range of political choices, but that within these limits such choices do exist. Having chosen different types of political machinery, Britain and

FIGURE 12.2 *Parliamentary Government, ca. 1980: The Slow Feedback Cycle*

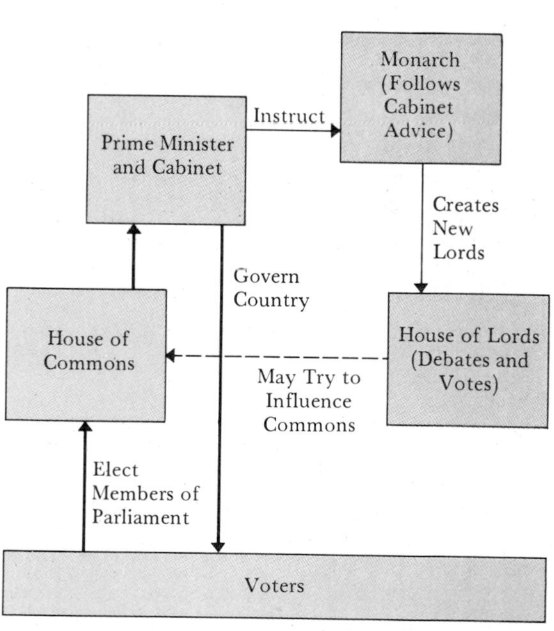

the United States have continued to face common problems: the struggle between conservatism and change and between the power of elites and broader political participation.

THE FROZEN DECADES, 1790–1832

A nation that has its own great revolution in relatively recent memory is unlikely to feel much need for another. Grandchildren and great-grand-children of revolutionaries tend to be somewhat conservative. In the second half of the eighteenth century, British politics was just that, in contrast to the incipient revolutionary changes going on in British industry and science.

The British system failed to respond to the needs of the American colonists, although the colonists might have seceded anyway. When the French Revolution broke out so much nearer to their island nation, the British for a moment faced

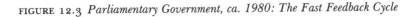

FIGURE 12.3 *Parliamentary Government, ca. 1980: The Fast Feedback Cycle*

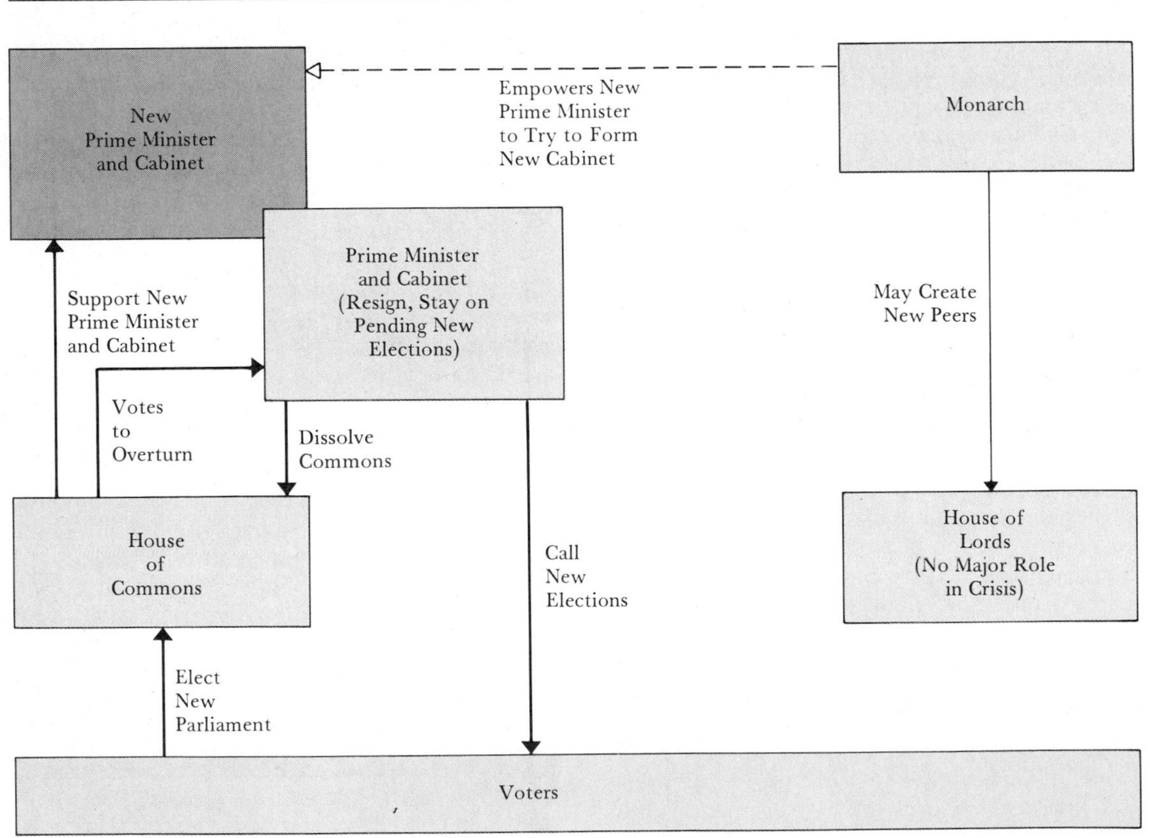

the possibility of a broader middle-class and lower-class revolution of their own. But within two years, as the revolution became more radical and violent, English public opinion switched toward opposition to the French Revolution and democratic agitation was silenced at home. This change in the public mood was accomplished in part by the deliberate political strategy of the British elites.

One of the intellectual architects of this strategy of counterrevolution was Edmund Burke. Burke emphasized that the French Revolution was godless. By exaggerating the case, he built a bridge between the privileged and established Church of England and the underprivileged Protestant sects. The latter included the Presbyterians, Methodists, and other small Protestant groups whose members had been treated as citizens of lesser right and prestige. In the name of religion, but really in the interests of a more general conservatism, differences among Protestant denominations were played down.[3]

THE GREAT REFORMS, 1832–1918

From 1790 to 1825 the British economy and technology changed quickly, but the British political system remained almost frozen. After 1825, conservatism began to wane. The first trade unions were legalized, and the first political organizations began to function in opposition to the government.

Within a relatively few years, in 1832, the *Reform Bill* was pushed through the Parliament. It had been opposed to the last moment by Napoleon's nemesis, the Duke of Wellington, who, like many military heroes, had become a conservative political leader after his victory. By 1832 the "Iron Duke" was out of a job and England was getting a new constitutional settlement through the enfranchisement of the middle class, the abolition of urban "rotten boroughs" and "pocket boroughs," and the enfranchisement of new cities such as Liverpool and Birmingham. The English working class in the towns got the vote a generation later, in 1867. The writer Thomas Carlyle compared the enfranchisement of laborers to "shooting Niagara," because he felt it was so dangerous to give working men the vote. In 1885 the rural laborers were enfranchised. In 1918, by a somewhat unchivalrous piece of legislation, women over thirty got the vote; in 1928 the British decided to entrust the ballot also to women between twenty-one and thirty.

Changes in the right to vote went hand in hand with social change. After 1832 the first wave of labor unrest, known as the Chartist movement, went through England, leaving in its wake the first factory inspection acts. With Tory help a labor-conservative coalition was formed at the time against liberal factory owners of the laissez-faire school of thought. This resulted in 1851 in the first limitation of working time, the ten-hour law. After 1889 the first great dock-workers' strike and the second wave of labor unrest followed, bringing with them the rise of the unskilled workers and the mass trade unions. The Independent Labour Party was founded in 1893 and the Labour Party in 1900. The first avowedly socialist government took office as a minority in 1924; the first absolute Labour majority was won in 1945, the second in 1964, the third in 1966.

[3]In Ireland this strategy was carried even further, perhaps far beyond Burke's intentions. The English royal house made a deliberate alliance with the Presbyterians of Ulster. The first Irish patriotic and revolutionary leaders had all been Protestants. Now, in the late 1790s, the *Orange Order* was founded in order to woo away the Protestants from the cause of Irish independence. Deliberately, members of Protestant sects were given privileges and special ties to the British establishment to divide them from the poorer Catholic Irish in the south of the island. The price of this successful, but divisive, strategy was still being felt nearly two hundred years later in the still unresolved bloodshed and intermittent civil war in British-ruled and Protestant-dominated Northern Ireland.

THE NEW REFORMS, 1945–80

During the decades 1870–1920, Britain's overseas empire had been greatly enlarged. There had been much agitation for *imperialism,* the policy aimed at making the empire even bigger. Conservatives and radicals agreed that such an empire was indispensable to private enterprise at home. From this, Conservatives concluded that empire was good, and radicals decided that private enterprise should be curbed or abolished.

The Exit from Empire. "I have not become His Majesty's First Minister to preside over the dissolution of the British Empire," growled Sir Winston Churchill during World War II. His successors, the Labour government, did just that—and turned their policy into a success. Said Prime Minister Clement Attlee in 1947 to a crowded Albert Hall audience celebrating the beginning of Indian independence, "this is the proudest day in British history."

During its history the English state has performed a succession of changing tasks. Its first task was to consolidate the Norman conquest; its second, to unify the British Isles into a single political and economic system. Its third task, lasting from the sixteenth to the eighteenth century, was the conquest of the seven seas and the acquisition of beachheads from Bombay and Calcutta to Gibraltar and Halifax. The fourth task, continuing from the mid-eighteenth through the nineteenth century, was the conquest of vast inland areas and populations in Asia and Africa and the establishment of the largest empire the world had ever seen. In 1911, when King George V of England was crowned king-emperor of India, the sun did not set on his dominions and more than 500 million people lived under the British flag. Britain's victory in World War I added new countries and peoples in the oil-rich Near East to the lands under British control. "Wider yet and wider may thy bounds be set," ran a popular hymn of those years; "God who made thee mighty, make thee mightier yet." But during the heyday of imperial expansion, domestic economic growth was neglected. British capital was sent overseas, and equipment in many industries at home was allowed to become obsolete.

After World War II, Britain faced a radically new task. The days of empires were ending, but not all imperial nations were aware of this fact. Britain's government and people met this new challenge with the same courage with which they met the Battle of Britain. They cooperated with local nationlists to organize in rapid succession the independence of India, Pakistan, Burma, and Egypt. In the next two decades there followed the independence of most of British Africa, Cyprus, Malaya, and the islands of the Caribbean.

At certain times and places the British resisted political independence, and fighting broke out between local nationalists, on the one hand, and British troops and sometimes British settlers, on the other. Malaya, Kenya, and Cyprus, the British opposition to the establishment of Israel in 1948, and the short-lived Suez War in alliance with Israel and France against Egypt in 1956 are all examples of such conflicts. But if one adds up all such fighting, one still must conclude that never before in human history had so many people received their independence with so little resistance from their former rulers. Britain moved faster into the postimperial age than did France, Belgium, the Netherlands, Portugal, and a large part of American public opinion.

The British adjustment was smoothed by the *commonwealth* concept. The term harks back to the government of England in Cromwell's day, but the word was applied widely to Britain's relations with its former colonies only from the 1920s onward. The substance of the new arrangements was developed from the nineteenth century on, at first under other names. In 1867, Britain granted to Canada the status of a dominion, which implied far-reaching rights of internal self-government. Between the 1890s and the 1920s, Canada's rights of dominion were extended to include control over foreign trade, immigration, military matters, and eventually external affairs. During the same period *dominion status* was extended to Australia, New Zealand, and the Union of South Africa. From the 1920s on, it became increasingly clear that nonwhite territories would also become self-governing and that the Commonwealth would become an organization of equals. After World War II, this happened in the sense that the former dominions became sovereign and the old notion of dominion status disappeared. The newly sovereign countries, such as India and Pakistan, chose to accept Commonwealth membership, side by side with the former dominions. At the end of the 1970s the Commonwealth of Nations included thirty-six sovereign states and their dependencies, comprising close to 1 billion people.

Today, Commonwealth membership implies mainly arrangements for political consultation, financial cooperation, and somewhat freer mobility of persons. There are also sentimental ties: some Commonwealth members have retained the British monarch as their symbolic head, although others, like India and Ghana, have become republics.

As the Commonwealth loosened and the empire was dissolved, they became less important issues for British politics at home. The majority of British voters recognized that the empire was impracticable to maintain at any tolerable cost. Their aspirations shifted toward building, as William Blake's popular hymn put it, a new "Jerusalem in England's green and pleasant land."

A New Start at Home. After 1945 the new Jerusalem of the Labour government began with years of stiff austerity. Many of the former sources of income from the old empire were gone, as were many British foreign assets that had been spent during the war. British industry had to be reconverted to peacetime production. Maintenance of equipment deferred for six war years had to be made up, and so, too, did the neglect of several preceding decades in mining and other industries. War damage had to be repaired in London, Coventry, Birmingham, and other cities and new housing constructed for returning soldiers and their families.

The Labour government attacked these tasks by a great expansion of governmental powers. Mining, gas and electricity, railways and other inland transport, and the iron and steel industry were *nationalized* and partly re-equipped. Public control over land use was strengthened by new planning legislation that eventually led to the building of twenty-five new towns. Finally, a comprehensive *National Health Service* was created, giving every person present in the British Isles—including visiting American businesspeople and students—a claim to free medical care whenever needed. Together, these measures did much to modernize the British economy and social structure.

The Two-Party Pendulum. By the early 1950s voters had grown tired of austerity with its prolonged rationing and holding back of consumer goods. In this mood they returned Conservative governments until the mid-1960s. These governments made greater concessions to middle-class consumers and to the private business sector. To some extent, they permitted the entire population to consume more, even at the risk of hurting Britain's competitive position in the world market. At the same time they accepted the nationalization of coal, railroads, and health services as part of their own policies and created a series of new universities. These actions made British conservatism very different from what goes by the name "conservatism" in the United States.

After more than a decade of Conservative relaxation, however, the voters—particularly the younger ones—once again became concerned about inequality and immobility in the country's social and economic life. In their view, members of the old establishment still had too many privileges, while contributing too little to the modernization and welfare of the nation. Accordingly, they elected a majority Labour government in 1964 and increased its majority in 1966. Some reform legislation followed, but soon Britain's declining export position and the weakness of its currency became the focus of government attention, while inflation advanced at home. The Labour government soon found itself resisting wage increases, trying to prohibit strikes in key sectors of employment, and increasing some charges to users of the National Health Service—policies rather similar to those proposed by the Conservatives. In the 1970 elections Labour lost heavily among voters under forty-five and sixty-five or over, among the middle class, and among the unskilled and the very poor, though keeping most of its traditional support among skilled workers, the forty-five to sixty-four age group, and the lower middle class. Though a good part of Labour's losses were due to nonvoting rather than to a shift to the Conservatives, the voting changes were large enough to bring a Conservative government under Prime Minister Edward Heath to power.

Electoral changes, however, did little to solve fundamental problems. British exports continued to lag, the currency remained weak in the foreign exchange markets, and there were continuing inflationary pressures. The Heath government tried to cope with these problems mainly by resisting wage increases wherever it could. The confrontation came in coal mining. A Labour government had nationalized the mines after 1945, to the relief of their owners, and the Conservatives had accepted this nationalization as permanent. Mining equipment, formerly antiquated, had been somewhat modernized in the late 1940s, and miners' wages had improved, but miners still felt badly disadvantaged in comparison with the bulk of British labor in the early 1970s. In late 1973 they went on strike, and the Heath government tried to break it, actually closing down much of British industry to operate for no more than three days a week, in hopes that this would turn the public mood against the strikers. Many Conservative voters were predictably indignant against the miners, but few—if any—of them volunteered to apply for their jobs. Not only Labour Party voters, but also many other British people felt that mining was hard, dangerous, and unpleasant work and that the miners deserved better treatment. Eventually the miners won. Prime Minister Heath resigned with his government in 1974 and a year later gave up the leadership of his party.

In the meantime, an election in October 1974 returned the Labour Party to office with a hair-thin majority in Parliament. In that election Labour won by gaining strongly among voters forty-five to sixty-four years of age (who had experienced the depression-ridden 1930s as teenagers) and by making lesser gains among nonunion labor, the middle class, and both skilled and unskilled workers. The party held its own among trade union members, the twenty-five to forty-four age group, and the lower middle class, but still they lost a small, but ominous, 2 percent among voters aged eighteen to twenty-four—those born in the 1950s and, thus, the generation whose votes they would need in the future. Another danger sign was the decline in Labour's share in votes cast from about 43 percent in 1970 to 39 percent in October 1974; only the large Conservative decline from 46 to 36 percent exceeded this decrease. A third warning was the transitory rise in strength of the Liberals and other third parties (like the nationalists), from 11 to 25 percent over the same period.

Nonetheless, it was a victory for the Labour Party and it returned them to power with an implied mandate to avoid bitter head-on confrontations with major groups of workers and their unions. Although later by-elections and the defection of one member of Parliament (MP) took away the party's three-seat margin of majority, a Labour Cabinet remained in office until 1979, headed first by Harold Wilson and after 1976 by James C. Callaghan as prime minister and supported during that time by the minor party votes of the Liberals, the Scottish Nationals, and the Welsh Nationalists (Plaid Cymru).

Since 1974, Britain has undergone a severe period of "double-digit" inflation, up to 25 percent, followed by a phase of the *social contract,* an arrangement between the Labour government and the trade unions, in which the latter agreed for three years to limit annual wage increases in general to 4.5 percent. On the whole, this contract was respected until 1977. Inflation declined to a single-digit rate, but remained well above the social contract's 4.5 percent limit on wage increases, so that workers' real wages declined. By 1978, workers felt that such wage ceilings without corresponding and effective price ceilings were no longer acceptable. Unions refused to renew the contract, and workers in many industries and service fields went out on strike, even without union authority, in order to win higher wages. In several important cases they did win them, raising thereby once more the specter of rapid inflation. The Conservatives called for a new election as the Callaghan government tried to hold on, relying on its capacity to work out a compromise with the unions. This compromise involved a new compact with the unions, limiting annual wage raises to 5 percent.

But it was not enough to satisfy the British electorate, as the Conservative Party succeeded in forcing Callaghan to call for a general election in May 1979. In that election the Conservatives were resoundingly returned to power with a majority of seventy seats in Parliament. The new prime minister, Margaret Thatcher, was able to use the issues of rising prices and taxes to score impressive gains among working-class voters, especially among skilled manual workers. The Tories also captured a large bloc of the last election's Liberal supporters and, for the first time since World War II, led Labour among new electors. Surprisingly, however, the professional classes, the traditional backbone of the Conservatives, gave only slightly more support to the party than in the last election. Margaret Thatcher has announced a new, more austere budget and tax policy in an attempt to cut inflation and raise productivity. How well this new policy will work remains to be seen.

The pendulum swings of voter support between relaxation and reliance on the forces of the market under the Conservatives, on the one hand, and modernization and planning under Labour, on the other, are likely to continue. The two major parties have much common ground because of the peculiar social structure of modern Britain. Only 3 percent of the work force remains in agriculture, which is not enough to provide a basis for a significant party. More than 90 percent of all workers are wage or salary earners, and manual workers outnumber white-collar employees by a ratio of two to one. No party can win without the wage and salary earners' vote. Up to two-thirds of the workers generally vote Labour, but in May 1979 the number was only about 49 percent, still enough to furnish nearly 80 percent of the Labour Party's vote. Almost two of every five workers, however, voted Conservative—enough to give the "working-class Tories" almost half of all votes cast for the Conservative Party. Among the middle and professional classes, about 60 percent voted Conservative in May 1979, furnishing most of the rest of the Conservative votes. One of five middle-class voters cast his or her ballot for Labour in 1974, and another one-fifth voted Liberal, furnishing over one-half of that party's vote. The middle-class and professional supporters of Labour often decide close elections and are an important source of expertise and leadership on Labour's side.[4] The net shift in votes in 1979 from Labour to the Conservatives was 5.2 percent, and the social structure of the electoral basis of the two major parties does not seem to have changed greatly. (See also Table 12.2.)

[4]The Liberals, successors to the ancient Whigs, played an important role from 1832 to 1924, but since then have remained somewhat less significant, earning under 14 percent of the vote in the national election of 1979. Labour has taken their place in the two-party system.

Under a system of proportional representation the Liberals would do somewhat better in gaining seats. When such a system is used, legislative seats are allocated in proportion to the votes received by each party, in contrast to the majority principle, according to which the strongest candidate in each district is declared the victor. Varieties of proportional representation exist in West Germany, whereas majority voting is the prevailing law in Britain and the United States.

TABLE 12.2 *Social Structure and Voting by Party, October 1974*

Social Group	Approximate % of population*		% of total votes cast (% of each group's vote) CONSERVATIVE	LIBERAL	LABOUR	TOTAL†
Upper middle and middle class	18	40	(55) 22	(21) 8	(20) 8	(96) 38
Lower middle class	22					
Manual workers	58		(24) 14	(18) 11	(53) 31	(95) 56
Total			36	19	39	95

*See Table 12.1, above.
†This table omits the almost 7 percent of votes cast for other parties, mainly Scottish and Welsh Nationalists.

Source: D. Butler and D. Kavanagh, *The British General Election of October 1974* (London: Macmillan, 1975).

Swings Within Each Party. A similar pendulum swing may be at work within each major party. At present there are two kinds of Conservatives. One kind is highly traditional, nationalistic, nostalgic for empire, hostile to nonwhites and, indeed, to most foreigners, and sympathetic to the government of South Africa and to the white minority in Zimbabwe Rhodesia. Such Conservatives are strong in rural party organizations, among retired officers, and also among small businesspeople and lower-middle-class enclaves in urban industrial areas. This right wing of the party supported the Suez War in 1956 and the racist policies of the former Cabinet minister Enoch Powell, who was disavowed by the leadership of his party. In 1979 he was a member of Parliament for the Unionist Party of Northern Ireland, a militantly Protestant group at the geographic and political periphery of the Conservative Party. The other wing of the Conservative Party (exemplified by former Prime Minister Edward Heath) favors modernization, reform, economic integration with Europe, cooperation with the nonwhite countries of the Commonwealth, and a continuation of the more moderate policies of the welfare state. The Conservative Party leadership has to maneuver between both wings and try to keep them together, a task facilitated by the British tradition of strong party discipline in Parliament and the country. For a short time the current party leader, Margaret Thatcher, tried to do this by incorporating some of Powell's attacks on nonwhite immigration into her own rhetoric, but then muted this theme in her successful 1979 campaign.

The Labour Party has its own internal divisions. Its left wing is concerned with the ideology of socialism and advocates further nationalization of industry. It stresses class interests and the working-class character of the party. It favors planning and distrusts the play of forces in the market. It opposes increased defense spending and the remnants of empire, demands sharp measures against Rhodesia and South Africa, rejects the concept of the Cold War, and is uneasy about Britain's alliance with the United States. This wing draws much of its support from the disadvantaged regions of Britain, such as Wales and Scotland, as well as from a minority of intellectuals. The right wing of the Labour Party is stronger in London and the South of England and among many of the better-paid groups of labor and public employees as well as among a majority of intellectuals. Right-wing leaders stress evolution and pragmatism, more reliance on market forces and consumer interests, greater cooperation with the United States and Western Europe, greater caution toward nationalization of industries, and further expansion of the public sector. They stress common interests among the classes and urge restraint in the further wage demands of the trade unions.

The Labour Party leadership, like its Conservative counterpart, must manage to work with both wings of its party and, for this purpose, makes heavy use of party discipline. As an added complication, the big trade unions, which for a long time cared little about ideology, insist on frequent wage increases. These unions command large blocs of votes at the party conference, and the Labour leadership cannot afford to quarrel too seriously with the Trade Union Congress, any more than the Conservative leadership can afford to quarrel too seriously with the financial interests in the City of London and industrial interests throughout the country.

In this continuing contest between the major parties and their allies among the interest groups, the basic domestic arrangements about the distribution of economic wealth, political power, social status, educational opportunity, and the future directions of British society and culture have become the main stakes of British politics.

THE STAKES OF BRITISH POLITICS

By the early 1970s the leverage of government on the British body politic had become powerful indeed. Already in the Britain of 1960, much as today, "one person in four was in public employment of some kind. This is six times as many as before 1940."[5] In 1979, taxes at all levels of government, together with national insurance contributions, had risen to 40 percent of the GNP, but public expenditure, already at 51 percent of national income in 1969, was officially reported at 62 percent in 1976.[6] Some of these fluctuations may have been due to inflation, but the public sector in Britain now seems close to one-half of the GNP—no matter which party is governing.

Conservative governments in the mid-1950s and early 1960s and the government of Prime Minister Edward Heath from 1970 to 1974 have made little headway in reversing this long-term trend. Indeed, the acceptance after 1945 by the Conservatives of the bulk of the Labour Party's welfare state program with its greatly expanded scope of services—and of much of the public employment entailed by them—has been an essential element in the British political consensus of the last four decades. Together with the monetary powers wielded by the Treasury—that heir to the exchequer of olden days—and with the available legal powers over land use and employment policies, the size and scope of this public sector offer to any British government an array of powerful instruments to influence the social, economic, and political course of the nation.

[5]Judith Ryder and Harold Silver, *Modern English Society: History and Structure, 1850–1970* (London: Methuen, 1970), p. 178. Such employment in publicly owned enterprises and public agencies is often underreported because of the scattering of the data. B. M. Russett et al., *World Handbook I,* reports only 11 percent of the working-age population—corresponding to 16 percent of all wage and salary earners—as employed in the public sector (pp. 25, 70).

[6]Samuel H. Beer, "The British Political System," in S. H. Beer and A. B. Ulam, eds., *Patterns of Government: The Major Political Systems of Europe,* 3rd ed. (New York: Random House, 1974), p. 293; Central Statistical Office *Annual Abstract of Statistics, 1977* (London: HMSO, 1977), pp. 341, 344.

But for what aims and policies are these powers to be used?

What National Role for Britain? In the early 1980s, two generations after their "finest hour" in World War II, the British people have not yet decided where they want to go. They have given up most of their empire, but they are reluctant to let go of their role as a world power even though it is becoming largely imaginary in comparison to the much greater resources of the United States and the Soviet Union.

Britain under Conservative leadership entered the *European Common Market* in 1973, and in a unique referendum in 1975, over 67 percent of the votes cast supported this policy (which is still more popular among a large part of its elites); but public opinion does not seem to be ready to accept any more directly political steps toward European integration.

Another possibility would be to concentrate primarily on domestic modernization, technological development, and economic growth, but this is difficult for a country with Britain's large and continuing roles as a world banker and investor, side by side with its continuing dependence on a vigorous export sector to pay for its needed imports of food and other goods. In these matters Britain's future self-definition and world role are at stake—its choice between the dangers of underachievement and overcommitment. Eventually, by commission or omission, British politics within the next decade or two may decide the fate of its people for a much longer time.

How Much Economic Growth? Some parts of these larger decisions are already at stake here and now. How much economic growth do the British people want, how fast, in what direction, and by what means? Their nation has grown less than most other major industrial countries. Their absolute gross national product has been overtaken by those of Japan, West Germany, France, the Soviet Union, and China. Their per capita GNP, too, has lagged and is now below the French, West German, and Soviet levels.

One obstacle to growth has been the British workers' choice of strikes and wage increases for their own trades at the expense of growth of the national economy as a whole, because they fear that they might not get a fair share of the latter. Moreover, British workers often prefer to work at their own pace, with time out for tea and without stressful adjustments to new technologies. This may have improved their health, but not the outmoded equipment in some of their plants or the average per capita income in their country.

The British press, in large part identified with the business community's point of view, has heavily publicized the British workers' technological conservatism and their propensity to strike. (The latter, in fact, is no higher than the average in other countries; see Table 12.6, below.) What has been less often noted is the silent strike of British financiers and investors that began in the 1960s, if not earlier. British owners of wealth have been reluctant to invest in many branches of industry, fearing that these might be nationalized without adequate compensation or made unprofitable by too high wages and too low *productivity* (market value of output per employee). As a result, British industries often have less modern equipment, and the remarkable ingenuity of British scientists and engineers often fails to be applied and to bear fruit in production. These failures, in turn, tend to restrict Britain's exports and foreign exchange earnings, to promote inflation, and to keep real wages low in comparison with those in other countries.

Although these troubles are visible to many, each side tends to blame the other for them. Whenever the Conservatives rule, Labour complains of social injustice; whenever Labour holds office, Conservatives complain of lack of economic motivation. Economic growth seems to the Conservatives to require more inequality, but social peace and justice seem to Labour to demand more equality, both in meeting human needs and in enjoying the better things in life. At heart this problem is common to all modern industrial societies, but in Britain it seems now to be posed particularly clearly. Perhaps the British people will find a better answer to it in the future; they need it urgently.

Thus far, they are just wrestling with the questions. Should Britain shift its energies toward an all-out effort at economic growth in order to regain its lost lead? Or should the people accept the economic slowdown as part of the price for continuing far-flung military and political commitments? Or should they take a more skeptical view of international power and military reputation and concentrate, somewhat like the Scandinavians, on the quality of their lives—on health, leisure, culture, and greater political and social equality and harmony—even without trying to catch up with, say, Sweden's high per capita income figures?

More Equality or Less? In any case, do the British people want more equality at home? They did reduce inequality to a significant extent between 1940 and 1955, when the share of the top 10 percent of income receivers fell from 38 to 30 percent of the nation's total income.[7] Since then, that share dropped more slowly, reaching about 25 percent before taxes and 21.5 percent after taxes in 1974–75. Moreover, individuals and some occupational groups have continued to rise or fall within it. Some aspects of the latter kind of shifts are presented in Table 12.3.

This unresolved problem has arisen even more sharply in regard to many health and welfare services. Here the adherents of equality, and the Labour Party, have generally favored a principle of *universalism,* a flat rate of benefits or service being offered equally to all, in order to avoid the stigma of charity or poverty, the humiliation of the applicants' being subjected to means tests (tests to prove their poverty), and also to avoid the bureaucratic costs of administering such a system of controls. But such flat rates of service for all will be very expensive, if they are to meet middle-class standards, or else they will be rejected by many middle-class persons as inadequate to their own needs and expectations. Accordingly, Conservatives have steadily urged services according to a principle of *selectivity:* offered free only to the needy, they are offered for pay to everybody else, preferably through private agencies operating in a market.

A third proposal has come from an academic expert, the late Professor Richard M. Titmuss, and has been publicized by the Fabian Society. He advocated a two-tier system of flat-rate universalist service standards for all as a base and framework, supplemented by additional amounts and kinds of services provided for those whose *needs* are greatest, without a test for the means that they may or may not have. This, Titmuss argued, will free the recipients and their children from the social stigma of poverty and failure and from the feelings of personal inadequacy and inferiority in their own minds. In American terms, this proposal would amount to replacing the question of whose "fault" it is that a case of medical or other needs arises—the fault of the individual, of society, or of the physical and technological environment—by the principle of "no fault" insurance against such needs, paid for by all members of society through taxes and, hence, in accordance with their ability to pay. The proposal leaves unanswered many questions of detail, and it raises, of course, major questions of ideology or principle. On the technical side it probably can be worked out; but in regard to values and a general sense of political and cultural direction, political decisions will have to be made by voters, elites, and the political

[7]See Table 5.1, above; and S. E. Finer, "Great Britain," in R. C. Macridis, ed., *Modern Political Systems: Europe,* 4th ed. (Englewood Cliffs, N.J.: Prentice-Hall, 1978), p. 45, tables 2.8 and 2.9 with references.

TABLE 12.3 *Shifts in Real Purchasing Power, 1938–75*

Job	Wage earnings (£) for 1975	Purchasing power as a percentage of 1938
UPPER AND MIDDLE CLASSES		
Airline pilot	11,200	111
Civil servant, assistant secretary	9,825	77
Doctor, general practitioner	8,485	93
University professor	7,740	75
Solicitor	6,000	102
Accountant (aged thirty)	3,800	109
Civil servant, executive officer	3,032	75
Graduate schoolmaster	2,955	91
Bank clerk	2,730	120
Shop assistant	1,510	116
MANUAL WORKERS		
Miner	3,690	263
Engine driver	3,400	165
Bus driver	3,287	149
Factory worker	3,070	190
Railman	2,540	227
Agricultural worker	1,980	204
British Average	2,900	

Source: S. E. Finer and M. Steed, "Politics of Great Britain," in R. C. Macridis, ed., *Modern Political Systems: Europe,* 4th ed. Central Statistical Office, *Annual Abstract of Statistics: 1977* (London: HMSO, 1977), calculated from table 6.24. Adapted by permission of Prentice-Hall, Inc., Englewood Cliffs, N.J., 1978.

parties through which their political efforts are channeled.[8]

So far, none of the three competing approaches to welfare policy has fully prevailed, neither flat-rate universalism, nor means-test selectivity, nor Titmuss's two-tier system of "positive discrimination" in favor of needs, not lack of means. Some compromises have been reached but every vote for the Labour Party promotes some efforts toward greater equality, whereas every electoral victory of the Conservatives, such as that in 1979, will move welfare policies somewhat in the opposite direction. Whether old people will get their eyeglasses and false teeth from the National Health Service without charge, as they did for a time, or whether they will have to pay for them or else prove their poverty will thus hinge on a series of political decisions.

[8]Richard M. Titmuss, *Commitment to Welfare* (London: Allen and Unwin, 1968), pp. 113–37, especially pp. 122–23, 134–35.

The need for such decisions might be eliminated, however, if both major parties should come to agree that Britain's economic position is so strained that payments from old people for many health and welfare services are indispensable, as both parties were beginning to agree during the late 1960s in the last years of the Labour government of Prime Minister Harold Wilson. In that case the stakes of politics seemed to contract. Voters, at least in the short run, were left without a real choice in regard to this range of issues; and the motivation of some of them to take part in politics was apt to be reduced. By 1974 this trend was reversed, and the Labour program stressed again its socialist beliefs. But some ebb and flow of opinion within and between the major parties seem likely to continue.

One Work Force or Two? Underpaid Service Jobs and Immigrant Labor. Another question at stake in British politics, as in those of several other highly developed industrial countries, is whether there is to be one work force or two. As real wages rise, the low-paid and often unpleasant jobs in many *service occupations*—garbage collectors, street cleaners, dishwashers, hospital orderlies, laundry workers, and the like—will tend to be deserted by the next generation of workers, who are finding more attractive opportunities in other occupations.

This exodus of local labor creates a problem and an option among ways to meet it. Either local service labor is to be lured back by means of higher pay and better working conditions, at a substantial increase in average service cost; or these service jobs are to be mechanized in large part, by means of substantial capital investments in new machinery, also at the price of higher service costs; or the service is to be cut back and partly neglected, through lack of personnel and equipment, at the cost that such neglect entails.

Finally, the service may henceforth be performed by cheap foreign labor, specially recruited from some of the poorest and least developed countries and regions in the world, such as, say, *nonwhite immigrants* from Pakistan and the West Indies, in the case of Britain. This keeps the service relatively cheap, except for some costs resulting from the lack of skill and cultural familiarity on the part of the newcomers. But it piles up other social costs: housing; schooling; the necessity perhaps of coping with major differences of culture and sometimes of language; the risks and costs of ethnic and racial conflicts; and, in short, the whole range of costs of acculturation. Thus far, British working-class and lower-middle-class voters have tended to oppose such immigration, while some other sectors of opinion have favored it. In early 1979, large strikes of hospital workers for higher wages alarmed the British public, and substantial wage increases had to be conceded. Cheap foreign labor in such service occupations might seem to some observers to offer one way of keeping costs down, but there is a social and political price.

Here, as in the case of equal versus unequal health and welfare services, technical specialists may eventually discover more attractive options. Cultural changes may produce shifts in popular values and priorities and perhaps also in the values of a part of the elite, therefore changing the probabilities of acceptance or rejection of this or that proposed solution. In the end, however, it will be the political process by which the decisions will be produced.

What Kind of Morality and Culture? Last, but not least, the stakes of British politics now include a good deal of the future cultural orientation of the country. Whether children will be lawfully beaten in government-supported schools—traditionalists approve, while reformers protest—may in time make a difference to British culture. So may the new tolerance for homosexual behavior under a law passed in the late 1960s, which permits it in private and among "consenting adults." The abolition of the death penalty for all crimes except treason, piracy, and certain military offenses is another portent of cultural and ethical change, and so are the changes in the legal and actual treatment of conscientious objectors. The abolishing or lessening of censorship of plays and films and the weakening of the obscenity laws may be seen as an increase in human freedom or else as a step toward the moral and cultural pollution of unwilling cities and neighborhoods where people wish to raise their children in a less sex-oriented environment. Some voters tend to react to all these changes with intense fear and resentment, seeing in them the downfall of order, morals, and authority; others hail all such changes as improvements; still others try to discriminate among them; but all must use politics to get the changes they desire, once they can agree on what they want.

Which Package of Policies? The six stakes just named—extent of public services and size of public sector, overall policy goals, rate of economic growth with levels of prices and employment, degrees of social and economic inequality, integrated or segregated recruitment of unskilled service workers, traditional or change-oriented culture patterns—are all interdependent; and most of them depend heavily on the level of available means and capabilities. A backward, stagnant, or declining economy can support neither an ambitious world role, nor a high and rising level of real wages, nor a vigorous program of domestic services. An inadequate level of real wages and welfare services cannot be distributed justly, on either equal or unequal terms, and the resulting inadequacies and injustices will be resented. An embittered and disgruntled work force, ever ready to engage in spontaneous slowdowns or take bribes, is unlikely to contribute much to economic growth or to encourage the private or public investment indispensable to growth. A culture oriented toward mass consumption, self-expression, permissiveness, and quick pleasures—rather than toward thrift, hard work, and the steadfast striving for more distant goals—is less likely to favor the accumulation of savings, capital, and skills and, hence, less likely to permit much economic growth. But a stagnant or inadequate level of real wages and social services, in turn, juxtaposed with the continuous demonstration of high living and consumption standards on television and in the other mass media, is likely to engender more frequent frustrations and social conflicts between labor and the middle classes, among different groups of labor, and between native labor and recent immigrants, particularly those from nonwhite countries. But a country that becomes known for treating nonwhites badly—or for treating them conspicuously less well than in the past—cannot maintain in the long run a commercial or political world role that also depends inevitably on the trust and good will of the nonwhite peoples and countries, which make up more than two-thirds of humankind.

These facts of multiple interdependence limit severely the choices among policies that are likely to be practicable, for one cannot choose policies one by one and hope realistically for their success. British voters would have to choose whole packages—viable configurations—of several such policies, all at once and in proportion and timed sequence to each other. Such viable configurations are relatively rare and hard to find. They must be discovered or invented, and much of this job has yet to be done.

The result is a seeming paradox. For a long time the size and importance of the stakes of British politics have tended to move a larger part of the British people toward political participation. But in recent years the ineffectiveness of many isolated policies, the lack of effective choice on some issues, the lack of plausible and workable overall patterns of policy, and the resulting apparent unresponsiveness and intractability of the British political and social system have left much of the British population frustrated and less inclined to participate in politics than they were earlier.

THE CHANGES IN POLITICAL PARTICIPATION

The broadening of political participation in Britain during the nineteenth and twentieth centuries has been a model case of its kind. The widening of the franchise is shown in Table 12.4.

As the right to vote widened, so did the numbers and proportions of those who actually voted. In 1874, actual voters numbered 1.6 million, or 53 percent of those who had the right to vote. A century later, in May 1979, actual voters totaled 40.1 million, or 76 percent of registered voters.

This change in the scale of participation brought with it a change in the scale of politics. In 1874 almost 30 percent of all constituencies (that is, electoral districts) for the House of Commons were uncontested. Some of these were multimember constituencies, with up to four elected. In the contested constituencies the average vote per constituency was about 8,000, regardless of the number of members to be elected from it. In 1979 all constituencies were contested, and the average vote in each was about 49,400.[9]

The state of political participation in Britain during the last decade is indicated by some data presented in Table 12.5.

The long-term increase in political participation has not continued during the last quarter century. Turnout of voters at general elections fell from 84 percent in 1950 to 76 percent in 1979. This decline in turnout was paralled by a decline in party preference. The proportion of those who replied "Don't know" to the annual Gallup poll question about which party they would vote for rose from an average of 13 percent in 1947–55 to 16 percent for 1956–67 and to 20 percent for 1968–71, but had declined to 11 percent by December 1975, perhaps in response to the greater variety of minor parties now represented in Parliament. An index of volatility in party attachment showed a similar trend: in 1965–71 it averaged about double the level that it had been in 1947–64 among Conservative voters and about five times as much as it had been in the earlier period among Labour sympathizers. Trade union membership as a proportion of the work force also declined in recent years. It had risen from 11 percent of the total employed population in 1892 to 42 percent in 1953, then declined somewhat to 38 percent in 1967. However, it rose to 46 percent in 1975, more than twice the level of 22 percent union participation in the United States.[10]

At the same time, strikes increased. The total striker days per five-year period averaged 2.2 million in 1947–56, rising slightly to 3.6 in 1957–66, then shooting up to 23.8 million for 1967–70 and to 55 million in 1972–76. Even so, in 1967–76, there were fewer strikes in Britain than in the United States, Italy, and Canada[11] (see Table 12.6).

One proposed explanation of the strike waves

TABLE 12.4 *Enfranchised Voters as a Percentage of the Population over Twenty Years of Age*

Year	Percentage
1831	5
After 1832 (first Reform Act)	7
After 1867 (second Reform Act)	16
After 1884 (third Reform Act)	29
After 1918 (vote for women over thirty)	74
After 1928 (Equal Franchise Act)	97

Source: Judith Ryder and Harold Silver, *Modern English Society: History and Structure, 1850–1970* (London: Methuen, 1970), p. 74, with reference to S. Gordon, *Our Parliament* (London: Cassell, 1964).

[9]Beer, "The British Political System," p. 243; and from data in D. Butler and D. Kavanagh, *The British General Election of October 1974* (London: Macmillan, 1975), p. 293–94.

[10]Beer, "The British Political System," pp. 286, 310–13; U.S. Department of Labor, Bureau of Labor Statistics, *Handbook of Labor Statistics: 1977* (Washington, D.C.: U.S. Government Printing Office, 1977).

[11]Beer, "The British Political System," p. 286; interview of British Foreign Minister David Owen, *Der Spiegel* (Hamburg), February 12, 1979, p. 118.

TABLE 12.5 *Political Interest and Participation in Britain, 1963–76*

Total electorate	100 %
Total number voting in general election (1974)*	73
People who read and discuss politics*	56
People who participate in at least some (nonvoting) political activity*	56
Members of voluntary associations†	47
Knowledgeable‡ citizens	42
Party members‡	25
Activists in voluntary associations†	13
Local party activists‡	0.5
Influential elected and nominated officers, local and central government‡	0.1

Sources:
*S. E. Finer and M. Steed, "The Politics of Great Britain," in R. C. Macridis, ed., *Modern Political Systems: Europe,* 4th ed. (Englewood Cliffs, N.J.: Prentice-Hall, 1978).
†Gabriel Almond and Sidney Verba, *The Civic Culture* (Princeton: Princeton University Press, 1965).
‡S. E. Finer, "Great Britain," in R. C. Macridis and R. E. Ward, eds., *Modern Political System: Europe,* 3rd ed. (Englewood Cliffs, N.J.: Prentice-Hall, 1972).

TABLE 12.6 *Strikes: Days Lost per 1,000 Employees, 1967–76*

Canada	1,906
Italy	1,824
U.S.A.	1,349
Britain	788
Federal Republic of Germany	56

Source: Interview of British Foreign Minister, David Owen, *Der Spiegel* (Hamburg), February 12, 1979, p. 118

has been the increased affluence of many workers, which lets them afford to go on strike more often, but weakens their identification with any more ideological working-class appeal and, hence, with the Labour Party. Another explanation has pointed to a general weakening of organizational discipline, particularly among younger workers, vis-à-vis both management and unions; most of the strikes after 1966 were not authorized, but arose spontaneously. Power, it was said, had moved from central union headquarters all the way down to the shop floor, where shop stewards were elected and strike votes taken. A third consideration might be that British labor has tended at some times in the past to alternate political and industrial action. If the government or the political system proved unresponsive to the workers' demands, they would resort to strikes; if strikes were unsuccessful, they would shift their effort back into politics.

If elements of all three explanations should contain some truth, then labor-based political and social conflicts and activities may well continue for a longer time than was expected in the prosperity-oriented climate of the 1950s. In that case, British politics might continue to show the marks of a cycle in which periods of convergence between the two major parties would be accompanied by some decline in voting turnout, but this eventually would be followed by the rise of new issues or the revival of old ones, the renewal of political conflicts, and a new increase in political participation. Each turn of this cycle would then put its own strains and stresses on the processes and machinery of government.

THE POLITICAL SYSTEM: ITS SELF-STEERING PROCESS AND MACHINERY

A considerable part of the British political system and its major institutions in the context of their historical development have been described in earlier sections of this chapter. There we encountered the Crown; Parliament with its two Houses, the Lords and the Commons; the prime minister and the Cabinet; and the major political parties, Conservative (or Tory) and Labour, and the formerly major and now minor party, the Liberals, the successors to the Whigs. Here it should suffice to state some of the main characteristics of the system as it works today.

The Location of Power: The Prime Minister and the Cabinet. The main power, so far as short-range or crisis decisions are concerned, is in the hands of the prime minister and the Cabinet. Since the prime minister has the power to appoint and dismiss Cabinet members or to change their assignments, it is his or her will that counts far more than any other. The prime minister is also the leader of his or her party in Parliament and in the nation. If rebellious members of that party in Parliament should break discipline by voting against his or her policy on some important issue, they would be unlikely to be renominated by the local party organization and re-elected by the voters unless backed by very strong popular feeling and/or local interests. Most often, their political careers would be finished. Ordinarily, therefore, the prime minister in office is likely to prevail over Parliament and over any opposition within his or her own party or in the country. Parliamentary acts and decisions, in turn, are likely to be executed by the civil service and the armed forces and obeyed by the vast majority of the population.

When Compliance Fails: The Civil War in Ulster. The most notable exception to this state of affairs was the refusal in 1912 of the Protestant population in Northern Ireland—or *Ulster*—to accept "home rule" for Ireland as a whole, which would have subordinated them to the Roman Catholic majority in the rest of that island. Their defiance, entailing the threat of civil war, was backed by a large part of the Conservative Party and unofficially by some members of the armed forces, which had numerous officers from the Protestant parts of Ulster. At that time the government retreated from home rule; British and Protestant power remained paramount until the Civil War of 1918–21 brought independence to the twenty-six counties of the South, which eventually became today's Ireland. However, the tight rule of the Protestant two-thirds majority was maintained through an autonomous regime in the remaining six counties of Northern Ireland. In the late 1960s the Roman Catholic minority there had become as intransigent and defiant as their Protestant neighbors. A new guerrilla-type civil war ensued. By the late 1970s over 1,200 persons had been killed; British troops were occupying Ulster; British direct rule had been restored; but neither troops nor government found much voluntary obedience and support from either Protestants or Catholics in that strife-torn section. The tragedy of Ulster reveals how much of the domestic power of the British government depends not merely on the procedures, but also on the substance of its decisions.

More peaceful—but no less clear-cut—examples of these limits on popular compliance come from the field of industrial relations. The general strike of 1926, called by the unions, had been forbidden by the Conservative government of the day, but the workers went on strike anyway. For nine days much of British business and industrial activity was paralyzed, until the workers went back. They had failed to win their goals, but had succeeded in demonstrating their freedom of action. Lesser strikes in the 1960s and 1970s, against explicit prohibitions of the Labour government of prime ministers Harold Wilson and James C. Callaghan, taught the same lesson—that government, without strong popular backing, could not compel reliable compliance with its commands against large, concentrated, and highly motivated opposition groups.

Power as the Consonance of Many Actors. Power in the British political system, therefore, is not the exclusive property of any one of its components, even the most influential. Rather, power in Britain is a result of a consonant and mutually supportive relationship among the major actors. That prime minister is powerful indeed who is backed by the Cabinet, by a strong majority in Parliament, and by his or her party's organization, members, and voters throughout the country; accepted by the main interest groups; critized—although not sabotaged—by the other major party acting as "loyal opposition" or even supported by it under a coalition agreement; and overwhelmingly supported by public opinion. Such was Prime Minister Winston Churchill's power from June 1940 to July 1945. By contrast, a prime minister is much weaker in a crisis if two of the Cabinet ministers resign, if an appreciable part of the parliamentary party is in revolt, if the opposition party is mounting a major attack, if public opinion in the country is split down the middle, if important member nations of the Commonwealth threaten to secede, and if the major foreign powers oppose his or her policy. This remarkable combination of handicaps confronted Prime Minister Sir Anthony Eden (later Lord Avon) in the Suez crisis of 1956. It was followed by his resignation and by the abandonment of the policy of military intervention that he had espoused.

Information Channels to the Government. Many aspects of the British political system seem designed to make sure that the government will propose only laws and policies that will in fact be widely supported and overwhelmingly obeyed. This is made more likely by the elaborate procedures of public hearings, commissions of enquiry, and confidential consultations with interest groups before any important legislation is introduced and enacted.

One major system of channels of information is composed of the large and well-organized interest groups. On the manufacturing employers' side these form the *Confederation of British Industry* (CBI), formed in 1965 through the merger of three smaller bodies. The CBI now includes 180 trade associations, 12,500 firms, and a highly professional staff of about 300 officials. Merchants, insurance houses, truckers, and the like are organized locally in about 100 Chambers of Commerce and nationally in the *Association of British Chambers of Commerce* (ABCC), representing about 60,000 firms. Both the CBI and the ABCC are very influential in the shaping of pending legislation and administrative practices. Farmers are organized in the still influential *National Farmers Union* (NFU) with about 200,000 members. A "bosses' trade union," the *Institute of Directors,* has over 40,000 members and looks after the interests of business executives in regard to legislation about corporate taxes, death duties, and the like. Not surprisingly, all these organizations are closest to the Conservatives.

On the side of labor, and allied with the Labour Party, there is the *Trade Union Congress* (TUC) with 10.4 million members, about 39 percent of the work force, and about 95 percent of all union members. Also allied with the Labour Party is the *Cooperative Party,* which is the political arm of over 1,200 cooperative societies and includes about 90 percent of the membership of the *Cooperative Union.* The latter, through its 565 affiliated retail distributive societies, has a total membership of over 12 million and accounts for about 9 percent of national retail sales. The TUC is a major force in the Labour Party, where each member union has a bloc vote corresponding to the size of its membership. Accordingly, the union vote accounts for a large majority of votes at the party's annual convention; and many Labour members of Parliament are sponsored by unions. Compared to the TUC, the Cooperative Party's representation and influence within the Labour Party are considerably smaller.

Professional organizations are less closely linked to either of the major parties. The British Medical Association (BMA) with 84 percent of general practitioners, the National Union of Teachers (NUT) with 85 percent of teachers in state schools, and the National and Local Government Officers' Association negotiate with and put pressure on each party and government in accordance with their understanding of the interests of their members.

Much of the influence of interest groups is exercised through the day-to-day contact with legislators and administrators, the furnishing of detailed information, the representation of viewpoints and of expectable responses from the membership and from the general public and the probable practical response to this or that proposed wording of a law. As a result, most of the legislation introduced by a government has been cleared with all major interest groups before it reaches Parliament; and additional amendments or deletions may be made there in accordance with the desires of some interest groups. Thus, the final act of Parliament is likely to be the result of negotiations and compromises with all major groupings.

As in other countries, the power of large, well-financed, and permanently organized groups threatens to overshadow the needs or desires of weaker or less well organized groups. In Britain, however, there has been in recent years a notable increase in the numbers, strength, and activity of *voluntary associations,* founded more or less spontaneously by groups of citizens in order to deal with particular policy issues. Combining the methods of publicity, legislative lobby, endorsement of parties or candidates, and sometimes dramatic semilegal direct action in the streets, such organizations have had a number of successes. At the start of the 1960s the Campaign for Nuclear Disarmament (CND), advocating unilateral renunciation of nuclear weapons, came close to capturing the Labour Party. In 1970 the Fair Cricket Campaign (FCC) and the Stop-The-Seventies-Tour (STST) brought about the cancellation of a proposed tour by the white, South African cricket team, as a protest against the conspicuously discriminatory race policies of that country. The Howard League for Penal Reform was effective in bringing about the abolition of the death penalty. The Homosexual Law Reform Society played a part in the repeal of most of the laws penalizing homosexuality. An organization called SHELTER drew attention to the plight of homeless persons and families. Founded in 1966, it had raised by 1969 about £2 million (about $5 million) and had provided homes for three thousand persons. "In 1960, the first Association for the Advancement of State Education was set up; by 1966 there were 120. . . . In the early sixties, membership in the [long-established] National Union of Students . . . grew rapidly from 150,000 to nearly 400,000." By 1977 they had grown to 700,000 members.[12]

Altogether, this new activity in an array of voluntary organizations brought a new element into politics, perhaps a counterweight to the bureaucratization of the old established major parties and interest groups.

Local self-assertion merged with a new ethnic self-assertion in a rise of Celtic nationalism. The Scottish National Party had polled less than 1 percent of the vote in Scotland in 1959. but in October 1974 its share of the vote there rose to almost 31 percent, and it won eleven seats in Parliament. However, it lost almost all of them in 1979 when many of its voters shifted back to Labour. The Welsh Nationalist Party also grew rapidly during the 1960s. In 1974, with 35,000 members, it received 11.1 percent of the vote in Wales and three seats in Parliament. Depending on the votes of these parties, the Labour government proposed schemes of administrative *devolution* for Scotland and Wales, in order to shift an array of powers to assemblies elected by the voters of each country.[13] In 1979 these arrangements were tested by referendum votes in each country. They were rejected by the voters of Wales (only 20 percent of those voting—or just 11 percent of the total electorate—favored devolution whereas the voters of Scotland evinced no clear preference for or against the proposed scheme (52 percent voted yes, constituting only 34 percent of the electorate).

[12]Beer, "The British Political System," pp. 320–21; *Directory of British Associations, 1977–78* (Kent, England: C.B.D. Research Ltd., 1977).

[13]Scotland and Wales are called "countries," and athletic events between their teams and England's are called "international" in Britain.

This was followed by significant losses of support for both nationalist parties in the 1979 general election. The Scottish National Party lost nine of its eleven seats, as its share of the Scottish vote dropped by half (to 16 percent); and the Welsh Nationalist Party lost one of its three seats, taking only 8.1 percent of the vote in Wales. Whether these results signal the ebbing of ethnic self-assertion in Great Britain or merely a temporary downswing remains to be seen.

Another system of information channels is offered by Parliament itself. Members of Parliament come from over six hundred constituencies, each small enough to permit them to remain in touch with local opinion. Within each constituency there is, as a rule, at least one local organization of each of the two major parties, and in many constituencies there are local party agents on an honorary or professional basis. These parties and agents transmit local views and concerns not only to the sitting member of Parliament, but also to the national headquarters of their party. Each MP, in turn, has the right to direct *questions in Parliament* to the government and to particular ministers in it; and the government is obligated to furnish an answer in the House of Commons, before an audience of MPs who do not take kindly to evasions. In this manner, specific cases of alleged wrong done to some individual can be raised, as well as larger questions of administrative practice and public policy. The weekly question period in the Commons gets wide attention from the public and the press, and political reputations have been made or broken through the manner in which ministers answered the questions put to them in Parliament.

The practices about which the ministers are likely to be questioned in this manner are most often those of the civil service; and it is the civil service of the departments for which the ministers are responsible that must brief them on the facts and considerations they need to know for their answers.

A Continuing Support: The Civil Serivce. The cohesion and effectiveness of the British government are provided by the civil service. Relatively new in British history, the civil service is a child of the great liberal reforms of the nineteenth century. Earlier, many offices, including commissions in the army, were sold for cash. Private companies, such as the East India Company until 1857, governed large territories through their employees.

When the inefficiencies of the old system became intolerable at home as well as in the colonies, the civil service system took its place. Its members were recruited by open competitive examinations and were to be promoted strictly on the grounds of merit, in contrast to the old practices of patronage and bribery. The civil service thus became a channel for the rise of many of the brightest sons of the British middle classes—even though civil servants with an upper-class background tended to have a better chance to reach its highest levels. For nearly a century British civil servants ran the empire; after 1945 they superintended its replacement by new independent nations.

In the British system, civil servants are expected to remain politically neutral. With equal efficiency they are to serve Conservative ministers in encouraging private enterprise and Labour ministers in nationalizing it. In exchange for such political self-denial they enjoy permanence of tenure. Ministers come and go, but the permanent undersecretaries in their ministries remain. In practice this often means that the policy of the ministries also remains constant, and only the minister's signature changes. From their long experience, civil servants in each department of the government develop "the departmental view," which no minister will override lightly. To this extent the civil servants—most notably those of the Treasury—actually govern the country.[14] (This

[14]Many of them are trained at Oxford or Cambridge. Loyal members of the latter university are fond of saying, "Oxford may speak for England, but Cambridge runs it."

practice, as we recall, contrasts with the arrangements in the United States under which a large number of top-level federal jobs are defined as policy making, to be staffed and restaffed at the discretion of each president.)

Though civil servants are influential and respected, their real income has declined. In 1975 their salaries bought only about three-quarters of what they had bought in 1938 when the Great Depression had kept goods and services cheap. These workers, too, in increasing numbers are choosing the path of militant unionism and the weapon of the strike. In late February 1979 a strike by 1,300 civil servants, including code clerks, computer operators, court clerks, and airport customs officials, provoked the conservative *Daily Telegraph* to the sensational statement that civil servants "have declared war on the government"; this remark then was duly headlined in the American press.[15] The civil servants may have a just grievance, and so may the public for being deprived of their services. In the end, both sides probably will succeed in keeping their tempers, and Britain will muddle through to another tolerable compromise solution.

New Institutions: Mixed Boards and Public Corporations. Civil servants in Britain work well not only with politicians and fellow bureaucrats, but also with businesspeople, trade union leaders, scientists, and technicians. They do so on numerous *mixed boards,* of which the London Passenger Transport Board is an early and successful example. Set up in 1933 by a Conservative government, this board, now called the London Transport Executive, brings together representatives of the government, the county of London, and the former private subway, bus, and streetcar companies that were merged into a single transport system for greater London. The system is managed by the board, which plans new lines, construction, and investments and sets the rates and conditions for service. It also acts as a board of directors, appointing managers and supervising their work.

Boards of this type straddle the line between public and private enterprise. They are expected to look out for the interests of stockholders and bondholders, thousands of employees, and millions of passengers or other consumers and also for the interests of the cities and of national development. Nowadays similar boards function in other countries, such as the New York Port Authority in the United States or the Northeast Swiss Power Stations in Switzerland. Britain, however, has gone furthest in developing this type of organization. Judging from the quality of London transport, which is clean, fast, dependable, and very pleasant to use, the system has been a success.

Another successful type of mixed authority, linking a plurality of public bodies, is the *University Grants Committee.* This body brings civil servants together with representatives of the universities for the purpose of distributing government subsidies among the universities in a way that protects both the institutions and their scholars from political pressures.

Finally, Britain has created a whole series of *public corporations* to manage various publicly owned services. These, too, provide for the representation of several public organizations and interests. They range from the British Broadcasting Corporation (BBC) and British Airways Corporation (BA), both set up by Conservative governments before World War II, to such creations of Labour governments as the National Coal Board, the Electricity Generating Board, and the Electricity Council. In 1967 the Labour government set up an Industrial Reorganization Corporation with $360 million capital to stimulate mergers in private industry; and the Land Commission was created to buy land for public purposes. Like the civil service, these various organizational devices contribute an array of stable machinery to aid the government in meeting its growing responsibilities, and this general trend is likely to continue under either major party.

[15]"Civil Servants 'Declare War' in Britain," *Boston Globe,* February 26, 1979, p. 4.

ACCOMPLISHMENTS AND UNFINISHED BUSINESS: AN INTERIM SCORE

In the generation in which 500 million people have become independent from British rule, the average Englishman has grown one inch taller than his father. The British people also have become better educated, better nourished, better housed, and longer lived.[16] Polls show the greater popularity of the National Health Service, and both major parties vie in promising to improve it further. With less than half of the per capita income of the United States, British life expectancy is higher.

Today Americans read in their newspapers mostly of the things that Britain has not done or that are difficult for it—much as the British are informed mainly about America's worst foibles, follies, and sometimes tragedies. Americans do not read of the things that Britain has done. The jet engine is a British invention. The decisive tube that made radar possible was brought from Britain to the United States by Sir Henry Tizard in World War II. Penicillin is a British contribution. In the mid-1960s eighteen Nobel Prize winners were teaching at Cambridge University alone. Britain, as we saw, is ahead of the United States in new towns and town planning, in national health services, and in the large-scale use of nuclear energy for peacful purposes. The British have doubled enrollment in their universities, as have the Americans. They have kept a good deal of their high quality work still going, better than in the United States, and they have struggled with many of their problems more successfully. Although they have their problems with racial differences, they are developing legal instruments to fight discrimination. After a long period of rigidity, they now have more humane laws about drugs and homosexuality than in the United States and yet have a much lower crime rate. Their streets are cleaner and safer to walk in. What they often lack in science and technology is large-scale application. Very often an invention is developed in England and applied in the United States.

This slowness in applying innovations on a large scale seems due at least as much to the attitude of managers and investors as to labor's distrust of innovations that might abolish some existing jobs. There is a general reluctance to make large investments in new equipment and facilities, both in the private and in the public sectors. The main circular road around London, the airport at Heathrow, the construction of a large number of modern office buildings and apartment houses—all these projects seem well behind in London, compared with their counterparts that have been completed or are under construction in Paris. Statistics confirm this picture. The British per capita income is lagging well behind that of France or West Germany and shows no signs of catching up.

The Search for Partnership Abroad. After the 1890s a British-American alliance began to grow, and in World War II it reached its peak. As late as 1949, American and British pilots flew their planes side by side to break Stalin's blockade of Berlin, and still later, a British brigade fought alongside United States troops in the Korean War. But although the two countries remained allied (with fourteen others) in the North Atlantic Treaty Organization (NATO), the "special relationship" of Britain to the United States faded in the 1950s.

By the 1960s United States leaders were paying little attention to their British allies, who were told of completed American policy decisions rather than being consulted about them in advance. Since the decisions involved matters of life and death for

[16]Deaths of infants under one year old, per 1,000 live births in the United Kingdom, numbered 150 in 1870–72; 110 in 1910–12; and 67 in 1930–32. In 1942 the death rate was 53, but in 1952 it had been reduced to 29 and in 1968 to 19. In less than one century, it had thus been cut by seven-eighths. About 800,000 children were born each year in 1870–72 and again in 1968. But in the latter year, more than 100,000 children's lives were saved in comparison to the earlier period (Ryder and Silver, pp. 143, 311, 314).

both countries, as in the Cuban crisis of 1962, the British were unenthusiastic about their new state of dependence. "Annihilation without representation," as the British historian Arnold Toynbee said earlier, "is unfair." At present, Britain still needs the alliance with the United States, but it also needs to regain a greater sense of equality and independence—a greater measure of control over its own fate.

The ties to the Commonwealth cannot give Britain this power. The Commonwealth countries that are predominantly white—Canada, Australia, and New Zealand—continue to accept British exports, immigrants, and capital on favorable terms and to supply Britain with cheaper food and raw materials to the extent that the transitional arrangements after Britain's entry into the Common Market in 1973 permit them to do so. The nonwhite Commonwealth nations, from Bangladesh to Jamaica, furnish Britain with cheap labor and an increase in racial and housing problems within the limits of Britain's tightening legislative and administrative curbs on immigration. South Africa furnishes some gold transactions, useful to the ailing British currency, at the price of grave political conflict over South African and Rhodesian race discrimination. But all these ties are no longer adequate. On balance, Commonwealth relations are becoming, to most of the British, a matter of the past more than of the future.

Yet Britain cannot see any promise in a policy of isolation. It has sought, therefore, to tie its economy, and perhaps in time its politics, to those of Western Europe. Such a policy of *European integration* may sound fine in general, but has become awkward in specifics. Joining the European Common Market may mean higher food prices for British consumers, sharper competition for British industry and labor, and less freedom of decision for British voters and their government. Even though Britain has belonged to the Common Market since 1973, many of these problems are nowhere near solution. Britain's new role in European and world affairs still has to be defined.

Some Enduring Assets. Britain's agenda for change seems impressive, but so are the nation's resources. The economic growth rate, the balance between exports and imports, inflation and the value of the pound, the process of planning for rapid technological progress, the removal of class or caste lines, the balanced growth of science and the humanities and the integration of these "two cultures"—all are weak points in Britain. Yet, in a very important way, Britain has managed to be innovative and still remain cohesive. It can function under tremendous strains, as it did in the Battle of Britain in 1940, and it can come up with new and sometimes very surprising ideas. New ideas and new dreams still are being generated in British universities. On the level of recent popular culture, young Britons gave the world much of the early hippie movement, the Beatles' contribution to rock and roll, and the miniskirt.

The British people's strange and happy combination of tremendous persistence and unceasing innovativeness—their insistence on being both innovative and coherent—suggests that their social and political system may repay deeper study. The British are trying to build a new social order while keeping much of their old culture and habits. This may seem impossible to do, but the British are not likely to stop trying. Though they will be harder to imitate than most other nations, the world can still learn from them.

KEY TERMS AND CONCEPTS

establishment
gentlemen
public schools
four-layer culture
wildcat strikes
Celts
Saxons
Normans
exchequer
common law
institution

tradition of enquiry
Domesday Book
Magna Carta
Royal Commission
law of primogeniture
member of Parliament
burgher
cross-class coalition
the Crown
divine right theory
roundheads
cavaliers
revolution
parliamentary government
House of Lords
House of Commons
Cabinet
party discipline
Whigs
Tories
Conservative Party
Liberals
Labour Party
parliamentary party
national party
whips
free votes
prime minister
Orange Order
Reform Bill of 1832
imperialism
Commonwealth
dominion status
nationalization of industries
National Health Service
the two-party pendulum
social contract
European Common Market
productivity
universalism versus selectivity in social services
service occupations and nonwhite immigrants
Ulster
Trade Union Congress
voluntary associations
devolution
questions in Parliament
mixed boards
University Grants Committee
public corporations
European integration

ADDITIONAL READINGS

Beer, S. H. "The British Political System." In S. H. Beer and A. Ulam, eds. *Patterns of Government: The Major Political Systems of Europe.* 3rd ed. New York: Random House, 1974. PB

———. *British Politics in a Collectivist Age.* Rev. ed. New York: Random House (Vintage), 1969. Note especially last chapter. PB

Blondel, J. *Voters, Parties and Leaders.* Harmondsworth: Penguin Books, 1963. PB

Butler, D., and D. Kavanagh, *The British General Election of October 1974.* London: Macmillan, 1975.

Butler, D., and J. Freeman, *British Political Facts, 1900–1968.* 3rd ed. New York: St. Martin's, 1968.

Butler, D., and M. Pinto-Duschinsky. *The British General Election of 1970.* London: Macmillan, 1971.

Butler, D., and D. Stokes. *Political Change in Britain: Forces Shaping Electoral Choice.* 2nd ed. New York: St Martin's, 1976. PB

Cole, G. D. H., and R. Postgate. *British Common People, 1745–1945.* London: Methuen, 1965. PB

Finer, S. *Anonymous Empire.* 2nd ed. London: Pall Mall Press, 1966. PB

———, and M. Steed. "Politics in Britain." In R. C. Macridis, ed., *Modern Political Systems: Europe.* 4th ed. Englewood Cliffs, N.J.: Prentice-Hall, 1978.

MacInnis, C. *City of Spades.* London: MacGibbon and Kee, 1958. PB

Mackenzie, R. T. *British Political Parties.* 2nd ed. New York: Praeger, 1964.

Osborne, J. *Look Back in Anger.* New York: Bantam, 1967. PB

Rose, R. *Governing Without Consensus: An Irish Perspective.* Boston: Beacon Press, 1971. PB
———. *Influencing Voters.* London: Faber, 1971.
———. *Politics in England.* Boston: Little, Brown, 1974. PB
Russell, B. *Autobiography.* 2 vols. Boston: Atlantic Monthly Press, Little, Brown, 1967 and 1968. PB
Ryder, J., and H. Silver. *Modern English Society: History and Structure, 1850–1970.* New York: Barnes and Noble, 1977. PB
Sampson, A. *The New Anatomy of Britain.* New York: Stein and Day, 1973. PB
Sillitoe, A. *Saturday Night and Sunday Morning.* New York: New American Library, 1973. PB
Titmuss, R. M. *Commitment to Welfare.* Winchester, Mass.: Allen and Unwin, 1976.
Verney, D. V. *British Government and Politics: Life Without a Declaration of Independence.* New York: Harper & Row, 1976. PB
Wilson, H. *The Labour Government, 1964–1970.* London: Penguin, 1974. PB

PB = *available in paperback*

XIII

France

The French people have dazzled and baffled their neighbors for centuries. They have acquired so many reputations that almost everyone has an image of the French, but the different images do not easily fit together.

THE MANY IMAGES OF FRANCE

Perhaps the best-known image of the French between 1789 and 1960 has been one of individualism, unrest, ceaseless change, and infinite variety. "Two Frenchmen are a political party," goes an old saying, "and three Frenchmen are a constitutional crisis." Even the French have wondered about themselves. Asked President de Gaulle, "How can you govern a country that has 247 kinds of cheese?"

Time and again in the last two centuries French governments have fallen by revolution. Even in periods of constitutional government, change has been the rule, not the exception. During the period from 1945 to 1961 the average tenure of a French chief executive was eight months. Some foreign observers were tempted to think that if one did not like a particular French government, one had only to wait a while, but a French proverb seemed even more accurate: the more it changes, the more it stays the same. Yet, this first picture may now be out of date. After 1961, French politics seemed to become remarkably stable. President de Gaulle stayed in office for eight years; and his successor, Georges Pompidou, held office for almost five years, until his death in April 1974. Pompidou's successor, Valéry Giscard d'Estaing, by 1979 had completed the first five years of his seven-year term, still representing the same majority coalition of moderate-to-conservative parties.

An entirely different image is that of the orderly French. This image sees the French as precise, logical, and bureaucratic. Indeed, their public gardens appear to have been designed with ruler and compass, as long, straight vistas emerge between shrubs and trees that have been neatly clipped into shape. Their scholars are famous for close "explications of texts," their thinkers for bold Cartesian logic,[1] their writers for French lucidity. Their provincial middle classes are known for their conservatism and the housewives and *rentiers*—people who live on fixed incomes from pensions or investments—for their thrift.

A third image focuses on the segmentation of French life. Changes in practices and habits rarely spill over quickly from one sector of activities to another. Often they stay confined to one aspect of life, leaving much of the rest unchanged. Their orderliness makes the French put many things into compartments, including themselves. Individuals tend to join mostly those voluntary associations that fit their own social group, in contrast to Americans, whose associations tend to cut across such boundaries. "The French," concludes Duncan MacRae, "are both principled and impervious to persuasion." The "typical" French landscape, observes Geoffrey Gorer, "is divided into contrasting segments . . . modified by human handiwork. The world of ideas is similarly compartmentalized. . . ." In such compartments, life can be lonely. "In no other country," says André Siegfried, "can one feel so utterly alone as in France where people barricade themselves in their homes as if they were fortresses." Neither the charms of French conversation in salons and cafés nor the eloquence of French orators and writers can overcome the divisions separating individuals from individuals and groups from groups.

A fourth image pictures the French as a nation of doubters. A medieval French monk, Peter Abelard, invented the scholastic method of reasoning, which lines up contradictory authorities on both sides of every question. Centuries later, Descartes introduced the Cartesian technique: to doubt everything as deeply as possible, so that only the simplest and most self-evident propositions will survive. And the skeptical smile on the death mask of Voltaire, the great satirist who made such merciless fun of the tyrannies, follies, and dogmas of his time, was called "the smile of France" by the writer Victor Hugo.

A fifth image dwells on French elegance and taste, imagination and creativity. France has long furnished the models for both designer clothing and ideas. In the arts, from modern painting to motion pictures, France has given the world the word and concept of *avant-garde*—the vanguard that does today what slower folk will do tomorrow. French technological pioneering since 1945 is reflected in such well-known jet aircraft as the Caravelle, the supersonic fighter plane Mirage, and the supersonic intercontinental passenger plane Concorde, the last of which was developed jointly with Britain. Other examples are the innovative automobile Citröen DS 21 and the exploration of the underwater world by Jacques Cousteau. French thinkers have excelled not only in their logic, but also in what the mathematician Pascal called the *esprit de finesse,* the spirit of subtlety that lives on among French scientists and existentialist philosophers.

A related image portrays France as the country of the good life. "To live like God in France" is a wistful German phrase for the utmost in wellbeing. The French gourmet is a renowned expert on good food and wine, and French has long been the language of love, even for some English and German writers.

A final image of the French is one of courage, loyalty, and pride. From the Crusades and Joan of Arc to the Battle of Verdun in World War I and the underground resistance in World War II, this tradition has stayed alive.

[1]The term is derived from the name of the French philosopher René Descartes (1596–1650), who has been widely considered the chief representative of the French intellectual tradition. Similarly, Georg Wilhelm Hegel (1770–1831) has been seen as typical of German thought, Giambattista Vico (1668–1744) of Italian ideas, Jeremy Bentham (1748–1832) of the British empirical tradition, and Thomas Jefferson (1743–1826) of the wide-ranging thought of the United States. However, no one person can completely represent the style of thought of an entire country.

Each of these images is one-sided and somewhat overdrawn. Yet each contains some truth. Taken together, they tell us something of France's complexity and of its capacity to produce surprises. How has one people acquired so many reputations, and how do all these traits work together in a single political system?

The French themselves have sometimes wondered which is the real France. Some of their writers have stressed the distinction between *le pays légal,* the legal France, divided by disputes about politics and laws, and *le pays réel,* the real country, held together by a profound unity of tradition and culture. If we are to find this real country, then, history must help us seek the answer.

The Heritage of Central Monarchy. The French were the first people on the Continent—and, after England, the second in Europe—to achieve a modern absolute monarchy for a large territorial state. Their centralized government was a work of art, will, and ruthless power. The English got their unified monarchy a little earlier, but as late as the fifteenth century two kings were fighting each other for England's one crown. England was not yet well centralized in the 1470s when Louis XI and his equally absolutist successors were putting France together. The first task of the English state was to consolidate a foreign conquest—that of England by the Normans. The first task of the French state was to prevent a foreign conquest—that of France by the English. A period of unscrupulousness was necessary for the successful completion of this task, but its rulers' politics of organized murder and cruelty eventually gave France a higher degree of civic peace, unity, and power than other countries in Europe had at that time.

The Weakness of Self-Government in the Cities. One decisive choice was made by the French, perhaps unconsciously. The French cities, feeling too weak to balance the power of the nobles and the countryside, backed the king and central monarchy. They did so to the point of yielding much of their powers of self-government to the royal administration. As a result, France has had less of a tradition of decentralized, urban self-government than has Germany or England. For backing the king, the bourgeois of the French cities won much of what they had hoped to receive from him: security, order, and protection for their businesses.[2]

By 1630 the French monarchy had obtained wide support. In many other countries, such as Germany, the church opposed a strong central government. But in France and Spain it backed central government that, in turn, supported Roman Catholicism as the national religion. After the Reformation many of the more independent-minded cities and nobles became Protestant. When they were defeated by the Catholics in alliance with the monarchy, local and provincial self-government was defeated, too.

Continuing Centralization. The church in the France of the seventeenth century was led by a political genius, Cardinal de Richelieu, one of the great practitioners of power politics of all time. It was Richelieu who conceived the idea that the main interest of Catholic France was to destroy the power of Catholic Spain. This could be done best, he felt, through intervening in the war between

[2]In exceptional situations when the burghers of a city tried to cling to self-government, they were mercilessly suppressed. In the sixteenth century the city of Bordeaux (which had been English for a time and had less of a tradition of submission to the French Crown) rose in defense of its ancient liberties. A royal army besieged the city and forced its capitulation. When the burghers killed a representative of the king, the royal army beheaded the civil consul in retaliation. The consul, who was executed for vindicating the rights of the citizens against the king, had an interesting name: Guillotin. He was beheaded by hand. More than two centuries later, another man named Guillotin, a doctor of medicine, developed a machine for beheading people that would make the process faster, more reliable, and he thought, more humanitarian; in the French Revolution his invention was applied to the king and many nobles.

Protestants and Catholics in Germany, where the Hapsburgs were uniting the resources of Austria and Spain on the Catholic side. If the French Catholic king would back the Protestant king of Sweden with money and persuade him to intervene on the Protestant side in Germany, these actions would weaken the Hapsburgs. Richelieu's maneuver succeeded brilliantly. The Swedes invaded Germany, and the Protestants and Catholics fought each other to a standstill. By 1648 two-fifths of the German people—8 million out of 20 million—had perished.

For Germany and central Europe the hundred-year period after 1620 was a century of devastation and decline. In French history books, however, this period is called *Le Grand Siécle*—The Great Century. During these years France became the leading power of Europe, and the fruits of Richelieu's work were reaped by Louis XIV—the king who so simply said, "The state—that is I." From about 1680 to 1780, France was the most brilliant, the richest, and the leading country of Europe, losing to England on the high seas, but outshining all other nations in most other respects. Throughout this period it remained predominant both as a power and as a model of official culture and elite behavior on the Continent.

Within France, Louis XIV broke the last resistance of the provincial nobles and at the same time laid the foundations of French leadership in taste and fashion. He built the most splendid palace of his time at Versailles and made the nobles reside there. He thus turned noblemen into courtiers. Far from their estates in the provinces, they had less power and were more dependent on the favor of the king. At court they were almost constantly in each other's company, and they were encouraged to compete not only in court intrigues and love affairs, but also in luxury and elegance. Court taste and court speech became the single standard for the nation. The results of this centralization have never been reversed. Isolated at Versailles, the nobles became assimilated in a common style of life and thought, but estranged from most of the rest of France. The legacy of this class division has lingered, too.

Even today, after the French monarchy has been swept away by a chain of revolutions, its heritage lives on. French administration has remained highly centralized, as authority flows from the top down. So has French culture. Paris is still the center of almost everything that is important in France—the arts, sciences, mass media, education, business, finance, and politics. Messages and ideas from the provinces count for little, unless their proponents move to Paris first.

In France a relatively modern centralized state was established before the Industrial Revolution and before any political middle-class revolution like those in England and the United States. Later, the effects of the French Revolution and the Napoleonic age further strengthened the power of the state and its machinery, modernizing it somewhat by increasing its claims to legitimacy and popular support. The result was a strong bureaucratic state that remained somewhat authoritarian in its dealings with its people and somewhat remote from them.

The Distance Between Government and People. Communications also move most often from the top down. They flow from government to the bureaucracy; from bureaucrats and party leaders to the people; from professors to students; and from Parisian designers and avant-garde artists to consumers. Little information, if any, flows upward in return.

The little people—workers, peasants, shopkeepers, taxpayers, soldiers, and voters—may resent this situation, but they are unlikely to be heard or heeded. The best they can do is to build defenses for themselves. They defend their individuality and their privacy. They distrust all government. If government is far away, they prefer to keep it there. They limit it legally whenever they can; and they evade it at every opportunity. Voltaire expressed the attitude of many French citizens in classic form when in the face of the powerful central monarchy he quietly announced that he

FIGURE 13.1 *Twelve French Political Regimes, 1788-1978*

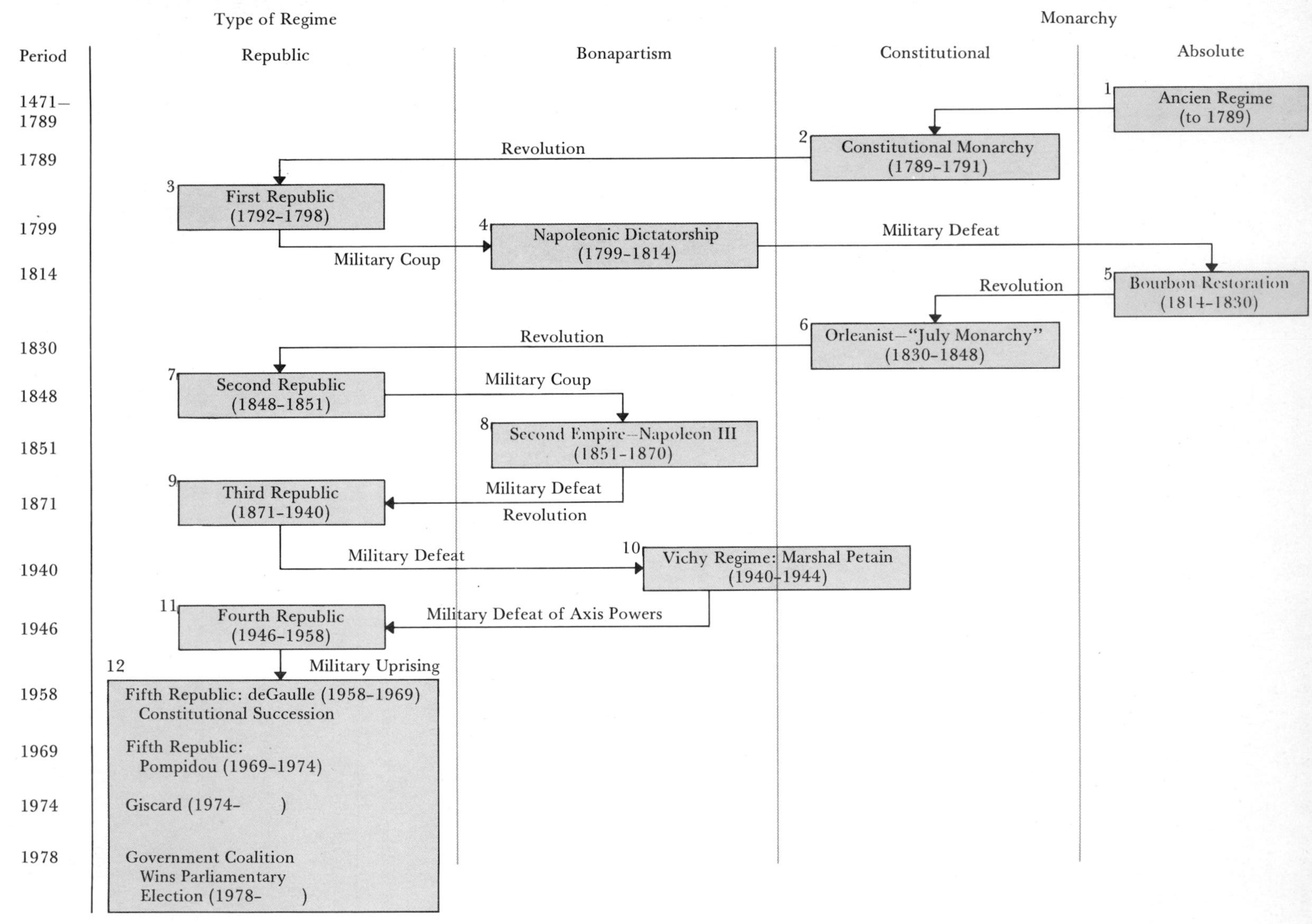

Source: From data in R. C. Macridis, "Politics of France," in R. C. Macridis and R. E. Ward, eds., *Modern Political Systems: Europe,* 4th ed., 1978. Adapted by permission of Prentice-Hall, Inc., Englewood Cliffs, N.J.

was going home to "cultivate his garden," that is, withdraw to private life.

Millions of French people are still doing so, at least in a figurative sense. They keep out of politics in ordinary times and, thus, make the moderate center of political opinion seem weaker than it is. But they return to political activity when stirred by unusual events, making politics in France—as shown in Figure 13.1—often more exciting and less predictable than anywhere else.

The Heritage of Revolution. It is hard to imagine just how rigid the French monarch and social system had become by the 1780s and how long it took to gather the forces that were to transform France and, in due time, the world. In 1789, France finally exploded in revolution. The French did not revolt against Louis XV, a bad ruler, but rose against Louis XVI, who was no worse than eighteenth-century monarchs generally were. If France could not be governed under a ruler of Louis XVI's quality, then something was fundamentally wrong with the system and would have to be changed. In this sense the revolts against Charles of England and Louis XVI of France involved the same need: to change a system, not a person.

From the king on down, the French people then showed another trait that has endured—their resistance to compromise. After the English revolution and the return of the monarchy, even Charles II accepted a bill of rights voted by Parliament. James II was driven out when he refused to compromise further; and two years later England got another monarch, William of Orange, whose reign led to the Act of Toleration. In the end the English monarchy gave in gracefully to the need for making concessions to the demands for constitutional government. The Bourbon kings of France were different. Of them it was said then and later that they never forgot and they never learned.

The French tried to establish a constitutional monarchy in 1791 with Louis XVI as monarch. But Louis refused to accept any constitutional limits to his power. He secretly corresponded with other absolute rulers of Europe (some of whom were his relatives) to persuade them to make war against France and restore him as absolute ruler. The correspondence was discovered and the king put on trial as a traitor before the National Assembly. Maximilien de Robespierre, the radical leader of the Jacobin Party,[3] displaying brilliant French logic, made the decisive point for the prosecution. If the king were innocent, he pointed out, then he was by the grace of God the absolute king of France; he had rightfully tried to organize the subjection of his rebellious subjects; and those sitting in the assembly were themselves rebels and traitors who ought to be beheaded. If, on the other hand, the assembly were truly representative of the French nation, then the king was a traitor to his country and it was he who had to be beheaded. Accepting this logic, the members of the assembly voted predictably. The king was beheaded and the *First Republic* established.

In this case logic was used to prevent compromise rather than permit it. This tactic revealed its greatness and strength as well as its long-run one-sidedness in the events that followed. Six European countries invaded France after the king's execution in 1793. But the war had already been started by the moderate Girondist government of France which had come to power under the First Republic in 1792.[4] It had started the war in the hope that a foreign war would increase national unity. The Girondists turned out to be grievously mistaken and perished for their folly. They started a war that they could not conduct

[3]The *Jacobins* were the main radical party of the French Revolution. Centered in Paris, they got their name from one of their early meeting places, a former monastery of Saint James, whom the French called Saint Jacques (i.e., Saint Jacob). Their ranks included members of the prosperous middle class as well as professional people and poor artisans.

[4]The *Girondists* became the main moderate party of the revolution by 1792. Strongest in the provinces, they were named after the Gironde, a fertile plain in southern France. Their members included the well-to-do of the smaller towns.

successfully, yet that became vital to the French people once it had begun. The Jacobins, the most radical middle-class leaders, took power under Robespierre in 1793 and mobilized the entire French nation.

The Nation in Arms. In one year France brought 1.3 million men under arms in fourteen armies and thereby changed the scale of warfare in Europe. This could not have possibly been done by an unpopular draft. The only way of getting 5 percent of the French people into uniform was through the voluntary support of large numbers of the French people. This voluntary support made possible the enforcement of the laws of the Republic. It seemed as if Rousseau's "general will" had taken armed shape.[5] Robespierre and the Jacobins seemed to be executing his ideas. Backed by a large part of the people, they were forcing the French populace to be "free." They did so with relentless logic and frequent cruelty. The city of Lyon rose against the central government and was destroyed by a republican army. The general in charge reported back to Paris, "Lyon rose against the Republic. Lyon is no more."

Revolutionary France was marked by extremisms of all sorts. The conservatives thought the republicans mad. The republicans, in turn, thought the conservatives to be walking corpses, people of the dead past. Each side felt that its opponents had no right to live. For a time there was a law that made it a crime to fall under suspicion.

If divisiveness and intolerance were extreme, so too were the heroism and efforts of the people. The Parisians descended to the cellars of Paris to scrape saltpeter deposits from the walls to get enough ammunition to blast the armies of the European monarchs out of France. In Paris alone, there were 243 open-air forges to make cast-iron cannon. The revolution first produced the massed artillery that later made Napoleon's military reputation.

The French soldiers fought with high morale; they did not run away in the field or in battle. Unlike the involuntary soldiers of the European monarchs, they did not need to fight in conspicuous uniforms and to march in close order into enemy fire so that their sergeants could keep an eye on them. The French soldiers fought against the royal armies in open skirmish lines, firing from whatever cover they found, and then attacked in massed columns. They won, and in the process they changed the art of war in their epoch.

The Politics of Revolution. But though they won foreign battles, they could not agree on how to run France. Not all the French favored the revolution. Not only aristocrats but also many of their servants, friends, or more loyal peasant subjects bitterly opposed the republican regime. The republican government tried to crush all resistance by public execution in a deliberate campaign of *terror*—much as the Bourbon kings had publicly executed those who resisted them or defied their laws. But soon the revolutionists turned against one another with the same ruthlessness that they had used against their enemies.

The Republic introduced rigid price controls to help the poor, which then turned the middle class (which had been part of the original Jacobin movement) against the more radical Jacobins. The very radical Jacobins—"the enraged," as they were called—also rose against the more moderate radicals, as the very conservative Jacobins had.

Robespierre thus had to fight enemies on both flanks. At first he used the radicals to behead the moderates. Then he used the surviving moderates to destroy the radicals. Danton on his right and Hébert on his left both died under the guillotine. But soon Robespierre himself was attacked and put to death by those who feared that their own gains from the revolution might now be in danger.

Robespierre had not been an extreme terrorist. In fact, he had cut down the executions in the provinces, brought all the trials to Paris, and reduced the indiscriminate killing. But when he was sentenced and executed, the whole responsi-

[5] Rousseau's views were discussed in Chapter 4, above.

bility for the terror was put on him even by those who themselves had led executions. When one provincial leader of the terror, who had voted against Robespierre, was reminded in the French assembly of his own share in the killings, he looked straight at his colleagues and answered, "Robespierre's grave is big enough to bury our differences in."

There followed a period of domestic relaxation and corruption, called *Thermidor,* and a period of government by five directors. Under this regime, called the *Directory,* the call rose for more freedom for speculators and for more law and order against the poor. The foreign wars continued. Quietly, the nation was getting ready to hand over its problems to a general.

The General Who Set a Precedent. The French in times of crisis have tended to turn to a general as their savior—Cavaignac in 1848; MacMahon in 1875; Foch in 1914; Pétain in 1940; de Gaulle in 1940, 1944, and 1958. But more than once they lived to regret it. The general who finally stepped forward to fill the role during France's revolutionary period was a young Corsican, Napoleon Bonaparte. As a Corsican, he understood revolutions well because Corsica had had its own revolution against Genoa, which had ended only when the island became French in 1768. By 1798, Napoleon's mastery of French was rapidly improving, though he still spoke it with an Italian accent. Earlier, he had helped the Directory come to power by beating down the last radical flare-up in Paris. He had then won a victorious campaign in Italy that had made him a popular hero. Now, in 1798, he made himself master of the Republic. It was an inside job, done with the help of some members of the government; two of the five directors helped bring about Napoleon's seizure of power. This occurred on the famous *eighteenth of Brumaire,* as the date was called in the French revolutionary calendar.

By 1800, Napoleon had made himself consul and the dictatorship had been formalized. In 1804 he had himself crowned emperor of the *First Empire.* At his coronation Napoleon took the crown out of the pope's hands and put it on his own head. Napoleon's vast self-confidence kept growing, while his judgment worsened. Like other rulers of great power, he lost critics and gained "yes men."

He led France into an unending series of wars—and ultimate disaster. After his fall there was a revulsion against war in France and much of Europe. This made it possible to restore many of the old dynasties in Italy and elsewhere and the Bourbons in France. People wanted quiet. There followed a period of withdrawal to family life and of distrust of politics.

More Revolutions, More Generals. The next generation rose again in revolution in 1830. France became a liberal monarchy. The subversive colors of red, white, and blue became official once again and replaced the lily of the Bourbons. The new constitutional king advised the middle classes: "Enrich yourselves, gentlemen!" And they did, abundantly.

The next wave of revolution swept through France in 1848. It included the poor, the lower middle class, and the working class, many of whom felt that they were becoming not richer, but poorer. The *Second Republic* was set up, but the 1848 uprisings promptly produced a split between labor and the middle classes. The middle classes rallied to a new general, Cavaignac, who led the bloody suppression of the labor revolt in Paris. In 1851 the conservative, military republic was replaced by a new monarchy—the *Second Empire* under Napoleon III, the first Napoleon's nephew.

The Second Empire lasted twenty years, marked by mixed speculation, prosperity, demagogy, and minor foreign wars, until it led France into a big war that ended disastrously. Once again Paris rose, this time with the first labor government, the communist-anarchist-oriented Paris Commune, which established itself for a few weeks before being beaten down by soldiers from the rest of France, most of them peasant sons in uniform. The other France, the conservative France, asserted its power. All subsequent French regimes show marks of its influence.

The France That Resists Change. France has produced many revolutions and many conservative reactions. Its revolutions flare up in Paris and a few other big cities and industrial areas. Its conservatism is supported by wealthy minorities in these centers, but draws its main strength from the small towns and the countryside.

More Proprietors, Fewer Babies. After 1800, French peasants became patriotic and conservative. It is this France that used to change slowly, that still furnishes many officers and soldiers, and that has given the nation its reputation for conservatism. The French Revolution, by making the peasants proprietors, had given them something to conserve. The revolution also led to a long slowdown in the growth of population. This happened because in time the new laws of property had an effect on the number of new babies. The revolutionary laws of the Jacobins abolished feudalism and gave the peasants land. These laws, later organized into a systematic legal code by Napoleon, also declared that all brothers in a family had the same right to the land, and therefore the farm had to be divided among all sons. But the more sons, the smaller a piece of land would remain for each and the poorer each would be. If a peasant did not want his land to be divided and his sons impoverished, he had to limit their number. Many peasants took to marrying later in life; those who already knew methods of birth control now had a stronger motive to practice it; and those who did not know now had a motive to learn.

Throughout much of the next 140 years the population of France grew more slowly than that of any other major country. The practice of birth control had begun in the last years of the Bourbons, but the slowdown of population proceeded under all forms of French government in the nineteenth century, and there was a further slowdown after 1870. The French population, which had been 25 million in the 1780s, was 40 million in 1913 and only 53 million in 1978. Limiting the growth of population proved conservative in its effects, it preserved more of the status quo.

France is still one of the more slowly growing countries in the world, but it is now one of the faster growing countries of Europe. More recent laws subsidize babies through family allowances. Also, fewer people live on farms, and more French men and women want more children. Now, as in the past, legislation must come together with a change in human motives if the habits of millions of people are to be changed. In France habits changed slowly until the mid-1960s; but since then, habit changes in many aspects of life have accelerated. By 1979 these changes had not yet found any major expression in the political system; but as they continue to accumulate, the pressures on the political system will be growing also, and political adjustments are quite likely to occur within the next decade.

Conservative Social and Economic Practices. Throughout the nineteenth and early twentieth centuries the French social structure underwent little change. With more peasant proprietors, more people stayed in the country than streamed into the cities. Fewer people moved into industry. To this day, the proportions of industrial workers, of city dwellers, and of wage and salary earners all are lower in France than in Germany or Britain (see Table 13.1).

Thus, the proclivities of French peasants to stay where their parents had been, and where they liked it, went together with the proclivities of the French middle class to slow down the growth of industry and labor in order to minimize the likelihood of further social revolutions.

For the same reasons, French governmental policies were aimed at preserving a high proportion of small entrepreneurs in industry and commerce, as well as of independent artisans, in both

TABLE 13.1 *Some Conservative Aspects of the French Social Structure, 1975*

	A Percentage of resident population in cities above 100,000	B Percentage of resident population in localities under 100,000	C Percentage of self-employed and family members among work force	D Percentage of labor force employed in agriculture
United Kingdom	72	28	7	3
United States	65	35	9	4
Japan	56	44	28	12
German Federal Republic	52	48	9	6
France	41	59	18	11
Soviet Union	33	67	0	22
China	11*	89	0	85†

Sources: Columns A and B are from C. L. Taylor and M. C. Hudson, *World Handbook of Political and Social Indicators,* 2nd. ed. (New Haven: Yale University Press, 1972), p. 219; and *United Nations Demographic Yearbook, 1976,* figures calculated from table 8. Note: The Taylor and Hudson figures are 1960 data and are for metropolitan areas above 100,000. *The Demographic Yearbook,* on the other hand, lists only cities over 100,000 (except for the U.S., for which metropolitan data is given). Because the population of metropolitan areas is a better guide of urbanization, in those instances in which the 1960 metropolitan area population exceeds the 1975 city population (the case for the U.K. and China), the 1960 Taylor and Hudson data is used (see discussion in Taylor and Hudson, p. 201).

Columns C and D are from *Yearbook of Labour Statistics, 1977* (Geneva: International Labour Organization), table 2B, with two exceptions: column C, United Kingdom: *Annual Abstract of Statistics, 1977* (London: Central Statistical Office of the United Kingdom), p. 151; column D, China: *National Basic Factbook, July 1, 1978* (Central Intelligence Agency, p. 38.)

*Data for China is for cities and metropolitan areas taken from census returns in 1953, 1957, and 1970.

†Data for China is for 1966.

towns and countryside. As late as 1975, the self-employed made up as much as 18 percent of the French work force, a higher proportion than in most industrial countries. The power and influence of the self-employed middle class were multiplied by several conditions. In the countryside its members became assimilated to the rural viewpoint, and in turn its small businesspeople, notaries, and lawyers furnished leadership not only to agriculturists, but also to a large part of the entire rural population. This included, in 1976, the 30 percent of the population who lived in communities of less than 2,000 inhabitants and, presumably, a part of the small-town population as well. In addition, this rural population is strongly overrepresented in the French political system. Finally, the self-employed middle class, through family ties and social life, has assimilated many of the middle-level salaried employees and technicians to its own outlook in social relations, economic policies, politics, and culture. Small businesspeople, though often backward in terms of economics and technology, thus have exercised a greater influence in France than in most other major countries.

A Strong Middle Class, a Weak Political Center. The proagricultural bias of the French has left its mark on modern-day France. In the mid-1970s manual workers in France still were only 37 percent of the work force, compared with 47 percent in Germany and with about 56 percent in England. Although workers can be highly militant in France and about half of them tend to vote for the Communist Party, all workers are a permanent minority. Marx's prediction that the proletariat would become the great majority of society has been contradicted by the development of France, the country where the theory of class politics and the class struggle was invented.

The French class structure, in fact, has remained remarkably rigid. Within the work force, in the 1970s, the 37 percent of workers—even with another 6 percent added by service personnel—were outnumbered: the large middle class, both salaried and self-employed, included government officials and officers in the armed forces and constituted 45 percent; and the farmers and farm workers formed another 10 percent. Within the middle class, small businesspeople, artisans, and petty investors predominated until the 1950s and marked its political style. Since many of these middle-class people, like peasants, are keenly interested in keeping what they have, this slow-changing French social structure has not lent itself to sweeping restructuring or basic reform.

Only in the 1950s and 1960s did the pace of economic and political change begin to quicken. Until then, the France that resisted change prevailed over all internal challenges.

The Third Republic: A Paradise for Legislators. The *Third Republic,* which lasted from 1875 to 1940, bore the marks of this change-resisting social structure. It was a government deliberately designed to be strong in foreign affairs and against the poorer French people at home, but to be weak in relation to the upper middle class in town and country.

The government of the Third Republic, like that of the United States, was divided into three branches. Its president, however, was much weaker and its legislature, the National Assembly, much stronger than their American counterparts. The legislature consisted of two chambers, of which the lower, called the Chamber of Deputies, was the more important; but the upper chamber, the Senate, also had a significant share of power, which it often exercised in defense of property rights. The president of the republic was elected by the legislature, not by the people. Like the king of England, the president was to reign, but not to rule. Presidential powers were ceremonial rather than real. The actual head of the executive branch of government was the premier, or prime minister, who, as in Britain, could remain in office only with the backing of a majority in the Chamber of Deputies. Unlike the British counterpart, however, the French premier did not have the power to dissolve the legislature and call for new elections.

The legislators, thus, had most of the power. They could at any time overthrow any premier by a vote of "no confidence" without having to answer for their actions to the voters. For the length of the legislative term of four years, members of the legislative majority were virtually irremovable as long as they themselves did not vote for new elections. In effect, though the premier and the Cabinet were responsible to the legislators, the legislators between elections were responsible to no one.

This arrangement provided not only for a weak president and a succession of weak premiers, but also for a multiplicity of weak political parties and temporary political factions. A legislator who broke party discipline had little to fear from his or her party as long as the next election was some years away. The rural and local character of much of French politics, and the strength of local notables and the self-employed middle class, combined with the individualism of many French voters to make the weakness of nationwide political parties and government into a tradition. According to this tradition, members of the French middle class often did not scruple to evade direct taxes by filling out false tax returns, nor did they hesitate to take their money out of France and speculate against the currency of their own country whenever it seemed profitable or they happened to dislike the policies of the government. As a rule the assembly refused to pass effective legislation that would have ensured full collection of direct taxes or a real control of French currency. Under such conditions a government could not control the world of finance, but a financial panic could easily bring down a government.

Though French political leadership was often unstable, French administration remained the mainstay of the state. While legislators played political games, civil servants ran the country. The French civil service, even more than the British, has a great tradition and commands high prestige to this day. Its top administrators, such as the Inspectors of Finance, are still drawn from the *"great schools"*—the École Normale Supérieure, the École Polytechnique, and the École Nationale d'Administration—which are more selective and more highly respected than even the country's greatest universities.[6] Throughout all governmental crises the French civil service has kept the country going.

Like all bureaucrats and technocrats, the French civil servants cannot create policies. They can only administer the policies of others. In the 1930s the Third Republic failed to produce policies adequate for the times. The depression divided labor from the upper middle class: workers demanded more welfare; proprietors, less public spending. Soon members of the French right began to mutter that they would prefer the rule of the German government under Hitler to any native left-of-center government in France. French Communists, in turn, in September 1939 refused to support the French middle-class government. At both ends of the political spectrum the French people disliked domestic opponents more than they disliked foreign enemies.

The Third Republic collapsed after brief and ineffective resistance against the Nazi invasion of France in 1940 and was succeeded by a conservative and authoritarian regime under the aged Marshal Pétain, a pathetic figurehead, and the unscrupulous Premier Pierre Laval, a willing collaborator of the Nazis. Calling itself the "French state" and located at the resort of *Vichy,* this regime was a puppet of the German occupying power. It was swept away by the invasion of the Allies in 1944, when a new republic was formed.

Promptly, most of the old political parties reappeared. Members of several of them had been active in the underground *Resistance* movement against the Nazi occupiers, which boasted a record of suffering and heroism; and some of these now emerged as candidates for leadership. But some who had avoided taking any risks during the occupation or had prudently waited to join the winners after the liberation also retained their influence or even increased it, and so did some outright collaborators with the Nazis, after having benefitted by amnesty in the 1950s. Even more important, the party system and the social structure persisted.

[6]The recruitment into these great schools was based on achievement, particularly on the student's record in the system of French academic high schools, the *lycées.* In practice, the *lycées* were open to the children of the upper bourgeoisie and of the middle class, whose home background equipped them with the skills, habits, and motivations to succeed in schools of this type and whose families could afford to support them during the last years of their secondary education and often thereafter. But this track through the academic high schools to the universities and elite institutions remained much less open to children of peasants and was nearly closed to children of working-class background. For all these children a second, parallel system of education had developed, stressing practical skills, but making a higher-level career quite unlikely. More definitely than in other advanced countries, with the possible exception of Britain, the career opportunities of many people were already set, on the day they entered their first job, by the type of secondary and higher education they had received or missed.

The Fourth Republic: Fast Economic Growth with Small Political Changes. The *Fourth Republic,* which lasted from 1944 to 1958, in many ways resembled the Third. There were the same irresponsible legislature, weak parties, weak presidents, and quick-changing premiers as in the Third Republic. General de Gaulle, who was elected its first president, tried to be strong, but failed, and withdrew to private life. Politics-as-usual followed, but some of its content changed.

The leaders of the Republic placed more emphasis on economic planning and on social justice and welfare legislation. Several industries were nationalized, including mining, aircraft, and part of the automobile industry. (When overtaken on the road by a new Renault car, made in a state-owned factory, one might reconsider the timeworn notion of "creeping socialism.") There also were marked improvements in health and welfare benefits, in access to higher education, and in special assistance to families with children.

But in economic life the high degree of economic inequality persisted, among regions as well as among social strata; and in politics the same game of musical chairs was being played by nearly the same small group of *ministrables*—politicians eligible for Cabinet seats. The policies of the Fourth Republic only rarely departed from those of the Third. To be sure, the Fourth Republic accepted as general and distant goals the Atlantic community and the unification of Europe and joined a number of important European organizations, including NATO, the European Coal and Steel Community (ECSC), EURATOM, and, most important, the European *Common Market*—the developing customs union of France, West Germany, Italy, the Netherlands, Belgium, and Luxembourg. During these same years, however, France rejected membership in the proposed European Defense Community (EDC) and the European Political Community (EPC). In other matters the Fourth Republic moved further away from its European partners. It continued to send its soldiers to fight for the preservation of an empire that could not be preserved. Embittered officers and soldiers returned from Indochina, and soon even larger numbers found themselves in a war in Algeria that the Fourth Republic could neither win nor end.

Overcommitment Abroad and Reorganization at Home. In foreign policy between 1880 and 1920, France had been successful to the point at which it had taken up commitments beyond its strength. By the 1920s France was the ruler of North Africa, the ruler of a part of the Middle East (both Syria and Lebanon), the ruler of Indochina, and the ruler of a substantial part of sub-Saharan Africa. From then on, as these countries and populations became politically active, France was involved in one bloody war after another. In 1920 to subjugate the Syrians the French killed 20,000 people in the bombardment of Damascus. From 1925 to 1927 they fought in Morocco. After 1945 they killed thousands of people in Morocco and Madagascar while trying to restore French rule. And they fought nine years in Indochina, from 1945 to their defeat at Dien Bien Phu in 1954.

The End of Empire. The force requirements for maintaining the empire became increasingly larger than the capabilities of metropolitan France. Yet the ties of the French elites, the French business community, and the French middle class to the empire were stronger in those days than the present ties of America's industrial and business groups overseas. The French middle class got more jobs out of the empire, French industry and commerce more sales, and the French military establishment more command posts than do comparable interests in the United States today. Thus, the eventual rejection of empire by the French set a significant precedent for all large nations.

Algeria: A Choice and a Decision. Blind acceptance of the theory of *economic determinism*—the simple view that economic facts and interests determine everything—would expect to find France still in Algeria. But what happened in France in the 1950s and early 1960s is a case study of how a large, modern country broke with its tradition of empire by refusing to carry on endlessly a frustrating military campaign. The country also broke economically from imperial policy, by shifting many of its economic efforts from policing the Casbah[7] to modernizing France. Finally, the country also broke morally with colonialism. The war in Algeria had led to massacres, torture, and a decline of exactly those moral values that the defense of France was supposed to maintain. As these atrocities became known, French intellectuals, students, and some members of the armed forces spoke out in protest, often at considerable risk to themselves. France could not remain civilized, cultured, and humane, they insisted, and still continue the Algerian War in the way it was being waged in the mid-1950s.

Reorganization at Home. In late 1957 and early 1958, French public opinion turned against the Algerian War. Individuals had protested earlier in increasing numbers, but by now public opinion poll returns had to be treated as state secrets "so as not to give comfort to the enemy." In May 1958 the French army took action against the Fourth Republic, which the former had long accused of supplying inadequate backing in the war. Aircraft and paratroopers moved from Algeria and Corsica against the mainland of France, and they received indications of support from the police and from the conservative parties. Moderates and members of the left called for mass demonstrations in defense of the Republic. Intense negotiations led to a quick compromise, once again disguised as strong-man rule.[8] The government of the day legally handed over power to a former president of the Fourth Republic and hero of the Resistance, Charles de Gaulle. De Gaulle had the confidence of the military and was acceptable to the left, who remembered that during his presidency Communists had sat in the French Cabinet. The right expected him to keep Algeria French; the left and an increasing number of persons in the center expected him to take France out of Algeria.

Often before in French history, factions of the right and left had balanced each other with incompatible desires and approximately equal strengths, with the richer classes calling for order and the poorer ones for change, and all demanding a stronger government to give them what they wanted. Out of such conditions *Bonapartism* had been born, exhibiting a skillful blend of military force and sweeping promises of social betterment. Under both Napoleons more and more force and less and less betterment had followed. Would Charles de Gaulle prove to be just another Bonapartist general?

This time the outcome was different. Appointed premier on May 31, 1958, de Gaulle soon obtained full powers to govern absolutely for six months. Changing the imperial policies of nearly a century also involved changing the French domestic political system that had produced them. Therefore, during the six-month interval of absolute rule de Gaulle had a constitution drafted. When it was submitted to a direct popular vote, a referendum of the French people, they overwhelmingly endorsed it. De Gaulle reassured the military by well-chosen ambiguities that he would hold Algeria, while quietly preparing to concede its independence to its Arab majority.

At the same time he announced an accelerated program of nuclear weapons development for the purpose of making France a nuclear power independent of all others. This program for an independent French *force de frappe*—a nuclear striking force—split the French military. Technology-minded officers now parted company with their still empire-minded colleagues. To many new-style military professionals, nuclear weapons were more

[7]The Casbah was the native quarter of the city of Algiers.
[8]For details, see James Meisel, *The Fall of the Republic* (Ann Arbor: University of Michigan Press, 1962).

TABLE 13.2 *Approximate Annual Averages of French Industrial Production, 1909–76*

	1909–38 (during the Third Republic)			
	A 1909–13	B 1925–29	C 1934–38	D Increase, ca. 1911–36 100 (C-A)/A
Aluminum (thousand tons)	14	29	51	264% 10.6% per annum
Merchant marine (million tons)	2.3	3.3	2.9	26% 1.0% per annum
Automobiles (thousands)	45	254	227	404% 16.2% per annum
Electricity (billion kWh)	—	16	21	(31% 3.4% per annum)†
Steel (million tons)	5	10	6	20% 0.8% per annum
Average annual increase for the measures of industrial production				7.2%‡

Source: From data in R. C. Macridis, "France," in R. C. Macridis and R. E. Ward., eds., *Modern Political Systems: Europe,* 3rd ed., 1972, and 4th ed., 1978. Adapted by permission of Prentice-Hall, Inc., Englewood Cliffs, N.J.
*Because the time period covered by certain data overlaps the Fourth and Fifth Republics, these data are used for the computation of the percentage increase for both Republics.
†Change 1925–29 to 1934–38 only.
‡Aluminum, merchant marine, automobiles, and steel only.

important than Algeria. They continued to support de Gaulle, even after his new policy in Algeria became visible. During this critical period some of the colonialist military faction tried to assassinate de Gaulle (they succeeded in assassinating several minor opponents of the war); and they conspired in a secret army organization, *OAS,* to overthrow the de Gaulle government.

The matter was ultimately decided in part by the response of the French enlisted troops in Algeria, who acted much as their relatives in France had acted when they voted in the referendum on de Gaulle's constitution. They had obeyed their commanders in the Algerian War, but now they refused to move against the government. In 1962 the Algerian War was formally ended. Thereafter nearly a million French were evacuated from Algeria, primarily to France, where in the 1960s most of them became integrated with the mainland French. In the meantime the machinery of de

1948–58 (during the Fourth Republic)			1958–70 (during the Fifth Republic)		1969–76 (Fifth Republic after de Gaulle)	
E	F*	G	H	I	J	K
1948–52	1955–59	Increase, ca. 1950–57 100 (F-E)/E	1967–70	Increase, ca. 1958–69 100 (H-F)/F	1975–76	Increase, ca. 1969–76 100 (J-H)/I[H]
75	218	191% 27.3% per annum	371	70% 6.4% per annum	175	33% 4.6% per annum
2.7	4.5	67% 9.6% per annum	6.0	33% 3.0% per annum	8.5	56% 8.0% per annum
286	1,283	349% 49.9% per annum	2,100	64% 5.8% per annum	3,100	48% 6.9% per annum
41	70	71% 10.1% per annum	132	89% 8.1% per annum	680	83% 11.9% per annum
9	15	67% 9.6% per annum	23	53% 4.8% per annum	27	17% 2.4% per annum
		21.3%		5.6%		6.8%

Gaulle's Fifth Republic had begun to work—as it would continue working into the 1970s after his retirement.

A New Start Toward Change. During the 1950s the French economy began to grow at a faster rate than it had experienced for many years, and this growth continued during the 1960s and early 1970s. Some data for typical products are shown in Table 13.2.

The entire time spanned by the data in Table 13.3, 1909–76, can be divided into three periods, corresponding to the political regimes of the Third, Fourth, and Fifth French Republics, respectively; and we can then compute for each period the rough rate of annual growth for the average of five indicators of industrial growth.

The results are a little surprising. Our first period, 1909–38, falls under the regime of the Third French Republic (1875–1940), and the rate of industrial growth averages about 7 percent per year. Our second period, 1948–59, falls under the

Fourth Republic (1944–58), during which General de Gaulle held political power only briefly, as president from 1944 to 1947, but during which France benefited substantially from United States economic aid under the Marshall Plan and other programs, as well as from the efforts of the French people themselves at material reconstruction. During this period the average annual rate of increase in our industrial indicators was as high as 21 percent. This period, despite its political and military difficulties, seems to have been the time of the most rapid growth of industry and of basic productive equipment. The third period, 1959–70, after General de Gaulle's return to power, appears to have returned to a slower rate of growth in our industrial indicators, roughly 6 percent per year, but these increases now occurred on a much higher basis—a basis created in large part during the preceding period. This is largely a period under the political regime of the Fifth Republic, and much of it falls under the regime of General de Gaulle, who returned to the presidency for the period 1958–69. During this period President de Gaulle received credit not only for the preservation of national unity, the end of the Algerian War, and the promotion of French independence and prestige in world affairs, but also for the economic progress and modernization that actually were largely the fruits of the economic development that had taken place under his predecessors. After de Gaulle's retirement and death, French industry grew at nearly 7 percent per year, and the Gaullists continued to claim credit for the economic prosperity and growth that had materialized under his administration.

No matter who claims credit for the economic changes, they were a visible fact in the 1960s and 1970s. Their scale and their speed were beginning to change the social structure of France at a faster pace than ever before.

Each year during the late 1960s, about 1 percent of the French work force shifted out of agriculture and into nonagricultural occupations, and in 1971–75 this shift accelerated to 2 percent per year. By 1975, persons employed in agriculture accounted for only 10 percent of registered voters; but middle-level white-collar employees had increased to 13 percent. There were still 9 percent self-employed "heads of enterprises," usually small ones, and another 7 percent in management positions and in the free professions, such as medicine and the law. Finally, there were the "inactives," most often people in retirement. (See Table 13.3.)

A similar shift has been under way from the countryside to the big cities. By 1975 as many as 44 percent of the French voters were living in cities of over 100,000 inhabitants, including the Paris agglomeration where 16 percent of the French people are now concentrated. Another 18 percent of the French now live in cities of between 10,000 and 100,000 inhabitants, and still another 10 percent live in small towns with populations between 2,000 and 10,000, so the French are now altogether a 73 percent urban people. The shift to the cities is continuing, perhaps at a rate of 0.6 percent per year, and small country towns and middle-sized cities are moving toward the next higher classes of population size.[9]

The increases in the share of the residents of big cities, of persons in nonagricultural occupations, and in the general level of education and exposure to mass media should tend toward increasing the share of change-oriented voters in the electorate. Some other trends, however, may work in the opposite direction. The growing share of white-collar employees and professional people in the French electorate is now 22 percent; together with the 9 percent self-employed *patrons* of nonagricultural enterprises—to whom they are linked through many social conventions, habits, and associations, as well as often through ties of family

[9]From data in "Données sociales: Édition 1978," *Les Collections de INSEE* (Paris: Institut National de la Statistique et des Études Économiques, 1978), p. 8. There are some small discrepancies between the data given here and elsewhere in the text and those given in Table 13.2 in this chapter. These are due to the different base years and sometimes to the somewhat different definitions of "city," "locality," etc. in the various sources used.

TABLE 13.3 *Registered Voters by Occupation*

	Millions	% of work force	% of voters
Registered voters	35.2		100
Total work force	21.1	100	60
A. Employers and self-employed (businesspeople, merchants, industrialists, artisans, and members of liberal professions)		10	6
Top managerial and administrative		6	4
Middle managerial and administrative		13	8
Farmers (employers and self-employed)		8	5
Subtotal		37	22
B. Clerical and subordinate (managerial, administrative, white-collar)		16	10
C. Workers		37	22
Service personnel		6	4
Farm workers		2	1
Subtotal		45	27
D. Other		2	1
Total A–D		100	61
E. Voters not in work force (housewives, retirees, etc.)		—	40
Grand Total		100	100

All figures rounded.

Source: From data in R. C. Macridis, "Politics of France," in R. C. Macridis, ed., *Modern Political Systems: Europe,* 4th ed., 1978, pp. 106–07. Adapted by permission of Prentice-Hall, Inc., Englewood Cliffs, N.J.

or neighborhood—they total 32 percent of the electorate, just about equal to the share of workers. In another five or ten years this white-collar and professional share is likely to be larger, easily outweighing any shrinkage that might occur during the same period among the self-employed.

Another trend is also at work to reduce the proportion of workers among the French electorate. It is the growing tendency to employ foreign workers in many occupations requiring heavy, boring, or ill-paid work, both in manufacturing and in the service trades. For these jobs, increasingly unpopular with French workers, foreign workers are imported from Spain, Portugal, and the Arab countries and to some extent from black Africa, so that some factories and some working-class neighborhoods are taking on a new look. There are about 3 million foreigners in France, and perhaps 2 million of these may be working for wages. They are accepted as members by the labor unions, but, being foreigners, they cannot vote. In effect, this might mean that of, say, 12 million workers in France, only 10 million are defined as "French" and have the right to vote—or that about one-sixth of the real industrial work force of the country is in effect disfranchised. Since the inflow of foreign labor is continuing and since no one at present seems to be making any major effort to let these people share in the right to vote, this development may continue to weaken the influence of labor and of parties oriented toward expanding social welfare and promoting social change.

Another trend favoring for a time at least a measure of social conservatism is the doubling of real wages from 1955 to 1975 and the rapid diffusion of durable consumer goods and higher living standards. In 1974 as many as 63 percent of French householders owned automobiles, as opposed to only 14 percent a quarter century earlier. Television sets already were in 82 percent of French households, and 88 percent had refrigerators; washing machines were found in 69 percent. Many French families now may feel that they have more to lose than was the case in earlier decades.

A Cohesive Ruling Class. Finally, the "directing class," (which to a large extent is the ruling class in France)—less than the top 1 percent of the population on a scale of power over the lives of others—has remained remarkably cohesive. Excluding all writers, artists, scholars, and members of the free professions from *Who's Who in France*—that is, all those persons of note who do *not* hold positions of economic, political, administrative, or military power—a team of French sociologists compared large samples of the rest, the power holders in France, for 1954, 1964, and 1974.[10] The power holders are an elite primarily by virtue of the positions they hold and not necessarily by any special talents demonstrated in competition with newcomers from other social groups, for they are themselves a tightly knit social group, closed in on itself. They are recruited from the same social setting, from among the same social class, which almost no outsiders penetrate. Consequently, the children possess the same social characteristics as their parents: in some cases they simply change their professions or their sectors.[11]

Within this ruling group there are subgroups: the private and the public sectors. And within the latter there are subelites such as the military or the one formed by the five *"great bodies of the state"*: the *Council of State (Conseil d'État)*, the *Court of Accounts*, the *General Inspection of Finances*, the *Corps of Prefects*, and the *Diplomatic Service*. "But this separation of functions does not break the original social unity of the ruling class," commented the sociologists in their study.[12]

Two cartoons sum up the situation. Whereas in earlier times three persons were playing at the poker table—a general, a frock-coated financier, and a dark-suited technocrat—now there is a single person standing before a mirror. Which of his three suits—general's uniform, banker's coat, or technical expert's suit—shall he put on next?

It follows that the French state is not simply dominated by big business, nor does it rule business as an impartial arbiter. Rather, the different sectors are held together by the uninterrupted circulation of the directing personnel from one position to another, assuring the cohesion of the whole directing class; and this top class, according to the authors of the study, has been increasing its social distance from the rest of French society.

[10]Pierre Birnbaum et al., *La Classe dirigeante française* (Paris: Presses Universitaires de France, 1978). All data in this section are from this study.

[11]Ibid., p. 187.

[12]Ibid.

Within this persistent basic pattern there have been some limited changes. The proportion of *patrons*—that is, owner-managers—has been declining; that of salaried managers, strongly increasing. Many of these managers, however, are sons or daughters of *patrons,* who later succeed to the ownership of the family firm; others remain managers by profession. Still other managers are former *patrons* who have become presidents or directors-general, as well as stockholders, of their enterprises after a juridical and financial merger or reorganization. A growing number of high officials and managers of public enterprises move up during later stages in their career into high positions in the private sector, as do many of the military. The increasing demand for highly competent and technically skilled managers throughout the private sector continues to foster this mobility of top personnel from the public into the private sector. Altogether, these developments have produced an elite of decision makers who are more favorable to technological innovation, but not necessarily to social, economic, and political reform.

A Politics of Countervailing Trends. Together, these mutually opposing currents of social and economic change have produced something of a paradox: a country of rapid change in economics, technology, consumption standards, the scale of higher education, population growth, and patterns of settlement, all of which are combined with a remarkable picture of near immobility in politics. The distribution of votes and seats for the National Assembly that emerged from the 1973 and 1978 elections closely resembled that of the previous and similar election of 1967. After that election, in 1968, about 6 percent of the French had moved temporarily to the right in a "law and order" reaction against the French students' revolt of May 1968, producing under the majority voting system of the Fifth Republic a Gaullist landslide majority of assembly seats. By 1973 that wave of emotion had passed; Socialists and Communists had agreed on a moderate "common program" of the left, and the small Party of Socialist Unity (PSU) declared that, though not endorsing this program, it would support the candidates of this "common front" in run-off elections. Most of the right had united behind the "majority" coalition led by President Pompidou and the Gaullist Party; and the result at the end of the election seemed to be a nearly complete return to the distribution of voting power in the National Assembly that had existed in 1967. In March 1978 the Common Front again presented itself to the voters. In the municipal elections of 1977 its candidates had done so well that one might have expected it to win in 1978. But voting for the mayor of one's city is not the same thing as voting for those who will assume control of one's nation. Communists and Socialists had quarreled during the last six months before the election; their Common Front no longer seemed credible. Just as the parties of the left found it hard to compromise among themselves, so did the parties of property find it hard to compromise with any of the leftist parties when the substantive demands of labor were raised. Instead, the governing majority appealed to the fear and caution of the voters; and it won once more.

Yet, at a deeper level France may now be moving toward broader and more fundamental political changes than those that were evident on the surface in the 1970s. The large currents of social, psychological, and economic change were likely to continue, but they were not so likely to balance or cancel each other's political effects to the degree that they had done in those years. The popular vote for the leftist parties had risen from 44 percent in 1967 to 46 percent in 1973 and to 49 percent in 1978. Well beyond a preference for any one party or coalition, there was clear evidence of a widespread demand for change, for social reform, and for a more equitable distribution of incomes, career openings, access to education, opportunities for participation in decisions at one's work place and at all levels of one's community, from neighborhood to municipality, to region, and nation. The leftist coalition had stressed these demands, but the governments of presidents Pompidou and Giscard responded by accepting in general terms this emphasis on change at the same time that they offered the government coalition as a better instrument for devising and carrying out the specific reforms required. In 1978 the government coalition got 46 percent of the votes on the first ballot, and its main opponents, the supporters of the common program of the left, won 45 percent. On the second ballot the government coalition got 50.5 percent of the vote, and the leftist coalition got 49.3 percent. However, thanks to the peculiarities of the electoral system, the government coalition emerged with 57 percent of the assembly seats.

But government and press agreed that the elections had revealed a serious demand for change, despite conditions of continuing prosperity and freedom, and that President Giscard's promise of reforms, televised on the day before the final popular balloting, was made in response to a real popular desire. Five years earlier, on the eve of the 1973 election, President Pompidou had made a similar promise on television. The day after that election, a cartoonist drew Marianne, the symbol of France, speaking to President Pompidou. She had tied a knot into the national flag "to remind you of your promise"; if leaders should forget, the nation would remember. More people did remember in 1978, but enough voters preferred once again the old promise of moderate reforms to any more radical experiments.

What these reforms would be, whether the Gaullist Party and its allies or, indeed, the French political system itself would be capable of designing them and putting them into effect—all this could be revealed only by the future. What seemed clear in 1978 was that the need and the demand for reforms were recognized and shared in one form or another by a majority of the electorate. These needs, demands, and aspirations, too, have now become part of the stakes of French politics for the years ahead.

THE STAKES OF FRENCH POLITICS

At many times the stakes of French politics have been unusually high. At the time of the Great Revolution, in 1789–93, they included the freedom and property of the peasants and the middle class; the power, property, and necks of the aristocracy; the worldly power and position of the church; the entire character and structure of French society; and the direction of its further evolution. In 1793–1800 the stakes included the security of middle-class property and enterprise; the claims of the poorer classes; the rise of military dictatorship; and the beginning of a policy of vast military conquest abroad.

From 1800 to 1940, conflicts about these stakes would recur. Middle-class and peasant property rights against working-class claims for a more equitable distribution of income and welfare; a monarchic versus a republican form of government; a powerful church versus the separation of church and state; civilian versus military rule; absolutism or dictatorship versus constitutional government; priority for domestic improvements versus military power politics in Europe or colonial expansion—all these were repeatedly at hazard in the political struggles and, with them more than once, the character and future of the country. France saw a kind of short-lived communist government, the Paris Commune of 1871, long before Communist governments won power in Russia or China. A modern Communist Party has been strong in France since about 1920; should it win power at the national level, much in French life would change once more, even though the Party has promised (in case of an electoral victory) to respect the rules of French multiparty democracy and to give up its share of the government if a future election should go against it. The disinclination of many French voters to trust this promise and to take any risk played a significant role in the re-election of a progovernment majority—albeit a reduced one—to the National Assembly in the 1973 and 1978 elections.

Another stake of politics from 1870 to 1945 was

the fate of two major regions, Alsace and Lorraine, which had been annexed by Germany from 1871 to 1918 and again from 1940 to 1945, after having been French since the late seventeenth century or even earlier. An even larger stake during World Wars I and II and again since 1945 has been the political and economic independence of the entire country, first vis-à-vis German attempts at conquest and occupation; and, from the late 1940s into the 1980s, against the spreading hegemony of the two superpowers of the period, the Soviet Union and the United States. Large issues of this kind have been ever present in the minds of some French people, and in intermittent crises they have aroused much larger numbers to political interest and activity.

At a less basic level the French political system today controls directly about 40 percent of the gross domestic product that passes through the public sector (including all levels of government), as well as the social security and health insurance systems and the turnover of the nationalized industries. This same public sector employs about 12 percent of the work force of the country. Indirectly, the political system controls an even larger part of the economy through its fiscal and credit politices and through its system of *indicative planning*—that is, noncompulsory plans based on careful economic forecasts and then negotiated among the government's civil service, the relevant private business firms and interest groups, the labor unions, and the regional and municipal authorities concerned. How and in what direction are all these governmental powers to be used? For growth or stagnation; inflation or deflation; price stability or full employment; greater or less social, educational, and economic inequality; more paternalistic authority or broader and more genuine participation in decision making in private industry as well as in public administration? All these elements are involved in the stakes of day-to-day politics and stimulate people to participate in them.

THE PARTICIPANTS IN POLITICS

Political participation for a large part of the French people is more intermittent than it is in some other highly developed countries, such as Britain or the German Federal Republic. Though the local prefects concentrate a good deal of power in their hands, they are appointed from Paris, and they depend somewhat less on the political decisions of the local voters and somewhat more on the plans, orders, and regulations of the central government. The French state and its administrative machinery were created in the days of the Bourbon kings and to an even greater extent during the empire of the first Napoleon, before industrialism, autonomous interest-group representation, and sustained civic participation in politics had become major aspects of public life. The national administration in France keeps functioning, therefore, whether or not most citizens take the trouble to be active in politics. Indeed, it is public unrest and activity, such as the student revolt and industrial strikes of May 1968, that is more disturbing to the quiet work of the civil service, which can continue unhampered in the face of public apathy or inactivity.

Voting Habits. French voters turn out fairly regularly. About 18 to 20 percent stay at home in most elections or referenda, as they did again in 1978. In rare moments of crisis, the portion of abstainers may decline to about 15 percent, and in equally rare times of unusual apathy it may rise to 25 percent. Another 2 percent, more or less, spoil their ballots or cast blank ones.

Nonvoters are more frequent among women, particularly among women living alone, such as the unmarried, the widowed, or the divorced; among French citizens of foreign origin, such as Muslim Algerians; and among members of religious minorities, such as Protestants (and nonpracticing Catholics), in contrast to practicing Catholics, who traditionally have tended to identify more closely with the nation. Abstention from voting—abstentionism—is also high among groups relatively isolated from the outside world, perhaps by geography or by language, as in the Breton-speaking parts of Brittany, and among individuals poorly integrated in their social environment, such as the ill, the handicapped, the old, and the politically alienated. The latter included the Poujadists in 1958 on the right and the adherents of extreme leftist or anarchist groups on the left.[13]

In the case of a referendum on a topic remote from the immediate concerns of French voters, the proportions of abstentions and blank or spoiled ballots may become very high. The referendum of April 1972 on the enlargement of the European Economic Community had been planned by President Pompidou as a nationwide vote in favor of European integration, as well as of his own cautious policy moves in that direction. Almost 40 percent of the voters did not trouble to vote, and the favorable two-thirds majority among the valid votes cast represented just about 40 percent of the registered voters, while a little more than 20 percent voted in opposition.[14]

Campaign Activity and Party Work: Notables and Militants. A second form of participation—sustained activity in political campaigns—is relatively rare. Among the political right and center, permanent party cadres—that is, core personnel—are small and consist mostly of local notables; dues-paying party members are nonexisting or unimportant; and the wider circle of habitual or potential adherents of the party is mobilized only at election time. French political parties of this type can grow very quickly across a few elections and then decline again. This was the case of the Catholic-centrist MRP between 1946 and 1962; the Gaullist Party, which declined between 1951 and 1956 and later continued to rise between 1956 and 1968; and the short-lived Poujadist party, whose demagogic and militantly pro-small-business appeal in the mid-1950s was followed by its collapse in 1958 and its loss of political significance thereafter.

Membership parties with larger bodies of regularly organized members are the Communists and, to a lesser extent, the Socialist Party and a much smaller Party of Socialist Unity (PSU). In 1975 the Socialists had about 200,000 dues-paying members, although their votes totaled about 3.2 million in 1968, 4.5 million in 1973, and nearly 6.5 million in 1978—perhaps 32 for each party member.[15] The party members are organized in local sections that elect delegates—one for every twenty-five—to the Party Congress, the highest authority of the party in all matters. In practice, party secretaries, local government functionaries, and parliamentarians have a larger share of influence, but the scope for discussion and participation in decision making by the membership is not inconsiderable.

A drawback of this broader participation is that the faithful and long-established members, to say nothing of many party functionaries, do not welcome newcomers to the party, if the latter are looking for a chance to make a political career. When in 1944 and 1945 many younger people, including former members of the Resistance, tried to join the Socialist Party for their political career, they were rebuffed; and by 1951 the party had the oldest parliamentary delegation in the National Assembly. In the late 1960s and 1970s, under the leadership of François Mitterand, this pattern changed; and in the 1973 and 1978 elections a number of young and conspicuously able Socialist legislators were elected.

The French Communist Party has a larger membership and expects more activity from it, but

[13]Philippe Braud, *Le Comportement électoral en France* (Paris: Presses Universitaires de France, 1973), p. 42, with reference to Alain Lancelot, *L'Abstentionnisme électoral en France* (Paris: Colin, 1968), pp. 171 et seq., 184, 205 et seq., 213, 217 et seq.

[14]Jean Stoetzel and Alain Girard, *Les Sondages d'opinion publique* (Paris: Presses Universitaires de France, 1973), pp. 92–93.

[15]Macridis, "Politics of France," p. 140; *Keesing's Contemporary Archives* (London), November 24, 1978. These are first-ballot votes. On the second ballot, one week later, the Socialists got 7.2 million votes.

keeps most of the real decision-making power within a narrower circle of persons. It had the support of nearly 6 million voters in 1978, compared to 5 million in 1946, 1951, 1967, and 1973. In other elections between these dates Communist votes rose as high as 5.5 million in 1956 and declined as low as 3.9 million in 1958, but on the whole its voting strength and its share of the electorate—about 17 percent of the registered voters and 21 percent of valid votes cast in 1978—have remained remarkably stable.

Behind the nearly 6 million Communist voters stand approximately 400,000 dues-paying party members—perhaps one for every fifteen voters. (The figure reported officially by the Party in 1969 was 473,000, but generally well-informed observers consider this figure unrealistically high.) Among the 400,000 members there are perhaps about 30,000 *militants,* roughly 7 percent of the total membership. Militants engage in more sustained and active work for the party; and many may strive to rise eventually through the party hierarchy. Among the militants, in turn, there are about 10,000 *cadres,* or skeleton staff, who work full-time for the party as secretaries and as members of higher-level bureaus or else as leaders of trade unions and similar mass organizations. At the center of the cadres and of the French party, then, is the leadership of about 100 persons, including the members of its politburo, secretariat, and central committee.

It has been pointed out that the influence of the Soviet Union on the policies of the French Communist Party adds an element of unreality to the notion that its members participate in any meaningful sense in the making of important policy decisions. "The Communists," the French Socialist leader Guy Mollet remarked some years ago, "are not Left but East"—a tune that he later was to change.

For times, indeed, have somewhat changed. The Communists protested in the 1960s against Soviet prison sentences for the dissident writers Sinyavsky and Daniel, and copies of the French Communist daily, *L'Humanité*, were confiscated in Moscow. Later, the French party criticized the Soviet invasion of Czechoslovakia in 1968; and it has generally moved away from too close conformity with Soviet views and nearer to the views and feelings of its French members and voters. Unlike the Italian Communist Party, however, the French Communist Party by early 1979 had not yet changed its inner structure. It was still being run from the top down, with rank-and-file members having little influence on major policy decisions. Nonetheless, by 1973 the Socialist Party, including Guy Mollet, had accepted the Communists, who had qualified their emphasis on the class struggle, as allies for a Common Program that favored free elections to decide on future governments. For the Communists this seemed a major departure from earlier doctrines, which had rejected "bourgeois democracy" and extolled the "dictatorship of the proletariat." Some observers saw in it an example of the cumulative influence of the French political environment on the Communist Party, moving it toward its eventual political transformation.[16] Even so, the uneasy Common Front of Socialists and Communists together was distrusted and rejected by sufficiently many French voters to fail in its bid for a majority of seats in the 1978 elections to the National Assembly.

To the extent that such a transformation of the Communist Party should actually materialize, it would bring back about one-fifth of the French into a more genuine communication with the rest of the country. At the same time, it would make their political potential available for coalitions in

[16]For a somewhat overstated account, see André Laurens and Thierry Pfister, *Les Nouveaux Communistes* (Paris: Stock, 1973); but see also François Borella, *Les Partis politiques dans la France d'aujourd'hui* (Paris: Seuil, 1973), pp. 169–202; Maurice Duverger, *Le Cinquième République,* 4th ed. (Paris: Presses Universitaires de France, 1968), pp. 197–203. See also *Programme commun de Gouvernement du Parti communiste française et du Parti socialiste (27 juin 1972)* (Paris: Editions Sociales, 1972).

favor of continued modernization and far-reaching social reforms. Only the future can tell whether such a development will occur and whether it will make political participation broader and more meaningful across the entire spectrum of political parties and tendencies in France. If such a development should occur, it would have to start within the framework of the institutions of the Fifth Republic as they were developed under President de Gaulle and his successors, presidents Georges Pompidou and Valéry Giscard d'Estaing. It is these institutions that we now must briefly survey.

THE PROCESS AND MACHINERY OF POLITICS: THE SELF-STEERING OF THE FRENCH POLITICAL SYSTEM

The Fifth Republic: All Power to the Executive. The *Fifth Republic* was designed to avoid the weaknesses of its predecessors. Major executive powers were given to the president, not to the premier. Its president is strong and is elected directly by the people. Like the president of the United States, he is fully independent of the legislature. Under the Constitution, as it finally emerged in the early 1960s, his legal powers are much greater than those of the American counterpart. The French President has the legal right to dissolve the assembly at will; the only limit is that it can be done only once each year. The president nominates the premier and thus can control this official and the Cabinet. The president may call a referendum, issue decrees having the force of law, or declare a state of emergency and "take the measures commanded by . . . circumstances" (Article XVI of the French Constitution). At no time is this individual responsible to the assembly.

The Constitution describes the president as the "arbiter," charged with making the ultimate decision among conflicting interests and policies. During de Gaulle's term in office he also took on the role of "guide" to the nation. As de Gaulle stated flatly in 1964, "The President elected by the nation is the source and holder of the power of the state." Backed by a large and growing staff, the office of the presidency has become the center of policy making in both foreign and domestic matters (see Figure 13.2).

In 1973, Prime Minister Pierre Messmer, himself a retired general, stated bluntly that if the alliance of the left should win a majority of seats in the National Assembly, President Pompidou would use the full constitutional powers of his office to prevent a Socialist-Communist government from taking charge. Similar predictions were made, less explicitly, for President Giscard's policy in case of a leftist majority emerging from the 1978 elections. In both years the voters did not take the risk. The majority was still preserved, and the old Gaullist coalition and regime seemed likely to endure (see Figure 13.5).

The structure of the Fifth Republic looks much like that of the Third and Fourth, but the relative powers of its various organs have changed. There still are a two-chamber legislature, a premier and Cabinet, a president, and a system of courts. A few details have been added, but the real power has shifted.

The role of the premier and the Cabinet is weaker vis-à-vis the president, but stronger vis-à-vis the National Assembly. The premier and Cabinet members are appointed by the president, whom no legislative vote can overthrow. The legislature technically may force the Cabinet's resignation, but its powers are much less than they were under the Third and Fourth Republics. Usually a Cabinet can be toppled only through a motion of censure, which requires an absolute majority of the members, so that blank ballots and abstentions count *for* the administration. In actuality, the Cabinet is an instrument of the president, carrying out the policies he or she determines. Some of the key ministers, such as those of foreign affairs and defense, often work with the president without much intervention from the premier. All

Cabinet decrees require the signature of the president for their validity.

A Shackled Legislature. The legislature consists of two chambers, the more important one being the *National Assembly* of 491 members (1978) who are elected directly by the people for five-year terms. A change in electoral law has given the strongest party a disproportionately large share of seats, which works to the great advantage of the Gaullist Party. But legislative seats mean less than they used to.

The Assembly legislates on all matters of law, but these are enumerated restrictively by the Constitution, which leaves all other matters to the *rule-making power*—the power to issue binding regulations—of the executive branch. Even the enumerated law-making powers may be delegated to the executive branch by an *organic law*—that is, a law which affects the Constitution and is

FIGURE 13.2 *Modern Constitutional Structure in France*

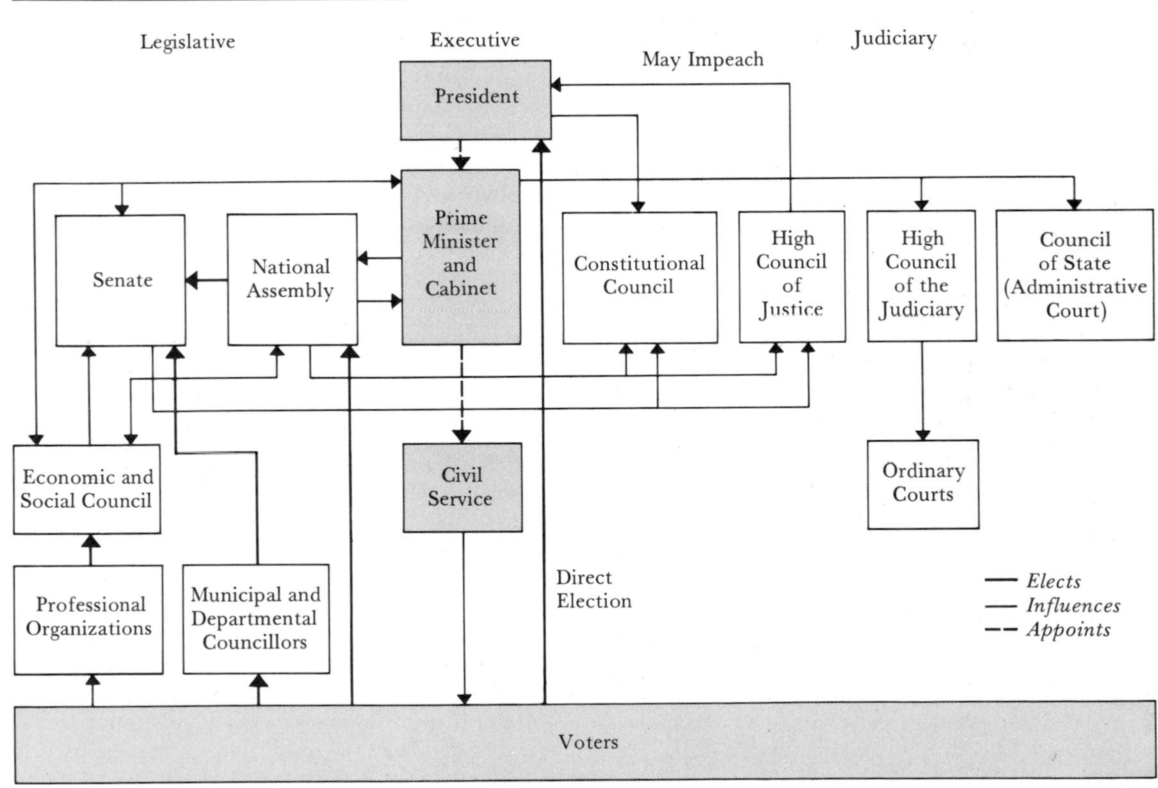

Source: R. C. Macridis, "France," in R. C. Macridis and R. E. Ward, eds., *Modern Political Systems: Europe,* 2nd ed., 1968. Adapted by permission of Prentice-Hall, Inc., Englewood Cliffs, N.J.

passed by a majority of the members of both houses. The Assembly's order of business is determined by the administration. The Assembly may have no more than six committees and may not meet for more than six months each year. Most important, the French legislature has lost the power of the purse; it no longer controls money. The executive alone draws up the budget and puts it before the Assembly. Any motion in the Assembly to reduce taxes or other government receipts or to increase government spending for any purpose is automatically out of order. If the Assembly fails to approve the government's budget within seventy days, it may be made public by executive decree, which makes it law.

The *Senate*'s 283 members are elected indirectly by municipal and departmental councilors and representatives of the cities. Those directly involved in electing senators number about 110,000, more than half of them representing small villages of less than 3,000 inhabitants. Encompassing only one-third of the French population, these villages through their representatives elect a majority of the Senate. Towns of over 100,000, constituting over 40 percent of the French people, elect only every fifth senator. As a result, the Senate overwhelmingly represents rural and small-town France.

The Senate, however, has few powers. Though a bill can become law only if passed in identical form by both houses, the real decision in the case of disagreement lies in the hands of the premier, who is primarily an instrument of the president. If the premier wishes a bill to pass he or she convenes a conference committee, which represents both the Assembly and the Senate, to seek agreement on its contents. Should they fail to agree and the premier likes the Assembly's version of the bill, he or she may simply resubmit it to the Assembly. A bill passed twice by the Assembly can override a senatorial veto and become law. Thus, in such cases, the Senate has merely the power to delay. If the premier, however, does not like the Assembly version, he or she can refuse to convene the conference committee. The bill then dies, and the Senate has exercised an absolute veto—thanks to the premier.

Senators are chosen for nine years, and one-third stand for re-election every three years. The Senate was intended to serve as a source of advice and mild delay and as a potential ally of the government against a recalcitrant Assembly. Actually, it has worked the other way: after the 1962 elections the new Assembly threw its support behind the Gaullist government and the Senate turned against it. The adherents of de Gaulle did well among the mass electorate and, with their allies, soon captured a majority of the Assembly (see Figure 13.3). Owing to weak local organization, however, they failed to take the Senate.

The Senate has continued to represent the entrenched power structures of local governments, which have remained strongholds of the traditional political parties. The Senate has also continued to represent a preference of the French voters to keep their traditional parties alive, at least at the local level, perhaps in readiness for some future return to the national scene. In the meantime the Senate remains a bulwark of opposition to the administration. It has rejected a large number of government bills that then have had to be repassed over its veto by the Assembly. By the late 1960s the weakness of the Senate was evident; ministers stopped attending its debates and answering written or oral questions from its members.

A Sidelined Judiciary. Other divisions of the government have still less political power. The Constitutional Council supervises elections and referenda and decides disputes about them. It passes also on the constitutionality of any bill or treaty before promulgation, but only at the request of the president, premier, president of the National Assembly, or president of the Senate. Once a bill has become law, the council can judge its constitutionality only in restricted cases and on request of the government. Judicial review in France is, thus, radically weaker and narrower than in the United States. The courts in general are independent, but lack power to nullify or modify laws or administrative actions.

A Lasting Reality: The Civil Service. Death and taxes are inevitable, goes an old saying. And, since the rise of modern tax-collecting states, with the taxes come the officials to collect them and to administer their disbursement. Three figures may indicate the importance of the French bureaucracy: about 40 percent of the French gross national product passes through the public sector; about 2.4 million people are employed there; and about 10,000 take part in formulating policy and directing its execution.[17]

French administration is organized, like the British, under ministries. The most important of these are the Ministry of the Interior, the Ministry of Finances, and the Ministry of Foreign Affairs. The Ministry of the Interior is in charge of the police and of all general administration throughout the country, including all departmental and local units of government. It appoints, transfers, and can remove by secret decision and at will the key official in charge of the administration of each

[17]Macridis, "Politics of France," p. 128.

FIGURE 13.3 *French Voter Opinion, 1960*

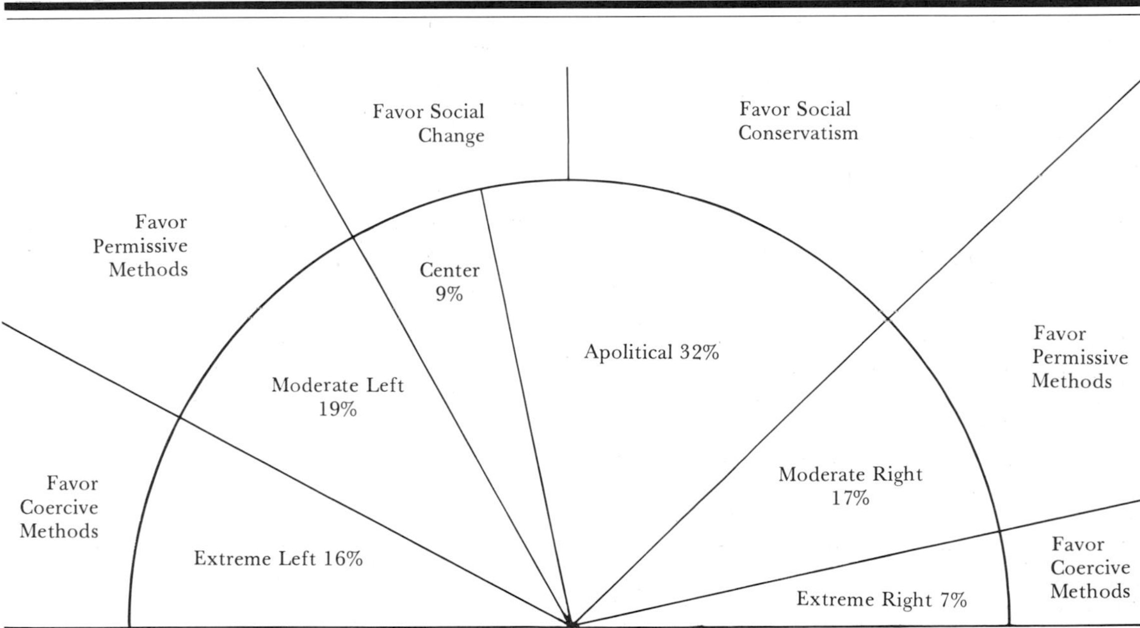

Source: R. C. Macridis, "France," in R. C. Macridis and R. E. Ward, eds., *Modern Political Systems: Europe,* 2nd ed., 1968. Adapted by permission of Prentice-Hall, Inc., Englewood Cliffs, N.J.

of the ninety departments: the *prefect.* The *Corps of Prefects* forms one of the five great bodies—*les grands corps*—of the French state. In 1978 a group of several hundred provincial *notables*—or prominent citizens—were asked, "Who exercises power in the province?" Almost all of them answered "the prefect." When asked to name several power holders, their answers produced the rankings shown in Table 13.4.

The mayor—*le maire*—of any of the 36,000 French communes is elected, but then must represent not only that municipality, but also the state. The mayor's decisions regarding the local budget and local taxation must be approved by the prefect; in some other matters the prefect can order the mayor to act in certain ways. If the latter fails to obey, he or she may be suspended or dismissed by an executive order of the prefect. This *tutelage* of the central government over all municipal authorities ensures a high degree of uniformity of administration throughout France. The powers of the elected General Council of each department are much weaker; the centralized and bureaucratic chain of command prevails.[18]

The second key ministry, that of finance, has a similar centralizing function. It prepares the budget, draws up estimates, collects taxes, and to some extent controls spending. Working within it, but often reaching beyond its boundaries by its actions, is the *General Inspection of Finances,* another of the great bodies of the state. It attracts many of the ablest candidates, as its officials do not merely inspect tax collections and expenditures; they actually take part in drawing up many kinds of legislation. Many of them eventually move on to higher office elsewhere; some are "detached" for service with other governmental agencies without losing their connection with the General Inspection.

The third key ministry is that of foreign affairs. The diplomats working under its direction form another of the great bodies of the state.

Three other bureaucratic agencies are counted among the great bodies, the most important of these being the *Council of State.* Since the days of Napoleon, this body, containing its own hierarchy of about two hundred high-level officials and a larger number of lower-ranking ones, has had two functions: first, to advise the head of the state and/or the government on matters of public policy and legislation and, second, to resolve conflicts within the administration. Over time, this second task has made the Council of State a quasi-judicial body, and it has played an important part in offering citizens a recourse against arbitrary bureaucratic acts.

Another great body is the *Court of Accounts.* Its members, like judges, cannot be removed from their positions; otherwise, it functions as part of

TABLE 13.4 *Who Exercises Power in the Province: Percentage of Mentions by Notables, 1978*

Prefect (appointed)	90
President of the General Council (elected)	66
Director of the chief regional or local daily newspaper	44
Mayor of the principal town or city (elected, but removable by the Minister)	28
Deputy (member of the National Assembly)	25
President of the Chamber of Commerce and Industry	23
Paymaster General	13
Senator	6
Responsible departmental functionary of a major political party	3
Responsible departmental functionary of a major labor union	3

Source: From data in *L'Express,* November 25, 1978, pp. 40–41.

[18] Ibid.

the administrative machinery, not of the judiciary. The fifth great body is the *Diplomatic Service*. And, finally, the *Supreme Administrative Court—la cour de cassation*—is sometimes considered a sixth great body. It has final power to confirm or annul the decisions of administrative agencies.

The recruitment of all these high civil servants is remarkably uniform. Most of them, perhaps 90 percent, come from the upper middle and middle classes. Many are the children of civil servants. Their main channel of entry is through the great schools, chiefly the *École Nationale d'Administration* (see p. 403, above). Access to these schools requires stiff competitive written examinations; similar skills are indispensable for graduating with the necessary high rank in class; and middle-class children almost exclusively have the educational background for such performance. The result is a proud and competent top-level bureaucracy, open in theory, but largely closed in fact.

To a great extent this bureaucracy is permanent. Civil servants generally are secure in their jobs and careers. Ministers come and go, but civil servants remain, unless those of high rank choose the option of *pantouflage,* or the "putting on of bedroom slippers"—that is, lucrative high-level employment in the private sector. Here the permanence of the civil service shades into the remarkable persistence of the larger French managerial and ruling class. The civil service, the army, and the larger ruling elite form a heavy counterweight to the changing contest among the political parties of the *right, left,* and *center* that has been moving France this way and that during nearly two centuries.

Another Enduring Reality: The Parties. In the United States and Britain the main constitutional arrangements are older than the parties. In France most of the parties are older than its several constitutions. The fundamental political divisions go back to the Revolution of 1789. Those French people who favored and accepted that revolution and the separation of church and state formed the left of the political spectrum; those whose sympathies lay with the monarchy and the unity of church and state formed the political right. The original terms "left" and "right" derive from the seating order of deputies in a past French legislature—a seating order that later became customary in many European parliaments. In the course of time the terms have acquired other connotations. Parties on the left tend to favor workers and the poor as well as political and social change—by radical and revolutionary methods if they are far to the left and by more moderate reforms if they are closer to the center. Parties on the right tend to favor tradition, property, and privilege as well as the interests of the well-to-do and of substantial citizens in town and countryside. Parties in the center usually seek compromises between these wings and are often paralyzed by immobilism and attacked by both sides.

In France a whole imagery has grown up around the unremitting contest between left and right. "Left is where the heart is," states a French saying; the right is seen as the side closest to the pocketbook. But although these general political tendencies seem perennial in France, issues and problems do change. New policies must be devised to cope with them and new coalitions formed to put these policies to work. In 1946, after World War II, 46 percent of all registered French voters cast their votes for parties of the left, 20 percent for parties of the center, 10 percent for parties of the right, and nearly 24 percent did not vote at all. By the second round of voting in 1978 the left had shrunk to 49.3 percent of the vote; the old center had split, one group joining the coalition of the left (2 percent) while most of the rest merged with the government coalition. President Giscard's center-right *Union for Democratic France (UDF),* which also included most of the former Conservative Independent candidates, won the support of 23 percent of the voters. Further to the right, but still moderate, a new party—the Gaullists—had risen to collect 26 percent of the electorate. The extreme right declined to 3 percent and the nonvoters to 18 percent. Still another 1.5 percent of the votes cast was provided by scattered minor allies of the government coalition, totaling about 50.5 percent of the votes cast, enough to win a majority of seats in the Assembly (see Table 13.5).

For a long time the strongest group on the left was the Communist Party. Their main support comes from workers and, to a lesser extent, from intellectuals, white-collar workers, and even some peasants. From 1920 to 1967 they were stronger than the Socialists. Nowadays they represent nearly a fifth of all eligible French voters and nearly a fourth of those who actually vote. Since 1968 the Socialists have been stronger than the Communists. They have lost much of their former following among manual workers and now get most of their support from public officials, teachers, and other white-collar groups, whose share in the work force is expanding. More moderate than the Communists and Socialists were the Radical Socialists, who were in fact neither radical nor socialist. They were strong defenders of republican traditions, of the memories and symbols of the French Revolution, and of strict separation of church and state. Opposition to any influence of the clergy on parties and education long united the Radical Socialists, Socialists, and Communists as a coalition of laypersons' parties or of the left. In 1935–37 these three parties supported the government of the *Popular Front,* although the Communists had no Cabinet representation in it. In 1944–47 the Communists did sit in the Cabinet, which then included not only the left, but also the followers of General de Gaulle and all other groups who had resisted the Nazi occupation. By 1973 most Radicals had entered a federation with the Socialists (UGSD).

Some Radicals of a more conservative outlook had joined the Gaullists or other parties in the government coalition. Most of the former Radicals, however, moved to a new center party, the *Réformateurs,* led by Jean Lecanuet, who leaned toward the Pompidou majority, and by J. J. Servan-Schreiber, who was critical of it. At the center a moderate Catholic party emerged in 1946, the Popular Republican Movement, or MRP. This party favored public support for Catholic schools, family allowances and other welfare legislation, and respect for republican and democratic traditions. By 1973 it had shrunk, and most of its members had changed their party name to Center for Democracy and Progress (CDP) and had become part of the government coalition. All these center parties had more or less disappeared by 1978, most of their voters going to Giscard's UDF. In effect, most centrist voters had moved to the moderate right. One new "nonpolitical" center party, the Ecologists, received 3 percent of the votes in the first round of voting in 1978, but lost almost all its voters to the right and left coalitions in the decisive second round.

To the right are those French citizens who oppose welfare legislation and nonmilitary public spending. Still further to the right are those who have never fully accepted the Revolution of 1789 and the Republics that followed from it. Here one finds some of the remnants of the French nobility, many officers' families, monarchists, and the more tradition-minded Catholics who found the MRP too liberal. The candidates they vote for are often called Independents. In recent years the Gaullist Party in coalition with the Independents has brought many of these voters back toward the political center and to support of the Fifth Republic, which embodies Gaullist policies. By 1978 most of them had been absorbed into the Gaullist Party under Jacques Chirac or, at least, into the progovernment majority. In addition, French individualism has produced a multitude of political splinter groups that often disappear after one or two elections and are fairly negligible in size.

In French society the middle class is strongest, but in French politics the center seems weak. The politically active French are on the right and left. In the middle are the politically passive—often about one-fifth of the electorate. As a result French politics is often deadlocked. People often stay out of politics until they begin to feel that something must be done.

As in other modern countries, only more so, French politics tends to oscillate between immobilism and emergency. When many different interest groups or parties stop or frustrate each other, the result is either immobility and widespread apathy or a willingness to hand things over to a strong leader who can mobilize the otherwise apathetic nonvoters. Then the center becomes significant. The strong leader, a Bonapartist or Gaullist, sometimes can win the support of former nonvoters, together with that of the center and the moderate right, to form a majority. That person is then a compromise candidate and coalition builder who manages not to look like one. Such a strategy worked for the two Napoleons and for de Gaulle, too—for a time. In recent years it has worked again for President Giscard, but this time in a low-pressure style.

Ordinarily, much of French politics works through compromises among the parties, despite the reluctance of many French people to make compromises or to draw attention to them. Some need to compromise is built into the French electoral system. French elections come in two stages. On election day voters cast their *first ballot* for the candidate whom each prefers. If no candidate wins an absolute majority, a run-off election follows: voters cast a *second ballot* for the compromise candidate whom they find most acceptable among contestants.

These compromise choices determine much of the composition of the legislature. The multiplicity of parties makes it necessary to form coalitions, since often no party wins a clear majority. Usually, adherents of a party of the left vote for the candidate of some other party of the left; and there is similar mutual support among the parties of the right. Similar alliances are formed sometimes among the center parties; and Communists vote sometimes for moderate left candidates, but the voters in the latter sector may or may not reciprocate. Many refused to do so in 1968. And in 1978, after several months of quarrels between Communists and Socialists, these reservations among the more moderate Socialist voters may have contributed toward limiting the leftist coalition to 49 percent of the vote and a minority of Assembly seats. In the March 1978 elections to the district councils, the parties of the Common Front, or the more or less united parties of the left, won over 54 percent of the vote, most of the gains going to the Socialists. It seems likely that a number of middle-of-the-road or float voters were more willing at that time to trust the left with power on the local level, but not with national office. The results in votes are shown in Table 13.5; the results in seats in the National Assembly, in Figure 13.5.

Despite these deals and shifts and many others like them, the basic pattern of French politics had remained fairly constant in recent decades. About one-fifth of the French voters usually stayed at home or spoiled their ballots. About one-third normally voted left: about half for the Communists and the other half for the more moderate left parties. Another third voted for the center and the right. Among these voters, those close to the center preferred the moderate Catholic MRP; those well toward the right voted for candidates who called themselves independents or moderates; the extreme right has been insignificant in most postwar elections. The lion's share of votes on the moderate right—more than one-third—went in recent years to the Gaullists. Furthermore, about every fifth voter was and still is likely to abstain from voting.

There is a *floating vote* of 10 to 20 percent of the electorate. In some years most of this vote floats left, as in 1946 and 1973, or to the moderate right, as in 1968, or it divides almost evenly, as in 1978. In other years 10 percent may go all the way to the extreme right, as in 1956; and in still other years a similar number may increase the body of abstainers, as in 1962. Table 13.6 permits us to trace such changes. They add up to a sequence of kaleidoscopic changes on the surface produced by the floating fifth that may conceal the stable political habits of four-fifths of the French voters. The stability of the many voters and the intermittent volatility of the few have marked French politics under the Third, Fourth, and Fifth Republics

TABLE 13.5 *Three Aspects of French Voting: Abstainers, Parties, Candidates*

A. FRENCH LEGISLATIVE VOTES BY PARTIES, 1946–78

Year	Total registered voters (millions)	(%)	Valid votes cast (%)	Abst. & void (%)*	Comm. & Prog. (%)	Soc. & Left Soc. (%)	Rad. (%)	Reform-ists (%)	MRP† (%)	UDF "Giscardians" (%)	Gaullists (%)	Ind. & Mod. (%)	Ext. Right (%)	Others (%)
1946	25.1	100	76.5	23.5	21.9	13.5	11.2	—	20.3	—	—	10.4	—	0.4
1951	24.5	100	78.0	22.0	20.1	11.0	8.8	—	9.8	—	16.7	10.6	—	0.4
1956	26.8	100	79.5	20.5	20.5	11.9	10.4	—	9.0	—	3.0	12.3	10.1	0.4
1958	27.7	100	75.8	22.4	14.1	11.6	9.7	—	8.7	—	13.0	14.8	2.5	—
1962	27.5	100	68.7	33.4	14.5	8.4	5.5	—	5.8	—	21.1	9.1	0.7	—
1967	28.3	100	78.5	21.3	17.6	14.8	—	—	10.2	—	30.0	3.9	0.7	—
1968	28.3	100	78.5	21.4	15.7	16.6‡	—	—	8.1	—	34.3	3.2	0.4	—
1973	29.7	100	79.0	21.0	19.5‡	20.2	—	10.0	3.0	—	19.6	6.0	2.2	—
1978 (Round 1)	35.2	100	81.1	18.9	16.7	18.3	1.7	—	—	17.4	18.6	1.9	2.4	4.4
1978 (Round 2)	31.0	100	82.2	17.8	15.3	23.3	2.0	—	—	20.1	21.5	1.0	—	0.2
						40.6					42.6			

B. PRESIDENTIAL ELECTIONS, 1965–74

						Mitterand						de Gaulle		
1965 (second ballot)	28.2	100	82.2	17.8		37.4						44.8		
1969 (first ballot)	28.8	100	77.2	22.8	16.6	18.1	3.9				33.9	2.8	—	1.8
						Poher						Pompidou		
1969 (second ballot)	28.7	100	64.6	35.4		27.4						37.2		
1974 (first ballot)	30.6	100	84.1	15.9		36.3		—	—	—	15.3	27.4	0.2	4.9
						Mitterand						Giscard		
1974 (second ballot)	30.6	100	86.1	13.9		42.4						43.7		

Sources: Data for 1946–73 from R. C. Macridis, "France," in R. C. Macridis and R. E. Ward, eds., *Modern Political Systems: Europe,* 2nd ed., 1968. Also from *Le Monde,* June 17, 1969, and March 6, 1973. For Assembly elections 1978: *Keesing's Contemporary Archives,* November 24, 1978, pp. 29322–23. Data for 1974–78 from R. C. Macridis, "Politics of France," in R. C. Macridis, ed., *Modern Political Systems: Europe,* 4th ed., 1978. Adapted by permission of Prentice-Hall, Inc., Englewood Cliffs, N.J.

*The slight discrepancies reflect the lack of uniform treatment of void ballots in French voting statistics. Such errors are always smaller than 0.7 million votes.

†The MRP was succeeded by other centrist groupings: *Centre démocrate* (1967); *Centre Progrès et Democratie moderne* (1968); and *Réformateurs* (1973).

‡A small leftist group, the Party of Socialist Unity, followed a more radical line in 1973 and was counted, therefore, as a Communist ally in that year, despite some sectarian disputes between the two parties. Earlier, in 1968, it had been counted as a Socialist ally, and the addition of its votes and that of other Socialist splinter groups made the Socialist vote in this table appear larger than the Communist vote in that year. In 1973 and 1978 the Socialists and Communists entered the elections with a common program, but with separate candidates for the first ballot. They had agreed, however, to withdraw their candidates from the race for the second round of balloting in favor of that candidate of the left who had received the most votes in the first round; and the PSU later joined this agreement. In the 1974 presidential election, the Socialists, Communists, and Radicals entered the election with a common program.

alike. In 1977 and 1978, despite some bickering, the *Common Program* of Communists and Socialists still held, and the floating vote went largely to the left, bringing it within 1 percent of a majority. If this alignment should endure, French politics may enter a new epoch.

Successes and Surprises. The entire Constitution of the Fifth Republic (see pp. 416-20) seemed custom-tailored to fit the imposing figure of President de Gaulle, and from 1958 to 1969 he wore his responsibilities well. During these years France acquired a great deal of prosperity, many new buildings and much productive equipment, a temporary surplus in its foreign trade, and a good deal of prestige. French technology moved forward. Acquiring a significant striking force, France became one of the world's nuclear powers. Through the development of its civilian jet plane, the Caravelle; its high-speed fighter plane, the Mystère; and the British-French supersonic plane, the Concorde, France joined the leaders of world aviation. French planning organizations were well staffed, forward-looking, and often effective. French scientists won Nobel Prizes, and the government took steps to safeguard the development of a national computer industry. The enrollment in French universities grew by leaps and bounds—from about 142,000 in 1952–53 to about 706,000 in 1975—and new universities were added.

Suddenly, some of the new policies backfired. In the years prior to 1968, thousands of students had grown resentful at the overcrowded universities. Even where new buildings had been built, old authoritarian methods of instruction had remained; and the more numerous the students became, the dimmer seemed their chances for future employment. Even where jobs did promise to be available, they appeared dull and unattractive in a country whose trappings of grandeur and reforms hid so much that was still stodgy and traditional.

When students struck and occupied the universities in May 1968, workers soon joined them for reasons of their own. Inflation had eaten into their wages, which both private employers and public authorities had been reluctant to increase. "The pennies, Charlie, the pennies!" workers in the streets had cried out at President de Gaulle, but to no avail. A wave of strikes soon closed factories. Some intellectuals were delighted. "You have created new possibilities," the best-known French philosopher, Jean-Paul Sartre, told a student leader. But the solid majority of the French was shocked.

After a wage increase was granted, the workers went back to their jobs. Their unions and the Communist Party showed no interest in revolution and condemned the radical students as adventurers. In the "election of fear" of June 1968, French voters gave de Gaulle an increased majority. Only 6 percent of the vote shifted from the left and center to the right, but under the French electoral system this was enough to produce a landslide in the Assembly (see Figure 13.4). Politically, de Gaulle had won (see Table 13.5).

In terms of economics he had lost, however. Once again French speculators and investors took their money out of the country. The surplus in international payments turned into a deficit. The national currency, the franc, became shaky. Inflation continued and increasingly hurt the *rentiers,* salaried employees, civil servants, and large parts of the middle class. These more conservative groups joined with labor and the intellectuals in a common resentment against de Gaulle's high-handed personal leadership, which each group now blamed for its troubles. In the spring of 1969, when de Gaulle tried to put through an administrative reform providing for greater regional autonomy, he found the legislature reluctant to cooperate. As before, he presented his plan to the people in a referendum. This time he lost. A majority of voters rejected not only his plan, but in effect his personal regime. The president resigned and returned to his home in a small village. The Fifth Republic, however, survived its creator.

A NEW FRANCE

At the end of the 1950s France had to choose what kind of country it wished to become. In following General de Gaulle, not toward what some thought he had promised—keeping Algeria French—but toward what he did in response to the will of the French people—ending the Algerian War—the French to a significant degree chose their own course. France today is no longer tied to its empire and is therefore a much more modern country than it was twenty years ago.

France still has larger shares of its population working in agriculture, living in small towns, and remaining self-employed than does Germany or Britain. But the French occupational structure is now changing more quickly. In the decade 1966–76 approximately 7 percent of the French work force has shifted from agricultural to nonagricultural pursuits, compared with shifts of only 4 percent in the German Federal Republic and 1 percent in Britain. In 1973, French agriculture comprised only 5 percent of the electorate. Even

FIGURE 13.4 *French National Assembly, 1968*

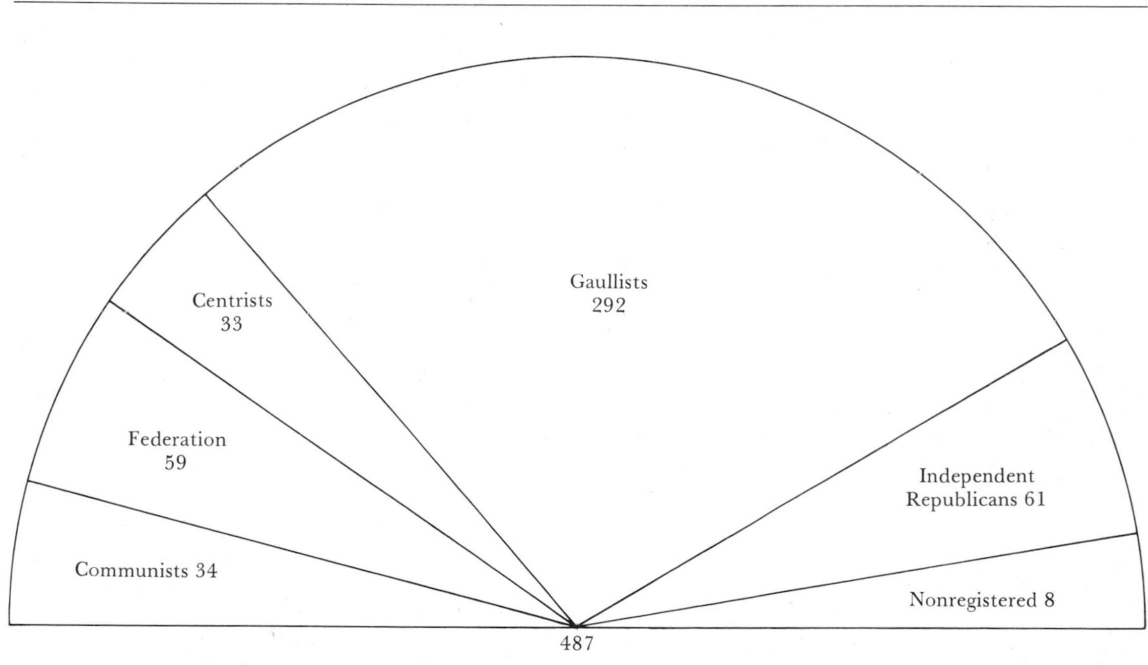

Source: R. C. Macridis, "France," in R. C. Macridis and R. E. Ward, eds., *Modern Political Systems: Europe,* 2nd ed., 1968. Adapted by permission of Prentice-Hall, Inc., Englewood Cliffs, N.J.

counting nonvoting teenagers and foreign laborers working on farms, agriculturists amounted to about one-ninth of the work force in 1975, and they may decline to one-twelfth in the early 1980s. If so, French politics will become very different from what it has been.

France is already in many ways a different country from what it used to be. It still has a social structure that makes unity difficult and a political culture that encourages distrust of government and withdrawal from politics. President Georges Pompidou, who in 1969 succeeded General de Gaulle, continued the policies of his predecessor, showing greater suavity of style, but no major change in substance; and his successor, President Giscard, followed suit in still more elegant style. As early as the mid-1960s, elite surveys had elicited the opinion that much of the Fifth Republic would survive General de Gaulle. The responses further indicated that the French elites wanted France to be an ally of the United States, but not a satellite.

Some of the more pessimistic French at that time forecast that, after General de Gaulle, everything in politics would be for sale. If this had turned out to be true, domestic and foreign interests with the greatest purchasing power might have picked up new political concessions. Ten years later, by early 1979, they had not yet done so. Perhaps there is less for sale in the French politics of growing mass participation than both native and foreign observers suspected. French technological and industrial development, French monetary policy, and modern French big business enterprise, no less than French intellectual life and public opinion—all are likely to respond to French national needs and pressures more fully than to any appeals from abroad whether they come from the United States, the Soviet Union, Western Europe, or the world of multinational corporations.

What is likely to be new in French politics in the 1980s is the sustained demand for structural reforms. These may include a partial redistribution of incomes and perhaps of patterns of authority in many situations of daily life. France has had such waves of reforms before: in 1789–99 during and after the French Revolution; in 1934–37, when Popular Front majorities legislated social security and the five-day workweek; and in 1944–46, when social services were expanded and important industries nationalized, such as electric power, mining, and segments of the automobile and aircraft industries. Perhaps another wave of social reforms and experiments is coming again—but when, and led by whom, we cannot tell as yet.

A poll published in February 1979 offers some glimpses of the things that have remained stable in French political opinion, together with some of the changes that have occurred and that may still be continuing.[20]

What is enduring is national pride: 60 percent of the respondents define themselves as French, as opposed to defining themselves by their age (38 percent), their profession (35 percent), their social class (31 percent), or their sex (24 percent). For two-thirds of all respondents one of the greatest assets of their country is the French language, "which is a language of culture and is spoken in vast regions of the world." National symbols—the national anthem, *La Marseillaise;* the red, white, and blue national flag, the *tricolore;* and the Fourteenth of July, the national feast day commemorating the storming of the Bastille prison in 1789, which marked the start of the French Revolution—have kept "the same value as before" for a clear majority (56 percent); only a strong minority (39 percent) now considers them "a bit outmoded."

As for France itself, they identify it first of all with liberty (61 percent), tolerance (33 percent), and generosity (29 percent); all these are mentioned even more often by the adherents of President Giscard's party. A smaller number add equality (17 percent) and greatness (12 percent), but only 5 percent mention *mesure,* that is, a sense of proportion. As to its faults, the most conspicuous to 24 percent of the respondents is *chauvinism,*

[19]Louis Harris, in *L'Express,* February 17, 1979, pp. 32–38. All following data in this chapter are from this survey.

FIGURE 13.5 *French National Assembly: (a) 1973; (b) 1978*

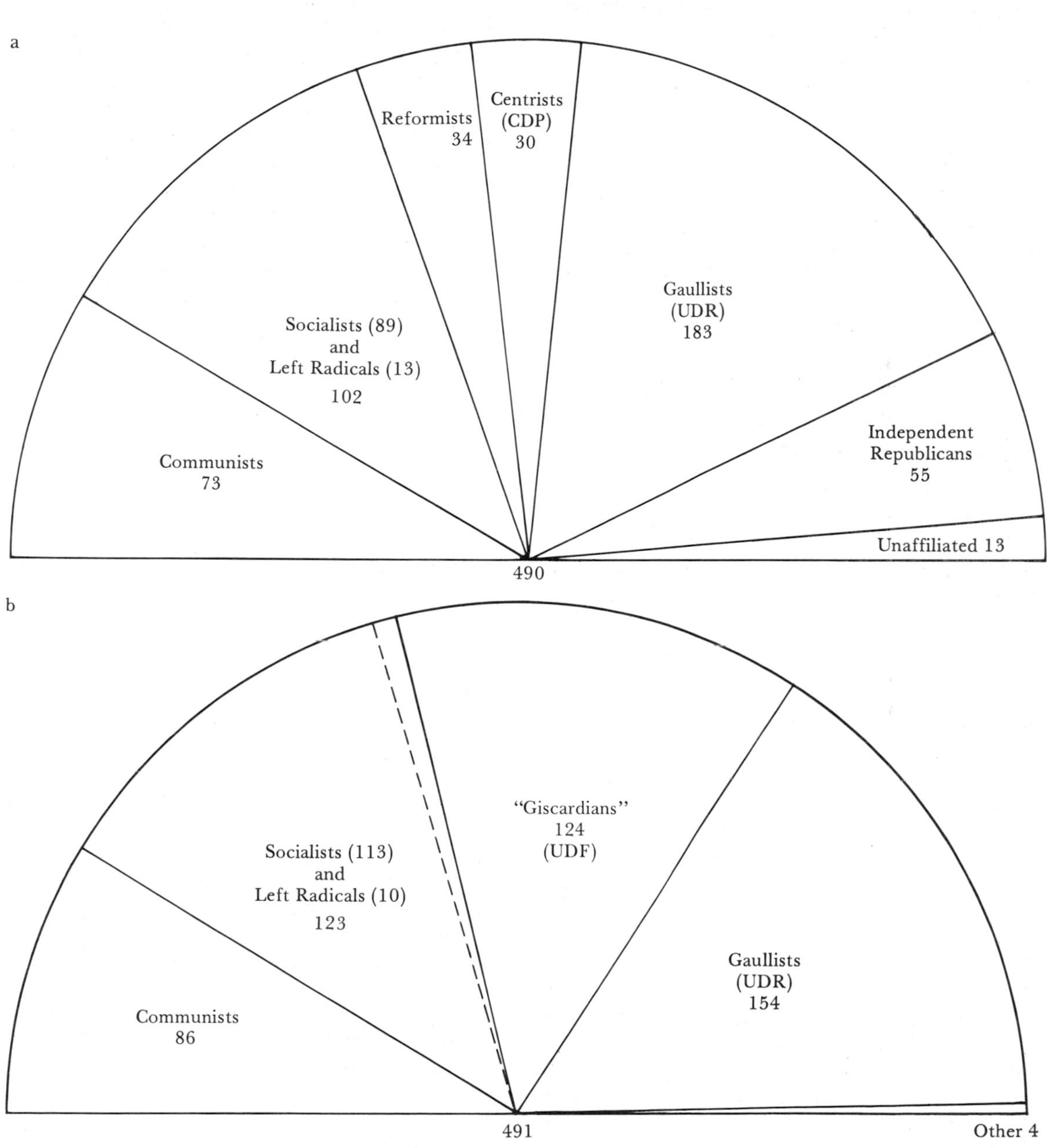

Source: *Keesing's Contemporary Archives,* April 23-29, 1973, p. 2584T, and November 24, 1978, p. 29323.

exaggerated nationalism that downgrades other nations in order to exalt one's own. Other faults are more rarely mentioned: pretentiousness (13 percent), futility (4 percent), and imperialism (4 percent).

Among the countries of the world France is now seen as occupying "an honorable middle position," in regard to both culture (65 percent) and technology (74 percent). Only one-fifth still sees it "as one of the leading countries of the world" in its culture, and only one-eighth has a similarly high opinion of its technology. Nearly two-thirds see something else as more important. A clear majority, 54 percent, think that "superior nations" ought *not* to run the world, and nearly two-thirds (63 percent) agree with this statement: "The political power of France matters little, for what makes it strong is that it has permitted and still permits the work of great writers, scholars, and artists."

In other respects the French remain divided. Nearly one-half think that French prestige is continuing to decline (46 percent), but nearly the same proportion disagree (44 percent). Class divisions are seen as persisting. "A French worker is more similar to a worker of another country than to a French employer," say 59 percent. Exactly 50 percent see France as invaded by "undesirable foreigners" who are not needed and should be sent back where they came from, but a strong minority—38 percent—oppose this view.

Similar divisions appear vis-à-vis international politics. Perceptions of foreign threats are scattered, the worst being seen in Communism (20 percent), population growth in the Third World (19 percent), the Arabs (17 percent), multinational corporations (16 percent), regional separatism (10 percent), and "supranational Europe" (7 percent). There is somewhat more unity about who are "the friends of France," but the answer shows a surprising change. Germany is now the most popular, gaining 33 percent of all mentions and followed at some distance by the United States (22 percent) and Britain (16 percent); in earlier decades the United States and Britain led the field. Though the Communist Party had won 21 percent of the valid votes cast in March 1978, only 2 percent in the 1979 poll named the Soviet Union as a friend of France.

Underlying many of these views is a common and persistent desire to maintain the independence of their country. The atomic bomb, says a strong plurality (45 percent), should be used exclusively to defend the national territory of France; only about one-fourth would be willing to use it also to defend its allies in the event of an attack on their territories. (Here French feelings for their friends show some limits.) Every major social class sees itself as the one most strongly committed to defend French national independence, and the same applies to all major parties, but the middle class (38 percent), the working class (37 percent), the Socialist Party (31 percent), and the Gaullists (31 percent) rank highest. Least trusted as defenders of national independence are "the big bourgeoisie" (17 percent) and the Communists (18 percent).

Finally, what about "the great tasks for the future"? Highest ranking is, surprisingly enough, "to transform the understanding *(les rapports)* among persons and nations" (32 percent), followed by "aid to underdeveloped countries" (19 percent). Lower-ranking tasks are "building Europe" (12 percent), "accelerating scientific and technical progress" (10 percent), "building socialism" (9 percent), and "building the liberal society" (8 percent). Together, these six tasks should offer a wide field for the discussions and experiments in which France often has excelled.

In the past France has been the experimental laboratory of the Western world. From the thirteenth century to the intellectual and scientific ferment of the present, the French have tried out more ideas than any other people. Often they have not innovated as much in practice as in thought. But what the French now try to do both in thought and in practice may continue to be of decisive importance for the entire Western world.

KEY TERMS AND CONCEPTS

rentiers
avant-garde
esprit de finesse
Le Grand Siècle
Jacobins
First Republic
Girondists
the terror
Thermidor
Directory
eighteenth of Brumaire
First Empire
Second Republic
Second Empire
Third Republic
great schools
Vichy regime
Resistance
Fourth Republic
ministrables
Common Market
economic determinism
Bonapartism
force de frappe
OAS
great bodies of the state
patrons
indicative planning
abstentionism
militants
cadres
Fifth Republic
National Assembly
rule-making power
organic law
Senate
prefect
Corps of Prefects
notables
maire
tutelage
General Inspection of Finances
Council of State
Court of Accounts
Diplomatic Service
Supreme Administrative Court
École Nationale d'Administration
pantouflage
right
left
center
Gaullists
Union for Democratic France
Popular Front
first ballot
second ballot
floating vote
common program
tricolore
chauvinism

ADDITIONAL READINGS

Aron, R. *France: Steadfast and Changing.* Cambridge: Harvard University Press, 1960.

Brinton, C. *The Americans and the French.* Cambridge: Harvard University Press, 1968.

———. *A Decade of Revolution, 1789–1799.* New York: Random House, 1965. PB

Crozier, M. *The Bureaucratic Phenomenon.* Chicago: University of Chicago Press, 1967. PB

Ehrmann, H. W. *Politics in France.* Boston: Little, Brown, 1968. PB

———. "French Communism: Theory and Practice," in *Problems of Communism,* May-June 1978, pp. 58–64.

Grosser, A. "Nothing but Opposition." In R. Dahl, ed., *Political Opposition in Western Democracies.* New Haven: Yale University Press, 1968. PB

Hoffmann, S., ed. *In Search of France.* Cambridge: Harvard University Press, 1963. PB

MacRae, D., Jr. *Parliament, Parties and Societies in France, 1946–1958.* New York: St. Martin's, 1967.

Macridis, R. C. "France." In R. C. Macridis, ed., *Modern Political Systems: Europe.* 4th ed. Englewood Cliffs, N.J.: Prentice-Hall, 1978.

———. "Pompidou and the Communists." *Virginia Quarterly,* vol. 45, no. 4 (1969), pp. 579–94.

Métraux, R., and M. Mead. *Themes in French Culture: A Preface to a Study of French Community.* Stanford, Calif.: Hoover Institute Series D, no. 1, 1954.

Wylie, L. *Village in the Vaucluse.* Cambridge: Harvard University Press, 1974. PB

For Those Who Can Read Some French:

Braud, P. *Le Comportement électoral en France.* Paris: Presses Universitaires de France, 1977.

Birnbaum, P., et al. *La Classe dirigeante française.* Paris: Presses Universitaires de France, 1978.

Duverger, M. *Le Cinquième République.* 4th ed. Paris: Presses Universitaires de France, 1974.

Escoube, P. *Les Grands corps de l'État.* Paris: Presses Universitaires de France, 1971.

Fauré, E. *Pour un nouveau contrat social.* Paris: Fayard, 1977.

Giscard d'Estaing, V. *Democratie française.* Paris: Fayard, 1976.

Lancelot, A. *L'Absentionnisme électoral en France.* Paris: Colin, 1968.

Laroque, A. *Les Classes sociales.* Paris: Presses Universitaires de France, 1972.

Laurens, A., and T. Pfister. *Les Nouveaux Communistes.* Paris: Stock, 1973.

Monod, J., and Ph. de Castelbajac. *L'Aménagement du territoire.* 2nd ed. Paris: Presses Universitaires de France, 1973.

Peyrefitte, A. *La Mal française.* Paris: Plon, 1976.

Stoetzel, J., and A. Girard. *Les Sondages d'opinion publique.* Paris: Presses Universitaires de France, 1973.

PB = *available in paperback*

XIV

The German Federal Republic

"To be German means to do a thing for its own sake," runs an old German saying. For good or ill, the German people often have committed themselves thoroughly to whatever they were doing at the time—to the admiration, astonishment, or horror of their neighbors. German diligence and orderliness are renowned. "In a German train," goes another saying, "not only the conductor is on duty but the passengers as well." Yet two thousand years earlier, the Roman historian Tacitus called the ancient Germans incurably undisciplined and lazy. How did a people of such great gifts go through such changes in its character?

Like the British, French, and American political systems, the various regimes by which Germany has been governed have had their roots in part in the political culture of the country. Such roots may reflect images of conflict or cooperation, hierarchy or equality, that have become embodied in the things people take for granted. These images lodge in people's minds even if they are not explicitly discussed as formal political problems.

German technology is much like that of the United States, the Soviet Union, Britain, France, and other advanced countries. But German history often has been radically different, and so has German politics. German politics cannot be understood by looking only at German institutions or day-to-day events, for all these have changed too often in this century. To discern what German politics means and how it works, we must know something of its origins and its past.

THE NATURE AND BACKGROUND OF GERMAN POLITICS

The present German Federal Republic is among the world's youngest political systems. It came into being only in 1949. But it governs three-quarters of one of the oldest peoples of Europe. In a sense the German people is even older than the English people. When the German people emerged, when the word *teutiscus*, or "German," was first used early in the ninth century, no Norman had yet come to England. Through a thousand years of history there has been a German people, but this people has lived in a united national state for less than eighty years. Today's divided Germany rings with the echoes of this past.

The Forming of the German People: Six Centuries of Expansion. German history differs radically from that of other major nations. While the English, French, and Russians each spent most of their histories as subjects of a single centralized state, the Germans spent most of their past as subjects either of a vaguely defined empire or of many princes. The German people was put together in a 250-year period of unification and expansion between roughly 750 and 1000 A.D., which was followed by another four centuries of further expansion. But all these centuries produced no unified German state. At first, German expansion moved southward with the expeditions of the Frankish emperors. This expansion was formalized on Christmas Day, 800 A.D., when the roughneck Frankish leader Charlemagne had himself crowned emperor of the Romans by the pope. In exchange for this political service Charlemagne made his troops available to the Papacy in the triangular war in southern Italy involving the Roman Catholic church, the Greek Byzantine Empire, and Muslim power. The Franks were called in by the Papacy to decide the outcome. A monk of Ravenna, reporting the scene when the Frankish army arrived, called it incredible. The soldiers, he said, were covered with iron from head to foot—a stream of iron flowing into Italy. The stream of iron moved northward and eastward as well as southward. Cities that today are in the middle of Germany were a thousand years ago frontier fortresses against Slavs and pagans. Later, and still more eastward, East Prussia was a province carved out by conquest.

Eventually some of the Slavic and Lithuanian non-German natives of these regions were exterminated; all survivors were subjugated, and most of their descendants were assimilated. Today many of the German family names in Eastern Europe clearly show their Slavic origin. Thus, despite all legends of the purity of the so-called Aryan race, the German people is as racially mixed as any of the peoples forming the great nations of the world.

The expansion came to a stop in 1410, when for the first time a Polish army defeated the German crusaders in the Battle of Tannenberg. Earlier, a foray farther east had been stopped in 1242 by the Russians under Alexander Nevski, to the pleasure of a later generation of Soviet motion picture makers. (Both these battles were omitted or played down in German textbooks. German children, too, were taught that their nation hardly ever lost a war.) But a large part of the country south of the Baltic Sea remained German.

The First German Empire. The first German empire, which began in 800 A.D. with the crowning of Charlemagne, was styled the *Holy Roman Empire of the German Nation.* Much of German history records how authority tried to forge one country, but reality created several. For its first forty-two years, the Holy Roman Empire, however, was not an entirely German state. It included both French-speaking and German-speaking people. Just as every German schoolchild is taught that Charlemagne was a German, every French child is taught that, of course, he was a Frenchman. According to the Dutch, both are mistaken, since obviously he was Dutch. In fact, these nationalities were not yet sharply distinguished in Charlemagne's day. In 832, some years after his death, the Synod of Tours ordered priests in the empire to preach in the "popular language." But what was considered to be the popular language was strikingly different in different regions.

In 842 the grandsons of Charlemagne divided his empire. Their armies met at Strasbourg and in preference to a war swore loyalty, each to its respective new ruler. One army swore in French loyalty to the king of the West Frankish Empire, which then became France; another army swore in German to the East Frankish ruler for the part of the empire that eventually became Germany.

Though Charlemagne had failed to bring about any lasting unity between France and Germany, he did more perhaps than even his successors in unifying Germany. His main methods were authority and force. In thirty years of warfare Charlemagne subjugated the *Saxons,* tamed them, and Christianized the survivors with a sword. Many of the surviving Saxons were assimilated forcibly. A number of places in South Germany contain the word "Saxon" in their name. These at one time were settlements of deported and transplanted Saxon populations who had been put into the Frankish countryside for faster fusion with the *Franks.*

This drive prevented the rise of two nationalities, Saxon and Frankish. Instead they became one people. Early in the tenth century Henry I was the first ruler from a Saxon dynasty to become emperor of Germany. First he was king and then proceeded to have himself crowned emperor, wearing Frankish dress and ordering his Saxon noblemen to take Frankish wives.

By the end of the tenth century the Saxon emperors Otto I, II, and III had successively led their armies again and again into Italy and built up the first powerful and splendid empire, based on a combination of German military manpower and Italian money and resources. The Holy Roman Empire was rarely holy and only intermittently Roman, but it was an empire much of the time. From 1000 to 1268 it legally and symbolically claimed power and suzerainty over all of Christendom. Its emperor was the leading symbol of secular authority in the Western world. Emotionally and intellectually it was supposed to be a world government: the vision of an empire of the world in Dante's famous book on universal monarchy was its intellectual swansong. But, many Germans remembered it in later ages as a German empire, and they derived from this memory an image of German world leadership and a claim to its renewal.

In actual fact the empire, splendid as its symbols were, was a political and organizational self-deception. It had no orderly administration. It had no means of collecting taxes and no permanent body of officials. It drew its administrators, its scant supply of literate personnel, its financial revenues, and over one-half of its military manpower from the church. More than half of the knights who rode with the emperors on the Italian expeditions held church lands and were subjects of the bishops or archbishops of the church. Since most of their money and administrative personnel came from the church, German emperors felt that controlling the church in Italy was vital. Forty times in three hundred years, German armies rode into Italy to enforce the German emperor's control over the Papacy, for to lose control of the pope meant to lose within a few years control of the German bishops. And to lose control of the bishops meant to lose money, administration, and effective power over the empire.

The Revolution of the Pope. Some thoughtful historians have argued that the popes were the first revolutionaries of Western history. According to this view, the first European revolution took place in the mind of a single man—Pope Gregory VII. In the year 1075, Gregory VII in a memo to himself, called *Dictatus Papae,* wrote that the pope and the church must never be subject to the emperor, but that the emperor ought to be subject to the pope. This stupendously bold document was the outcome of a hundred years of ferment in the church, but thenceforth the Papacy did everything it could to make the church free from secular domination. The hymn *Veni Creator Spiritus* (Come, Creative Spirit) became to the church what *La Marseillaise* became to the French Revolution eight hundred years later.

The Papacy made an alliance with the Italian cities. The city-states agreed to furnish the Papacy with militias, and in 1176 these militias defeated the imperial army at Legnano. For the first time a noble army of armor-clad aristocrats had been beaten in pitched battle by troops of European cities. Emperor Frederick Barbarossa barely escaped with his life, and German power in Italy never fully recovered.

The wars went on. The German princes north of the Alps became more and more unwilling to supply manpower and money for an increasingly hopeless effort to subjugate Italy by German force. The church called in Norman knights, and Normans from France and southern Italy under the house of Anjou became formidable allies of the pope. The last Hohenstaufen prince to try to rule Italy and to regain the imperial title, Duke Conradin of Swabia, was defeated, captured, and in 1268 beheaded in the public square at Naples with the obvious approval of the church. This church-inspired revolution of the thirteenth century was the first revolution to behead a monarch.

A GERMANY OF MANY STATES

Germany remained without a ruler until 1273 and theN lived for three hundred years as a shadow empire with no emperor in effective control. For the empire it was a period of profitable anarchy, but within the smaller regions there was a good deal of order. The real units of government were a number of territorial principalities and of sovereign city-states. Perhaps one-tenth of the German people lived in well-governed and increasingly prosperous city-states. Outside the city-states the countryside remained under the rule of nobles, and the labor of the peasants made German land increasingly cultivated and fertile. Organizations of cities, such as the Hanseatic League, carried German merchants all over eastern Europe and gave them special privileges in Venice and London. Not until the sixteenth century were German merchants in London reduced to the level of English merchants in the eyes of English law.

A substantial part of Germany was under clerical domination. What is today the Rhineland was largely under the rule of the archbishops of Cologne, Trier, and Mainz; they had the effective equivalents of church-states, which they administered in their capacity as secular rulers. Medieval Germany would have been a nightmare for an adherent of a centralized modern state, but it worked for two and one-half centuries, economically as well as culturally.

The Reformation and the Religious Split. The prosperity of Germany created a middle class and increasingly self-conscious and self-confident princes who grew ever more critical of the ceaseless demands of the Roman church for more money. In the meantime Italy likewise lived under prosperous anarchy. The Italian city-states flourished, fought, and produced some of the world's outstanding treasures of art. The Papacy eventually fell into the hands of a line of fabulous bankers and art collectors, the Medici, who made up in refinements and expensiveness of taste what they might have lacked in simple piety.

The German princes also acquired the expensive tastes of Renaissance rulers, together with growing needs for money to pay for bureaucrats and mercenaries. The princes wanted to keep the silver from the German mines in their own country and spend it for their own purposes. At the same time, sincere young German monks felt disturbed by the contrast between the abnegation demanded of them and the self-indulgence they saw in Rome. They were less critical of their own princes.

Martin Luther was perhaps the outstanding example of the profoundly conscience-driven revolutionist who relied on the German princes for protection. Very soon the princes discovered that Luther's doctrines could be highly profitable for rulers who wished to keep more money and power in their own hands, while finding good, respectable theological reasons for taking over the properties of the church.

Luther's doctrines on ecclesiastical purity—the desire that the church should not be rich and arrogant, the importance of practicing Christian virtues, the value of translating the Bible so that the people themselves could read what it said, and the establishment of services in the popular language—appealed not only to the urban middle classes, but also to the peasants. And when the peasants rose, their demands became a mixture of social revolution, populism, and fundamentalism. One of the peasant songs said, "Naught shall prevail but Holy Writ!" In sum, there was to be no canon law, no ecclesiastic rules; scripture was to be directly read and literally interpreted, and this would be sufficient to run everybody's lives. This is a view that still survives in some rural communities in the Bible Belt of the United States, stretching from Georgia to Kansas.

Authority Defeats the Peasants. In Germany at that time this kind of fundamentalism meant war against the monasteries and the church. It meant plunder and violence and, in response, the ferocious repression of the peasants by the nobles. The actions of the nobles had the blessings not only of the Catholic church, but of Martin Luther, too. It was Luther who wrote in 1525 in a pamphlet addressed to the nobles and entitled *Against the Robbing and Murdering Hordes of Peasants,* "Dear Beloved Gentlemen: There is no time in which one could deserve better of heaven by killing, hanging, burning, and piercing people through than now." He urged the nobles to do this to the peasants and restore order.

It was done to the peasants with devastating thoroughness. The victory of authoritarianism over the Saxons in Charlemagne's day was now paralleled by a second victory of authoritarianism over the peasants in Luther's day. Germany began to stagnate—politically, culturally, and economically—after the victory of the nobles and princes over its peasants; and soon the princes began to win victories over the self-governing powers of many of Germany's cities.

Germany became a plurality of authoritarian princely states. The princes who ruled the seven largest had the right to elect the emperor, and they became one of the world's smallest, though most corrupt, electorates. Records show how the imperial crown of Germany was bought for cash in 1530. Charles V of Spain used the gold streaming in from the plunder of the New World and from the massacres of the natives of Mexico and Peru to bribe the German electors at the imperial diet into electing him emperor, but he had to borrow additional sums to make up the full price demanded by the electors.

Religious War, Devastation, and a Legacy of Fear. The *Reformation* led to wars between Catholic and Protestant princes, spurred on by zealous theologians on both sides. Germany suffered. It ceased to be the source for the exercise of power over foreign countries and became a theater for power exercised from abroad. Spanish money and later Spanish armies strengthened the Counter Reformation and the Catholic princes in their war against the Protestants. In 1555 a compromise was reached in the *Religious Peace of Augsburg,* establishing the doctrine of *cuius regio eius religio* (whoever rules the land has the right to determine the religion). It was freedom for the prince, but not for his subjects. They had to accept his religion or, with luck, get out. Ever since, some German regions have remained Protestant and others Catholic; and German politics often has reflected this diversity.

The Peace of Augsburg lasted about half a century. There were disagreements within both camps whether this uneasy peace ought to last. One of the lesser-known chapters of European history is the struggle between the doves and hawks among Protestants and Catholics alike, which ended in the defeat of the peace factions on both sides. Soon after this, the victory of the hard-liners on both sides led to an increase in political warfare throughout Europe.

The worst explosion occurred in Germany in the *Thirty Years' War*. Foreign armies entered in the name of religion and stayed to fight for power. German princes on both sides abetted them. The war was fought without mercy. In its course, two-fifths of the German people perished. Germany, which had entered the war with 20 million inhabitants, left it with 12 million.

The trauma of Germany was lasting, leaving in its political culture a legacy of fear and distrust of foreigners. Foreign armies had made Germany the expendable battlefield for the conflicts of European power politics. But the Germans' fear and distrust of others was combined with a fear and distrust of themselves. At least half or more of the soldiers who had plundered and devastated Germany were Germans recruited in the name of the pure gospel of Protestantism or for the sake of the one and exclusive church. Either way they had been paid intermittently by their mercenary captains and had received permission to plunder and torture the population. The Thirty Years' War, thus, was as much an act of self-destruction as an act of destruction by other stronger, better-organized, and more ruthless neighboring states.

A more subtle damage preceded the war and continued after it. For a hundred years following the discovery of America, the world's trade routes had been shifting from the Mediterranean to the Atlantic seaboard. Italy and Germany—to a large extent the centers of the medieval world—were becoming the backwaters of the emerging modern age. German cities had stopped growing by the middle of the sixteenth century, and Germany was stagnating much as a river valley whose water supply is drying up. The Germans had no clear awareness of what was happening to them. They only had a vague feeling that unidentified, secret, alien forces were doing harm to them, and the fear of such anonymous threats to the German people became another theme in their political culture.

Two German Remedies: Discipline and Work. After 1648, when the military and the economic misfortunes had reached their peak, the surviving Germans worked their way back to security under the rule of various absolute princes. They saved themselves through discipline and diligence. Authoritarianism scored a third victory. The most typical political entity to emerge in this period was the principality of Brandenburg, "the sandbox of the empire," as it was called, having poor soil and few natural resources, but an incredible ability for organization, discipline, and hard work. Later it was said of Brandenburg that it had starved itself into greatness.

The key legal change was the introduction of compulsory personal service. The peasants not only owed services to the nobles on their fields in spring, summer, and fall, but from the seventeenth century onward they also had to work indoors under supervision, spinning, weaving, and producing useful commodities. Work became a German form of emotional therapy and eventually the basis of restored prosperity. Tireless work habits, thoroughness, and order became characteristics of the German people.

The Miracle of German Culture. Authoritarianism did not affect all aspects of German life. Despite devastation and oppression, there arose in the second half of the seventeenth century a great culture with a deeply humanist tradition in science, poetry, and music. Hermann Hesse in his book *The Glass Bead Game* suggests that perhaps the rise of German music was one effort toward psychological and cultural healing; music put the souls of a people together again after their lives had been shattered.

The eighteenth century brought a continuation of both German traits, authoritarianism and humanism. There was absolutism under efficient cynical rulers like Frederick the Great, who wrote, "I take what I want. There will always be plenty of professors to justify what I do," and who on another occasion asserted that "prostitutes and professors can always be procured." What Frederick did not take into account was that

Germany might yet produce other scholars who would do more to put the skids under monarchies than those whom he had procured to justify his exploits. The same German university culture that produced Leibniz and Goethe eventually produced Marx, Freud, and Einstein, the three men who destroyed the pillars of so many of the world's former beliefs.

Whereas German politics remained absolutist and authoritarian, German culture became increasingly liberal and humanist. The work and outlook of Lessing, Kant, Mozart, Beethoven, and Goethe shows that every one of these thinkers was a liberal. Each believed in the free development of the personality of every individual, and each thought that government ought to serve this end. Lessing and Mozart were freemasons, and Kant and Beethoven were both self-confessed Jacobins—friends and admirers of the French Revolution—in their political sympathies and in their writings. Kant said, "I admire Rousseau. He straightened me out." But the silent majority of the German people remained obedient to their princes.

LIBERTY OR UNION: GERMANY'S LONG DILEMMA

In France and Britain the main struggles for popular liberties occurred within nation-states that were already unified. Likewise, "Liberty and Union—one and inseparable!" is an old slogan in American history. Germany's many states, by contrast, offered neither liberty nor union. For the German people the choice of which goal to seek first, liberty or union, was always difficult and sometimes tragic.

A Revolutionary Era. The issue was first posed by the example of the French Revolution, which found Germany politically and economically unprepared. Napoleon's armies overran Germany easily; the vaunted Prussian armies collapsed, proving hopelessly obsolete before the French onslaught. Soon the French occupied Berlin. But under the noses of the occupying government German nationalism grew faster, and the German economy changed. In Prussia the civil service was reformed, the cities got partial self-government, and the University of Berlin was founded. In 1813 a wave a nationalism swept through Germany, inspiring the Germans to play a major role in destroying the Napoleonic armies in the military actions between 1813 and 1815.

There followed an age of utter tiredness with war and revolution. There were now over thirty German states, heirs of several hundred still smaller ones that they had swallowed. The average German man preferred to withdraw into his family and to delight in the solid comfort of his furniture. The drowsy man in stocking cap and nightshirt became the German cartoonists' symbol for the mood of their fellow citizens. It was an age of princes restored to nearly absolute rule over obedient middle-class burghers who held that to be quiet was every citizen's first duty.

Romanticism and an Unsuccessful Revolution. After 1830 the popular mood began to change. A combination of liberalism, nationalism, and *romanticism* came to the fore. The uprising of the Greeks against the sultan of Turkey attracted some German volunteers. Hand in hand with a growing interest in nationalism came an increase in romanticism. The first generation of romantics already had created the new images and concerns of romanticism: the love of the night and of the feelings for emotion, the thirst for intellectual powers, and the longing to transcend limits. Now the movement grew and broadened. Those contemporaries who thought romanticism was a movement of mere irrationality grossly underestimated its intellectual performance. Great philosophers like Hegel and Schopenhauer also belonged to that trend; as its last offshoot, so did Nietzsche with his vision of man and superman. The social critics coming out of the romantic decades—Engels, Marx, and others—were to prove intellectually and politically formidable. Most of the romantics, however, favored German union ahead of liberty or social change. Even the romantic movement was less individualistic in Germany than in France, Britain, or America. Family structure, too, may have played a role in the long history of German submissiveness to authority. In many countries families were large and extended. They included aunts and uncles and cousins, and they habituated the younger people to the authority of their elders and of the larger group. In the United States, Britain, France, the Netherlands, and Scandinavia, however, individualism and romantic love set many young people free from this authority. Mobility and travel to distant places tended to have the same effect. When industrialization and mass politics came to prevail in these countries, individualism and a spirit of criticism and pluralism were already well established in the thoughts and feelings of many individuals and showed up to some extent in all social classes. But in Germany—and even more so in Russia, China, and Japan—individualism spread only at a later date, over many more years, and among more limited sectors of the population. When industry and mass politics came to these countries, the great majority of their peoples still was used to submitting to the will of some collective and to the authority of its leaders, although by this time they might accept the new authority of a monarch, leader, party, or central committee instead of the old authority of family and elders. In Japan, China, and Russia this authoritarian and collectivist psychological heritage was perhaps still stronger, but among many Germans until 1945 it was strong enough to mark their political behavior.

The revolution that broke out in Germany in 1848 was the century's high point in the struggle for liberty, but it was another failure. Some cities rose, but they were small; some students, small craftsmen, and workers from the few factories of the time manned the barricades. But many of the handicraftsmen in the cities were not interested in revolution. Germany was still overwhelmingly agrarian and the lot of the peasants had been considerably improved since the days of Luther and the Thirty Years' War. When in 1848 most remnants of feudal oppression were abolished by timely reforms, most of the peasants remained conservative. Their sons in soldiers' uniforms helped suppress the 1848 revolution. In the cities the new factory owners had gotten into deep conflicts with their few factory workers and felt that revolution would make factory labor unmanageable.[1] Throughout Germany the revolution was beaten easily, and the middle class turned again to authoritarian leadership, partly to keep the working class in order and partly to maintain a strong army against foreign rivals.

Middle-class Germans sought, first, stability, and they were willing to submit to authority to get it. Second, they wanted wealth and power, and they sought union as the path to these. Only last they wanted liberty—and they sacrificed it readily whenever stability or union seemed at stake.

Throughout the nineteenth century the German middle class felt that it needed strong military protection against foreign rivals, but it never trusted its own competence to perform the great military operations. It believed that a first-class military power required aristocratic officers and generals. This is one of the sharp differences between German political culture, on the one hand, and French, British, or American, on the other.

Union from Above. In the 1850s and 1860s, Germany was transformed economically through the

[1]One should remember that European industry was built up in the first half of the nineteenth century by denying industrial workers the right to vote and by putting all the economic sacrifices on their first and second generations. This is quite different from modern economic development, where in most developing countries industrial labor cannot be treated in the way British, French, and German labor was treated between 1820 and 1848.

establishment of a railroad network and rapid acceleration of industrial growth. By the end of the 1860s, Germany was producing more steel and coal than France.

When Germany finally was unified in 1870-71, it resulted in the fourth major victory of authoritarianism in Germany history. Things greatly longed for by generations of Germans—unification of their country, equality before the law, and more rights for the middle classes and even for the common people—came as a gift of authority. Prussia, the most authoritarian state, and Bismarck, its Iron Chancellor and the faithful servant of its monarch, brought it about. Bismarck's ruthless moves of power politics and brilliant manipulation of alliances were all undertaken without major parliamentary or popular participation in making decisions. Most Germans gratefully accepted the results. Throughout the next four decades stability and power seemed assured. Thereafter, Germany was to become the most bellicose and unstable power in western Europe.

SEVENTY-FOUR YEARS OF UNITY

Germany was united from 1871 to 1945. During this short time—less than three generations—the country went through three forms of government and two world wars.

The Failure of Steering and the Slide into World War I. The almost unlimited capacity of the Germans to trust their government made it easy for them to go wholeheartedly into World War I. In 1914, however, other people trusted their own governments no less uncritically, and this made the coming of war more certain. Other governments on both sides shared responsibility for the war, but the German failures of realistic political decision and self-control were among the worst of the great powers.

The German people loyally supported a government and a political system that in the end proved incapable of self-steering. The German government failed to understand the danger of the world war to which its own decisions were leading. It grossly underrated the numbers, strength, and determination of the foreign enemies it was acquiring; and it failed to see the character of the war into which it was blundering and the consequences that this war would produce.

Blind leadership found blind obedience. After the German government had decided to go to war against France, it announced on August 3, 1914, that French aircraft had dropped bombs on Nuremberg. This announcement, we know now, was a lie. The commander of Nuremberg knew nothing of this alleged attack. The German press, nevertheless, published it, and the German people believed their leaders. They thought themselves attacked, and they produced 3 million poems expressing their patriotic fervor in the first nine months of the war. Never in the history of humanity was so much bad poetry produced by so many people in so short a time.

The sacrifices of the German people were vast. At the village of Langemark in Belgium, it takes a bus forty-five minutes to go past the cemetery that contains the graves of four regiments of student volunteers who were used up by the German military command in 1914 in mass infantry attacks against British machine guns. The using up of manpower continued for four years. In the end, the war was lost, the empire collapsed in revolution, and the emperor escaped to Holland where he lived in retirement—as the richest citizen of Germany. He kept his properties while the German people experimented with their first republic.

Between Revolution and Authority: The Weimar Republic. In November 1918 a revolution ended the war and created a German republic. Later its constitution was drafted by a convention in the small town of Weimar, famed for memories of the poets Goethe and Schiller and safely distant from the country's restless industrial centers. From this birthplace of its constitution it became known as the *Weimar Republic* (1919–33).

Throughout its fourteen-year existence the Weimar Republic could only rarely count on a republican and democratic majority among its people. The republic's main parties were the Social Democrats, who put democracy ahead of socialism and averaged about 20 percent of the vote; the Catholic Center Party, which represented about 13 percent; the liberal Democrats, who averaged nearly 10 percent until 1930 and then dropped to 2 percent; and, on the moderate right, the German People's Party, which averaged about 18 percent until 1928, but dropped to 3 percent by 1930. Together, these moderate parties commanded a majority of the voters until 1928. On the radical left the Communists averaged 11 percent. On the far right the conservative German Nationalists averaged another 11 percent until 1930, and the National Socialists (Nazis) held about 5 percent. From 1920 to 1930 roughly one-fifth of German voters steadily abstained from voting (see Table 14.1).

Most often the republic remained torn between the conservatism and authoritarianism of strong groups on the right and the revolutionary impatience of a minority on the extreme left. This struggle in the end strengthened the right-wing reaction.

But during the first few years left-wing uprisings were most conspicuous. Karl Liebknecht, the first member of the German Reichstag (the lower house of parliament) who had voted in 1914 against war credits (that is, in effect, against allocating money for the war), was one of a small group of radicals who from 1917 on were sympathetic to the Russian Revolution. Another was Rosa Luxemburg, one of the most brilliant women in politics of any time. They were leaders of the Spartacist League, which thought that a quick uprising in Berlin in January 1919 could win Germany for communism without going through the long and tedious process of gaining the consent and support of a majority of the German people.[2]

The uprising was quickly beaten down by troops returned from the front. A new army, the Reichswehr, was recruited largely among nationalist and military circles, and Liebknecht and Luxemburg were murdered by some of its soldiers in January 1919. A series of other radical uprisings followed—in 1919 in Bavaria, in 1920 in the Rhineland, in 1923 in Thuringia, and in 1923 at Hamburg. All were bloodily repressed. The leadership of the small German Communist Party believed that it was unimportant whether an uprising succeeded or not. Coups, combat, and uprisings were expected to have great educational value for the workers, revolutionizing them by their example. A number of left-wing leaders perished in these actions. On the whole, the *Putsch period*—the time of armed coups by small groups from 1919 to 1923—disorganized and split German labor without producing any major successes for the radicals.

Meanwhile, moderate labor and middle-class groups turned for protection to conservatives and nationalists, who became entrenched in the army. Under the new democratic constitution, social reforms were enacted, but soon the German government let the currency decline in value. German industry discovered that one could profit from inflation, and by 1923 the shock of World War I, which had expropriated the holdings of many members of the German middle class, was reinforced by another catastrophe: runaway inflation that wiped out the savings of countless others.

Many voters again turned to authority. In 1925 they chose as president the leading representative of German militarism in World War I, Field Marshal Paul von Hindenburg. This was the fifth victory of authoritarianism. Hindenburg was elected by a minority of voters. By insisting on running on a separate ticket, the Communist candidate, Ernst Thälmann, made it possible for Hindenburg

[2]Although Liebknecht and Luxemburg personally disapproved of the uprising and considered it unwise, they loyally supported the action when the majority of the organization voted for it.

to be elected rather than the moderate candidate, a Catholic politician with the surprising name of (Wilhelm) Marx. Hindenburg became president through Thälmann's insistence on not supporting the more liberal candidate. Later, in 1932, Democrats and Socialists united with conservatives for Hindenburg's re-election as a lesser evil than the election of Adolf Hitler to the presidency. They were soon to regret their success. Hindenburg appointed Hitler chancellor in January 1933. Authoritarianism triumphed a sixth time (see Table 14.2). Hitler promptly became dictator, suppressing all parties but his own. Soon he ordered Thälmann's arrest and subsequent murder. Many of the moderates also were murdered by Hitler's regime. History can be more tragic than the stage.

Government by a Death Cult: The Nazi Period. During the 1920s a small group of right-wing extremists was organized by Hitler under the name of the National Socialist German Workers' Party. Its main ideas were laid down in 1924 in Hitler's book *Mein Kampf.* This book extolled war as the be-all and end-all of politics. War, according to Hitler, was eternal and inevitable. Nations were determined by race, he said, and were destined to struggle perpetually against each other for survival like other species of animals in a world of insufficient food supplies. It was the duty of the German people to fight against all other nations and to turn itself into a *master race,* subjugating or exterminating all rivals, who, in any case, were "inferior" by definition. Jews were to be the first—but not the last—marked for extermination. For the master race the only honorable alternative to victory was death, either in combat or by suicide.

Death and its symbols were made psychologically attractive by the Nazis. Skulls and crossbones formed part of the insignia of Hitler's black-clad Elite Guard; honorable death was glorified in more than half the songs in the Nazi official songbook. Hitler tried to practice what he preached. Facing defeat at the end of World War II, he gave orders for the destruction of Germany. Many Nazi leaders ended their lives by suicide; Hitler ordered an aide to kill him and burn his body.

How could such an insane set of beliefs win the support of the German people? It happened in the four short years between 1929 and 1933 when the explosive legacies of German history and politics reached their peak under the impact of a worldwide depression.

After World War I and the great inflation, the Depression of 1929 was the third of the major catastrophes within a dozen years to hit the German middle class. German political culture once again showed its unfortunate tendency of reaching toward extremes in times of crisis. As before, the more conservative people in Germany moved toward authoritarianism, while the more radical shifted toward extreme radicalism. In the United States the opposite happened: the depression was answered by a series of reform efforts, aimed at preserving not only property rights, but also human rights, and at serving human needs. In England, too, Keynesian economic theory was applied, preserving both welfare spending and private enterprise. In Germany, however, rigid and outdated policies were put ahead of people. Even the Catholic Center Party advocated an extreme response to the depression: cutting public spending, lowering wages, and reducing the power of trade unions.

Hurt by the deepening depression, the masses of the middle class moved far to the right. In particular, the lower middle class flocked to Adolf Hitler's National Socialist German Workers' Party, which until 1930 had been only a minor far right sect. From 1930 on, however, Hitler received massive financial and press support from big business groups. Some feared communism; others wanted "order" and a curb on democratic labor unions; still others expected profits from rearmament or even greater profits from war and the

TABLE 14.1 *Electoral Shares of German Parties and Groupings, 1871–1976 (by approximate percentage of all eligible voters)*

	1871	1912	Jan. 1919	June 1920	May 1924	May 1928	Sept. 1930	Nov. 1932
Citizens entitled to vote (in millions)	7.7	14.4	36.8	36.0	38.4	41.2	43.0	44.4
Valid votes cast (in millions)	3.9	12.2	30.4	28.2	29.3	30.8	35.0	35.5
1. Far Right:								
Nazis					5	2	15	26
Conservatives	12	11	8	13	19	14	10	7
2. Moderate Right:			DVP					
National Liberals (1919–33:DVP)	15	12	4	11	6	6	3	2
Subtotal Right	*27*	*23*	*12*	*24*	*30*	*22*	*28*	*35*
3. Progressives and Democrats (1928: State Party)	8	10	16	7	6	10	9	2
4. Center and Bavarian Peoples Party	10	14	16	14	13	11	12	12
5. Particularists	4	9	1	1	1	1	1	2
Subtotal Center	*22*	*33*	*33*	*22*	*20*	*22*	*22*	*16*
6. Social Democrats	2	29	32	17	15	22	20	16
Independent Social Democrats			6	13	1			
7. Communists				2	10	8	11	13
Subtotal Left	*2*	*29*	*38*	*32*	*26*	*30*	*31*	*29*
8. Nonvoters	49	15	17	22	25	26	19	20
Total	100	100	100	100		100	100	100

[1]The FDP share of valid votes cast was 5.8 percent, well above the 5 percent minimum required by the "threshold clause" of the electoral law.
[2]Includes 2 percent invalid votes.
[3]After 1969 the minimum age for voters had been lowered from 21 to 18 years.
[4]The FDP share of valid votes was 8.4 percent; thus the distance from the 5 percent threshold was enlarged. This was effected by much more use of splitting between the first and the second ballot of each voter, similar to 1961.
[5]Includes 0.7 percent invalid votes.
[6]Includes 0.8 percent invalid votes.

Mar. 1933	Aug. 1949	Sept. 1953	Sept. 1957	Sept. 1961	Sept. 1965	June 1969	Nov. 1972	Oct. 1976
44.7	31.2	33.1	35.4	37.4	38.5	38.7	41.4[3]	42.1
39.3	24.5	28.5	31.1	31.3	32.6	33.0	37.4	37.8
39								
7								
	DP and DRP			NDP	2	4	0.5	0.3
	4	4	4	1				
1								
47	*4*	*4*	*4*	*1*	*2*	*4*	*0.5*	*0.3*
	FDP							
2	9	9	6	11	8	5[1]	7.6[4]	7.1
	CDU/CSU							
12	24	36	43	38	40	39.5	40.5	43.7
0	13	7	5	2	—	8	0.1	
14	*49*	*52*	*54*	*51*	*48*	*44.5*	*48.2*	*50.8*
16	22	25	27	31	33	36.5	41.5	38.3
11	4	2		1			0.3	0.6
27	*26*	*27*	*27*	*32*	*33*	*36.5*	*41.8*	*38.9*
12	24	17	15	16	16	15[2]	9.5[5]	10.1[6]
100		100	100	100	100	100	100.0	100.0

Sources: K. W. Deutsch, "The German Federal Republic," in R. C. Macridis, ed., *Modern Political Systems: Europe,* 4th ed., 1978. Adapted by permission of Prentice-Hall, Inc., Englewood Cliffs, N.J.; German Consulate, Boston, Mass.; for 1972.
Süddeutsche Zeitung, November 21, 1972; for 1976, International Centre for Parliamentary Documentation, *Chronicle of Parliamentary Elections* 11 (July 1, 1976–June 30, 1977).

TABLE 14.2 *Six Authoritarian Victories in German History*

1. Charlemagne subjugates the Saxons, 764–814.
2. Luther and the princes smash the Peasants' War, 1525.
3. Absolute princes rule over Germany's recovery after the Thirty Years' War, 1648–1701.
4. Prussia and Bismarck unite Germany, 1862–71.
5. German voters elect Hindenburg president, 1925.
6. Hindenburg appoints Adolf Hitler chancellor, 1933.

Similar tables of authoritarian victories could be compiled for other nations. For Britain and France, however, they would have to be interspersed with major revolutions and popular reforms. The triumphs of German authoritarianism were more frequent, bigger, and less relieved by democratic triumphs.

conquest of a new empire. The Protestant middle-class parties lost most of their supporters to the Nazis, but nine-tenths of the Catholic Center Party's voters remained faithful. The Center Party, however, decided not to collaborate any longer with liberal or socialist groups and joined forces with the right. This decision led to the voluntary dissolution of the Center Party in 1933 and was followed by a concordat between Hitler and the Vatican—which the Nazis later violated.

On the left, workers remained cool to Hitler. Both the Social Democrats and Communists kept nine-tenths of their voters. They continued to oppose the Nazis, often at the cost of their lives. The main sources of Nazi voting strength came from the middle classes, the rural population and the newly mobilized former nonvoters. Outside the ballot box some of the military, like some business leaders, were useful to the Nazis.

The Nazi empire, according to its leaders, was to last a thousand years. It had a six-year period of arms prosperity and cheap victories over weaker or more timid opponents, followed by World War II. From 1942 to 1945 a series of military defeats brought on the complete collapse of Nazi Germany. Those upper- and middle-class groups that had supported Hitler in the belief of serving either Germany or their own group interests now discovered that the war was destroying Germany, as well as their own lives, their homes, and their children.

By the end of the war almost all major German cities were leveled. Today, guidebooks point out the few exceptions, such as Heidelberg, where most of the houses were left standing. The Nazis' projected thousand-year rule had shrunk to twelve. It left behind hundreds of thousands of tortured and murdered Germans, millions of dead German soldiers, half a million German civilian war dead, 6 million slaughtered Jews; another 60 million lives lost in World War II, and a Germany in ruins.

The Temporary Disappearance of a German State, 1945–49. For a time after the war there was no German government and no German political system. Germany was divided into four zones of occupation, each occupied and governed by the military forces of one of the chief Allied powers—Britain, France, the United States, and the Soviet Union. Berlin, conquered by the Soviet army in 1945 and then located deep in the Soviet zone of occupation, was similarly divided into four sectors, each under one of the four powers, with a joint Allied *Kommandatura* that was to decide common problems in the city by unanimous vote.

For a time, Germans had no share in the governing of their occupied country. Soon, however, the envisaged cooperation among the four Allies quickly dwindled and gave way to the Cold War. Each side, in gradually restoring some political life in the part of Germany it controlled, took care to establish the institutions and parties it found congenial. The Western Allies, who by 1948 had merged their zones, encouraged democratic parties and, particularly under United States influence, encouraged private business enterprise and forbade any major nationalization of industry. In this manner, important long-term decisions about the basic structure of the German economy and political system were made, as a result of the international situation of the late 1940s. By their decisions about currency, industrial property, trade union structure, and the social welfare system, the Western Allies established in the western parts of Germany the foundations for a pluralistic and democratic political system, but also eventually for a significant degree of concentration of private wealth and economic power. The effect of these decisions helped later to make the Federal Republic somewhat more conservative and to keep the Social Democratic Party out of the national government longer than might otherwise have been the case.

The Soviet Union, in its own zone of occupation, did the opposite. It established what in effect soon became the one-party rule of a reconstituted Communist Party, even though the latter had been renamed *Socialist Unity Party of Germany (SED)* and augmented by a merger with a part of the local Social Democrats, brought about under considerable Soviet pressure. Two nonsocialist parties were also permitted a nominal existence, but without any real autonomy or power. This effective one-party system in politics was supplemented in time by Soviet-type institutions in economics, such as nationalizing of all major industrial establishments, central planning, and eventually replacing of individual or family farming by agricultural production cooperatives *(LPGs)*. In politics a Soviet-type dictatorship was established, dependent on the Soviet Union and leaving little or no room for free discussion or dissent.

Another Try: The German Federal Republic. Out of the ruins of World War II and the quarrels of the victorious powers there emerged by 1949 two postwar Germanys: a Communist-ruled *German Democratic Republic (GDR),* encompassing one-quarter of the German population, in the east, and a *German Federal Republic (GFR),* embracing three-quarters of the German people, in the west.

In some respects, the German Federal Republic represented an attempt to restore an element of continuity with the German past and particularly with the Weimar Republic. It repudiated the Hitler regime, but defined itself as the successor to its legal and moral obligations, such as the eventual paying of indemnities to victims of Nazism and their families. At the same time, however, the German Federal Republic is in some ways very different from all the German political systems that preceded it.

In order to understand the changing stakes of politics in that republic, as well as the patterns of participation in its political life, it is perhaps best to reverse our usual sequence of analysis and to take first a look at its new institutions, processes, and machinery of government.

THE PROCESS AND MACHINERY OF POLITICS IN THE GERMAN FEDERAL REPUBLIC

The Federal Republic was created in 1949 out of the British, French, and American zones of occupation with major economic and political assistance from the United States. The main effort for the success of the Federal Republic has come from its own people, who worked hard and kept their heads. In the last thirty years, for the first time, Germans have reacted more often by moving toward the middle than toward the extremes. The far right and far left parties in West Germany are small. In 1976, Communist votes amounted to about 0.7 percent; neo-Nazi National Democratic Party (NDP) votes were about 0.3 percent. Each of these percentages could probably be much increased under the right conditions, such as an economic depression, but the far right is not likely to exceed 15 percent, even under favorable circumstances, and the far left not much more than 5 percent.

A New Party System. The important news came from nearer to the middle of the political spectrum (see Table 14.1, above). To the right of center a new party has arisen, the *Christian Democratic Union (CDU),* with an affiliate in Bavaria, the *Christian Social Union (CSU),* which caters to local sentiment in that state, but otherwise acts most often as part of the CDU. The CDU/CSU is a successor to the Catholic Center Party, but it appeals explicitly also to Protestant voters. From the beginning of the Federal Republic it has been the chief party of the middle class in town and country, and it has received generous financial support from industry. Further, it has been the main political voice of farmers and rural laborers and of people with very high and very low incomes, the latter being mainly pensioners and dependent family members from the countryside. The CDU/CSU also attracts proportionately more votes from those over sixty, from women, and from those Catholics and Protestants who regularly attend church.

The CDU/CSU's share of the electorate has grown steadily, mainly at the expense of smaller middle-class splinter groups and parties. It includes on the one hand most of the former moderate right, leaving only the extreme fringe to the NDP. On its left wing it attracts a significant contingent of votes from Catholic trade unionists and from city dwellers in the industrial Rhine-Ruhr area. Some prominent CDU/CSU leaders, like former Chancellor Georg Kiesinger and former President Heinrich Lübke, once were minor members of the Nazi Party, but the CDU/CSU commitment to constitutional and democratic government has held firm for three decades since 1949.

The only other surviving middle-class party of any importance is the *Free Democratic Party (FDP),* which attracted 7.6 percent of valid votes cast in 1976. Apart from its smaller size, the FDP differs from the CDU/CSU in three respects. On the issues of education and culture it is secular, if not slightly anticlerical. If favors greater separation of church and state, whereas the CDU/CSU defends public support for denominational schools and public collection of taxes for the church. It is more hostile to censorship, whereas the CDU/CSU is more willing to invoke the powers of the state in enforcing the moral views of the church. On most such issues the views of the FDP place it to the left of the CDU/CSU. Second, in foreign affairs and problems of German unification the FDP favors a more conciliatory policy toward the countries of the Soviet bloc, including East Germany. Here, too, the FDP stands to the left of the CDU/CSU. Third, in economic matters the FDP has long been to the right of the CDU/CSU. It has been more favorable to the viewpoint of employers and management, less sympathetic to wage increases and welfare spending, and more often opposed to government intervention in economic life. For this reason, the FDP has received much of its financial support from the same industrial and business interests as the CDU/CSU.

Throughout the Federal Republic the FDP has drawn votes from the free professions, civil servants, employers, and a minority of churchgoing Protestants. The party also used to attract regional support from northern Germany, some of it conservative, and from southern Germany, much of it traditionally liberal.

By the end of the 1960s some of the conservative support for the FDP was disappearing. More conservative supporters of the FDP were switching to the CDU/CSU in reaction to the party's trying to gain ground among younger and more liberal voters. This shift in its electoral base has placed the party somewhat more clearly to the left of the CDU/CSU. At the same time, the introduction of government subsidies for political parties has given the FDP a new source of income and reduced its dependence on business and industry as sources of funds. Together, these changes have made it easier for the FDP to form a coalition with the Social Democrats, and they may continue to influence FDP policies throughout the 1980s.

To the left of center stands the *Social Democratic Party (SPD),* the direct successor of the Social Democratic Party of the old empire and the

Weimar Republic. In contrast to the record during the Weimar era, the SPD now receives practically all the votes of labor and of the left of center, which it no longer has to share with the Communist Party, which has been insignificant since 1949 and outlawed since 1953. Throughout the 1960s and 1970s the SPD moved from its old class appeal to workers and toward a new image as a progressive party for the entire people of the Federal Republic. During this period the party reduced its emphasis on nationalization and public ownership and stressed instead indirect economic policies aimed at combining economic growth, full employment, and comprehensive welfare with the flexibility of a free market. Appealing to the ambition of most Germans to own a car, one SPD poster in the 1960s showed the party's initials on an automobile license plate.

The party's new look has paid off in votes. German white-collar voters who did not identify themselves as proletarians have been quite willing to see themselves as progressives. The 1969 and 1972 elections brought the party a substantial gain in votes, placing it only a short distance behind the CDU/CSU. This opened the way to a coalition with the FDP, which made Gustav Heinemann the first Social Democratic president since 1925 and Willy Brandt the first Social Democratic chancellor since 1930. In the elections of 1972, this coalition substantially increased its majority, and it kept a slightly reduced majority in the 1976 election.

Together, these three parties—SPD, FDP, and CDU/CSU—have formed a new party system, which is in contrast to the many parties of the Weimar era. The two major parties, CDU/CSU and SPD, in 1976 polled more than 91 percent of all votes cast, winning 92 percent of seats in the Bundestag, the directly elected chamber of the national legislature. Many observers have assumed, therefore, that the Federal Republic is on its way to a two-party system and that the days of the FDP are numbered. Despite a decade of such predictions and a low vote in the 1969 elections, the FDP appears alive and well; this was confirmed by the results of some state-level elections in early 1979. The FDP offers a significant alternative for those voters who are dissatisfied with the CDU/CSU but unwilling to give up a distinctive middle-class identity. By voting for the FDP, these voters can support a coalition with the Social Democrats without having to entrust their political fate completely to the latter. Being small, the FDP also can offer quicker-rising public careers to younger persons of political talent, in contrast to the much less hospitable bureaucracy of the two major political parties. So long as these conditions persist, the Federal Republic's "two-and-a-half-party" system may well endure.

A New Type of Federalism. The organization of the Federal Republic is laid down in the *Basic Law.* Passed in 1949, it is a constitution in fact, though not in name. Theoretically, it is to remain valid until "a constitution comes into effect which has been freely decided upon by the German people," that is, after the hoped-for German reunification. Actually, the Basic Law is entering the fourth decade of its validity and is now considered permanent by most West Germans.

The Basic Law created a new variety of federalism. Under its provisions the federal government in Bonn has direct control of only a few matters, chiefly foreign affairs, defense, federal finances, the postal, telegraph, and telephone services, and the railroads. A second group of tasks of government belongs exclusively to the nine *Länder,* which are similar to states in the United States or provinces in Canada. The Länder directly control all matters of education, from grade schools to universities. They, and not Bonn, are responsible for most of the police power and for whatever regulations are required to ensure freedom of the press. Moreover, they own and control the radio and television media (except for one competing network established in the 1960s). The Länder also have most of the administrative machinery of the country. A third group of governmental responsibilities is given to the national government and the Länder concurrently. Here the Länder may legislate, unless federal legislation supersedes their actions. Fourth, the Länder, in addition to their own tasks, carry out all federal laws and regulations, except those few directly executed by the federal government (see Table 14.3).

The Federal Government in Operation. The most powerful office in the federal government is that of the *chancellor*. This individual appoints and dismisses, in effect, all Cabinet members; in these matters, the president is bound to follow the chancellor's proposals. In case of war or emergency the chancellor, not the president, becomes commander in chief of the armed forces. Generally, the chancellor guides public policy. Within the limits of the Basic Law he or she assigns jurisdiction among the ministries. He or she cannot be impeached and can be overthrown only if a legislative majority agrees on a successor.

Konrad Adenauer of the CDU/CSU was the first chancellor. In his long and strong administration from 1949 to 1963 he set many patterns for the office. His CDU/CSU successor, Ludwig Erhard (1963–66) was not as successful, and neither was the CDU/CSU leader Georg Kiesinger, who served as chancellor of a "great coalition" government by the two major parties, CDU/CSU and SPD (1969–72). In 1972 a new and victorious socialist-liberal coalition of SPD and FDP made Willy Brandt chancellor, with high hopes for a new policy toward East Germany in foreign affairs and reforms in domestic politics. The changes in foreign policy took place, but the internal reforms lagged. Inflation and unemployment got slightly—but disquietingly—worse, and the policy toward the GDR was criticized for having brought fewer improvements than expected. At the same time, Chancellor Brandt seemed to be losing control of some of the day-to-day operations of his administration, and one of his aides was arrested—and later convicted—as a spy for the GDR. In the resulting scandal Brandt lost support from a part of his own party, the SPD, and found it necessary to resign. His successor, Helmut Schmidt, also from the SPD, has created once again the image of a strong chancellor in effective control of his party and his administration. He has continued most of Brandt's policies at home and abroad, but has modified Brandt's emotional and socialist appeal by a deliberate stress on pragmatism, efficiency, and the capacity to get things done—an ability that many German voters like. By early 1979, polls showed the popularity of the SPD to be in the 40 percent range, and Schmidt as a chancellor had the approval of over 60 percent of the voters.

The *president* is, primarily, a figurehead. In emergencies, however, certain presidential powers can be important. In some conflicts between chancellor and Bundestag, the president decides whether to call new elections. By that decision, the chancellor can thus be strengthened or forced out of office at the discretion of the president.

Federal legislation is carried out by a two-chamber legislature. One house, the *Bundestag*, is the main source of federal legislation. It is so much more important than the other that we might well speak of a one-and-a-half chamber system, as in Britain and France, where power has shifted to the directly elected chamber of each legislature. Vis-a-vis the executive, however, the Bundestag has less power than the House of Commons, but more than the French National Assembly. Work in the Bundestag is carried on largely in committees, and it is controlled by the parliamentary party caucuses, called *fractions*. Party discipline is tight.

The second chamber, the *Bundesrat*, or Federal Council, consists of delegates from the Länder governments. The delegation from each Land votes as a unit and follows its government's instructions. Thanks to the Bundesrat's share of legislative power, major laws and emergency laws cannot be enacted without state consent. Moreover, several states are set up in a manner that practically assures them a socialist government or else a coalition government with socialist participa-

TABLE 14.3 *Initiation and Execution of Laws*

	INITIATION OF LEGISLATION BY:		
Execution through:	Federation	Länder	Both concurrently
Federation	Foreign affairs, defense, federal finances		
Länder	Most other federal legislation	Education, press, communications, police	Sphere of concurrent legislation

tion. The city-states of Hamburg and Bremen are examples; Hesse is another. Thus there is a built-in balance between Christian Democratic states like Bavaria and the Social Democratic ones. Finally, Bundesrat members are backed by the strong bureaucracies of their Länder, whose members may differ in view from the federal administration. This makes the Bundesrat stronger than it appears on the surface, and it leads to passage of better laws.

In the process of making laws, nearly two-thirds of all bills are initiated by the federal government (see Figure 14.1). Most of the rest are started by the Bundestag. The Bundesrat initiates roughly eight laws in a hundred. A sequence of committee reports, three readings by the Bundestag, and, when needed, joint conference committee proceedings ensures careful scrutiny of each measure.

The West German court system provides for judicial independence, protection for human rights, and some limited judicial review of government actions. In this last respect, German courts have fewer powers than those in the United States, but more than those in Britain and France.

Political Innovation. To govern is to invent, says political theorist Carl J. Friedrich. The German Federal Republic thus far has lived up to this principle. Its political life has been characterized by at least seven political innovations new to Germany, and all of them have continued to work.

The first is the high degree of *federalism* that has given major powers to the states of the Federal Republic, together with the Bundesrat. State execution of federal laws, concurrent jurisdiction of states and the federal government, and the blend of cooperation and competition between the two bureaucracies make the West German system a new contribution to modern government.

Second, there is the *constructive vote of "no confidence."* The West German government is parliamentary in form, similar to the English; and, as in France, it may be overthrown by a vote of "no confidence." However, in a slight variation, as we have seen in Chapter 8, the government can overthrow a prime minister (whom the Germans call chancellor in memory of Bismarck and of the earlier empire of medieval days) only if they can agree on a new one. In other words, a government cannot be overthrown in West Germany by a negative majority. Rightly or wrongly, this requirement has worked and seemingly has given

FIGURE 14.1 *The Passage of Ordinary Bills in the German Federal Republic*

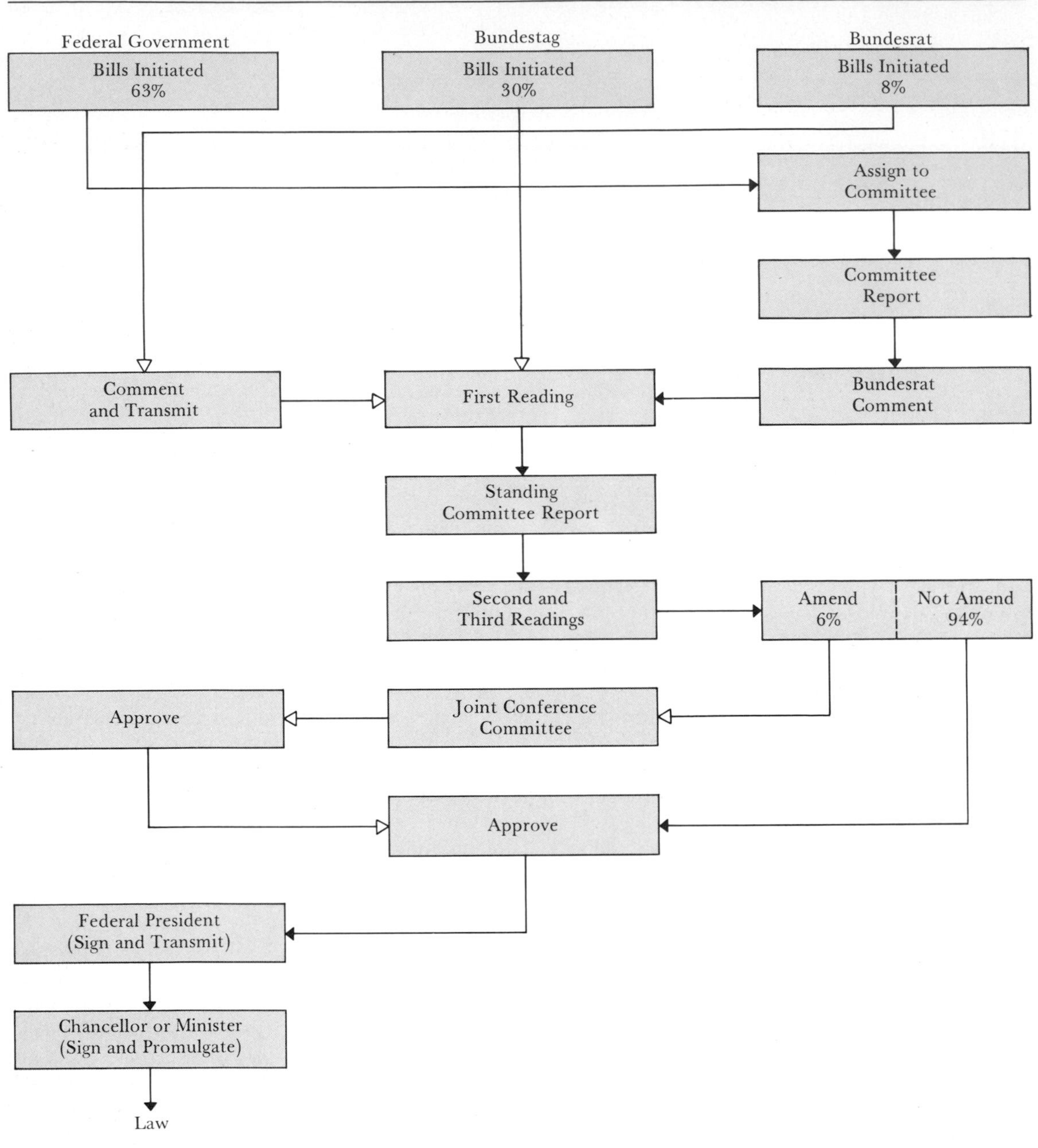

Source: K. W. Deutsch, "The German Federal Republic," in R. C. Macridis, ed., *Modern Political Systems: Europe,* 14th ed. (1978), adapted by permission of Prentice-Hall, Inc., Englewood Cliffs, N.J.; and Heinz Rausch, *Bundestag und Bundesregierung* (Munich: H. C. Beck, 1976).

West Germany more stability than is enjoyed by the political systems of most other large continental countries.

The third innovation is the *threshold clause.* A party that receives less than 5 percent of the total vote in the national election gets no seat in parliament unless it obtains a very strong representation in a particular region.

Fourth, there is a *two-track voting system.* The West German electoral system combines majority voting with proportional representation. One-half of the members of parliament are elected in single-member constituencies that each can carry by being personally known to the voters. The other half is elected by *party slate;* voters cast a ballot for the entire list by brand name, so to speak. Each list is drawn up by the party, often reflecting in effect the views of its national and regional bureaucracy. If the voters trust the party, they cast their ballot for the election of the whole slate of candidates. If not, they may vote for the slate of another party, or they may refuse to vote for any slate and vote only for a single candidate. Every West German voter, therefore, has one ballot for an individual in the district and one for an entire slate of candidates chosen by the party. The result is that some reasonably obstreperous individuals can get elected by having political strength of their own, yet the parties can also maintain cohesion. In fact, parties and party bureaucracies are more powerful than individuals under this system.

Fifth, West Germany is the first country in the world that has systematically provided *public financing of competitive political parties.* This innovation has somewhat loosened the dependence of parties on their financiers. Until the 1960s the same major business organization subsidized the Christian Democrats and the so-called Free Democratic Party. As a result the two parties never voted against each other on important matters. Under the new party finance system the Free Democrats no longer have to echo the more numerous Christian Democrats. They have their own money and have used it to vote independently for the new president of West Germany, Gustav Heinemann, and to choose their coalition partners on the state and federal levels.

The sixth innovation, the civilian defense commissioner *(ombudsman),* involves the military sector, which is itself one of the stakes of German politics and which we shall discuss in detail in the following section.

The seventh innovation is the *indexing* of social security payments, maternity and disability payments, and the like *to the cost of living.* As the index of the cost of living rises, so do these payments, semi-automatically, albeit with a six-month delay.[3] This compensates the persons getting these payments for most of the effects of inflation, and it still has permitted the German Federal Republic to have one of the lowest inflation rates among all the world's market-economy countries. Several other countries adopted this practice later, but the Federal Republic was among the first to do so.

When all is said and done, what difference can all these innovations make? What is there still to be decided by German voters and in German politics? How large and how meaningful are the stakes of the West German political process?

THE STAKES OF GERMAN POLITICS

In few other countries have the stakes of politics changed as often and as rapidly during the last half-century as they have in Germany. In 1930, the stakes included success or failure in combating the depression; in 1933, the choice between democracy and dictatorship; in 1939-43, participation in an attempt at world conquest; in 1944 and early 1945, timely surrender before total destruction; in late

[3]The law requires each time an enabling vote from the Bundestag to let the automatic increase come into effect. Ordinarily, it would take a bold politician to vote "no" on such occasions. One such increase was suspended, however, by vote of the government coalition in the Bundestag in 1978.

1945 and early 1946, a minimum of food, fuel, and shelter for survival.

Some other matters no longer were at stake in German politics. The unity or division of the country, its territory and boundaries, its economic and social order, and its basic political institutions—all these were decided by the victorious Allies. When the German Federal Republic began to function in 1949, all these decisions had been already made. Whatever German politics in 1949 and the early 1950s were to decide would have to be decided within these constraints.

The first problems that faced all political groups in the Federal Republic after 1949 were economic reconstruction and the resettlement of 10 million German refugees and expellees from Eastern Europe. Both tasks were met with remarkable success, thanks to a combination of German diligence and political stability and American aid. The next task was economic growth, and in this respect the Federal Republic, with an annual per capita growth rate of over 6 percent during the 1950s, was one of the leaders of the Western world. During the 1960s the pace slowed, but remained close to a respectable 5 percent, and the per capita income of the Federal Republic overtook that of both France and Britain. Even with its slower growth rate of 2.9 percent in 1970–77, the Federal Republic maintained its lead and increased it slightly compared to Britain.

Throughout the more than thirty years since the stabilization of the mark in 1948, price stability was maintained to a notable degree. Gradual inflation, common to all Western countries, remained tolerable, as the Federal Republic experienced one of the lowest inflation rates in the Western world. Since 1973, civil service salaries and many social benefits for the general population have been tied to the cost of living through indexing for automatic adjustment. The Republic also has had an excellent record in modernizing its technology. Management and unions usually have cooperated in smoothing the introduction of new machines and methods.

The problem of finding new markets for German industry to replace its traditional outlets in Eastern Europe, now under Communist rule, was solved by finding new markets in the United States and particularly in the European Common Market. West German governments steadfastly supported the increasing economic integration of Europe. Although this integration has remained gradual and partial and made relatively little progress in the 1960s, its importance for the Federal Republic's economy has been great.

By the end of the 1960s the Federal Republic had grown so prosperous that Chancellor Brandt's government found it advisable to revalue the national unit of currency, the mark, upward by about 10 percent—a step almost unparalleled in the Western world since 1930. In 1973 the mark was revalued upward by another 10 percent in relation to the devalued United States dollar and the currencies that remained tied to it. Another 2 percent revaluation came in the fall of 1979. From 1970 to early 1979, the mark has risen against the dollar from a value of $0.27 to $0.56. The earlier undervaluation of the mark had aided German exports. Whether the present higher valuation of the German mark would hurt exports is not yet certain.

Reunification or Détente: The Choice of an "Eastern Policy." Other problems have proved far less manageable. German reunification has remained a widely held desire, but as a matter of practical politics it has receded to a more distant future. For over twenty years governments in the Federal Republic's capital of Bonn have refused to recognize the Communist-ruled German Democratic Republic, hoping that it would collapse and that its Soviet backers would withdraw. Nothing of the sort has happened. The westward flight of nearly 200,000 East Germans per year from 1949 to 1961 was reduced to a trickle by the building of a heavily guarded wall between the Communist and Western-ruled sectors of Berlin. Despite its unpopular government the GDR has had an economic growth rate similar to that of the Federal Republic, even though its per capita income and, particularly, its consumer standards have remained below those of its Western neighbor. Nonetheless, by 1970 both Germanys were prosperous and growing. Also by 1970, both the American and West German governments seemed agreed that confrontation tactics had brought the German problem no nearer to solution and seemed willing to try new approaches through negotiations with the Soviet Union and the GDR.

By 1973 the new approaches had borne fruit. The two "German states"—the GFR and GDR—had recognized each other as such, even though the GFR refused to accord the GDR all diplomatic formalities due a foreign power, because, in the GFR view, Germans could not be foreigners to each other. The GDR continued to demand full formal recognition in accordance with international law, but the substance of the quarrel had been settled in large part. A new Berlin Agreement gave the West Berliners somewhat easier access to the GDR, where many had relatives; and it also provided for easier and more elaborately guaranteed land communications between the Federal Republic and West Berlin by road and rail across the territory of the GDR. The latter had received full diplomatic recognition from France, Britain, and many other countries; United States recognition came in 1974; and the two German states applied for membership in the United Nations and were accepted there in 1973. West Germany had formally accepted the Oder-Neisse boundary of Poland, and the Bundestag had ratified the treaty. Chancellor Willy Brandt had received the Nobel Prize for Peace, and his coalition had won a clear-cut victory in the elections of November 1972, which gave it a larger and presumably safer majority in the Bundestag. A long-standing source of German and worldwide insecurity, the eastern frontiers of Germany, seemed to have been settled in a peaceful manner, and the same *Ostpolitik,* or "Eastern policy" was continued by Brandt's successor, Chancellor Helmut Schmidt.

A Continuing Problem: Armament and Arms Control. Clearly, West Germany's political opinion on the eastern territories has shifted, and the approach used by chancellors Brandt and Schmidt thus far has been a success. But we do not know how it will succeed in the future in containing further and heavier rearmament or in other critical areas. The character and size of the German military sector continue to be one of the stakes of German politics. Germany was supposed to be disarmed after World War II, but the Federal Republic was rearmed to a limited degree in the 1950s, in response to American pressure more than any domestic West German demand. In 1977–78 about 3.3 percent of the West German gross national product went into defense spending. (The German Democratic Republic had comparable rearmament, in proportion to its smaller size, under the watchful eyes of the Soviet Union.)

West German armament is limited under the Pacts of Paris of 1955. West Germany is barred from having or procuring nuclear weapons, chemical weapons, or bacterial weapons. Some West German politicians, such as CSU leader Franz Josef Strauss, have demanded that West Germany be given the formal right to possess any kind of weapons against any possible adversary. That is, Strauss has demanded qualitative equality with the Soviet Union and the United States. However, the West Germans have not won this right. Most of the other West German leaders do not demand it, and West German voters have not shown any interest in pushing rearmament. In 1969 the new coalition government of Chancellor Willy Brandt agreed to sign the *Non-Proliferation Treaty,* renouncing nuclear weapons, and the treaty was ratified in 1971.

The West German armies are under civilian supervision, reinforced by the sixth innovation—this one borrowed from Sweden. This innovation consists in a *civilian defense commissioner,* to hear and investigate complaints, an ombudsman, as the Swedes call him. In West Germany the ombudsman is a parliamentary commissioner to whom soldiers can complain directly. There is also an important office of internal leadership within the armed forces that tries to educate the soldiers to think of themselves as citizens in uniform.

Such special institutions may be needed, because the political behavior of the military posed major problems to earlier German governments. Under the Weimar Republic the military was far more nationalistic and militaristic than the majority of the voters. It acted as "a state within the state" and contributed to the overthrow of the constitutional regime. The government and major parties of the Federal Republic were concerned to prevent a repetition of these events. As late as the mid-1950s, one-tenth of West German poll respondents between the ages of fifteen and twenty-five professed open admiration for Hitler. But in another poll only 10 percent of German young men of military age said that they would consider military service as a career. These two groups are likely to overlap. The Germans who are drafted into the army for a short period constitute a cross section of public opinion. But those who volunteer to become the professional noncommissioned and commissioned officers may well be more nationalistic and more militaristic in outlook than the average German. In opinion polls in the middle and late 1960s about 33 percent of respondents agreed that "we ought to have again a single strong national party that really represents the interests of all strata of our people." Also, in elections in the 1960s, small garrison towns showered significantly more votes on the neo-Nazi party than did similar small towns where no troops were stationed. We do not know whether this will be a greater problem in the future or whether civilian democracy in the Federal Republic will somehow digest, absorb, and control it.

The Question of Social Structure. As some industrial societies become richer, questions of social, educational, and economic inequality seem to become more salient to a part of their population. Just this seems to have occurred in the German Federal Republic. Despite its prosperity, inequalities of *income* have remained high, the top 10 percent of income receivers getting over 41 percent of the total income—a higher share than in eleven other countries for which we have data. Inequalities of *wealth* in the GFR, as almost everywhere, are much higher, for the lower-income groups rarely can save enough to accumulate sizable cash savings or to acquire any substantial amount of tangible property or real estate. By 1971, available data showed that less than 4 percent of all households in the GFR owned 32 percent of all net wealth, but as much as 75 percent of all productive wealth.[4]

The government of the GFR has a good deal of leverage to reduce this relative high degree of inequality and to bring it down to the level found in Scandinavia or Britain, if enough of the influential political groups and actors should so desire. In 1977 the total income of the public sector in West Germany accounted for 56 percent of national income, and public sector employment amounted to 10 percent of the work force.[5] Here again, the potential stakes of politics are high.

A final stake of politics may be what is sometimes called the "quality of life." In West Germany this problem has become linked in part with the conflict between generations. These are troubles that the Federal Republic shares with other Western countries, but in its own case have become particularly acute. Impoverished by the war, a generation of Germans concentrated their thoughts and efforts on restoring material prosperity and later on increasing it. Now a generation of young Germans is in revolt against what seems to be an excessive preoccupation with material gain. In their eyes the moral authority of their

[4]See Table 5.1, p. 126, above; and tables and graphs in K. W. Deutsch, "The German Federal Republic," in Macridis, *Modern Political Systems: Europe,* pp. 243–45.

[5]*Germany, June 1978: O.E.C.D. Economic Surveys* (Paris: Organization for Economic Cooperation and Development, 1978); and Statistisches Bundesamt, Wiesbaden, *Statistisches Jahrbuch für Bundesrepublik Deutschland, 1978.* (Stuttgart: Kohlhammer Verlag, 1978).

elders is more suspect than in any other country: what did their parents do during the years of Hitler's crimes? German student protest has been more vehement than elsewhere, and poll results suggest that nearly two-thirds of young Germans between the ages of fifteen and twenty-one sympathize with these protests. Whatever the cause of this unrest, it can hardly have been excessively permissive education. Most German families are still authoritarian and few German parents ever become followers of Dr. Spock.

Rising German discontent—of the young as well as of some of their elders—has extended to the political parties and to the machinery of government. The late 1960s saw the growth of a new political movement, the *Extra-Parliamentary Opposition (APO),* which included many writers and other intellectuals and was highly critical of all three major parties. Before the 1969 and 1972 elections, however, prominent writers like Günter Grass campaigned to swing the votes of the discontented behind the candidates of the SPD, and they succeeded to a large extent. In the 1976 election the practice continued.

From Discontent to Terrorism. In the 1970s acute discontent declined among the many, but became extreme among a few. Small numbers of people, mostly in their twenties and early thirties, found normal professions and politics unpromising or unattractive and resorted to conspiracy and *terrorism.* Their language and ideology were borrowed from the anarchist and Marxist far left, but their actions reminded many people of the right-wing student assassins of the early 1920s who had killed such statesmen of the Weimar Republic as the Catholic leader Matthias Erzberger and the Liberal Walter Rathenau.

This time, terrorism began with attacks on banks and department stores to get money for the terrorist organization. Those who conducted these raids, in the name of a vague "proletarian revolution" did not hesitate to kill real workers—salespeople, bank clerks, and drivers—who got in their way. Some were soon caught and sentenced to long prison terms, but others, remaining at large, then tried to kidnap hostages to force the release of these prisoners. In 1977 they killed a prominent hostage, Hans Martin Schleyer, president of the German Employers Association and a former SS member, when the Schmidt government refused a bargain of this kind. Another victim, banker Jürgen Ponte, was killed in the same year when he resisted his kidnappers, one of whom was his own goddaughter.

The German terrorists had allies in small groups in other countries and also ties with Palestinian terrorist groups. Through the latter they arranged in October 1977 the kidnapping of a large German tourist plane with its crew and passengers: 106 men, women, and children. The lives of these people, they announced, were to be bartered for the freedom of some prominent convicted terrorists, imprisoned in the maximum security prison at Stammheim in Baden-Würtemberg in southern Germany. The plane was flown first to Baghdad, where one pilot was killed for having tried to escape at the airport, and then continued to Mogadishu in Somalia, while the German government negotiated with the terrorists.

But the Schmidt government did not surrender. With Somalia's permission a hand-picked troop of German border guards stormed the plane at night, dazzled the kidnappers with a strong source of light, and killed or wounded all of them before they could harm the hostages. When the surviving crew and all the passengers returned to Germany, millions watched their rousing welcome on television, and Chancellor Schmidt's popularity rose higher than ever. Many people felt that if the German government had given in to the terrorists' demands, the people of the Federal Republic might have been at the beginning of a new journey into fear—a journey toward government by the gun—as taken by an earlier generation of Germans in the 1930s and early 1940s.

But with the triumph at Mogadishu there came a tragedy at Stammheim. It was announced that three well-known terrorists imprisoned there had committed suicide on learning of the final failure of the airplane hijacking. Some underground groups, claiming that the three had been murdered by the West German authorities, threatened revenge through further attacks on West German passenger flights. In fact, no major attacks of this kind occurred. Among young and old, students, workers, and intellectuals, opinion swung decisively against the terrorists, and thus far it has remained overwhelmingly opposed to them. A careful investigation, in which international experts participated, produced overwhelming evidence that the three prisoners had indeed committed suicide, coordinated by radio sets and carried out with weapons smuggled into their cells with the connivance of prison guards who had been intimidated by threats against their families. Also revealed was a remarkable laxity in the actual conduct of the prison, which had contributed to the tragic outcome.

The three dead were buried by their families and friends in a major cemetery near Stuttgart in a public ceremony attended by more than a thousand people and carried on television. The CDU mayor of Stuttgart, Manfred Rommel (son of a World War II general whom Hitler had forced to commit suicide) had given his permission. Over two thousand years earlier the Greek poet Aeschylus, in his play *Antigone,* had told the Athenians that every dead person has the right to a decent burial—even an enemy of the state. At Stuttgart in 1977, although many would have liked to see the public funeral forbidden, Aeschylus's view prevailed.

What had the terrorists imagined they were doing? As they became more expert in plotting ambushes and handling guns and explosives, they became more primitive in their political ideas. Some naive souls saw themselves as "urban guerrillas" whose bold and violent deeds would add courage to the long-seething anger of downtrodden peasants and urban poor, in West Germany just as in the poorest Latin American republic, and would thus spark the long-awaited revolution of the masses. Even in poor countries this theory of the triggering or *excitatory terror* most often has remained a dream. In the prosperous, orderly, and welfare-oriented German Federal Republic it was political madness.

Other terrorists professed a more complex theory. True, they admitted, German workers, peasants, and the general run of the people had no desire for revolution now. But the rulers and leaders, together with the upper and middle classes, could be provoked by terrorism so that they would overreact and install an overtly fascist dictatorship. Such a fascist regime, they reasoned, would soon stumble into some catastrophe and become so unpopular that then a left-wing revolution would follow—on the rebound.

This theory of *provocative terror* was dubious in its morality. It proposed to manipulate millions of people like billiard balls or chess pawns, to use terror and killings to move them this way and that without their own knowledge. It was no less dubious in its realism. The last installation of a right-wing dictatorship in Germany—Hitler's in 1933—had led not to a revolution, but only to vast destruction and suffering. The overwhelming majority of people in the Federal Republic would have nothing to do with all these theories.

Most of the terrorists believed and acted as they did out of despair. They despaired of being effective in democratic politics, of ever making a worthwhile contribution in a regular profession or career, of ever getting a real share in the intellectual, cultural, and political leadership of their country and of their own generation. Despairing of the efficacy of persuasion, they turned to the gun and to any theory that seemed to justify its use.

Each young person who turns to terrorism is a loss to democracy, perhaps most often a loss from despair. Is such despair inevitable, even for a gifted few? Whether the political system of the Federal Republic will manage to draw such persons and such forces of discontent into new programs of constructive change remains a major question for the 1980s. Clearly, this decade will continue to test the republic's capacity for political creativity and innovation in the realm of civic and political participation.

PARTICIPATION IN POLITICS

During most of the national elections in the Weimar Republic, from 1920 through 1932, between one-fifth and one-fourth of the eligible voters did not bother to cast their votes. Only at times of major excitement, in early 1919 and 1933, did voting participation rise to 83 and 88 percent, respectively, most of the increase going to the left in the first year and to the far right in the second. In neither case did the moderate parties of the center benefit much from the newly mobilized voters, and these voters, in turn, soon reverted to apathy after 1919 and to the posture of obedient followers after 1933.

Changes in Voting Behavior. In the Bonn Republic, voting behavior has been very different. Only in the first general elections in August 1949 did 24 percent of the eligible voters stay at home. Already in 1953, however, voting participation had risen to 83 percent, and from then on it increased steadily until its peak, thus far, of 90.5 percent in 1972. The victory of the Brandt-Scheel socialist-liberal coalition in that year was endorsed by the highest voter participation in any free general election in German history, whereas this same election reduced the share of the votes cast for the extremist parties on the far right, such as the NDP, and on the far left, such as the Communists, to insignificance. In the 1976 election, participation remained high at nearly 90 percent; the socialist-liberal coalition was confirmed in office and the share of votes for extremist parties on the right and left was further reduced. (See Table 14.1, above.)

Increases in participation went hand in hand with changes in attitude. Women in Germany for a long time had been far less concerned with politics than men and, when they did vote at all, had voted more often on the conservative side. In the Federal Republic, women's votes thus had been a major asset to the CDU/CSU ticket until the late 1960s. By 1972, however, this attitude had changed: for the first time in that year the SPD received the same proportion of votes among women as it did among the general electorate. In particular, it appeared that the younger women, those under thirty or thirty-five, had departed from the voting habits of their older sisters. In 1976 this trend continued, and the shares of the two major parties in the women's vote remained similarly close.

The lowering of the voting age to eighteen years has worked in the same direction. The young voters have thus far resisted the temptation to withdraw into extremism, perfectionism, or indifference and have cast their votes where they counted, in the choice between the major parties nearer to the political center and, thus, in the decision between the two major trends of policy that the two contending sides—the socialist-liberal coalition and the CDU/CSU—represented.

Other Channels of Political Participation. The changes in voting habits at the federal level have clear implications for the Land and municipal elections, which come at different times in each Land, and they may well enhance the importance of the activities of the political parties and their members, who now have to respond to the newly enhanced political interests and concerns of these new strata of voters.

The SPD has about 1 million party members, roughly 1 for every 16 votes; and their membership dues furnish about 46 percent of the party's income. In the CDU/CSU local party members are less important. There are only 810,000 of them, little more than 1 for every 44 votes; and their dues account for only 25 percent of the CDU/CSU income. This situation is similar to that prevailing in the FDP, whose 80,000 members—about 1 for every 27 voters—pay dues that yield about 15 percent of its income. Correspondingly, nationwide interest groups—such as the trade unions, consumers' cooperatives and municipal enterprises for the SPD, and private financial, industrial, business, and farming interests for the CDU/CSU and FDP—are important sources of support for all parties, but the dependence of these last two parties on interest group support and financing is markedly greater. All parties, however, have become less dependent on interest group support under the new Party Finance Law, which provides them with public subsidies in proportion with their share in the electoral vote (see p. 453).

Some age groups are more likely than others to use the parties as channels of participation. Persons of fifty years or older constitute 47 percent of the membership of the CDU/CSU and 50 percent or more of the members of the SPD. In the latter party, about 24 percent of the members are under the age of thirty-four. Recent and current recruitment efforts of the SPD may modify this picture. Of new party members who entered since 1967, five out of ten are under thirty; and there has been a 30 percent increase in the under-thirty age group during a ten-year period.

In addition, each major party has a youth organization affiliated with it as a source of current support and future membership, talent, and potential leadership. The SPD's Young Socialists (*Jungsozialisten* or, abbreviated, *Jusos*) number almost 300,000. The CDU/CSU's *Junge Union* is somewhat smaller with about 214,000 members; and the youth group of the FDP is smaller still. Neo-Nazi youth groups, more or less clandestine, were estimated in 1979 to have 1,000–2,000 members—enough to desecrate some cemeteries, but not enough to count in politics. All major youth groups tend to outgrow the status of passive echoes of the views of their elders. They attempt to formulate policy proposals more in line with the views of their members; and these policies tend to be more change-oriented and radical and less concerned with considerations of cost, feasibility, and support or opposition from existing interests. The result is recurrent clashes between each youth organization and the leadership of its adult party, which usually tends to win out in such disputes, for each youth organization depends on its party not only for financial support, but also for political influence, career opportunities for active members, and a general link to political reality. Each party, in turn, must make some compromises with its unruly youth organization, if it is not to handicap its own political future.

An increasing role in the political push-and-pull within each party is played by its local organization at the municipal, constituency, and Land levels. It is at the constituency level that many nominations for the Bundestag are decided, even though in the absence of any American-style primaries only about 3 percent of the party members participate directly in the nominating process. Though national party headquarters have the power to put candidates of their choice in safe places on their lists of candidates—from which lists one-half of the Bundestag is elected (see p. 453)—the provision of 248 relatively small constituencies for the other half of all Bundestag mandates has shifted political power to some extent downward from the national party leadership to the constituency level, where younger or more reform-minded party members sometimes may have a better chance to make their views prevail.

Old Interest Groups in the New Party System. Under the political system of the Federal Republic most of the old interest groups have survived. Only the large landowners have lost the power they enjoyed in the days of Bismarck and in the Weimar era. Most of the large estates were in East Germany and were expropriated by the Communists. Those landowners who escaped to the German Federal Republic had to make new lives for themselves in business, the armed forces, or the civil service.

Business interests in the Federal Republic have

proved far more durable. Factories and enterprises were rebuilt after World War II, often with Marshall Plan aid. By the mid-1950s the Federation of German Industries (BDI) and similar organizations were again powers in the politics of the Federal Republic. Farm groups, too, soon became well organized and influential again, but their electoral weight has been gradually reduced by the steady migration from the country into the towns. The civil service continued to function and soon was serving the Federal Republic as routinely as many of its members had served the Hitler regime. Over 160,000 civil servants discharged by the Allies after the fall of the Nazis, most often because of Nazi ties, were back on their jobs by late 1953. Nearly all civil servants and public employees, regardless of their politics, are members of strong professional organizations that press effectively for their salaries, security, and other interests.

German labor is also strongly organized. In the Weimar Republic labor was divided among Catholic, Nationalist, and more or less Social Democratic trade unions; in the Federal Republic, all wage earners' labor groups have merged into the German Confederation of Trade Unions (DGB), which, with 7.2 million members, includes about 34 percent of all wage and salary earners. The DGB is a unitary organization. There are no important unions outside it. It is organized by industries, not crafts, and it makes use of a highly legalized system of industrial relations to a much greater extent than is the case in most other Western industrial countries. The DGB is also the republic's largest organization of white-collar employees and civil servants, exceeding by a moderate margin its competition, the specialized organization of white-collar employees (DAG).

Four major interest groups remain: the military, the mass media, the churches, and the universities. The military is less powerful than under either the empire or even the Weimar Republic. Although the armed forces have nearly 500,000 members, their leaders have thus far stayed out of German politics. The mass media have been more liberal for the most part than the average German. Radio and television are for the most part publicly owned, but control of them is largely decentralized among the states. A powerful and somewhat nationalistic newspaper chain has sprung up under the leadership of Axel Springer, but other newspapers and magazines remain diversified and vigorous. The Protestant and Catholic churches continue to exercise political influence, sometimes through direct pronouncements, but more often through lay organizations responsible to their leadership. The universities have expanded greatly, but are now so poorly organized to look after their interests that their traditional self-government is in danger of being ground down between state control from above and student protest from below.

THE GERMAN PERFORMANCE

Almost an entire generation has passed since the Nazi tyranny and its total collapse and defeat marked the time when German political development had brought itself to the point of self-destruction. After that fateful break in continuity it had been foreign, not German, decisions that set the framework for the start of reconstruction and the emergence of two new German states. As time has passed, each state has repaired the physical damages of the war and outgrown the economic levels of the prewar period. Never in their history have the German people been as prosperous as they are now, and never have they turned in a more impressive peacetime economic performance.

At the same time, they have outgrown much of the emotional and ideological heritage of the Nazi past. Anti-Semitism, militarism, dreams of dictatorship and renewed conquests survive on the fringes of the political system, but they have been decisively weakened at its heart. In 1979 the television movie entitled *Holocaust,* dramatizing the fate of Jewish victims of Nazi mass murder, was watched by 16 to 18 million German viewers. Their overwhelming positive response to its anti-Nazi message confirmed once more how much Germany has changed. It would take a very unusual combination of political and economic circumstances to revive German fascism once more as a formidable danger. The very sensitivity and vigilance of many Germans, as well as of Germany's neighbors, against any revival of Nazi-type ideas or actions make such a revival more unlikely.

These economic and political successes have given rise to new problems, some of them involving unfinished business from the past. The German Democratic Republic now has to try to make a Soviet-type bureaucratic socialism work at an economic and technological level as high as or higher than that of the Soviet Union itself. But the GDR, like the Soviet Union, will have to do this in the face of the continuing difficulties created by the practices of dictatorship and tightly enforced ideological conformity, which do not accord well with the rising education, technological, and intellectual levels of its own population.

In the Federal Republic the institutions of pluralistic democracy have made it easier to manage the problems of a more educated and potentially more politically active population and of higher levels of prosperity. But many structural problems have remained under the prosperous surface. Great concentration of wealth and economic power, a high degree of social and economic inequality, the continuing partial self-closure of some professional groups, such as the West German judiciary, the high ranks of the civil service, and perhaps the military—all will continue to pose potentially serious problems in the 1980s.

The mass recruitment of cheap foreign labor from underdeveloped countries to fill the lowest-paying and least desirable jobs in the West German occupational structure will pose a growing set of problems. Today there are about 2.5 million foreign workers employed in West Germany. They may join unions and vote in elections for factory councils, but they cannot vote on any level of government—local, state, or national. But if one-tenth more of West German labor is legally defined as "foreign" and automatically disfranchised, the remaining German workers may well become a permanent minority in their own country. They may gain somewhat in economic terms from the cheaper labor of their "foreign" colleagues, if the latter remain concentrated in jobs and services that are supplementary rather than competitive to those staffed by German labor. But the German workers, their unions, and their political parties may pay for it with the loss of a part of their electoral and political power base. The problem might be solved by a law similar to the British Nationality Act of 1947, which gave Irish citizens the right to vote in British elections after working only six months in the United Kingdom; but thus far neither the SPD nor any other major party or labor union seems to have given the problem much consideration.

Like other pluralistic democracies, the German Federal Republic offers only relatively poor political opportunities to groups that have little power or are poorly organized, no matter how urgent their needs and concerns may appear to their members. Such groups then must choose between accepting the rules of the game (and perhaps being disregarded or underrepresented for a long time) or else using more unconventional and drastic means, including confrontation tactics, occupations, disruptions, and even force in order to compel attention, raise the self-confidence of their own constituents, and wrest concessions from other interest groups and from the public authorities.

If these tactics succeed, however, they may generate among those who use them the expectation that more pressure will produce more benefits. The leaders of the formerly underrepresented group now may be tempted to overreach themselves and to provoke massive hostile reactions not only from other groups and the government, but also from general public opinion, including many of their own former sympathizers and potential allies.

This has been one of the problems of the minority of radical critics—mainly students and other young people—in the Federal Republic. Their use of attention-getting overstatements sometimes has escalated to the casual or even deliberate employment of untruths and slander against individuals who disagree with them; confrontation tactics have grown into deliberate disruption and the use of force. Such efforts to produce better universities or a better society in the name of some high-sounding ideology, but by means of force and fraud, raise once again the issue of the relationship of means and ends and of the feedback effects from the former on the latter. It is an issue that has arisen more than once in Germany during the last two generations, and the young Germans may have to meet it yet again.

A Problem of Means and Ends: The Decree Concerning Radicals. For a time it seemed as if the second strategy of the terrorists—the provocation strategy (see p. 458, above)—might have at least partial success. Opinion was indeed aroused against them, within the ruling socialist-liberal coalition as well as in the conservative opposition party, the CDU/CSU. From 1974 onward, the latter, following the usual strategy of conservative opposition parties in such situations, accused the government of weakness and clamored for stronger repressive and preventive action. All radicals on the left side of the political spectrum, they argued, ought to be suspected as potential terrorist "sympathizers" who collectively formed a kind of social and cultural background out of which the actual terrorists arose and from which they drew moral and practical support. Critical writers, such as Heinrich Böll, a Catholic and a Nobel Prize winner, were then accused of having prepared the ground for bomb throwers and murderers. By late 1977 this new public mood of intolerance seemed to be reaching ominous proportions.

In the meantime, the federal government, still under the chancellorship of Willy Brandt in 1974, produced the *Decree Concerning Radicals,* as it became known in public discussion, which ordered the investigation of all public officials or applicants for employment as officials if they could be suspected, for any reason, of lacking loyalty to "the fundamental libertarian-democratic order" of the Federal Republic. By 1979 more than 500,000 persons had been subjected to investigation and hearings under this decree. Fewer than 500—or less than 1 in 1,000—were then denied employment as a result of this procedure and, so far as is known, not a single terrorist was. Rather, a primary school teacher and a railroad engineer were denied employment for being overt members of one or another Communist or radical organization. The investigations had labored like a mountain, it might seem, and produced a few mice.

But people are not mice. More than one-half million people had been presumed guilty and made to bear the burden of having to prove their innocence, often at considerable cost in time, money, human relations, and peace of mind. This practice contrasted with the principle of innocent until proved guilty, which is normal in Anglo-American—and ordinarily also in West German—law.

The threat of being denied employment in any job as an official was serious in the Federal Republic, where the public sector of the economy is large and many more job holders are classified as officials *(Beamte)*, than is the case in many other Western countries. In many fields—from grade school teaching to telephone, telegraph, and railroad work—practically no jobs exist outside the public sector. Denial of employment as a public official in such situations was equivalent to effectively prohibiting the rejected candidates from exercising the vocation or profession for which they often had spent years preparing themselves. Even for innocent persons the fear of such an outcome was not to be taken lightly. The West German investigations were more sweeping and, for a time, less controlled by legal safeguards than the security programs for "sensitive" defense-related jobs in the United States, except perhaps at the time of Senator Joseph McCarthy in the early 1950s.

From 1974 to early 1979 the federal political police—the "Service for Protection of the Constitution" *(Verfassungsschutz)*—was routinely asked for any derogatory information, evaluated or unevaluated, in its files about any person under investigation. Police organizations in Germany, as in the United States, keep in their files all kinds of tips, hearsay, rumor, gossip, and accusations made out of spite, although these are not evidence admissible in court. In the West German investigations of the 1970s, however, they were permitted, and it was left to persons under investigation to disprove them if they could.

Moreover, certain details and standards of these investigations sometimes seemed to be made of rubber, stretchable in various directions. Of one registered member of the neo-Nazi NDP party the authorities said that it did not necessarily follow that he agreed with the antidemocratic statements in the platform of his party. Members of far-left parties or organizations rarely, if ever, benefited from such leniency. The federal decree was carried out by the Länder under the German form of federalism (see pp. 449–51, above), and its execution varied widely with the political climate from Land to Land, more temperate under socialist-liberal administrations, as in Bremen or Hessen, and more zealous in conservative states, such as Bavaria.

On the whole, these investigations caught no terrorists, intimated some radicals and dissidents and many more people closer to the middle of the political spectrum, and alienated and radicalized a not inconsiderable minority among the young. Demonstrations resounded in the streets and at universities against the *Berufsverbot,* or the "ban on exercising one's profession," which was the critics' name for what government spokespeople called the *Radikalenerlass,* or the Decree Concerning Radicals. Some critics did not mention that similar bans on public or professional employment for dissenters were common practice in the neighboring Communist-ruled German Democratic Republic. Others did mention it and found it one more reason to consider the practice distasteful.

Ultimately, cooler heads prevailed. Even among the earlier supporters of the decree, many turned away from it as doing more harm than good to democratic government. In early 1979 the federal policy was modified. Routine requests for information from the Service for the Protection of the Constitution were abolished, and the rights of persons under investigation were somewhat strengthened and their appeals to the courts facilitated. Much would still depend on how the new policy would be implemented by the various states, but it seemed clear that the German Federal Republic in 1979 was far from turning into the right-wing dictatorship that some of the terrorists had hoped to bring about.

Another Experiment in Means and Ends. All politics is an experiment in means and ends, but in Germany that experiment often has been more stressful and more tragic than in many other countries. Some of the most serious problems of Western civilization at high levels of industrialization and technology have occurred in Germany. In the 1920s Germany was the most educated country in continental Europe; it had the biggest university system and the greatest intellectual traditions. Yet it fell into the worst and most murderous barbarism under the Nazis. Universities can be, as they have been in Germany, centers of humanity and enlightenment. But they can become centers of brutality and barbarism. As late as 1950 the three most pro-Nazi sections of the West German population were the peasants, the long term veterans of World War II, and the Ph.D.'s. The new generation of West German students is different in its political aims from its parents' generation. Though it often professes left-of-center views, it has sometimes resorted to violent means. One hopes that it can remain different in the methods that it considers acceptable.

Swiss writer Friedrich Dürrenmatt put these

words in the mouth of a survivor of a Nazi concentration camp: "One tells us today one should forget these things, particularly in Germany, and that other countries, too, have had their cruelties and atrocities. I refuse to forget them because I am a human being. As a human being I refuse to distinguish between good peoples and bad peoples and to distinguish between virtuous and wicked nations. But I must distinguish between good persons and bad persons, and I must distinguish between those who inflict pain and those who suffer it. I refuse to make a distinction among any of those who like to torture people. They all have the same eyes."

What Dürrenmatt wrote in Switzerland is now being widely read in Germany. With luck it will be remembered—in Germany and in other countries.

KEY TERMS AND CONCEPTS

Holy Roman Empire of the German Nation
Saxons
Franks
Dictatus Papae
Reformation
Religious Peace of Augsburg
cuius regio eius religio
Thirty Years' War
romanticism
union from above
Weimar Republic
Putsch period
master race
Socialist Unity Party (SED)
German Democratic Republic (GDR)
German Federal Republic (GFR)
Christian Democratic Union/Christian Social Union (CDU/CSU)
Free Democratic Party (FDP)
Social Democratic Party (SPD)
Basic Law
Länder
chancellor
president
Bundestag
fractions
Bundesrat
federalism
constructive vote of "no confidence"
threshold clause
two-track voting system
party slate
public financing of political parties
ombudsman
indexing to the cost of living
Ostpolitik
Non-Proliferation Treaty
Extra-Parliamentary Opposition (APO)
terrorism
excitatory terror
provocative terror
Jungsozialisten
Junge Union
Decree Concerning Radicals

ADDITIONAL READINGS

Böll, H. *Billards at Half-Past Nine.* New York: Avon, 1975. PB

———. *Group Portrait with Lady.* New York: Avon, 1974. PB

Brzezinski, Z. *Alternative to Partition: For a Broader Conception of America's Role in Europe.* New York: McGraw-Hill, 1965. PB

Dahrendorf, R. *Society and Democracy in Germany.* Garden City, N.Y.: Doubleday. 1969. PB

Deutsch, K. W. "The German Federal Republic." In R. C. Macridis, ed., *Modern Political Systems: Europe.* 4th ed. Englewood Cliffs, N.J.: Prentice-Hall, 1978.

Dürrenmatt, F. *The Physicists.* New York: Samuel French, 1963.

———. *The Visit: A Tragicomedy.* New York: Grove, 1962.

Goldman, G. "The German Political System." In S. H. Beer and A. Ulam, eds., *Patterns of Government.* New York: Random House, 1973. PB

Grass, G. *Dog Years.* Greenwich, Conn.: Fawcett World Library, 1969. PB

———. *From the Diary of a Snail.* New York: Harcourt Brace Jovanovich, 1973.

———. *The Tin Drum.* New York: Random House, 1971. PB

Grosser, A. *Germany in Our Time: A Political History of the Postwar Years.* New York: Praeger, 1971. PB

Hesse, H. *Steppenwolf.* New York: Modern Library, 1963. PB

Hitler, A. *Mein Kampf.* Translated by R. Manheim. Boston: Houghton Mifflin, 1943. PB

Montgomery, J. D. *Forced to Be Free.* Chicago: University of Chicago Press, 1957.

Weber, M. *The Protestant Ethic and the Spirit of Capitalism.* New York: Scribner's, 1930. PB

PB = *available in paperback*

XV

Japan

EDWIN O. REISCHAUER

The Japanese see themselves and are often seen by others as a unique people. Certainly, they have had an extremely distinctive history, developing from an isolated tribal society into a leading industrialized nation, outdistanced in economic production only by the world's two larger superpowers, the United States and the Soviet Union. Over time and particularly during the past century and a half, Japan has changed more rapidly and more significantly than most other countries. It stands out today among the major industrialized democracies as the only one with a non-Western cultural background and, therefore, with probably the most distinctive patterns of organization and operation.

During the process of change the Japanese have often developed close parallels to the attitudes, institutions, and procedures of other nations. They consciously imitated the Chinese political system in ancient times, unconsciously paralleled medieval European feudalism in a later period, and then adopted modern Western political models in recent years. But at the same time, certain distinctive Japanese traits have shown a remarkable degree of persistence, giving a special quality to Japanese institutions that were basically like those of other countries. These points of similarity and dissimilarity make of Japanese politics and government a particularly interesting area for comparative study.

THE ARENA OF POLITICS

Most countries have established their identities and borders only over a long time and with difficulty. In the case of Japan, however, geography made this easy, for the Japanese islands form a clearly defined geographic unit. The example of Japan's great neighbor, China, which consolidated itself into a centralized state at an early date, also encouraged Japan to see itself as a united nation. It is no accident that the three existing countries of the world that first emerged in essentially their present geographic shape and with their present people and language were China in the third century B.C. and then its two neighbors, Korea and Japan, in the sixth and seventh centuries A.D.

The basic problem facing the Japanese has been not their own identity or unity, but rather their relationship or lack of it with the rest of the world. During most of their history they have lived in comparative isolation from other lands, experiencing only sporadic periods of intense interaction with foreign peoples. Today, however, their heavy industrialization and their large population of 115 million people, living on a narrow geographic base that is poor in most natural resources, force them to rely for their very existence on a vast interchange of goods with virtually all parts of the world. No other large country is more dependent economically on the outside world or more vulnerable to the vagaries of international trade. In this sense, the Japanese are now the world's most global people, facing multiple and complex problems of international relations for which their traditional isolation has ill prepared them.

The Ethnic Unit. Throughout its history Japan has been characterized by a relatively high degree of *cultural homogeneity*—that is, a high degree of linguistic and cultural similarity among the people throughout the country. As early as the seventh century, the Japanese, who then occupied the western two-thirds of the island chain, seem to have been relatively homogeneous for that period in history. And over the years the culturally distinct and more primitive people of the northern third of the islands were pushed back or absorbed. Their remnants, the Ainu of the northern island of Hokkaido, now number only a few thousand and are on the verge of total absorption. They constitute, thus, more of a cultural curiosity than a political problem.

The Japanese islands are strung out over a long distance and are broken up into many small pockets by rugged mountainous terrain. Throughout most of Japanese history the country was not well unified politically, but was divided into many relatively autonomous feudal domains. It is not surprising, therefore, that dialect differences existed in the Japanese language and the local customs sometimes differed sharply. But the distinction between the Japanese and all their neighbors was much greater. This was true even of the Koreans, who come closest to the Japanese in language and in early culture. From the seventh century on, Japan was always seen as a political and cultural unit, sharply distinguished from its neighbors.

The differences among the Japanese in dialects and customs, moreover, are no more pronounced than those among the Germans, who inhabit a much more consolidated piece of terrain. The contrast of the Japanese with the peoples of the British Isles is marked. Even though the British Isles are much less mountainous than Japan and spread out over only 600 miles (in contrast to 1,200 miles of the main islands of Japan, or 2,000 miles if Okinawa in the south is included), their inhabitants still remain divided into two language groups, four national traditions, and two religions. Although it has almost twice the population of the British Isles, Japan has no comparable divisions of language or national tradition, and the multiple religions of Japan—native Shinto; the many sects of Buddhism, a religion derived from India by way of China and Korea; and, more recently, Christianity—have been the source of political discord only for brief spells in the now distant past.

Up until the seventh century there was a flow of people from the Korean peninsula into Japan, but since then there has been almost no infusion of outside blood. The only significant foreign minority in Japan today consists of about 600,000 Koreans, who are the residue of a large number of forced laborers brought to Japan from its Korean colony during World War II. Though in large part culturally assimilated, they are discriminated against by the Japanese and, in resentment, form a troublesome political minority, quarreling among themselves and with the Japanese government over relations with the two mutually hostile regimes in Korea. Somewhat less than half as many Chinese, largely from Japan's former colony of Taiwan, form a smaller and less contentious minority, whereas other foreigners are so few and usually so physically distinct as to be considered complete outsiders only temporarily residing in Japan.

Another minority group is larger and provides a source of even greater problems than the Koreans, but it is not physically distinct or culturally very different. It consists of the descendants of the semioutcasts of feudal times, once largely known as *eta,* but now normally called *burakumin,* meaning "people of [special] hamlets." The *burakumin* are ethnically indistinguishable from other Japanese and have enjoyed legal equality since 1871, but they remain subject to strong social prejudice and discrimination. Living largely in the western half of Japan, they often constitute an explosive element in local politics there.

The strongly centralized political and educational systems of the past century, the tight network of modern communications, and the spread of the mass media, such as television, have in recent generations made the Japanese very much more homogeneous than they ever were before. Probably no other country of comparable size and population has achieved as high a degree of homogeneity as contemporary Japan.

Relations with the Outside World. Japan's geographic isolation has made problems of foreign relations a secondary concern at most times in the past. One early period of important foreign contacts was the seventh to the ninth centuries, when the government embarked on an ambitious effort to adopt the centralized political institutions and most of the higher culture of China, which at that time was probably the most advanced nation in the world. Between 607 and 838 a series of large formal embassies was dispatched to China, serving as a major vehicle for obtaining the necessary knowledge from the continent.

Then followed several centuries of virtually no contact with the outside world, broken finally in 1274 and 1281 by two massive, though unsuccessful, invasions by the Mongols, who had recently overrun China and most of the known world as far west as the Middle East and Russia. These were the only foreign onslaughts the Japanese were ever to experience before World War II. Japan was saved from the Mongols less by its few doughty warriors than by adverse weather conditions. The *kamikaze,* or "divine wind," a fortuitously timed typhoon, strengthened the Japanese in their belief that their land was unique and divine.

At about this time Japanese warrior-traders began to sail abroad, taking by the sword what they could not obtain by trade. These piratical adventurers gradually extended their sphere from Korea to the coasts of China and then to Southeast Asia. This period of activity abroad culminated in 1592 and 1597 in two great Japanese invasions of Korea. These were the only military expeditions dispatched abroad by the Japanese government between the seventh and the late nineteenth centuries. Thus, Japan had for more than a thousand years a record of almost uninterrupted peace with the outside world—a record that few other peoples can match.

In the meantime, Europeans had reached Japan in the middle of the sixteenth century, bringing with them Christianity and firearms. Both proved popular in Japan, but the government came to view Christianity as involving dangerous foreign loyalties that threatened the stability of the native feudal system, which had only recently been consolidated at the national level. Therefore, it stamped out the new religion, abandoning in the process a lucrative trade with the outside world and plunging Japan into almost complete isolation. A small Chinese merchant community and an outpost of Dutch traders in the western port of Nagasaki were Japan's only important contacts with the outside world between 1638 and 1853.

In isolation Japan enjoyed prolonged peace and a rich cultural flowering. It developed great cities, a complex central government, and an advanced money economy, but it fell technologically behind the West. By the mid-nineteenth century it faced an Occident that was now well into the Industrial Revolution and incomparably stronger than the European powers that the Japanese had driven away in the seventeenth century. From this point on, Japan's foreign relations, which had hitherto been relatively unimportant, became the dominant force in shaping the destiny of the nation.

The superior military and economic technology of the West threatened to reduce the Japanese to the colonial or semicolonial bondage already forced by Europe on most non-Western lands. The few Japanese scholars who had been studying Western science through Dutch books had received little encouragement, but now they realized that they must catch up in technology and win security from the West and political equality with it. This effort necessitated a thorough restructuring of their political and social institutions, but in the end the Japanese proved successful, becoming by the early twentieth century one of the major modern industrial and military powers and standing on a footing of legal equality with the West.

In the process, Japan had fought and won wars with China in 1894–95 and Russia in 1904–5. Through these conflicts it had obtained the beginnings of an empire—like those of the West—in Taiwan, Korea, and South Manchuria. Modern industry had also made Japan dependent on the resources and markets of foreign areas. Starting as a reliance on foreign cotton, wool, and minerals, such as iron ore, this dependence grew in time to include energy resources, such as oil and coal, most mineral resources, and even food.

In the aftermath of World War I the Japanese faced a choice: they could seek economic security through a further expansion of empire or instead they could rely on a peaceful world system of open trade, accepting the dictum of the United States and the European powers that the age of empire—or, rather, the age of acquiring new empires—was now at an end. Initially, the Japanese accepted the second option, but the economic stagnation of the 1920s and the Great Depression that followed convinced some of them that they had been duped by the Western powers, which already had won their empires. The result was a return to imperial expansion in the *Manchurian Incident* of 1931 and the China War of 1937. Rising nationalism, however, had indeed brought an end to the age of overseas empires. Japan bogged down in the quagmire of Chinese nationalism and, in attempting to escape from it, fell into the catastrophe of World War II.

Japan emerged from this war in 1945 as a thoroughly destroyed nation, shorn of empire and controlled by a nominally Allied, but largely American, army of *occupation* under General Douglas MacArthur. Its future, particularly its economic viability, seemed dubious, and it was subjected by the American occupation to a sweeping series of political, social, and economic reforms. However, the Japanese political and social systems were reinvigorated by these reforms and sprang back to life. And the nation, permitted by the Americans to enter freely into world trade again, began a rapid industrial recovery and new growth that soon came to be called an economic miracle. By the late 1960s Japan had become the third largest economic unit in the world, and in the course of the 1970s it became evident that this was one of the most stable and successful of all the modern industrial democracies.

This stable and affluent new Japan, however, remains completely dependent on the outside world. More than 90 percent of the energy that it consumes comes from abroad—most of it in the form of oil from the Persian Gulf. Almost all the natural resources used in industry must be imported, and much of its food comes from the United States, Canada, and Australia. To pay for all these imports, it must export its manufactures to all areas of the globe, particularly to the lands of the West, which are best able to purchase the advanced products of modern industry that Japan turns out in great abundance. Japan thus relies entirely on the maintenance of a huge worldwide trade. Its vital lines of supply extend far beyond any military defense that Japan itself could conceivably provide. Its worldwide trade can be preserved only by world peace and an open world trading system. There could be no sharper contrast than that between contemporary Japan's complete dependence on world trade and the state of isolated self-sufficiency in which its people lived only 150 years ago.

THE DEVELOPMENT OF POLITICAL INSTITUTIONS

The political system of Japan has varied greatly over its millennium and a half of existence, but certain elements and characteristics have persisted to become part of Japan's modern political and social system. It is these features inherited from the past that account for much of Japan's extraordinary success in modern times and the distinctive way in which its society and political system operate in comparison with those of other modern industrial democracies.

The Heritage of Early Japan. The earliest Japanese political system of which we know much was that of the fifth and sixth centuries. It was characterized by a number of hereditary clanlike units, known as *uji;* they had a considerable degree of autonomy under the largely religious authority of a so-called imperial clan, from which the modern Japanese emperors are descended. Controls were loose, but legitimate political authority was seen as deriving from the emperors, who have been accepted as the fountainhead of legitimacy ever since. Usually their role has been more as symbol or puppet than as actual ruler, but they have served as a powerful reminder of the identity and unity of the Japanese nation.

The *uji* system was one of hereditary authority. The role of heredity in the transmission of power, privilege, and wealth remained paramount in all succeeding political systems until comparatively recent times, and even today some vestiges of it remain. The Japanese have also always had a strong sense of *hierarchy,* or rank. Even today, in a basically very egalitarian society, positions are carefully graded by age, length of service, education, and the like. Leadership in almost all fields, however, is now determined not by birth, but by education, success in various types of qualifying examinations, and performance on the job.

It was the *uji* system that the Japanese tried to make over between the seventh and ninth centuries into a centralized bureaucratic state on the Chinese model. Eventually the effort foundered, as the taxable public lands disappeared into privately held, tax-free estates and the central organs of government atrophied for lack of financial support and functions. But a considerable residue lingered on after this period, influencing the rest of Japanese history.

The concept of Japan as a unified state had been greatly strengthened. A capital city, the modern Kyoto, had been created; it remained the recognized national capital until 1868. The position of the emperor as temporal ruler of a centralized state as well as religious leader had been strengthened in theory, if not in practice. The concept of rule by a civil bureaucracy based on educational attainment had become familiar, even though it was not maintained. The Japanese had also imbibed a number of ideas from the Confucian tradition of China: that the state was supreme in society, that good government was an exercise in moral leadership more than a matter of military power, that education was important for the training of superior leaders, and that government service was the highest goal of the superior man.

Though many of the Chinese concepts and institutions seem to have been lost sight of in the feudal age that followed, some of them later re-emerged to help shape the modern Japanese state. So also did a lesson from the early attempt to borrow from China. In the nineteenth century the Japanese were already well aware that many useful things could be learned from abroad and thus were gaining a head start over other non-Western societies, most of which came to this realization only in the twentieth century.

The Feudal Heritage. The Chinese-style centralized bureaucratic state of the seventh to ninth centuries gradually dissolved into a feudal system, which went through a series of phases that historians now see as the only close parallels to Western feudalism anywhere outside Europe. In the first phase, local warrior bands formed in the provinces to protect the private estates, which the weakened central government could no longer defend. Clashes between contending bands of warriors grew until the late twelfth century, when the captain of one such band won effective control over the whole nation, including the imperial court. Taking the title of generalissimo, or *shōgun,* he and his successors ruled Japan with reasonable effectiveness through their hereditary military retainers, or *samurai,* scattered throughout the private estates of the nation as stewards, or managers.

This first feudal regime was overthrown in the fourteenth century and was succeeded by a new feudal system, in which a hereditary line of *shōgun* attempted with less success to control the country through a number of territorial lords, who came to be known as *daimyō.* During the almost incessant warfare of this period, particularly from the late fifteenth century to the end of the sixteenth, political conditions in Japan most closely resembled those of high and late feudalism in Europe.

In the late sixteenth century three successive conquerors succeeded in reuniting Japan and restoring order. The third managed to perpetuate from 1600 to 1867 the rule of his *Tokugawa* family from its castle headquarters in what is now the city of Tokyo. The Tokugawa *shōgun* ruled about a quarter of the land directly, but left the remainder divided into 265 or more semiautonomous feudal domains, each of which had its own *daimyō* lord and his *samurai* retainers.

The heritage of more than seven centuries of feudal rule has had a profound influence on modern Japan. Its strong military traditions made its people clearly aware of Western military superiority in the nineteenth century and encouraged them to build up their own capabilities, until Japan became one of the great powers of modern times. The Spartan self-discipline of the feudal warriors gave to the modern Japanese their superb sense of self-discipline, which has made them capable of prodigious feats in many fields. The strong bonds of loyalty demanded by a feudal system were susceptible to being developed into a fanatical sense of loyalty to the emperor as the symbol of the state or, more generally, to the Japanese nation as a whole.

Five other less predictable results of the feudal experience also proved equally or even more important to modern Japan. First, throughout the feudal age, but particularly in the Tokugawa period, the *shōgun* and *daimyō* were often mere figureheads, like the emperors, and effective leadership was exercised by councils of their retainers. So the Japanese became accustomed to look not to personal or charismatic leaders, but to group leadership. During the Tokugawa period, in fact, they developed a sort of bureaucratic form of rule, even though the make-up of the bureaucracy was basically determined by hereditary class.

Second, the Tokugawa period was a time of complete order and stability. With the establishment of national isolation in 1638, Japan settled into a prolonged period of peace that was not broken until 1863, after its doors had been forced open again by the Western powers. This was a long-lasting experience of peace and stability that no other large nation has known in modern times. The Japanese became accustomed to orderly processes of law and an administration that was not arbitrary, but instead was based on precedent and known regulations. They came to take for granted the existence of law and order. All this undoubtedly helped them to pass through the great wrenching changes of modern times with a minimum of domestic disorder.

Third, the Tokugawa system, though outwardly characterized by feudal division and autonomy, was in actuality quite centrally controlled. One of the chief means of achieving this centralization was the system of *alternate attendance* of the *daimyō* at the *shōgun*'s capital: all *daimyō* had to leave their wives and heirs as hostages at the *shōgun*'s capital, and they personally had to spend alternate years in residence there and in their own domains. The costs of maintaining large residences at the capital and of moving with their great retinues each year, back and forth between the capital and their domains, forced all the *daimyō* to produce cash exports to the rest of Japan to pay for these expenses. This situation made all of Japan into a single great market and greatly developed the economy. The congregation of much of the political leadership at the capital also helped to unify the nation intellectually. A measure of the relative advancement of the economy, as well as of education in Japan, is the estimate that by the middle of the nineteenth century some 45 percent of men and 15 percent of women were literate—figures not far below the more advanced lands of the West at that time.

Complete domestic peace and order, an established and predictable system of rule, and a nationwide unified economy combined to permit the merchant and later the peasant classes to engage in long-range entrepreneurial activities, a fourth outcome of the feudal experience. Such entrepreneurial habits and skills proved extremely valuable to the Japanese when in the nineteenth century they were forced to open up to world trade and had to compete economically with the technologically more advanced lands of the Occident.

Finally, under feudalism the Japanese acquired habits of group identity and skills in group cooperation that have served them well in modern times. Under the Tokugawa the two most important groupings were the feudal domains for the ruling *samurai* class and the autonomous peasant villages for the bulk of the population. Most *samurai* were gathered into the capital towns of their domains, leaving the villagers free to run their own affairs, as long as they maintained order and paid their taxes. Neither the domain nor the autonomous village has survived into the modern era, but the Japanese have transferred the attitudes and skills developed in them to more modern groupings, such as the local community or the work unit of factories and business organizations. This sense of belonging to and working through a group, in contrast to the Western emphasis on the individual as the basic unit, has perhaps helped the Japanese to pass through the great social and political upheavals of modern times and the traumatic transformation from a rural agrarian people to an urban industrial society with less sense of alienation and disorder than most Western peoples.

The Creation of a Modern State. The nineteenth-century Japanese had a sophisticated and advanced civilization, inferior to the West only in technology, and they inherited from the past many attitudes and skills that would prove useful in modern times. Their feudal political and social structure, however, was not sufficiently flexible or centralized to meet the challenge posed by the West. Within a few years of the opening of Japan by an American naval expedition in 1853–54, the Japanese were thrown into a frenzied effort to find effective means to fend off Western economic and military dominance.

Groups of iconoclastic younger *samurai* from some of the greater domains of western Japan, particularly Satsuma and Choshu, banded together around the ancient symbolic figure of the emperor, overthrew the Tokugawa regime in 1868, and installed themselves as a new "imperial" government at the old Tokugawa capital, now renamed Tokyo. This epoch-making revolution is usually called the *Meiji Restoration,* named for the reign period of the new boy emperor, which lasted from 1868 until 1912, and for the theory that imperial rule was being restored.

The new leaders saw that the old feudal disunity of autonomous domains and hereditary classes would have to be replaced by a new political and social unity. By 1871 they had abolished the domains and by 1876 had stripped away all hereditary powers and privileges from the *samurai* class, which constituted 6 or 7 percent of the population. Most of the new leaders, of course, emerged from the *samurai* class, which hitherto had monopolized all leadership, but the bulk of the *samurai,* unable to accommodate themselves to the new conditions, sank into anonymity as mere commoners.

The new leaders saw themselves as returning to the imperial rule of early times, but they did so only in the pretense that the emperor was ruling and in the restoration of old names for some of the new institutions. In actuality, they established a sort of rule by council, much like the system of Tokugawa times, and then in a piecemeal and pragmatic fashion they introduced Western institutions that were seen as helping to produce a strong nation that could withstand the West.

They developed a modern navy and a modern army to replace the Tokugawa class army. For the navy they quite naturally chose the British model; for the army, first the French and then the German models. They created a modern monetary and tax system, and after an experiment with the decentralized American banking system they adopted a centralized banking system based on that of Belgium. For local government they followed the centralized French model with some Prussian overtones. For the judicial system and the civil service they used German models, which they adapted and perfected for their own needs. Modern ministries were created one at a time, and eventually in 1885 the ministers at the top were grouped together into a modern type of cabinet under a prime minister. In reality the new Cabinet was simply the old council of former *samurai* leaders organized together under a new name.

In education the new leaders followed the trends of the time in Europe, but in some ways forged ahead in creating a more uniform system than any Western nation then had. They early decreed elementary education for all children, girls as well as boys, and eventually by 1907 did get all of them into schools. At the intermediate level they created various technical schools, in order to produce men of more advanced skills, and a more strictly academic track leading to the state universities, which were to produce the leadership for the nation. Since all these schools were wide open to talent, the new educational system began rapidly to erase the class lines of feudal times.

The Development of Constitutional Government. The new Japanese leaders, noting that the most advanced nations of the West had constitutions and parliaments, saw elements of modern power in these institutions. They also were aware that within the large former *samurai* class were many persons who were restive at their loss of a share in political leadership and that among the other classes there were rising men who also hungered for a share in power. For these two reasons and because of their own eagerness to end the period of experimentation and to return to an established permanent system, like that of the Tokugawa, they decided to have the emperor grant a constitution that would define an unchanging, new system of government, including a popular national assembly. The final decision on this was made in 1881, and the constitution, usually called in English the *Meiji Constitution,* was promulgated in 1889.

According to the Meiji Constitution, the emperor was not only sovereign, but actually "sacred and inviolable." In theory all power emanated from him, but in reality he could do nothing without the advice and consent of his ministers and the laws passed by the new assembly. The leaders who created the constitution obviously assumed that they themselves would make the decisions for the emperor, as other councils had done for titular leaders in Japan for close to a millennium, but they failed to specify this in the constitution. They probably just took it for granted and may have assumed that their own group, by now known as the *genrō*, or "elder statesmen," would be self-perpetuating. If so, they were quite wrong. They also failed to realize the extent to which the Japan that they had set in rapid motion would inevitably continue to change. They had urgently begun to industrialize Japan in order to protect it from foreign manufactures and to give it the economic foundations needed for military strength. Now the rapid spread of industrialization and universal education were creating a new Japan and a new Japanese people that could not easily be contained within the centralized pattern of rule they had devised.

The *genrō*, after experimenting for a decade with elected assemblies in local governments, created through the constitution a popular national assembly, called the *Diet*. This body was carefully limited in its electorate and powers. It consisted of a House of Peers, modeled on the British House of Lords, and a House of Representatives, elected only by the higher taxpayers. Together the two houses had the power to pass on taxes, budgets, and other legislation. The *genrō* thought of the Diet as a safe way to share a modicum of power with others, to permit a safety valve for the expression of discontent, and to build up the sort of popular support for the government that the countries of Europe seemed to derive through their parliaments.

In practice, however, the Diet proved a great disappointment to the leaders. From the start the House of Representatives proved hostile to the Cabinet, which they correctly saw as being dominated by men from Satsuma and Choshu, the two former feudal domains that had taken the lead in the Meiji Restoration. The leaders also found that they had given away more power to the Diet than they had intended. Their German advisors had assured them that they could keep control of the national purse strings by a provision in the constitution permitting the use of the previous year's budget if the Diet failed to vote a new one. In actuality, the previous year's budget was never enough at this time of rapid economic growth and could suffice for an extra year only with great difficulty. Constrained by fear of the Westerners' contempt if Japan failed in its borrowed Occidental institutions and worried that this in turn would result in the refusal of the West to accept Japan as a legal equal, the leaders did not take the otherwise simple course of revising the constitution that they had themselves drawn up. Instead they resigned themselves to living with it.

As a result, the period between 1889 and the 1920s was one of constant struggle between the Diet and the Cabinet and of rapid parliamentary evolution, comparable to the historic growth of the British Parliament. The Diet, taking advantage of its control over the budget, steadily increased its powers. Parties like those in the West appeared, winning their way into the Cabinet and steadily increasing their membership in it. Finally in 1918 it was decided that the prime ministership itself should be given to the head of the leading parliamentary party, and Japan embarked on more than a decade of largely party Cabinets. The electorate also had been steadily increased, and in 1925 all adult males were given the vote. Meanwhile many of the liberal tendencies then current in the West had begun to spread throughout Japan, too.

The original *genrō* eventually died off, the last in 1924, leaving only one later member to represent, with greatly diminished strength, their old role as the spokesmen for a theoretically all-powerful emperor. This situation revealed another major flaw in the 1889 Constitution. The *genrō* had themselves created the modern Japanese military as well as the civil government, and they originally were in full control of both, but their bureaucratic and parliamentary successors did not have comparable powers over the military, which claimed to be answerable only to the emperor. When a sharp division occurred on foreign policy over the advisability of depending on open world trade or returning to empire building through military conquest, this lack of central control permitted the army to act on its own in the Manchurian Incident in 1931 and the China War in 1937. Such military activism was strongly backed by many young officers who were inspired by concepts derived from Japanese warrior traditions, as well as by ideas derived from European Fascism (see Chapter 4, above). These young zealots did not shrink from assassination to further their policies. Wartime conditions and the early successes in this return to imperial aggrandizement made it possible for the military to infiltrate and gradually win dominance over the civil government, until by 1941, at the outbreak of war with the United States, the Cabinet and civil government were little more than adjuncts to the military.

Both the rapid evolution toward a British type of parliamentary government during the first four decades after 1889 and the sudden shift to military control of the government in the 1930s occurred as perfectly legal and constitutional developments. Both were made possible because of the ambiguity and vagueness of the Meiji Constitution regarding the key point of who in fact was to exercise the vast theoretical powers of the emperor.

Reform and a New Start. The American military occupation of Japan at the end of World War II might have seemed a poor way to sponsor healthy political growth and an almost certain way to inspire a violent nationalistic reaction. Instead, the sweeping reforms carried out by the occupation helped clear the ground for a sturdy flowering of the parliamentary form of government that the Japanese had themselves been developing up through the 1920s, and despite much resentment at the temporary American dominance over the nation, the foreign-led reforms produced no major nationalistic or reactionary response.

The chief reason for this surprising outcome was that both the mass of the Japanese people and the American planners wished to see Japan develop in the same direction. The war had proved that Japan could not find economic security in empire, but must rely on peace and an open trading world. Revolted by the carnage and suffering of war and convinced that only world peace would give them a chance of survival, the Japanese turned abruptly from being the fierce warrior nation of recent years and became instead the world's most ardent and sincere pacifists. Disgusted with the follies and the heavy-handed indoctrination of their military leaders, they wanted no more dictators, but rather a return either to the parliamentary rule of the 1920s or, as the more radical envisioned, some more utopian socialist regime.

The American occupation forces arrived well prepared with plans worked out in Washington during the war. These were designed to help make Japan a more peaceful and democratic land, just as the Japanese themselves wished. The plans wisely called not for the introduction of American forms of democracy, but for the strengthening of the British parliamentary system, with which the Japanese were already familiar. They also advocated supplementary social and economic reforms to create a stronger base for a democratic form of government. The reforms were carried out with great dramatic flair by General MacArthur in his position as *Supreme Commander for the Allied Powers (SCAP)*. MacArthur actually exceeded his instructions when in February 1946 he had his staff draft a new constitution for Japan. After some small emendations and formal acceptance by the Japanese government, this replaced the Meiji Constitution in May 1947.

The new constitution, though, basically following the lines of Washington planning, corresponded to the hopes of most Japanese. It relegated the emperor in theory, as well as in practice, to a purely symbolic role and made the Diet the supreme "organ of state power." The House of Representatives, which remained unchanged, now was given the power to elect the prime minister from among its members, and the House of Peers was supplanted by a purely elected *House of Councilors.* Local governments were given more autonomy, and all their chief officials were made elective. The constitution guaranteed a detailed list of human rights, and the courts were assigned the duty of seeing that laws and government rulings did not infringe on them. Women were given the vote, and family control over adult members of the family was eliminated. Perhaps most surprising of all, Article IX of the constitution renounced forever the right to make war and maintain military forces. The Japanese ever since have enthusiastically called this document the *Peace Constitution.*

In addition to the constitution, many other reforms were carried out. The great financial, trading, and industrial combines, which were known as the *zaibatsu* and had grown up under prewar policies of fostering rapid economic development, were entirely dissolved, though their great component corporations, which had once been slated for breakup, were subsequently allowed to continue in existence. Labor unions were encouraged and soon embraced over 7 million members. All military officers and most higher civil officials were purged from positions of public responsibility. A sweeping land reform was carried out, outlawing absentee ownership of agricultural land, limiting the size of individual holdings (in most cases to a maximum of about ten acres), and transferring through virtual confiscation most of the 45 percent of the land worked by tenant farmers to the hands of these former tenants.

In education, compulsory schooling was extended to nine years, efforts were made to eliminate indoctrination and encourage independent thinking, and the various tracks of education were unified in the American manner into a single track that would make all students eligible for the next higher level. With Japan's subsequent rise to economic affluence, the Japanese may by now have become the world's best-educated people. More than 90 percent of its young people go through the extremely rigorous twelve years of education leading to graduation from senior high school—probably the world's record—and close to 40 percent go on for some higher education, a figure exceeded only in the United States.

The occupation reforms were concentrated largely in the early years. Between 1947 and 1949 the American authorities, distressed by the failure of Japan to recover economically and worried by the growing Cold War with the Soviet Union elsewhere in the world, began to put more emphasis on economic recovery and to slow down reform programs, which had already for the most part been completed. The Japanese have called this change of emphasis the *"reverse course."* Actually, little in the reform program was reversed, except for the abandonment of the plan to break up large corporations, a relaxation of the purge measures, the outlawing of strikes by public employees, the creation of a paramilitary police reserve, and a shift from friendly tolerance of Communists to open harassment.

After the end of the occupation in 1952 the conservative Japanese government then in power continued the "reverse course" somewhat further, despite the vehement opposition of the parties of the left. It dropped the purge measures completely, reconsolidated in part the control of the central government over the police and education, and changed the police reserve into the small, but more clearly military, *Self-Defense Forces (SDF).* At the time of the peace treaty it also entered into the *Mutual Security Treaty* with the United States, which gave Japan protection, but left American bases and troops in the country. All this happened in the 1950s, and thereafter the "reverse course" went no further. Although the conservatives had hoped to amend the constitution by eliminating the no-war clause and restoring theoretical sovereignty to the emperor, they eventually had to give up these plans as politically unfeasible.

Animosities and suspicions derived from the prewar and wartime experience between left and right, however, dominated Japanese politics for two or more decades after the war. The leftists, generally known as the *progressives,* feared that the conservatives wished to turn the clock back to the prewar system of the 1930s. They also felt that the security treaty, far from giving Japan security, might embroil it in war. The conservatives feared that the progressives were aiming at making Japan a communist country. Mutual fear made both sides battle desperately over what would have otherwise seemed to be small and relatively innocuous differences of opinion or organization. Large public demonstrations and confrontations in the halls of government were the order of the day.

In time these fears and animosities began to ease. The postwar economic miracle made the Japanese for the first time in their history a relatively affluent people. The economic pie had grown enormously and was divided more equally than in most other countries. A recent study shows that among the industrialized democracies Japan, next to Sweden and Australia, has the least discrepancy of income between the richest and the poorest members of society. The security treaty with the United States and the existence of American bases and the Japanese Self-Defense Forces have not embroiled Japan in foreign wars or lessened the prevailing pacifist mood. Much of the old style of political confrontation developed in the 1950s lingers on, but the parties of left and right and still more the voters who support them have drawn closer together, and the new concerns—about foreign trade and the domestic clash between economic growth and the quality of life—engender less sharp divisions in politics.

The progressives throughout have strongly supported the reforms of the occupation, while decrying the alliance with the United States. The conservatives throughout have championed a close alliance with the United States, while regretting what they felt had been the excesses of the occupation reforms. Gradually, however, both sides have coalesced in firm support of the existing political system embodied in the 1947 Constitution. Few constitutions in the world have more complete or enthusiastic popular support.

The Japanese today enjoy an extraordinarily stable and fully accepted political system. It is basically defined in the 1947 Constitution and its supporting legislation. They are based largely on the parliamentary evolution that took place in Japan between 1889 and the 1920s, which in turn was an outgrowth of the efforts to modernize the Japanese government between 1868 and the promulgation of the Meiji Constitution. Finally, this modernized Japanese government incorporated some of the political attitudes, habits, and skills that the Japanese had developed over the preceding millennium and a half. Thus, there is a long and significant history lying behind Japan's present political system. This gives us all the more reason to believe that it will remain relatively solid and stable in the future.

THE MACHINERY AND PROCESSES OF GOVERNMENT

The Diet. At the center of Japanese politics is the Diet (see Figure 15.1). Floating vaguely above it is the symbolic figure of the emperor, while the bureaucracy and local government operate partly in subordination to it, partly in tandem with it. But the Diet is supreme—by constitutional definition "the highest organ of state power" and "the sole law-making organ."

The transference of sovereignty in the 1947 Constitution from the emperor to the Japanese people was a shattering blow for some old-fashioned, conservative Japanese. In the Meiji Constitution the emperor had been described not only as the holder of all sovereignty, but as a "sacred and inviolable" figure, deriving his authority from his "lineal succession unbroken for ages eternal." According to the new constitution he is now no more than "the symbol of the State and of the unity of the people." The Japanese as a whole and the imperial family, too, have adjusted to the change with little or no regret. The new definition has simply brought theory into line with what had been in fact age-old practice.

The emperor himself was never a contender for

FIGURE 15.1 *Government Structure of Japan*

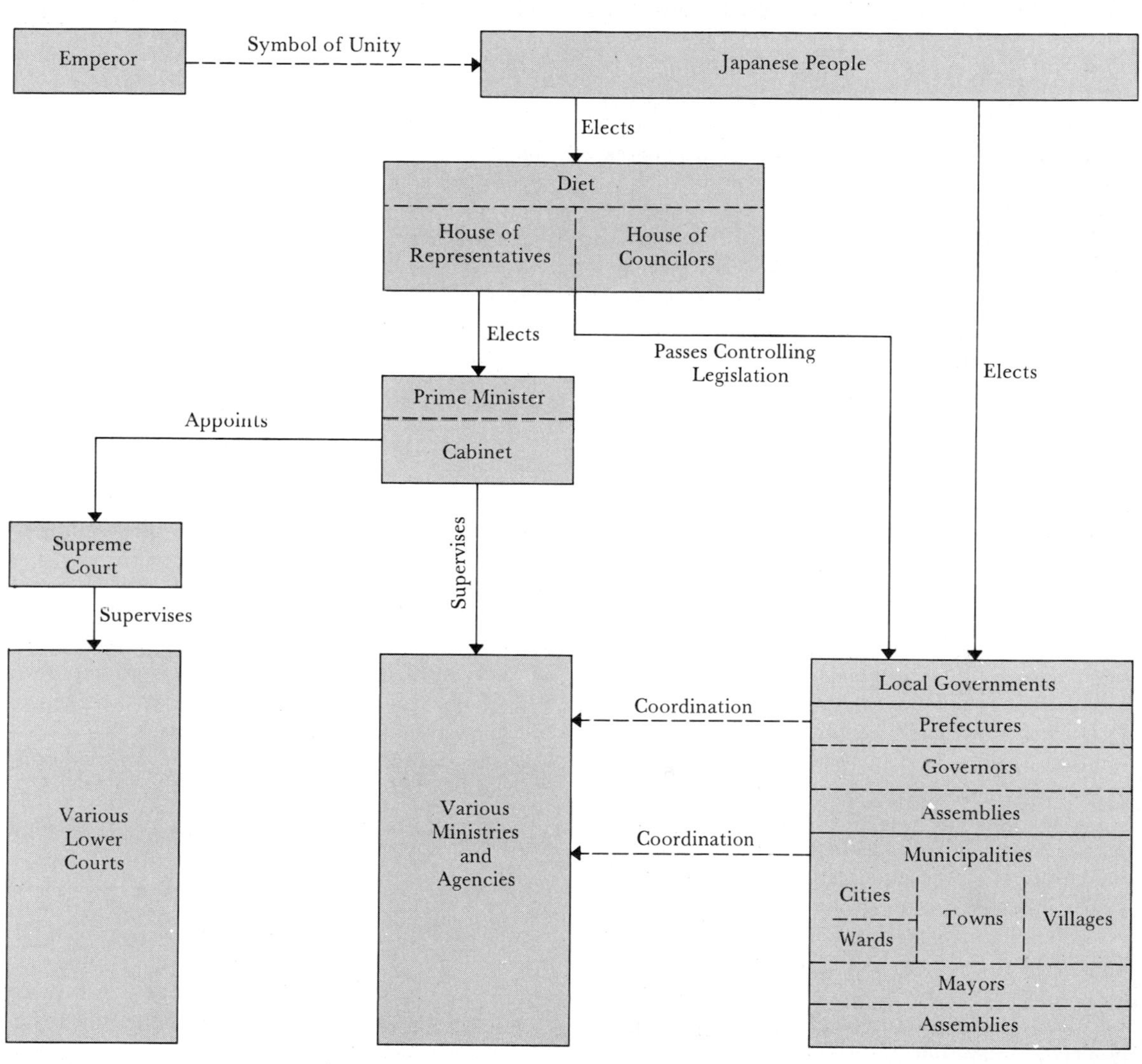

power with the Diet, and all those organs that were, because of their claim to speak in his name, have been eliminated. The *genrō* have long since ceased to exist: the sole remaining member died in 1940. Other august bodies that were beyond Diet control, such as the Privy Council, have been abolished. The military, which was the branch of state that had successfully challenged and largely destroyed parliamentary power in the 1930s, exists only in attenuated form. The Self-Defense Forces, which now substitute for the old army and navy, are relatively small, having only a strength of about 250,000 persons and a budget that absorbs less than 1 percent of Japan's gross national product. (Comparable figures are 3 to 5 percent in most Western European countries, around 6 percent in the United States, and between 10 and 20 percent in the Soviet Union and several highly militarized nations.) The SDF by law are under strict civilian control, enjoy only the lukewarm toleration of most Japanese, and carefully eschew any sign of exercising political influence. A measure of their political insignificance is that although the conservative party in power has long wished to raise the Defense Agency, which supervises the SDF, to the status of a Defense Ministry, this move has never seemed worth the risk of the determined political opposition that it would face.

The Diet is not only the sole source of law in Japan, but it also has the right to choose the prime minister. Theoretically, both houses of the Diet jointly select this official from among their memberships, but since the will of the lower house prevails in case of disagreement between them, it is the House of Representatives that in fact elects the prime minister, so far always from its own membership. The prime minister selects the rest of the Cabinet, but since this individual is elected by the Diet, which can elect a new prime minister at any time, he or she in no sense has independent powers comparable to those of an American president. In fact, the prime minister and Cabinet are merely a sort of executive committee operating on behalf of the Diet.

Both Diet houses are elected, but by differently constituted electorates and for different terms, as is the case of the American Congress. Half of the 252-member House of Councilors is elected every three years for a six-year term. Of the total, 100 are elected from the nation at large; this means that a mere 2 percent of the vote can elect 1 councilor among the 50 who win in each election. The remaining 152 are elected from each of Japan's forty-seven prefectures, which correspond to our states. The smallest prefecture elects 1 each time, and the most populous elects 4. This difference in the number of councilors per prefecture, ranging from 2 to 8, is far less than their differences in population. The most populous is at a 5-to-1 disadvantage compared to the least populous, but this is much less than the 75-to-1 discrepancy in the most extreme case in the American Senate.

The representatives of the lower house are elected for a four-year term according to a system established in 1925 and called the *middle-size electoral district system.* Between three and five representatives are elected from each electoral district, but each voter can cast only one ballot for one specific candidate, not a party. It is a unique system among the major legislatures of the world and, as we shall see, has a profound influence on the conduct of electoral politics in Japan. Like the electoral system for the upper house, it produces a certain degree of proportional representation, because minority groups can win some seats. Thus, 20 percent of the vote cast for a candidate in a five-seat district ensures his or her election. The system also produces more stable results than occur in other nations. In the Anglo-American one-seat, winner-take-all system a shift of a small percentage of the votes in a large number of electoral districts can bring a change of landslide proportions. In the Japanese system a similar change would produce only a small change, reducing, for example, a majority party's representation in a five-seat district merely from three to two.

The size of the House of Representatives, set in 1925 at 466, continued into the postwar period, but then was slowly increased to allow for the return in 1972 of Okinawa as Japan's forty-seventh prefecture and to compensate slightly for the great demographic changes that were taking place as people left the countryside and swarmed into the larger cities, which were given a few additional seats. In 1976 the size of the lower house was set at 511, elected from 130 districts. This still leaves discrepancies of as great as 4-to-1 voters per representative. Court rulings have pointed out that this is a sort of political discrimination not permitted by the constitution, but, unlike the American courts in their "one man one vote" rulings, the Japanese courts left it up to the Diet to take the necessary corrective action, which it has shown little inclination to do.

The House of Representatives only rarely lives out its full four-year term. In the British manner it can pass a vote of "no confidence" against the Cabinet, forcing the prime minister either to resign or to dissolve the lower house. In fact, this has occurred only twice, in 1948 and 1953, but what does happen frequently is that the prime minister voluntarily dissolves the lower house at some time short of its full four years, forcing a new general election; this, in turn, necessitates a new selection of a prime minister by the Diet. The reason for dissolving the lower house usually is to take advantage of a situation that appears more propitious for the prime minister's party than the end of the full four-year term may prove to be.

Both houses elect their own officers and have their own rules and precedents of procedure. Each is divided into sixteen committees, corresponding for the most part to the ministerial subdivisions of the government, and these are divided into various subcommittees. The system was modeled on that of the United States, but in fact operates quite differently. While the American congressional committees serve as major organs for the investigating of problems and the drafting of legislation, these functions are mostly performed elsewhere in the Japanese system. The Japanese Diet committees do pass on all legislation before it goes to a full, or plenary, session of the house, and sometimes they amend the draft laws. But primarily these committees serve as a first arena for public partisan debate, in which the oppostition parties can question, or interpellate, the government ministers and their assistants who are sponsoring the proposed legislation. The objective is more to embarrass the party in power or delay the legislative process rather than to shape legislation, though sometimes emendations do result. The large budget committee of fifty members is the chief arena for this process of *interpellation.* The whole procedure bears more resemblance to British parliamentary processes than to American.

The lower house has superior powers over the upper. Not only does it elect the prime minister, but it can override the upper house with a two-thirds vote. Since the party composition of the two houses has always been about the same and the party in power has never had a two-thirds majority, this situation has never in fact arisen. On certain types of legislation the House of Representatives can take action without the concurrence of the House of Councilors. The budget passed by the lower house, to which it must be presented first, goes into effect if the upper house fails to take concurrent action within thirty days. This same provision applies to the ratification of treaties. Amendments to the constitution, however, require positive action by two-thirds of the members of both houses and then a majority vote in a national referendum. Not surprisingly, there have been no amendments, just as the Meiji Constitution was never amended during its fifty-eight-year existence.

The Bureaucracy. The executive branch of government is headed by the prime minister and the Cabinet that he or she chooses. The Cabinet is made up of the ministers of the twelve regular ministries and the heads of a few agencies, who are appointed Cabinet members as ministers without portfolio. The ministries are regarded as having varying degrees of importance. The Finance Ministry, which has chief responsibility for the budget, unquestionably ranks at the top, and the Ministry of Foreign Affairs has always been important, whereas the *Ministry of International Trade and Industry (MITI),* has loomed very large since the war because of its key role in the spectacular economic development of the nation. The agencies are administrative units that rank slightly below the ministries, but will be lumped together with them hereafter, for convenience. Among those agencies that normally carry Cabinet membership for their directors are the Defense, Environment, Economic Planning, and Science and Technology agencies. The chief Cabinet secretary and the head of the prime minister's office, which gathers under it a miscellany of administrative functions in much the same way as the executive office in Washington does, are also Cabinet members.

The ministers (including the agency directors) are virtually all politicians, drawn from the membership of the ruling party in the Diet. So also are the one or two parliamentary vice ministers (or vice directors) for each ministry (or agency). Their function of liaison between the bureaucracy and the Diet is largely nominal, and they exist primarily to create more high-sounding titles to be passed around among the politicians. Even the ministers (and directors) hold their posts normally for only a year or two and thus have little chance to learn about their respective ministries or to establish firm control over them.

The actual operation of the bureaucracy takes place quite apart from these politicians nominally at its top. Starting with the adoption in 1885 of a perfected form of the German civil service system, the Japanese have built up an extremely efficient, dedicated, honest, and highly professional bureaucracy. The original concept was that all graduates of the government universities would qualify for membership, but from the start more judges were needed than the universities could supply, so special examinations were held for these positions. Soon it was discovered that too many university graduates were being turned out to be accommodated in the other posts. As a result, examinations came to be required for all positions. In 1900 the top bureaucratic posts were sealed off from all those who had not passed the examinations, thus protecting the Japanese bureaucracy from what they felt to be the corrupting influence of the political spoils system practiced in the United States. By the 1920s the whole system had taken on its contemporary shape. Candidates, qualified by graduation from either government or private universities, took examinations for admission into the various ministries or other bureaucratic branches of government, and a select few were chosen each year for a career of service in that particular branch of government.

Because of the traditional Japanese emphasis on government service, the cream of the Japanese educational system has tended to go into the bureaucracy, making it a very elite corps with high prestige, as is the case in many of the democracies of Western Europe, though not in the United States. The bulk of the high bureaucrats have traditionally come from Tokyo University, and this is still the case, at least for the older members. This situation probably results not so much from the fact that Tokyo University professors devised the examinations, as from the fact that a large percentage of the ablest students from all over Japan (or at least those most skilled in taking examinations) gain admission into this most prestigious of Japanese universities by passing its stiff entrance examinations.

Once accepted into the government, the new bureaucrat has career-long security and is promoted more or less routinely by seniority. The most capable at each age level are given the most important and interesting jobs open to that level and thus are groomed for the top jobs, which only a few will hold. Eventually one member of each age cohort is selected for the top bureaucratic job of *administrative vice minister* (or vice director). This is the person who really runs the ministry (or agency). His or her peers, usually still in their early fifties, must then retire. To supplement their retirement pay, they usually must seek post-retirement employment, commonly as advisers in industry or in various governmental supervisory agencies. Promotion up and out is relatively rapid, bringing individuals of two or more decades of professional experience—but still in the prime of their vigor—to the top bureaucratic posts. This often provides a marked contrast to the American system with regard to both age and professionalism.

The bureaucracy, including that of local government entities, extends far beyond the higher civil service described above. It includes large numbers of secretaries, clerks, specialists, and local officials; all workers for the national railway system and certain government monopolies, like tobacco; all police officers; and teachers in all government schools, from the elementary grades through the university. All these varied functionaries and specialists achieve their posts through a diversity of educational qualifications and sometimes special examinations, but they are to be distinguished from the higher civil service.

The prestige, professionalism, and relative independence of this higher civil service gives it a comparatively large role in government. Each ministry, comprised of a stable and self-confident group of professionals, tends to have its own policies on matters that concern it. These are worked out by negotiation and compromise between the various component units and factional groupings within the ministry. Naturally, nothing can be achieved unless the politicians of the Diet are willing to pass the necessary legislation, and the bureaucrats must, therefore, trim their sails to parliamentary winds, but they still feel free to differ with the prime minister and Cabinet in a way that few American bureaucrats would dare.

The bulk of the drafting of all legislation, usually after extensive consultations and negotiations, is done by the bureaucracy, not by the legislators, as is the American tradition. Most laws are usually framed in general terms, leaving room for interpretation by the bureaucracy when putting them into effect. While the courts watch carefully to see that individual rights guaranteed in the constitution are not transgressed, they do not take the lead in making rulings to implement legislation or the constitution, as they sometimes do in the United States. There are also fewer outside regulatory bodies deciding how laws should be implemented; and, as a result, the bureaucracy is allowed greater scope in making decisions on implementation. Thus, from the original deciding on policy, through the drafting of legislation, to the implementing of it, the Japanese bureaucracy plays a larger role than its American counterpart.

Standing close to the bureaucracy, but in a sense remaining distinct from it, are certain other bodies. A relatively autonomous Board of Audit keeps a careful eye on all financial matters, and the National Personnel Authority sees to the honest and fair functioning of the bureaucracy itself. The court system, which since its inception in the Meiji period has prided itself on its independence from the rest of government and on its strict adherence to legal principles, is nonetheless constituted along much the same lines as the rest of the bureaucracy.

The members of the Supreme Court are selected by the Cabinet, but must be confirmed by popular vote at the next general election and every ten years thereafter. This confirmation by popular vote sounds enlightened, but has proved meaningless so far, because the justices are not sufficiently well known to the public. The Supreme Court is vested with the rule-making authority for all lesser courts and thus supervises the whole system. However, persons qualify for the judiciary in much the same way that they do for the higher civil service. A few hundred are selected each year by rigorous examinations from among university graduates and then are put through a two-year training program conducted by the Japanese Legal Training and Research Institute. On the completion of this course, successful candidates then choose between careers as judges, public prosecutors, or lawyers.

After experimenting somewhat with the Anglo-Saxon jury system, the Japanese decided it was too erratic and opted instead for a system in which the decisions as well as the sentences are determined by the judge. Trials are conducted according to the continental European system of having the judge direct the inquiry, rather than by the adversary system conducted between lawyers, as in the American tradition. On the whole, the Japanese judicial system operates with honesty, fairness, and reasonable efficiency.

Local Government. Japan is divided into forty-seven *prefectures,* which are analogous to American states but have much less autonomy. Curiously, there is no single word for "prefecture" in Japanese, the forty-seven being divided into one *tō* ("metropolis"), one *dō* ("circuit"), two *fu* ("urban prefectures"), and forty-three *ken* ("ordinary prefectures"). In population the prefectures average over 2 million each, but there are great discrepancies among them, and most are closer to Rhode Island or Massachusetts in geographic size than the larger American states. Each prefecture is completely divided into municipal units known as cities, towns, or villages, depending on the size of their populations. The nine largest cities are subdivided into administrative wards, which are much larger than American city wards, but smaller than the boroughs of New York. Tokyo itself is unusual in having no city government, but the twenty-three wards that constituted the prewar city of Tokyo have the status of "special cities," though with less autonomy from the prefectural government (Tokyo metropolis) than other municipalities.

Before World War II all these local units had popularly elected assemblies with very restricted powers. The assemblies selected the mayors, who had to be approved by the national administration. The linchpin in the whole system of local government was the prefectural governor, who was a bureaucrat appointed by the Home Ministry of the central government, and most of the work of local administrations was simply to carry out the tasks assigned to them by Tokyo.

A major political objective of the American occupation was to increase *local autonomy,* which was seen by the Americans as a key ingredient of democracy. The postwar constitution decrees that the chief executive officer of all local public entities, meaning both the governors and the mayors, must be popularly elected. Greatly increased powers of taxation and other authority for local affairs were given to the various types of assemblies and chief executives. The strong control over local government by the prewar Home Ministry was sharply curtailed, and its duties were broken up to some extent. The new Police Agency, for example, took over control of police matters. The remaining functions of the Home Ministry were assigned to a greatly weakened administrative authority, at first known as the Autonomy Agency, but later upgraded to become the *Autonomy Ministry.*

The American efforts to create strong local self-government fell far short of the goal. Japan is simply too small a country geographically and the people too accustomed to centralized government to adapt themselves easily to the American concepts of local government derived from a very different geographic situation and historical tradition. In addition, the local tax base proved inadequate for much autonomy of action, and local governments have remained heavily dependent on financial support from the national government.

After the end of the occupation some of the powers given to the local administrations were actually restored to the central government, despite the strong opposition of the political left. A police system divided into independent municipal units and prefectural rural police had proved inefficient and too costly. In 1954 it was reconsolidated into a prefectural police system under close national supervision. A largely decentralized educational system under elected municipal and prefectural boards of education also did not win general popular confidence. In 1956 a compromise system was adopted, in which locally appointed boards of education replaced the elected ones and were placed under careful Ministry of Education guidance. Local administrations also slipped back into the old position of devoting most of their energies to nationally determined and funded programs; governors and mayors came to spend much of their time in Tokyo, lobbying for local interests with the central government; and bureaucrats of the central government ministries were dispatched for lengthy periods of service in the local governments in order to gain practical experience in their respective fields and to strengthen the links between central and local governments.

Local administrations, thus, are far from being as independent as those of the United States, but they do have considerably more autonomy than similar bodies in a still more centralized democracy, like France, which originally was Japan's major model for modern local government. Local elective politics for governors, mayors, and ward, municipal, and prefectural assemblies is extremely lively, giving a strong foundation for national electoral politics. Local government bureaucracies sometimes enjoy equal or better financial treatment than the national bureaucracy and are rising in relative prestige. One reason for this is the increasing importance of local government, as problems of pollution, urban crowding, social services, and the environment, all of which have a strong local component, have in recent years begun to loom large on the national political docket. Actions on these problems taken by local governments have often led the way toward later action on a national scale, showing the influence and significance that local government is capable of achieving.

POLITICAL PARTICIPATION AND THE PARTY SYSTEM

However perfect the machinery of government may be, the true test of a country's political system is its efficiency in actual operation. Three things are required of it. First, it must be effective in making necessary political decisions and maintaining order. Second, it should allow the people as a whole to feel a sense of participation and, at least in a democracy, actually participate in a meaningful way in the decision-making process. Finally, it must be able to steer itself by means of a successful feedback system that allows it to respond to external stimuli resulting from new or changing conditions.

The premodern Tokugawa government of Japan met the first criterion of making decisions and maintaining order, but had little sense of popular participation, except for the limited *samurai* class, and in its later years proved notably weak in responding to a changing environment. The various intermediate regimes between the Meiji Restoration and World War II continued to meet the first criterion, but handled the other two with only varying degrees of success. Japanese politics today, however, seem to measure up quite well in all three respects.

Popular Participation and Electoral Politics. In ancient and feudal Japan a vast gulf existed between the rulers and the ruled. This was epitomized by the phrase *"kanson-minpi"*: "the officials honored, the people despised." Today, despite the relatively high prestige of the higher civil service, bureaucrats are seen not as a superior class nor as distant imperial officers, but as public servants, and they are held to extremely exacting standards of honesty and hard work. Elected politicians, who are a modern phenomenon and were never very highly regarded, are looked on with as much contempt as respect, as is common in most modern democracies. In any case, no one has any doubt that they are the representatives, not the rulers, of the people.

The shift in attitude toward those in authority is particularly marked in the case of the police, who not long ago were greatly feared as well as respected. The postwar police have gone out of their way to change this image. They act with restraint and without arrogance. Established in small local "police boxes," where two or more are always on duty or are out on patrol of their area on foot, they take pains to establish themselves as trusted members of the local community. The intimacy and mutual respect between the residents of the community and their local police produce close cooperation. As a result, Japan has one of the lowest crime rates among major industrial nations, and the statistics are tending to fall rather than rise. In addition, almost no crimes go unsolved, which is hardly the situation in the United States.

However important attitudes may be, the key to popular participation in a democracy is a meaningful electoral system. Although completely unknown in traditional Japan, elections have been held for local assemblies since 1879 and for the national Diet since 1890 and are now a thoroughly familiar and central element of the political system. All persons above the age of twenty have the right to vote for all those who have the power to make both local and national political decisions. These are the members of the prefectural, municipal, and ward assemblies, the mayors of municipalities, the governors of prefectures, and the members of the two houses of the Diet, which in turn selects the prime minister.

The Japanese take their duties as voters very seriously. Like the voters in most other advanced democracies, many of them are cynical about the results of electoral politics and are critical of politicians. The bulk of the voters, in fact, disdain to associate themselves with any particular party, insisting on their status as political independents. Still, when it comes time to vote, they pour out in large numbers. For national elections, their voting rates are likely to be 75 percent or more of those eligible, in contrast to the rates of 55 percent or less that are common in the United States. They also show discrimination in the elections they respond to. More vote in elections for the more powerful lower house of the Diet than for the less important upper house. Voting rates run highest in the less urbanized areas, and the highest ratios of all are found in local assembly or mayoral elections in less urbanized areas, where the candidates are more likely to be personally known and the issues more directly felt. This situation contrasts with that in the United States, particularly in urban areas, where elections for national office commonly draw many more voters than elections for the welter of local elective positions.

Voting in Japan started with local elections, first in rural areas and then in the cities, and the early restricted electorates, made up of those who paid the highest taxes, were largely well-to-do farmers who paid the land tax, the major direct tax of that time. Gradually the tax restrictions were lowered, but it was not until 1925 that the bulk of male urban dwellers got the vote, and their first chance to exercise it came in 1928, just before the Manchurian Incident began to swing Japan from parliamentary leadership to military dictatorship. As a result, early electoral politics in Japan had largely rural roots, and urban Japanese voters became a significant electoral force only after the war.

Strongly personalized tendencies have always been combined with the rural roots of Japanese electoral politics. In any small community the known personal qualities of a candidate are likely to loom larger than the party label under which he or she may stand. This is particularly the case in Japan, where personal relationships have always been strongly emphasized. Between 1890 and 1925 several different electoral systems were used in national elections, but candidates always ran as individuals rather than as members of a party slate.

Since 1925 the middle-size electoral district system has further emphasized the importance of the individual. Since three to five persons are elected from each district, a candidate from a major party is usually forced to run against one or more other candidates from his or her own party; and these fellow party members are in a sense the most important competition, because they are likely to appeal to the same type of voter. It is necessary, therefore, for each candidate to establish his or her own image and own electoral machine. Somewhat the same situation exists in prefectural, municipal, or ward assembly elections, in which the same multiseat electoral district system exists or, in the case of smaller units, all candidates run at large against all the rest.

Because of the necessity of running as individuals, virtually all candidates in local elections originally ran as independents on their own personal reputations and contacts. Today there is still a large preponderance of such independents in smaller municipalities, even though most of them are actually supporters of the conservative party in power. Over time, however, there has been a growing tendency for politicians at the national and prefectural levels and in the more heavily urbanized communities to adopt party labels. This is because adequate personal contacts are difficult to maintain in the larger units or under the less intimate conditions of modern urban life. A party label helps to establish the candidate's political stand and image. As a result, there have been virtually no true independents in the Diet for some time, though some pseudoindependents do win seats at each election for special reasons. Independents have also become almost equally rare in prefectural and large urban assemblies and exist in large numbers only in the assemblies of small cities, towns, and villages.

Governors and mayors form something of a special case. Since only one person can be elected to each post, a candidate normally faces no competition from other members of the party, so it might seem natural to use the party label. But this is not needed for party members and is felt to run the risk of driving away some otherwise prospective supporters. In some cases, also, the support of other parties is necessary to win election. This is particularly true of the various opposition parties, which are all too small to elect a candidate on their own strength and must rely on a coalition of parties. As a consequence, governors and mayors frequently are nominal independents, though normally it is well known which party or parties were behind their election. Once elected, they tend to have considerable political longevity, since their relatively weak powers save them from the frequent dilemma their American counterparts face in an electorate that simultaneously demands more services and less taxation. Governors and mayors in their fourth or fifth consecutive four-year terms are not at all uncommon.

In any of the multiseat electoral systems existing in Japan each candidate must secure an adequate share of his or her party's vote in the district. Traditionally, this was done by building up a strong base in one part of the electoral district. The traditional Japanese village, now downgraded to the status of an unofficial hamlet incorporated into an expanded administrative village, town, or even city, was always a tightly knit social group. The villagers from the start realized that they would have more political clout—that is, they would be more likely to elect a candidate to represent their interests—if they agreed to vote in unison for one person. Some ambitious, locally strong candidate would put together an adequate number of such voting blocs to win election to the municipal assembly; a series of such groups would be put together for a seat in the prefectural assembly; and a grouping of these larger units would combine for a Diet seat. A local base of this sort, called a *jiban,* usually constituted a geographically continguous area within the electoral district that could be counted on to deliver the bulk of its vote to a local figure of prominence. A strong *jiban* of this sort—an "iron" *jiban,* as it was called—might persist for a long time, being passed from a politician to his or her political heir, who might well be a son by birth or adoption or perhaps a nephew.

In the highly urbanized Japan of today such localized or "vertical" *jiban* are hard to maintain. There is not sufficient community solidarity in an urban environment, and even in the countryside a large percentage of farm dwellers actually commute to nearby towns and factories to work. Other connections and loyalties have superseded the old village solidarity, and the bloc system of voting has therefore seriously eroded.

To adjust to this change, politicians have developed what is called the "horizontal" *jiban:* a base spread more evenly throughout the whole electoral district. The key organ of this sort of *jiban* is the *kōenkai,* or personal "support society." Because of the strict limitations set by Japanese electoral laws, which keep electoral campaigning to specified short periods, sharply restrict activities, and set very modest budgets, the *kōenkai* cannot admit to being the election organizations that they in fact are. Instead, they pose as cultural and educational societies that maintain a year-round program of enlightening activities, such as informative lectures by the prospective candidate, supporters from within the district, and political friends from national or prefectural politics. The *kōenkai* aim in particular at specific voting blocs within the district, usually having special divisions for women, young people, farmers, workers, and the like.

The above description applies particularly to the politicians of the conservative party in power, which is the continuation of the major prewar parties and is deeply entrenched in rural Japan. It applies less or not at all to the politicians of the smaller opposition parties, who rely to a greater extent on the voters in cities, where the old vertical *jiban* is quite impossible to establish and even the *kōenkai* system is difficult to maintain. These politicians usually depend on groupings like labor unions for their support or on the appeal of their respective ideologies, made clear by the party labels they must use. As Japanese society steadily becomes more urbanized and depersonalized, the old personal type of politics will no doubt decline still further, and politics by party organization and ideology is likely to become even more the rule.

Parties. While independents still linger on in local politics, the Japanese parties have a long history (see Figure 15.2). By the 1870s and 1880s two party lines began to form around two former members of the oligarchic ruling group who, breaking with the others, demanded a larger political role for former *samurai* and others excluded from meaningful participation in the political system. It was in part to meet these demands that a Diet was created through the Meiji Constitution, and it was people from these political lines who dominated the Diet from its inception in 1890 and successfully battled the Cabinet for a larger share in power. The older of the two lines originally called itself the Jiyūtō, which literally means "freedom party," but has been more tactfully translated as the Liberal Party. In 1900, parts of it merged with elements in the bureaucracy to form the Seiyūkai, which can be translated as "the association of political friends." The Seiyūkai was the dominant party most of the time until the 1930s. The other political line had a more checkered career and changed names frequently. In 1927 it eventually settled on the name of Minseitō, which means "people's government party."

The military forced all the parties to disband in 1940 and join a loose organization called the Imperial Rule Assistance Association, but with Japan's defeat in 1945 the old parties sprang back to life at once, the Seiyūkai under its early name of Liberal Party and the Minseitō alternating between the names of Progressive Party and Democratic Party. These two revived prewar parties dominated postwar politics, and when they saw the rising opposition vote of the left as a dangerous challenge, they merged in 1955 to form the *Liberal Democratic Party (LDP),* which has been in power in the national government ever since.

Partly as a result of the Russian Revolution of 1917 and the liberal ideas that swept Europe after World War I, various leftist intellectual stirrings took place in Japan in the 1920s and penetrated the labor movement. A small Communist Party was founded in 1922, but it was soon suppressed and its leaders either imprisoned or driven into exile. A socialistic Farmer-Labor Party was formed in 1925, and from it was spawned a variety of short-lived parties, which usually divided into two or three mutually contentious lines. Eventually in

FIGURE 15.2 *Political Parties of Japan*

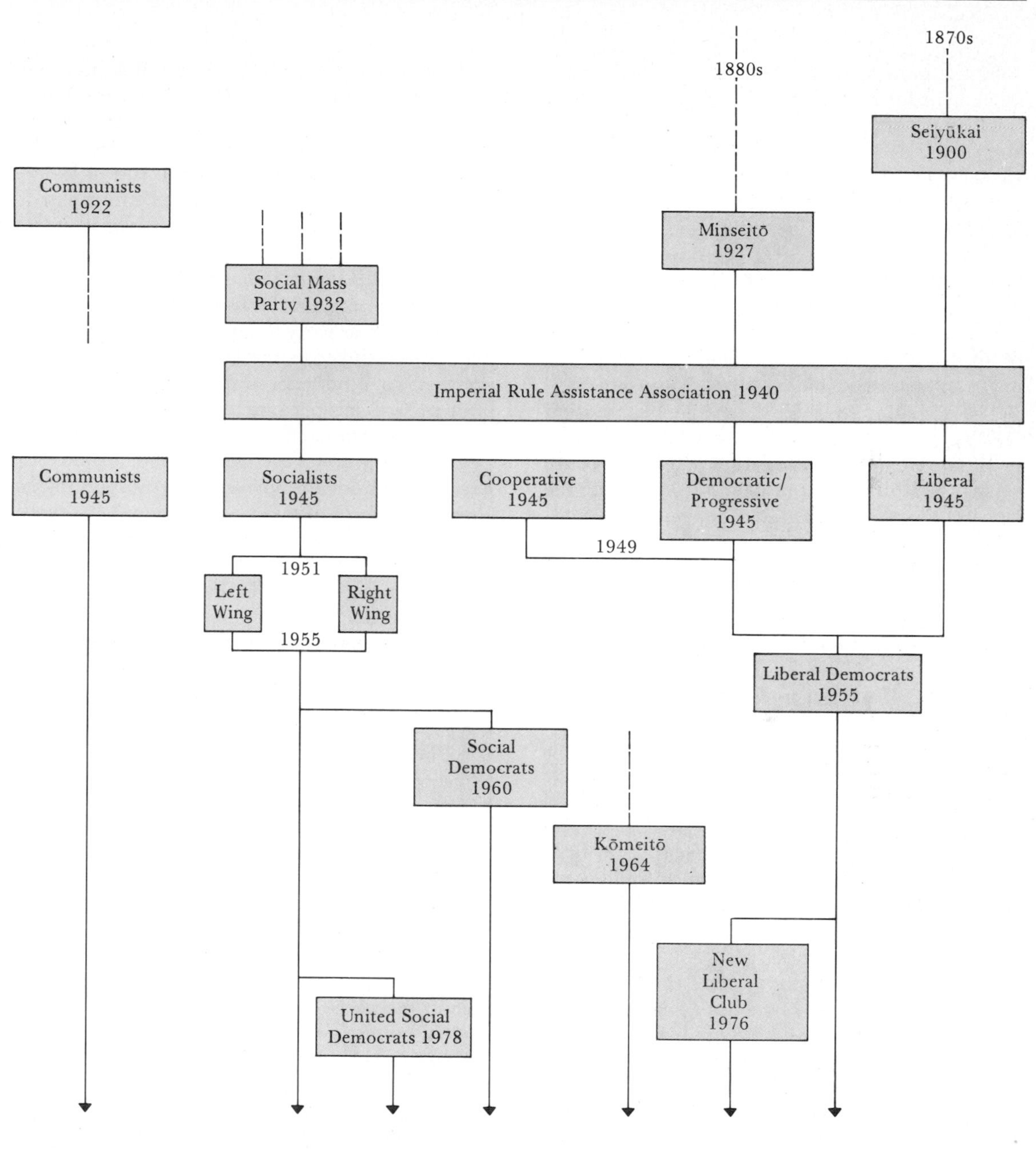

1932 the more moderate elements of the socialist movement formed the Social Mass Party; it won a small, but rapidly rising, vote until it, too, was absorbed in 1940 into the Imperial Rule Assistance Association.

After the surrender in 1945 the parties of the left also came back to life. Emerging from prison or returning from exile in the Soviet Union or China, the communists re-established their now legal *Communist Party (JCP),* while the Social Mass Party was resurrected under the forthright name of the *Socialist Party (JSP).* The divisions of the 1920s still persisted among the Socialists, however. Between 1951 and 1955 the party split into left and right wings, and in January 1960 the more moderate elements of the former right wing broke off again, this time permanently, to form the *Democratic Socialist Party (DSP).*

The disturbed conditions after the war also gave birth to a welter of new parties, but none had much significance except the Cooperative Party, which merged into the Democrats in 1949 and, thus, into the LDP in 1955. The only postwar party of lasting importance is the *Kōmeitō* (sometimes called the Clean Government Party), which gradually came into being between 1955 and 1964, when it adopted its present name. It is unusual in having started as the political wing of a religious organization called the *Sōka Gakkai,* which is an offshoot of Buddhism.

More recently, other parties have split off from the older ones, but their long-range influence is doubtful. In 1976 a few younger LDP Diet members left their party to form the *New Liberal Club,* which with new recruits did very well in the election for the lower house in December 1976, but was less successful in the upper-house election in July 1977 and won only four seats in the lower-house election of October 1979. In 1978 an even smaller group of moderate Socialists left their party to form a United Social Democratic Party but won only two seats in the 1979 election.

Party Support. The LDP, as the inheritor of the two traditional party lines that go back all the way to the 1870s and 1880s, is strong in rural Japan. It is known as the party of the farmers, but this fact is of declining significance. Even though rural Japan has a disproportionately high share of Diet representation, farmers themselves have shrunk from about half of the population at the end of World War II to less than 15 percent today, and many of these people are also engaged in nonagricultural jobs. The LDP is also known as the party of big business, called the *zaikai,* or "the financial world." This is because the LDP is the most conservative and probusiness party in Japan, providing spectacularly successful economic leadership, and because most of its economic support comes from big business, which is permitted to make contributions to political parties in the same way as labor unions.

The LDP, however, cannot depend on big business or even the farmers for the bulk of its voting strength. This must come from those members of the general public who see it as the party best able to direct the nation's affairs. The greatest strength of the LDP has always been the pragmatism and lack of dogmatism of its politicians. They are ready to accept a large government role in business or a drift toward a welfare state, as long as the measures taken appear popular and practical. In fact, the dilemma and frustration of the opposition parties have resulted from the LDP's readiness to co-opt their most popular and workable policies, while projecting the image of being the only party with the practical experience that will enable them to carry these policies out effectively.

The Socialist Party relies heavily on organized labor for financial support, votes, and leadership. In particular, it depends on *Sōhyō,* the largest of the labor federations, which has more than 4.5 million members. The Sōhyō unions are largely made up of government and white-collar workers, such as teachers and petty functionaries in the national and local governments, who tend to constitute the radical wing of the labor movement, since the best way they have to achieve their goals is to exert direct influence on the government.

The Democratic Socialists depend to a large extent on *Dōmei,* a labor federation of slightly over 2 million members, largely from blue-collar unions in private industry. These form the more moderate wing of the labor movement, concentrating on bargaining over wages and working conditions with their private employers and on avoiding disruptive strikes for fear of hurting the competitive position of their respective companies, with which they usually have lifetime employment.

The Kōmeitō draws its support largely from members of the Sōka Gakkai. These tend to be lower-income city dwellers who, lacking affiliation with large companies or other prestigious bodies, have joined the religion as a means of finding a group with which to identify. As an opposition party, Kōmeitō takes a generally leftist stance against the LDP, but its membership is actually rather conservative, coming on the whole from the less educated, more old-fashioned, and more traditional sectors of urban society.

The Communists rely for their support on certain labor unions and the small, but determined, band of communist believers. Since they are tightly and efficiently organized, they also attract many of the floating voters of the larger metropolitan areas, who, though not necessarily attracted by Communist policies, use the party to register a protest vote against what they feel are the unsatisfactory conditions of contemporary urban life. Some of the urban floating vote also goes to Kōmeitō, since it, too, is seen as a well-organized, effective party.

The conservatives, united since 1955 as the LDP, have dominated politics throughout the postwar period. The only partial break in their rule was during a period from May 1947 to October 1948, when there were two Socialist-Democratic-Cooperative coalition Cabinets, one led by a moderate Socialist called Katayama. The long dominance of the LDP has made the other parties very bitter and induced them to assume the stance of a permanent uncooperative opposition. Some people have described Japanese politics not as a two-party system, but as a "party-and-a-half" system. The Marxist background of most of the opposition parties has widened the division between them and the LDP, and memories of prewar and wartime oppression of the left have contributed to a deep suspicion and hostility toward the party in power. Thus, a serious cleavage has existed in postwar Japanese politics between the conservative camp of the ruling LDP and the so-called progressive camp of the opposition. This confrontation was particularly marked in the years immedately after the end of the American occupation and began to fade only in the early 1970s.

During the postwar period the LDP vote and number of seats in the Diet have both slowly eroded. The conservative parties won their highest proportion of the popular vote in 1952 with 66 percent, but thereafter the LDP vote slowly declined, until by 1967 it was 49 percent and in 1976 only 46 percent, even including the New Liberal Club defectors. With the aid of some independents and the division of the opposition into a number of parties, the LDP has maintained a bare majority in the two houses of the Diet, but not enough in recent years to be in full command of all Diet committees. This slow shift in votes away from the conservatives appears to have been largely the result of demographic changes: an increase in the number of urban residents, a movement of the labor force from agriculture to manufacturing and service industries, rising educational standards, and generational changes, all of which have favored the progressives over the conservatives.

The Socialist Party was once expected to succeed the LDP as the majority party, but it has gradually faded as other opposition parties came on the scene. It reached its high point in popular votes at 33 percent in 1958, but in 1979 was down to less than 20 percent. The Communists and Kōmeitō each get around 10 percent of the vote; the DSP, somewhat less.

The decline of the LDP vote seems to have slowed down or stopped of late, and it appears possible that the party may maintain its slim margin for some time into the future. If it does not, many people have assumed that a coalition of the progressive parties would take over, but this is most unlikely. There are deep historical fissures between the Communists and the Socialists, within the JSP itself, and between these parties of the left and Kōmeitō and the DSP in the center. Meanwhile the issues that once divided the conservatives and progressives have faded to a large extent, and the voters for all of the parties have tended to drift toward the center on most issues, dragging their parties with them. If the LDP can no longer rule alone, it seems probable that at first an informal and then possibly a formal coalition will be worked out with the parties of the center. It is also possible that eventually a reshuffling of parties might take place to produce a large new ruling party that is nearer the center of the political spectrum and consists of the Kōmeitō, the DSP, the bulk of the LDP, and probably some moderate elements from the JSP.

In any case, ever since the 1976 and 1977 elections for the lower and upper houses, a sort of informal coalition has existed between the LDP and the center parties, which separately lend the LDP support from time to time on controversial issues. The LDP, moreover, is careful to make as much of its legislation as possible acceptable to the other opposition parties. Thus, whatever the trend in votes may be over the next few years, there seems little reason to believe that the balance of political opinion or power in Japan will shift radically either to the left or to the right.

Party Organization. Most Japanese consider themselves political independents, not tied to parties—an attitude that is becoming increasingly common in the United States, too. But many Japanese do get involved in party politics, and most vote with fair consistency for one party or another. The contrast between small formal party membership and wide party support is particularly marked in the case of the LDP.

The core of the LDP consists of the party members who are elected to the two houses of the Diet (see Figure 15.3). They constitute the bulk of the delegates to the party convention, which is held on average every two years and elects the party president and the other party officers. These include at times a vice president, if there happens to be a suitable candidate, but the second most important party post is that of *secretary general,* the person who oversees the running of the party while the president is running the Cabinet and government. Other important party positions are the chairs of the party's *Executive Council* and the Policy Affairs Research Committee. Tbe party president is always elected prime minister by the LDP majority in the lower house, and this official and other party leaders choose the Cabinet ministers and the various party committees that supervise the operations of both the government and the party.

This preponderance of control of the party by the LDP members of the Diet and the prevalence of independents at the lowest grassroots levels have given rise to a picture of the LDP as an inverted pyramid or a "ghost party," for it has a clear head, but only shadowy feet. This, however, is not a correct representation of the situation. Beneath the core of Diet members are the local groups of LDP politicians, who are would-be or elected assembly members, mayors, or governors in prefectural and municipal governments, and below them, the many *kōenkai* of politicians in national and local politics. Through the latter, very large numbers of people become directly involved in LDP politics.

In the autumn of 1978, moreover, a new primary system for the selection of the party president was introduced in order to get more grassroots participation. Party members who had paid their dues or made other financial contributions voted by prefectures for candidates for the party presidency, and the final selection was then made by the party Diet members between the two candidates with the highest votes. More than 1.3 million votes were cast, and, in this case at least, the popular vote proved decisive in determining a change in December 1978 in the presidency and prime ministership from Fukuda to Ōhira. Still, this primary vote represents only a little more than 5 percent of the vote that the LDP can count on in national elections, showing how the majority of voters hang back from making a clear party commitment.

One surprising feature of Japanese politics and especially of the LDP is that even though most successful members of the Diet get elected on the basis of their own individual images and personal electoral machines, they adhere to a system of strict party discipline, almost always voting in unison, once they are congregated together in the Diet. In the United States, where candidates have strong local roots and are elected in large part on their own personal strength (as in Japan), there is little semblance of party discipline in Congress,

FIGURE 15.3 *Decision-Making Organs of the Japanese Government and the Liberal Democratic Party*

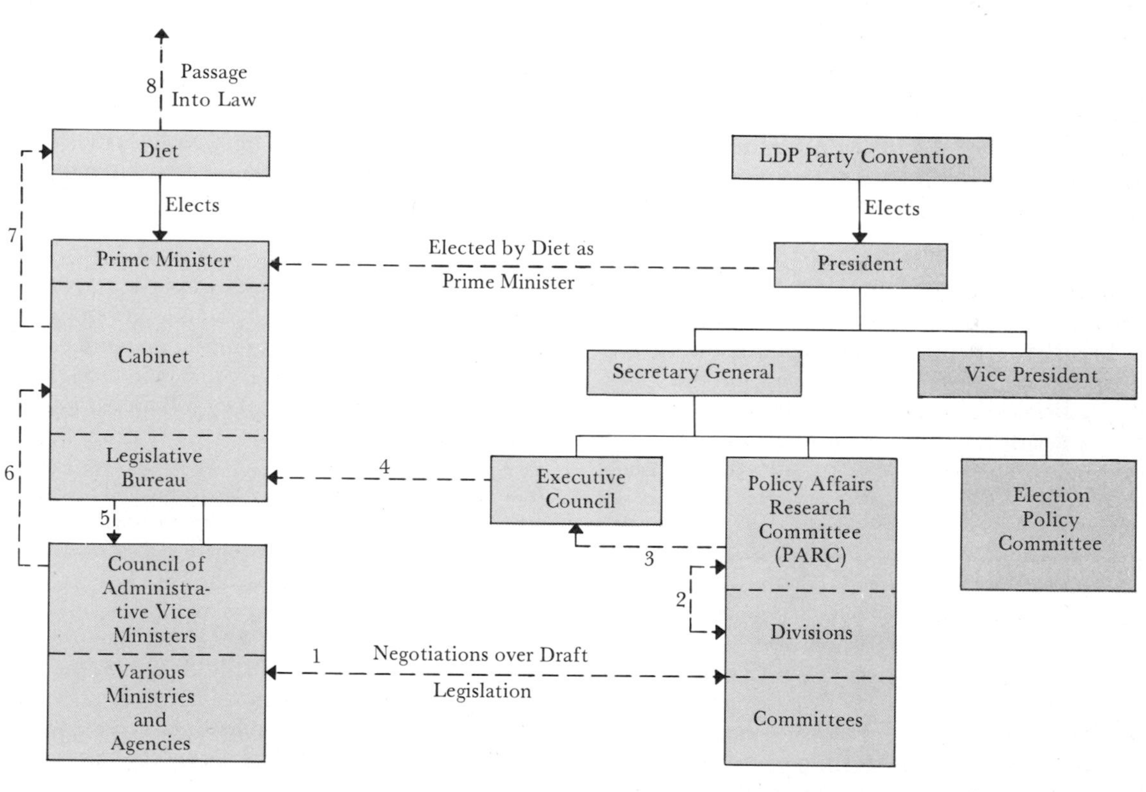

TABLE 15.1 *Hypothetical Results of Unbalanced and Balanced LDP Voting*

	UNBALANCED LDP VOTE		BALANCED LDP VOTE	
Parties	Vote	Results	Vote	Results
LDP	110,000	Elected	80,000	Elected
LDP	52,000		68,000	Elected
LDP	48,000		62,000	Elected
DSP	53,000	Elected	53,000	
Komeito	58,000	Elected	58,000	
JSP	70,000	Elected	70,000	Elected
JCP	60,000	Elected	60,000	Elected

and each member votes according to his or her own conscience or interests. On the other hand, in countries that have strong party discipline, candidates are usually elected not because of personal strength, but because of the party they represent, and frequently they have only weak ties with their constituencies. The Japanese ability to combine strong personal electoral politics with strict party discipline at the parliamentary level is unusual and offers a measure of their skill in group organization.

A particularly difficult problem for the LDP is the selection of candidates to run for the lower house of the Diet. In the middle-sized three-to-five-seat districts, if too many LDP candidates run or the vote is distributed too unevenly between them, the LDP may win fewer seats than its number of votes would entitle it to. Table 15.1 presents a hypothetical example, showing how this might work in a five-seat district in which one of the LDP candidates is extremely popular and runs away with too large a proportion of the votes. Similarly, if the LDP runs too many candidates, there can be the same sort of disastrous results, as Table 15.2 illustrates.

It is obviously imperative to spread out the votes between the party candidates and to avoid running too many, but this is not easy to accomplish. There is no primary system to select candidates, and there are many ambitious local LDP politicians who are eager to run for the Diet and have been building up their local support with this objective in mind. The way in which this problem is solved is through the party's Election Policy Committee, which has the duty of deciding on the number of candidates and the specific individuals in each electoral district. Sometimes disappointed would-be nominees, confident of their electoral strength and unwilling to accept the committee's decision, will defy it by running as nominal independents. If they succeed, replacing in all probability one of the party's regular candidates, they will almost always rejoin the party at once.

One feature of the LDP is that virtually all of its Diet members are divided into *factions.* These are informal clubs led by prominent politicians, who usually are striving for the party presidency and prime ministership. The factions are almost universally condemned as being disruptive of party unity, but their very persistence shows that they do have a function. They usually do not represent ideological differences and thus are in no sense miniparties, as they are sometimes called. While the leaders do vary in their political stances, the

TABLE 15.2 *Hypothetical Results of Voting for Four and Three LDP Candidates*

	FOUR LDP CANDIDATES		THREE LDP CANDIDATES	
Parties	Vote	Results	Vote	Results
LDP	60,000	Elected	76,000	Elected
LDP	52,000		68,000	Elected
LDP	50,000		66,000	Elected
LDP	48,000			
DSP	53,000	Elected	53,000	
Komeito	58,000	Elected	58,000	
JSP	70,000	Elected	70,000	Elected
JCP	60,000	Elected	60,000	Elected

members of their factions normally spread over the whole range of political opinion in the party.

The factions actually serve many functions. Of course, they are useful to the leaders as a base for their efforts to exert influence in the party and eventually to achieve the party presidency. For the members, too, the factions are of help in a variety of ways. A factional alignment may have aided a Diet member originally in getting the nomination of the party. It is likely to be a source of extra campaign funds beyond those provided by the party, and the ability to raise political funds is, therefore, a prime requisite for a successful faction leader. In the Diet the faction's meetings serve as a sort of seminar for the new members and a device by which members of the party leadership keep in touch with rank-and-file sentiment. So the factions are useful in helping the party reach a consensus that can serve as the basis for a unified vote in the Diet. The factions also help their members attain the coveted positions of committee chairs, parliamentary vice ministers, and eventually Cabinet members.

To be at all effective, a faction must have at least ten or twenty members in the two houses of the Diet; but if it grows much beyond eighty or ninety members, it is likely to become unwieldy and run the risk of division. Since the factions are so important in the operation of the LDP at the Diet level, it is necessary that there be a certain factional balance in Cabinet appointments, in other government and party posts, and particularly in key bodies such as the Executive Council, the Policy Affairs Research Committee, and the Election Policy Committee.

Many of the leaders of LDP factions in recent years have been members of the Diet who originally served in the bureaucracy. In fact, the Japanese government has been led by prime ministers of such background during the better part of the post–World War II era. The list of former bureaucrats who became prime minister is impressive: Shidehara (1945–46), Ashida (1948), Yoshida (1946–47, 1948–54), Kishi (1957–60), Ikeda (1960–64), Satō (1964–72), Fukuda (1976–78), and Ōhira (1978–). Bureaucrat-politicians have predominated because the bureaucracy has traditionally drawn a high percentage of the most talented citizens, and when it became evident at the end of the war that the Diet was the center of power, quite a few of them shifted from the bureaucracy to electoral politics and then achieved the highest post because of their native ability and deep knowledge of the working of government. It is doubtful, however, that the bureaucratic leadership of the LDP will continue far into the future. Two of the recent prime ministers, Miki (1972–74) and Tanaka (1974–76), did not have this background, and increasing numbers of the LDP Diet leaders are emerging from lifetime careers in local and national politics.

Most of the other parties have organizations more or less comparable to that of the LDP, except that they do not have the problem of dividing up government positions, since they are not in power, and, with the exception of the Socialists, they are all too small to have major factional divisions or to face the problem of running more than one candidate in a lower-house electoral district. In the case of the JSP, its drastic loss of lower-house seats from 140 to 90 between 1967 and 1969 was directly caused by its overoptimistically running too many candidates in 1969.

The Communists and the Kōmeitō are the most tightly organized of the parties and have proportionately larger official memberships than the others. Both have a clear-cut and strong leadership. The Kōmeitō is financially supported primarily by the Sōka Gakkai and the Communist Party primarily by its newspaper, *Akahata* ("Red Flag"), which has a daily circulation of several hundred thousand and a Sunday circulation of close to 2.5 million.

The JSP and DSP depend heavily both for funds and for votes on the Sōhyō and Dōmei labor federations, respectively. Representatives of the JSP's prefectural and local organizations, in which Sōhyō often plays a major role, make up the bulk of the membership at the party's conventions, where the party chairperson and other top officials are selected. Since Sōhyō and the other local activists tend toward the left, the results of these conventions often show a leftward drift; but since the JSP must also appeal to more moderate voters to elect its candidates, at times of national elections the party often swings back toward the center. Ever since the war the JSP has been plagued by factionalism, which, being based on ideological differences, is very disruptive in a way that the LDP factions are not. Always lying beneath the surface and sometimes breaking to the top, a rather sharp cleavage between left and right exists within the Socialist Party, and at times a rather clear center group can be identified as well.

THE SELF-STEERING SYSTEM

The Decision-Making Process. The Japanese traditionally have preferred consensus, whenever possible, rather than simple majority decisions. They show this tendency throughout their society, including big business, where decisions are usually arrived at after lengthy consultation up and down the chain of command and not simply by a few top executives. The same applies to government and the whole political process.

The central core of decision-making organs in politics consists of the bureaucracy and the Diet—more specifically, the party in power. The bureaucracy, of course, is divided into a number of ministries and agencies, each with its own area of authority, which it jealously guards, and its own policies, hammered out between its many functional divisions and internal groups with differing opinions. The LDP is similarly divided into various factions and occasional policy groupings that transcend factional lines. Between these two bodies and their various elements, it is no simple task to work out draft legislation that will receive majority Diet support and thus become law.

One key organ in achieving this result is the *Policy Affairs Research Committee (PARC)* of the LDP. It has seventeen divisions, which correspond to the major divisions of the bureaucracy, and beneath these some fifty-five committees (as of 1978) that work on issues of interest to specific political pressure groups. Individual LDP Diet members belong to two of the divisions of PARC, but can attend any of the committees they wish, thus having a say at this lowest level of national decision making on any legislation in which they have an interest. The various ministries and agencies come up with draft legislation, but only after intensive intraministry consultations and, when appropriate, interministry negotiations and also with an eye to prevailing opinions in the Diet and among the public. Similarly, the committees and divisions of PARC, reflecting the interests of LDP Diet members and their readings of their constituents' desires, produce their own suggestions for legislation. After careful negotiations between the bureaucratic and the PARC groups concerned, draft legislation is produced, which then goes through a long process of scrutiny and emendation.

Draft laws must first win approval of PARC as a whole and then the party's Executive Council, both of which are factionally balanced groups. Then they are passed to the Legislative Bureau under the Cabinet, which clears them through the Council of Administrative Vice Ministers, the group in day-to-day control of the various branches of the bureaucracy, to be sure that there are no bureaucratic problems remaining. The draft legislation is then ready for adoption by the Cabinet and presentation to the Diet, where, after all this careful work, it is assured of LDP support and, therefore, probable passage.

Such broad LDP and bureaucratic consensus, however, cannot always be achieved by this process. In such cases it is usually up to the leaders of the LDP to make the decisions. Here the faction system has its value, because the leaders, in close touch with the members of their respective factions, can judge what sort of compromise can win general approval. Sometimes the leaders meet informally as faction heads to make these decisions, but at other times they may get together more formally as the occupants of the top party posts. Occasionally a prime minister has to make the decision alone, despite the risk that members of the party may subsequently repudiate this decision and unseat him.

Throughout this interplay between the LDP and the bureaucracy in drawing up draft legislation, both sides are mindful of public opinion and the attitudes of the opposition parties. Unpopular laws may lose votes in the next election, and legislation that the opposition parties disapprove of bitterly will require a lot of time for passage through the Diet. In fact, the chief tactic that the opposition employs in the Diet is attempting to delay action both in the committees and at the plenary sessions. Though time is strictly allotted for the debate of each issue, the opposition hopes that through interpellation they can trick an LDP minister into some unwise remark that can, for example, be interpreted as denigrating democracy, human rights, or popular sovereignty. They then can blow this remark up into a new issue that must be debated, using up valuable Diet time in the process.

Earlier, in the 1950s and most notably during the great Mutual Security Treaty debate of the spring of 1960, the opposition also used cruder methods, such as keeping the speaker bottled up in his office by force, disrupting sessions by fisticuffs, boycotting sessions, and demanding innumerable procedural votes and then dragging these out as long as possible. The LDP would respond to these delaying tactics by "ramming through" legislation, as it was called, through trickery or force. For example, the key vote in the 1960 debate was taken by suddenly calling a session and taking a voice vote before the opposition realized what was happening.

Such undignified parliamentary procedures are now rare, but the ability of the opposition parties to delay and sometimes block legislation by uncooperative tactics remains strong. In large part, this is because of the traditional preference of the Japanese for consensus decisions. They tend to sympathize with the minority and feel it should have its full say and, if possible, a share in the decision. The Japanese are quick to condemn what they call "the tyranny of the majority," though none would prefer "the tyranny of the minority." The net result is that only a few truly controversial bills can be passed in any one session of the Diet. This makes it necessary for the LDP to make the maximum number of its draft laws noncontroversial and to limit the controversial elements of the others as much as it can. As a result, the opposition parties have a much larger role in the decision-making process than is usually realized. In recent years, as the representation of the LDP in the Diet has gradually shrunk to virtual equality with the opposition parties, the influence of the latter has naturally grown, producing an increase in consultations with them during the drafting process and more emendations of draft laws at their instigation during Diet debate.

Pressure Groups. Japanese voters, of course, exercise ultimate control over the political decision-making process through their election of members of the Diet and, at a lower level, the members of the local governments, but the public also exercises its influence more directly. Throughout Japanese society there are special interest or *pressure groups* that seek to influence political decisions that concern them.

One particularly powerful and well organized group has exerted such great influence that it has drawn special attention. In fact, some observers have felt that it should be regarded as part of the inner decision-making core of the Japanese political system. This is big business, or the *zaikai.* It is closely integrated through a number of bodies, the chief of which is the Keidanren, the Association of Economic Organizations. Big business naturally had a major role in Japan's amazing postwar industrial expansion. During the 1950s and 1960s, when rapid economic growth was the central Japanese concern, it played a very influential part in establishing economic policies, together with the LDP politicians and the bureaucrats, and in putting these into effect in cooperation with the bureaucracy. This situation has given rise to descriptions of Japanese politics as being in the hands of a triumvirate made up of the LDP, the bureaucracy, and the *zaikai.* The residence of most of the members of all three groups in Tokyo, the graduation of many of them from Tokyo University, a certain degree of intermarriage between them, and the movement of some bureaucrats after retirement into business positions or politics all tended to confirm this picture.

This triumvirate model, however, is basically misleading. It never applied to most policy fields, but only to matters of industrial economic growth—the area of interest to the *zaikai.* It has also proved much less correct even in this area during the 1970s than before. As rapid economic growth produced serious problems of pollution and overcrowding in the cities, the interests of LDP politicians and of bureaucrats began to diverge from those of big business executives. Sensitive to the demands of the public, the politicians and bureaucrats became concerned with pollution controls, the quality of life, social security, and other matters that conflicted with economic growth. The *zaikai,* of course, remains as certainly one of the most influential pressure groups, but it is now and has always been merely one among many.

Pressure groups are found in almost all realms of Japanese life. Through their huge cooperatives the farmers exert a great deal of political influence and with the aid of the LDP, which depends on their vote, have managed to get a system of agricultural price supports that has given rural Japan a full share in the affluence that industry has brought the country. The labor federations and their component unions are also large and powerful pressure groups, though they normally stand in an adversary relationship with the LDP and seek to achieve their ends through the opposition parties. Smaller groups such as doctors, dentists, and other professional people have more restricted, but still effective, pressure groups, as do other bodies of citizens that center around interests other than strictly economic ones.

Pressure groups get their voices heard in a variety of ways. Most ministries and other bureaucratic agencies have several *shingikai,* or advisory boards, made up of experts or concerned individuals from among the public who are expected to give advice on legislation or serve as sounding boards for legislative proposals. More important, the various pressure groups establish direct contacts with the branches of the bureaucracy and the committees in PARC that are concerned with the problems of interest to them. In addition, they naturally work on individual Diet members and enlist them as the champions of their respective causes. When they feel the LDP will not aid them, they work through the opposition parties and their Diet members.

Pressure groups also attempt to affect political decisions directly through popular *demonstrations.* During the turbulent early postwar years, marches and other demonstrations in the streets were to be seen everywhere, and the word *demo,* a short form of the English "demonstration," became one of the most frequently used words in the Japanese vocabulary. At times of political excitement, as during the security treaty debate in 1960, demonstrations brought out several hundred thousand people into the streets of Tokyo and became quite unruly. Even today pressure groups of all types are prone to stage street marches, usually in very orderly fashion, or to call at government offices and vociferously present their demands.

Violence as a means of exerting political pressure, however, has usually proved counterproductive. In the early postwar years, occasional acts of violence by the extreme left tended to drive away voters, and similar acts of violence by the extreme right have always met universal condemnation. When the student radical movements in the late 1960s became increasingly violent, they also lost all popular support and in a sense placed themselves outside of the meaningful Japanese political spectrum.

Often direct popular pressures are exerted by larger bodies transcending the usual special interest groups. In the early postoccupation years such movements, called *citizens' movements (shimin undō),* were commonly sponsored by the opposition parties and supported particular political causes. These movements frequently concentrated on showing opposition to the presence of American bases and military personnel in Japan. They would call attention to unpleasant incidents involving the American military, and they also helped build anti-American feelings through demonstrations against nuclear weapons, particularly on August 6, the anniversary of the dropping of the atomic bomb on Hiroshima.

In more recent years such citizens' movements have been replaced for the most part by what are called *local residents' movements (jūmin undō).* These are concerned largely with local matters, such as pollution, crowding, factory and road construction, nuclear power plants, and other such problems of modern urban life, and they normally try to avoid involvement in party politics. These local residents' movements have been quite successful in drawing the attention of local governments and, eventually, the attention of the national government as well.

The Mass Media. An outstanding feature of Japanese politics is the extremely large role of the mass media, especially newspapers, since the Japanese are avid readers and consumers of news in all forms. There are two national television networks and four or five commercial ones covering Japan. Weekly and monthly magazines number in the hundreds and are available everywhere. Newspapers, however, loom largest as purveyors of news and shapers of public opinion. There are three national dailies with upwards of 5 million in circulation, two others only slightly smaller, four regional newspapers of around 1 million each, and many smaller publications. Almost without exception, all these papers maintain high standards of detailed and accurate reporting on both national and international news. The Japanese are probably better served by the press in terms of news reporting than any other major nation, and collectively the newspapers exert an influence on public opinion and through it on politics that is possibly unmatched elsewhere in the world.

Most of the newspapers pride themselves on being politically neutral. They sit in judgment on politics, as it were, and through their huge circulations help determine the public response. Much of Japanese politics, especially what goes on under public scrutiny in the Diet, is determined by fears or hopes regarding the way it will be reported by the press and, thus, will affect popular attitudes and future votes. Newspapers are still influenced by their formative years, when they saw themselves as critics of an all-powerful government. This makes them tend to be especially critical of any group in political power. On the whole, this is a salutary situation, though at times criticism of the government has been carried to extremes, unduly arousing political passions.

One unusual aspect of the Japanese mass media is the so-called *press club*. A press club is a group of reporters from the various papers, wire services, magazines, and networks which concentrates on one particular branch of government, political party, or leading politician. Press clubs develop a special privileged relationship with their specific institution or person, which results in a far more detailed knowledge of what is going on politically than most journalists in other countries can obtain. At the same time, the press clubs also develop a sort of symbiotic relationship with their subject. The latter provides them with news, but they in turn serve as mouthpieces for their subject's views. This situation induces the members of the press clubs to hang back from investigative reporting or exposés that would damage this relationship and result in cutting off their source of information. So the press club system has its weaknesses as well as its strengths.

On the whole, however, the Japanese mass media and especially the newspapers provide the public with more copious and more accurate news than do the mass media of other countries, and they play a more important role as critics of government and shapers of public opinion. Together with the vigorous direct participation in politics of pressure groups and local residents' movements, they provide Japanese politics with ample feedback, which combines with the whole electoral process to produce a successful self-steering system.

THE STAKES OF POLITICS

If one looks back over the vast political, economic, and social changes the Japanese have been through during the past 150 years, one can see that much is at stake in the way the political process works in Japan. This is no unchanging society, but one that has been in almost constant ferment for the last four or five generations. Only in recent years have there been signs that some stability has been reached for the first time since the middle of the nineteenth century, when pressures from the outside world set Japan off in rapid motion.

The Political System. Between 1853 and the end of World War II the key question was how Japan was to be governed, and for several years after the war this question still remained uppermost in Japanese minds. Both the Japanese people and the American occupation authorities were determined that the virtual dictatorship of the military during the war years should be ended, but there was a wide divergence of opinion between those Japanese who felt that only a slight modification of the parliamentary system of the 1920s would be adequate and those who wanted to see a fully communist or socialist system in which the proletariat clearly ruled.

People divided into conservative and progressive camps. The very terminology showed the degree of hostility and suspicion that lay between them. The progressives feared that the conservatives were trying to turn the clocks back to the militarism and suppression of individual freedoms of the prewar system. The conservatives felt the progressives to be impractical zealots who would wreck Japan economically and sacrifice its national character.

In this atmosphere almost any policy dispute might blow up to crisis proportions. Such was the case in the somewhat theoretical disagreement over whether the emperor or the people possessed sovereignty and the rather technical problem of the degree to which the central government should exercise control over the police and education. The recentralization of some police controls during the 1950s was seen as a step toward the recreation of a police state and was met with frenzied opposition. The appointment, rather than election, of school boards and the institution of teacher rating systems and courses on ethics were seen as preparations for the use of education to indoctrinate the people, as before the war. The political powers of organized labor were also matters of bitter contention. The use of the general strike was outlawed as running the risk of chaos and revolution, and the right of government workers to strike was also denied. One of the most fiercely contested issues was whether Japan, in view of Article IX of the constitution, had the right to maintain the Self-Defense Forces.

As the postwar system gradually stabilized and people became accustomed to it, many of these issues either disappeared or dwindled in significance. But some still remain very much alive. A running battle continues between the Japan Teachers Union and the Ministry of Education over a wide variety of matters concerning the organization of schools and the textbooks and other contents of education. The right of government workers to strike is hotly maintained by their unions and the parties that back them, and strikes of this sort do in fact occur. Most of the opposition parties continue to disapprove officially of the Self-Defense Forces, though public opinion has gradually swung to their support at their present, very modest levels of strength, and the issue, therefore, is no longer a major one.

On the whole, the Japanese people seem content with the basic nature of their postwar political system as well as the social and economic systems that lie behind it. Opinion polls reveal that 90 percent of them consider themselves to be middle class; in fact, 60 percent describe themselves as the middle of the middle class. They like their egalitarian system in which good education is fully available to everyone and produces an educational meritocracy that runs the nation. They constantly complain, however, of the pressures of educational competition and the "examination hell" that this system imposes on their children. Few would want or can even imagine any political setup other than their present electoral and parliamentary system. Except for tiny fringes at the extreme left and right, there is complete support for and great pride in the Peace Constitution and a strong determination not to change it in any way, however slight, for fear of opening the door to more significant changes.

This does not mean that there is not disenchantment with the way in which the political system sometimes operates. The supporters of the opposition parties feel that there is something unfair about a situation in which their parties seem destined to remain out of power. Throughout society there is a feeling that politics is dirty and politicians corrupt. Too much in politics seems to depend on the lavish use of money, and clearly politicians are breaking the spirit—if not the letter—of the law in their free use of money and large-scale electoral campaigns disguised as educational and cultural activities. Occasionally the whole nation is rocked by a scandal, when some particularly large or blatant use of money in elections or other political dealings comes to light or is suspected to exist. Complex bureaucracies often seem insensitive to personal and local needs, although there is little reason to think that bureaucrats are dishonest or corrupt, in contrast to conditions in many countries. Thus, there is a large pot of political issues that is constantly boiling away, raising incessant political controversies, but in recent years none of these issues has really concerned the basic make-up of the Japanese political system. In fact, the Japanese political system at present seems to be one of the most stable and secure in the whole world.

Foreign Relations. Ever since 1853, Japan's relationship with the outside world has been the chief force behind the rapid change in political, economic, and social conditions, and so, quite naturally, foreign relations have frequently been the major area of political controversy. This was true in the great transformation of 1868 and during the tremendous convulsions surrounding World War II and is still the case today. Since the war, divisions over foreign policy have been more basic and persistent than controversies over the political system itself.

The conservatives, though irritated by their having to accept aspects of the American reforms and by MacArthur's having drafted their postwar constitution, have felt throughout that a close relationship with the United States was necessary for both economic and security reasons. The progressives have feared that this association would endanger Japan by embroiling it in the Cold War and in what they felt was the inevitably aggressive and imperialistic foreign policy of the world's largest capitalist country. They have also felt that this association with "American imperialism" would strengthen domestic "monopoly capitalism," thus precluding Japan from the possibility of building a socialist system. The progressives preferred a policy for Japan of unarmed neutrality or, in the case of the extreme left, of open alignment with the Communist powers.

Since the American bases and military personnel in Japan and the Mutual Security Treaty offered tangible targets of attack, and since the natural distaste for the presence of foreign forces on Japanese soil easily stirred nationalistic feelings, the opposition forces found these issues the easiest to exploit in their battles with the conservatives. As a result, the alignment with the United States was at the heart of the controversy between the left and right in Japan throughout the 1950s and 1960s. Every opposition party condemned the security treaty and advocated the withdrawal of American troops from Japan, though with varying degrees of vehemence and with different timetables in mind. Public opinion surveys also showed a preponderance of sentiment for this side. The conservative government, however, held staunchly to the American alignment as absolutely necessary for Japan.

Beneath this violent conflict over relations with the United States, however, there existed a broad, but largely unconscious, consensus over foreign policy. Even the conservatives wished to limit Japan's involvement in international controversies as far as possible and concentrate instead on establishing friendly relations with all countries, Communist or non-Communist alike, and on developing Japanese trade with all parts of the world in this way. Japan was extremely successful in this policy. It made reparations settlements with its neighbors in Southeast Asia, which laid the groundwork for later great export markets in these countries. It became a major trading partner for both the Soviet Union and China—in fact, China's largest trading partner. At the same time, of course, the bulk of its trade remained with the Western nations and the countries economically associated with them.

Japan's policy of maintaining a low profile in world politics and concentrating on the development of its own trade had widespread support at home, but brought it some criticism from abroad. The United States complained at times of Japan's lukewarm cooperation and the "free ride" it was taking at the expense of American defense efforts. De Gaulle once contemptuously called the Japanese prime minister a "transistor salesman." Later, when the Japanese economy had grown powerful, the Japanese were accused of being merely "economic animals." The developing nations, especially those of Southeast Asia, became bitter about Japan's failure to provide them with more aid, whereas the industrial nations of the West, including the United States, became incensed over the imbalance of trade in Japan's favor and the flood of Japanese industrial goods that threatened parts of their own economies. Still, Japan's postwar foreign policy did prove eminently successful in removing that nation from the line of fire in most international controversies, allowing it to keep its own military expenditures to a minimum, and laying the basis for its extraordinary growth to economic affluence and its present position as the third largest economic power in the world.

Even the one area of formerly bitter debate in Japan, foreign policy, has shrunk in importance in recent years. There are many reasons why this has happened, but perhaps the most fundamental has been the rift between the Soviet Union and China, which became progressively more evident and irreversible after 1960. Fearful and resentful of each other, these two important neighbors of Japan began to seek better relations with both the United States and Japan and to give tacit approval to the Japanese-American military alliance, thus undermining the arguments of the opposition parties.

Clearly, the intimate connection with the United States had not led to the dire results formerly predicted by the left. The Cold War faded, and a détente developed in American relations with both the Soviet Union and China. Nixon's visit to China in 1972 made the Japanese feel free to go a step beyond the United States in establishing full diplomatic relations with China more than six years before the United States did so and to sign a full peace treaty with China in 1978. The United States also promised in 1969 to give back political control over Okinawa, Japan's forty-seventh prefecture, and did return the islands in 1972, before Japanese resentments over this lost province reached the boiling point. Meanwhile the American military presence in Japan was gradually declining in size and visibility. The Vietnam War, which had revolted most Japanese and given credence to assertions that the United States was an inevitably imperialistic nation, also died away gradually in the early 1970s.

For all these reasons, the problem of the American alliance slowly faded as a political issue in Japan. The public came to accept it, not with enthusiasm, but as a matter of course. Some of the opposition parties formally shifted to a less hostile stand on the security treaty, and none saw fit to make it a major issue in the elections for the lower and upper houses in 1976 and later. In its place, foreign economic relations arose as the major foreign problems, but on these, unlike the issue of the American connection, no clear-cut political divisions between left and right have emerged.

Economic and Social Issues. Since the opposition parties in Japan stem largely from Marxist origins, one might assume that fundamental economic issues would lie at the heart of political controversy in Japan, but this has not been the case. In the early years after the war some labor unions attempted to get control of industry, and some Communist and Socialist adherents appeared committed to trying to establish a socialist economy, but these conditions did not last long. At first the problems of mere economic survival overshadowed everything else, and, in any case, control by the American occupation precluded the possibility of a serious experiment with a socialist economy. Later, the land reform program and economic recovery through private industry guided by government planning proved so successful that, unlike the situation in many other countries, little push developed in Japan for government ownership of industry or the collectivization of agriculture.

Almost all Japanese felt that the first task was to restore the economy and help it to grow as quickly as possible. Here was another area of very broad consensus, and it was difficult to fault the general strategy of the government once economic recovery began to pick up speed after 1950. Even the parties of the left gradually settled into tacit acceptance of the existing economic system and came to concentrate on attempting to correct its imperfections rather than on overturning it. They tried to do this through advocating a more equitable division of the economic rewards of the system, strengthening competition through supporting fair trade legislation, and championing small business against big business. In other words, the parties of the left seemed more intent on making the free enterprise system work well than on creating a truly socialist alternative.

Unlike the sharply drawn battle lines over foreign policy that existed in the early postwar years, political contests over economic and social matters have usually seemed more like myriad small skirmishes in a guerrilla war. While accepting the conservative policy of concentrating on expanding the economic pie as a whole, the opposition parties fought constantly for a more equal division of its slices. While approving in general of the postwar political and social system, the progressives found countless issues on which to attack the government's disregard of the needs or rights of some particular group. The opposition parties saw themselves in particular as the defenders of the many human rights guaranteed by the constitution. These, of course, are so sweeping as to raise many difficult problems of interpretation and implementation. There is plenty of room for disagreement, and political conflict of this sort continues unabated.

The conservatives themselves, however, have become increasingly committed to full support of constitutional rights, and during most of the 1950s and 1960s economic growth was so rapid that the individual slices of the economic pie automatically grew at a very satisfactory rate. In time, Japanese personal incomes in monetary terms rose to the levels of Western Europe and the United States and were more equitably divided between rich and poor in Japan than in most Western lands. Thus, no fundamental clash ever developed over the basic economic issues, though extraordinarily high prices in Japan, because of the scarcity of space and resources, made the Japanese in fact less affluent than the monetary figures would suggest.

The late 1960s and the 1970s, however, saw the emergence of a new set of economic and social problems. Rapid economic growth in Japan's limited terrain was beginning to cause serious overcrowding and pollution, especially in metropolitan areas, and a dangerous degradation of the natural environment. Housing was scarce and terribly crowded in cities. Many people were forced to commute long distances to work each day—often between one and two hours each way. Urban streets were glutted with traffic, and commuter train lines and subways, though numerous and excellent, were crowded beyond capacity. Air and water pollution became serious hazards to health and produced in some cases spectacularly injurious ailments, such as the famous Minamata disease from mercury poisoning, which was caused by eating contaminated fish. Continued rapid economic growth that worsened these conditions was seen as lowering the quality of life rather than enhancing it.

The Japanese have developed a concept broader than pollution, which they called *kōgai,* or "public nuisance." *Kōgai* includes not just the ordinary types of air and water pollution, but also "sound pollution" from airports, highways, and railways, undue crowding of every sort, and even the obstruction of the individual's access to sunshine, which figures importantly in Japan in wintertime heating and in year-round drying of laundry. The Japanese have also proved very sensitive to the dangers of nuclear radiation, and constant battles rage over the locating of nuclear power plants, which are important for an energy-poor country.

Long concentration on economic growth at the expense of other matters also produced social foundations woefully inadequate for the ponderous economic machine that they now bear. Public services, such as sewage systems, lagged far behind those of other modern industrial societies, as did the social security system. This latter weakness was all the more serious because of a changing age structure in the Japanese population. Birth control, which had swept Japan since the war, had made the two-child family typical and had brought population growth down to about 1 percent per year, with zero growth being a predictable result before long. Simultaneously, life expectancy in Japan had risen rapidly, until it surpassed that of Sweden as the highest in the world. All this meant a rapidly aging population and a new problem of caring for the aged, since crowded urban living conditions were ruling out the traditional method of accommodating the elderly as live-in grandparents.

Japan in the 1970s thus faced a whole new series of economic and social issues, such as pollution controls, compensation for those injured by pollution, limitations on factory and road construction that were seen as undesirable by the local community, increased retirement and social security benefits, and free medical care, especially for the aged. As we have already noted, many of these issues were brought to public attention largely by local citizens' movements and local governments, which in the metropolitan areas were commonly in the hands of the progressive parties by the late 1960s. The courts also played a key role in several landmark decisions in the early 1970s, which established that polluters must pay for the damage they cause.

These various issues could well have produced a new fundamental split between the opposition parties, representing the urban population, and the LDP, representing the interests of big business and rural people, who were less concerned by *kōgai* issues. Both the LDP and the bureaucracy, however, proved sensitive to these problems—the LDP, no doubt, because of the votes that were at stake. They co-opted the issues at the national level and together with the opposition parties began working vigorously on their solution. Japan quickly established and enforced stringent limitations on the emission of pollutants and the first system in the world for making those who produced pollution compensate those who suffered from it. Social security, retirement benefits, and free medical care, especially for the elderly, have also been rapidly expanded in recent years.

The oil crisis growing out of the Arab-Israeli War in the autumn of 1973 and the resultant quadrupling of oil prices was a particularly severe shock to Japan, which depends for close to three-quarters of its total energy resources on imported oil, most of it from the Persian Gulf. The growth of the economy in real terms tumbled in a single year from 11 percent to less than zero and then recovered to only around 6 percent. No major country suffered a worse economic blow, and it is a measure of Japan's stability that it withstood it without any serious political or social tremors. In fact, in some ways the oil shock was a blessing in disguise, since it came just at a time when the country was considering a shift from high growth policies to a greater emphasis on social services and the quality of life. The enforced economic slowdown made this shift more natural and less controversial. The complete lack of panic in Japan and easy accommodation to the second oil shock of rising prices and shortages in 1978 and 1979 show that resources-poor Japan has prepared itself better to deal with such energy problems than have the United States and some other industrial countries.

Myriad specific problems remain, however. Most of the decisions will require tradeoffs between conflicting interests and must be made through budgetary decisions that involve controversies among the various branches of the bureaucracy and also among the many different pressure groups. As in most advanced democratic countries, budgetary changes tend to be slow, complex, and sharply contested. Here lies a vast area of continuing political controversy, but there is no broad chasm in Japanese politics over these problems, nor do they threaten the basic stability of the political system.

UNRESOLVED PROBLEMS

Japanese government and society present on the whole a picture of great efficiency and stability that is hard to match elsewhere. The country does, of course, face a great number of problems, but the Japanese appear to be quite capable of handling them in a satisfactory manner. They need to do a great deal to improve the social underpinnings of their tremendously efficient economy. High land prices, intolerable crowding, and countless other urban problems pose vast difficulties. But there is no reason to fear that the Japanese will not tackle these with reasonable effectiveness within the severe constraints imposed on them by geography. Viewed in purely domestic terms, few countries seem to be in as sound shape as Japan. But when one looks abroad, the situation is by no means as reassuring.

The country is extremely vulnerable to unfavorable external conditions. It must have a huge flow of trade in and out of the islands simply to live. For this commerce there must be general world peace and a strong international trading system, both of which depend less on the Japanese themselves than on the actions of other nations. Japan could not conceivably protect by military means the foreign sources of food, energy, and raw materials on which it depends, the markets that must pay for these imports, or even the life lines of its world trade. To try to develop military power of a sort that could defend even a small proportion of these vital economic interests would probably do much more harm than good, for this would frighten Japan's trading partners, making them more hostile, and it would put a heavy burden on the Japanese economy and an intolerable strain on internal political consensus.

Japan cannot even defend itself in a nuclear age. The people, quite wisely, are determined not to build a nuclear force themselves. In part, this is because of their unique experience with nuclear weapons. On August 6, 1945, when the Japanese government was known to be trying to find a way to surrender, a single American atomic bomb wiped out the whole city of Hiroshima. Whether or not this bombing was justified in order to convince die-hard Japanese militarists that the war was indeed lost, there was certainly no justification for the dropping three days later of a second bomb, which destroyed the city of Nagasaki.

Japanese attitudes, however, are not based merely on their historical memories. Japan is so small and crowded that it could not survive a first attack by nuclear weapons. To have any security, it must rely through the security treaty on the American nuclear umbrella—a position the people have slowly and reluctantly come to accept—and beyond that on the maintenance of world peace by those who possess nuclear weapons. How best Japan itself can contribute to the maintenance of this world peace is a question that the Japanese have not yet answered fully, but it will undoubtedly be a problem of growing importance to them in the future.

The maintenance of a healthy and growing world trading system is a matter of equal concern, because without it the whole world will no doubt stagnate and Japan will eventually be plunged into catastrophe. This is a problem that presses more immediately on Japan, because economically it is the third largest superpower and because its rate of economic growth—more rapid than that of the other great industrial nations—and its somewhat distinctive economic organization have made it appear, at least to others, as creating major disturbances in the world economic system. Japan's large balance-of-trade surplus, especially with the United States, and its inundation of foreign markets with advanced industrial goods, such as motorcycles, electronic equipment, automobiles, and steel, have raised great anxieties abroad, again particularly in the United States.

For some years now, such economic problems have recurrently risen to crisis proportions, and each crisis has become progressively more severe as the Japanese economy grew in relative size. The result normally has been strong political repercussions, including demands for retaliatory protectionist trade policies. If this cyclical pattern is allowed to continue and grow worse, the outcome may well be just such restrictionist measures. These in turn could easily set off a trade war and a downward spiral of international trade, ultimately leading to disastrous results for everyone. The stagnant world trade of the 1920s and the economic collapse at the end of that decade, which led eventually to worldwide tragedy, are sobering reminders of the dangers of such a course.

These economic problems that revolve around Japan are the product of Japanese successes more than failures. They derive in part from a very efficient economic system in which mutual trust and close coordination between government and business permit a smooth transformation from inefficient, declining industries to strong, growing ones. They are also based on some fundamental Japanese characteristics: a strong work ethic, possibly the highest educational levels in the world, deeply entrenched habits of saving and reinvesting, and superb skills at organization and cooperation. The Japanese economy has undoubtedly become one of the most efficient in the whole world.

Another reason for the recurrent frictions between Japan and its trading partners is that the Japanese economy is geared somewhat differently from those of the other advanced industrialized nations. Japanese business executives are less concerned with the profits that their companies make than with their size, growth, and market share. Their own salaries are less affected by profits than in the West, and they derive more of their rewards in psychological terms from the importance of their posts. In other words, they are more like bureaucrats. In addition, they finance their businesses through bank loans at fixed interest rates more often than through equity capital. They also regard their employees as being permanent members of the company who should never be fired, if that is at all possible. For all these reasons they are less concerned with quarterly profits (which in the West are the way to attract capital) and are more interested in the maintenance of or increase in rates of production.

All this gives the Japanese entrepreneur a much longer time horizon in planning for expansion and also strong incentives not to cut down on production, even during periods of recession. As a result, when a recession brings reduced production in the West in order to maintain profits, the Japanese economy, despite a slackening of domestic demand, tries to continue at full blast, channeling an even greater proportion of its product abroad and thus compounding the problems there. In the past, times of crisis in international trade have usually been ameliorated by Japan's eventually adopting so-called *voluntary controls* on certain exports, but only after political damage had been done and anxieties and ill will had been raised on both sides. In the future a system will be needed to restrict these economic crises before they come to the political boiling point.

Trade with the other industrialized nations, thus, is an area of many extremely difficult problems that demand immediate attention. But so also is the field of economic relations with the so-called developing nations. Here are to be found some of the greatest problems for the future of the whole world. The developing nations and particularly Japan's neighbors in Southeast Asia feel, with considerable bitterness, that Japan has been stingy in its aid to them and often unfair in its economic dealings. These relations with the developing world demand far greater attention by the Japanese people and more decisive action, not only for the sake of the developing nations themselves, but equally for the future of Japan and the stability of the world.

Unfortunately, the Japanese do not seem as well prepared to work on their problems of foreign economic relations as on domestic problems. Their long isolation and sense of being unique and separate from the outside world may make them somewhat insensitive to the viewpoints of others. Their language—which is sharply different from those of all the countries of importance to them, with the single exception of Korea—stands as a massive barrier to easy communication with others. A century and a quarter of scrambling madly to catch up to a technologically more advanced Occident and the realization of their present complete dependence on world trade make them feel that they must have a thick economic cushion and that other countries should realize this. Indeed, the terms of trade in the future are sure to turn against them in a world of limited agricultural land and natural resources, of which they themselves possess so little.

So the Japanese will continue to face a multitude

of domestic problems that require constant political attention and some much more crucial and difficult decisions on foreign policy. Obviously, they will have to maintain an efficient system for making policy decisions. They also will need strong, farseeing leadership. In particular, they will have to develop and display a level of diplomacy and leadership in world affairs that has been notably lacking in the past.

KEY TERMS AND CONCEPTS

cultural homogeneity
burakumin
Manchurian Incident
occupation
uji
hierarchy
shōgun
samurai
daimyō
alternate attendance
Meiji Restoration
Meiji Constitution
genrō
Diet
Supreme Commander for the Allied Powers (SCAP)
House of Councilors
Peace Constitution
zaibatsu
"reverse course"
Self-Defense Forces (SDF)
Mutual Security Treaty
progressives
middle-size electoral district system
interpellation
Ministry of International Trade and Industry (MITI)
administrative vice minister
prefectures
local autonomy
Autonomy Ministry
jiban
kōenkai
Liberal Democratic Party (LDP)
Communist Party (JCP)
Socialist Party (JSP)
Democratic Socialist Party (DSP)
Kōmeitō
Sōka Gakkai
New Liberal Club
Sōhyō
Dōmei
secretary general
Executive Council
factions
Policy Affairs Research Committee (PARC)
pressure groups
zaikai
demonstrations
citizens' movements
local residents' movements
press clubs
kōgai
voluntary controls

ADDITIONAL READINGS

Austin, L., ed. *Japan: The Paradox of Progress.* New Haven: Yale University Press, 1976.
Baerwald, H. *Japan's Parliament.* New York: Cambridge University Press, 1974.
Burks, A. W. *The Government of Japan.* New York: Crowell, 1972. PB
Campbell, J. *Contemporary Japanese Budget Policies.* Berkeley and Los Angeles: University of California Press, 1977.
Curtis, G. *Election Campaigning Japanese Style.* New York: Columbia University Press, 1971.
Destler, Sato, Clapp, and Fukui. *Managing an Alliance: The Politics of U.S.-Japan Relations.* Washington, D.C.: Brookings Institution, 1976. PB
Emmerson, J. K. *Arms, Yen and Power: The Japanese Dilemma.* New York: Dunellen, 1971.

Fukui, H. *Party in Power: The Japanese Liberal-Democrats and Policy Making.* Berkeley and Los Angeles: University of California Press, 1970.

Ike, N. *Japanese Politics: Patron Client Democracy.* New York: Knopf, 1972. PB

———. *A Theory of Japanese Democracy.* Boulder, Colorado: Westview Press, 1978.

Kawai, K. *Japan's American Interlude.* Chicago: University of Chicago Press, 1960.

Langdon, F. *Politics in Japan.* Boston: Little, Brown, 1967. PB

McNelly, T. *Politics and Government in Japan.* Boston: Houghton Mifflin, 1972. PB

Maruyama, M. *Thought and Behaviour in Modern Japanese Politics.* London and New York: Oxford University Press, 1969. PB

Packard, G. *Protest in Tokyo: The Security Treaty Crisis of 1960.* Princeton: Princeton University Press, 1966.

Patrick, H., and H. Rosovsky, eds. *Asia's New Giant: How the Japanese Economy Works.* Washington, D.C.: Brookings Institution, 1976. PB

Pempel, T. J., ed. *Policymaking in Contemporary Japan.* Ithaca, N.Y.: Cornell University Press, 1977.

Reischauer, E. O. *Japan: The Story of a Nation.* New York: Knopf, 1974. PB

———. *The Japanese.* Cambridge: Harvard University Press, 1977. PB

Richardson, B. *The Political Culture of Japan.* Berkeley and Los Angeles: University of California Press, 1974.

Scalapino, R., ed. *The Foreign Policy of Modern Japan.* Berkeley and Los Angeles: University of California Press, 1977. PB

Steiner, K. *Local Government in Japan.* Palo Alto, Calif.: Stanford University Press, 1965.

Stockwin, J. A. A. *Japan: Divided Politics in a Growth Economy.* New York: Norton, 1975.

Thayer, N. *How the Conservatives Rule Japan.* Princeton: Princeton University Press, 1968.

Tsuneishi, W. M. *Japanese Political Style.* New York: Harper & Row, 1966. PB

Tsurutani, T. *Political Change in Japan.* New York: McKay, 1977.

Vogel, E. *Japan as No. 1: Lessons for America.* Cambridge: Harvard University Press, 1979. PB

Vogel, E., ed. *Modern Japanese Organization and Decision-Making.* Berkeley and Los Angeles: University of California Press, 1975. PB

Ward, R. E. *Japan's Political System.* Englewood Cliffs, N.J.: Prentice-Hall, 1978. PB

———, ed. *Political Development in Modern Japan.* Princeton: Princeton University Press, 1978.

Watanuki, J. *Politics in Postwar Japanese Society.* Tokyo: Tokyo University Press, 1977.

PB = *available in paperback*

XVI

The Chinese People's Republic

ROY HOFHEINZ, JR.

China presents the greatest challenge to any comparative analysis of politics and government. The sheer weight of its population makes China the largest of the world's nations. It is estimated at nearly one billion—more than all of Europe and almost a quarter of all humankind. One of China's provinces, Szechwan in the rich upper valley of the Yangtze River, is roughly the size of Britain, France, or Germany. China is more than a nation among nations: it is at one time a continent, a state, and an idea.

THE NATURE AND BACKGROUND OF CHINESE POLITICS: A CONTINUITY OF IMAGE AND ARENA

The political idea of China is older than the idea of a unified Europe. Other ancient kingdoms—such as those of Egypt, Persia, Rome, and India—spawned at the beginning of the Iron Age and disappeared within a few centuries; but the Chinese successfully maintained their centralized government through many periods of disorder for more than two millennia. Though the structure of the government, its relationship to the population, and to some extent its informing ideology have changed from dynasty to dynasty, the concept of China as an indivisible political-cultural unit remains far more alive than the often expressed idea of a reunified Europe.

As vast as China's size have been its sufferings since the mid-nineteenth century. Two gigantic cataclysms, the Taiping Rebellion (1850–64) and the Anti-Japanese War and Civil War (1937–49), were perhaps the most murderous conflicts in human history. Each of these wars snuffed out the lives of more people than are living today in such small states as Holland, Nigeria, or Vietnam. Whereas the Russian, French, and American revolutions built up over a period of years to culminate in a brief period of violence that was soon terminated by a return to normalcy, the Chinese chaos—in the form of banditry, "warlordism," social degeneration, and administrative disintegration—lasted for decades. It is for good reason that the Chinese Communists speak not of a Chinese "revolution," but of several phases of China's "revolutionary civil wars," which ended only with the establishment of the People's Republic of China on October 1, 1949. The startling recurrence of civil disorders during the Great Proletarian Cultural Revolution of 1966–67, though only the tiniest of ripples in comparison with the great tidal waves of the past, reminds us of the history of China's recent political turmoil.

In addition to the size, longevity, and recent instability of China's political system, analysts must face a frustrating "inscrutability gap" in dealing with this vast nation. The distance between Chinese culture and language and our own has led many to assume incorrectly that the "wily Orientals" are somehow unfathomable—that they "always do things upside down," in the words of missionary W. Dyer Ball. The obvious differences between East and West make it easy to jump to misleading conclusions about the Chinese, based often on wrong or oversimplified views of our own Western political system. This heritage of ignorance and error is easily strengthened by very real gaps in our knowledge about China, caused in part by China's recent disorder, which make collection of data difficult, and in part by the lack of a tradition of making information public in China. It is fair to say that we know far less of China, in those realms of knowledge useful to political analysis, than we do of any other of the world's major nations. This inscrutability should not lead us to think that politics is absent from the Chinese scene or that the government in China fails to perform functions similar to those of governments in America, Europe, or the Soviet Union.

"Traditional" and "Modern" Politics. In recent years, with the emergence into the world political system of so many new nations, it has become fashionable to speak of the difference between "traditional" and "modern" political systems. *Modern* (or *developed*) *systems* have elections, parliaments, codified laws, political parties, rationalized public administrations, and centralized, integrated national governments. Their citizens are politically conscious, believe in their ability to affect their fates through political action, and are capable of being mobilized for politically relevant action on short notice. By contrast, *traditional systems* lack these elements of modern politics. Monarchs are absolute; governors are patrimonial; officials are privately corrupt; the populace is sharply stratified between literate city dwellers and illiterate peasants; and citizens are considered mere subjects. Certainly there is a great deal of truth and usefulness to these two opposed ideal types of political systems.[1] But just as modern British parliamentary democracy depends in large degree on the deference to royal authority and the system of social class that we know to be traditional in England, the elements of tradition in non-Western countries such as China may play a critical role in shaping modern institutions.

China is no exception to this pattern of the *"modernity of tradition."* Indeed, for many centuries after the "discovery" of China (ca. 1272) by the Italian explorer Marco Polo (1254?–1324?), the Chinese were considered to be more advanced and progressive in political matters than the Europeans. As late as the middle of the nineteenth century, when the renowned British reformer Sir Charles Trevelyan was searching for a model on which to reform the British civil service, he turned to China, which since the eighth century had possessed a system of official *entrance examinations* by which entrants to the career of mandarin were recruited. (The *mandarins* were the bureaucratic administrators of the empire.) Europeans could not fail to marvel at the prolonged unity of the Chinese state, at the extensive network of official

[1]The father of much political development theory of this type is the German sociologist Max Weber.

bureaucracy, at the relative openness of competition for public office, which contrasted so sharply with eighteenth-century European practice. In our own day we can still look back to traditional China for examples of attitudes and practices that seem modern to us. The implicit faith in the value of education, the distrust of hereditary privilege, the belief that officials should be aware of the moral and environmental impact of their decisions—all these were part of the broad tradition of Confucian statecraft.

The long heritage of Chinese statecraft did not, however, originate with *Confucius* (551–479 B.C.). Indeed, the founder of Confucianism taught that he was merely rediscovering and extending the "way" *(tao)* of emperors of ancient times whose lineage myths supposedly extended forty-five thousand years into the past. Likewise, the tradition that bears his name includes many philosophical and practical elements unfamiliar or alien to Confucius, a moralist and itinerant adviser to the kings of a divided China. Whereas Confucius stressed the importance of proper ethical and social behavior according to one's station in life, his follower *Mencius* (373–288 B.C.) made emperors responsible for the well-being of their subjects and gave those subjects the implicit right to overthrow their ruler when he failed to provide for their livelihood. In turn, other ancient Chinese political theorists offered alternatives to the Confucian-Mencian notions of social and political order. The *Legalist (fa-chia) school* of the third century B.C. emphasized the importance of law and administrative fiat in assuring order; and the *Taoist philosophers* doubted that any political system could function without the existence of innate, natural, unconscious harmonies among people.

The variety of Chinese political thought is as great as that in the West, and so, too, is the complexity of Chinese political practice during the historical era. But in several important respects there is a continuity in the Chinese political tradition that dates from shortly after the unification of China in 221 B.C. by the great First Emperor of the Ch'in dynasty, Shih-huang-ti. Three important elements define this core of the Chinese political tradition.

First, there is the consciousness of the inseparability of political and social, economic, or moral matters. At the heart of Confucius's concept of proper behavior is the notion of *social relationships (lun),* which are all pictured as forming a coherent single unit. Thus the relationship between ruler and subject is analogous to that between neighbor and neighbor, brother and brother, husband and wife, and especially parent and child. Rulers are most effective when they rule not by brute power, but by the example of their propriety in preserving relationships. The ideal emperor is the most perfectly filial son: a great Manchu emperor, Ch'ien-lung, honored his "sacred mother" with innumerable poems, elaborate palaces, and extravagant tours of China's scenic southern wonders, but never once visited the scene of fourteen disastrous Yangtze floods.[2] Far from discrediting him, Ch'ien-lung's piety toward his ancestor gave him leverage over those bureaucrats who were in charge of flood control and other matters. He consciously used his exemplary behavior in human relationships as proof of his legitimacy as ruler of the Chinese state.

In accordance with this notion of the unity of all human relationships, the Chinese tradition assumed the *unity of public and private realms.* It made no distinction between them, and thus in principle it permitted the government to intervene at will in all matters, somewhat similar to the overlapping powers of church and secular government in medieval Europe. A vast portion of the codified laws of the Chinese state pertained not to public concerns, but to what we would regard today as private matters: the regulation of behavior toward parents or of proper clothing and coiffure: the Manchu dynasty (1644–1911), for example, ruled that all subjects would shave their foreheads and

[2]Harold L. Kahn, *Monarchy in the Emperor's Eyes: Image and Reality in the Ch'ien-Lung Reign* (Cambridge: Harvard University Press, 1971).

wear their hair long and plaited into a queue. Likewise, the judicial system itself functioned in civil matters less as a system of adversary proceedings than as one of role-patterned mediation. The best judges were those who understood the importance not of principle, but of compromise. In criminal cases punishments fell often as much on the innocent as on the guilty, as judges strove to teach all subjects to handle their conflicts without resort to the law.

Whereas the imperceptible merging of private and public matters appears to grant great powers to the emperors and officialdom, in fact the absolute despotism of Chinese rulers often conflicted directly with the needs of society. If the emperor was the parent of society, he had to provide for society's basic needs. His failures, as measured by the extent of hunger or disorder in the realm, diminished his virtue in the eyes of his subjects. Chinese political philosophy, from the time of Mencius onward, provided an escape valve for revolutionary sentiment: the theory that emperors enjoy their *divine mandate (t'ien-ming)* as long as they continue to rule a peaceful and well-fed realm. Unlike Western absolute despots, Chinese emperors were not protected from the turmoils of their society by an airtight theory. Loyalty to the state was compatible with resisting—and overthrowing—grossly unsuccessful emperors. The permanence of the Chinese state, thus, included cycle after cycle of dynastic rise and fall. When modern visitors to China remark on the extent of government interference in private lives, on the pervasiveness of organization in China, on the lack of dividing lines between politics and everything else, they are inadvertently describing the constant features of the Chinese political structure over the ages.

Officialism and Officials: The Scholar-Bureaucrats. The second enduring characteristic of the Chinese tradition was *officialism.* The legalist school, which stood behind the reforms of the First Emperor, insisted that he reward his loyal followers not by giving them land, as had been the practice, but by assuring them territories to rule in his name. Thus, the Chinese state from its earliest times embodied restraints against the development of feudalism that helped erode and dissolve the Roman Empire. By turning potential feudatories into the salaried minions of a central government, the Ch'in emperor established the world's longest-lasting permanent bureaucracy.

To be sure, the Confucian bureaucrat was a far cry from Max Weber's idealized "legal-rational" officeholder. The weakness of administrative law subjected him to the arbitrary whim of emperors. (The Ch'ien-lung type of emperor with a flip of his vermilion-colored brush could condemn hundreds of lifelong public servants to death because they had made mistakes in penmanship.) The ideal of all-round moral and ethical perfection for the scholar-bureaucrat limited his ability to master specialized subjects. Confucian stress on personal relationships, and on sincerity of character rather than performance, made corruption and personal indulgence the rule rather than the exception. But, for all these faults, the Chinese bureaucracy was a remarkably long-lived and effective political machine.

Its effectiveness depended on a combination of several characteristics. Access into the civil service was rigorously controlled by a system of examinations established as early as the Sui dynasty (589–618 A.D.). While these examinations in later years tended to stress artistic and classical literary skills more than statecraft, they assured at least a minimum of education and literacy among the official class. Officialdom was divided into an extensive territorial hierarchy that reached down to the county *(hsien)* level, as well as into specialized ministries in the imperial capital. Rigorous "rules of avoidance" prevented officials from being assigned to their own home districts in order to limit the temptations of corruption; their meager salaries ($300 or so by the nineteenth century) could be supplemented by "honesty encouragement" fees that were hundreds of times larger in amount.

Imperial attacks on officialdom (in this, as in other matters, Chairman Mao Tse-tung was able to draw on a long tradition) were balanced against a long tradition of remonstrance and censorial criticism, which on occasion might reach as high as the imperial person himself. Chinese officials, in essence, represented not just the bureaucracy, but the entire elite of literate society, which considered itself an independent body of scholarly custodians of public ethics. This tradition—with its polarity between a professionalized, expert staff of clerks and a critical, ambitious, and somewhat independent pool of aspiring moral engineers—finds strong reflections in China's present-day handling of its official cadre class.

Practicality and Humanism. The third characteristic of the Chinese tradition is what we might call *humanism.* A society that stresses social relationships naturally avoids uncompromising absolutes. The transcendental religions of the Middle East and of South Asia, which encourage the denial of self and the realities of this world, are not found in the Chinese scene. Even when they employ supernatural concepts, as in the case of Taoism or Maitreyan Buddhism, Chinese religions are profoundly immanent and practical—on the human (and not the divine) scale.

In contrast with the absolute Christian concept of love, the Confucian ideal of *jen,* or benevolence, emphasizes the relativism of affection. The Chinese tradition of humanism assumes that human beings naturally care more for those with whom they are in *socially determined* contact. This tradition differs sharply from Western "individualism"—an expression that, when translated into Chinese, sounds overly personalistic and selfish. Although the orthodox tradition of Confucianism frowns on private coalitions of interest—since groups such as secret societies, merchant guilds, or religious sects may potentially threaten the bureaucratic state and the social order—the heterodox tradition of humanism positively encourages such coalitions. Indeed, for many modern Chinese it is the "little tradition" of humanism, as exemplified in the popular novels of bandit kingdoms or socio-religious bands, that demonstrates the powerful traditional Chinese drive to human solidarity. This characteristic of the folk culture, which in China is more democratic, egalitarian, and iconoclastic than the more forbidding orthodoxy of Confucianism, lies behind many of the striking features of modern Chinese politics.

THE DIMENSIONS OF A REVOLUTION

Of course, the present is not just a reflection of the past. There has been a revolution in China far more profound than any of the previous dynastic changes. Lost is the purity of the Chinese concept of a world order with Peking at its center. Though Lin Piao, Mao's erstwhile successor-designate, spoke in 1965 of Peking as the center of the "world revolution," the People's Republic has since joined the United Nations. No longer is the Chinese state content with less than 2 percent of the national product or staffed by fewer than thirty thousand cadres. Chinese subjects, though perhaps no more able to chart their own course than before, are not any more the illiterate "stupid people" despised by their gentry protectors. The "People's Middle Kingdom," to use John Fairbank's phrase, is a vastly different political system from that of the ancient empire. What are the dimensions of the political change that produced the present government of China?

The Impact of the West. To a considerable degree the political history of modern China can be described as a response to the West. Whereas other nations studied in this volume developed their national political systems without the direct interference of foreign powers, China's modern history is one of constant challenge by the European and American states. Despite the fierce independence of the Chinese and the strength of their political tradition, modern China still owes much to the outside world for its present system of government, as well as for the changes that brought it about.

The Western nations came to China unannounced and largely unwelcome. Appearing in the Pacific at about the same time as the discovery of America, European traders seeking spices and tea were soon followed by European navies protecting trade, by colonists seeking new homes, and by missionaries seeking converts to the European religions and way of life. Many Asian nations succumbed to the tides of European empire building—the Spice Islands to Holland, India and Burma to England, Indochina to France. But China's enormous size, its distance from the European centers, and its domestic political cohesiveness combined with the naturally balancing rivalries of the great powers to prevent a takeover by any one Western nation.

Instead, the Chinese follow their famed nationalist leader Sun Yat-sen (1888–1925) in calling China a "semicolony" during the nineteenth century. China was not a full colony even though tiny Western detachments could destroy Chinese armed forces at will. Each of a number of small, but humiliating, defeats brought new concessions from the increasingly inept Chinese ruling dynasty—itself a dynasty of foreign rulers from inner Asia. The Opium War of 1840–42, while forcing the Chinese government to accept the importation of debilitating narcotics, established also the right of foreigners to claim permanent enclaves on Chinese soil. The present British colony of Hong Kong is, along with the Portuguese colony of Macao across the bay from it, the last vestige of the enclave system of the nineteenth century. The Anglo-Chinese War of 1860 extracted from the Chinese the right to declare major trading centers, even along the inland rivers, to be official "treaty ports"; this was sanctified by what the Chinese have since termed the "unequal treaties" signed by the old dynasty and the West. Within these new enclaves Westerners were subject to laws and to court systems different from those of ordinary Chinese. The Boxer Rebellion of 1900, the result of an ill-conceived Chinese imperial attempt to side with an antiforeign politico-religious movement known as the Boxers (from their practice of the Chinese martial arts), demonstrated the incapacity of the traditional, unreformed government to resist determined Western military power and brought a new wave of foreign investment in mining and railroad concessions throughout the Chinese subcontinent.

Yet, through all these humiliations the Chinese continued to grope for adequate responses to Western incursion. Early resistance came from upright mandarins who resented, among other things, the "barbarian" habit of opium smoking. Then military commanders sought to reform China's war-making capacity by importing new technology. By the 1860s a new school of "self-strengthening" *(tzu-ch'iang)* had arisen to urge that China's social fabric would have to be toughened (along traditional lines, to be sure) to meet the Western challenge. By 1898 those who urged reform from within were able to gain a brief moment of power in Peking and to force through important changes in the domestic constitution, changes that, when later put into effect, would restrain rampant official corruption, refocus priorities on military resistance, increase the pool of Western knowledge, and restrain the selfish and ineffectual imperial monarchy that had ruled since 1644. The *Revolution of 1911*, which overthrew the Manchu dynasty and declared China a republic, marked the end of a century of domestic turmoil over the way to respond to the Western challenge.

Much of the Chinese political scene of the early twentieth century derived from the clash between the potent old tradition and the new styles of Western power. The new republic, having open political parties, elections, and national and provincial legislatures, very quickly succumbed to older forms of rule; by 1916 the nominal president, Yuan Shi-kai, attempted unsuccessfully to restore the monarchical system with himself as emperor. A new breed of rulers, Western in their command of military force and their ruthless pursuit of power in their territories, but Eastern in their strong belief in personal loyalty and stern moralism, sprang up to rule in province after province as central power continued to erode. These "warlords" *(chün fa)* benefited from an unprecedented militarization of Chinese society, which increased the number of men in arms nearly a hundredfold between 1900 and the 1940s. The Japanese invasion of China after 1937 thus marked the last in a century-long series of foreign intrusions. And the two Chinese forces who combated them, the Nationalists and the Communists, likewise were the modern descendants of the official, scholarly, intellectual, and mass antiforeign movements that had convulsed China for almost two centuries.

Western Ideas in Chinese Garb. Perhaps the most obvious dimension of China's modern revolution is the introduction of political concepts and practices from the West. The very longevity and apparent permanence of the traditional state encouraged a resistance to European ideas and attitudes more powerful than that encountered by the European intrusion of capital and armed forces into China in the nineteenth century. Unlike Japan, Thailand, Turkey, and many other non-Western countries, the Chinese resisted Western notions to the extent of hampering China's ability to defend itself or even to maintain domestic order. After first rejecting all European influence as uncivilized and barbarian, the Chinese in turn attempted to limit contacts with Westerners, while privately employing Europeans and Americans as advisers to the government. But the growth of trade, especially in the treaty ports of the China coast after the Opium War of 1840–42, and the expansion of missionary activities after their legalization in 1858 made contact between the West and ordinary Chinese subjects inevitable. Western ideas such as national sovereignty and constitutionalism followed in the footsteps of the missionaries, traders, and arms sellers.

What made China's response to these ideas unique was the way in which the Chinese channeled them into their view of the nation's needs. Popular participation in government, for example, became a slogan during and after the abortive Reform Movement of 1898, but not because of any widespread clamor of popular interests for the vote. Rather, the proponents of constitutions argued that only through collective action that involved and changed the people could China strengthen its military might and repel such potential aggressors as the Japanese. Likewise, only after the victory of the Russian Communists in 1917, which demonstrated the power of Marxist ideas to build the state and resist external aggression, did Chinese intellectuals turn to the serious study of socialism. Political parties and parliaments, tried several times in the decade after the Revolution of 1911, proved uniformly impotent to solve the basic problem of China in the twentieth century: the construction of a national government that would be rich and strong enough to control domestic disorder and resist external pressures.

The history of the *May Fourth Movement of 1919* illustrates the fate of transplanted Western ideas in twentieth-century China. That movement originated among a new generation of students, who were the first to emerge since the abolition of the traditional examination system in 1905 and who felt that China's national interests were being betrayed by a government that continued to deal with expansive Japanese imperialism. This new generation thought of itself as modern and called itself variously the "new culture movement" or the "new tide" or "new youth." It demanded many changes from traditional Chinese practice: abandoning the classical style of writing for the popular language, encouraging freedom from familial and other social restraints on the younger generation, relaxing restrictions on political organization and protest. But although European and American heroes such as Bertrand Russell or John Dewey were models at the start of the movement, and although "democracy and science" were the main themes of one phase of the cultural and literary outpouring after 1917, by the early 1920s these heroes and themes had become discredited; they were no more capable than parliaments and parties of solving China's problem as the Chinese perceived it.

Marxism-Leninism, Chinese Style. Nor was the answer Marxism-Leninism. Many still regard the growth of the Chinese Communist Party after its formation in 1921 by a splinter group from the May Fourth Movement as further evidence of the Westernization of Chinese politics. But in fact it took the success of Lenin's revolution to make Chinese aware of the great European Marxist tradition. The founders of the Chinese Communist Party (CCP), Ch'en Tu-hsiu and Li Ta-chao, knew nothing of socialism until that time, but were quickly converted when they saw how rapidly Lenin had turned Russia from an invaded and disordered land into an independent and outspoken nation. The history of the CCP after 1921 showed how readily the Chinese would discard essential elements of Leninism in order to further their goal of unifying and building a new China. Western ideas were indeed important in China's transformation, but less as models for Chinese behavior than as symptoms of a deeper drive to regenerate China's proud national existence.

The earliest Chinese Communists proved far too faithful to the *Soviet model of Leninism.* Lenin had taught them that in the "semicolonial" areas of the world, like China, Communist parties had to ally themselves first with the representatives of the bourgeois class of their own nation. The Chinese proletariat, after all, numbered less than one-half of 1 percent of the Chinese population. After Lenin's death Stalin interpreted the "national bourgeoisie" in China to mean the *Kuomintang*—the party of Sun Yat-sen, which in late 1922, after a decade of resistance to the post-1911 parliamentary system, had finally gained a foothold in the southern province of Kwangtung. The Communists dutifully contributed their full energies to building the Kuomintang, only to find after Sun's death that they were constructing their own nemesis. By 1927 the powerful Nationalist army of the Kuomintang, now led by Chiang Kai-shek, backed by landowners, middle class, and business interests, and fortified by Soviet advice and arms, had turned on the Communists and crushed their hopeful mass organizations in a bloody massacre that shaped the survivors' outlook for decades.

Out of this debacle rose the party of Mao Tse-tung. Mao, a young Hunanese intellectual who had studied in Peking University during the May Fourth period, helped found the *Chinese Communist Party* in 1921, served dutifully as a Kuomintang bureaucrat in Canton, and in late 1926 deeply imbibed the local peasants' enthusiasm for the "National Revolution" in his home province of Hunan. Voicing the attitudes of the Communist wing of the Kuomintang toward the collective potential of the *peasantry,* Mao declared in his famous *Report on the Peasant Movement in Hunan* that "the peasantry represents 70 per cent of the power of the revolution"—a view that brought him into conflict with the more orthodox Leninist Ch'en Tu-hsiu. During the disastrous months of August and September 1927, Mao led a series of hapless uprisings against Kuomintang power in Hunan and retreated with the remnants of his "worker-peasant Red Army" into the mountain fastness of southeastern Hunan. From this tiny force grew the powerful People's Liberation Army, which twenty years later would sweep back into Hunan on its way to victory.

In those two decades Mao developed both a strategy and a body of practice for the Chinese revolution that peculiarly suited Chinese conditions. He demanded and got independence of his troops from the interference of Moscow and the urban-based Chinese Communist Central Committee. He resisted the demands of his superiors to waste his forces in futile attacks on the cities, outlining instead a strategy of building base areas in the remote mountains and in the broad countryside. After he gained full power over the Party during his army's heroic *Long March* (1934–35), which took them through thousands of miles of the interior, he moderated in his village work Moscow's hard-line "class struggle" doctrines, which had lost the party considerable support. During the Anti-Japanese War of 1937–45, (the Chinese name for World War II), Mao developed a delicate balancing strategy of a *united front* with all anti-Japanese elements (including Chiang's Kuomintang) that permitted him to expand his party manyfold. Each of these tactical and strategic innovations strained his relations with his superiors in Moscow, but admirably suited his overarching goal of revolutionary victory.

Chinese Communism during these revolutionary years developed a distinctive style of political interaction with the Chinese population. Mao's troops contrasted sharply with those of the warlords and the Nationalist central government at Nanking and later wartime Chungking: they were disciplined, mostly literate, and above all politically conscious. Red Army practice emphasized inner-party democracy and forthrightness. Military goals yielded to political. The masses—most often the peasants—deserved considerate treatment in regard to their property, their families, and their customs and beliefs, because they were needed to support the Communist army in the countryside. Soldiers and their political officers had to be all-round, independent fighters capable of long periods of separation from central Communist authority.

Many of these practices reached maturity during 1936–40, the period when the Party Politburo resided in the remote northwestern town of Yenan. In many ways *the Yenan experience*—characterized by its comradely small-town warmth, its fierce sense of national purpose, its new discovery of unsuspected support among broad segments of the peasant population in northern China—represents today a golden age of the Chinese Communist past. Most Chinese Communist leaders today retain much of the antiurban, anti-intellectual, antibureaucratic, and, above all, strongly nationalistic outlook they acquired during their revolutionary struggles. With these memories and this outlook the Chinese Communists at the end of the civil war in 1949 found themselves the rulers of the largest and oldest country and people in the world.

The Causes of the Chinese Revolution. China's revolution, which produced the People's Republic of China in October 1949, was at least as enormous an event as any of the great European revolutions—the English of the seventeenth century, the French of the eighteenth, the Russian of the early twentieth. It took longer to occur—nearly a century of violence preceded it—and spilled more blood than any other revolution. Yet the causes of this event are often obscured behind arguments for one side or the other in the civil wars of China in the first half of this century or behind more abstract arguments about the nature of the good society. Some will single out the misbehavior of foreigners on Chinese soil, or the exploitation of the common peasantry by an irresponsible landlord class, or the rise of new ideas of democracy or egalitarianism, as the major cause of the Chinese revolution. We may all agree that Western "imperialism" had its bad aspects or that warlords did not treat their common subjects generously, but still fail to understand the rise of the Communist Party to power.

The Chinese Communist Party differed enormously from the Soviet Communist Party of Lenin in its history, its personnel, and especially in its sources of support. Lenin's party was a conspiratorial offshoot of intellectual socialists trained in the European political tradition. Lenin came to power in October 1917 almost by accident: his "party" of a few thousand members proved more adept at parliamentary politics and more ruthless about seizing dictatorial powers than any other force in St. Petersburg. Insofar as any real mass support for Lenin's coup of 1917 was required, it came largely from organized urban workers, as well as from war-weary soldiers and sailors, while the rural masses of Russia remained silent either from ignorance or from deliberate abstention. While the ravages of World War I and the incompetence of the czarist government gave Lenin's party the chance it needed, the leadership of the Russian Revolution fell to him in part by chance, as well as by dint of the hard work and organization that had prepared his followers to seize that chance when it came. Only after November 1917 did the peasants' desire to seize the land (and the soldiers' eagerness to end the war against the superior German artillery) add that large mass support that the regime of Lenin's party needed in order to survive.

By contrast, the Chinese party, which sought for thirty years to build a Leninist party and to follow the footsteps of their Russian comrades, took a different course entirely. Since China had no real proletariat, except in a few large cities that governments or warlords could easily control, the Chinese Communists had to turn quite early to building a rural organization. China in the early twentieth century had no national center such as Moscow, so that power could not simply be seized at the capital and extended over the rest of the country, as in Russia. Finally, the disorders that overwhelmed the Manchu dynasty in 1911 were far more extensive than the problems of the czar, who until his fall in 1917 still commanded a nationwide bureaucracy and a national army. Communists in China were forced to overthrow not just a national state apparatus, but hundreds of local power holders and petty militarists.

The Chinese Communist Party, which began as a small but independent subset of the Nationalist Party and grew from perhaps fifty thousand in 1927 to a giant army of millions by 1949, conquered China as an army, not as a purely political force. To be sure, much of the credit for the idea of a Communist "party-army" must be given to Soviet advisers to the Chinese in the 1920s; but after 1927, Mao Tse-tung built his Red Army into a formidable military-political weapon.

The Red Army (called the People's Liberation Army after 1945) built its bases largely among the peasantry and often in easily defensible, remote regions of the vast Chinese countryside. It was not until the late 1940s that the Communists began to translate their real military power into nationwide administrative control. But this fact should not obscure the reality of Communist skills in the Chinese political arena. The Red Army under Mao Tse-tung showed an uncanny ability to voice the desires of a large number of ordinary Chinese. Mao's party openly declared war on Japan long before the Nationalist leader, Chiang Kai-shek, dared to do so. The Red Army, though often relying on doctrinaire theories and heavy-handed methods, still convinced the populace that it supported the desire of many villagers to be free from the multiple squeezes of usury, rack-rents and uncontrolled violence. The Communist Party by World War II had indisputably won over to its side the independent and antiestablishment voices of the new Chinese intellectual elite. When liberation came in 1949, there was no question that the vast majority of Chinese welcomed the chance to build their nation in peace. The Communist Party's skill in enlisting and utilizing popular aspirations in the game of politics was probably the most important cause of the Chinese Revolution of 1949.

THE STAKES OF CHINESE POLITICS: THE FUTURE CHARACTER OF CHINESE SOCIETY

As in the Soviet Union, so in today's post-revolutionary China do the stakes of politics include not merely some allocations of desired values, but the structure and development of the entire society and of much of its culture. Further, the attempted redesign of human society in China, as in Russia, also involved attempts to establish a new image of the human personality, of relations among the sexes and the generations, and of life in the family, village, and place of work. At stake also was the economic infrastructure of railroads, roads, and ports; the social infrastructure of schools, hospitals, and laboratories; and the future organization, equipment, and performance of factories and farms. The Chinese Revolution by 1949, like the Russian Revolution by 1917, was becoming a huge attempt to remake an entire society by means of politics; and for a time almost everything in China, as earlier in Russia, became political.

The First Decade of Communist Rule: Efforts to Apply the Soviet Model. Certainly the Communists had been only a small part of the Chinese political system of the first half of this century. The population of the China that they won over in October 1949 was much larger than their membership, though by that date the CCP already numbered about 4.5 million members and was about the same size as the Communist Party of the Soviet Union.

Also, some elements of modernization had come into being before the Communists came to power. For nearly forty years the central government of China, under constantly changing leadership, had groped falteringly for formulas to build a new China. At least seven constitutions had come and gone since 1907. A large and moderately successful central bureaucracy had come into being under Chiang Kai-shek's national government in the 1930s. The Kuomintang, while remaining a party supported primarily by the well-to-do classes of the cities and some landowners in the countryside, had expanded its membership to become an extensive political organization, resembling in many of its features the European Fascist parties of that era. Above all, the Chinese people in the republican era, despite the extent of the chaos that surrounded them, had begun to create the basis for a modern economy in the cities and the rudiments of a nationwide communications system that would be helpful in integrating the nation after 1949.

China's revolution of 1949 resembled the Russian events of 1917 only because China, too, was a poor, non-Western country ravaged by war and famine. The differences were striking: China's political traditions were rich and highly developed, its Communist party far more mature and experienced in ruling, its social fabric far more torn by a century of disorder than even that of wartime Russia. And yet, despite these differences, in the decade after 1949 the Chinese Communist government exerted every effort to engineer a society and government that closely resembled the Soviet Union's. "We must lean to one side," said Chairman Mao Tse-tung in a famous speech in 1949, in order to build a "new democratic dictatorship" on the Soviet model.

Already in this first decade there were signs that the Chinese would not be fully satisfied with a mere carbon copy of Soviet government and politics—the Stalinist variety. *Mao's theory of "democratic dictatorship"* expanded Lenin's, including the massive peasantry of China (some 85 percent of the population) as partners in rule. But Russian quickly replaced English as the major foreign language taught in Chinese schools, and translations from the Russian represented a significant proportion of the output of Chinese presses in the first decade after 1949.

The new institutions built to replace Nationalist organizations closely resembled the Russian models: the Communist Party dominated an extensive state apparatus of pyramidal shape; a modicum of regional autonomy was encouraged for regions where China's minority populations lived; the educational establishment was centralized in a group of institutes located largely in Peking; the new and vastly expanded press system, in which the *People's Daily (Jen-min Jih-pao)* was the central organ, even imitated the formats and style of *Pravda* and *Izvestia.* The Constitution of the People's Republic of China, promulgated in September 1954, and the Rules of the Communist Party of China, drawn up in 1956, codified many of these Soviet-style structures. The Russian model for the 1950s encouraged the Chinese to centralize their bureaucracy, mechanize their agriculture, concentrate on heavy industrial production, and build watertight divisions among specialized ministries and organizations.

While Russia was moving in the mid-1950s toward limited political de-Stalinization—though retaining Stalin's stress on the primacy of heavy industry—the Chinese departed more fundamentally from Stalinism, even though they continued to speak more favorably of him as a political leader of the Soviet Union. Already by 1955 the Chinese had decided to abandon the Stalinist pattern of preceding rural collectivization with the mechanization of agriculture. Mao Tse-tung startled the Russians by announcing first in 1955 that China would soon be totally collectivized (a point that the Soviet Union has still not reached) and then in 1958 that Chinese agriculture was rapidly approaching the stage of communism—in which all property would be owned by the state acting through local territorial units called *communes*. The Chinese argued that these units, with around twenty thousand people in each, would replace not only the favored Russian collective farm *(kolkhoz)*, but the organs of local government as well. Despite an angry Khrushchev's warning that the Russians had tried such experiments in the 1920s and failed, the Chinese by late 1958 had grouped virtually their entire rural and urban population into these new units, which promised to hasten the arrival of communism by caring for infants and the elderly, by shouldering the main burden of military training, and by providing for each member according to his or her needs and the commune's ability to pay. Although very shortly thereafter the Maoist leaders had to back off from their rasher claims, because of material lacks and bureaucratic failures, still the people's commune (though now around seven thousand members in size) remains China's basic local unit of political and economic power.

The Chinese likewise developed to a far higher art than the Soviets the technique of the campaign *(yun-tung)* as a device for drumming up support for party policy. "Rectification campaigns" *(cheng-feng yun-tung)*, aimed at bringing party members and cadres (a more common term in China than in Russia) into line, took place virtually every year. In one of these, the Hundred Flowers Campaign of 1956, Mao Tse-tung seemed almost to encourage active criticism of Communist Party members by students, writers, and professors. In military policy China after 1957 de-emphasized the Soviet-style development of massive conventional forces in favor of guerrilla-like local militia training, which paid off in increased local discipline and productiveness.

All these phenomena suggested that Chinese leaders would not remain satisfied by merely imitating Soviet practices and institutions. Indeed, the open break in diplomatic and party relations with Moscow, which followed bitter public denunciations in 1960, climaxed a period of increasing dissatisfaction in Peking with playing second fiddle to the heirs of Stalin in Russia. The favorable atmosphere for Russian borrowing lasted even more briefly than the half-century of receptiveness to American and European ideas and practices that had preceded it.

Yet the fact that the Chinese explicitly reject the more corrupt and "revisionist" elements of Soviet practice—bureaucratism, hedonism, "great-nation chauvinism," and so on—should not blind us to the parallels between Chinese and Russian nation building after their respective revolutions.

Reintegrating a National Arena of Politics. First, the Chinese, like Lenin, had to reintegrate a ravaged society. In China this task of national unification was initially more difficult, whereas in Russia the cultural and economic dominance of the two main cities of Moscow and Leningrad made imposition of control over the provinces relatively easy. Chinese politics had been polycentric for decades, as each province's tens of millions of people had been governed solely by their resident warlord, or *tuchün*. The proclamation of the People's Republic in Peking began the process of building central political structures in China. Real power remained in the hands of *military administrative committees* in the six major regions of China until the formation in 1954 of the State Council under Premier Chou En-lai. Yet existence of the People's Liberation Army, nearly five million strong, made these regional committees (which corresponded to the garrison regions of each) relatively easy to coordinate. It was the political military—virtually the entire Central Committee of the CCP in 1949 had combat experience in the revolution—who cemented together the new government and kept order during the difficult period of transition. Civilian governments, staffed by former army commissars, party leaders, and a smaller number of non-Communist former Kuomintang bureaucrats, assumed power in the provinces only after this period of tutelage. From 1949 to the present the Communist government has preserved essentially the same regional structure, sometimes allowing it formal representation as a level of state authority (1949–54), sometimes relying on the party regional bureaus (1954–66), and sometimes preserving only the twelve great military regions (after 1966). But regional and provincial variety, in some years greater than in others, has flourished since 1949 only with the tolerance of central officials, who now command far more power over their regional subordinates than ever before.

Within two years of 1949 the income passing from the provinces to Peking through the budget, to pick an example, had multiplied by a factor of ten. Railway construction in the first decade more than doubled the track mileage linking Peking with the provinces and roughly quadrupled the amount of interprovincial trade. Central policy discouraged the use of nonstandard Chinese dialects in party and government meetings and supported extensive teaching of the Peking dialect. The system of *autonomous regions* for minority nationalities, such as the Uighurs in Sinkiang, the Mongols in Inner Mongolia, and the various Thai populations in southwestern Yunnan, did not permit the formation of separate Communist parties for each nationality (as in the Russian case). A number of rectification campaigns during the 1950s were aimed at rooting out "localism" among party cadres and ensuring the absolute authority of the central line. When the Cultural Revolution broke out in 1966, it was virtually certain that China would not fall apart again into groupings by warlord or region, simply because earlier integration efforts had been so exhaustive.

The Development of Political Participation. The second task of the early years was participation building. The Communists' victory came largely as a result of their success in involving China's rural population in their cause. The first decade after 1949 saw a participation explosion in China on an unprecedented scale. Certainly, the Russian Communists discovered quite early the advantage of mass mobilization for their political goals. But the transformation of Chinese mass attitudes to government after 1949 was by all accounts more striking because the vast majority of Chinese had been so systematically excluded from the political process until that date.

"Participation" is not the word that the Chinese use to describe their process of involving the masses. They prefer time-honored Leninist phrases like "democratic centralism" or the "mass line." But the essence of their practice closely resembles what political scientists call participation in other nations. The *mass line* involves three major elements, each of which binds the ordinary citizen more closely to the new political structures that the CCP created after 1949.

First is the *awareness* of government and policy. Whereas ordinary Chinese in pre-Liberation China (as the old society is often called today) either knew nothing of their government or feigned ignorance in the hope of avoiding taxes and other complications, the Communists demanded that every citizen understand how the government affected him or her. Under the pressure of Communist cadres and organizers, public matters came to occupy a larger portion of the consciousness of the ordinary worker or farmer.

Second, there was much wider *sharing* in the output of government. The citizen of the new system, at least in the early stages of the post-1949 transformation, benefited from the ploughing under of the old order. Carrying out land reform in the countryside, remolding urban businesses and factories, and reforming the legal structure to favor the working classes gave millions of Chinese a sense of real participation in the process of reconstruction and economic growth during the 1950s and that sense of participation through sharing is still widely perceived in China today.

Finally, after sharing came *joining*. The new government explicitly demanded that, in return for the real interests gained from the revolution, the citizenry be willing to participate actively in the new society. Private associations such as clans, religious societies, and business corporations came under sharp attack in the first few years and by 1956 had been virtually eliminated from China. In their place, cadres built myriad *public associations:* women's associations, professional societies, labor unions bearing the official seal of approval, and especially the Communist Youth League and the Chinese Communist Party. Some data are shown in Figure 16.1.

As a result, the weekly schedule of ordinary people soon filled with innumerable public meetings to discuss public problems and to learn the government's policies. Participation in this last sense carried with it an obligation of civic responsibility that was not uniformly welcomed. But there was no denying that by the end of the 1950s the Chinese Communists had generated participation on a vast scale and that the effect of this newfound sense of belonging to a new nation was irreversible.

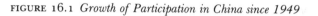

FIGURE 16.1 *Growth of Participation in China since 1949*

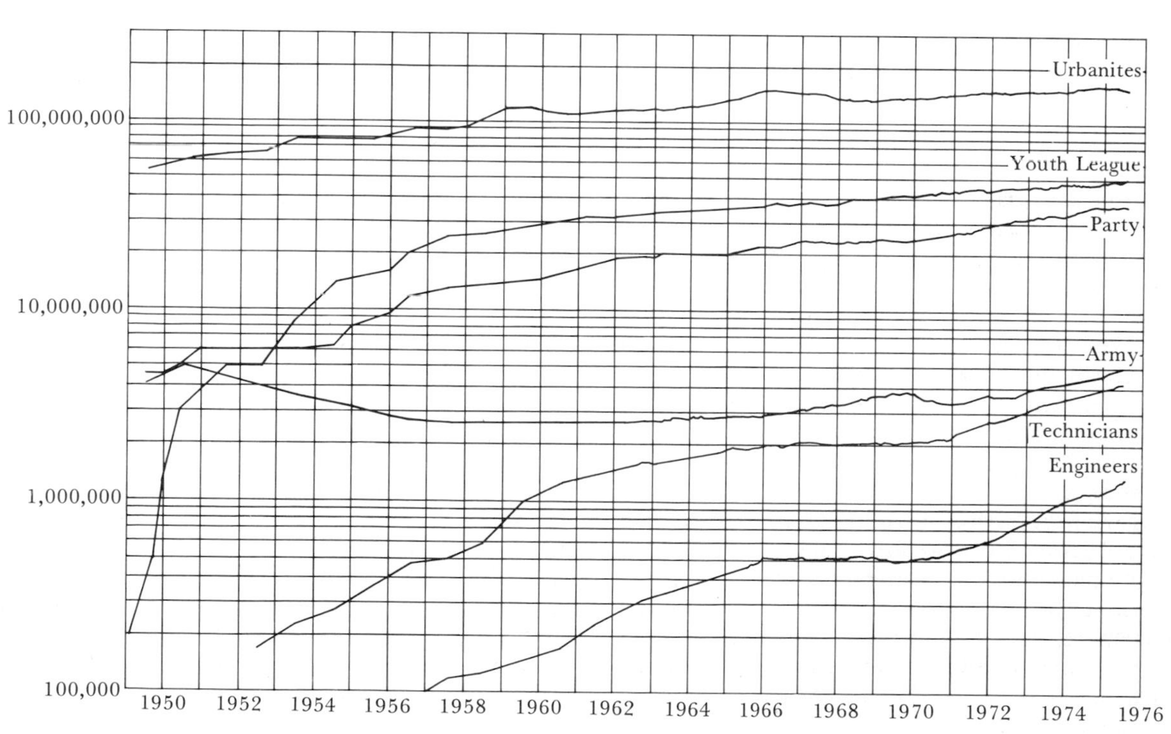

Institution Building: A New Machinery of Politics. The third task of the first decade was institution building. Though there was no lack of institutions in premodern and transitional China, the Communist government came to power determined to undermine and destroy what it regarded as the corrupt and evil political organs of the oppressive and exploiting ruling classes. The extensive government, armies, and parties of the pre-Communist era fell almost at one blow in 1949–50 and were replaced by the Communists' own version—which in many instances closely resembled the old institution, but with new personnel.

The new central, provincial, and local government built after 1949 very often included a number (though always a small minority) of officials held over from the Kuomintang government, individuals who had successfully remolded themselves to fit the revolutionary image. Some of these people, like several of the ministers in Chou En-lai's new State Council of 1954, had shifted their allegiance to the Communists at a key point in the last days of the struggle for power. In other cases, non-Communist politicians were kept on to indicate the new government's tolerance of non-party "democratic personages" in the government during the transition period.

But the lion's share of official positions fell to new people, those whose loyalty to the new system was unquestioned. Staffing these positions required a massive recruitment campaign that swelled the ranks of the Youth League and the Party in the 1950s. By 1958 the CCP, with 17 million members, had become the largest organized political elite in the world.

The Chinese Communist Party of the 1950s was closely modeled in structure on the Communist Party of the Soviet Union under Stalin. The 1956 Party Rules provided for a Politburo; a Central Committee with a Secretariat and several Departments; and provincial, district, and local party committees outside Peking. Elections to higher-level party committees followed the same democratic-centralist pattern of nomination from below and confirmation from above. In theory and in the rules, the Party stood apart from the even larger body of state employees and state government organizations, though the Party was intended to be the guiding and policy-making force in government at all levels, as in the Soviet Union. But what was striking about Chinese Communist institutional structures after 1949 was their rapid growth and their flexibility within the letter of the rules.

After 1958, however, many of the new institutions, including the Communist Party, were to be tested severely once more by major strains and pressures for another round of revolutionary restructuring.

FROM "GREAT LEAP FORWARD" TO "GREAT PROLETARIAN CULTURAL REVOLUTION"—THE MAOIST DECADE

One of the great paradoxes of modern politics is that those groups who most prominently claim to represent impersonal forces of history or society so often evolve into the personal followings of single, powerful leaders. This process, which Michael Walzer has so admirably described in his book about the Puritan revolution in seventeenth-century England (see pp. 362–64, above) is justified in the Leninist tradition by the theory of the dictatorship of the proletariat. Since, in Lenin's view, the working class of any nation may be misled by faulty leadership or selfish economic interest into betraying the true cause of revolution, it must be represented by a core or vanguard of professionals who see farther and clearer than others. In the Russian case this status of near-sainthood was always reserved for the Party, not for the leader himself, despite the worship of Lenin after his death. Even as he systematically decimated the ranks of top leaders to heighten his personal power, Stalin never implied that the idea of the vanguard party ought to be challenged. Mao Tse-tung, the leader of the Chinese Communist Party from 1935 until 1976, came perilously close to undermining the idea of a vanguard Communist Party organization in the decade between 1958 and 1968.

There were five elements to Mao's programs during this decade, each of which could be traced back to his own personal revolutionary experience before 1949 and to his distrust of Soviet imports into China. First, his so-called *Great Leap Forward* of 1958, while it promised all-round rapid advances in China's First Five-Year Plan, in fact reoriented Chinese economic policy away from urban industrial growth to a stress on rural industry and agriculture. Decentralization of power to local party committees in the provinces, reliance on large-scale labor-intensive rural projects, and creation of huge politico-economic units called *People's Communes,* having thousands of members—all these added up to an extensive *ruralization* of China's development plan.

Second, beginning with the Great Leap, Mao increasingly stressed the importance not of material wealth, but of will, strength of character, and especially political loyalty in building the new socialist China—a *voluntarism* that dated back to guerrilla days when an iron will was the best weapon of the Red Army soldier.

Third, *antibureaucratism* became a major theme of government propaganda, especially after the overenthusiastic (and economically disastrous) exertions of the Great Leap came under criticism from lower-level party authorities who had to carry them out.

Fourth, Mao increasingly turned to the People's Liberation Army as the model for the *remilitarization* of a China that had become too complacent, he thought, after revolutionary victory.

Finally, Mao turned his energies against the growing signs of disaffection with his policies among the intellectual class, which, a decade earlier, had been his strong supporter. The *proletarianization of culture*—by which he meant the purging of corrupt "bourgeois" works of art as well as the silencing of vocal critics of his politics (who were accused of "taking the capitalist road")—became the slogan that launched China's great purge of 1966–67, known as the *Great Proletarian Cultural Revolution.*

All five of these Maoist policies of the 1960s placed great strain on the new institutions of Party and state that had been so carefully built up during the 1950s. They would have been impossible to impose on China without the enormous prestige enjoyed by the Party's great leader. We need not believe that "the great helmsman," Chairman Mao, actually swam fifteen kilometers in sixty-five minutes in the turbid Yangtze in his seventy-third year, as the Chinese press reported,[3] in order to recognize that his personal influence was, for a time, more potent than that of his party.

But bureaucracies die hard, and the Chinese are as adept as any people at protecting the entrenched interest of officialdom. The Cultural Revolution was hailed as a massive onslaught against the inequities and privilege of the cadres of party and government. Yet the signs are clear that it merely substituted one group of cadres for another and, indeed, that virtually all the discredited "capitalist roaders in authority" have made striking comebacks since 1967.

The impact of the Maoist decade was greater in the less tangible fields of style and rhetoric than in major structural change. In the 1970s the rebuilt Chinese Communist Party was less preoccupied with formal rules of promotion and demotion, had fewer desk-bound officials, and extended farther into the countryside than a generation earlier. Education, ever the esteemed path to mobility in China, became more open to people from less privileged backgrounds (around two-thirds of high school pupils in the 1960s still came from cadre or "free professional" backgrounds); and certainly intellectuals, and especially writers and artists, tread more warily within earshot of authority. And yet, despite Maoism, the process of

[3]*China Quarterly,* no. 28 (October–December 1966), pp. 149–52.

governing China continues to require an enormous amount of paperwork, communications skills in high degree, and dedicated professional civil servants.

NEW DEPARTURES IN OLD PATTERNS: CHINA AFTER MAO

Chairman Mao's death in September 1976 brought to a close a remarkable reign. But like the passing of Stalin in 1953, it opened the floodgates of rapid change as Chinese leaders adjusted to new priorities. To ease the transition, Mao's successors pushed forward a much younger man, fiftyish Hua Kuo-feng, to take on his ceremonial roles, indicating the need for youth in government. Considerable real power remained, however, in the hands of an old guard of revolutionaries of Mao's generation, many of whom felt a need to moderate the stridency of late Maoist policy. Beginning scarcely a month after Mao's death, the successors, led by Teng Hsiao-p'ing, turned against Mao's closest personal aides, including his widow, and launched a new program of rapid modernization.

Many aspects of this drive seemed new and striking to observers accustomed to Maoist China. Economic rationality, including the emphasis on planning as far ahead as the twenty-first century, came to be stressed instead of revolutionary fervor. High standards of training and performance seemed to be preferred over political purity and proper worker-peasant-class origin. Teng Hsiao-p'ing's slogan of "Seek the truth from the facts" supplanted Mao Tse-tung's cry of "Rebellion is justified." And, most surprising of all, China began to open its doors to students and experts and to establish extensive commercial ties with the capitalist world, even choosing to end a three-decade-old diplomatic separation from the United States by mutual recognition on January 1, 1979.

Yet the new departures suggested echoes of the past and confirmed underlying patterns in the governance of China. The state Constitution of 1978, for example, drew heavily on the Constitution of 1956, which Teng Hsiao-p'ing had helped to shape. New economic plans, with their heavy stress on science and technology and on military preparedness, seemed to be extensions of the planning efforts of the 1950s. The careful preservation of the image of Mao, concurrent with a rejection of his policies, resembled the delicate de-Stalinization of Russia, about which the Chinese had been deeply concerned. The new stress on democracy did not move far beyond the essentially centralized notions of rule that had dominated the political systems of Communist parties in power since Lenin. Even the turn to the West and to the United States was justified as a tactical move necessary to deal with the "main enemy"—this time the Soviet Union on China's north. The events of the 1970s show how difficult it is for a nation, especially one so large and so deeply steeped in tradition as China, to break away from old paths. This recent sluggishness makes all the more remarkable China's about-face of 1949 and suggests that true revolutions are by nature short-lived political phenomena.

SOME RESULTS—AND SOME UNRESOLVED PROBLEMS

The performance of governments must be judged in the light of the problems that governments face. On this test, the first three decades of Chinese Communist rule must be counted as a great success.

Three Areas of Accomplishment. First, government succeeded in stopping a century or more of disorder and civil warfare and imposed peace on a weary population. By 1951 all China, except the offshore island province of Taiwan, rested easily in the control of new rulers committed to rooting out disruptive elements.

Second, the self-destructive tendencies of inflation, excessive urbanization, and overpopulation that have plagued other Asian societies in this century had to be curbed. By 1960, China had reduced the net reproduction rate to around 2 percent, had eliminated currency instability, and had actually reversed the flow of population into the cities by using the tactic of compulsory rustication *(hsia-fang)*.

Finally, the national economy had to be not only revived, but actually transformed to meet the requirements of an ever growing population and the desires of a nation-building elite. The Chinese government, deciding after 1960 on a strategy of "agriculture as the root, and industry as the main branch," has presided over growth in these two sectors ranging from 2 to 7 percent per year, with an average of perhaps 5 percent. In contrast to the situation thirty years ago, the Chinese economy is now no longer dependent on foreign loans, imports, and advice. "With one's own strength alone can one be victorious" is a classic Chinese expression that has now become a standard and ubiquitous slogan.

Some Continuing Economic Problems. The post-Mao Chinese government has decided on a dramatic scheme of modernization of the economy. In the economic sphere China remains, in Mao Tse-tung's words, "poor and blank." Farm families in model villages still earn less than ten dollars a month in cash income. Productivity in farms and factories is still far below that of non-Communist Chinese economies such as those smaller and more manageable ones of Hong Kong and Taiwan, where market forces, rather than state plans, determine business decisions, and where the international economy with its technology and buying power still has an important impact. Despite tremendous efforts to bring modernization to China's vast countryside, villagers are still far less literate, less well educated, and less well fed and clothed than are urban dwellers.

In the industrial sphere, despite three decades of effort, China has yet to join the modern world. Nearly two decades of political vacillation have left the managerial elite uncertain about the future, the working population relatively unskilled, and the industrial plant outmoded. Ambitious plans call for importing capital goods worth almost as much as the national debt of the United States by the year 2000, but China's exports are too few at present to finance even a more modest program. The younger generation of workers, deprived of consumer goods for years, now seeks higher wages at the same time as rural dwellers are being promised a better living standard. The top-heavy Chinese political system is still unprepared for the clamor caused by rising expectations, even if the target of 8–10 percent annual industrial growth can be achieved.

Education continues to be a major problem for the Chinese system. The Soviet-style elitist educational structure of universities and research institutes gave way in the 1960s to a great expansion in mass education, including high quotas for relatively unprepared, but politically reliable, rural youth. The turmoil of the "Gang of Four" period of the early 1970s created an extended hiatus in higher education and research that ended only after Mao's death. Striking plans to send tens of thousands of Chinese abroad to fill the resulting generation gap have been cut back for want of foreign exchange to pay for them and in hopes of satisfying political critics who fear excessive foreign influence.

Recurring Political Strains: Generations, Regions, and Civil-Military Relations. The death of Mao Tse-tung has left serious tensions in the Chinese system. In his last years Mao used his great personal esteem to undermine the authority of the Communist Party bureaucracy. Yet the very officials who replaced him are unable to abandon easily the symbol of Mao as the great helmsman of the Chinese revolution without undermining their own legitimacy. Hua Kuo-feng attempted to imitate Mao's style, even his haircut, to gain acceptance as the successor. China thus faces a classical problem described by Max Weber: how to "routinize the charisma" of a lost leader.

In part the problem is generational. The present members of the Politburo have an average age of over seventy and share the common experience of guerrilla warfare, one that does not help them to deal with critical economic, educational, and international tasks. This generation finds it hard to understand the demands of the younger, technocratic group that is managing China's modernization. Younger people, for their part, remember little of the days when personal sacrifice for the revolution was a necessity. Many expect to be given substantial responsibility while still junior. Mao Tse-tung's reliance on young Red Guards for support in 1966 has not been forgotten.

In part the problem is regional, since few of the current top leadership came from China's most industrialized regions, such as Shanghai and Liaoning. In a developing nation such as China, regions develop differently, and less advanced provinces such as Szechwan or Honan have a strong stake in a political system that redistributes the benefits of growth. It may be no accident that such provinces have been well represented in the Politburo. China remains divided by many dialects (though the written Chinese language is common to all) and by many nationalities—most of these in China's sensitive border regions. Regional unity in China is now, as it always has been, a matter of high political priority.

Another tension in the political system is that between civilian and military rule. This dichotomy is an element of the classical tradition that stressed rule by the word (*wen,* or "written culture") over the weapon (*wu,* or "military force"). Yet behind the changes in political vocabulary, style, and leadership in China since liberation has stood the inexorable power of the People's Liberation Army, now the unchallenged masters of domestic security. The army stood behind the authority of Chairman Mao through the tumultuous Cultural Revolution despite blows to its own integrity, and the army swung behind Hua Kuo-feng at the critical moment of Mao's death.

The experimental army intervention in politics in the late 1960s left a legacy that would be familiar in other developing countries: professional military members, with their natural concern for discipline and order, may be natural leaders in times of crisis when these virtues are essential. But they cannot, while remaining military members, sustain the workings of a complex political system. Fewer than 3 million soldiers cannot make governing decisions for nearly half as many villages and retain their organized fighting strength. The Communist Party, grown to 36 million by 1979, can provide the personnel and the day-to-day presence to do that job. At the same time, China's leaders may feel they continue to need the stamina and the imputed objectivity of the loyal military to overcome the tendencies toward sloth and selfishness that they abhor. Military strength will be particularly needed around China's periphery and in the provinces, where local diversity demands firm control of peace keeping forces.

It might be worth remembering, however, that thus far in all Communist-ruled countries civilian party rule has remained predominant, in contrast to many less developed countries in the non-Communist world, where military dictatorships have been common. If the Chinese People's Republic should at some future time fall under military rule, this would not be a new thing in China's long history, but it would be a new departure in the shorter history of the Communist world, where dictatorships have been essentially party-based and civilian.

Developing a Role for China in World Politics. The final residual problem for China is its position in world affairs. To be sure, China is not yet a "superpower" (to use Chou En-lai's derogatory term for the United States and the Soviet Union), nor is it likely to become one in the near future. China has a smaller land army than that of the United States and virtually no air force or navy, except for coast defense vessels and conventional submarines. While Chinese weapons experts have developed and tested fission and fusion bombs (more than a dozen tests since the first in 1964) and are on their way to deploying short- and medium-range delivery systems, the Chinese industrial plant cannot sustain full-scale conventional war in the way that the Soviet Union, Japan, or the United States might. China's problem is not so much to build up strength for offensive warfare, but rather to act on the world stage in order to minimize the likelihood of being isolated and attacked by potential enemies. China's strategy of playing one potential enemy against another coincides with Mao Tse-tung's tactical approach to guerrilla warfare as much as it does with classical Chinese strategic concepts. A million Russian troops on China's northern border, stationed there since the Sino-Soviet split broke into brief open warfare in mid-1969, symbolize the need to develop a flexible, multifaceted diplomacy. The recent turn toward a reconciliation with the United States after a quarter century of hostility suggests that the Chinese have learned much about the world since challenging the United Nations in the Korean War (1950–54). Perhaps the United States, too, has learned something of China's real intentions and capacities.

At the same time, the task of fitting China into the world system of nations will not be easy, even though China itself poses little real military, economic, or political threat to the other large nations. The province of Taiwan, occupied by ethnic Chinese of several dialects and ruled by Mao Tse-tung's ancient ally-turned-rival, Chiang Kai-shek, remains an international issue despite Chinese and American attempts to defuse it. President Carter's recognition of the government of the People's Republic of China as the legitimate government of China has left Taiwan without diplomatic status, but it remains a nation-sized political unit, being 16 million strong and wielding considerable influence in the world economy. In addition, there is British-ruled, Chinese-run Hong Kong; and in Singapore and throughout Southeast Asia reside 20 million ethnic Chinese who possess great economic power. The world's third largest economy, that of Japan, vastly overshadows the still essentially rural nation of China and will continue affecting the nations on the rim of Asia. The legacy of China's break with Soviet communism, having such deep geopolitical, ideological, and cultural roots, may last many years. It is doubtful that newly reforged bonds with America, which historically has been sympathetic to China's causes, will work miracles in the arduous job of bringing a quarter of humankind into a peaceful world arena.

KEY TERMS AND CONCEPTS

modern (or developed) political systems
traditional political systems
"modernity of tradition"
entrance examinations
mandarins
Confucius
Mencius
legalist school
Taoist philosophers
social relationships as model
unity of public and private realms
divine mandate of the emperor
officialism
humanism
Revolution of 1911
May Fourth Movement of 1919
Leninism (Soviet model)
Kuomintang
Chinese Communist Party (CCP)
Mao's view of peasantry
Long March of 1934–35
united-front strategy
the Yenan experience
Mao's theory of "democratic dictatorship"
communes
military administrative committees
autonomous regions
mass line

public associations
Great Leap Forward of 1958–59
people's communes
ruralization
voluntarism
antibureaucratism
remilitarization
proletarianization of culture
Great Proletarian Cultural Revolution of 1966–67

ADDITIONAL READINGS

Barnett, A. D., ed. *Chinese Communist Politics in Action.* Seattle: University of Washington Press, 1969. PB

Bennett, G., and R. Montaperto. *Red Guard: The Autobiography of Dai Hsiao-ai.* Garden City, N.Y.: Doubleday, 1971. PB

Karnow, S. *Mao and China: From Revolution to Revolution.* New York: Viking Press, 1972.

Lewis, J. W., ed. *Party Leadership and Revolutionary Power in Communist China.* London: Cambridge University Press, 1970.

Orleans, L. *Every Fifth Child: The Population of China.* Stanford, Calif.: Stanford University Press, 1972.

Scalapino, R. *Elites in the People's Republic of China.* Seattle: University of Washington Press, 1972. PB

Schram, S. *Mao Tse-tung: A Political Biography.* Baltimore: Penguin Books, 1968. PB

———. *The Political Thought of Mao Tse-tung.* Rev. ed. New York: Praeger, 1969. PB

Schurmann, F. *Ideology and Organization in Communist China.* 2nd ed. Berkeley and Los Angeles: University of California Press, 1968. PB

Schwartz, B. I. *Communism and China: Ideology in Flux.* Cambridge: Harvard University Press, 1968. PB

Smedley, A. *The Great Road.* New York: Monthly Review Press, 1956. PB

Snow, E. *Red Star over China.* Rev. ed. New York: Grove Press, 1968. PB

Solomon, R. *Mao's Revolution and Chinese Political Culture.* Berkeley and Los Angeles: University of California Press, 1971. PB

Terrill, R. *Eight Hundred Million: The Real China.* New York: Dell, 1972. PB

U.S. Congress, Joint Economic Committee. *Chinese Economy Post-Mao.* Washington, D.C.: U.S. Government Printing Office, 1978.

PB = *available in paperback*

XVII

The World of the Emerging Nations

In the world of today, most states are young. Of the 153 present-day states for which data have been collected, less than one-sixth are older than the American Revolution. More than one-half came into existence only after 1925; more than one-fourth became independent only after 1959. Except for the 21 nation-states that were already sovereign in 1775, all the remaining 132 states have been emerging nations at some time during the last two hundred years. (Figure 17.1 summarizes the record.)[1]

Accordingly, *emerging nations* can be defined as populations of countries that have only relatively recently acquired a status of formal political *sovereignty;* a significant amount of the modern political and administrative *machinery and institutions;* and some relatively widespread popular habits of mutual communication, compliance, and loyalty vis-à-vis their government and a significant portion of their compatriots. But the emerging nations also have many other things in common, beginning with their departure from what their populations and societies were like before they began to move at a faster pace toward modernity.

THE STARTING POINT: TRADITIONAL SOCIETIES

There has been a good deal of recent research and writing on traditional societies, some of it being of high quality; and yet in the world of the 1970s

[1]See data in C. L. Taylor and M. C. Hudson, *World Handbook of Political and Social Indicators,* 2nd ed. (New Haven: Yale University Press, 1972), pp. 26–29, table 2.1. The identities of many of these emerging nations and the approximate period of their emergence are indicated on the maps in Chapter 5 above, Figures 5.1 through 5.4, and some aspects of this change in the number of modern states are discussed in that chapter, on pp. 112–28.

FIGURE 17.1 *Emerging Modern Nations, 1776–1978.*

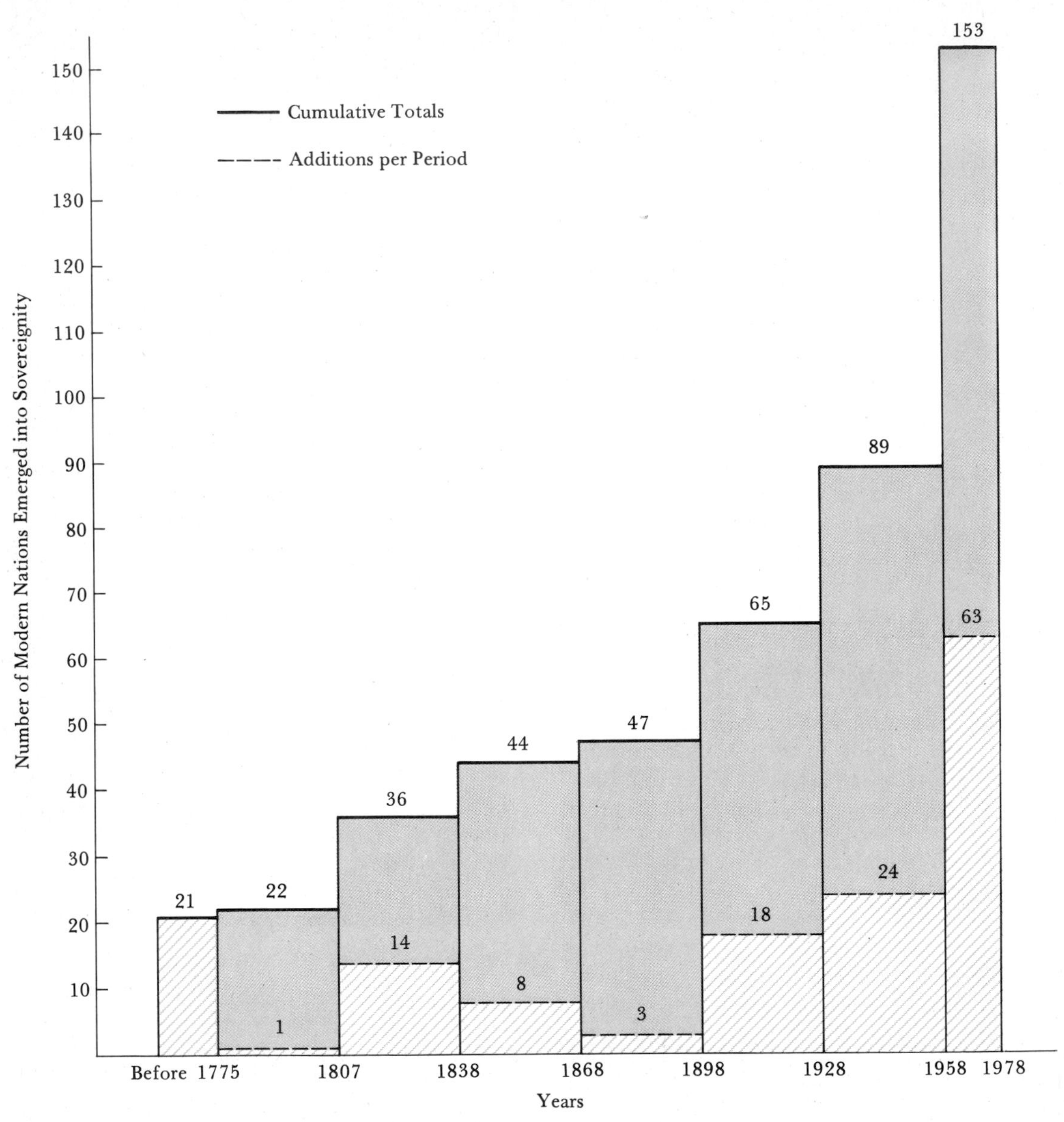

Sources: 1775–1973: C.L. Taylor and M.C. Hudson, *World Handbook of Political & Social Indicators,* 2nd ed. (New Haven: Yale University Press, 1972), pp. 26–29. 1973–78: John Paxton, ed., *Statesman's Yearbook 1978–1979* (London: Macmillan Press, 1978), p. viii–xii, 10–11.

there are hardly any countries left that could be called entirely traditional. What we now call a *traditional society* is in fact most often a construct—that is, an image put together from many elements found scattered among different real-life countries. Few countries, if any, now correspond to this full-fledged *ideal type* that is supposed to have all these traits together and none that would not fit in with them.

Until recently, perhaps only Chad, Ethiopia, Malawi, Nepal, and possibly Burundi and Rwanda were reasonably close to this picture, even though some of these now have been shaken by "Marxist" revolutions. There is reason to think, however, that the number of countries of this type was larger even twenty years ago and still larger fifty or a hundred years ago. There is evidence that at some time in the past every country went through a stage when its life was governed largely by tradition; and substantial elements of a traditional society can still be found in over a hundred countries in the present-day world.

What, then, is this traditional society, and what are its major elements and features that still survive in so many places? To answer these questions, we shall first consider what the different wholly or partly traditional societies tend to have in common, so that we can perceive them as belonging to one type; and then we shall examine some of the very important major differences among them and their influence on the different patterns of politics, society, and culture that succeeded each traditional society.

What Traditional Societies Have in Common. The first characteristic of a traditional society—there were only about a dozen left in 1976—is its poverty: a per capita income of $120 or less at 1976 prices. *Early transitional societies,* which are partly traditional and of which there are about fifty-six, are also poor, but somewhat less so; per capita incomes range from $120 to about $900 in 1976 terms. *Advanced traditional societies* have higher per capita incomes, ranging from just over $900 in 1976 (Tunisia and Turkey) to about $3,000 (Portugal, Iran, and Greece). In 1976 there were about twenty-five countries in this category; and each of these had preserved some lesser, but still substantial, elements and aspects of the traditional society within its system. The next richer category, the *industrialized societies,* includes about seventeen countries with 1976 per capita incomes ranging from $3,000 to $6,000; representative nations are Italy, Finland, Czechoslovakia, and the Soviet Union. In these countries only minor elements of the traditional society have survived the process of industrialization.

Finally, there are about eleven very highly developed countries, whose 1976 per capita incomes vary from $6,100 for Australia to about $7,900 for the United States, $8,700 for Sweden, and $8,900 for Switzerland. In these countries, industrialization is largely completed: new industries are more likely to replace older ones than to take the place of preindustrial pursuits, such as traditional handicrafts or agriculture. In these countries, also, there is a rapid growth of service industries, of professional and white-collar employment, of secondary and higher education, of computer technology and automation, and generally of information-processing occupations and industries. Some observers have called such societies *postindustrial.* For reasons set forth more fully in Chapter 20, perhaps a more positive description would be to call them countries entering the *information revolution*—the next great wave of change after the classic industrial revolution that these countries have already more or less completed. In the countries in this last group only vestiges of traditional enclaves, habits, and institutions have survived, and even most of these small remnants seem to dwindle fast.

A schematic overview of these five groups, with their income ranges and the countries that belong to each, is presented in Table 17.1.

The typical traditional society is not only poor; it is predominantly rural. In most countries of this type relatively few people live in cities of any size, and very few—usually less than 10 percent—live in cities of more than 100,000 inhabitants. The

TABLE 17.1 *Traditional, Transitional, Industrialized, and High-Information Societies, ca. 1975*

A. STRUCTURE	1 GNP per cap. ca. 1976	2 % Econ. growth p.a. per cap. 1970–76	3 % Work force in agric. ca. 1975	4 % Urban (100,000) ca. 1975	5 Pop. growth ca. 1970–76	6 Pop. total (million) ca. 1976	7 For. trade (imp. & exp.) as % of GNP ca. 1975	8 Concentration: of export receiving countries (index) ca. 1975	9 Concentration: of commodities exported (index) ca. 1975
TRADITIONAL SOCIETIES									
Ethiopia	100	0.2	84	5.3	2.6	29	21	10	20
Malawi	130	3.2	89	4.2	2.9	5	59	18	24
EARLY TRANSITIONAL SOCIETIES									
India	140	0.5	69	9.8	2.1	620	12	11	6
Pakistan	180	1.1	59	16.2	3.0	71	28	10	21
Egypt	280	3.1	54	33.9	2.3	38	54	17	20
Ghana	370	0.7	58	14.4	2.9	10	27	12	38
China	370	4.3	68	—	1.7	836	—	—	—
Nigeria	400	5.4	62	11.3	2.6	77	55	14	88
Bolivia	510	3.4	55	22.7	2.7	6	49	12	—
ADVANCED TRANSITIONAL SOCIETIES									
Cuba	840	−0.5	31	31.3	1.7	9	101	—	75
Chile	1050	−2.3	24	48.9	1.8	10	32	9	56
Mexico	1060	1.7	45	32.9	3.5	62	15	71	5
Brazil	1300	7.4	46	38.9	2.8	110	20	10	11
Argentina	1580	1.8	16	55.5	1.3	26	18	7	17
Yugoslavia	1750	5.8	50	12.6	0.9	21	36	11	6
Iran	1660	13.3	46	43	2.9	33	55	12	94
INDUSTRIALIZED SOCIETIES									
Soviet Union	2800	3.1	26	35.7	0.9	257	11	7	16
Poland	2880	5.3	39	19.7	0.9	34	26	—	11
Italy	3220	2.0	19	28.7	0.8	56	47	10	9
United Kingdom	4180	1.7	3	62.6	0.1	56	46	6	10
Saudi Arabia	4420	9.5	66	25.6	3.0	9	102	9	100
HIGH-INFORMATION SOCIETIES (POSTINDUSTRIAL)									
Japan	5090	3.9	20	57.8	1.3	113	23	10	17
France	6730	3.3	14	44.5	0.7	53	34	9	9
West Germany	7510	2.0	7	34.5	0.2	62	40	6	12
United States	7880	1.7	4	71.8	0.8	215	14	11	10
Canada	7930	3.5	8	54.9	1.3	23	42	63	8
Sweden	9030	2.1	8	27.5	0.3	8	53	8	11
Switzerland	9160	0.5	8	30.4	−0.2	6	50	7	13

TABLE 17.1 *(cont'd)*

B. COMMUNICATION	10 % Adult literacy ca. 1970	11 Higher education enrolment per 100,000 ca. 1975	12 Newspaper circulation per 1,000 ca. 1975	13 Radios per 1,000 ca. 1975	14 TV per 1,000 ca. 1975	15 Telephones per 1,000 ca. 1975	16 Physicians per 100,000 ca. 1975	17 Infant deaths per 1,000 live births ca. 1975	18 Inequality index: sectoral (Gini) ca. 1970	19 Central govt. expend. as § of GNP 1975	20 Defense expend. as % of GNP 1975	21 Milit. partic. per 1,000 work age pop. ca. 1975
TRADITIONAL SOCIETIES												
Ethiopia	6	23	2	6	1	2	1	84	—	13	3.8	3.4
Malawi	22	23	2	21	0	4	2	151	47	13	0.7	1.9
EARLY TRANSITIONAL SOCIETIES												
India	33	559	16	22	0	3	24	122	48	9	3.3	5.0
Pakistan	15	163	—	27	2	3	25	124	33	11	6.3	14.1
Egypt	44	1212	21	132	16	13	21	101	43	25	11.7	19.0
Ghana	30	92	51	82	3	6	10	156	—	12	1.6	4.1
China	—	—	—	15	1	—	—	—	—	—	11.01	8.4
Nigeria	15	52	9	23	2	2	7	—	—	13	4.6	8.2
Bolivia	63	921	35	282	0	9	48	77	—	13	2.7	6.8
ADVANCED TRANSITIONAL SOCIETIES												
Cuba	85	872	5	155	63	30	86	27	—	—	6.1	22.7
Chile	88	1460	—	144	73	43	43	56	51	13	4.3	18.1
Mexico	74	879	—	278	82	49	53	48	58	11	0.9	3.2
Brazil	66	993	39	60	97	31	44	—	57	10	2.2	7.6
Argentina	93	2351	154	379	177	79	212	59	44	10	2.3	9.9
Yugoslavia	84	1853	89	166	131	61	117	40	35	—	4.5	19.3
Iran	37	405	24	229	51	24	39	139	50	17	8.6	24.0
INDUSTRIALIZED SOCIETIES												
Soviet Union	100	1903	397	390	216	67	288	28	—	—	—	27.7
Poland	98	1701	248	174	180	76	172	25	26	—	—	19.2
Italy	94	1775	113	218	215	264	198	21	—	14	2.8	14.1
United Kingdom	99	1247	388	626	317	376	134	16	34	22	5.0	9.8
Saudi Arabia	2	295	11	11	14	18	40	—	—	12	5.8	20.2
HIGH-INFORMATION SOCIETIES (POSTINDUSTRIAL)												
Japan	98	2024	526	546	234	410	114	10	39	11	0.9	3.2
France	99	1963	214	316	268	261	147	10	52	15	4.0	17.4
West Germany	99	1355	312	323	307	318	195	20	39	21	3.6	12.6
United States	99	5228	287	1416	566	697	158	16	42	19	6.0	15.5
Canada	99	3588	235	742	412	576	172	15	33	20	2.0	5.2
Sweden	100	1962	572	380	348	654	156	8	39	25	3.2	14.1
Switzerland	99	990	402	296	267	599	176	12	—	13	1.9	5.8

Sources: Except as otherwise noted data are from C. L. Taylor, *World Handbook of Political and Social Indicators*, 3rd ed. (New Haven: Yale University Press, forthcoming); cols. 1, 2, 5, and 6 are from World Bank, World Atlas (Washington, D.C.: World Bank, 1978); and col. 18 is from S. Jain, *Size Distribution of Income* (Washington, D.C.: World Bank, 1975).

overwhelming majority of the work force, 80 or 85 percent, is engaged in agricultural or pastoral occupations. The nonagricultural occupations are weak and static in numbers, often segmented into specialties, disinclined to free communication across professional or status boundaries, and inhospitable to any large or rapid change or innovation. What communication there is remains largely within the conventional channels of family, locality, ritual, occupational specialty, and social class. There is little geographic or social mobility. Most people stay where they are—in their locality, their station in society, their culture and subculture, their old memories, and their old ways of thinking, feeling, and acting.

Both birth rates and death rates used to be high and tended to remain so; many people—infants, children, and young adults—passed through their short lives quickly. There often still is much interest in tombs, charnel houses, cemeteries, funerals, and other commemorative ceremonies for the dead. Population then used to grow very slowly or not at all, for the many deaths—from disease, malnutrition, neglect of effective health care and infant care, infections in childbirth or after accidents—all mounted up to balance the high rate of births.

But even in traditional societies, parents did not like traditional death rates among their children. With the coming of modern medicine and public health, death rates were pushed down, although birth rates remained traditionally high. Thus, population often doubled within a generation, requiring twice as much food and making many traditional practices untenable. In this way many traditional societies began to disrupt themselves.

Rates of change and social learning remained low. Arts, crafts, methods of technology, styles of art, rituals of religion, and doctrines of science or philosophy changed but slowly, if at all. Where there was large change, it often occurred over the period of about one century, as in the spread of maize in the seventeenth and eighteenth centuries in Turkey and Italy, the spread of potatoes in much of northern Europe, the spread of maize and millet in eighteenth-century China, or the spread of manioc—the plant from which tapioca is prepared—through much of precolonial Africa. Where large changes proceeded more quickly, they usually remained limited to a sector of life, as in the acceptance of a new religious ritual or a sectarian doctrine, or in a change of dynasty, or in the conquest of a region. Even today, many of these changes have remained on the surface of society. Daily life for most people continues as before.

In a static or slow-changing social and natural environment, experience is the most valuable form of knowledge and conservatism the safest strategy of action. Habits and prejudices, once acquired, have a good chance of proving useful as well as convenient. Memories, habits, traditions, and long-established institutions are likely to become part of the local community and family patterns and the personality structures of many individuals living in such a society.

Together, these patterns interlock and reinforce one another, preserving what all traditional societies have in common: an established way of life with its adaptation to local conditions and its ignorance of more distant facts; its depth of traditions and its narrowness of choices; its apparent mood of stability and security, and its real anxieties and fears, high rates of death, hunger, and disease; its persistence through centuries and its pervasive resistance to all major change.

What counts is not the age of a tradition, but its power over the lives of people and its resistance to change, once it has become established. Traditions can be established very quickly, for they are the result of combinations of memories and patterns of behavior that need not depend for their effectiveness on the speed or slowness with which they were put together. Sparta, Islam, such sects as the Sikhs of India or the Hutterites and some other groups in the United States—all go back to a certain act or brief period of foundation; but, once founded, they proved remarkably persistent and often came soon to conform to the pattern of smaller or larger traditional societies. Other traditional societies go back to a brief and lively period of immigration or of transition to a new type of agriculture; yet after the change has been adopted, a traditional society may emerge and last for a long time.

Such a traditional society is rarely found today in anything like its pure form. Even the small tribes with Stone Age cultures, which anthropologists still can find and study, are beginning to change. During the last twenty-five years tribesmen in remote South Sea Islands, as Margaret Mead reported, have begun to change their loincloths for factory-made cotton pants; and in other parts of the world formerly tradition-bound peasants have turned into guerrilla fighters for some form of social revolution.

But if traditional societies are being infected by elements of change, many changing and developing countries are shot through with elements of conservatism and tradition in many sectors and aspects of their lives. Here we find the conservative peasants and other rural voters; the traditional-minded artisans; the groups of devout believers in a supposedly unchanging religion and its hallowed ritual; the local folk distrustful of strangers and things new; and those who feel that what was good enough in the past will remain equally good enough for them in the future.

When we recall the proposition of the sociologist Talcott Parsons (see pp. 145–46) that every social system needs to maintain its own patterns and needs certain persons and institutions to perform this function of *pattern maintenance,* we can see readily that even in rapidly developing countries and societies some traditional elements will survive and often contribute to this pattern-maintaining function. Conversely, those persons and institutions that maintain cultural patterns and transmit them to the next generation—the women, the family, and the educational system in many countries—will at the same time also tend to preserve and transmit elements of an older traditional culture and society.

The content of this traditional culture and social system, however, may differ very much between one country and another. It is only when they are viewed from a great distance—both intellectual and emotional—that all traditional societies look alike. In reality the differences among them are often profound, and these can have major effects on the probable speed and character of their eventual development.

Some Major Differences Among Traditional Societies. Traditional societies differ profoundly in their productivity labor, in their technologies and economies, in their capacity to produce concentrations of wealth at least in some localities or sectors, and in the level of their intellectual and artistic culture.

Some traditional societies derive their livelihood mainly from gathering, hunting, or fishing, such as the Eskimos, various Indian tribes in South America, and some primitive tribes in Africa, Asia and Oceania. Other traditional societies live mainly on livestock raising and related pastoral activities, such as many nomadic Bedouin tribes, the Mongolian herdspeople in both Outer (Soviet) and Inner (Chinese) Mongolia, the Masai tribe in Kenya, and certain Somali tribes. More often, even very poor traditional societies practice some primitive forms of agriculture, nomadic or sedentary, yielding just enough food to permit survival on a basis of more or less equal poverty.

Where agriculture is steadier and more efficient, its surplus product—beyond the subsistence needs of the producer—is large enough to support other occupations, and most often entire social classes, such as warriors and landlords, scribes, priests, builders and artists, rulers, tax collectors and administrators, artisans, merchants, and moneylenders. Where the soil is fertile and well watered by rains or irrigation, the climate favorable, and the crop-plants relatively high yielding, traditional societies have developed into elaborate class systems and states, religious establishments and doctrines, monuments of art and architecture, warlike aristocracies, monarchies and armies, often expanding into empires holding sway over neighboring poorer regions and populations. Such have been, broadly speaking, the traditional cultures of ancient Egypt, Mesopotamia, and Iran; of the rice and grain fields of India, Burma, Vietnam, Thailand, and China; and of the grain fields of medieval Europe. Temples and cathedrals, palaces and monuments, aqueducts and roads, large enterprises of conquest and great works of art—all testify to what a traditional society can do under such favorable circumstances. But it is well to remember that these glories most often involved directly less than 5 or 10 percent of the population and that the great mass of the people went on living and dying in the same poverty-stricken and unchanging monotony, generation after generation.

Today, most of the traditional empires are gone, Nepal being the most prominent of the few holdouts. Saudi Arabia, Libya, Yemen, Rwanda, Burundi, and Tibet still were largely traditional societies as late as the late 1940s; but since then, the impact of oil, aviation, automobile transport, modern weapons, and the competing modern ideologies of commercialism, nationalism, and Communism have set them on the pathways of accelerating social and political development. Ethiopia, Somalia, Guinea, Iraq, Laos, and Cambodia—all were ruled by more or less revolutionary regimes, often calling themselves Marxist, but sometimes quarreling bitterly among themselves and even fighting undeclared, but bloody, wars with each other.

The division of labor already existent within the traditional society and culture may make a major difference to the subsequent development of the country. Are the people, both men and women, habituated to sustained and diligent labor, as in most of the cultures of South, Southeast, and East Asia? Or is agriculture still a primitive affair, left largely to women, while men are habituated to spending much of their time on hunting, fishing, cattle raising, participating in local and tribal politics, and perhaps perpetrating raids, cattle thefts, and petty warfare—as well as on gossiping, smoking, and indulging in plain idleness? Clearly, men already used to doing steady and dependable work are more likely to adjust well to industrial employment and big-city life. On the other hand, those more accustomed to relying on the labor of their womenfolk, while themselves remaining idle between bouts of hunting, politicking, or fighting, would be more likely to become paupers, drunks, or criminals in modern urban and industrial society. The first type of culture requires relatively little learning for the shift from the steady work of advanced traditional wheat or rice culture to the steady work needed by industry; the second type of culture may require a much greater effort of social learning and psychic readjustment for a similar transition to modernity.

A related difference is the presence or absence of highly developed handicraft skills, and perhaps of home industries, in the traditional society. Chinese, Japanese, and Hindu craftsmen were renowned for their patience and skill in many different trades and crafts. Competence in the production of high-quality textiles, metals, and carvings in ivory, wood, or stone offers potential resources of skill and habits of care and accuracy for the later growth of industry. Let us remember the marvelous steel swords of medieval Japan, the famed Damascene steel of early medieval Syria, and the wood carvings and icons of the village craftsmen of medieval and early modern Russia.

Related to this is the extent to which a traditional culture already has taught the population some of the merchant's skills and virtues: the ability to read, write, and calculate numbers accurately; to save, to learn, and generally to work for distant goals; and to develop a high degree of accuracy and dependability in dealing with money, time, and contractual obligations. In the cultures of the Japanese and the Chinese and among such trading castes or peoples as the Parsees, the Jains, and the Marwaris of India, the Armenians and Greeks in the eastern Mediterranean and the Ottoman Empire, the Syrian and Lebanese traders in Muslim

Africa, the Scots in seventeenth- and eighteenth-centry Britain, the Ibo people in Nigeria, the Bamilike tribe in Cameroon, and the Jews in medieval Eastern Europe—in the cultures and traditions of each of these groups was a merchant strain that prepared them for a faster and more successful transition to modernity, albeit sometimes at the cost of making them unpopular with their less successful neighbors. Other traditional cultures may teach people a different set of skills, less well suited to success in industrial, commercial, bureaucratic, or scientific occupations: the warriors' preference for the virtues of the sword over those of the book and the pen; their contempt for the merchants' thrift and care; their alternation between the austerity of warfare or the hunt and the wealth expended on days of feasting or victory; their delight in physical prowess and their disdain for paperwork, study, and examinations; their reliance on intuitive judgment and their distrust of explicit rules and reasoned explanations; and their respect for past deeds and heroic ancestors and their relative lack of interest in any changes in the future.

Accordingly, members of some soldierly or religiously oriented cultures, such as the Muslim or the Spanish Catholic, have particular difficulties in the transition to modernization. Muslims in colonial India and Nigeria often did less well in British civil service examinations than did their Hindu or Ibo competitors. In the American high schools in Hawaii, according to some reports, the children of Filipino workers often have done less well than their fellow students of Chinese or Japanese ancestry who were recruited from the same occupational groups and social strata.

Something similar may even apply to entire countries. Bruce Russett and his collaborators found that Muslim countries, and also Catholic countries, appeared to perform less well on a number of indicators of social and economic development and of political modernization than the average of all countries of the world. Historians similarly record that most Spanish-speaking or Muslim Arab countries have been deficient in many aspects of social and economic development during the last four hundred years.[2]

It is interesting to note that many economists and political leaders of developing countries in Eastern Europe and East and South Asia, from the political left as well as the right, have stressed the capacity of such countries to achieve their political and economic independence and development

[2]In about 1960, countries with a higher percentage of Muslims tended to have—as indicated by the positive or negative percentage coefficient of correlation after each variable—higher rates of birth (46), natural population growth (41), and infant death (22). They had more of their work force occupied in agriculture (44), spent a larger share of their incomes on defense (21), and had smaller shares of urban population (−30) and urban growth (−42). They were marked by lower levels of per capita income (−44), capital formation (−38), income growth (−32), literacy (−64), public school enrollment (−54), higher education (−31), and general government revenue (−42) and expenditure (−34). They also had less industry (−40), shorter life expectancy of the population (−45), fewer physicians (−40) and hospital beds (−37), and fewer mass media (−46 to −26 on five indicators), but they also had slightly lower levels of income inequality (−23).

Countries with a higher percentage of Roman Catholics, compared with all countries, tended to have higher levels of income inequality (47) and to keep it even after taxes (46). They also showed greater inequality in landholdings (40), and a larger proportion of their wage and salary earners was unemployed (42). But they were less agricultural in income (−25) and employment (−23); their per capita incomes tended to be higher (31), and so were their levels of literacy (34), higher education (33), school enrollment at the primary and secondary levels (21), and mass media saturation—such as by radio (35), newspapers (29), television (23), and motion pictures (22). Their rates of birth, population growth, and economic growth did not differ significantly from those of the rest of the world, but relative to their population they had fewer marriages (−34) and more physicians (37) and hospital beds (29) and, nonetheless, higher rates of death (29) and infant death (32).

This does not necessarily mean of course, that Islam or Catholicism caused these conditions, which may have existed in some of these lands before their present religions were adopted.

For data, see B. M. Russett et al., *World Handbook of Political and Social Indicators* (New Haven: Yale University Press, 1964), pp. 286–87.

primarily by their own efforts. By contrast, significant numbers of economists and political representatives from countries of Spanish Catholic or Muslim Arab culture, and most often from leftist groups, have tended to put forward theories of imperialism and *neocolonialism,* which asserted or implied that the underdevelopment of these countries was due primarily to conditions outside their borders and that their own people could not be expected to be primarily responsible for the success or failure of their own emancipation. There are some exceptions even among the countries of Muslim or Ibero-American tradition. Where indigenous movements have had some success, as in Mexico, Cuba, and recently Iran, the chances for independence and development by national efforts are seen in a more favorable light.

More subtle differences among traditional societies exist in regard to many values and attitudes that are apt to be crucial for the success or failure of rapid social, political, and economic modernization. Some nations and cultures put stress on *achievement motivation;* that is, they treat heroism, great deeds, victory in contest and feats of skill, gains in wealth, or the production of substantial or outstanding works of art, architecture, or economic construction as things to be admired and desired. Similarly, societies differ in their evaluation of manual labor and also of steady and persistent work, of reliability and truth, of accuracy and accountability. European craftsmen were traditionally proud of working with their hands, whereas high-caste Hindus were taught by the traditions of their caste system to disdain and avoid manual work. Some traditional societies teach people to value the future and to work for distant goals; others teach them to live for the past or the present, to persist in playing age-old social roles, or else to snatch every brief moment of happiness as soon as they can. Some traditions teach trust and cooperation, whereas others may teach mistrust and the expectation and practice of betrayal and deceit, often outside the circle of one's family, but sometimes even within it.

Related to these differences are the different levels of desire for and competence in the organization and conduct of autonomous small groups holding real powers of decision over at least some activities or aspects of life that truly matter to the people concerned. And related to these, in turn, is the desire for self-government on the local, regional, or national level, as in the case of the self-governing cities of much of medieval western Europe, and later of the American colonies and the United States, and of the self-governing town councils—the *cabildos*—found in parts of Latin America. Other forms of self-government may develop on the basis of craft or occupation (as in the medieval European guilds) or for groups of religious believers (as in the congregations of certain Protestant denominations in seventeenth-century Britain). Once developed within the framework of a still wholly or largely traditional society, such skills, habits, and institutions of *group solidarity and self-government* may then be available for the faster and more thorough social and political growth of the country in which they exist.

Other conditions that developed within the traditional society may also greatly influence the effects of the cultural values, attitudes, and institutions just mentioned. Geographic proximity to large markets tends to favor the more rapid emancipation of the peasantry. Peasants learn quickly to use money and to adapt at least some of their produce to the market; landlords discover that if the peasants are left free to do this, they will earn more money, of which the landlord then can get a share in the form of rent. Under such conditions individual freedom, economic rationality, and political self-government have a relatively good chance to develop quickly.

Being located a great distance from the nearest major market tends to have the opposite effect. Peasants then will depend on intermediaries to buy, transport, and market their products; and these intermediaries are likely to find it less trouble to deal with a few landlords than with many peasants. Once landlords form a coalition against the peasants, they are likely to profit and grow stronger and to exploit the peasants more. Serfdom, peonage, chattel slavery, and half-forced contract labor have developed under such conditions, and the introduction of worldwide markets and shipping services has sometimes made these conditions even worse. Cases in point include the spread and tightening of serfdom in sixteenth- and seventeenth-century Prussia, Poland, and Russia; the growth of slave labor between 1810 and 1860 in the cotton kingdom of the South of the United States; and the growth and partial persistence of the plantation system in colonial Latin America, Indonesia, Malaysia, and Indochina.

Even within these traditional or semitraditional societies of unfree labor there are differences. Chattel slavery tends to weaken or destroy family ties and solidarity, since individuals can be sold away at any time. Peonage may at least respect family ties, but it usually ignores or suppresses the formal or informal solidarity and self-government of villages. Only serfdom, though it denies freedom to the individual, tends to leave both families and village communities intact. In this latter case, therefore, the eventual shift to economic development, the process of social and political modernization, and the emancipation of the people by their own efforts should tend to be relatively easier and quicker.

Another critical set of conditions inherited from the traditional society is the extent of *ethnic, linguistic, cultural, and religious diversity or uniformity* and, hence, the ease or difficulty of communication and cooperation among different elements of the population. Pakistan and China had in 1965 similar low per capita incomes, but China had inherited from its long premodern past a much higher degree of cultural and linguistic unity. By 1979, Pakistan had broken in two: a new state, Bangladesh, of over 80 million population who were almost entirely Bengali-speaking; and a much diminished rump state, still called Pakistan, but in fact limited to the former West Pakistan. The over 70 million inhabitants of Pakistan belong to several different ethnic language groups that have remained separated from one another, despite their common Muslim religion, by continuing difficulties in the way of broad social communication, cooperation, and civic solidarity. During the same fourteen years, 1965–79, China passed through its Great Proletarian Cultural Revolution and then through a period of attempted economic modernization, emerging stronger and apparently more united than before. It is natural for the Chinese Communist government to claim credit for this success. It is likewise natural for the dictatorial military government of Zia ul-Hag that ruled Pakistan in 1979 to be blamed for the country's continuing difficulties. But, in fact, the Chinese rulers may well have been helped—and the Pakistani generals hindered—by the different ethnic and linguistic traditions of the two countries.

THE IMPACT OF MODERNITY

Whatever the heritage of a country from its traditional past and whatever the extent to which elements—or even major patterns—from its past have survived intact, sooner or later every society and culture in today's world is likely to be challenged and changed by the impact of modernization. This impact is likely to be uneven. It will interfere with some sectors and practices of the traditional society much more than with others. It may destroy or transform some, bring others into being, and leave still others largely undisturbed.

The sources of modernity, likewise, are not spread uniformly over the country or throughout the society. They are concentrated in particular localities, groups, practices, and institutions, which thus play a key role in the modernizing process.

Domestic Sources of Modernization. An underlying source of *modernization* consists in some increase in the productivity of labor—more ample crops, more abundant livestock, a greater catch of fish, a special material to be gathered or hunted (such as amber or ivory), or a special product of handicraft (such as textiles or metal goods)—that now can become objects of trade. Such trade may be local, from one village to another or from several villages to a nearby marketplace; or else it may be long-distance trade, moving some local product to a distant market, either directly or through a chain of intermediaries. The more trade increases in volume, the larger the number and diversity of persons and localities involved in it, and the greater the efficiency of transport that permits the involvement of relative strangers, the more likely it is that people eventually will find it convenient to trade for money rather than to exchange goods or services in kind. Growing productivity and transport thus tend to produce growing trade; growing trade tends to produce an increasing *monetization* of economic life; and money and monetization are powerful solvents of past habits and traditions.

At the same time, increasing productivity also permits an increase in the division of labor. Even the poor peasants in a village in India often produce enough food to support some village artisans, such as a blacksmith or a barber, who serve their needs. Or such artisans may serve several villages, visiting each in turn. Other artisans, such as weavers, may live in a village and spend some or all of their time producing goods to sell in nearby markets or to traders for sale in more distant ones. In this manner there arises, in the midst of a rural and agricultural society, a small, but growing, nonagricultural population, a population gaining its livelihood mainly from nonagricultural work.

As the number of people in nonagricultural occupations grows, some of them will move closer to a marketplace where their services and products are more in demand and, hence, can be exchanged or sold on more favorable terms. This concentration of nonagricultural occupations in combination with a market constitutes one major element in the economic and social character of a city.

A *marketplace,* in turn, usually requires a location at a crossroads, a ford, a bridge, the head of a caravan trail, or some similar *node of transportation,* where travelers and merchants stop to rest, take on supplies, perhaps also change their means of transport, and repackage their loads and goods. But a *market* as an economic institution is primarily a place or region within which the decisions of many buyers and sellers are closely interdependent, so that when one seller charges more, prospective customers can quickly survey whatever alternative offers are available to them, and when one seller raises or lowers the price, all others can quickly learn about it and decide whether or not to follow suit. In this sense a market is made primarily not by geography, but by transport and communication. The markets for wheat and oil are worldwide and have been so for many decades, thanks to cables and power-driven ships. Other markets may be confined to a few villages and a small market town that serves them or, as sometimes happens, exploits them.

But a market also has some political requirements. It requires a high probability of peace and of security for merchants and customers and their money and goods. It also needs some law, or, rather, a high probability that contract obligations will be fulfilled and debts will be paid. Within many countries, merchants and market towns are, therefore, among the first to press for stronger local government that can assure a high degree of local "law and order." They are also likely to support the development of a strong central government that will ensure safety on the highways and waterways between the different cities and that will credibly promise to enforce contract obligations throughout the country.[3]

Some political and economic centers of this sort

[3]To be sure, markets and money also function on the level of the international system, where there is no central world government to protect property and enforce laws and contract obligations. Such world trade and finance, however, function often less reliably, and they operate only with greater difficulties, risks, and costs. Private international trading and financial interests often are found among the supporters of a stronger system of international law and limited or general world government.

may arise in premodern times and only later become centers for the spread of industry and the eventual transformation of their countries. Cairo in Egypt, Baghdad in Iraq, Teheran in Iran, Moscow in the Soviet Union, Warsaw in Poland, Mexico City in Mexico, Peking and Nanking in China, and Addis Ababa in Ethiopia are centers of this kind.

Wherever they keep growing on a sufficiently large scale, markets and money thus tend to mobilize people from their old habits and their local isolation. They promote a trend toward stronger and more effective government and, more often than not, toward political and administrative centralization as well. But the same mobilizing and modernizing process also promotes the rise of local and regional centers and activities; and these, in turn, generate demands for local and regional political autonomy and political power. In this manner the spread of money and the rise of markets will tend to foster both the growth of central governments, eager to monopolize power, and the rise of local and minority movements increasingly determined to resist them. Far from being a smooth pathway toward ever larger and more perfect integration, the road of economic and political modernization more often leads to growing political conflicts.

Cities also are gateways to modernity in another sense. Within their shelter there arise new occupations and new social classes, and these, in many countries, tend to organize themselves eventually for the pursuit of political power. In medieval Europe growing numbers of urban merchants and artisans were followed by the rise of guilds and often by the entry of these guilds and their members into political activity. Under more modern conditions factories, rather than artisans, and large corporations, rather than small merchants, have been the main carriers of economic modernization. But these larger firms, too, have tended to pursue their interests also in the field of active politics; and their workers and clerical employees have tended to form or join labor unions and to support labor-oriented parties and, thus, to enter deeply into politics of such different countries as Finland, Argentina, Bolivia, Ghana, and Japan. The spread of money and markets, the growth of cities and industry, and the increase of artisans, workers, and white-collar employees have to some degree transformed society and politics in every part of the world: first in northwestern Europe and the United States; later in central, Mediterranean, and Eastern Europe and in Latin America; still later in China and India; and most recently in the Arab world and in black Africa.

External Bridgeheads of Modernity. In many countries, as in much of Western Europe, this process of modernization has grown autonomously. It was initiated mainly from domestic centers, and it has been sustained and enhanced mainly by domestic personnel and resources. In other countries, such as the Soviet Union and Japan, minor or transitory foreign centers, organizations, and individuals supplied some of the initiative, but the main developments were soon taken over and carried further by native and internal elements. In still other countries the main economic and financial activities have remained much longer concentrated in foreign hands, as in much of black Africa and Latin America; or at least the main commercial, industrial, and banking firms have remained foreign-owned and foreign-controlled, directly or indirectly, even though the large majority of low-level and middle-level personnel eventually came to be recruited from native—and much cheaper—labor. This latter pattern is still characteristic of much of Latin America, Asia, parts of Africa, and to a lesser degree even of parts of southern Europe.

Bridgehead Cities. In many cases, money, modern commerce, banking, transport, and industry all tend to be concentrated in a few foreign or foreign-dominated economic centers. These are usually located at the geographic periphery of the developing countries, usually at a port city, often of relatively recent origin. Examples are Bombay and Calcutta in India; Shanghai and Canton in

China; Hong Kong, just off the Chinese coast; Singapore at the tip of the Malaysian peninsula; Buenos Aires in Argentina; San Salvador, Bahia, and later Rio de Janeiro in Brazil; Oran in Algeria; Accra in Ghana; Lagos in Nigeria; Zanzibar and Dar es Salaam in Tanzania; and there are many more.

In other cases a foreign-dominated city may be established deeper inland, first as an administrative and military center, perhaps later becoming a commercial, financial, and industrial one as well. Such has been the role of Santiago in Chile, Lima in Peru, Delhi in India, Nairobi in Kenya, Salisbury in Rhodesia, and Lusaka in Zambia.

Direct Foreign Rule. Often the impact of foreign-dominated geographic bridgeheads of modernity is supplemented or surpassed by that of direct foreign conquest and administration, followed by a substantial inflow of foreign settlers, as in Mexico, Peru, and elsewhere in much of Latin America; in the Union of South Africa; in Kenya and Rhodesia; in Algeria, Tunisia, and the Malagasy Republic (Madagascar). Such direct intrusion of foreign rule and foreign settlers tends to accelerate some aspects of the modernization process, such as the inflow of foreign capital, skills, and innovation; but it often tends to slow down other aspects of the same process, such as the development of skilled middle-level and higher-level native personnel in government, finance, industry, and large-scale commerce; and it may slow down the process of local capital formation and investment, if foreign businesspeople and settlers get most of the higher salaries and profits and remit much of them back to their home countries.

Indirect Rule. Methods of indirect rule tend to be slower in spreading technical innovations and economic, political, cultural, and social change. Under this system a foreign power would leave a native sultan, rajah, sheikh, or tribal chieftain, usually with his entourage, in charge of the province, district, or tribe that traditionally had been under his authority, on condition that he henceforth would maintain a type of "law and order" and a general state of affairs favorable to the operations of foreign business interests, and sometimes to foreign settlers, and perhaps also to the strategic interests of the "protecting power"—with the latter often taking charge of all foreign political trade relations, major military matters, and, often, taxation and public finance. In exchange for his collaboration, the native ruler could henceforth count on the military and police support of the foreign power, not only against neighboring tribes or rulers, but also—and sometimes primarily—against his own subjects. In the past native chieftains could be deposed more or less freely by the members of the tribe whenever they became sufficiently unpopular. But they now became virtually irremovable, thanks to the backing of the seemingly invincible machine guns, cannon, and airplanes of the foreign power.

Usually these arrangements were extended to the priests or teachers of the locally established religion, who were protected against critics, heretics, or major religious rivals and who were aided, directly or indirectly, in their suppression. (Christian missionaries most often made so few converts that the power of the established religion and of its priests, teachers, or, among animist tribes, its witch doctors was not seriously threatened.) Similarly, indirect rule would protect the power and privileges of local landowners, high castes of priests or warriors, rich merchants or moneylenders, and the like. By this method, warmly advocated by the political philosopher Edmund Burke (see Chapter 4), the foreign power not only avoided provoking popular resistance by upsetting native traditions and culture, but it actually changed the relationships of political power within the native community by making an alliance with its most powerful elements and giving them a vested interest in collaboration.

Past examples of indirect rule include the British rule of important parts of India through maharajahs and similar local rulers such as those of Travancore, Baroda, Hyderabad, and Kashmir. The Indian Republic was established in 1947, and by the early 1970s many of Britain's formal and economic claims and privileges had been abolished. Other examples are afforded by British rule through local and tribal chiefs in Ghana; through emirs and other rulers in northern Nigeria; through sheikhs of small, but oil-rich, sultanates or tribal territories in the Arab peninsula, such as Kuwait, Qatar, and Oman; and British backing for larger monarchies, such as Jordan and Saudi Arabia. In the last-named countries, the United States since the mid-1950s has become associated in the support of these regimes, but, as the 1973 oil crisis and succeeding events have shown, with less control over their actual behavior and their internal politics.

Though indirect rule slows down some aspects of modernization and perpetuates some old forms of oppression, injustice, and neglect, it still preserves a larger pool of native leadership talent. It offers more opportunities than does direct rule for the training and employment of new skilled native personnel; and it preserves a larger, deeper, and more varied stock of native cultural memories and symbols. At the same time, it avoids some of the worst effects of foreign conquests: the expulsion, in one form or another, of many natives from their land holdings—tribal, familial, or individual—and their replacement by white settlers who then tend to become bitter-end fighters against native equality and emancipation. The bloodshed that accompanied the eventual winning of independence of Kenya, Algeria, and Madagascar—all countries that then had many white settlers—contrasts with the relatively bloodless transition to independence of such countries as Morocco and Iraq, which earlier had been under indirect rule, and of Ghana, Sierra Leone, Senegal, and the Ivory Coast, all of which had few, if any, white settlers.

But formal political independence does not end the process of social and political modernization. In some cases, rather, it marks the beginning; in others, the gathering of speed and strength. But how can we gauge the speed and strength of this process, and how can we estimate its probable outcome?

SOCIAL MOBILIZATION VERSUS CULTURAL ASSIMILATION: A RACE FOR THE DESTINY OF COUNTRIES

Developing countries—and let us recall once again that in some sense all countries today are developing—are being transformed by three broad types of processes: (1) processes of *growth,* both demographic and economic, which increase the number of persons or of their material possessions without changing immediately the structure of the society and the proportions among its elements; (2) processes of social *mobilization;* and (3) processes of *assimilation.* The interplay among these three types of processes of social change goes far toward setting the choices of politics and the conditions under which political decisions must be made. Each type of process, therefore, deserves closer examination.

Processes of Growth. In most countries in the world the population increases at a rate of about 2 percent per year, and this is also the approximate mean and median growth rate for all 153 countries for which we have data. At this rate, if this growth should continue, the population of the world, and of each country, should double in about 35 years.

In many of the less highly developed countries, population growth is higher. While the crude birth rate for a country near the median in the world, such as Brazil, is still a nearly traditional 38 per thousand, the death rate in that country already has been brought down to a nearly modern 9 per thousand, leaving a net population increase of as much as 29 per thousand. At this rate, typical of many countries at this stage of *demographic transition,* there will be twice as many Brazilians within about 24 years (not counting any future immigrants). Large developing countries such as India, Indonesia, and the United Arab Republic are in the same situation. The general problem of the demographic transition as many demographers see it, is illustrated in Figure 17.2.

As the curves of the birth and death rates scissor apart because of an early fall in the death rate at a relatively early stage of development (represented, perhaps, by a 20 percent literacy level), the rate of population growth—which is roughly proportional to the distance between them—rises steeply and then often remains high, at 3 percent and more, until a much higher level of development. There, however, perhaps in the neighborhood of 80 percent literacy, birth rates in most countries start dropping sharply. (Venezuela offers a conspicuous exception, as shown in Figure 17.2). At high levels of development—with 90 percent literacy or more—birth rates then tend to be as low as 2 percent or less, and the rate of population growth goes down again to 1 percent or even 0.5 percent or less.

If a country had to start nearly from scratch, such as Upper Volta in Africa, and if it progressed no fáster than the average of countries in the recent past, it might require about seventy or eighty years to get to the 80 percent literacy level. Of these years, if it behaved like many other countries in the past, it would spend about fifty years in the period of high population growth at 3 percent per year or more; and in the absence of major upheavals, epidemics, wars, or famines it should settle down at the end of this half-century with 80 percent literacy or better—and presumably with other corresponding indicators of development—but with a population that is four times larger.

Fortunately, most countries do not have quite so far to go. India is today about 36 percent literate (the figure was 28 percent around 1965); China is now 90 percent literate or better; and the world average in 1975 was 73 percent for 140 countries. For much of humankind in the emerging countries, therefore, the transition period of high population growth is likely to be over within the next thirty years or early in the next century. The populations of these countries may well double during this period, but thereafter their growth might slow down very much. China's population growth is already reported to be down to 1.7 percent per year. For most other developing countries, however, the next doubling of their populations between, say, 1975 and 2000 probably cannot be stopped by any morally or politically acceptable method (and probably not by a practicable one, in any case).

Then what will this rapid population growth in the developing countries—even if it should remain limited to about 2.5 percent per year and, hence, to a doubling period of twenty-eight years—do to the countries in which it continues to take place?

It would be tempting to answer that it would do nothing much. We might imagine that such growth simply means more people filling the same kind of roles within the same social structures. But this would almost certainly be an error.

World population, in round figures, has grown in recent decades at about 2 percent per year; per capita income at about 3 percent; aggregate income, again as a world average, at about 5 percent; and world consumption of energy also at 5 percent. But the total amount of *potential* interactions, relationships, conflicts, and collisions has grown roughly in proportion to the square of this last figure (1.05), which equals about 1.10, or 10 percent more per year. If we assume that less than one-half of this potential traffic, clutter, and hustle actually materializes, we must expect an annual increase of about 7 percent in many kinds of traffic and communications and in demands for a wide variety of services from all kinds of public and private agencies. In fact, this is what we actually find.[4]

[4]For data on telephone traffic, air travel, and other service loads that grow at about 7 percent per year, see Manfred Kochen and Karl W. Deutsch, "Toward a Rational Theory of Decentralization: Some Implications of a Mathematical Approach," *American Political Science Review* 63 (September 1969), 734–49, and especially p. 748 n. 16.

FIGURE 17.2 *Population Growth at Different Stages of Development: A Schematic Sketch*

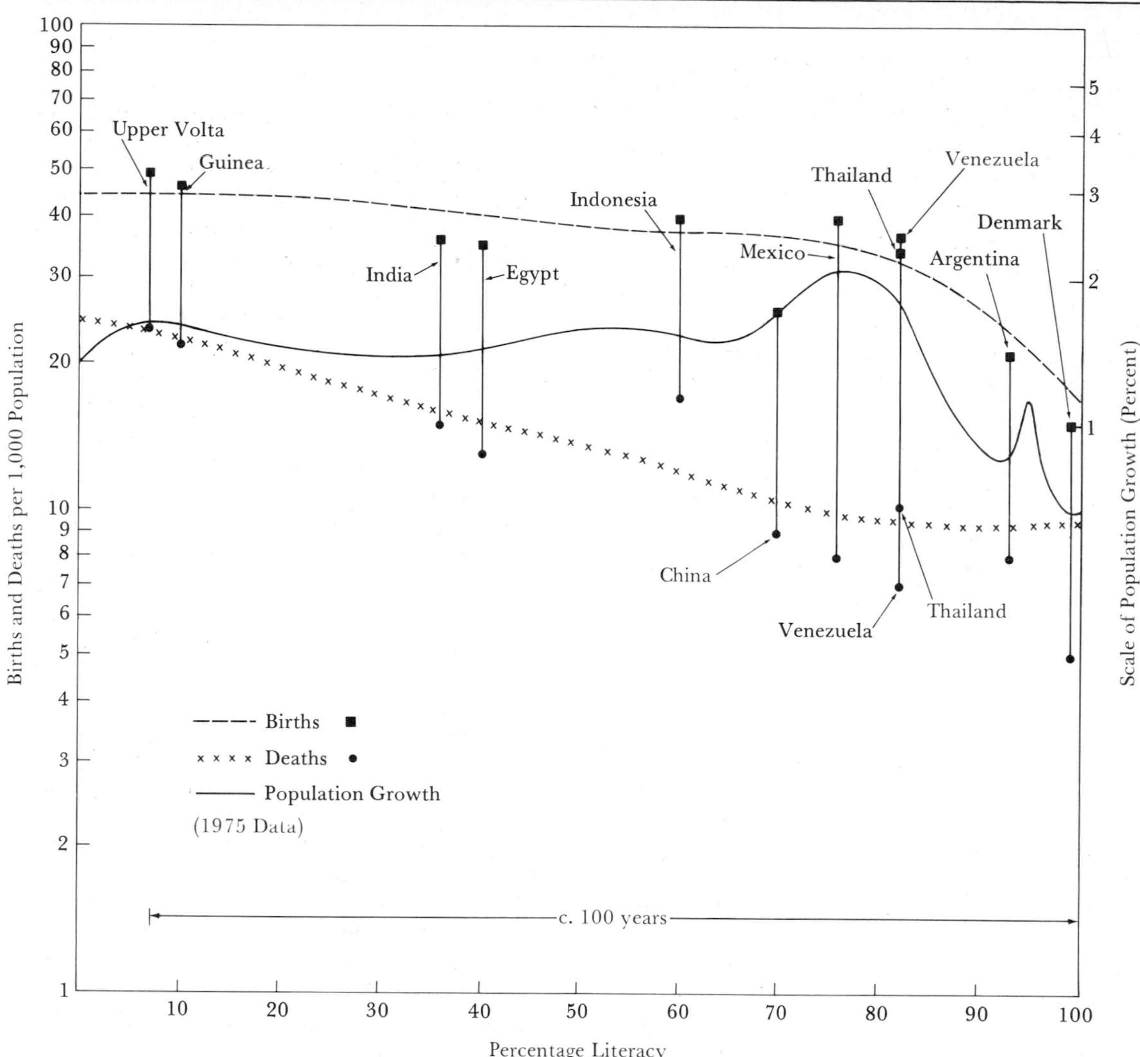

Note 1: The composite curve indicates the general process. Birth and death rates of particular countries are scattered around it, as shown.
Note 2: Other indicators of development will give substantially the same result as literacy does.
Note 3: The time scale of 100 years is based on the estimated annual shift into literacy of 1 per cent of the population, and corresponding speeds of modernization in other respects. At slower rates of modernization, the demographic transition might take longer, and the resulting population increase would be higher.

Sources: For birth and death rates and percentage population growth: *World Development Report, 1978* (Washington: World Book, 1978), table 15, pp. 104–5. For percentage literacy: Ruth Leger Sivard, *World Military and Social Expenditures, 1978* (Leesburg, Va: WMSE Publications, 1978) p. 24–28.

More people require more housing, streets, water, and utilities; more energy and fuels; more food, metals, and materials. Providing all these over the next thirty years will be almost impossible without many rearrangements in economic, social, and political practices and institutions. The growth in our sheer weight of numbers will work as a poorly directed, but powerful, engine for change and reform.

Pressures from Migration. In certain sectors the impact of demographic growth will be reinforced, or even overshadowed, by the *impact of migration.* About 0.15 percent long-term foreign immigrants per year were reported in about 1960 for such countries as the United States, Britain, France, and West Germany; about 0.1 percent for Argentina and Brazil; but between 1.2 and 1.8 percent for Australia, Canada, and Venezuela. By the late 1906s the proportions had risen slightly to 0.2 percent for the United States and France and to 0.4 percent for the United Kingdom.[5] Short-term migrants and foreign "guest workers" greatly exceed these percentages in many countries; and the figures for *internal migration,* from villages to towns and cities, from towns to large cities, and from city to city, do so still more. The houses, wells, streets, and sewers—such as they may be—left behind by migrants from a town or district losing population become largely useless, while in the fast-growing regions and areas where the migrants congregate, a mounting demand is generated for new housing, utilities, and infrastructure installations such as hospitals and schools. Often the demand is not met. Guest workers in Western Europe are often housed badly; the inhabitants of the shantytowns on the fringes of many big cities in Latin America, Asia, and Africa are housed worse; and the potential for political discontent and the pressures for change increase—and are apt to continue to do so.

The movement of people into cities can be measured. On an average for the world about 0.4 percent of the population of each country has been moving each year into cities of more than 100,000 inhabitants. In many countries the figures are higher; and additional people are moving into the smaller towns of between 2,000 and 20,000 population and into the middle-sized ones of between 20,000 and 100,000. This entire movement is very hard to stop—if anybody wanted to do that—and it, too, keeps generating political pressures, slowly, but steadily.

But the process of development not only mobilizes some people's bodies for migration. It also mobilizes larger numbers for changes of occupation, even though not all of them may change their residence; and it mobilizes still larger numbers for new forms of communications and for new dimensions of imagination and thought.

Changes of Occupation. Every year, on the average about 0.6 percent of the work force in the developing countries leaves its employment in agriculture and shifts to nonagricultural pursuits. A smaller, but substantial, number—perhaps 0.4 percent per year—moves from self-employment or family-type work into wage-earning or salaried positions; but only about 0.2 percent per year move into employment in industry. By now, almost one-half of humankind—47 percent in 1977—has ceased to work in agriculture.[6] This vast change in the occupational structure of most countries will continue to be a major and unceasing force for political and social change for the next half-century or more.

Changes in Communication. Modern life is penetrating most regions of the world with ever new demonstrations of human powers and possibilities. Every airplane overhead demonstrates that people can fly. Every truck, jeep, or station wagon passing on the road or through a village demonstrates a

[5]Russett et al., *World Handbook I,* p. 233; *United Nations Demographic Yearbook, 1970* (United Nations, 1971), pp. 754–55.

[6]*FAO Production Yearbook, 1977,* vol. 31 (Food and Agriculture Organization, United Nations, 1978), pp. 61–62.

new scale of speed and power. Every advertising poster, every show window, every mail-order catalog, and every market with factory-made goods demonstrates the possibility of new riches. Every hospital, pharmacy, or patent medicine sales outlet demonstrates that diseases, far from being ordained by fate, might be cured by human effort—which governments might have to organize. And every bit of money, every coin that people touch, and every purchase or sale for money that they learn to make introduces them to a world of possible rationality and calculation and to the possibility of having to deal, seriously and continuously, with a succession of relative strangers.

Such demonstration effects reach each year perhaps an additional 2.5 percent of the population of many developing countries, and monetization—the use of money—reaches in such countries each year perhaps a new 2 percent of all inhabitants and perhaps a new 1 percent of all activities, pushing back the realm of subsistence economy, barter, and work within the family.

The *impact of mass media* works in the same direction. About 2 percent of the population of many countries enter the radio audience each year; about 0.5 percent of families per year are newly reached by newspapers and periodicals; 0.7 percent of families start watching television. (This is again an average figure; in richer countries television has been spreading faster.) Still others are reached first by motion pictures. The new film industries of India, Japan, the Arab world, and China are adding to the mass impact of the older ones of the United States, Western Europe, and the Soviet Union.

Still more important in its depth impact is the spread of literacy, which now proceeds at an average rate of about 2 percent per year. This, at least, is the proportion of the population over age fifteen that is being added each year to the proportion already literate. Since many ten- to fourteen-year-olds also are learning to read, in greater proportions than their elders, the total shift into literacy among the population ten years of age and older may well be even higher. Most of this rapid rise in literacy is occurring in the Far East and the Near East; in southern Asia, Latin America, and Africa current changes are much slower.[7]

On this basis we may then say that for many countries the shift from 5 to 10 percent literacy (the level of Ethiopia, Upper Volta, or Guinea) to about 95 percent (the level of Italy and China) can be accomplished within two or three generations, as indicated on the time scale on Figure 17.2.

The mobilization into literacy is a more fundamental change, since it opens so many different sources of stimulation and information to people, and since it tends to support and enhance autonomous thought and activity more than mere passive participation in the mass media audience could do. What is most important for the political effects of the mass media on political development is not so much how they compete with one another, but rather how they supplement and reinforce one another in mobilizing the imagination and aspirations of a growing number of individuals.

This ability to imagine oneself at different places and in different social roles is—as the social scientist Daniel Lerner has pointed out—a major internal aspect of social mobilization.[8] It takes place within the mind of each individual, but it also can occur within the small worlds of many families and groups. To imagine oneself a sailor or a cowpuncher, a monarch or a revolutionary, a factory worker or a business executive, a detective or a criminal, a colonel or a spy—all this one learns from books, films, plays on the stage or in the streets, newspapers, radio, and television. But once a person has learned it, his or her intellectual and emotional worlds—and the world of perceived political possibilities and choices—will never be the same.

[7]From data in Ruth Legar Sivard, *World Military and Social Expenditures, 1974* and *1978* (Leesburg, Va: WMSE Publications, 1974 and 1978).

[8]See Daniel Lerner, *The Passing of Traditional Society* (New York: Free Press, 1956).

The Interlocking Processes of Social Mobilization: A Composite Picture. It should be clear from the preceding paragraphs that the various components of *social mobilization* tend to grow at different speeds. Yet, with only rare exceptions they all operate in one and the same direction. They are clearly correlated with each other. If one indicator—such as per capita income—grows, then other indicators—such as literacy or the proportion of radios or physicians to the population—will also grow. It seems legitimate, therefore, to look at them as different indicators of one and the same underlying process. A closer look confirms this view, for we find that these processes tend to reinforce each other, often in the form of amplifying feedback systems. Increased literacy will increase the expectable audience of newspapers, and the availability of interesting newspapers and periodicals will increase the motivation to become literate. A news story in the press may stimulate curiosity to find out what happened next and to find out more quickly from the radio; and a short news item on the radio may stimulate interest to read more about it in the papers. Demonstration and mass media effects stimulate the desire for money to buy some of the new things seen or shown; and money buys more opportunities to watch or listen to such demonstrations and such media. It would be tedious to list all such interlocking relationships, but they are numerous and their effects are real.

How quickly, then, does the whole interlocking bundle of processes of social mobilization operate in the course of development? For an overall answer in terms of rough estimate our indicators have been arranged in Table 17.2 in rank order of their speed.

For the eleven indicators in the table we may thus assume a median rate of shift of 0.7 percent per year, or 7 percent per decade. For particular countries that are less highly developed, we might use the spread of literacy as a general indicator of the process of social mobilization; and in the case of more highly developed countries, the speed of the spread of television might serve the same purpose. Finally, for some countries in the intermediate range an average of the diffusion rates of literacy and television might be most indicative. All these considerations will leave us with a basic or overall rate of social mobilization of about 0.9 percent per year for most of the countries about midway in the course of development.

This last qualification is worth noting. Countries that are still almost entirely traditional have, of course, only slow *rates of mobilization*, as indicated by the spread of literacy and similar indicators. Very highly developed countries, on the other hand, usually have not many people left to mobilize (for example, to learn to read), so that their indicators also will be low. It is mainly in the range between 10 and 90 percent of literacy, or of other indicators, that rates of mobilization will be as fast as or faster than indicated by our average and median values.

The scheme in Figure 17.3 illustrates this point. It should be noted that the growth of industrial employment in the 1970s has slowed down in many countries, adding the strains of greater unemployment or underemployment to those of the mobilizing process.

Social mobilization makes people more available for change. It does so by inducing them or teaching them to change their residence, their occupations, their communications, their associates, and their outlook and imagination. It gives rise to new needs, new aspirations, new demands and capabilities. But all these new patterns of behavior may disunite a population or unite it. They can make people more similar or more different. They may produce cooperation or strife, integration or secession. To learn to judge the probable outcome in each case, we must now turn our attention to the problem of assimilation.

Assimilation: The Concept and the Process. Assimilation is a special case of social learning. It is the learning of habits of behavior that are so similar to the habits of another person, or a group, that the behavior of the *assimilated* person cannot be distinguished readily or reliably from that of the person

TABLE 17.2 *The Speed of Social Mobilization in Developing Countries: A Rank Order of Indicators*

Indicator or process	Percentage of rate of shift of population per year		
A. MOBILIZATION WITHOUT NECESSARY CHANGE OF RESIDENCE OR OCCUPATION			
1. Exposure to demonstration effects	2.5†		
2. Use of money	2.0†		
3. Radio audience*	2.0	Median A: 2.0	
4. Literacy	2.0		
5. Television audience*	0.7		
6. Newspaper audience*	0.5		Median A + B = 0.6
B. MOBILIZATION WITH CHANGE OF OCCUPATION OR RESIDENCE			
7. Nonagricultural occupations	0.5		
8. Migrations (internal and/or external)	0.5†	Median B: 0.4	
9. Urbanization (cities over 100,000)	0.4		
10. Wage or salaried employment	0.4		
11. Industrial employment	0.2		

*Newspaper audiences were calculated at 3 readers per copy, or 3 persons of reading age per household; radio and television audiences were computed at 4 listeners or watchers per instrument. Saturation levels for newspapers were thus put at 333 per 1,000 population; for radio and television, at 250. Shifts were then computed as percentages of each saturation level.
†Estimated.

Sources: Taylor and Hudson, *World Handbook II.* Russett et al., *World Handbook I.* Ruth Legar Sivard, *World Military and Social Expenditures, 1974* and *1978* (Leesburg, VA.: WMSE Publications, 1974 and 1978), pp. 25–29. *UNESCO Statistical Yearbook, 1974,* p. 770; *1976,* p. 921. *FAO Production Yearbook, 1977,* p. 61. *U.N. Demographic Yearbook, 1970,* pp. 480f.; *1971,* pp. 382f.; *1973,* pp. 388f. *I.L.O. Yearbook of Labor Statistics, 1972,* pp. 44f.; *1977,* pp. 52f.

or group to whom he or she has become assimilated. Assimilation is, therefore, a matter of degree. People's behavior may be more or less similar, more or less easily distinguishable by themselves or by outside observers. Nonetheless, there is a critical threshold in assimilation to a group, a culture, or a people. This threshold is marked by the *ability to pass* as a member of the group. In somewhat more technical terms, an assimilated member of a long-established group has passed this threshold if anyone's judgments about the membership of this person will have the same distribution of errors as would be found in such judgments about any other member of the group.

The same reasoning applies to the degree of assimilation among two or more groups. A group is assimilated to another if its members can no longer be distinguished effectively from their counterparts in the other group.

Dimensions of Assimilation. Assimilation can occur in regard to many different aspects of behavior. Eight among these are outstanding for their political significance: assimilation of (1) language; (2) culture; (3) ethnicity with its social associations, organizational memberships, and family connections; (4) aspirations; (5) capabilities; (6) attainments; (7) civic compliance; and (8) political loyalties.

Any two or more of these aspects of behavior, or even all of them, of course, may coincide in some particular case and work in the same direction. To the extent that they do so, they will tend to reinforce each other and form an interlocking structure that may be stronger than the sum of its components. Anyone who has learned to speak habitually American English, perhaps even without an accent; who has become steeped in American childhood memories, education, and culture; who has entered deeply into the old-stock American community in terms of personal friendships, social associations, ties of intermarriage, and family connections; who has learned to have American aspirations and values, such as those of mobility, equality, success, and wealth; who has developed the capabilities needed and valued in American culture, such as competence, efficiency, capacity for hard work, skill, energy, persistence, initiative, a talent both for self-direction and for cooperation with others, together with a reasonably discriminating capacity for showing trust and being trusted; who has attained the characteristic level of rewards of American culture in terms of health, wealth, knowledge, and respect; who obeys laws in the manner most other Americans do; and who will actively support American interests and institutions to the same degree as other citizens do—such a person will indeed have become an American.

FIGURE 17.3 *How the Speed of Further Social Mobilization Changes with the Levels Already Attained: A Schematic Presentation*

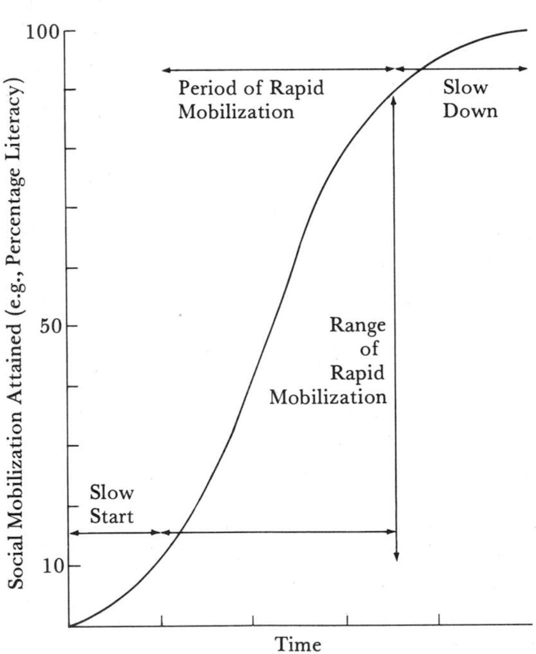

Note: The changing slope of the curve represents the changing speeds of further mobilization.

Similar checklists for these eight dimensions of assimilation could be made for the assimilation to British, French, German, Japanese, Soviet, or Chinese Communist culture.

Assimilation and Marginality. In many actual cases, however, assimilation may not proceed equally in all dimensions. Individuals may learn the vocabulary and grammar of a language, but retain a distinctive accent; they may acquire American work habits, but remain ignorant of much of American culture; or they may come to share American aspirations of wealth and status, but fall short of the American standards of skill, competence, initiative, efficiency, and self-direction in sustained hard work. Still others may be fully assimilated in terms of both aspirations and capabilities, but may continue to avoid and discourage intermarriage outside their smaller ethnic or religious group, and they may tend to keep their closest friendships and major social ties within its confines.

Wherever assimilation in one or more of these dimensions is absent, or where the degree of assimilation in two or more of these dimensions differs substantially, there we are likely to find groups that have remained *marginal* in the community toward which their uneven and incomplete steps of assimilation had been directed.

Assimilation and Acceptance. Success in some dimensions of assimilation, moreover, does not depend only on the efforts of groups or persons making them. In regard to language, culture, and capabilities, the existing speech habits and culture patterns may ease their task or make it much more difficult. Entry into an ethnic community through intermarriage, family connections, friendship ties, and social associations depends on the *social acceptance* of the would-be assimilant by the members of the group. Even more critically, and sometimes tragically, the assimilation of attainments even by highly skilled and hard-working outsiders or by members of minority groups may depend critically on the absence of *discrimination,* explicit or implied. Members of the established in-group or the favored ethnic or social group would have to be willing to accept the work and other contributions of the would-be assimilants on equal terms, and these terms themselves would have to avoid any concealed form of actual discrimination.[9]

The outcome of the process of assimilation, and the different forms and degrees of merging or marginality that it is likely to produce in various cases, will thus depend on the interplay of assimilation in all eight dimensions and also on the interplay of efforts at assimilation and acceptance within some of them. Often this interplay tends to have a major effect on the motives for making continued efforts at assimilation (or else for abandoning them) and for learning or unlearning assimilated habits.

Motives for Assimilation or Disassimilation. Why should people try to unlearn old habits and endeavor to learn new ones? And even if they made no conscious efforts of this kind, why should they learn these new habits, anyway?

We have said that assimilation is a form of social learning. Like all learning, it requires a drive—a need or imbalance—that will tend to move the person, group, or learning system away from its present state and toward some "preferable" or "goal" state in which this actor's inner drive or disequilibrium will be reduced (see Chapter 7, pp. 155–58). People who are assimilating do so, first of all, because in their unassimilated state they lack something that they need. This missing something may be physical or emotional security, as in the case of refugees; or economic or social opportunity, as in the case of many economically motivated immigrants; or better chances in employment, career, or business, which are available to the speakers of the favored language and members of the favored ethnic group; or the greater richness of knowledge, beauty, and prestige that a more highly developed language and culture may offer. Others may be moved by the desire to belong to a stable and well-identified group and to be accepted by it; this motive has been measured by the psychologist Daniel McClelland under the name of *need for affiliation.* Or there may be a combination of several needs, deficiencies, or hungers that drive persons or groups to forsake a part of their earlier identity and to enter the pathway of assimilation.

Another element of social mobilization may be even more crucial. It is the presence or absence of

[9]Examples are "On this program all fashion models and television announcers, black or white, must have thin lips and long straight hair"; or "Any employee, man or woman, will be discharged in case of pregnancy"; or "Each candidate for this scholarship must prove that he or she has only American-born grandparents."

rewards for assimilation and the terms and conditions under which they are available. If relatively moderate efforts at and small increments in some dimensions of assimilation are positively and readily rewarded materially and emotionally, these rewards will tend to reinforce the behavior and elicit further efforts at learning. If there continue to be no such rewards, or if they are forthcoming only after discouragingly long delays and under difficult conditions, most people are likely to reduce or give up further efforts at assimilation, and they may even unlearn some or much of the assimilated habits already acquired.

In such cases the process may reverse, for there may also be *rewards* available from *differentiation and secession:* from setting up one's own distinctive group, from striving for its independence from the dominant language, nation, or country, or even for striving for its predominance. If the ruling nationality fails to reward assimilation, and if it lets its language and culture become associated with repeated experiences of frustration and oppression, while the different language and culture of a submerged group remain attractive and rewarding to them and their fellows, then the members may unlearn some of their assimilated ways, and their children may do so even more. They all may then prefer to strengthen the distinctiveness, language, cultural cohesion, and political solidarity of their own, still disadvantaged group and to struggle for its independence and power in the future.

Experience has shown that attempts by the government to penalize such behavior are likely to make matters worse, often tending to produce more resentment than genuine compliance and loyalty. In this manner some Algerian *évolués*—Arabs who are assimilated to French language and culture—of the 1930s, such as Ferhat Abbas, were disappointed by continuing French privilege and unresponsiveness and eventually turned into leaders of the Arab-oriented Algerian independence movement in the 1950s.

Similarly, the partial assimilation of many Jews in the Soviet Union to the Russian language and to Soviet culture and political loyalty during the 1920s and early 1930s was reinforced for a time by the granting of equal rights, by the successes of economic modernization, and by the threat of Hitler's Germany. The process was eventually reversed for at least some of them, however, by Stalin's persecutions and later by the continued frustration of the rising aspirations and self-confidence of many Soviet Jews who found top positions more often barred to them, as they saw it, than to their non-Jewish competitors. Perhaps also the rising attractiveness of the new state of Israel, between its victorious war against Egypt in 1967 and the indecisive Egyptian attack of 1973, was a contributing factor. Since other Soviet Jews have continued to identify themselves culturally, politically, and emotionally with the Soviet Union, the social learning processes of assimilation and dissimilation seem to have divided what was earlier a relatively more homogenous community of Soviet Jews.

In each specific case the outcome of the learning process of assimilation will depend on the interplay of specific conditions and processes along the various major dimensions that were surveyed above. In order to enable each of us to study any such case more thoroughly by ourselves, it will be helpful to take a closer look at least at some of the balances or imbalances among the rates of change in these different dimensions.

The Imbalance Between Social Mobilization and Assimilation. Most is known, perhaps, about the assimilation of language groups. They are more easily identified; the language spoken habitually, or customarily in their homes, can be ascertained. With the spread of systems of military conscription and public education, the language that soldiers or schoolchildren actually speak and understand acquires obvious public importance. Students of education and of *social linguistics*—that is, of the ways in which the use of language and the arrangements of society influence each other—have contributed a rich store of studies and data.

The picture that emerges from all this information is in some ways surprising, for it shows the remarkably low speed of *linguistic assimilation* of larger settled populations to any other language. The average rate of their shift to the favored or predominant language is only about 0.15 percent per year ±0.25: that is, between 0.4 percent per year under the most favorable conditions and −0.1 per year under the least favorable ones.[10] In the latter case, therefore, linguistic assimilation will be reversed, and people will actually shift away from the language of the favored group and back into the language of the disfavored one, albeit slowly.

Even at best, then, the average speed of linguistic assimilation is less than one-half of that of the shift into literacy, which now is about 2.0 percent per year, and under more normal circumstances it will be only about one-sixth of the latter. In any case it will be much less than the rate of entry into the radio audience or into the circle of users of money. It is much slower, in short, than many of the processes of social mobilization; the latter, therefore, will tend to produce in many multilingual countries growing numbers of mobilized, but linguistically unassimilated, people. If linguistic shift should move at its normal speed of 0.15 percent per year, it will be also less than half as fast as the shift into wage or salaried employment, which moves on the average at 0.4 percent per year. It also will be less than one-half of the shift to big-city residence and to urban residence in general, which normally occurs at an annual 0.4 percent, and less than one-fourth the shift out of agriculture into nonagricultural occupations. Everywhere these discrepancies will give rise to mobilized, but nonassimilated, groups, displaying potential for linguistic and political conflict.

Something similar will hold for the spread of radio, newspapers, and other mass media into the countryside. Of every five or six rural people mobilized into the mass media audience, only one will be likely to learn the predominant language. The other four or five will furnish a ready-made public for a new literature and mass culture in the formerly submerged popular language or languages and an array of new writers, reporters, editors, and publishers in those newly risen idioms. The spread of school enrollment and literacy tends to have similar effects, since most of the new reading and schooling has to be for the unassimilated population and their children; it has to be done in their native language, by teachers who know it well and are recruited, ever more often, from this native group itself. The teachers, like the editors and writers, soon tend to become available as the intellectuals and potential spokespeople and leaders of the formerly submerged nationality groups, often in a struggle against their privileged neighbors.

Similar quantitative imbalances exist among other dimensions of assimilation. The assimilation of aspirations spreads almost as fast as the results of demonstration effects and membership in mass media audiences—that is, at speeds of between 0.5 and 2.5 percent per year, or at a median annual rate of about 1.5 percent. But the assimilation of capabilities proceeds much more slowly, at best at the rate of entry into urban, salaried, or industrial occupations. In short, aspirations in developing countries or among emerging peoples tend to collect about three times as fast as capabilities.

This three-to-one ratio of speeds—when and where it is a fact—has some striking implications. A schematic example is shown in Figure 17.4.

If the spread of modern aspirations throughout the population of some country (or the members of some ethnic group) should take about 40 years, then the corresponding period for assimilation of capabilities by the entire population will be 120 years. During this period many members of the population will experience a real gap between aspirations and capabilities, and their numbers will grow quickly. Already after the first 10 years one-sixth of the population, and after 20 years one-third of the people, will have greater aspirations than capabilities. From the thirtieth to the

[10]K. W. Deutsch, *Tides Among Nations* (New York: Free Press, 1977), pp. 304–06.

FIGURE 17.4 *A Quick Learning of Aspirations versus Slower Learning of Capabilities: A Schematic Presentation*

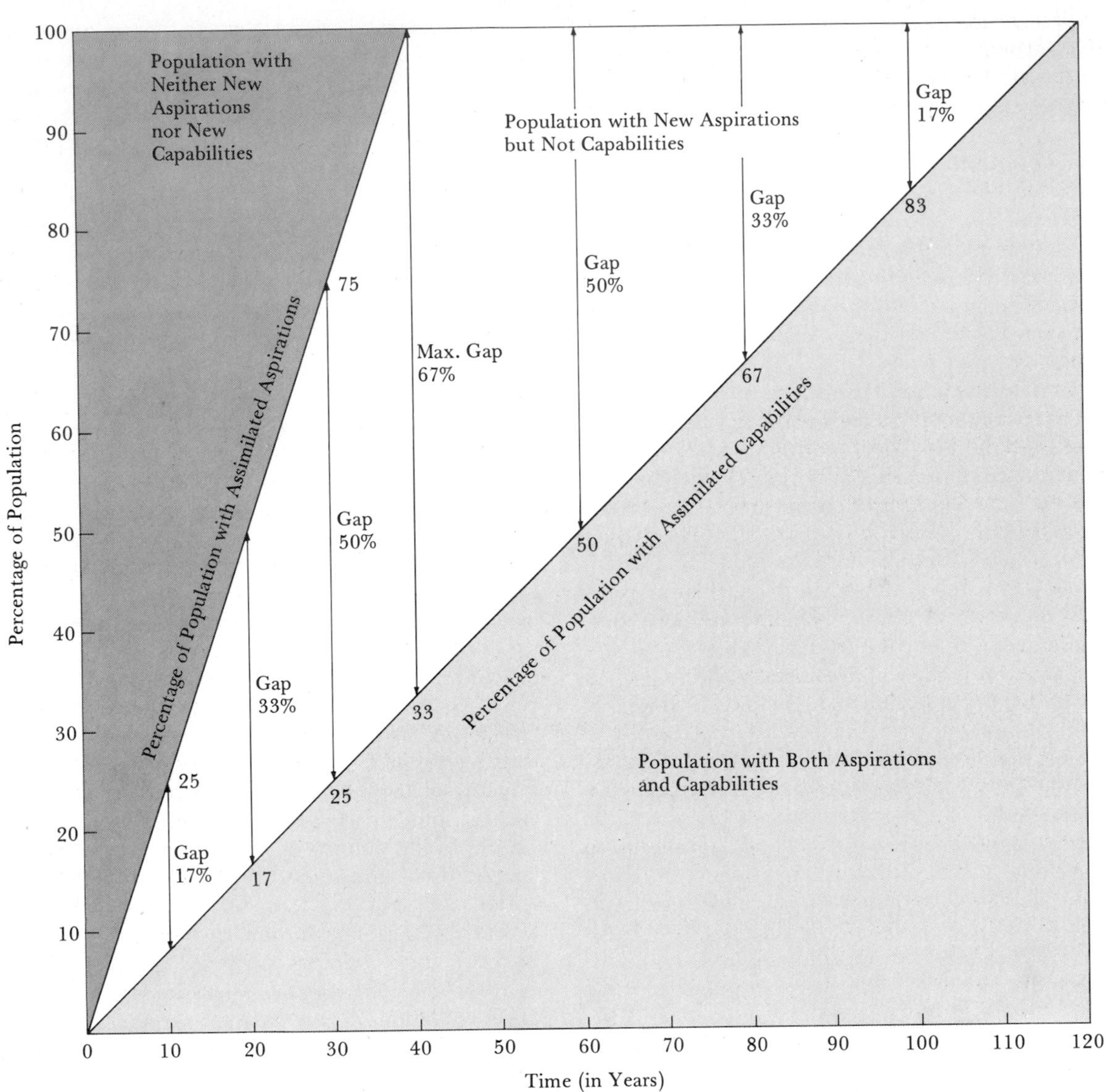

Assumptions: Rate of assimilation: of aspirations, 2.5 per cent per annum; of capabilities, 0.83 per cent per annum.
Note: If the speeds of both assimilation rates were cut in half, all time periods would double but the vertical dimensions of the diagram would remain unchanged. The maximum gap would still be 67 per cent, but it would be reached in 80 years, not 40, and a gap of 33 per cent or more would persist not for 90 years but for 180.

sixtieth year a majority of them will feel the gap; in the fortieth year the maximum number, two-thirds of the population, will be reached. These are not good prospects for political stability.[11]

The Payoff: The Assimilation of Attainments. Aspirations and capabilities produce attainments in different values. If equality among groups, races, or nations is desired, then we shall want to know the size of the gap in major values between the relevant groups, the current rates of assimilation for each value, and the approximate time within which assimilation in regard to each is expected to be accomplished, perhaps to the extent of bringing the distribution of each value in one group of people so close to that in the other group that the remaining distance between the two distributions will be less than one standard deviation. (If the standard deviations of the two distributions should differ significantly, we might agree to choose the smaller one.

Even a brief look at the data suggests that some of these processes of assimilation of attainment might take a long time. The gap between average black and white earnings in the United States in 1977 was about 100:57; if some past rates of change should continue, it may be closed within about fifty or sixty years. But the gap between the wealth of the highly developed countries and the poverty of much of the emerging world would take, even at best, more than one hundred years to close, if an international action to that end were begun today—one large enough to redistribute each year about 4 or 5 percent of world income—and if it did so in the most effective manner. This is unlikely to happen just now—although it may come to pass within the lifetime of today's students—and under current practices the huge income gaps among rich and poor nations seem likely to persist for centuries.

The large gaps in levels of health, life expectancy, and educational attainment are closing somewhat more quickly among nations, and they have become smaller within many of them. But within the United States the smaller gap of about 8 percent between white and black life expectancies and the gap between white and black years of completed education—about 4 percent in 1977, or fourteen years, as opposed to thirteen and one-half—seem to have changed but little in the last ten years; and these percentage figures ignore any differences in the quality of the health care and schooling actually available to blacks and whites. Yet the assimilation of such material attainments might well be achieved within the next thirty to fifty years, should a serious political effort in that direction be resumed. Internationally, too, levels of health might be brought fairly close together, at Western levels or higher ones, within the next half century. Differences in educational levels among nations might be reduced considerably within the next one or two centuries. The linguistic diversity of the world, however, including notably the emerging nations, seems likely to remain large for at least 200 years, and more likely for about 600 or 700 years, if present rates of linguistic assimilation should continue.

Finally, rates of intermarriage among blacks and whites in the United States were so low up to the 1950s and early 1960s that it was calculated by Michael Leiserson that assimilation in regard to intermarriage in the United States—that is, making interracial marriages about as frequent as could be expected from a model of random pairing—would take more than 900 years to reach. To be sure, rates of intermarriage can change strikingly, from less than 3 percent to more than 30 percent within about thirty years, as they did

[11]Slower rates of assimilation of aspirations and capabilities would make matters worse, as long as the 3:1 ratio between the two rates remained. Cutting all speeds in half, 1.25 percent per year for the spread of aspirations and 0.42 percent for that of capabilities, would merely double the length of the whole process, including the duration of the period of very large gaps between the population with new aspirations and the much smaller one that would have new capabilities as well. A more than 50 percent gap would then persist not for thirty, but for sixty years.

among some Jewish groups in the United States between the 1920s and the 1950s. In the world at large, however, most of the 950 million Chinese, the 630 million Indians, and the over 300 million black Africans south of the Sahara are overwhelmingly likely to marry within their own respective racial groups. Even though smaller subgroups, such as some African tribes, may come to experience much higher rates of intermarriage with other tribes in their countries, the large racial divisions of humankind—Far Eastern, southern Asian, and black African in particular—are likely to persist for another 500 or 1,000 years or still longer.

The major languages and races of the world will not be wiped out any time soon by assimilation. It is unrealistic to expect them to merge quickly. What can be done is to help to improve relations among them and to improve the position of the diverse individuals, lovers, friends, and families within each language group or race, providing them with full opportunities to reach out for human ties beyond their boundaries.

AN OVERVIEW OF POLITICS IN THE EMERGING COUNTRIES

We have traced at some length several characteristics of the emerging countries: their incomplete transition from tradition to modernity; their partial dependence on the particular content of the traditional cultural, social, and economic heritage; and the race among the several processes of fundamental change, particularly that between the processes of social mobilization and linguistic, cultural, and political assimilation, which does so much to set the conditions for the political development of each country.

Now we shall turn to the basic political issues and decisions in the emerging countries. We cannot treat these countries here in the manner of the seven states that have been discussed earlier in this book in relative detail. The emerging nations are too numerous and too diversified for that. But a brief look at a few major issues may aid the reader in analyzing one or another of these emerging nations on his or her own.

The first issue in almost every such country has been *independence,* usually from some colonial power, sometimes also from indirect forms of foreign hegemony and military, political, and financial control.

The second general issue is *stability:* how to preserve the property, interests, and positions of the dominant elements within the national territory or in the national society. These dominant elements and institutions may be landowners, bankers, merchants, or manufacturers, native or foreign (in which case the stability and independence issues may be in conflict). Or they may be the leaders, party members, and officials of a Communist regime, with their state-owned industries, collective institutions, and vivid desire to keep their regime, its institutions, and development plans from being overthrown.

The third issue is *development* itself—the change from poverty to prosperity, illiteracy to widespread education, an obsolete technology to a modern one, inefficiency to competence, high death rates to low ones, national impotence to national power. The emphasis on this or that element in the mixture may vary, but the basic thrust remains the same, and it goes far in determining what politics is all about.

The Stakes of Politics. In many developing countries the stakes of politics are at times almost all-encompassing. They include the independence of the country, or its continuation in colonial status, or its relapse into a colonial position or into some disguised form of dependence—military, political, or economic—in what is now sometimes called a pattern of *neocolonialism.*

At stake in some critical periods may also be the social order of the country. Is it to be Communist or anti-Communist (and, hence, probably capitalist in its economic orientation)? Or is it to be a search for a "third force," a form of African socialism, or an Indian or Asian variety thereof? Which class or classes are to rule or to have the most influence? Which regions and which ethnic groups are to have the best opportunities for getting influence and favors in politics, economics, and social life?

The entire character of the national culture—as well as the national language—may be at stake in domestic affairs. So may be the country's relationship to the great international alliance systems in its military and foreign policy and, hence, its probable sources and amounts of foreign economic aid.

Compared to these large decisions, the ordinary spoils of politics in an emerging country do not loom very large. Government taxation, expenditure, and employment in such countries are not large, although they may be important because of the scarcity of other opportunities.

Once the social structure and political culture of an emerging country have been set, the life chances of many individuals and their degree of expectable social mobility will have been determined in large part with them.

One set of major stakes, however, is likely to recur. It is the issue of civilian or military government, of *constitutionalism or authoritarian dictatorship.* When the military take power in an emerging country, they often do so in the name of stability—that is, in the defense of property and the present highly unequal distribution of social and economic opportunities and status. Military governments that promote even modest social and political reforms are relatively rare. There are, however, some exceptions: Kemal Atatürk's regime in the Turkey of the 1920s; the military or semimilitary regimes of Mexican revolution, from General Venustiano Carranza in 1917 to Lázaro Cárdenas in the 1930s; the current military regime in Peru; and the Argentine regime of General Juan Perón and its offshoot, the *Peronista* party that won an Argentine election of 1973, but has been kept out of power by the current military dictatorship headed by General Videla. All these military governments were involved in reforms and efforts at limited social change that were not trivial.[12] Whether these developments will prove significant enough to change in the future the predominantly conservative role of the military in the emerging nations remains to be seen.

The Participants in Politics. Whether reform-oriented or conservative, most military governments tend to restrict political participation, often very sharply. Military leaders are most often elitists. By instinct and training they tend to think most often in terms of *chain of command*—in which orders and rewards flow from the top down, and only reports are expected to flow up—and not in terms of popular participation.

Nonetheless, the politics of the emerging countries has been marked generally by a large increase in popular participation. Among the population aged twenty years and older, perhaps 2 percent per year shifted from nonvoting to voting in major elections between the late 1950s and the mid-1960s, reaching an average value of 72 percent for the latter period. Certainly in many countries such an act of voting was more a public affirmation of support for the government than a genuine choice, but even this symbolic participation did suggest that the views and acts of ordinary men and women counted for something.

Mass participation in developing countries, even

[12]The temporary participation of Chilean army leaders in President Salvador Allende's Marxist-oriented government in the winter of 1972–73 and the orderly return to a fully civilian cabinet in the spring of 1973 seemed for a time to point in the same direction. In September 1973, however, a right-wing group of military, naval, and air force generals overthrew the government; forced the few loyalist army leaders, such as General Carlos Prats Gonzalez, out of office and into exile; and established a dictatorship. Estimates of the number of people killed in the coup varied from *Newsweek*'s 2,700 in the first two weeks to the *New York Times*'s estimate on October 25, 1973, that 2,000 lives had been lost; the latter number may be low since the *Times* had reported very little about events in northern Chile, including such towns as Antofagasta and Iquique, where adherents of the Allende government had been numerous.

in one-party regimes, also means experience in a relatively wide range of organizations, such as a political party, trade unions, farmers' and women's organizations, youth groups and students' organizations (even though they are often state-sponsored), consumers' or producers' cooperatives, and many more. From participating in these a significant part of the population learns the basic skills of political activity: to speak publicly, to work in a committee, to conduct a meeting, to propose a motion, to take a vote, and to perform other participatory functions.

This gradually increasing pool of politically experienced personnel is likely eventually to confront any authoritarian or military regime in their country, and the shifting balance between politically mobilized and traditionally inert groups may in time increase the chances of the civilians and the partisans of high participation to prevail.

Elite participation in many developing countries has some peculiarities. First, elites tend to be small, in line with the modest level of general wealth and of secondary and higher education. Second, they are often divided between pronationalist and proforeign interests and factions. Third, many of them are bilingual and bicultural, as one part of the personality is connected with the native language and culture and the other with some foreign language, literature, and sector of civilization. Thus, in an age of rising nationalism it is a part of the elite that is becoming marginal in its own country.

The peasants may be behind the urban groups in their rates of social mobilization and political participation, but the spread of money and other aspects of social mobilization tends to remind many peasants of the pressure of their rents and taxes, as exacted by landlords and governments. Even more, it may remind them of the importance of the question of land ownership and land reform. In time, and in the absence of reforms, peasants may begin to develop radical movements, particularly if conscription has taught some of them military skills.

If demands for change from the city and the countryside should become synchronized, in the name of nationalism, Communism, or a combination of the two, then the combined movement may well carry the day or, at least, force the overburdened government to call in foreign aid, which may or may not be forthcoming.

Perhaps the governments most successful in meeting these problems without falling under major foreign influence or native military rule have been those that have undertaken major land reforms and other changes, either with the help of a democratic coalition, as did India, or with the early help of a foreign occupying power, as did Japan in the late 1940s, or else with the aid—and at the cost—of a major revolution, as did China in 1949.

The Arena and Images of Politics. Only a few of the emerging countries have territories that have been well defined by forces and processes internal to them. More often they have inherited the boundaries drawn for administrative or political convenience by foreign colonial rulers, as in the cases of India, Pakistan, Argentina, Nigeria, and Ghana. Others have as their core some territory of a premodern state or kingdom (China, Thailand, Iran, Ethiopia). Finally, the territory and identity of some emerging countries have been the result of a major revolution, counterrevolution, or civil war (Bangladesh, North and South Korea, Vietnam, Uruguay).

Despite their varied origins the territories of the emerging nations most often make some *geographic sense*. Colonial powers often found it convenient to run their boundaries through more or less unpopulated territories, such as mountains, deserts, or jungles, and even the native wars and revolutions often stopped at these natural barriers. Other pieces of land, however, remained long in dispute between two or more nations. Moreover, some governments took to ransacking the archives in search of documents that could be used to develop a claim on a certain long-lost piece of territory or to discover an "unredeemed" group of fellow ethnics or compatriots, unfortunately now still under foreign yoke. China has raised such territorial claims or semiclaims based on old maps, and Thailand has discovered large numbers of unredeemed Thais on the far side of its borders in Burma, China, and Indochina. The great majority of African states have decided—probably wisely—not to press territorial disputes and claims against each other. The disputes between Algeria and Morocco over desert lands suspected of bearing oil and between Kenya and Somalia over pasture lands are two of the exceptions.

The territory of the state has for many developing countries a symbolic function as starting point for the hoped-for development of loyalties to the nation. As in seventeenth- and eighteenth-century Europe, so now in the emerging world it is *patriotism*—the solidarity of all those living in a country—that precedes ethnic nationalism, the solidarity of those belonging to an ethnic group. In many emerging countries, such as Kenya, Nigeria, India, and even Peru, there is no one ethnic group comprising all or most inhabitants. Loyalty in such countries has grown, if at all, around a territory, perhaps a heritage of history, and probably a way of life attractive and rewarding enough to encourage the learning of common loyalties.

Ideologies alone will not suffice. A proclaimed commitment to Islam did not preserve the unity of Pakistan. Communist Serbs and Communist Croats have quarreled repeatedly in Yugoslavia. More fundamental political theories seem to have emerged only in a few places. Certainly the ideas of Mao Tse-tung in China, of Mahatma Gandhi and Jawaharlal Nehru in India, perhaps of Fidel Castro and the late Che Guevara in Cuba deserve some serious attention, regardless of how much one might disagree with them on many points. But a richer flow of political theories from the emerging countries may be yet to come.

EMERGING POLITICAL SYSTEMS: THEIR STEERING, MACHINERY, AND PROCESSES

Many emerging nations had to make their start with the mere rudiments of a modern political system. Most of them inherited a foreign-directed civil service from their immediate colonial past. In the case of traditionally independent countries, such as China, Thailand, Ethiopia, Turkey, and Iran, there were elements of a premodern, or even partly modernized, administrative staff. Such countries, as well as the former colonies, had some soldiers and police officers, and some schools, teachers, and public health officials. Much of this top- and middle-level personnel was foreign, but there were some middle-level and many lower-level native clerks, who often had good talents and training.

The first task of most governments of the emerging countries after 1945 was to keep operating. This meant recruiting some new nationalistic native personnel and retaining the services of irreplaceable foreign experts. And this in turn meant getting money to pay these soldiers, police officers, and bureaucrats and continuing to get such money for some time.

Some of this money came from abroad, most often from one or the other of the competing superpowers, the United States and the Soviet Union. Sometimes both sides paid. Between 1946 and 1975, India got about $9 billion from the United States, or about $15.00 per capita over thirty years (about $0.50 per head per year). And during 1954-76 it also got over $2 billion from the Soviet Union, or over $4.00 per capita. This brought its total take to $11 billion, an average of less than $0.75 per Indian per year. Egypt got over $1.3 billion from the Soviet Union and nearly as much from the United States, yielding a total of about $3.00 per Egyptian per year. Iran, Afghanistan, Greece, Turkey, and Tunisia also got substantial amounts from both sides; but the American aid was much larger to Greece, Turkey, and Tunisia than the Soviet contribution. Other countries had only one large benefactor: Cuba between

1961 and 1975 got over $4.7 billion from the Soviet Union, about $4.00 annually per Cuban. China got much more total aid from the Soviets—more than $16 billion—but this amounted only to $2.00 per person per year, and no further aid followed. Massive American aid, but no Soviet aid, has been going to Jordan, Israel, and Liberia.

Other short-term tasks were to collect taxes and to maintain essential government services. As these matters were dealt with successfully, national independence could at least begin to take on meaning.

Other tasks have to be started soon, but involve middle-term policy commitments of about five to fifteen years. Here we find the perennial problem of encouraging domestic capital formation and the inflow and investment of foreign capital, while trying to discourage capital flight or withdrawals. Another middle-term task is to win popular support and eventually to consolidate it into firm habits, loyalties, and institutions.

The long-term tasks (fifteen to twenty-five years) of the government are, then, to deal with some of the basic structural problems of development. *Quantitative modernization* can be measured simply by noting by how much the national performance has improved according to any one or a few indicators, considering each indicator in isolation from all others. *Qualitative modernization* can be judged, on the contrary, by noting the relationships and balances—or imbalances—among the different sectors, elements, and dimensions of development.

Here the government must develop an intelligent policy for dealing with the center-periphery problem, since central regions and populations tend to be more favored, prosperous, and quick to develop, leaving the periphery districts and their population more and more behind. Related to this is the problem of what Gunnar Myrdal has called the *backwash effect,* that is, the draining away of mobile capital, skilled personnel, and money from the peripheral and poorer districts and the concentrating of these mobile factors of production in the central or otherwise already advanced regions. This process is the opposite of the *spread effect,* so confidently predicted by the classical economists; they felt that wealth and would spread out gradually from any area of early concentration until the entire country had been made more or less uniformly prosperous.

Other long-term and structural problems are related to those just named. As population grows, as migration from the countryside proceeds, and as people are trying to move out of agriculture into urban and industrial employment, it turns out that all these changes require large amounts of capital—to construct the housing, the social infrastructure, and the factories and work places to house and employ these migrants. Wherever capital formation and investment fall short of these needs, there will appear a *marginal* population for whom there are no machines, work places, housing, and other facilities available.

Another long-term problem is likewise related to capital formation. It takes capital to build a factory or bridge where an engineer can be employed or to build and equip a laboratory where a scientist can work. Lacking such capital, a society will force its intellectual talent into the capital-extensive occupations, such as law and journalism.

All such problems can only be indicated here. Some emerging nations have been facing them for many years. How have they performed?

THE PERFORMANCE OF THE EMERGING NATIONS

The emerging nations are so different that it seems hard, if not impossible, to arrive at any kind of common judgment about all of them. Yet, two facts may be noted as a first indication. First, not a single emerging nation has done so badly as a sovereign state since 1947 that it had to go out of existence. And, second, more states have emerged into independence—and with less bloodshed, relative to the numbers of states and people involved—since 1947 than during any other thirty-year period in history.

On the whole, most of these new states have promoted health care, reduced general death rates and child mortality, and spread mass education—at all levels—faster and farther than did the colonial administrations that preceded many of them.

Finally, many of these emerging nations have made at least a beginning in self-government. They have carried it forward, to some extent, at the level of the nation, the locality, and the smaller voluntary groups and organizations.

Fifty years ago, many seasoned observers would have called impossible what many of these new nations in fact have done already. Their record to date is mixed, uneven, contradictory. But, withal, it is the story of one of humankind's great beginnings.

KEY TERMS AND CONCEPTS

emerging nations
traditional societies
ideal type
early transitional societies
advanced transitional societies
industrialized societies
postindustrial societies
information revolution
pattern maintenance
neocolonialism
achievement motivation
bases for group solidarity and self-government
ethnic, cultural, linguistic, and religions conditions
process of modernization
monetization
marketplace
node of transportation
market
bridgeheads of modernity
direct foreign rule vs. indirect foreign rule
processes of growth
demographic transition
impact of migration
internal migration
impact of mass media
interlocking process of social mobilization
rates of mobilization
concept and process of assimilation
dimensions of assimilation
marginality
assimilation and acceptance
motives for assimilation
need for affiliation
rewards for assimilation
differentiation and secession
social linguistics
linguistic assimilation
assimilation of attainments
independence, stability, and development
constitutionalism vs. authoritarian dictatorship
chain of command
mass participation
elite participation
geographic origins of states
patriotism
quantitative modernization
qualitative modernization
backwash vs. spread effect

ADDITIONAL READINGS

Apter, D. *The Politics of Modernization.* Chicago: University of Chicago Press, 1965. PB

Black, C. E. *The Dynamics of Modernization.* New York: Harper, 1967. PB

Deutsch, K. W. *Nationalism and Its Alternatives.* New York: Knopf, 1969.

———. *Nationalism and Social Communication.* Rev. ed. Cambridge: MIT Press, 1966. PB

Emerson, R. *From Empire to Nation.* Boston: Beacon Press, 1962. PB

Fanon, F. *The Wretched of the Earth.* New York: Grove Press, 1965. PB

Foltz, W. J. *From French West Africa to the Mali Federation.* New Haven: Yale University Press, 1965.

Galtung, J. "A Structural Theory of Imperialism." *Journal of Peace Research,* July 1971.

Hartz, L., et al. *The Founding of New Societies.* New York: Harcourt, 1969. PB

Hudson, M. C. *The Precarious Republic.* New York: Random House, 1968.

Huntington, S. P. *Political Order in Changing Societies.* New Haven: Yale University Press, 1968. PB

Johnson, C. *Revolutionary Change.* Boston: Little, Brown, 1964. PB

Kohn, H. *The Idea of Nationalism.* New York: Macmillan, 1944. PB

McAlister, J. T. *The Vietnamese and Their Revolution.* New York; Harper & Row, 1970.

Merritt, R. L., and S. Rokkan. *Comparing Nations.* New Haven: Yale University Press, 1966. PB

Perham, M. *The Colonial Reckoning.* London and Westport, Conn.: Greenwood Press, 1976.

Pye, L. *Aspects of Political Development.* Boston: Little, Brown, 1966. PB

Race J. *War Comes to Long An.* Berkeley and Los Angeles: University of California Press, 1971. PB

Regmi, M. C. *A Study in Nepali Economic History 1768–1846.* New Delhi: Manjusri Publishing House, 1971.

Russett, B. M., et al. *World Handbook of Political and Social Indicators.* New Haven: Yale University Press, 1964.

Safran, N. *Israel: The Embattled Ally.* Cambridge: Harvard University Press, 1978.

Stephens, H. *The Political Transformation of Tanganyika, 1920–67.* New York: Praeger, 1968.

Taylor, C. L., and M. C. Hudson. *World Handbook of Political and Social Indicators.* 2nd ed. New Haven: Yale University Press, 1972.

PB = *available in paperback*

XVIII

Some Developing Countries: Poor to Almost Rich

What we can say about developing countries in general will rarely be true about one country in particular. They are too different. Even looking at a few emerging countries briefly gives an impression of their diversity. The people of each country have endured different experiences, faced different conditions, and chosen different actions by which to make their fates.

For these brief sketches, seven countries have been chosen. Two are located in Africa: Egypt and Nigeria. Two others belong to Asia: India and Iran. Three are in Latin America (to be dealt with in the following chapter): Brazil, Mexico, and Cuba. The last of these, Cuba, belongs to a different social and economic system. The development of these countries varies widely. Their per capita GNPs in the mid-1970s ranged from $150 in India to $1930 in oil-rich Iran. Their urban populations ranged from 20 percent of the total population in India to 63 percent in Mexico. Similar contrasts hold for their accomplishments in education and health. Literacy ranged from 25 percent in Nigeria to 82 percent in Mexico and 83 percent in Cuba. Life expectancy at birth varied from a short forty-one years in Nigeria to sixty-three and seventy years, respectively, in Mexico and Cuba.

Behind these statistical signposts are memories of ancestral peoples and nations: the ancient cultures of Egypt, India, and Iran; the old culture of Nigeria-Benin; the Indian and Spanish heritage of Mexico; the colonial history of Cuba; and the mingled colonial and pioneering history of Brazil. Throughout their histories, these countries have made political choices that have either reinforced their social and economic fates or else changed them. We begin with those countries that have the furthest to go in their economic development, as indicated by their per capita GNP.

INDIA: THE SECOND-LARGEST COUNTRY IN THE WORLD

India is the poorest of the countries discussed in this chapter. In 1976, its per capita GNP was only $150, only 20 percent of its population lived in towns, and only 35 percent of its work force was in occupations outside agriculture, forestry, and fishing. But 30 percent of its 1976 population was literate, compared with only 17 percent in 1951. Life expectancy at birth in 1976 was fifty-three years, an improvement by a dozen years since the 1950s, and by about twenty-one years since the last decade of British rule. How did so much improvement become possible in so vast and poor a country? To seek an answer, we must first look at India's history and at her human, cultural, and political resources.

One of India's assets is its sheer size. Next to China, India is the largest of the world's developing countries. In 1978, its population was 656 million; in 1980, it is likely to be close to 700 million. Geographically, it covers most of a subcontinent. It is the home of one of the oldest continuous cultural traditions of humankind, covering about 3,500 years, from the Bronze Age to the nuclear age. Politically, it has been both independent and almost unified only twice: once in about 250 B.C. under King Ashoka, who ruled two-thirds of the subcontinent, and again since 1947, after the secession of Pakistan.

A Grid of Transportation Routes. India's transportation routes have lasted longer than her changing political regimes. They have provided a means of national communication that has held India together over the centuries. The routes form a diamond standing on its southern tip at Cape Comorin where the Arabian Sea and the Bay of Bengal meet, with a blunt northern tip in the western Himalayas and the valley of Kashmir. The long Indian coast of the Arabian Sea forms the southwest side of the diamond and the coast of the Bay of Bengal forms the southeast one, with coastal shipping along each of these. The northwest side of the grid is marked by the Indus River that flows from the western Himalayas southwestward to form with its tributaries the fertile "five-stream land," the Punjab, and then continues to the sea. The diamond is completed by the valley of the huge Ganges River that flows eastward along the Himalayas and then southward into the Bay of Bengal near Calcutta.

Most major Indian cities lie either at or near the seacoasts, such as Surat, Bombay, Madras, and Calcutta, or on the big rivers and their tributaries. India's capital, Delhi, lies at the junction of two such tributaries of the Ganges River on the land-bridge where the distance between the river systems of the Indus and Ganges is smallest. In much of the interior, away from the river systems, communications are poor, most soils not fertile, and populations thinly settled. There are the high plains of the Deccan, high mountains and large tracts of jungle. In the Deccan, are some old principalities, such as Hyderabad and Mysore, and some considerable cities of more recent importance such as Nagpur and Bangalore.

Ancient Conquest from the North: The Heritage of Caste. Far beyond the major cities and transportation routes, Indian culture has penetrated deeply almost everywhere on the subcontinent. Polished stone tools were used in India before 3000 B.C. and the Bronze Age began there well before it did in China. A decisive change came with the gradual conquest of India between 2000 and 1200 B.C. by the Aryans, light-skinned invaders from the north who spoke Indo-European languages. They pushed back, subjected, and in part absorbed the darker-skinned Dravidian-speaking inhabitants.

By 1200 B.C., a common language, Sanskrit, had emerged in northern India, with an oral literature of religion and law. The modern languages of northern India, such as Hindi (spoken by about 35 percent of the population), Urdu, Bengali, Marathi, and Gujarati, are descended from Sanskrit and are still mutually intelligible. But in the south, the old Dravidian languages, quite different from the Indo-European ones, have continued in such modern forms as Telugu, Kannada, and Malayalam.

Laws and religion were written down in Sanskrit in about 1000 B.C. in the *Vedas,* of which the *Rigveda* was the most important. They embodied the code of a patriarchal agricultural society, dominated by the conquerors. Between 800 and 550 B.C., the Aryans expanded their conquests eastward to Bihar, and the Vedic rules of *caste* were elaborated and made more stringent.

The Sanskrit word for caste, *Varna,* means "color." Four main castes were delineated and continue to exist today. Topmost were the priests, or *brahmans,* as the guardians of knowledge, writing, and religion. Second ranked the noble warriors, or *kshatriyas;* and third were the commonalty *(vaisyas)* of artisans and peasants. Still below these three castes were the serfs *(sudras),* the non-Aryan descendants of the conquered, separated from the three higher castes by taboos of ritual, cleanliness, and food. In time, a respectable caste of merchants *(banyas)* was added above the *sudras,* and among the latter an unfortunate group of outcasts, or "untouchables" *(pariahs),* were separated out. The untouchables were charged with the most undesirable and infection-prone occupations, such as tanning, sweeping, cleaning, and removing carrion and excrement. Eventually it was taught that even the shadow of an untouchable would defile the food of an upper-caste Hindu. Despite many subcastes, the system of four main castes has persisted.

The caste system has lasted so long because it linked conquest, language, and, originally, physical appearance with the social division of labor. A somewhat similar division of labor among priests, warriors, and peasants persisted in medieval and early modern Europe for a thousand years. Moreover, castes and subcastes offered social niches in which newly conquered or converted tribes could be integrated and even their tribal cults and deities could be accommodated. In this manner, Hindu culture united its believers not in a uniform nationality and creed, but rather in a vast mosaic that preserved and even sharpened their differences.

To believing Hindus, caste was unchangeable. No one could escape from the caste of birth, except by losing it and becoming an outcast to be shunned by all. Fate was to be borne in patience, not to be mastered by action. At best, peace of mind could be reached through contemplation. A doctrine of reincarnation developed, according to which everyone would be reborn in a higher or lower caste, or even in animal form, depending on the merits or demerits they accumulated in their current life. Efforts to escape one's caste counted as demerits, to be punished by rebirth at lower stations in one's lives to come. This doctrine was gradually supplemented by child marriages, polygamy, and the burning of widows. The latter practice was only ended by the British government in the nineteenth century.

These doctrines and practices reinforced each other. They did not destroy the profound spiritual elements of Hinduism as a religion, but they often distorted it into a system of social stability without parallel in history. For three thousand years, kings and kingdoms came and went but the caste system remained.

Alternatives to Caste. Castes did not remain without resistance. About 500 B.C., the Jain sect and shortly thereafter Buddhism arose, offering alternatives to the harsh caste rule of the brahmans. Both religions survived as minorities in India. (Buddhism eventually spread in various forms to Ceylon, Burma, Tibet, China, and Japan, where its influence has endured.) Almost two thousand years later, the Muslim conquerors offered a creed that promised the brotherhood of all believers. In East Bengal and elsewhere in India, some low-caste Hindus accepted the promise and converted to Islam. Later, some Muslim rulers of small Indian principalities converted to Hinduism, perhaps hoping to ensure high-caste status for themselves and their descendants.

Other Hindus turned against both caste and Muslim pressure. In the Punjab, a fifteenth-century religious order, the Sikhs, turned into a thoroughly militarized sect in the seventeenth century and eventually also into a people. The order had started out both proclaiming monotheism and Muslim-Hindu fellowship and opposing priestly rule and caste restrictions. In time, it became a formidable anti-Muslim military force, as well as a thriving community whose bearded and turbaned men have remained a conspicuous part of India's military and economic life.

All these religious groups have persisted, and so have other sects. Jains, Marwari Hindus, and Parsees (an offshoot of the old Persian Zoroastrian religion) all are prominent in business and finance. Sikhs, Rajput Hindus, and the Gurkhas from Nepal, all once classed by the British as "martial races," still have their share in the armed services.

Across these divisions, modern industry has created masses of both industrial workers with their labor unions and employers and businesspeople with their class interests. There are large and small landowners, farmers, and peasants, and they all press for the political representation of their interests. Language, ethnicity, religion, caste, class occupations, and geography thus make India's politics rich and complex.

Through the years, India most of the time was made up of small monarchies and principalities, most often under native rulers. Sometimes, some regions were ruled by Muslim conquerors, such as the Moghul emperors who united parts of India from the sixteenth through the end of the eighteenth century without being able to prevent the step-by-step conquest of India by foreign powers.

A New Conquest by the West. In 1498, the Portuguese sailor Vasco da Gama opened a sea route from Europe to India. In 1660, after establishing earlier footholds at Surat and Madras, the English set up a fortified trading post where the city of Bombay is today. In 1690, they founded Calcutta.

They organized these areas not as a foreign state but as a commercial corporation, the English East India Company, which had been chartered in 1600 and continued to be backed by British naval and military power. In addition to its monopoly of trade with Britain, the company came to exercise political and military powers in India, whereas other European powers, mainly the Portuguese, Dutch, and French, eventually were defeated and expelled or confined to small enclaves.

In the eighteenth century, able officials of the company, such as Robert Clive and later Warren Hastings, intervened in the wars between local Indian rulers. Those siding with the English eventually won, but the company gained most of the power. Clive and Hastings conquered large and populous territories for the company, such as Bengal, and enriched themselves greatly in the process. Despite famines among the native population, pickings were easy for the conquerors. "I was astonished," Hastings later said, "at my own moderation."

Individuals took little in comparison to what the company collected. In the territories that it controlled directly, taxes, called revenue, were levied on the peasantry through local landowners, called *Zamindars,* who also functioned as tax collectors. This arrangement left deep traces in India's social structure. British people functioned increasingly as magistrates and judges. After 1793, Indians were excluded from all higher posts. In other regions, the company ruled indirectly through agreements with local rulers, who put themselves under British protection. They and their subjects then paid for this protection in one form or another.

Directly and indirectly, vast amounts of wealth were transferred to Britain during the eighteenth and nineteenth centuries. British rule brought an end to local wars and, from the second half of the nineteenth century onward, important improvements in transportation, public health, and education. Whether India would have done better or worse under her native rulers is a matter British and Indian scholars still dispute.

The British conquest continued between 1785 and 1819. Much of south India and the lands of the Marathas behind Bombay were conquered, and the rulers of Hyderabad and Rajputana put their large territories under British protection. In the 1840s and 1850s, most of the rest of northern

India, including Sindh, the Punjab, and Delhi, were occupied. This occupation substantially completed the British conquest of India.

After controlling foreign trade and taxes on land, the British entered India's internal market. British rule kept it open to the products of British industry. As the Industrial Revolution progressed, cheap British machine-made goods wiped out some of the handicraft industries in India. Industry in Manchester was prospering, but, as one British governor reported in 1834, "the bones of the Indian weavers are bleaching in the plains of the Deccan."

For more than two centuries, the company had been both a large business enterprise and a big government. By the late 1850s, the combination became untenable. In 1857, a vast uprising shattered the company's rule throughout much of the subcontinent. It started among the company's Muslim mercenaries but spread quickly to the general population, with Hindus joining in. In many places, British people and their families were massacred or became victims of atrocities. Eventually British regular troops suppressed the uprising. They tied rebel leaders to the mouths of British cannon, which tore them to pieces. The British called the uprising "The Great Mutiny." Indian schoolchildren are taught today that it was a war of liberation. Although it was defeated, there are now monuments to it in Indian cities.

The events of 1857 fundamentally changed the political system of India. The British government replaced the company as the political and administrative power. Educational reforms were started and universities founded, construction of a railroad network was begun, a civil service was organized. Within one hundred years, Thomas Babington Macaulay wrote in his famous *Minute on Educational Reform in India* that the subcontinent would be transformed. As it turned out, he was right.

The lower ranks of government administration became filled with native clerks. Hindus competed best in the examinations for these civil service posts. Muslims for a time were distrusted by the British who remembered the mutiny of 1857. The railroad eventually proved too small for the country's needs, but in the meantime it transformed the subcontinent. Famines became rarer as food supplies could be moved, but five million lives were lost in 1876–78 in a famine in Deccan, and another two million died in widespread famines in 1896–1900. Even so, the population grew, and the towns and cities grew faster. By the mid-1880s, British-ruled India was a different country from what it had been in the days of the company.

A New India Begins. But as India changed, more Indians began to think of national unity and independence. In 1885, the Indian National Congress was founded, uniting Muslims and Hindus in their demands for more Indian self-government. Bal G. Tilak, Gopal K. Gokhale, and later Mohandas K. Gandhi became major political leaders. Muslims came to demand a larger share of public jobs and other opportunities and to fear their minority status in a Hindu-dominated self-governing India. The British administration now welcomed Muslim aspirations, and in 1906 the All-India Muslim League was founded and Mohammed Ali Jinnah became a prominent Muslim leader.

Gandhi's and Nehru's Congress party tried to keep Hindus and Muslims together. Indian self-government was to be secular: Religion and the state were to be kept separate. At all times, some Muslim leaders held prominent offices in the congress, side by side with Hindus, but other Muslims feared that majority rule would give power and privilege to Hindus. As the British conceded increasing self-rule to India during the first half of the twentieth century, they insisted on separate electoral rolls (registers of voters) for Muslims and Hindus, with separate shares of the elective offices assigned to each. The Muslim League welcomed this. Congress and other critics saw it as deliberate support of religious separatism, in accordance with the ancient tactic of "divide and rule." Still others considered it adaptation to political reality.

When India became independent in 1947, the

regions with Muslim majorities seceded, except Kashmir, and formed the new state of Pakistan, first as a self-governing British dominion with Mohammed Ali Jinnah as its governor-general. Jinnah died in 1948, and Pakistan became an Islamic republic in 1950. In 1971, it broke up into two states: Bangladesh to the east of India and today's Pakistan to the west, each with more than seventy million inhabitants, still including some Hindu minorities. Today, more Muslims are living as a minority in India than in either of these Muslim states—more than 11 percent of India's population, or perhaps seventy-seven million.

Partition (separation) in 1947 had a high cost in blood. An estimated one million lives were lost in riots and massacres, sometimes carried out with the connivance of the police on both sides of the new border. Debtors killed creditors, peasants attacked landlords, workers rioted against employers, wherever the new cleavage of nationality was added to the old "communal" one of religion. There had been smaller communal riots in the past, and if the size of the catastrophe of 1947 had been foreseen and safeguarded against, many lives could have been saved. No adequate protection of minorities was offered on either side of the border. Leaders of the congress had denied the danger, preferring to believe in the unity of India. Muslim leaders had been preoccupied with setting up their new country. The British government, withdrawing its troops and leaving the unprotected minorities behind, may have considered their responsibility ended; some British officials, relieved to be rid of a thankless job, may have felt that such riots would merely confirm their belief in India's incapacity for self-government.

Despite the lives lost, and the ten million or more refugees exchanged between India and Pakistan, this pessimism proved unwarranted. India, Pakistan, and Bangladesh all are functioning as states today. But the Pakistan-Bangladesh partition in 1971 once again claimed many lives; *communalism* remains a political problem, and bloody communal riots between Hindus and Muslims in India were reported in the summer of 1979.

The Vast Stakes of Indian Politics. Perhaps more is at stake in the politics of India than in those of most other countries. India is the largest noncommunist country in the world, but in two states, Kerala and West Bengal, Communist parties have participated in coalitions that formed state governments. India, almost unique among the world's large emerging nations, has been under a democratic and constitutional government since independence, but this, too, has come under strain. The problems of caste in political, social, and economic life, of persistent poverty, of occasional famine such as that in the Ganges Plain in 1967, and of population growth demand political action.

The life and death of millions affect and are affected by politics in India. Public health and life expectancy, famines and epidemics or their avoidance depend on public policy. Many issues press for political decisions: economic development; its orientation toward industry or agriculture; the interests of Indian and foreign corporations, of Indian big business, small business, labor unions, and the unemployed, of landowners, big famers, small peasants, and the landless rural poor, of the highly educated, the merely literate, and the illiterate majority. And so do many matters of family and personal life, of custom and culture press for political decisions—matters that in other countries are settled and stable. Which caste rules to reject and which ones to obey? With whom to eat or not to eat? What dowry to pay to the husband of one's daughter? Arrange a marriage between children? How many children to have? Accept sterilization, practice contraception, or let marriage and nature take their course? Politics in India has thus acquired greater intensity and personal relevance than is found in the politics of many other countries.

Political Participation. By the mid–nineteenth century, British conquests had enlarged the domain of direct and indirect British rule, and population growth worked in the same direction. Modernization, particularly from the 1850s onward, enlarged the scope of government. Decade after decade, more decisions had to be made concerning more people than ever before. The growing administrative burden in India, together with rising wages and living standards in Britain, made British clerks more expensive and required hiring ever larger numbers of Indian clerical employees. In this manner, Indians increasingly participated in the administrative process.

It also became prudent to ask at least some Indians more formally for their opinion and advice. Under the rule of the company, the governor-general of India had created in 1853 an appointed legislative council to advise him. After the Government of India Act of 1858, the governor-general became a viceroy, British administration replaced that of the company, the viceroy's administration was enlarged in 1861, and similar councils on the provincial level were added in 1862. The appointees serving on these bodies included a small share of Indians, picked by the British from among the more cooperative members of the Indian elites. In the early 1880s, Lord Ripon, a liberal viceroy, introduced local self-government. But a further reform that would have permitted Indian judges in outlying areas to try Europeans was defeated by the fierce opposition of British residents. In the early 1890s, the legislative councils were further enlarged and their powers increased. Henceforth, their "nonofficial" European and Indian members were to be nominated by local bodies, so that tacitly these members were elected. By the Morley-Minto Act of 1909, the legislative councils were again greatly increased and given increased power. Several provincial councils now had elected majorities, but Hindu and Muslim voters had separate electoral rolls, and the more substantial class of citizens was restricted from voting.

Further reforms came in 1918 after the presentation of the Montague-Chelmsford report to parliament, with the announced aim of developing self-governing institutions in India, but the report was denounced as unsatisfactory by many Indian leaders. Despite these protests, its recommendations were enacted through the Government of India Act of 1919. Henceforth 70 percent of the council members were to be elected. However, according to a principle of dyarchy (double rule), important matters (such as defense, police, and finance) were "reserved" for the provincial governor and the appointed British members of the executive council; the less important (such as education, health, and agriculture) were to be "transferred" to the Indian members. The franchise (right to vote) was still limited by property qualifications. In 1932, the franchise was extended to members of the "depressed classes"—the untouchables whom Gandhi renamed *harijans* (children of God), the name by which they are known officially in India today. The *harijans* themselves already had begun to organize politically. They became important allies of Gandhi and of the Indian National Congress. Today their leaders play a significant part in Indian politics, and there are special quotas reserved for *harijan* students at Indian universities.

In 1935, another Government of India Act—sometimes called in Britain the India Bill—gave wider autonomy to the provincial legislatures but reserved emergency powers for the governors (who remained British). A two-chamber central legislature at Delhi was created, consisting of a "council of state" with 34 elected and 26 appointed members and a "legislative assembly" of 40 appointed members and 105 members elected by the provincial assemblies. Defense, foreign affairs, and certain financial powers remained under the governor-general and hence in British hands. Under these provisions, Britain in 1939 took India into World War II, without real Indian consent. Until its independence in 1947, India had no universal and equal suffrage, nor full control over its military and financial affairs.

The story of the gradual increase of self-government in India is also a story of Indian political pressure and opposition. Through occasional riots and sustained peaceful political organization, through economic and political strikes and large campaigns of nonviolent civil disobedience, millions of Indians learned to act in politics and to struggle for their rights. A generation of Indian political leaders, including Mahatma Gandhi and Jawaharlal Nehru, became graduates of British jails. They symbolized readiness for self-sacrifice to their people.

In the end, increasing self-government and political opposition may have worked together. The slow extension of Indian self-government by the British rulers gave India three generations of political experience within a constitutional order. Motilal Nehru was an important political leader in the 1920s, demanding dominion status for India, similar to the very large degree of self-government already then enjoyed by Canada and Australia. His son, Jawaharlal Nehru, was the prime minister of independent India from 1947 to 1964. Nehru's daughter, Indira Gandhi (for whom in the early 1930s when she was still a teenager, he had written in jail a long version of world history[1]) was prime minister from 1966 to 1977, and was again reelected in 1980. At the same time, it was through their own growing efforts, organization, struggle, and readiness to sacrifice that Indians developed the self-confidence and the moral and political capabilities for sustained self-government and independence with constitutional democracy.

During much of the three-generation period, 1885–1977, the National Congress was India's major political party. Outside of today's Pakistan and Bangladesh, it was also the chief vehicle of effective political participation. In 1977, this period ended. After two years of Indira Gandhi's emergency rule, with its stringent economic controls and suspension of many civil rights, the Congress party was defeated. The many minor parties, as well as the factions of her opponents, united in the new Janata party, led by a conservative elder statesman, Morarji Desai. The Janata party won the 1977 election; Desai became prime minister; and emergency rule was lifted.

By mid-1979, however, the Janata coalition had broken apart. Its diverse elements had included socialists, the Jan Sangh, a party of Hindu nationalists, the Lok Dal, a north Indian peasant party, and the anti-Indira wing of the old Congress party. Having gained their negative goal of defeating Indira Gandhi's unpopular emergency regime, they lacked agreement on a positive program. After a number of prominent figures resigned from the government, Prime Minister Desai lost his parliamentary majority. In August a caretaker government was formed, and in January 1980, new elections were held, which returned Indira Gandhi to power.

Certain political realities that have prevailed in the recent past seem likely to remain. Voting participation in national elections has remained above 55 percent of all adults since 1962, higher than in the United States. Extremist parties of the right and left are small, and civil rights have remained popular. The Muslim and *harijan* minorities have remained strong; the linguistic diversity is ineradicable, particularly between north and south. In foreign affairs, no major political group wishes to change India's policy of nonalignment with the great power blocs, West and East. It is within all these facts, that India's future politics will take its course.

Some Stable Images of Indian Politics. To the relatively stable limits of current Indian politics, we must also add some images in Indian political thought. The first of these is the vastness and unity of India and the depth of the attachment of many people to it. India is seen as the great mother. The cry *"Jai Hind!"* ("Long live India!") still appeals to millions.

A second image comes from outside India, but has become part of the national tradition. It is the British idea of government by discussion, of playing by parliamentary rules, of respect for individuals and civil rights. Members of the Indian elite for two generations learned civilized politics at elite British schools like Eton and Harrow and at the universities of Cambridge and Oxford, where

[1] J. Nehru, *Glimpses of World History* (London: Longmans Green, 1935).

their families sent them to be educated. The image is still alive for many of India's leaders today, even though it is becoming more remote for the new generation of Indian politicians, some of whom come from nonelite strata.

A third image stems from the unique Indian tradition created, or at least developed by, Mohandas K. Gandhi who was called *Mahatma* ("great soul") even in his lifetime. It reaches back to the old Indian religious tradition of the holy man who lives in poverty but enjoys general respect and has great moral influence. Gandhi also drew on Thoreau's ideas of civil disobedience and Tolstoy's ideas of pacifism and nonviolence. As Gandhi developed his political philosophy, nonviolence became more powerful, both as a moral philosophy and a political strategy. Large campaigns of *ahimsa* (nonviolence) and *satya-graha* (truth force) forced Britain to concessions and at the same time reduced the intensity of conflicts among various groups of Indians themselves.

To this day, success in Indian politics requires a moral basis. A would-be leader must be something of a wise and holy person to win one of the highest offices. A woman must have, or seem to have, a similar stature through the example of her own life and family background. By contrast, the politics of Machiavelli with its single-minded pursuit of power, even by force and fraud has little charm for most Indians. Their intellectuals know that amoral ruthlessness was proclaimed by the Indian writer Kautilya in a handbook for rulers, *Artha-sastra,* more than a thousand years earlier—and that it had not worked very well. Gandhi, Nehru, Lal Bahadur Shastri (prime minister in 1964–66), Indira Gandhi, Morarji Desai, and the socialist opposition leader, Jayaprakash Narayan, have all clung to this anti-Machiavellian position of personal moral leadership in addition to their interest in power. For many years to come probably every successful successor of these leaders will find it advisable to do the same.

The Arena of Indian Politics. Indian traditions thus far have tended to work against any further disintegration or secession because of geography or language. India in its present borders is still widely perceived as a unit. China's occupation in 1962 of an almost empty strip of territory near the disputed and poorly marked border of Tibet aroused a remarkable amount of popular indignation.

Territorial unity has been supported by federalism and by respect for regional languages. In the 1920s, Mahatma Gandhi induced the Congress party to delimit its regional organizations according to language and no longer according to either traditional or British-imposed administrative divisions. After independence in 1947, several states in the federation of India still cut across language boundaries, but by the early 1960s their boundaries had been redrawn to conform to the language of their population. The British terms *dialect* and *vernacular* have been replaced officially by the term *regional language.* Most university education at the undergraduate level since the 1970s has been offered in these regional languages—even though it takes fourteen of them to reach 90 percent of India's population.

In its scope, India's government is more comprehensive than those of many other developing countries. It has accepted responsibility for guiding family planning, much of the economy, mass education, public health, agricultural development, and a host of other matters. It has many governmental organizations and institutions at the levels of village, district, city, state, and federation. The performance of these institutions and the political experience they have made possible may have held Indian politics together.

Self-Steering in Politics. Within its large territory, though, how does the government find out what has to be done? Perhaps the most important channel between the population and the government is the political parties. In second place are perhaps the labor unions, and third the press. After many years of rule since 1947, the Congress party became more rigid and less responsive in the 1970s. Other political parties, the actions by labor unions, and the criticism by the press all became more persuasive. These combined pressures split the Congress party and defeated it in the elections of 1977.

In addition to the political parties, labor unions, and the press, a private opinion research organization conducts political surveys of limited reliability. There are also many excellent government surveys of such matters as economic life, popular habits of spending, investment and consumption, health and social patterns. These are carried out by the Indian Statistical Office and other public institutions. They are repeated and their results stored, as memories to help steer the Indian political system in the future.

The government has many other channels to the people. A direct channel functions through legislation and the administrative machinery. Another works through the state-owned radio and television system, and a third through the political parties currently represented in the government and supporting its policies. Finally, the government also has some influence on the press. It can create news that the latter must report, and it can often induce the press to back its policies.

The Process and Machinery of Government. According to one school of thought, India belongs to the *soft states* of the world; that is, the decisions of its government have only a small chance of being carried out. Inefficiency, black markets, the poverty of many clerks and officials, the resulting petty corruption in private and public life, and the large-scale corruption at higher levels of society and politics all contribute to this result. The inertia of age-old customs and beliefs together with the rigidity of a large bureaucracy make the system immobile.

Another view sees Indian government as surprisingly effective in running things from day to day, in carrying out large reforms, and in guiding the country through major stresses and changes.

The truth most likely rests somewhere in between. There are many small frustrations, often due to poverty. Stamps sometimes are stolen from letters that were supposed to be posted. Official permits sometimes take a long time to obtain and only money speeds them up. But the country on the whole has grown and improved in income, nourishment, health, and education—more than a really soft state could have accomplished.

One key to India's success is the civil service. Introduced by the British in the nineteenth century, it offered at least some opportunities to a small number of gifted Indians. Their access to its higher ranks was small indeed, but not too small to permit the development of an Indian administrative elite and tradition, oriented toward British standards. Since independence, a large civil service has been built, staffed almost entirely by Indians and maintaining the morale and the standards of this tradition.

The Performance of the Indian Political System. No other country on earth is at once so poor, so large, and yet so democratic in the rights it grants to its citizens. Independent India by mid-1979 has been a constitutional country for nearly one-third of a century, without real interruption. Even during Indira Gandhi's "state of emergency," people retained the right and capacity to organize politically and to defeat in an honest election that state of emergency and the government that had imposed it.

India in 1980 has more than ten times as many university students as it had during its days under British rule. Mass literacy has doubled and there are four times as many children in school. The gain of almost a decade in average life expectancy speaks for itself.

A street scene I saw in Bombay has become a symbol of India for me. A heavy cart with wooden disks for wheels, was drawn there by a tired buffalo, but it was overtaken by two buses, one on each side, and these were marked "Indian Atomic Energy Commission." India's past is weighty, but her future is open.

NIGERIA: THE FIRST LARGE BLACK STATE

Nigeria's cultural heritage is an old one from several ancient kingdoms. Modern Nigeria, however, is the child of a short history. For several years prior to 1900, a coastal region near the past and present capital, Lagos, was administered by a private business corporation under British protection. Direct British colonial administration of this region commenced in 1900, and by 1914 the territories of present-day Nigeria were united under it.

A major reason for this territorial merger seems to have been convenience of river transportation. The great river Niger forms a pattern like the letter Y and links three major regions that differ in their peoples, languages, cultures, and in some cases geographic conditions. The coastal regions of the southeast and southwest are hot, moist rain forests, suitable for agriculture. The north is drier, with extended grasslands, suitable for cattle raising and horseback riding, and crossed by extended caravan trails. The main peoples are the Yoruba in the southwest, which includes Lagos, the Ibo in the southeast, and Hausa in the far north. Each people has a different language developed from a combination of local dialects. Both Yorubas and Ibos still practice traditional religions of their older cultures, but in more recent times Christian and to a lesser degree Muslim converts also have become significant.

The north is Muslim, with elements of Arab cultural influence. Its main languages are Hausa and Fulani. Its society and politics are still characterized by aristocratic and feudal traditions, supported by a traditional governing class and local rulers. This society contrasts with the more urban and decentralized political culture of the Yorubas and even more with the egalitarian, commercial, and competitive traditions of the Ibos. A multitude of smaller groups, languages, and religions supplement these three major groups and seems likely to persist.

Growth Toward Independence. The Yorubas of the southwest and the Ibos of the southeast relatively quickly took to education, commerce, social mobility, and eventually to labor unions, political parties, and aspirations for independence from Britain. The north for a long time tended to remain proud, traditional, illiterate, socially conservative, and more or less content with British rule. Not surprisingly, British colonial administrators, both military and civilian, felt comfortable with northern nobles who rode horseback and played polo and uncomfortable with the argumentative lawyers and politicians from the steamy coastal regions.

From 1914 to the 1950s, Nigeria's population grew, and so did its cities and towns and the nonagricultural occupations within them. The use of money increased, as did literacy, mails, and the mass media audience. During World War II, local industries multiplied. More soldiers and officers were trained, and some went overseas to aid the British war effort. After 1945, there was an increase in labor unions, newspapers, and political agitation, demanding more self-government and the eventual end of foreign rule.

By the later 1950s, Britain was ready to concede legal independence to Nigeria and to replace colonial rule by the more indirect means of economic and political influence. But Britain wanted the country to stay together and expected the conservative north to exert a stabilizing influence throughout the country as well as encourage the confidence of foreign investors. The federal independence constitution of Nigeria deliberately favored the north. It assigned to the north a larger number of peoples so as to give it a majority of the population, electorate, legislature, and armed forces of the new federation that was formally established in 1960.

Within a few years, regional rivalries and political instability threatened the very existence of the federation. The effective head of government was a northerner, Prime Minister Abubaker Tafawa Balewa. Southerners counted on the advantages of their own peoples in education and commercial and technical skills to shift the social, economic, and political leadership to them eventually. Particularly for the Ibos, these expectations soon seemed to come true. Their businesses prospered. Their young men came out on top in the competition for the better jobs in the railroad and telegraph services, in much of public administration throughout the country, and even in the military services.

In January 1966, a military coup instigated by a group of predominantly Ibo officers overthrew Prime Minister Balewa's northern-dominated government. A military government under Major-General Johnson Aguiyi-Ironsi, an Ibo, was established. In July, however, anti-Ibo violence started in the north and culminated in another military coup under General Yakubu Gowon. During these events, thousands of Ibos were massacred in the north, while thousands of propertyless survivors fled back to the Ibo homeland in the southeast.

Ibo opinion now turned in favor of secession. This trend was reinforced by the recent discovery of substantial oil deposits in the Ibo-dominated Eastern Region. These promised considerable economic benefits, either for all Nigeria and under its military government or else for an independent Ibo state, should it succeed in keeping the oil fields for itself. But if the oil discoveries promised an economic reward for Ibo secession, they also promised a reward to the Nigerian government for preventing secession.

The result was civil war that lasted thirty months, from May 1967 until January 1970. The Ibos declared the independence of their region, called it Biafra, and established a government headed by Odumegwu Ojukwu. They asked for foreign aid, both military and humanitarian, while hinting that they might express their gratitude in economic concessions to helpful foreign firms and countries. The Nigerian government blockaded Biafra, causing much starvation and eventually conquering the entire region. During the civil war, Biafra received some aid from France, Portugal (then still under a conservative and procolonialist dictatorship), and South Africa, as well as from scattered firms and groups in other countries. Nigeria, however, retained the diplomatic recognition and actual support of Britain, the United States, the Soviet Union, and most other countries, and with it access to vital military and economic supplies. In the end, about one million people had perished in the civil war. But the unity of Nigeria was preserved.

Before the civil war, Nigeria's army had numbered about twenty thousand. At its end, it had grown tenfold, to about two hundred and fifty thousand. Since then it has shrunk, but its political influence has persisted. All Nigerian governments since 1970 have been military, similar to governments in many other Black African states.

Government leaders continued to change. In July 1975, General Gowon was deposed while out of the country at a conference of the Organization of African Unity (OAU) at Kampala, Uganda. His place was taken by Brigadier General Ramat Muhammad. Less than a year later, Muhammad was assassinated and Lieutenant General Olusegun Obasanjo became the head of government.

Policy and Politics in the Eighties. Nigeria at the start of the 1980s has a population of more than seventy million. Its government is federal and constitutional in form, but an authoritarian military regime in substance. The old three regions, north, southeast, and southwest, have been replaced by twelve states, in the hope of reducing the likelihood of conflicts among large regions. After suppressing the attempt at secession, the Nigerian military government embarked on a policy of reconciliation, permitting the return from abroad of many Ibo refugees, including some political leaders.

A return to civilian rule and free parliamentary elections was scheduled to take place some time in 1979. In June 1979, the former leader of the attempted Biafran secession, Odumegwu Ojukwu, announced from his exile in the Ivory Coast his intention to run for a seat in the Nigerian parliament. Whether he will be permitted to run, whether he will be elected and seated, and how the new parliament will function all remain to be seen.

The oil fields have been developed and their output has grown. They have already paid for much of the cost of the civil war. In 1978, they yielded about three million barrels of oil per day, furnished 14 percent of the oil exports to the United States, and contributed substantially to the financial stability and relative prosperity of the country—which still has remained poor.

In the 1980s, Nigerian politics remains independent from foreign rule, both in form and in substance. Domestic politics, rather than foreign influence, has the largest share in determining the distribution of incomes, investments, and career opportunities among different regions, language groups, and peoples. It determines the size, intensity, and nature of development efforts as well. Class politics thus far has been less salient; religious conflicts have not been prominent.

Political participation is limited. With an average per capita income of $403 in 1978 and with only 25 percent of the population literate (in 1962), 26 percent urban (in 1960), and 98 percent in nonagricultural occupations (in 1950), much of the population is still uninvolved in politics. In addition, the military government keeps a watchful eye on political organizations, intellectuals, and students of all kinds.

After World War II, several political parties and leaders began to appear, and the multiparty system has remained alive. The National Congress of Nigerian Citizens (N.C.N.C.), led by Nnamdi Azikiwe, was strongest in the Ibo region but soon also won adherents in other areas. In Yoruba country, a party under Obafemi Awolowo became prominent. In the north, the Muslim landowners, traditional emirs and local rulers such as the Sardauna of Sokoto, remained the real powers behind politics.

In October 1979, military government announced that Nigeria was to return to civilian rule, and that elections were to be held. In June 1979, a dispatch from Lagos had reported five parties admitted to the electoral contest, out of an original fifty-two would-be contenders. Two parties had a northern geographic base and a Hausa and Muslim orientation: the relatively left-of-center party, led by Aminu Kano and drawing much of its support from the city of Kano; and the Great Nigerian People's party under Waziri Ibrahim, a multimillionaire who made his fortune in the arms business during the civil war. A third party, the National party, with some conservative middle-class support from all parts of the country, was led by Shehu Shagari and considered a favorite to win. Finally, there were the two old regional groupings: the United Nigeria party of Obafemi Awolowo, "the uncrowned king of the Yorubas," and the adherents of the other grand old man of Nigerian politics, the seventy-four-year-old Ibo leader and first president of Nigeria, Nnamdi Azikiwe, called "Zik." As evidence of their integrity, all candidates were required to publish their income tax returns for the preceding three years. Only Awolowo did so in complete form. Zik's returns were incomplete, and the other contenders thus far have published none.[2]

The elections were to take place in five stages, with the last scheduled for October 1979. By July, no party had won a majority, but the National party had won a plurality of votes, as expected. By August, Shehu Shagari had won the presidential election, again as expected, but the three smaller parties alleged voting frauds in some crucial states and wanted the election results set aside. Only the runner-up candidate, Obafemi Awolowo, was reported to be noncommittal on this issue. Whether all the elections actually will be completed, whom they will make president, whether the military will respect their results, and what government will emerge from them—these questions are still unanswered.

Despite these uncertainties, Nigerians rightly look on their country as the largest state in Black Africa and as the only one with the potential of becoming a middle-sized power within the next ten or twenty years. Nigeria has sometimes acted

[2]*Der Tagesspiegel,* Berlin (West), June 24, 1979, p. 31, with reference to the *Nigerian Herald.*

as a speaker for Black Africa, as in its opposition to the racist regimes of South Africa and Rhodesia during the 1970s.

Nigeria's political system is still weakly integrated. Civic loyalty and skills, communication channels between government and governed, administrative accountability and efficiency are still incompletely developed. Even so, Nigeria's performance since the Biafran war deserves respect. Since that time, there has been relatively little bloodshed or repression, measured by the size of the country and the standards of many other developing nations. Economic gains have been matched by gains in education, symbolized by such universities as those of Lagos and Ibadan. Starting from a heritage of poverty and severe interregional cleavages in colonial days, Nigeria in the 1970s has done better than many observers expected.

EGYPT: A MIXTURE OF NATIONALISM AND POPULAR OBEDIENCE

Egypt is a very poor country. Its per capita GNP in 1976 was $280, ranking well below Nigeria's $330 for the same year. Average gross domestic product per capita during 1965–75 grew in real terms only by 0.8 percent per year, and not much of that reached the poorer strata of the population. Yet Egypt ranks much higher on other indicators of development. Its 1976 population was 45 percent urban; 48 percent of its work force was in nonagricultural occupations; and 40 percent of its population over ten years old was literate. Average life expectancy in 1975 was fifty-two years, a gain of seven years since 1960.

For most practical purposes, Egypt is the Nile Valley—a thin strip of highly fertile land running north from the border of the Sudan to the Nile delta at the shore of the Mediterranean Sea. This is where the important cities are, as well as almost the entire rural population. The rest of the country is mostly desert.

Organized government has existed in the Nile Valley for more than four thousand years. Yet its political system seems poorly developed: there is no strong tradition of democracy, nor of efficient government. It has left a legacy of obedience and political passivity among most of the people.

The First Three Thousand Years. Government in ancient Egypt meant water. Kings and their officials directed the construction and maintenance of the extensive dams that were indispensable for irrigation. Priests alone could predict the day when spring would come and the flood waters of the Nile, fed by the melting snow from far-off mountains, would cover the fields with water and fertilizing mud. Together, kings, officials, and priests formed an irrigation bureaucracy that people did not dare to disobey for many centuries.

A Succession of Conquerors. Later conquerors—Assyrians, Babylonians, Greeks, Romans, and Byzantines—found an easy prey in the rich country and its obedient people. Capital cities changed often, both under native and foreign dynasties. So long as taxes were collected, it mattered little in what city the rulers chose to spend them by setting up their court there. After 332 B.C., when Alexander the Great conquered Egypt and founded the city of Alexandria, first Greek gods and later Roman ones replaced the old Egyptian ones. For a time, Alexandria led the ancient world in commerce and learning. Greek and Roman laws became practiced. Egypt served as a granary for imperial Rome, and from the fourth century A.D. on, the country became Christian in religion and Byzantine in administration.

Greek and Roman influence decreased with the Muslim conquest after A.D. 639. The conquerors spoke Arabic. In 712, they founded the city El-Kahira, "the victorious," today's Cairo. More Arabs moved into the country and merged with the local population. By about 950, more than one-half of the inhabitants of Egypt spoke Arabic. By about 1350, this proportion had risen to about 90 percent. The mass of the people had become Muslim and Arabic, and it remains so today.

New regimes evolved—Seldjuks, Mamelukes, and Turks. But now they, too, belonged to the world of Islam. Twice the court of the sultans of Egypt became a brilliant center of Muslim culture: once in about A.D. 1000 under the Fatimid dynasty, and again about two centuries later under Sultan Saladin. Early in the sixteenth century, Portuguese fleets cut off Egypt's trade through the Red Sea with India. For a while, an impoverished Egypt fell under the direct administration of the Ottoman Empire under a governor, later called viceroy. The Mamelukes remained noble landowners; the peasants, the *fellaheen*, continued to work for whomever was in power.

After more than a thousand years of Islam, Western influences broke into Egypt. In 1798, General Napoleon Bonaparte of the French republic landed with an army and defeated the Mameluke cavalry in the Battle of the Pyramids. "Forty centuries are looking upon you," he exhorted his soldiers. He conquered the country, only to find his sea lanes to France cut by the British navy. He had to evacuate his army and return the country to the Ottoman Empire in 1801.

But the country was no longer quite the same. French and English trade and influence remained and grew. Its sultan, now a Turkish viceroy, had more money and could borrow still more. From 1805 to 1848, a strong viceroy, Mehemet Ali of Albanian extraction, began to modernize the country. In the 1820s and 1830s, he raised a strong army and offered to help the Turkish sultan reconquer Greece. The scheme was stopped by the threat of French and British intervention, but it was the first time in centuries that anyone had tried to project Egyptian military power beyond its borders.

Mehemet Ali's successors, particularly his grandson Ismail (1863–79), focused their attention on administrative reforms, roads, railroads, and new dams, financed largely by foreign loans, albeit with high costs in usurious interest and discount rates. Inefficiency and corruption continued among the domestic elite of landowners and bureaucrats. When Civil War in the United States pushed up the price of cotton, long-staple cotton planting was introduced in Egypt with British aid. When cotton prices fell again after the Civil War was over, England wanted Egypt to continue as an additional source of cotton for the British textile industry. More loans to Egypt were forthcoming, but at ever stiffer terms. French business interests pushed the old project of a Suez Canal toward realization. The canal opened in 1869, putting Egypt once more on the main trade route to India and the Far East. The French Suez Canal Company, however, ran out of money in 1875, after France had been weakened by its defeat in the Franco-Prussian war of 1870–71. In 1877, the British government bought up the khedive's share and became the company's largest shareholder. Now Britain was the chief creditor of Egypt, and Egypt was becoming unable to pay.

Expansion, Militarization, and Indebtedness. In the meantime, Egypt expanded its political and military power in Africa. Between 1865 and 1879, it occupied the Red Sea coast; completed the conquest of the Sudan begun in the 1820s; and waged an inconclusive war with Ethiopia. All this activity pushed Egypt more deeply into debt and financial dependence on foreign powers. But just as economic developments strengthened Egypt's middle class, so the military actions produced new strata of Egyptian officers, soldiers, and bureaucrats. They resented Egypt's dependence and became increasingly ready to respond to appeals for a new Egyptian nationalism.

In 1876, a British and a French controller were appointed in charge of Egypt's finances, leading to a brief Anglo-French condominium in the interest of the creditors. Two years later, an Englishman was made minister of finance and a Frenchman minister of public works. When that foreign-dominated government fell after a demonstration of army officers in 1879, perhaps encouraged by the viceroy Ismail, the Turkish sultan deposed Ismail under pressure by the European powers. Ismail was replaced by his more pliable son, Tewpik. In 1880, a new Law of Liquidation (of Egypt's debts) provided that all surplus should go toward repaying the debts, regardless of the country's other needs.

Early Nationalism and British Occupation. In 1881, the Egyptian officers forced the appointment of a nationalist, Mahmud Sami, as war minister and, in early 1882, the appointment of a nationalist ministry. The nationalists were led by Ahmed Arabi, called "Arabi Pasha." They were inspired by the famous modernizing Muslim teacher Jamal-ud-Din el-Afghani, who since 1871 had preached resistance to the West and the necessary adoption of Western political methods for defense.

Britain and France intervened. In May 1882, their warships appeared before Alexandria, ostensibly in support of the khedive against his nationalist government. An Anglo-French ultimatum forced the resignation of the government, but the khedive soon had to call them back into office. In June, riots in Alexandria killed some fifty Europeans. According to some, the khedive instigated the riots to force European intervention in his favor. Within weeks, the British navy bombarded Alexandria, landed troops, and occupied Cairo. Arabi surrendered and was eventually banished to Ceylon. Egypt remained under British occupation from 1882 until 1956.

British Rule Becomes Indirect. The legal forms changed. Egypt remained nominally subject to the sultan of Turkey until 1914, when it was declared a British protectorate. Khedive Abbas Hilmi was deposed, replaced by his uncle Hussein Kamil, with the title of sultan, and by Sultan Ahmed Fuad after Kamil's death in 1917. In 1922, Britain unilaterally terminated the protectorate. Egypt was declared independent; Fuad took the title of king. In 1923, a relatively liberal constitution was promulgated. It was suspended in 1928, replaced by a less democratic one in 1930, but restored in 1935. In 1937, Egypt became a member of the League of Nations. In fact, British power remained dominant, but gradually Egypt became somewhat stronger.

A Second Wave of Nationalism. During the same decades, popular nationalism mounted. A nationalist party, Wafd, grew rapidly during World War I. When in 1919 the British deported Saad Zaghlul Pasha and other nationalist leaders to Malta to keep them from going to the Paris peace conference, a national insurrection followed. British troops put it down. Zaghlul returned in 1921, was deported again in the same year, returned once more in 1923, and became prime minister in early 1924. Large anti-British riots continued in 1922, 1924, 1930, 1933, and 1935. But as elections and some press freedom were permitted, the nationalists turned to the polls. They won a string of victories in the elections of 1923, 1925, 1929, 1933, and 1936, were eclipsed by internal dissensions and government pressure in 1938 and 1945, but again won an overwhelming majority in 1950. Mass nationalism had come to stay. All that might change were its leaders and channels of expression.

British power was eroding. Twice, in 1924 and 1928, a British ultimatum forced major concessions on the Egyptian government, followed by the resignation of its prime minister. King Fuad accepted British advice to suspend consitutional liberties and used Britain as an ally to preserve his power within the country. After his death in 1936, he was succeeded by his sixteen-year-old son Farouk, who did not seek to usurp power but won publicity as a fat, fun-loving playboy. In his reign, Egypt moved to the threshold of real independence and modernity.

In 1936, a treaty between Egypt and the United Kingdom obligated Britain to withdraw all troops from the country, except for ten thousand men in the Suez Canal zone, and to permit both the return of Egyptian troops to the Sudan and the unrestricted immigration of Egyptians to that country. The same treaty established a twenty-year alliance between Egypt and Britain.

In 1937, a British military mission arrived to advise the Egyptian government on that task. Soon, the first modern officer training courses were begun and, in 1938, universal military training was instituted. All this preparation took place in the face of the mounting threat of World War II. When the war came in 1939, however, the Egyptian government did not enter it. Its army did not fight, even when German and Italian armies moved toward Cairo in 1940 and 1942. Britain, on the contrary, did fight on Egyptian soil, controlling its territory, ports, and resources. British troops drove east from El Alamein in October 1942, meeting in the spring of 1943 with the American army in Tunisia, and ending the German and Italian military presence in North Africa. The Egyptian government finally declared war on the Axis in February 1945 and thus formally qualified as a member of the United Nations. In the same year, the League of Arab States was established, with headquarters in Cairo.

In 1946, Britain withdrew her forces from Egypt. The new Egyptian army, in alliance with troops from other Arab states, invaded Israel in 1948. It was defeated in that war, gaining for Egypt only the Gaza strip of 150 square miles and several hundred thousand Palestinian Arabs and refugees.

The Egyptian Revolution: Nasserism. Younger officers returning from the war blamed the monarch, the politicians, and the old elites for the weakness of their country and conspired to bring about a change. In 1952, King Farouk was overthrown. Soon his property was placed in state custody, the titles *bey* and *pasha* were abolished, and all political parties, including the Wafd, were dissolved, to be replaced in early 1953 by a single Liberation Rally. In June 1953, Egypt was proclaimed a republic, with General Naguib its president and prime minister. In 1954, Naguib was ousted by Lieutentant-Colonel Gamal Abdel-Nasser who became prime minister and, in 1956, president.

Populist in domestic politics, Nasser first tried to get aid from both the United States and the Soviet Union. He was rebuffed in 1956 by U.S. Secretary of State John Foster Dulles, who refused U.S. aid for a projected high dam at Aswan. That dam was completed with Soviet aid. Egypt embarked on a pro-Soviet course in foreign policy that lasted for eighteen years.

In 1956, Nasser nationalized the Suez Canal. In the ensuing dispute over his decision, Britain, France, and Israel initiated a war against Egypt. The Egyptian troops in the Sinai were defeated by the Israelis, but the main strength of the Egyptian army held out in Egypt proper. British and French landings won no decisive successes. The opposition of the Soviet Union, of the United States, of a large part of the Commonwealth and the British Labour party, and much of British public opinion soon brought the war to an end. Nasser was left more or less a victor.

In domestic affairs, Nasser developed a policy of Arab socialism, under which he strove to drive out major foreign business firms, to nationalize banks, various industries, and services, but to leave room for small and middle-sized Egyptian businesses, artisans, and farmers. This policy led to slow economic growth, much bureaucratic regulation, recurrent difficulties with currencies and credits, and an almost constant tug of war within the government party between adherents of the public and the private sectors.

In foreign affairs, Nasser aimed at national greatness. He stressed pan-Arabism and strove to make Egypt, the most populous of the Arabic-speaking countries, the leader of the Arab world. Pan-Arabism required accepting the independence of the Sudan, something earlier Egyptian governments had opposed. This policy still left Egypt free to promote its influence, by radio broadcasts and in other ways, among the populations in Africa south of the Sahara. At the same time, Egypt under Nasser became the major adversary of Israel, encouraging Arab guerrilla attacks on Israel from neighboring Arab states. Other Arab states, particularly Syria, followed the same policy. But in the 1950s and 1960s, Egypt's size and power supplied the main strength of the Arab coalition that refused to recognize Israel's existence.

In 1958, Syria and Egypt joined to form the United Arab Republic (UAR), with which Yemen became associated. The Syrian elites, particularly landowners, at that time felt threatened by movements demanding radical social changes; federation with Egypt and Nasser's moderate social policies seemed to promise more protection for their interests. The union at first was superficial. Nasser was president of the UAR, but the governments, armies, and administrations of Syria and Egypt remained separate. When efforts were made to merge them, it soon appeared that the Egyptians, five times more numerous than the Syrians, would hold most top jobs in the proposed joint army and administration. Efforts to nationalize Syrian industries within the UAR offered similar prospects. The Syrian elites became more afraid of the Egyptians than they had been of their own people. In 1961, the Syrian army revolted and restored Syria's independence. In the same year, Nasser dissolved Egypt's association with Yemen, denouncing the rule of the latter as reactionary. Civil war in Yemen followed. From 1962 to 1967, Nasser sent forty thousand Egyptian troops to that country to support the pro-Nasser faction there, with indifferent success.

The Six Days' War. Nasser tried to keep his role as leader of the Arab opposition to Israel's existence. He ordered threatening troop movements, encouraged increased guerrilla activity, and closed the Strait of Tiran from the Red Sea to the Israeli port of Elath. In June 1967, Israel responded by a "preemptive" attack on Egypt, Syria, and Jordan, defeating all three within six days. Egypt lost the Gaza Strip and the entire Sinai peninsula to Israeli occupation, as well as the much-needed revenues from the Suez Canal, which became the border between the Egyptian and Israeli military positions and was closed to traffic.

By late 1967, Nasser's pan-Arabism had failed, and his policy of alignment with the Soviet Union and its allies, begun in 1955, had won no substantial successes since the later 1950s. His domestic policies had not done much better. Armaments and war had depleted Egypt's resources. Western currencies and credits were scarce or unavailable. Egyptian entrepreneurs wanted more freedom; workers demanded more power for their unions. Economic growth was disappointing. Many people leaving agriculture and moving to the cities found little housing and no jobs. And the army resented the memory of its defeat by Israel in 1967. When Nasser died in 1970, the country was ready for a change.

A New Course: Anwar el Sadat. The change came step by step after Nasser's vice president and ancient associate, Anwar Sadat, succeeded to his office. Sadat tightened his grip on the government party and the government-controlled mass media, arresting some cabinet members in 1971 on charges of conspiracy. He played down Nasser's Arab socialism and made some economic concessions to business and the middle class. He strengthened the army and built up its modern equipment, largely with Soviet aid. Then, when he had accumulated a stock of Soviet arms, he dramatically reversed a major part of Egypt's foreign policy. In 1972, he ordered all Soviet advisers, military and civilian, to leave the country and soon began to work to improve relations with the United States and the other Western powers.

The October War of 1973. At the same time, he stepped up war preparations against Israel. On October 6, 1973, during Judaism's highest holiday, the Egyptian army struck. It crossed the Suez Canal quickly and broke through the Israeli defense lines there—something Israeli experts had considered impossible. Egypt's attack was synchronized with an attack by Syria, and during the first few hours it seemed a triumph for the Arab cause. Within a very few days, however, the Israeli army and air force stopped the Egyptian and Syrian tanks with heavy losses, drove a salient across the canal into the Egyptian mainland, and threatened to cut off an Egyptian force of twenty thousand. When the United States and the Soviet Union imposed a cease-fire, Egypt claimed victory. The

Israelis claimed that they would have won a victory within a few more days, but no one could have known how a protracted war would have ended. When the war did end, Israel had lost 2,500 young men out of her small population of less than three million, and Egypt and Syria had lost larger numbers out of a joint population that was about fifteen times larger. Serious, too, were the economic costs, both for Israel and its larger but poorer adversaries. In blood and treasure, both sides had become poorer. Until well into the 1980s, any further round of warfare seemed likely to produce nothing more than another such stalemate.

In November 1977, Sadat again reversed Egyptian policy. In a dramatic gesture, he flew to Jerusalem to address the Knesset and undertake serious negotiations for a peace treaty between Egypt and Israel that would end thirty years of conflict between the two countries. The move had been prepared on both sides with the aid of the United States. It meant that Egypt was prepared to adjust, at least temporarily, its position of leadership among the Arab nations as well as some of its past commitment to the Palestinian Arabs. In exchange, Egypt expected to gain the return of the Sinai peninsula and the Gaza Strip, occupied by Israel since the 1967 war; a lightening of the burdens of repeated wars and war preparations; an increase in Western private investment; and substantial economic and military aid from the United States.

The negotiations on the draft treaty were mainly completed in late 1978 at Camp David in the United States, with the personal participation of President Carter. Ratification by both countries followed. In 1979, Prime Minister Begin visited Egypt and was cheered by friendly crowds. In November 1979, a substantial part of the Sinai peninsula was to be returned to Egypt and full diplomatic relations between Egypt and Israel were to be in effect. Eventually, Palestinian Arabs on the left bank of the Jordan River, occupied by Israel since the 1967 war, were to be given a degree of self-government. But in October 1979, the Israeli and Egyptian positions on this matter were still far apart and the negotiations seemed to be dragging on. In the wording of the Camp David agreements, occupation of the left bank was a matter separate from all others. Its outcome would carry great political and moral importance for Sadat's prestige both inside and outside Egypt.

In the meantime, Sadat was bitterly criticized in the Arab world for having broken its solidarity and having recognized Israel. The Arab league expelled Egypt and removed its headquarters from Cairo to Tunis—a move Egypt refused to recognize. Most Arab governments broke diplomatic relations with Egypt; Saudi Arabia and other oil-rich states cut off their subsidies. To what extent the United States and other Western countries would replace these sources of income was not yet clear. Nor did it seem clear how solid Sadat's support within Egypt would remain, particularly if his efforts on behalf of the Palestinians should fail. If Egyptian nationalism should become more Egyptian than pro-Arab, Sadat might succeed. If Nasser's pan-Arabism should prevail, Sadat's difficulties might well increase.

The High Stakes of Egyptian Politics. By the fall of 1979, the stakes of Egyptian politics had become high indeed. At risk were war or peace with Israel; greater militarization of the country or more civilian development; more or less land and equipment for most peasants and their children; deepening poverty or new industrial growth and investment; nonalignment in foreign policy or membership in either the Western or the Eastern bloc.

In time, even the basic social order of the country would be decided by the outcome of its politics. Would private enterprise dominate and, with it, petty traders, partisans, and peasants? Or would a strong national ruling class of big and middling bankers, businesspeople, and landowners emerge victorious, strengthened by kinship ties to high-level bureaucrats and military officers? Would it become a market economy dominated by multinational corporations? Or would Egypt once more move toward a more collective and centrally planned social and economic system? And would whatever future pattern that might emerge still be considered Arab socialism? Would social and economic inequality decline or would most peasants still stay *fellaheen*? In all these respects, the fate of the Egyptian people still hangs in the balance at the beginning of the 1980s, almost thirty years after the officers' revolution of 1952.

The Narrowness of Political Participation. The revolution of 1952 made the politics of modern Egypt, but it was made by a few officers, not by the mass of the people. Although 44 percent literate, the Egyptian people have no choice among political parties, no truly autonomous organizations, no substantial power of political decision making. They can say "yes" to governmental policies and candidates, cheer them in the streets, or keep silent. And most of them do not appear to mind. When labor unions in the few industrial plants demand higher wages or more rights and are suppressed, when students are arrested or newpapers censored, the rest of the country does not stir.

Only religion offers an indirect outlet for expression. Muslim theologians, worshipers at mosques, teachers and students at religious universities such as Al Azhar in Cairo, inevitably form groups to discuss ideas, although most often traditional or fundamentalist ones. The "Muslim brotherhood" *(Ikhwan)* could have become a political spearhead for such trends and have been held responsible for some acts of terrorism. Currently, they are suppressed. The underground strength they may have kept is hard to measure.

An Uncertain Arena. Just what are Egypt's boundaries at the start of the 1980s?

Southward: The Sudan. Even in 1850 B.C. Nubia, including part of the Sudan, was part of the Egyptian empire, and it remained so for centuries. Many Egyptians, from the 1820s on, considered the Sudan to be part of their country or at least part of its legitimate sphere of expansion. They had expected the Anglo-Egyptian condominium over the Sudan to be replaced by Egyptian dominance in one form or another. By the mid 1950s, these prospects had become remote. The Sudan had its own government, army, and administrative state machinery. This Sudanese state was dominated by the Arab-speaking and Muslim population of Khartoum and the north, but only grudgingly obeyed by many of the black inhabitants of the south who spoke African tribal languages and professed animist religions or else Christianity. Neither northerners nor southerners showed any inclination to accept Egyptian rule. Rather, the Sudan counted as an Arab state and, under the policies of the Arab league, Egypt was bound to respect its sovereignty.

Westward: Libya. To the west, the former Italian colonies of Tripoli and Cyremaica became the Arab state of Libya. From the sixteenth to the nineteenth century, both Egypt and Libya were closely united under the Ottoman Empire, until Egypt's occupation by the British in 1882 and Libya's conquest by Italy in 1911. Libya's population in 1952 found itself in a sovereign pro-Western monarchy under a Sanusi leader who called himself King Idris I.

In 1969, Idris was overthrown by an officers' revolution, led by twenty-seven-year-old Colonel Muammar el-Qaddafi, who became the new head of state. A stridently nationalistic and leftist republic was established, with only about 2.5 million inhabitants but a remarkable degree of oil-based wealth, and with Arab unity and hostility to Israel as major elements in its foreign policy. In the name of Arab unity, Libya signed an agreement in 1971 to form a three-nation federation of Arab republics, but nothing came of the project. Since then, Libya has alternated between offers of unity with Egypt, sometimes going as far as offering to merge the two countries, and angry accusations and threats against Sadat's government for its allegedly insufficient zeal in pressing the Arab cause against Israel. Egyptian responses thus far have been cautious or negative, despite the lure of small Libya's oil riches for Egypt's large but poor economy. Whether Libya will remain forever separate from Egypt, no one now can say.

Eastward: The Sinai, Palestine, and Israel. The sparsely inhabited Sinai peninsula has been a part of Egypt since ancient times. Before 1800 B.C., a pharaoh reorganized Egyptian mining operations there.

Palestine's links to Egypt are almost as old. The country was conquered by Egypt in about 1470 B.C. and held more or less effectively until about 1100 B.C. Later, both Palestine and Egypt were conquered by the Arabs and Islam, ruled for some centuries by the caliphs of the empire of Islam, and belonged to the Ottoman Empire. From 1918 to 1946, both countries in effect were under British control, in one form or another.

In the war of 1948 against Israel, Egypt acquired the Gaza Strip with some Palestinian refugees but lost it again to Israeli occupation in the war of 1967. The restoration of the strip to Egyptian sovereignty was one of the topics of negotiation between Egypt and Israel in late 1979.

For Arab solidarity, Egypt would be obliged to support the claims of the Palestinian Arabs against Israel. Nasser did so with vigor and at great cost; Sadat has continued to do so, albeit more moderately and without thus far making peace with Israel dependent on the satisfaction of these claims. From the viewpoint of pan-Arab nationalism, Egypt should continue to seek mergers with other Arab states, not only with Libya and the Sudan, but also with Syria, Yemen, Jordan, Lebanon, and eventually even with Saudi Arabia and Iraq. Finally, from the viewpoint of Islamic solidarity, as propagated by the Muslim brotherhood, Egypt should champion the cause of Islam against Israel and against the Christian minority in Lebanon.

None of these viewpoints is currently prevailing over all others in Egypt, nor would a policy based on any one of them be likely to succeed. They mean that the arena of Egyptian politics is not sharply delineated. In particular, to the east and north, the boundary between Egyptian domestic politics and the politics of the Palestinian Arabs, Syria, Jordan, and Lebanon is less sharply and solidly drawn than in most modern nation states. Any Egyptian government could be strengthened by success in these areas, any major failure there could threaten its stability.

The Changing Images of Egypt. One answer to the question "What is Egypt?" depends on the answer to another question: "Who are the Egyptians?" Are they mainly the descendants of the people of the ancient empire and the pyramids, towering over the centuries long before Islam? Or are the ties of the Arabic language stronger than those of ancestry and of the land in the Nile Valley? Or is the religion of Islam in its Sunni form the strongest source of identity for most Egyptians? Finally, how many people see themselves as members of a class, whether peasants in the country or workers in the few industrial districts of the cities. How many take seriously the visions of a new social order, Arab or otherwise?

At present, Egypt's leaders try to appeal to all these images. Nasser stressed the images of pan-Arabism and socialism; Sadat balanced these themes somewhat with appeals to Egyptian interest and to Islam. Which image or combination of images will prevail in the future politics of Egypt still seems an open question.

Political System and Administration. Channels of communication from the government to the people appear strong, through the radio and to a lesser extent the press. Feedback channels from the people to the government seem weak. The one-party system, government control of the media, the strong military and police, the weakness of labor unions, students, and intellectuals, and the absence of autonomous peasant organizations not only keep the people quiet, they keep the government ill informed about the people's feelings.

If President Sadat has been able thus far to steer his country through a zigzagging path of policy changes, it has been in part because government broadcasts have been loud, political participation small, and political apathy great. But these are dwindling assets—if indeed they are assets at all. Industrial, social, and economic modernization will erode them.

Egypt's underdevelopment is lessening. One area showing signs of improvement is the administration. Despite such high-sounding titles as *pasha, bey,* and *effendi,* the foreign image of Egyptian administrators for well over a century has been one of lassitude, laziness, inefficiency, and corruption. *Baksheesh,* the Arab word for a gratuity or bribe needed to get anything done, long has been notorious. But the old titles are gone and contemporary Egyptian administration has proved more effective than some foreigners had anticipated.

When Egypt took over the Suez Canal in 1956, many foreign observers predicted that it would fail to maintain the canal and that Egyptian pilots would be incapable of guiding the larger ships through it. Egyptians proved competent in coping with all these tasks. Similarly, in the October war of 1973, the organization and discipline of the Egyptian army and its logistic support proved to be more effective than most foreigners had expected. More than once, Egypt's administration has passed a severe test of performance.

The Performance of the Egyptian Political System. Since the revolution of 1952, nutrition, health, and life expectancy have significantly improved. Banks and industries, government agencies and the military function tolerably well under Egyptian personnel and management. And President Sadat's government has been able, thus far, to move away from recurrent warfare to a search for peace that in the fall of 1979 appeared serious and sincere. As in many other developing countries, the outcome of all these policies is still open—but there is room for hope.

IRAN: SPLENDOR, OIL, AND REVOLUTION

Iran is the richest of the developing countries sketched in this chapter. In 1975, its per capita income of $1660 put it ahead of Argentina. But the low levels of its literacy, industrialization, and access to higher education, its high infant mortality rate, and its high index of economic inequality suggest how incomplete and uneven its economic and social development has been.

The case of Iran is a case of religion and the state, of dictatorship and revolution. Tensions between religion and the state have been recurring for many centuries. In our century, Iran has had three revolutions: an incomplete middle-class one in 1905, an authoritarian "revolution from above" by the two Pahlavi shahs from 1925 to 1978, and the revolution of 1979 that is not yet completed.

At the start of the 1980s, we cannot study Iran the way we can study most other countries. Ordinarily, a country changes so slowly that we can study its structures as if they were standing still, and its processes as if they were highly repetitive. We can sketch maps of their political system. But for contemporary Iran, we need not maps but a film—a film that reaches far back into the past where changes came from and suggests where some of them may be going.

This section will say little, therefore, about Iran's current administration, laws, and institutions, since they may change significantly within a year or two. But it will deal with Iran's history and the recurring conflicts that once more broke into the open in 1979.

An Ancient Culture of Contrasts and Refinement. Iran (until 1935 called Persia) is one of the oldest civilizations in the world. It is one of the world's first regions where agriculture was developed and refined. A Bronze Age culture existed there before 2000 B.C. The ancient Indo-Europeans or Aryans settled in Iran before 1800 B.C.; some of them went on to invade India. The cultivation of peaches and the use of houses were known in Iran before they became known to the Greeks. Persian cooking, together with that of China and France, is considered one of the three great cooking traditions of the world. Sophistication and refinement, imagination and curiosity have been described as continuous elements in Iranian culture.

Throughout its history, except during the last sixty years, the borders of Iran have been fluid. At various times, Armenia, Azerbaijan, and parts of today's Iraq have belonged to it, as have Afghanistan, Khwa, and Bukhara. Many movements and leaders have come from these lands, but the regions around Shiraz, Isfahan, Qum, and Tehran always have been its core.

The country is variegated, even in its central regions. There are plains and towering mountains, deserts and fertile gardenlike valleys. Much of the country depends on irrigation, and the peasants in these areas have depended on the landowning nobles who controlled the distribution of the water. No single river, like the Nile in Egypt, provided a permanent basis for a central government and perpetual obedience to it. Mountain peoples and tribes in the plains have always been ready to resist governmental authority if it became too onerous. The interplay of all these elements has led to strangely mixed events. In some periods of their history, Iranians have obeyed absolute rulers; but more than once, revolutionary movements have shaken the country.

A History of Grandeur and Catastrophes. Political systems in Iran have been discontinuous. One period of imperial glory lasted a little over two hundred years. It began in about 550 B.C., when Cyrus the Great took power in the Iranian kingdom of Media, conquered Lydia and Babylonia, and founded the Persian Empire, which stretched from the Indus River to the Mediterranean from the Caucasus mountains to the Indian Ocean. His son, Cambyses, conquered Egypt. His successors, Darius I and Xerxes, tried to conquer Greece but failed. Yet the Greeks were so impressed by the size of the empire and its capabilities that their victories seemed to them won against overwhelming odds. At that time, the empire was centralized, divided into twenty provinces, each under a royal governor, or *satrap.* The king himself had four residences, at Persepolis, Susa, Ecbatana, and Babylon. Good roads, with stations for royal messengers, permitted regular communications within the empire. The king could raise vast armies and amass and spend large treasures. The rulers professed the Zoroastrian religion, according to which a single god of light fights against a single god of darkness and evil. Conquered tribes and people were left free to worship their own deities. Belief in the Devil and religious tolerance thus may have ancient Iranian precedents.

Decline set in after 450 B.C., with struggles for the throne, assassinations, and civil war. Within three years, between 334 and 331 B.C. the ruler of Macedonia, Alexander the Great, aided by troops from nearly all the Greek cities, conquered the entire empire. After Alexander's death, it was divided among his generals and a period of partial Greek cultural dominance began. About a century later, the Parthians expanded their rule into Iran. They were splendid horsemen and archers, who had adopted an Indo-European language in place of their earlier Turanian tongue. By 138 B.C., their empire covered most of present-day Iran and beyond. Beating off Roman efforts at conquest, their rule lasted more than three hundred years, but without, it seems, any cultural accomplishments.

A second period of Iranian greatness followed, between A.D. 226 and 651 under the Sassanian dynasty. Son of a vassal-king of the Parthian Empire in Fars-Persia proper, Ardashir I defeated the last Parthian ruler and conquered several neighboring regions. He created a strong centralized state, supported by the priesthood (called *Magi*) of the Zoroastrian religion. The privileges of the Magi were restored. Under his successors, the empire expanded and fought Rome to a stand-off. By A.D. 380, the empire had reached a peak of its power.

Recurrent Tensions Between Religion and State. During this period and in the ups and downs that followed, religion and the state were sometimes in alliance. Already in about A.D. 275, the new sect of

Manicheanism was outlawed and its founder Mani executed. Christians were sometimes tolerated but more often persecuted; the Magi were once persecuted but more often favored. A communistic sect following the doctrines of Mazdak was supported by a king, Kobad, whom the nobles then deposed. When Kobad returned to power in A.D. 501, he turned against Mazdak. The Mazdakites were massacred in A.D. 523.

A new peak of Iranian power and royal splendor occurred between A.D. 531 and 628 under the kings Anushirwan the Just (Chosroes I) and Khushru Parviz (Chosroes II). It was ended by the murder of Khushru by his own troops, followed by struggles and assassinations, and succeeded by the Muslim conquest of the country between 639 and 651. Persia became part of the empire of the Arab caliphs, who ruled most often from Damascus and later from Baghdad.

Social revolts sometimes led by priests—Magi or Muslim—kept recurring in Persia and in the caliphate: the Zindigs in Khorasan and western Persia after 775; the Khurramites, led by the Magian Babek, from Azerbaijan after 813 until Babek's defeat and execution in 838; the slave uprising of the Zanj rebellion (869–883); and the revolt of the Carmathians (891–906), who temporarily took Mecca. All these revolts of the poor were defeated but they may have left memories rather different from those of the more obedient people of Egypt.

On a higher social level, a Persian cultural revival began under Arab rule. With the caliphs now ruling from newly founded Baghdad (around 762), Persian culture and refinement soon permeated the court and the lifestyle of the elite, even though Arabic remained the predominant language there. In the tenth century, Persian was revived as a literary language, particularly in the eastern Persian province of Khorasan at the court of the local Saffarid dynasty and their successors, the Samanids and Ghaznawids. Eventually, these rulers extended their power over modern Persia. At the court of the greatest of them, Mahmud the Idol-Breaker, the great Persian poet Firdausi flourished about A.D. 1000 and so did the physician and philosopher Ibn Sīna, whom the West called Avicenna. At that time, Islam and Persian culture spread to parts of northern India.

There followed conquests by Seldjuk Turk and Mongol rulers. For a time, Persian intellectual life flourished again in the days of the ruler Malik Shah (1073–1092) and the mathematician and poet Omar Khayyam. Underground, below the surface of changing rulers of the Near East, from Persia to Syria, the traditions of dissident sects and rebel movements lived on as secret societies. In 1090, a formidable sect was founded at the mountain stronghold of Alamut in northern Persia. They relied on secrecy and political murders, and they used hashish (a stronger variety of marijuana). Accordingly, they were called "hashish eaters," *hash-shāhshīn* in Arabic, from which the word *assassin* in several European languages derives. Western crusaders and Near Eastern rulers fell to their daggers, until the grandson of Jenghis Khan, Hulagu, exterminated the sect in 1256.

A century of provincial rulers, called *Il-Khans,* under the Mongols followed. Then Timur, the vizier (minister) of such a ruler, overthrew his master and embarked on a vast career of conquest. He conquered Persia, Baghdad, Mesopotamia, all the lands between Moscow and the Great Wall of China, invaded India, and sacked Delhi, inflicting numerous cruelties. His son, Shah Rukh, ruled in splendor over eastern Persia and parts of central Asia for nearly half a century (1404–1447). Once again conquest followed, this time by the Turkomans, and there were further dynastic conflicts. But then came a bigger change.

In a spectacular turn of events in 1500, Iran got a national ruler and a national dynasty, the first in many centuries. This striking change depended on a rearrangement between the two contending forces—religion and state—that so often had been in conflict throughout Iranian history.

Shi'ism: A Dissident Tradition in Islam. The faith preached by the Prophet Muhammad after A.D. 622 had been revolutionary in many ways. Its sign had been the curved sword, later sometimes misunderstood as the crescent. Where it conquered, it swept away the wealth of the Byzantine church and the tax collectors of the Byzantine state. Muslims usually were armed and free from taxes; only non-Muslims had to pay them for tolerance and protection. Islam had no highly organized church to accumulate land and wealth. Its law, the Koran, protected the property of artisans, merchants, peasants, and landholders, but forbade lending at interest. It commanded simple living without alcohol or luxuries, made almsgiving a duty, and proclaimed the brotherhood of all believers. The doctrine soon became more accommodating to the interests of the powerful and rich, and at times more tolerant of luxury and ostentatious display. But time and again, as in Christianity, some sect would raise the old demands for a return to Muslim virtue, simplicity, and justice.

Islam had to have a single military leader, the caliph, against the world of infidels. The caliph had to be a legitimate successor of the Prophet, a requirement that became the formal point of division between Islam and its main sects.

After the death of the Prophet Muhammad, each of the first four "orthodox" caliphs attained the office of head of the Muslim state, commander-in-chief of the armies, and supreme judge either through election or by appointment by the predecessor, or by some combination of both. Once in office, each caliph was still bound by the Koran, the traditional sayings of the Prophet *(hadith)*, as well as by custom and public opinion. The second caliph, Omar, under whose reign Persia had been conquered, was murdered by a Persian slave. The third caliph, Othman of the Omayyad family of Mecca was resented by the Hashimite family of Mekka, accused of nepotism, and murdered at Medina.

Eventually Ali, cousin and son-in-law of the Prophet Muhammad, was elected caliph. Like the Prophet himself, Ali was of the Hashimite family, and some partisans of the Omayyads accused him of complicity in Othman's murder. The Omayyad governor of Syria, Muawiya, rose against him. After an inconclusive battle, the two claimants submitted to arbitration, which in 658 gave the caliphate to Muawiya. Ali refused to accept the decision, which might have reflected the majority view of Arab notables. He insisted on his claim, based on his belonging to the house of the Prophet and hence on divine right. Among his own army, however, twelve thousand of the most radical, called *Kharijites,* rose against him claiming that by submitting to arbitration he had already betrayed their cause. They wanted to submit to no caliph, but only to the "Lord alone." Ali dispersed them, had eighteen holdouts killed, and was murdered three years later (661) by a Kharijite. Muawiya became caliph and moved the seat of government to Damascus, where his successors ruled as the Omayyad dynasty of caliphs to A.D. 750.

Ali's older son submitted to Muawiya and was allowed to live in comfort at Medina. Eight years later, he was poisoned. According to Persian tradition, this was done on Muawiya's orders. In 680, Ali's younger son, Husayn, was invited by the Beduins of Kufa in Iraq to assert his hereditary title to the caliphate. Betrayed by the Kufans, he was slain in the battle of Kerbela. The power of the Omayyads was safe for a time, but Ali, Hasan, and Husayn became more powerful as martyrs than they had ever been in life.

Their adherents did not give up. Called *Shi'ites* (partisans), they became the chief religious opposition party in Islam. To this day, perhaps 85 percent of the world's Muslims adhere to the orthodox tradition of Islam, the *sunna,* and are *Sunnites.* Their faith accepts the outcomes of ancient Arab politics, the decisions of the caliphs, and the age-old influence of the elites of the Arab and Turkish world. Sunnis form the vast majority of Muslims in the Arabian peninsula, Egypt, North Africa, and almost all Muslim countries—but not in Persia. There Shi'ism, the religion of the underdogs in those ancient sectarian struggles, has lived on.

Shi'ites believe that only the descendants of Ali are the divinely appointed hereditary successors to the caliphate. They believe that this supreme authority consists less in the secular power of the caliph over government and armies and more in the caliph's role as *imām* (spiritual leader) of the faithful. The main branch of the Shi'ites counts twelve such *imāms,* ending with Mohammed al-Muntazar ("the unexpected one") who in 878 as a boy vanished in a mosque in Iraq. Since then, according to Shi'ite tradition, he has lived on as "the hidden *imām*" among the people, to appear on the last day as the *Mahdi* ("the divinely guided one") to bring an era of universal Islam prosperity and peace. Until then, governments are only provisionally legitimate and kings are akin to usurpers. At best, a monarch may be called a "shadow of the imām" by the Shi'ite priests, if they approve of him and his actions. But they may choose to give this approval or to withhold it.

For more than eight hundred years after the deaths of Ali and Husayn, the Shi'ite religion lived on as a heresy. It was disclaimed by the Sunni governments of all Muslim countries, at best tolerated, but often persecuted and driven underground. In these centuries, the Shi'ites developed their doctrine of *dissimulation*: It is lawful for Shi'ites to deny their faith and to profess outwardly any other religion that may protect them from persecution. "Even the recording angel withdraws," goes a saying, "when two Shi'ites meet."

With the martyrs Ali and Husayn, Shi'ism extolled the losers in a power struggle. Its adherents often kept an emotional distance from the strong, the successful, the rich—and from the Arab rulers and elites, particularly the Omayyad caliphs. This made Shi'ism particularly appealing to the people of Iran, where Shi'ite uprisings repeatedly occurred. According to a Persian tradition, Husayn married the daughter of the last Sassanid king, Yezdigird, so that Husayn's descendants are legitimized both as heirs of the Persian kings and as descendants of the Prophet. It was in eastern Iran, in the province of Khorasan, that the black banner of the Abbasid claimants to the caliphate was raised. It was under the Abbasid caliphs at Baghdad that Persian culture rose again to prominence. But Shi'ism itself had to survive as best it could, remote from government.

It did so by developing a stronger organization of its clergy than the majority branch of Islam, the Sunnis, had. Islam has no ordained priests, supernaturally different from mere lay people, as many Christian denominations have. Its clergy differs from lay people only by its learning. But among Shi'ites to this day, these preachers and teachers of religion, called *mullahs*—their number estimated today at somewhere under twenty thousand—are highly respected and strongly organized. A *mullah* who studies the religious law or theology may become a *mujtahid,* if accepted by the established *mujtahids.* A *mujtahid* has the right to give individual views on religious problems (which under Islam may include almost everything in law, politics, economics, and society.) *Mujtahids* are expected to give views within the Shi'ite tradition. As Sunnis, they would be much less free to decide, since under that faith both tradition and the law give less leeway and are seen as fixed. Even under the shahs, the *mujtahids* have had much prestige and influence among the populace. At the start of the 1980s, Iran had perhaps 1000 *mujtahids.* A few of the *mujtahids* may rise through further study and exemplary conduct to the rank of *ayatollah.* In 1979, Iran had about twenty *ayatollahs,* of whom only four held the supreme title of *ayatollah al-ozma.* In late 1979, one of these was murdered. Another, Ayatollah Khoi, is the most highly respected of the four, but he is ninety-four years old, lives at Karbala in Iraq, and thus far has kept out of politics. This leaves only two top-ranking *ayatollahs,* Ruhollah Khomeini and Shariat Madari. The latter is the spiritual leader of the Turkic-speaking Shi'ites of Azerbaijan, and a potential rival to the influence of Ayatollah Khomeini in that region and perhaps elsewhere in Iran. Throughout the centuries, this organizational and emotional power of Shi'ism has been reinforced through pilgrimages to the sacred Shi'ite cities of Mashhad, Ardebil, and Qum. The last of these has been called "the Rome of the Shi'ites." In A.D. 1500, Shi'ism became the state religion of Persia.

The Shi'ite Monarchy, 1500–1924. Ismail, the leader of a war band, began to establish his power in Persia at about 1500. His ancestry was mixed, chiefly Turkoman and Greek. On his father's side, he was descended from a line of chiefs of a small monastic military state at the town of Ardabil in Azerbaijan. One of their ancestors had been a shaykh Safi, from whom the Safarids derived their name. Safi and his heirs also claimed descent from Caliph Ali. The dervish order that was the backbone of the state of Ardabil was fanatically devoted to Shi'ism. Ismail's father reorganized these dervishes, many recruited from Turkoman tribes in the region, into a powerful military organization, known as "red-heads" from the color of their headdresses. Besides, Haydar was the son-in-law of Uzun-Hasan, head of one of the main Turkoman tribes who had expanded his power over a large part of Persia and had given his daughter from a Greek princess to Haydar as a wife. Despite these assets, Haydar was defeated and killed by the chief of another Turkoman tribe; but Ismail, after several years in hiding, assembled a band of followers, defeated the rival tribe, and conquered Tabriz where he had himself proclaimed shah. He made Shi'ism the state religion and conquered all of Persia. At that time and even today, the bonds of religion were stronger than the links of language. To be a Shi'ite was to be a Persian, even though people in Azerbaijan might speak a Turkic language and the people in Khuzistan, near today's Iraq, might speak Arabic. The new state did not turn these populations into Persian speakers, but with the help of Shi'ism it assimilated them into Persian culture. (How deeply this assimilation has been, the last decades of our own century may have to show.)

Even so, the new state was the first truly Persian one in many centuries. It was Persian in the religion, culture, geography, and language of most inhabitants. Yet it had its ups and downs. After Ismail's rule followed years of war against Irbegs and Turks and quarrels about the successions with executions and assassinations. But under Shah Abbas the Great (1587–1629), another period of splendor and prosperity followed, not only in economic and military matters but also in cultural affairs. Then came decline, rivalries for the throne, and wholesale executions once more.

In 1711, Afghanistan seceded, defeated the Persian troops, and became an independent state. In the 1720s, the Afghans took Ispahan and an Afghan ruler, Mahmud, became shah. Russia and Turkey made an agreement for the dismemberment of Persia. But a Safarid prince, Tahmasp, called for national resistance and was aided by a powerful tribal chief, Nadir Kuli of Khorasan. By 1730, the Afghans were defeated and expelled. Tahmasp became shah, but Nadir soon deposed him and in 1736 became shah himself.

Nadir Shah was the last spectacular military conqueror to rule Iran. He led a Persian army to the conquest and sack of Delhi, the capital of the Moghul Empire in India, with a vast massacre and immense booty. But, returned to Iran, the conqueror became miserly in guarding his loot. He turned against Shi'ism. His attempts to stamp it out provoked growing unrest, and in 1747 Nadir, "hated by all," was assassinated by one of his own tribespeople.

After a humane rule by Karim Khan 1750–79, the Qajarite dynasty came to power in 1794 and held it until 1925. The first Qajarite ruler was cruel, the rest mediocre. Throughout the nineteenth century, absolutism and traditionalism predominated. Reforms were slow and few, and the royal finances were troubled. Foreign influences, particularly British and Russian, penetrated and eventually divided the country into spheres of influence. Yet foreign penetration was not deep. The people and the national culture and economy slowly became consolidated. There were no bloody succession struggles within the royal family, nor any other powerful claimants to the throne. Succession became orderly, by inheritance, and Shah Nasir-ud-Din ruled without major challenge for nearly a half century (1848–96). Persia's boundaries toward Turkey were to be demarcated, according to a treaty concluded in 1823 and confirmed in 1847; the task actually was concluded in 1914. The border toward Afghanistan was defined in 1872.

In 1878, a Persian Cossack brigade was organized under Russian officers. Russian influence grew rapidly from the 1880s on. British and Russian financiers competed at the court. In 1890, the government granted a concession for tobacco production and export, which aroused so much religious and popular opposition that the concession had to be canceled. Six years later, Shah Nasir-ud-Din was assassinated.

Under his successor, Muzaffar-ud-Din, the Qajar monarchy was engulfed by revolution. Foreign loans increased. In 1901 a New Zealander, William K. d'Arcy, won a concession to explore for oil throughout most of the country promising the government £20,000, the same amount in shares, and 16 percent of the future profits. But only in 1908 was a major oil field found. Anglo-Persian Oil Company, forerunner of today's British Petroleum Company (BP), was founded in 1909 and took over d'Arcy's concession.

In the meantime, Persian finances were getting worse. In 1900 and 1902, Russia, through a bank it controlled, granted large loans to the shah. These loans were to replace past and future British loans, and were to be secured by part of Persia's customs. In addition, Russia got a road concession and a new Persian tariff favoring it over Britain. In 1903, Persian customs were put under the control of a foreigner, M. Naus, a national of Belgium.

Popular opposition to the absolute monarchy had been growing since at least 1890. Religious leaders and the commercial classes objected to taxes, corruption, government inefficiency, and the privileges of foreigners. Since the shah was leaning toward Russia, British influence also was brought to bear against him.

The Persian revolution began in December 1905, perhaps encouraged by the Russian revolution of that year, which had forced the tsar to move toward constitutional government. In July 1906, twelve thousand revolutionaries, including merchants and religious leaders, took refuge on the grounds of the British legation in Tehran, and a group of the *mujtahids* left for Qum. The shah had to yield to popular pressure. He dismissed his chief minister, unpopular for corruption and favoring foreigners, and agreed to call a national assembly. In the words of the shah's rescript (decree), it was to be "an assembly of delegates elected by the Princes, the Mujtahids, the Quajar family, the nobles and notables, the Landowners, the merchants and the guilds . . . formed . . . by election of the classes above mentioned."[3]

The *majlis* met in October and produced a liberal monarchical constitution. The shah signed it, but died a few days later.

His son, Mohammed Ali Shah, tried to circumvent the constitution and bring back the old order. He appointed a reactionary minister, Atabegi-Azam, who was assassinated in August 1907. In December, the shah tried a coup d'état, which provoked a popular uprising in several regions. The shah had to yield but tried again in 1908. With the help of the Russian legation and the Russian-officered Persian Cossack brigade, the shah closed the *majlis* and had many liberal leaders killed. He controlled Tehran but the people of Tabriz in the north rose against him. A deadlock followed until, in March 1909, Russian troops occupied Tabriz for the shah and brutally suppressed the rebels. In June, a leader of the southern and pro-British Bakhtiar tribe marched on Tehran to defend the constitutional regime, took the city in July, and deposed the shah in favor of his twelve-year-old son, Sultan Ahmad Shah, who ruled as a figurehead until 1925.

In reality, power in Iran had been divided between Tsarist Russia and Britain. In 1907, the two countries agreed to a compromise on Persia as part of Russia's joining Britain and France in the Triple Entente, preparing for the possibility of the war against Germany that came in 1914. Britain was to remain in southeastern Persia where the oil was; the northern half of the country was to be a Russian sphere; and a central belt was available for concessions granted to either side. The agreement also reaffirmed the independence and integrity of Persia. Few Persians at the time believed these

[3]Cited in Sir Percy Sykes, *A History of Persia*, vol. 2 (London: Macmillan, 1915), p. 509.

promises, but in surprising ways history made them come true.

From 1909 to 1914, Russian influence prevailed in the north and in the center. In 1914, Persia declared its neutrality in World War I but could not enforce it. On occasion, Turkish and Russian fought each other on Persian soil. In 1915, with Russia in difficulties in its war against Germany and Austria, German influence grew in Tehran. Allegedly to counter this influence, the Russians invaded northern Persia in November, while in early 1916 Sir Percy Sykes organized the South Persia Rifles and later in the year marched northeast to Isfahan, which the Russians were already occupying, and then to Shiraz, the heart of Persia. The foreign contest for Persia seemed at a peak.

In March 1917, the Turks withdrew from Persia after their defeat by British and Indian troops at Baghdad; in November, following the Bolshevik revolution, the Russians began to withdraw. Only the British stayed, sent troops into northern Persia, and organized a flotilla into the Caspian Sea. In 1919, an Anglo-Persian agreement was drawn up to seal the British ascendancy. Under it, Persia's independence and integrity were formally reconfirmed, but in fact its government would have remained largely dependent on Britain.

The *majlis* refused to convene to ratify this agreement. In May 1920, the Bolsheviks, victorious from Russia's civil war, sent their Caspian fleet to take the Persian cities of Enseli and Resht, to occupy most of the province of Gilan on the shore of the Caspian, and to set up there the short-lived Soviet republic of Gilan (1920–21). The Persian Cossack brigade under its anti-Bolshevik Russian officers fought them with some initial success but then was driven back in defeat. The British tried to reorganize it, but in 1921 British forces began to withdraw from Persia in response to British troubles elsewhere and a war-weary domestic attitude. Persia's chance for greater independence had come. One officer took it.

The Monarch as Dictator: The Pahlavi Rulers, 1925–79. Reza Khan, an officer in the Persian Cossack brigade, engineered the dismissal of the Russian officers, took up negotiations with the writer and reformer Zia ud-Din, and marched with three thousand Cossacks on Tehran for a coup d'état. On February 21, 1921, he set up a new government with Zia ud-Din as prime minister and himself as minister of war, commander-in-chief, and the real holder of power. The new government at once dropped the unratified treaty with Britain. Five days later, it concluded a treaty with the Soviet government. The latter, hoping to destroy the British ascendancy, agreed to evacuate the country; cancel all debts, concessions, and special privileges; and turn over all Russian property in Persia without compensation. In October, the Soviet republic of Gilan was ended and the province brought back under the authority of Tehran. A treaty of peace and friendship with Turkey linked Persia to the revolutionary nationalist regime of Mustafa Kemal in that country. Reza Khan's regime was on the way to consolidation.

Reza followed up on his first successes. From 1922 on, an American economic expert named Dr. Arthur C. Millspaugh, was given wide powers to reorganize Persia's finances. In 1923, Reza took over the premiership and the Ahmad Shah Qajar left for Europe, never to return. Agitation in the following year for a republic on the Turkish model was opposed by the Shi'ite leaders and Reza. Also in 1924, Reza's government subdued the Bakhtiar chiefs in southeastern Persia, not far from the oil fields that had made the chiefs almost independent with the aid of the Anglo-Persian Oil Company and the British government. Most of Persia was now under government control.

In 1925, Reza was voted dictatorial powers, and later in the year he had himself proclaimed shah. He took the pre-Islamic name Pahlavi from the Old Persian and ruled as Reza Shah Pahlavi until 1941. Under his rule, Iran went through a drastic face-lifting operation. Modernization was announced for many sectors of life, was promoted seriously in some, and succeeded in a few. Since the Shi'ite leaders opposed many reforms, the shah turned against them and gave his regime a secular cast. He promoted pre-Islamic memories and symbols as a base for a new nationalism and as a counterweight to Shi'ite influence. Women were encouraged to discard the veil and, among the small urban upper middle classes, many did so. The entire country was renamed Iran in 1935. A new judicial system was introduced in 1928, modeled on the French and greatly reducing the jurisdiction and the power of the *mujtahids'* religious courts.

There were also some material successes. A trans-Iranian railroad from the Caspian to the Persian gulf was begun in 1927 and completed in 1939. The lines of the Indo-European Telegraph Company within the country were taken over by the government. The oil concession to d'Arcy and his successor, the Anglo-Persian Oil Company, was canceled and replaced in 1933 by a new concession more favorable to Persia. And there were various plans for improvements in the countryside, in health and education, and in the lifestyle of a small elite.

For Iran as a whole, most of these reforms remained cosmetic. The life of the peasants, then still a majority of the people, changed hardly at all. The life of small artisans in the towns and cities and of the small merchants in the bazaars did not change much more. Neither did corruption, or the power of money and connections in administration, or the application of the law change. The industrial working class remained small, even including those working in the oil fields, who remained in poverty.

Foreign Occupation and a Precarious Constitutional Interlude. During World War II, Iran's independence once more was temporarily submerged. After Nazi Germany attacked the Soviet Union in June 1941, Iranian neutrality (on which Reza Shah insisted) would have blocked one of Russia's last supply lines from Britain and the United States. In August, British and Soviet forces entered Iran and established there a regime that would cooperate with them. Reza Shah abdicated and was replaced by his son, Mohammed Reza Pahlavi, who for a time governed under a constitution. Under the new shah, Iran declared war on Germany in 1943, but British troops continued to hold the south of the country, and Soviet troops the north, including Tehran. When the Allied leaders, Franklin D. Roosevelt, Winston Churchill, and Joseph Stalin, met at Tehran in 1943, Stalin was host.

In 1945, after the surrender of Germany, the government of Iran requested Britain, the United States, and the Soviet Union to withdraw their forces from the country. Withdrawal was promised by these powers for March 1946, but in November 1945 the Communist-led Tudeh ("masses") party organized an uprising in Azerbaijan and then set up a Soviet-type regime there. Armed government intervention was prevented by the continued presence of Soviet troops, but pressure from the United States, Britain, and the United Nations brought a change. Iran and Russia agreed on the withdrawal of all Russian troops (completed by May 1946) as well as on reforms in Azerbaijan and the setting up of a Soviet-Iranian oil company for northern Iran. In June, government troops reoccupied Azerbaijan without serious resistance.

As the image of preponderant American power emerged in the first postwar years, and as the United States replaced Britain as the leading Western power in the Near and Middle East, the shah moved to a pro-American orientation. An agreement with the United States provided for an American military mission and purchases of United States military equipment. The new *majlis,* elected with a progovernment majority, canceled the Soviet oil agreement. In 1949, the Tudeh party was banned; the constitution was revised to give the shah the power to dissolve parliament; a seven-year plan of economic development was announced, to be directed by American specialists; and a new agreement with the Anglo-Iranian Oil Company was drawn up, so as to give the government a somewhat larger share of the profits. A prosperous royal dictatorship seemed just ahead.

A Brief Swing to the Left: The Mossadegh Regime. The next political developments occurred in the opposite direction. From mid-1951 on, the United States was engaged in the Korean war. American attention and resources available for other parts of the world were likely to decline, and the demand for oil would rise. In April 1951, the *majlis* made the leader of the non-Communist leftist National Front, Mohammed Mossadegh, prime minister. His government promptly nationalized the oil industry. Britain and the British management of the Anglo-Iranian Oil Company resisted nationalization by all means short of war. They involved the International Court of Justice, withdrew all British technicians from the oil fields, and eventually organized a worldwide boycott of Iranian oil. Arab monarchies increased their oil output, partly replacing Iran's share. From the United States, President Truman in July 1951 sent a personal message to Iran to urge a compromise. In early 1952, United States military aid to Iran was suspended for almost four months. Mossadegh resigned in July. A pro-Western premier replaced him for five days but was overthrown in bloody rioting. Mossadegh returned to power, and parliament voted him dictatorial powers. In October, he broke diplomatic relations with Britain, but could not overcome the economic pressure of the international oil boycott.

In the spring of 1953, Western power rose. In Russia, Stalin died and his successors were busy with domestic politics. The Korean war was winding down. In the United States, President Eisenhower had come into office. Events moved quickly. On June 26, the Korean armistice was signed; on June 29, President Eisenhower informed Mossadegh that no further aid would be granted until the oil dispute with Britain was settled. On August 16, Mohammed Reza Shah tried to dismiss Mossadegh and then fled to Iraq, which then still had a pro-British government. Three days later, Mossadegh was overthrown by a coup backed by the Tehran police and some military, led by General Fazollah Zahedi, the shah's earlier choice for premier. Various employees of the U.S. Central Intelligence Agency (CIA) later claimed credit for having engineered the coup and its success.

After three more days, on August 22, the shah was back in Tehran. Two weeks later, the United States made a grant of $45 million to Iran. Mossadegh had been arrested, and later was tried and jailed. Soon diplomatic relations with Britain were restored, negotiations for a new oil agreement started, and parliament dissolved. In early 1954, police and troops suppressed antigovernment demonstrations, and the government announced a great electoral victory. A new oil agreement was concluded with a consortium of major American, British, and continental oil companies, with a substantial increase in Iran's share of the profits.

The Shah in Full Power. Mohammed Reza Shah was now firmly established. For the next quarter century, he controlled parliament and the entire state. Iran as a whole grew richer, and the shah and his family got richer even faster. Some wealth fostered new industries, some of them at first state-owned. If they were profitable, many were then sold to the private sector. Often they ended up as the personal property of the shah, his family, or his favorites. After 1973, Iran became a member of the Organization of Petroleum Exporting Countries (OPEC), and the price of oil on the world market rose to four and later five times what it had been. The country, and even more so the shah, grew richer still.

Some of the wealth was spent on extravagant display. An elegant city of tents was built for the 2,500-year anniversary of King Darius near the ruins of Persepolis, one of his capital cities. Thousands of members of the international elite were entertained there in elaborate festivities. Other wealth purchased the shah a 25-percent share in the West German steel firm of Friedrich Krupp and Company.

Another large part of the new wealth was spent on armed forces, armaments, and the police. Iran was to become a naval power in the Gulf of Persia. Destroyers and other war vessels were ordered from abroad. Claims were raised for various territories in the Persian gulf, such as the oil-rich Bahrein Islands and other small states. The shah and his government kept recalling the greatness of the empire of King Darius in 500 B.C. and its territorial extensiveness. Should it not be Iran's destiny to rise again to similar greatness? In any case, the army was well equipped with tanks and the strong air force with modern fighter planes.

The United States encouraged some of this spending on armaments. After the secession of Bangladesh in 1971, Pakistan had ceased to be a major military power in the Middle East. Shouldn't Iran take its place to restore pro-Western power in the region? And if Iran spent a part of its oil wealth on costly American weapons, wouldn't this help the U.S. balance of payments and the international value of the dollar? In the end, it was the shah who made the decisions, but his allies did little if anything to dissuade him.

Other expenditures went to the police. There was a local police, a national gendarmerie, and a dreaded secret political police, known as SAVAK. American advice on efficient technical police work was sought and sometimes accepted, but it was merged with long-standing oriental practices of cruelty and torture. The result was a long succession of atrocities and the popular hatreds they provoked.

The people remained poor. The shah's extravagant expenses and displays did nothing for them; even as spectacles they were alien to their tradition. What could the ancient pagan empire mean to the mass of devout Muslims? What good did the shah's purchase of stock in a German steel firm do for Iranian villages? In 1975, Iran's per capita income was more than six times as high as that of Egypt; but inequality in Iran was substantially higher, Iran's rates of literacy and higher education were lower, and her rate of infant mortality exceeded that of Egypt by more than one-third.

The shah's political system was destroying itself. The growing number of workers—larger in 1979 than they had been in the days of Mossadegh—were angered by the suppression of effective labor unions and labor parties, and by the inflationary rise in the cost of living. Peasants remained poor, but now could see what they were missing. Bazaar merchants and artisans felt harassed by government regulations and the often corrupt way in which these were administered. The professional and upper middle classes, too, had grown and felt frustrated by censorship, a police regime, and an inefficient authoritarian bureaucracy—and so did many of the clerks and bureaucrats themselves. Since the shah claimed the power to decide everything, he was blamed by everyone for all results.

In addition, the shah continued his father's course of head-on collision with religion. He opposed the Shi'ite community, whose priests had a long tradition of judging critically the legitimacy of a shah. Now many of them became his enemies. And among many of the newly mobilized ex-villagers, who in recent decades had moved into the poorer quarters of rapidly growing cities and oil fields, religion had retained its hold. Indeed, in the bewildering new environment in which they now found themselves, these ex-villagers thirsted for clear, simple, and undoubted authority. Many of them offered a potential following for a movement of religious fundamentalism. Such a movement did develop and it too turned against the shah.

While the storm gathered, the shah's public relations personnel denied it and he may have done so himself. Even foreign scholars and experts kept writing with admiration about the stability of his regime and the great progress occurring under it. Foreign powers joined in the chorus of admiration. Britain and the United States saw him as an ally and supported him accordingly. Continental European businesspeople saw him and his country as good credit risks and customers. The Soviet Union in the mid-1960s signed a trade agreement, bought Iranian natural gas, and undertook a steel mill near Isfahan. The shah was elaborately welcomed on visits to the Soviet Union and other Soviet bloc states and was given honorary degrees by some of their universities, just as he received similar honors from some major universities in the United States.

Of Mohammed Reza Shah's five predecessors since the beginning of revolutionary agitation in

1890, four had been overthrown, assassinated, or exiled. Yet in the 1970s, few observers took the trouble to remember history. Critics in Iran were silenced by SAVAK or, if lucky, driven into exile. Iranian students abroad were watched by police agents sent to keep them under control. The CIA had promised the shah in the 1960s not to have any contacts with the opposition, and it seems that they kept their word; the opposition may have seemed to them unimportant anyway. It all seemed safe—and then the roof fell in.

The Revolution of 1979. Some of the cracks in the structure had been growing for more than a decade. In the 1960s and 1970s, agitation against the shah had been growing among Iranian students abroad. Some religious leaders had been living in exile, such as the Ayatollah Ruhollah Khomeini in Paris. And a small but growing body of critical technical experts, including some economists and engineers, had found employment abroad or were living there on private incomes.

In 1978, opposition became visible in Iran, and it came from all sides. Agitation, strikes, riots all increased. Police arrests and cases of SAVAK torture multiplied; troops fired into crowds. It has been estimated that government repression in 1978 and 1979 killed several thousand people. Funerals of the victims sometimes turned into demonstrations. Popular antagonism was reaching a critical point. Suppressing it by the shah's forces became as difficult as rubbing ice cubes dry with a towel; the harder the rubbing, the more moisture produced.

In 1979, unrest reached its peak. Bazaar merchants and artisans shut their shops. Workers at the oil refinery at Abadan went on strike, and so did the employees at the Iranian central bank. Students walked out from their classes. Bankers, business managers, professional men, and their emancipated wives and daughters turned against the shah. So did the Communists from the Tudeh party, long outlawed but living underground, turn against him, even though the press and radio of the Soviet Union for a long time avoided any criticism of the monarch. *Mullahs* and *mujtahids* preached against the shah, and the words of the Ayatollah Khomeini from Paris, condemning the shah, were spread through the land.

Most of SAVAK stayed reliable. But the common soldiers were the sons, brothers, and cousins of the peasants, artisans, and laborers from whose families they had been recruited. They, too, were Shi'ites, and the voice of religious leaders, speaking from the sacred city of Qum, meant more to them than that of the shah journeying abroad or recalling the pagan glories of Persepolis. Even officers remembered their ties to the middle classes from among whom many had come. When air force officers still seemed likely to obey the shah's orders to act against the rebels, their mechanics immobilized their planes. Later on, many younger officers and cadets, like the mechanics, joined the revolution.

The shah first tried to order repression. When this failed, he went abroad but avoided formal abdication. Before he left, his orders had escalated the bloodshed and the consequent hatred. When President Carter permitted him to come to the United States for medical treatment, Iranian hatred became focussed also on the United States.

The new government demanded his extradition to put him on trial for what were now seen as his crimes. Some religious leaders pronounced that anyone who murdered the shah would act justly and please God—a sentiment in line with Iran's long history of pious assassinations. The Ayatollah Khomeini shared this view. When in late October 1979 it seemed that the shah might have cancer, the unforgiving old priest was reported as saying he hoped that was the case. In early November, students occupied the United States embassy in Tehran and held fifty of its personnel as hostages in defiance of diplomatic immunity for the professed purpose of forcing the United States to return the shah to Iran for trial and also to repatriate the wealth of the shah that in their view had been acquired illegally.

The Ayatollah Khomeini endorsed the action of the students and their refusal to negotiate until the shah was returned. President Carter, in turn, backed by united American public opinion, refused to negotiate about anything else until all the hostages were released. A unanimous vote by the United Nations Security Council confirmed the illegality of Iran's holding diplomats and embassy personnel as hostages and demanded their unconditional release, but the council further urged patience and caution on all parties so as to avoid war.

The Iranian revolution of 1979 throws doubt on the assumption that modern weapons make uprisings hopeless and governments irresistible. Weapons systems are also human systems. Tanks and airplanes need people to operate them and still more people to maintain them and to furnish them with fuel, spare parts, and other supplies. When enough people of different backgrounds all become hostile to government and are able to coordinate their efforts, the government will fall despite its arms. This is what happened to the shah's regime. It was the most heavily armed among the Muslim states, but inside its armor it was dying. The Pahlavi dictatorship fell because it had become incompatible with Iran's present social structure, religion, and past history. What will take its place?

The Current Political System. Most of what can be written in late October 1979 about Iran may no longer be true in the early 1980s. Revolutions bring rapid changes, and Iran's revolution is not finished. But real revolutions also cannot quite be reversed, and the Iranian revolution of 1979 seems genuine enough. Which of the changes it has brought so far are likely to endure?

The Higher Stakes of Politics. Between 1954 and 1978 few important things, if any, could be decided by politics outside the royal palace. Major matters seemed to be fixed: the power of the monarch; the powerlessness of religion and most interest groups; the obedience of the army and police; the subordination of peasants, workers, clerks, and intellectuals; the wealth of landowners and the few big business firms, many of them foreign.

Now almost everything is at stake. Banks and large industries have been nationalized; they may stay so or they may be returned to private ownership. Some peasants are holding their own land; others are tenants. One kind of land reform could make more peasants into competing property owners; another could push them into cooperatives or collectivization. The economy could be developed or left to stagnate, linked more closely to the world market or isolated from it. The country as a whole might move more toward a free market system or toward central planning. Politically, it might move toward combining dictatorship or democracy with either of these economic patterns. Or it might seek some combination of a few big industries, particularly oil and petrochemicals, with an economy of small peasants, artisans, and merchants.

Much of Iranian culture is at stake, too. Now that the religious leaders have much power, they must make decisions about economics, politics, the law, education, and daily life, and they will increasingly be seen as responsible for them. At the moment, one seventy-five-year-old leader, the Ayatollah Khomeini, has the chief voice, but different leaders will favor different policies in time.

Already the revolution has wiped out many of Reza Shah's legal reforms and returned a great deal of judicial power to the *mujtahids.* Which way will their decisions go, year after year? Once the Shi'ite community of priests has moved from the sidelines to the center of decision making—even if only for a time—that community of priests will never be the same again.

Also at stake are health, education, and the rights of women. Emancipated women are few. They supported the revolution, but now they may be forced back to the household and to wearing the veil in accordance with Muslim tradition. Already the segregation of the sexes has been imposed on all schools. Will education and health care be oriented toward science and modernity or toward tradition and religion? And will lay persons or priests run these activities?

In its foreign policy, will Iran move toward cooperation with the Soviet bloc, as Iraq has done, will it restore the weakened links with the West, or will it try for a more or less genuine nonalignment? What level of armaments will Iran choose, and where will they come from?

In politics, will the secular parties dwindle or will they survive and grow stronger? Which ones will gain—the liberal pro-Western groups, such as that of Prime Minister Bakhtiar who won office early in the revolution but then went into exile? Or the Communists of the Tudeh party, which has returned to a legal existence, no one knows for how long. Or will it be the partisans of the shah, secular in culture, technocrats in economics, conservatives in matters of politics and social services? Or will Iran become an ever-tightening religious dictatorship? Each of these outcomes still seems possible.

The Increase in Political Participation. Genuine revolutions bring new masses of people into political activity. Dispatches in 1979 spoke of demonstrations by hundreds of thousands of people, and of meetings by one million. Even if these reports were exaggerated, they show that participation has changed.

Most of this increased participation has occurred in the large cities, those with more than 100,000. These cities contained 47 percent in 1978 (43 percent in 1975) of the people of Iran. There, almost all strata seem to have become active participants—students, industrial workers, professional people, clerks, artisans, and bazaar merchants.

Little activity has been reported from the villages and the agricultural sector, which in 1978 employed 42 percent of the work force. This may have been due to a lack of reporting, or the peasants may have remained passive, or their stirrings may be yet to come.

The Threatened Arena of Politics. Throughout its history, Iran's borders have been fluid. In the revolution of 1979 and its consequences, they may become fluid again.

The Kurdish minority in western Iran is demanding autocracy; some of them are demanding secession from Iran and a sovereign Kurdish state. The Kurds are settled astride the mountainous borders between Iraq, Turkey, and Iran. Their nationalism has brought them into conflict with all three governments, though usually not at the same time. When Iran and pro-Soviet Iraq quarreled, the shah supported the Kurds against Iraq and so sometimes did the United States. Currently, the Kurds have risen in some cities against Ayatollah Khomeini's Islamic republic, perhaps with some covert aid from Iraq, or the West, or both, despite their differences.

The Iranian army, though weakened by the revolution, has occupied much of Iran's Kurdish districts. So have Khomeini's "revolutionary guards." Since most Kurds are Sunnis, Iran's Shi'ite-led revolution has little appeal to them and the conflict has become bitter. According to press reports, about six hundred persons in Iranian Kurdistan have been executed, mostly by the revolutionary guards, but nearly always by the order of special courts. Near the end of October 1979, however, the Ayatollah Khomeini ordered a halt to any further executions, and offered the Kurds limited autonomy. Whether Iran will keep its Kurdish regions or whether they will secede and establish a new state, only the future can show.

Another minority region is Khuzistan in southwest Iran. Its population is Arab speaking and in large part professes the Sunni faith. Khuzistan contains the main oil fields of Iran. Since the triumph of the revolution at Tehran, some pipelines and refineries have been sabotaged. The Tehran government blames these incidents on counterrevolutionaries and foreign agents, but some Western observers have been inclined to see in them signs of an awakening Arab nationalism there. If so, at least some nationalists probably would accept any foreign aid they could get for their struggle. It would be a bitter one, since any Iranian government would fight hard to keep the oil fields and with them the current mainstay of the nation's wealth. The Western powers would hardly welcome a prolonged civil war in Khuzistan; it would reduce the flow of Iranian oil to the world market and further drive up the price of oil. The fate of this part of Iran's political arena, too, lies hidden in the future.

A third minority area, in the long run perhaps the most important, is that inhabited by the 5 million *Azerbaijanis* who speak a Turkic language. They live in the north around the city of Tabriz and extending up to the border of the Soviet Union's Republic of Azerbaijan. Smaller groups of them, often economically prosperous, live in many major cities of Iran. They are Shi'ite by religion but have been jealous of their distinctiveness and desirous of autonomy. Their religious leader, Ayatollah Shariat Madari, has been the only top-ranking cleric to challenge Ayatollah Khomeini's authority. In December 1979 aroused adherents of Madari and the secular *Khalg* party occupied the Tabui broadcasting station and held it for bargaining during negotiations with the central government.

As for the shah's hopes for Iranian expansion to include Bahrein and perhaps Kuwait and some other territories on the Gulf of Persia, they are currently dead. A counterrevolutionary nationalist regime, however, if one should come to power in Iran at some later time, might revive these ambitions once again. Or the current regime might at some future time decide to do so.

Which Revolutionary Image for Iran? The Pahlavi shahs and their followers tried to establish an image of a powerful modern Iran, rich, well armed, and continuing the heritage of the pre-Islamic empire of the ancient Persian kings. The small Westernized elite wanted their country to develop toward a modern Western-style constitutional regime, open to moderate foreign investment favoring domestic private enterprise. The Communists presumably wanted to make Iran a Soviet-style "people's republic."

By early November 1979, a different image emerged. Iran was declared an Islamic republic, based on the authority of the Koran. This name echoes the title of Pakistan as an Islamic state. But whereas Pakistan has been ruled mostly by its military dictators, Iran's republic is currently ruled by its Shi'ite clergy. In such a state, according to Shi'ite tradition, it should be the religious leaders who set the goals and limits for the policies, watch over their execution, and correct any deviation from the course that the clergy has been setting. On this issue, many ayatollahs are agreed. They supported the revolution and, in December 1979, they supported Khomeini's leadership.

But momentum carried events further. Most people find it easier to look to a person as a leader, and partly as a model for imitation, than to interpret and follow any more abstract political program or theological doctrine. In times of great change, when people find that many of their old habits no longer apply and that they must find and learn new ones, they look for a personal leader rather than for a party platform or a book. In such situations, they seek a leader with *charisma*—a personal grace that makes someone seem naturally prominent and admirable in the follower's eyes. For them, wherever that person sits is the head of the table.

In the summer and fall of 1979, Khomeini became such a charismatic leader. His ascendancy over the people is without parallel in the last seventy years of Persian history. Mehdi Bazargan, the prime minister appointed by Khomeini, said in an interview in Tehran ". . . his relationship with the masses is in fact very special in that he and they think in the same way and speak the same language—a nod and they understand each other."[4]

This image of the charismatic leader can be found in the transition phases of many revolutions in other times and countries. In Iran, however, a special element has become linked to it, no one knows for how long, but with great potential power while it lasts. This is the Shi'ite doctrine of the *imām*.

On October 26, 1979, it was reported from

[4]"Bazargan Calls Khomeini Primitive—But a Genius," *International Herald Tribune* (October 31, 1979), p. 1, cols. 2–7. The interview was described as "recent."

Tehran that, according to the state radio, millions took part in a "march of solidarity with *Imām* Khomeini." The mass rallies had been called by the clergy to denounce the government of Premier Bazargan and to call for a far-reaching purge. According to the press report, the crowd at Tehran shouted "Khomeini the idol smasher is the Imām of our people."[5]

This is the most exalted role available in all Iranian history and culture. Can Khomeini take it seriously? The hidden *imām* was believed to be so pure that his body cast no shadow, but Khomeini's body does. The hidden *imām* is to come back as a savior; calling Khomeini the *imām* implies vast expectations. While Khomeini himself has not made any explicit claim to this most exalted role, he has not objected to Iranian radio and television frequently using the title *imām* for him in such a way as to imply and hint at just such mounting expectations. Can he live up to these expectations or must he sooner or later disappoint his followers? Is this vast overstatement of the capacities of an individual—any individual—a prelude to his fall?

In December 1979 a new constitution for Iran was voted in by plebiscite, after the holiest week of the Shi'ite year, devoted to the passionate remembrance of the martyrs Ali and Glusayn, and following the stirring up of further passions by the occupation of the American Embassy, the mass demonstrations of support in Tehran and other cities, and the tense confrontation with the United States—and after all these events had been duly amplified by Iranian and foreign radio and television (including prime-time telecasts in the United States). Never before had Iran received so much attention in the world.

The constitution seems to have passed overwhelmingly in Tehran and central Iran. In Azerbaijan 80 percent of the voters seem to have boycotted the plebiscite, data from other minority areas were not yet available. The constitution made Khomeini the *faghi*—the supreme religious leader, with power to depose the prime minister and the cabinet, and to decide about war and peace. In effect, it made him dictator.

Perhaps there may be no turning back for Khomeini and for some of the clergy who pushed his image to such extremes. But revolutions have a way of continuing beyond their charismatic stage. If they are not crushed, some of the great changes that they brought will remain, and people will turn to the less dramatic but not less important task of making them work in day-to-day practice.

So far, the Iranian revolution has produced two channels of political communication and power, each backed by different social groups and interests. Much will depend on which of these two sets prevails.

Two Competing Systems of Political Communication and Power. The Iranian revolution gave rise to an alternative network of communication and decision making that competed with the official bureaucracy of the state that had developed under the shah. Its basis was the old network of mosques and *mullahs,* of preaching and pilgrimages. But in the 1970s, this old network carried new political messages. They carried complaints from the mass of people to the *mullahs* and *ayatollahs,* and they carried their appeal and instructions to the masses. Through this feedback process, clergy and people learned to respond to each other on matters of burning interest to both of them: the oppressive regime of the shah and what to do about it.

Then came groups of lay people forming an association with the mosques and the clergy. They passed on the messages of the Ayatollah Khomeini from his Paris exile to the Iranian people. Here were then recruited some of the people who later staffed the revolutionary committees, the revolutionaries that were to parallel the old authorities at the local district and provincial level, and the revolutionary militia that would eventually parallel and replace much of the shah's police and regular army.

Other elements, too, in time joined these parallel structures. Leftist groups, some trade unionists,

[5]"Islamic Clergy Denounces Premier, Calls for Purge," United Press International in *International Herald Tribune* (October 27–28, 1979), p. 1, cols. 3–4.

and others did so, but the preponderant influence and power has remained with the religious and populist elements that accept Khomeini's leadership. By early November 1979, Khomeini seemed well established as the *de facto* head of the state, and he proclaimed himself commander-in-chief of the armed forces.

Compared to these new channels and structures (Khomeini and the clergy, the revolutionary councils and committees, and the revolutionary courts), the older authorities (the secular government, the professional military officers, and the regular courts of justice) retained only a shadow of their former power. Without Khomeini's backing, they could not count on the obedience of the civilians and soliders. The prime minister, Mehdi Bazargan, complained about this situation, and about "the deplorable state in which the army, police and security forces find themselves, all of them indispensable bodies for establishing law and order. Since the people consider them a . . . threat left over from the imperial regime, we have not succeeded in putting them in shape."[6]

The dual structure of power and political communication in Iran is not likely to last. The clergy and the revolutionary authorities either will permeate and take over the government and army, or else they will be replaced by them. And there are attacks by outright counterrevolutionaries, as well as by extremists of the left. Thus far, six close associates of Khomeini have been assassinated, and more may follow. The future character of Iranian politics is yet to be decided.

The Performance of Iran. Iran is one country but it has had two radically different political regimes, that of the shah and that of the revolution. Together, their performances are the performances of the country.

The "white revolution" of the Pahlavi shahs since 1924 brought the country some modernity, mainly in the oil industry, some other industrial sectors, and some big cities. It made Iran one of the richest of the developing countries, with a per capita income of $1660 in 1975 and $2180 in 1977. It awed its smaller neighbors by large armaments and dazzled the world by lavish displays and well-financed public relations. It built some highways and railroads, and it encouraged the growth of a small industrial working class. A Westernized section of the professional, upper, and middle classes sent their sons abroad to study at Western universities. Their wives and daughters began to demand new rights for women that went beyond the narrow limits granted them by Muslim tradition.

But the shahs who reformed Iran's technology did not reform its society in any depth. Iran's Gini index of inequality remained at 50 percent in 1975, among the highest of the countries for which we have such data. Even with its oil wealth, Iran's per capita income was still so low that this inequality was bringing real suffering to those many at the short end of it. The infant death rate in the first year after birth in 1975 was 139 per thousand, substantially worse than the rates for Pakistan, India, Egypt, and Ethiopia. Life expectancy in Iran averaged fifty years, no better than that for India, a vastly poorer country. Of its adults in 1970, 63 percent were illiterate. No other large- or middle-sized country shows such contrasts between wealth and backwardness.

To preserve these contrasts, repression was needed. Since the start of the unrest in 1978 alone, the shah's troops, police, and political police (SAVAK) killed and tortured thousands. Since his fall, revolutionary tribunals have executed over six hundred. The legacy of the royal dictatorship has turned into a legacy of bloodshed.

Positive results of the revolution have been slow in coming. Iran is now less dependent on any foreign country, more fully in possession of its industries, utilities, and mineral resources. But in late 1979, the output of all these was much lower than it had been under the shah. Machinery is in danger of going unrepaired; security in streets and homes is less; some revolutionary tribunals are no less arbitrary and unpredictable than SAVAK

[6]Interview, *International Herald Tribune* (October 31, 1979), p. 5, cols. 1–4.

used to be. A new Islamic view of what may be printed has led to a censorship in some ways as narrow-minded as the one that existed under the shah. The women in many places have to struggle against being pushed back into seclusion and having to wear the veil. The costs of the revolution are here for all to see, but so far not many achievements promised by the revolution have taken shape. The coming years may yet bring some of the achievements hoped for, or they may bring bloodier conflicts and catastrophies either within Iran or through conflict with other countries. For good or ill, the country's future is open and hopeful but at the same time full of risk and danger for itself and the peace of the world.

KEY TERMS AND CONCEPTS

India:
Punjab
Aryans
Sanskrit
Hindi
Dravidian languages
Vedas
caste *(varna)*
brahmans
kshatriyas
banyas
sudras
untouchables *(pariahs, harijan)*
Sikhs
East India Company
"The Great Mutiny" of 1857
National Congress
Mohandas K. Gandhi (Mahatma Gandhi)
All-India Muslim League
Mohammed Ali Jinnah
Pakistan
Bangladesh
communalism
depressed classes
Jawaharlal Nehru
Indira Gandhi
Janata party
Morarji Desai
Jan Sangh party
Indian National Congress
Mahatma
nonviolence
"truth force"
"vernacular" vs. "regional language"
"soft states"
civil service
state of emergency

Nigeria:
Yoruba
Ibo
Hausa
Fulani
Nnamdi Azikwe
Abuaker Talewa
Yakubu Gowon
Biafra
Odumegwu Ojukwu
Obafemi Awolowo
Shehu Shagari

Egypt:
fellaheen
Ottoman Empire
Mehemet Ali
khedive
Suez Canal
Arabi Pasha
Jamal-ud-Din el-Afghani
protectorate
indirect rule
Wafd
King Fuad
King Farouk
Mohammed Naguib
Liberation Rally
Gamal Abdel-Nasser
Nasserism
Suez War, 1956

Arab socialism
Pan-Arabism
United Arab Republic (UAR)
Six Days' War, 1967
Anwar el Sadat
October War, 1973
Camp David agreements, 1978
Arab League
Muslim brotherhood *(Sanusi)*
the Sudan
Sunni
pasha
bey
effendi
baksheesh

Iran:
Achamenian dynasty, 550–331 B.C.
satrap
Zoroastrian religion
Sassanian dynasty
Magi
Caliphs
Assassins *(hash-shāhshīn)*
Il-Khans
Timur
Shi'ism
Islam
Koran *(Q'uran)*
caliph
Ali
Omayyad dynasty
Husayn
sunna
Sunnites, Sunnis
imām
Mahdi
doctrine of dissimulation
tallebe
mullah
mujtahid
ayatollah
ayatollah uzma
Ayatollah Ruhollah Khomeini
Ayatollah Shariat Madari
Qajarite dynasty, 1794–1925
Persian Cossack brigade, 1878
Anglo-Persian Oil Company
Persian revolution, 1905
Bakhtiar tribe
British-Russian agreement, 1907
South Persia Rifles, 1916
Anglo-Persian agreement, 1919
Soviet Republic of Gilan, 1921
Reza Khan
Reza Shah Pahlavi
Pahlavi dynasty, 1925–79
Trans-Iranian railroad, 1927–39
British-Soviet occupation, 1941
Mohammed Reza Shah Pahlavi, 1943–79
Tudeh party
Azerbaijan People's Republic, 1945–46
National Front
Mohammed Mossadegh
International oil boycott, 1952–53
CIA-assisted coup, 1953
Organization of Petroleum-Exporting Countries (OPEC), 1973
SAVAK
Kurds
Khuzistan
Iranian Revolution, 1979
Revolutionary Guards
Azerbaijan, Azerbaijanis (in Iran)
Azerbaijan, Republic of, in Soviet Union
Khalg party
Constitution of 1979
faghi
Qum, holy city of
Shah Abbas the Great, 1587–1629
Nadir Shali, 1736–47

ADDITIONAL READINGS

India:

Appadorai, A., ed. *Documents on Political Thought in Modern India.* Vol. 1. New York: Oxford University Press, 1974.

Bhagwati, J. and T. N. Srinivasan. *Foreign Trade Regimes and Economic Development: India.* New York: Columbia University Press, 1976.

Bose, N. *The Structure of Hindu Society.* Columbia, Mo.: South Asia Books, 1976.

Brecher, M. *Succession in India: A Study in Decision-Making.* London: Oxford University Press, 1966.

Bueno de Mesquita, B. *Strategy, Risk and Personality in Coalition Politics: The Case of India.* Cambridge: Cambridge University Press, 1975.

Chatterji, S. K. *Indo-Aryan & Hindi.* Rev. and enl. 2d ed. Calcutta: Firma K. L. Mukhopadhyay, 1960.

———. *Languages and Literatures of Modern India.* Calcutta: Bengal Publishers, 1963.

Cohen, S. P. and R. L. Park. *India: Emergent Power?* New York: Crane-Russak, 1978. PB

Desai, A. R. *Recent Trends in Indian Nationalism,* 2d ed. New York: International Publications Service, 1974.

Eldersveld, S. and A. Bashiruddin. *Citizens and Politics: Mass Political Behavior in India.* Chicago: University of Chicago Press, 1978.

Erickson, E. H. *Gandhi's Truth: On the Origins of Militant Non-Violence.* New York: Norton, 1970. PB

Frankel, F. R. *India's Green Revolution: Political Costs of Economic Growth.* Princeton, N.J.: Princeton University Press, 1971.

Gandhi, M. K. *An Autobiography: The Story of My Experiments with Truth.* Boston: Beacon Press, 1957.

———. *Collected Works.* 70 vols. Delhi: Ministry of Information and Broadcasting, 1958.

———. *The Essential Gandhi: An Anthology Edited by Louis Fischer.* New York: Random House, 1962.

———. *The Gandhi Reader.* Edited by Homer Jack. Bloomington: Indiana University Press, 1956.

———. *Thoughts on National Language.* Ahmedabad: Navajivan Publishing House, 1956.

Harrison, S. *India: The Most Dangerous Decades.* Princeton, N.J.: Princeton University Press, 1960.

Karve, I. *Kinship Organization in India.* 3d ed. New York: Asia Publishing House, 1965.

Kothari, R. *State and Nation Building: A Third World Perspective.* Columbia, Mo.: South Asia Books, 1976.

———, ed. *Caste in Indian Politics.* Atlantic Highlands, N.J.: Humanities Press, 1970.

Lamb, B. *India: A World in Transition.* New York: Praeger, 1975. PB

Maddison, A. *Class Structure and Economic Growth: India and Pakistan Since the Moghuls.* New York: Norton, 1972.

Mehta, V. *The New India.* New York: Penguin, 1978. PB

Mukherjee, R. K. *Social Indicators.* Columbia, Mo.: South Asia Books, 1975.

Narain, I. *Election Studies in India.* Columbia, Mo.: South Asia Books, 1978.

Nayar, B. *Minority Politics in the Punjab.* Princeton, N.J.: Princeton University Press, 1966.

———. *National Communication and Language Policy in India.* New York: Praeger, 1969.

Nehru, J. *Selected Works.* 11 vols. Columbia, Mo.: South Asia Books, 1972–78.

———. *The Unity of India.* London: Drummond, 1941.

———. *An Autobiography.* London: Bodley Head, 1953.

———. *Glimpses of World History.* New York: John Day, 1942.

———. *The First Sixty Years.* Condensed ed. 2 vols. Edited by D. Norman. London: Bodley Head, 1965.

Singh, T. *Poverty and Social Change: With a Reappraisal.* 2d ed. Westport, Ct.: Greenwood Press, 1975.

Singh, Y. *Social Stratification and Change in India.* Columbia, Mo.: South Asia Books, 1978.

Srinivas, M. N. et al. *Dimensions of Social Change in India.* Columbia, Mo.: South Asia Books, 1978.

Subrahamanayam, K. *Self-Reliance and National Resilience.* Columbia, Mo.: South Asia Books, 1975.

Veit, L. A. *India's Second Revolution: The Dimension of Development.* New York: McGraw, 1976.

Weiner, M. *Politics of Scarcity: Public Pressure and*

Political Response in India. Chicago: University of Chicago Press, 1962.

——— ed. *Electoral Politics in the Indian States: Party Systems and Cleavages.* Vol. 4. Columbia, Mo.: South Asia Books, 1976.

Nigeria:

Coleman, J. S. *Nigeria: Background to Nationalism.* Berkeley: University of California Press, 1971.

Luckhman, R. *Nigerian Military: A Sociological Analysis of Authority and Revolt, 1960–67.* New York: Cambridge University Press, 1971. PB

Melson, R. and H. Wolfe, eds. *Nigeria: Modernization and the Problems of Communalism.* Lansing: Michigan State University Press, 1971.

Ostheimer, J. M. *Nigerian Politics.* New York: Harper & Row, 1973. PB

Peace, A. J. *Choice, Class and Conflict: A Study of Southern Nigerian Factory Workers.* Atlantic Highlands, N.J.: Humanities Press, 1979. PB

Shatz, S. P. *Nigerian Capitalism.* Berkeley: University of California Press, 1978.

Sklar, R. *Nigerian Political Parties: A Study of the Political Parties of the First Republic.* New York: NOK Publishers, 1980. PB

Wayas, J. *Nigeria's Leadership Role in Africa.* Atlantic Highlands, N.J.: Humanities Press, 1979.

Egypt:

Baker, R. W. *Egypt's Uncertain Revolution under Nasser and Sadat:* Cambridge: Harvard University Press, 1978.

Berger, M. *Bureaucracy and Society in Modern Egypt.* Princeton, N.J.: Princeton University Press, 1957.

Binder, L. *In a Moment of Enthusiasm: Political Power and the Second Stratum in Egypt.* Chicago: University of Chicago Press, 1978.

Bowie, R. *Suez 1956.* New York: Oxford University Press, 1974. PB

Hussein, M. *Class Conflict in Egypt, 1945–1970.* New York: Monthly Review Press, 1973.

Mabro, R. *The Egyptian Economy, 1952–1972.* New York: Oxford University Press, 1974.

———. *The Industrialization of Egypt, 1939–73,* New York: Oxford University Press, 1976.

O'Brien, P. *Revolution in Egypt's Economic System: From Private Enterprise to Socialism, 1952–65.* New York: Oxford University Press, 1966.

Richmond, J. *Egypt in Modern Times.* New York: Columbia University Press, 1969, 1977.

Safran, N. *Egypt in Search of Political Community: An Analysis of the Intellectual and Political Evolution of Egypt, 1804–1952.* Cambridge: Harvard University Press, 1961.

Vatikiotis, P. J. *Nasser and His Generation.* New York: St. Martin, 1978.

Waterbury, J. *Egypt: Burdens of the Past, Options for the Future.* Bloomington: Indiana University Press, 1978.

Iran:

Ahmad, Eqbal et al. "The Explosion in the Moslem World: A Round Table on Islam." In *The New York Times* (December 11, 1979), A16–17.

Amuzegar, J. *Iran: An Economic Profile.* Washington, D.C.: Middle East Institute, 1977.

Brockelmann, C. *History of the Islamic Peoples.* New York: Putnam, 1960. PB

Frye, R. N. *Persia.* Rev. ed. London: Allen and Unwin, 1968.

Ghirshman, R. *Iran.* New York: Penguin, 1978. PB

Graham, R. *Iran.* New York: St. Martin's Press, 1979. PB

Halliday, F. *Iran: Dictatorship and Development.* New York: Penguin, 1979. PB

Sykes, P. M. *A History of Persia,* 2 vols. London: Macmillan, 1915, and in Iran/Persia series, New York: Gordon Press, 1976.

Wilber, D. *Iran: Past and Present,* 8th ed. Princeton: N.J.: Princeton University Press, 1976. PB

PB = *available in paperback*

XIX

The Political Development of Cuba, Mexico, and Brazil: Three Latin American Cases

VAN R. WHITING, JR.

Among the world's developing countries, those of Latin America occupy a special position. In some of them, the rich live in luxury while the poor live at near-starvation levels of poverty; in all, poverty and underdevelopment distinguish them in absolute wealth, in human welfare, and in standards of constitutional freedom from the industrial countries of Europe and North America. Foreign powers have heavily influenced their history, boundaries, traditions, and economies. The predominant languages and cultures of these countries are Western, derived from Spain and Portugal; the pre-existing Indian civilizations were largely absorbed or wiped out.

The Latin American nations won their independence in the nineteenth century, most often by successful revolutions, long before many Asian and African nations became independent (see maps on pp. 113–16). Since independence, their elites and their economies have been more thoroughly influenced by Britain, France, and the United States. Western science, technology, and literature as well as mass immigration have been available to them, although these resources have not by themselves produced development. In short, the countries of Latin America represent a combination of developed and "Third World" conditions and traditions, with Indian, Latin-Iberian, Northern European, American, and in some cases African, elements intermingling and combining into new patterns. The political development of the countries of the region reflects this diversity and uniqueness.

The three countries chosen for this chapter—Cuba, Mexico, and Brazil—are richer than most other countries in Asia, Africa, and Latin America, and their politics have been more stable for the last fifteen years or more. They are countries of different sizes and traditions. One country (Mexico) has a strong Indian heritage and the two others have African traditions. Cuba largely depends on a one-crop economy based on sugar, Brazil on a broadly diversified economy, and Mexico on its considerable natural riches, including oil. All are closely tied to the United States by geography, strategy, and past or present economic links. They include one egalitarian, Communist-ruled dictatorship, one growth-oriented, anticommunist military regime, and one nationalist democratic regime dominated by a single party. All three countries now are striving for economic development and real national independence; between them, they exemplify most of the political patterns found in Latin America.

CUBA: THE SOCIALIST "PEARL OF THE ANTILLES"

The republic of Cuba is a nation of islands. As the largest of the Greater Antilles chain, the "pearl of the Antilles" is located in the Caribbean just south of Florida. The rich soil and warm climate have long been conducive to growing tobacco and sugar cane, thus providing a base for the Cuban economy and a dependence on foreign markets that even socialism has not been able to escape. Agricultural monoculture (dependence on one crop) is only the most constant aspect of Cuba's dependence, leading to another: the dependence on foreign powers. Despite a strong tradition of national pride, Cuba was subject to the Spanish Crown until the uprising of 1895 and the Spanish-Cuban-American War of 1898. After Cuba's formal independence, the United States first ruled then indirectly dominated the island. Since the revolution of 1959, Cuba has been beholden to the Soviet Union. The first socialist nation in the Western hemisphere, Cuba has since 1975 assumed a more active role in the world—especially by sending troops to Africa. The small nation has captured the attention of the world more than once in recent years.

History Prior to the Revolution. Cuba was discovered by Christopher Columbus on his maiden voyage in 1492. The Spanish quickly vanquished the few primitive Indians native to the island, and by 1539 established Cuba as a minor colony of Spain. The Spanish *conquistadores* (conquerors) put most of their energies into searching for gold in the richer Indian empires in Mexico and Peru; for a time Cuba was neglected. For most of the sixteenth and seventeenth centuries and into the eighteenth, Cuba was an underpopulated and relatively unimportant Spanish colony, devoted to tobacco farming and cattle raising. Havana was a meeting place for ships and sailors. But in the middle of the eighteenth century, plantation agriculture, sugar production, and the importation of African slaves all began to expand. In the seventy-six years that followed the brief British occupation of Havana in 1763, more than six times as many slaves (some five thousand per year) were imported to Cuba than in the preceding 250 years. In that time, whites relatively declined from a majority to a minority of the island population.[1] The independence of most of Spanish America in the early 1800s left Cuba, with its new importance as a major sugar producer, as Spain's richest colony. Finding outlets for growing trade with the United States, the planter elite, observing slave revolts in nearby Haiti, remained politically loyal to Spain. Their loyalty earned Cuba the sobriquet *"la isla siempre fiel"*—the ever-faithful isle.

Though the British had ended their slave trade in 1807, the existence of slavery elsewhere (especially in the United States) meant that the Cubans could get slaves without trouble. By about 1840, nearly 80 percent of the Cuban labor force was slave labor. Forty years later, by 1880, slavery was in decline. Changes in the technology of the sugar industry, the end of slavery elsewhere, and the immigration of whites, Chinese, and Indians from Mexico's Yucatán peninsula had reduced the

[1]Franklin W. Knight, *Slave Society in Cuba During the Nineteenth Century* (Madison: University of Wisconsin Press, 1970), pp. 10, 22.

number of slaves to less than one-quarter of Cuba's total work force.

Even in the ever-faithful isle there were those who sought independence from Spain. Bloody though unsuccessful struggles for independence were fought in the Ten Years' War from 1868 to 1878 and in the "little war" of 1880; together they took over 200,000 lives. Trade between Cuba and the United States nevertheless increased. Cubans resented the mother country's control more and more, and in 1895 the independence struggle broke out again. With the intellectual inspiration of the patriot José Martí and the fighting skill of soldiers such as Máximo Gómez, Calixto García, and Antonio Maceo (all experienced in the Ten Years' War), three more years of war ensued. Martí himself was killed in the first weeks of fighting.

The United States, which before the American Civil War had tried to purchase Cuba from Spain, intervened in 1898 when the U.S.S. *Maine* was sunk in Havana harbor. The result was the misnamed "Spanish-American War."[2] In a quick victory over Spain, the United States acquired Puerto Rico and the Philippines and dominated Cuba. From 1898 to 1902, the United States ruled Cuba with military governors. To the constitution of 1901 was added an amendment by Senator O. H. Platt of Connecticut (the Platt Amendment) by which Cuba limited its ability to make foreign treaties or to contract foreign loans; the United States was granted a naval station (still existing at Guantánamo) and the right to intervene to protect "life, property, and individual liberty." In effect, Cuba was a U.S. protectorate.

When in 1906 the first president of Cuba, Tomas Estrada Palma, called on the United States to protect his re-elected government from rebel opposition, President Theodore Roosevelt agreed to send troops to govern Cuba. He then appointed Charles Magoon governor of Cuba for three years. U.S. troops were in Cuba again in 1917 to prop up President Mario García Menocal at the time of the United States' entry into the First World War; this time they stayed five years. The fifth Cuban president after independence, Gerardo Machado (ruling from 1925 to 1933), used dictatorship and repression to counter unrest caused by the fall of sugar prices and to enrich himself and his family. His firing on students triggered a broadly-based revolt which forced him to resign in 1933. After Sumner Welles, U.S. ambassador to Cuba, failed to install a new president there, the United States pulled back from its imperial policy, abrogating the Platt Amendment in 1934. Notably, there was a surplus of sugar in the U.S. market that year. The United States would no longer try to dictate who should rule Cuba—or so they said.

Sergeant Fulgencio Batista took advantage of the 1933 revolt against Machado and dominated politics in Cuba for the next eleven years. With the backing of the army, Batista was the power behind the president until 1940, and himself president from 1940 to 1944. During his presidency, he supervised the modernization of much of the country's roads and public works. But after two terms out of office (during the moderate but corrupt administrations of Ramón Grau San Martín, 1944–1948, and Carlos Prío Socarras, 1948–1952), Batista came back to power through a coup, this time as a dictator. As such, he ruled for another six and a half years, directly or through a shadow president.

The United States, no longer imposing direct rule on Cuba, lobbied there for its business interests and generally supported a strong central government.[3] U.S. foreign direct investment grew in importance in mining and manufacturing, in railroads and tourism. The economies of Cuba and the United States were tied closely together.

The most recent period in Cuba's history is

[2]The war is properly named the Spanish-Cuban-American War, since Spain and Cuba had already been at war for three years before the United States got involved. See Philip S. Foner, *The Spanish-Cuban-American War and the Birth of American Imperialism.* (New York: Monthly Review Press, 1972).

[3]For a comparison of U.S. imperialism to 1933 and "hegemony" from 1933 to 1958, see Jorge I. Domínguez, *Cuba: Order and Revolution* (Cambridge: Harvard University Press, 1978), chaps. 2 and 3.

overshadowed by Fidel Castro. Even during his days as a law student, Castro was active in student and party politics. After the coup of March 1952, which returned Batista to power, a band of about 170 young rebels, convinced that only insurrection would throw off Batista's oppressive rule, attacked the army barracks at Moncada on July 26, 1953. (This attack later provided the name for the revolutionary "26th of July movement.") Many of the rebels were killed; Castro was captured and put on trial. His defense speech at the closed trial has become famous under the title, "History will absolve me!"

Released from jail in a general amnesty in 1955, Castro went to Mexico to organize and train for armed resistance. Returning to Cuba on the yacht *Granma,* arriving on December 2, 1956, the small band led by Fidel Castro (and including the Argentinian Ernesto "Ché" Guevara) began a guerrilla war in the Sierra Maestra mountains with the quiet support of the peasantry. The general disillusionment with Batista among the middle class and the army, as well as among peasants, students, and workers helped speed the success of the movement. Within two years and one month, the movement triumphed and Batista fled. Castro took power on January 1, 1959.

Fidel Castro was probably not a Communist or a Socialist when he came to power. However, he had a radical vision of land reform and the restructuring of society, and soon his policies brought him into conflict with the United States. Besides proceeding with an extensive land reform that hurt large American landowners, Cuba expropriated numerous North American industrial enterprises, mining firms, oil companies, hotels, and utilities. Matters moved toward a collision. Possible compensation agreements worked out by the U.S. Ambassador Phillip W. Bonsal were turned down by Washington. Cuba continued to attack the United States verbally, most noticeably in Fidel's speech before the United Nations in September 1960. In the United States, Castro was attacked as a Communist and his government opposed long before he declared, "I am a Marxist-Leninist." During their last year in office, President Dwight Eisenhower and Vice President Richard Nixon considered various plans of action against Cuba, including the one that was later followed. Less than four months after John F. Kennedy took office, in April 1961, the Central Intelligence Agency (CIA) sponsored an abortive invasion by about 1200 Cuban exiles at the "Bay of Pigs." The invaders were killed or captured; 2,500 CIA agents within Cuba as well as tens of thousands of other opponents of the regime were imprisoned, although many were held only briefly.[4] This victory helped Castro consolidate his position.

On December 2, 1961 (the anniversary of the landing of the *Granma*), Castro announced his commitment to Marxism-Leninism. In January 1962, Cuba was expelled from the Organization of American States (OAS). Then, in October of that year, U.S. intelligence detected the construction of nuclear missile sites in Cuba and the presence of Soviet-built nuclear missiles. The Cuban Missile Crisis involved a face-off between the United States and the Soviet Union over Cuba. By firm but careful diplomacy and the imposition of a naval blockade of the island, the United States succeeded in getting the Soviet Union to remove the missiles and to agree not to place offensive weapons in Cuba in the future. (This brief *blockade*, which physically impeded entrance or exit from Cuba, should be distinguished from the long-lasting trade *embargo*, which forbids the direct sale of goods to Cuba by U.S. firms.) As its part of the agreement, the United States undertook not to support any further invasions of Cuba. So far, both the United States and the Soviet Union have kept their word. If there had been any doubt before, it was clear after the Bay of Pigs and the Cuban Missile Crisis that Cuba was a revolutionary socialist country and that the island enjoyed the economic and military support of the Soviet Union.

[4]Hugh Thomas, *The Cuban Revolution* (New York: Harper & Row, 1977), pp. 581, 587.

The Stakes of Politics in Cuba. The revolution has changed the stakes of politics in Cuba. Politics still affects in important ways the welfare of the Cuban people, their participation in government, and the position of Cuba in the international sphere. Under a socialist dictatorship, these factors have taken on new meanings.

The revolutionary regime has brought changes in the ownership of land and other productive facilities, and in the distribution of wealth and property. These changes mean that most Cubans are assured basic standards of food, shelter, clothing, health, and education. Above basic welfare, however, difficulties begin. Two questions significantly affect the welfare of most individuals: economic growth (or lack of growth) and the allocation of material goods and services. As long as the economy does not grow, there is little chance for improving the material well-being of the people. Though Cuban workers may have enough food and may have roughly the same living space, or access to recreation facilities, or pairs of shoes as a writer or school teacher or government official, the limited overall growth of the economy restricts variety in their material possessions and improvement in their standard of living. Many people have only one pair of shoes; for many years the houses of Havana went unpainted. Scarce resources were used elsewhere in the economy.

Recent state policies may make more goods available to some and not to others. Since about 1970, material incentives have rewarded those who work more or more productively, according to the socialist principle, "From each according to his abilities, to each according to his work." Not by a long shot has Cuba arrived at communism, that is, an economy of abundance in which all would receive according to need. As long as Cuba is a society of scarcity, the tension between incentives for growth and distribution for equity will not easily be resolved.

Other policies may also affect the distribution of goods in the society. Cubans living in the United States may bring gifts to their relatives in Cuba, or buy gifts for them with dollars in special stores. The policy of rapprochement with the "Cuban Community Abroad" adopted in late 1978 introduces unequal access to material goods that conflicts with the egalitarian goals of the revolution.

At stake in socialist Cuba is also the amount and kind of popular participation in the government. New forms of popular participation have been accepted since the new socialist constitution was adopted in 1976. Participation is limited, however, to those who agree with the basic policies of the government. In a regime based on the controlled mobilization of the people, tension will continue to surround participation in formulating policy as well as in discussing and carrying out policies already formed.

Finally, the military and diplomatic position of Cuba in the world is a major issue for Cuban politics. The advantages of continued dependence on the Soviet Union may decrease as Soviet aid decreases and payments on past aid come due. Similarly, access to advanced technology and a large nearby market makes relations with the United States an issue that will recur in Cuba's foreign affairs. The role of Cuba in the Third World is an issue that not only involves the prestige of the nation; when Cuban troops fight in Africa—estimated at various times at a total of between 20,000 and 50,000—the lives of Cuban soldiers are the most graphic stakes of politics.

Participants in Politics. Cuba is a mobilized socialist society. Participation in the political system involves the majority of the population, since most people come into contact with a mass political organization at their school, at their workplace, or in their community. Of course, not all these members are activists. Another organization groups together the activists in Cuba: the Communist party.

Mass organizations in Cuba exist for workers, peasants, youth, and women; there are also community organizations in which all are encouraged to participate. Workers as well as peasants participate in mobilized mass organizations, which are effective at educating Cubans about new policies and goals of the revolutionary government. New ideas also filter upward from the mass discussions, though the revolutionary leadership decides which suggestions to accept. The Cuban Labor Confederation (CTC) brings workers to assemblies to discuss major new laws or proposals; there are also smaller meetings at the factory level for local issues. Anywhere from 60 to 90 percent of the members attend the assemblies, and government proposals are typically approved by overwhelming majorities. Since most participants support proposed policies, only the negative votes are counted. It thus becomes significant if 1, 2, or 3 percent of the voters disapprove a proposal.

Major policy proposals are discussed by nearly everyone, not just workers. Such discussions have been held for the 1971 law on vagrancy (to combat excessive absenteeism); the 1975 family code (including rules on marriage, the family, and parenthood); and the 1979 penal code. But the most massive discussions were about the 1976 constitution. In those discussions, perhaps six million people participated (often on several occasions) in a country whose total population is just under ten million. In the first discussion in 1975, 88.5 percent of the participants approved the draft constitution without any changes; about 10 percent supported amendments proposed by 16,000 (0.25 percent) participants around the country; less than 2 percent opposed it altogether. In the 1976 referendum of the proposed new constitution, 98 percent of all registered voters participated; 97.7 percent of them approved.[5] Under its terms, however, Cuba remains a one-party dictatorship and any organized opposition is illegal.

All such participation activities, as well as the voting for representatives to organizations and to the new "Assemblies of Peoples' Power," provide information to the Cuban people, increase the likelihood of their commitment to the government, and gather suggestions from many people. In the countryside, the National Association of Small Peasants (ANAP) has changed from a lobbying group for farmers in the early 1960s to an organization for controlled mass participation in the 1970s. It is now easier for information about government decisions to reach the peasants, but more difficult for their input to matter in policy making. Some changes do get made in response to peasants' wishes, however; for example, peasants on small private farms (still allowed in Cuba) can join private cooperatives instead of state farms and can sell some of their produce privately.[6]

Perhaps the best-known and certainly the largest of Cuba's mass organizations are the Committees for the Defense of the Revolution (CDRs). Founded in 1960, the CDRs were a security apparatus, organized in every community to observe and denounce counterrevolutionary activity. At the time of the Bay of Pigs invasion, the CDRs complemented the work of the armed forces at *Playa Giron* (the beach bordering the Bay of Pigs) and made possible the mass detention of suspected subversives. Since 1960, the membership of the CDRs has increased from less than one million to almost five million and their functions have become more mundane. Denunciations now are more likely to focus on the parents of school truants or on apprehending common criminals. Effective mass public health campaigns, literacy and education drives, neighborhood improvement, and voluntary labor as well as political vigilance are all functions of the CDRs.

Although women still hold only a small percentage of elected offices, the Cuban revolution has explicitly recognized the equality and importance of women. A steadily increasing proportion of women are integrated into the paid work force (28 percent in 1975), but that is probably due to the

[5]Domínguez, *Cuba*, pp. 299–302. Unless otherwise noted, data in this section and the following on the party are from this source.

[6]Most tobacco, one-quarter to one-half of various fruits and vegetables, and 18 percent of sugar cane were produced privately in 1975. Domínguez, *Cuba*, p. 452.

general modernization of the economy and the society (a process taking place in capitalist as well as socialist societies). The Federation of Cuban Women (FMC) brings together women who work for pay and those who do not; its membership has gone from a scant 17,000 in 1961 to over two million in 1975—approximately 80 percent of the adult female population. In addition to education, training, and health care services, the FMC organizes volunteer labor in the sugar harvest and elsewhere. Perhaps most important for the working mothers, it operates approximately seven hundred day-care centers. Women are gaining importance in national politics, in part at Fidel Castro's insistence. He has declared it a priority.

Like workers and peasants, both male and female, children also participate in mass organizations. Although membership is optional, nearly 99 percent of Cuban school children belong to the *Pioneers*. Like the other mass organizations (and like the Boy Scouts elsewhere), the Pioneers help socialize the children to patriotism and loyalty. Educational functions and recreational incentives, such as organized vacations, also encourage participation. Similar organizations exist at the high school level. In addition, all young people spend two years of compulsory service in the army. Many serve in the Army of Working Youth, which engages more in civilian than in military work.

Cuba is a highly integrated society by American standards. A country with a history of slavery, Cuba has a white majority with a large black and mulatto minority. As before, there are still few blacks at the highest levels of government. However, all services and institutions are open to blacks and whites alike. Black and white children play together on the beaches near Havana, and black couples honeymoon at the luxurious Havana Riviera Hotel, which had been beyond their reach in earlier days.

The Communist Party of Cuba. Before the revolution, Cuba's Communist party (the PSP) was quite independent of the 26th of July movement. In the first years of the revolution, the old Communist party assumed more importance. It united with the 26th of July movement and the Revolutionary Directorate of university students in the Integrated Revolutionary Organization (ORI). Then the Communist leader, Anibal Escalante, was sent off in 1962 to Prague, Czechoslovakia, for "sectarianism" in what came to be called the first "Escalante affair." ORI evolved into the United Party of the Socialist Revolution (PURS) in 1963, and into the new Communist Party of Cuba (PCC) in 1965. In 1967, Escalante, having returned from Eastern Europe, tried again to take control of the party and was arrested, tried, and imprisoned as the leader of a pro-Soviet "microfaction." After years in prison, he was released sometime before his death in the mid-1970s. Although after 1970 Cuba developed closer ties with the Soviet Union, it was because Castro, not other leaders, decided it should be so.

Though the party was weak through the 1960s, it has grown to become the leading political organization of the country. By about 1975 there were over 200,000 party members in Cuba (up from about 15,000 in 1962 and 100,000 in 1970). There are over one hundred members of the central committee; the direction of the party is in the hands of the small secretariat and political bureau.

Politics in Cuba is highly centralized. The Communist party is still both small and centralized. Authority in the mass organizations is centralized at the national level. Although few leaders of mass organizations at the local level are party members, the party can and does exercise authority over promotion criteria and leadership selection in the mass organizations. Although the party is young, having held its First Party Congress only in 1975, it is the most powerful ruling group in Cuba.

Images of Politics. Castro is the leader of the Cuban revolution and in many respects he himself is its leading symbol. Since the days in the Sierra Maestra, he has been the principal actor and the principal spokesperson for Cuba. One of the most vivid political experiences for many Cubans is to gather in the Plaza of the Revolution with hundreds of thousands or even one million fellow citizens to hear a speech by their president—an experience that happens with considerable frequency. Fidel Castro is a charismatic leader. With his beard and green army fatigues, he himself symbolizes the revolution.

Anti-imperialism is a recurring theme in Cuban politics. The image of Cuba as a small but valiant David facing the giant Goliath ninety miles to the north is implicitly evoked in references to the relations between Cuba and the United States. The defeat of U.S.–supported forces at the Bay of Pigs validated this image. The external threat to the nation posed by "Yankee imperialism" provides a galvanizing external force that facilitates nationalist celebrations of Cuba's strength and autonomy. It also demands increased sacrifice. The Soviet Union, never having challenged the Cubans by force, is also more distant and therefore less threatening. Given Cuba's location, it is unlikely that the Soviet Union would be able to dominate Cuba against the wishes of her leaders. Therefore, imperialism rather than socialist dependence provides the more vivid image.

The Cuban revolution is young by world standards. In the 1960s, the image of the new man and the new woman were held up to Cubans as images of the new society they were trying to build. Cuba was seen as being on the forefront of history, perhaps the first nation to cross the bridge from socialism to communism. That period of radical idealism, relying on the commitment of the people to moral rather than material incentives and on spontaneity and enthusiasm rather than on discipline and organization, ended with the failure of the year-long push to harvest ten million tons of sugar in 1970. Although the harvest was large, it did not reach the goal, and the disruptions in the rest of the economy were massive. Since that year, the government has emphasized institutionalization of the revolution. Institutions like the party, popular assemblies, and the courts have been strengthened. There has been a partial return to material incentives, in an effort to increase production and productivity. Still, for many who remember participating in the revolution and defending the island against foreign attack, the Cuban revolution is still youthful. They are hopeful and willing to sacrifice in a way that citizens in more mature socialist countries are not.

Finally, Cuba aspires to a position of leadership in the Third World. In the 1960s, under the influence of "Ché" Guevara, Cuba exported the revolution. In addition to ideological support it provided arms and money to Communist parties and insurrectionist movements throughout Latin America. This support ended, however, with the death of Ché and his small group of Cuban followers in the jungles of Bolivia in 1967, following upon their failure to win effective peasant support in that region and their defeat by a CIA-directed antiguerrilla campaign. Cuba has also supported independence movements and struggles for national self-determination. Rather than Cuban volunteers acting as individuals, the Cuban state now gives official support and military assistance at the invitation of foreign governments. The Cubans consider this international solidarity to be "paying their debt to humanity." They are returning the fraternal support they received when they were vulnerable and under attack.

In the 1970s, Cuba turned to Africa, a continent where many Cubans have ancestral roots. It is easier for the Cubans to be seen as leaders by elites in the poorer countries of Africa than in the relatively more developed countries of Latin America. For their part, Cubans know their ancestors left Africa as slaves; they see themselves returning as liberators. When Cuban soldiers return home, their austere society seems comfortable by comparison to the hardships they have experienced in the African countries they have visited.

Cuba has sought international leadership, not only by military and economic aid to Angola and other African nations, but also, in 1979, as a leader of the Nonaligned Movement. Cuba hosted the sixth summit meeting of the Nonaligned Movement in Havana in September 1979. At that time,

Castro tried to move the group toward a position hostile to the United States and more positive to the Soviet Union. Despite his fiery rhetoric, Castro had little success in this effort. Most major nations in the movement preferred to continue the tradition set by Marshal Tito of Yugoslavia, as well as by India, of maintaining independence from both major powers. Although Cuba will hold the chairmanship of the movement for three years after 1979, it is unlikely to have a major impact on the policies of the major nonaligned countries.

For many people, Cuba's image is darkened by the lack of individual freedom, particularly for intellectuals.[7] Cuba's most effective leadership is by example, a revolutionary regime with relatively high levels of social welfare and equity at home. It is these achievements in satisfying basic needs rather than an alliance with the socialist bloc that make Cuba an attractive model for the Third World. One U.S. academic returning from Cuba summarized his impressions this way: "If you lived in the bottom two-thirds of most developing countries, you would rather live in Cuba." Of course, those who influence politics in such countries are more likely to be in the top third, and would not prefer to live in Cuba.

The Political Arena. Since Cuba is an island, the territorial definition of its political arena should be straightforward. And so it is. Yet the recurring dependence on the great powers leaves several open questions about Cuba's sovereignty over Cuban territory. At the time of the Bay of Pigs invasion, Cuban exiles, with the support of a foreign intelligence agency, attempted to overthrow the Cuban government from the outside. The United States has confirmed that CIA agents have made continued attempts on the life of Fidel Castro. Although these attempts failed, the threat of direct foreign intervention has helped strengthen the nationalism and unity of Cuba.

A large community of Cubans live in the United States, which further extends the arena of politics. From 1960 to 1974, nearly 600,000 Cubans left the island. Nearly one-third left in the first three years; most came to the United States.[8] For years the Cuban expatriates, many of whom were property owners, government officials, or professionals, acted as a threat to the survival of the Cuban revolution. In addition to invasion attempts, bombings, and other acts of terrorism, many Cubans lobbied against normalizing relations. However, by 1979 the Cuban government changed its policy on the Cuban community abroad, making it possible for large numbers of expatriates to visit their relatives in Cuba for the first time since their departure. In the first half of that year, approximately fifty thousand Cubans returned home as tourists. The maneuver of bringing Cubans in the United States into the political arena has been partially successful: In June 1979, a committee of Cuban-Americans presented ten thousand signatures to the U.S. government requesting normalized relations with Cuba.[9]

The most blatant illustration of the divided political arena is the U.S. naval base at Guantánamo. Claimed by the government of Cuba and retained by the United States as a perpetuation of early treaty rights, the base is a constant reminder to the Cubans that they do not control all the territory of the island. The mock landing of marines on the beaches of Guantánamo as a show

[7]From 1973 on, very few of Chile's refugees from the right-wing dictatorship of General Augusto Pinochet chose to go to Cuba. The great majority preferred to go to Spain, Mexico, Italy, or France where they could enjoy the comfortable lifestyle and intellectual freedom they had known in Chile. Of course, Cuba did not invite large-scale migration from Chile.

[8]Domínguez, *Cuba,* p. 140.

[9]The Cuban community in the United States is itself deeply divided. Many Cubans continue to visit their homeland from the United States. However, one of those who participated in the negotiations to make the trips possible was assassinated in late 1979 by extremists who oppose any contact with Cuba while Fidel Castro is in power.

of U.S. force in October 1979, after the announcement that Soviet combat troops were in Cuba, was an angry demonstration of U.S. ability to intervene militarily in Cuba if necessary to confront the Soviet Union—an ability that was never in doubt.

Besides the base at Guantánamo, uncertainty about the Cuban arena has at times existed with regard to Cuba's airspace and her territorial waters. The airspace has been an area of conflict when the United States has conducted surveillance overflights of the island by U-2 "spy planes," a practice that President Carter renewed in the fall of 1979. The Soviet Union uses Cuba as a communications intelligence base for its own purposes, though with the permission of the Cubans.

Not all issues involving the political arena have resulted in conflict between the United States and Cuba. Both the treatment of hijackers who fly to Cuba and the definition of fishing rights in territorial waters shared by Cuba and the United States have been negotiated to amicable solutions.

In the summer and fall of 1979, there was a period of unpleasantness between the United States and Cuba when the United States announced the presence in Cuba of a Soviet military unit of about three thousand soldiers. Both the USSR and Cuba said the troops had been there for seventeen years, and the United States later admitted that the troops had probably been in Cuba "at least" since 1975. In fact, ground troops were not covered by the U.S.–Soviet agreements reached after the missile crisis; their "discovery" in 1979 was thus a somewhat artificial issue. Nevertheless, Cuba's link to Soviet military goals and operations and the U.S. naval base at Guantánamo remain continuing exceptions to the integrity of Cuba's political arena.

The Cuban Political System. The political system of Cuba is composed of three parallel structures: the Cuban Communist party; the apparatus of the state, including all the ministries and functional divisions within the state; and the structures of "popular power" *(poder popular),* that is, the elected organs authorized in the 1976 constitution. The party provides the leadership and the direction necessary for managing the politics and the economy. It is the transmission belt for decisions made at the top; it provides the *cadres* (party activists) with the correct interpretation of current government policy. The ministries and special committees are set up along functional lines to carry out the day-to-day business of the society. The council of ministers brings together, under the direction of the prime minister, Fidel Castro, all the heads of the various ministries: foreign affairs, foreign trade, electricity, public health, education, sugar industry, and so on. The council of state on the other hand is an organ of the national assembly, which carries out the legislative functions of the assembly during the greater part of the year when the assembly is not in session. Castro is both its president and head of state.

What is most striking about the party leadership, the council of ministers, and the council of state is that many of the members overlap, holding positions in several or all. Three individuals stand out from the rest: Fidel Castro, his brother Raúl Castro, and Carlos Raphael Rodríguez. Fifteen other leaders make up a small group—an interlocking directorate—occupying the major posts in the Cuban political system. All these eighteen people hold several important decision-making positions and constitute the highest political elite of the country. Most of these leaders, like Fidel and Raúl Castro, were active fighters with the rebel army in the 1950s. Direct participation in the revolution is still a major legitimating factor for the political elite.

The Communist party is an effective mechanism for steering the government in the desired political direction. The voters, and the agencies, supposedly have autonomy at the local level. It is nonetheless the party that indicates the direction for policy and action.

Although the political steering mechanism operating through the party is strong, the mechanisms for feedback from the people are relatively weak. Some feedback is obtained from the suggestions put forward in the mass organizations. Unlike more open systems, newspapers and other mass media are a relatively poor source of feedback to the government since they are tightly controlled. Although specific complaints about poor goods and services are aired in the press, nothing critical of the regime can be included on television, on the radio, or in books and pamphlets with mass circulation.

The principal unsolved problem of the political system is succession. Rule by Fidel and Raúl Castro has provided continuity over time, but there is neither experience nor a proven mechanism for converting to a new leadership should something happen to the current president and prime minister. By now, however, Cuba seems sufficiently consolidated to cope with any such successor problem. Under a successor, some of Fidel's policies might change but the basic character of the regime seems likely to endure. In the meantime, the great concentration of power in the hands of one man and the small group surrounding him means that decisions can be made easily within that group. Controversies can be resolved by the president and changes in direction can be made relatively rapidly. However, much of the learning that takes place in the system occurs inside the head of Fidel Castro. The consultative mechanisms of the mass organizations and research undertaken by the Ministry of Internal Demand provide some input from the people as to their likes and dislikes. But the strictly controlled press and the limitation on political expression mean that the political leaders are unlikely to hear significantly divergent views.

The State Machinery. For the first decade after the Cuban revolution, there was almost no separation of functions in the state. Executive discretion was almost unlimited, and though much was made of frequent conversations and discussions by Fidel with broad groups of the population, the government was in fact run by a handful of men. The same executive group legislated new laws and took responsibility for their implementation. Justice was dispensed through a varied and changing court system, which for a time gave prominence to the so-called popular tribunals made up of lay rather than professional judges. The country functioned practically without a constitution and the number of law students in the universities dropped to almost nothing.

By 1970, after the failure of the ten-million-ton sugar harvest, a period of institutionalization that continued through the seventies began to formalize and differentiate the powers of government. The Communist party, with closer links to the enlarged mass organizations, became a vital and functioning socialist party organization, responsible for the formulation and general direction of policy. Under the constitution of 1976 and following several years of experiments in the province of Matanzas, popular assemblies were organized and elected at the municipal, provincial, and national levels. These assemblies and the council of state, operating at the national level during the recess of the national assembly, discuss and legislate laws and regulations. These laws are always based on the general direction set by the party, but include the suggestions and proposals of its own working committees, of the council of ministers, the council of state, and of various other organizations with the capacity to propose new legislation.

As part of institutionalization, law once again became an important area to study. Lawyers are trained to work as prosecutors in the renovated court system, to work as defense counsel in collective law offices around the country, and to work as legal counsel in the expanding offices of state enterprise. From graduating classes numbering eight or ten students, the law school of the University of Havana now trains some five hundred lawyers per year. Regular channels for the protest of abuses or the discussion of problems have been established, so that appeals to Castro or letters to the editor of national journals, though they persist, are less necessary than they once were. As the socialist regime in Cuba has become more stable and institutionalization proceeds, the political machinery becomes more differentiated and a separation of powers, though still modest, has begun to emerge.

Performance of the Political System. The Cuban revolution has done well for the people that supported it. Especially for the poorest members of the society, the redistributive measures and the socialization of the economy have resulted in dramatic increases in overall well-being. Although overall income (per capita GNP) was relatively low, about $800 per capita in 1975, most people had the necessities of life. Literacy was almost universal, probably the highest of any country in Latin America. Other indicators shown in Table 17.1 likewise ranked Cuba as an advanced transitional society, moving toward industrialization. Also impressive is the improvement in such indicators as infant mortality, which was at twenty-seven per thousand in 1975 and has continued to drop, thus approaching the levels of health found in advanced industrial societies. Indeed, the free provision of education and health care and the subsidized provision of other services, such as transportation, day care, and housing, have meant that the broad mass of the Cuban population live much more comfortably than do citizens of other countries with a similar per capita GNP.

Nevertheless, the mobilized and equitable socialist system has not increased the overall levels of production. Growth has been negligible for many years, resulting in stagnating welfare increases. Improvements have tended to go to more qualified and skilled technical sectors of the population and to members of the bureaucracy. Socialism has leveled the society; this equality has left some intellectuals and bureaucrats dissatisfied. Their services are needed, especially given the massive emigration of professionals after the revolution, so distribution of goods and services through bureaucratic channels, particularly through the workplace, has been unequal. This same system has meant that more subtle pressures for conformity can now be brought into play. Whereas once dissidents might be detained or imprisoned, there are now economic disincentives to dissidence.

The mobilizational arts, such as dance, theatre, and cinema, have flowered in Cuba. Perhaps more than in other socialist countries, the graphic arts have also been highly developed. Yet the intellectual freedom of artists, writers, teachers, and university professors is constrained in a socialist regime. Subversive art is not tolerated. Nevertheless, Cuba seems to be more open in this respect than many other socialist countries.

In the international sphere, Cuba is looking for a position as leader of the Third World, while maintaining its allegiance to the Soviet Union. There is also a strong interest in resuming economic relations with the United States to take advantage of natural trading economies offered by geography and to gain access to U.S. technology. Both the United States and Cuba are interested in eventually returning to normal diplomatic relations. Steps in this direction were taken in the mid-1970s leading to the establishment of diplomatic interest sections (in the Czech embassy in Washington and in the Swiss embassy in Havana), but further moves have been chilled by the United States due to the presence of Cuban troops in Africa and the 1979 flap over Soviet troops in Cuba.

In the long run, improved ties and normalized relations are likely. Cuba already has diplomatic relations with 117 countries, and consular relations with 2 others. The United States, for its part, has found the way to normal relations with China, the Soviet Union, and other socialist countries. More than four hundred U.S. firms have held talks with the Cubans in Havana, and many of them conduct business through their overseas subsidiaries. Educational, cultural, and artistic ties have increased. Ironically, however, these moves have partially eased the pressures for rapid normalization of diplomatic relations.

A number of outstanding problems remain to be

solved. The Cuban-American community remains divided on the advisability of renewed relations with Cuba under Castro, and an active minority is violently opposed. Many in the United States are concerned about political prisoners in Cuba, though many have recently been released; that issue has diminished in importance. The compensation of U.S. firms expropriated after the revolution remains a more difficult problem, but one that the two governments could solve with good faith. Most intractable are the problems in the international sphere. Cuba refuses to tie its foreign policy in Africa or elsewhere to U.S. wishes, and the United States has been unwilling to negotiate its naval base in Guantánamo or to drop the embargo. These circumstances mean that although there will be increasing visits by Cuban-Americans, by scholars and students, and by other American tourists to Cuba, and increased trade with the overseas subsidiaries of U.S. companies, the normalization of diplomatic relations between the United States and Cuba, though likely in the long run, was in 1979 still a distant goal.

MEXICO: CONTRASTS OF WEALTH AND POVERTY ON THE U.S. BORDER

"Mexico is the country of inequality," said the German traveler and scientist Alexander von Humboldt in the eighteenth century. From the time before Columbus when the *Méxica* (or *Azteca*) tribe dominated the Indians of the central valley, to the Spanish colonial period when fabulous silver wealth made white men rich while Indians starved, to the rule of the dictator Porfirio Díaz at the end of the nineteenth century, to the oil-rich days of the present, Mexican society has been one of the most unequal in the world.[10] Nor is the contrast of wealth and poverty confined to within the national boundaries. The northern border of Mexico, stretching from Tijuana and San Diego on the Pacific Ocean through Matamoros and Brownsville near the Caribbean, separates a proud and struggling people from one of the wealthiest and most powerful nations on earth. As the emerging nation closest to the United States, Mexico offers a dramatic example of the problems of the world's developing countries.

A Tradition of Three Cultures. Mexico is an Indian empire and Spanish colony fused in a *mestizo* nation. (*Mestizos* are people of mixed Indian and Spanish blood.)

Before the conquest of New Spain, Mexico was one of the two ancient centers of Indian civilization in the New World. (Peru, with its Inca masters, was the other.) In the fifteenth century, the Aztec tribe had consolidated its rule over its various subjects, from west of the capital Tenochtitlán, where Mexico City now stands, east to the Caribbean coast at Veracruz. All the tribes paid tribute to their common masters, who used a common language, *Nahuatl,* to communicate with the dominated peoples.

When Hernán Cortés landed near Veracruz in 1519, the technology of his army (including horses, crossbows, and artillery), his lust for gold, and the dissatisfaction of the subject tribes enabled him to conquer the Méxica tribe in only two years. The linguistic skills of Malinche, the Indian mistress of Cortés, aided greatly in the conquest, giving rise to the derogatory term *malinchista* referring to those Mexicans who prefer things foreign.

The Spaniards imposed their language, their religion, and their economic interests on the Indians. Hispanic culture, colonialism, and Catholicism were all new to the Indians and disastrous for their old civilization. Scholars have suggested that in the first century or so after the conquest (from 1519 to 1650), at least six-sevenths of the Indian population of Central America was decimated by new diseases and other hardships

[10]See column 18 of Table 17.1. The 0.58 Gini index of inequality given there shows Mexico as the most unequal of the countries considered.

brought by their new masters.[11] Those who survived were ruled by administrators appointed by the Spanish Crown, but their daily contact was more likely to be with the priests and friars who baptized literally millions of Indians, bringing them the Catholic faith and Spanish culture.

With their former shrines and temples everywhere destroyed and replaced by Spanish churches, the Indians adopted the saints and symbols of the new religion as their own, often creating unique forms of folk Catholicism such as the glorification of the Virgin of Guadalupe. The Spanish language, however, was only partially adopted. Indeed, although the friars were charged by the Crown with both converting Indians and teaching them Hispanic language and culture, the friars in the sixteenth and seventeenth centuries imitated the Aztecs before them and converted the Indians either in Nahuatl or in their native tongues.

Indians became Catholics and learned enough Spanish to labor on the extensive landholdings (*haciendas*) of the Spanish elite or in the gold and silver mines, which provided Spain with the greatest wealth to come out of the New World. Not only did the Indians in Mexico have to give their labor under conditions of peonage (near-servitude), but they also paid an individual tribute (tax) for being Indians. By the end of the eighteenth century fully two-thirds of Spain's revenues came from Mexico.[12] But colonialism was not to last, and from the combination of a long history of Aztec civilization with three centuries of Spanish colonialism, a new people—the mestizos—and a new nation emerged.

[11]Eric Wolf, *Sons of the Shaking Earth: The People of Mexico and Guatemala—Their Land, History and Culture* (Chicago: The University of Chicago Press, 1959), p. 195. Other scholars give more drastic estimates: "Within less than a century the population of central Mexico shrank from approximately twenty-five millions to under two millions; the tropical coasts became the disease-ridden wastes that they have remained until recent decades." Woodrow Borah and Sherburne F. Cook, "Why Population Estimates are Important in the Interpretation of Mexican History," in *Latin America: A Historical Reader*, ed. Lewis Hanke (Boston: Little, Brown and Company, 1974), p. 119.

A Stormy Independence: Defining the Nation-State Arena. The first revolts for independence from Spain, led by the parish priests Miguel Hidalgo and José María Morelos, were violently repressed and ended in failure. But as Spain lost power in Europe and turned liberal, more conservative *creoles*[13] in Mexico established an independent Mexican monarchy on September 16, 1821. Two years later a republic was declared. Slavery was abolished, though it had never been very important in Mexico. The conditions of the Indians were scarcely improved; they lived on under their village chiefs, known to the Indians as *caciques,* and increasingly under the control of the landowners. The Spaniards left for Cuba or returned to Spain, the creoles fought among themselves for political control of the country, and with the protection of the Monroe Doctrine, American and British investors replaced the Spanish as bankers and mine-owners. Local landowners and former army officers, now also called caciques (bosses), built up local bases of power. But at the national level there was no unity. Two issues divided the country: whether there would be a strong central government or decentralized provinces (federalism), and whether or not the new state would control the Church.

During the generations of uncertainty that followed independence, the arena of politics in Mexico changed dramatically, and in a way that is often forgotten in the United States, though never in Mexico. Settlers from the United States moved to Texas, and although the Mexican Generalísimo Antonio Lopez de Santa Anna fought several battles to keep Texas, badly defeating the Ameri-

[12]John Lynch, *The Spanish-American Revolutions, 1808–1826* (New York: W. W. Norton, 1973), p. 303.

[13]*Creoles* were Spaniards born in the New World, in contrast to the *mestizos,* who were of mixed Spanish and Indian heritage.

can settlers at the Alamo in 1836, the territory nevertheless separated from Mexico and became an independent republic. In 1845, Texas was admitted to the Union by the United States. Mexico went to war, again under the leadership of Santa Anna. But the American army that invaded through Veracruz eventually took Mexico City, despite the resistance of the Mexican "boy heroes," young cadets still honored today for dying rather than surrendering to the foreign army. These events have left very different images of heroes and villains in the collective memories of the two countries. Youngsters in the United States learn to "Remember the Alamo!" whereas Mexicans honor the boy soldiers who died opposing the invading army. Each side remembers those who died valiantly defending their territory.

In the conqueror's settlement in 1848, Mexico lost what is today California, Arizona, and New Mexico, amounting, with Texas, to half its territory. The United States expanded to the Pacific, increasing its own size by two-thirds.[14] The new border ran through an unpopulated wasteland to meet the Rio Grande, which flowed down past Texas to the Gulf of Mexico.

By the 1850s, the outer boundaries of Mexico had largely been fixed, but sovereignty had not yet been attained, either domestically or internationally. Since independence, various Indian groups had revolted, seeking autonomy and a return to the traditional patterns of their village life. These included both the Yaqui tribe in what is now northern Mexico and the independent Maya on the Yucatan peninsula. It had taken the Spanish a generation to conquer the Maya in the sixteenth century. In 1847, the Maya revolted again in the so-called Caste War of Yucatan. Although such revolts were contained, this regional and local diversity still exists in the loyalty of many Mexicans to the region and section from which they originated: their *patria chica*, or "little homeland." In a country of few recent immigrants from other countries, these ties resemble the ties immigrant groups elsewhere may feel to the habits and traditions of "the old country."

International status as a sovereign state was slow in coming. Besides the war and territorial losses to the United States, Mexico also had to contend with attempts at domination by the French. The French had briefly occupied Veracruz in 1838 in the so-called Pastry War, touched off by a French baker's claim for damages suffered in a previous civil disturbance. In 1861, while the United States was involved in its own Civil War, Spain, France, and Great Britain jointly landed troops in Veracruz, partly in an effort to enforce debt collection on the shaky government led by President Benito Juárez, a Zapotec Indian from Oaxaca, who had finally replaced Santa Anna. The French, without the British or Spanish, decided to march on Mexico City, which they occupied in 1863. Under the tutelage of Napoleon III and with the support of the Pope, Mexico was ruled as an empire by foreign monarchs, Maximilian of Hapsburg (Austria) and his wife Carlota, until 1867. With the Civil War in the United States over and with Napoleon unwilling to invade North America again, Juárez was able to depose and execute Maximilian. (Carlota was exiled and later went mad.) There was no popular support in Mexico for the foreigners.

The defeat of this empire by Juárez and the republican general Porfirio Díaz helped pull the nation together. Reforms limiting the economic power of the Church and the federalist republic first outlined in the liberal constitution of 1857 were finally implemented. Yet the country had lost half its territory and had become impoverished by the nearly constant wars since 1810.

Economic Modernization and Authoritarian Rule: The Porfiriato. Five years after Juárez died in 1872, Porfirio Díaz came to power by force of arms, though with considerable popular support. He remained as president from 1877 (except for one term, 1880–84) until the Mexican revolution deposed him in 1911. His presidency is called the *Porfiriato*. As Europe increasingly embraced free

[14]Robert H. Ferrell, *American Diplomacy* (New York: W. W. Norton, 1959), p. 106.

trade, Mexico under Díaz entered a period of economic modernization. With the help of British banks and British and American investment companies, and with the ideological underpinnings of positivism, extensive railroad lines were built and gold, silver, copper, and lead mining expanded. Especially in the northern city of Monterrey, the manufacture of steel, textiles, beer, and other products proceeded apace. Roads were built, telephones introduced, and ports expanded. Foreign trade doubled and doubled again. After the turn of the century, oil became an increasingly rich line of production.

The price of this growth was repression. With the help of the rural police (*rurales*), Díaz controlled with force the unrest that accompanied the intrusion of modernizing capitalism into the traditional countryside. The liberal reforms that broke up large Church landholdings were also used to force the sale of community property (*ejidos*) in the villages. Through these reforms and by concessions to private interests and speculators, the formerly public lands concentrated in the hands of large private landholders during the *Porfiriato* amounted to over one-quarter of the total area of the republic. Over three-quarters of the population lived in the countryside, and over half of these residents were tied to the large haciendas. Concentration of land and wealth was as great as it had ever been in Mexico.

The Mexican Revolution. The Mexican revolution, which began in 1910, ranks with the later Russian and Chinese revolutions as one of the major political upheavals of this century. It was costly and bloody. Haciendas and railroads were captured, recaptured, and often burned; many peasant soldiers lost their lives in the battles and skirmishes. The first rebel, Francisco I. Madero, took as his slogan in 1910: *"Effective Suffrage, No Re-election."* This motto is still a key to understanding the Mexican political system and has increasingly become an ideal for other governments in Latin America.

Díaz fell, and Madero became president during 1911–12. The peasant leader Emiliano Zapata challenged Madero, demanding the restoration of the village *ejido* lands to the peasants. After a military coup in 1913 led to Madero's assassination, the military failed to repress a constitutionalist revolt led by Venustiano Carranza in 1914. Then Carranza and one of his generals, Alvaro Obregón, joined forces against Zapata in the south and Pancho Villa in the north in 1915–16. Sufficient order was established to write the constitution of 1917, which laid the bases for extensive land reform, for the protection and encouragement (and control) of the labor movement, and for some limitation of foreign ownership of land, water, or minerals.

The revolution had its share of international as well as domestic conflict. By the time the United States entered World War I, President Wilson had twice authorized the invasion of Mexican territory. U.S. troops occupied Veracruz in 1914 in response to a supposed affront to the dignity of the United States, and troops under Pershing advanced into northern Mexico in retaliation for Pancho Villa's border raids.

The leaders of the revolution, Madero, Zapata, and Carranza, had all been killed by 1920, but the foundations for stability had been laid. During the 1920s, under the official or unofficial guidance of Plutarco Elías Calles, Mexico was able to lessen the factionalism of the military leaders of the revolution, survive a three-year rebellion of Church-inspired Christian reaction (the *Cristero* war), and begin to incorporate workers and peasants into national political participation through the foundation in 1929 of the National Revolutionary party, the forerunner of the dominant party of today.

The consolidation of the revolution was completed by the powerful and popular president Lázaro Cárdenas, who held office from 1934 to 1940. Under his leadership, the Mexican system took on the institutional form it has maintained, with some modifications, since those years.

Cárdenas is still remembered as the greatest of Mexico's presidents since the revolution. As the worldwide depression resulted in economic hardship and unemployment in Mexico, Cárdenas responded in a way that won him the affection of the people and the approval of many historians. He confronted the manipulations of Calles and established the precedent of an independent president whose great power is limited by relinquishing the position to a successor after six years. The principle of "no re-election" was institutionalized in fact as well as in form. The extensive distribution of land to the peasantry, applying the promises of the 1917 constitution, incorporated the rural dwellers (*campesinos*) into national political life, though the efforts of collectivization of the *ejidos* never attained economic success.

The commitment of Cárdenas to the Mexican system is revealed by the fact that he kept the rural peasants organized separately from the urban workers who had joined together in the Federation of Mexican Labor (CTM) headed by the leftist Vicente Lombardo Toledano. Thus, the CTM did not become an autonomous political force. Rather, it became one of the mainstays of the national party, the party of the Mexican Revolution, as it was renamed in 1938. This party was in turn reformed and renamed the Institutional Revolutionary party (PRI) in 1946.

The Oil Expropriation. Lázaro Cárdenas is best remembered for his nationalization of the oil industry. Though raw materials have now been reclaimed from foreign companies by many governments around the world, in 1938 such a step was highly unusual. Within Mexico, however, it had ample precedent. Article 27 of the Mexican constitution of 1917 had laid the groundwork by establishing that natural resources belong to the nation. In the early 1920s, when Mexico was the world's third largest producer of petroleum, the United States and Mexico had clashed over oil. U.S. oil interests influencing the administration of Warren G. Harding (later implicated in the Teapot Dome scandal) were able to prevent for three years the American recognition of the government of Alvaro Obregón (president of Mexico from 1920 to 1924). Obregón finally agreed in writing that Article 27 of the constitution would not be applied retroactively to oil companies that had drilled their wells before 1917. The United States then recognized the government of Mexico in 1923.

Nevertheless, two years later the U.S. Secretary of State Frank B. Kellogg put Mexico "on trial before the world" for not giving sufficient protection to U.S. nationals. President Calles finally reached agreement in 1927 when Calvin Coolidge sent Dwight Morrow to Mexico as the new ambassador. Calles extended the concessions of the oil companies beyond the earlier fifty-year limit, and the United States recognized the sovereignty and jurisdiction of the Mexican government to resolve any future disputes with American companies.

This precedent was important when a new conflict arose in the 1930s. A labor conflict resulted in a wage settlement imposed on the oil companies by an arbitration board and upheld on appeal by the Mexican Supreme Court. When the companies ignored the court order, Cárdenas nationalized the foreign oil companies. Britain broke off diplomatic relations, but with the earlier U.S. recognition of Mexico's sovereignty, with President Franklin D. Roosevelt's noninterventionist "good neighbor policy," and with the threat of Hitler in Europe urging hemispheric unity, the United States agreed to accept the nationalization if a compensation agreement could be negotiated.

Sinclair Oil settled with Cárdenas in 1940 for $8.5 million. Without explicitly stating whether the compensation included oil in the ground, the joint U.S.–Mexico settlement commission finally reached agreement in November 1941 (after Cárdenas had left office). The other U.S. companies received $24 million (plus 3 percent interest from 1938). The last payment was made on schedule in 1947; no longer did anyone contest that the oil belonged to Mexico.[15]

The Stakes of Politics in Mexico. In modern Mexico, the stakes of politics are less likely than in the past to be a matter of life or death, but the stakes are still high. The sovereignty and independence of the country have been assured, and most of the residents of the country feel themselves part of the nation and proud of their revolutionary heritage, though that pride is often tempered by a skepticism about results and a cynicism about the meaning of the revolution today. The political system, legitimized by the revolution and resting on a strong president, has proved remarkably stable, especially when compared to other developing countries.

The true issue in Mexico is development: the political problem of providing the conditions for economic growth, while making the benefits from that growth available to all the people rather than to just the elite and the middle class. The population, which reached 66 million in 1978, has been growing since 1960 at an average of 3.5 percent per year, one of the highest rates of population growth in the world (even though that rate is finally beginning to slow). High population growth means that the entire economy—all goods and services, including food production, transportation, schools, health facilities, housing construction—must grow at that rate just to maintain satisfaction of the society's needs. Any improvements require either much higher growth rates or policies distributing the goods and services in a more equitable way. The rapid growth of the population in recent years has made a "population pyramid" that is very wide at the base: There are many more young people than middle-aged or older people. Thus, with fully half the population under fifteen years of age, there is a special strain in two crucial areas: education and jobs. Unless these challenges can be met, the considerable accomplishment of stable civilian rule that has so distinguished Mexico may once again come into question.

The Participants in Politics. Not everyone participates equally in politics in Mexico. Mexico is ruled by a political and economic elite. The middle classes receive some benefits and have varying degrees of access to this elite. The same is true, though to a lesser extent, for organized workers and peasants. There is a large group of rural workers and urban marginals who are not organized, have no access to the elite, and receive few if any benefits.

The political elite in Mexico has been called the "revolutionary family" or the "revolutionary coalition." Originally composed of those who actually participated in the revolution, it now includes those who occupy the political offices, from the president, the president's cabinet and staff; directors of state-owned industries and banks; state governors; officials of the major party (PRI); and ambassadors, senators, and deputies. These people are likely to have a similar upper- or middle-class background and to have received their education at the national university, often in law or another professional specialization. The economic elite is made up of the owners and executives of large firms in banking, insurance, manufacturing, and agriculture. More likely to have been trained in expensive private schools and universities than members of the political elite, these individuals are able to influence politics through the organizations that represent their industries and that have officially sanctioned consultative status with the government. They also influence politics through intermediary groups such as lawyers or ex-politicians and directly through personal contact with the political elite at political and social functions.

Members of the middle class, who may be small

[15]The British companies did not reach any agreement until 1947, when they settled for $130 million. See Lorenzo Meyer, *Mexico y los Estados Unidos en el Conflicto Petrolero (1917–1942)* (Mexico: El Colegio de Mexico, 1972), pp. 449–461. See also Howard F. Cline, *The United States and Mexico* (Cambridge: Harvard University Press, 1967), pp. 248–249.

business owners or administrative workers in business or government, will have little influence on decisions, but can often obtain a job, gain a benefit, or cut through red tape thanks to a friend or relative (or the friend of a friend, or the relative of a relative) who is in a position to help them out. The middle classes, like the elite, can often afford to pay bribes (the *mordida*, or "bite") when necessary or convenient. Workers or peasants may occasionally have access to that kind of influence, but they are more likely to have to rely on their representative organizations, the leaders of which can influence political decisions and distribute benefits. The landless, unorganized rural worker and the recent migrant to the city who is unemployed or has only occasional marginal work have almost no chance of influencing politics. They may benefit from one government program or another from time to time, or they may rarely organize for a brief time with their neighbors to request the provision of a supply of water or the closing of an open sewer. These unemployed and underemployed workers and peasants constitute at least a third of the population. Monolingual Indians, now only about 6 percent of the population, also figure among the politically marginal.

Images of Mexico. The Mexican revolution is still a powerful symbol of the nation. As with other nations that have undergone such a societal upheaval, the revolution at once represents the high ideals that men and women died for, and the fearful specter of a conflict that pitted citizen against citizen. Today, as the last living participants in the war become octogenarians, the rhetoric of Mexico as a revolutionary nation is more vivid than the reality. Land reform, the great aspiration of the revolution, has come to a halt in the absence of new expropriations of the illegally large landholdings, the *neolatifundia*. The official labor organizations are more efficient at enforcing wage guidelines than at obtaining new benefits for the workers. The oil expropriation, with its base in the constitution, is still remembered on the national Day of Economic Independence. But the benefits of oil wealth are yet to reach the people.

Despite these realities that tarnish the image of the revolution, Mexicans remain committed to the nation.[16] Though few Mexicans expect results from the political system, they remain loyal to the symbols of the nation—especially against any challenge from the outside. In dealing with the United States, the Mexican president expects Mexico to be treated with all the respect due any important nation, and in this he has the full support of his people. Now that Mexico has petroleum in exportable quantities, the United States is beginning to pay more attention to Mexico. Unfortunately, this misses the point: Mexico wants to be treated as an equal for itself, not for its oil.

The image of Mexico at home may be that of a society with a revolutionary heritage, and bilaterally one of equality, but regarding other developing countries Mexico's self-image is one of leadership. President Luís Echeverría Alvarez (1970–76) was a spokesman for the New International Economic Order and sponsored the Charter of Economic Rights and Duties of States before the United Nations. President José Lopez Portillo similarly hoped to establish Mexican leadership in the energy field when he visited the United Nations in 1979 to propose a world energy order under U.N. auspices.

The Arena with a Permeable Border. Mexico lost half her territory in the last century, and was invaded by the French and by the United States on more than one occasion. Those days are gone, and Mexico's territory is probably safe from direct foreign threats. Furthermore, Mexico practices what it preaches: A staunch defender of nonaggression and nonintervention, Mexico has no designs or claims on the territory of other nations.

[16]This contrast is revealed in interviews conducted in the 1960s by Gabriel A. Almond and Sidney Verba, *The Civic Culture* (Boston: Little, Brown and Company, 1965), p. 203, as well as in more recent surveys.

The long border between Mexico and the United States means that the line between Mexican and U.S. political arenas is sometimes blurred. Many of the twin border cities have grown up together, moving from village to town to city with an international border between the two parts. These twin cities share commerce and industry (merchants accept both dollars and pesos); they also share common problems such as crime control, waste disposal, and pollution.

With such a long and busy frontier, unwanted movement of people is difficult if not impossible to control. Unemployment is high in Mexico and U.S. employers are anxious to get low-paid, hard-working, and nonunionized workers. Thus there is a steady flow of illegal migrants (also called "undocumented workers") from Mexico to the United States. The same conditions have encouraged the establishment of border industry—U.S.-owned plants on the Mexican side of the border to assemble textiles or electronic equipment. These plants employ unskilled Mexican workers, usually young women, who work for less than one-quarter the minimum wage in the United States. More than four hundred firms have set up shop as part of the Border Industrialization Program, in which the Mexican government suspends restrictions on foreign ownership and on exports and imports that apply to foreign firms located elsewhere in Mexico. The six major border towns have grown from a combined population of less than one-half million in 1950 to over 2.5 million in 1979. Trade, investment, migration, border towns—all these make the U.S.–Mexican border a unique and difficult region. In that zone, the United States and Mexico have a small part of their political arenas in common.

The Process of Politics. Mexico has a presidential system, and the country's major political event is the election of the president every six years. Because one party dominates the system, however, this election does not have the same significance as presidential elections in countries with democratic elections. The candidate of the official party, the PRI, has always won, ever since the party was founded; in 1976, José Lopez Portillo obtained 94.4 percent of the vote. More significant in this situation is the level of participation: In the 1976 presidential election, 69 percent of eligible voters actually went to the polls; in the congressional elections of 1979, that proportion fell below the 50 percent mark. For about fifty years, the PRI candidate for president has been selected from among the cabinet ministers; usually the candidate is a man who has served as a state governor or senator prior to joining the cabinet. Although opinions from the worker, peasant, and "popular" sectors of the party are solicited, and surely from the private sector as well, the outgoing president effectively names his successor.

Three parties of the Right and Center Right for years have competed weakly with the PRI for the presidency, for seats in the congress, and for state governorships. Of these conservative parties, the National Action party (PAN) is strongest, with an electoral base in the north of Mexico. With the 1977 political reform, three new parties of leftist persuasion were given official recognition. The Mexican Communist party (PCM), a moderate Communist party of eurocommunist persuasion, has some strength in urban areas, especially Mexico City. According to the reform, one-quarter of the seats in the Chamber of Deputies will be reserved for opposition parties.[17] In this way, though the relative power of the PRI will be diluted, the system as a whole should be strengthened.

This cooptation of the opposition into the system, as with past and present cooptation into the PRI, is used to supplement the selective repression of opposition by the police and the army. The army massacre of at least fifty student demonstrators in 1968 and the wounding of some five hundred others in the Plaza of Three Cultures

[17]One opposition party on the Left, the Socialist Workers' party (PST) did not participate in the reform. Its leader, Heberto Castillo, is a well-known columnist in a major Mexican weekly newsmagazine, *Proceso*.

is only the most striking use of force in recent times.[18] Peasant leaders frequently disappear forever when they violate the rules of the game. There were some guerrilla groups active both in the country and in the city in the early 1970s, such as the sectarian Communist League of the 23rd of September, but although crimes are sometimes still attributed to them, most of them were killed or captured by the end of the decade.

The Machinery of Administration. The political process in Mexico has been effective at coopting and controlling the organized political energies of the people. The traditions of the Mexican revolution, moreover, have absorbed the loyalties of most Mexicans. The presidency in Mexico is strong compared to other political institutions. In contrast, the actual administration of politics is neither as efficient nor as effective as one might expect from such a centralized system. Mexico is a soft state, even though the *scope* of state actions and the *domain* of state concerns are both large.

Although concentrating decision-making power in the president makes the adoption of policy relatively easy compared to other systems in which the legislature has a more significant role and in which the courts exercise some real control, the same concentration often impedes effective implementation of adopted policies. Members of the bureaucracy charged with implementing and administering announced policies hesitate to act firmly if they have any doubts about the desires or intentions of either the president or their bureaucratic superiors. Everyone looks upwards before acting. Thus the president's speech of today is taken as an indication of whether or not to implement the policy of yesterday.

Elites representing economic interests or other parts of the bureaucracy can also impede effective implementation. Since these elites have access to those with political power at higher levels, lower- and middle-level bureaucrats are unlikely to implement a policy that would negatively affect a powerful friend of their superiors. Exceptions are also made for one's own friends and relatives, and not a few in the bureaucracy make new friends easily, for the right amount of cash.

This ineffectiveness in implementation is complicated by the inefficiency in hiring and promotion. Since one's position depends on loyalty to one's superior rather than to an agency or its mission, a change of administrator often means that an entire team or *equipo* will change as well. Good superiors will take "their people" with them to the new job. Both the old office and the new office are robbed of continuity in day-to-day operations. It is a good system for making friends and contacts who may later help with a favor or a job; it is not a very good system for accomplishing the business of government.

Some recent changes may help to improve administration. There is now a national school for public administration. More use is now being made of the resources of academic institutions such as El Colegio de México (a research and teaching institute that offers graduate degrees and sponsors research, increasingly on government projects). As an aid to more effective administration in foreign affairs, several centers for the study of the United States have finally been established, at the Center for Economic Research and Training (CIDE), a government-supported institute in Mexico City, at El Colegio de México, and at the National University.

System Performance and Problems. The Mexican political system has well served the interests of the economic elites and it has maintained the significant benefits of peace and political stability. Increasing networks of roads and highways as well as the expansion of mass communications have brought more and more of the population into contact with the modern world. Literacy has

[18]Judith Adler Hellman, *Mexico in Crisis* (New York: Holmes and Meier, 1978), p. 142. These are the most conservative casualty figures. Other sources estimate that 200 to 400 students were killed in the 1968 massacre.

continued to increase, if slowly, reaching approximately 82 percent in 1978. Economically, the policies of "import-substitution industrialization" that favored large national and foreign firms have led to a positive rate of economic growth in both total and per capita terms. Gross domestic product per capita has averaged 2.3 percent growth per year since 1960.

These positive aspects of the Mexican system have had their costs: The price of growth has increased inequality. The very processes of modernization have led to an increased migration to the cities, especially to Mexico City, now a megalopolis of at least thirteen million (the world's second largest metropolitan area after New York) with a growth rate of 5 percent per year. Infant mortality had increased to 56 per thousand live births by 1978, according to Mexican government data given to the Inter-American Development Bank.[19] Although the average calories per capita potentially available in the country have increased, the shortage of food for the most needy groups has meant an increase in malnutrition. Likewise, the growth in overall GNP has been accompanied by a worsening in the income distribution. The growth of manufacturing industries has led to a balance of payments deficit due to the importation of intermediate and capital goods, and the dependence on foreign loans to finance growth has made Mexico, with Brazil, one of the greatest debtor nations in the world.

In its relations with the United States, Mexico has continued to be dependent in spite of the discovery of large quantities of oil and natural gas that promise to make Mexico a major energy producer. As Table 17.1 shows, nearly three-quarters (71 percent) of Mexico's trade is concentrated with one partner, the United States. The United States also provides a major labor market for millions of Mexico's unemployed. In its defense, Mexico has found oil. When the U.S. government vetoed a gas agreement reached by Mexico with some U.S. firms, Mexico switched its domestic industry to gas and will only sell the surplus. Before President Lopez Portillo met President Carter in Washington in the fall of 1979, a gas agreement was signed for the small residual amounts, at prices much higher than those which were vetoed the year before.

Internationally, oil will increase Mexico's bargaining power and will make it less likely that the "colossus of the north" will simply ignore its southern neighbor as it so often has done in the past. Domestically, the income from oil will buy some time. But it will also raise the expectations of those who travel the new roads to the oil fields. If oil contributes to growth but not equity, if Mexico continues to be the country of inequality, as it was in the days of great silver wealth, then the half-century-old stability of the Mexican system may find its future elsewhere than in the peace of one-party politics.

Several outcomes are possible. The changes in the rules for political participation resulting in the legalization of new parties may result in a more pluralistic, multiparty system with legitimate channels for real participation by greater numbers of people. However, these reforms are more likely to consolidate the existing system than to transform it. On the other hand, the tensions produced by growth without improved income distribution may result in popular unrest and a consequent increase in repression on the part of the armed forces. The army in Mexico lost influence after the 1920s and 1930s in terms of budgets and official positions held by military officers. However, their budget has been increased in recent years as has their autonomy. If the young officers trained at the new Colegio Militar in the south of Mexico City should decide that they are more qualified to maintain internal order than the civilian political leaders provided for under the constitution, Mexico may see, within the next ten years, military intervention or increased military participation in decision making. With the tensions produced by Mexico's new oil wealth, it is unlikely that the present system

[19]Inter-American Development Bank, *Economic and Social Progress in Latin America, 1978* (Washington, D.C.: Inter-American Development Bank, 1978), p. 322.

will be able to continue without structural and institutional changes.

BRAZIL: THE "LAND OF THE FUTURE" UNDER MILITARY RULE

Brazil is a large country by any standard, and its rapid rate of growth in recent years led Brazil to be held up as a model of development for poor countries. Brazil ranks fifth in the world in area; it occupies half of the continent of South America, includes every extreme of climate, and is larger than the continental United States excluding Alaska. In population Brazil ranks sixth in the world, with over 115 million people, and growing at 2.8 percent per year. In total gross domestic product (GDP) Brazil ranks ninth among the countries of the world. Yet, because of the uneven pattern of growth and the concentration of wealth, Brazil is still an underdeveloped country: it ranks only forty-third (in 1976) when its national production is ranked on a per capita basis.[20]

The rapid growth and capital accumulation that have taken place in Brazil have been termed "the Brazilian miracle." The country's GDP grew at 4.8 percent per year from 1960 to 1976 (see Table 17.1). However, this figure hides the fact that from 1967 to 1973 Brazil grew at 10.3 percent annually, one of the highest rates in the world and has grown more slowly since then. The absolute level of production achieved by the country from the days of the colony until 1967 was doubled in less than ten years. This growth was a success story for only some Brazilians, however; much of Brazil was left behind. The modern steel and glass architecture in the new inland capital of Brasilia and the huge agro-industrial projects in the Amazon basin contrast sharply with both poverty and malnutrition in the northeast of Brazil and squalor in the *favelas* (shantytowns) of Rio de Janeiro and São Paulo.

[20]Figure 6.8 on page 141 shows the intersection of the world's most populous countries with the world's richest countries. Although not one of the five major "superpowers," by 1979 Brazil would have moved into that "big power" intersection.

Early History of Brazil. Brazil was discovered in 1500 by the Portuguese explorer Pedro Cabral, who was looking for India. Yet strangely enough, it belonged to Portugal, through an agreement with Spain, even before the South American continent was discovered! In that agreement, the "Tordesillas Line" was drawn 370 leagues west of the Cape Verde Islands, with Portugal owning anything discovered east of that division. Brazil was further explored by Amerigo Vespucci in 1501–02 during his second voyage to the New World. At that time, perhaps a million Indians, broken into small and dispersed tribes, were scattered throughout the huge territory. In the early years, Brazil's chief export was brazilwood, though later gold and diamonds were discovered and sugar, cotton, and coffee became primary export commodities.

Other colonial powers did not concede the huge colony to Portugal without a struggle. Portugal had to fight with the Dutch and the French as well as the English to establish clear dominion over the territory. The French established missions along the Amazon River in the seventeenth century and the British attacked coastal towns. The Dutch, with their Dutch West Indies Company, were perhaps the most aggressive contenders. It was not until 1654 that the Portuguese defeated them, signing a peace treaty in 1661.

Slavery was introduced early into Brazil and raiding parties from São Paulo explored the interior of the colony in search of slaves. Black slaves from Africa, eventually numbering in the millions, were also imported. Sugar plantations using slave labor predominated on the vast landholdings in the seventeenth and eighteenth centuries; Brazil was a sugar economy.

Both the Portuguese and the Africans who came to Brazil were for the most part single men. The absence of immigrant women ensured that the Brazilian population was from the beginning a thorough mixture of races. Early in the twentieth century the sociologist Gilberto Freyre popularized the importance of the mixture of three races—Indian, European, and African—in his book, *The Masters and the Slaves.* These men of mixed blood were the principal adventurers *(bandeirantes)* who pushed the Brazilian frontier westward, especially after 1650.

The most unique aspect of Brazilian history is its constitution as a monarchy. It was the only colony in the Americas to preserve the institution of monarchy after separating from the mother country. With the colonial reforms of the Portuguese minister Pombal after 1750 and in spite of an unsuccessful revolutionary attempt by the nationalist Tiradentes (Joaquim José da Silva Xavier—"the toothpuller") in 1789, Brazil remained close to the parent country. When Napoleon set out to invade Portugal in 1809, Prince João (John) fled to Brazil and established the Portuguese monarchy at Rio de Janeiro.

By that time, Brazil had a population of approximately three million, already larger than that of Portugal. In the new monarchy, Prince João issued decrees encouraging trade, banking, agriculture, and industry. He also encouraged the expansion of Brazil north to French Guyana and south toward Rio de la Plata. At a time when Spanish America was shaken by wars of independence, Brazil was ruled by a foreign monarch. No violent break with the past marked Brazil's birth as a nation.

In 1822, Prince João returned to Portugal and left the government of Brazil in the hands of his son, Dom Pedro. The Portuguese *cortes* attempted to control Brazil once again from the mother country, but in 1822 Dom Pedro, with the support of the Brazilians, issued a declaration called the *Grito de Ypiranga* (Cry of Ypiranga), proclaiming the independence of Brazil. Dom Pedro became the constitutional emperor of the new monarchy, reigning as Pedro the First. For a number of years, politics in Brazil was unsettled, with provincial revolts and warfare between Brazil and Argentina (resulting in 1828 in the independence of Uruguay). In 1840, Pedro's fourteen-year-old son came to power as Pedro II. Throughout his rule, until 1889, Brazil continued to develop rapidly. Railroads were built, coffee production grew in importance as well as sugar production, and rubber was introduced in the Amazon. Britain replaced Portugal in the nineteenth century as the major sea power, and as Brazil's principal trading partner. Brazilian coffee and other exports paid for British manufactures imported to Brazil.

Brazil expanded to the west and the southwest, joining in a Triple Alliance with her old enemies Argentina and Uruguay in a five-year war against Paraguay from 1865 to 1870. Given its size, perhaps the most amazing thing about Brazil is that it was able to remain unified as a single country. Unlike the Spanish-American countries, Brazil was concerned not with loss of territory or foreign domination, but with the expansion and consolidation of its own rule. The experience as a monarchy during most of the nineteenth century also established a long tradition of powerful executive rule handling all the functions of government.

Between 1870 and 1890, while coffee production for export grew, the abolition of slavery proceeded by stages. Since slavery did not provide enough workers for the coffee plantations, it was hoped that free labor would meet the demand for workers. In 1871, all children born to slaves were declared free. In 1885, slaves attained their freedom at the age of sixty-five. Finally in 1888, the so-called Golden Law abolished slavery for good. Though agriculture, mining, industry, and trade continued to expand rapidly, the dependence on coffee and rubber markets abroad led to economic instability and frequent overproduction.

During the same period, republicanism began to grow and the Republican party was formed in 1870. By 1889, the army overthrew the emperor and declared a republic. Political inexperience and economic pressures led to frequent turnover among the presidents of the new republic, with the changeover often at the instigation of the army. Nevertheless, some reforms were adopted. Church and state were separated at least nominally, and in 1891 a constitution was adopted. The rebellious province on Rio Grande do Sul, having rebelled in 1891, revolted for the second time in 1893–95. But the government of the republic was able to keep the nation together, in spite of regional competition and political rivalries. Economic growth continued, and with the disruption of world trade by World War I, Brazil began to develop a domestic industry based on a strategy of import substitution.

In 1930 Getulio Vargas, then governor of Rio Grande do Sul, led a swift and successful revolution and came to power. With the populist support of workers and with urban interests opposed to the landed oligarchy, Vargas was able to control a populist state in Brazil from 1930 to 1945. In 1934, a new constitution increased the centralization of the government and reduced regional conflicts. Vargas was elected president under the constitution.

In 1937, Vargas proclaimed a new constitution giving himself dictatorial powers over the organization of the society and the economy. Labeling this new regime the *Estado Novo* (New State), Vargas instituted an elitist and paternalistic government, which set the pattern for Brazilian politics in the modern period. Participation by workers and peasants was carefully controlled by the state. The Estado Novo was based on the support of the military, the collaboration of business, the legitimacy of the Catholic Church, and the control of the people.

During the thirties, both the Communist party and the Fascist middle-class movement (the *Integralistas*) grew in power. But although Brazilian politics had some elements in common with the European totalitarian regimes, Brazil entered World War II on the side of the Allies. Brazil, in fact, was the only Latin American country to send ground troops to Europe. The close coordination of the United States and Brazilian militaries and the intense group experience of the officers in the Brazilian Expeditionary Force (FEB) were formative elements in the attitudes of the military men who would later take power in 1964.

In 1945, Vargas was forced to resign and War Minister General Enrico Dutra was elected president, as head of the Social Democratic party. Yet another constitution was drawn up and when elections were again held in 1950, Getulio Vargas was once again elected, this time on a platform of populist and democratic social reforms. Four years later, in August 1954, Vargas was forced to resign. Defeated and threatened by the armed forces, he took his own life. Since his death, he has become a national hero; the main thoroughfare in Rio de Janeiro bears his name.

After Vargas came a period of constitutional democracy in which many parties contended in reasonably honest elections. In 1955, Juscelino Kubitschek won the presidency with João Goulart as his vice-president. They took office in 1956 and ruled for five years, during which time the capital of the country was moved in 1960 to the new city of Brasilia in the interior of the country. The next president, Jânio da Silva Quadros, came to power in 1961, but resigned after less than seven months, saying that he could not accomplish the reforms necessary for the country. João Goulart, also vice president to Quadros, succeeded to the presidency, despite the opposition of the Brazilian military. From 1962 to 1964, Goulart instituted a massive distribution of federal lands to the peasantry, responded to workers' demands, nationalized basic industries, and expropriated private landholdings. But "Jango," as Goulart was called, was a weak president. Inflation ran rampant, and the Brazilian military (as well as many United States officials) feared an even greater shift to the left. In April 1964, while Goulart was out of the country, the presidency was declared vacant and the military took power.

The military immediately repressed the Left, and especially the Communists. In 1965, General Castello Branco assumed dictatorial powers as the head of the military government. In a series of "Institutional Acts," the military, with the support of the United States, the Church, and the owners of land and property, moved to institutionalize their rule. Under the constitution of 1967 and especially the Fifth Institutional Act of 1968, the military gave the president extensive powers to declare a state of siege, to remove officials from office, and to suspend political freedoms.

The Stakes of Politics in Brazil. Just as Brazil is a big country, the stakes of its politics loom large as well. The political process in the coming years will determine who rules, what kind of development will take place, who will benefit from that development, and what growth will mean for the country. Because of Brazil's importance in the region, and increasingly in the world, these stakes matter not only to Brazilians but to neighbors and international allies as well.

The first question raised by politics in Brazil is whether the military government that has ruled since 1964 will continue in power, or whether civilian participation in running the country will increase. Unlike the traditional pattern of military intervention in Latin America, the military in Brazil has every appearance of being in power to stay. After fifteen years, a regular rotation in the presidency has evolved and a carefully controlled party system has been developed to legitimate the military rule. For most of their rule, the military has effectively controlled workers, labor, peasants, students, and even the private sector. It will be important to see whether the limited liberalization seen in 1979 will result in greater real participation in government or, rather, merely an improved stability for the military regime.

Although Brazil continues to depend on international capital and the international system for its development, there is no disputing the fact that it has developed. At stake in the future is the kind of development and its direction: whether development will be capital-intensive, benefiting large corporations owned by multinationals, large private firms, and state enterprises competing on the world markets and benefiting from cheap labor in Brazil, or whether development will include the poor and unemployed marginal people left out at present.

Who controls the economy may depend on the power of the state, and particularly of state-owned enterprises, relative to the power of national, private capital—sometimes called the "national bourgoisie"—and of transnational corporations, often from the United States.[21] At stake for the mass of the population is whether they will participate in (and benefit from) the growth of the economy that has so distinguished Brazil from its Third World neighbors. Evidence is clear that the present pattern of economic growth is increasing inequality.

Political decisions will influence the national and international implications of economic growth and development for Brazil. Will Brazil become less dependent on foreign capital, foreign markets, and foreign firms or will it increase its dependence on these external factors? Significant regional disparities exist between the industrialized cities and regions in the south, the large, barely explored tracts of jungle in the Amazon, and the rural poverty in the northeast. Will these contrasts be exacerbated or improved with development?

Finally, how will the present developmental model and the present political system affect Brazil's future role in the world? Will Brazil become a world power? Will the development of nuclear energy be confined to peaceful purposes or will Brazil try to join the superpowers armed with nuclear weapons? Will Brazil expand its influence in South America? Will it become involved in the politics of Portuguese-speaking Africa? Or will it turn inward and find its challenges in developing its own people and resources, building on that strength to become a self-confident and powerful nation?

The Participants in Brazilian Politics. Who participates in politics in Brazil? We may start the list

[21]Peter Evans has studied who controls the economy and how in *Dependent Development: The Alliance of Multinational, State, and Local Capital in Brazil* (Princeton: Princeton University Press, 1979).

with those who rule the country—the military and the technocrats who support them—followed by those who run the ever-growing number of state-owned enterprises. (Some call these state managers the "state bourgoisie.") We should also consider industrialists and large landowners as well as workers, peasants, and marginals. The Catholic Church is also a political force that cannot be overlooked in today's Brazil.

The military clearly holds the controlling positions in government. Since 1964, they have permanently assumed responsibility for the political direction of the country, as opposed to their earlier pattern of merely handling the transitions between alternating civilian governments. By the 1960s, the Brazilian military had accepted many aspects of U.S. military training, particularly the importance of maintaining internal security—that is, security from threats to public order originating inside the nation rather than coming from a foreign country. The logical consequence of this new mission, as Alfred Stepan has argued, was a new professionalism that led to the military's remaining in power rather than alternating with civilian rule.[22] A generation of military officers, who shared fighting experience in Europe during World War II and had close ties to the United States military, studied together at the Higher War College, and forged a new military ideology that distinguished the 1964 coup from earlier military coups in Brazilian history. Once in power, the military ended political parties and relied on technocrats, rather than on civilian politicians, to accomplish the business of government.

The military has agreed that economic growth is a primary goal of the regime. Thus, the managers of large enterprises, be they multinational, national, or state-owned, stand to benefit from the military rule. Even though businesspeople, too, are organized in state-promoted, corporate representative bodies, their influence is much greater than that of workers or peasants. Both large landowners and industrial elites are able to organize separate pressure groups outside the formal state-authorized groups and are thus able to exercise a leverage that is not allowed workers and peasants.

The workers and peasants are restricted to the organizations set up by the state in their name; they are repressed if they attempt to go outside those organizations. The workers, organized in official unions, or *sindicatos,* are controlled by leaders screened by both the government and the police. Collective bargaining and the right to strike—two tools fundamental to the defense of labor interests—have been severely limited in Brazil. Similarly, peasants are greatly constrained in what they can do to lobby for their interests.

The Church in Brazil is historically linked to the government in an organic way that is rare in Latin America. The state allows it to perform certain roles in society, such as education, which the state subsidizes. As an institution, the Church has been primarily a conservative force, legitimatizing the government. Although the Church has provided refuge against the worst abuses of military repression and protected some of its victims, still it has accepted an alliance with the military in its own institutional interests. Its ability to protest has been limited, hence it has implicitly supported the government.

Political parties in Brazil today are very different from other parties we may know. The military power has its own party known as Arena *(Aliança Renovadora Nacional).* There is also an officially authorized opposition party, Movimento Democratica Brasileiro (MDB). According to one Brazilian, one party says "yes" to the government, while the other says "yes, sir." More recently,

[22]These arguments are elaborated in Alfred Stepan, "The New Professionalism of Internal Warfare and Military Role Expansion," in Alfred Stepan (ed.), *Authoritarian Brazil: Origins, Policies, and Future* (New Haven: Yale University Press, 1973), pp. 47–65. See also his more complete study, *The Military in Politics: Changing Patterns in Brazil* (Princeton, N.J.: Princeton University Press, 1971).

however, the MDB has become associated with some degree of genuine opposition.

Despite the existence of opposition, the structure of representation is such that in the 1978 election, out of twenty-three Senate seats open to direct election, the opposition MDB was awarded only eight senate seats, though it won 46.8 percent of the vote. Arena, on the other hand, received 34.7 percent of the vote, yet received fifteen seats, plus twenty-one out of twenty-two seats in the senate allocated by an electoral college rather than by direct vote! Thus, with 35 percent of the direct vote in 1978, the party in power, Arena, received 80 percent of the senate seats.

Images of Brazil. Brazil has long seen itself as an important and aggressive world actor. This was strikingly demonstrated in June 1926, when the country withdrew from the League of Nations after failing to obtain a seat on the Permanent Council. When the United States refused to sell nuclear technology in the 1970s, Brazil reached an agreement with West Germany. Brazil maintains a large army with military expenditures reaching approximately 9.4 percent of the federal budget. It has moved into the direct manufacture of conventional arms and military supplies, and increasingly sells military equipment abroad.

Brazilian society sees itself as an integrated society. The image that most Brazilians, black and white, hold of their country is of a nonprejudiced society. Unlike the situation in the United States, there is not a sharp boundary between black and white in Brazil. Most whites believe that they have no prejudice and that any dark-skinned Brazilians in a lower economic or social position are there because of some personal, rather than social, handicap. Many blacks also accept that view, so that they may underestimate their own real potential. But even these blacks hope for greater opportunities for their children. They tend to support a more open society and increased pluralization of the political system. More recently, some Brazilian blacks have begun to champion Afro-Brazilian culture, paralleling the "black power" movement in the United States.

Politically, the most common image of Brazil held by social scientists is that of a corporatist state. Though it may sound like it, *corporatism* does not refer to modern corporations. Rather, it refers to the organization of society along functional lines, that is, by industries or occupations, with employers and employees organized separately within each. The corporatist sees society as a unit, with workers, peasants, the Church, businesspeople, students organized as functional parts much as legs, arms, head, and heart function in a human body. This all-encompassing, holistic, and nonconflicting vision of society is an alternative to individualistic, liberal views as well as to Marxist views based on class conflict. Whereas the liberal and the Marxist see the state as acting in response to interest groups or dominant classes, the corporatist subordinates interest groups as well as class-based organizations to the state.

In this unifying view, then, the state has considerable autonomy in dealing with private groups and classes in the society. More than that, the state actually organizes and controls the organizations and groups through which functional groups may participate. Thus, the state controls and authorizes labor unions, peasant federations, and workers' associations. Likewise, the state has a special relationship with the Roman Catholic Church, within whose traditions the corporatist ideal was developed. Given both the paternalistic authority found in Brazilian society since it was a colony, and the strong influence of the Catholic Church, integrated with the state more in Brazil than elsewhere in Latin America, the corporatist image for a time seemed realistic to many Brazilians. In practice, corporatist notions in Brazil have tended to discourage major reforms and to limit the pursuit of separate interests, particularly by disadvantaged groups and classes.

Another image of politics in Brazil was coined by the Argentine scholar, Guillermo O'Donnell: the "bureaucratic-authoritarian" state. In a bureaucratic-authoritarian regime, high levels of popular mobilization combine with import-substitution industrialization (the replacement of imports with locally manufactured goods) and a structural economic crisis follows. That crisis encourages the replacement of civilian political authority with military technical and bureaucratic authority.

In 1964, several factors combined with import-substitution industrialization to precipitate a military coup in Brazil: a rapid rise in popular political participation in the 1950s and early 1960s; the threat of large-scale land reform, which implied weakening economic and political power among the landed elites; an increase in class-based organizations; and violent political activity, which threatened the military's monopoly on force. Perhaps a structural crisis of the economy stimulated political change, but it was political participation and class conflict that determined the rate and timing of the change. Once the military broke the previous pattern of civilian rule and mass political participation, the state took control of popular organizations. The technocratic elites (sometimes called a "technocracy")—those whose jobs involve modern technology—exercise power.

These four images of Brazil all represent aspects of current Brazilian reality. Brazil is a powerful nation aspiring to be a major actor in the world. It has succeeded in bringing together citizens of different racial and ethnic backgrounds. The state is organized along corporatist lines; that is, it directs and controls organizations for different functional groups in the society. Its character may be described as bureaucratic-authoritarian: A repressive, controlled authoritarian regime is governed by a bureaucratic, technocratic group of rulers, rather than by a single, charismatic leader or a democratic plurality.

Brazil: The Arena of Politics. The enormous size of Brazil has already been pointed out: 8.5 million square kilometers and a population estimated to grow to 200 million by the year 2000. In contrast to many developing countries, there have been no successful challenges to Brazilian sovereignty. Rather, Brazil responded to such challenges in the eighteenth and nineteenth centuries by expanding. Such has been the force of Brazilian expansion that some countries worry about being overwhelmed by their giant neighbor. Brazil directly borders every country in South America except Chile and Ecuador. As Brazil's regional trade and investment expands, especially with Paraguay, Uruguay, and Bolivia, some critics suggest that Brazil is becoming a "subimperialist" power. It is clear that Brazil is likely to become involved in any regional disputes that may occur. For example, Brazil has an interest in a Bolivian outlet to the sea, since Brazil could indirectly benefit. The recent development of the world's largest hydroelectric plant on the Paraná River may affect the flow of the river and bring Brazil into conflict with Argentina. As a regional power, Brazil may increase or decrease conflict. It was reported by some observers that recent tensions between Argentina and Chile were moderated because of the possibility that greater conflict would bring Brazilian involvement.

Still, the internal frontier poses more immediate problems for Brazil. First, the government must incorporate the Indians of the interior into national life without eliminating them. Second, it must meet the sheer physical challenge of conquering and cultivating for human use the enormous potential of the Amazon basin. Whether this area is developed by nationals, by the state, or by foreigners will influence the future political arena. Daniel Ludwig, one of the richest men in the United States, has begun to operate a million-acre farm for growing selected hardwoods in the Amazon region. Likewise, foreign mining firms have been allowed to exploit and develop untapped mineral resources.[23] This reliance on, or partnership, with foreign capital and technology is sure to

[23]There is a serious danger that this type of industrial development will disrupt the fragile ecology of the Amazon, which is still only partially understood. See H. O'Reilly Steinberg, "Development and Conservation," in Karl W. Deutsch, ed., *Ecosocial Systems and Ecopolitics* (Paris: UNESCO, 1977), pp. 337–358.

speed the development of those resources, but if control of those resources passes outside the country, the political arena will be narrowed.

The Process of Politics and the State Machinery in Brazil. As described in the section on participation in Brazilian politics, the political system in Brazil is tightly controlled from the top by military leaders. There are strict controls on the press and on the opposition. Even when these are slightly relaxed, discussion is only allowed within clear limits. Fundamental criticisms of the leaders and of the system, although tolerated in private, are not allowed in the mass media. A government council supervises all radio and television broadcasting. The partial opening has provided the military with improved feedback on sources of popular discontent and possible sources of opposition without allowing that opposition any increase in power or participation in political decision making. Thus, the military remains the group that steers the country. The rest of the society follows its lead.

This mobilized society, led by the military, is very efficient at accomplishing some tasks, particularly the organization and direction needed for rapid economic growth. It is growth that provides the only legitimacy for the regime in power. Opposition to the regime is controlled and, when necessary, repressed.

Although there is no pretense that the president of Brazil is popularly elected, the military has succeeded in finding a formula for regular succession to the presidency. The first four military presidents were officially elected by the Congress. The first president, General Humberto Castello Branco, was replaced in 1967 by Marshal Artur de Costa e Silva. When he was taken ill, Congress selected General Emílio Garrastazu Médici, who ruled until General Ernesto Geisel took office in 1974 for a five-year term. According to the procedure in effect at present, the president is selected by an "electoral college" of municipal councillors for a six-year term. The first president selected under these rules was General João Baptista Figueiredo, who took office in March of 1979. Presidents cannot immediately succeed themselves in office.

The Senate and the Chamber of Deputies were directly elected (by literate voters over the age of 18) until 1977, when the election for one-third of the Senate was to be selected by the electoral college. The allocation of seats for deputies is by total population, not number of voters. Rural areas with large populations but few voters usually favor the government candidates. Because of restrictions, about 40 percent of the adult population is ineligible to vote. The military has devised a system acceptable to its own members. But by manipulation of electoral rules, restrictions on political parties, and control of the press, radio, and television, the degree of real competition in Brazilian politics is most limited.

However, tensions are building. The image of the military as capable of accomplishing any economic feat is made questionable by a rising inflation rate, and corruption and scandals within the military likewise tarnish their technocratic image. Competition from state-owned enterprises run by the military has weakened the support of private businessmen for military rule. The Catholic Church, in response to the repression of the people, has organized grassroots movements with the leadership of Bishop Dom Heldar Camara. The unions, in spite of controls by the government, have re-emerged as significant pressure groups, with a number of strikes in 1978 and 1979, particularly in the crucial automobile industry.

In 1979, in a much discussed *Abertura* (democratic opening), several political leaders from the days before the 1964 coup were allowed to return to the country, most notably Leonel Brizola and Miguel Arraes, both former leaders of the opposition parties. Although it is unlikely that the Communist party will be allowed to function openly, the Labor party (Partido Trabalhista Brasileiro) may be allowed to function under Brizola's lead. Similarly since the *Abertura,* some strike activity has been permitted. But as the 1978 election shows, even if this opening absorbs organizational energy and provides a safety valve for some discontent, it is not likely to result in any truly open competition among political parties in Brazil.

Performance of the Political System. The inequality of Brazilian society shows both in the high figures of the Gini index of inequality and, even more dramatically, in the figures of infant mortality, which reflect the welfare of the poorer segments of society. The figures indicate that ninety to one hundred infants per thousand live births die in their first year. The contrasts and the similarities between Brazil and Cuba are striking. In Brazil, the military has taken power, encouraged high rates of economic growth and reconcentration of wealth, and maintained levels of poverty for large groups of the population. Dissidents have been repressed with violence. In Cuba, with a centrally planned economy, the state has mobilized to gain support for the regime through policies of distribution rather than policies of growth. Cuban society, then, is much more equal than Brazilian society and health and welfare standards are higher, but Brazil has been able to grow much more rapidly than Cuba.

The Brazilian regime has done best in mobilizing the society for high rates of economic growth, rather than in protecting human lives. They have attracted foreign investment through transnational corporations and have enabled the country to qualify for high rates of foreign lending. With a 1978 foreign debt of 42 billion dollars, Brazil is the developing country with the highest level of absolute foreign indebtedness. The success of its controls and austerity, as well as repression, in maintaining political tranquillity depends on a high level of economic growth. At the very high levels of growth that Brazil has been able to achieve, some "trickle-down" improves the standard of living for much of the population, even if their relative share of total income has declined. Were this growth to slow or to halt and the well-being of workers, middle-class employees, and marginal people to deteriorate, the stability of the regime would be called into question. The military would be likely to return to more repression, which characterized its earlier years.

Brazil has been quite successful in achieving national unity, but it remains to be seen whether the alliance of national, state and foreign capital will be successful in such ambitious projects as developing the Amazon region. It also remains to be seen whether Brazil will assume a position of leadership in Latin America or in Africa based on its economic successes. There are indications that the Brazilian government will continue to resist complete dependence on the United States and will try to diversify its trading partners and political allies. But the huge foreign debt requires both more capital from abroad and more access to foreign markets. Payments on the foreign debt in 1978 were equivalent to two-thirds of Brazil's export earnings. It seems likely that Brazil will continue to pursue a high-growth strategy, allying state capital with foreign firms. Likely also is that Brazil's poor will continue to suffer and will only benefit when some of the new wealth happens to trickle down their way.

The Hopes for "Decompression". During the second half of the 1970s, an increasing number of Brazilians, including some thoughtful members of the military, sought ways to bring about a "decompression" of the Brazilian political system. By this they meant a relaxation of repression and political controls, and more freedom for political parties, the press, and various interest groups, including labor unions. How to achieve this without precipitating civil strife and frightening away the foreign capital required for the success of the "Brazilian model of development" has so far been unresolved. Labor unions have increasingly exercised their right to strike, led by the automobile workers in São Paulo, in spite of the removal from office of the more militant labor leaders by the government. Some small steps towards liberalization have been taken under Presidents Ernest Geisel and João Baptista Figueiredo; under the 1979 amnesty even the communist Carlos Luís Prestes was allowed to return from his exile in Moscow. The political *abertura* will probably be limited and controlled. But popular pressure, and the electoral strength of the opposition in the MDB, argue for decompression. The examples of peaceful exits from dictatorships in Portugal, Spain, and Greece may encourage Brazil's military rulers to risk some further cautious steps in that direction.

KEY TERMS AND CONCEPTS

Cuba:

Pearl of the Antilles
sugar monoculture
conquistadores
the ever faithful isle
"Spanish American War"
Platt Amendment
Fulgencio Batista
26th of July Movement
yacht *Granma*
Bay of Pigs invasion
Cuban Missile Crisis
the United States blockade
trade embargo
society of scarcity
Cuban troops in Africa
Committees for the Defense of the Revolution (CDRs)
Communist party of Cuba
Ernesto (Ché) Guevara
Non-Aligned Movement
Cuban community abroad
U.S. naval base at Guantánamo Bay
Fidel Castro and Raúl Castro
the socialist constitution of 1976
institutionalization of the revolution
"History Will Absolve Me"

Mexico:

Aztecs (*Méxica* Indians)
Nahuatl language
colonialism
mestizo
creole
liberal reforms of Benito Juárez
Colossus of the North
"Effective Suffrage, No Re-Election"
PRI (Institutional Revolutionary Party)
Lázaro Cárdenas
land reform
1938 oil expropriation
PEMEX *(Petroleos Mexicanos)*
population pyramid
mordida
peonage
Cristero revolt
Mexican American War of 1848
Luís Echeverría Alvarez (1970–76)
José Lopez Portillo (1976–82)
haciendas

Brazil:

regional power
the Brazilian Empire
corporatism
dependent development
Estado Novo
sindicatos
bandeirantes
bureaucratic-authoritarianism
"moderator model" of the Brazilian military (pre-1964)
national, transnational, and state-owned firms
ARENA and MDB (national political parties)
technocrats, technocracy
infant mortality
"trickle-down" improvement of standard of living
Brazilian model of development
capital accumulation; growth versus equity
import-substitution industrialization
decompression

ADDITIONAL READINGS

Cuba:

Bonachea, R. E. and P. V. Nelson, eds. *Cuba in Revolution.* New York: Doubleday, 1972. PB

Castro, F. *Fidel Castro Speaks.* Edited by M. Kenner and J. Petras. New York: Grove Press, 1970. PB

Dominguez, J. I. *Cuba: Order and Revolution.* Cambridge: Harvard University Press, 1978.

Fagen, R. *The Transformation of Political Culture in Cuba.* Stanford: Stanford University Press, 1969.

González, E. *Cuba Under Castro: The Limits of Charisma.* Boston: Houghton Mifflin, 1974. PB

Goodseel, J. N., ed. *Fidel Castro's Personal Revolution in Cuba: 1959–1973.* New York: Knopf, 1975. PB

Knight, F. W. *Slave Society in Cuba during the Nineteenth Century.* Madison: University of Wisconsin Press, 1970. PB

Mesa, L. C. *Cuba in the 1970s: Pragmatism and Institutionalization.* Albuquerque: University of New Mexico Press, 1974. PB

O'Connor, J. *The Origins of Socialism in Cuba.* Ithaca, N.Y.: Cornell University Press, 1970.

Thomas, H. *The Cuban Revolution.* New York: Harper & Row, 1977. PB

Zeitlin, M. *Revolutionary Politics and the Cuban Working Class.* New York: Harper & Row, 1970. PB

Mexico:

Almond, G. A. and S. Verba. *The Civic Culture: Political Attitudes and Democracy in Five Nations.* Boston: Little Brown, 1965.

Baird, P. and E. McCaughan. *Beyond the Border: Mexico and the U.S. Today.* New York: North American Congress on Latin America, 1979.

Bazant, J. *A Concise History of Mexico from Hidalgo to Cárdenas, 1805–1940.* New York: Cambridge University Press, 1977.

Brandenburg, F. R. *The Making of Modern Mexico.* Englewood Cliffs, N.J.: Prentice-Hall, 1964.

Brenner, A. *The Wind that Swept Mexico.* New York: Harper & Row, 1943.

Cline, H. F. *The United States and Mexico.* Rev. ed. Cambridge: Harvard University Press, 1967.

Cosia Cillegas, D. et al. *A Compact History of Mexico.* Trans. M. M. Urquidi. Mexico: El Colegio de Mexico, 1974.

Eckstein, S. *The Poverty of Revolution: The State and the Urban Poor in Mexico.* Princeton, N.J.: Princeton University Press, 1977.

Gonzalez Cassanova, P. *Democracy in Mexico.* Trans. D. Salti. New York: Oxford University Press, 1970.

Grindle, M. S. *Bureaucrats, Politicians, and Peasants in Mexico: A Case Study in Public Polity.* Berkeley: University of California Press, 1977.

Hansen, R. D. *The Politics of Mexican Development.* Baltimore: Johns Hopkins University Press, 1971.

Helman, J. A. *Mexico in Crisis.* New York: Holmes and Meier, 1978.

Herring, H. *A History of Latin America from the Beginnings to the Present,* 3d ed. New York: Knopf, 1968.

Lewis, O. *Five Families: Mexican Case Studies in the Culture of Poverty.* New York: Basic Books, 1959.

Lynch, J. *The Spanish American Revolutions, 1808–1826.* New York: Norton, 1973.

Meyer, L. *Mexico and the United States in the Oil Controversy, 1917–1942.* Trans. M. Vasconcellos. Austin: University of Texas Press, 1977.

Meyer, M. C. and W. L. Sherman. *The Course of Mexican History.* New York: Oxford University Press, 1979.

Padgett, L. V. *The Mexican Political System,* 2d ed. Boston: Houghton Mifflin, 1976.

Reyna, J. L. and R. S. Weinert, eds. *Authoritarianism in Mexico.* Philadelphia: ISHI, 1977.

Smith, P. H. *Labyrinths of Power—Political Recruitment in Twentieth Century Mexico.* Princeton: Princeton University Press, 1979.

Stevens, E. P. *Protest and Response in Mexico.* Cambridge: MIT Press, 1974.

Wolf, E. *Sons of the Shaking Earth: The People of Mexico and Guatemala Their Land, History, and Culture.* Chicago: University of Chicago Press, 1959.

Womack, J. *Zapata and the Mexican Revolution.* New York: Vintage Books, 1968.

Brazil:

Burns, E. B. *A History of Brazil.* New York: Columbia University Press, 1970.

Davis, S. H. *Victims of the Miracle: Development and the Indians of Brazil.* New York: Cambridge University Press, 1977.

Della Cava, R. "Catholicism and Society in Twentieth-Century Brazil." *Latin American Research Review,* 9, No. 1 (1976), 7–50.

Erickson, K. P. *The Brazilian Corporative State and Working-Class Politics.* Berkeley: University of California Press, 1977.

———. "Brazil: Corporatism in Theory and Practice." In *Latin American Politics and Development,* edited by H. J. Wianda and H. F. Kline. Boston: Houghton Mifflin, 1979, 144–181.

Evans, P. *Dependent Development: The Alliance of Multinational, State, and Local Capital in Brazil.* Princeton: Princeton University Press, 1979.

Haring, C. H. *Empire in Brazil: A New World Experiment with Monarchy.* Cambridge: Harvard University Press, 1958. PB

Mericle, K. S. "Corporatist Control of the Working Class: Authoritarian Brazil Since 1964." In *Authoritarianism and Corporatism in Latin America,* edited by J. M. Malloy. Pittsburgh: University of Pittsburgh Press, 1977.

Mendonca de Barros, J. R. and D. H. Graham. "The Brazilian Economic Miracle Revisited: Private and Public Sector Initiative in a Market Economy." *Latin American Research Review* 13, No. 2 (1978), 5–37.

Jaquaribe, H. *Economic and Political Development: A Theoretical Approach and a Brazilian Case Study.* Cambridge: Harvard University Press, 1968.

Leff, N. H. *Economic Policy-Making and Development in Brazil, 1947–1964.* New York: Wiley, 1968.

Robock, S. H. *Brazil: A Study in Development Progress.* Lexington, Mass.: D.C. Heath, 1975.

Roett, R., ed. *Brazil in the Seventies.* Washington, D.C.: American Enterprise Institute for Public Policy Research, 1976.

Schmitter, P. C. *Interest Conflict and Political Change in Brazil.* Stanford: Stanford University Press, 1971.

Skidmore, T. E. *Politics in Brazil, 1930–1964: An Experiment in Democracy.* New York: Oxford University Press, 1967.

Stepan, A., ed. *Authoritarian Brazil: Origins, Policies, and Future.* New Haven: Yale University Press, 1973.

———. *The Military in Politics: Changing Patterns in Brazil.* Princeton, N. J.: Princeton University Press.

PB = *available in paperback*

PART III

TODAY AND TOMORROW

XX

The Unfinished Business of Politics

During World War II the story was told of an American business executive who said that he would work as hard as possible to end the war and then would shoot himself in order not to have to live in the postwar world. He was by no means the last person to be afraid of the future.

Explicit efforts by writers to imagine the future have produced some outstanding nightmares. Aldous Huxley's *Brave New World* suggested a world in which people were produced artificially in chemical solutions and "decanted" from assembly lines. Later they were taught in their sleep to repeat endlessly basic indoctrination and to retain a sense of class snobbery. They swore by the name of Ford and the secret sign of the Model T and were encouraged to indulge every whim and desire, including the abundant use of sex and drugs, provided that they did not indulge any desire for freedom.

Another nightmare, even worse than Huxley's, was George Orwell's *1984*. In Orwell's world people lived in a totalitarian society in the midst of artificial squalor, dirtiness, and poverty. They were subjected to constant censorship and surveillance by their government and were indoctrinated by the state in daily "two-minute hate" exercises against a supposed national enemy with whom they were engaged in endless but inconclusive warfare. Orwell's book, like Huxley's, was exaggerated and yet to many postwar readers horribly believable, since it projected into the future some of the most menacing and unpleasant features of their own day and age.

When writers and politicians consciously tried to forecast the future in friendlier terms, their vision seemed a positive utopia. The postwar world, they predicted, was to be a world of peace, abundance, and steady progress within the confines of dependable law. People believed many of these hopes. A Soviet worker in 1936, in the first Moscow superdelicatessen, the Gastronome, was eyeing the various attractions and buying a small parcel. Asked whether he were in the habit of buying here, he laughed and replied, "Oh, no, I couldn't possibly afford it, but I come here once every month to buy something in order to get accustomed to the living standard that we'll enjoy in a few years." Over forty years have passed since then and even at best this workman is still waiting for some of the abundance which he had hoped for then.

The politics of the present, and perhaps of the years ahead, seems characterized by a feeling of great fear—a vague dread of impending major changes. (This is not only a modern phenomenon. The French peasants on the eve of the revolution experienced a similar "great fear.")

All of us are now living in that fearsome postwar world. Many of the readers of this book will have been born into it. At the same time they will have been born into a period in which familiar symbols of the past have taken on additional importance. In 1952, when the first hydrogen bombs were tested by the United States at Bikini in the Pacific, a fashion of coonskin caps swept the country. The homely garments which American pioneers had worn more than a hundred years earlier were worn by children, youngsters, and at least one presidential candidate. At a time when the energy of the sun was exploded on earth for the first time by human hands, people suddenly began reaching back to some familiar symbol of a safe, more stable, and more dependable past. This, too, was a kind of utopia.

Though the positive utopias have proven no more accurate or believable than the negative ones, there is another kind of utopia which may be the most unrealistic, indeed the most utopian, of all. That is the utopia that suggests that the world will stay as it is.

THE GREAT CURRENTS OF CHANGE

We know that the future will not resemble the fantasies of evil or abundance which people entertained in the last decades. But in many decisive ways it will be much different from the present. The changes the world has lived through in the last half-century have been gigantic and the changes to come in the next thirty years are almost certain to be larger still.

In the coming years perhaps the first need of a political system will be to preserve a sense of identity and continuity for its people. In growing up we undergo a great many changes but we can cope with each of them because of a sense of self, a sense of personality. That is to say, we have a sense of something within us that continues through every change we experience from infancy through adolescence to adulthood. Identity means the applicability of memories, both our own and those of others around us. When these memories no longer apply to us, our identity has changed. Something similar holds for groups, communities, and nations. Their members need a sense of identity, a sense of continuous growth, and a sense of belonging in order to face the dangers, the opportunities, and the tasks of reorientation which they will encounter.

In the future, the world will look very different from the way it used to. Many of the old landmarks—old governments, old institutions, old beliefs—will have disappeared. Since it was these landmarks toward which we oriented ourselves in the past, the future will impose a continuous task of reorientation. But the only landmark we will need to preserve will be our sense of who we are—our sense of identity as a group, as a people, and as a country.

For a long time the world will be inhabited by many stubbornly different peoples, each with its own culture, institutions, and social system. The Russians will remain Russians; the Americans, Americans; the Germans, Germans; and to the English, of course, there will always be an England. But someday there will come a decisive and ever-increasing orientation toward the values of humankind. It is possible that some future generation will paraphrase President John F. Kennedy's words and say, "Do not ask what mankind has done for your country, but ask what your country can do for mankind." To reach this point, however, a sense of country, of nation, and of individual and collective selfhood will have had to be maintained in the midst of great changes. To help humankind, we must know who we are and where we are, and we must be in charge of ourselves.

But we shall have to keep our identity in a world that has changed beyond a point of no return. All continents contain watersheds. These are mountain ranges somewhere in the interior where all the water that falls on one side of them runs toward one ocean and all that falls on the other side runs toward another ocean. In North America, the Rocky Mountains is such a watershed; the rain falling on its eastern slopes runs to the Atlantic, while the rain falling on its western slopes runs to the Pacific. In driving across the American continent, when we come to the place marked "continental divide," even though the dividing line itself is invisible and the peaks and the high plateau at that point may look ordinary, we sense that we have indeed moved from the America of the Atlantic to the America of the Pacific.

There are similar *watersheds* in history. All the events that happened before them belong largely to one age in the history of humankind. Most of the events afterward belong to a new age and lead to a new kind of historic pattern. The world is crossing such a watershed now. Or, more exactly, it has crossed a watershed in the forty years from 1940 to 1980. Several changes in those decades have become irreversible.

For the first time in history humankind has the possibility to commit suicide as a species. Individuals have taken their own lives during many ages. But never before has it been possible for all humankind to end its own life. Nearly two thousand years ago, the Roman Emperor Caligula expressed his regret that humankind did not have a single neck so that he could cut it off at one stroke. Caligula died a frustrated man, but what he could not do then, modern physics has enabled us to do today. An all-out war, exploding large numbers of nuclear weapons, can end all or most of civilized life, and quite possibly all life on this planet.

But if the manufacture of death has reached unprecedented heights of effectiveness and power, so has the growth of life. The world's population at the beginning of the 1980s is growing at a rate that will double its numbers every thirty-five years. Six to seven billion human beings are expected to live on this planet by the end of the century. Human reproduction has become a vast power, a vast problem, and, more slowly, an increasing responsibility of both individuals and government.

The growing numbers of people and the growing power of the mechanical and chemical devices at their service have begun to change the physical quality of life. The more than a million automobiles in use in the Los Angeles area have put a dense pile of smog over the city, and it is little comfort to its inhabitants to reflect that replacing the automobiles with their equivalent in horsepower—a quarter of a billion horses—would only make the place smell worse. The sheer numbers of people, and the amounts of energy, fire, smoke, chemicals, and waste fluids, have produced effects which are qualitatively, as well as quantitatively, new. Rivers have become poisonous to fish and human beings. The sun has begun to pale over many industrial cities, and the carbon dioxide that has been deposited in the atmosphere by machines has become so great that some scientists fear a permanent change in the earth's climate. In some ways all these are different aspects of one and the same process: humankind's growing too big and too powerful for its own old habits.

The difference between poverty and riches has persisted. Among a few countries the difference has narrowed. In others it has widened. But though the gap between poor and rich is an old story, now for the first time many millions of people in the poor nations are gaining access to enough science, technology, and power to do something about it. What they will do—whether it will be peaceful and constructive or warlike and violent—is not yet certain.

What many countries have done is to try accelerating their rate of economic growth. On the average, the per capita income of humankind has been growing at a rate of 2 percent a year. Together with the 2 percent growth rate of world population, this has meant a total annual growth of 4 percent of world income, or a doubling of humankind's output of material goods and services approximately every eighteen years. In richer countries, a faster growth in the gross national product and a slower growth in population have produced a higher per capita growth rate of as much as 3 percent a year. (All these are long-run growth rates; for a few years, or even a decade, many countries have grown faster, and in times of recession or depression, more slowly.) Taking into account the significantly higher economic base of the richer countries, it is probable that differing growth rates alone will not reduce significantly the gap between poor and rich peoples for many decades to come.

Clearly, too, the disproportions among countries will no longer be evened out by the methods of the nineteenth century. For the first time in history, mass migration on a global scale has stopped. The few emigrants from a few countries who still make their way into the small state of Israel or the few hundreds of thousands of refugees from Cambodia and Vietnam are less than a drop in the lake. In the nineteenth century over 60 million people left Europe for new overseas homes. Nothing of the sort seems likely or even possible in the last decades of the twentieth century. People are penned in by the frontiers of their own states and by the unwillingness of other states to receive large numbers of immigrants.

This means that rich, relatively empty countries, such as the United States, Canada, the Soviet Union, and Australia, face poor, crowded ones, such as India, Bangladesh, China, Egypt, or Indonesia's main island of Java. Other countries are both poor and empty. They have abundant land but lack capital and humanpower; Brazil, Argentina, and much of Latin America, the islands of Borneo and New Guinea, the Union of South Africa, and much of the rest of Africa all fit this description. Finally, a few countries are both rich and crowded. Lacking land, they have more than enough capital to make up for the shortage of square miles. Great Britain, Germany, Belgium, the Netherlands, and Japan all have proved that people can make a living in densely populated countries if they have enough machines and enough skills to use them.

The redistribution of the world's land resources, by political change, purchase, or mass migration, may become a political question in the future. But the redistribution of capital is likely to be more important. It is possible that just as in the first half of the twentieth century the idea of an income tax became accepted in all advanced countries, an international income tax within the international system may yet become a major political issue. If the experience of national income taxes is any guide, the idea will first be shrugged off as impossible, then denounced as outrageous, still later resisted as intolerable, and finally accepted as normal.

The majority of humankind is now literate for the first time since writing was invented. The crossover seems to have occurred in the mid-1950s. In terms of absolute numbers, of course, there are probably more illiterates in the world now than there were a hundred years ago because the numbers of people have increased. But the relative decline of illiteracy has continued so that today perhaps only 30 percent of the world's population of ten years and older still cannot read or write. By the end of the century this proportionality will have been reduced to only a quarter of humankind.

In most parts of the world, the importance of cities has decisively increased. During the 1970s the majority of humankind had become urban in residence and nonagricultural in occupation. In many highly developed countries, cities used to be surrounded by the countryside. Now the countryside is becoming surrounded by cities. Even in such formerly agricultural countries as Mexico, Brazil, and Peru a majority of inhabitants already live in towns and cities. Everywhere in the world the rural population and the farmers and peasants are becoming a minority, and the influence of their conservatism is dwindling. (In this respect, suburbanites will not replace them.) The effects of this change on world politics are bound to be profound.

Nearly everyone can now be reached by mass media of communication. Indeed the majority of the urban and industrial part of the world can probably be reached within a few days. In 1969 perhaps one-half of humankind may have heard within less than a month that men had walked on the moon. And those walks on the moon foreshadowed another irreversible change—the opening of the age of interplanetary travel.

THE INFORMATION REVOLUTION

More generally, the industrial revolution of the nineteenth and early twentieth centuries has been followed by an information revolution. This revolution has had two aspects. First, it has increased the number of people working in information-processing industries of all kinds, from clerks and librarians to telegraph and telephone operators, and to operators of computing machines and other devices. During the 1950s through the 1970s between 0.5 percent and 1 percent of the work force in advanced countries shifted into these information-processing occupations every year. At the same time, in the highly advanced countries, the number of production-line workers and their proportion in the work force did not increase. More and more mechanical and muscular jobs on the production line came to be handled by automation. So did some of the mechanical work of adding numbers or keeping clerical records. On the whole, the demand for human beings in the information-processing occupations continues to increase. By the end of the century we will have more people occupied with manipulating symbols, items of knowledge, and pieces of paper than we will have working on farms, in mines, or on production lines.

The other aspect of the information revolution has been the increasing intellectualization of society. All industrial growth requires ever more raw materials and other ingredients. If industrial processes remain unchanged but are carried out on a larger scale, the demand for raw materials will increase and the rarer materials will go into short supply. Production will become more expensive and eventually will slow down. This is what is called the *law of diminishing returns.* The only answer to the law of diminishing returns is new inventions. People must discover new ways for making the goods they need. They must use other materials or use them in different proportions in order to break the bottlenecks of scarcity among the materials in short supply. In addition to inventions, there will be need for *innovations,* for changes of habits among millions of people to make them actually act in line with the new techniques.

Without a constant stream of invention and innovation the vast machinery of technology in all countries will slowly grind to a stop. As economies and populations grow, the need for invention and innovation increases and hence the need for the kind of people who produce them. The people who produce invention and innovation are the kind we often call *intellectuals.* They are people who are in the habit of using abstract ideas and symbols in many fields. Not only are they in the habit of thinking critically, of taking all patterns of knowledge to pieces, looking at each piece separately, and deciding which ones to keep and which to reject, they also think combinatorially. That is, they put different pieces of knowledge together in new patterns. Dissociation—breaking old knowledge into smaller pieces—and recombination—putting the pieces together into a new pattern—are the essential processes of creative thought. In the economies of the future such creative thought will not be a luxury but a necessity. The kind of people who produce it, the intellectuals, and the conditions that enable them to produce it, including security and freedom, will also be necessities.

An even greater strain on humankind will be the speed of these information changes. The number of scientific papers published in the world doubles every fifteen years. More than half of the sales of the world's largest chemical corporation, Du Pont, some years ago concerned goods that had not been known ten years before.

Rapid change, however, creates a gap between generations. Where a society changes hardly at all, parents know much more than their children. There is relatively little to learn and the parents have more time to learn it; experience counts, with little else necessary. Where change occurs a little faster, the children learn some things their parents have not learned. Parents and children now share many memories that are sufficiently alike for them to understand each other, but sufficiently different to make conversation interesting. If, however, society changes very fast, many of the experiences of the parents seem irrelevant to the children, and many experiences of the children are unknown to their elders. This accounts in part for some of the communication gap between parents and children which was discovered in recent years not only in the United States but in many other highly developed countries. The appearance in rapid succession of a "beat generation," a "hippie generation," a "militant generation," and a "me generation"—and who knows what next—is a symptom of an underlying process that is deeper and broader than many observers have suspected.

The rapidity of change bewilders old and young alike. How are they to orient themselves in the world and in their society? Their plight is reminiscent of the story of troops on a ship which was torpedoed at night in World War II. The soldiers, crew, and chaplain took their lifebelts and started swimming; and the chaplain, to cheer the men on, called out in a loud voice, "Forward, men, forward!" Out of the darkness came a plaintive plea, "But Father, which way is forward?"

If one does not know which way is forward, one would dearly like a map that provides a simple answer. When experiences follow too quickly and are too different from each other to be an easily understandable guide, one may learn to distrust the testimony of the past. Rather, one looks for simplified maps of the present or future. One looks for ideologies and seeks something simple to cling to—such as the pronouncements or the name of one's favorite politician in the West, or the thoughts of the late Mao Tse-tung in China.

Distrust of experience, fear of highly developed technology, and impatience with the sustained thought needed to understand complex processes and systems, all add up to the risk of massive intellectual failure. Risking a failure to understand the complex and dangerous reality now facing it, humankind may find itself confronted by a still more complex and more dangerous reality as the years go on. If we distrust anything that seems too complicated, we may be unable to deal with the realities we cannot avoid. And one cannot understand a complicated system or process without, at least for a time, accepting some information on trust. A master of political deception, Adolf Hitler, wrote in his book *Mein Kampf* that there were two kinds of people who were easiest to fool: those who believe everything they read and those who believe nothing. If Hitler were alive today, he might suspect that he would find some new easy victories among those who are approaching the age of the computer with a Stone Age cast of mind.

A PLURALITY OF POLITICAL CHANGES

Our age of physical and intellectual dangers is also an age of growing intellectual resources. For the first time in centuries, humankind again has a plurality of social systems existing at approximately the same level of technology. Indeed, the difference between the social systems of private enterprise and communism is more profound in some respects than were the differences among, say, medieval Europe, medieval Mexico, and medieval China. And each of these different social systems has many variants. Today there are at least four kinds of communism in the world: Russian, Chinese, Yugoslavian, and Vietnamese—and North Korean may turn out to be a fifth. There are a number of different kinds of capitalism in the world, most of them alloyed in varying proportions with the institutions of the welfare state. The systems of the United States, Britain, France, Canada, and many other countries are examples. Finally, there are countries whose societies, although based predominantly on private enterprise, have both large public sectors and governments that avowedly favor democratic socialism. (In 1980, the German Federal Republic, Denmark, Norway, and Austria were examples of such societies.) This means that for many different policies we can find experiences in a plurality of social systems and institutions. We can not only make an experiment in a single country by keeping its social order unchanged, but we can also observe how a particular law works in the context of several different social systems, whenever such a law, or a law similar to it, has been enacted in several countries belonging to different systems.

One of the most important changes in the world has been the change in political participation and political culture. At the beginning of the 1960s, voting statistics available from one hundred countries comprising more than two-thirds of the world's population showed that among more than two billion people, nearly 60 percent of adults were in the habit of voting. Additional countries which had not published their statistics, such as Malaysia and China, were known to use voting on a large scale. By 1980, more than one-half of the world's population (and more than three-fifths, if mainland China is included) had engaged in a vote of some kind. Never before in history had there been voting participation on so grand a scale.

To be sure, not every vote in every country means the same thing. We know that in some countries an election is a choice among genuine alternatives, such as different candidates and different parties, while in other countries it is mainly an appeal by the government for some expression of popular support or loyalty. On this last and highly restricted level, the 1960s and 1970s marked the first time that the governments of the majority of humankind came back every few years to almost all of their adults for a symbolic confirmation of their actions.

The increase in voting is not the only form in which political participation has increased. In traditional countries today, as well as in medieval Europe in the past, the activists in politics number far less than 1 percent of the population. In some countries they now number 3 percent, and in others still more, rising to 5 percent, and under special conditions even 10 percent of the population. Something similar has happened in the increase of autonomous groups, both large organizations and small groups, which take action in many aspects of social life having political significance. Industrial workers the world over now join labor unions; farmers in many countries are organized in farm organizations; interest groups for businesspeople and management have arisen in a number of places. In general, the political activity of autonomous small groups as well as of large organizations is much larger than ever.

Moreover, many of these groups and movements are primarily oriented not only to pursuit of the routine interests of their members but also to the bringing about of some more far-reaching kind of change in their society. All the organizations of the black people in the United States are working to produce such far-reaching changes in the country's race relations as well as far-reaching changes in the living conditions of its black people. The labor organizations try to produce far-reaching changes in the living conditions of industrial workers. The farm organizations try to make the life of farmers more secure and less burdened by the hazards of weather, the market, and the workings of the interest rate than the farmer's lot has been for many centuries.

Agents of change, both public and private, are at work in the world today on a larger scale and in a greater variety than ever before. A hundred years ago people used to debate whether the world could be changed; fifty years ago they debated whether change was desirable; today they mainly debate how change can best be accomplished.

Since so many people have become active in society and politics, the basis of the great empires has declined. Empires grew out of the apathy of the many that made possible the rule by the few. If the millions in a country care nothing about politics, a few thousand soldiers brought there over land or by ship can seize control. Or a small militant minority may govern the country, perhaps aided by foreign loans or other economic ties. And the majority continue to live in their villages not caring what happens in the strange world of politics far above their heads.

For centuries, the many have been at the mercy of the few. Now that pattern is changing. With many people entering the process of politics, outside intervention becomes ever less effective. Every year sees foreign loans, foreign ambassadors, or even foreign armies less able than formerly to exercise control over a distant country. This is the shift that has liquidated the great colonial empires. It has also frustrated the ambitions of those who thought that the old imperial powers had merely suffered a failure of nerve, leaving the world in waiting for a new, brasher, or more confident power to fill the supposed vacuum. Ever more often, there is no power vacuum. No longer can the world be governed from a distance—either by a conqueror, an ideology, or a world police officer. The issue is not who shall succeed to these jobs, for the fact is that these jobs have been abolished.

Something similar has happened to paternalistic government. The days when a government could do things for its people and expect them to remain duly passive and grateful are disappearing. More and more it has become necessary to do things *with* people rather than merely *for* them. When the Founding Fathers of the United States said that governments obtained their powers from the consent of the governed, they were well ahead of their time. Today the world is catching up with them. George Orwell's nightmare vision of the totalitarian world of 1984 has turned out to have been completely false. Striking as his satire was in its day, and still is in ours, effective as it has been in picking up details and particular features of the political follies of humankind, it has completely misrepresented the mainstream of political development.

In country after country the inclination to take people for granted has become increasingly impracticable. Rather, it has become important to consider the responses of those affected by a public policy and to include their reactions in the planning of the policy. This is true in the running of housing projects, in the renewal of cities, in the development of educational systems, and in the operation of great universities as well as factories. Abraham Lincoln's notion of "government of the people, by the people, for the people" must now be pronounced with a heavy stress on the word "by."

Any one of these great currents of change may undergo brief and limited reversals. At times or places the trend might head toward less participation; people might leave the towns or be forced to leave them, as happened in Cambodia in the 1970s, and find themselves again scattered in the countrysides. Travel might again become more difficult and hazardous. Mass media might become scarce, and people might pay less attention to their contents. The information revolution might be halted and people once again become impoverished in knowledge and by objects competing for other attention. In some places the clocks of history might run backward for a time. But the analysis of politics should enable us to distinguish the mainstream of a river from the eddies at its fringes. Such eddies can be powerful and lead to whirlpools in which people can drown. They should never be underestimated. Yet in the end it is still crucial to distinguish the eddy from the stream.

THE AGENDA FOR THE FUTURE

The most dangerous thing the world today can do is to continue politics as usual. If we should traverse the 1980s and 1990s merely repeating the ideas and policies of the first third of the century, the dangers would be great indeed. There is a special reason for these dangers. Through most ages of human history the main decision-makers have been mature individuals who collected their experiences and proved their competence before they reached the age of fifty. But their main image of the world was formed in most cases at the time they were twenty. Anyone born in America between 1900 and 1909 formed his or her images of the world in the days of Coolidge and Hoover. In Germany, they were formed in the era of President Hindenburg; in France, in the days of the conservative French governments of the 1920s; and in Russia, in the days of the coming to power of Joseph Stalin. In Britain, they were formed in the days of the conservative government of Stanley Baldwin and the abortive general strike of the British unions.

The first nuclear explosions occurred in 1945. Very few leaders of today were either young enough or flexible enough in their thinking to be able to accept the full significance of nuclear weapons and nuclear energy, not only in their thought processes, but also in their feelings, down to the very marrow of their bones. As a result, we are in 1980 still governed by the only generation of statesmen that will ever have the power to control nuclear weapons but who have not *fully* internalized the significance of the new changes. Most of the statesmen who come to power in the 1980s will be people who were less than twenty years old in 1945 and who will have accepted the nuclear age fully. To these people war and empire no longer seem things to be sought seriously because the impracticality of nuclear war will be obvious to them.

When gasoline pumps were originally introduced across the United States, they had to be manned by a generation of attendants who had already developed the habit of smoking, and an occasional attendant might smoke near his gas pump on a hot summer day. Such attendants are no longer with us. In one way or the other, they have been replaced by a generation of attendants who have learned not to smoke near a gasoline pump. Very likely the world will be governed in the next two decades by a generation of politicians who will have learned to be as careful around nuclear weapons as gas station attendants are around their pumps.

The most dangerous thing next to a nuclear war would be to try to press all humankind into the mold of a single ideology. At the present state of our social sciences all utopias are only half thought out at best. The governments of the Communist-ruled countries do not fully understand either the economics, the politics, or the sociology of communism, even though they understand enough to stay in power. In the private-enterprise countries, too, inflation, unemployment, and recession, as well as the larger economic and social trends are not fully understood by either management or unions, or governments or voters. In these respects, much of the Cold War of past decades was a competition in exporting ignorance. Future efforts to force poorly understood institutions hastily upon larger and larger parts of humankind are likely to lead to worse disappointments and dangers.

In the meantime it is perhaps safer to see whether we know what we do *not* want or what dangers or conditions we must abolish. Perhaps the first emergency task will be to *abolish war*. Either we abolish all-out war or it will abolish us. Though limited war is increasingly unrewarding and impractical it may continue for a time. Yet it seems safe to say that it will rarely bring its participants the rewards they expect. Civil wars may be harder to cope with. Much as we can hope to abolish all-out war and restrict limited wars, eventually even abolishing the latter, too, it does not seem likely that we shall succeed during the next several decades in abolishing civil wars and revolutions among the local populations of many countries. Too many backward institutions, too many ideological and religious conflicts, too much impatience and intolerance, and too much poverty make it unlikely that all political and social change will be peaceful for the rest of the century. What seems more reasonable to hope for is the limiting of civil wars and revolutions to the populations directly involved. Very likely the factions in such wars will call on like-minded allies for ideological and strategic advice as well as for various types of economic aid or military hardware. But people can at least aim at restricting to a minimum or actually banning the sending of troops into foreign countries by any power, be it Russia, China, the United States, or any of their smaller allies.

Another emergency task will be the *abolition of hunger*. Many millions still go to bed hungry every night. Indian villages every year record the deaths of people from "general weakness," a polite phrase for starvation. Hunger can be abolished in our time through the use of better strains of food plants and better methods of cultivation and through the large-scale shipments of food supplies and farm tools to countries in need of such aid. For the same purpose, a great deal of technical and educational help can be given to countries to teach them to grow more of their own food supplies. For the last twenty years humankind has been in a race between increasing numbers and the difficulty of growing more food. By 1980, luckily, humankind may have pulled a little ahead; food supplies have grown a little faster than world population.

To unite the nations of the world and help them in the struggle against hunger will not be a luxury but a necessity. Any nation, Communist or non-Communist, that holds large reserves of land but refuses either to accept large-scale immigration or to grow food for the hungry will court annihilation on the day when the hungry peoples acquire nuclear weapons and rise up in desperation. That day is not yet here. But just as bicycles, machine guns, and airplanes have spread around the world and are now being used by Ethiopians, Paraguayans, and Burmese, as well as by members of most other nations, so nuclear weapons will be virtually available by the end of the century to many countries, large and small, rich and poor. Some will obviously have more of them than others, but even some poor and small nations will have enough of these instruments of destruction to do terrible damage if they should despair of enough food. Clearly, humankind can no longer afford to drive any substantial part of its family to desperation.

Beyond the immediate need to reduce and end hunger lies the more far-reaching goal of *eliminating poverty*. Even under the best of circumstances, this could well take three generations. The average income of the world is between $1,500 and $1,600 per capita at 1979 prices, and very unevenly distributed. On the average, per capita income has been growing at 2 percent per year, and as we know, doubling every thirty-five years. If we could accelerate this growth rate to 3 percent a year and a corresponding doubling time of only twenty-three years, and if the United States dollar henceforth should remain stable, average income would be close to $3,000 for the world early in the next century and close to $6,000 by its third decade. It would have reached a level higher than the United States enjoyed in the days of President Hoover. Another twenty-three years later, in the fifth decade of the twenty-first century, it ought to be at a level of about $12,000 (all in 1979 dollars, to be sure), higher than per capita income in the United States today. In terms of the average income of the world, poverty may well by then have been abolished.

But how could income be distributed in such a way as to benefit the poor classes and nations? A basic principle of economics is that of *marginal utility*. It teaches us that if you offer a very thirsty person one drink of water he or she will make great sacrifices to get it. If you offer that person two glasses of water, the second glass may be worth less to him or her, and if you offer the tenth glass of water he or she may say, "Thank you, I no longer need it."

Perhaps something similar may apply to income in terms of goods and services. When the United States was poorer, wage disputes between labor and management often were bloody. People died on picket lines. Since the income of the United States has become high, labor disputes ordinarily no longer involve the shedding of blood or the loss of life. Many leaders of major labor unions now resemble the corporate executives with whom they are negotiating, and many of the skilled people in unions, particularly those in well-organized skilled occupations, consider themselves members of the middle class. Is it possible to think that some reaction of this kind may develop during the next three generations on a worldwide scale?

So long as the United States was poorer, the idea of a federal income tax was bitterly resisted. It was considered both unconstitutional and unfair. As the American people became richer their objections to paying income tax declined. Now they are so used to paying income tax that grumbles have become perfunctory. On the international scale, nations that consider themselves relatively poor may object to paying an income tax for the benefit of their poorer neighbors. But when nations feel rich enough to send some of their citizens to the moon they may be willing to pay some taxes for their neighbors on this planet. It could even be thought that the truly rich countries of the world, the United States, Britain, France, West Germany, Japan, and by now the Soviet Union, owe the rest of humankind a good deal in back taxes. In the next decades they will have become ready to acknowledge the obligation and start making payments.

How much could such payments accomplish? The task, as we indicated, is to increase the annual rate of growth of per capita income from 2 percent to 3 percent. That is, we must add 1 percent to the growth of income for most countries of the world. To add 1 percent to the income of a country requires an investment of about 4 percent. It takes roughly between three dollars and four dollars invested once to add one dollar to annual income in a national economy. The amount needed is approximately the arms budgets of the world today, which run at 7 percent of world income. If we could cut the armament bill of the world in half and increase economic aid by the amount saved, we would be far on the way toward abolishing the ancient curse of poverty. Dwight D. Eisenhower was the first American president to make a proposal of this kind.

On a smaller scale, many countries can reduce poverty by doing a better job in integrating their large citites. The politics of big cities have become more like international relations, as their populations have become recruited from many races and ethnic groups. The more we become skilled in integrating our cities, the more we may develop some of the skills needed to help integrate the world.

The instruments for doing most of these things will still be the governments of our nation-states. These include all levels of the machinery of government—local, state, and national. Beyond them, we shall make use of regional organizations such as the Common Market in Western Europe and the United Nations with all its specialized agencies, as well as the many nongovernmental international organizations such as the International Red Cross.

The rule according to which all these instruments will have to be used is the principle of the *self-determination of peoples.* Insofar as the population of an area is a people—a cohesive group of persons capable of communicating and cooperating with each other with a high degree of solidarity—its members are likely to demand their rights to demonstrate their capacity and take their fate into their own hands.

Perhaps the most important task for national states, national governments, and entire peoples will be the effort to increase their *cognitive capabilities.* The nations of the world are like a fleet of ships crossing a foggy sea full of currents and icebergs. Both in the relations of nations among one another, which require the avoidance of war, and of peoples toward their natural environment, which require a more effective control of science and technology, they need to know much more than they now know in order to act in a way that prevents destroying themselves. In the United States and other Western countries this could also include an increase in *integrative capabilities*—that is, in the capabilities to enable people of different races, languages, religions, and geographic and other background conditions to work together effectively.

Two more problems appear on the urgent agenda for the twenty-first century. The first of these concerns *population growth.* We already have learned the importance of taking some responsibility for the seemingly automatic increase in our numbers. But most of the world's troublesome adults for the next twenty years have already been born. Hundreds of millions of peasants around the world will not change their habits quickly, and their babies will keep coming until they do. There is one comforting thought in this reflection. About one child in a thousand is born with intelligence at what is conventionally called the "genius level." If we get another three billion people in the world, we should find another three million living geniuses among them. The world could well use some of that talent and some of it will be used.

Another set of problems facing us in the next decades and in the next century will be how to cope with the opportunities and dangers of the great breakthroughs in science and technology that have been made in our own time or that are now in the making.

THE INCREASE OF HUMAN CAPABILITIES: SEVEN RECENT BREAKTHROUGHS IN SCIENCE AND TECHNOLOGY

The great changes have already started. We are now in the midst of them, although sometimes it takes an effort to realize where we are and what is happening around us.

The most obvious change is the change in *speed.* In the mid-1920s, propeller-driven planes carried their passengers at about 180 kilometers per hour. In the late 1940s, the fastest experimental jet aircraft flew ten times as fast, at about 1800 kilometers per hour. In the 1960s and 1970s, astronauts flew ten times faster still, at 18,000 kilometers per hour, in rocket-powered space capsules and space laboratories. This latest speed, one hundred times faster than that of the 1920s, was greater than "escape velocity," that is, fast enough to overcome the gravitational attraction of earth and to permit human beings to enter outer space and thus signal the beginnings of the age of interplanetary transportation.

This breakthrough points to a second one. This second breakthrough is humanity's conquest of *new habitations*—new places in which to live and work—on the bottom of the sea, in laboratories in outer space, and eventually on other moons and perhaps planets of our solar system. Always before in the history of humankind, when people have entered a radically new environment—a new world—they have brought back from it discoveries that have had a profound influence on life at home. When Columbus sailed to the New World in search of spices, gold, and silver, no one expected that maize and potatoes would transform the agriculture of the old world. Yet they did. Similarly in the twenty-first century the impact of the age of seabed mining and space navigation will be felt in every country.

In a third breakthrough, *new energy sources* have become available from nuclear fission, with dangerous byproducts, but safer and cleaner sources of energy from nuclear fusion, and perhaps most important in the long run, new energy sources from solar energy are being actively developed.

In a fourth broad advance, chemistry and biochemistry have given us *new materials,* such as synthetic fibers, new *antibiotic drugs,* and drugs altering the state of a person's mind, which can be used for healing but equally well can be abused.

In a fifth and perhaps fateful breakthrough, molecular biology has created the possibility of *DNA-manipulation,* that is, the production of controlled changes in the genetic code—and hence in the hereditary constitution—of micro-organisms and eventually of plants and animals. In 1979 already one genetically altered bacillus was producing insulin—vitally important for patients suffering from diabetes—of acceptable quality and with the prospect of radically lower costs. Sooner or later, the step from changing the genetic constitution of micro-organisms to changing the hereditary characteristics of food-plants will be taken—with far-reaching effects on world food supplies. As another aspect of the same scientific development, the possibility of genetic repairs, even in human beings, appears on the horizon now, with all the hopes and promises, but also the ethical problems, that it would imply.

If these five breakthroughs mainly have tended to increase human material powers, the sixth and seventh tend primarily to enhance humanity's powers of awareness and of thought. For the sixth breakthrough has been our beginnings at use of the entire *electro-magnetic spectrum*—from microwaves to very long ones—as a source of our perceptions. For millions of years, living organisms on our planet have developed cells sensitive to that narrow portion of that spectrum that we call "light." In this manner crabs, fish, insects, reptiles, birds, and mammals all have developed eyes of one kind or another. But in this century, human beings have started to use radio and radar waves, radio astronomy, infrared light, polarized light, ultraviolet light, ultrashort waves, microwaves, electron microscopes, x-rays, and x-ray scanners as sources of information. We now can "see" tiny molecules and crystalline structures, vast distant galaxies and previously unknown "quasars" and "radio stars," that is, sources of interstellar radio emission. It is as if humanity had acquired half-a-dozen sets of new eyes during the last few decades.

How can we make sense out of the many new things that we can see? It is here, as in many other matters, that the seventh breakthrough comes into play. It is the development of large *computers* that permit us to deal with much larger amounts of information much faster and more effectively than before. The progressive *miniaturization* of such computers through transistors and microcircuits is making them steadily more mobile and available in many new uses. The literature of computer programs and procedures—the *"software"*—is becoming larger and more important than the *"hardware"* of the machines themselves, reminiscent of the process whereby the totality of printed books and periodicals has become bigger than the totality of printing presses. Together, hardware and software are developing into new systems of *auxiliary intelligence.* It is as if we had added collectively a new layer of grey cells to our brains. Nothing comparable has happened in our history since the inventions of writing and counting, or perhaps even of speech, thousands of years ago.

What is new about these breakthroughs is not only the size of each of them but the fact that they all have come together, mainly during the last half-century. Never before in history has there been so short a period with so many large changes coming so close together. Their effects are reinforcing each other already now, and they will do so still more in the future.

Each of these breakthroughs, and all of them together, offer a great aid to our power of thinking and acting. But they are not and cannot be a substitute for human thought and human action. What we think about them and what we do about them is still in our own heads and hands.

It is patent nonsense to say that we do not know whether there is "progress." Its results and its problems are staring us in the face. But it is meaningful to ask whether we like what is happening before our eyes, and more to the point, whether we can cope with our vast new problems and powers, or whether they will blindly destroy our happiness and our chances of survival.

Here the question comes back to ourselves. We cannot act well together if we cannot also make sense of our lives as individuals. Perhaps the twenty-first century will also be the age of *personal self-determination,* much as our own has been the century of the growing self-determination of entire peoples. We may do more in exploring the *inner space* of the human mind and spirit, and we may become more effectively mindful of the feelings and emotions of every individual. This will also involve some continuing changes in the position of women and the young in many countries and cultures. It may also be necessary to develop more devices for defending individual freedom and controlling governments by means of checks and balances.

Constitutional government may turn out to be neither an old-fashioned remnant of some Western middle-class tradition nor a luxury that only a few rich countries can afford. Freedom of the individual and freedom of opinion are essential parts of freedom in the search for knowledge, and the search for knowledge is an indispensable element in humankind's search for security and livelihood. Systems of government that are respectful of the individual, protective of minorities, and permissive of new discoveries and individuals' changing their minds about them, will be a necessity for the future growth of humankind. Where constitutional government and individual freedom already exist, it may be worthwhile to guard and develop these traditions and guarantees now, because all humankind will need them someday in the future.

We have no control over what our descendants will do in the next century. But we have an inescapable responsibility for what we ourselves do today and tomorrow. The fate of humankind is a do-it-yourself project.

ADDITIONAL READINGS

Bell, D. *The Coming of the Post-Industrial Society.* New York: Basic Books, 1973.

Brown, H., et al. *The Next Hundred Years: Man's Natural and Technological Resources.* New York: Viking Press, 1963. PB

Deutsch, K. W. "Social and Political Convergence in Industrializing Countries," in N. Hammond, ed., *Social Science and the New Societies.* East Lansing, Mich.: Michigan State University, 1973. Pp. 95–115.

Emerson, R. *From Empire to Nation.* Boston: Beacon Press, 1962. PB

Harrington, M. *Socialism* (especially pp. 421–456). New York: Bantam Books, 1973. PB

Heilbroner, R. L. *Between Capitalism and Socialism.* New York: Random House (Vintage), 1970. Pp. 79–114. PB

Huxley, A. *Brave New World.* New York: Harper, 1932. PB

Kahn, H., and A. J. Wiener. *The Year 2000: A Framework for Speculation.* New York: Macmillan, 1967.

Lasswell, H. D. "The World Revolution of Our Time," in H. D. Lasswell and D. Lerner, eds., *World Revolutionary Elites.* Cambridge, Mass.: MIT Press, 1965.

Lowi, T. *The End of Liberalism.* New York: Norton, 1969.

Mende, T. *From Aid to Re-Colonialization.* New York: Pantheon, 1973.

Orwell, G. *1984.* New York: Harcourt, 1949. PB

Perloff, H. S. *The Future of the U.S. Government: Toward the Year 2000.* New York: Braziller, 1971.

Platt, J. *The Step to Man.* New York: Wiley, 1966.

Sakharov, A. D. *Progress, Coexistence, and Intellectual Freedom.* New York: Norton, 1969. PB

Shepard, P., and D. McKinley, eds. *The Subversive Science.* Boston: Houghton Mifflin, 1969. PB

Simon, P. *The Politics of World Hunger.* New York: Harper's Magazine Press, 1973.

Toffler, A. *Future Shock.* New York: Random House, 1970. PB

Ward, B., and R. Dubos. *Only One Earth.* New York: Norton, 1972. PB

Wiener, N. *The Human Use of Human Beings.* Boston: Houghton Mifflin, 1954. PB

PB = *available in paperback*

INDEX

BCDEFGHIJ-H-8210

3 6289 00216513 9